Collins Discovery World Atlas

Collins
An imprint of HarperCollinsPublishers
77–85 Fulham Palace Road
London
w6 8jb

First Published 2004
Originally published as Collins World Atlas Illustrated
Edition 2003

Printed in Italy

British Library Cataloguing in Publication Data.
A catalogue record for this book is available from
the British Library.

ISBN 0 00 719089 1

RH11820 Imp 001

All mapping in this atlas is generated from Collins
Bartholomew digital databases. Collins Bartholomew,
the UK's leading independent geographical information
supplier, can provide a digital, custom, and premium
mapping service to a variety of markets.
For further information:
Tel: +44 (0) 141 306 3752
e-mail: collinsbartholomew@harpercollins.co.uk

We also offer a choice of books, atlases and maps that
can be customized to suit a customer's own
requirements. For further information:
Tel: +44 (0) 141 306 3209
e-mail: business.gifts@harpercollins.co.uk

or visit our website at: www.collinsbartholomew.com

everything clicks at www.collins.co.uk

Collins

Collins
Discovery
World
Atlas

Contents

Map Symbols

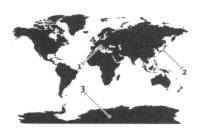

Southern Europe   1

Japan   2

Antarctica   3

Settlements

Population	National capital	Administrative capital	Other city or town
over 10 million	**BEIJING** ◉	**Karachi** ◉	**New York** ◉
5 million to 10 million	**JAKARTA** ✧	**Tianjin** ◉	**Nova Iguaçu** ◉
1 million to 5 million	**KĀBUL** ✧	**Sydney** ◉	**Kaohsiung** ◉
500 000 to 1 million	**BANGUI** ✧	Trujillo ◉	Jeddah ◉
100 000 to 500 000	WELLINGTON ✧	Mansa ◎	Apucarana ◎
50 000 to 100 000	PORT OF SPAIN ✧	Potenza ○	Arecibo ○
10 000 to 50 000	MALABO ✧	Chinhoyi ○	Ceres ○
under 10 000	VALLETTA ✿	Ati ○	Venta ○

    ▨ Built-up area

Boundaries

▬▬▬ International boundary

▪▬▪▬▪ Disputed international boundary or alignment unconfirmed

▬▬▬ Administrative boundary

• • • • • Ceasefire line

Miscellaneous

- - - - - National park

· · · · · · Reserve or Regional park

✿ Site of specific interest

▭▭▭▭ Wall

Land and sea features

Desert

Oasis

Lava field

1234 △ Volcano height in metres

Marsh

Ice cap or Glacier

Escarpment

Coral reef

1234 Pass height in metres

Lakes and rivers

Lake

Impermanent lake

Salt lake or lagoon

Impermanent salt lake

Dry salt lake or salt pan

123 Lake height surface height above sea level, in metres

River

Impermanent river or watercourse

‖ Waterfall

— Dam

| Barrage

Relief

Contour intervals and layer colours

Height metres
6000 –
5000 –
4000 –
3000 –
2000 –
1000 –
500 –
200 –
0 –
below sea level –
0 –
200 –
2000 –
4000 –
6000 –

Depth

1234 △ Summit height in metres

-123 Spot height height in metres

123 Ocean deep depth in metres

Transport

▬▬▶ - - - - - Motorway (tunnel; under construction)

▬▬▬ - - - - - Main road (tunnel; under construction)

▬▬▬ - - - - - Secondary road (tunnel; under construction)

· · · · · · · · Track

▬▬▬ - - - - - Main railway (tunnel; under construction)

▬▬▬ - - - - - Secondary railway (tunnel; under construction)

▬▬▬ - - - - - Other railway (tunnel; under construction)

▬▬▬ Canal

✈ Main airport

✈ Regional airport

SPOT

Space Shuttle

IKONOS

Satellite imagery - The thematic pages in the atlas contain a wide variety of photographs and images. These are a mixture of terrestrial and aerial photographs and satellite imagery. All are used to illustrate specific themes and to give an indication of the variety of imagery available today. The main types of imagery used in the atlas are described in the table below. The sensor for each satellite image is detailed on the acknowledgements page.

Main satellites/sensors

Satellite/sensor name	Launch dates	Owner	Aims and applications	Internet links	Additional internet links
Landsat 4, 5, 7	July 1972–April 1999	National Aeronautics and Space Administration (NASA), USA	The first satellite to be designed specifically for observing the Earth's surface. Originally set up to produce images of use for agriculture and geology. Today is of use for numerous environmental and scientific applications.	geo.arc.nasa.gov landsat.gsfc.nasa.gov	asterweb.jpl.nasa.gov earth.jsc.nasa.gov earthnet.esrin.esa.it
SPOT 1, 2, 3, 4, 5 (Satellite Pour l'Observation de la Terre)	February 1986–March 1998	Centre National d'Etudes Spatiales (CNES) and Spot Image, France	Particularly useful for monitoring land use, water resources research, coastal studies and cartography.	www.cnes.fr www.spotimage.fr	earthobservatory.nasa.gov eol.jsc.nasa.gov modis.gsfc.nasa.gov
Space Shuttle	Regular launches from 1981	NASA, USA	Each shuttle mission has separate aims. Astronauts take photographs with high specification hand held cameras. The Shuttle Radar Topography Mission (SRTM) in 2000 obtained the most complete near-global high-resolution database of the earth's topography.	science.ksc.nasa.gov/shuttle/countdown www.jpl.nasa.gov/srtm	seawifs.gsfc.nasa.gov topex-www.jpl.nasa.gov visibleearth.nasa.gov www.rsi.ca
IKONOS	September 1999	Space Imaging	First commercial high-resolution satellite. Useful for a variety of applications mainly Cartography, Defence, Urban Planning, Agriculture, Forestry and Insurance.	www.spaceimaging.com	www.usgs.gov

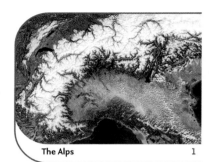

The Alps | 1

Amsterdam, Netherlands | 2

Italy | 3

Europe		Area sq km	Area sq miles	Population	Capital	Languages	Religions	Currency
ALBANIA		28 748	11 100	3 166 000	Tirana	Albanian, Greek	Sunni Muslim, Albanian Orthodox, Roman Catholic	Lek
ANDORRA		465	180	71 000	Andorra la Vella	Spanish, Catalan, French	Roman Catholic	Euro
AUSTRIA		83 855	32 377	8 116 000	Vienna	German, Croatian, Turkish	Roman Catholic, Protestant	Euro
BELARUS		207 600	80 155	9 895 000	Minsk	Belorussian, Russian	Belorussian Orthodox, Roman Catholic	Belarus rouble
BELGIUM		30 520	11 784	10 318 000	Brussels	Dutch (Flemish), French (Walloon), German	Roman Catholic, Protestant	Euro
BOSNIA-HERZEGOVINA		51 130	19 741	4 161 000	Sarajevo	Bosnian, Serbian, Croatian	Sunni Muslim, Serbian Orthodox, Roman Catholic, Protestant	Marka
BULGARIA		110 994	42 855	7 897 000	Sofia	Bulgarian, Turkish, Romany, Macedonian	Bulgarian Orthodox, Sunni Muslim	Lev
CROATIA		56 538	21 829	4 428 000	Zagreb	Croatian, Serbian	Roman Catholic, Serbian Orthodox, Sunni Muslim	Kuna
CZECH REPUBLIC		78 864	30 450	10 236 000	Prague	Czech, Moravian, Slovak	Roman Catholic, Protestant	Czech koruna
DENMARK		43 075	16 631	5 364 000	Copenhagen	Danish	Protestant	Danish krone
ESTONIA		45 200	17 452	1 332 000	Tallinn	Estonian, Russian	Protestant, Estonian and Russian Orthodox	Kroon
FINLAND		338 145	130 559	5 207 000	Helsinki	Finnish, Swedish	Protestant, Greek Orthodox	Euro
FRANCE		543 965	210 026	60 144 000	Paris	French, Arabic	Roman Catholic, Protestant, Sunni Muslim	Euro
GERMANY		357 022	137 849	82 476 000	Berlin	German, Turkish	Protestant, Roman Catholic	Euro
GREECE		131 957	50 949	10 976 000	Athens	Greek	Greek Orthodox, Sunni Muslim	Euro
HUNGARY		93 030	35 919	9 877 000	Budapest	Hungarian	Roman Catholic, Protestant	Forint
ICELAND		102 820	39 699	290 000	Reykjavík	Icelandic	Protestant	Icelandic króna
IRELAND, REPUBLIC OF		70 282	27 136	3 956 000	Dublin	English, Irish	Roman Catholic, Protestant	Euro
ITALY		301 245	116 311	57 423 000	Rome	Italian	Roman Catholic	Euro
LATVIA		63 700	24 595	2 307 000	Rīga	Latvian, Russian	Protestant, Roman Catholic, Russian Orthodox	Lats
LIECHTENSTEIN		160	62	34 000	Vaduz	German	Roman Catholic, Protestant	Swiss franc
LITHUANIA		65 200	25 174	3 444 000	Vilnius	Lithuanian, Russian, Polish	Roman Catholic, Protestant, Russian Orthodox	Litas
LUXEMBOURG		2 586	998	453 000	Luxembourg	Letzeburgish, German, French	Roman Catholic	Euro
MACEDONIA (F.Y.R.O.M.)		25 713	9 928	2 056 000	Skopje	Macedonian, Albanian, Turkish	Macedonian Orthodox, Sunni Muslim	Macedonian denar
MALTA		316	122	394 000	Valletta	Maltese, English	Roman Catholic	Maltese lira
MOLDOVA		33 700	13 012	4 267 000	Chişinău	Romanian, Ukrainian, Gagauz, Russian	Romanian Orthodox, Russian Orthodox	Moldovan leu
MONACO		2	1	34 000	Monaco-Ville	French, Monegasque, Italian	Roman Catholic	Euro
NETHERLANDS		41 526	16 033	16 149 000	Amsterdam/The Hague	Dutch, Frisian	Roman Catholic, Protestant, Sunni Muslim	Euro
NORWAY		323 878	125 050	4 533 000	Oslo	Norwegian	Protestant, Roman Catholic	Norwegian krone
POLAND		312 683	120 728	38 587 000	Warsaw	Polish, German	Roman Catholic, Polish Orthodox	Złoty
PORTUGAL		88 940	34 340	10 062 000	Lisbon	Portuguese	Roman Catholic, Protestant	Euro
ROMANIA		237 500	91 699	22 334 000	Bucharest	Romanian, Hungarian	Romanian Orthodox, Protestant, Roman Catholic	Romanian leu
RUSSIAN FEDERATION		17 075 400	6 592 849	143 246 000	Moscow	Russian, Tatar, Ukrainian, local languages	Russian Orthodox, Sunni Muslim, Protestant	Russian rouble
SAN MARINO		61	24	28 000	San Marino	Italian	Roman Catholic	Euro
SERBIA AND MONTENEGRO		102 173	39 449	10 527 000	Belgrade	Serbian, Albanian, Hungarian	Serbian Orthodox, Montenegrin Orthodox, Sunni Muslim	Serbian dinar, Euro
SLOVAKIA		49 035	18 933	5 402 000	Bratislava	Slovak, Hungarian, Czech	Roman Catholic, Protestant, Orthodox	Slovakian koruna
SLOVENIA		20 251	7 819	1 984 000	Ljubljana	Slovene, Croatian, Serbian	Roman Catholic, Protestant	Tólar
SPAIN		504 782	194 897	41 060 000	Madrid	Castilian, Catalan, Galician, Basque	Roman Catholic	Euro
SWEDEN		449 964	173 732	8 876 000	Stockholm	Swedish	Protestant, Roman Catholic	Swedish krona
SWITZERLAND		41 293	15 943	7 169 000	Bern	German, French, Italian, Romansch	Roman Catholic, Protestant	Swiss franc
UKRAINE		603 700	233 090	48 523 000	Kiev	Ukrainian, Russian	Ukrainian Orthodox, Ukrainian Catholic, Roman Catholic	Hryvnia
UNITED KINGDOM		243 609	94 058	58 789 194	London	English, Welsh, Gaelic	Protestant, Roman Catholic, Muslim	Pound sterling
VATICAN CITY		0.5	0.2	472	Vatican City	Italian	Roman Catholic	Euro

Dependent territories		Territorial status	Area sq km	Area sq miles	Population	Capital	Languages	Religions	Currency
Azores		Autonomous Region of Portugal	2 300	888	242 073	Ponta Delgada	Portuguese	Roman Catholic, Protestant	Euro
Faroe Islands		Self-governing Danish Territory	1 399	540	47 000	Tórshavn	Faroese, Danish	Protestant	Danish krone
Gibraltar		United Kingdom Overseas Territory	7	3	27 000	Gibraltar	Engllish, Spanish	Roman Catholic, Protestant, Sunni Muslim	Gibraltar pound
Guernsey		United Kingdom Crown Dependency	78	30	62 701	St Peter Port	English, French	Protestant, Roman Catholic	Pound sterling
Isle of Man		United Kingdom Crown Dependency	572	221	75 000	Douglas	English	Protestant, Roman Catholic	Pound sterling
Jersey		United Kingdom Crown Dependency	116	45	87 186	St Helier	English, French	Protestant, Roman Catholic	Pound sterling

Ganges Delta, India 1

Cyprus, eastern Mediterranean 2

Indian subcontinent 3

Asia		Area sq km	Area sq miles	Population	Capital	Languages	Religions	Currency
AFGHANISTAN		652 225	251 825	23 897 000	Kābul	Dari, Pushtu, Uzbek, Turkmen	Sunni Muslim, Shi'a Muslim	Afghani
ARMENIA		29 800	11 506	3 061 000	Yerevan	Armenian, Azeri	Armenian Orthodox	Dram
AZERBAIJAN		86 600	33 436	8 370 000	Baku	Azeri, Armenian, Russian, Lezgian	Shi'a Muslim, Sunni Muslim, Russian and Armenian Orthodox	Azerbaijani manat
BAHRAIN		691	267	724 000	Manama	Arabic, English	Shi'a Muslim, Sunni Muslim, Christian	Bahrain dinar
BANGLADESH		143 998	55 598	146 736 000	Dhaka	Bengali, English	Sunni Muslim, Hindu	Taka
BHUTAN		46 620	18 000	2 257 000	Thimphu	Dzongkha, Nepali, Assamese	Buddhist, Hindu	Ngultrum, Indian rupee
BRUNEI		5 765	2 226	358 000	Bandar Seri Begawan	Malay, English, Chinese	Sunni Muslim, Buddhist, Christian	Brunei dollar
CAMBODIA		181 035	69 884	14 144 000	Phnom Penh	Khmer, Vietnamese	Buddhist, Roman Catholic, Sunni Muslim	Riel
CHINA		9 584 492	3 700 593	1 289 161 000	Beijing	Mandarin, Wu, Cantonese, Hsiang, regional languages	Confucian, Taoist, Buddhist, Christian, Sunni Muslim	Yuan, HK dollar*, Macau pataca
CYPRUS		9 251	3 572	802 000	Nicosia	Greek, Turkish, English	Greek Orthodox, Sunni Muslim	Cyprus pound
EAST TIMOR		14 874	5 743	778 000	Dili	Portuguese, Tetun, English	Roman Catholic	United States dollar
GEORGIA		69 700	26 911	5 126 000	T'bilisi	Georgian, Russian, Armenian, Azeri, Ossetian, Abkhaz	Georgian Orthodox, Russian Orthodox, Sunni Muslim	Lari
INDIA		3 064 898	1 183 364	1 065 462 000	New Delhi	Hindi, English, many regional languages	Hindu, Sunni Muslim, Shi'a Muslim, Sikh, Christian	Indian rupee
INDONESIA		1 919 445	741 102	219 883 000	Jakarta	Indonesian, local languages	Sunni Muslim, Protestant, Roman Catholic, Hindu, Buddhist	Rupiah
IRAN		1 648 000	636 296	68 920 000	Tehrān	Farsi, Azeri, Kurdish, regional languages	Shi'a Muslim, Sunni Muslim	Iranian rial
IRAQ		438 317	169 235	25 175 000	Baghdād	Arabic, Kurdish, Turkmen	Shi'a Muslim, Sunni Muslim, Christian	Iraqi dinar
ISRAEL		20 770	8 019	6 433 000	Jerusalem (De facto capital. Disputed.)	Hebrew, Arabic	Jewish, Sunni Muslim, Christian, Druze	Shekel
JAPAN		377 727	145 841	127 654 000	Tōkyō	Japanese	Shintoist, Buddhist, Christian	Yen
JORDAN		89 206	34 443	5 473 000	'Ammān	Arabic	Sunni Muslim, Christian	Jordanian dinar
KAZAKHSTAN		2 717 300	1 049 155	15 433 000	Astana	Kazakh, Russian, Ukrainian, German, Uzbek, Tatar	Sunni Muslim, Russian Orthodox, Protestant	Tenge
KUWAIT		17 818	6 880	2 521 000	Kuwait	Arabic	Sunni Muslim, Shi'a Muslim, Christian, Hindu	Kuwaiti dinar
KYRGYZSTAN		198 500	76 641	5 138 000	Bishkek	Kyrgyz, Russian, Uzbek	Sunni Muslim, Russian Orthodox	Kyrgyz som
LAOS		236 800	91 429	5 657 000	Vientiane	Lao, local languages	Buddhist, traditional beliefs	Kip
LEBANON		10 452	4 036	3 653 000	Beirut	Arabic, Armenian, French	Shi'a Muslim, Sunni Muslim, Christian	Lebanese pound
MALAYSIA		332 965	128 559	24 425 000	Kuala Lumpur/Putrajaya	Malay, English, Chinese, Tamil, local languages	Sunni Muslim, Buddhist, Hindu, Christian, traditional beliefs	Ringgit
MALDIVES		298	115	318 000	Male	Divehi (Maldivian)	Sunni Muslim	Rufiyaa
MONGOLIA		1 565 000	604 250	2 594 000	Ulan Bator	Khalka (Mongolian), Kazakh, local languages	Buddhist, Sunni Muslim	Tugrik (tögrög)
MYANMAR		676 577	261 228	49 485 000	Rangoon	Burmese, Shan, Karen, local languages	Buddhist, Christian, Sunni Muslim	Kyat
NEPAL		147 181	56 827	25 164 000	Kathmandu	Nepali, Maithili, Bhojpuri, English, local languages	Hindu, Buddhist, Sunni Muslim	Nepalese rupee
NORTH KOREA		120 538	46 540	22 664 000	P'yŏngyang	Korean	Traditional beliefs, Chondoist, Buddhist	North Korean won
OMAN		309 500	119 499	2 851 000	Muscat	Arabic, Baluchi, Indian languages	Ibadhi Muslim, Sunni Muslim	Omani riyal
PAKISTAN		803 940	310 403	153 578 000	Islamabad	Urdu, Punjabi, Sindhi, Pushtu, English	Sunni Muslim, Shi'a Muslim, Christian, Hindu	Pakistani rupee
PALAU		497	192	20 000	Koror	Palauan, English	Roman Catholic, Protestant, traditional beliefs	United States dollar
PHILIPPINES		300 000	115 831	79 999 000	Manila	English, Pilipino, Cebuano, local languages	Roman Catholic, Protestant, Sunni Muslim, Aglipayan	Philippine peso
QATAR		11 437	4 416	610 000	Doha	Arabic	Sunni Muslim	Qatari riyal
RUSSIAN FEDERATION		17 075 400	6 592 849	143 246 000	Moscow	Russian, Tatar, Ukrainian, local languages	Russian Orthodox, Sunni Muslim, Protestant	Russian rouble
SAUDI ARABIA		2 200 000	849 425	24 217 000	Riyadh	Arabic	Sunni Muslim, Shi'a Muslim	Saudi Arabian riyal
SINGAPORE		639	247	4 253 000	Singapore	Chinese, English, Malay, Tamil	Buddhist, Taoist, Sunni Muslim, Christian, Hindu	Singapore dollar
SOUTH KOREA		99 274	38 330	47 700 000	Seoul	Korean	Buddhist, Protestant, Roman Catholic	South Korean won
SRI LANKA		65 610	25 332	19 065 000	Sri Jayewardenepura Kotte	Sinhalese, Tamil, English	Buddhist, Hindu, Sunni Muslim, Roman Catholic	Sri Lankan rupee
SYRIA		185 180	71 498	17 800 000	Damascus	Arabic, Kurdish, Armenian	Sunni Muslim, Shi'a Muslim, Christian	Syrian pound
TAIWAN		36 179	13 969	22 548 000	T'aipei	Mandarin, Min, Hakka, local languages	Buddhist, Taoist, Confucian, Christian	Taiwan dollar
TAJIKISTAN		143 100	55 251	6 245 000	Dushanbe	Tajik, Uzbek, Russian	Sunni Muslim	Somoni
THAILAND		513 115	198 115	62 833 000	Bangkok	Thai, Lao, Chinese, Malay, Mon-Khmer languages	Buddhist, Sunni Muslim	Baht
TURKEY		779 452	300 948	71 325 000	Ankara	Turkish, Kurdish	Sunni Muslim, Shi'a Muslim	Turkish lira
TURKMENISTAN		488 100	188 456	4 867 000	Ashgabat	Turkmen, Uzbek, Russian	Sunni Muslim, Russian Orthodox	Turkmen manat
UNITED ARAB EMIRATES		77 700	30 000	2 995 000	Abu Dhabi	Arabic, English	Sunni Muslim, Shi'a Muslim	United Arab Emirates dirham
UZBEKISTAN		447 400	172 742	26 093 000	Tashkent	Uzbek, Russian, Tajik, Kazakh	Sunni Muslim, Russian Orthodox	Uzbek som
VIETNAM		329 565	127 246	81 377 000	Ha Nôi	Vietnamese, Thai, Khmer, Chinese, local languages	Buddhist, Taoist, Roman Catholic, Cao Dai, Hoa Hao	Dong
YEMEN		527 968	203 850	20 010 000	San'ā'	Arabic	Sunni Muslim, Shi'a Muslim	Yemeni rial

Dependent and disputed territories		Territorial status	Area sq km	Area sq miles	Population	Capital	Languages	Religions	Currency
Christmas Island		Australian External Territory	135	52	1 560	The Settlement	English	Buddhist, Sunni Muslim, Protestant, Roman Catholic	Australian dollar
Cocos Islands		Australian External Territory	14	5	632	West Island	English	Sunni Muslim, Christian	Australian dollar
Gaza		Semi-autonomous region	363	140	1 203 591	Gaza	Arabic	Sunni Muslim, Shi'a Muslim	Israeli shekel
Jammu and Kashmir		Disputed territory (India/Pakistan)	222 236	85 806	13 000 000	Srinagar			
West Bank		Disputed territory	5 860	2 263	2 303 660		Arabic, Hebrew	Sunni Muslim, Jewish, Shi'a Muslim, Christian	Jordanian dinar, Israeli shekel

*Hong Kong dollar

Victoria Falls   1

Sinai Peninsula, Egypt   2

Africa		Area sq km	Area sq miles	Population	Capital	Languages	Religions	Currency
ALGERIA		2 381 741	919 595	31 800 000	Algiers	Arabic, French, Berber	Sunni Muslim	Algerian dinar
ANGOLA		1 246 700	481 354	13 625 000	Luanda	Portuguese, Bantu, local languages	Roman Catholic, Protestant, traditional beliefs	Kwanza
BENIN		112 620	43 483	6 736 000	Porto-Novo	French, Fon, Yoruba, Adja, local languages	Traditional beliefs, Roman Catholic, Sunni Muslim	CFA franc*
BOTSWANA		581 370	224 468	1 785 000	Gaborone	English, Setswana, Shona, local languages	Traditional beliefs, Protestant, Roman Catholic	Pula
BURKINA		274 200	105 869	13 002 000	Ouagadougou	French, Moore (Mossi), Fulani, local languages	Sunni Muslim, traditional beliefs, Roman Catholic	CFA franc*
BURUNDI		27 835	10 747	6 825 000	Bujumbura	Kirundi (Hutu, Tutsi), French	Roman Catholic, traditional beliefs, Protestant	Burundian franc
CAMEROON		475 442	183 569	16 018 000	Yaoundé	French, English, Fang, Bamileke, local languages	Roman Catholic, traditional beliefs, Sunni Muslim, Protestant	CFA franc*
CAPE VERDE		4 033	1 557	463 000	Praia	Portuguese, creole	Roman Catholic, Protestant	Cape Verde escudo
CENTRAL AFRICAN REPUBLIC		622 436	240 324	3 865 000	Bangui	French, Sango, Banda, Baya, local languages	Protestant, Roman Catholic, traditional beliefs, Sunni Muslim	CFA franc*
CHAD		1 284 000	495 755	8 598 000	Ndjamena	Arabic, French, Sara, local languages	Sunni Muslim, Roman Catholic, Protestant, traditional beliefs	CFA franc*
COMOROS		1 862	719	768 000	Moroni	Comorian, French, Arabic	Sunni Muslim, Roman Catholic	Comoros franc
CONGO		342 000	132 047	3 724 000	Brazzaville	French, Kongo, Monokutuba, local languages	Roman Catholic, Protestant, traditional beliefs, Sunni Muslim	CFA franc*
CONGO, DEMOCRATIC REP. OF		2 345 410	905 568	52 771 000	Kinshasa	French, Lingala, Swahili, Kongo, local languages	Christian, Sunni Muslim	Congolese franc
CÔTE D'IVOIRE		322 463	124 504	16 631 000	Yamoussoukro	French, creole, Akan, local languages	Sunni Muslim, Roman Catholic, traditional beliefs, Protestant	CFA franc*
DJIBOUTI		23 200	8 958	703 000	Djibouti	Somali, Afar, French, Arabic	Sunni Muslim, Christian	Djibouti franc
EGYPT		1 000 250	386 199	71 931 000	Cairo	Arabic	Sunni Muslim, Coptic Christian	Egyptian pound
EQUATORIAL GUINEA		28 051	10 831	494 000	Malabo	Spanish, French, Fang	Roman Catholic, traditional beliefs	CFA franc*
ERITREA		117 400	45 328	4 141 000	Asmara	Tigrinya, Tigre	Sunni Muslim, Coptic Christian	Nakfa
ETHIOPIA		1 133 880	437 794	70 678 000	Addis Ababa	Oromo, Amharic, Tigrinya, local languages	Ethiopian Orthodox, Sunni Muslim, traditional beliefs	Birr
GABON		267 667	103 347	1 329 000	Libreville	French, Fang, local languages	Roman Catholic, Protestant, traditional beliefs	CFA franc*
THE GAMBIA		11 295	4 361	1 426 000	Banjul	English, Malinke, Fulani, Wolof	Sunni Muslim, Protestant	Dalasi
GHANA		238 537	92 100	20 922 000	Accra	English, Hausa, Akan, local languages	Christian, Sunni Muslim, traditional beliefs	Cedi
GUINEA		245 857	94 926	8 480 000	Conakry	French, Fulani, Malinke, local languages	Sunni Muslim, traditional beliefs, Christian	Guinea franc
GUINEA-BISSAU		36 125	13 948	1 493 000	Bissau	Portuguese, crioulo, local languages	Traditional beliefs, Sunni Muslim, Christian	CFA franc*
KENYA		582 646	224 961	31 987 000	Nairobi	Swahili, English, local languages	Christian, traditional beliefs	Kenyan shilling
LESOTHO		30 355	11 720	1 802 000	Maseru	Sesotho, English, Zulu	Christian, traditional beliefs	Loti, S. African rand
LIBERIA		111 369	43 000	3 367 000	Monrovia	English, creole, local languages	Traditional beliefs, Christian, Sunni Muslim	Liberian dollar
LIBYA		1 759 540	679 362	5 551 000	Tripoli	Arabic, Berber	Sunni Muslim	Libyan dinar
MADAGASCAR		587 041	226 658	17 404 000	Antananarivo	Malagasy, French	Traditional beliefs, Christian, Sunni Muslim	Malagasy franc
MALAWI		118 484	45 747	12 105 000	Lilongwe	Chichewa, English, local languages	Christian, traditional beliefs, Sunni Muslim	Malawian kwacha
MALI		1 240 140	478 821	13 007 000	Bamako	French, Bambara, local languages	Sunni Muslim, traditional beliefs, Christian	CFA franc*
MAURITANIA		1 030 700	397 955	2 893 000	Nouakchott	Arabic, French, local languages	Sunni Muslim	Ouguiya
MAURITIUS		2 040	788	1 221 000	Port Louis	English, creole, Hindi, Bhojpurī, French	Hindu, Roman Catholic, Sunni Muslim	Mauritius rupee
MOROCCO		446 550	172 414	30 566 000	Rabat	Arabic, Berber, French	Sunni Muslim	Moroccan dirham
MOZAMBIQUE		799 380	308 642	18 863 000	Maputo	Portuguese, Makua, Tsonga, local languages	Traditional beliefs, Roman Catholic, Sunni Muslim	Metical
NAMIBIA		824 292	318 261	1 987 000	Windhoek	English, Afrikaans, German, Ovambo, local languages	Protestant, Roman Catholic	Namibian dollar
NIGER		1 267 000	489 191	11 972 000	Niamey	French, Hausa, Fulani, local languages	Sunni Muslim, traditional beliefs	CFA franc*
NIGERIA		923 768	356 669	124 009 000	Abuja	English, Hausa, Yoruba, Ibo, Fulani, local languages	Sunni Muslim, Christian, traditional beliefs	Naira
RWANDA		26 338	10 169	8 387 000	Kigali	Kinyarwanda, French, English	Roman Catholic, traditional beliefs, Protestant	Rwandan franc
SÃO TOMÉ AND PRÍNCIPE		964	372	161 000	São Tomé	Portuguese, creole	Roman Catholic, Protestant	Dobra
SENEGAL		196 720	75 954	10 095 000	Dakar	French, Wolof, Fulani, local languages	Sunni Muslim, Roman Catholic, traditional beliefs	CFA franc*
SEYCHELLES		455	176	81 000	Victoria	English, French, creole	Roman Catholic, Protestant	Seychelles rupee
SIERRA LEONE		71 740	27 699	4 971 000	Freetown	English, creole, Mende, Temne, local languages	Sunni Muslim, traditional beliefs	Leone
SOMALIA		637 657	246 201	9 890 000	Mogadishu	Somali, Arabic	Sunni Muslim	Somali shilling
SOUTH AFRICA, REPUBLIC OF		1 219 090	470 693	45 026 000	Pretoria/Cape Town	Afrikaans, English, nine official local languages	Protestant, Roman Catholic, Sunni Muslim, Hindu	Rand
SUDAN		2 505 813	967 500	33 610 000	Khartoum	Arabic, Dinka, Nubian, Beja, Nuer, local languages	Sunni Muslim, traditional beliefs, Christian	Sudanese dinar
SWAZILAND		17 364	6 704	1 077 000	Mbabane	Swazi, English	Christian, traditional beliefs	Emalangeni, South African rand
TANZANIA		945 087	364 900	36 977 000	Dodoma	Swahili, English, Nyamwezi, local languages	Shi'a Muslim, Sunni Muslim, traditional beliefs, Christian	Tanzanian shilling
TOGO		56 785	21 925	4 909 000	Lomé	French, Ewe, Kabre, local languages	Traditional beliefs, Christian, Sunni Muslim	CFA franc*
TUNISIA		164 150	63 379	9 832 000	Tunis	Arabic, French	Sunni Muslim	Tunisian dinar
UGANDA		241 038	93 065	25 827 000	Kampala	English, Swahili, Luganda, local languages	Roman Catholic, Protestant, Sunni Muslim, traditional beliefs	Ugandan shilling
ZAMBIA		752 614	290 586	10 812 000	Lusaka	English, Bemba, Nyanja, Tonga, local languages	Christian, traditional beliefs	Zambian kwacha
ZIMBABWE		390 759	150 873	12 891 000	Harare	English, Shona, Ndebele	Christian, traditional beliefs	Zimbabwean dollar

Dependent and disputed territories		Territorial status	Area sq km	Area sq km	Population	Capital	Languages	Religions	Currency
Canary Islands		Autonomous Community of Spain	7 447	2 875	1 694 477	Santa Cruz de Tenerife, Las Palmas	Spanish	Roman Catholic	Euro
Madeira		Autonomous Region of Portugal	779	301	242 603	Funchal	Portuguese	Roman Catholic, Protestant	Euro
Mayotte		French Territorial Collectivity	373	144	171 000	Dzaoudzi	French, Mahorian	Sunni Muslim, Christian	Euro
Réunion		French Overseas Department	2 551	985	756 000	St-Denis	French, creole	Roman Catholic	Euro
St Helena and Dependencies		United Kingdom Overseas Territory	121	47	5 644	Jamestown	English	Protestant, Roman Catholic	St Helena pound
Western Sahara		Disputed territory (Morocco)	266 000	102 703	308 000	Laâyoune	Arabic	Sunni Muslim	Moroccan dirham

*Communauté Financière Africaine franc

Sydney, Australia   1

Uluru (Ayers Rock), Australia   2

Oceania		Area sq km	Area sq miles	Population	Capital	Languages	Religions	Currency
AUSTRALIA		7 692 024	2 969 907	19 731 000	Canberra	English, Italian, Greek	Protestant, Roman Catholic, Orthodox	Australian dollar
FIJI		18 330	7 077	839 000	Suva	English, Fijian, Hindi	Christian, Hindu, Sunni Muslim	Fiji dollar
KIRIBATI		717	277	88 000	Bairiki	Gilbertese, English	Roman Catholic, Protestant	Australian dollar
MARSHALL ISLANDS		181	70	53 000	Delap-Uliga-Djarrit	English, Marshallese	Protestant, Roman Catholic	United States dollar
MICRONESIA, FEDERATED STATES OF		701	271	109 000	Palikir	English, Chuukese, Pohnpeian, local languages	Roman Catholic, Protestant	United States dollar
NAURU		21	8	13 000	Yaren	Nauruan, English	Protestant, Roman Catholic	Australian dollar
NEW ZEALAND		270 534	104 454	3 875 000	Wellington	English, Maori	Protestant, Roman Catholic	New Zealand dollar
PAPUA NEW GUINEA		462 840	178 704	5 711 000	Port Moresby	English, Tok Pisin (creole), local languages	Protestant, Roman Catholic, traditional beliefs	Kina
SAMOA		2 831	1 093	178 000	Apia	Samoan, English	Protestant, Roman Catholic	Tala
SOLOMON ISLANDS		28 370	10 954	477 000	Honiara	English, creole, local languages	Protestant, Roman Catholic	Solomon Islands dollar
TONGA		748	289	104 000	Nuku'alofa	Tongan, English	Protestant, Roman Catholic	Pa'anga
TUVALU		25	10	11 000	Vaiaku	Tuvaluan, English	Protestant	Australian dollar
VANUATU		12 190	4 707	212 000	Port Vila	English, Bislama (creole), French	Protestant, Roman Catholic, traditional beliefs	Vatu

Dependent territories		Territorial status	Area sq km	Area sq miles	Population	Capital	Languages	Religions	Currency
American Samoa		United States Unincorporated Territory	197	76	67 000	Fagatoga	Samoan, English	Protestant, Roman Catholic	United States dollar
Cook Islands		Self-governing New Zealand Territory	293	113	18 000	Avarua	English, Maori	Protestant, Roman Catholic	New Zealand dollar
French Polynesia		French Overseas Territory	3 265	1 261	244 000	Papeete	French, Tahitian, Polynesian languages	Protestant, Roman Catholic	CFP franc*
Guam		United States Unincorporated Territory	541	209	163 000	Hagåtña	Chamorro, English, Tapalog	Roman Catholic	United States dollar
New Caledonia		French Overseas Territory	19 058	7 358	228 000	Nouméa	French, local languages	Roman Catholic, Protestant, Sunni Muslim	CFP franc*
Niue		Self-governing New Zealand Territory	258	100	2 000	Alofi	English, Polynesian	Christian	New Zealand dollar
Norfolk Island		Australian External Territory	35	14	2 037	Kingston	English	Protestant, Roman Catholic	Australian Dollar
Northern Mariana Islands		United States Commonwealth	477	184	79 000	Capitol Hill	English, Chamorro, local languages	Roman Catholic	United States dollar
Pitcairn Islands		United Kingdom Overseas Territory	45	17	51	Adamstown	English	Protestant	New Zealand dollar
Tokelau		New Zealand Overseas Territory	10	4	2 000		English, Tokelauan	Christian	New Zealand dollar
Wallis and Futuna Islands		French Overseas Territory	274	106	15 000	Matā'utu	French, Wallisian, Futunian	Roman Catholic	CFP franc*

*Franc des Comptoirs Français du Pacifique

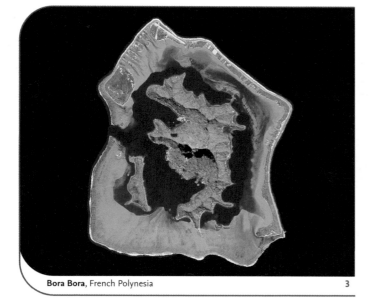

Bora Bora, French Polynesia   3

Mount Cook, New Zealand   4

The Pentagon, Washington DC, USA   5

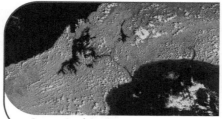

Panama Canal, Panama   6

Cuba, Caribbean Sea   7

North America

North America	Area sq km	Area sq miles	Population	Capital	Languages	Religions	Currency
ANTIGUA AND BARBUDA	442	171	73 000	St John's	English, creole	Protestant, Roman Catholic	East Caribbean dollar
THE BAHAMAS	13 939	5 382	314 000	Nassau	English, creole	Protestant, Roman Catholic	Bahamian dollar
BARBADOS	430	166	270 000	Bridgetown	English, creole	Protestant, Roman Catholic	Barbados dollar
BELIZE	22 965	8 867	256 000	Belmopan	English, Spanish, Mayan, creole	Roman Catholic, Protestant	Belize dollar
CANADA	9 984 670	3 855 103	31 510 000	Ottawa	English, French	Roman Catholic, Protestant, Eastern Orthodox, Jewish	Canadian dollar
COSTA RICA	51 100	19 730	4 173 000	San José	Spanish	Roman Catholic, Protestant	Costa Rican colón
CUBA	110 860	42 803	11 300 000	Havana	Spanish	Roman Catholic, Protestant	Cuban peso
DOMINICA	750	290	79 000	Roseau	English, creole	Roman Catholic, Protestant	East Caribbean dollar
DOMINICAN REPUBLIC	48 442	18 704	8 745 000	Santo Domingo	Spanish, creole	Roman Catholic, Protestant	Dominican peso
EL SALVADOR	21 041	8 124	6 515 000	San Salvador	Spanish	Roman Catholic, Protestant	El Salvador colón, United States dollar
GRENADA	378	146	80 000	St George's	English, creole	Roman Catholic, Protestant	East Caribbean dollar
GUATEMALA	108 890	42 043	12 347 000	Guatemala City	Spanish, Mayan languages	Roman Catholic, Protestant	Quetzal, United States dollar
HAITI	27 750	10 714	8 326 000	Port-au-Prince	French, creole	Roman Catholic, Protestant, Voodoo	Gourde
HONDURAS	112 088	43 277	6 941 000	Tegucigalpa	Spanish, Amerindian languages	Roman Catholic, Protestant	Lempira
JAMAICA	10 991	4 244	2 651 000	Kingston	English, creole	Protestant, Roman Catholic	Jamaican dollar
MEXICO	1 972 545	761 604	103 457 000	Mexico City	Spanish, Amerindian languages	Roman Catholic, Protestant	Mexican peso
NICARAGUA	130 000	50 193	5 466 000	Managua	Spanish, Amerindian languages	Roman Catholic, Protestant	Córdoba
PANAMA	77 082	29 762	3 120 000	Panama City	Spanish, English, Amerindian languages	Roman Catholic, Protestant, Sunni Muslim	Balboa
ST KITTS AND NEVIS	261	101	42 000	Basseterre	English, creole	Protestant, Roman Catholic	East Caribbean dollar
ST LUCIA	616	238	149 000	Castries	English, creole	Roman Catholic, Protestant	East Caribbean dollar
ST VINCENT AND THE GRENADINES	389	150	120 000	Kingstown	English, creole	Protestant, Roman Catholic	East Caribbean dollar
TRINIDAD AND TOBAGO	5 130	1 981	1 303 000	Port of Spain	English, creole, Hindi	Roman Catholic, Hindu, Protestant, Sunni Muslim	Trinidad and Tobago dollar
UNITED STATES OF AMERICA	9 826 635	3 794 085	294 043 000	Washington DC	English, Spanish	Protestant, Roman Catholic, Sunni Muslim, Jewish	United States dollar

Dependent territories	Territorial status	Area sq km	Area sq miles	Population	Capital	Languages	Religions	Currency
Anguilla	United Kingdom Overseas Territory	155	60	12 000	The Valley	English	Protestant, Roman Catholic	East Caribbean dollar
Aruba	Self-governing Netherlands Territory	193	75	100 000	Oranjestad	Papiamento, Dutch, English	Roman Catholic, Protestant	Arubian florin
Bermuda	United Kingdom Overseas Territory	54	21	82 000	Hamilton	English	Protestant, Roman Catholic	Bermuda dollar
Cayman Islands	United Kingdom Overseas Territory	259	100	40 000	George Town	English	Protestant, Roman Catholic	Cayman Islands dollar
Greenland	Self-governing Danish Territory	2 175 600	840 004	57 000	Nuuk	Greenlandic, Danish	Protestant	Danish krone
Guadeloupe	French Overseas Department	1 780	687	440 000	Basse-Terre	French, creole	Roman Catholic	Euro
Martinique	French Overseas Department	1 079	417	393 000	Fort-de-France	French, creole	Roman Catholic, traditional beliefs	Euro
Montserrat	United Kingdom Overseas Territory	100	39	4 000	Plymouth	English	Protestant, Roman Catholic	East Caribbean dollar
Netherlands Antilles	Self-governing Netherlands Territory	800	309	221 000	Willemstad	Dutch, Papiamento, English	Roman Catholic, Protestant	Netherlands guilder
Puerto Rico	United States Commonwealth	9 104	3 515	3 879 000	San Juan	Spanish, English	Roman Catholic, Protestant	United States dollar
St Pierre and Miquelon	French Territorial Collectivity	242	93	6 000	St-Pierre	French	Roman Catholic	Euro
Turks and Caicos Islands	United Kingdom Overseas Territory	430	166	21 000	Grand Turk	English	Protestant	United States dollar
Virgin Islands (U.K.)	United Kingdom Overseas Territory	153	59	21 000	Road Town	English	Protestant, Roman Catholic	United States dollar
Virgin Islands (U.S.A.)	United States Unincorporated Territory	352	136	111 000	Charlotte Amalie	English, Spanish	Protestant, Roman Catholic	United States dollar

South America

South America	Area sq km	Area sq miles	Population	Capital	Languages	Religions	Currency
ARGENTINA	2 766 889	1 068 302	38 428 000	Buenos Aires	Spanish, Italian, Amerindian languages	Roman Catholic, Protestant	Argentinian peso
BOLIVIA	1 098 581	424 164	8 808 000	La Paz/Sucre	Spanish, Quechua, Aymara	Roman Catholic, Protestant, Baha'i	Boliviano
BRAZIL	8 514 879	3 287 613	178 470 000	Brasília	Portuguese	Roman Catholic, Protestant	Real
CHILE	756 945	292 258	15 805 000	Santiago	Spanish, Amerindian languages	Roman Catholic, Protestant	Chilean peso
COLOMBIA	1 141 748	440 831	44 222 000	Bogotá	Spanish, Amerindian languages	Roman Catholic, Protestant	Colombian peso
ECUADOR	272 045	105 037	13 003 000	Quito	Spanish, Quechua, other Amerindian languages	Roman Catholic	US dollar
GUYANA	214 969	83 000	765 000	Georgetown	English, creole, Amerindian languages	Protestant, Hindu, Roman Catholic, Sunni Muslim	Guyana dollar
PARAGUAY	406 752	157 048	5 878 000	Asunción	Spanish, Guaraní	Roman Catholic, Protestant	Guaraní
PERU	1 285 216	496 225	27 167 000	Lima	Spanish, Quechua, Aymara	Roman Catholic, Protestant	Sol
SURINAME	163 820	63 251	436 000	Paramaribo	Dutch, Surinamese, English, Hindi	Hindu, Roman Catholic, Protestant, Sunni Muslim	Suriname guilder
URUGUAY	176 215	68 037	3 415 000	Montevideo	Spanish	Roman Catholic, Protestant, Jewish	Uruguayan peso
VENEZUELA	912 050	352 144	25 699 000	Caracas	Spanish, Amerindian languages	Roman Catholic, Protestant	Bolívar

Dependent territories	Territorial status	Area sq km	Area sq miles	Population	Capital	Languages	Religions	Currency
Falkland Islands	United Kingdom Overseas Territory	12 170	4 699	3 000	Stanley	English	Protestant, Roman Catholic	Falkland Islands pound
French Guiana	French Overseas Department	90 000	34 749	178 000	Cayenne	French, creole	Roman Catholic	Euro

The current pattern of the world's countries and territories is a result of a long history of exploration, colonialism, conflict and politics. The fact that there are currently 193 independent countries in the world – the most recent, East Timor, only being created in May 2002 – illustrates the significant political changes which have occurred since 1950 when there were only eighty two. There has been a steady progression away from colonial influences over the last fifty years, although many dependent overseas territories remain.

The shapes of countries and the pattern of international boundaries reflect both physical and political processes. Some borders follow natural features – rivers, mountain ranges, etc – others are defined according to political agreement or as a result of war. Some are still subject to dispute between two or more countries, and many remain undefined on the ground.

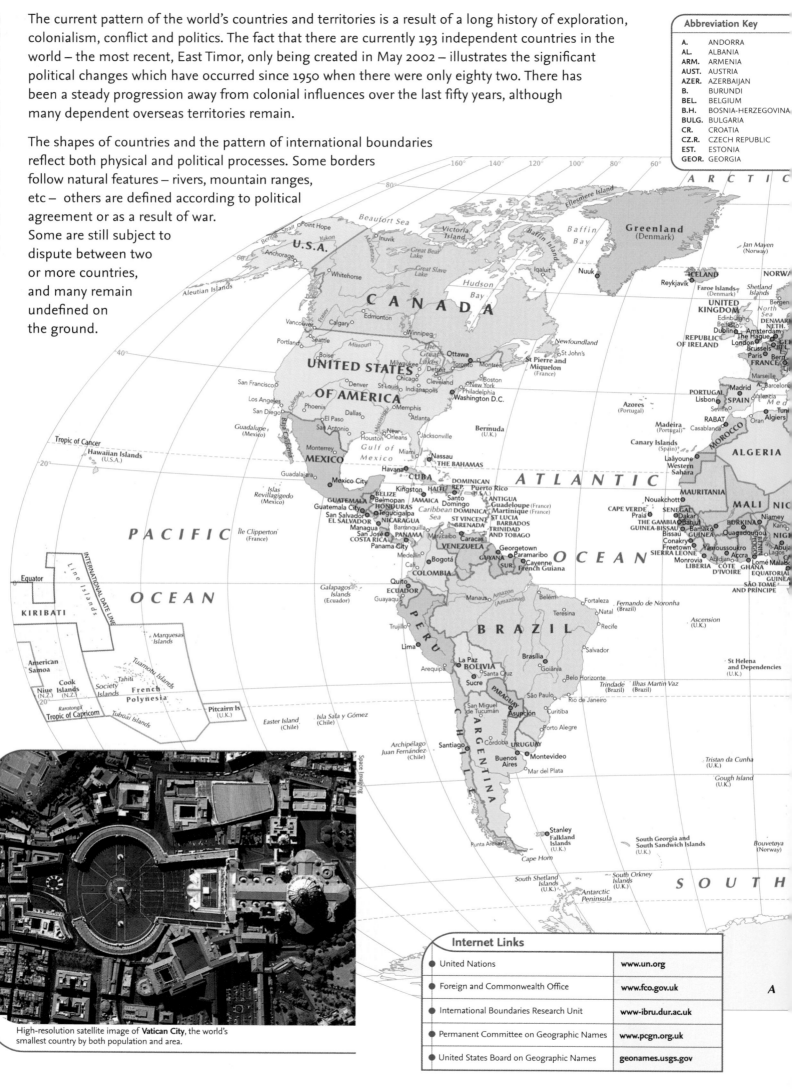

High-resolution satellite image of **Vatican City**, the world's smallest country by both population and area.

Internet Links	
● United Nations	**www.un.org**
● Foreign and Commonwealth Office	**www.fco.gov.uk**
● International Boundaries Research Unit	**www.ibru.dur.ac.uk**
● Permanent Committee on Geographic Names	**www.pcgn.org.uk**
● United States Board on Geographic Names	**geonames.usgs.gov**

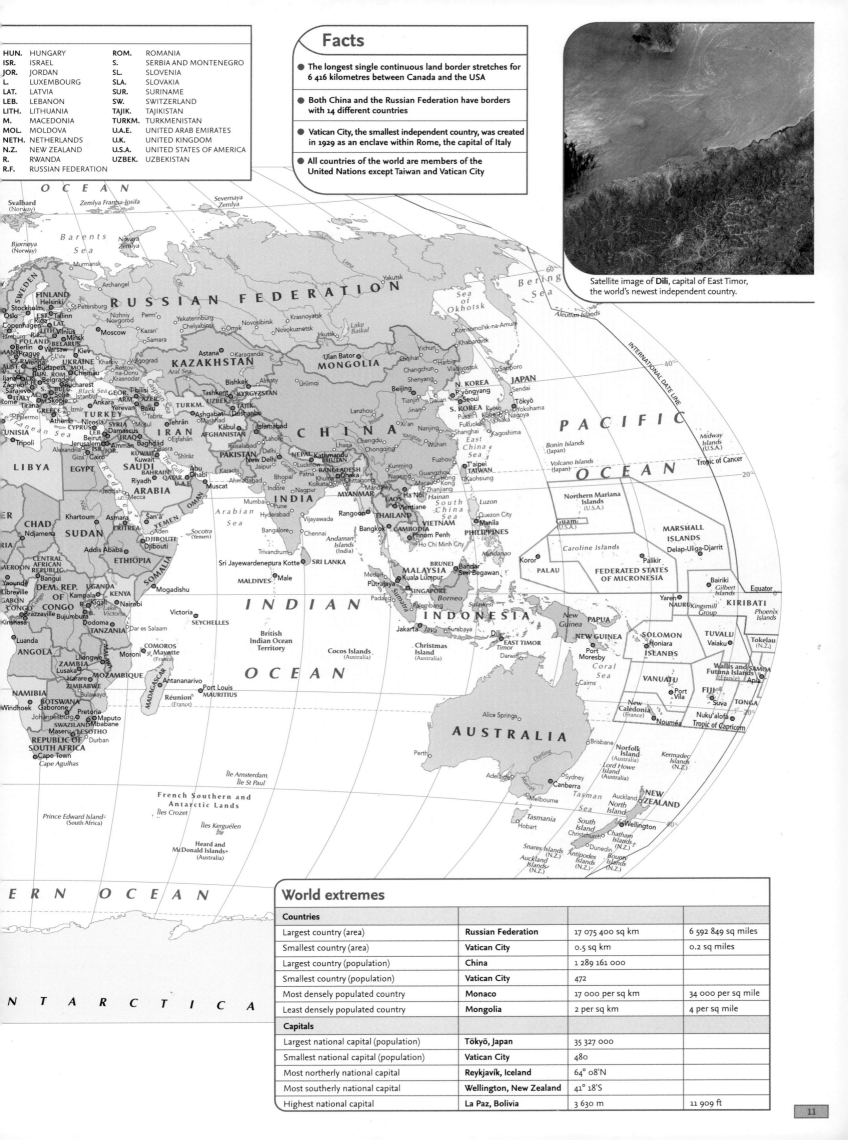

HUN.	HUNGARY	ROM.	ROMANIA	
ISR.	ISRAEL	S.	SERBIA AND MONTENEGRO	
JOR.	JORDAN	SL.	SLOVENIA	
L.	LUXEMBOURG	SLA.	SLOVAKIA	
LAT.	LATVIA	SUR.	SURINAME	
LEB.	LEBANON	SW.	SWITZERLAND	
LITH.	LITHUANIA	TAJIK.	TAJIKISTAN	
M.	MACEDONIA	TURKM.	TURKMENISTAN	
MOL.	MOLDOVA	U.A.E.	UNITED ARAB EMIRATES	
NETH.	NETHERLANDS	U.K.	UNITED KINGDOM	
N.Z.	NEW ZEALAND	U.S.A.	UNITED STATES OF AMERICA	
R.	RWANDA	UZBEK.	UZBEKISTAN	
R.F.	RUSSIAN FEDERATION			

Facts

● The longest single continuous land border stretches for 6 416 kilometres between Canada and the USA

● Both China and the Russian Federation have borders with 14 different countries

● Vatican City, the smallest independent country, was created in 1929 as an enclave within Rome, the capital of Italy

● All countries of the world are members of the United Nations except Taiwan and Vatican City

Satellite image of **Dili**, capital of East Timor, the world's newest independent country.

World extremes

Countries			
Largest country (area)	**Russian Federation**	17 075 400 sq km	6 592 849 sq miles
Smallest country (area)	**Vatican City**	0.5 sq km	0.2 sq miles
Largest country (population)	**China**	1 289 161 000	
Smallest country (population)	**Vatican City**	472	
Most densely populated country	**Monaco**	17 000 per sq km	34 000 per sq mile
Least densely populated country	**Mongolia**	2 per sq km	4 per sq mile
Capitals			
Largest national capital (population)	**Tōkyō, Japan**	35 327 000	
Smallest national capital (population)	**Vatican City**	480	
Most northerly national capital	**Reykjavík, Iceland**	64° 08'N	
Most southerly national capital	**Wellington, New Zealand**	41° 18'S	
Highest national capital	**La Paz, Bolivia**	3 630 m	11 909 ft

The earth's physical features, both on land and on the sea bed, closely reflect its geological structure. The current shapes of the continents and oceans have evolved over millions of years. Movements of the tectonic plates which make up the earth's crust have created some of the best-known and most spectacular features. The processes which have shaped the earth continue today with earthquakes, volcanoes, erosion, climatic variations and man's activities all affecting the earth's landscapes.

The total topographic range of the earth's surface is nearly 20 000 metres, from the highest point Mount Everest, to the lowest point in the Mariana Trench. Major mountain ranges include the Himalaya, the Andes and the Rocky Mountains, each of which give rise to some of the world's greatest rivers. In contrast, the deserts of the Sahara, Australia, the Arabian Peninsula and the Gobi cover vast areas and each provide unique landscapes.

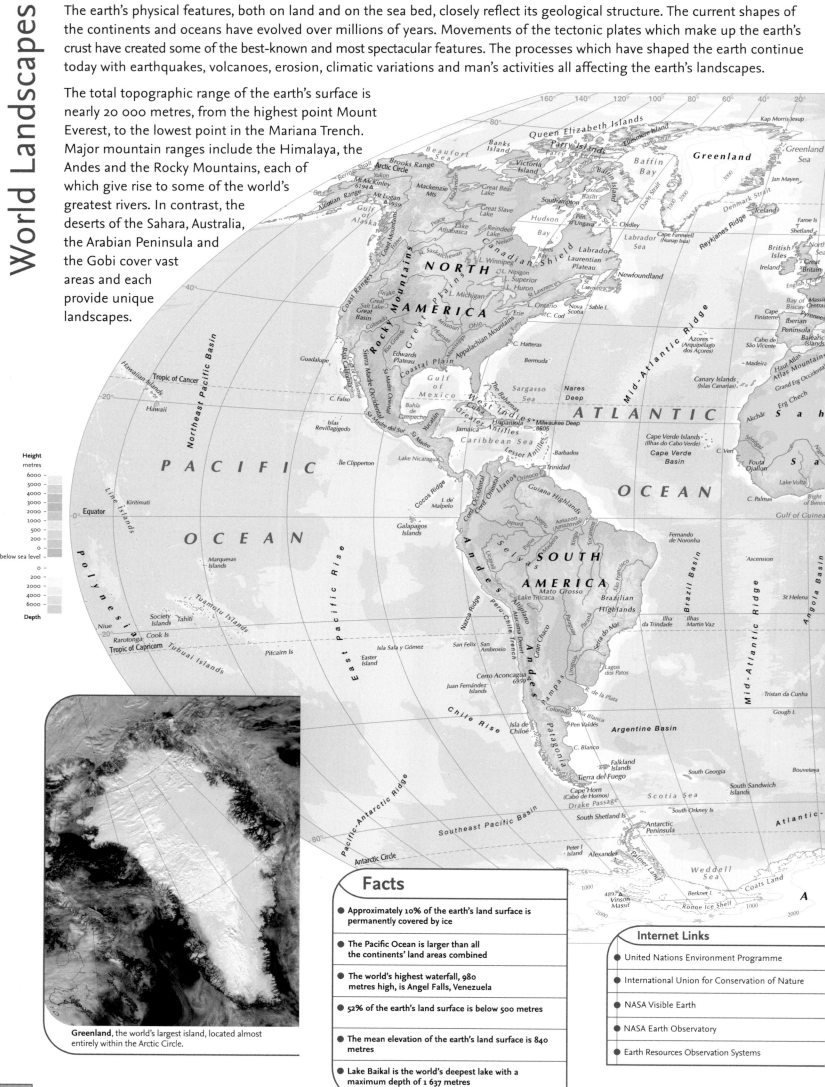

Greenland, the world's largest island, located almost entirely within the Arctic Circle.

Facts

- Approximately 10% of the earth's land surface is permanently covered by ice

- The Pacific Ocean is larger than all the continents' land areas combined

- The world's highest waterfall, 980 metres high, is Angel Falls, Venezuela

- 52% of the earth's land surface is below 500 metres

- The mean elevation of the earth's land surface is 840 metres

- Lake Baikal is the world's deepest lake with a maximum depth of 1 637 metres

Internet Links

- United Nations Environment Programme
- International Union for Conservation of Nature
- NASA Visible Earth
- NASA Earth Observatory
- Earth Resources Observation Systems

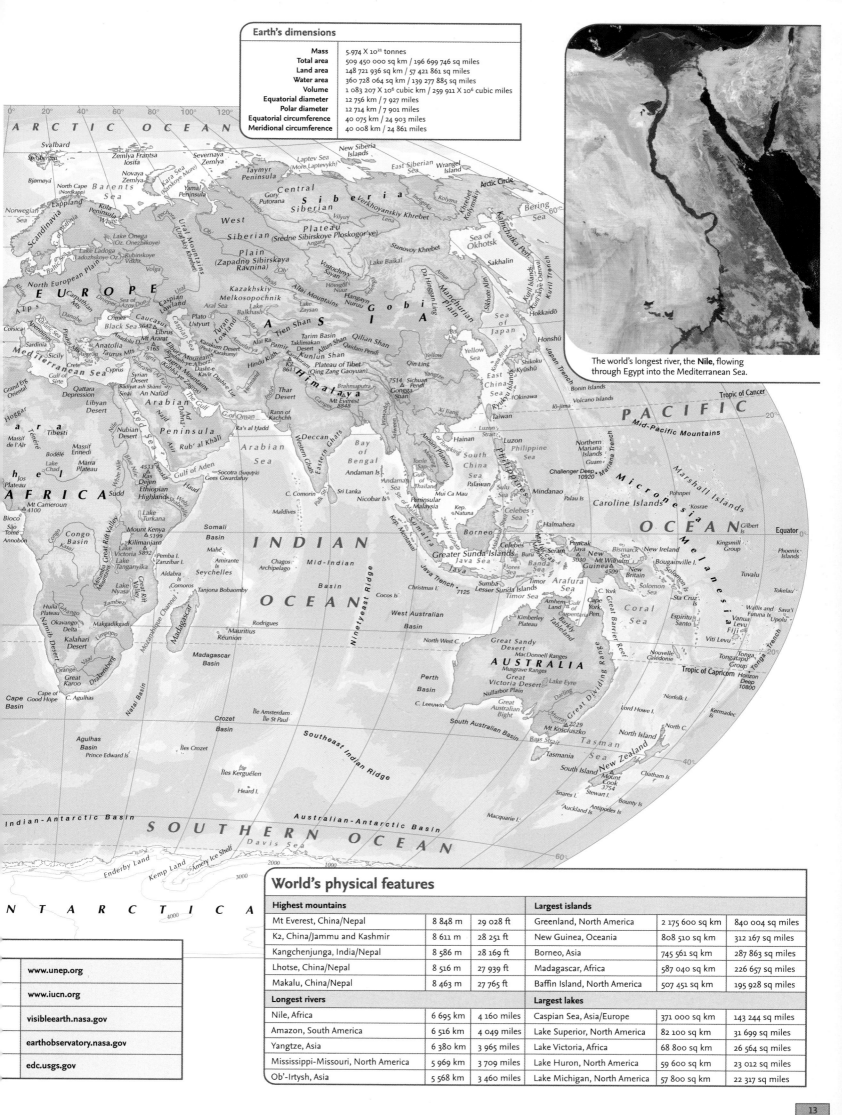

Mass	5.974 X 10²¹ tonnes
Total area	509 450 000 sq km / 196 699 746 sq miles
Land area	148 721 936 sq km / 57 421 861 sq miles
Water area	360 728 064 sq km / 139 277 885 sq miles
Volume	1 083 207 X 10⁶ cubic km / 259 911 X 10⁶ cubic miles
Equatorial diameter	12 756 km / 7 927 miles
Polar diameter	12 714 km / 7 901 miles
Equatorial circumference	40 075 km / 24 903 miles
Meridional circumference	40 008 km / 24 861 miles

The world's longest river, the **Nile**, flowing through Egypt into the Mediterranean Sea.

www.unep.org

www.iucn.org

visibleearth.nasa.gov

earthobservatory.nasa.gov

edc.usgs.gov

World's physical features

Highest mountains			Largest islands		
Mt Everest, China/Nepal	8 848 m	29 028 ft	Greenland, North America	2 175 600 sq km	840 004 sq miles
K2, China/Jammu and Kashmir	8 611 m	28 251 ft	New Guinea, Oceania	808 510 sq km	312 167 sq miles
Kangchenjunga, India/Nepal	8 586 m	28 169 ft	Borneo, Asia	745 561 sq km	287 863 sq miles
Lhotse, China/Nepal	8 516 m	27 939 ft	Madagascar, Africa	587 040 sq km	226 657 sq miles
Makalu, China/Nepal	8 463 m	27 765 ft	Baffin Island, North America	507 451 sq km	195 928 sq miles
Longest rivers			**Largest lakes**		
Nile, Africa	6 695 km	4 160 miles	Caspian Sea, Asia/Europe	371 000 sq km	143 244 sq miles
Amazon, South America	6 516 km	4 049 miles	Lake Superior, North America	82 100 sq km	31 699 sq miles
Yangtze, Asia	6 380 km	3 965 miles	Lake Victoria, Africa	68 800 sq km	26 564 sq miles
Mississippi-Missouri, North America	5 969 km	3 709 miles	Lake Huron, North America	59 600 sq km	23 012 sq miles
Ob'-Irtysh, Asia	5 568 km	3 460 miles	Lake Michigan, North America	57 800 sq km	22 317 sq miles

Earthquakes and volcanoes hold a constant fascination because of their power, their beauty, and the fact that they cannot be controlled or accurately predicted. Our understanding of these phenomena relies mainly on the theory of plate tectonics. This defines the earth's surface as a series of 'plates' which are constantly moving relative to each other, at rates of a few centimetres per year. As plates move against each other enormous pressure builds up and when the rocks can no longer bear this pressure they fracture, and energy is released as an earthquake. The pressures involved can also melt the rock to form magma which then rises to the earth's surface to form a volcano.

The distribution of earthquakes and volcanoes therefore relates closely to plate boundaries. In particular, most active volcanoes and much of the earth's seismic activity are centred on the 'Ring of Fire' around the Pacific Ocean.

Facts

- Over 900 earthquakes of magnitude 5.0 or greater occur every year
- An earthquake of magnitude 8.0 releases energy equivalent to 1 billion tons of TNT explosive
- Ground shaking during an earthquake in Alaska in 1964 lasted for 3 minutes
- Indonesia has more than 120 volcanoes and over 30% of the world's active volcanoes
- Volcanoes can produce very fertile soil and important industrial materials and chemicals

Earthquakes

Earthquakes are caused by movement along fractures or 'faults' in the earth's crust, particularly along plate boundaries. There are three types of plate boundary: constructive boundaries where plates are moving apart; destructive boundaries where two or more plates collide; conservative boundaries where plates slide past each other. Destructive and conservative boundaries are the main sources of earthquake activity.

The epicentre of an earthquake is the point on the earth's surface directly above its source. If this is near to large centres of population, and the earthquake is powerful, major devastation can result. The size, or magnitude, of an earthquake is generally measured on the Richter Scale.

Deadliest earthquakes, 1900–2003

Year	Location	Deaths
1905	**Kangra**, India	19 000
1907	west of **Dushanbe**, Tajikistan	12 000
1908	**Messina**, Italy	110 000
1915	**Abruzzo**, Italy	35 000
1917	**Bali**, Indonesia	15 000
1920	**Ningxia Province**, China	200 000
1923	**Tōkyō**, Japan	142 807
1927	**Qinghai Province**, China	200 000
1932	**Gansu Province**, China	70 000
1933	**Sichuan Province**, China	10 000
1934	**Nepal/India**	10 700
1935	**Quetta**, Pakistan	30 000
1939	**Chillán**, Chile	28 000
1939	**Erzincan**, Turkey	32 700
1948	**Ashgabat**, Turkmenistan	19 800
1962	**Northwest Iran**	12 225
1970	**Huánuco Province**, Peru	66 794
1974	**Yunnan** and **Sichuan Provinces**, China	20 000
1975	**Liaoning Province**, China	10 000
1976	central **Guatemala**	22 778
1976	**Hebei Province**, China	255 000
1978	**Khorāsān Province**, Iran	20 000
1980	**Ech Chélif**, Algeria	11 000
1988	**Spitak**, Armenia	25 000
1990	**Manjil**, Iran	50 000
1999	**Kocaeli (İzmit)**, Turkey	17 000
2001	**Gujarat**, India	20 000
2003	**Bam**, Iran	26 271

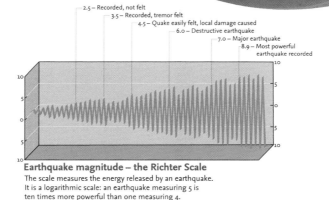

2.5 – Recorded, not felt
3.5 – Recorded, tremor felt
4.5 – Quake easily felt, local damage caused
6.0 – Destructive earthquake
7.0 – Major earthquake
8.9 – Most powerful earthquake recorded

Earthquake magnitude – the Richter Scale

The scale measures the energy released by an earthquake. It is a logarithmic scale: an earthquake measuring 5 is ten times more powerful than one measuring 4.

Extensive damage caused by major earthquake centred on **Bam, Iran** in December 2003.

Labels on globe (first map): Mt St Helens, Kilauea, El Chichónal, Guatemala, Soufrière Hills, Nevado del Ruiz, Galeras, Huánuco, Chillán, Volcán Llaima

NORTH AMERICAN PLATE
PACIFIC PLATE
COCOS PLATE
CARIBBEAN PLATE
SOUTH AMERICAN PLATE
NAZCA PLATE
SCOTIA PLATE

Labels on globe (second map): Ech Chélif
SOUTH AMERICAN PLATE

- ⊕ Deadliest earthquake
- ● Earthquake of magnitude 7.5 or greater
- ○ Earthquake of magnitude 5.5 – 7.4
- ▲ Major volcano
- ▲ Other volcano

Volcanoes

The majority of volcanoes occur along destructive plate boundaries in the 'subduction zone' where one plate passes under another. The friction and pressure causes the rock to melt and to form magma which is forced upwards to the earth's surface where it erupts as molten rock (lava) or as particles of ash or cinder. This process created the numerous volcanoes in the Andes, where the Nazca Plate is passing under the South American Plate. Volcanoes can be defined by the nature of the material they emit. 'Shield' volcanoes have extensive, gentle slopes formed from free-flowing lava, while steep-sided 'continental' volcanoes are created from thicker, slow-flowing lava and ash.

Lava flow from **Mt Etna, Sicily, Italy** threatens the town of Zafferana Etnea.

Major volcanic eruptions, 1980–2002

Volcano	Country	Date
Mt St Helens	USA	1980
El Chichónal	Mexico	1982
Gunung Galunggung	Indonesia	1982
Kilauea	Hawaii	1983
Ō-yama	Japan	1983
Nevado del Ruiz	Colombia	1985
Mt Pinatubo	Philippines	1991
Unzen-dake	Japan	1991
Mayon	Philippines	1993
Galeras	Colombia	1993
Volcán Llaima	Chile	1994
Rabaul	Papua New Guinea	1994
Soufrière Hills	Montserrat	1997
Hekla	Iceland	2000
Mt Etna	Italy	2001
Nyiragongo	Democratic Republic of Congo	2002

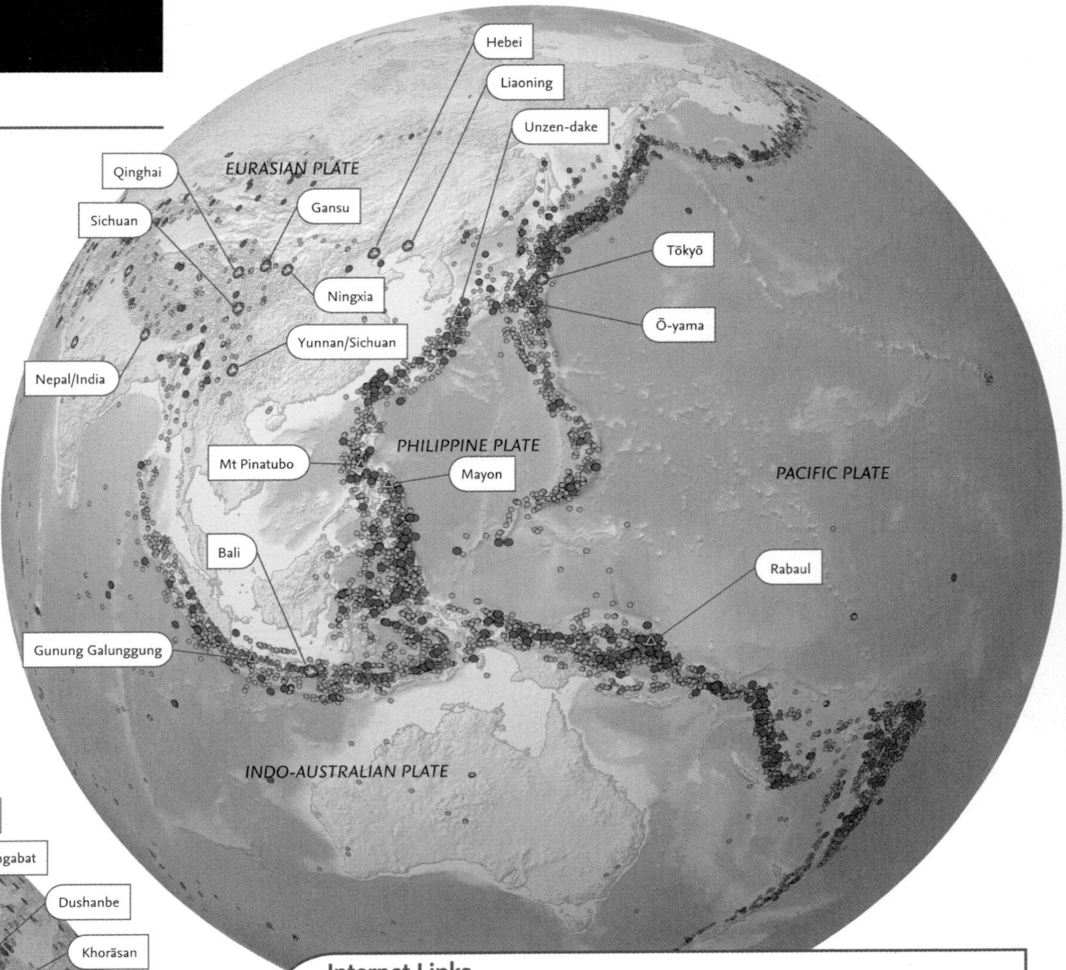

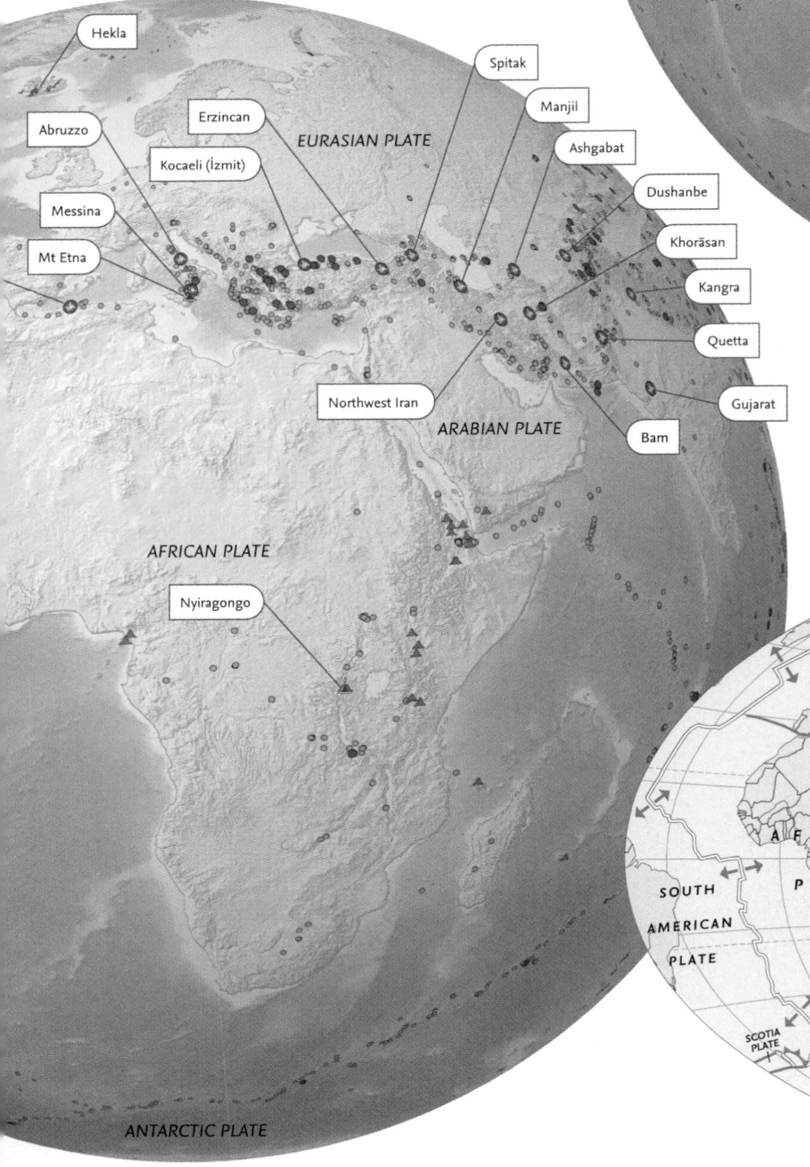

Internet Links

●	USGS National Earthquake Information Center	neic.usgs.gov
●	USGS Volcano Information	volcanoes.usgs.gov
●	British Geological Survey	www.bgs.ac.uk
●	NASA Natural Hazards	earthobservatory.nasa.gov/NaturalHazards
●	Volcano World	volcano.und.nodak.edu

Plate boundaries

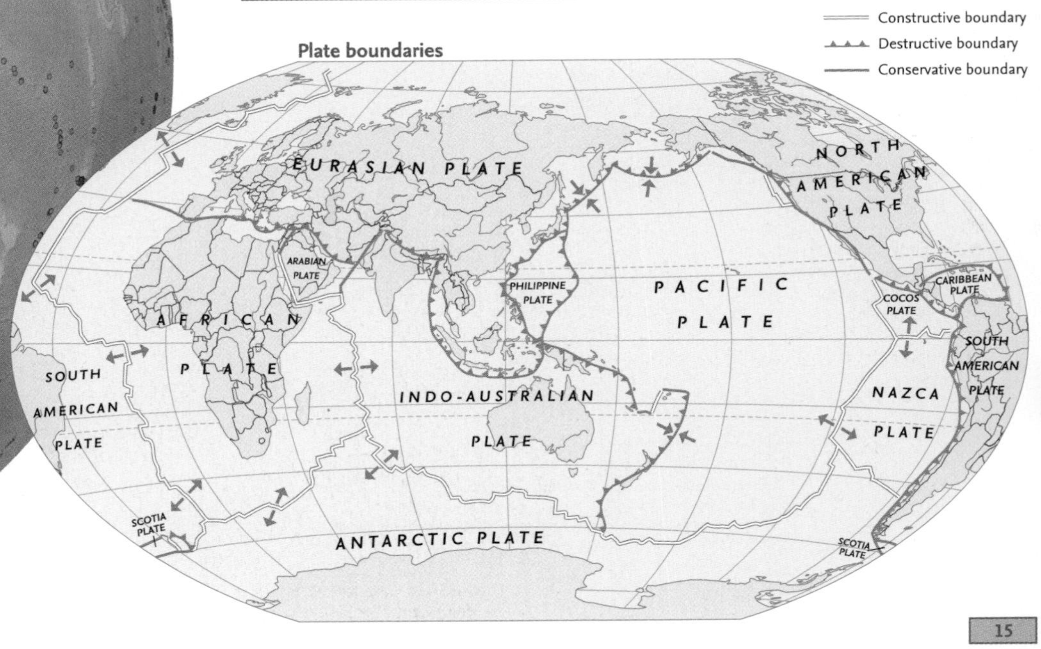

Constructive boundary
Destructive boundary
Conservative boundary

The climate of a region is defined by its long-term prevailing weather conditions. Classification of Climate Types is based on the relationship between temperature and humidity and how these factors are affected by latitude, altitude, ocean currents and winds. Weather is the specific short term condition which occurs locally and consists of events such as thunderstorms, hurricanes, blizzards and heat waves. Temperature and rainfall data recorded at weather stations can be plotted graphically and the graphs shown here, typical of each climate region, illustrate the various combinations of temperature and rainfall which exist worldwide for each month of the year. Data used for climate graphs are based on average monthly figures recorded over a minimum period of thirty years.

World Statistics: see pages 154–160

Tropical storm Dina, January 2002, northeast of Mauritius and Réunion, Indian Ocean.

Weather extremes

Highest recorded temperature	**57.8°C/136°F** Al'Azīzīyah, Libya (September 1922)
Hottest place - annual mean	**34.4°C/93.6°F** Dalol, Ethiopia
Driest place - annual mean	**0.1mm/0.004 inches** Atacama Desert, Chile
Most sunshine - annual mean	**90%** Yuma, Arizona, USA (over 4000 hours)
Lowest recorded temperature	**-89.2°C/-128.6°F** Vostok Station, Antarctica (July 1983)
Coldest place - annual mean	**-56.6°C/-69.9°F** Plateau Station, Antarctica
Wettest place annual mean	**11 873 mm/467.4 inches** Meghalaya, India
Greatest snowfall	**31 102 mm/1 224.5 inches** Mount Rainier, Washington, USA (February 1971 – February 1972)
Windiest place	**322 km per hour/200 miles per hour** (in gales) Commonwealth Bay, Antarctica

Facts

- Arctic Sea ice thickness has declined 4% in the last 40 years
- 2001 marked the end of the La Niña episode
- Sea levels are rising by one centimetre per decade
- Precipitation in the northern hemisphere is increasing
- Droughts have increased in frequency and intensity in parts of Asia and Africa

Climate change

In 2001 the global mean temperature was 0.63°C higher than that at the end of the nineteenth century. Most of this warming is caused by human activities which result in a build-up of greenhouse gases, mainly carbon dioxide, allowing heat to be trapped within the atmosphere. Carbon dioxide emissions have increased since the beginning of the industrial revolution due to burning of fossil fuels, increased urbanization, population growth, deforestation and industrial pollution. Annual climate indicators such as number of frost-free days, length of growing season, heat wave frequency, number of wet days, length of dry spells and frequency of weather extremes are used to monitor climate change. The map highlights some events of 2001 which indicate climate change. Until carbon dioxide emissions are reduced it is likely that this trend will continue.

❶ Warmest winter recorded in **Alaska and Yukon**.
❷ Third warmest year on record in **Canada**.
❸ Severe rainfall deficit in **northwest USA**.
❹ Costliest storm in US history was tropical storm **Alison**.
❺ Extreme summer drought in **Central America**.
❻ Strongest hurricane to hit Cuba since 1952 was **Michelle**.

⓮ Continued drought in area around **Horn of Africa**.
⓯ Widespread minimum winter temperatures near -60°C in **Siberia and Mongolia**.
⓰ 1998 drought continues in **Southern Asia**.
⓱ Severe drought and water shortages in **Northern China, Korean Peninsula and Japan**.
⓲ Extensive flooding in September caused by Typhoon **Nari**.
⓳ Severe flooding August to October in **Vietnam and Cambodia**.

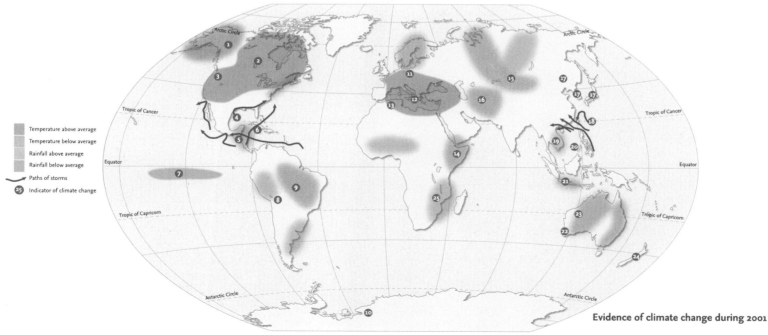

▢	Temperature above average
▢	Temperature below average
▢	Rainfall above average
▢	Rainfall below average
⌒	Paths of storms
㉕	Indicator of climate change

Evidence of climate change during 2001

❼ End of **La Niña** episode.
❽ Severe flooding in **Bolivia**.
❾ Normal rainy season hit by drought in **Brazil**.
❿ Longer lasting ozone hole than previous years in **Antarctica**.
⓫ Worst flooding since 1997 in **southwest Poland and Czech Republic**.
⓬ Temperatures 1°–2°C above average for 2001 in **Europe and Middle East**.
⓭ Severe November flooding in **Algeria**.

⓴ Severe flooding causes more than 400 deaths when four tropical cyclones, **Durian, Yutu, Ulor and Toraji** made landfall in July.
㉑ Major flooding in February on **Java**.
㉒ Driest summer on record in **Perth**.
㉓ Cooler and wetter than normal in **Western Australia**.
㉔ One of the driest summers recorded in **New Zealand**.
㉕ Severe flooding February to April in **Mozambique, Zambia, Malawi and Zimbabwe**.

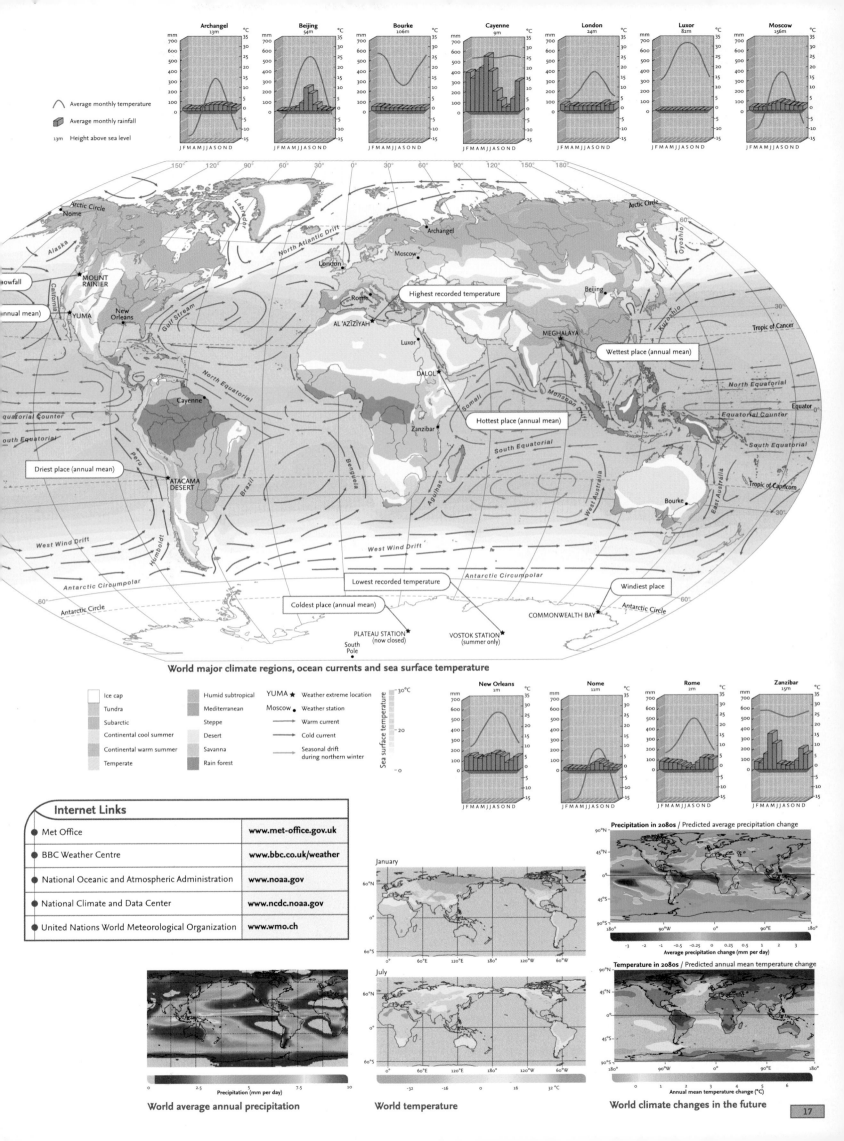

Archangel 13m

Beijing 54m

Bourke 106m

Cayenne 9m

London 24m

Luxor 82m

Moscow 156m

Average monthly temperature

Average monthly rainfall

13m   Height above sea level

World major climate regions, ocean currents and sea surface temperature

	Ice cap		Humid subtropical	YUMA ★	Weather extreme location
	Tundra		Mediterranean	Moscow ●	Weather station
	Subarctic		Steppe	→	Warm current
	Continental cool summer		Desert	→	Cold current
	Continental warm summer		Savanna	→	Seasonal drift during northern winter
	Temperate		Rain forest		

Sea surface temperature

New Orleans 1m

Nome 11m

Rome 2m

Zanzibar 15m

Internet Links

● Met Office	**www.met-office.gov.uk**
● BBC Weather Centre	**www.bbc.co.uk/weather**
● National Oceanic and Atmospheric Administration	**www.noaa.gov**
● National Climate and Data Center	**www.ncdc.noaa.gov**
● United Nations World Meteorological Organization	**www.wmo.ch**

January

July

Precipitation in 2080s / Predicted average precipitation change

Average precipitation change (mm per day)

Temperature in 2080s / Predicted annual mean temperature change

Annual mean temperature change (°C)

Precipitation (mm per day)

World average annual precipitation

World temperature

World climate changes in the future

The oxygen- and water- rich environment of the earth has helped create a wide range of habitats. Forest and woodland ecosystems form the predominant natural land cover over most of the earth's surface. Tropical rainforests are part of an intricate land-atmosphere relationship that is disturbed by land cover changes. Forests in the tropics are believed to hold most of the world's bird, animal, and plant species. Grassland, shrubland and deserts collectively cover most of the unwooded land surface, with tundra on frozen subsoil at high northern latitudes. These areas tend to have lower species diversity than most forests, with the notable exception of Mediterranean shrublands, which support some of the most diverse floras on the earth. Humans have extensively altered most grassland and shrubland areas, usually through conversion to agriculture, burning and introduction of domestic livestock. They have had less immediate impact on tundra and true desert regions, although these remain vulnerable to global climate change.

Evergreen needleleaf forest	
Evergreen broadleaf forest	
Deciduous needleleaf forest	
Deciduous broadleaf forest	
Mixed forest	
Closed shrubland	
Open shrubland	
Woody savanna	
Savanna	
Grassland	
Permanent wetland	
Cropland	
Urban and built-up	
Cropland/Natural vegetation mosaic	
Snow and Ice	
Barren or sparsely vegetated	
Water bodies	

Snow and ice, Spitsbergen, Svalbard, inside the Arctic Circle.

World land cover
Map courtesy of IGBP, JRC and USGS

Urban, La Paz, Bolivia.

Land cover

The land cover map shown here was derived from data aquired by the Advanced Very High Resolution Radiometer sensor on board the polar orbiting satellites of the US National Oceanic and Atmospheric Administration. The high resolution (ground resolution of 1km) of the imagery used to compile the data set and map allows detailed interpretation of land cover patterns across the world. Important uses include managing forest resources, improving estimates of the earth's water and energy cycles, and modelling climate change.

Internet Links

World Resources Institute	www.wri.org
World Conservation Monitoring Centre	www.unep-wcmc.org
United Nations Environment Programme (UNEP)	www.unep.org
IUCN The World Conservation Union	www.iucn.org
Land Cover at Boston University	geography.bu.edu/landcover/index.html

Top 20 protected areas by size

Rank	Protected area	Country	Size (sq km)	Designation
1	Greenland	Greenland	972 000	National Park
2	Rub' al Khālī	Saudi Arabia	640 000	Wildlife Management Area
3	Great Barrier Reef Marine Park	Australia	344 360	Marine Park
4	Northwestern Hawaiian Islands	United States	341 362	Coral Reef Ecosystem Reserve
5	Amazonia	Colombia	326 329	Forest Reserve
6	Qiangtang	China	298 000	Nature Reserve
7	Macquarie Island	Australia	162 060	Marine Park
8	Sanjiangyuan	China	152 300	Nature Reserve
9	Cape Churchill	Canada	137 072	Wildlife Management Area
10	Galapagos Islands	Ecuador	133 000	Marine Reserve
11	Northern Wildlife Management Zone	Saudi Arabia	100 875	Wildlife Management Area
12	Ngaanyatjarra Lands	Australia	98 129	Indigenous Protected Area
13	Alto Orinoco-Casiquiare	Venezuela	84 000	Biosphere Reserve
14	Vale do Javari	Brazil	83 380	Indigenous Area
15	Ouadi Rimé-Ouadi Achim	Chad	80 000	Faunal Reserve
16	Arctic	United States	78 049	National Wildlife Refuge
17	Yanomami	Brazil	77 519	Indigenous Park
18	Yukon Delta	United States	77 425	National Wildlife Refuge
19	Aïr and Ténéré	Niger	77 360	National Nature Reserve
20	Pacifico	Colombia	73 981	Forest Reserve

Great Barrier Reef, Australia, the world's 3rd largest protected area.

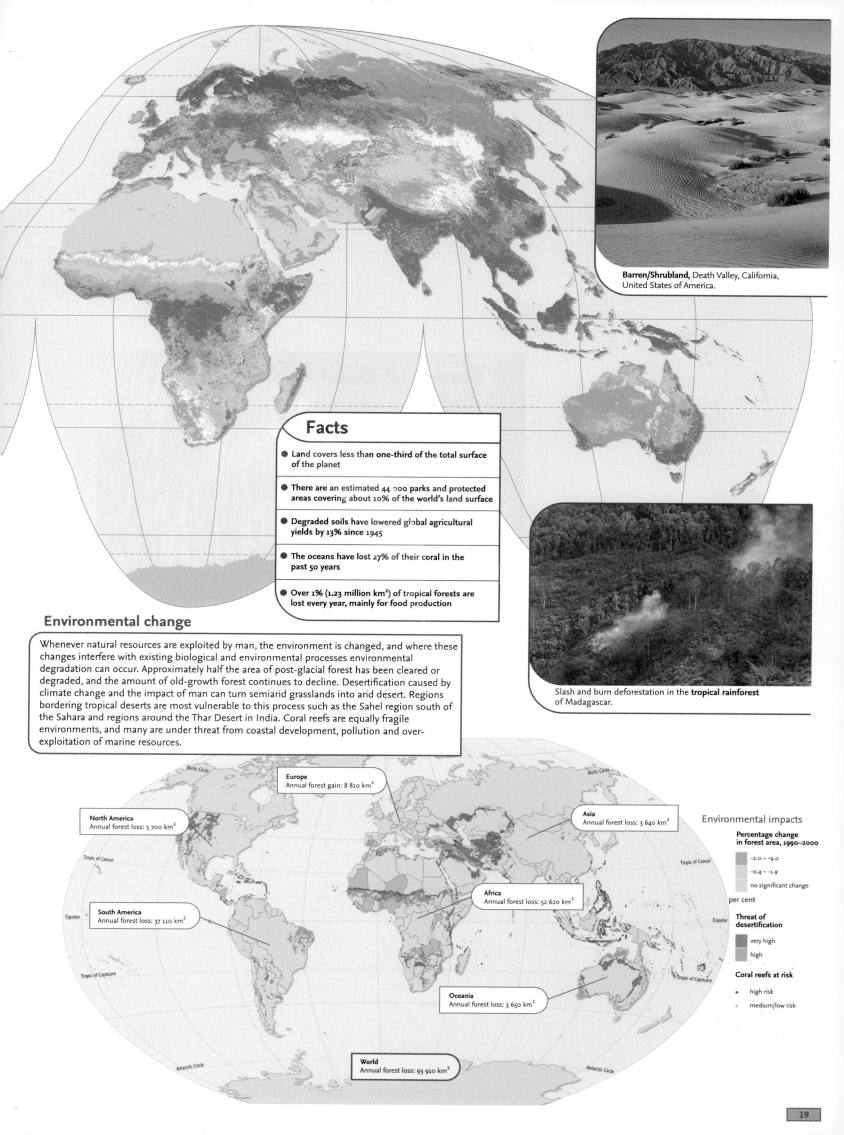

Barren/Shrubland, Death Valley, California, United States of America.

Facts

- Land covers less than **one-third of the total surface of the planet**

- There are an estimated 44 000 parks and protected areas covering about 10% of the world's land surface

- Degraded soils have lowered global agricultural yields by 13% since 1945

- The oceans have lost 27% of their coral in the past 50 years

- Over 1% (1.23 million km²) of tropical forests are lost every year, mainly for food production

Environmental change

Whenever natural resources are exploited by man, the environment is changed, and where these changes interfere with existing biological and environmental processes environmental degradation can occur. Approximately half the area of post-glacial forest has been cleared or degraded, and the amount of old-growth forest continues to decline. Desertification caused by climate change and the impact of man can turn semiarid grasslands into arid desert. Regions bordering tropical deserts are most vulnerable to this process such as the Sahel region south of the Sahara and regions around the Thar Desert in India. Coral reefs are equally fragile environments, and many are under threat from coastal development, pollution and over-exploitation of marine resources.

Slash and burn deforestation in the **tropical rainforest** of Madagascar.

Europe
Annual forest gain: 8 810 km²

North America
Annual forest loss: 5 700 km²

Asia
Annual forest loss: 3 640 km²

Africa
Annual forest loss: 52 620 km²

South America
Annual forest loss: 37 110 km²

Oceania
Annual forest loss: 3 650 km²

World
Annual forest loss: 93 910 km²

Environmental impacts

Percentage change in forest area, 1990–2000

-2.0 – -9.0
-0.4 – -1.9
no significant change

per cent

Threat of desertification

very high
high

Coral reefs at risk

- high risk
- medium/low risk

After increasing very slowly for most of human history, world population more than doubled in the last half century. Whereas world population did not pass the one billion mark until 1804 and took another 123 years to reach two billion in 1927, it then added the third billion in 33 years, the fourth in 14 years and the fifth in 13 years. Just twelve years later on October 12, 1999 the United Nations announced that the global population had reached the six billion mark. It is expected that another three billion people will have been added to the world's population by 2050.

world statistics: see pages 154–160

Facts

- The world's population is growing at an annual rate of 76 million people per year

- Today's population is only 5.7% of the total number of people who ever lived on the earth

- It is expected that in 2050 there will be more people aged over 60 than children aged less than 14

- More than 90% of the 70 million inhabitants of Egypt are located around the River Nile

- India's population reached 1 billion in August 1999

Top 20 countries by population, 2003

Rank	Country	Population
1	China	1 289 161 000
2	India	1 065 462 000
3	United States of America	294 043 000
4	Indonesia	219 883 000
5	Brazil	178 470 000
6	Pakistan	153 578 000
7	Bangladesh	146 736 000
8	Russian Federation	143 246 000
9	Japan	127 654 000
10	Nigeria	124 009 000
11	Mexico	103 457 000
12	Germany	82 476 000
13	Vietnam	81 377 000
14	Philippines	79 999 000
15	Egypt	71 931 000
16	Turkey	71 325 000
17	Ethiopia	70 678 000
18	Iran	68 920 000
19	Thailand	62 833 000
20	France	60 144 000

Top 20 countries by population density, 2003
(persons per square kilometre)

Rank	Country	Population density
1	Monaco	17 000
2	Singapore	6 656
3	Malta	1 247
4	Maldives	1 067
5	Bahrain	1 048
6	Bangladesh	1 019
7	Vatican City	944
8	Barbados	628
9	Taiwan	623
10	Nauru	619
11	Mauritius	599
12	South Korea	480
13	San Marino	459
14	Tuvalu	440
15	Comoros	412
16	Netherlands	389
17	Lebanon	350
18	India	348
19	Belgium	338
20	Japan	338

Population distribution

The world's population in mid-2003 had reached 6 301 million, over half of which live in six countries: China, India, USA, Indonesia, Brazil and Pakistan. Over 80% (5 098 million) of the total population live in less developed regions. As shown on the population distribution map, over a quarter of the land area is uninhabited or has extremely low population density. Barely a quarter of the land area is occupied at densities of 25 or more persons per square km, with the three largest concentrations in east Asia, the Indian subcontinent and Europe accounting for over half the world total.

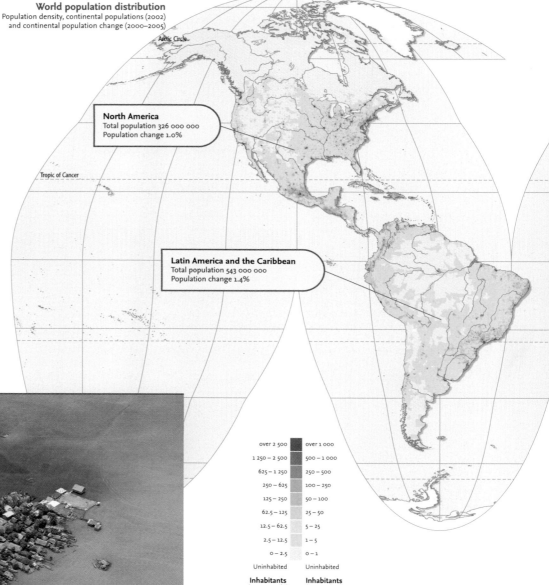

World population distribution
Population density, continental populations (2002) and continental population change (2000–2005)

Arctic Circle

Tropic of Cancer

North America
Total population 326 000 000
Population change 1.0%

Latin America and the Caribbean
Total population 543 000 000
Population change 1.4%

Inhabitants (per sq mile)	Inhabitants (per sq km)
over 2 500	over 1 000
1 250 – 2 500	500 – 1 000
625 – 1 250	250 – 500
250 – 625	100 – 250
125 – 250	50 – 100
62.5 – 125	25 – 50
12.5 – 62.5	5 – 25
2.5 – 12.5	1 – 5
0 – 2.5	0 – 1
Uninhabited	Uninhabited

Kuna Indians inhabit this congested island off the north coast of Panama.

Population change by country, 2000–2005
Average annual rate of population change (per cent) and the top ten contributors to world population growth (net annual addition)

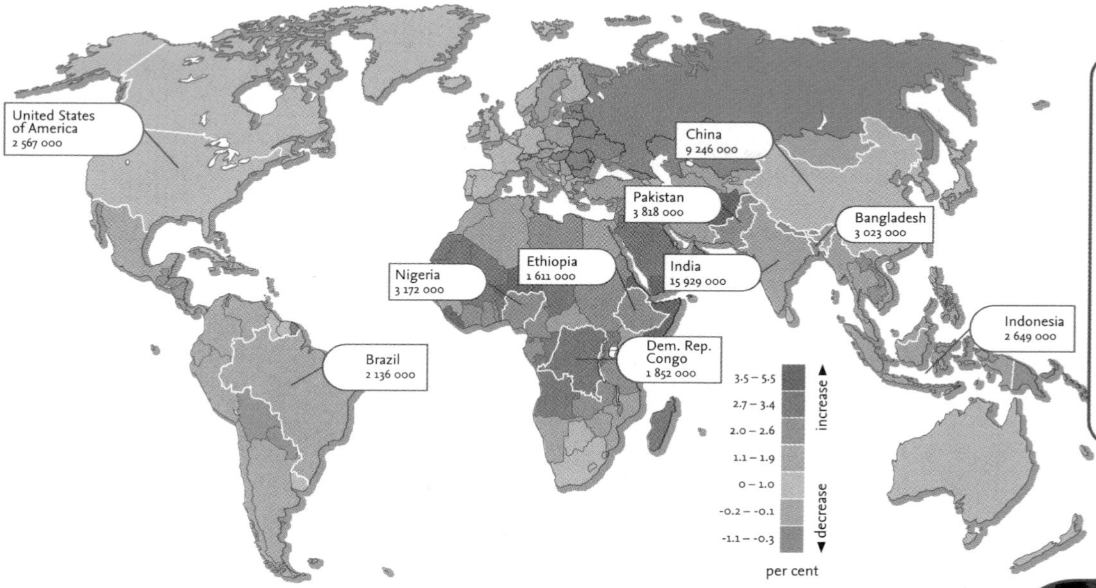

United States of America 2 567 000
China 9 246 000
Pakistan 3 818 000
Bangladesh 3 023 000
Nigeria 3 172 000
Ethiopia 1 611 000
India 15 929 000
Indonesia 2 649 000
Brazil 2 136 000
Dem. Rep. Congo 1 852 000
3.5 – 5.5
2.7 – 3.4
2.0 – 2.6
1.1 – 1.9
0 – 1.0
-0.2 – -0.1
-1.1 – -0.3
increase
decrease
per cent

World population change

Population growth since 1950 has been spread very unevenly between the continents. While overall numbers have been growing rapidly since 1950, a massive 89 per cent increase has taken place in the less developed regions, especially southern and eastern Asia. In contrast, Europe's population level has been almost stationary and is expected to decrease in the future. India and China alone are responsible for over one-third of current growth. But most of the highest rates of growth are to be found in Sub-Saharan Africa with Liberia and Sierra Leone experiencing the highest percentage increases in population between 2000 and 2005. Until population growth is brought under tighter control, the developing world in particular will continue to face enormous problems of supporting a rising population.

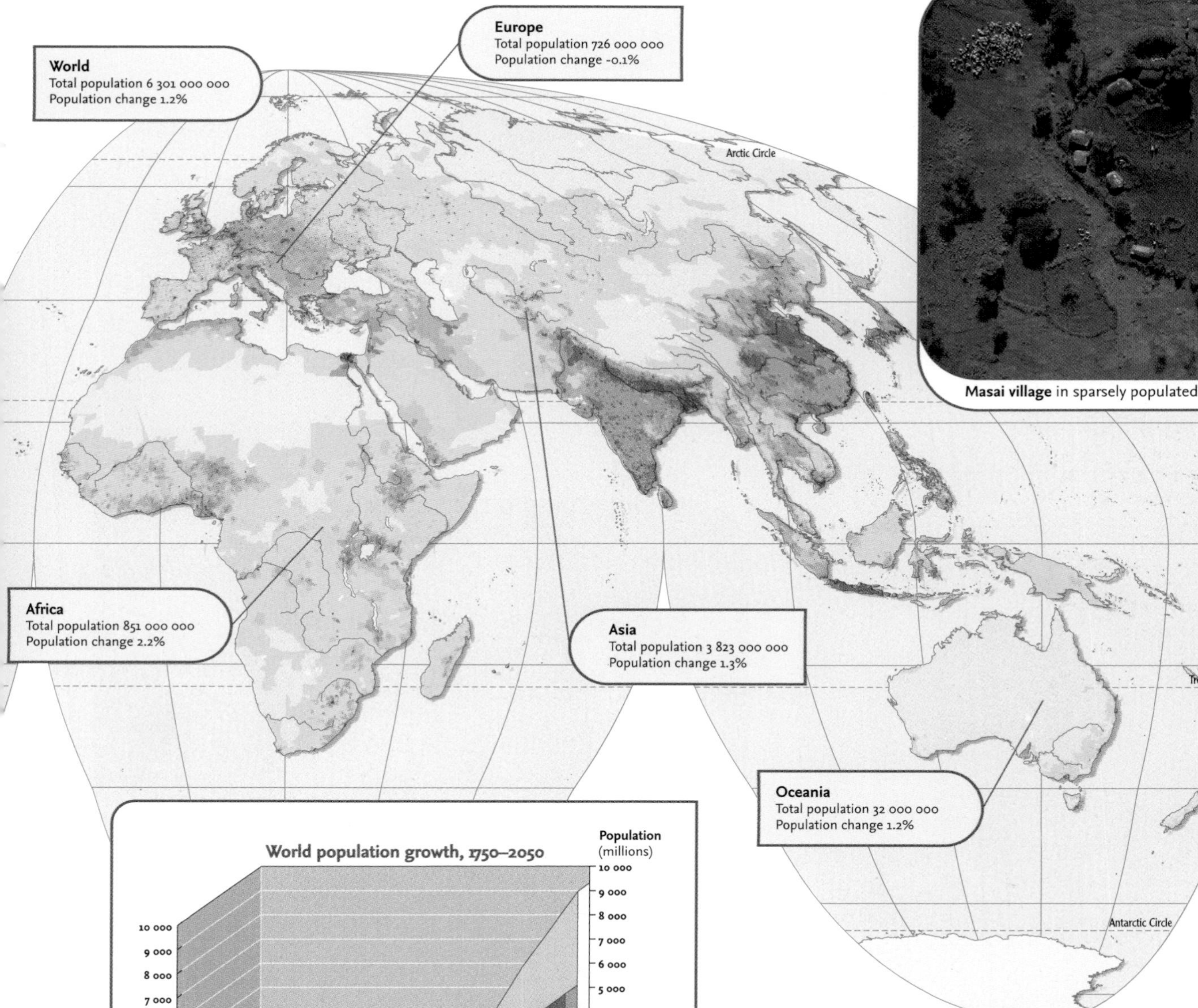

World
Total population 6 301 000 000
Population change 1.2%
Europe
Total population 726 000 000
Population change -0.1%
Arctic Circle
Africa
Total population 851 000 000
Population change 2.2%
Asia
Total population 3 823 000 000
Population change 1.3%
Equator
Tropic of Capricorn
Oceania
Total population 32 000 000
Population change 1.2%
Antarctic Circle

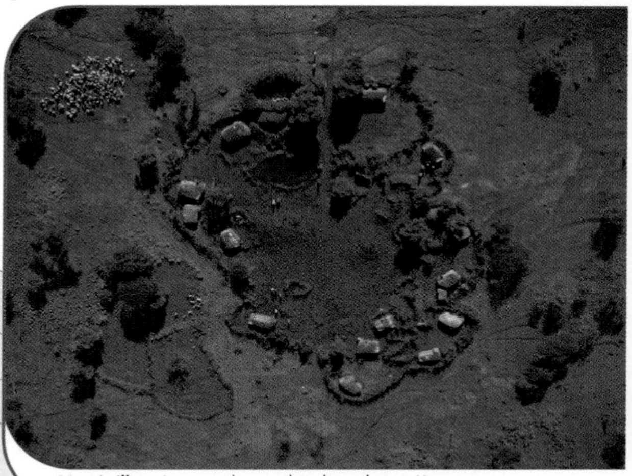

Masai village in sparsely populated southwest Kenya.

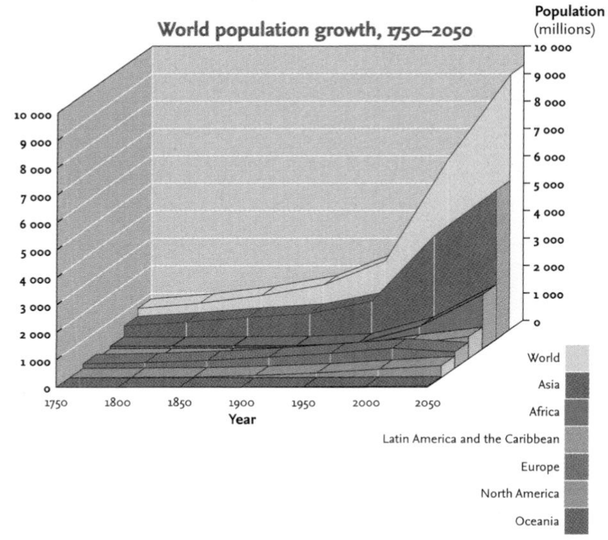

World population growth, 1750–2050
Population (millions)
10 000
9 000
8 000
7 000
6 000
5 000
4 000
3 000
2 000
1 000
0
1750
1800
1850
1900
1950
2000
2050
Year
World
Asia
Africa
Latin America and the Caribbean
Europe
North America
Oceania

Internet Links

United Nations Population Information Network	**www.un.org/popin**
US Census Bureau	**www.census.gov**
UK Census	**www.statistics.gov.uk/census2001**
Population Reference Bureau Pop Net	**www.popnet.org**
Socioeconomic Data and Applications Center	**sedac.ciesin.columbia.edu**

World Urbanization and Cities

The world is becoming increasingly urban but the level of urbanization varies greatly between and within continents. At the beginning of the twentieth century only fourteen per cent of the world's population was urban and by 1950 this had increased to thirty per cent. In the more developed regions and in Latin America and the Caribbean seventy per cent of the population is urban while in Africa and Asia the figure is less than one third. In recent decades urban growth has increased rapidly to nearly fifty per cent and there are now 387 cities with over 1 000 000 inhabitants. It is in the developing regions that the most rapid increases are taking place and it is expected that by 2030 over half of urban dwellers worldwide will live in Asia. Migration from the countryside to the city in the search for better job opportunities is the main factor in urban growth.

World Statistics: see pages 154–160

Facts

- Cities occupy less than 2% of the earth's land surface but house almost half of the human population

- Urban growth rates in Africa are the highest in the world

- Antarctica is uninhabited and most settlements in the Arctic regions have less than 5 000 inhabitants

- India has 32 cities with over one million inhabitants; by 2015 there will be 50

- London was the first city to reach a population of over 5 million

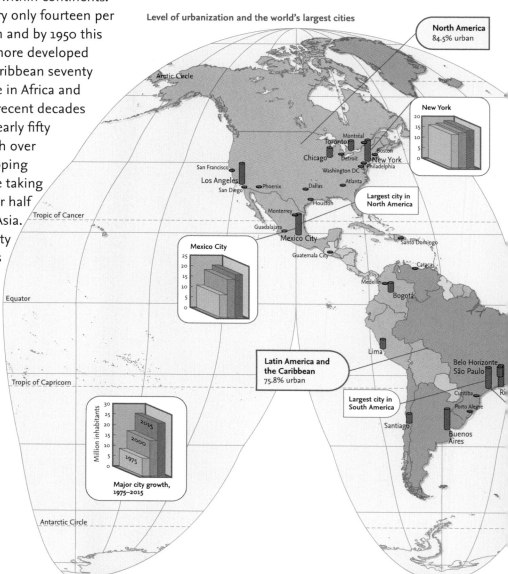

Level of urbanization and the world's largest cities

North America
84.5% urban

New York

Largest city in North America

Mexico City

Latin America and the Caribbean
75.8% urban

Largest city in South America

Major city growth, 1975–2015

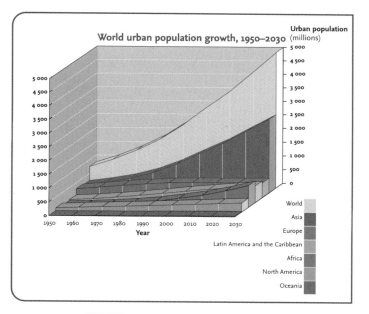

World urban population growth, 1950–2030

Urban population (millions)

World
Asia
Europe
Latin America and the Caribbean
Africa
North America
Oceania

Characteristic high-rise development and densely packed low-rise buildings in **Tōkyō**, the world's largest city.

Internet Links

United Nations Population Division	www.un.org/esa/population/unpop.htm
United Nations World Urbanization Prospects	www.un.org/esa/population/publications/wup2003/2003WUP.htm
United Nations Population Information Network	www.un.org/popin
The World Bank - Urban Development	www.worldbank.org/urban/
City Populations	www.citypopulation.de

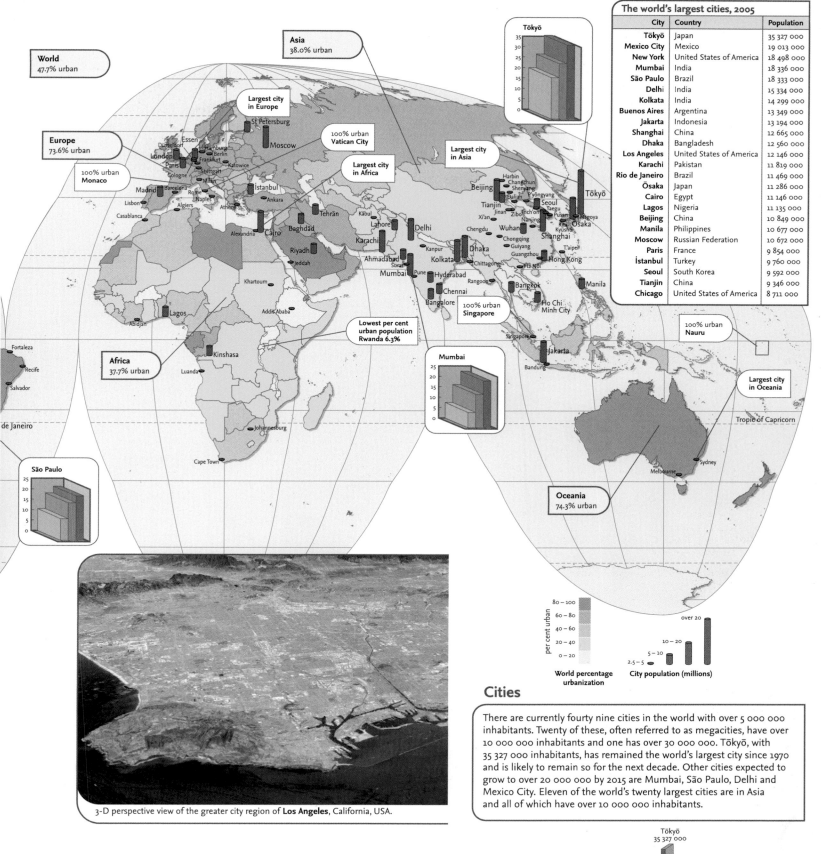

Tōkyō

The world's largest cities, 2005

City	Country	Population
Tōkyō	Japan	35 327 000
Mexico City	Mexico	19 013 000
New York	United States of America	18 498 000
Mumbai	India	18 336 000
São Paulo	Brazil	18 333 000
Delhi	India	15 334 000
Kolkata	India	14 299 000
Buenos Aires	Argentina	13 349 000
Jakarta	Indonesia	13 194 000
Shanghai	China	12 665 000
Dhaka	Bangladesh	12 560 000
Los Angeles	United States of America	12 146 000
Karachi	Pakistan	11 819 000
Rio de Janeiro	Brazil	11 469 000
Ōsaka	Japan	11 286 000
Cairo	Egypt	11 146 000
Lagos	Nigeria	11 135 000
Beijing	China	10 849 000
Manila	Philippines	10 677 000
Moscow	Russian Federation	10 672 000
Paris	France	9 854 000
İstanbul	Turkey	9 760 000
Seoul	South Korea	9 592 000
Tianjin	China	9 346 000
Chicago	United States of America	8 711 000

World 47.7% urban

Asia 38.0% urban

Largest city in Europe

Europe 73.6% urban

100% urban **Vatican City**

Largest city in Africa

100% urban **Monaco**

Largest city in Asia

Largest city in Africa

Lowest per cent urban population **Rwanda 6.3%**

Africa 37.7% urban

100% urban **Singapore**

Mumbai

100% urban **Nauru**

Largest city in Oceania

Tropic of Capricorn

Oceania 74.3% urban

São Paulo

3-D perspective view of the greater city region of **Los Angeles**, California, USA.

per cent urban
- 80 – 100
- 60 – 80
- 40 – 60
- 20 – 40
- 0 – 20

World percentage urbanization

City population (millions)
- over 20
- 10 – 20
- 5 – 10
- 2.5 – 5

City population (millions)

Cities

There are currently fourty nine cities in the world with over 5 000 000 inhabitants. Twenty of these, often referred to as megacities, have over 10 000 000 inhabitants and one has over 30 000 000. Tōkyō, with 35 327 000 inhabitants, has remained the world's largest city since 1970 and is likely to remain so for the next decade. Other cities expected to grow to over 20 000 000 by 2015 are Mumbai, São Paulo, Delhi and Mexico City. Eleven of the world's twenty largest cities are in Asia and all of which have over 10 000 000 inhabitants.

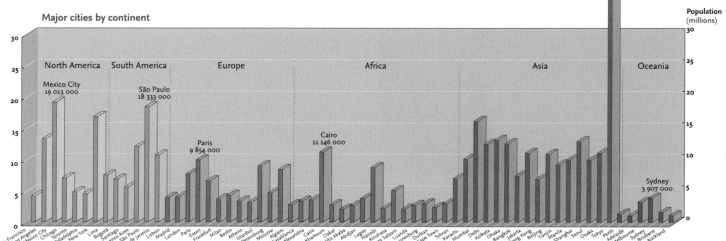

Major cities by continent

Tōkyō 35 327 000

Population (millions)

North America · South America · Europe · Africa · Asia · Oceania

Mexico City 19 013 000

São Paulo 18 333 000

Paris 9 854 000

Cairo 11 146 000

Sydney 3 907 000

Increased availability and ownership of telecommunications equipment since the beginning of the 1970s has aided the globalization of the world economy. Over half of the world's fixed telephone lines have been installed since the mid-1980s and the majority of the world's internet hosts have come on line since 1997. There are now over one billion fixed telephone lines in the world. The number of mobile cellular subscribers has grown dramatically from sixteen million in 1991 to well over one billion today.

The internet is the fastest growing communications network of all time. It is relatively cheap and now links over 140 million host computers globally. Its growth has resulted in the emergence of hundreds of Internet Service Providers (ISPs) and internet traffic is now doubling every six months. In 1993 the number of internet users was estimated to be just under ten million, there are now over half a billion.

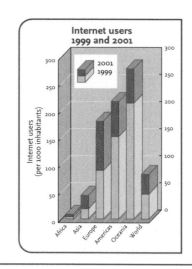

Internet users 1999 and 2001

| | 2001 |
| | 1999 |

Internet users (per 1000 inhabitants)

Africa, Asia, Europe, Americas, Oceania, World

Internet Links	
● OECD Information and Communication Technologies	**www.oecd.org**
● Telegeography Inc.	**www.telegeography.com**
● International Telecommunication Union	**www.itu.int**

Internet users per 1 000 inhabitants

- over 200
- 150 – 200
- 100 – 149
- 10 – 99
- 0 – 9
- no data

Major interregional internet routes

- 0.0 – 0.9
- 1.0 – 4.9
- 5.0 – 24.9
- 25.0 – 125.0

∘ London

Internet hub cities, 2001

Internet users and major Internet routes

A visualization of **global internet traffic**. Each line represents the path of a data probe sent to specific internet locations.

The Internet

The Internet is a global network of millions of computers around the world, all capable of being connected to each other. Internet Service Providers (ISPs) provide access via 'host' computers, of which there are now over 140 million. It has become a vital means of communication and data transfer for businesses, governments and financial and academic institutions, with a steadily increasing proportion of business transactions being carried out on-line.

Top 20 Internet Service Providers (ISPs)		
Internet Service	**Web Address**	**Subscribers (000s)**
AOL (USA)	www.aol.com	20 500
T-Online (Germany)	www.t-online.de	4 151
Nifty-Serve (Japan)	www.nifty.com	3 500
EarthLink (USA)	www.earthlink.com	3 122
Biglobe (Japan)	www.biglobe.ne.jp	2 720
MSN (USA)	www.msn.com	2 700
Chollian (South Korea)	www.chollian.net	2 000
Tin.it (Italy)	www.tin.it	1 990
Freeserve (UK)	www.freeserve.com	1 575
AT&T WorldNet (USA)	www.att.net	1 500
Prodigy (USA)	www.prodigy.com	1 502
NetZero (USA)	www.netzero.com	1 450
Terra Networks (Spain)	www.terra.es	1 317
HiNet (Taiwan-China)	www.hinet.net	1 200
Wanadoo (France)	www.wanadoo.fr	1 124
AltaVista	www.microav.com	750
Freei (USA)	www.freei.com	750
SBC Internet Services	www.sbc.com	720
Telia Internet (Sweden)	www.telia.se	613
Netvigator (Hongkong SAR)	www.netvigator.com	561

Satellite communications

International telecommunications use either fibre-optic cables or satellites as transmission media. Although cables carry the vast majority of traffic around the world, communications satellites are important for person-to-person communication, including cellular telephones, and for broadcasting. The positions of communications satellites are critical to their use, and reflect the demand for such communications in each part of the world. Such satellites are placed in 'geostationary' orbit 36 000 km above the equator. This means that they move at the same speed as the earth and remain fixed above a single point on the earth's surface.

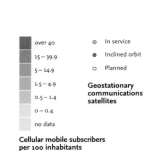

Cellular mobile subscribers per 100 inhabitants

- over 40
- 15 – 39.9
- 5 – 14.9
- 1.5 – 4.9
- 0.5 – 1.4
- 0 – 0.4
- no data

Geostationary communications satellites
- ○ In service
- ● Inclined orbit
- ○ Planned

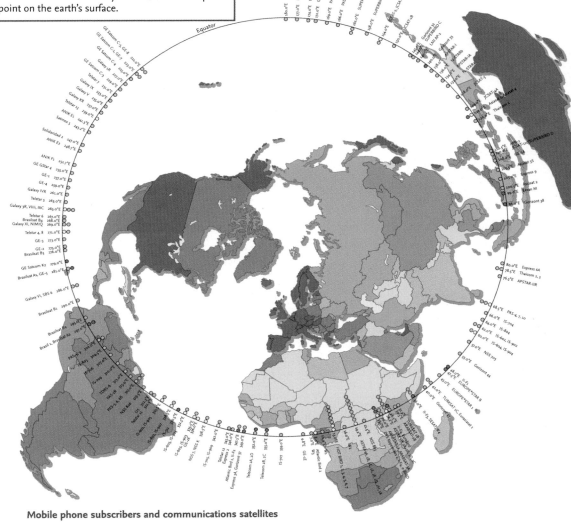

Mobile phone subscribers and communications satellites

Facts

- Luxembourg has the world's highest density of telephone lines per person with more telephones than Bangladesh – a country with more than 300 times as many people.

- Fibre-optic cables can now carry approximately 20 million simultaneous telephone calls

- The first transatlantic telegraph cable came into operation in 1858

- The internet is the fastest growing communications network of all time and now has over 140 million host computers

- Sputnik, the world's first artificial satellite, was launched in 1957

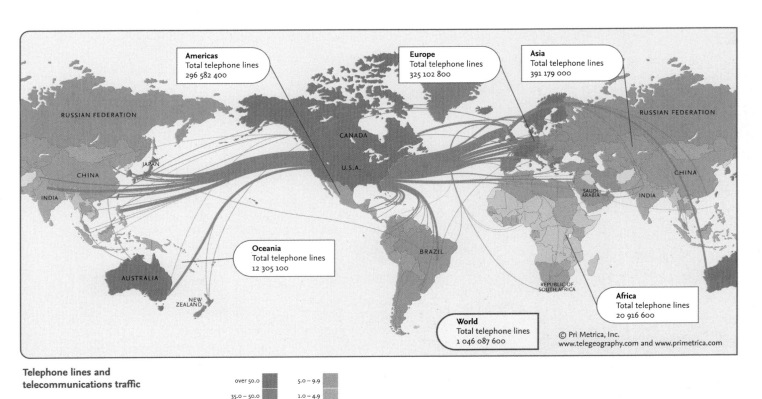

Americas
Total telephone lines
296 582 400

Europe
Total telephone lines
325 102 800

Asia
Total telephone lines
391 179 000

Oceania
Total telephone lines
12 305 100

Africa
Total telephone lines
20 916 600

World
Total telephone lines
1 046 087 600

© Pri Metrica, Inc.
www.telegeography.com and www.primetrica.com

Telephone lines and telecommunications traffic

Telephone lines per 100 inhabitants
- over 50.0
- 35.0 – 50.0
- 15.0 – 34.9
- 10.0 – 14.9
- 5.0 – 9.9
- 1.0 – 4.9
- 0 – 0.9
- no data

Traffic flows
5 000   2 500   1 000   100
Million minutes of telecommunications traffic (mMiTTs)

World Social Indicators

Countries are often judged on their level of economic development, but national and personal wealth are not the only measures of a country's status. Numerous other indicators can give a better picture of the overall level of development and standard of living achieved by a country. The availability and standard of health services, levels of educational provision and attainment, levels of nutrition, water supply, life expectancy and mortality rates are just some of the factors which can be measured to assess and compare countries.

While nations strive to improve their economies, and hopefully also to improve the standard of living of their citizens, the measurement of such indicators often exposes great discrepancies between the countries of the 'developed' world and those of the 'less developed' world. They also show great variations within continents and regions and at the same time can hide great inequalities within countries.

World Statistics: see pages 154–160

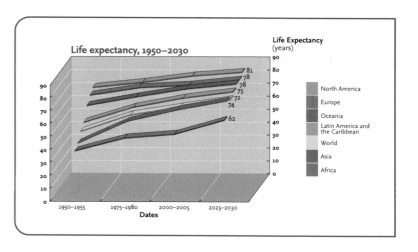

Life expectancy, 1950–2030

Life Expectancy (years)

- North America
- Europe
- Oceania
- Latin America and the Caribbean
- World
- Asia
- Africa

Internet Links

United Nation Development Programme	www.undp.org
World Health Organization	www.who.int
United Nations Statistics Division	unstats.un.org
United Nations Millennium Development Goals	millenniumindicators.un.org

UN Millennium Development Goals
From the Millennium Declaration, 2000

Goal 1	Eradicate extreme poverty and hunger
Goal 2	Achieve universal primary education
Goal 3	Promote gender equality and empower women
Goal 4	Reduce child mortality
Goal 5	Improve maternal health
Goal 6	Combat HIV/AIDS, malaria and other diseases
Goal 7	Ensure environmental sustainability
Goal 8	Develop a global partnership for development

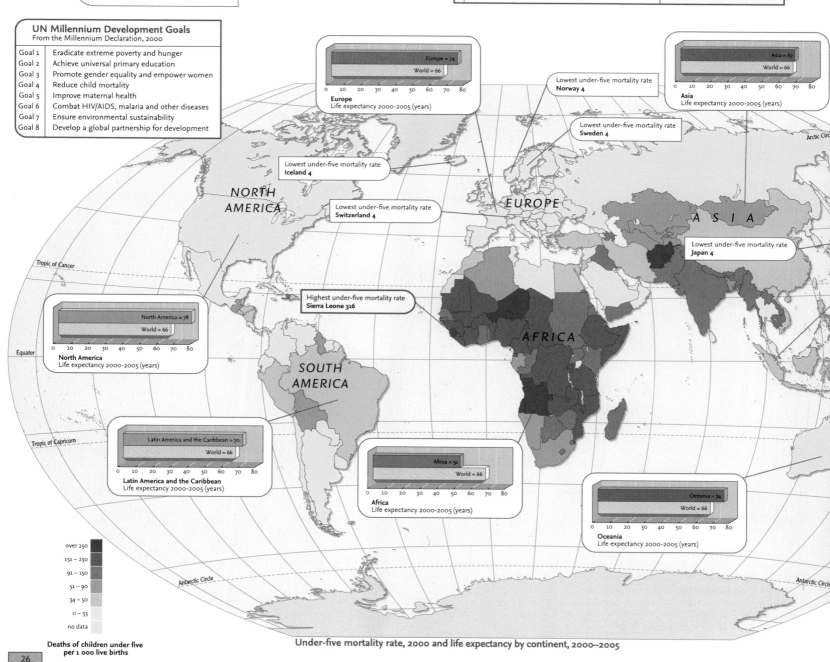

Under-five mortality rate, 2000 and life expectancy by continent, 2000–2005

Deaths of children under five per 1 000 live births
- over 250
- 151 – 250
- 91 – 150
- 52 – 90
- 34 – 50
- 0 – 33
- no data

Outdoor education at a school in Bahia state, northeast Brazil.

Literacy rate, 2002
Percentage of population aged 15–24 with
at least a basic ability to read and write

per cent
96 – 100
86 – 95
66 – 85
41 – 65
0 – 40
no data

Measuring development

Measuring the extent to which a country is 'developed' is difficult, and although there have been many attempts to standardize techniques there is no universally accepted method. One commonly used measure is the Human Development Index (HDI), which is based on a combination of statistics relating to life expectancy, education (literacy and school enrolment) and wealth (Gross Domestic Product – GDP).

At the Millennium Summit in September 2000, the United Nations identified eight Millennium Development Goals (MDGs) which aim to combat poverty, hunger, disease, illiteracy, environmental degradation and discrimination against women. Forty eight indicators have been identified which will measure the progress each country is making towards achieving these goals.

Facts

- Of the 10 countries with under-5 mortality rates of more than 200, 9 are in Africa

- Many western countries believe they have achieved satisfactory levels of education and no longer closely monitor levels of literacy

- Children born in Nepal have only a 12% chance of their birth being attended by trained health personnel, for most European countries the figure is 100%

- The illiteracy rate among young women in the Middle East and north Africa is almost twice the rate for young men.

Doctors per 100 000 people
Number of trained doctors per 100 000 people

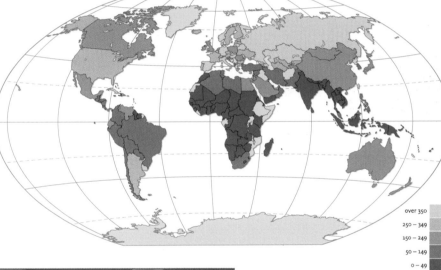

over 350
250 – 349
150 – 249
50 – 149
0 – 49
no data

Lowest under-five mortality rate
Singapore 4

Tropic of Cancer

Equator

Tropic of Capricorn

OCEANIA

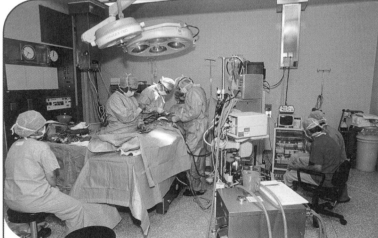
High class **health care facilities** such as these are not available in many parts of the world.

Human Development Index (HDI), 2002	
Top 10	
Rank	**Country**
1	Norway
2	Sweden
3	Canada
4	Belgium
5	Australia
6	USA
7	Iceland
8	Netherlands
9	Japan
10	Finland
Bottom 10	
Rank	**Country**
164	Mali
165	Central African Republic
166	Chad
167	Guinea-Bissau
168	Ethiopia
169	Burkina
170	Mozambique
171	Burundi
172	Niger
173	Sierra Leone

Health and education

Perhaps the most important indicators used for measuring the level of national development are those relating to health and education. Both of these key areas are vital to the future development of a country, and if there are concerns in standards attained in either (or worse, in both) of these, then they may indicate fundamental problems within the country concerned. The ability to read and write (literacy) is seen as vital in educating people and encouraging development, while easy access to appropriate health services and specialists is an important requirement in maintaining satisfactory levels of basic health.

The globalization of the economy is making the world appear a smaller place. However, this shrinkage is an uneven process. Countries are being included in and excluded from the global economy to differing degrees. The wealthy countries of the developed world, with their market-led economies, access to productive new technologies and international markets, dominate the world economic system. Great inequalities exist between and also within countries. There may also be discrepancies between social groups within countries due to gender and ethnic divisions. Differences between countries are evident by looking at overall wealth on a national and individual level.

World Statistics: see pages 154–160

The City, London, the world's largest financial centre.

Regional distribution of wealth

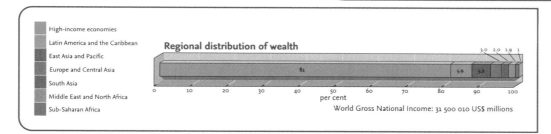

High-income economies
Latin America and the Caribbean
East Asia and Pacific
Europe and Central Asia
South Asia
Middle East and North Africa
Sub-Saharan Africa

3.0 2.0 1.9 1

81   5.9 5.2

0   10   20   30   40   50   60   70   80   90   100
                              per cent

World Gross National Income: 31 500 010 US$ millions

Facts

- The City, one of 33 London boroughs, is the world's largest financial centre and contains Europe's biggest stock market

- Half the world's population earns only 5% of the world's wealth

- During the second half of the 20th century rich countries gave over US$1 trillion in aid

- For every £1 in grant aid to developing countries, more than £13 comes back in debt repayments

- On average, The World Bank distributes US$30 billion each year between 100 countries

Personal wealth

A poverty line set at $1 a day has been accepted as the working definition of extreme poverty in low-income countries. It is estimated that a total of 1.2 billion people live below that poverty line. This indicator has also been adopted by the United Nations in relation to their Millennium Development Goals. The United Nations goal is to halve the proportion of people living on less than $1 a day in 1990 to 14.5 per cent by 2015. Today, over 80 per cent of the total population of Ethiopia, Uganda and Nicaragua live on less than this amount.

Percentage of population living on less than $1 a day

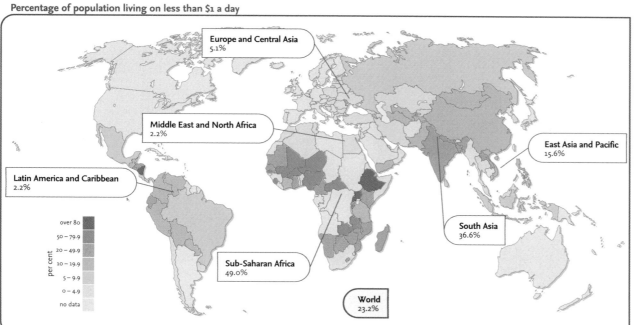

Europe and Central Asia
5.1%

Middle East and North Africa
2.2%

Latin America and Caribbean
2.2%

East Asia and Pacific
15.6%

South Asia
36.6%

Sub-Saharan Africa
49.0%

World
23.2%

per cent
- over 80
- 50 – 79.9
- 20 – 49.9
- 10 – 19.9
- 5 – 9.9
- 0 – 4.9
- no data

Gross National Income per capita

Highest

Rank	Country	US$ 2001
1	Luxembourg	41 770
2	Switzerland	36 970
3	Japan	35 990
4	Norway	35 530
5	United States	34 870
6	Denmark	31 090
7	Iceland	28 880
8	Sweden	25 400
9	United Kingdom	24 230
10	Netherlands	24 040

Lowest

Rank	Country	US$ 2001
150	Mozambique	210
151	Chad	200
152	Eritrea	190
153	Tajikistan	170
154	Malawi	170
155	Niger	170
156	Guinea-Bissau	160
157	Sierra Leone	140
158	Burundi	100
159	Ethiopia	100

Key economic indicators by region	World	High-income economies	East Asia and Pacific	Europe and Central Asia	Latin America and The Caribbean	Middle East and North Africa	South Asia	Sub-Saharan Africa
Gross National Income (US$ millions)	31 500 010	25 506 410	1 649 435	930 455	1 861 820	601 270	615 596	317 045
Gross National Income per capita (US$)	5 170	27 680	1 060	2 010	3 670	2 090	440	470
Gross Domestic Product (US$ millions)	31 283 840	25 103 680	1 664 211	986 652	1 943 350	no data	615 307	315 269
Gross Domestic Product growth (annual %, US$ millions)	1.41	1.07	5.49	2.50	0.42	no data	4.39	3.00
Aid per capita received (US$)	9.64	1.99	4.68	22.91	9.67	15.63	3.13	20.42
External debt, total (US$ millions)	no data	no data	632 953	499 344	774 418	203 785	164 375	215 794
Official development assistance and official aid received (US$ millions)	58 369	1 887	8 463	10 867	4 987	4 609	4 241	13 453
Total debt service (US$ millions)	no data	no data	92 730	74 902	179 221	24 921	14 517	12 342

Gross National Income per capita

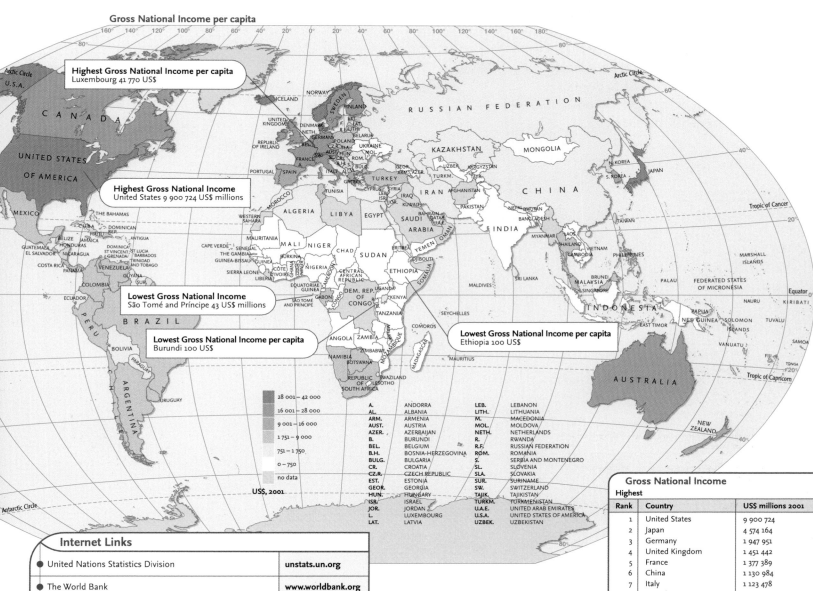

Highest Gross National Income per capita
Luxembourg 41 770 US$

Highest Gross National Income
United States 9 900 724 US$ millions

Lowest Gross National Income
São Tomé and Príncipe 43 US$ millions

Lowest Gross National Income per capita
Burundi 100 US$

Lowest Gross National Income per capita
Ethiopia 100 US$

28 001 – 42 000
16 001 – 28 000
9 001 – 16 000
1 751 – 9 000
751 – 1 750
0 – 750
no data

US$, 2001

A.	ANDORRA
AL.	ALBANIA
ARM.	ARMENIA
AUST.	AUSTRIA
AZER.	AZERBAIJAN
B.	BURUNDI
BEL.	BELGIUM
B.H.	BOSNIA-HERZEGOVINA
BULG.	BULGARIA
CR.	CROATIA
CZ.R.	CZECH REPUBLIC
EST.	ESTONIA
GEOR.	GEORGIA
HUN.	HUNGARY
ISR.	ISRAEL
JOR.	JORDAN
L.	LUXEMBOURG
LAT.	LATVIA

LEB.	LEBANON
LITH.	LITHUANIA
M.	MACEDONIA
MOL.	MOLDOVA
NETH.	NETHERLANDS
R.	RWANDA
R.F.	RUSSIAN FEDERATION
ROM.	ROMANIA
S.	SERBIA AND MONTENEGRO
SL.	SLOVENIA
SLA.	SLOVAKIA
SUR.	SURINAME
SW.	SWITZERLAND
TAJIK.	TAJIKISTAN
TURKM.	TURKMENISTAN
U.A.E.	UNITED ARAB EMIRATES
U.S.A.	UNITED STATES OF AMERICA
UZBEK.	UZBEKISTAN

Internet Links

United Nations Statistics Division	unstats.un.org
The World Bank	www.worldbank.org
International Monetary Fund	www.imf.org
Organisation for Economic Co-operation and Development	www.oecd.org

Measuring wealth

One of the indicators used to determine a country's wealth is its Gross National Income (GNI). This gives a broad measure of an economy's performance. This is the value of the final output of goods and services produced by a country plus net income from non-resident sources. The total GNI is divided by the country's population to give an average figure of the GNI per capita. From this it is evident that the developed countries dominate the world economy with the United States having the highest GNI. China is a growing world economic player with the sixth highest GNI figure and a relatively high GNI per capita (US$890) in proportion to its huge population.

Rural homesteads, **Sudan** – most of the world's poorest countries are in Africa.

Gross National Income

Highest

Rank	Country	US$ millions 2001
1	United States	9 900 724
2	Japan	4 574 164
3	Germany	1 947 951
4	United Kingdom	1 451 442
5	France	1 377 389
6	China	1 130 984
7	Italy	1 123 478
8	Canada	661 881
9	Spain	586 874
10	Mexico	550 456

Lowest

Rank	Country	US$ millions 2001
150	Solomon Islands	253
151	Dominica	224
152	Comoros	217
153	Vanuatu	212
154	Guinea-bissau	202
155	Tonga	154
156	Palau	132
157	Marshall Islands	115
158	Kiribati	77
159	São Tomé and Príncipe	43

The world's biggest companies

Rank	Name	Sales (US$ millions)
1	Wal-Mart Stores	256 330
2	BP	232 570
3	ExxonMobil	222 880
4	General Motors	185 520
5	Ford Motor	164 200
6	DaimlerChrysler	157 130
7	Toyota Motor	135 820
8	General Electric	134 190
9	Royal Dutch/Shell Group	133 500
10	Total	131 640

World Conflict

Geo-political issues shape the countries of the world and the current political situation in many parts of the world reflects a long history of armed conflict. Since the Second World War conflicts have been fairly localized, but there are numerous 'flash points' where factors such as territorial claims, ideology, religion, ethnicity and access to resources can cause friction between two or more countries. Such factors also lie behind the recent growth in global terrorism.

Military expenditure can take up a disproportionate amount of a country's wealth – Eritrea, with a Gross National Income (GNI) per capita of only US$190 spends over twenty seven per cent of its total GNI on military activity. There is an encouraging trend towards wider international cooperation, mainly through the United Nations (UN) and the North Atlantic Treaty Organization (NATO), to prevent escalation of conflicts and on peacekeeping missions.

Facts

- There have been nearly 70 civil or internal wars throughout the world since 1945
- The Iran-Iraq war in the 1980s is estimated to have cost half a million lives
- The UN are currently involved in 15 peacekeeping operations
- It is estimated that there are nearly 20 million refugees throughout the world
- Over 1 600 UN peacekeepers have been killed since 1948

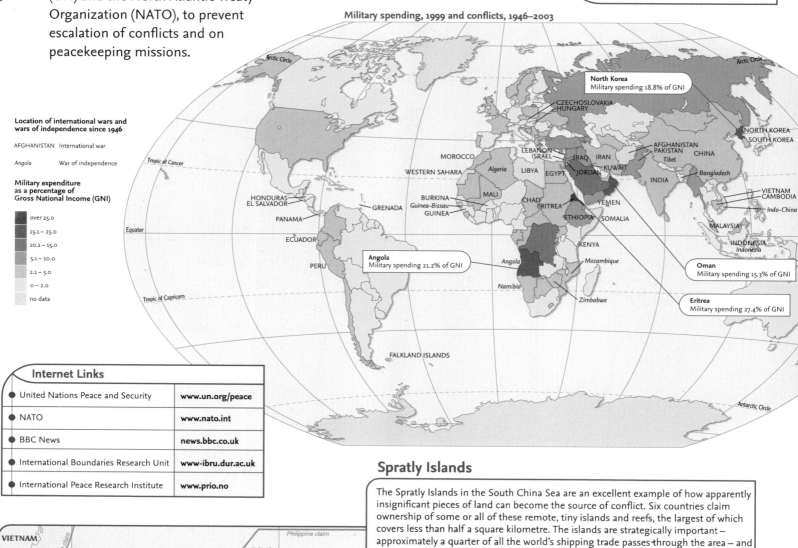

Military spending, 1999 and conflicts, 1946–2003

Location of international wars and wars of independence since 1946

AFGHANISTAN   International war

Angola   War of independence

Military expenditure as a percentage of Gross National Income (GNI)

- over 25.0
- 15.1 – 25.0
- 10.1 – 15.0
- 5.1 – 10.0
- 2.1 – 5.0
- 0 – 2.0
- no data

North Korea Military spending 18.8% of GNI
Angola Military spending 21.2% of GNI
Oman Military spending 15.3% of GNI
Eritrea Military spending 27.4% of GNI

Internet Links

United Nations Peace and Security	www.un.org/peace
NATO	www.nato.int
BBC News	news.bbc.co.uk
International Boundaries Research Unit	www-ibru.dur.ac.uk
International Peace Research Institute	www.prio.no

Spratly Islands

The Spratly Islands in the South China Sea are an excellent example of how apparently insignificant pieces of land can become the source of conflict. Six countries claim ownership of some or all of these remote, tiny islands and reefs, the largest of which covers less than half a square kilometre. The islands are strategically important – approximately a quarter of all the world's shipping trade passes through the area – and ownership of the group would mean access to 250 000 square kilometres of valuable fishing grounds and sea bed believed to be rich in oil and gas reserves. Five of the claimant countries have occupied individual islands to endorse their claims, although there appears little prospect of international agreement on ownership.

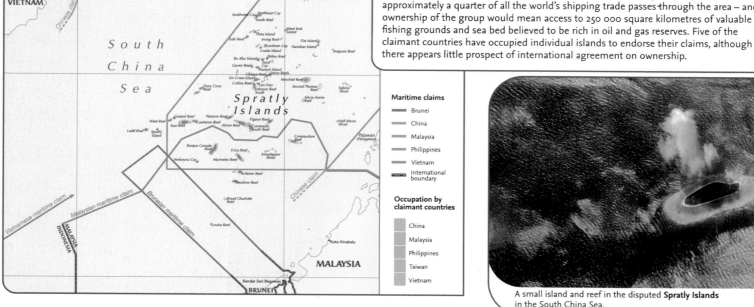

Maritime claims
- Brunei
- China
- Malaysia
- Philippines
- Vietnam
- International boundary

Occupation by claimant countries
- China
- Malaysia
- Philippines
- Taiwan
- Vietnam

A small island and reef in the disputed **Spratly Islands** in the South China Sea.

Terrorist incidents, 1998–2003

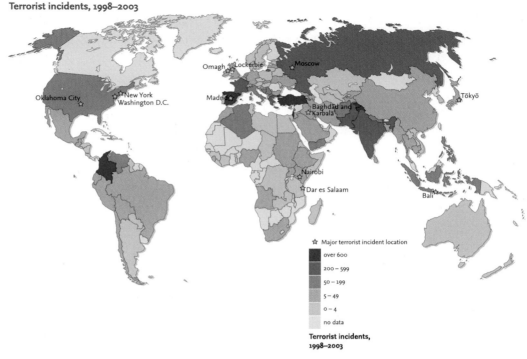

Investigators inspect wreckage outside the Neve Shalom synagogue, **Istanbul, Turkey** after car bombs killed 20 people and injured more than 250.

☆ Major terrorist incident location

	over 600
	200 – 599
	50 – 199
	5 – 49
	0 – 4
	no data

Terrorist incidents, 1998–2003

Global terrorism

Terrorism is defined by the United Nations as "All criminal acts directed against a State and intended or calculated to create a state of terror in the minds of particular persons or a group of persons or the general public". The world has become increasingly concerned about terrorism and the possibility that terrorists could acquire and use nuclear, chemical and biological weapons. One common form of terrorist attack is suicide bombing. Pioneered by Tamil secessionists in Sri Lanka, it has been widely used by Palestinian groups fighting against Israeli occupation of the West Bank and Gaza. In recent years it has also been used by the Al Qaida network in its attacks on the western world.

Major terrorist incidents

Date	Location	Summary	Killed	Injured
December 1988	Lockerbie, Scotland	Airline bombing	270	5
March 1995	Tōkyō, Japan	Sarin gas attack on subway	12	5700
April 1995	Oklahoma City, USA	Bomb in the Federal building	168	over 500
August 1998	Nairobi, Kenya and Dar es Salaam, Tanzania	US Embassy bombings	257	over 4000
August 1998	Omagh, Northern Ireland	Town centre bombing	29	330
September 2001	New York and Washington D.C., USA	Airline hijacking and crashing	2752	4300
October 2002	Bali, Indonesia	Car bomb outside nightclub	202	300
October 2002	Moscow, Russian Federation	Theatre siege	170	over 600
March 2004	Baghdad and Karbalā', Iraq	Suicide bombing of pilgrims	181	over 400
March 2004	Madrid, Spain	Train bombings	191	1800

Middle East politics
Changing boundaries in Israel/Palestine, 1922–2003

West Bank
Population
97% Palestinian Arab
610 000 refugees

West Bank
Security
18% of land under Palestinian control
23% of land under Palestinian civil control and joint security control
59% of land under Israeli control

Gaza
Population
98% Palestinian Arab
865 000 refugees

Gaza
Security
60% of land under Palestinian control
40% of land under Israeli control or settlement

Security fence along the **Egypt/Gaza** border near Rafiah.

The Middle East

The on-going Israeli/Palestinian conflict reflects decades of unrest in the region of Palestine which, after the First World War, was placed under British control. In 1947 the United Nations (UN) proposed a partitioning into separate Jewish and Arab states – a plan which was rejected by the Palestinians and by the Arab states in the region. When Britain withdrew in 1948, Israel declared its independence. This led to an Arab-Israeli war which left Israel with more land than originally proposed under the UN plan. Hundreds of thousands of Palestinians were forced out of their homeland and became refugees, mainly in Jordan and Lebanon. The 6-Day War in 1967 resulted in Israel taking possession of Sinai and Gaza from Egypt, West Bank from Jordan, and the Golan Heights from Syria. These territories (except Sinai which was subsequently returned to Egypt) remain occupied by Israel – the main reason for the Palestinian uprising or 'Intifada' against Israel. The situation remains complex, with poor prospects for peace and for mutually acceptable independent states being established.

–·–·–	International boundary
–×–×–	Disputed International boundary
·····	Ceasefire line
―――	British Mandate Boundary 1922-1948
▬▬▬	Israel Boundary 1948
▨	Land occupied by Israel 1967
Jenīn □	Main Palestinian towns

With the process of globalization has come an increased awareness of, and direct interest in, issues which have global implications. Social issues can now affect large parts of the world and can impact on large sections of society. Perhaps the current issues of greatest concern are those of national security, including the problem of international terrorism (see World Conflict pages 30–31), health, crime and natural resources. The three issues highlighted here reflect this and are of immediate concern.

The international drugs trade, and the crimes commonly associated with it, can impact society and individuals in devastating ways; scarcity of water resources and lack of access to safe drinking water can have major economic implications and causes severe health problems; and the AIDS epidemic is having disastrous consequences in large parts of the world, particularly in sub-Saharan Africa.

Internet Links	
● UNESCO	**www.unesco.org**
● UNAIDS	**www.unaids.org**
● WaterAid	**www.wateraid.org.uk**
● World Health Organization	**www.who.int**
● United Nations Office on Drugs and Crime	**www.unodc.org**

The drugs trade

The international trade in illegal drugs is estimated to be worth over US$400 billion. While it may be a lucrative business for the criminals involved, the effects of the drugs on individual users and on society in general can be devastating. Patterns of drug production and abuse vary, but there are clear centres for the production of the most harmful drugs – the opiates (opium, morphine and heroin) and cocaine. The 'Golden Triangle' of Laos, Myanmar and Thailand, and western South America respectively are the main producing areas for these drugs. Significant efforts are expended to counter the drugs trade, and there have been signs recently of downward trends in the production of heroin and cocaine.

Soldiers in **Colombia**, a major producer of cocaine, destroy an illegal drug processing laboratory.

The international drugs trade
Main producers and trafficking routes for opiates (opium, morphine, heroin) and cocaine

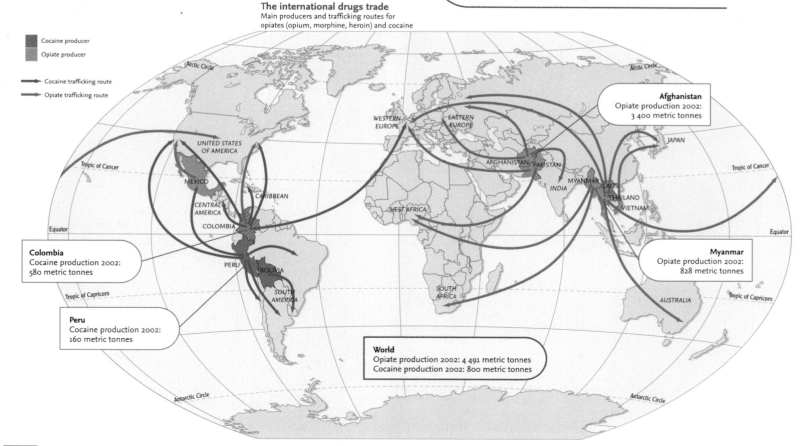

- Cocaine producer
- Opiate producer
- → Cocaine trafficking route
- → Opiate trafficking route

Afghanistan
Opiate production 2002:
3 400 metric tonnes

Colombia
Cocaine production 2002:
580 metric tonnes

Peru
Cocaine production 2002:
160 metric tonnes

Myanmar
Opiate production 2002:
828 metric tonnes

World
Opiate production 2002: 4 491 metric tonnes
Cocaine production 2002: 800 metric tonnes

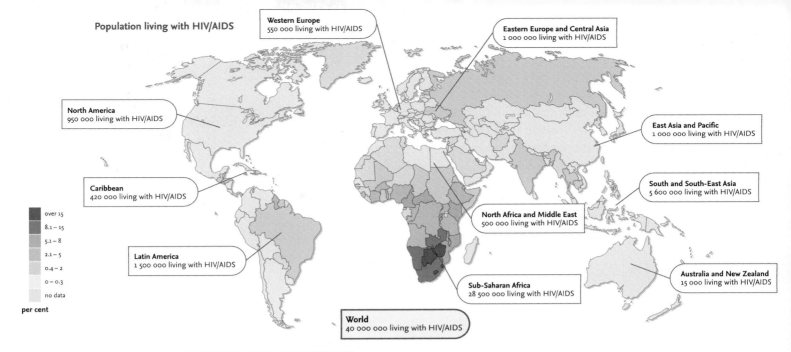

Population living with HIV/AIDS

Western Europe
550 000 living with HIV/AIDS

Eastern Europe and Central Asia
1 000 000 living with HIV/AIDS

North America
950 000 living with HIV/AIDS

East Asia and Pacific
1 000 000 living with HIV/AIDS

Caribbean
420 000 living with HIV/AIDS

South and South-East Asia
5 600 000 living with HIV/AIDS

North Africa and Middle East
500 000 living with HIV/AIDS

Latin America
1 500 000 living with HIV/AIDS

Australia and New Zealand
15 000 living with HIV/AIDS

Sub-Saharan Africa
28 500 000 living with HIV/AIDS

World
40 000 000 living with HIV/AIDS

over 15
8.1 – 15
5.1 – 8
2.1 – 5
0.4 – 2
0 – 0.3
no data

per cent

Protect your children. Teach them about AIDS

AIDS poster in **Zambia**, one of the countries worst affected by the AIDS epidemic.

Aids epidemic

With over 40 million people living with HIV/AIDS (Human Immunodeficiency Virus/Acquired Immune Deficiency Syndrome) and more than 20 million deaths from the disease, the AIDS epidemic poses one of the biggest threats to public health. The UNAIDS project estimated that 5 million people were newly infected in 2003 and that 3 million AIDS sufferers died. Estimates into the future look bleak, especially for poorer developing countries where an additional 45 million people are likely to become infected by 2010. The human cost is huge. As well as the death count itself, more than 11 million African children, half of whom are between the ages of 10 and 14, have been orphaned as a result of the disease.

Access to safe water, 2000
Percentage of population with access to improved drinking water

91 – 100
66 – 90
51 – 65
31 – 50
0 – 30
no data

per cent

Facts

- The majority of people infected with **HIV**, if not treated, develop signs of AIDS within 8 to 10 years

- One in five developing countries will face water shortages by 2030

- Over 5 million people die each year from water-related diseases such as cholera and dysentery

- Estimates suggest that 200 million people consume illegal drugs around the world

Water resources

Water is one of the fundamental requirements of life, and yet in some countries it is becoming more scarce due to increasing population and climate change. Safe drinking water, basic hygiene, health education and sanitation facilities are often virtually nonexistent for impoverished people in developing countries throughout the world. WHO/UNICEF estimate that the combination of these conditions results in 6 000 deaths every day, most of these being children. Currently over 1.2 billion people drink unclean water and expose themselves to serious health risks, while political struggles over diminishing water resources are increasingly likely to be the cause of international conflict.

Domestic use of **untreated water** in Kathmandu, Nepal.

World Change

Many parts of the world are undergoing significant changes which can have widespread and long-lasting effects. The principal causes of change are environmental – particularly climatic – factors and the influence of man. However, it is often difficult to separate these causes because man's activities can influence and exaggerate environmental change. Changes, whatever their cause, can have significant effects on the local population, on the wider region and even on a global scale. Major social, economic and environmental impacts can result from often irreversible changes – land reclamation can destroy fragile marine ecosystems, major dams and drainage schemes can affect whole drainage basins, and local communities can be changed beyond recognition through such projects.

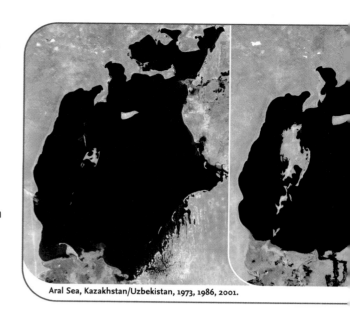

Aral Sea, Kazakhstan/Uzbekistan, 1973, 1986, 2001.

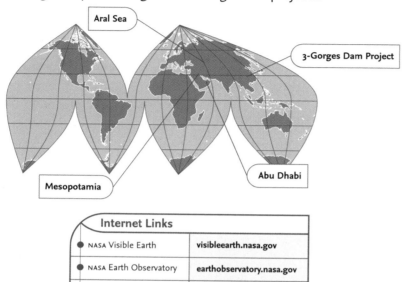

Aral Sea
3-Gorges Dam Project
Mesopotamia
Abu Dhabi

Internet Links	
● NASA Visible Earth	**visibleearth.nasa.gov**
● NASA Earth Observatory	**earthobservatory.nasa.gov**
● USGS Earthshots	**earthshots.usgs.gov**

Man-made change

Human activity has irreversibly changed the environment in many parts of the world. Major engineering projects and the expansion of towns and cities create completely new environments and have major social and economic impacts. The 3-Gorges Dam project in China will control the flow of the Yangtze river and generate enormous amounts of hydro-electric power. During its construction, millions of people were relocated as over 100 towns and villages were inundated by the new reservoir.

The city of Abu Dhabi, capital of the United Arab Emirates, has been built largely on land reclaimed from The Gulf. From a small fishing village it has grown, through a dramatic re-modelling of the coastline, into a major city.

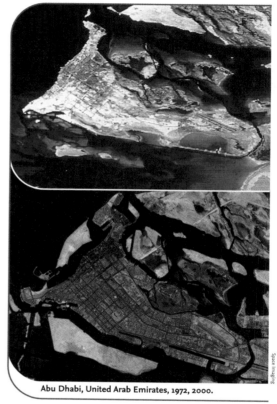

Abu Dhabi, United Arab Emirates, 1972, 2000.

Part of the **Yangtze** river, China, in the region of the 3-Gorges, before construction of the new reservoir.

The **3-Gorges Dam** under construction.

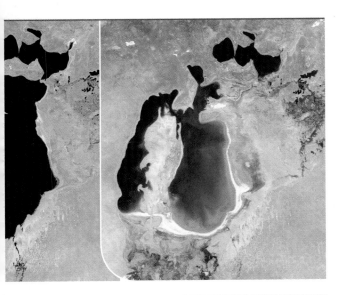

Environmental change

Water resources in certain parts of the world are becoming increasingly scarce. The Aral Sea in central Asia was once the world's fourth largest lake but it now ranks only tenth after shrinking by almost 40 000 square kilometres. This shrinkage has been due to climatic change and to the diversion, for farming purposes, of the major rivers which feed the lake. The change has had a devastating effect on the local fishing industry and has caused health problems for the local population.

The marshlands of Mesopotamia in Iraq have also undergone significant change. It is estimated that only 7 per cent of these ecologically valuable wetlands now remain after systematic drainage of the area and upstream diversion of the Tigris and Euphrates rivers.

Facts

- Earth-observing satellites can now detect land detail, and therefore changes in land cover, of less than 1 metre extent

- Over 90 000 square kilometres of precious tropical forest and wetland habitats are lost each year

- The surface level of the Dead Sea has fallen by 16 metres over the last 30 years

- Hong Kong International Airport, opened in 1998 and covering an area of over 12 square kilometres, was built almost entirely on reclaimed land

Mesopotamian marshlands, Iraq, 1973. Large areas of dense marsh vegetation show as dark red.

Mesopotamian marshlands, Iraq, 2000. Vast areas of former marshland now appear as grey-green areas of sparse vegetation or bare ground.

Europe, the westward extension of the Asian continent and the second smallest of the world's continents, has a remarkable variety of physical features and landscapes. The continent is bounded by mountain ranges of varying character – the highlands of Scandinavia and northwest Britain, the Pyrenees, the Alps, the Carpathian Mountains, the Caucasus and the Ural Mountains. Two of these, the Caucasus and Ural Mountains define the eastern limits of Europe, with the Black Sea and the Bosporus defining its southeastern boundary with Asia.

Across the centre of the continent stretches the North European Plain, broken by some of Europe's greatest rivers, including the Volga and the Dnieper and containing some of its largest lakes. To the south, the Mediterranean Sea divides Europe from Africa. The Mediterranean region itself has a very distinct climate and landscape.

Iceland in winter, one of Europe's largest islands.

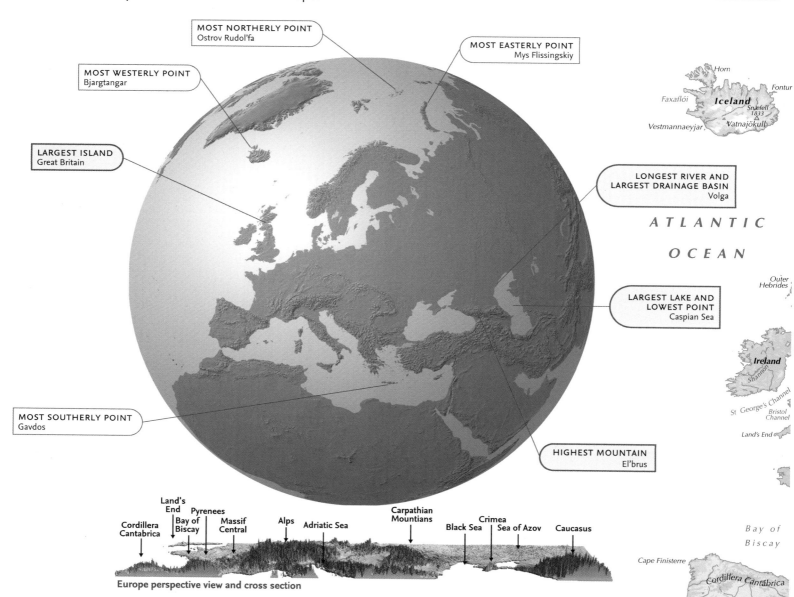

MOST NORTHERLY POINT
Ostrov Rudol'fa

MOST EASTERLY POINT
Mys Flissingskiy

MOST WESTERLY POINT
Bjargtangar

LARGEST ISLAND
Great Britain

LONGEST RIVER AND LARGEST DRAINAGE BASIN
Volga

LARGEST LAKE AND LOWEST POINT
Caspian Sea

MOST SOUTHERLY POINT
Gavdos

HIGHEST MOUNTAIN
El'brus

ATLANTIC

OCEAN

Cordillera Cantabrica | Land's End | Bay of Biscay | Pyrenees | Massif Central | Alps | Adriatic Sea | Carpathian Mountians | Black Sea | Crimea | Sea of Azov | Caucasus

Europe perspective view and cross section

Europe's greatest physical features

Highest mountain	El'brus, Russian Federation	5 642 metres	18 510 feet
Longest river	Volga, Russian Federation	3 688 km	2 292 miles
Largest lake	Caspian Sea	371 000 sq km	143 243 sq miles
Largest island	Great Britain, United Kingdom	218 476 sq km	84 354 sq miles
Largest drainage basin	Volga, Russian Federation	1 380 000 sq km	532 818 sq miles

Europe's extent

Total Land Area	9 908 599 sq km / 3 825 710 sq miles
Most northerly point	Ostrov Rudol'fa, Russian Federation
Most southerly point	Gavdos, Crete, Greece
Most westerly point	Bjargtangar, Iceland
Most easterly point	Mys Flissingskiy, Russian Federation

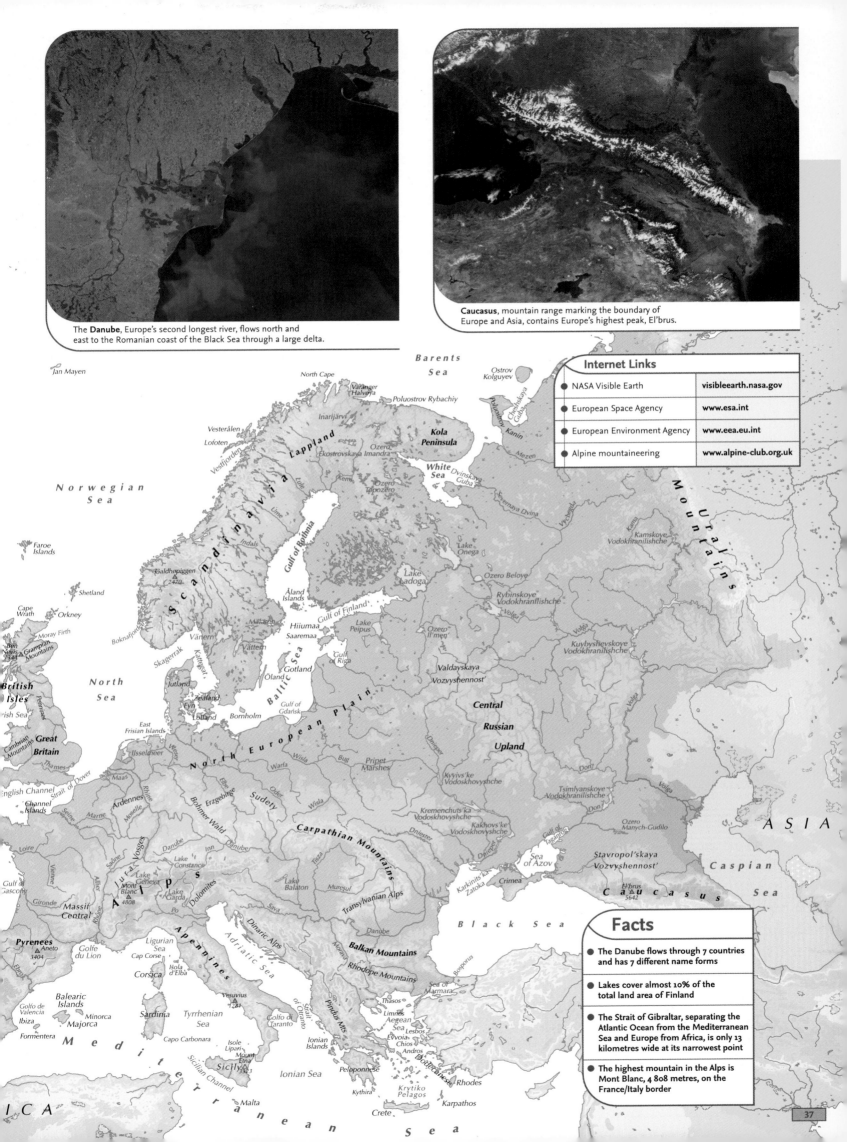

The **Danube**, Europe's second longest river, flows north and east to the Romanian coast of the Black Sea through a large delta.

Caucasus, mountain range marking the boundary of Europe and Asia, contains Europe's highest peak, El'brus.

Internet Links	
● NASA Visible Earth	**visibleearth.nasa.gov**
● European Space Agency	**www.esa.int**
● European Environment Agency	**www.eea.eu.int**
● Alpine mountaineering	**www.alpine-club.org.uk**

Jan Mayen

North Cape

B a r e n t s
S e a

Ostrov
Kolguyev

Varanger
Halvøya
Poluostrov Rybachiy

Vesterålen

Inarijärvi

Poluostrov Kanin

Chëshskaya Guba

Lofoten

L a p p l a n d

**Kola
Peninsula**

Ekostrovskaya Imandra

Ozero Imandra

**White
Sea**

Dvinskaya
Guba

Mezen

N o r w e g i a n
S e a

S c a n d i n a v i a

Lule

Kemi

Ozero
Topozero

Severnaya Dvina

Vychegda

Faroe
Islands

Galdhøpiggen
2470

Ume

Lake
Onega

Ozero Beloye

Kamskoye
Vodokhranilishche

Shetland

Indals

Åland
Islands

Lake
Ladoga

Rybinskoye
Vodokhranilishche

Kama

M o u n t a i n s

Cape
Wrath

Orkney

Boknafjorden

Vänern

Gulf of Finland

Lake
Peipus

Ozero
Il'men'

Volga

U r a l

Moray Firth

Ben
Nevis
1344

Grampian
Mountains

Skagerrak

Kattegat

Mälaren

Hiiumaa
Saaremaa

Gulf
of Riga

Valdayskaya
Vozvyshennost'

Kuybyshevskoye
Vodokhranilishche

N o r t h
S e a

Vättern

Gotland

Öland

Volga

**British
Isles**

Jutland

Zealand

B a l t i c   S e a

Central

Russian

Tsimlyanskoye
Vodokhranilishche

Irish Sea

Pennines

Cambrian
Mountains

Fyn

Lolland

Bornholm

Gulf of
Gdańsk

Upland

Don

Volga

**Great
Britain**

Thames

East
Frisian Islands

N o r t h   E u r o p e a n   P l a i n

Wisla

Bug

Pripet
Marshes

Kyvivs'ke
Vodoskhovyshche

Don

English Channel

Channel
Islands

Ijsselmeer

Weser

Warta

Oder

Wisla

Kremenchuts'ka
Vodoskhovyshche

Kakhovs'ke
Vodoskhovyshche

Gulf of
Taganrog

Ozero
Manych-Gudilo

A S I A

Seine

Maas

Ardennes

Rhine

S u d e t y

Dnieper

Dniester

Dnieper

Marne

Moselle

Böhmer Wald

Erzgebirge

Elbe

C a r p a t h i a n   M o u n t a i n s

Sea of
Azov

Stavropol'skaya
Vozvyshennost'

C a s p i a n

Loire

Vienne

Danube

Inn

Danube

Lake
Constance

Saône

J u r a

V o s g e s

Lake
Geneva

Mont
Blanc
4808

A l p s

Lake
Garda

Dolomites

Tisza

Lake
Balaton

Mureşul

Sava

Po

Transylvanian Alps

Karkinits'ka
Zatoka

Crimea

Sea
of
Taganrog

El'brus
5642

C a u c a s u s

S e a

Gulf of
Gascony

Rhône

Gironde

Massif
Central

Pyrenees
Aneto
3404

Ebro

A p e n n i n e s

Ligurian
Sea

Cap Corse

A d r i a t i c   S e a

Dinaric Alps

Danube

Balkan Mountains

Danube

Morava

B l a c k   S e a

Golfe
du Lion

Corsica

Isola
d'Elba

Rhodope Mountains

Bosporus

Facts

Balearic
Islands

Golfo di
Valencia

Minorca

Sardinia

*Tyrrhenian
Sea*

Capo Carbonara

Vesuvius
1281

Isole
Lipari

Golfo di
Taranto

Pindus Mts

Sea of
Marmara

Thasos

Limnos

*Aegean
Sea*

Lesbos

Evvoia
Chios

Andros

● The Danube flows through 7 countries and has 7 different name forms

● Lakes cover almost 10% of the total land area of Finland

● The Strait of Gibraltar, separating the Atlantic Ocean from the Mediterranean Sea and Europe from Africa, is only 13 kilometres wide at its narrowest point

Ibiza

Majorca

Formentera

Sicily

Mount
Etna
3323

Strait
of Otranto

Ionian Sea

Peloponnese

Kythira

Dodecanese

Rhodes

Karpathos

● The highest mountain in the Alps is Mont Blanc, 4 808 metres, on the France/Italy border

I C A

Malta

Sicilian Channel

Krytiko
Pelagos

Crete

M e d i t e r r a n e a n
S e a

Europe Countries

The predominantly temperate climate of Europe has led to it becoming the most densely populated of the continents. It is highly industrialized, and has exploited its great wealth of natural resources and agricultural land to become one of the most powerful economic regions in the world.

The current pattern of countries within Europe is a result of numerous and complicated changes throughout its history. Ethnic, religious and linguistic differences have often been the cause of conflict, particularly in the Balkan region which has a very complex ethnic pattern. Current boundaries reflect, to some extent, these divisions which continue to be a source of tension. The historic distinction between 'Eastern' and 'Western' Europe is no longer made, following the collapse of Communism and the break up of the Soviet Union in 1991.

Paris, the capital of France and Europe's largest capital city with 9 630 000 residents.

LEAST DENSELY POPULATED COUNTRY
Iceland

MOST NORTHERLY CAPITAL
Reykjavík

LARGEST CAPITAL
Paris

SMALLEST COUNTRY (AREA AND POPULATION)
Vatican City

LARGEST COUNTRY (AREA AND POPULATION)
Russian Federation

HIGHEST CAPITAL
Andorra la Vella

SMALLEST CAPITAL
Vatican City

MOST SOUTHERLY CAPITAL
Valletta

MOST DENSELY POPULATED COUNTRY
Monaco

Facts

- The European Union was founded by six countries: Belgium, France, Germany, Italy, Luxembourg, and the Netherlands. It now has 25 members

- The newest members of the European Union joined in 2004: Cyprus, Czech Republic, Estonia, Hungary, Latvia, Lithuania, Malta, Poland, Slovakia, and Slovenia

- Europe has the 2 smallest independent countries in the world – Vatican City and Monaco

- Vatican City is an independent country entirely within the city of Rome, and is the centre of the Roman Catholic Church

ATLANTIC

OCEAN

REPUBLIC OF IRELAND
Dublin

Bay of Biscay

Cape Finisterre · A Coruña
Bilbao
Oporto · Douro · Salamanca
Madrid
Lisbon · PORTUGAL · Tagus · SPAIN
Cabo de São Vicente · Seville · Córdoba
Cádiz · Málaga · Cartagena
Str. of Gibraltar · Gibraltar

Brest

Azores (Portugal)

Reykjavík · ICELAND

Bosporus, Turkey, a narrow strait of water which separates Europe from Asia.

Europe's capitals

Largest capital (population)	Paris, France	9 854 000
Smallest capital (population)	Vatican City	480
Most northerly capital	Reykjavík, Iceland	64° 39'N
Most southerly capital	Valletta, Malta	35° 54'N
Highest capital	Andorra la Vella, Andorra	1 029 metres 3 376 feet

A F

Europe (excluding Russian Federation) percentage of total population and land area

Legend: Population, Land area

per cent (0 – 16 scale)

Countries (x-axis): Ukraine, France, Spain, Sweden, Germany, Finland, Norway, Poland, Italy, UK, Romania, Belarus, Greece, Bulgaria, Iceland, Serb. and Mont., Hungary, Portugal, Austria, Czech Rep., Rep. of Ireland, Lithuania, Latvia, Croatia, Bosnia-Herz., Slovakia, Estonia, Denmark, Netherlands, Switzerland, Moldova, Belgium, Albania, Macedonia, Slovenia, Luxembourg, Andorra, Malta, Liechtenstein, San Marino, Monaco, Vatican City

Europe's countries

Largest country (area)	Russian Federation	17 075 400 sq km	6 592 812 sq miles
Smallest country (area)	Vatican City	0.5 sq km	0.2 sq miles
Largest country (population)	Russian Federation	143 246 000	
Smallest country (population)	Vatican City	472	
Most densely populated country	Monaco	17 000 per sq km	34 000 per sq mile
Least densely populated country	Iceland	3 per sq km	7 per sq mile

Belgrade, the capital of Serbia and Montenegro, stands at the junction of the Danube, Europe's second longest river, and the Sava river.

Internet Links

● European Union	**europa.eu.int**
● UK Foreign and Commonwealth Office	**www.fco.gov.uk**
● CIA World Factbook	**www.cia.gov/cia/publications/factbook**

Conic Equidistant Projection

1:10 000 000

0   100   200   300   400 miles

0   100   200   300   400   500   600 km

Europe
Northern Europe

Europe
Western Russian Federation

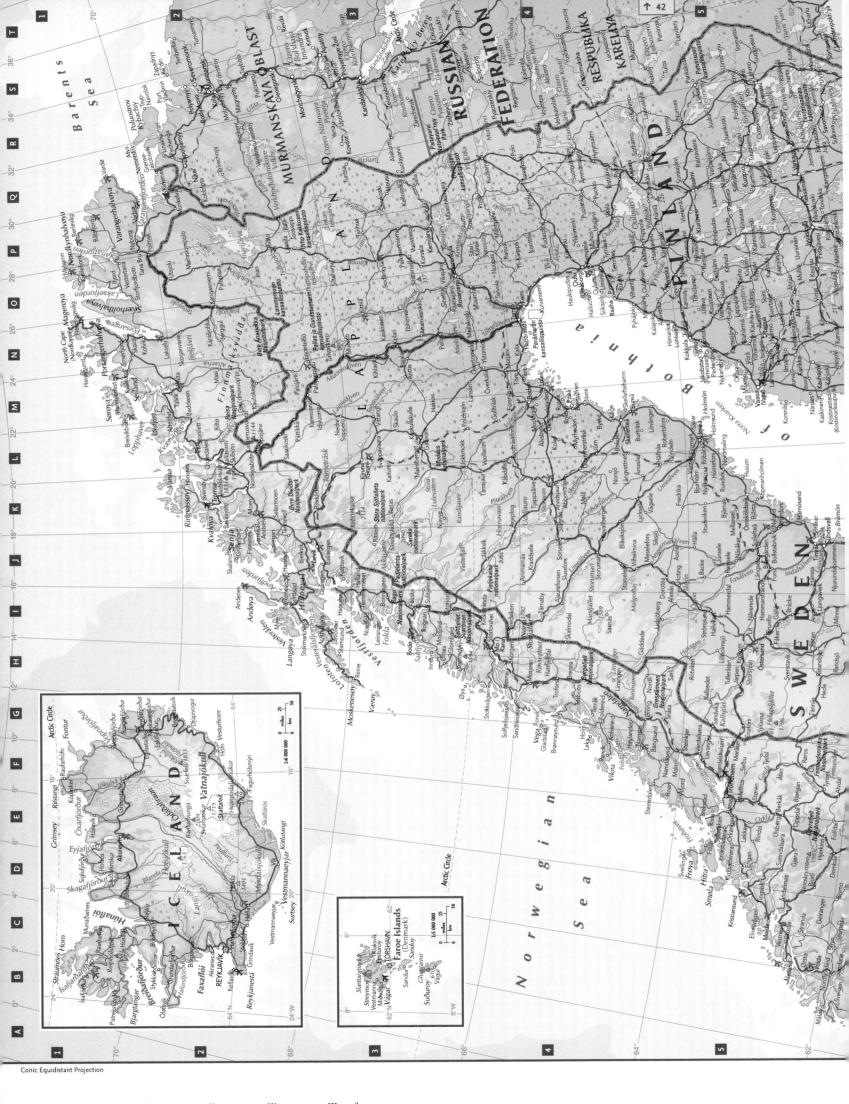

Barents Sea

MURMANSKAYA OBLAST

RUSSIAN FEDERATION

Karel'skiy Bereg

RESPUBLIKA KARELIYA

FINLAND

LAPLAND

SWEDEN

Gulf of Bothnia

Norwegian Sea

North Cape

Arctic Circle

Arctic Circle

ICELAND

Vatnajökull

REYKJAVÍK

Faxaflói

Hunaflói

Grímsey

Vestmannaeyjar

Surtsey

1:6 000 000

0   25   50 miles
0   25   50 km

Faroe Islands
(Denmark)

TÓRSHAVN

Streymoy

Vágar

Suðuroy

Sandoy

1:5 000 000

0   25   50 miles
0   25   50 km

Conic Equidistant Projection

1:5 000 000

0   50   100   150 miles

0   50   100   150   200   250 km

Conic Equidistant Projection

1:5 000 000

| | 0 | 50 | 100 | 150 | miles |

| | 0 | 50 | 100 | 150 | 200 | 250 | km |

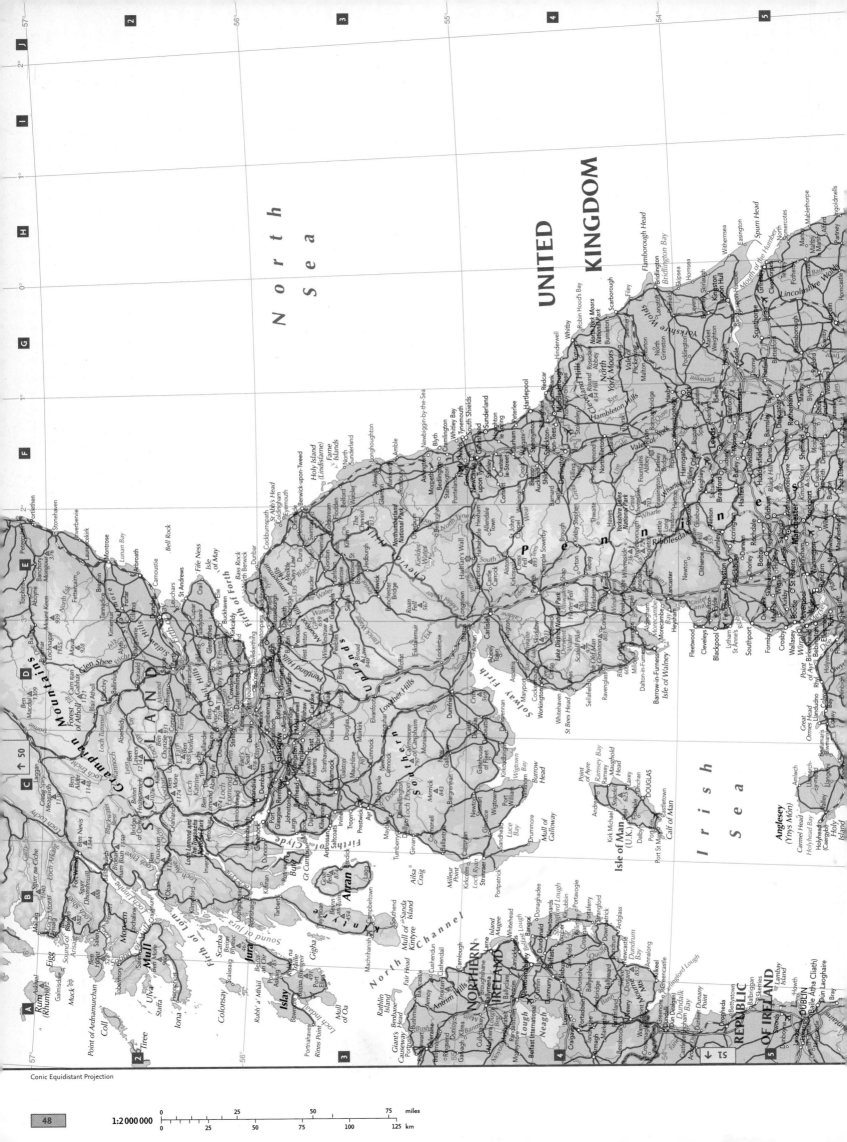

North Sea

UNITED

KINGDOM

Irish Sea

North Channel

NORTHERN IRELAND

REPUBLIC OF IRELAND

SCOTLAND

Grampian Mountains

Southern Uplands

Pennines

Conic Equidistant Projection

1:2 000 000

0   25   50   75   miles

0   25   50   75   100   125   km

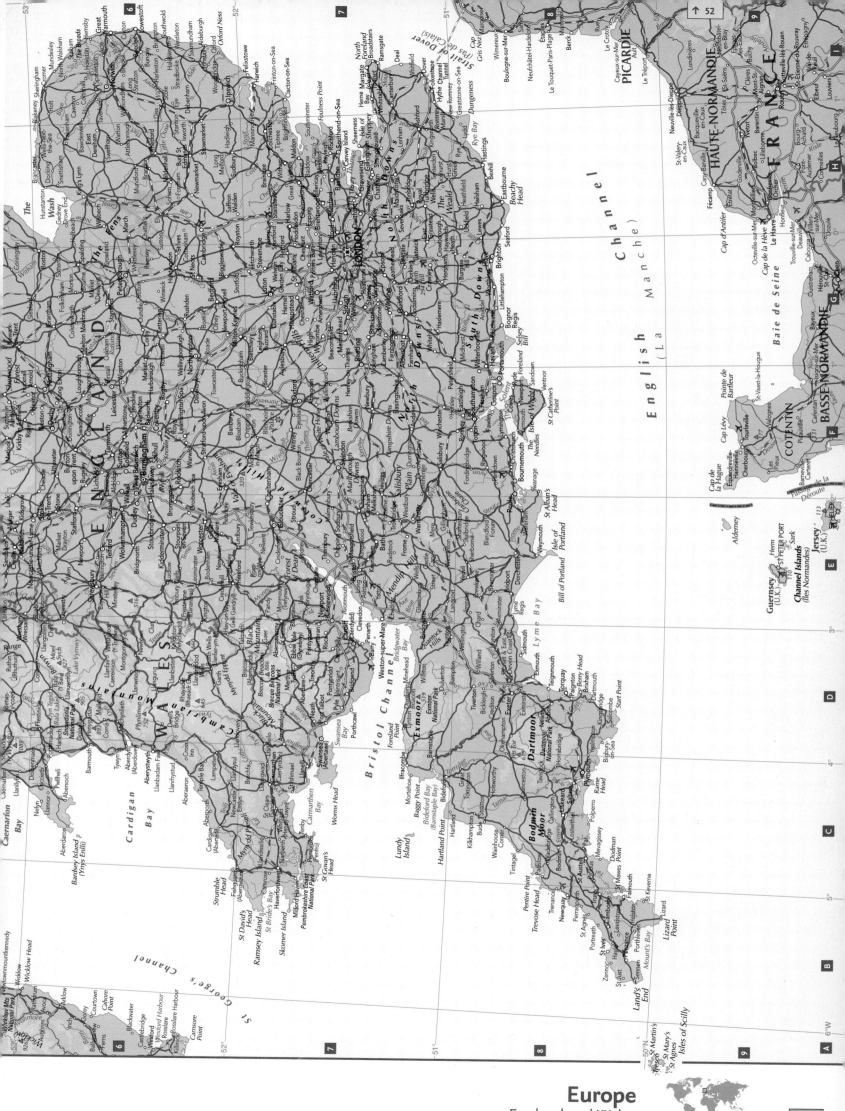

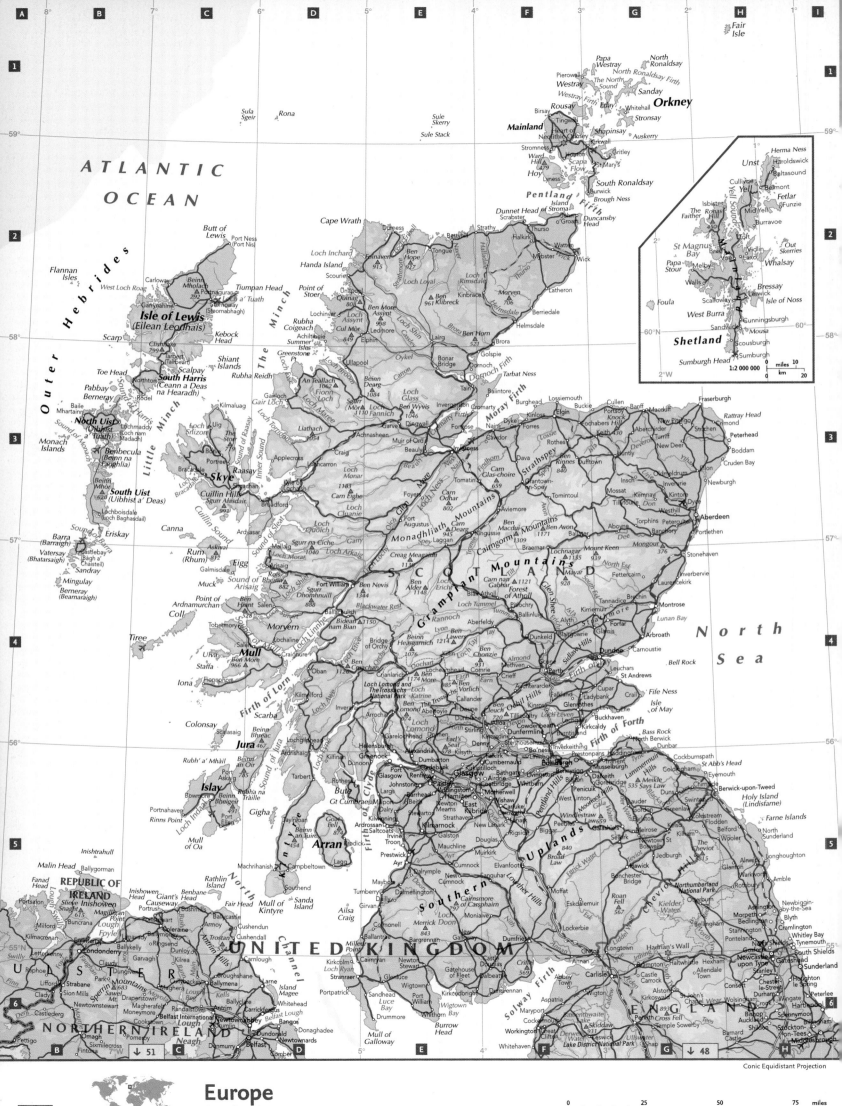

Europe
Scotland

1:2 000 000

Conic Equidistant Projection

50

Conic Equidistant Projection

1:2 000 000

Conic Equidistant Projection

1:2 000 000

Conic Equidistant Projection

1:10 000 000

0   100   200   300   400 miles
0   100 200 300 400 500 600 km

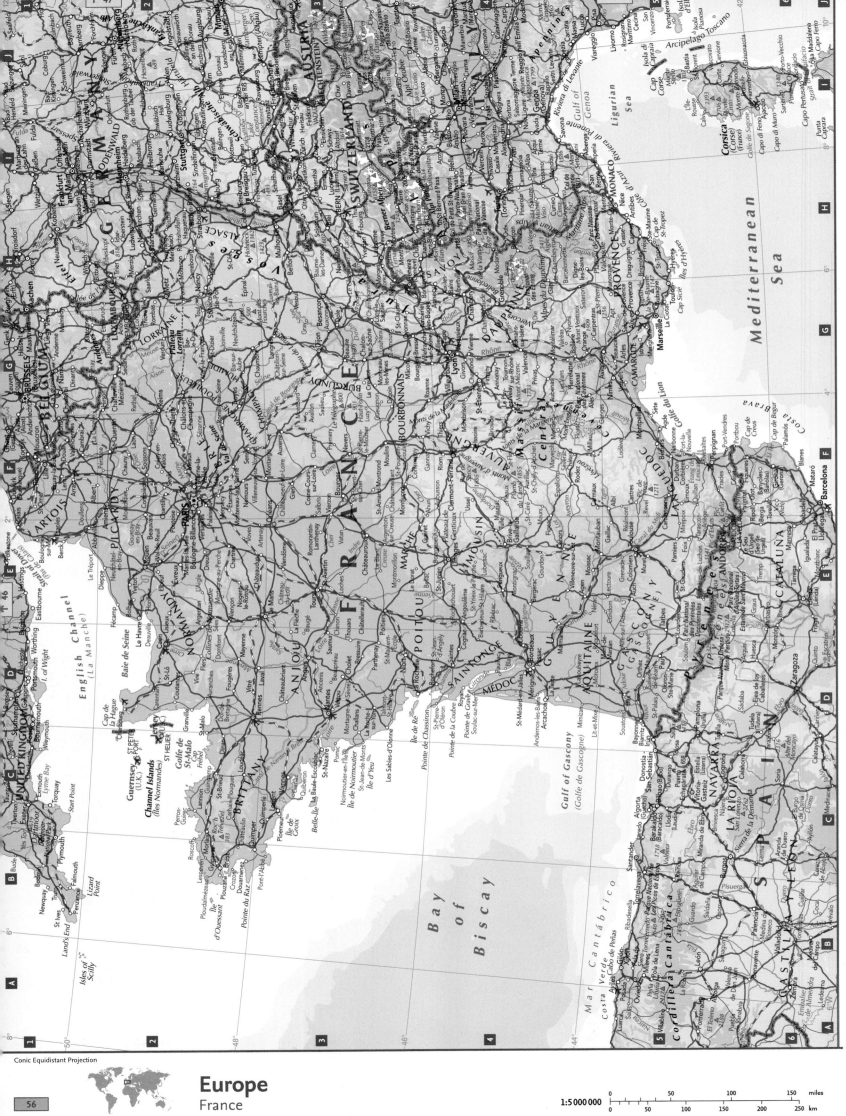

Europe
France

Conic Equidistant Projection

1:5 000 000

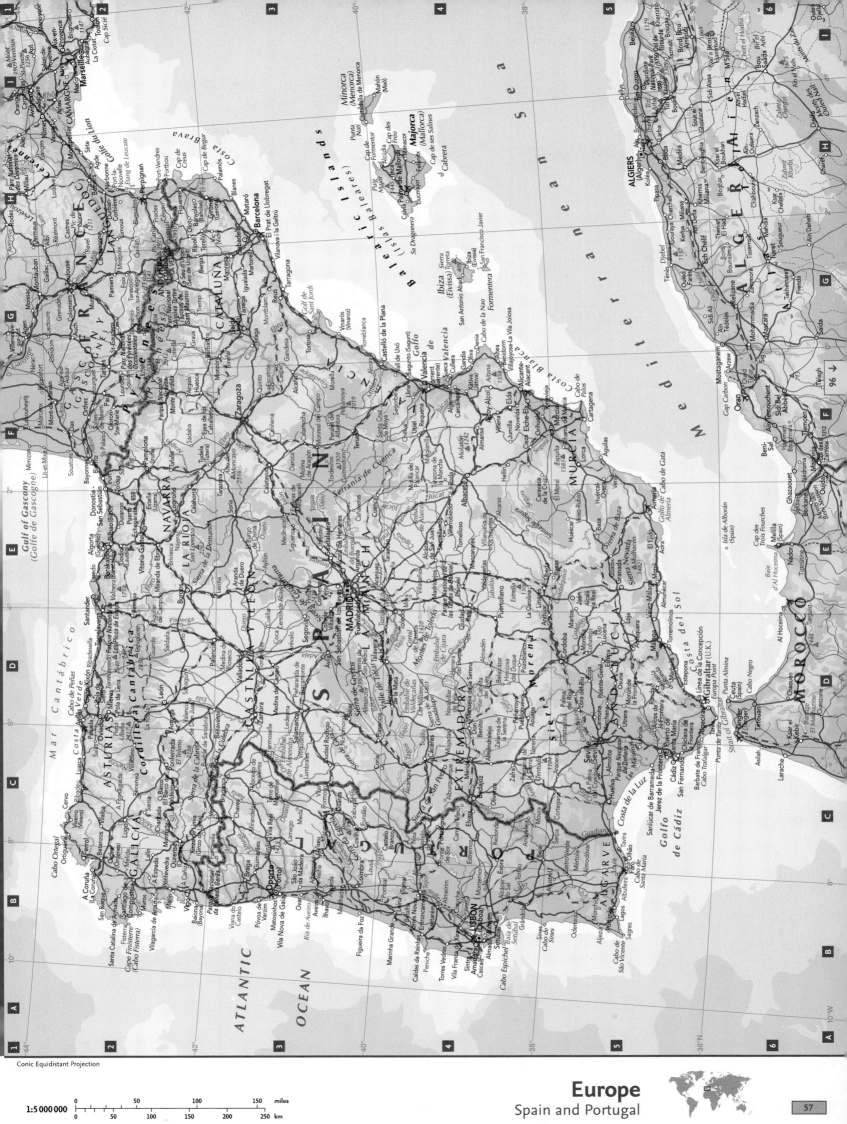

Conic Equidistant Projection

1:5 000 000

Conic Equidistant Projection

1:5 000 000

| 0 | 50 | 100 | 150 | miles |

| 0 | 50 | 100 | 150 | 200 | 250 km |

Asia is the world's largest continent and occupies almost one-third of the world's total land area. Stretching across approximately 165° of longitude from the Mediterranean Sea to the easternmost point of the Russian Federation on the Bering Strait, it contains the world's highest and lowest points and some of the world's greatest physical features. Its mountain ranges include the Himalaya, Hindu Kush, Karakoram and the Ural Mountains and its major rivers – including the Yangtze, Tigris-Euphrates, Indus, Ganges and Mekong – are equally well-known and evocative.

Asia's deserts include the Gobi, the Taklimakan, and those on the Arabian Peninsula, and significant areas of volcanic and tectonic activity are present on the Kamchatka Peninsula, in Japan, and on Indonesia's numerous islands. The continent's landscapes are greatly influenced by climatic variations, with great contrasts between the islands of the Arctic Ocean and the vast Siberian plains in the north, and the tropical islands of Indonesia.

Ice and snow covered peaks of the volcanic mountains on the **Kamchatka Peninsula**, northeast Russian Federation.

Facts

- 90 of the world's 100 highest mountains are in Asia

- The Indonesian archipelago is made up of over 13 500 islands

- The height of the land in Nepal ranges from 60 metres to 8 848 metres

- The deepest lake in the world is Lake Baikal, Russian Federation, which is over 1 600 metres deep

Asia's physical features

Highest mountain	Mt Everest, China/Nepal	8 848 metres	29 028 feet
Longest river	Yangtze, China	6 380 km	3 965 miles
Largest lake	Caspian Sea	371 000 sq km	143 243 sq miles
Largest island	Borneo	745 561 sq km	287 861 sq miles
Largest drainage basin	Ob'-Irtysh, Kazakhstan/Russian Federation	2 990 000 sq km	1 154 439 sq miles
Lowest point	Dead Sea	-398 metres	-1 306 feet

Internet Links

● NASA Visible Earth	**visibleearth.nasa.gov**
● NASA Earth Observatory	**earthobservatory.nasa.gov**
● Peakware World Mountain Encyclopedia	**www.peakware.com**
● The Himalaya	**himalaya.alpine-club.org.uk**

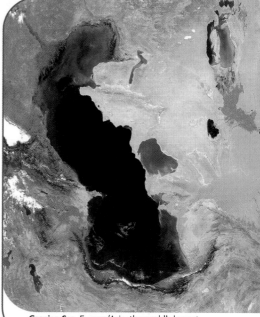

Caspian Sea, Europe/Asia, the world's largest expanse of inland water.

MOST EASTERLY POINT
Mys Dezhneva

MOST NORTHERLY POINT
Mys Arkticheskiy

LARGEST DRAINAGE BASIN
Ob'-Irtysh

LARGEST LAKE
Caspian Sea

MOST WESTERLY POINT
Bozcaada

LOWEST POINT
Dead Sea

HIGHEST MOUNTAIN
Mt Everest

LONGEST RIVER
Yangtze

LARGEST ISLAND
Borneo

MOST SOUTHERLY POINT
Pamana

Hahajima-rettō
Bonin Islands
Volcano Islands

Mediterranean Sea
Cyprus
Caucasus
Caspian Sea
Turan Lowlands
Tien Shan
Tarim Basin
Plateau of Tibet
Gobi
Yellow Sea
Sea of Japan
Honshu

Asia perspective view and cross section

CIFIC
CEAN

Asia's extent

TOTAL LAND AREA	45 036 492 sq km / 17 388 686 sq miles
Most northerly point	Mys Arkticheskiy, Russian Federation
Most southerly point	Pamana, Indonesia
Most westerly point	Bozcaada, Turkey
Most easterly point	Mys Dezhneva, Russian Federation

Palau Islands

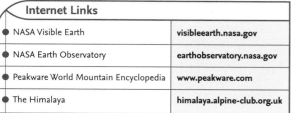

Jazirah Doberai
Puncak Jaya ▲ 5030
New Guinea
Kepulauan Aru
Kepulauan Tanimbar
Arafura Sea

The **Yangtze**, China, Asia's longest river, flowing into the East China Sea near Shanghai.

With approximately sixty per cent of the world's population, Asia is home to numerous cultures, people groups and lifestyles. Several of the world's earliest civilizations were established in Asia, including those of Sumeria, Babylonia and Assyria. Cultural and historical differences have led to a complex political pattern, and the continent has been, and continues to be, subject to numerous territorial and political conflicts – including the current disputes in the Middle East and in Jammu and Kashmir.

Separate regions within Asia can be defined by the cultural, economic and political systems they support. The major regions are: the arid, oil-rich, mainly Islamic southwest; southern Asia with its distinct cultures, isolated from the rest of Asia by major mountain ranges; the Indian- and Chinese-influenced monsoon region of southeast Asia; the mainly Chinese-influenced industrialized areas of eastern Asia; and Soviet Asia, made up of most of the former Soviet Union.

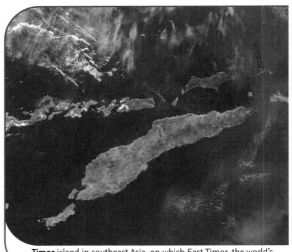

Timor island in southeast Asia, on which East Timor, the world's newest independent state, is located.

Facts

- **Over 60% of the world's population live in Asia**

- **Asia has 11 of the world's 20 largest cities**

- **East Timor is Asia's newest independent country – founded in May 2002**

- **The Korean peninsula was divided into North Korea and South Korea in 1948 approximately along the 38th parallel**

62

Internet Links

● UK Foreign and Commonwealth Office	www.fco.gov.uk
● CIA World Factbook	www.odci.gov/cia/publications/factbook
● Asian Development Bank	www.adb.org
● Association of Southeast Asian Nations (ASEAN)	www.aseansec.org
● Asia-Pacific Economic Cooperation	www.apecsec.org.sg

Asia's countries

Largest country (area)	Russian Federation	17 075 400 sq km	6 592 812 sq miles
Smallest country (area)	Maldives	298 sq km	115 sq miles
Largest country (population)	China	1 289 161 000	
Smallest country (population)	Palau	20 000	
Most densely populated country	Singapore	6 656 per sq km	17 219 per sq mile
Least densely populated country	Mongolia	2 per sq km	4 per sq mile

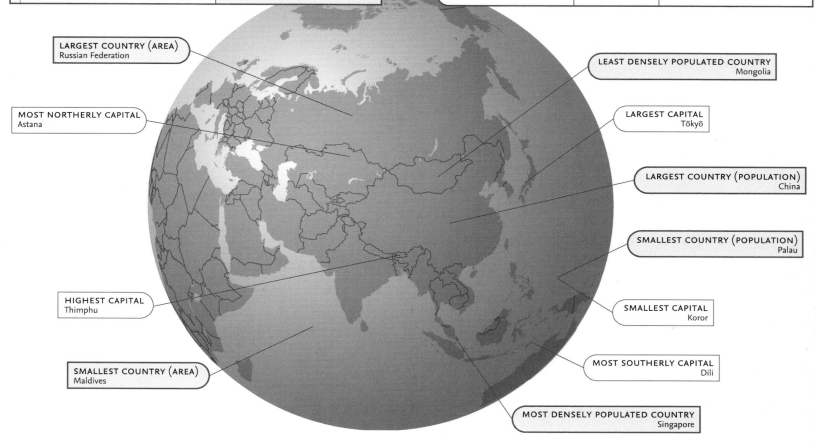

LARGEST COUNTRY (AREA)
Russian Federation

LEAST DENSELY POPULATED COUNTRY
Mongolia

MOST NORTHERLY CAPITAL
Astana

LARGEST CAPITAL
Tōkyō

LARGEST COUNTRY (POPULATION)
China

SMALLEST COUNTRY (POPULATION)
Palau

HIGHEST CAPITAL
Thimphu

SMALLEST CAPITAL
Koror

MOST SOUTHERLY CAPITAL
Dili

SMALLEST COUNTRY (AREA)
Maldives

MOST DENSELY POPULATED COUNTRY
Singapore

Different land use patterns help identify the borders between **Egypt**, **Israel** and **Gaza** in this space shuttle photograph.

Bonin Islands (Japan)

Volcano Islands (Japan)

Koror
PALAU

Jayapura

New Guinea

Asia (excluding Russian Federation) percentage of total population and land area

per cent

China 34
India 30
28

Population
Land area

China, India, Kazakhstan, Saudi Arabia, Indonesia, Iran, Mongolia, Pakistan, Turkey, Myanmar, Afghanistan, Yemen, Thailand, Turkmenistan, Uzbekistan, Iraq, Japan, Malaysia, Vietnam, Oman, Philippines, Laos, Kyrgyzstan, Syria, Cambodia, Nepal, Bangladesh, Tajikistan, North Korea, South Korea, Jordan, Azerbaijan, UAE, Georgia, Sri Lanka, Bhutan, Taiwan, Armenia, Israel, Kuwait, Qatar, Lebanon, Cyprus, Brunei, Bahrain, Singapore, Palau, Maldives

Asia's capitals

Largest capital (population)	Tōkyō, Japan	35 327 000
Smallest capital (population)	Koror, Palau	14 000
Most northerly capital	Astana, Kazakhstan	51° 10'N
Most southerly capital	Dili, East Timor	8° 35'S
Highest capital	Thimphu, Bhutan	2 423 metres 7 949 feet

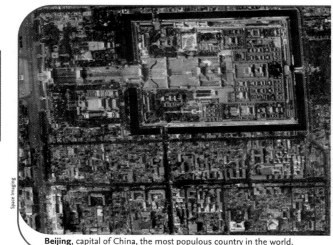

Space Imaging

Beijing, capital of China, the most populous country in the world.

Conic Equidistant Projection

64

1:20 000 000

| 0 | 200 | 400 | 600 miles |

| 0 | 200 | 400 | 600 | 800 | 1000 km |

Asia
Northern Asia

Albers Conic Equal Area Projection

1:20 000 000

0   200   400   600   miles
0   200 400 600 800 1000 km

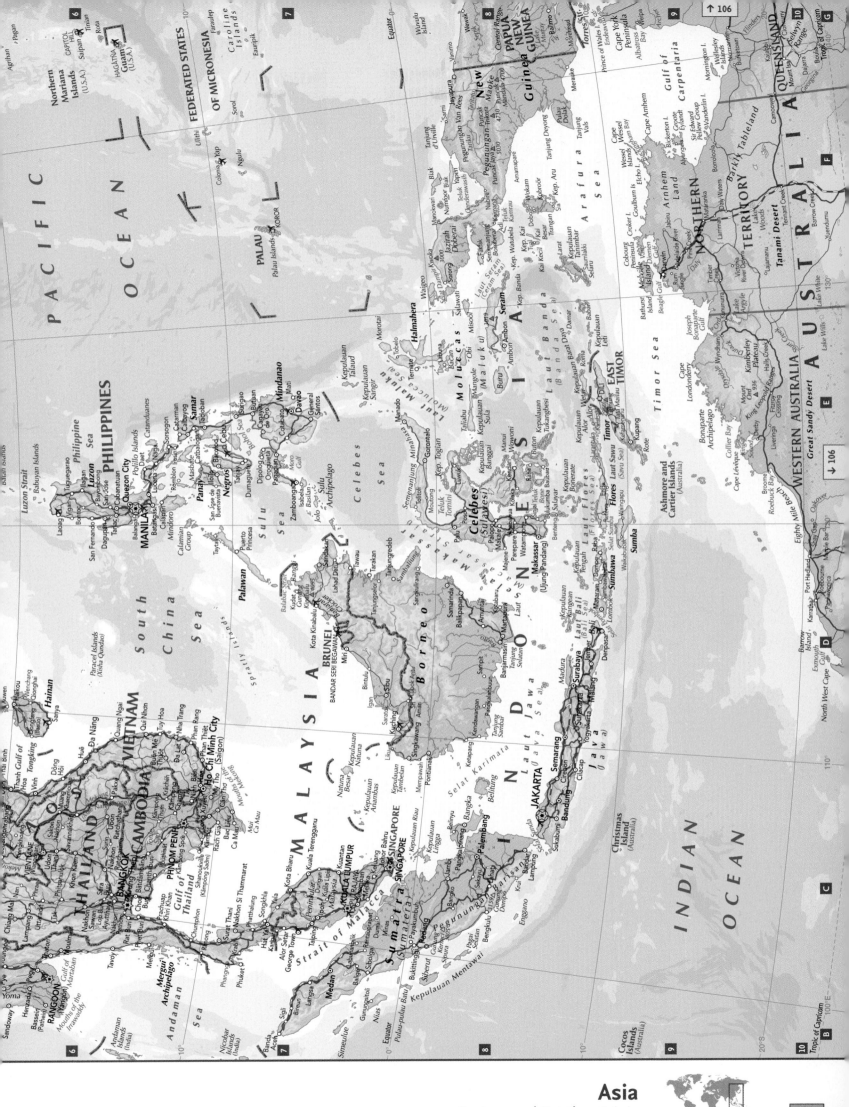

Asia
Eastern and Southeast Asia

Haitan Dao
T'AIPEI
Chilung
Keelung
Sakishima-shotō
Ryukyu Islands
(Nansei-shotō) (Japan)
Hsinchu
Ilan
Fengyüan
Changhua
Hualien
Chiai Yü Shan
3950
Okino-Daitō-jima
Kita-lō-jima
Volcano Islands
(Kazan-rettō)
(Japan)
Minami-
Iō-jima
(Japan)

TAIWAN
T'ainan
T'aitung
Tropic of Cancer

Kaohsiung
Lan Yü

Bashi Channel
Itbayat
Batan
Islands
Batan

Okino-Tori-shima
(Japan)
Farallon
de Pajaros
(Uracas)
Maug
Islands

Babuyan
Calayan
Babuyan Islands
Fuga
Luzon Strait
Asuncion

Laoag
Babuyan Channel
Agrihan

P A C I F I C
Pagan

Bangued
Tuguegarao
Philippine
Sea
Alamagan
Guguan

Vigan
Bontoc
Ilagan
Northern
Mariana
Islands
(U.S.A.)
Sarigan

San Fernando
Santiago
Bayombong
Anatahan
Farallon
de Medinilla

Baguio
Dagupan
Baler
O C E A N
Luzon
San Jose
Cabanatuan
CAPITOL HILL
Saipan

Tarlac
Polillo Islands
Tinian
Aguijan

Olongapo
Quezon City
Rota

Balanga
MANILA
San Pablo
Daet
HAGÅTÑA
Guam
(U.S.A.)

Nasugbu
PHILIPPINES
Catanduanes

Batangas
Lucena
Naga
Virac

Mount
Calapan
Lopez
Iriga
Legaspi

Mamburao
2585 Marinduque
Burias
Sorsogon

Mindoro
Sibuyan
Sea
Irosin
Laoang

Roxas
Romblon
Masbate
Catarman

Cuyo
Islands
Barboza
Roxas
Masbate
Calbayog

San Jose de
Buenavista
Iloilo
Gadiz
Samar
Tacloban

Bago
Bacolod
Leyte
Ormoc
Baybay

Dumaran
Negros
2450
Maasin
Dinagat

Cauayan
Carcar
Bohol
Tanjay
Cebu
Surigao
Siargao

Dumaguete
Bohol Sea
Tandag

Dipolog
Cagayan
de Oro
Butuan

Sea
Orquieta
Iligan
Bislig

Ozamiz
Lake
Lanao
Malaybalay

Pagadian
Mindanao

Zamboanga
Cotabato
Mount
2954
Davao
Davao
Mati

Basilan
Isabela
Norala
Digos
Gulf
Cape San
Agustin

Jolo
General Santos
Malita

Sulu Archipelago
Sarangani
Islands

FEDERATED STATES

Colonia
Yap
Fais
Gaferut

Ngeruangel
Ngulu
Sorol
OF MICRONESIA
West
Fayu
Pikelot
Namonuito

PALAU
Palau Islands
Eil Malk
KOROR
Angaur
Faraulep
Woleai
Olimarao
Lamotrek
Elato
Satawal
Puluwat
Pulap

Sonsorol
Islands
Eauripik
Ifalik
Pulusuk

Pulo Anna
Merir
C a r o l i n e
I s l a n d s

Tobi
Helen
Helen
Reef

Celebes
Sea

Kepulauan
Nanusa

Karakelong
Kepulauan
Talaud
Niampak
Tahuna
Salibabu
Kaburuang

Sangir
Manado
1784
Kepulauan
Sangir

Tahulandang
Siau
Tanjung Sopi
Morotai

Semenanjung Minahasa
Bitung
Susupu
Daruba

Tolitoli
Tondano
Gebe
Waigeo

Gunung
Oroamas
Gorontalo
Kotamobagu
Loloda
1635
Ternate
Halmahera

Moutong
Marisa
Bogani Nani
Wartabone
National Park
Akelamo

Equator

Teluk
Tomini
Tomali
Togian
Kepulauan Togian
Laut Halmahera
(Halmahera Sea)
Ninigo
Group

Gunung
Lokilalaki
2610
Batudaka
Togian
Pangkalsiang
Labuha
Bacan
Gam
Bisa
Selat Dampir
Kwoka
Kaironi
Sorong
3000
Manokwari
Numfoor
Biak
St Matthias
Group
Tabalo
Mussau
Island

Poso
Ampoa
Luwuk
Laiwui
Obi
Rajaampat
Temiabuan
Sajam
Num
Pom
Yapen
Supiori
Rümberpon
Rori
Tanjung
d'Urville
Teba
Hermit
Islands
Admiralty Islands
Rambutyo
Island

Tenteno
Kolonedale
Kepulauan
Sula
Mangole
Misool
Tg Winsop
Jazirah Doberai
2939
Serui
Tanjung
Aua
Island
Wuvulu Island
Pelleluhu Is
Manus Island
Lorengau

Taliabu
Leksula
Faktak
Kep.
Pisang
Aranda
Modan
Teluk
Cenderawasih
Marine National Park
Bismarck
Archipelago

Celebes
(Sulawesi)
Banggai
Kepulauan
Banggai
Buru
Wahai
2252
Rufufiru
Asori
Pegunungan Van Rees
272
Jayapura
Vanimo
Sissano
Kairiru I.
Schouten Islands
Mussau
Island

Palopo
Bahomonte
Seram
3019
Manusela
National Park
Bomberai
Selasi
Pegunungan
3892
Sarmi
Ansudu
Demta
Lumi
Bewani
Maprik
Wewak
Witu Islands

Malili
Kolaka
Wowoni
Fogi
Ambalau
Ambon
Undur
Faktak
Kaimana
Teluk
5030
Maoke
Pk Jaya
4730
4595
4700
Green
River
Ambunti
Sepik
Watam
Manam I.
Mount
Kanangio
Bismarck
Sea

Kendari
Raha
Buton
Kepulauan
Gorong
Nusawulan
Teluk
Kamrau
Amamapare
Gunung Lorentz
National Park
Puncak
Mandala
Jayawijaya
Central Ra
Wabag
Mt Hagen
Karkar Island
8038

Watampone
Manui
Buru
Kepulauan
Banda
Kepulauan
Watubela
New
Tembagapura
Puncak
Yamin
3711
Lake
Kopiago
Tari
Mendi
4359
Madang
Long I.

Teluk
Bone
Sinjai
Wawalindu
2799
Wangiwangi
Kepulauan
Lucipara
Kai Besar
Kep.
Tayandu
Kola
Agats
Guinea
Mulia
Wabag
Goroka
Bulolo
Umboi
New
Britain

Bulukumba
Siumpu
Kepulauan
Tukangbesi
Laut Banda
(Banda Sea)
Tual
Dobo
Benjina
Kobroör
Wokam
Kai Kecil
Muting
PAPUA
Mount
4509
Anepmete
Walingai
Kandrian
Finschhafen

Benteng
Salayar
Trangan
Kepulauan Aru
NEW GUINEA
Kaiapit
4359
4107
Lae
Morobe

Laut Flores
(Flores Sea)
Kep.
Bonerate
Molu
Larat
Kepulauan Tanimbar
Tanjung Deyong
Lake
Murray
3719
Kratke
Bulolo
Cape
Ward Hunt

Tanjung Kapondai
Kepulauan
Barat Daya
Damar
Watubela
Yamdena
Tanjung Vals
Yomuka
Pulau
Dolak
Kurik
Boigu I.
Torres
Wasua
Balimo
Aramia
Kikori
Kerema
Mount
Victoria
4071
Pondetta

Ruteng
2420
Komba
Kepulauan Alor
Wetar
Roma
Moa
Sermata
Leti
Babar
Seru
Arafura
Sea
Merauke
Weam
Morehead
Daru
Kiwai Island
Bula
Cape
Nelson

Maumere
Bajawa
Selat Wetar
Gunung Tata Mailau
2960
DILI
Selat
Solor
Atambua
Atauro
Kefamenanu
Komoran
Tanjung
Deyong
Morehead
Tais
Bereina
Hisiu
Hood
Point
Kwikila

Flores
Waingapu
Lembata
EAST TIMOR
Soe
Timor
Prince of
Wales Island
Moa Island
PORT MORESBY
Owen
Stanley Ra.
3676
Abau

Sumba
Waikabubak
Kupang
EAST TIMOR
Badu Island
Ashmore Reefs
Endeavour
Strait

Ngalu
Savu
Raijua
Baun
Rote
T i m o r
S e a
Cape Van
Diemen
Croker Island
Gobourg Peninsula
Cape
Wessel
Wessel
Islands
Cape York
Great Barrier Reef
Marine Park
(Far North Section)
Jardine River
National Park
Cape Grenville

Ashmore and
Cartier Islands
(Australia)
Bathurst Island
Mitchell Point
Melville I.
Maningrida
Elcho I.
AUSTRALIA
Mapoon
Bramwell

Asia
Southeast Asia

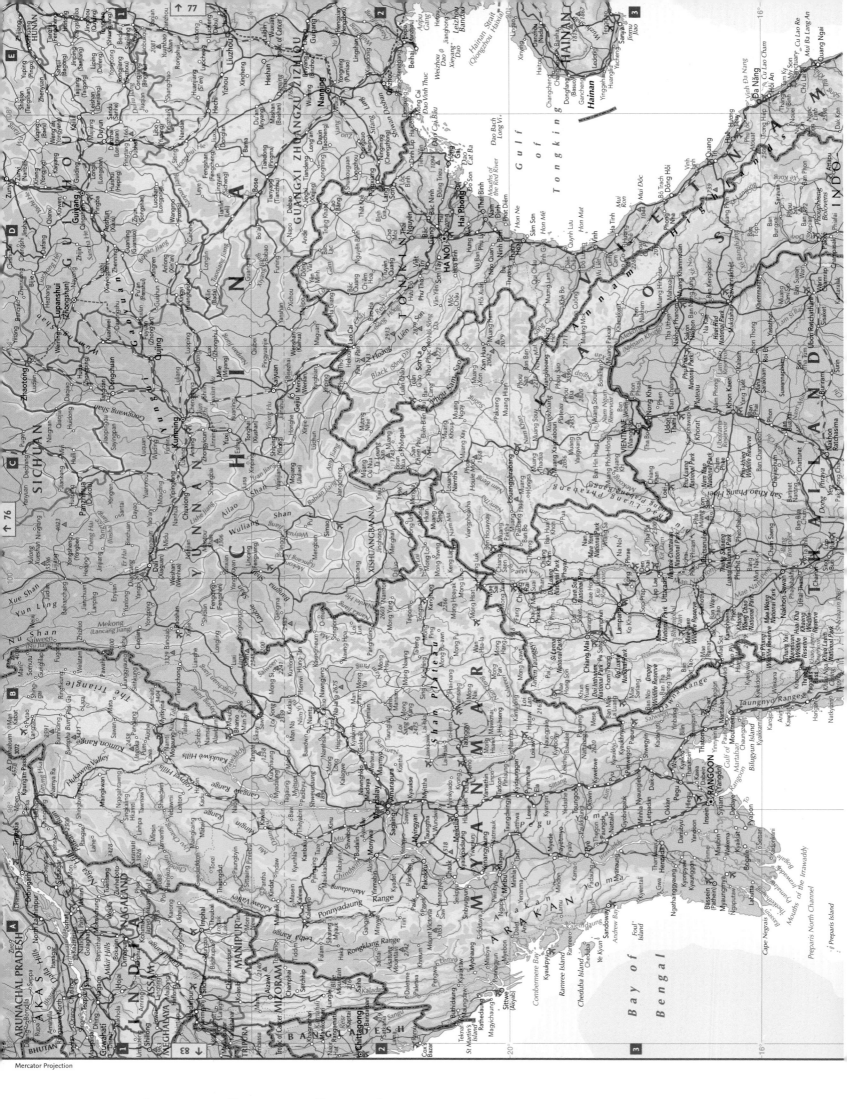

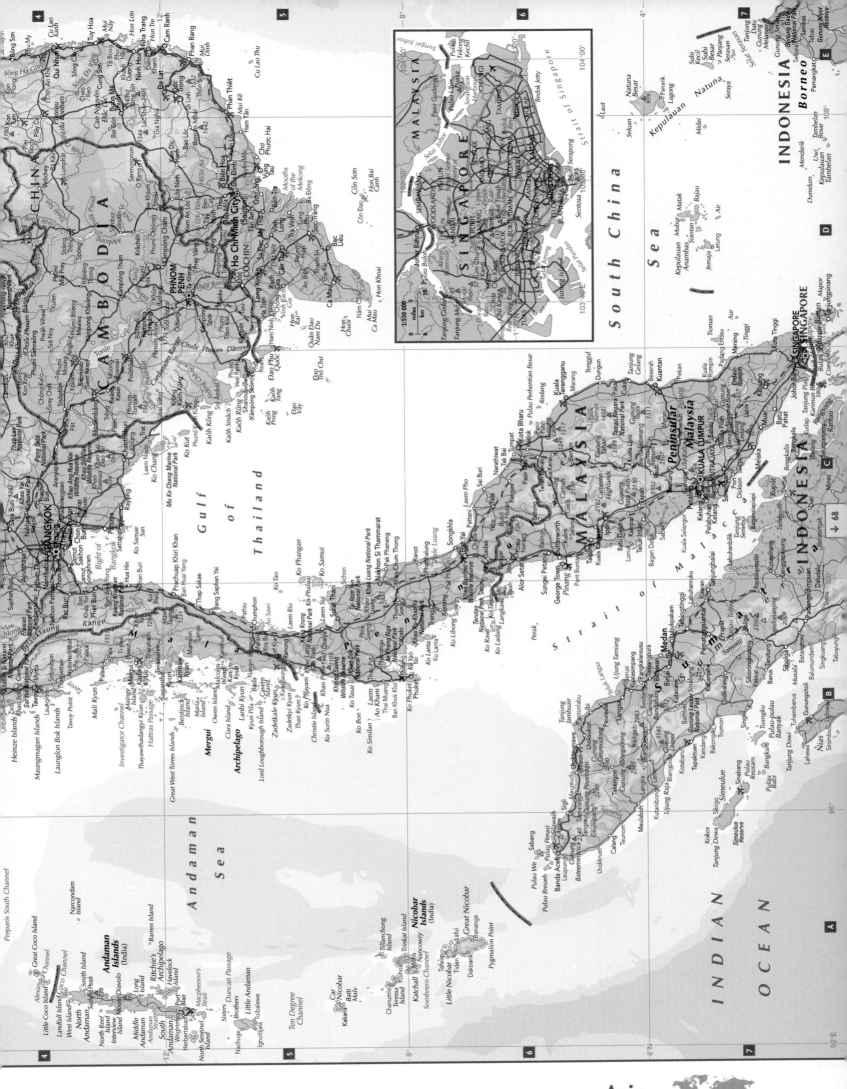

Asia

Myanmar, Thailand, Peninsular Malaysia and Indo-China

Albers Conic Equal Area Projection

1:15 000 000

Asia

Eastern Asia

H

G

F

E

D

C

B

A

1   2   3   4

Sea of Okhotsk
(Okhotskoye More)

Sakhalin

SAKHALINSKAYA OBLAST'

Zapadno-Sakhalinsk Khrebet

Tatarskiy Proliv

La Pérouse Strait

Sóya-misaki

Hokkaidō

RUSSIAN FEDERATION

Amurskiy liman

Khrebet Yam Alin'

KHABAROVSKIY KRAY

Khabarovsk

Komsomol'sk-na-Amure

YEVREYSKAYA AVTONOMNAYA OBLAST'

Birobidzhan

PRIMORSKIY KRAY

Lake Khanka

Vladivostok

AMURSKAYA OBLAST'

Blagoveshchensk

Khrebet

Bol'shoy Khingan

HEILONGJIANG

CHINA

Harbin

Qiqihar

Daqing (Anda)

Fuyu

NEI MONGOL ZIZHIQU

Da Hinggan Ling

Changchun

JILIN

Shenyang

LIAONING

CHITINSKAYA OBLAST'

Conic Equidistant Projection

1:7 000 000

0   100   200   miles
0   100   200   300   400   km

ADMINISTERED BY RUSSIAN FEDERATION, CLAIMED BY JAPAN

Kuril'skiye Ostrova
(Kuril Islands)

Asia

Japan, North Korea and South Korea

Conic Equidistant Projection

1:7 000 000

0   100   200   miles

0   100   200   300   400 km

Albers Conic Equal Area Projection

1:20 000 000

| 0 | | 200 | | 400 | | 600 miles |
| 0 | 200 | 400 | 600 | 800 | 1000 km |

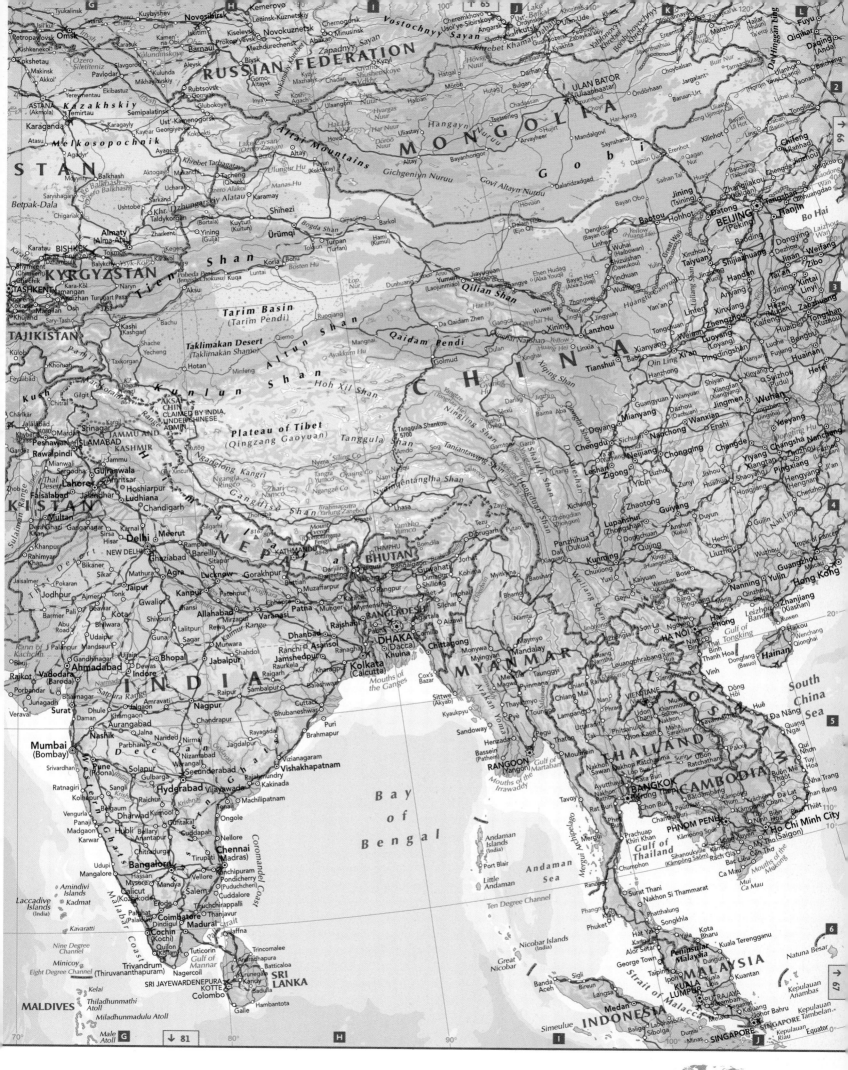

Albers Equal Area Conic Projection

1:13 000 000

| 0 | 100 | 200 | 300 | 400 | 500 miles |

| 0 | 100 | 200 | 300 | 400 | 500 | 600 | 700 | 800 km |

Asia
Southern Asia

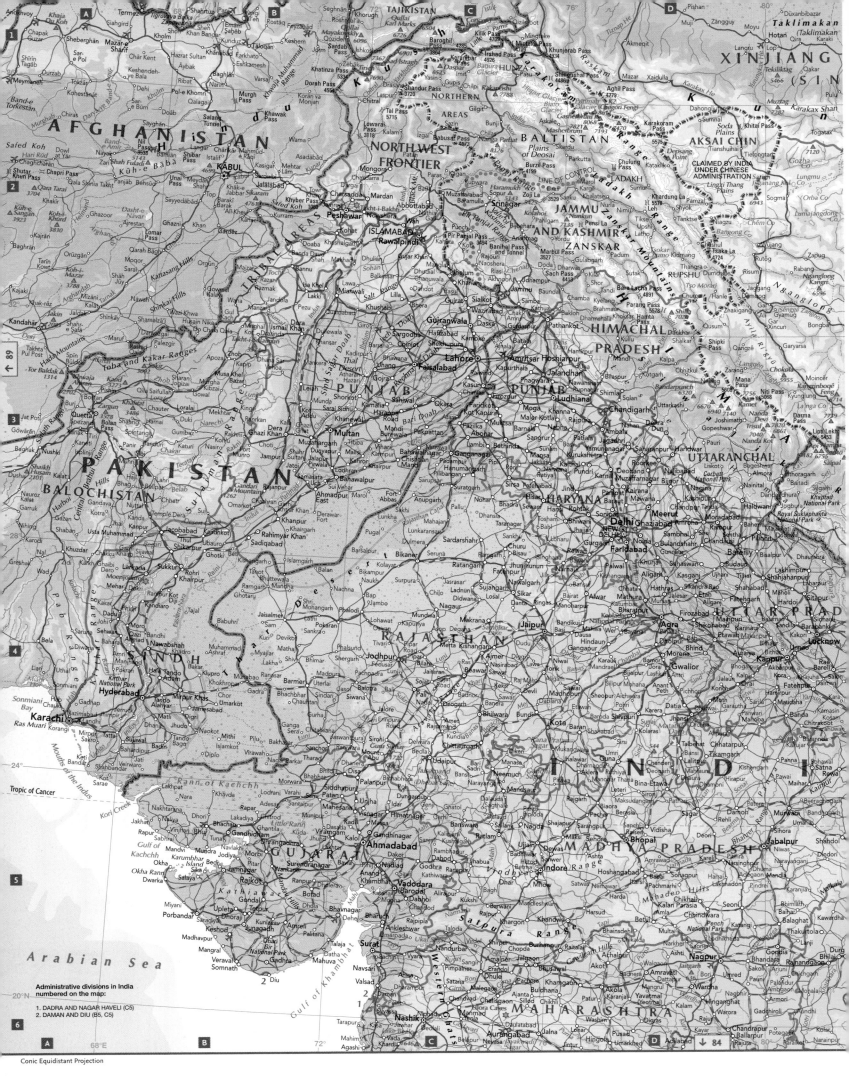

Conic Equidistant Projection

Administrative divisions in India numbered on the map:

1. DADRA AND NAGAR HAVELI (C5)
2. DAMAN AND DIU (B5, C5)

1:7 000 000

| 0 | 100 | 200 | miles |
| 0 | 100 | 200 | 300 | 400 | km |

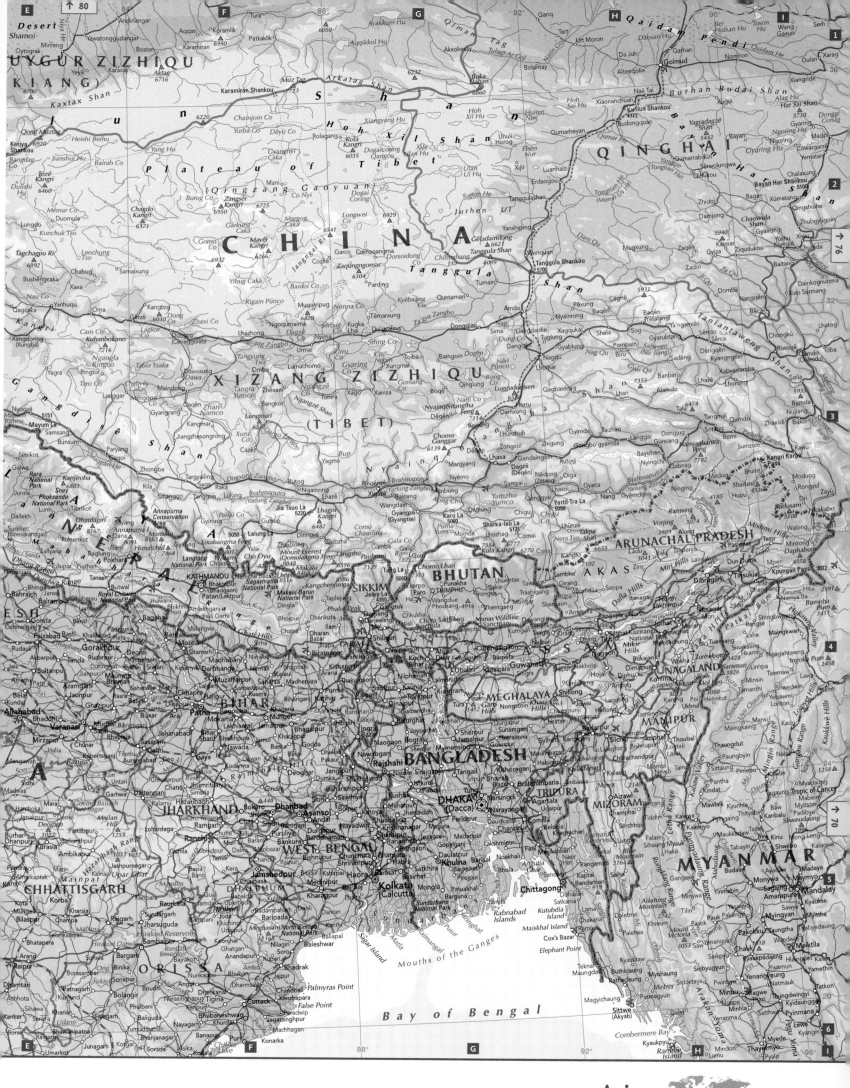

Asia
Northern India, Nepal, Bhutan and Bangladesh

83

Asia
Southern India and Sri Lanka

Conic Equidistant Projection

1:7 000 000

Administrative divisions in India
numbered on the map:

1. DADRA AND NAGAR HAVELI (B1)
2. DAMAN AND DIU (A1, B1)
3. PONDICHERRY (C4)

**Mediterranean
Sea**

CYPRUS

SYRIA

LEBANON

BEIRUT
(Beyrouth)

DAMASCUS
(Dimashq)

IRAQ

Syrian Desert
(Bādiyat ash Shām)

WEST
BANK

Tel Aviv-Yafo

JERUSALEM
(Yerushalayim)
(El Quds)

GAZA

ISRAEL

JORDAN

AMMAN

Port Said
(Būr Sa'īd)

BŪR SA'ĪD

SAUDI
ARABIA

EGYPT

SHAMAL SĪNĀ'

JANŪB SĪNĀ'

Conic Equidistant Projection

1 : 3 000 000

```
0        25        50        75        100   miles
0    25    50    75    100   125   150   175 km
```

Asia
Middle East

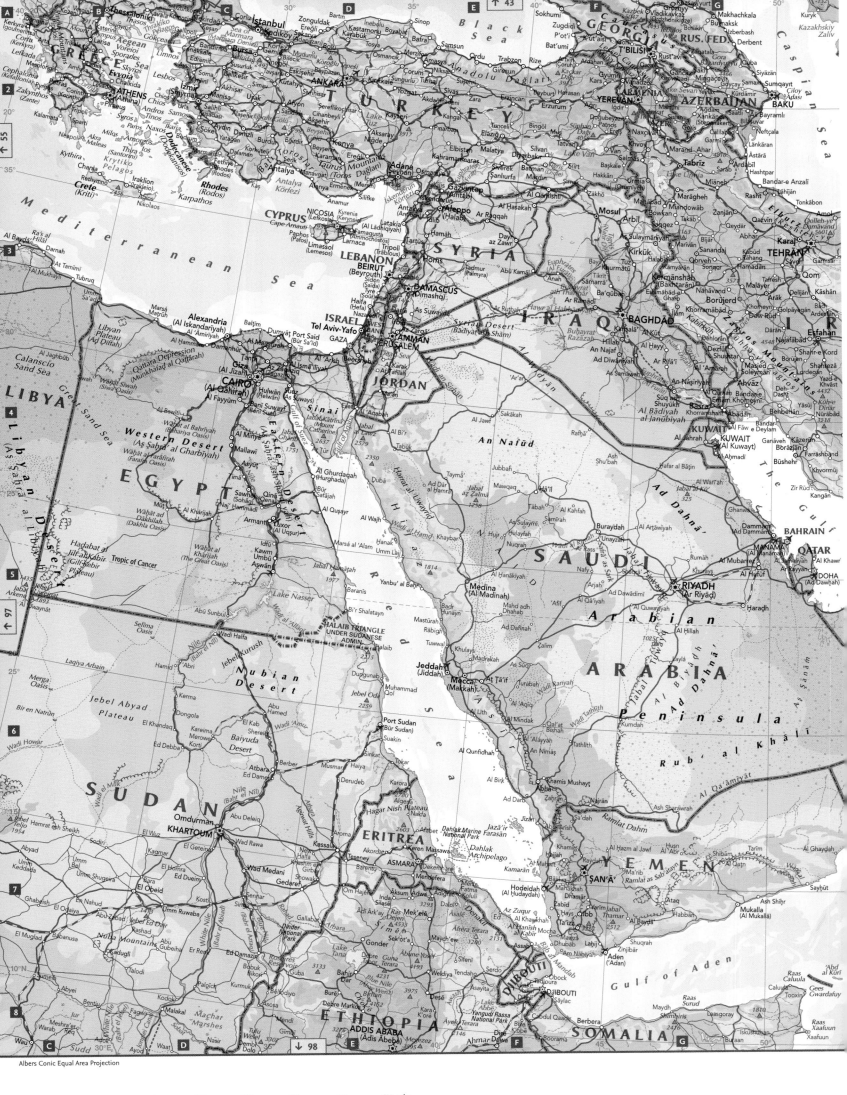

Albers Conic Equal Area Projection

1:13 000 000

| 0 | 100 | 200 | 300 | 400 | 500 miles |

| 0 | 100 | 200 | 300 | 400 | 500 | 600 | 700 | 800 km |

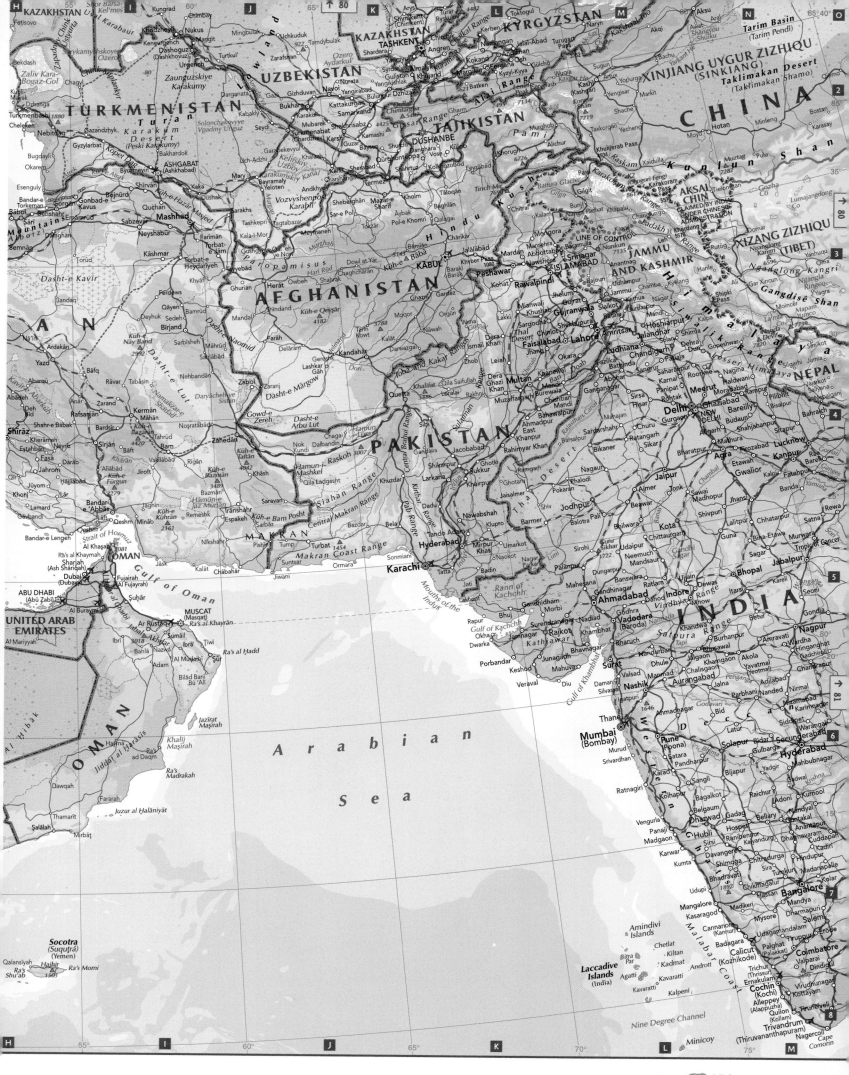

Conic Equidistant Projection

1:7 000 000

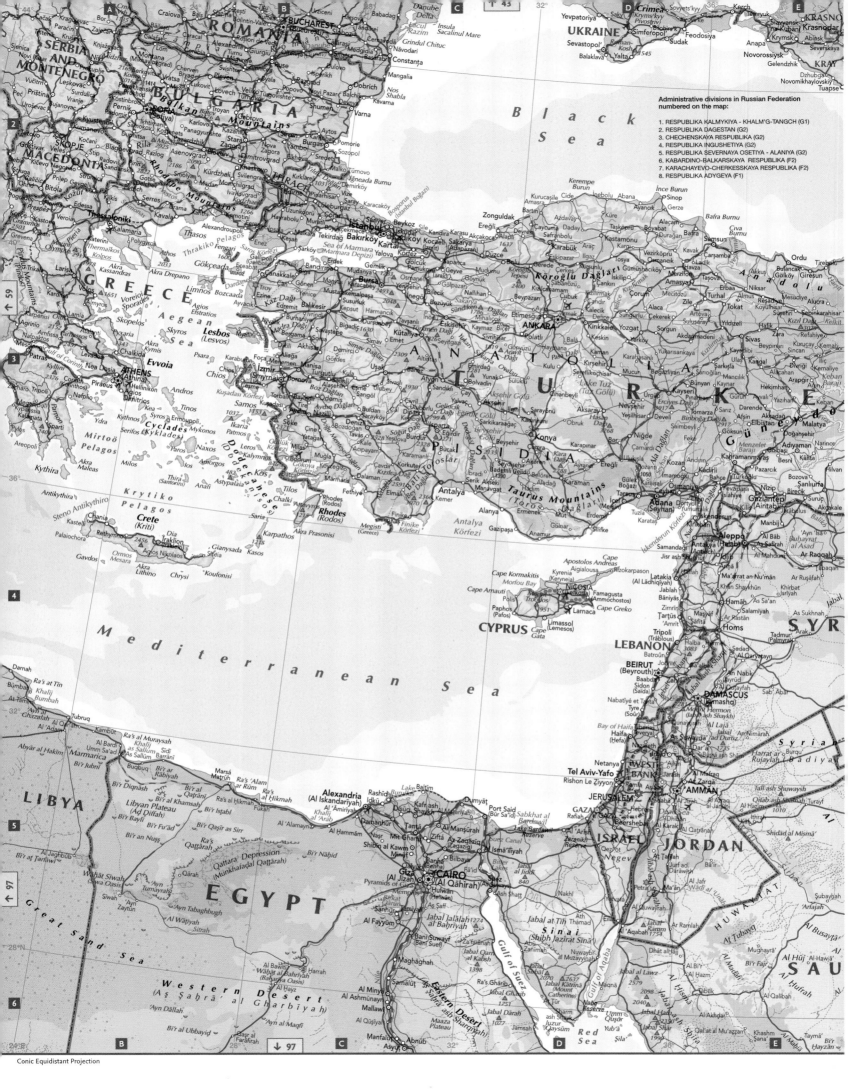

Conic Equidistant Projection

1:7 000 000

miles
0   100   200

km
0   100   200   300   400

Africa Landscapes

Some of the world's greatest physical features are in Africa, the world's second largest continent. Variations in climate and elevation give rise to the continent's great variety of landscapes. The Sahara, the world's largest desert, extends across the whole continent from west to east, and covers an area of over nine million square kilometres. Other significant African deserts are the Kalahari and the Namib. In contrast, some of the world's greatest rivers flow in Africa, including the Nile, the world's longest, and the Congo.

The Great Rift Valley is perhaps Africa's most notable geological feature. It stretches for nearly 3 000 kilometres from Jordan, through the Red Sea and south to Mozambique, and contains many of Africa's largest lakes. Significant mountain ranges on the continent are the Atlas Mountains and the Ethiopian Highlands in the north, the Ruwenzori in east central Africa, and the Drakensberg in the far southeast.

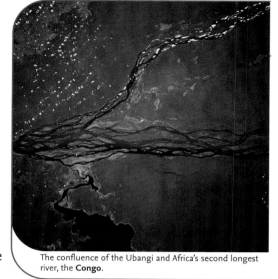

The confluence of the Ubangi and Africa's second longest river, the **Congo**.

Africa's extent

TOTAL LAND AREA	30 343 578 sq km / 11 715 655 sq miles
Most northerly point	La Galite, Tunisia
Most southerly point	Cape Agulhas, South Africa
Most westerly point	Santo Antão, Cape Verde
Most easterly point	Raas Xaafuun, Somalia

Internet Links

● NASA Visible Earth	**visibleearth.nasa.gov**
● NASA Astronaut Photography	**eol.jsc.nasa.gov**
● Peace Parks Foundation	**www.peaceparks.org**

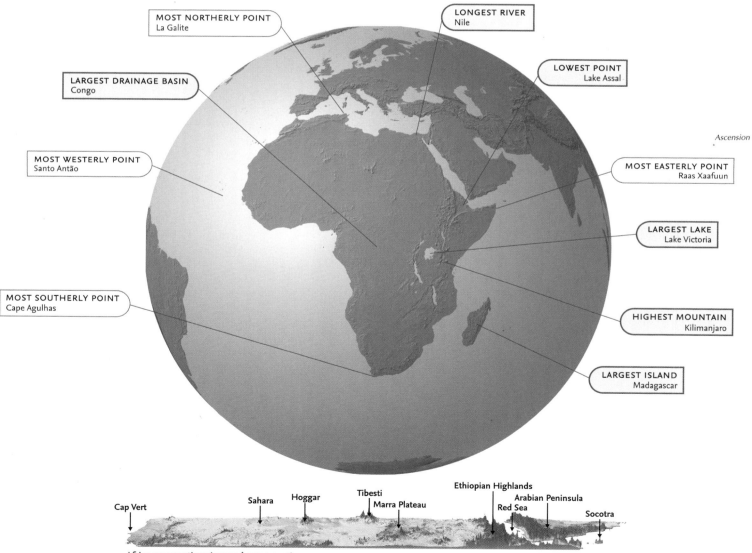

MOST NORTHERLY POINT
La Galite

LONGEST RIVER
Nile

LARGEST DRAINAGE BASIN
Congo

LOWEST POINT
Lake Assal

MOST WESTERLY POINT
Santo Antão

MOST EASTERLY POINT
Raas Xaafuun

LARGEST LAKE
Lake Victoria

MOST SOUTHERLY POINT
Cape Agulhas

HIGHEST MOUNTAIN
Kilimanjaro

LARGEST ISLAND
Madagascar

Cap Vert · Sahara · Hoggar · Tibesti · Marra Plateau · Ethiopian Highlands · Arabian Peninsula · Red Sea · Socotra

Africa perspective view and cross section

Madeira

Canary Islands
Tenerife
Gran Canaria

Cape Verde Santo Antão
Boa Vista
Ilhas dos Cabo Verde
Fogo Santiago
Cap Vert

Akchâr

Aoukâr

Sénégal

Gambia

Fouta Djallon

Ascension

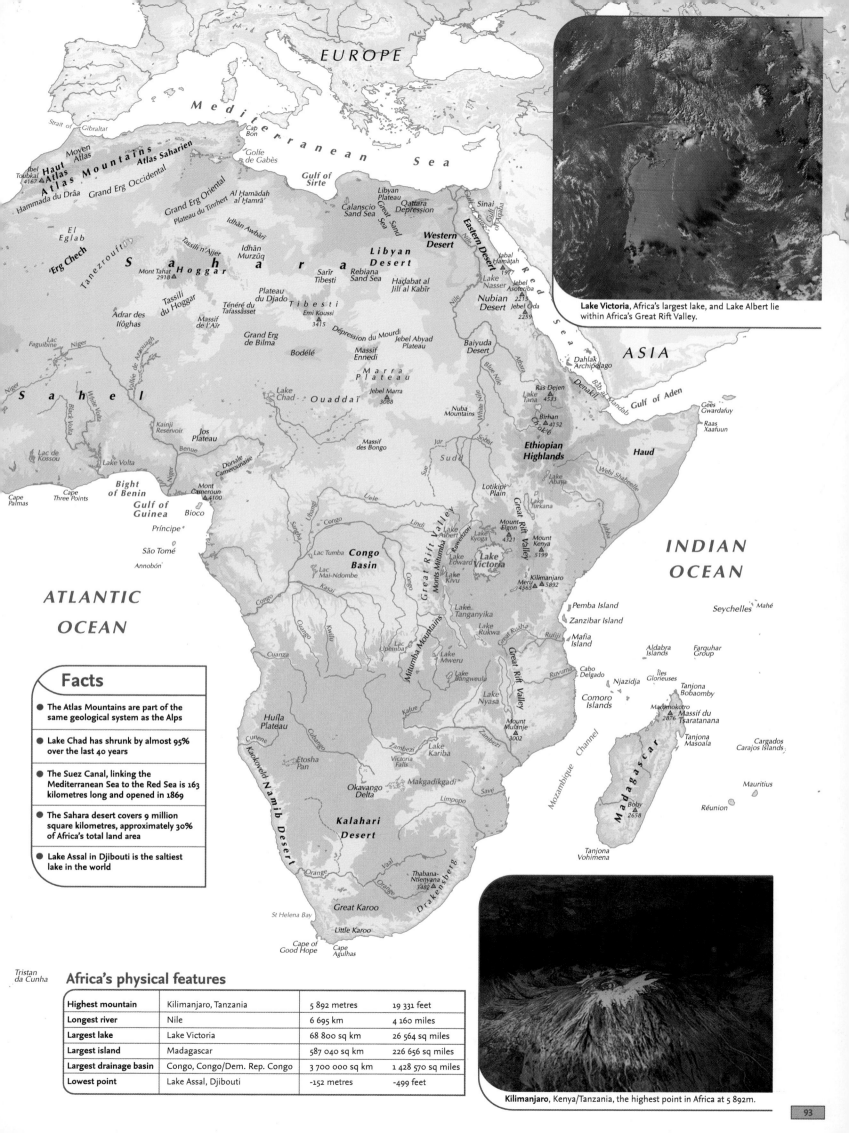

EUROPE

Strait of Gibraltar

M e d i t e r r a n e a n   S e a

Cape Bon

Golfe de Gabès

Gulf of Sirte

ASIA

Gulf of Aden

Gêes Gwardafuy

Raas Xaafuun

ATLANTIC OCEAN

INDIAN OCEAN

Moyen Atlas
Jbel Toubkal 4167
Haut Atlas
A t l a s   M o u n t a i n s
Atlas Saharien
Hammada du Drâa
Grand Erg Occidental

El Eglab
'Erg Chech
Tanezrouft
Grand Erg Oriental
Plateau du Tinrhert
Al Hamādah al Ḥamrāʾ
Libyan Plateau
Calanscio Sand Sea
Great Sand Sea
Qattara Depression
Western Desert
Eastern Desert
Sinai
Gulf of Suez
Gulf of Aqaba
Jabal Ḥamāṭah 1917

S a h a r a
Tassili n'Ajjer
Idhân Awbârî
Idhân Murzûq
Mont Tahat 2918
H o g g a r
Sarīr Tibesti
Rebiana Sand Sea
Libyan Desert
Ḥaḍabat al Jilf al Kabīr
Nubian Desert
Jebel Asoteriba 2215
Jebel Oda 2259
Lake Nasser

Tassili du Hoggar
Adrar des Ifôghas
Ténéré du Tafassasset
Massif de l'Aïr
Plateau du Djado
Grand Erg de Bilma
T i b e s t i
Emi Koussi 3415
Dépression du Mourdi
Jebel Abyad Plateau
Baiyuda Desert
Red Sea
Dahlak Archipelago
Bâb al Mandab
Denakil

Lac Faguibine
Niger
Vallée de Azaouagh
Bodélé
Massif Ennedi
M a r r a   P l a t e a u
Lake Chad
Ouaddaï
Jebel Marra 3088
Nuba Mountains
Ethiopian Highlands
Lake Tana
Ras Dejen 4533
Choke 4152
Birhan
Haud

S a h e l
White Volta
Black Volta
Kainji Reservoir
Jos Plateau
Lac de Kossou
Lake Volta
Benue
Niger
Dorsale Camerounaise
Massif des Bongo
Jur
Sue
Sudd
Sobat
Blue Nile
Atbara
White Nile
Lake Abaya

Cape Palmas
Cape Three Points
Bight of Benin
Gulf of Guinea
Mont Cameroun 4100
Bioco
Príncipe
São Tomé
Annobón
Ubangi
Uele
Lindi
Congo
Lotikipi Plain
Lake Turkana
Great Rift Valley
Mount Elgon 4321
Lake Albert
Ruwenzori
Lake Kyoga
Mount Kenya 5199

Sangha
Congo
Lac Tumba
Lac Mai-Ndombe
Congo Basin
Kasai
Monts Mitumba
Lake Edward
Lake Kivu
Lake Victoria
Meru 4565
Kilimanjaro 5892

Cuango
Kwilu
Lac Upemba
Mitumba Mountains
Lake Tanganyika
Lake Mweru
Lake Rukwa
Great Ruaha
Rufiji
Pemba Island
Zanzibar Island
Mafia Island
Seychelles Mahé

Cuanza
Lake Bangweulu
Ruvuma
Cabo Delgado
Aldabra Islands
Farquhar Group
Njazidja
Íles Glorieuses
Comoro Islands
Tanjona Bobaomby

Huíla Plateau
Kafue
Lake Nyasa
Mount Mulanje 3002
Maromokotro 2876
Massif du Tsaratanana
Tanjona Masoala

Kaokoveld
Cunene
Cubango
Etosha Pan
Zambezi
Victoria Falls
Lake Kariba
Great Rift Valley
Mozambique Channel
M a d a g a s c a r
Boby 2658
Cargados Carajos Islands
Mauritius

N a m i b   D e s e r t
Okavango Delta
Makgadikgadi
Limpopo
Savé
Tanjona Vohimena
Réunion

Kalahari Desert
Orange
Vaal
Orange
Thabana-Ntlenyana 3482
Drakensberg

St Helena Bay
Great Karoo
Little Karoo
Cape of Good Hope
Cape Agulhas

Tristan da Cunha

Lake Victoria, Africa's largest lake, and Lake Albert lie within Africa's Great Rift Valley.

Facts

- The Atlas Mountains are part of the same geological system as the Alps
- Lake Chad has shrunk by almost 95% over the last 40 years
- The Suez Canal, linking the Mediterranean Sea to the Red Sea is 163 kilometres long and opened in 1869
- The Sahara desert covers 9 million square kilometres, approximately 30% of Africa's total land area
- Lake Assal in Djibouti is the saltiest lake in the world

Africa's physical features

Highest mountain	Kilimanjaro, Tanzania	5 892 metres	19 331 feet
Longest river	Nile	6 695 km	4 160 miles
Largest lake	Lake Victoria	68 800 sq km	26 564 sq miles
Largest island	Madagascar	587 040 sq km	226 656 sq miles
Largest drainage basin	Congo, Congo/Dem. Rep. Congo	3 700 000 sq km	1 428 570 sq miles
Lowest point	Lake Assal, Djibouti	-152 metres	-499 feet

Kilimanjaro, Kenya/Tanzania, the highest point in Africa at 5 892m.

Africa Countries

Africa is a complex continent, with over fifty independent countries and a long history of political change. It supports a great variety of ethnic groups, with the Sahara creating the major divide between Arab and Berber groups in the north and a diverse range of groups, including the Yoruba and Masai, in the south.

The current pattern of countries in Africa is a product of a long and complex history, including the colonial period, which saw European control of the vast majority of the continent from the fifteenth century until widespread moves to independence began in the 1950s. Despite its great wealth of natural resources, Africa is by far the world's poorest continent. Many of its countries are heavily dependent upon foreign aid and many are also subject to serious political instability.

Cape Verde, North Atlantic Ocean, a small group of islands lying 500 kilometres off the coast of west Africa.

Madeira (Portugal)

Canary Islands (Spain)

Laâyoune

WESTERN SAHARA

Nouâdhibou

MAURITANIA
Nouakchott

CAPE VERDE
Praia

St-Louis
Dakar SENEGAL Kayes
Banjul Kaolack
THE GAMBIA
Bissau
GUINEA-BISSAU GUINEA
Conakry Kankan
Freetown
SIERRA LEONE
Monrovia
LIBERIA

MOST NORTHERLY CAPITAL
Tunis

LARGEST CAPITAL
Cairo

LARGEST COUNTRY (AREA)
Sudan

LARGEST COUNTRY (POPULATION)
Nigeria

HIGHEST CAPITAL
Addis Ababa

SMALLEST CAPITAL
Victoria

Ascension (U.K.)

SMALLEST COUNTRY (AREA AND POPULATION)
Seychelles

LEAST DENSELY POPULATED COUNTRY
Namibia

MOST DENSELY POPULATED COUNTRY
Mauritius

MOST SOUTHERLY CAPITAL
Cape Town

Internet Links

UK Foreign and Commonwealth Office	www.fco.gov.uk
CIA World Factbook	www.odci.gov/cia/publications/factbook
Southern African Development Community	www.sadc.int
Satellite imagery	www.spaceimaging.com

Africa percentage of total population and land area

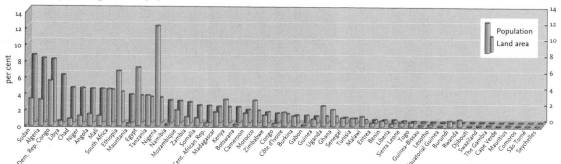

Facts

- Africa has over 1 000 linguistic and cultural groups
- Only Liberia and Ethiopia have remained free from colonial rule throughout their history
- Over 30% of the world's minerals, and over 50% of the world's diamonds, come from Africa
- 9 of the 10 poorest countries in the world are in Africa

94

EUROPE

Mediterranean Sea

Strait of Tangier
Gibraltar
Rabat
Casablanca
Beni Mellal
arrakech
Fès
Sidi Bel
Abbès
Oran
Ech
Chélif
Algiers
Skikda
Annaba
Constantine
Tunis
Bejaia
Béchar
Laghouat
Sfax
Gabès
TUNISIA
Tripoli
Mişrâtah
Gulf of
Sirte
Benghazi
Al Baydâ'
Alexandria
Port Said
Tanța
Giza
Cairo
Suez

MOROCCO
Atlas Mountains

ALGERIA

LIBYA

Libyan Desert

EGYPT

Sahara

Al Minyâ
Asyûṭ
Qinâ
Luxor
Aswân
Lake
Nasser
Nile
Red Sea

ASIA

Space Imaging

Cairo, capital of Egypt and the largest city in Africa with 11 146 000 inhabitants.

MALI

Niger
Gao

NIGER

Agadez

CHAD

Abéché

Lake
Chad
Ndjamena

SUDAN

Port Sudan

Omdurman
Khartoum
Wad Medani
El Obeid
ERITREA
Asmara
Gedaref
Mek'elê
Bahir Dar

DJIBOUTI
Djibouti
Berbera
Hargeysa

Gulf of Aden

égou
Mopti
Bamako
bo-Dioulasso
BURKINA
Ouagadougou
Zinder
Sokoto
Kano
Maiduguri
Maroua
Niamey

BENIN
TOGO
CÔTE
Bouaké
Yamoussoukro
Tamale
Parakou
Zaria
Kumo
NIGERIA
Abuja
Sarh
Moundou

Ngaoundéré
Bossangoa
Bouar

CENTRAL
AFRICAN REPUBLIC

Wau
Juba

Addis Ababa
Dirê
Dawa

ETHIOPIA

SOMALIA

Mogadishu

GHANA
Ibadan
Ogbomosho
Kumasi
Lomé
Accra
D'IVOIRE
Abidjan
Cape
Coast
Lagos
Porto-
Novo
Onitsha
Warri
Port Harcourt
Uyo
CAMEROON
Nkongsamba
Yaoundé
Malabo
Douala

Bangui

DEMOCRATIC

KENYA

UGANDA
Kampala
Kisumu
Nakuru
Mount
Kenya
5199
Nairobi

Kismaayo

Gulf of
Guinea
SÃO TOMÉ AND PRÍNCIPE
São Tomé
EQUATORIAL
GUINEA
Libreville
Port-Gentil

GABON
Franceville

REPUBLIC

CONGO

Congo
Mbandaka

Kisangani

RWANDA
Bukavu
Kigali
BURUNDI
Bujumbura

Mwanza
Lake
Victoria
Arusha
Kilimanjaro
5895

INDIAN

OCEAN

Victoria

SEYCHELLES

ATLANTIC

OCEAN

OF

Bandundu
Brazzaville
Pointe-Noire
CABINDA
(Angola)
Kinshasa
Matadi
Kasai
Kikwit
CONGO
Kananga
Mbuji-Mayi
Kamina
Kigoma
Kalemie
Tabora
Dodoma
Lake
Tanganyika
TANZANIA
Mbeya
Iringa
Tanga
Zanzibar
Dar es Salaam
Zanzibar Island

Aldabra
Islands

Luanda
Cuanza

St Helena
and Dependencies
(U.K.)

Lobito
Benguela
ANGOLA

Namibe
Lubango
Huambo

Likasi
Lubumbashi
Solwezi
Mansa
Kasama
Chingola
Ndola
Chípata
Kabwe
Lake
Nyasa
MALAWI
Lilongwe
Blantyre

COMOROS
Moroni
Pemba
Mayotte
(France)
Nacala
Nampula
Mahajanga

Antsiranana

ZAMBIA
Mongu
Lusaka

Livingstone

Tete

MOZAMBIQUE

Quelimane

Mozambique Channel

MADAGASCAR

Toamasina
Antananarivo

Port Louis
MAURITIUS

Réunion
(France)

Etosha
Pan

NAMIBIA

Okavango
Delta
Windhoek

Francistown

Chitungwiza
Harare
ZIMBABWE
Gweru
Bulawayo
Mutare
Beira

Inhambane

Fianarantsoa

Toliara

Namib Desert

BOTSWANA
Gaborone

Johannesburg
Carletonville
Soweto
Pretoria
Xai-Xai
Maputo
Mbabane
SWAZILAND

Kimberley
Bloemfontein

LESOTHO
Maseru

Durban

Orange

REPUBLIC OF
SOUTH AFRICA

Cape
Town
Khayelitsha
Cape of
Good Hope
Cape
Agulhas
Port Elizabeth
East London

Space Imaging

Cape Town, legislative capital of the Republic of South Africa and the most southerly African capital city.

Africa's countries

Largest country (area)	Sudan	2 505 813 sq km	967 494 sq miles
Smallest country (area)	Seychelles	455 sq km	176 sq miles
Largest country (population)	Nigeria	124 009 000	
Smallest country (population)	Seychelles	81 000	
Most densely populated country	Mauritius	599 per sq km	1 549 per sq mile
Least densely populated country	Namibia	2 per sq km	6 per sq mile

Africa's capitals

Largest capital (population)	Cairo, Egypt	11 146 000
Smallest capital (population)	Victoria, Seychelles	30 000
Most northerly capital	Tunis, Tunisia	36° 46'N
Most southerly capital	Cape Town, Republic of South Africa	33° 57'S
Highest capital	Addis Ababa, Ethiopia	2 408 metres 7 900 feet

95

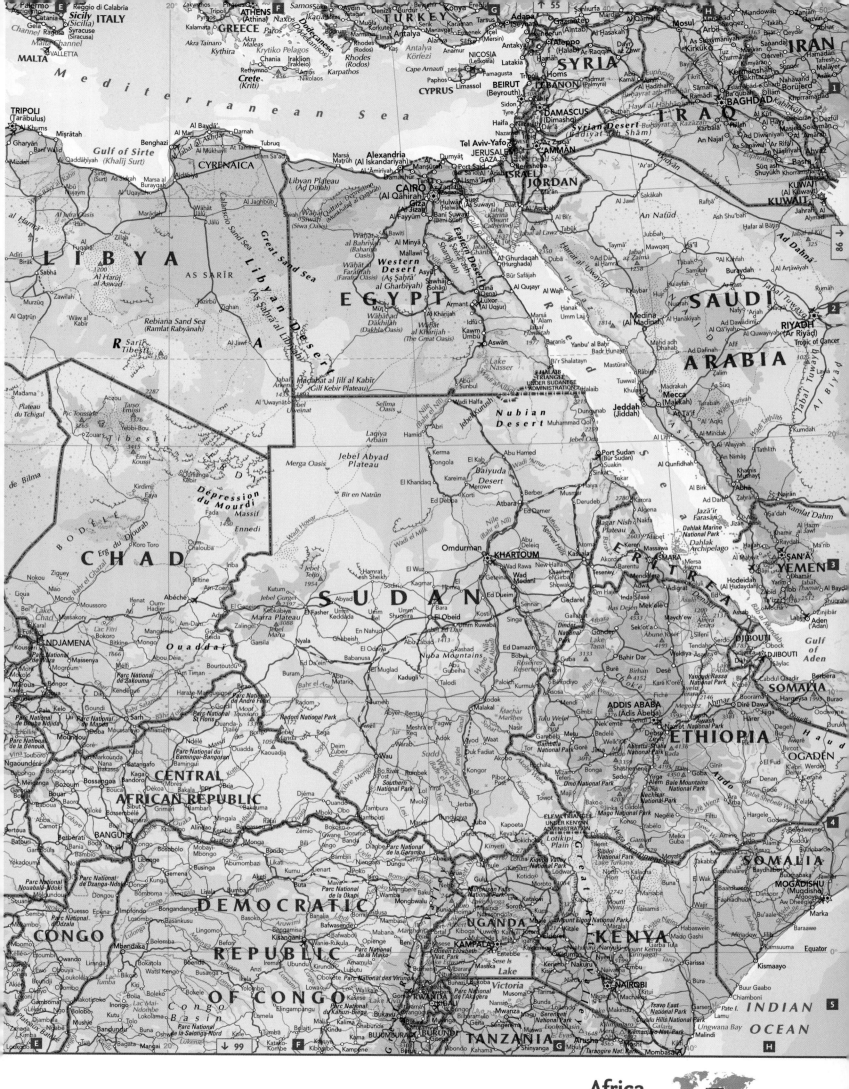

Africa
Central and Southern Africa

99

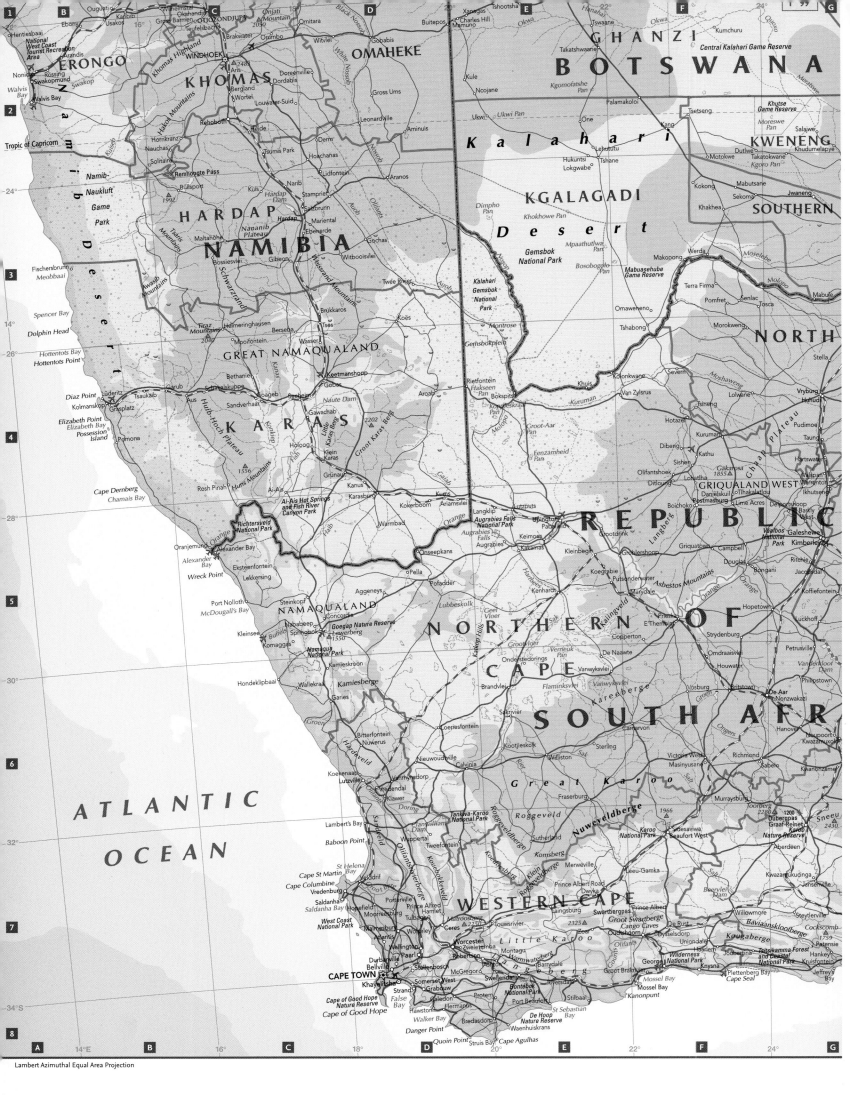

Lambert Azimuthal Equal Area Projection

1:5 000 000

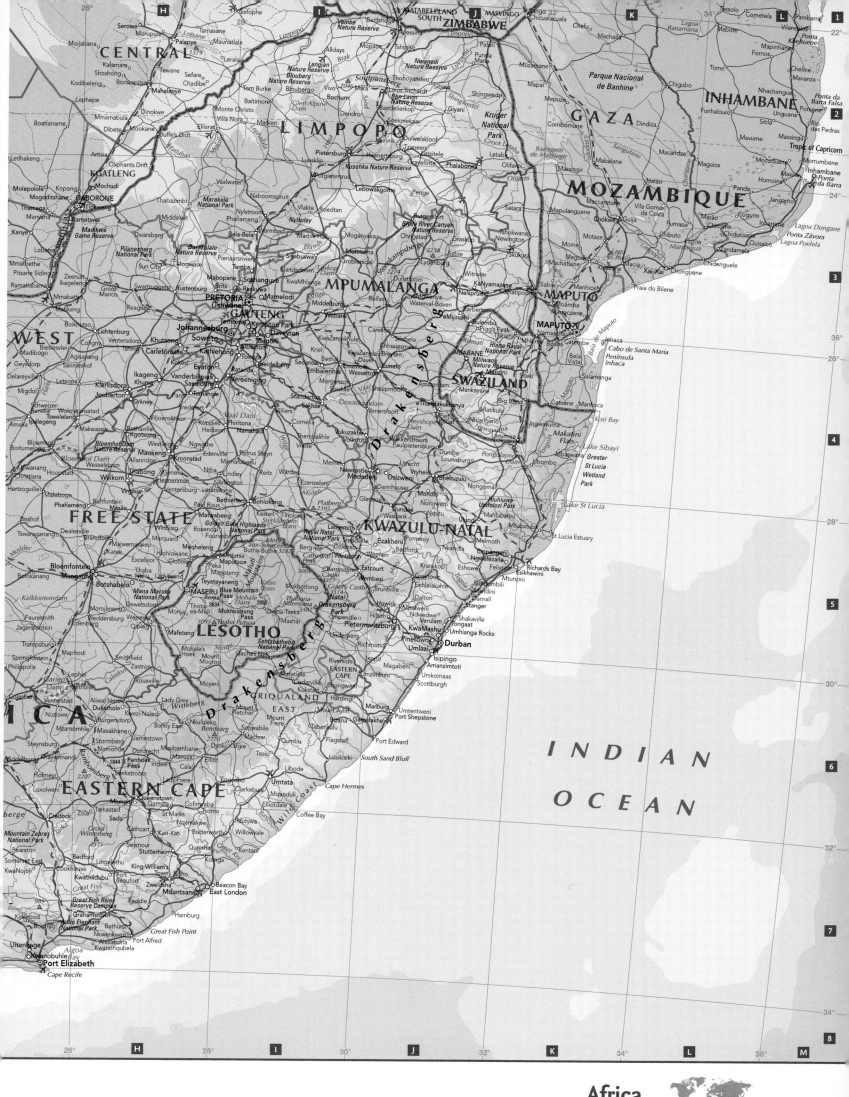

Africa
Republic of South Africa

Oceania comprises Australia, New Zealand, New Guinea and the islands of the Pacific Ocean. It is the smallest of the world's continents by land area. Its dominating feature is Australia, which is mainly flat and very dry. Australia's western half consists of a low plateau, broken in places by higher mountain ranges, which has very few permanent rivers or lakes. The narrow, fertile coastal plain of the east coast is separated from the interior by the Great Dividing Range, which includes the highest mountain in Australia.

The numerous Pacific islands of Oceania are generally either volcanic in origin or consist of coral. They can be divided into three main regions of Micronesia, north of the equator between Palau and the Gilbert islands; Melanesia, stretching from mountainous New Guinea to Fiji; and Polynesia, covering a vast area of the eastern and central Pacific Ocean.

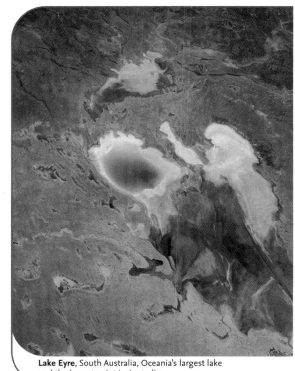

Lake Eyre, South Australia, Oceania's largest lake and the lowest point in Australia.

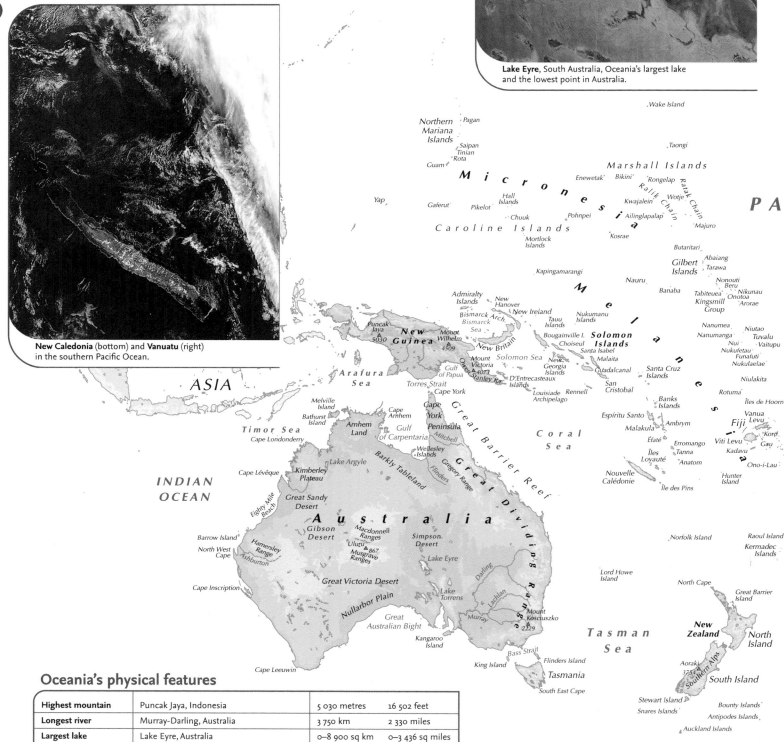

New Caledonia (bottom) and **Vanuatu** (right) in the southern Pacific Ocean.

Oceania's physical features

Highest mountain	Puncak Jaya, Indonesia	5 030 metres	16 502 feet
Longest river	Murray-Darling, Australia	3 750 km	2 330 miles
Largest lake	Lake Eyre, Australia	0–8 900 sq km	0–3 436 sq miles
Largest island	New Guinea, Indonesia/Papua New Guinea	808 510 sq km	312 166 sq miles
Largest drainage basin	Murray-Darling, Australia	1 058 000 sq km	408 494 sq miles
Lowest point	Lake Eyre, Australia	-16 metres	-53 feet

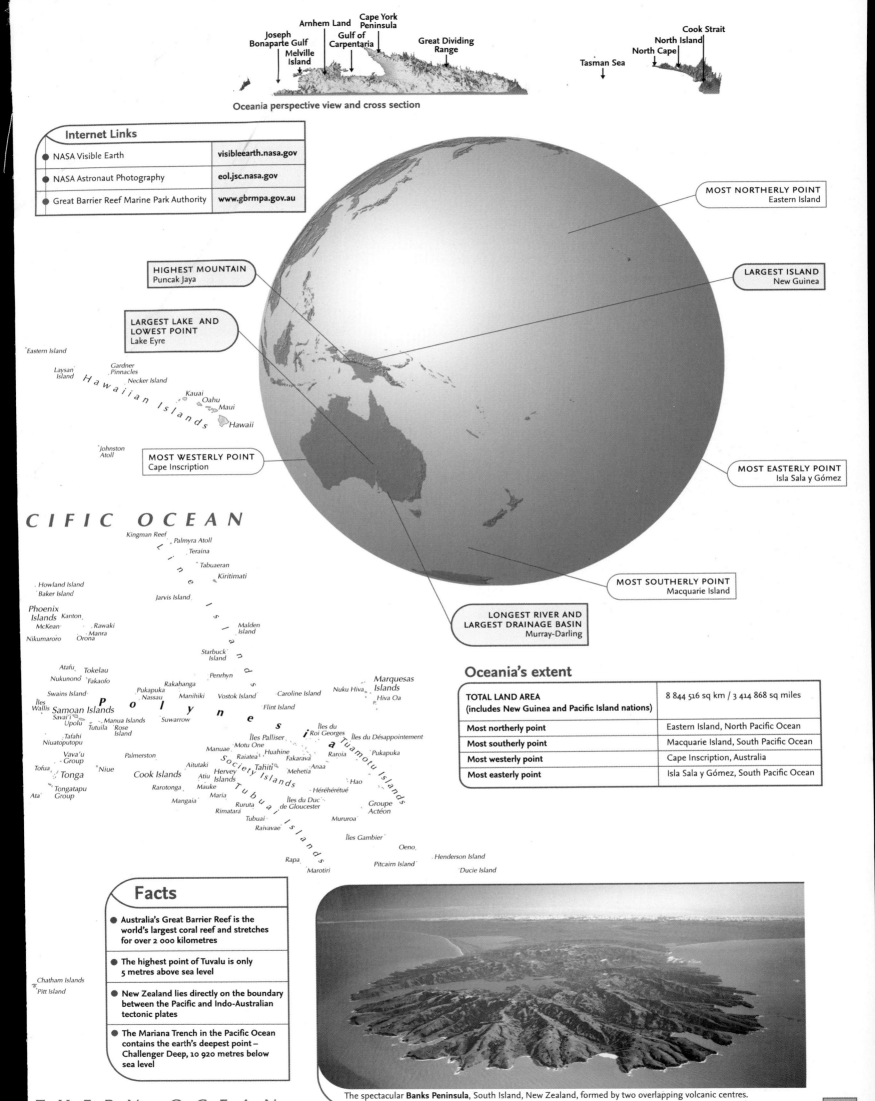

Oceania perspective view and cross section

Labels on cross section: Joseph Bonaparte Gulf, Melville Island, Arnhem Land, Gulf of Carpentaria, Cape York Peninsula, Great Dividing Range, Tasman Sea, North Cape, North Island, Cook Strait

Internet Links

● NASA Visible Earth	visibleearth.nasa.gov
● NASA Astronaut Photography	eol.jsc.nasa.gov
● Great Barrier Reef Marine Park Authority	www.gbrmpa.gov.au

MOST NORTHERLY POINT Eastern Island

LARGEST ISLAND New Guinea

HIGHEST MOUNTAIN Puncak Jaya

LARGEST LAKE AND LOWEST POINT Lake Eyre

MOST WESTERLY POINT Cape Inscription

MOST EASTERLY POINT Isla Sala y Gómez

MOST SOUTHERLY POINT Macquarie Island

LONGEST RIVER AND LARGEST DRAINAGE BASIN Murray-Darling

CIFIC OCEAN

Eastern Island, Laysan Island, Gardner Pinnacles, Necker Island, Kauai, Oahu, Maui, Hawaii, *Hawaiian Islands*, Johnston Atoll

Kingman Reef, Palmyra Atoll, Teraina, Tabuaeran, Kiritimati, *Line Islands*, Howland Island, Baker Island, Phoenix Islands, Kanton, McKean, Rawaki, Manra, Orona, Nikumaroro, Jarvis Island, Malden Island, Starbuck Island, Atafu, Tokelau, Nukunono, Fakaofo, Rakahanga, Penrhyn, Swains Island, Pukapuka, Nassau, Manihiki, Vostok Island, Caroline Island, Îles Wallis, *Samoan Islands*, Savai'i, Upolu, Manua Islands, Rose Island, Suwarrow, Flint Island, Tutuila, *Polynesia*, Tafahi, Niuatoputopu, Îles du Roi Georges, Îles du Désappointement, Nuku Hiva, *Marquesas Islands*, Hiva Oa, Manuae, Motu One, Îles Palliser, Vava'u Group, Palmerston, Raiatea, Huahine, Anaa, Raroia, Pukapuka, Tofua, Tonga, Niue, Cook Islands, Aitutaki, Tahiti, Fakarava, *Society Islands*, *Tuamotu Islands*, Atiu, Hervey Islands, Mehetia, Hao, Rarotonga, Mauke, Maria, Hérehérétué, Ata, Tongatapu Group, Mangaia, Ruruta, Îles du Duc de Gloucester, *Tubuai Islands*, Rimatara, Tubuai, Mururoa, Groupe Actéon, Raivavae, Îles Gambier, Rapa, Marotiri, Oeno, Pitcairn Island, Henderson Island, Ducie Island

Chatham Islands, Pitt Island

Oceania's extent

TOTAL LAND AREA (includes New Guinea and Pacific Island nations)	8 844 516 sq km / 3 414 868 sq miles
Most northerly point	Eastern Island, North Pacific Ocean
Most southerly point	Macquarie Island, South Pacific Ocean
Most westerly point	Cape Inscription, Australia
Most easterly point	Isla Sala y Gómez, South Pacific Ocean

Facts

- Australia's Great Barrier Reef is the world's largest coral reef and stretches for over 2 000 kilometres

- The highest point of Tuvalu is only 5 metres above sea level

- New Zealand lies directly on the boundary between the Pacific and Indo-Australian tectonic plates

- The Mariana Trench in the Pacific Ocean contains the earth's deepest point – Challenger Deep, 10 920 metres below sea level

The spectacular **Banks Peninsula**, South Island, New Zealand, formed by two overlapping volcanic centres.

THERN OCEAN

Oceania Countries

Stretching across almost the whole width of the Pacific Ocean, Oceania has a great variety of cultures and an enormously diverse range of countries and territories. Australia, by far the largest and most industrialized country in the continent, contrasts with the numerous tiny Pacific island nations which have smaller, and more fragile economies based largely on agriculture, fishing and the exploitation of natural resources.

The division of the Pacific island groups into the main regions of Micronesia, Melanesia and Polynesia – often referred to as the South Sea islands – broadly reflects the ethnological differences across the continent. There is a long history of colonial influence in the region, which still contains dependent territories belonging to Australia, France, New Zealand, the UK and the USA.

Wellington, capital of New Zealand and the most southerly national capital in the world.

Tasmania, a small Australian island state, separated from the mainland by the Bass Strait.

Facts

- Over 91% of Australia's population live in urban areas
- The Maori name for New Zealand is Aotearoa, meaning 'land of the long white cloud'
- Auckland, New Zealand, has the largest Polynesian population of any city in Oceania
- Over 800 different languages are spoken in Papua New Guinea

Internet Links

UK Foreign and Commonwealth Office	www.fco.gov.uk
CIA World Factbook	www.odci.gov/cia/publications/factbook
Geoscience Australia	www.ga.gov.au

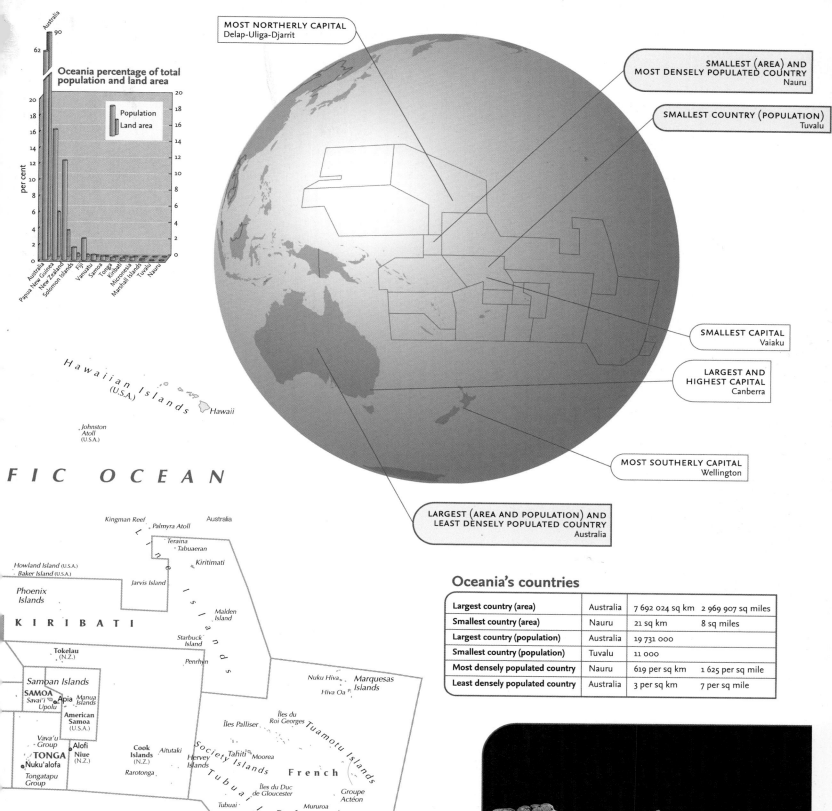

Oceania percentage of total population and land area

Legend: Population / Land area

(Bar chart with countries: Australia, Papua New Guinea, New Zealand, Solomon Islands, Fiji, Vanuatu, Samoa, Tonga, Kiribati, Micronesia, Marshall Islands, Tuvalu, Nauru; per cent axis 0–20, with Australia values at 90 and 62)

MOST NORTHERLY CAPITAL
Delap-Uliga-Djarrit

SMALLEST (AREA) AND MOST DENSELY POPULATED COUNTRY
Nauru

SMALLEST COUNTRY (POPULATION)
Tuvalu

SMALLEST CAPITAL
Vaiaku

LARGEST AND HIGHEST CAPITAL
Canberra

MOST SOUTHERLY CAPITAL
Wellington

LARGEST (AREA AND POPULATION) AND LEAST DENSELY POPULATED COUNTRY
Australia

F I C   O C E A N

Hawaiian Islands (U.S.A.)
Hawaii

Johnston Atoll (U.S.A.)

Kingman Reef
Palmyra Atoll
Australia
Teraina
Tabuaeran
Kiritimati

Howland Island (U.S.A.)
Baker Island (U.S.A.)

Phoenix Islands

Jarvis Island

Malden Island

K I R I B A T I

Line Islands

Starbuck Island

Tokelau (N.Z.)

Penrhyn

Samoan Islands
SAMOA
Savai'i   Apia   Manua Islands
Upolu
American Samoa (U.S.A.)

Nuku Hiva   Marquesas Islands
Hiva Oa

Îles du Roi Georges
Tuamotu Islands

Vava'u Group   Alofi
TONGA   Niue (N.Z.)
Nuku'alofa
Tongatapu Group

Cook Islands (N.Z.)
Aitutaki
Rarotonga

Îles Palliser
Society Islands
Tahiti   Moorea
Hervey Islands
F r e n c h

Tubuai Islands
Îles du Duc de Gloucester
Groupe Actéon
Tubuai
Mururoa
P o l y n e s i a
Îles Gambier

Pitcairn Is (U.K.)
Henderson Island
Pitcairn Island

Rapa

Chatham Islands (N.Z.)

Oceania's countries

Largest country (area)	Australia	7 692 024 sq km	2 969 907 sq miles
Smallest country (area)	Nauru	21 sq km	8 sq miles
Largest country (population)	Australia	19 731 000	
Smallest country (population)	Tuvalu	11 000	
Most densely populated country	Nauru	619 per sq km	1 625 per sq mile
Least densely populated country	Australia	3 per sq km	7 per sq mile

Oceania's capitals

Largest capital (population)	Canberra, Australia	387 000	
Smallest capital (population)	Vaiaku, Tuvalu	5 100	
Most northerly capital	Delap-Uliga-Djarrit, Marshall Islands	7° 7'N	
Most southerly capital	Wellington, New Zealand	41° 18'S	
Highest capital	Canberra, Australia	581 metres	1 906 feet

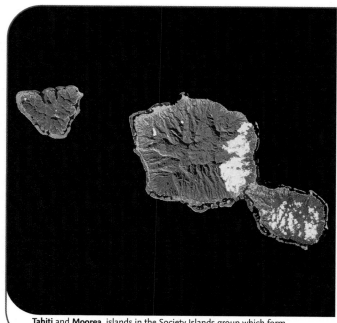

Tahiti and **Moorea**, islands in the Society Islands group which form part of the dependent territory of French Polynesia.

O C E A N

INDONESIA

Celebes Sea

Borneo
Equator

Celebes
(Sulawesi)

Makassar
(Ujung Pandang)

Laut Maluku
(Molucca Sea)

PAPUA

Bismarck Archipelago

NEW GUINEA

New Guinea

PAPUA

PORT MORESBY

Laut Banda
(Banda Sea)

Arafura Sea

Torres Strait

Gulf of Papua

EAST TIMOR

INDIAN OCEAN

Ashmore and Cartier Islands
(Australia)

Timor Sea

Arnhem Land

Gulf of Carpentaria

Cape York Peninsula

Coral Sea Islands Territory
(Australia)

Great Barrier Reef

Kimberley Plateau

Great Sandy Desert

NORTHERN TERRITORY

Tanami Desert

Barkly Tableland

QUEENSLAND

WESTERN

AUSTRALIA

Gibson Desert

Simpson Desert

Great Dividing Range

Tropic of Capricorn

Great Victoria Desert

SOUTH AUSTRALIA

Brisbane

Nullarbor Plain

NEW SOUTH WALES

Perth

Great Australian Bight

Sydney

Canberra
A.C.T.

VICTORIA

Melbourne

Bass Strait

TASMANIA

Hobart

South East Cape

Lambert Azimuthal Equal Area Projection

1:20 000 000

0   200   400   600 miles
0   200   400   600   800   1000 km

Oceania
Australia, New Zealand and Southwest Pacific

Lambert Azimuthal Equal Area Projection

1:8 000 000

| 0 | 100 | 200 | 300 | miles |

| 0 | 100 | 200 | 300 | 400 | 500 | km |

Oceania
Western Australia

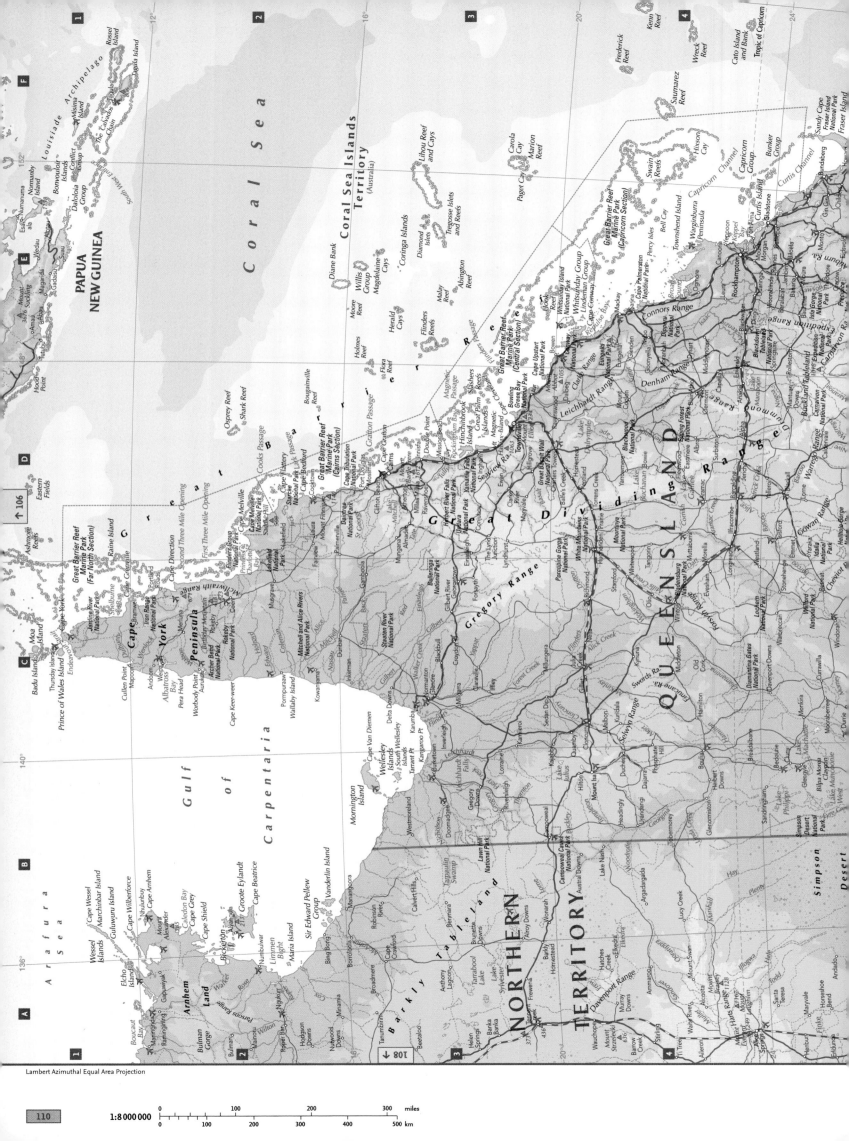

Louisiade Archipelago
Rossel Island
Tagula Island
Misima Island
The Calvados Chain
Bonvouloir Islands
Daloloia Group
Normanby Island
Conflict Group
Wedau
Magaidou
Suau
Mount 3676 Suckling
Amau
Tufi
Tubu

PAPUA NEW GUINEA

Hood Point
Eastern Fields

Ashmore Reefs

C o r a l   S e a

Coral Sea Islands Territory (Australia)

Diane Bank
Willis Group
Magdelaine Cays
Holmes Reef
Flora Reef
Herald Cays
Flinders Reefs
Moore Reef
Malay Reef
Diamond Islets
Coringa Islands
Tregosse Islets and Reefs
Lihou Reef and Cays
Carola Cay
Marion Reef
Frederick Reef
Kenn Reef
Saumarez Reef
Wreck Reef
Cato Island and Bank
Sandy Cape Fraser National Park
Fraser Island

Osprey Reef
Shark Reef
Bougainville Reef

Raine Island
Cape Grenville

Great Barrier Reef Marine Park (Far North Section)

G r e a t   B a r r i e r   R e e f

Great Barrier Reef Marine Park (Capricorn Section)
Swain Reefs
Hixson Cay
Pager Cay
Capricorn Group
Bunker Group
Curtis Channel
Capricorn Channel

Thursday Island
Prince of Wales Island
Cape York
Endeavour Strait

Cape York Peninsula

Iron Range National Park
Rokeby National Park
Archer Bend National Park
Lakefield National Park

Flinders Group National Park
Cape Melville National Park
Starcke National Park
Cape Flattery
Cooktown
Cape Bedford
Cape Tribulation
Port Douglas
Mossman
Cairns
Great Barrier Reef Marine Park (Cairns Section)
Green Island

G u l f   o f   C a r p e n t a r i a

Cape Van Diemen
Wellesley Islands
Mornington Island
Cape Keer-weer
Pormpuraaw
Wallaby Island
Kowanyama

QUEENSLAND

Great Dividing Range

Gregory Range

NORTHERN TERRITORY

Barkly Tableland

Simpson Desert

Arnhem Land

A r a f u r a   s e a

Wessel Islands
Cape Wessel
Marchinbar Island
Cape Arnhem
Elcho Island
Cape Wilberforce

Groote Eylandt
Sir Edward Pellew Group

Lambert Azimuthal Equal Area Projection

1:8 000 000

0   100   200   300 miles
0   100   200   300   400   500 km

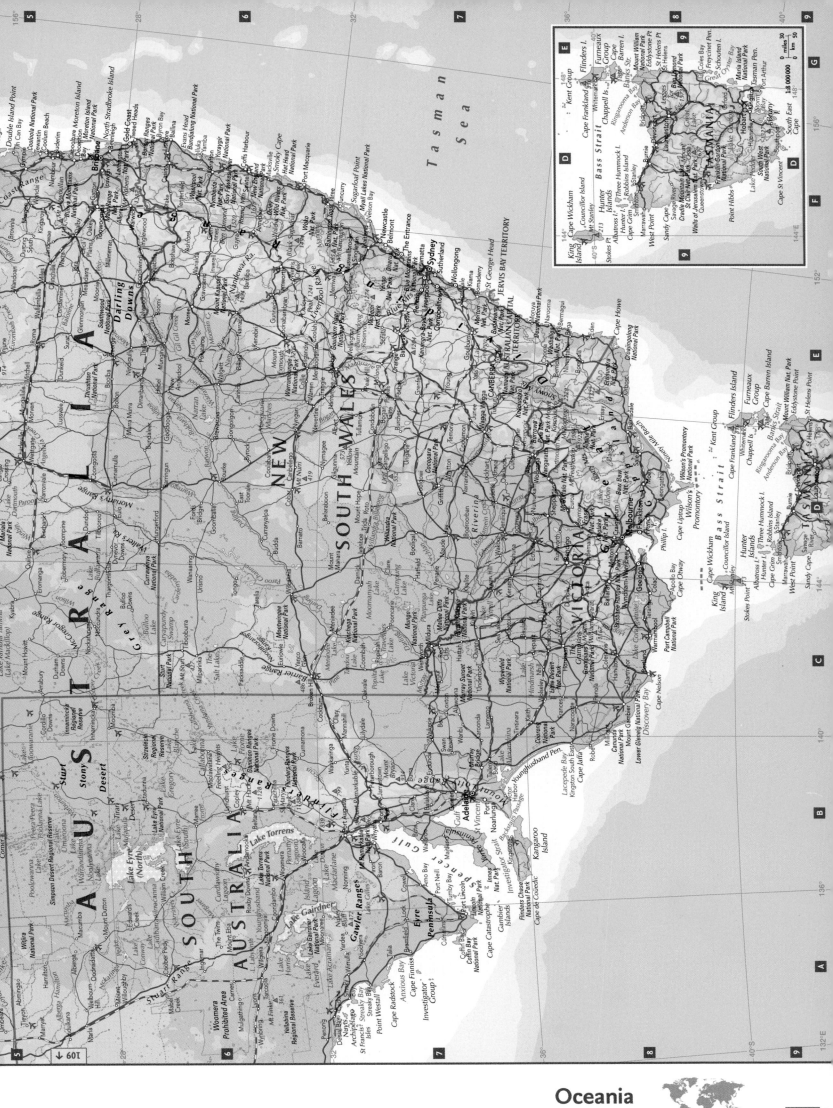

Oceania
Eastern Australia

Oceania
Southeast Australia

Lambert Azimuthal Equal Area Projection

1:5 000 000

| miles | 0 | 50 | 100 | 150 |
| km | 0 | 50 | 100 | 150 | 200 |

Oceania
New Zealand

North America, the world's third largest continent, supports a wide range of landscapes from the Arctic north to sub-tropical Central America. The main physiographic regions of the continent are the mountains of the west coast, stretching from Alaska in the north to Mexico and Central America in the south; the vast, relatively flat Canadian Shield; the Great Plains which make up the majority of the interior; the Appalachian Mountains in the east; and the Atlantic coastal plain.

These regions contain some significant physical features, including the Rocky Mountains, the Great Lakes – three of which are amongst the five largest lakes in the world – and the Mississippi-Missouri river system which is the world's fourth longest river. The Caribbean Sea contains a complex pattern of islands, many volcanic in origin, and the continent is joined to South America by the narrow Isthmus of Panama.

Internet Links	
● NASA Visible Earth	**visibleearth.nasa.gov**
● U.S. Geological Survey	**www.usgs.gov**
● Natural Resources Canada	**www.nrcan-rncan.gc.ca**
● SPOT Image satellite imagery	**www.spotimage.fr**

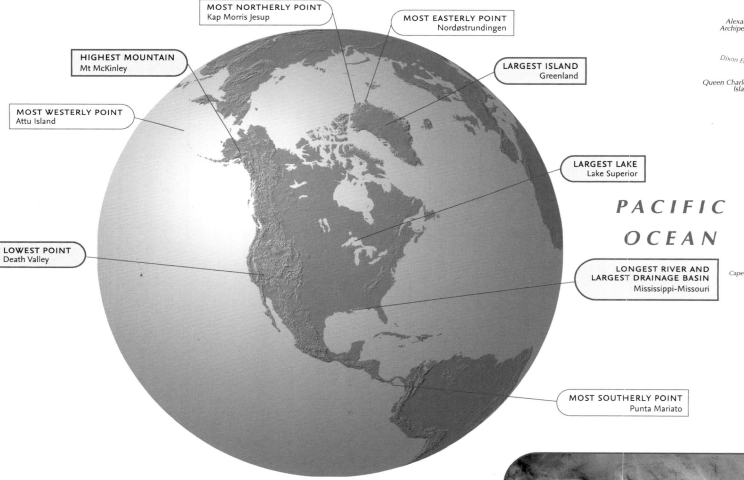

MOST NORTHERLY POINT
Kap Morris Jesup

MOST EASTERLY POINT
Nordøstrundingen

HIGHEST MOUNTAIN
Mt McKinley

LARGEST ISLAND
Greenland

MOST WESTERLY POINT
Attu Island

LARGEST LAKE
Lake Superior

LOWEST POINT
Death Valley

LONGEST RIVER AND LARGEST DRAINAGE BASIN
Mississippi-Missouri

MOST SOUTHERLY POINT
Punta Mariato

PACIFIC OCEAN

Coast Ranges · Rocky Mountains · Great Plains · Lake Michigan · Lake Huron · Lake Erie · Chesapeake Bay · Appalachian Mountains · Long Island · Cape Cod · Nova Scotia

North America perspective view and cross section

North America's physical features

Highest mountain	Mt McKinley, USA	6 194 metres	20 321 feet
Longest river	Mississippi-Missouri, USA	5 969 km	3 709 miles
Largest lake	Lake Superior, Canada/USA	82 100 sq km	31 699 sq miles
Largest island	Greenland	2 175 600 sq km	839 999 sq miles
Largest drainage basin	Mississippi-Missouri, USA	3 250 000 sq km	1 254 825 sq miles
Lowest point	Death Valley, USA	-86 metres	-282 feet

North America's longest river system, the Mississippi-Missouri, flows into the Gulf of Mexico through the **Mississippi Delta**.

North America's extent

TOTAL LAND AREA (including Hawaiian Islands)	24 680 331 sq km / 9 529 076 sq miles
Most northerly point	Kap Morris Jesup, Greenland
Most southerly point	Punta Mariato, Panama
Most westerly point	Attu Island, USA
Most easterly point	Nordostrundingen, Greenland

The **Grand Canyon**, Arizona, USA, the world's largest and most spectacular land canyon.

Facts

- Devon Island, Canada, is the world's largest uninhabited island
- Canada has the longest coastline of any country in the world
- Lake Superior is the world's largest freshwater lake
- Over 320 000 square kilometres of the USA is protected for conservation purposes

The **Yucatán peninsula**, Mexico, divides the Gulf of Mexico from the Caribbean Sea.

North America has been dominated economically and politically by the USA since the nineteenth century. Before that, the continent was subject to colonial influences, particularly of Spain in the south and of Britain and France in the east. The nineteenth century saw the steady development of the western half of the continent. The wealth of natural resources and the generally temperate climate were an excellent basis for settlement, agriculture and industrial development which has led to the USA being the richest nation in the world today.

Although there are twenty three independent countries and fourteen dependent territories in North America, Canada, Mexico and the USA have approximately eighty five per cent of the continent's population and eighty eight per cent of its land area. Large parts of the north remain sparsely populated, while the most densely populated areas are in the northeast USA, and the Caribbean.

Washington DC, a leading international political centre and capital city of the United States.

LARGEST COUNTRY (POPULATION)
United States of America

LARGEST (AREA) AND LEAST DENSELY POPULATED COUNTRY
Canada

MOST NORTHERLY CAPITAL
Ottawa

SMALLEST COUNTRY (AREA AND POPULATION)
St Kitts and Nevis

MOST DENSELY POPULATED COUNTRY
Barbados

LARGEST AND HIGHEST CAPITAL
Mexico City

SMALLEST CAPITAL
Belmopan

MOST SOUTHERLY CAPITAL
Panama City

North America's capitals

Largest capital (population)	Mexico City, Mexico	19 013 000	
Smallest capital (population)	Belmopan, Belize	9 000	
Most northerly capital	Ottawa, Canada	45° 25'N	
Most southerly capital	Panama City, Panama	8° 56'N	
Highest capital	Mexico City, Mexico	2 300 metres	7 546 feet

North America percentage of total population and land area

- Population
- Land area

per cent

Canada 40, USA 58, 22, 20, 39

Canada, USA, Mexico, Nicaragua, Honduras, Cuba, Guatemala, Panama, Costa Rica, Dominican Rep., Haiti, Belize, El Salvador, The Bahamas, Jamaica, Trinidad and Tobago, Dominica, St Lucia, Antigua and Barbados, Barbados, St Vincent and Grenadines, Grenada, St Kitts and Nevis

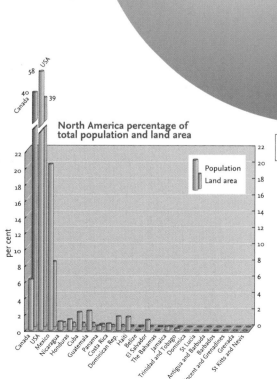

The cities of **El Paso**, USA, and **Ciudad Juarez**, Mexico, are located on the Rio Grande which forms part of the USA/Mexico border.

North America's countries

Largest country (area)	Canada	9 984 670 sq km	3 855 103 sq miles
Smallest country (area)	St Kitts and Nevis	261 sq km	101 sq miles
Largest country (population)	United States of America	294 043 000	
Smallest country (population)	St Kitts and Nevis	42 000	
Most densely populated country	Barbados	628 per sq km	1 627 per sq mile
Least densely populated country	Canada	3 per sq km	8 per sq mile

Point Hope, Bering Strait, St Lawrence Island, Nome, **U.S.**, **ALASKA**, Fairbanks, Mount McKinley 6194, Anchorage, Valdez, Aleutian Islands, Alaska Peninsula, Kodiak Island, Gulf of Alaska, Alexander Archipelago, Queen Charlotte Islands

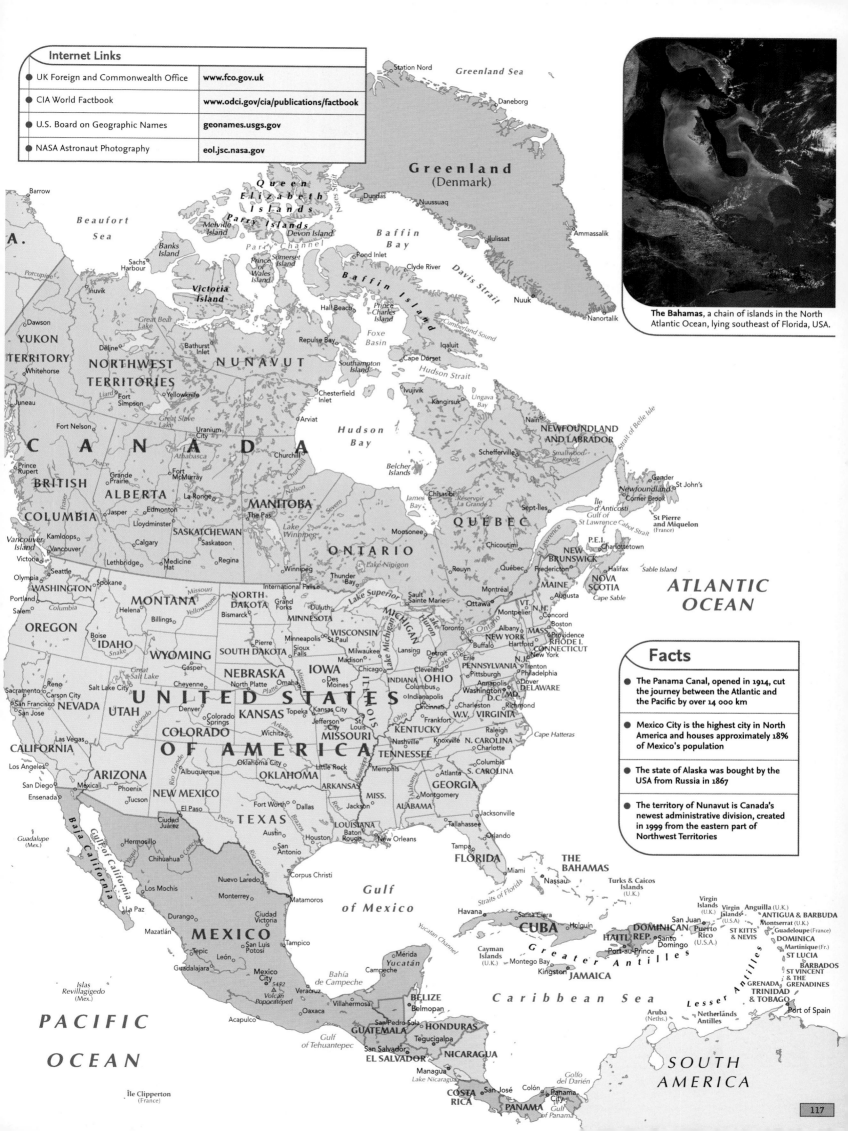

The Bahamas, a chain of islands in the North Atlantic Ocean, lying southeast of Florida, USA.

Greenland Sea

Station Nord
Daneborg

Greenland
(Denmark)

Nuussuaq
Dundas

Ammassalik

Ilulissat

Nuuk

Nanortalik

Beaufort
Sea

Barrow

Queen
Elizabeth
Islands

Parry Islands

Baffin
Bay

Melville
Island

Devon Island

Banks
Island

Sachs
Harbour

Porcupine

Inuvik

Prince
of
Wales
Island

Somerset
Island

Pond Inlet

Clyde River

Davis Strait

Baffin Island

Dawson

Victoria
Island

Parry Channel

Hall Beach

Prince
Charles
Island

YUKON
TERRITORY

Whitehorse

Déline

Yellowknife

Great Bear
Lake

NORTHWEST

Bathurst
Inlet

N U N A V U T

Repulse Bay

Foxe
Basin

Iqaluit
Cape Dorset

Cumberland Sound

Juneau

TERRITORIES

Fort
Simpson

Liard

Chesterfield
Inlet

Ivujivik

Hudson Strait

Prince
Rupert

Fort Nelson

Great Slave
Lake

Athabasca

Uranium
City

Arviat

Kangirsuk

Ungava
Bay

Nain

NEWFOUNDLAND
AND LABRADOR

Strait of Belle Isle

C A N A D A

Churchill

Hudson
Bay

Belcher
Islands

Schefferville

Smallwood
Reservoir

Gander

Newfoundland

St John's

BRITISH

Grande
Prairie

Fort
McMurray

Peace

Nelson

Chisasibi

Reservoir
La Grande 2

Corner Brook

ALBERTA

La Ronge

James
Bay

Sept-Iles

Île
d'Anticosti

St Pierre
and Miquelon
(France)

COLUMBIA

Jasper

Edmonton

Lloydminster

SASKATCHEWAN

The Pas

Severn

Gulf of
St Lawrence

Cabot Strait

Vancouver
Island

Kamloops

Calgary

Saskatoon

Moosonee

QUÉBEC

Chicoutimi

P.E.I.
Charlottetown

Vancouver

Lethbridge

Medicine
Hat

Regina

Lake
Winnipeg

ONTARIO

Lake Nipigon

Rouyn

Québec

Fredericton

NEW
BRUNSWICK

Halifax

Sable Island

Victoria

Winnipeg

Thunder
Bay

Montréal

NOVA
SCOTIA

Seattle

Spokane

International Falls

Lake Superior

Sault
Sainte Marie

Ottawa

Augusta

Cape Sable

ATLANTIC
OCEAN

Olympia

WASHINGTON

MONTANA

Missouri

NORTH
DAKOTA

Grand
Forks

Duluth

Lake Huron

Toronto

Lake Ontario

Montpelier

N.H.
Concord

Portland

Salem

OREGON

Boise

IDAHO

Helena

Billings

Bismarck

MINNESOTA

Lake Michigan

MICHIGAN

Lake Erie

Buffalo

Albany

Boston

MASS.

Providence
RHODE I.

Columbia

Snake

WYOMING

Casper

Pierre

SOUTH DAKOTA

Minneapolis
St Paul

WISCONSIN

Milwaukee
Madison

Lansing

Detroit

Cleveland

Erie

PENNSYLVANIA

Hartford

CONNECTICUT

New York

N.J.

Trenton

Sacramento

Reno

Great
Salt Lake

Salt Lake City

Cheyenne

North Platte

Omaha

Des
Moines

IOWA

Chicago

INDIANA

OHIO

Columbus

Pittsburgh

Philadelphia

DELAWARE

Dover

San Francisco

Carson City

NEVADA

UTAH

Denver

Platte

NEBRASKA

U N I T E D   S T A T E S

ILLINOIS

Indianapolis

Cincinnati

Washington
D.C.

Annapolis

MD.

San Jose

Colorado
Springs

KANSAS

Topeka

Kansas City

St
Louis

Frankfort

Richmond

CALIFORNIA

Las Vegas

COLORADO

Colorado

O F   A M E R I C A

Jefferson
City

MISSOURI

Ohio

KENTUCKY

W.V.

VIRGINIA

Raleigh

Cape Hatteras

Los Angeles

Arkansas

Wichita

Nashville

Knoxville

N. CAROLINA

Charlotte

Columbia

San Diego

ARIZONA

Albuquerque

Mexicali

Phoenix

Tucson

NEW MEXICO

OKLAHOMA

Oklahoma City

Little Rock

ARKANSAS

Memphis

Mississippi

Atlanta

S. CAROLINA

GEORGIA

Ensenada

Rio Grande

El Paso

TEXAS

Pecos

Fort Worth

Dallas

Jackson

MISS.

Alabama

ALABAMA

Montgomery

Jacksonville

Guadalupe
(Mex.)

Gulf of California

Hermosillo

Chihuahua

Ciudad
Juárez

Rio Grande

Conchos

Brazos

Austin

San
Antonio

LOUISIANA

Houston

Baton
Rouge

New Orleans

Tallahassee

FLORIDA

Orlando

Tampa

Baja California

Yaqui

La Paz

Los Mochis

Nuevo Laredo

Corpus Christi

Gulf
of Mexico

Miami

THE
BAHAMAS

Nassau

Turks & Caicos
Islands
(U.K.)

Durango

Ciudad
Victoria

Monterrey

Matamoros

Straits of Florida

Havana

Santa Clara

Virgin
Islands
(U.K.)

Virgin
Islands
(U.S.A)

Anguilla (U.K.)

ANTIGUA & BARBUDA

Mazatlán

Tampico

Yucatan Channel

CUBA

Holguín

San Juan

DOMINICAN
REP.

Puerto
Rico
(U.S.A.)

Montserrat (U.K.)

Guadeloupe (France)

Tepic

León

San Luis
Potosí

Cayman
Islands
(U.K.)

HAITI

Santo
Domingo

ST KITTS
& NEVIS

DOMINICA

Guadalajara

MEXICO

Mérida

Campeche

Bahía
de Campeche

Montego Bay

Port-au-Prince

Greater Antilles

Martinique (Fr.)

ST LUCIA

Islas
Revillagigedo
(Mex.)

Mexico
City

5452
Volcán
Popocatépetl

Veracruz

Villahermosa

Oaxaca

Kingston

JAMAICA

BARBADOS

ST VINCENT
& THE
GRENADINES

Acapulco

Yucatán

BELIZE

Belmopan

Caribbean Sea

Lesser Antilles

GRENADA

TRINIDAD
& TOBAGO

PACIFIC

San Pedro Sula

GUATEMALA

HONDURAS

Tegucigalpa

Aruba
(Neths.)

Netherlands
Antilles

Port of Spain

Gulf
of Tehuantepec

San Salvador

EL SALVADOR

NICARAGUA

OCEAN

Managua

Lake Nicaragua

Golfo
del Darién

SOUTH
AMERICA

Île Clipperton
(France)

COSTA
RICA

San José

Colón

PANAMA

Panama
City

Gulf of Panama

Lambert Conformal Conic Projection

1:16 000 000

North America

Canada

Conic Equidistant Projection

1:7 000 000

North America
Western Canada

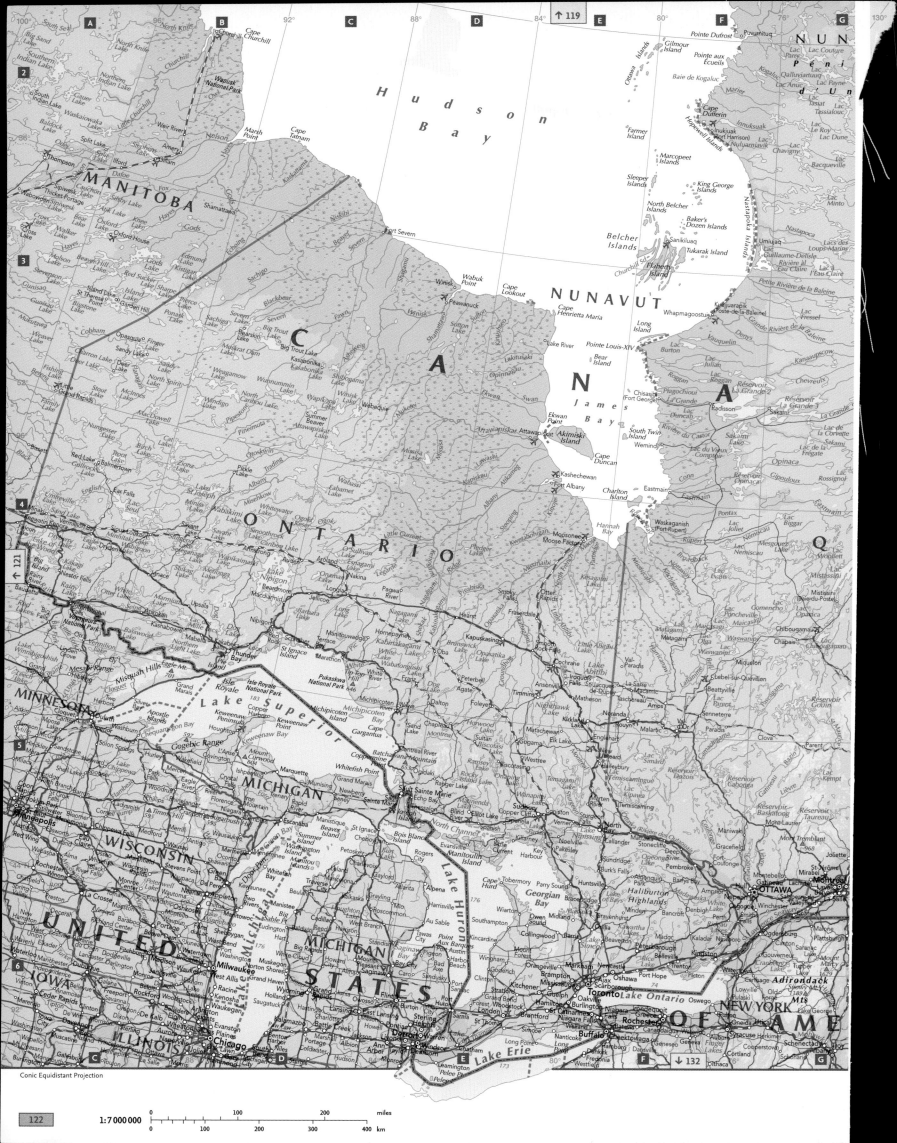

Conic Equidistant Projection

1:7 000 000

LABRADOR

Labrador Sea

NEWFOUNDLAND AND LABRADOR

Labrador

QUÉBEC

CANADA

Ungava Bay

Gulf of St Lawrence

NEWFOUNDLAND AND LABRADOR

Newfoundland

Péninsule de Gaspé

Monts Notre Dame

QUÉBEC

NEW BRUNSWICK

PRINCE EDWARD ISLAND

NOVA SCOTIA

MAINE

VERMONT

NEW HAMPSHIRE

AMERICA

ATLANTIC OCEAN

Gulf of Maine

Bay of Fundy

St Pierre and Miquelon (France)

ST-PIERRE

North America
Eastern Canada

123

Lambert Conformal Conic Projection

1:12 000 000

0   100   200   300   400   miles
0 100 200 300 400 500 600 700 km

Lambert Conformal Conic Projection

1:7 000 000

0   100   200   miles

0   100   200   300   400 km

PACIFIC

OCEAN

CALIFORNIA

NEVADA

UNIT

OF

BAJA CALI
M

Lambert Conformal Conic Projection

1:3 500 000

0   50   100   miles

0   50   100   150   200 km

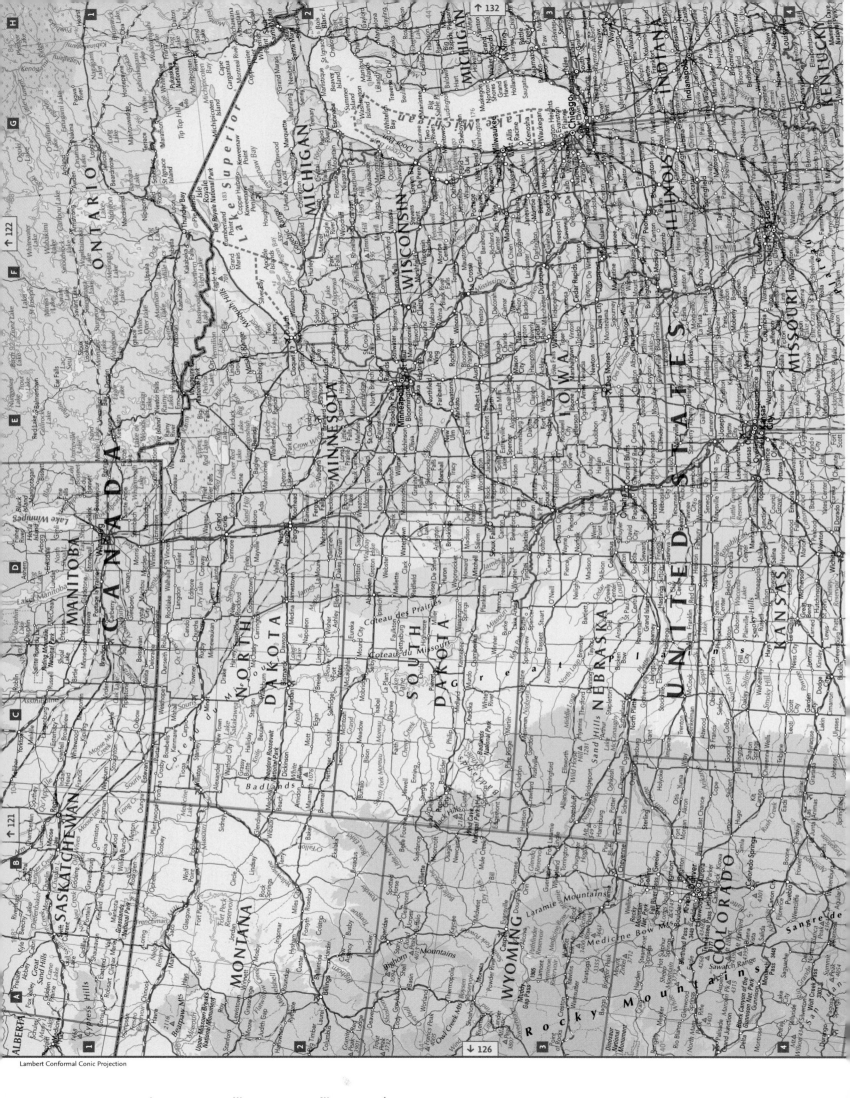

Lambert Conformal Conic Projection

1:7 000 000

| 0 | 100 | 200 | miles |

| 0 | 100 | 200 | 300 | 400 | km |

States in the U.S.A.
numbered on the map:

1. CONNECTICUT (F3)
2. DELAWARE (F4)
3. MASSACHUSETTS (F3)
4. RHODE ISLAND (G3)

Lambert Conformal Conic Projection

132

1:7 000 000

0   100   200   miles
0   100   200   300   400 km

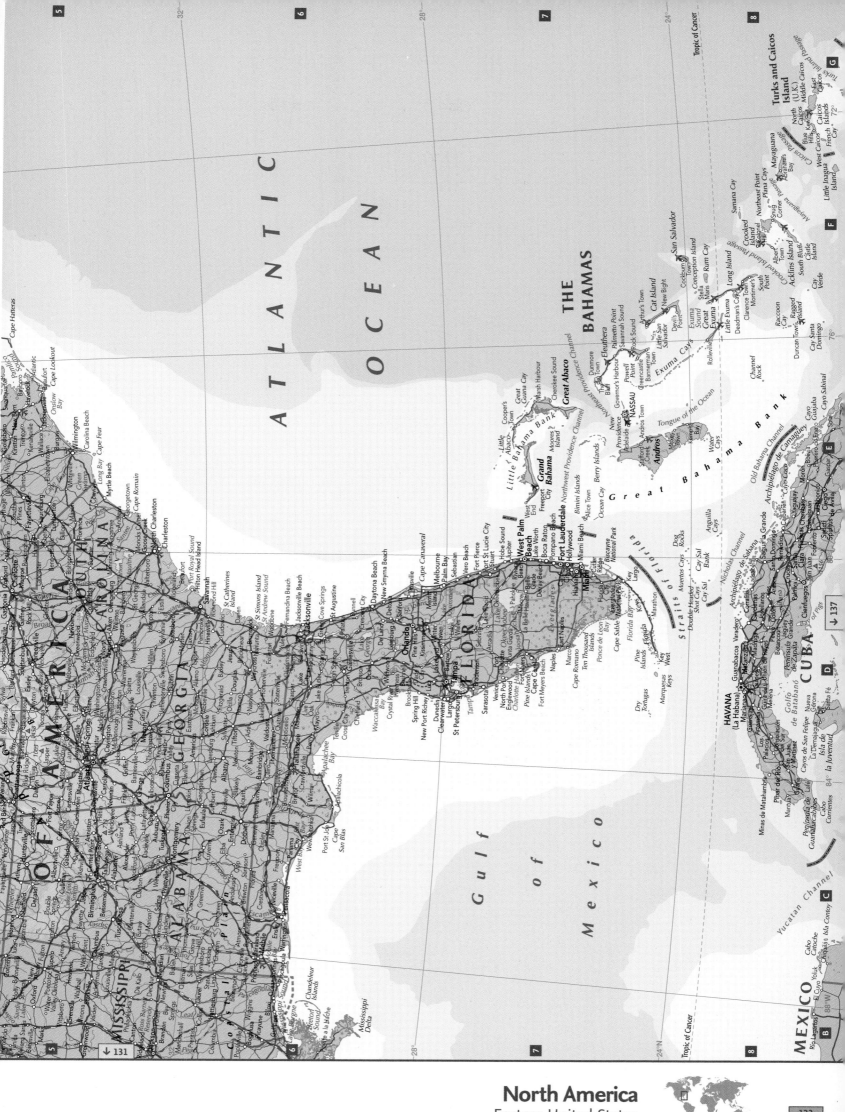

North America
Eastern United States

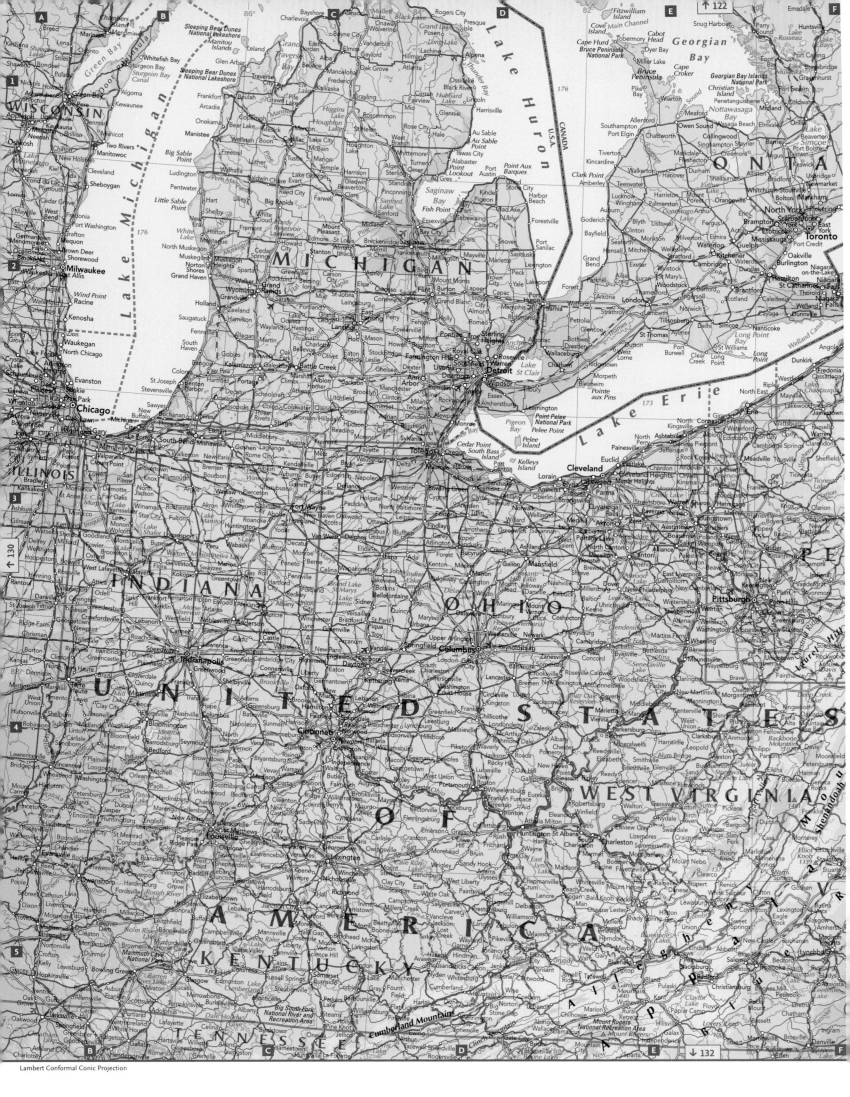

Lambert Conformal Conic Projection

1:3 500 000

0   50   100   miles

0   50   100   150   200 km

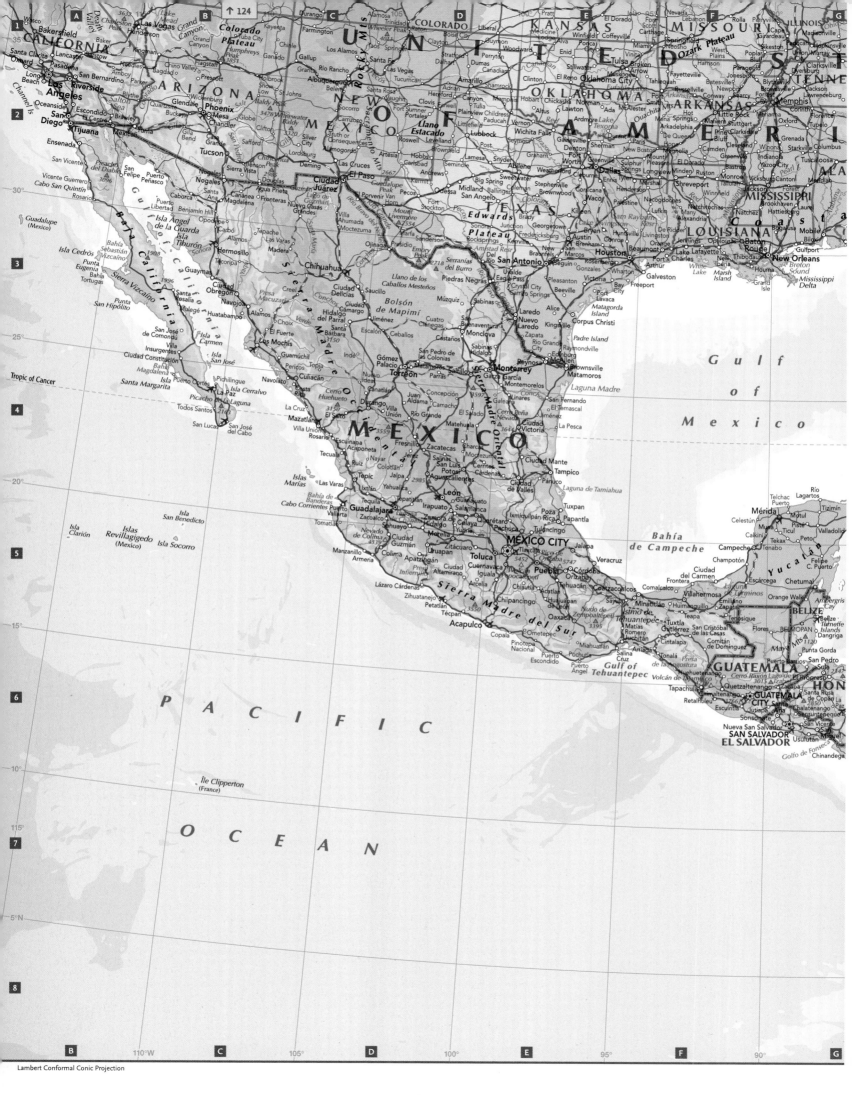

Lambert Conformal Conic Projection

1:14 000 000

0   200   400   miles
0   200   400   600   800 km

North America
Central America and the Caribbean

South America is a continent of great contrasts, with landscapes varying from the tropical rainforests of the Amazon Basin, to the Atacama Desert, the driest place on earth, and the sub-Antarctic regions of southern Chile and Argentina. The dominant physical features are the Andes, stretching along the entire west coast of the continent and containing numerous mountains over 6 000 metres high, and the Amazon, which is the second longest river in the world and has the world's largest drainage basin.

The Altiplano is a high plateau lying between two of the Andes ranges. It contains Lake Titicaca, the world's highest navigable lake. By contrast, large lowland areas dominate the centre of the continent, lying between the Andes and the Guiana and Brazilian Highlands. These vast grasslands stretch from the Llanos of the north through the Selvas and the Gran Chaco to the Pampas of Argentina.

South America's largest lake, **Lake Titicaca**, high in the Andes on the border between Bolivia and Peru.

South America perspective view and cross section

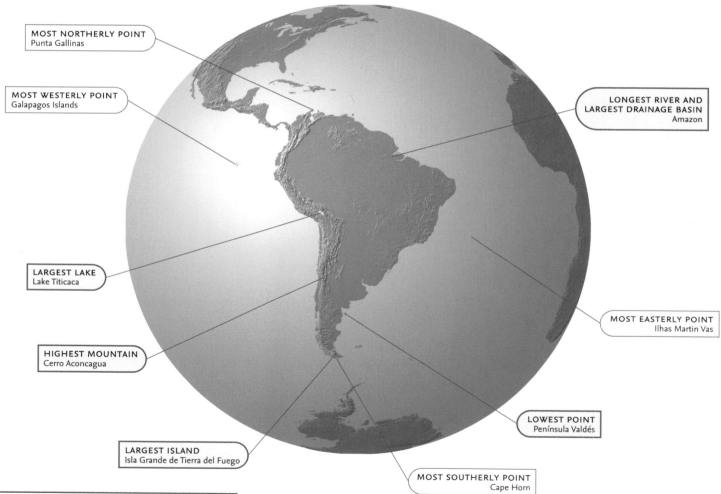

MOST NORTHERLY POINT
Punta Gallinas

MOST WESTERLY POINT
Galapagos Islands

LONGEST RIVER AND LARGEST DRAINAGE BASIN
Amazon

LARGEST LAKE
Lake Titicaca

MOST EASTERLY POINT
Ilhas Martin Vas

HIGHEST MOUNTAIN
Cerro Aconcagua

LOWEST POINT
Península Valdés

LARGEST ISLAND
Isla Grande de Tierra del Fuego

MOST SOUTHERLY POINT
Cape Horn

Internet Links

NASA Visible Earth	**visibleearth.nasa.gov**
NASA Astronaut Photography	**eol.jsc.nasa.gov**
World Rainforest Information Portal	**www.rainforestweb.org**
Peakware World Mountain Encyclopedia	**www.peakware.com**

South America's physical features

Highest mountain	Cerro Aconcagua, Argentina	6 959 metres	22 831 feet
Longest river	Amazon	6 516 km	4 049 miles
Largest lake	Lake Titicaca, Bolivia/Peru	8 340 sq km	3 220 sq miles
Largest island	Isla Grande de Tierra del Fuego, Argentina/Chile	47 000 sq km	18 147 sq miles
Largest drainage basin	Amazon	7 050 000 sq km	2 722 005 sq miles
Lowest point	Península Valdés, Argentina	-40 metres	-131 feet

Caribbean Sea

NORTH AMERICA

PACIFIC OCEAN

ATLANTIC OCEAN

Isla Grande de Tierra del Fuego, South America's largest island, situated at the southernmost tip of the continent.

South America's extent

TOTAL LAND AREA	17 815 420 sq km / 6 878 534 sq miles
Most northerly point	Punta Gallinas, Colombia
Most southerly point	Cape Horn, Chile
Most westerly point	Galapagos Islands, Ecuador
Most easterly point	Ilhas Martin Vas, Atlantic Ocean

Facts

- Water flow along the Amazon is over 1 500 times that of the River Thames

- Cerro Aconcagua, 6 959 metres, is the highest point in the western hemisphere

- The Amazon rainforest supports approximately half of all the world's living species

- The Pantanal in Brazil is the largest area of wetland in the world

- The world's driest desert is the Atacama, where only 1mm of rain may fall as infrequently as once every 5–20 years

Confluence of the **Amazon** and **Negro** rivers at Manaus, northern Brazil.

French Guiana, a French Department, is the only remaining territory under overseas control on a continent which has seen a long colonial history. Much of South America was colonized by Spain in the sixteenth century, with Britain, Portugal and the Netherlands each claiming territory in the northeast of the continent. This colonization led to the conquering of ancient civilizations, including the Incas in Peru. Most countries became independent from Spain and Portugal in the early nineteenth century.

The population of the continent reflects its history, being composed primarily of indigenous Indian peoples and mestizos – reflecting the long Hispanic influence. There has been a steady process of urbanization within the continent, with major movements of the population from rural to urban areas. The majority of the population now live in the major cities and within 300 kilometres of the coast.

Rio de Janeiro, third largest city in Brazil and the capital until 1960 when the status of capital was transferred to Brasília.

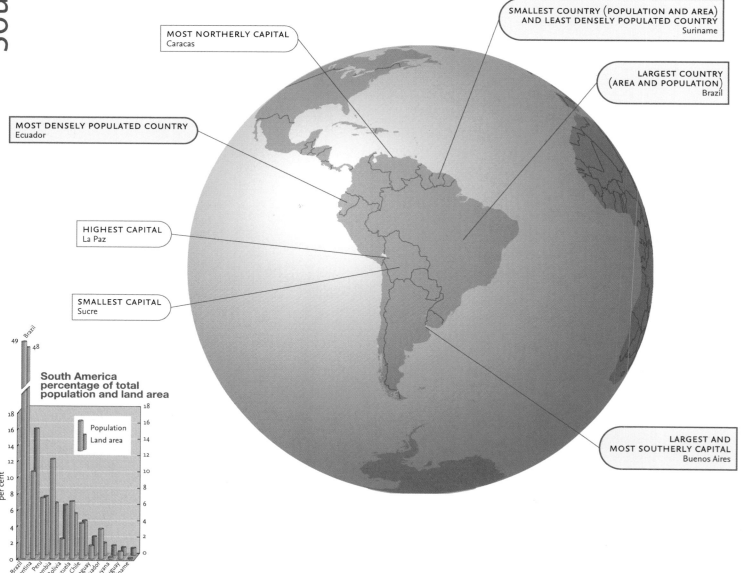

SMALLEST COUNTRY (POPULATION AND AREA) AND LEAST DENSELY POPULATED COUNTRY
Suriname

MOST NORTHERLY CAPITAL
Caracas

LARGEST COUNTRY (AREA AND POPULATION)
Brazil

MOST DENSELY POPULATED COUNTRY
Ecuador

HIGHEST CAPITAL
La Paz

SMALLEST CAPITAL
Sucre

LARGEST AND MOST SOUTHERLY CAPITAL
Buenos Aires

South America percentage of total population and land area

Population
Land area

per cent

Brazil · Argentina · Peru · Colombia · Bolivia · Venezuela · Chile · Paraguay · Ecuador · Guyana · Uruguay · Suriname

South America's countries

Largest country (area)	Brazil	8 514 879 sq km	3 287 613 sq miles
Smallest country (area)	Suriname	163 820 sq km	63 251 sq miles
Largest country (population)	Brazil	178 470 000	
Smallest country (population)	Suriname	436 000	
Most densely populated country	Ecuador	48 per sq km	124 per sq mile
Least densely populated country	Suriname	3 per sq km	7 per sq mile

South America's capitals

Largest capital (population)	Buenos Aires, Argentina	13 349 000	
Smallest capital (population)	Sucre, Bolivia	183 000	
Most northerly capital	Caracas, Venezuela	10° 28'N	
Most southerly capital	Buenos Aires, Argentina	34° 36'S	
Highest capital	La Paz, Bolivia	3 630 metres	11 909 feet

NORTH AMERICA

Punta Gallinas

Barranquilla
Cartagena
Maracaibo
Cabimas
Maracay
Caracas
Cumaná
Barquisimeto
Valencia
Ciudad
Bolívar
Montería
San Cristóbal
Puerto
Ayacucho
Georgetown
Medellín
Tunja
VENEZUELA
Paramaribo
Ibagué
Bogotá
GUYANA
Cayenne
Cali
COLOMBIA
SURINAME
French
Guiana
Isla de Malpelo
(Colombia)
Neiva
Guaviare
Boa Vista
Orinoco
Branco

Esmeraldas
Quito
Caquetá
Japurá
Represa
de Balbina
Amazon
Mouths of
the Amazon
Manta
ECUADOR
Putumayo
Manaus
Santarém
Belém
Guayaquil
Cuenca
Amazon
Tonantins
Iça
Xingu
Tapajós
São
Luís
Parnaíba
Iquitos
Juruá
Represa
Tucuruí
Fortaleza
Sullana
Marañón
Yavarí
Carauari
Purus
Madeira
Maraba
Teresina
Natal
Chiclayo
Ucayali
Cruzeiro do Sul
B R A Z I L
João Pessoa
Trujillo
Pucallpa
Porto
Velho
Teles Pires
Xingu
Araguaia
Tocantins
Floresta
Recife
Rio Branco
Jiparaná
Iriri
Tapajós
Juàzeiro
PERU
PACIFIC
OCEAN
Huancayo
Puerto
Maldonado
Guaporé
Aripuanã
Juruena
Arinos
São Francisco
Maceió
Callao
Lima
Ica
Cusco
Beni
Lago
de San Luis
Trinidad
Cuiabá
Aracaju
Juliaca
Lake
Titicaca
Mamoré
BOLIVIA
Goiânia
Brasília
Salvador
Ilhéus
Arequipa
La Paz
Cochabamba
Santa Cruz
Pantanal
Paranaíba
Patos de Minas
Uberaba
Teófilo
Otôni
Arica
Sucre
Potosí
Campo
Grande
Araçatuba
Ribeirão
Preto
Belo
Horizonte
Vitória
Iquique
Tarija
Paraguay
PARAGUAY
Pedro Juan
Caballero
Paranapanema
Campinas
Nova Iguaçu
Grande
Antofagasta
San Salvador
de Jujuy
Pilcomayo
São
Paulo
Rio de Janeiro
Maringá
San Miguel
de Tucumán
Teuco
Asunción
Iguaçu
Foz do Iguaçu
Curitiba
Copiapó
Formosa
Resistencia
Corrientes
Encarnación
Posadas
Florianópolis
Catamarca
Salado
Santa
Maria
La Rioja
Santa Fé
Uruguay
Paraná
Concordia
Paysandú
Lagoa
dos Patos
Porto Alegre
ATLANTIC
OCEAN
San
Juan
Córdoba
Rosario
Paraná
Rio Grande
Cerro
Aconcagua
6959
Mendoza
San Luis
Valparaíso
Santiago
San Rafael
Buenos Aires
La Plata
Montevideo
Talca
URUGUAY
Río de la Plata
Concepción
Chillán
ARGENTINA
Santa
Rosa
Colorado
Bahía
Blanca
Mar del Plata
Valdivia
Neuquén
Negro
Viedma
Puerto Montt
Isla de Chiloé
Patagonia
Trelew
Archipiélago
de los Chonos
Comodoro
Rivadavia
Golfo de
San Jorge
Punta Medanosa
Falkland
Islands
(U.K.)
Bahía Grande
Puerto Natales
Río Gallegos
Stanley
Punta Arenas
Isla Grande
de Tierra del Fuego
Ushuaia
Cape Horn

CHILE

Galapagos Islands
(Ecuador)

Galapagos Islands, an island territory of Ecuador which lies on the equator in the eastern Pacific Ocean over 900 kilometres west of the coast of Ecuador.

Facts

- South America is often referred to as 'Latin America', reflecting the historic influences of Spain and Portugal

- The largest city in each South American country is the capital, except in Brazil and Ecuador

- South America has only 2 landlocked countries – Bolivia and Paraguay

- Chile is over 4 000 kilometres long but has an average width of only 177 kilometres

Falkland Islands, an overseas UK territory in the South Atlantic Ocean.

South Georgia
(U.K.)

South America
Northern South America

BOLIVIA

PARAGUAY

BRAZIL

Belo Horizonte

Nova Iguaçu

Rio de Janeiro

São Paulo

Santos

ASUNCIÓN

Curitiba

Córdoba

Rosario

URUGUAY

BUENOS AIRES

MONTEVIDEO

SANTIAGO

A R G E N T I N A

Mar del Plata

Bahía Blanca

A T L A N T I C

O C E A N

P A T A G O N I A

Golfo
San Matías

Golfo de
San Jorge

Falkland Islands
(U.K.)

West Falkland
Weddell Island

STANLEY

East Falkland

Beauchene
Island

Cape Horn

Tropic of Capricorn

Shag
Rocks

South Georgia
(U.K.)

Lambert Azimuthal Equal Area Projection

South America
Southern South America

1:14 000 000

0   200   400 miles

0   200   400   600   800 km

1:7 000 000

0   100   200 miles

0   100   200   300   400 km

Between them, the world's oceans and polar regions cover approximately seventy per cent of the earth's surface. The oceans contain ninety six per cent of the earth's water and a vast range of flora and fauna. They are a major influence on the world's climate, particularly through ocean currents. The Arctic and Antarctica are the coldest and most inhospitable places on the earth. They both have vast amounts of ice which, if global warming continues, could have a major influence on sea level across the globe.

Our understanding of the oceans and polar regions has increased enormously over the last twenty years through the development of new technologies, particularly that of satellite remote sensing, which can generate vast amounts of data relating to, for example, topography (both on land and the seafloor), land cover and sea surface temperature.

The Oceans

The world's major oceans are the Pacific, the Atlantic and the Indian Oceans. The Arctic Ocean is generally considered as part of the Atlantic, and the Southern Ocean, which stretches around the whole of Antarctica is usually treated as an extension of each of the three major oceans.

One of the most important factors affecting the earth's climate is the circulation of water within and between the oceans. Differences in temperature and surface winds create ocean currents which move enormous quantities of water around the globe. These currents re-distribute heat which the oceans have absorbed from the sun, and so have a major effect on the world's climate system. El Niño is one climatic phenomenon directly influenced by these ocean processes.

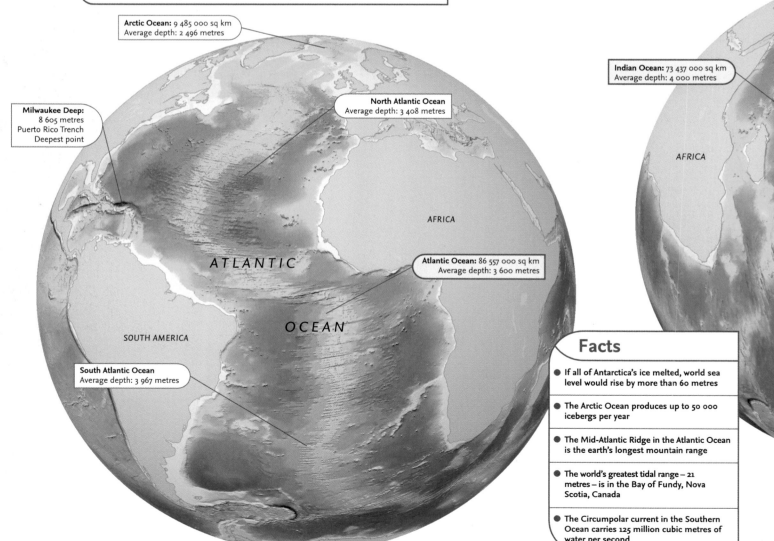

Pacific Ocean
World's largest ocean: 166 241 000 sq km
Average depth: 4 200m

North Pacific Ocean
Average depth: 4 573 metres

NORTH AMERICA

PACIFIC OCEAN

Challenger Deep: 10 920 metres
Mariana Trench
Deepest point

AUSTRALIA

South Pacific Ocean
Average depth: 3 935 metres

Arctic Ocean: 9 485 000 sq km
Average depth: 2 496 metres

North Atlantic Ocean
Average depth: 3 408 metres

Indian Ocean: 73 437 000 sq km
Average depth: 4 000 metres

AFRICA

Milwaukee Deep:
8 605 metres
Puerto Rico Trench
Deepest point

AFRICA

ATLANTIC

Atlantic Ocean: 86 557 000 sq km
Average depth: 3 600 metres

OCEAN

SOUTH AMERICA

South Atlantic Ocean
Average depth: 3 967 metres

Facts

- If all of Antarctica's ice melted, world sea level would rise by more than 60 metres

- The Arctic Ocean produces up to 50 000 icebergs per year

- The Mid-Atlantic Ridge in the Atlantic Ocean is the earth's longest mountain range

- The world's greatest tidal range – 21 metres – is in the Bay of Fundy, Nova Scotia, Canada

- The Circumpolar current in the Southern Ocean carries 125 million cubic metres of water per second

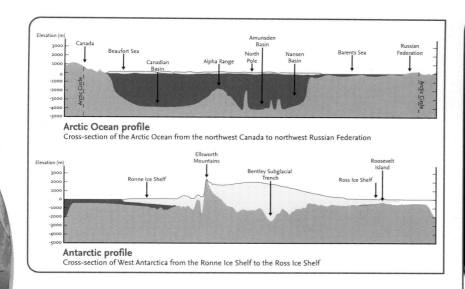

Arctic Ocean profile
Cross-section of the Arctic Ocean from the northwest Canada to northwest Russian Federation

Antarctic profile
Cross-section of West Antarctica from the Ronne Ice Shelf to the Ross Ice Shelf

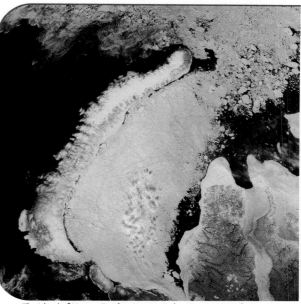

The island of **Novaya Zemlya**, Russian Federation, prevents the Kara Sea (right) from being affected by the warming influence of the Gulf Stream in the Atlantic Ocean and the Barents Sea (left).

Internet Links

● National Oceanic and Atmospheric Administration	**www.noaa.gov**
● Southampton Oceanography Centre	**www.soc.soton.ac.uk**
● British Antarctic Survey	**www.bas.ac.uk**
● Scott Polar Research Institute (SPRI)	**www.spri.cam.ac.uk**
● The National Snow and Ice Data Center (NSIDC)	**nsidc.org**

Polar Regions

Although a harsh climate is common to the two polar regions, there are major differences between the Arctic and Antarctica. The North Pole is surrounded by the Arctic Ocean, much of which is permanently covered by sea ice, while the South Pole lies on the huge land mass of Antarctica. This is covered by a permanent ice cap which reaches a maximum thickness of over four kilometres. Antarctica has no permanent population, but Europe, Asia and North America all stretch into the Arctic region which is populated by numerous ethnic groups. Antarctica is subject to the Antarctic Treaty of 1959 which does not recognize individual land claims and protects the continent in the interests of international scientific cooperation.

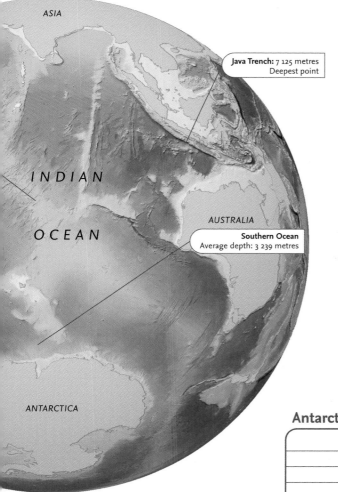

Java Trench: 7 125 metres
Deepest point

Southern Ocean
Average depth: 3 239 metres

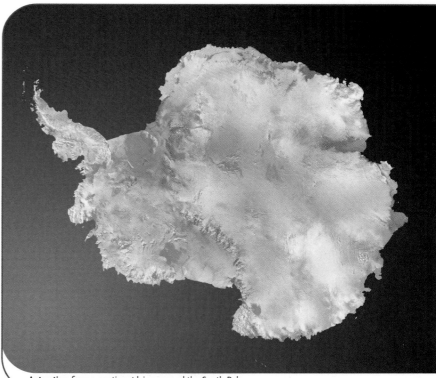

Antarctica, frozen continent lying around the South Pole.

Antarctica's physical features

Highest mountain: Vinson Massif	4 897 m	16 066 ft
Total land area (excluding ice shelves)	12 093 000 sq km	4 669 292 sq miles
Ice shelves	1 559 000 sq km	601 954 sq miles
Exposed rock	49 000 sq km	18 920 sq miles
Lowest bedrock elevation (Bentley Subglacial Trench)	2 496 m below sea level	8 189 ft below sea level
Maximum ice thickness (Astrolabe Subglacial Basin)	4 776 m	15 669 ft
Mean ice thickness (including ice shelves)	1 859 m	6 099 ft
Volume of ice sheet (including ice shelves)	25 400 000 cubic km	10 160 000 cubic miles

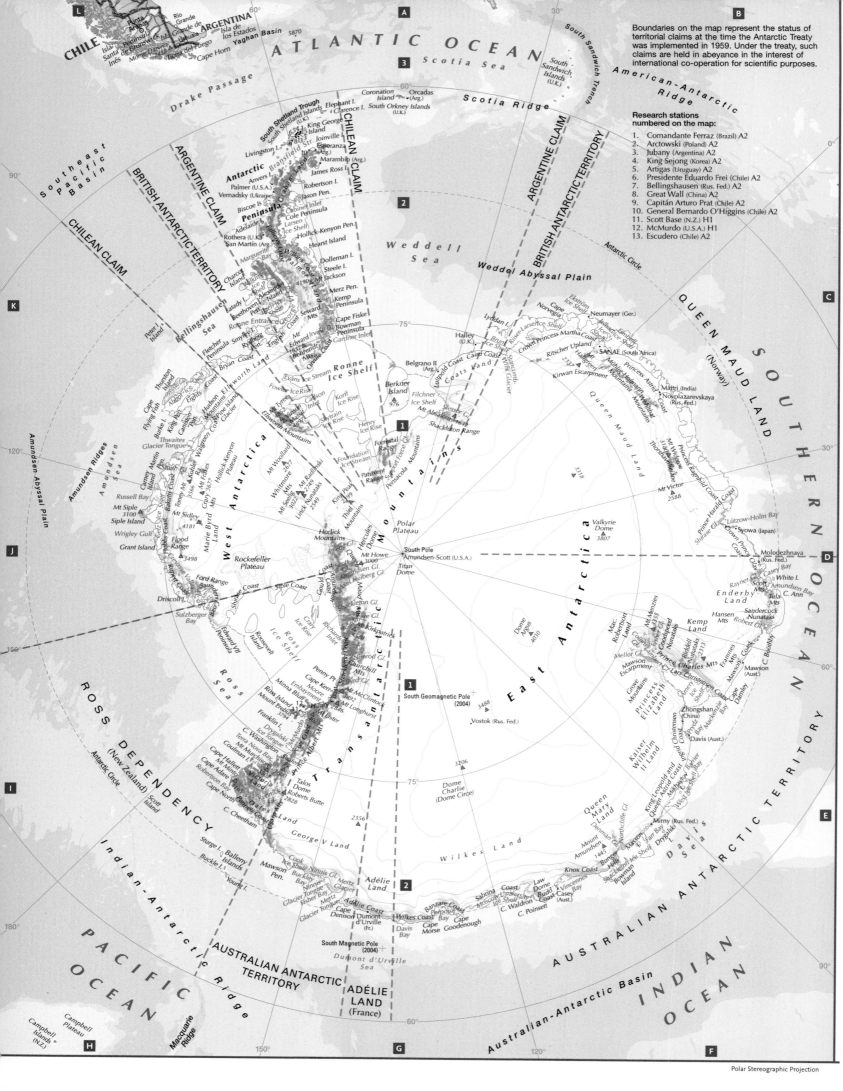

Antarctica

ATLANTIC OCEAN

Scotia Sea

South Sandwich Islands (U.K.)

American-Antarctic Ridge

Research stations numbered on the map:

1. Comandante Ferraz (Brazil) A2
2. Arctowski (Poland) A2
3. Jubany (Argentina) A2
4. King Sejong (Korea) A2
5. Artigas (Uruguay) A2
6. Presidente Eduardo Frei (Chile) A2
7. Bellingshausen (Rus. Fed.) A2
8. Great Wall (China) A2
9. Capitán Arturo Prat (Chile) A2
10. General Bernardo O'Higgins (Chile) A2
11. Scott Base (N.Z.) H1
12. McMurdo (U.S.A.) H1
13. Escudero (Chile) A2

CHILE · ARGENTINA

Drake Passage

Scotia Ridge

Southeast Pacific Basin

ARGENTINE CLAIM

BRITISH ANTARCTIC TERRITORY

CHILEAN CLAIM

Antarctic Peninsula

Weddell Sea

Weddel Abyssal Plain

Antarctic Circle

ARGENTINE CLAIM

BRITISH ANTARCTIC TERRITORY

QUEEN MAUD LAND

SOUTHERN OCEAN

Bellingshausen Sea

Ronne Ice Shelf

Filchner Ice Shelf

Berkner Island

Ellsworth Mountains

Transantarctic Mountains

Polar Plateau

South Pole
Amundsen-Scott (U.S.A.)

West Antarctica

East Antarctica

Queen Maud Land

Amundsen Sea

Amundsen Abyssal Plain

Marie Byrd Land

Ross Ice Shelf

Ross Sea

ROSS DEPENDENCY (New Zealand)

Victoria Land

South Geomagnetic Pole (2004)

Vostok (Rus. Fed.)

Dome Charlie (Dome Circe)

Wilkes Land

Queen Mary Land

Davis Sea

AUSTRALIAN ANTARCTIC TERRITORY

Indian-Antarctic Ridge

Macquarie Ridge

PACIFIC OCEAN

AUSTRALIAN ANTARCTIC TERRITORY

South Magnetic Pole (2004)

Dumont d'Urville Sea

ADÉLIE LAND (France)

George V Land

Adélie Land

Australian-Antarctic Basin

INDIAN OCEAN

Antarctica

1:26 000 000

| 0 | 200 | 400 | 600 | 800 | 1000 miles |

Polar Stereographic Projection

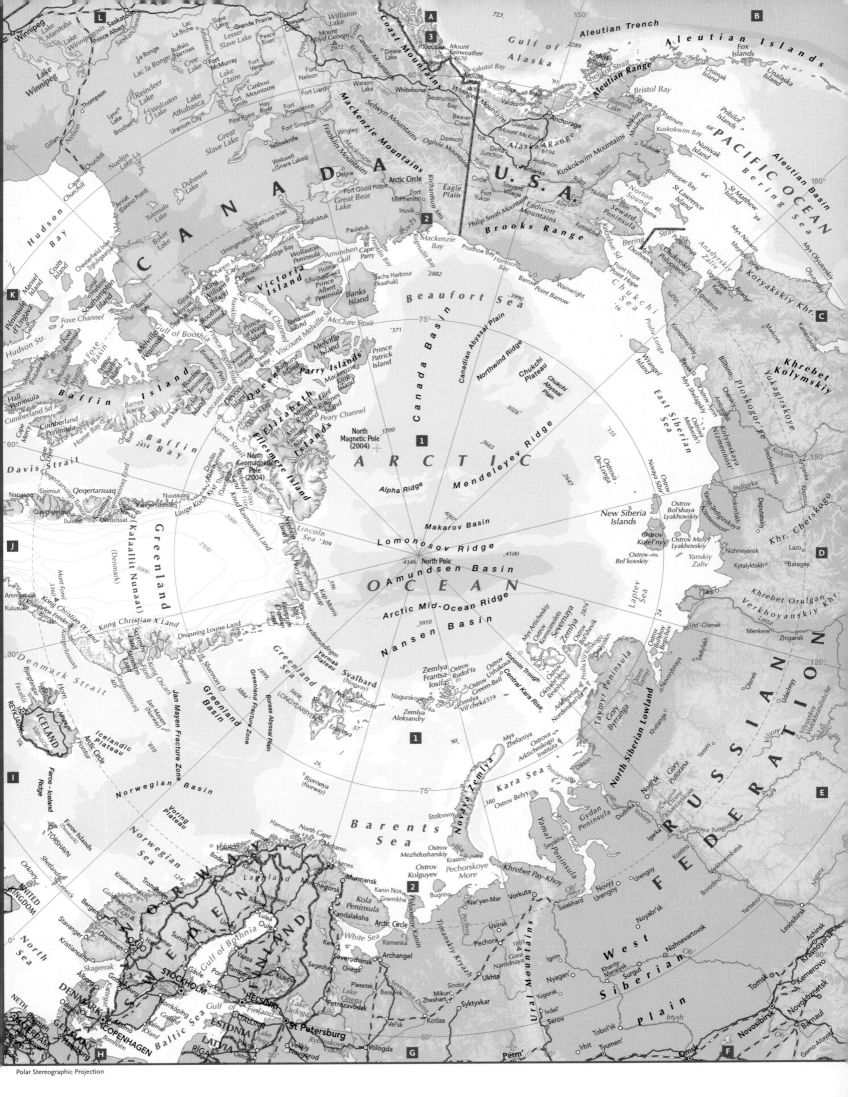

The Arctic

Polar Stereographic Projection

1:26 000 000

| 0 | 200 | 400 | 600 | 800 | 1000 miles |

| 0 | 200 | 400 | 600 | 800 | 1000 | 1200 | 1400 | 1600 km |

World Statistics

	Population						Economy					
	Total population	Population change (%)	% urban	Total fertility	Population by age (000s) 0–14	Population by age (000s) 65 or over	2050 projected population	Total Gross National Income (GNI) (US$M)	GNI per capita (US$)	Total debt service (US$)	Debt service ratio (% GNI)	Aid receipts (% GNI)	Military spending (% GNI)
WORLD	6 301 000 000	1.2	47.7	2.7	1 814 525	418 420	9 322 251 000	31 500 010	5 170	...	...	...	2.3
AFGHANISTAN	23 897 000	3.7	22.3	6.8	9 466	619	72 267 000	...	...	...	...	...	...
ALBANIA	3 166 000	0.6	42.9	2.3	939	184	3 905 000	4 236	1 230	27 000 000	0.7	8.5	1.3
ALGERIA	31 800 000	1.8	57.5	2.8	10 554	1 248	51 180 000	50 355	1 630	4 466 500 096	8.8	0.3	4.0
ANDORRA	71 000	4.1	92.2	...	...	...	193 000	...	...	...	...	...	...
ANGOLA	13 625 000	3.0	34.9	7.2	6 326	373	53 328 000	6 707	500	1 204 499 968	25.4	8.1	21.2
ANTIGUA AND BARBUDA	73 000	0.3	37.1	...	...	...	73 000	621	9 070	...	...	1.5	...
ARGENTINA	38 428 000	1.2	88.3	2.4	10 265	3 592	54 522 000	260 994	6 960	27 345 100 800	9.9	...	1.6
ARMENIA	3 061 000	0.1	67.2	1.1	898	327	3 150 000	2 127	560	43 000 000	2.2	11.2	5.8
AUSTRALIA	19 731 000	1.0	91.2	1.8	3 927	2 346	26 502 000	383 291	19 770	...	...	...	1.8
AUSTRIA	8 116 000	-0.1	67.4	1.2	1 343	1 256	6 452 000	194 463	23 940	...	...	...	0.8
AZERBAIJAN	8 370 000	0.6	51.8	1.5	2 330	546	8 897 000	5 283	650	180 900 000	3.7	2.9	6.6
THE BAHAMAS	314 000	1.2	88.9	2.3	90	16	449 000	...	...	...	...	0.1	...
BAHRAIN	724 000	1.7	92.5	2.3	180	19	1 008 000	...	...	...	...	...	8.1
BANGLADESH	146 736 000	2.1	25.6	3.6	53 190	4 291	265 432 000	49 882	370	789 699 968	1.7	2.4	1.3
BARBADOS	270 000	0.4	50.5	1.5	55	28	263 000	...	...	...	...	...	0.5
BELARUS	9 895 000	-0.4	69.6	1.2	1 904	1 357	8 305 000	11 892	1 190	232 200 000	0.8	0.1	1.3
BELGIUM	10 318 000	0.1	97.4	1.5	1 771	1 744	9 583 000	239 779	23 340	...	...	...	1.4
BELIZE	256 000	1.9	48.1	2.9	87	10	392 000	718	2 910	66 100 000	8.6	1.9	1.6
BENIN	6 736 000	2.8	43.0	5.7	2 907	172	18 070 000	2 349	360	76 700 000	3.6	10.6	1.4
BHUTAN	2 257 000	2.6	7.4	5.1	891	88	5 569 000	529	640	6 600 000	1.3	11.6	...
BOLIVIA	8 808 000	2.2	62.9	3.9	3 300	334	16 966 000	8 044	940	661 600 000	8.2	5.8	1.8
BOSNIA-HERZEGOVINA	4 161 000	1.1	43.4	1.3	753	393	3 458 000	5 037	1 240	334 000 000	7.2	16.2	4.5
BOTSWANA	1 785 000	0.5	49.4	3.9	649	44	2 109 000	5 863	3 630	68 000 000	1.3	0.6	4.7
BRAZIL	178 470 000	1.2	81.7	2.2	49 077	8 760	247 244 000	528 503	3 060	62 787 600 384	11.0	0.1	1.9
BRUNEI	358 000	1.8	72.8	2.5	105	11	565 000	...	...	...	...	...	4.0
BULGARIA	7 897 000	-1.0	67.4	1.1	1 252	1 282	4 531 000	12 644	1 560	1 189 200 000	10.2	2.7	3.0
BURKINA	13 002 000	3.0	16.9	6.8	5 617	375	46 304 000	2 395	210	54 700 000	2.5	14.0	1.6
BURUNDI	6 825 000	3.0	9.3	6.8	3 023	182	20 219 000	692	100	21 400 000	3.2	13.8	7.0
CAMBODIA	14 144 000	2.4	17.5	4.8	5 749	367	29 883 000	3 329	270	31 400 000	1.0	12.6	4.0
CAMEROON	16 018 000	2.1	49.7	4.7	6 411	545	32 284 000	8 723	570	561 900 032	6.8	4.7	1.8
CANADA	31 510 000	0.8	78.9	1.6	5 882	3 875	40 407 000	661 881	21 340	...	...	...	1.4
CAPE VERDE	463 000	2.1	63.5	3.2	168	20	807 000	596	1 310	16 100 000	2.9	17.0	0.9
CENTRAL AFRICAN REPUBLIC	3 865 000	1.6	41.7	4.9	1 599	150	8 195 000	1 006	270	14 100 000	1.5	7.9	2.8
CHAD	8 598 000	3.1	24.1	6.7	3 663	247	27 732 000	1 597	200	26 300 000	1.9	9.6	2.4
CHILE	15 805 000	1.2	86.1	2.4	4 328	1 090	22 215 000	66 915	4 350	6 162 599 936	9.0	0.1	3.0
CHINA	1 289 161 000	0.7	36.7	1.8	316 838	87 428	1 462 058 000	1 130 984	890	21 728 299 008	2.0	0.2	2.3
COLOMBIA	44 222 000	1.6	75.5	2.6	13 806	1 993	70 862 000	82 017	1 910	5 170 599 936	6.6	0.2	3.2
COMOROS	768 000	2.9	33.8	5.0	304	19	1 900 000	217	380	2 700 000	1.3	9.3	...
CONGO	3 724 000	3.0	66.1	6.3	1 396	101	10 744 000	2 171	700	42 800 000	1.9	1.5	3.5
CONGO, DEMOCRATIC REPUBLIC OF	52 771 000	3.3	30.7	6.7	24 846	1 465	203 527 000	...	...	24 800 000	...	...	14.4
COSTA RICA	4 173 000	2.0	59.5	2.7	1 302	205	7 195 000	15 332	3 950	649 900 032	4.4	0.1	0.5
CÔTE D'IVOIRE	16 631 000	2.1	44.0	4.6	6 745	495	32 185 000	10 259	630	1 020 300 032	11.8	3.7	0.8
CROATIA	4 428 000	0.0	58.1	1.7	840	658	4 180 000	20 366	4 550	2 437 400 064	13.0	0.3	3.3
CUBA	11 300 000	0.3	75.5	1.6	2 377	1 072	10 764 000	...	...	...	...	...	1.9
CYPRUS	802 000	0.8	70.2	1.9	181	90	910 000	...	...	...	...	...	3.4
CZECH REPUBLIC	10 236 000	-0.1	74.5	1.2	1 686	1 421	8 429 000	54 108	5 270	4 773 499 904	9.5	0.9	2.3
DENMARK	5 364 000	0.2	85.1	1.7	971	798	5 080 000	166 345	31 090	...	...	...	1.6
DJIBOUTI	703 000	1.0	84.2	5.8	273	20	1 068 000	572	890	13 500 000	2.4	12.5	4.3
DOMINICA	79 000	-0.1	71.4	...	...	...	72 000	224	3 060	10 200 000	4.3	6.4	...
DOMINICAN REPUBLIC	8 745 000	1.5	66.0	2.7	2 805	359	11 960 000	18 955	2 230	520 800 000	2.8	0.3	0.7
EAST TIMOR	778 000	3.9	7.5	3.9	317	20	1 410 000	...	...	...	...	...	...
ECUADOR	13 003 000	1.7	63.4	2.8	4 278	594	21 190 000	15 952	1 240	1 276 099 968	10.3	1.2	3.7
EGYPT	71 931 000	1.7	42.7	2.9	24 004	2 808	113 840 000	99 406	1 530	1 813 400 064	1.8	1.3	2.7
EL SALVADOR	6 515 000	1.8	61.5	2.9	2 235	312	10 855 000	13 088	2 050	373 700 000	2.9	1.4	0.9
EQUATORIAL GUINEA	494 000	2.8	49.3	5.9	200	18	1 378 000	327	700	5 300 000	1.1	...	3.2
ERITREA	4 141 000	4.2	19.1	5.3	1 608	106	10 028 000	792	190	3 300 000	0.5	25.3	27.4
ESTONIA	1 323 000	-1.1	69.4	1.2	247	200	752 000	5 255	3 810	427 600 000	9.3	1.4	1.5
ETHIOPIA	70 678 000	2.4	15.9	6.8	28 414	1 859	186 452 000	6 767	100	139 400 000	2.2	11.1	8.8
FIJI	839 000	1.1	50.2	3.0	271	28	916 000	1 755	2 130	30 100 000	2.1	2.0	2.0
FINLAND	5 207 000	0.1	58.5	1.6	933	773	4 693 000	124 171	23 940	...	...	...	1.4
FRANCE	60 144 000	0.4	75.5	1.8	11 098	9 462	61 833 000	1 377 389	22 690	...	...	...	2.7
GABON	1 329 000	2.5	82.3	5.4	494	72	3 164 000	3 990	3 160	467 900 000	11.0	0.3	2.4
THE GAMBIA	1 426 000	2.4	31.3	4.8	525	40	2 605 000	440	330	18 600 000	4.5	12.4	1.3
GEORGIA	5 126 000	-0.5	56.5	1.4	1 077	680	3 219 000	3 097	620	116 900 000	3.8	5.3	1.2

Social Indicators						Environment				Communications				
Infant mortality rate	Life expectancy M	Life expectancy F	Literacy rate (%)	Access to safe water (%)	Doctors per 100 000 people	Forest area (%)	Annual change in forest area (%)	Protected land area (%)	CO_2 emissions	Telephone lines per 100 people	Cellular phones per 100 people	Internet connections per 1 000 people	International dialling code	Time zone
83	**63.9**	**68.1**	**...**	**82**	**...**	**29.6**	**-0.2**	**6.4**	**...**	**17.2**	**15.6**	**82.3**	**...**	**...**
257	43.0	43.5	...	13	...	2.1	...	0.3	0.0	...	...	...	...	+4.5
31	70.9	76.7	98.2	97	129	36.2	-0.8	2.9	0.5	5.0	8.8	2.5	355	+1
65	69.9	73.3	90.4	89	85	0.9	1.3	2.5	3.6	6.0	0.3	1.9	213	+1
7	...	...	...	100	...	...	...	...	...	43.8	30.2	89.7	376	+1
295	44.5	47.1	...	38	8	56.0	-0.2	6.6	0.5	0.6	0.6	4.4	244	+1
15	...	...	...	91	114	20.5	...	...	5.0	47.4	31.8	65.2	1 268	-4
21	70.6	77.7	98.6	...	268	12.7	-0.8	1.8	3.8	21.6	18.6	80.0	54	-3
30	70.3	76.2	99.8	...	316	12.4	1.3	7.6	0.9	14.0	0.7	142.1	374	+4
6	76.4	82.0	...	100	240	20.1	-0.2	7.0	17.7	52.0	57.8	372.3	61	+8 to +10.5
5	75.4	81.5	...	100	302	47.0	0.2	29.2	7.9	46.8	80.7	319.4	43	+1
105	68.7	75.5	...	78	360	13.1	1.3	5.5	4.9	11.1	8.0	3.2	994	+4
18	65.2	73.9	97.4	97	152	84.1	...	...	6.1	40.0	19.7	55.0	1 242	-5
16	72.1	76.3	98.6	...	100	...	14.9	...	29.1	24.7	42.5	198.9	973	+3
82	60.6	60.8	52.1	97	20	10.2	1.3	0.7	0.2	0.4	0.4	1.1	880	+6
14	74.5	79.5	...	100	125	4.7	...	...	5.9	46.3	10.6	37.4	1 246	-4
20	62.8	74.4	99.8	100	443	45.3	3.2	6.3	6.0	27.9	1.4	41.2	375	+2
6	75.7	81.9	...	...	395	22.2	-0.2	2.8	9.9	49.3	74.7	280.0	32	+1
41	73.0	75.9	98.2	92	55	59.1	-2.3	20.9	1.8	14.4	11.6	73.8	501	-6
154	52.5	55.7	55.5	63	6	24.0	-2.3	6.9	0.1	0.9	1.9	3.9	229	+1
100	62.0	64.5	...	62	16	64.2	...	21.2	0.5	2.0	...	3.6	975	+6
80	61.9	65.3	96.3	83	130	48.9	-0.3	14.2	1.5	6.2	9.0	14.6	591	-4
18	71.3	76.7	...	...	...	44.6	...	0.5	1.2	11.1	5.7	11.1	387	+1
101	38.7	37.4	89.1	95	24	21.9	-0.9	18.0	2.4	9.3	16.7	15.4	267	+2
38	64.7	72.6	93.0	87	127	64.3	-0.4	4.4	1.8	21.8	16.7	46.6	55	-2 to -5
7	74.2	78.9	99.5	...	85	83.9	-0.2	...	17.1	24.5	28.9	104.5	673	+8
16	67.1	74.8	99.7	100	345	33.4	0.6	4.5	5.7	35.9	19.1	74.6	359	+2
198	47.0	49.0	36.9	42	3	25.9	-0.2	10.4	0.1	0.5	0.6	1.7	226	GMT
190	39.8	41.4	66.1	78	...	3.7	-9.0	5.3	0.0	0.3	0.3	0.9	257	+2
135	53.6	58.6	80.1	30	30	52.9	-0.6	15.8	0.1	0.3	1.7	0.7	855	+7
154	49.3	50.6	94.4	58	7	51.3	-0.9	4.4	0.1	0.7	2.0	3.0	237	+1
6	76.2	81.8	...	100	229	26.5	...	9.1	15.5	65.5	32.0	435.3	1	-3.5 to -8
40	67.0	72.8	89.2	74	17	21.1	9.3	...	0.3	14.3	7.2	27.5	238	-1
180	42.7	46.0	69.9	70	4	36.8	-0.1	8.2	0.1	0.3	0.3	0.5	236	+1
198	45.1	47.5	69.9	27	3	10.1	-0.6	9.0	0.0	0.1	0.3	0.5	235	+1
12	73.0	79.0	99.0	93	110	20.7	-0.1	18.7	4.1	23.9	34.0	200.2	56	-4
40	69.1	73.5	98.2	75	162	17.5	1.2	6.2	2.5	13.8	11.2	26.0	86	+8
30	69.2	75.3	97.2	91	116	47.8	-0.4	8.2	1.7	17.1	7.6	27.0	57	-5
82	59.4	62.2	59.0	96	7	4.3	-4.3	...	0.1	1.2	...	3.4	269	+3
108	49.6	53.7	97.8	51	25	64.6	-0.1	4.5	0.6	0.7	4.8	0.2	242	+1
207	51.0	53.3	83.7	45	7	59.6	-0.4	4.3	0.1	0.0	0.3	0.1	243	+1 to +2
12	75.0	79.7	98.4	95	141	38.5	-0.8	14.2	1.4	23.0	7.6	93.4	506	-6
173	47.7	48.1	67.6	81	9	22.4	-3.1	5.2	0.9	1.8	4.5	4.3	225	GMT
9	70.3	78.1	99.8	...	229	31.9	0.1	7.4	4.5	36.5	37.7	55.9	385	+1
9	74.8	78.7	99.8	91	530	21.4	1.3	17.2	2.2	5.1	0.1	10.7	53	-5
7	76.0	80.5	99.8	100	255	18.6	3.7	...	7.9	64.3	46.4	221.6	357	+2
5	72.1	78.7	...	...	303	34.1	...	15.8	11.5	37.4	65.9	136.3	420	+1
5	74.2	79.1	...	100	290	10.7	0.2	32.0	10.1	72.3	73.7	447.2	45	+1
146	...	...	85.7	100	14	0.3	...	...	0.6	1.5	0.5	5.1	253	+3
16	...	...	...	97	49	61.3	-0.7	...	...	29.1	1.6	77.8	1 767	-4
48	64.4	70.1	91.7	86	216	28.4	...	31.3	2.5	11.0	14.7	21.5	1 809	-4
...	49.2	50.9	...	...	...	34.3	-0.6	...	...	...	...	...	670	+9
32	68.3	73.5	97.5	85	170	38.1	-1.2	42.6	2.2	10.4	6.7	25.4	593	-5
43	68.2	71.9	71.3	97	202	0.1	3.3	0.8	1.7	10.3	4.3	9.3	20	+2
40	67.7	73.7	89.0	77	107	5.8	-4.6	0.2	1.0	9.3	12.5	8.0	503	-6
156	52.4	55.6	97.4	44	25	62.5	-0.6	0.0	0.6	1.5	3.2	1.9	240	+1
114	51.1	53.7	72.0	46	3	13.5	-0.3	4.3	...	0.8	...	2.6	291	+3
21	65.8	76.4	99.8	...	297	48.7	0.6	11.1	12.1	35.2	45.5	300.5	372	+2
174	42.8	43.8	57.2	24	...	4.2	-0.8	5.0	0.0	0.5	0.0	0.4	251	+3
22	68.1	71.5	99.2	47	48	44.6	-0.2	1.1	0.9	11.0	9.3	18.3	679	+12
5	74.4	81.5	...	100	299	72.0	...	5.5	10.4	54.8	77.8	430.3	358	+2
5	75.2	82.8	...	...	303	27.9	0.4	13.5	6.3	57.4	60.5	263.8	33	+1
90	53.1	55.1	...	86	...	84.7	...	2.7	2.4	3.0	20.5	13.5	241	+1
128	45.7	48.5	60.0	62	4	48.1	1.0	2.0	0.2	2.6	3.2	13.5	220	GMT
29	69.5	77.6	...	79	436	43.7	...	2.8	1.0	15.9	5.4	4.6	995	+4

World Statistics

	Population							Economy					
	Total population	Population change (%)	% urban	Total fertility	Population by age (000s) 0 – 14	65 or over	2050 projected population	Total Gross National Income (GNI) (US$M)	GNI per capita (US$)	Total debt service (US$)	Debt service ratio (% GNI)	Aid receipts (% GNI)	Military spending (% GNI)
GERMANY	82 476 000	0.0	87.7	1.3	12 739	13 453	70 805 000	1 947 951	23 700	...	...	...	1.6
GHANA	20 922 000	2.2	36.4	4.2	7 901	627	40 056 000	5 731	290	471 800 000	9.4	11.5	0.8
GREECE	10 976 000	0.0	60.3	1.2	1 598	1 862	8 983 000	124 553	11 780	...	...	...	4.7
GRENADA	80 000	0.3	38.4	...	...	...	105 000	368	3 720	12 000 000	3.2	4.7	...
GUATEMALA	12 347 000	2.6	39.9	4.4	4 965	404	26 551 000	19 559	1 670	438 000 000	2.3	1.4	0.7
GUINEA	8 480 000	1.5	27.9	5.8	3 592	226	20 711 000	3 043	400	133 000 000	4.5	5.0	1.6
GUINEA-BISSAU	1 493 000	2.4	32.3	6.0	521	43	3 276 000	202	160	6 200 000	3.1	37.7	2.7
GUYANA	765 000	0.2	36.7	2.3	233	38	504 000	641	840	115 600 000	17.5	16.3	0.8
HAITI	8 326 000	1.6	36.3	4.0	3 305	302	13 982 000	3 887	480	41 700 000	1.0	5.4	...
HONDURAS	6 941 000	2.3	53.7	3.7	2 682	216	12 845 000	5 922	900	578 099 968	10.0	7.8	0.7
HUNGARY	9 877 000	-0.5	64.8	1.2	1 689	1 460	7 486 000	48 924	4 800	7 945 900 032	18.0	0.6	1.7
ICELAND	290 000	0.7	92.7	1.9	65	33	333 000	8 201	28 880	...	...	...	...
INDIA	1 065 462 000	1.5	27.9	3.0	337 921	50 096	1 572 055 000	474 323	460	9 694 000 128	2.1	0.3	2.5
INDONESIA	219 883 000	1.2	42.1	2.3	65 232	10 221	311 335 000	144 731	680	18 771 900 416	13.2	1.2	1.1
IRAN	68 920 000	1.4	64.7	2.8	26 302	2 364	121 424 000	112 855	1 750	3 438 200 064	3.3	0.1	2.9
IRAQ	25 175 000	2.7	67.4	4.8	9 554	659	53 574 000	...	...	...	...	...	5.5
IRELAND, REPUBLIC OF	3 956 000	1.0	59.3	2.0	820	431	5 366 000	88 385	23 060	...	...	...	1.0
ISRAEL	6 433 000	2.0	91.8	2.7	1 706	596	10 065 000	...	...	...	...	...	8.8
ITALY	57 423 000	-0.1	67.1	1.2	8 216	10 396	42 962 000	1 123 478	19 470	...	...	...	2.0
JAMAICA	2 651 000	0.9	56.6	2.4	810	186	3 816 000	7 264	2 720	643 400 000	9.2	0.2	0.8
JAPAN	127 654 000	0.1	78.9	1.3	18 694	21 826	109 220 000	4 574 164	35 990	...	...	...	1.0
JORDAN	5 473 000	2.8	78.7	4.3	1 968	137	11 709 000	8 786	1 750	669 200 000	8.0	6.8	9.2
KAZAKHSTAN	15 433 000	-0.4	55.8	2.0	4 364	1 109	15 302 000	20 146	1 360	1 839 500 032	10.8	1.2	0.9
KENYA	31 987 000	1.9	34.4	4.2	13 331	869	55 368 000	10 309	340	481 000 000	4.7	5.0	1.9
KIRIBATI	88 000	1.3	38.6	...	...	...	138 000	77	830	...	...	21.8	...
KUWAIT	2 521 000	2.6	96.1	2.7	599	42	4 001 000	...	...	...	...	...	7.7
KYRGYZSTAN	5 138 000	1.2	34.3	2.3	1 670	297	7 538 000	1 386	280	173 200 000	14.2	17.8	2.4
LAOS	5 657 000	2.3	19.7	4.8	2 256	184	11 438 000	1 650	310	41 900 000	2.5	17.1	2.0
LATVIA	2 307 000	-0.6	59.8	1.1	421	357	1 744 000	7 719	3 260	561 600 000	7.8	1.3	0.9
LEBANON	3 653 000	1.6	90.1	2.2	1 089	212	5 018 000	17 585	4 010	1 821 200 000	10.5	1.2	4.0
LESOTHO	1 802 000	0.7	28.8	4.5	799	85	2 478 000	1 127	550	65 800 000	5.7	3.7	2.6
LIBERIA	3 367 000	5.5	45.5	6.8	1 244	83	14 370 000	...	...	700 000	...	...	1.2
LIBYA	5 551 000	2.2	88.0	3.3	1 795	179	9 969 000	...	...	...	...	...	...
LIECHTENSTEIN	34 000	1.1	21.5	...	...	...	39 000	...	...	...	...	...	...
LITHUANIA	3 444 000	-0.2	68.6	1.2	719	494	2 989 000	11 401	3 270	906 000 000	8.1	0.9	1.3
LUXEMBOURG	453 000	1.2	91.9	1.8	81	63	715 000	18 550	41 770	...	...	...	0.8
MACEDONIA (F.Y.R.O.M.)	2 056 000	0.3	59.4	1.5	460	203	1 894 000	3 445	1 690	161 300 000	4.6	7.7	2.5
MADAGASCAR	17 404 000	2.8	30.1	5.7	7 143	481	47 030 000	4 170	260	92 700 000	2.4	8.1	1.2
MALAWI	12 105 000	2.2	15.1	6.3	5 239	332	31 114 000	1 778	170	58 700 000	3.5	24.9	0.6
MALAYSIA	24 425 000	1.7	58.1	2.9	7 575	918	37 850 000	86 510	3 640	5 967 200 256	7.2	0.1	2.3
MALDIVES	318 000	3.0	28.0	5.4	127	10	868 000	578	2 040	19 900 000	3.8	4.7	...
MALI	13 007 000	2.9	30.9	7.0	5 235	454	41 724 000	2 280	210	97 200 000	4.3	15.6	2.3
MALTA	394 000	0.4	91.2	1.8	79	48	400 000	...	...	...	...	...	0.8
MARSHALL ISLANDS	53 000	...	66.0	...	...	...	85 000	115	2 190	...	...	56.6	...
MAURITANIA	2 893 000	3.0	59.1	6.0	1 176	84	8 452 000	974	350	100 300 000	11.0	23.3	4.0
MAURITIUS	1 221 000	0.8	41.6	1.9	298	72	1 426 000	4 592	3 830	553 299 968	12.7	0.5	0.2
MEXICO	103 457 000	1.4	74.6	2.5	32 770	4 671	146 652 000	550 456	5 540	58 258 698 240	10.4	...	0.6
MICRONESIA, FEDERATED STATES OF	109 000	2.4	28.6	...	...	...	269 000	258	2 150	...	...	39.5	...
MOLDOVA	4 267 000	-0.3	41.4	1.4	993	400	3 577 000	1 399	380	135 400 000	10.0	9.1	0.5
MONACO	34 000	0.9	100.0	...	...	...	38 000	...	...	...	...	...	...
MONGOLIA	2 594 000	1.1	56.5	2.3	892	96	4 146 000	962	400	29 200 000	3.1	23.7	2.1
MOROCCO	30 566 000	1.8	56.1	3.0	10 355	1 238	50 361 000	34 555	1 180	3 332 699 904	10.3	1.3	4.3
MOZAMBIQUE	18 863 000	1.8	33.3	5.9	8 037	591	38 837 000	3 747	210	87 500 000	2.5	24.8	2.5
MYANMAR	49 485 000	1.2	28.1	2.8	15 806	2 193	68 546 000	...	...	87 000 000	...	...	7.8
NAMIBIA	1 987 000	1.7	31.4	4.9	768	66	3 663 000	3 520	1 960	...	...	4.4	2.9
NAURU	13 000	2.3	100.0	...	...	...	26 000	...	...	...	...	...	...
NEPAL	25 164 000	2.3	12.2	4.5	9 455	859	52 415 000	5 879	250	99 700 000	1.8	7.2	0.8
NETHERLANDS	16 149 000	0.3	89.6	1.5	2 902	2 165	15 845 000	385 401	24 040	...	...	...	1.8
NEW ZEALAND	3 875 000	0.7	85.9	2.0	867	441	4 439 000	47 632	12 380	...	...	...	1.2
NICARAGUA	5 466 000	2.6	56.5	3.8	2 162	155	11 477 000	...	...	300 200 000	14.2	25.7	1.2
NIGER	11 972 000	3.6	21.1	8.0	5 401	218	51 872 000	1 953	170	28 300 000	1.6	11.5	1.2
NIGERIA	124 009 000	2.6	44.9	5.4	51 300	3 471	278 788 000	37 116	290	1 009 299 968	2.7	0.5	1.6
NORTH KOREA	22 664 000	0.7	60.5	2.1	5 902	1 315	28 038 000	...	...	...	...	...	18.8
NORWAY	4 533 000	0.4	75.0	1.7	883	687	4 880 000	160 577	35 530	...	...	...	2.2
OMAN	2 851 000	3.3	76.5	5.5	1 119	63	8 751 000	...	...	864 099 968	...	...	15.3

Social Indicators						Environment				Communications				
Infant mortality rate	Life expectancy M	Life expectancy F	Literacy rate (%)	Access to safe water (%)	Doctors per 100 000 people	Forest area (%)	Annual change in forest area (%)	Protected land area (%)	CO$_2$ emissions	Telephone lines per 100 people	Cellular phones per 100 people	Internet connections per 1 000 people	International dialling code	Time zone
5	75.0	81.1	...	...	350	30.7	...	26.9	10.1	63.5	68.3	364.3	49	+1
102	56.0	58.5	92.1	73	6	27.8	-1.7	4.6	0.2	1.2	0.9	1.9	233	GMT
6	75.9	81.2	99.8	...	392	27.9	0.9	3.6	8.1	52.9	75.1	132.1	30	+2
26	...	...	...	95	50	14.7	0.9	...	1.9	32.8	6.4	52.0	1 473	-4
59	63.0	68.9	80.3	92	93	26.3	-1.7	16.8	0.9	6.5	9.7	17.1	502	-6
175	48.0	49.0	...	48	13	28.2	-0.5	0.7	0.2	0.3	0.7	1.9	224	GMT
215	44.0	46.9	60.9	56	17	60.5	-0.9	0.0	...	1.0	...	3.3	245	GMT
74	58.0	66.9	99.8	94	18	78.5	-0.3	0.3	2.2	9.2	8.7	109.2	592	-4
125	50.2	56.5	66.2	46	8	3.2	-5.7	0.3	0.2	1.0	1.1	3.6	509	-5
40	63.2	69.1	84.2	88	83	48.1	-1.0	6.0	0.8	4.7	3.6	6.2	504	-6
9	67.8	76.1	99.8	99	357	19.9	0.4	7.0	5.8	37.4	49.8	148.4	36	+1
4	77.1	81.8	...	...	326	0.3	2.2	9.5	7.6	66.4	82.0	679.4	354	GMT
96	63.6	64.9	74.1	84	48	21.6	0.1	4.4	1.1	3.4	0.6	6.8	91	+5.5
48	65.3	69.3	98.0	78	16	58.0	-1.2	10.1	1.2	3.7	2.5	18.6	62	+7 to +9
44	68.8	70.8	94.8	92	85	4.5	...	5.1	4.7	16.0	2.7	6.2	98	+3.5
130	63.5	66.5	45.3	85	...	1.8	...	<0.1	3.7	...	...	...	964	+3
6	74.4	79.6	...	...	219	9.6	3.0	0.9	10.3	48.5	72.9	233.1	353	GMT
6	77.1	81.0	99.5	...	385	6.4	4.9	15.5	10.1	47.6	80.8	230.5	972	+2
6	75.5	81.9	99.8	...	554	34.0	0.3	7.3	7.2	47.1	83.9	275.8	39	+1
20	73.7	77.8	94.5	92	140	30.0	-1.5	0.1	4.3	19.7	26.9	38.5	1 876	-5
4	77.8	85.0	...	...	193	64.0	...	6.8	9.0	59.7	58.8	454.7	81	+9
34	69.7	72.5	99.5	96	166	1.0	...	3.3	3.0	12.7	14.4	40.9	962	+2
75	59.6	70.7	...	91	353	4.5	2.2	2.7	8.2	11.3	3.6	6.2	7	+4 to +6
120	48.7	49.9	95.8	57	13	30.0	-0.5	6.0	0.3	1.0	1.6	16.0	254	+3
70	...	...	...	48	...	38.4	...	...	0.3	4.0	0.5	25.0	686	+12 to +14
10	74.9	79.0	93.1	...	189	0.3	3.5	1.5	26.3	24.0	24.8	101.5	965	+3
63	64.8	72.3	...	77	301	5.2	2.6	3.5	1.3	7.7	0.5	10.6	996	+5
105	53.3	55.8	73.3	37	24	54.4	-0.4	0.0	0.1	0.9	0.5	1.8	856	+7
21	65.7	76.2	99.8	...	282	47.1	0.4	12.5	3.2	30.8	27.9	72.3	371	+2
32	71.9	75.1	95.6	100	210	3.5	-0.4	0.5	3.9	19.5	21.3	85.8	961	+2
133	37.5	35.1	91.1	78	5	0.5	...	0.2	...	1.0	1.5	2.3	266	+2
235	54.6	56.7	71.7	...	...	31.3	-2.0	1.2	0.1	...	...	...	231	GMT
20	70.7	74.8	97.0	72	128	0.2	1.4	0.1	7.2	10.9	0.9	3.6	218	+2
11	...	...	...	...	...	46.7	1.2	...	...	...	...	...	423	+1
21	67.6	77.7	99.8	...	395	31.9	0.2	9.9	4.2	31.3	25.3	67.9	370	+2
5	74.6	80.9	...	...	272	...	...	...	18.0	78.3	96.7	226.6	352	+1
26	71.4	75.8	...	...	204	35.6	...	7.1	6.1	26.4	10.9	34.3	389	+1
139	52.5	54.8	81.5	47	11	20.2	-0.9	1.9	0.1	0.4	0.9	2.1	261	+3
188	39.6	39.0	72.5	57	...	27.2	-2.4	8.9	0.1	0.5	0.5	1.7	265	+2
9	70.6	75.5	97.9	...	66	58.7	-1.2	4.6	5.4	19.9	30.0	239.5	60	+8
80	68.3	67.0	99.2	100	40	3.3	...	...	1.3	10.1	6.8	37.0	960	+5
233	51.1	53.0	69.9	65	5	10.8	-0.7	3.7	0.1	0.4	0.4	2.6	223	GMT
6	75.9	81.0	98.7	100	261	n.s.	...	...	4.7	53.0	35.4	252.6	356	+1
68	...	...	...	...	...	...	...	...	...	6.0	0.1	12.9	692	+12
183	50.9	54.1	49.6	37	14	43.9	...	1.7	1.2	0.7	0.3	2.6	222	GMT
20	68.4	75.8	94.3	100	85	7.9	-0.6	...	1.5	25.6	25.0	131.7	230	+4
30	70.4	76.4	97.2	88	186	28.9	-1.1	3.4	3.9	13.7	21.7	36.2	52	-6 to -8
24	...	...	...	...	...	21.7	-4.5	...	...	8.3	...	33.8	691	+10 to +11
33	62.8	70.3	99.8	92	350	9.9	0.2	1.4	2.3	15.4	4.8	13.7	373	+2
5	...	...	...	100	...	...	...	...	...	...	...	...	377	+1
78	61.9	65.9	99.6	60	243	6.8	-0.5	11.5	3.3	4.8	7.6	15.6	976	+8
46	68.3	72.0	69.6	80	46	6.8	...	0.7	1.2	3.9	15.7	13.2	212	GMT
200	37.3	38.6	62.8	57	...	39.0	-0.2	6.0	0.1	0.4	0.8	0.7	258	+2
110	53.8	58.8	91.4	72	30	52.3	-1.4	0.3	0.2	0.6	0.0	0.2	95	+6.5
69	48.9	49.0	92.3	77	30	9.8	-0.9	12.9	0.0	6.6	5.6	25.2	264	+2
30	62.5	68.0	...	100	...	68.2	...	2.6	10.3	...	...	...	850	+9
100	60.1	59.6	62.8	88	4	27.3	-1.8	7.6	0.1	1.3	0.1	2.5	977	+5.75
5	75.6	81.0	98.3	100	251	11.1	0.3	5.7	10.4	62.1	73.9	329.2	31	+1
6	75.3	80.7	...	...	218	29.7	0.5	23.4	7.9	47.1	62.1	280.7	64	+12
45	67.2	71.9	72.3	77	86	27.0	-3.0	7.0	0.7	3.1	3.0	9.9	505	-6
270	45.9	46.5	24.4	59	4	1.0	-3.7	7.7	0.1	0.2	0.0	1.1	227	+1
184	52.0	52.2	88.5	62	18	14.8	-2.6	3.3	0.7	0.4	0.3	1.8	234	+1
30	62.5	68.0	...	100	...	68.2	...	2.6	10.3	...	...	...	850	+9
4	76.0	81.9	...	100	413	28.9	0.4	6.5	7.6	72.0	82.5	596.3	47	+1
14	70.2	73.2	98.5	39	133	0.0	5.3	16.1	8.8	9.0	12.4	45.8	968	+4

World Statistics

	Population							Economy					
	Total population	Population change (%)	% urban	Total fertility	Population by age (000s)		2050 projected population	Total Gross National Income (GNI) (US$M)	GNI per capita (US$)	Total debt service (US$)	Debt service ratio (% GNI)	Aid receipts (% GNI)	Military spending (% GNI)
					0 – 14	65 or over							
PAKISTAN	153 578 000	2.5	33.4	5.1	59 021	5 195	344 170 000	59 637	420	2 856 600 064	4.8	1.1	5.9
PALAU	20 000	2.1	69.3	…	…	…	39 000	131	6 730	…	…	…	…
PANAMA	3 120 000	1.4	56.5	2.4	…	…	4 262 000	9 532	3 290	928 400 000	9.9	0.2	1.4
PAPUA NEW GUINEA	5 711 000	2.2	17.6	4.3	1 929	117	10 980 000	3 026	580	304 500 000	8.3	7.2	1.1
PARAGUAY	5 878 000	2.5	56.7	3.8	2 173	191	12 565 000	7 345	1 300	330 000 000	4.4	1.1	1.1
PERU	27 167 000	1.6	73.1	2.6	8 567	1 238	42 122 000	52 147	2 000	4 305 299 968	8.3	0.8	2.4
PHILIPPINES	79 999 000	1.9	59.4	3.2	28 395	2 670	128 383 000	80 845	1 050	6 736 699 904	8.5	0.7	1.4
POLAND	38 587 000	-0.1	62.5	1.3	7 395	4 685	33 370 000	163 907	4 240	10 290 299 904	6.6	0.9	2.1
PORTUGAL	10 062 000	0.1	65.8	1.5	1 672	1 563	9 006 000	109 156	10 670	…	…	…	2.1
QATAR	610 000	1.5	92.9	3.3	151	9	831 000	…	…	…	…	…	10.0
ROMANIA	22 334 000	-0.3	55.2	1.3	4 095	2 986	18 150 000	38 388	1 710	2 340 800 000	6.4	1.2	1.6
RUSSIAN FEDERATION	143 246 000	-0.6	72.9	1.1	26 123	18 170	104 259 000	253 413	1 750	11 670 700 032	4.9	0.7	5.6
RWANDA	8 387 000	2.1	6.3	5.8	3 370	200	18 523 000	1 884	220	35 000 000	2.0	18.3	4.5
SAMOA	178 000	0.3	22.3	4.2	65	7	223 000	260	1 520	8 500 000	3.6	11.6	…
SAN MARINO	28 000	1.1	90.4	…	…	…	30 000	…	…	…	…	…	…
SÃO TOMÉ AND PRÍNCIPE	161 000	1.8	47.7	…	…	…	294 000	43	280	4 400 000	10.1	79.5	1.0
SAUDI ARABIA	24 217 000	3.1	86.7	5.5	8 735	602	59 683 000	…	…	…	…	…	14.9
SENEGAL	10 095 000	2.5	48.2	5.1	4 176	236	22 711 000	4 726	480	228 000 000	5.3	9.8	1.7
SERBIA AND MONTENEGRO	10 527 000	-0.1	51.7	1.6	2 113	1 381	9 030 000	…	…	177 400 000	2.1	…	5.0
SEYCHELLES	81 000	1.3	64.6	…	…	…	145 000	…	…	17 400 000	3.0	3.0	…
SIERRA LEONE	4 971 000	4.5	37.3	6.5	1 949	128	14 351 000	726	140	42 600 000	6.9	29.0	3.0
SINGAPORE	4 253 000	1.7	100.0	1.5	878	291	4 620 000	…	…	…	…	…	4.8
SLOVAKIA	5 402 000	0.1	57.6	1.3	1 054	615	4 674 000	20 028	3 700	2 590 000 128	13.8	0.6	1.8
SLOVENIA	1 984 000	-0.1	49.1	1.1	316	277	1 527 000	19 447	9 780	…	…	0.3	1.4
SOLOMON ISLANDS	477 000	3.3	20.2	5.3	200	12	1 458 000	253	580	9 100 000	3.2	24.0	…
SOMALIA	9 890 000	4.2	27.9	7.3	4 209	211	40 936 000	…	…	…	…	…	…
SOUTH AFRICA, REPUBLIC OF	45 026 000	0.8	57.7	2.9	14 734	1 545	47 301 000	125 486	2 900	3 859 599 872	3.1	0.4	1.5
SOUTH KOREA	47 700 000	0.7	82.5	1.5	9 740	3 305	51 561 000	447 698	9 400	23 204 999 168	5.1	…	2.9
SPAIN	41 060 000	0.0	77.8	1.1	5 874	6 767	31 282 000	586 874	14 860	…	…	…	1.3
SRI LANKA	19 065 000	0.9	23.1	2.1	4 976	1 186	23 066 000	16 294	830	737 500 032	4.6	1.7	4.7
ST KITTS AND NEVIS	42 000	-0.7	34.2	…	…	…	34 000	283	6 880	19 600 000	7.1	1.4	…
ST LUCIA	149 000	1.1	38.0	2.5	47	8	189 000	628	3 970	40 300 000	6.0	1.6	…
ST VINCENT AND THE GRENADINES	120 000	0.6	56.0	…	…	…	138 000	312	2 690	15 400 000	4.9	2.0	…
SUDAN	33 610 000	2.3	37.1	4.5	12 474	1 071	63 530 000	10 346	330	61 000 000	0.6	2.3	4.8
SURINAME	436 000	0.4	74.8	2.1	127	23	418 000	709	1 690	…	…	…	1.8
SWAZILAND	1 077 000	0.9	26.7	4.4	385	32	1 391 000	1 388	1 300	23 600 000	1.6	1.0	1.5
SWEDEN	8 876 000	-0.1	83.3	1.3	1 609	1 541	7 777 000	225 894	25 400	…	…	…	2.3
SWITZERLAND	7 169 000	-0.1	67.3	1.4	1 194	1 147	5 607 000	266 503	36 970	…	…	…	1.2
SYRIA	17 800 000	2.5	51.8	3.7	6 612	507	36 345 000	16 608	1 000	343 600 000	2.2	1.0	7.0
TAIWAN	22 548 000	0.7	36.7	…	…	…	…	…	…	…	…	…	…
TAJIKISTAN	6 245 000	0.7	27.7	2.9	2 397	279	9 763 000	1 051	170	87 500 000	9.3	15.3	1.3
TANZANIA	36 977 000	2.3	33.3	5.0	15 800	857	82 740 000	9 198	270	216 700 000	2.4	11.2	1.4
THAILAND	62 833 000	1.1	20.0	2.0	16 742	3 282	82 491 000	120 872	1 970	14 016 499 712	11.6	0.5	1.7
TOGO	4 909 000	2.6	33.9	5.4	2 004	142	11 832 000	1 279	270	29 600 000	2.5	5.5	1.8
TONGA	104 000	0.4	33.0	…	…	…	125 000	154	1 530	4 100 000	2.6	12.1	…
TRINIDAD AND TOBAGO	1 303 000	0.5	74.5	1.5	323	86	1 378 000	7 249	5 540	500 200 000	7.5	…	1.4
TUNISIA	9 832 000	1.1	66.2	2.1	2 809	554	14 076 000	20 051	2 070	1 900 000 000	10.2	1.2	1.8
TURKEY	71 325 000	1.3	66.2	2.3	20 021	3 847	98 818 000	168 335	2 540	21 135 800 320	10.5	0.2	5.3
TURKMENISTAN	4 867 000	1.9	44.9	3.2	1 783	202	8 401 000	5 236	950	…	…	0.7	3.4
TUVALU	11 000	1.3	53.2	…	…	…	16 000	…	…	…	…	…	…
UGANDA	25 827 000	3.2	14.5	7.1	11 466	586	101 524 000	6 286	280	159 300 000	2.6	13.1	2.3
UKRAINE	48 523 000	-0.9	68.0	1.1	8 840	6 849	29 959 000	35 185	720	3 660 699 904	11.9	1.7	3.0
UNITED ARAB EMIRATES	2 995 000	1.7	87.2	2.9	678	71	3 709 000	…	…	…	…	…	4.1
UNITED KINGDOM	58 789 194	0.2	89.5	1.6	11 272	9 359	58 933 000	1 451 442	24 230	…	…	…	2.5
UNITED STATES OF AMERICA	294 043 000	0.9	77.4	1.9	61 507	34 831	397 063 000	9 900 724	34 870	…	…	…	3.0
URUGUAY	3 415 000	0.7	92.1	2.3	827	430	4 249 000	19 036	5 670	1 313 100 032	6.8	0.1	1.3
UZBEKISTAN	26 093 000	1.4	36.6	2.3	9 022	1 163	40 513 000	13 780	550	898 700 032	12.1	1.4	1.7
VANUATU	212 000	2.5	22.1	4.3	83	6	462 000	212	1 050	2 200 000	1.0	20.4	…
VATICAN CITY	472	…	100.0	…	…	…	1 000	…	…	…	…	…	…
VENEZUELA	25 699 000	1.8	87.2	2.7	8 227	1 075	42 152 000	117 169	4 760	5 846 099 968	4.9	0.1	1.4
VIETNAM	81 377 000	1.3	24.5	2.3	26 070	4 178	123 782 000	32 578	410	1 303 200 000	4.2	5.4	…
YEMEN	20 010 000	4.1	25.0	7.6	9 188	423	102 379 000	8 304	460	221 400 000	3.0	3.5	6.1
ZAMBIA	10 812 000	2.1	39.8	5.7	4 850	307	29 262 000	3 336	320	185 600 000	6.7	28.7	1.0
ZIMBABWE	12 891 000	1.7	36.0	4.5	5 709	403	23 546 000	6 164	480	471 400 000	6.6	2.6	5.0

Socal Indicators						Environment				Communications				
Infant mortality rate	Life expectancy		Literacy rate (%)	Access to safe water (%)	Doctors per 100 000 people	Forest area (%)	Annual change in forest area (%)	Protected land area (%)	CO₂ emissions	Telephone lines per 100 people	Cellular phones per 100 people	Internet connections per 1 000 people	International dialling code	Time zone
	M	F												
110	61.2	60.9	58.7	90	57	3.1	-1.5	4.7	0.7	2.4	0.6	3.5	92	+5
29	...	...	...	79	...	76.1	...	...	...	...	...	...	680	+9
26	...	...	97.0	90	167	38.6	-1.6	18.8	2.1	14.8	20.7	31.7	507	-5
112	56.8	58.7	76.9	42	7	67.6	-0.4	<0.1	0.5	1.4	0.2	28.1	675	+10
31	68.6	73.1	97.3	78	110	58.8	-0.5	3.4	0.9	5.1	20.4	10.6	595	-4
50	67.3	72.4	97.1	80	93	50.9	-0.4	2.7	1.1	7.8	5.9	115.0	51	-5
40	68.0	72.0	98.8	86	123	19.4	-1.4	4.8	1.0	4.0	13.7	25.9	63	+8
10	69.8	78.0	99.8	...	236	29.7	0.2	9.1	8.3	29.5	26.0	98.4	48	+1
6	72.6	79.6	99.8	...	312	40.1	1.7	6.6	5.5	42.7	77.4	349.4	351	GMT
16	69.4	72.1	95.3	...	126	0.1	9.6	...	85.7	27.5	29.3	65.6	974	+3
22	66.5	73.3	99.7	58	184	28.0	0.2	4.6	4.1	18.3	17.2	44.7	40	+2
22	60.0	72.5	99.8	99	421	50.4	...	3.1	9.8	24.3	3.8	29.3	7	+2 to +12
187	40.2	41.7	84.9	41	...	12.4	-3.9	13.8	0.1	0.3	0.8	2.5	250	+2
26	66.9	73.5	99.8	99	34	37.2	-2.1	...	0.8	5.6	1.7	16.7	685	-11
6	...	...	...	...	...	...	...	...	...	...	...	...	378	+1
75	...	...	...	...	47	28.3	...	...	0.5	3.6	...	60.0	239	GMT
29	71.1	73.7	93.6	95	166	0.7	...	2.3	14.4	14.5	11.3	13.4	966	+3
139	52.5	56.2	52.9	78	8	32.2	-0.7	11.1	0.4	2.5	4.0	10.4	221	GMT
20	70.9	75.6	...	98	...	28.3	-0.1	3.3	...	22.9	18.7	56.2	381	+1
17	...	...	...	...	132	66.7	...	...	2.5	26.7	55.2	112.5	248	+4
316	39.2	41.8	...	57	7	14.7	-2.9	1.1	0.1	0.5	0.6	1.4	232	GMT
4	75.9	80.3	99.8	100	163	3.3	...	4.7	21.0	47.1	72.4	605.2	65	+8
9	69.8	77.6	...	100	353	45.3	0.9	22.1	7.1	28.8	39.7	120.3	421	+1
5	72.3	79.6	99.8	100	228	55.0	0.2	5.9	7.4	40.1	76.0	300.8	386	+1
25	67.9	70.7	...	71	14	88.8	-0.2	0.0	0.4	1.6	0.2	4.3	677	+11
225	47.4	50.5	...	...	...	12.0	-1.0	0.3	0.0	...	...	...	252	+3
70	42.5	42.3	91.8	86	56	7.3	-0.1	5.4	8.3	11.4	21.0	70.1	27	+2
5	71.8	79.1	99.8	92	136	63.3	-0.1	6.9	7.8	47.6	60.8	510.7	82	+9
5	75.4	82.3	99.8	...	424	28.8	0.6	8.4	6.3	43.1	65.5	182.8	34	+1
19	69.9	75.9	97.1	77	36	30.0	-1.6	13.3	0.4	4.3	3.8	7.9	94	+6
25	...	...	...	98	117	11.1	-0.6	...	2.5	56.9	3.1	51.6	1 869	-4
19	71.1	76.4	...	98	47	14.8	-4.9	...	1.3	...	...	...	1 758	-4
25	...	...	...	93	88	15.4	-1.4	...	1.4	22.0	2.1	30.9	1 784	-4
108	57.6	60.6	79.1	75	9	25.9	-1.4	3.4	0.1	1.4	0.3	1.8	249	+3
33	68.5	73.7	...	82	25	90.5	...	4.5	5.2	17.6	19.1	33.0	597	-3
142	35.8	34.8	91.2	...	15	30.3	1.2	...	0.4	3.1	6.5	13.7	268	+2
4	77.6	82.6	...	100	311	65.9	...	8.1	5.5	73.9	79.0	516.3	46	+1
4	75.9	82.3	...	100	323	30.3	0.4	25.7	5.9	71.8	72.4	404.0	41	+1
29	70.6	73.1	88.3	80	144	2.5	...	0.0	3.3	10.9	1.2	3.6	963	+2
...	...	...	...	...	...	...	...	...	...	57.3	96.6	349.0	886	+8
73	65.2	70.8	99.8	60	201	2.8	0.5	4.1	0.8	3.6	0.0	0.5	992	+5
165	50.1	52.0	91.6	68	4	43.9	-0.2	14.6	0.1	0.4	1.2	8.3	255	+3
29	67.9	73.8	99.0	84	24	28.9	-0.7	13.8	3.2	9.4	11.9	55.6	66	+7
142	51.1	53.3	77.4	54	8	9.4	-3.4	7.6	0.2	1.0	2.0	10.7	228	GMT
21	...	...	...	100	...	5.5	...	...	1.2	9.9	0.1	10.2	676	+13
20	72.5	77.2	99.8	90	79	50.5	-0.8	6.0	17.4	24.0	17.3	92.3	1 868	-4
28	70.8	73.7	94.3	80	70	3.1	0.2	0.3	2.4	10.9	4.0	41.2	216	+1
45	68.0	73.2	96.9	82	121	13.3	0.2	1.3	3.2	28.5	30.2	37.7	90	+2
70	63.9	70.4	...	...	300	8.0	...	4.1	5.7	8.0	0.2	1.7	993	+5
53	...	...	...	...	...	...	...	...	...	...	...	...	688	+12
127	45.3	46.8	80.3	52	...	21.0	-2.0	7.9	0.1	0.3	1.4	2.7	256	+3
21	62.7	73.5	99.9	98	299	16.5	0.3	1.6	7.0	21.2	4.4	11.9	380	+2
9	74.1	78.4	91.5	...	181	3.8	2.8	...	32.4	39.7	72.0	339.2	971	+4
6	75.7	80.7	...	100	164	11.6	0.6	20.4	9.2	58.8	78.3	399.5	44	GMT
8	74.6	80.4	...	100	279	24.7	0.2	13.1	19.8	66.5	44.4	499.5	1	-5 to -10
17	71.6	78.9	99.3	98	370	7.4	5.0	0.3	1.8	28.3	15.5	119.0	598	-3
67	66.8	72.5	99.7	85	309	4.8	0.2	1.8	4.5	6.6	0.3	5.9	998	+5
44	67.5	70.5	...	88	12	36.7	0.1	...	0.3	3.4	0.2	27.4	678	+11
...	...	...	...	...	...	...	...	...	...	...	...	...	39	+1
23	70.9	76.7	98.2	83	236	56.1	-0.4	35.4	6.7	11.2	26.4	52.8	58	-4
39	66.9	71.6	97.3	77	48	30.2	0.5	3.0	0.6	3.8	1.5	4.9	84	+7
117	60.7	62.9	67.8	69	23	0.9	-1.9	0.0	0.9	2.2	0.8	0.9	967	+3
202	42.6	41.7	89.1	64	7	42.0	-2.4	8.5	0.2	0.8	0.9	2.4	260	+2
117	43.3	42.4	97.6	83	14	49.2	-1.5	7.9	1.2	1.9	2.4	7.3	263	+2

Definitions

Indicator	Definition
Population	
Total population	Interpolated mid-year population, 2003.
Population change	Percentage annual rate of change, 2000–2005.
% urban	Urban population as a percentage of the total population, 2001.
Total fertility	Average number of children a women will have during her child-bearing years, 2000–2005.
Population by age	Population in age groups 0–14 and 65 or over, in thousands, 2000.
2050 projected population	Projected total population for the year 2050.
Economy	
Total Gross National Income (GNI)	The sum of value added to the economy by all resident producers plus taxes, less subsidies, plus net receipts of primary income from abroad. Data are in U.S. dollars (millions), 2001. Formerly known as Gross National Product (GNP).
GNI per capita	Gross National Income per person in U.S. dollars using the World Bank Atlas method, 2001.
Total debt service	Sum of principal repayments and interest paid on long-term debt, interest paid on short-term debt and repayments to the International Monetary Fund (IMF), 2000.
Debt service ratio	Debt service as a percentage of GNI, 2000.
Aid receipts	Aid received as a percentage of GNI from the Development Assistance Committee (DAC) of the Organization for Economic Co-operation and Development (OECD), 2000.
Military spending	Military-related spending, including recruiting, training, construction, and the purchase of military supplies and equipment, as a percentage of Gross National Income, 1999.
Social Indicators	
Infant mortality rate	Number of deaths of children aged under 5 per 1 000 live births, 2000.
Life expectancy	Average life expectancy, at birth in years, male and female, 2000–2005.
Literacy rate	Percentage of population aged 15–24 with at least a basic ability to read and write, 2002.
Access to safe water	Percentage of the population with sustainable access to sources of improved drinking water, 2000.
Doctors	Number of trained doctors per 100 000 people, most recent year figures obtained.
Environment	
Forest area	Percentage of total land area covered by forest.
Change in forest area	Average annual percentage change in forest area, 1990–2000.
Protected land area	Percentage of total land area designated as protected land.
CO_2 emissions	Emissions of carbon dioxide from the burning of fossil fuels and the manufacture of cement, divided by the population, expressed in metric tons, 1998.
Communications	
Telephone lines	Main telephone lines per 100 inhabitants, 2001.
Cellular phones	Cellular mobile subscribers per 100 inhabitants, 2001.
Internet connections	Internet users per 1 000 inhabitants, 2001.
International dialling code	The country code prefix to be used when dialling from another country.
Time zone	Time difference in hours between local standard time and Greenwich Mean Time.

Main Statistical Sources	Internet Links
United Nations Statistics Division	unstats.un.org/unsd
World Population Prospects: The 2002 Revision and World Urbanization Prospects: The 2001 Revision, United Nations Population Division	www.un.org/esa/population/unpop
United Nations Population Information Network	www.un.org/popin
United Nations Development Programme	www.undp.org
Organisation for Economic Cooperation and Development	www.oecd.org
State of the World's Forests 2001, Food and Agriculture Organization of the United Nations	www.fao.org
World Development Indicators 2002, World Bank	www.worldbank.org/data
World Resources 2000–2001, World Resources Institute	www.wri.org
International Telecommunication Union	www.itu.int

Introduction to the index

The index includes all names shown on the reference maps in the atlas. Each entry includes the country or geographical area in which the feature is located, a page number and an alphanumeric reference. Additional entry details and aspects of the index are explained below.

Name forms

The names policy in this atlas is generally to use local name forms which are officially recognized by the governments of the countries concerned. Rules established by the Permanent Committee on Geographical Names for British Official Use (PCGN) are applied to the conversion of non-roman alphabet names, for example in the Russian Federation, into the roman alphabet used in English.

However, English conventional name forms are used for the most well-known places for which such a form is in common use. In these cases, the local form is included in brackets on the map and appears as a cross-reference in the index. Other alternative names, such as well-known historical names or those in other languages, may also be included in brackets on the map and as cross-references in the index. All country names and those for international physical features appear in their English forms. Names appear in full in the index, although they may appear in abbreviated form on the maps.

Referencing

Names are referenced by page number and by grid reference. The grid reference relates to the alphanumeric values which appear on the edges of each map. These reflect the graticule on the map – the letter relates to longitude divisions, the number to latitude divisions. Names are generally referenced to the largest scale map page on which they appear. For large geographical features, including countries, the reference is to the largest scale map on which the feature appears in its entirety, or on which the majority of it appears.

Rivers are referenced to their lowest downstream point – either their mouth or their confluence with another river. The river name will generally be positioned as close to this point as possible.

Alternative names

Alternative names appear as cross-references and refer the user to the index entry for the form of the name used on the map.

For rivers with multiple names - for example those which flow through several countries - all alternative name forms are included within the main index entries, with details of the countries in which each form applies.

Administrative qualifiers

Administrative divisions are included in entries to differentiate duplicate names - entries of exactly the same name and feature type within the one country - where these division names are shown on the maps. In such cases, duplicate names are alphabetized in the order of the administrative division names.

Additional qualifiers are included for names within selected geographical areas, to indicate more clearly their location.

Descriptors

Entries, other than those for towns and cities, include a descriptor indicating the type of geographical feature. Descriptors are not included where the type of feature is implicit in the name itself, unless there is a town or city of exactly the same name.

Insets

Where relevant, the index clearly indicates [inset] if a feature appears on an inset map.

Alphabetical order

The Icelandic characters Þ and þ are transliterated and alphabetized as 'Th' and 'th'. The German character ß is alphabetized as 'ss'. Names beginning with Mac or Mc are alphabetized exactly as they appear. The terms Saint, Sainte, etc, are abbreviated to St, Ste, etc, but alphabetized as if in the full form.

Numerical entries

Entries beginning with numerals appear at the beginning of the index, in numerical order. Elsewhere, numerals are alphabetized before 'a'.

Permuted terms

Names beginning with generic geographical terms are permuted - the descriptive term is placed after, and the index alphabetized by, the main part of the name. For example, Mount Everest is indexed as Everest, Mount; Lake Superior as Superior, Lake. This policy is applied to all languages. Permuting has not been applied to names of towns, cities or administrative divisions beginning with such geographical terms. These remain in their full form, for example, Lake Isabella, USA.

Gazetteer entries and connections

Selected entries have been extended to include gazetteer-style information. Important geographical facts which relate specifically to the entry are included within the entry in coloured type.

Entries for features which also appear on, or which have a topical link to, the thematic pages of the atlas include a reference to those pages.

Abbreviations

admin. dist.	administrative district	IL	Illinois	plat.	plateau		
admin. div.	administrative division	imp. l.	impermanent lake	P.N.G.	Papua New Guinea		
admin. reg.	administrative region	IN	Indiana	Port.	Portugal		
Afgh.	Afghanistan	Indon.	Indonesia	pref.	prefecture		
AK	Alaska	Kazakh.	Kazakhstan	prov.	province		
AL	Alabama	KS	Kansas	pt	point		
Alg.	Algeria	KY	Kentucky	Qld	Queensland		
AR	Arkansas	Kyrg.	Kyrgyzstan	Que.	Québec		
Arg.	Argentina	l.	lake	r.	river		
aut. comm.	autonomous community	LA	Louisiana	reg.	region		
aut. reg.	autonomous region	lag.	lagoon	res.	reserve		
aut. rep.	autonomous republic	Lith.	Lithuania	resr	reservoir		
AZ	Arizona	Lux.	Luxembourg	RI	Rhode Island		
Azer.	Azerbaijan	MA	Massachusetts	Rus. Fed.	Russian Federation		
b.	bay	Madag.	Madagascar	S.	South, Southern		
Bangl.	Bangladesh	Man.	Manitoba	S.A.	South Australia		
B.C.	British Columbia	MD	Maryland	salt l.	salt lake		
Bol.	Bolivia	ME	Maine	Sask.	Saskatchewan		
Bos.-Herz.	Bosnia-Herzegovina	Mex.	Mexico	SC	South Carolina		
Bulg.	Bulgaria	MI	Michigan	SD	South Dakota		
c.	cape	MN	Minnesota	sea chan.	sea channel		
CA	California	MO	Missouri	Serb. and Mont.	Serbia and Montenegro		
Cent. Afr. Rep.	Central African Republic	Moz.	Mozambique	Sing.	Singapore		
CO	Colorado	MS	Mississippi	Switz.	Switzerland		
Col.	Colombia	MT	Montana	Tajik.	Tajikistan		
CT	Connecticut	mt.	mountain	Tanz.	Tanzania		
Czech Rep.	Czech Republic	mts	mountains	Tas.	Tasmania		
DC	District of Columbia	N.	North, Northern	terr.	territory		
DE	Delaware	nat. park	national park	Thai.	Thailand		
Dem. Rep. Congo	Democratic Republic of Congo	N.B.	New Brunswick	TN	Tennessee		
depr.	depression	NC	North Carolina	Trin. and Tob.	Trinidad and Tobago		
des.	desert	ND	North Dakota	Turkm.	Turkmenistan		
Dom. Rep.	Dominican Republic	NE	Nebraska	TX	Texas		
E.	East, Eastern	Neth.	Netherlands	U.A.E.	United Arab Emirates		
Equat. Guinea	Equatorial Guinea	NH	New Hampshire	U.K.	United Kingdom		
esc.	escarpment	NJ	New Jersey	Ukr.	Ukraine		
est.	estuary	NM	New Mexico	U.S.A.	United States of America		
Eth.	Ethiopia	N.S.	Nova Scotia	UT	Utah		
Fin.	Finland	N.S.W.	New South Wales	Uzbek.	Uzbekistan		
FL	Florida	N.T.	Northern Territory	VA	Virginia		
for.	forest	NV	Nevada	Venez.	Venezuela		
Fr. Guiana	French Guiana	N.W.T.	Northwest Territories	Vic.	Victoria		
F.Y.R.O.M.	Former Yugoslav Republic of Macedonia	NY	New York	vol.	volcano		
g.	gulf	N.Z.	New Zealand	vol. crater	volcanic crater		
GA	Georgia	OH	Ohio	VT	Vermont		
Guat.	Guatemala	OK	Oklahoma	W.	West, Western		
HI	Hawaii	OR	Oregon	WA	Washington		
H.K.	Hong Kong	PA	Pennsylvania	W.A.	Western Australia		
Hond.	Honduras	Para.	Paraguay	WI	Wisconsin		
i.	island	P.E.I.	Prince Edward Island	WV	West Virginia		
IA	Iowa	pen.	peninsula	WY	Wyoming		
ID	Idaho	Phil.	Philippines	Y.T.	Yukon Territory		

1

3-y Severnyy Rus. Fed. 41 S3
5 de Outubro Angola see Xá-Muteba
9 de Julio Arg. 144 D5
25 de Mayo Buenos Aires Arg. 144 D5
25 de Mayo La Pampa Arg. 140 C5
26 Bakı Komissarı Azer. 91 H3
70 Mile House Canada 120 F5
100 Mile House Canada 120 F5
150 Mile House Canada 120 F4

A

Aabenraa Denmark see Åbenrå
Aachen Germany 52 G4
Aalborg Denmark see Ålborg
Aalborg Bugt b. Denmark see Ålborg Bugt
Aalen Germany 53 K6
Aalesund Norway see Ålesund
Aaley Lebanon see Aley
Aalst Belgium 52 E4
Aanaar Fin. see Inari
Aarhus Denmark see Århus
Aarlen Belgium see Arlon
Aars Denmark see Års
Aarschot Belgium 52 E4
Aasiaat Greenland 119 M3
Aath Belgium see Ath
Aba China 76 D1
Aba Dem. Rep. Congo 98 D3
Aba Nigeria 96 D4
Abacaxis r. Brazil 143 G4
Ābādān Iran 88 C4
Ābādeh Iran 88 D4
Ābādeh Ţashk Iran 88 D4
Abadla Alg. 54 D5
Abaeté Brazil 145 B2
Abaetetuba Brazil 143 I4
Abagnar Qi China see Xilinhot
Abaiang atoll Kiribati 150 H5
Abajo Peak U.S.A. 129 I3
Abakaliki Nigeria 96 D4
Abakan Rus. Fed. 72 G2
Abakanskiy Khrebet mts Rus. Fed. 72 F2
Abalak Niger 96 D3
Abana Turkey 90 D2
Abancay Peru 142 D6
Abariringa atoll Kiribati see Kanton
Abarkūh, Kavīr-e des. Iran 88 D4
Abarqū Iran 88 D4
Abarshahr Iran see Neyshābūr
Abashiri Japan 74 G3
Abashiri-wan b. Japan 74 G3
Abasolo Mex. 131 D7
Abau P.N.G. 110 E1
Abaya, Lake Eth. 98 D3
Ābaya Hāyk' l. Eth. see Abaya, Lake
Ābay Wenz r. Eth. 98 D2 see Blue Nile
Abaza Rus. Fed. 72 G2
Abba Cent. Afr. Rep. 98 B3
Abbasabad Iran 88 D3
'Abbāsābad Iran 88 E2
Abbasanta Sardinia Italy 58 C4
Abbatis Villa France see Abbeville
Abbe, Lake Djibouti/Eth. 86 F7
Abbeville France 52 B4
Abbeville AL U.S.A. 133 C6
Abbeville GA U.S.A. 133 D6
Abbeville LA U.S.A. 131 E6
Abbeville SC U.S.A. 133 D5
Abbey Canada 121 I5
Abbeyfeale Rep. of Ireland 51 C5
Abbey Town U.K. 48 D4
Abborrträsk Sweden 44 K4
Abbot, Mount Australia 110 D4
Abbot Ice Shelf Antarctica 148 K2
Abbotsford Canada 120 F5
Abbott NM U.S.A. 127 G5
Abbott VA U.S.A. 134 E5
Abbottabad Pak. 89 I3
'Abd al 'Azīz, Jabal hill Syria 87 F3
'Abd al Kūrī i. Yemen 86 H7
'Abd Allah, Khawr sea chan. Iraq/Kuwait 88 C4
Abd al Ma'asīr well Saudi Arabia 85 D4
Ābdānān Iran 88 B3
Abdollāhābād Iran 88 D3
Abdulino Rus. Fed. 41 Q5
Abéché Chad 97 F3
Abellinum Italy see Avellino
Abel Tasman National Park N.Z. 113 D5
Abengourou Côte d'Ivoire 96 C4
Åbenrå Denmark 45 F9
Abensberg Germany 53 L6
Abeokuta Nigeria 96 D4
Aberaeron U.K. 49 C6
Aberchirder U.K. 50 G3
Abercorn Zambia see Mbala
Abercrombie r. Australia 112 D4
Aberdare U.K. 49 D7
Aberdaron U.K. 49 C6
Aberdaugleddau U.K. see Milford Haven
Aberdeen Australia 112 E4
Aberdeen Hong Kong China 77 [inset]
Aberdeen S. Africa 100 G7
Aberdeen U.K. 50 G3
Aberdeen U.S.A. 130 D2
Aberdeen Lake Canada 121 L1
Aberdovey U.K. see Aberdyfi
Aberdyfi U.K. 49 C6
Aberfeldy U.K. 50 F4
Aberford U.K. 48 F5
Aberfoyle U.K. 50 E4
Abergavenny U.K. 49 D7
Abergwaun U.K. see Fishguard
Aberhonddu U.K. see Brecon
Abermaw U.K. see Barmouth
Abernathy U.S.A. 131 C5
Aberporth U.K. 49 C6
Abersoch U.K. 49 C6
Abertawe U.K. see Swansea
Aberteifi U.K. see Cardigan
Aberystwyth U.K. 49 C6
Abeshr Chad see Abéché
Abez' Rus. Fed. 41 S2
Āb Gāh Iran 89 E5
Abhā Saudi Arabia 86 F6
Abhar Iran 88 C2
Abiad, Bahr el r. Sudan/Uganda 86 D6 see White Nile

▶Abidjan Côte d'Ivoire 96 C4
Former capital of Côte d'Ivoire. 4th most populous city in Africa.

Abijatta-Shalla National Park Eth. 98 D3
Ab-i-Kavīr salt flat Iran 88 E3
Abilene KS U.S.A. 130 D4
Abilene TX U.S.A. 131 D5
Abingdon U.K. 49 F7
Abingdon U.S.A. 134 D5
Abington Reef Australia 110 E3
Abinsk Rus. Fed. 90 E1
Abiseo, Parque Nacional nat. park Peru 142 C5
Abitau Lake Canada 121 J2
Abitibi, Lake Canada 122 E4
Ab Khūr Iran 88 E3
Abminga Australia 109 F6
Abnūb Egypt 90 C6
Åbo Fin. see Turku
Abohar India 82 C3
Aboisso Côte d'Ivoire 96 C4
Aboite U.S.A. 134 C3
Abomey Benin 96 D4
Abongabong, Gunung mt. Indon. 71 B6
Abong Mbang Cameroon 96 E4
Abou Déia Chad 97 E3
Abovyan Armenia 91 G2
Aboyne U.K. 50 G3
Abqaiq Saudi Arabia 88 C5
Abraham's Bay Bahamas 133 F8
Abramov, Mys pt Rus. Fed. 42 I2
Abrantes Port. 57 B4
Abra Pampa Arg. 144 C2
Abreojos, Punta pt Mex. 127 E8
'Abri Sudan 86 D5
Abrolhos Bank sea feature S. Atlantic Ocean 148 F7
Abruzzo, Parco Nazionale d' nat. park Italy 58 E4
Absalom, Mount Antarctica 152 B1
Absaroka Range mts U.S.A. 126 F3
Abtar, Jabal al hills Syria 85 C2
Abtsgmünd Germany 53 J6
Abū aḍ Ḍuhūr Syria 85 C2
Abū al Ḥusayn, Qā' imp. l. Jordan 85 D3
Abū 'Alī i. Saudi Arabia 88 C5
Abū al Jirāb i. U.A.E. 88 D5
Abū 'Āmūd, Wādī watercourse Jordan 85 C4
Abū 'Arīsh Saudi Arabia 86 F6
Abu 'Aweigīla well Egypt see Abū 'Uwayqilah
Abu Deleiq Sudan 86 D6

▶Abu Dhabi U.A.E. 88 D5
Capital of the United Arab Emirates.

Abū Du'ān Syria 85 D1
Abu Gubeiha Sudan 86 D7
Abū Ḥafnah, Wādī watercourse Jordan 85 D3
Abu Haggag Egypt see Ra's al Ḥikmah
Abū Ḥallūfah, Jabal hill Jordan 85 C4
Abu Hamed Sudan 86 D6

▶Abuja Nigeria 96 D4
Capital of Nigeria.

Abū Jifān well Saudi Arabia 88 B5
Abū Jurdhān Jordan 85 B4
Abū Kamāl Syria 91 F4
Abu Matariq Sudan 97 F3
Abumombazi Dem. Rep. Congo 98 C3
Abu Musa i. The Gulf 88 D5
Abū Mūsá, Jazīreh-ye i. The Gulf see Abu Musa
Abunã r. Bol. 142 E5
Abunã Brazil 142 E5
Ābune Yosēf mt. Eth. 86 E7
Abū Nujaym Libya 97 E1
Abū Qa'ṭūr Syria 85 C2
Abū Rawthah, Jabal mt. Egypt 85 B5
Aburo mt. Dem. Rep. Congo 98 D3
Abu Road India 79 G4
Abū Rujmayn, Jabal mts Syria 85 D2
Abu Rûtha, Gebel mt. Egypt see Abū Rawthah, Jabal
Abū Sawādah well Saudi Arabia 88 C5
Abu Simbil Egypt see Abū Sunbul
Abū Sunbul Egypt 86 D5
Abū Ṭarfā', Wādī watercourse Egypt 85 A5
Abut Head hd N.Z. 113 C6
Abū 'Uwayqilah well Egypt 85 B4
Abu Zabad Sudan 86 C7
Abū Ẓabī U.A.E. see Abu Dhabi
Abūzam Iran 88 C4
Abū Zanīmah Egypt 90 D5
Abu Zenīma Egypt see Abū Zanīmah
Abyad Sudan 86 C7
Abyaḍ, Jabal al mts Syria 85 C2
Abyār al Hakīm well Libya 90 A5
Abydos Australia 108 B5
Abyei Sudan 86 C8
Abyssinia country Africa see Ethiopia
Academician Vernadskiy research station Antarctica see Vernadsky
Academy Bay Rus. Fed. see Akademii, Zaliv
Acadia prov. Canada see Nova Scotia
Acadia National Park U.S.A. 132 G2
Açailândia Brazil 143 I5
Acamarachi mt. Chile see Pili, Cerro
Acampamento de Caça do Mucusso Angola 99 C5
Acandí Col. 142 C2
A Cañiza Spain 57 B2
Acaponeta Mex. 136 C4
Acapulco Mex. 136 E5
Acapulco de Juárez Mex. see Acapulco
Acará Brazil 143 I4
Acaraú Brazil 143 J4
Acaray, Represa de resr Para. 144 E3
Acari, Serra hills Brazil/Guyana 143 G3
Acarigua Venez. 142 E2
Acatlan Mex. 136 E5
Accho Israel see 'Akko
Accomac U.S.A. 135 H5
Accomack U.S.A. see Accomac

▶Accra Ghana 96 C4
Capital of Ghana.

Accrington U.K. 48 E5
Ach r. Germany 53 L6
Achacachi Bol. 142 E7
Achaguas Venez. 142 E2
Achalpur India 82 D5
Achampet India 84 C2
Achan Rus. Fed. 74 E2
Achayvayam Rus. Fed. 65 S3
Acheng China 74 B3
Achhota India 84 D1
Achicourt France 52 C4
Achill Rep. of Ireland 51 C4
Achillbeg Island Rep. of Ireland 51 C4
Achill Island Rep. of Ireland 51 B4
Achiltibuie U.K. 50 D2
Achim Germany 53 J1
Achinsk Rus. Fed. 64 K4
Achit Rus. Fed. 41 R4
Achit Nuur l. Mongolia 80 H2
Achkhoy-Martan Rus. Fed. 91 G2
Achna Cyprus 85 A2
Achnasheen U.K. 50 D3
Acıgöl l. Turkey 59 M6
Acıpayam Turkey 59 M6
Acireale Sicily Italy 58 F6
Ackerman U.S.A. 131 F5
Ackley U.S.A. 130 E3
Acklins Island Bahamas 133 F8
Acle U.K. 49 I6

▶Aconcagua, Cerro mt. Arg. 144 B4
Highest mountain in South America.
South America 138–139

Acopiara Brazil 143 K5
A Coruña Spain 57 B2
Acqui Terme Italy 58 C2
Acra U.S.A. 135 H2
Acragas Sicily Italy see Agrigento
Acraman, Lake salt flat Australia 111 A7
Acre r. Brazil 142 E6
Acre Israel see 'Akko
Acre, Bay of Israel see Haifa, Bay of
Acri Italy 58 G5
Ács Hungary 47 Q7
Actaeon Group is Fr. Polynesia see Actéon, Groupe
Actéon, Groupe is Fr. Polynesia 151 K7
Acton Canada 134 E2
Acton U.S.A. 128 D4
Acungui Brazil 145 A4
Acunum Acusio France see Montélimar
Ada MN U.S.A. 130 D2
Ada OH U.S.A. 134 D3
Ada OK U.S.A. 131 D5
Ada WI U.S.A. 134 B2
Adabazar Turkey see Sakarya
Adaja r. Spain 57 D3
Adalia Turkey see Antalya
Adam Oman 87 I5
Adam, Mount hill Falkland Is 144 E8
Adamantina Brazil 145 A3
Adams IN U.S.A. 134 C4
Adams KY U.S.A. 134 D4
Adams MA U.S.A. 135 I2
Adams NY U.S.A. 135 G2
Adams, Mount U.S.A. 126 C3
Adams Center U.S.A. 135 G2
Adams Lake Canada 120 G5
Adams Mountain U.S.A. 120 D4
Adam's Peak Sri Lanka 84 D5
Adams Peak U.S.A. 128 C2

▶Adamstown Pitcairn Is 151 L7
Capital of the Pitcairn Islands.

'Adan Yemen see Aden
Adana Turkey 85 B1
Adana prov. Turkey 85 B1
Adana Yemen see Aden
Adapazarı Turkey see Sakarya
Adare Rep. of Ireland 51 D5
Adare, Cape Antarctica 152 H2
Adavale Australia 111 D5
Adban Afgh. 89 H2
Ad Dabbah Sudan see Ed Debba
Ad Ḍabbīyah well Saudi Arabia 88 C5
Ad Dafinah Saudi Arabia 86 F5
Ad Dahnā' des. Saudi Arabia 86 G5
Ad Dakhla W. Sahara 96 B2
Ad Damir Sudan see Ed Damer
Ad Dammam Saudi Arabia see Dammam
Addanki India 84 C3
Ad Dār al Ḥamrā' Saudi Arabia 86 E4
Ad Darb Saudi Arabia 86 F6
Ad Dawādimī Saudi Arabia 86 F5
Ad Dawḥah Qatar see Doha
Ad Dawr Iraq 91 F4
Ad Daww plain Syria 85 C2
Ad Dayr Iraq 91 G5
Ad Dibdibah plain Saudi Arabia 88 B5
Aḍ Ḍiffah plat. Egypt see Libyan Plateau

▶Addis Ababa Eth. 98 D3
Capital of Ethiopia.

Addison U.S.A. 135 G2
Ad Dīwānīyah Iraq 91 G5
Addlestone U.K. 49 G7
Addo Elephant National Park S. Africa 101 G7
Addoo Atoll Maldives see Addu Atoll
Addu Atoll Maldives 81 D12
Ad Duwayd well Saudi Arabia 91 F5
Ad Duwaym Sudan see Ed Dueim
Ad Duwayris well Saudi Arabia 88 C6
Adegaon India 82 D5
Adel GA U.S.A. 133 D6
Adel IA U.S.A. 130 E3

▶Adelaide Australia 111 B7
State capital of South Australia.

Adelaide r. Australia 108 E3
Adelaide Bahamas 133 E7
Adelaide Island Antarctica 152 L2
Adelaide River Australia 108 E3
Adele Island Australia 108 C3
Adélie Coast Antarctica 152 G2
Adélie Land reg. Antarctica 152 G2
Adelong Australia 112 D5
Aden Yemen 86 F7
Aden, Gulf of Somalia/Yemen 86 G7
Adena U.S.A. 134 E3
Adenau Germany 52 G4
Adendorf Germany 53 K1
Aderbissinat Niger 96 D3
Aderno Sicily Italy see Adrano
Adesar India 82 B5
Adhan, Jabal mt. U.A.E. 88 E5
Adh Dhāyūf well Saudi Arabia 91 G6
'Adhfā' well Saudi Arabia 91 F5
'Ādhirīyāt, Jibāl al mts Jordan 85 C4
Adi i. Indon. 69 I7
Ādī Ārk'ay Eth. 86 E7
Adige r. Italy 58 E2
Ādīgrat Eth. 98 D2
Adilabad India 84 C2
Adilcevaz Turkey 91 F3
Adin U.S.A. 126 C4
Adīrī Libya 97 E2
Adirondack Mountains U.S.A. 135 H1
Ādīs Ābeba Eth. see Addis Ababa
Adi Ugri Eritrea see Mendefera
Adıyaman Turkey 90 E3
Adjud Romania 59 L1
Adlavik Islands Canada 123 K3
Admiralty Island Canada 119 H3
Admiralty Island U.S.A. 120 C3
Admiralty Island National Monument - Kootznoowoo Wilderness nat. park U.S.A. 120 C3
Admiralty Islands P.N.G. 69 L7
Ado-Ekiti Nigeria 96 D4
Adok Sudan 86 D8
Adolfo L. Mateos Mex. 127 E8
Adolphus U.S.A. 134 B5
Adonara i. Indon. 108 C2
Adoni India 84 C3
Adorf Germany 53 M4
Adorf (Diemelsee) Germany 53 I3
Ado-Tymovo Rus. Fed. 74 F2
Adour r. France 56 D5
Adra Spain 57 E5
Adramyttium Turkey see Edremit
Adramyttium, Gulf of Turkey see Edremit Körfezi
Adrano Sicily Italy 58 F6
Adrar Alg. 96 C2
Adrar hills Mali see Ifôghas, Adrar des
Adraskand r. Afgh. 89 F3
Adré Chad 97 F3
Adrian MI U.S.A. 134 C3
Adrian TX U.S.A. 131 C5
Adrianople Turkey see Edirne
Adrianopolis Turkey see Edirne
Adriatic Sea Europe 58 E2
Adua Eth. see Ādwa
Adunara i. Indon. see Adonara
Adusa Dem. Rep. Congo 98 C3
Aduwa Eth. see Ādwa
Adverse Well Australia 108 C5
Ādwa Eth. 98 D2
Adycha r. Rus. Fed. 65 O3
Adyk Rus. Fed. 43 J7
Adzhiyan Turkm. 88 D2
Adzopé Côte d'Ivoire 96 C4
Aegean Sea Greece/Turkey 59 K5
Aegina i. Greece see Aigina
Aegyptus country Africa see Egypt
Aela Jordan see Al 'Aqabah
Aelana Jordan see Al 'Aqabah
Aelia Capitolina Israel/West Bank see Jerusalem
Aelönlaplap atoll Marshall Is see Ailinglapalap
Aenus Turkey see Enez
Aerzen Germany 53 J2
Aesernia Italy see Isernia
A Estrada Spain 57 B2
Āfabet Eritrea 86 E6
Afanas'yevo Rus. Fed. 42 L4
Affreville Alg. see Khemis Miliana
Afghānestān country Asia see Afghanistan
▶Afghanistan country Asia 89 G3
Asia 6, 62–63
Afgooye Somalia 98 E3
'Afīf Saudi Arabia 86 F5
Afiun Karahissar Turkey see Afyon
Åfjord Norway 44 G5
Aflou Alg. 54 E5
Afmadow Somalia 98 E3
Afogados da Ingazoira Brazil 143 K5
A Fonsagrada Spain 57 C2
Afonso Cláudio Brazil 145 C3
Āfrēra Terara vol. Eth. 86 F7
Africa Nova country Africa see Tunisia
'Afrīn Syria 85 C1
'Afrīn, Nahr r. Syria/Turkey 85 C1
Afşin Turkey 90 E3
Afsluitdijk barrage Neth. 52 F2
Afton U.S.A. 126 F4
Afuá Brazil 143 H4
'Afula Israel 85 B3
Afyon Turkey 59 N5
Afyonkarahisar Turkey see Afyon
Aga Germany 53 M4
Agadès Niger see Agadez
Agadez Niger 96 D3
Agadir Morocco 96 C1
Agadyr' Kazakh. 80 D2
Agalega Islands Mauritius 149 L6
Agana Guam see Hagåtña
Agara Georgia 91 F2
Agartala India 83 G5
Agashi India 84 B2
Agate Canada 122 E4
Agathe France see Agde
Agathonisi i. Greece 59 L6
Agats Indon. 69 J8
Agatti i. India 84 B4
Agboville Côte d'Ivoire 96 C4
Ağcabädi Azer. 91 G2
Ağdam Azer. 91 G3
Ağdaş Azer. 91 G2
Agdash Azer. see Ağdaş
Agde France 56 F5
Agdzhabedi Azer. see Ağcabädi
Agedabia Libya see Ajdābiyā
Agen France 56 E4
Aggeneys S. Africa 100 D5
Aggteleki nat. park Hungary 47 R6
Aghil Pass China/Jammu and Kashmir 82 D1
Agiabampo Mex. 127 F8
Agiguan i. N. Mariana Is see Aguijan
Ağın Turkey 90 E3
Aginskoye Rus. Fed. 72 G1
Aginum France see Agen
Agios Dimitrios Greece 59 J6
Agios Efstratios i. Greece 59 K5
Agios Georgios i. Greece 59 J6
Agios Nikolaos Greece 59 K7
Agios Theodoros Cyprus 85 B2
Agiou Orous, Kolpos b. Greece 59 J4
Agirwat Hills Sudan 86 E6
Agisanang S. Africa 101 G4
Agnes, Mount hill Australia 109 E6
Agnew Australia 109 C6
Agnibilékrou Côte d'Ivoire 96 C4
Agnita Romania 59 K2
Agniye-Afanas'yevsk Rus. Fed. 74 E2
Agra India 82 D4
Agrakhanskiy Poluostrov pen. Rus. Fed. 91 G2
Agram Croatia see Zagreb
Ağrı Turkey 91 F3
Agria Gramvousa i. Greece 59 J7
Agrigan i. N. Mariana Is see Agrihan
Agrigento Sicily Italy 58 E6
Agrigentum Sicily Italy see Agrigento
Agrihan i. N. Mariana Is 69 L3
Agrinio Greece 59 I5
Agropoli Italy 58 F4
Agryz Rus. Fed. 41 Q4
Ağsu Azer. 91 H2
Agua, Volcán de vol. Guat. 136 F6
Água Clara Brazil 144 F2
Aguadilla Puerto Rico 137 K5
Agua Escondida Arg. 144 C5
Agua Fria r. U.S.A. 129 G5
Agua Fria National Monument nat. park U.S.A. 129 G4
Aguanaval r. Mex. 131 C7
Aguanga U.S.A. 128 E5
Aguanus r. Canada 123 J4
Aguapeí r. Brazil 145 A3
Agua Prieta Mex. 127 F7
Aguaro-Guariquito, Parque Nacional nat. park Venez. 142 E2
Aguascalientes Mex. 136 D4
Agudos Brazil 145 A3
Águeda Port. 57 B3
Aguemour reg. Alg. 96 D2
Aguié Niger 96 D3
Aguijan i. N. Mariana Is 69 L4
Aguilar U.S.A. 127 G5
Aguilar de Campóo Spain 57 D2
Águilas Spain 57 F5

▶Agulhas, Cape S. Africa 100 E8
Most southerly point of Africa.

Agulhas Basin sea feature Southern Ocean 149 J9
Agulhas Negras mt. Brazil 145 B3
Agulhas Plateau sea feature Southern Ocean 149 J8
Agulhas Ridge sea feature S. Atlantic Ocean 148 I8
Ağva Turkey 59 M4
Agvali Rus. Fed. 91 G2
Ahaggar plat. Alg. see Hoggar
Āhangarān Iran 89 F3
Ahar Iran 88 B2
Ahaura N.Z. 113 C6
Ahaus Germany 52 H2
Ahipara Bay N.Z. 113 D2
Ahiri India 84 D2
Ahklun Mountains U.S.A. 118 B4
Ahlen Germany 53 H3
Ahmadabad India 82 C5
Aḥmadābād Iran 89 E3
Aḥmad al Bāqir, Jabal mt. Jordan 85 B5
Ahmadī Iran 88 E5
Ahmadnagar India 84 B2
Ahmadpur East Pak. 89 H4
Ahmar mts Eth. 98 E3
Ahmar Mountains Eth. see Ahmar
Ahmedabad India see Ahmadabad
Ahmednagar India see Ahmadnagar
Ahorn Germany 53 K4
Ahr r. Germany 52 H4
Ahram Iran 88 C4
Ahrensburg Germany 53 K1
Āhtäri Fin. 44 N5
Ahtme Estonia 45 O7
Ahu China 77 H1
Āhū Iran 88 C4
Ahun France 56 F3
Ahuzhen China see Ahu
Ahvāz Iran 88 C4
Ahwa India 84 B1
Ahwāz Iran see Ahvāz
Ai-Ais Namibia 100 C4
Ai-Ais Hot Springs and Fish River Canyon Park nature res. Namibia 100 C4
Aichwara India 82 D4
Aid U.S.A. 134 D4
Aidin Turkm. 88 D2
Aigialousa Cyprus 85 B2
Aigina i. Greece 59 J6
Aigio Greece 59 J5
Aigle de Chambeyron mt. France 56 H4
Aigües Tortes i Estany de Sant Maurici, Parc Nacional d' nat. park Spain 57 G2
Ai He r. China 74 B4
Aihua China see Yunxian
Aihui China see Heihe
Aijal India see Aizawl
Aikawa Japan 75 E5
Aiken U.S.A. 133 D5
Ailao Shan mts China 76 D3
Aileron Australia 108 F5
Ailinglabelab atoll Marshall Is see Ailinglapalap
Ailinglapalap atoll Marshall Is 150 H5
Ailly-sur-Noye France 52 C5
Ailsa Craig Canada 134 E2
Ailsa Craig i. U.K. 50 D5
Aimangala India 84 C3
Aimorés, Serra dos hills Brazil 145 C2
Aïn Beïda Alg. 58 B7
'Aïn Ben Tili Mauritania 96 C2
'Aïn Dâlla spring Egypt see 'Ayn Dāllah
Aïn Defla Alg. 57 H5
Aïn Deheb Alg. 57 G6
Aïn el Hadjel Alg. 57 H6
'Aïn el Maqfi spring Egypt see 'Ayn al Maqfī
Aïn el Melh Alg. 57 I6
Aïn Mdila well Alg. 58 B7
Aïn-M'Lila Alg. 54 F4
Aïn Oussera Alg. 57 H6
Aïn Salah Alg. see In Salah
Aïn Sefra Alg. 54 D5
Ainsworth U.S.A. 130 D3
Aintab Turkey see Gaziantep
Aïn Taya Alg. 57 H5
Aïn Tédélès Alg. 57 G5
Aïn Temouchent Alg. 57 F6
'Aïn Tibaghbagh spring Egypt see 'Ayn Tabaghbugh
'Ain Timeira spring Egypt see 'Ayn Tumayrah
'Ain Zeitûn Egypt see 'Ayn Zaytūn
Aiquile Bol. 142 E7
Air i. Indon. 71 D7
Airaines France 52 B5
Airdrie Canada 120 H5
Airdrie U.K. 50 F5
Aire r. France 52 E5
Aire, Canal d' France 52 C4
Aire-sur-l'Adour France 56 D5
Air Force Island Canada 119 K3
Airpanas Indon. 108 D1
Aisatung Mountain Myanmar 70 A2
Aisch r. Germany 53 L5
Aishihik Canada 120 B2
Aishihik Lake Canada 120 B2
Aisne r. France 52 C5
Aïssa, Djebel mt. Alg. 54 D5
Aitamännikkö Fin. 44 N3
Aitana mt. Spain 57 F4
Aït Benhaddou tourist site Morocco 54 C5
Aiterach r. Germany 53 M6
Aitkin U.S.A. 130 E2
Aiud Romania 59 J1
Aix France see Aix-en-Provence
Aix-en-Provence France 56 G5
Aix-la-Chapelle Germany see Aachen
Aix-les-Bains France 56 G4
Aiyina i. Greece see Aigina
Aiyion Greece see Aigio
Aizawl India 83 H5
Aizkraukle Latvia 45 N8
Aizpute Latvia 45 L8
Aizu-wakamatsu Japan 75 E5
Ajaccio Corsica France 56 I6
Ajanta India 84 B1
Ajanta Range hills India see Sahyadriparvat Range
Ajaureforsen Sweden 44 I4
Ajax Canada 134 F2
Ajayameru India see Ajmer
Ajban U.A.E. 88 D5
Aj Bogd Uul mt. Mongolia 80 I3
Ajdābiyā Libya 97 F1
a-Jiddét des. Oman see Ḥarāsīs, Jiddat al
'Ajlūn Jordan 85 B3
'Ajman U.A.E. 88 D5
Ajmer India 82 C4
Ajmer-Merwara India see Ajmer
Ajnala India 82 C3
Ajo U.S.A. 129 G5
Ajo, Mount U.S.A. 129 G5
Ajrestan Afgh. 89 G3
Akademii, Zaliv b. Rus. Fed. 74 E1
Akademii Nauk, Khrebet mt. Tajik. see Akademiyai Fanho, Qatorkŭhi
Akademiyai Fanho, Qatorkŭhi mt. Tajik. 89 H2
Akagera National Park Rwanda 98 D4
Akalkot India 84 C2
Akama, Akra c. Cyprus see Arnauti, Cape
Akamagaseki Japan see Shimonoseki
Akan National Park Japan 74 G4
Akaroa N.Z. 113 D6
Akas reg. India 76 B3
Akāshat Iraq 91 E4
Akbarābād Iran 91 I5
Akbarpur Uttar Pradesh India 82 E4
Akbarpur Uttar Pradesh India 83 E4
Akbaytal, Pereval pass Tajik. 89 I2
Akbaytal Pass Tajik. see Akbaytal, Pereval
Akbez Turkey 85 C1
Akçadağ Turkey 90 E3
Akçakale Turkey 85 D1
Akçakoca Turkey 59 N4
Akçakoca Dağları mts Turkey 55 N4
Akçakoyunlu Turkey 85 C1
Akçalı Dağları mts Turkey 85 A1
Akchâr reg. Mauritania 96 B3
Akchi Kazakh. see Akshiy
Akdağlar mts Turkey 59 M6
Akdağmadeni Turkey 90 D3
Akdere Turkey 85 A1
Akelamo Indon. 69 H6
Åkersberga Sweden 45 K7
Akersloot Neth. 52 E2
Aketi Dem. Rep. Congo 98 C3
Akgyr Erezi hills Turkm. see Akkyr, Gory
Akhali-Afoni Georgia see Akhali Ap'oni
Akhali Ap'oni Georgia 91 F2
Akhḍar, Al Jabal al mts Libya 97 F1
Akhḍar, Jabal mts Oman 88 E6
Akhisar Turkey 59 L5
Akhnoor Jammu and Kashmir 82 C2
Akhsu Azer. see Ağsu
Akhta Armenia see Hrazdan
Akhtarīn Syria 85 C1
Akhtubinsk Rus. Fed. 43 J6
Akhty Rus. Fed. 91 G2
Akhtyrka Ukr. see Okhtyrka
Aki Japan 75 D6
Akiéni Gabon 98 B4
Akimiski Island Canada 122 E3
Akishma r. Rus. Fed. 74 D1

Akita Japan 75 F5
Akjoujt Mauritania 96 B3
Akkajaure *l.* Sweden 44 J3
Akkerman Ukr. *see* **Bilhorod-Dnistrovs'kyy**
Akkeshi Japan 74 G4
'Akko Israel 85 B3
Akkol' *Akmolinskaya Oblast'* Kazakh. 80 D1
Akkol' *Atyrauskaya Oblast'* Kazakh. 43 K7
Akku Kazakh. 80 E1
Akkul' Kazakh. *see* **Akkol'**
Akkuş Turkey 90 E2
Akkyr, Gory *hills* Turkm. 88 D1
Aklavik Canada 118 E3
Aklera India 82 D4
Ak-Mechet Kazakh. *see* **Kyzylorda**
Akmeņrags *pt* Latvia 45 L8
Akmeqit China 82 D1
Akmola Kazakh. *see* **Astana**
Akmolinsk Kazakh. *see* **Astana**
Akobo Sudan 97 G4
Akobo Wenz *r.* Eth./Sudan 98 D3
Akokan Niger 96 D3
Akola India 84 C1
Akom II Cameroon 96 E4
Akonolinga Cameroon 96 E4
Akordat Eritrea 86 E6
Akören Turkey 90 D3
Akot India 82 D5
Akpatok Island Canada 123 I1
Akqi China 80 E3
Akra, Jabal *mt.* Syria/Turkey *see* **Aqra', Jabal al**
Akranes Iceland 44 [inset]
Åkrehamn Norway 45 D7
Akréréb Niger 96 D3
Akron *CO* U.S.A. 130 C3
Akron *IN* U.S.A. 134 B3
Akron *OH* U.S.A. 134 E3
Akrotiri Bay Cyprus 85 A2
Akrotirion Bay Cyprus *see* **Akrotiri Bay**
Akrotiriou, Kolpos *b.* Cyprus *see* **Akrotiri Bay**
Akrotiri Sovereign Base Area *military base* Cyprus 85 A2

▶**Aksai Chin** *terr.* Asia 82 D2
Disputed territory (China/India).

Aksaray Turkey 90 D3
Aksay China 80 H4
Aksay Kazakh. 41 Q5
Ak-Say *r.* Kyrg. 87 M1
Aksay Rus. Fed. 43 H7
Akşehir Turkey 59 N5
Akşehir Gölü *l.* Turkey 59 N5
Akseki Turkey 90 C3
Aksha Rus. Fed. 73 K2
Akshiganak Kazakh. 80 B2
Akshiy Kazakh. 80 E3
Akshukur Kazakh. 91 H2
Aksu China 80 F3
Aksu Kazakh. 80 E1
Aksu *r.* Tajik. *see* **Oqsu**
Aksu *r.* Turkey 59 N6
Aksuat Kazakh. 80 F2
Aksu-Ayuly Kazakh. 80 D2
Aksubayevo Rus. Fed. 43 K5
Āksum Eth. 86 E7
Aktag *mt.* China 83 F1
Aktas Dağı *mt.* Turkey 91 G3
Aktau Kazakh. 78 E2
Akto China 89 J2
Aktobe Kazakh. 78 E1
Aktogay *Karagandinskaya Oblast'* Kazakh. 80 E2
Aktogay *Vostochnyy Kazakhstan* Kazakh. 80 E2
Aktsyabrski Belarus 43 F5
Aktyubinsk Kazakh. *see* **Aktobe**
Akulivik Canada 119 K3
Akune Japan 75 C6
Akure Nigeria 96 D4
Akuressa Sri Lanka 84 D5
Akureyri Iceland 44 [inset]
Akusha Rus. Fed. 43 J8
Akwanga Nigeria 96 D4
Akxokesay China 83 G1
Akyab Myanmar *see* **Sittwe**
Akyatan Gölü *salt l.* Turkey 85 B1
Akyazı Turkey 59 N4
Akzhaykyn, Ozero *salt l.* Kazakh. 80 C3
Ål Norway 45 F6
'Alā, Jabal al *hills* Syria 85 C2
Alabama *r.* U.S.A. 133 C6
Alabama *state* U.S.A. 133 C5
Alabaster *AL* U.S.A. 133 C5
Alabaster *MI* U.S.A. 134 D1
Al 'Abṭīyah *well* Iraq 91 G5
Alaca Turkey 90 D2
Alacahan Turkey 90 E3
Alaçam Turkey 90 D2
Alaçam Dağları *mts* Turkey 59 M5
Alacant Spain *see* **Alicante-Alacant**
Alaçatı Turkey 59 L5
Aladağ Turkey 90 D3
Ala Dağlar *mts* Turkey 91 F3
Ala Dağları *mts* Turkey 90 D3
Al 'Adam Libya 90 A5
Al Aflāj *reg.* Saudi Arabia 88 B6
Alag Hu *l.* China 76 C1
Alagir Rus. Fed. 91 G2
Alagoinhas Brazil 145 D1
Alahärmä Fin. 44 M5
Al Aḥmadī Kuwait 88 C4
Alai Range *mts* Asia 89 H2
Ālaivān Iran 88 D3
Ālājah Syria 85 B2
Alajärvi Fin. 44 M5
Al 'Ajrūd *well* Egypt 85 B4
Alakanuk U.S.A. 118 B3
Al Akhḍar Saudi Arabia 90 E5
Alakol', Ozero *salt l.* Kazakh. 80 F2
Ala Kul *salt l.* Kazakh. *see* **Alakol', Ozero**
Alakurtti Rus. Fed. 44 Q3
Al 'Alamayn Egypt 90 C5
Al 'Alayyah Saudi Arabia 86 F6
Alama Somalia 98 E3
Al 'Amādīyah Iraq 91 F3
Alamagan *i.* N. Mariana Is 69 L3
Alamaguan *i.* N. Mariana Is *see* **Alamagan**
Al 'Amārah Iraq 91 G5
'Alam ar Rūm, Ra's *pt* Egypt 90 B5
'Alāmarvdasht *watercourse* Iran 88 D4
Alamdo China 76 B2
Alameda U.S.A. 128 B3
'Alam el Rûm, Râs *pt* Egypt *see* **'Alam ar Rūm, Ra's**
Al Amghar *waterhole* Iraq 91 G5
Al 'Āmirīyah Egypt 90 C5
Alamo *GA* U.S.A. 133 D5
Alamo *NV* U.S.A. 129 F3
Alamo Dam U.S.A. 129 G4
Alamogordo U.S.A. 127 G6
Alamo Heights U.S.A. 131 D6
Alamos *Sonora* Mex. 127 F7
Alamos *Sonora* Mex. 127 F8
Alamos *r.* Mex. 131 C7
Alamos, Sierra *mts* Mex. 127 F8
Alamosa U.S.A. 127 G5
Alamos de Peña Mex. 127 G7
Alampur India 84 C3
Alan Myanmar *see* **Myede**
Alanäs Sweden 44 I4
Åland *is* Fin. *see* **Åland Islands**
Aland *r.* Germany 53 L1
Aland India 84 C2
Al Andarīn Syria 85 C2
Åland Islands Fin. 45 K6
Alandur India 84 D3
Alanson U.S.A. 134 C1
Alanya Turkey 90 D3
Alapli Turkey 59 N4
Alappuzha India *see* **Alleppey**
Alapuzha India *see* **Alleppey**
Al 'Aqabah Jordan 85 B5
Al 'Aqīq Saudi Arabia 86 F5
Al 'Arabīyah as Sa'ūdīyah *country* Asia *see* **Saudi Arabia**
Alarcón, Embalse de *resr* Spain 57 E4
Al 'Arīsh Egypt 85 A4
Al Arṭāwīyah Saudi Arabia 86 G4
Alas, Selat *sea chan.* Indon. 108 B2
Alaşehir Turkey 59 M5
Alashiya *country* Asia *see* **Cyprus**
Al Ashmūnayn Egypt 90 C6
Alaska *state* U.S.A. 118 D3
Alaska, Gulf of U.S.A. 118 D4
Alaska Highway Canada/U.S.A. 120 A2
Alaska Peninsula U.S.A. 118 B4
Alaska Range *mts* U.S.A. 118 D3
Älät Azer. 91 H3
Alat Uzbek. 89 F2
Alataw Shankou *pass* China/Kazakh. *see* **Dzungarian Gate**
Al Atwā' *well* Saudi Arabia 91 F5
Alatyr' Rus. Fed. 43 J5
Alatyr' *r.* Rus. Fed. 43 J5
Alausí Ecuador 142 C4
Alaverdi Armenia 91 G2
'Alavī Iran 88 C3
Alavieska Fin. 44 N4
Alavus Fin. 44 M5
Alawbum Myanmar 70 B1
Alawoona Australia 111 C7
Alay Kyrka Toosu *mts* Asia *see* **Alai Range**
Al 'Ayn Oman 88 E6
Al 'Ayn U.A.E. 88 D5
Alayskiy Khrebet *mts* Asia *see* **Alai Range**
Al 'Azīzīyah Iraq 91 G4

▶**Al 'Azīzīyah** Libya 55 G5
Highest recorded shade temperature in the world.

Al Azraq al Janūbī Jordan 85 C4
Alba Italy 58 C2
Alba U.S.A. 134 C1
Al Bāb Syria 85 C1
Albacete Spain 57 F4
Al Badī' Saudi Arabia 88 B6
Al Bādiyah al Janūbīyah *hill* Iraq 91 G5
Al Bahrayn *country* Asia *see* **Bahrain**
Alba Iulia Romania 59 J1
Al Bajā' *well* U.A.E. 88 C5
Albājī Iran 88 C4
Al Bakhrā *well* Saudi Arabia 88 B5
Albanel, Lac *l.* Canada 123 G4
▶**Albania** *country* Europe 59 H4
Europe 5, 38–39
Albany Australia 109 B8
Albany *r.* Canada 122 E3
Albany *GA* U.S.A. 133 C6
Albany *IN* U.S.A. 134 C3
Albany *KY* U.S.A. 134 C5
Albany *MO* U.S.A. 130 E3

▶**Albany** *NY* U.S.A. 135 I2
State capital of New York.

Albany *OH* U.S.A. 134 D4
Albany *OR* U.S.A. 126 C3
Albany *TX* U.S.A. 131 D5
Albany Downs Australia 112 D1
Albardão do João Maria *coastal area* Brazil 144 F4
Al Bardī Libya 90 B5
Al Bāridah *hills* Saudi Arabia 85 D5
Al Baṣrah Iraq *see* **Basra**
Al Baṭḥa' *marsh* Iraq 91 G5
Al Bāṭinah *reg.* Oman 88 E5
Albatross Bay Australia 110 C2
Albatross Island Australia 111 [inset]
Al Bawītī Egypt 90 C5
Al Bayḍā' Libya 86 B3
Al Bayḍā' Yemen 86 G7
Albemarle U.S.A. 133 D5
Albemarle Island *Galápagos* Ecuador *see* **Isabela, Isla**
Albemarle Sound *sea chan.* U.S.A. 132 E5
Albenga Italy 58 C2
Alberche *r.* Spain 57 D4
Alberga Australia 111 A5
Alberga *watercourse* Australia 111 A5
Albergaria-a-Velha Port. 57 B3
Albert Australia 112 C4
Albert France 52 C5
Albert, Lake Dem. Rep. Congo/Uganda 98 D3
Albert, Parc National *nat. park* Dem. Rep. Congo *see* **Virunga, Parc National des**
Alberta *prov.* Canada 120 H4
Alberta U.S.A. 135 G5
Albert Kanaal *canal* Belgium 52 F4
Albert Lea U.S.A. 130 E3
Albert Nile *r.* Sudan/Uganda 97 G4
Alberto de Agostini, Parque Nacional *nat. park* Chile 144 B8
Alberton S. Africa 101 I4
Alberton U.S.A. 126 E3
Albert Town Bahamas 133 F8
Albertville Dem. Rep. Congo *see* **Kalemie**
Albertville France 56 H4
Albertville U.S.A. 133 C5
Albestroff France 52 G6
Albi France 56 F5
Albia U.S.A. 130 E3
Al Biḍah *des.* Saudi Arabia 88 C5
Albina Suriname 143 H2
Albino Italy 58 C2
Albion *CA* U.S.A. 128 B2
Albion *IL* U.S.A. 130 F4
Albion *IN* U.S.A. 134 C3
Albion *MI* U.S.A. 134 C2
Albion *NE* U.S.A. 130 D3
Albion *NY* U.S.A. 135 F2
Albion *PA* U.S.A. 134 E3
Al Biqā' *valley* Lebanon *see* **El Béqaa**
Al Bi'r Saudi Arabia 90 E5
Al Birk Saudi Arabia 86 F6
Al Biyāḍh *reg.* Saudi Arabia 86 G5
Alborán, Isla de *i.* Spain 57 E6
Ålborg Denmark 45 F8
Ålborg Bugt *b.* Denmark 45 G8
Albro Australia 110 D4
Al Budayyi Bahrain 88 C5
Albufeira Port. 57 B5
Al Buḥayrāt al Murrah *lakes* Egypt *see* **Bitter Lakes**
Albuquerque U.S.A. 127 G6
Al Burayj Syria 85 C2
Al Buraymī Oman 88 D5
Al Burj Jordan 85 B5
Alburquerque Spain 57 C4
Albury Australia 112 C6
Al Buṣayrah Syria 91 F4
Al Busayṭā' *plain* Saudi Arabia 85 D4
Al Bushūk *well* Saudi Arabia 88 B4
Alcácer do Sal Port. 57 B4
Alcalá de Henares Spain 57 E3
Alcalá la Real Spain 57 E5
Alcamo *Sicily* Italy 58 E6
Alcañiz Spain 57 F3
Alcántara Spain 57 C4
Alcantara Lake Canada 121 I2
Alcaraz Spain 57 E4
Alcázar de San Juan Spain 57 E4
Alcazarquivir Morocco *see* **Ksar el Kebir**
Alchevs'k Ukr. 43 H6
Alcobaça Brazil 145 D2
Alcoi Spain *see* **Alcoy-Alcoi**
Alcoota Australia 108 F5
Alcora Spain 57 F3
Alcova U.S.A. 126 G4
Alcoy Spain *see* **Alcoy-Alcoi**
Alcoy-Alcoi Spain 57 F4
Alcúdia Spain 57 H4
Aldabra Islands Seychelles 99 E4
Aldan Rus. Fed. 65 N4
Aldan *r.* Rus. Fed. 65 N3
Alde *r.* U.K. 49 I6
Aldeboarn Neth. *see* **Oldeboorn**
Aldeburgh U.K. 49 I6
Alder Creek U.S.A. 135 H2
Alderney *i.* Channel Is 49 E9
Alder Peak U.S.A. 128 C4
Aldershot U.K. 49 G7
Al Dhafrah *reg.* U.A.E. 88 D6
Aldingham U.K. 48 D4
Aldridge U.K. 49 F6
Aleg Mauritania 96 B3
Alegre *Espírito Santo* Brazil 145 C3
Alegre *Minas Gerais* Brazil 145 B2
Alegrete Brazil 144 E3
Alegros Mountain U.S.A. 129 I4
Aleksandra, Mys *hd* Rus. Fed. 70 E1
Aleksandriya Ukr. *see* **Oleksandriya**
Aleksandro-Nevskiy Rus. Fed. 39 I5
Aleksandropol Armenia *see* **Gyumri**
Aleksandrov Rus. Fed. 42 H4
Aleksandrov Gay Rus. Fed. 43 K6
Aleksandrovsk Rus. Fed. 41 R4
Aleksandrovsk Ukr. *see* **Zaporizhzhya**
Aleksandrovskiy Rus. Fed. *see* **Aleksandrovsk**
Aleksandrovskoye Rus. Fed. 91 F1
Aleksandrovsk-Sakhalinskiy Rus. Fed. 74 F2
Aleksandry, Zemlya *i.* Rus. Fed. 64 F1
Alekseyevka *Akmolinskaya Oblast'* Kazakh. *see* **Akkol'**
Alekseyevka *Vostochnyy Kazakhstan* Kazakh. *see* **Terekty**
Alekseyevka *Amurskaya Oblast'* Rus. Fed. 74 B1
Alekseyevka *Belgorodskaya Oblast'* Rus. Fed. 43 H6
Alekseyevka *Belgorodskaya Oblast'* Rus. Fed. 43 H6
Alekseyevskaya Rus. Fed. 43 I6
Alekseyevskoye Rus. Fed. 42 K5
Aleksin Rus. Fed. 43 H5
Aleksinac Serb. and Mont. 59 I3
Alèmbé Gabon 98 B4
Ålen Norway 44 G5
Alençon France 56 E2
Alenquer Brazil 143 H4
Alenuihaha Channel *HI* U.S.A. 127 [inset]
Alep Syria *see* **Aleppo**
Aleppo Syria 85 C1
Alert Canada 119 L1
Alerta Peru 142 D6
Alès France 56 G4
Aleşd Romania 59 J1
Aleshki Ukr. *see* **Tsyurupyns'k**
Aleşkirt Turkey *see* **Eleşkirt**
Alessandria Italy 58 C2
Alessio Albania *see* **Lezhë**
Ålesund Norway 44 E5
Aleutian Basin *sea feature* Bering Sea 150 H2
Aleutian Islands U.S.A. 118 A4
Aleutian Range *mts* U.S.A. 118 C4
Aleutian Trench *sea feature* N. Pacific Ocean 150 I2
Alevina, Mys *c.* Rus. Fed. 65 Q4
Alevişik Turkey *see* **Samandağı**
Alexander U.S.A. 130 C2
Alexander, Kap *c.* Greenland *see* **Ullersuaq**
Alexander, Mount *hill* Australia 110 B2
Alexander Archipelago *is* U.S.A. 120 B3
Alexander Bay *b.* Namibia/S. Africa 100 C5
Alexander Bay S. Africa 100 C5
Alexander City U.S.A. 133 C5
Alexander Island Antarctica 148 L2
Alexandra Australia 112 B6
Alexandra N.Z. 113 B7
Alexandra, Cape S. Georgia 144 I8
Alexandra Channel India 71 A4
Alexandra Land *i.* Rus. Fed. *see* **Aleksandry, Zemlya**
Alexandreia Greece 59 J4
Alexandretta Turkey *see* **İskenderun**
Alexandria Afgh. *see* **Ghaznī**
Alexandria Canada 135 H1

▶**Alexandria** Egypt 90 C5
5th most populous city in Africa.

Alexandria Romania 59 K3
Alexandria S. Africa 101 H7
Alexandria Turkm. *see* **Mary**
Alexandria U.K. 50 E5
Alexandria *IN* U.S.A. 134 C3
Alexandria *KY* U.S.A. 134 C4
Alexandria *LA* U.S.A. 131 E6
Alexandria *VA* U.S.A. 135 G4
Alexandria Arachoton Afgh. *see* **Kandahār**
Alexandria Areion Afgh. *see* **Herāt**
Alexandria Bay U.S.A. 135 H1
Alexandria Prophthasia Afgh. *see* **Farāh**
Alexandrina, Lake Australia 107 B7
Alexandroupoli Greece 59 K4
Alexis *r.* Canada 123 K3
Alexis Creek Canada 120 F4
Aley Lebanon 85 B3
Aleyak Iran 88 E2
Aleysk Rus. Fed. 72 E2
Alf Germany 52 H4
Al Farwānīyah Kuwait 88 B4
Al Fas Morocco *see* **Fès**
Al Fatḥah Iraq 91 F4
Al Fāw Iraq 91 H5
Al Fayyūm Egypt 90 C5
Alfeld (Leine) Germany 53 J3
Alfenas Brazil 145 B3
Alford U.K. 48 H5
Alfred *ME* U.S.A. 135 J2
Alfred *NY* U.S.A. 135 G2
Alfred and Marie Range *hills* Australia 109 D6
Al Fujayrah U.A.E. *see* **Fujairah**
Al Fuqahā' Libya 97 E2
Al Furāt *r.* Iraq/Syria 85 D2 *see* **Euphrates**
Alga Kazakh. 80 A2
Ålgård Norway 45 D7
Algarrobo del Aguilla Arg. 144 C5
Algarve *reg.* Port. 57 B5
Algeciras Spain 57 D5
Algemesí Spain 57 F4
Algena Eritrea 86 E6
Alger Alg. *see* **Algiers**
Alger U.S.A. 134 C1

▶**Algeria** *country* Africa 96 C2
2nd largest country in Africa.
Africa 7, 94–95

Algérie *country* Africa *see* **Algeria**
Algermissen Germany 53 J2
Algha Kazakh. *see* **Alga**
Al Ghāfāt Oman 88 E6
Al Ghammās Iraq 91 G5
Al Ghardaqah Egypt *see* **Al Ghurdaqah**
Al Ghawr *plain* Jordan/West Bank 85 B4
Al Ghayḍah Yemen 86 H6
Alghero *Sardinia* Italy 58 C4
Al Ghurdaqah Egypt 86 D4
Al Ghuwayr *well* Qatar 88 C5

▶**Algiers** Alg. 57 H5
Capital of Algeria.

Algoa Bay S. Africa 101 G7
Algoma U.S.A. 134 B1
Algona U.S.A. 130 E3
Algonac U.S.A. 134 D2
Algonquin Park Canada 135 F1
Algonquin Provincial Park Canada 135 F1
Algorta Spain 57 E2
Algueirao Moz. *see* **Hacufera**
Al Habakah *well* Saudi Arabia 91 F5
Al Ḥabbānīyah Iraq 91 F4
Al Ḥadaqah *well* Saudi Arabia 88 B4
Al Ḥadd Bahrain 88 C5
Al Hadhālīl *plat.* Saudi Arabia 91 F5
Al Ḥadīdīyah Syria 85 C2
Al Ḥadīthah Iraq 91 F4
Al Hadīthah Saudi Arabia 85 C4
Al Ḥaḍr Iraq *see* **Hatra**
Al Ḥafār *well* Saudi Arabia 91 F5
Al Ḥaffah Syria 85 C2
Al Haggounia W. Sahara 96 B2
Al Ḥajar al Gharbī *mts* Oman 88 E5
Al Ḥajar ash Sharqī *mts* Oman 88 E6
Al Ḥamād *plain* Asia 90 E5
Al Ḥamādah al Ḥamrā' *plat.* Libya 96 E2
Alhama de Murcia Spain 57 F5
Al Ḥamar Saudi Arabia 88 B6
Al Ḥamīdīyah Syria 85 B2
Al Ḥammām Egypt 90 C5
Al Ḥanākīyah Saudi Arabia 86 F5
Al Ḥanīsh al Kabīr *i.* Yemen 86 F7
Al Haniyah *esc.* Iraq 91 G5
Al Hariq Saudi Arabia 88 B6
Al Harrah Egypt 90 C5
Al Harūj al Aswad *hills* Libya 97 E2
Al Hasa *reg.* Saudi Arabia 88 C5
Al Ḥasakah Syria 91 F3
Al Hawi *salt pan* Saudi Arabia 85 D5
Al Ḥawjā' Saudi Arabia 90 E5
Al Ḥawṭah *reg.* Saudi Arabia 88 B6
Al Ḥayy Iraq 91 G4
Al Hayz Egypt 90 C5
Al Hazīm Jordan 85 C4
Al Ḥazm Saudi Arabia 90 E5
Al Ḥazm al Jawf Yemen 86 F6
Al Ḥibāk *des.* Saudi Arabia 87 H6
Al Ḥījānah Syria 85 C3
Al Ḥillah Iraq *see* **Hillah**
Al Ḥillah Saudi Arabia 86 G5
Al Ḥinnāh Saudi Arabia 98 E1
Al Ḥinw *mt.* Saudi Arabia 85 D5
Al Hirrah *well* Saudi Arabia 88 C6
Al Hīshah Syria 85 D1
Al Ḥismā *plain* Saudi Arabia 90 D5
Al Ḥiṣn Jordan 85 B3
Al Hoceima Morocco 57 E6
Al Ḥudaydah Yemen *see* **Hodeidah**
Al Ḥufrah *reg.* Saudi Arabia 90 E5
Al Hufūf Saudi Arabia 86 G4
Al Hūj *hills* Saudi Arabia 90 E5
Al Husayfin Oman 88 E5
Al Huwwah Saudi Arabia 88 B6
Ali China 82 D2
'Alīābād Afgh. 89 H2
'Alīābād *Golestān* Iran 88 D2
'Alīābād *Hormozgan* Iran 88 D4
'Alīābād *Khorāsān* Iran 89 F4
'Alīābād *Kordestān* Iran 88 B2
Alīābād, Kūh-e *mt.* Iran 88 C3
Aliağa Turkey 59 L5
Aliakmonas *r.* Greece 59 J4
Alibag India 84 B2
Äli Bayramlı Azer. 91 H3
Alicante Spain *see* **Alicante-Alacant**
Alicante-Alacant Spain 57 F4
Alice *r.* Australia 110 C2
Alice *watercourse* Australia 110 D5
Alice U.S.A. 131 D7
Alice, Punta *pt* Italy 58 G5
Alice Springs Australia 109 F5
Alice Town Bahamas 133 E7
Aliceville U.S.A. 131 F5
Alichur Tajik. 89 I2
Alichur *r.* Tajik. 89 I2
Alick Creek *r.* Australia 110 C4
Alifu Atoll Maldives *see* **Ari Atoll**
Al Ifzi'iyyah *i.* U.A.E. 88 C5
Aliganj India 82 D4
Aligarh *Rajasthan* India 82 D4
Aligarh *Uttar Pradesh* India 82 D4
Alīgūdarz Iran 88 C3
Alihe China 74 A2
Alījūq, Kūh-e *mt.* Iran 88 C4
'Alī Kheyl Afgh. 89 H3
Al Imārāt al 'Arabīyah at Muttaḥidah *country* Asia *see* **United Arab Emirates**
Alimia *i.* Greece 59 L6
Alindao Cent. Afr. Rep. 98 C3
Alingsås Sweden 45 H8
Aliova *r.* Turkey 59 M5
Alipura India 82 D4
Alipur Duar India 83 G4
Alirajpur India 82 C5
Al 'Irāq *country* Asia *see* **Iraq**
Al 'Īsāwīyah Saudi Arabia 85 C4
Al Iskandarīyah Egypt *see* **Alexandria**
Al Iskandarīyah Iraq 91 G4
Al Ismā'īlīyah Egypt 90 D5
Aliveri Greece 59 K5
Aliwal North S. Africa 101 H6
Alix Canada 120 H4
Al Jafr Jordan 85 C4
Al Jāfūrah *des.* Saudi Arabia 88 C5
Al Jaghbūb Libya 90 B5
Al Jahrah Kuwait 88 B4
Al Jamalīyah Qatar 88 C5
Al Jarāwī *well* Saudi Arabia 85 D4
Al Jauf Saudi Arabia *see* **Al Jawf**
Al Jawb *reg.* Saudi Arabia 88 C6
Al Jawf Libya 97 F2
Al Jawf Saudi Arabia 91 E5
Al Jawsh Libya 96 E1
Al Jaza'ir *country* Africa *see* **Algeria**
Al Jaza'ir Alg. *see* **Algiers**
Aljezur Port. 57 B5
Al Jībān *reg.* Saudi Arabia 88 C5
Al Jil *well* Iraq 91 F5
Al Jilh *esc.* Saudi Arabia 88 B5
Al Jithāmīyah Saudi Arabia 91 F6
Al Jīzah Egypt *see* **Giza**
Al Jīzah Jordan 85 B4
Al Jubayl *hills* Saudi Arabia 88 B5
Al Jubaylah Saudi Arabia 88 B5
Al Jufra Oasis Libya 97 E2
Al Julayqah *well* Saudi Arabia 88 C5
Aljustrel Port. 57 B5
Al Juwayf *depr.* Syria 85 C3
Al Kahfah *Al Qaşīm* Saudi Arabia 86 F4
Al Kahfah *Ash Sharqīyah* Saudi Arabia 88 C5
Alkali Lake Canada 120 F5
Al Karak Jordan 85 B4
Al Kāẓimīyah Iraq 91 G4
Al Khābūrah Oman 88 E6
Al Khalīl West Bank *see* **Hebron**
Al Khāliṣ Iraq 91 G4
Al Khārijah Egypt 86 D4
Al Kharj *reg.* Saudi Arabia 88 B6
Al Kharrārah Qatar 88 C5
Al Kharrūbah Egypt 85 A4
Al Khaṣab Oman 88 E5
Al Khatam *reg.* U.A.E. 88 D5
Al Khawkhah Yemen 86 F7
Al Khawr Qatar 88 C5
Al Khizāmī *well* Saudi Arabia 88 C5
Al Khums Libya 97 E1
Al Khunfah *sand area* Saudi Arabia 90 E5
Al Khunn Saudi Arabia 98 E1
Al Kifl Iraq 91 G4
Al Kir'ānah Qatar 88 C5
Al Kiswah Syria 85 C3
Alkmaar Neth. 52 E2
Al Kūbrī Egypt 85 A4
Al Kūfah Iraq 91 G4
Al Kumayt Iraq 91 G4
Al Kuntillah Egypt 85 B5
Al Kuṣūr *hills* Saudi Arabia 85 D4
Al Kūt Iraq 91 G4
Al Kuwayt *country* Asia *see* **Kuwait**
Al Kuwayt Kuwait *see* **Kuwait**
Al Labbah *plain* Saudi Arabia 91 F5
Al Lādhiqīyah Syria *see* **Latakia**
Allagadda India 84 C3
Allahabad India 83 E4
Al Lajā *lava field* Syria 85 C3
Allakaket U.S.A. 118 C3
Allakh-Yun' Rus. Fed. 65 O3
Allanmyo Myanmar *see* **Myede**
Allanridge S. Africa 101 H4
Allapalli India 84 D2
'Allāqī, Wādī al *watercourse* Egypt 86 D5
'Allâqi, Wâdi el *watercourse* Egypt *see* **'Allāqī, Wādī al**
Allardville Canada 123 I5
Alldays S. Africa 101 I2
Allegan U.S.A. 134 C2
Allegheny *r.* U.S.A. 134 F3
Allegheny Mountains U.S.A. 130 D5
Allegheny Reservoir U.S.A. 135 F3
Allen, Lough *l.* Rep. of Ireland 51 D3
Allendale U.S.A. 133 D5
Allendale Town U.K. 48 E4
Allende *Coahuila* Mex. 131 C6
Allende *Nuevo León* Mex. 131 C7
Allendorf (Lumda) Germany 53 I4
Allenford Canada 134 E1
Allenstein Poland *see* **Olsztyn**
Allensville U.S.A. 134 B5
Allentown U.S.A. 135 H3
Alleppey India 84 C4
Aller *r.* Germany 53 J2
Alliance *NE* U.S.A. 130 C3
Alliance *OH* U.S.A. 134 E3
Al Lībīyah *country* Africa *see* **Libya**
Allier *r.* France 56 F3
Al Lihābah *well* Saudi Arabia 88 B5
Allinge-Sandvig Denmark 45 I9
Al Liṣāfah *well* Saudi Arabia 88 B5
Al Lisān *pen.* Jordan 85 B4
Alliston Canada 134 F1
Al Līth Saudi Arabia 86 F5
Al Liwā' *oasis* U.A.E. 88 D6
Alloa U.K. 50 F4
Allons U.S.A. 134 C5
Allora Australia 112 F2
Allur India 84 D3
Alluru Kottapatnam India 84 D3
Al Lussuf *well* Iraq 91 F5
Alma Canada 123 H4
Alma *MI* U.S.A. 134 C2
Alma *NE* U.S.A. 130 D3
Alma *WI* U.S.A. 130 F2
Al Ma'ānīyah Iraq 91 F5
Alma-Ata Kazakh. *see* **Almaty**
Almada Port. 57 B4
Al Madāfi' *plat.* Saudi Arabia 90 E5
Al Ma'danīyāt *well* Iraq 91 G5
Almaden Australia 110 D3
Almadén Spain 57 D4
Al Madīnah Saudi Arabia *see* **Medina**
Al Mafraq Jordan 85 C3
Al Maghrib *country* Africa *see* **Morocco**
Al Maghrib *reg.* U.A.E. 88 D6
Al Mahākik *reg.* Saudi Arabia 88 C6
Al Mahdum Syria 85 C1
Al Maḥīā *depr.* Saudi Arabia 90 E6
Al Maḥwīt Yemen 86 F6
Al Malsūnīyah *reg.* Saudi Arabia 88 C5
Almalyk Uzbek. 80 C3
Al Manadir *reg.* Oman 88 D6
Al Manāmah Bahrain *see* **Manama**
Al Manjūr *well* Saudi Arabia 84 B6
Almanor, Lake U.S.A. 128 C1
Almansa Spain 57 F4
Al Manṣūrah Egypt 90 C5
Almanzor *mt.* Spain 57 D3
Al Mariyyah U.A.E. 88 D6
Al Marj Libya 97 F1
Almas, Rio das *r.* Brazil 145 A1
Al Maṭarīyah Egypt 90 D5

▶**Almaty** Kazakh. 80 E3
Former capital of Kazakhstan.

Al Mawṣil Iraq *see* **Mosul**
Al Mayādīn Syria 91 F4
Al Mazār Egypt 85 A4
Almaznyy Rus. Fed. 65 M3
Almeirim Brazil 143 H4
Almeirim Port. 57 B4
Almelo Neth. 52 G2
Almenara Brazil 145 C2
Almendra, Embalse de *resr* Spain 57 C3
Almendralejo Spain 57 C4
Almere Neth. 52 F2
Almería Spain 57 E5
Almería, Golfo de *b.* Spain 57 E5
Al'met'yevsk Rus. Fed. *see* **Al'met'yevsk**
Al'met'yevsk Rus. Fed. 41 Q5
Älmhult Sweden 45 I8
Almina, Punta *pt* Spain 57 D6
Al Mindak Saudi Arabia 86 F5
Al Minyā Egypt 90 C5
Almirós Greece *see* **Almyros**
Al Mish'āb Saudi Arabia 88 C4
Almodôvar Port. 57 B5
Almond *r.* U.K. 50 F4
Almont U.S.A. 134 D2
Almonte Spain 57 C5
Almora India 82 D3
Al Mu'ayzīlah *hill* Saudi Arabia 85 D5
Al Mubarrez Saudi Arabia 86 G4
Al Muḍaibī Oman 87 I5
Al Muḍairib Oman 88 E6
Al Muḥarraq Bahrain 88 C5
Al Mukallā Yemen *see* **Mukalla**
Al Mukhā Yemen *see* **Mocha**
Al Mukhaylī Libya 86 B3
Al Munbaṭiḥ *des.* Saudi Arabia 88 C6
Almuñécar Spain 57 E5
Al Muqdādīyah Iraq 91 G4
Al Mūrītānīyah *country* Africa *see* **Mauritania**
Al Murūt *well* Saudi Arabia 91 E5
Almus Turkey 90 E2
Al Musannāh *ridge* Saudi Arabia 88 B4
Al Musayyib Iraq 88 B3
Al Muwaqqar Jordan 85 C4
Almyros Greece 59 J5
Almyrou, Ormos *b.* Greece 59 K7
Alnwick U.K. 48 F3

▶**Alofi** Niue 107 J3
Capital of Niue.
Oceania 8, 104–105

Aloja Latvia 45 N8

Alon Myanmar 70 A2
Along India 83 H3
Alongshan China 74 A2
Alor i. Indon. 108 D2
Alor, Kepulauan is Indon. 108 D2
Alor Setar Malaysia 71 C6
Alor Star Malaysia see Alor Setar
Alost Belgium see Aalst
Aloysius, Mount Australia 109 E6
Alozero Rus. Fed. 44 Q4
Alpen Germany 52 G3
Alpena U.S.A. 134 D1
Alpercatas, Serra das hills Brazil 143 J5
Alpha Australia 110 D4
Alpha Ridge sea feature Arctic Ocean
153 A1
Alpine AZ U.S.A. 129 I5
Alpine TX U.S.A. 135 G2
Alpine TX U.S.A. 131 C6
Alpine WY U.S.A. 126 F4
Alpine Europe see Europe
Alpine National Park Australia 112 C6
Alps mts Europe 56 H4
Al Qa'āmīyat reg. Saudi Arabia 86 G6
Al Qaddāḥīyah Libya 97 E1
Al Qadmūs Syria 85 C2
Al Qāhirah Egypt see Cairo
Al Qā'īyah Saudi Arabia 86 F5
Al Qā'īyah well Saudi Arabia 88 B5
Al Qalībah Saudi Arabia 90 E5
Al Qāmishlī Syria 91 F3
Al Qar'ah Libya 90 B5
Al Qar'ah well Saudi Arabia 88 B3
Al Qar'ah lava field Syria 85 C3
Al Qardāḥah Syria 85 C2
Al Qarqar Saudi Arabia 85 C4
Al Qaryatayn Syria 85 C2
Al Qaşab Ar Riyāḍ Saudi Arabia 88 B5
Al Qaşab Ash Sharqīyah Saudi Arabia
88 C6
Al Qaṭīf Saudi Arabia 88 C5
Al Qaṭn Yemen 86 G6
Al Qaṭrānah Jordan 85 C4
Al Qaṭrūn Libya 97 E2
Al Qāysūmah well Saudi Arabia 91 F5
Al Qumur country Africa see Comoros
Al Qunayṭirah Syria 85 B3
Al Qunfidhah Saudi Arabia 86 F6
Al Qurayyāt Saudi Arabia 85 C4
Al Qurnah Iraq 91 G5
Al Quşaymah Egypt 85 B4
Al Quşayr Egypt 86 D4
Al Quşayr Syria 85 C2
Al Qūşīyah Egypt 90 C6
Al Qūşūrīyah Saudi Arabia 88 B6
Al Quṭayfah Syria 85 C3
Al Quwayʻ Saudi Arabia 88 B6
Al Quwayʻīyah Saudi Arabia 86 G5
Al Quwayrah Jordan 85 B5
Al Rabbād r. U.A.E. 88 D6
Alroy Downs Australia 110 B3
Alsace admin. reg. France 52 H6
Alsace reg. France 56 H2
Alsager U.K. 49 E5
Al Samīt well Iraq 91 F5
Alsask Canada 121 I5
Alsatia reg. France see Alsace
Alsek r. U.S.A. 120 B3
Alsfeld Germany 53 J4
Alsleben (Saale) Germany 53 L3
Alston U.K. 48 E4
Alstonville Australia 112 F2
Alsunga Latvia 45 L8
Alta Norway 44 M2
Alta, Mount N.Z. 113 B7
Altaelva r. Norway 44 M2
Altafjorden sea chan. Norway 44 M1
Alta Floresta Brazil 143 G6
Altai Mountains Asia 72 F3
Altamaha r. U.S.A. 133 D6
Altamira Brazil 143 H4
Altamura Italy 58 G4
Altan Shiret China 73 J5
Altan Xiret China see Altan Shiret
Alta Paraíso de Goiás Brazil 145 B1
Altar r. Mex. 127 F7
Altar, Desierto de des. Mex. 125 F6
Altavista U.S.A. 134 F5
Altay China 80 G2
Altay Mongolia 80 I2
Altayskiy Rus. Fed. 80 G1
Altayskiy Khrebet mts Asia see
Altai Mountains
Altdorf Switz. 56 I3
Altea Spain 57 F4
Alteidet Norway 44 M1
Altenahr Germany 52 G4
Altenberge Germany 53 H2
Altenburg Germany 53 M4
Altenkirchen (Westerwald) Germany
53 H4
Altenqoke China 83 H1
Altin Köprü Iraq 91 G4
Altınoluk Turkey 59 L5
Altınözü Turkey 85 C1
Altıntaş Turkey 59 N5
Altiplano plain Bol. 142 E7
Altmark reg. Germany 53 L2
Altmühl r. Germany 53 L6
Alto, Monte hill Italy 58 D2
Alto Chicapa Angola 99 B5
Alto del Moncayo mt. Spain 57 F3
Alto de Pencoso hills Arg. 144 C4
Alto Garças Brazil 143 H7
Alto Madidi, Parque Nacional nat. park
Bol. 142 E6
Alton CA U.S.A. 128 A1
Alton IL U.S.A. 130 F4
Alton MO U.S.A. 131 F4
Alton NH U.S.A. 135 J2
Altona Canada 120 F3
Altoona U.S.A. 135 F3
Alto Parnaíba Brazil 143 I5
Altötting Germany 47 N6
Altrincham U.K. 48 E5
Alt Schwerin Germany 53 M1
Altun Kübrī Iraq see Altin Köprü
Altun Shan mts China 80 G4
Alturas U.S.A. 126 C4
Altus U.S.A. 131 D5
Al Ubaylah Saudi Arabia 98 F1

Alucra Turkey 90 E2
Alūksne Latvia 45 O8
Alūm Iran 88 C3
Alum Bridge U.S.A. 134 E4
Al 'Uqaylah Libya 97 E1
Al 'Uqaylah Saudi Arabia see An Nabk
Al Uqṣur Egypt see Luxor
Alur India 84 C2
Al Urayq des. Saudi Arabia 90 E5
Al 'Urdun country Asia see Jordan
Alur Setar Malaysia see Alor Setar
'Ālūt Iran 88 B3
Aluva India see Alwaye
Al 'Uwayjā' well Saudi Arabia 88 C6
Al 'Uwaynāt Libya 86 B5
Al 'Uwayqīlah Saudi Arabia 91 F5
Al 'Uzayr Iraq 91 G5
Alva U.S.A. 131 D4
Alvand, Kūh-e mt. Iran 88 C3
Alvarães Brazil 142 F4
Alvaton U.S.A. 134 B5
Alvdal Norway 44 G5
Älvdalen Sweden 45 I6
Alvesta Sweden 45 I8
Ålvik Norway 45 E6
Alvik Sweden 44 J5
Alvin U.S.A. 131 E6
Alvinópolis Brazil 145 C3
Alvito Port. 57 C4
Älvsbyn Sweden 44 L4
Al Wafrah Kuwait 88 B4
Al Wajh Saudi Arabia 86 E4
Al Wakrah Qatar 88 C5
Alwar India 82 D4
Al Wari'ah Saudi Arabia 86 G4
Al Wāṭiyah well Saudi Arabia 90 B5
Alwaye India 84 C4
Al Widyān plat. Iraq/Saudi Arabia 91 F4
Al Wusayṭ well Saudi Arabia 88 B4
Alxa Youqi China see Ehen Hudag
Alxa Zuoqi China see Bayan Hot
Al Yamāmah Saudi Arabia 88 B5
Al Yaman country Asia see Yemen
Alyangula Australia 110 B2
Al Yāsāt i. U.A.E. 88 C5
Alyth U.K. 50 F4
Alytus Lith. 45 N9
Alzette r. Lux. 52 F5
Alzey Germany 53 I5
Amacayacu, Parque Nacional nat. park
Col. 142 D4
Amadeus, Lake salt flat Australia 109 E6
Amadjuak Lake Canada 119 K3
Amadora Port. 57 B4
Åmål Sweden 45 H7
Amakusa-nada b. Japan 75 C6
Amalia S. Africa 101 G4
Amaliada Greece 59 I6
Amalner India 82 C5
Amamapare Indon. 69 J7
Amambaí Brazil 144 E2
Amambaí, Serra de hills Brazil/Para.
144 E2
Amami-Ō-shima i. Japan 75 C7
Amami-shotō is Japan 75 C8
Amamula Dem. Rep. Congo 98 C4
Amanab P.N.G. 69 K7
Amangel'dy Kazakh. 80 C1
Amankeldi Kazakh. see Amangel'dy
Amantea Italy 58 G5
Amanzimtoti S. Africa 101 J6
Amapá Brazil 143 H3
Amarante Brazil 143 J5
Amarapura Myanmar 70 B2
Amareleja Port. 57 C4
Amargosa watercourse U.S.A. 128 E3
Amargosa Desert U.S.A. 128 E3
Amargosa Range mts U.S.A. 128 E3
Amargosa Valley U.S.A. 128 E3
Amarillo U.S.A. 131 C5
Amarillo, Cerro mt. Arg. 144 C4
Amarkantak India 83 E5
Amasia Turkey see Amasya
Amasine W. Sahara 96 B2
Amasra Turkey 90 D2
Amasya Turkey 90 D2
Amata Australia 109 E6
Amatulla India 83 H4
Amau P.N.G. 110 E1
Amay Belgium 52 F4
Amazar Rus. Fed. 74 A1
Amazar r. Rus. Fed. 74 A1
▶ Amazon r. S. America 142 F4
Longest river and largest drainage
basin in South America and 2nd
longest river in the world.
Also known as Amazonas or Solimões.
South America 138–139
World 12–13
Amazon, Mouths of the Brazil 143 I3
Amazonas r. S. America 142 F4 see
Amazon
Amazon Cone sea feature
S. Atlantic Ocean 148 E5
Amazónia, Parque Nacional nat. park
Brazil 143 G4
Ambajogai India 84 C2
Ambala India 82 D3
Ambalangoda Sri Lanka 84 D5
Ambalavao Madag. 99 E6
Ambam Cameroon 98 B3
Ambar Iran 88 E4
Ambarchik Rus. Fed. 65 R3
Ambarnyy Rus. Fed. 44 R4
Ambasa India see Ambassa
Ambasamudram India 84 C4
Ambato Ecuador 142 C4
Ambato Boeny Madag. 99 E5
Ambato Finandrahana Madag. 99 E6
Ambatolampy Madag. 99 E5
Ambatomainty Madag. 99 E5
Ambatondrazaka Madag. 99 E5
Ambejogai India see Ambajogai
Ambeno enclave East Timor see Ocussi
Amberg Germany 53 L5
Ambergris Cay i. Belize 136 G5

Ambérieu-en-Bugey France 56 G4
Amberley Canada 134 E1
Ambgaon India 84 D1
Ambianum France see Amiens
Ambikapur India 83 E5
Ambilobe Madag. 99 E5
Ambition, Mount Canada 120 D3
Amble U.K. 48 F3
Ambler U.S.A. 118 C3
Ambleside U.K. 48 E4
Amblève r. Belgium 52 F4
Ambo India 83 F5
Amboasary Madag. 99 E6
Ambodifotatra Madag. 99 E5
Ambohimahasoa Madag. 99 E6
Ambohitra mt. Madag. 99 E5
Amboina Indon. see Ambon
Ambon Indon. 69 H7
Ambon i. Indon. 69 H7
Amboró, Parque Nacional nat. park Bol.
142 F7
Ambositra Madag. 99 E6
Ambovombe Madag. 99 E6
Amboy U.S.A. 129 F4
Ambre, Cap d' c. Madag. see
Bobaomby, Tanjona
Ambrim i. Vanuatu see Ambrym
Ambriz Angola 99 B4
Ambrizete Angola see N'zeto
Ambrosia Lake U.S.A. 129 J4
Ambrym i. Vanuatu 107 G3
Ambunti P.N.G. 69 K7
Ambur India 84 C3
Am-Dam Chad 97 F3
Amded, Oued watercourse Alg. 96 C3
Amdo China 83 G2
Ameland i. Neth. 52 F1
Amelia Court House U.S.A. 135 G5
Amenia U.S.A. 135 I3
Amer, Erg d' des. Alg. 98 A1
Amereli India see Amreli
Americana Brazil 145 B3
American, North Fork r. U.S.A. 128 C2
American-Antarctic Ridge sea feature
S. Atlantic Ocean 148 G9
American Falls U.S.A. 126 E4
American Falls Reservoir U.S.A. 126 E4
American Fork U.S.A. 129 H1
▶ American Samoa terr. S. Pacific Ocean
107 J3
United States Unincorporated Territory.
Oceania 8, 104–105
Americus U.S.A. 133 C5
Amersfoort Neth. 52 F2
Amersfoort S. Africa 101 I4
Amersham U.K. 49 G7
Amery Canada 121 M3
Amery Ice Shelf Antarctica 152 E2
Ames U.S.A. 130 E3
Amesbury U.K. 49 F7
Amesbury U.S.A. 135 J2
Amet India 82 C4
Amethi India 83 E4
Amfissa Greece 59 J5
Amga r. Rus. Fed. 65 O3
Amgalang China 73 L3
Amgu Rus. Fed. 74 E3
Amguid Alg. 96 D2
Amgun' r. Rus. Fed. 74 E1
Amherst Myanmar see Kyaikkami
Amherst MA U.S.A. 135 I2
Amherst OH U.S.A. 134 D3
Amherst VA U.S.A. 134 F5
Amherstburg Canada 134 D2
Amherst Island Canada 135 G1
Amiata, Monte mt. Italy 58 D3
Amida Turkey see Diyarbakır
Amidon U.S.A. 130 C2
Amiens France 52 C5
'Āmij, Wādī watercourse Iraq 91 F4
Amīk Ovası marsh Turkey 85 C1
'Amīnābād Iran 88 D4
Amindivi atoll India see Amini
Amindivi Islands India 84 B4
Amini atoll India 84 B4
Amino Eth. 98 E3
Aminuis Namibia 100 D2
Amirābād Iran 88 B3
Amirante Islands Seychelles 149 L6
Amirante Trench sea feature Indian Ocean
149 L6
Amisk Lake Canada 121 K4
Amistad, Represa de resr Mex./U.S.A. see
Amistad Reservoir
Amistad Reservoir Mex./U.S.A. 131 C6
Amisus Turkey see Samsun
Amite U.S.A. 131 F6
Amity Point Australia 112 F1
Amla India 82 D5
Amlapura Indon. see Karangasem
Amlash Iran 88 C2
Amlekhganj Nepal 83 F4
Åmli Norway 45 F7
Amlia Island U.S.A. 118 A4
Amlwch U.K. 48 C5
▶ 'Ammān Jordan 85 B4
Capital of Jordan.
Ammanazar Turkm. 88 D2
Ammanford U.K. 49 D7
Ammānsaari Fin. 44 P4
'Ammār, Tall hill Syria 85 C3
Ammarnäs Sweden 44 J4
Ammaroo Australia 110 A4
Ammassalik Greenland 153 J2
Ammerland reg. Germany 53 H1
Ammern Germany 53 K3
Ammochostos Cyprus see Famagusta
Ammochostos Bay Cyprus 85 B2
Am Nābiyah Yemen 86 F7
Amne Machin Range mts China see
A'nyêmaqên Shan
Amnok-kang r. China/N. Korea see
Yalu Jiang
Amo Jiang r. China 76 D4
Amol Iran 88 D2
Amorbach Germany 53 J5
Amorgos i. Greece 59 K6

Amory U.S.A. 131 F5
Amos Canada 122 F4
Amourj Mauritania 96 C3
Amoy China see Xiamen
Ampani India 84 D2
Amparai Sri Lanka 84 D5
Amparo Brazil 145 B3
Ampasimanolotra Madag. 99 E5
Ampitheatre Australia 112 A6
Ampoa Indon. 69 G7
Amraoti India see Amravati
Amravati India 84 C1
Amrawad India 82 D5
Amreli India 82 B5
Amring India 83 H4
'Amrīt Syria 85 B2
Amritsar India 82 C3
Amroha India 82 D3
Amsden U.S.A. 134 D3
Åmsele Sweden 44 K4
Amstelveen Neth. 52 E2
▶ Amsterdam Neth. 52 E2
Official capital of the Netherlands.
Amsterdam S. Africa 101 J4
Amsterdam U.S.A. 135 H2
Amsterdam, Île i. Indian Ocean 149 N8
Amstetten Austria 47 O6
Am Timan Chad 97 F3
Amudar'ya r. Asia 89 F2
Amudaryo r. Asia see Amudar'ya
Amund Ringnes Island Canada 119 I2
Amundsen, Mount Antarctica 152 F2
Amundsen Abyssal Plain sea feature
Southern Ocean 152 J2
Amundsen Basin sea feature
Arctic Ocean 153 H1
Amundsen Bay Antarctica 152 D2
Amundsen Coast Antarctica 152 J1
Amundsen Glacier Antarctica 152 I1
Amundsen Gulf Canada 118 F2
Amundsen Ridges sea feature
Southern Ocean 152 J2
Amundsen-Scott research station
Antarctica 152 C1
Amundsen Sea Antarctica 152 K2
Amuntai Indon. 68 F7
Amur r. China 74 D1
also known as Heilong Jiang (China)
Amur r. Rus. Fed. 74 F1
'Amur, Wadi watercourse Sudan 86 D6
Amur Oblast admin. div. Rus. Fed. see
Amurskaya Oblast'
Amursk Rus. Fed. 74 E2
Amurskaya Oblast' admin. div. Rus. Fed.
74 C1
Amurskiy liman strait Rus. Fed. 74 F1
Amurzet Rus. Fed. 74 C3
Amvrosiyivka Ukr. 43 H7
Amyderya r. Asia see Amudar'ya
Am-Zoer Chad 97 F3
An Myanmar 70 A3
Anaa atoll Fr. Polynesia 151 K7
Anabanua Indon. 69 G7
Anabar r. Rus. Fed. 65 M2
Anacapa Islands U.S.A. 128 D4
Anaconda U.S.A. 126 E3
Anacortes U.S.A. 126 C2
Anadarko U.S.A. 131 D5
Anadolu Dağları mts Turkey 90 E2
Anadyr' Rus. Fed. 65 S3
Anadyr, Gulf of Rus. Fed. see
Anadyrskiy Zaliv
Anadyrskiy Zaliv b. Rus. Fed. 65 T3
Anafi i. Greece 59 K6
Anagé Brazil 145 C1
'Ānah Iraq 91 F4
Anaheim U.S.A. 128 E5
Anahim Lake Canada 120 E4
Anahuac Mex. 131 C7
Anahuac U.S.A. 131 E6
Anaimalai Hills India 84 C4
Anaiteum i. Vanuatu see Anatom
Anajás Brazil 143 I4
Anakie Australia 110 D4
Analalava Madag. 99 E5
Anamā Brazil 142 F4
Anambas, Kepulauan is Indon. 71 D7
Anamosa U.S.A. 130 F3
Anamur Turkey 85 A1
Anan Japan 75 D6
Anand India 82 C5
Anandapur India 83 F5
Anantapur India 84 C3
Anantnag India 82 C2
Anant Peth India 82 D4
Anantpur India see Anantapur
Ananyiv Ukr. see Anan'yiv
Anan'yiv Ukr. 43 F7
Anapa Rus. Fed. 90 E1
Anápolis Brazil 145 A2
Anár Fin. see Inari
Anār Iran 88 D4
Anardara Afgh. 89 F3
Anatahan i. N. Mariana Is 69 L3
Anatajan i. N. Mariana Is see Anatahan
Anatolia reg. Turkey 90 D3
Anatom i. Vanuatu 107 G4
Anaypazari Turkey see Gülnar
An Biên Vietnam 71 D5
Anbür-e Kalārī Iran 88 D5
Anbyon N. Korea 75 B5
Ancenis France 56 D3
Anchorage U.S.A. 118 D3
Anchorage Island atoll Cook Is see
Suwarrow
Anchor Bay U.S.A. 134 D2
Anchuthengu India see Anjengo
Anci China 77 G1
Anci, Salto waterfall Venez. see
Angel Falls
Ancona Italy 58 E3
Ancud Chile 144 B6
Ancud, Golfo de g. Chile 144 B6
Ancyra Turkey see Ankara
Anda Heilong. China see Daqing
Anda Heilong. China 74 B3
Andacollo Chile 144 B4

Andado Australia 110 A5
Andahuaylas Peru 142 D6
Andal India 83 F5
Åndalsnes Norway 44 E5
Andalucía aut. comm. Spain 57 D5
Andalusia aut. comm. Spain see Andalucía
Andalusia U.S.A. 133 C6
Andaman Basin sea feature Indian Ocean
149 O5
Andaman Islands India 71 A4
Andaman Sea Indian Ocean 71 A5
Andaman Strait India 71 A4
Andamooka Australia 111 B6
Andapa Madag. 99 E5
Andarāb reg. Afgh. 89 H3
Ande China 76 E4
Andegavum France see Angers
Andelle r. France 52 B5
Andenes Norway 44 J2
Andenne Belgium 52 F4
Andéramboukane Mali 96 D3
Anderlecht Belgium 52 E4
Andermatt Switz. 56 I3
Andernos-les-Bains France 56 D4
Anderson r. Canada 118 F3
Anderson AK U.S.A. 118 D3
Anderson IN U.S.A. 134 C3
Anderson SC U.S.A. 133 D5
Anderson TX U.S.A. 131 E6
Anderson Bay Australia 111 [inset]
Anderson Lake Canada 120 F5
Andes mts S. America 144 C4
Andfjorden sea chan. Norway 40 J2
Andhíparos i. Greece see Antiparos
Andikíthira i. Greece see Antikythira
Andilamena Madag. 99 E5
Andilanatoby Madag. 99 E5
Andīmeshk Iran 88 C3
Andímilos i. Greece see Antimilos
Andipsara i. Greece see Antipsara
Andırın Turkey 90 E3
Andirlangar China 83 I1
Andizhan Uzbek. 80 D3
Andkhoy Afgh. 89 G2
Andoany Madag. 99 E5
Andoas Peru 142 C4
Andogskaya Gryada hills Rus. Fed. 42 H4
Andol India 84 C2
Andong China see Dandong
Andong S. Korea 75 C5
Andongwei China 77 H1
Andoom Australia 110 C2
▶ Andorra country Europe 57 G2
Europe 5, 38–39
▶ Andorra la Vella Andorra 57 G2
Capital of Andorra.
Andorra la Vieja Andorra see
Andorra la Vella
Andover U.K. 49 F7
Andover NY U.S.A. 135 G2
Andover OH U.S.A. 134 E3
Andøya i. Norway 44 I2
Andrade U.S.A. 129 F5
Andradina Brazil 145 A3
Andranomavo Madag. 99 E5
Andranopasy Madag. 99 E6
Andreanof Islands U.S.A. 150 I2
Andreapol' Rus. Fed. 42 G4
Andreas Isle of Man 48 C4
André Félix, Parc National de nat. park
Cent. Afr. Rep. 98 C3
Andrelândia Brazil 145 B3
Andrew Canada 121 H4
Andrew Bay Myanmar 70 A3
Andrews SC U.S.A. 133 E5
Andrews TX U.S.A. 131 C5
Andreyevka Kazakh. 80 F2
Andria Italy 58 G4
Androka Madag. 99 E6
Andropov Rus. Fed. see Rybinsk
Andros i. Bahamas 133 E7
Andros i. Greece 59 K6
Andros Town Bahamas 133 E7
Andrott i. India 84 B4
Androscoggin r. U.S.A. 135 K2
Andselv Norway 44 K2
Andújar Spain 57 D4
Andulo Angola 99 B5
Anec, Lake salt flat Australia 105 E5
Anéfis Mali 96 D3
Anegada, Bahía b. Arg. 144 D6
Anegada Passage Virgin Is (U.K.) 137 L5
Aného Togo 96 D4
Aneityum i. Vanuatu see Anatom
Anemourion tourist site Turkey 85 A1
Anepmete P.N.G. 69 L8
Anet France 52 B6
Anetchom, Île i. Vanuatu see Anatom
Aneto mt. Spain 57 G2
Ānewetak atoll Marshall Is see Enewetak
Aney Niger 96 E3
Aneytioum, Île i. Vanuatu see Anatom
Anfu China 77 G3
▶ Angara r. Rus. Fed. 72 G1
Part of the Yenisey-Angara-Selenga,
3rd longest river in Asia.
Angarsk Rus. Fed. 72 I2
Angas Downs Australia 109 F6
Angatuba Brazil 145 A3
Angaur i. Palau 69 I5
Ånge Sweden 44 I5
Angel, Salto waterfall Venez. see
Angel Falls
Ángel de la Guarda, Isla i. Mex. 127 E7
▶ Angel Falls waterfall Venez. 142 F2
Highest waterfall in the world.
Ängelholm Sweden 45 H8

Angellala Creek r. Australia 112 C1
Angels Camp U.S.A. 128 C2
Ångermanälven r. Sweden 44 J5
Angers France 56 D3
Angikuni Lake Canada 121 L2
Angiola U.S.A. 128 C4
Angkor tourist site Cambodia 71 C4
Anglesea Australia 112 B7
Anglesey i. U.K. 48 C5
Angleton U.S.A. 131 E6
Anglo-Egyptian Sudan country Africa see
Sudan
Angmagssalik Greenland see Ammassalik
Ang Mo Kio Sing. 71 [inset]
Ango Dem. Rep. Congo 98 C3
Angoche Moz. 99 E5
Angohrän Iran 88 E5
Angol Chile 144 B5
▶ Angola country Africa 99 B5
Africa 7, 94–95
Angola IN U.S.A. 134 C3
Angola NY U.S.A. 134 F2
Angola Basin sea feature
S. Atlantic Ocean 148 H7
Angora Turkey see Ankara
Angostura Mex. 127 F8
Angoulême France 56 E4
Angra dos Reis Brazil 145 B3
Angren Uzbek. 80 D3
Ang Thong Thai. 71 C4
Anguang China 74 A3
▶ Anguilla terr. West Indies 137 L5
United Kingdom Overseas Territory.
North America 9, 116–117
Anguilla Cays is Bahamas 133 E8
Anguille, Cape Canada 123 K5
Angul India 84 E1
Angus Canada 134 F1
Angutia Char i. Bangl. 83 G5
Anholt i. Denmark 45 G8
Anhua China 77 F2
Anhumas Brazil 143 H7
Anhwei prov. China see Anhui
Aniak U.S.A. 118 C3
Aniakchak National Monument and
Preserve nat. park U.S.A. 118 C4
Anin Myanmar 70 B4
Anitápolis Brazil 145 A4
Anıtlı Turkey 85 A1
Aniva Rus. Fed. 74 F3
Aniva, Mys c. Rus. Fed. 74 F3
Aniva, Zaliv b. Rus. Fed. 74 F3
Anizy-le-Château France 52 D5
Anjadip i. India 84 B3
Anjalankoski Fin. 45 O6
Anjar India 82 B5
Anjengo India 84 C4
Anji China 77 G2
Anjir Avand Iran 88 D3
Anjoman Iran 88 E3
Anjou reg. France 56 D3
Anjouan i. Comoros see Nzwani
Anjozorobe Madag. 99 E5
Anjuman reg. Afgh. 89 H3
Anjuthengu India see Anjengo
Ankang China 77 F1
▶ Ankara Turkey 90 D3
Capital of Turkey.
Ankaratra mt. Madag. 99 E5
Ankazoabo Madag. 99 E6
Ankeny U.S.A. 130 E3
An Khê Vietnam 71 E4
Ankleshwar India 82 C5
Anklesvar India see Ankleshwar
Ankola India 84 B3
Ankouzhen China 76 E3
Anlong China 76 E3
Anlu China 77 G2
Anmoore U.S.A. 134 E4
An Muileann gCearr Rep. of Ireland see
Mullingar
Anmyŏn-do i. S. Korea 75 B5
Ann, Cape Antarctica 152 D2
Ann, Cape U.S.A. 135 J2
Anna Rus. Fed. 43 I6
Anna, Lake U.S.A. 135 G4
Annaba Alg. 58 B6
Annaberg-Buchholtz Germany 53 N4
An Nabk Saudi Arabia 85 C4
An Nabk Syria 85 C2
An Nafūd des. Saudi Arabia 91 F5
An Najaf Iraq 91 G5
Annalee r. Rep. of Ireland 51 E3
Annalong U.K. 51 G3
Annam reg. Vietnam 68 D3
Annam Highlands mts Laos/Vietnam
70 D3
Annan U.K. 50 F6
Annan r. U.K. 50 F6
'Annān, Wādī al watercourse Syria 85 D2
Annandale U.S.A. 135 G4
Anna Plains Australia 108 C4
▶ Annapolis U.S.A. 135 G4
State capital of Maryland.
Annapurna Conservation Area nature res.
Nepal 83 F3
Annapurna I mt. Nepal 83 E3
Ann Arbor U.S.A. 134 D2
Anna Regina Guyana 143 G2
An Nás Rep. of Ireland see Naas
An Nāşirīyah Iraq 91 G5
An Naşrānī, Jabal mts Syria   81 C3
Annean, Lake salt flat Australia 109 B6
Anne Arundel Town U.S.A. see Annapolis
Annecy France 56 H4
Anne Marie Lake Canada 123 J3
Annen Neth. 52 G1
Annette Island U.S.A. 120 D4
An Nimārah Syria 85 C3
An Nimāş Saudi Arabia 86 F6
Anning China 76 D3
Anniston U.S.A. 133 C5
Annobón i. Equat. Guinea 96 D5
Annonay France 56 G4
An Nu'mānīyah Iraq 91 G4

Asheboro U.S.A. 132 E5
Asher U.S.A. 131 D5
Ashern Canada 121 L5
Asheville U.S.A. 132 D5
Asheweig r. Canada 122 D3
Ashford Australia 112 E2
Ashford U.K. 49 H7
Ash Fork U.S.A. 129 G4

▶Ashgabat Turkm. 88 E2
Capital of Turkmenistan.

Ashibetsu Japan 74 F4
Ashikaga Japan 75 E5
Ashington U.K. 48 F3
Ashizuri-misaki pt Japan 75 D6
Ashkelon Israel see Ashqelon
Ashkhabad Turkm. see Ashgabat
Ashkum U.S.A. 134 B3
Ashkun reg. Afgh. 89 H3
Ashland AL U.S.A. 133 C5
Ashland ME U.S.A. 132 G2
Ashland NH U.S.A. 135 J2
Ashland OH U.S.A. 134 D3
Ashland OR U.S.A. 126 C4
Ashland VA U.S.A. 135 G5
Ashland WI U.S.A. 130 F2
Ashland City U.S.A. 134 B5
Ashley Australia 112 D2
Ashley MI U.S.A. 134 C2
Ashley ND U.S.A. 130 D2

▶Ashmore and Cartier Islands terr. Australia 108 C3
Australian External Territory.

Ashmore Reef Australia 108 C3
Ashmore Reefs Australia 110 D1
Ashmyany Belarus 45 N9
Ashqelon Israel 85 B4
Ash Shabakah Iraq 91 F5
Ash Shaddādah Syria 91 F3
Ash Shallūfah Egypt 85 A4
Ash Sham Syria see Damascus
Ash Shanāfiyah Iraq 91 G5
Ash Shaqīq well Saudi Arabia 91 F5
Ash Sharawrah Saudi Arabia 86 G6
Ash Shāriqah U.A.E. see Sharjah
Ash Sharqāţ Iraq 91 F4
Ash Shaţrah Iraq 91 G5
Ash Shaţţ Egypt 85 A5
Ash Shawbak Jordan 85 B4
Ash Shaybānī well Saudi Arabia 91 F5
Ash Shaykh Ibrāhīm Syria 85 D2
Ash Shiblīyāt hill Saudi Arabia 85 C5
Ash Shiḥr Yemen 86 G7
Ash Shu'āybah Saudi Arabia 91 F6
Ash Shu'bah Saudi Arabia 86 F4
Ash Shurayf Saudi Arabia see Khaybar
Ashta India 82 D5
Ashtabula U.S.A. 134 E3
Ashtarak Armenia 91 G2
Ashti Maharashtra India 82 D5
Ashti Maharashtra India 84 B2
Ashti Maharashtra India 84 C2
Ashtīān Iran 88 C3
Ashton S. Africa 100 E7
Ashton U.S.A. 126 F3
Ashton-under-Lyne U.K. 48 E5
Ashuanipi r. Canada 123 I3
Ashuanipi Lake Canada 123 I3
Ashur Iraq see Ash Sharqāţ
Ashville U.S.A. 133 C5
Ashwaubenon U.S.A. 134 A1
Asi r. Asia 90 E3 see 'Āşī, Nahr al
'Āşī r. Lebanon/Syria see Orontes
'Āşī, Nahr al r. Asia 90 E3
also known as Asi or Orontes
Āsīā Bak Iran 88 C3
Asifabad India 84 C2
Asika India 84 E2
Asilah Morocco 57 C6
Asinara, Golfo dell' b. Sardinia Italy 58 C4
Asino Rus. Fed. 64 J4
Asipovichy Belarus 43 F5
Asīr Iran 88 D5
'Asīr reg. Saudi Arabia 86 F5
Asisium Italy see Assisi
Askale Jammu and Kashmir 82 C2
Aşkale Turkey 91 F3
Asker Norway 45 G7
Askersund Sweden 45 I7
Askim Norway 45 G7
Askino Rus. Fed. 41 R4
Askival hill U.K. 50 C4
Asl Egypt see 'Asal
Aslanköy r. Turkey 85 B1
Asmar reg. Afgh. 89 H3

▶Asmara Eritrea 86 E6
Capital of Eritrea.

Āsmera Eritrea see Asmara
Åsnen l. Sweden 45 I8
Aso-Kuju National Park Japan 75 C6
Asonli India 76 B2
Asop India 82 C4
Asori Indon. 69 J7
Āsosa Eth. 98 D2
Asotin U.S.A. 126 D3
Aspang-Markt Austria 47 P7
Aspatria U.K. 48 D4
Aspen U.S.A. 126 G5
Asperg Germany 53 J6
Aspermont U.S.A. 131 C5
Aspiring, Mount N.Z. 113 B7
Aspro, Cape Cyprus 85 A2
Aspromonte, Parco Nazionale dell' nat. park Italy 58 F5
Aspron, Cape Cyprus see Aspro, Cape
Aspur India 89 I6
Asquith Canada 121 J4
As Sa'an Syria 85 C2
Assab Eritrea 86 F7
As Sabsab well Saudi Arabia 88 C5
Assad, Lake resr Syria see Asad, Buḩayrat al
Aş Şadr U.A.E. 88 D5
Aş Şafā lava field Syria 85 C3
Aş Şafāqis Tunisia see Sfax
Aş Şaff Egypt 90 C5
As Safīrah Syria 85 C1
Aş Şaḩrā' al Gharbīyah des. Egypt see Western Desert
Aş Şaḩrā' ash Sharqīyah des. Egypt see Eastern Desert
Assake-Audan, Vpadina depr. Kazakh./Uzbek. 91 J2
'Assal, Lac l. Djibouti see Assal, Lake

▶Assal, Lake Djibouti 86 F7
Lowest point in Africa.
Africa 92–93

Aş Şālihīyah Syria 91 F4
As Sallūm Egypt 90 B5
As Salmān Iraq 91 G5
As Salţ Jordan 85 B3
Assam state India 83 G4
Assamakka Niger 96 D3
As Samāwah Iraq 91 G5
As Samrā' Jordan 85 C3
Aş Şanām reg. Saudi Arabia 86 H5
As Sarīr reg. Libya 97 F2
Assateague Island U.S.A. 135 H4
As Sawādah reg. Saudi Arabia 88 B6
Assayeta Eth. see Āsayita
As Sayḩ Saudi Arabia 88 B6
Assen Neth. 52 G1
Assenede Belgium 52 D3
Assesse Belgium 52 F4
As Sidrah Libya 97 E1
As Sīfah Oman 88 E6
Assigny, Lac l. Canada 123 I3
As Sikak Saudi Arabia 88 C5
Assiniboia Canada 121 J5
Assiniboine r. Canada 121 L5
Assiniboine, Mount Canada 118 G4
Assis Brazil 145 A3
Assisi Italy 58 E3
Aßlar Germany 53 I4
Aş Şubayḩīyah Kuwait 88 B4
Aş Şufayrī well Saudi Arabia 88 B4
As Sukhnah Syria 85 D2
As Sulaymānīyah Iraq 91 G4
As Sulaymī Saudi Arabia 86 F4
Aş Şulb reg. Saudi Arabia 88 C5
Aş Şummān plat. Saudi Arabia 88 B5
Aş Şummān plat. Saudi Arabia 88 C6
As Sūq Saudi Arabia 86 F5
As Sūrīyah country Asia see Syria
Aş Şuwar Syria 91 F4
As Suwaydā' Syria 85 C3
As Suways Egypt see Suez
As Suways governorate Egypt 81 A4
Assynt, Loch l. U.K. 50 D2
Astakida i. Greece 59 L7
Astakos Greece 59 I5
Astalu Island Pak. see Astola Island

▶Astana Kazakh. 80 D1
Capital of Kazakhstan.

Astaneh Iran 88 C2
Astara Azer. 91 H3
Āstārā Iran 86 G2
Asterabad Iran see Gorgān
Asti Italy 58 C2
Astillero Peru 142 E6
Astin Tag mts China see Altun Shan
Astipálaia i. Greece see Astypalaia
Astola Island Pak. 89 F5
Astor r. Pak. 89 I3
Astorga Spain 57 C2
Astoria U.S.A. 126 C3
Åstorp Sweden 45 H8
Astrabad Iran see Gorgān
Astrakhan' Rus. Fed. 43 K7
Astrakhan' Bazar Azer. see Cälilabad
Astravyets Belarus 45 N9
Astrida Rwanda see Butare
Asturias aut. comm. Spain 57 C2
Asturias, Principado de aut. comm. Spain see Asturias
Asturica Augusta Spain see Astorga
Astypalaia i. Greece 59 L6
Asuncion i. N. Mariana Is 69 L3

▶Asunción Para. 144 E3
Capital of Paraguay.

Aswad Oman 88 E5
Aswān Egypt see Aswān
Aswān Egypt 86 D5
Asyūţ Egypt see Asyūţ
Asyūţ Egypt 90 C6
Ata i. Tonga 107 I4
Atacama, Desierto de des. Chile see Atacama Desert
Atacama, Salar de salt flat Chile 144 C2

▶Atacama Desert Chile 144 C3
Driest place in the world.

Atafu atoll Tokelau 107 I2
Atafu i. Tokelau 150 I6
'Aţā'iţah, Jabal al mt. Jordan 85 B4
Atakent Turkey 85 B1
Atakpamé Togo 96 D4
Atalándi Greece see Atalanti
Atalanti Greece 59 J5
Atalaya Peru 142 D6
Ataléia Brazil 145 C2
Atambua Indon. 108 D2
Ataniya Turkey see Adana
'Ataq Yemen 86 G7
Atâr Mauritania 96 B2
Atari Pak. 89 I4
Atascadero U.S.A. 128 C4
Atasu Kazakh. 80 D2
Ataúro, Ilha de i. East Timor 108 D2
Atáviros mt. Greece see Attavyros
Atayurt Turkey 85 A1
Atbara Sudan 86 D6
Atbara r. Sudan 86 D6
Atbasar Kazakh. 80 C1
Atchison U.S.A. 130 E4
Atebubu Ghana 96 C4
Ateransk Kazakh. see Atyrau
Āteshān Iran 88 D3
Āteshkhāneh, Kūh-e hill Afgh. 89 F3
Atessa Italy 58 F3
Ath Belgium 52 D4
Athabasca r. Canada 121 I3
Athabasca, Lake Canada 121 I3
Athalia U.S.A. 134 D4
'Athāmīn, Birkat al well Iraq 88 A4
Atharan Hazari Pak. 89 I4
Athboy Rep. of Ireland 51 F4
Athenae Greece see Athens
Athenry Rep. of Ireland 51 D4
Athens Canada 135 H1

▶Athens Greece 59 J6
Capital of Greece.

Athens AL U.S.A. 133 C5
Athens GA U.S.A. 133 D5
Athens MI U.S.A. 134 C2
Athens OH U.S.A. 134 D4
Athens PA U.S.A. 135 G3
Athens TN U.S.A. 132 C5
Athens TX U.S.A. 131 E5
Atherstone U.K. 49 F6
Atherton Australia 110 D3
Athies France 52 C5
Athina Greece see Athens
Athínai Greece see Athens
Athleague Rep. of Ireland 51 D4
Athlone Rep. of Ireland 51 E4
Athnā', Wādī al watercourse Jordan 85 D3
Athni India 84 B2
Athol N.Z. 113 B7
Athol U.S.A. 135 I2
Atholl, Forest of reg. U.K. 50 E4
Athos mt. Greece 59 K4
Ath Thamad Egypt 85 B5
Ath Thāyat mt. Saudi Arabia 85 C5
Ath Thumāmī well Saudi Arabia 88 B5
Athy Rep. of Ireland 51 F5
Ati Chad 97 E3
Aţīābād Iran 88 E3
Atico Peru 142 D7
Atikameg Canada 120 H4
Atikameg r. Canada 122 E3
Atik Lake Canada 121 M4
Atikokan Canada 119 I5
Atikonak Lake Canada 123 I3
Atka Rus. Fed. 65 Q3
Atka Island U.S.A. 118 A4
Atkarsk Rus. Fed. 43 J6
Atkri Indon. 69 I7

▶Atlanta GA U.S.A. 133 C5
State capital of Georgia.

Atlanta IN U.S.A. 134 B3
Atlanta MI U.S.A. 134 C1
Atlantic IA U.S.A. 130 E3
Atlantic NC U.S.A. 133 E5
Atlantic City U.S.A. 135 H4
Atlantic-Indian-Antarctic Basin sea feature S. Atlantic Ocean 148 H10
Atlantic-Indian Ridge sea feature Southern Ocean 148 H9

▶Atlantic Ocean 148
2nd largest ocean in the world.

Atlantic Peak U.S.A. 126 F4
Atlantis S. Africa 100 D7
Atlas Méditerranéen mts Alg. see Atlas Tellien
Atlas Mountains Africa 54 C5
Atlas Saharien mts Alg. 54 E5
Atlas Tellien mts Alg. 57 H6
Atlin Lake Canada 120 C3
Atmakur India 84 C3
Atmore U.S.A. 133 C6
Atnur India 84 C2
Atocha Bol. 142 E8
Atoka U.S.A. 131 D5
Atouat mt. Laos 70 D3
Atouila, Erg des. Mali 96 C2
Atqan China see Aqqan
Atrak r. Iran/Turkm. see Atrek
Atrak, Rūd-e r. Iran/Turkm. 88 D2
Atrato r. Col. 142 C2
Atrek r. Iran/Turkm. 88 D2
also known as Atrak, alt. Etrek
Atropatene country Asia see Azerbaijan
Atsonupuri vol. Rus. Fed. 74 G3
Aţ Ţafīlah Jordan 85 B4
Aţ Ţā'if Saudi Arabia 86 F5
Attalea Turkey see Antalya
Attalia Turkey see Antalya
At Tamīmī Libya 90 A4
Attapu Laos 70 D4
Attavyros mt. Greece 59 L6
Attawapiskat Canada 122 E3
Attawapiskat r. Canada 122 E3
Attawapiskat Lake Canada 122 D3
Aţ Ţawīl mts Saudi Arabia 91 E5
At Taysīyah plat. Saudi Arabia 91 F5
Attendorn Germany 53 H3
Attersee l. Austria 47 N7
Attica IN U.S.A. 134 B3
Attica NY U.S.A. 135 F2
Attica OH U.S.A. 134 D3
Attigny France 52 E5
Attikamagen Lake Canada 123 I3
Attila Line Cyprus 85 A2
Attleborough U.K. 49 I6
Attopeu Laos see Attapu
Attu Greenland 119 M3
Aţ Ţubayq reg. Saudi Arabia 85 C5

▶Attu Island U.S.A. 65 S4
Most westerly point of North America.

At Tūnisīyah country Africa see Tunisia
Aţ Ţūr Egypt 90 D5
Attur India 84 C4
Aţ Ţuwayyah well Saudi Arabia 91 F6
Atuk Mountain hill U.S.A. 118 A3
Åtvidaberg Sweden 45 I7
Atwater U.S.A. 128 C3
Atwood U.S.A. 130 C4
Atwood Lake U.S.A. 134 E3
Atyashevo Rus. Fed. 43 J5
Atyrau Kazakh. 78 E2
Atyraū admin. div. Kazakh. see Atyrauskaya Oblast'
Atyrau Oblast admin. div. Kazakh. see Atyrauskaya Oblast'
Atyrauskaya Oblast' admin. div. Kazakh. 41 Q6
Aua Island P.N.G. 69 K7
Aub Germany 53 K5
Aubagne France 56 G5
Aubange Belgium 52 F5
Aubenas France 56 G4
Aubergenville France 52 B6
Auboué France 52 F5
Aubrey Cliffs mts U.S.A. 129 G4
Aubry Lake Canada 118 F3
Auburn r. Australia 111 E5
Auburn Canada 134 E2
Auburn AL U.S.A. 133 C5
Auburn CA U.S.A. 128 C2
Auburn IN U.S.A. 134 C3
Auburn KY U.S.A. 134 B5
Auburn ME U.S.A. 135 J1
Auburn NE U.S.A. 130 E3
Auburn NY U.S.A. 135 G2
Auburn Range hills Australia 110 E5
Aubusson France 56 F4
Auch France 56 E5
Auche Myanmar 70 B1
Auchterarder U.K. 50 F4

▶Auckland N.Z. 113 E3
5th most populous city in Oceania.

Auckland Islands N.Z. 107 G7
Auden Canada 122 D4
Audenarde Belgium see Oudenaarde
Audo mts Eth. 98 E3
Audo Range mts Eth. see Audo
Audruicq France 52 C4
Audubon U.S.A. 130 E3
Aue Germany 53 M4
Auerbach Germany 53 M4
Auerbach in der Oberpfalz Germany 53 L5
Auersberg mt. Germany 53 M4
Augathella Australia 111 D5
Augher U.K. 51 E3
Aughnacloy U.K. 51 F3
Aughrim Rep. of Ireland 51 F5
Augrabies S. Africa 100 E5
Augrabies Falls S. Africa 100 E5
Augrabies Falls National Park S. Africa 100 E5
Au Gres U.S.A. 134 D1
Augsburg Germany 47 M6
Augusta Australia 109 A8
Augusta Sicily Italy 58 F6
Augusta AR U.S.A. 131 F5
Augusta GA U.S.A. 133 D5
Augusta KY U.S.A. 134 C4

▶Augusta ME U.S.A. 135 K1
State capital of Maine.

Augusta MT U.S.A. 126 E3
Augusta Auscorum France see Auch
Augusta Taurinorum Italy see Turin
Augusta Treverorum Germany see Trier
Augusta Vindelicorum Germany see Augsburg
Augusto de Lima Brazil 145 B2
Augustus, Mount Australia 109 B6
Auke Bay U.S.A. 120 C3
Aukštaitijos nacionalinis parkas nat. park Lith. 45 O9
Aulavik National Park Canada 118 G2
Auld, Lake salt flat Australia 108 C5
Auliye Ata Kazakh. see Taraz
Aulnoye-Aymeries France 52 D4
Aulon Albania see Vlorë
Ault France 52 B4
Aumale Alg. see Sour el Ghozlane
Aumale France 52 B5
Aundh India 84 B2
Aundhi India 84 D1
Aunglan Myanmar see Myede
Auob watercourse Namibia/S. Africa 100 E4
Aupaluk Canada 123 H2
Aur i. Malaysia 71 D7
Aura Fin. 45 M6
Auraiya India 82 D4
Aurangabad Bihar India 83 F4
Aurangabad Maharashtra India 84 B2
Aure r. France 49 F9
Aurich Germany 53 H1
Aurigny i. Channel Is see Alderney
Aurilândia Brazil 145 A2
Aurillac France 56 F4
Aurora CO U.S.A. 126 G5
Aurora IL U.S.A. 134 A3
Aurora MO U.S.A. 131 E4
Aurora NE U.S.A. 130 D3
Aurora UT U.S.A. 129 H2
Aurora Island Vanuatu see Maéwo
Aurukun Australia 110 C2
Aus Namibia 100 C4
Au Sable U.S.A. 134 D1
Au Sable Point U.S.A. 134 D1
Auskerry i. U.K. 50 G1
Austin IN U.S.A. 134 C4
Austin MN U.S.A. 130 E3
Austin NV U.S.A. 128 E2

▶Austin TX U.S.A. 131 D6
State capital of Texas.

Austin, Lake salt flat Australia 109 B6
Austintown U.S.A. 134 E3
Austral Downs Australia 110 B4
Australes, Îles is Fr. Polynesia see Tubuai Islands

▶Australia country Oceania 106 C4
Largest country in Oceania. Most populous country in Oceania.
Oceania 8, 104–105

Australian - Antarctic Basin sea feature Southern Ocean 150 C9
Australian Antarctic Territory reg. Antarctica 152 G2
Australian Capital Territory admin. div. Australia 112 D5
▶Austria country Europe 47 N7
Europe 5, 38–39
Austvågøy i. Norway 44 I2
Autazes Brazil 143 G4
Autesiodorum France see Auxerre
Authie r. France 52 B4
Autti Fin. 44 O3
Auvergne reg. France 56 F4
Auvergne, Monts d' mts France 56 F4
Auxerre France 56 F3
Auxi-le-Château France 52 C4
Auxonne France 56 G3
Auyuittuq National Park Canada 119 L3
Auzangate, Nevado mt. Peru 142 D6
Ava MO U.S.A. 131 E4
Ava NY U.S.A. 135 H2
Avallon France 56 F3
Avalon U.S.A. 128 D5
Avalon Peninsula Canada 123 L5
Avān Iran 91 G3
Avarau atoll Cook Is see Palmerston
Avaré Brazil 145 A3
Avaricum France see Bourges

▶Avarua Cook Is 151 J7
Capital of the Cook Islands, on Rarotonga island.

Avawam U.S.A. 134 D5
Avaz Iran 89 F3
Aveiro Port. 57 B3
Aveiro, Ria de est. Port. 57 B3
Āvej Iran 88 C3
Avellino Italy 58 F4
Avenal U.S.A. 128 C3
Avenhorn Neth. 52 E2
Avenio France see Avignon
Aversa Italy 58 F4
Avesnes-sur-Helpe France 52 D4
Avesta Sweden 45 J6
Aveyron r. France 56 E4
Avezzano Italy 58 E3
Aviemore U.K. 50 F3
Avignon France 56 G5
Ávila Spain 57 D3
Avilés Spain 57 D2
Avion France 52 C4
Avis U.S.A. 135 G3
Avlama Dağı mt. Turkey 85 A1
Avlama Dağı mt. Turkey 85 A1
Avlona Albania see Vlorë
Avnyugskiy Rus. Fed. 42 J3
Avoca Australia 112 A6
Avoca r. Australia 112 A5
Avoca Rep. of Ireland 51 F5
Avoca IA U.S.A. 130 E3
Avoca NY U.S.A. 135 G2
Avola Sicily Italy 58 F6
Avon r. England U.K. 49 E6
Avon r. England U.K. 49 E7
Avon r. England U.K. 49 F8
Avon r. Scotland U.K. 50 F3
Avon U.S.A. 135 G2
Avondale U.S.A. 129 G5
Avonmore r. Rep. of Ireland 51 F5
Avonmore U.S.A. 134 F3
Avonmouth U.K. 49 E7
Avranches France 56 D2
Avre r. France 52 C5
Avsuyu Turkey 85 C1
Avuavu Solomon Is 107 G2
Avveel Fin. see Ivalo
Avvil Fin. see Ivalo
A'waj r. Syria 85 B3
Awakino N.Z. 113 E4
Awālī Bahrain 88 C5
Awanui N.Z. 113 D2
Āwarē Eth. 98 E3
'Awārid, Wādī al watercourse Syria 85 D2
Awarua Point N.Z. 113 B7
Āwash Eth. 98 E3
Āwash r. Eth. 98 E2
Awa-shima i. Japan 75 E5
Āwash National Park Eth. 98 D3
Awasib Mountains Namibia 100 B3
Awat China 80 F3
Awatere r. N.Z. 113 E5
Awbārī Libya 96 E2
Awbeg r. Rep. of Ireland 51 D5
'Awdah well Saudi Arabia 88 C6
'Awdah, Hawr al imp. l. Iraq 91 G5
Aw Dheegle Somalia 97 H4
Awe, Loch l. U.K. 50 D4
Aweil Sudan 97 F4
Awka Nigeria 96 D4
Awserd W. Sahara 96 B2
Axe r. England U.K. 49 D8
Axe r. England U.K. 49 E7
Axedale Australia 112 B6
Axel Heiberg Glacier Antarctica 152 I1
Axel Heiberg Island Canada 119 I2
Axim Ghana 96 C4
Axminster U.K. 49 E8
Axum Eth. see Āksum
Ay France 52 E5
Ayachi, Jbel mt. Morocco 54 D5
Ayacucho Arg. 144 E5
Ayacucho Peru 142 D6
Ayadaw Myanmar 70 A2
Ayagoz Kazakh. 80 F2
Ayaguz Kazakh. see Ayagoz
Ayakkum Hu salt l. China 83 G1
Ayaköz Kazakh. see Ayagoz
Ayan Rus. Fed. 65 O4
Ayancık Turkey 90 D2
Ayang N. Korea 75 B5
Ayaş Turkey 90 D2
Āybak Afgh. 89 H2
Aybas Kazakh. 43 K7
Aydar r. Ukr. 43 H6
Aydarkul', Ozero l. Uzbek. 80 C3
Aydın Turkey 59 L6
Aydıncık Turkey 85 A1
Aydın Dağları mts Turkey 59 L5
Āyelu Terara vol. Eth. 86 F7
Ayer U.S.A. 135 J2
Ayers Rock hill Australia see Uluru
Ayeyarwady r. Myanmar see Irrawaddy
Ayila Ri'gyü mts China 82 D2
Áyios Dhimítrios Greece see Agios Dimitrios
Áyios Evstrátios i. Greece see Agios Efstratios
Áyios Nikólaos Greece see Agios Nikolaos
Áyios Yeóryios i. Greece see Agios Georgios
Aylesbury N.Z. 113 D6
Aylesbury U.K. 49 G7
Aylett U.S.A. 135 G5
Ayllón Spain 57 E3
Aylmer Ont. Canada 134 E2
Aylmer Que. Canada 135 H1
Aylmer Lake Canada 121 I1
'Ayn al 'Abd well Saudi Arabia 84 C4
'Ayn al Baidā' Saudi Arabia 85 C4
'Ayn al Bayḑā' well Syria 85 C2
'Ayn al Ghazalah well Libya 90 A4
'Ayn al Maqfī spring Egypt 90 C6
'Ayn Dāllah spring Egypt 90 B6
Ayní Tajik. 89 H2
'Ayn 'Īsá Syria 85 D1
'Ayn Tabaghbugh spring Egypt 90 B5
'Ayn Tumayrah spring Egypt 90 B5
'Ayn Zaytūn Egypt 90 B5
Ayod Sudan 86 D8
Ayon, Ostrov i. Rus. Fed. 65 R3
'Ayoûn el 'Atroûs Mauritania 96 C3
Ayr Australia 110 D3
Ayr Canada 134 E2
Ayr U.K. 50 E5
Ayr r. U.K. 50 E5
Ayr, Point of U.K. 48 D5
Ayrancı Turkey 90 D3
Ayre, Point of Isle of Man 48 C4
Aytos Bulg. 59 L3
Ayuthia Thai. see Ayutthaya
Ayutthaya Thai. 71 C4
Ayvacık Turkey 59 L5
Ayvalı Turkey 90 E3
Ayvalık Turkey 59 L5
Azak Rus. Fed. see Azov
Azalia U.S.A. 134 C4
Azamgarh India 83 E4
Azaouâd reg. Mali 96 C3
Azaouagh, Vallée de watercourse Mali/Niger 96 D3
Azaran Iran see Hashtrud
Azärbaycan country Asia see Azerbaijan
Azärbayjan country Asia see Azerbaijan
Azare Nigeria 96 E3
A'zāz Syria 85 C1
Azbine mts Niger see L'Aïr, Massif de
Azdavay Turkey 90 D2
▶Azerbaijan country Asia 91 G2
Asia 6, 62–63
Azerbaydzhanskaya S.S.R. country Asia see Azerbaijan
Azhikal India 84 B4
Aziscohos Lake U.S.A. 135 J1
'Azīzābād Iran 88 E4
Aziziye Turkey see Pınarbaşı
Azogues Ecuador 142 C4

▶Azores terr. N. Atlantic Ocean 148 G3
Autonomous region of Portugal.
Europe 5, 38–39

Azores-Biscay Rise sea feature N. Atlantic Ocean 148 G3
Azotus Israel see Ashdod
Azov Rus. Fed. 43 H7
Azov, Sea of Rus. Fed./Ukr. 43 H7
Azovs'ke More sea Rus. Fed./Ukr. see Azov, Sea of
Azovskoye More sea Rus. Fed./Ukr. see Azov, Sea of
Azraq, Bahr el r. Sudan 86 D6 see Blue Nile
Azraq ash Shīshān Jordan 85 C4
Azrou Morocco 54 C5
Aztec U.S.A. 129 I3
Azuaga Spain 57 D4
Azuero, Península de pen. Panama 137 H7
Azul, Cordillera mts Peru 142 C5
Azuma-san vol. Japan 75 F5
'Azza Gaza see Gaza
Azzaba Alg. 58 B6
Aẓ Ẓahrān Saudi Arabia see Dhahran
Az Zaqāzīq Egypt 90 C5
Az Zarbah Syria 85 C1
Az Zarqā' Jordan 85 C3
Az Zawr, Ra's pt Saudi Arabia 91 H6
Azzeffâl hills Mauritania/W. Sahara 96 B2
Az Zubayr Iraq 91 G5
Az Zuqur i. Yemen 86 F7

B

Baa Indon. 108 C2
Baabda Lebanon 85 B3
Ba'albek Lebanon 85 C2
Ba'al Hazor mt. West Bank 85 B4
Baan Baa Australia 112 D3
Baardheere Somalia 98 E3
Bab India 82 D4
Bābā, Kūh-e mts Afgh. 89 H3
Baba Burnu pt Turkey 59 L5
Babadağ mt. Azer. 91 H2
Babadag Romania 59 M2
Babadaykhan Turkm. 89 F2
Babadurmaz Turkm. 88 E2
Babaeski Turkey 59 L4
Babahoyo Ecuador 142 C4
Babai India 82 D5
Babai r. Nepal 83 E3
Bābā Kalān Iran 88 C4
Bāb al Mandab strait Africa/Asia 86 F7
Babanusa Sudan 86 C7
Babao Qinghai China see Qilian
Babao Yunnan China 76 E4
Babar i. Indon. 108 E1
Babar, Kepulauan is Indon. 108 E1
Babati Tanz. 99 D4
Babayevo Rus. Fed. 42 G4
Babayurt Rus. Fed. 91 G2
B'abdā Lebanon see Baabda
Bab el Mandeb, Straits of Africa/Asia see Bāb al Mandab
Babi, Pulau i. Indon. 71 B7
Babian Jiang r. China 76 D4
Babine r. Canada 120 E4
Babine Lake Canada 120 E4
Babine Range mts Canada 120 E4

Bābol Iran 88 D2
Bābol Sar Iran 88 D2
Babongo Cameroon 97 E4
Baboon Point S. Africa 100 D7
Baboua Cent. Afr. Rep. 98 B3
Babruysk Belarus 43 F5
Babstovo Rus. Fed. 74 D2
Babu China see Hezhou
Babuhri India 82 B4
Babusar Pass Pak. 89 I3
Babuyan i. Phil. 69 G3
Babuyan Channel Phil. 69 G3
Babuyan Islands Phil. 69 G3
Bacaadweyn Somalia 98 E3
Bacabal Brazil 143 J4
Bacan i. Indon. 69 H7
Bacanora Mex. 127 F7
Bacău Romania 59 L1
Baccaro Point Canada 123 I6
Băc Giang Vietnam 70 D2
Bacha China 74 D2
Bach Ice Shelf Antarctica 152 L2
Bach Long Vi, Đao i. Vietnam 70 D2
Bachu China 80 E4
Bachuan China see Tongliang
Back r. Australia 110 C3
Back r. Canada 121 M1
Bačka Palanka Serb. and Mont. 59 H2
Backbone Mountain U.S.A. 134 F4
Backbone Ranges mts Canada 120 D2
Backe Sweden 44 J5
Backstairs Passage Australia 111 B7
Bac Lac Vietnam 70 D2
Bac Liêu Vietnam 71 D5
Băc Ninh Vietnam 70 D2
Bacoachi Mex. 127 F7
Bacoachi watercourse Mex. 127 F7
Bacobampo Mex. 127 F8
Bacolod Phil. 69 G4
Băc Quang Vietnam 70 D2
Bacqueville, Lac l. Canada 122 G2
Bacqueville-en-Caux France 49 H9
Bacubirito Mex. 127 G8
Bād Iran 88 D3
Bada China see Xilin
Bada mt. Eth. 98 D3
Bada i. Myanmar 71 B5
Bad Abbach Germany 53 M6
Badagara India 84 B4
Badain Jaran Shamo des. China 80 J3
Badajoz Spain 57 C4
Badami India 84 B3
Badampaharh India 83 F5
Badanah Saudi Arabia 91 F5
Badanjilin Shamo des. China see Badain Jaran Shamo
Badaojiang China see Baishan
Badarpur India 83 H4
Badaun India see Budaun
Bad Axe U.S.A. 134 D2
Bad Bergzabern Germany 53 H5
Bad Berleburg Germany 53 I3
Bad Bevensen Germany 53 K1
Bad Blankenburg Germany 53 L4
Bad Camberg Germany 53 I4
Badderen Norway 44 M2
Bad Driburg Germany 53 J3
Bad Düben Germany 53 M3
Bad Dürkheim Germany 53 I5
Bad Dürrenberg Germany 53 M3
Bademli Turkey see Aladağ
Bademli Geçidi pass Turkey 90 C3
Bad Ems Germany 53 H4
Baden Austria 47 P6
Baden Switz. 56 I3
Baden-Baden Germany 53 I6
Baden-Württemberg land Germany 53 I6
Bad Essen Germany 53 I2
Bad Grund (Harz) Germany 53 K3
Bad Harzburg Germany 53 K3
Bad Hersfeld Germany 53 J4
Bad Hofgastein Austria 47 N7
Bad Homburg vor der Höhe Germany 53 I4
Badia Polesine Italy 58 D2
Badin Pak. 89 H5
Bad Ischl Austria 47 N7
Bādiyat ash Shām des. Asia see Syrian Desert
Badkhyzskiy Zapovednik nature res. Turkm. 89 F3
Bad Kissingen Germany 53 K4
Bad Königsdorff Poland see Jastrzębie-Zdrój
Bad Kösen Germany 53 L3
Bad Kreuznach Germany 53 H5
Bad Laasphe Germany 53 I4
Badlands reg. ND U.S.A. 130 C2
Badlands reg. SD U.S.A. 130 C3
Badlands National Park U.S.A. 130 C3
Bad Langensalza Germany 53 K3
Bad Lauterberg im Harz Germany 53 K3
Bad Liebenwerda Germany 53 N3
Bad Lippspringe Germany 53 I3
Bad Marienberg (Westerwald) Germany 53 H4
Bad Mergentheim Germany 53 J5
Bad Nauheim Germany 53 I4
Badnawar India 82 C5
Badnera India 84 C1
Bad Neuenahr-Ahrweiler Germany 52 H4
Bad Neustadt an der Saale Germany 53 K4
Badnor India 82 C4
Badong China 77 F2
Ba Đông Vietnam 71 D5
Badou Togo 96 D4
Bad Pyrmont Germany 53 J3
Badrah Iraq 91 G4
Bad Reichenhall Germany 47 N7
Badr Ḥunayn Saudi Arabia 86 E5
Bad Sachsa Germany 53 K3
Bad Salzdetfurth Germany 53 K2
Bad Salzuflen Germany 53 I2
Bad Salzungen Germany 53 K4
Bad Schwalbach Germany 53 I4
Bad Schwartau Germany 47 M4
Bad Segeberg Germany 47 M4
Badu Island Australia 110 C1
Badulla Sri Lanka 84 D5
Bad Vilbel Germany 53 I4
Bad Wilsnack Germany 53 L2
Bad Windsheim Germany 53 K5
Badzhal Rus. Fed. 74 D2
Badzhal'skiy Khrebet mts Rus. Fed. 74 D2
Bad Zwischenahn Germany 53 I1
Bae Colwyn U.K. see Colwyn Bay
Baesweiler Germany 52 G4
Baeza Spain 57 E5
Bafatá Guinea-Bissau 96 B3
Baffa Pak. 89 I3
Baffin Bay sea Canada/Greenland 119 L2
▶Baffin Island Canada 119 L3
2nd largest island in North America and 5th in the world.
World 12–13
Bafia Cameroon 96 E4
Bafilo Togo 96 D4
Bafing r. Africa 96 B3
Bafoulabé Mali 96 B3
Bafoussam Cameroon 96 E4
Bāfq Iran 88 D4
Bafra Turkey 90 D2
Bafra Burnu pt Turkey 90 D2
Bāft Iran 88 E4
Bafwaboli Dem. Rep. Congo 98 C3
Bafwasende Dem. Rep. Congo 98 C3
Bagaha India 83 F4
Bagalkot India 84 B2
Bagalkote India see Bagalkot
Bagamoyo Tanz. 99 D4
Bagan China 76 C1
Bagan Datoh Malaysia see Bagan Datuk
Bagan Datuk Malaysia 71 C7
Bagansiapiapi Indon. 71 C7
Bagata Dem. Rep. Congo 98 B4
Bagdad U.S.A. 129 G4
Bagdarin Rus. Fed. 73 K2
Bagé Brazil 144 F4
Bagerhat Bangl. 83 G5
Bageshwar India 82 D3
Baggs U.S.A. 126 G4
Baggy Point U.K. 49 C7
Bagh India 82 C5
Bàgh a' Chaisteil U.K. see Castlebay
Baghak Pak. 89 G4
Baghbaghū Iran 89 F2
▶Baghdād Iraq 91 G4
Capital of Iraq.
Bāgh-e Malek Iran 88 C4
Bagherhat Bangl. see Bagerhat
Bāghīn Iran 88 E4
Baghlān Afgh. 89 H2
Baghrān Afgh. 89 G3
Bağırsak r. Turkey 85 C1
Bağırsak Deresi r. Syria/Turkey see Sājūr, Nahr
Bagley U.S.A. 130 E2
Baglung Nepal 83 E3
Bagnères-de-Luchon France 56 E5
Bago Myanmar see Pegu
Bago Phil. 69 G4
Bagong China see Sansui
Bagor India 89 I5
Bagrationovsk Rus. Fed. 45 L9
Bagrax China see Bohu
Bagrax Hu l. China see Bosten Hu
Baguio Phil. 69 G3
Bagur, Cabo c. Spain see Begur, Cap de
Bagzane, Monts mts Niger 96 D3
Bahādorābād-e Bālā Iran 88 E4
Bahalda India 83 F5
Bahāmabād Iran see Rafsanjān
▶Bahamas, The country West Indies 133 E7
North America 9, 116–117
Bahara Pak. 89 G5
Baharampur India 83 G4
Bahardipur Pak. 89 H5
Bahariya Oasis oasis Egypt see Baḥrīyah, Wāḥāt al
Bahau Malaysia 71 C7
Bahawalnagar Pak. 89 I4
Bahawalpur Pak. 89 H4
Bahçe Adana Turkey 85 B1
Bahçe Osmaniye Turkey 90 E3
Baher Dar Eth. see Bahir Dar
Baheri India 82 D3
Bahia Brazil see Salvador
Bahia state Brazil 145 C1
Bahía Asunción Mex. 127 E8
Bahía Blanca Arg. 144 D5
Bahía Kino Mex. 127 F7
Bahía Laura Arg. 144 C7
Bahía Negra Para. 144 E2
Bahía Tortugas Mex. 127 E8
Bahir Dar Eth. 98 D2
Bahl India 82 C3
Bahlā Oman 88 E6
Bahomonte Indon. 69 G7
Bahraich India 83 E4
▶Bahrain country Asia 88 C5
Asia 6, 62–63
Bahrain, Gulf of Asia 88 C5
Bahrām Beyg Iran 88 C2
Bahrāmjerd Iran 88 E4
Baḥrīyah, Wāḥāt al oasis Egypt 90 C6
Bahuaja-Sonene, Parque Nacional nat. park Peru 142 E6
Baia Mare Romania 59 J1
Baiazeh Iran 88 D3
Baicang China 83 G3
Bai Canh, Hon i. Vietnam 71 D5
Baicheng Henan China see Xiping
Baicheng Jilin China 74 A3
Baicheng Xinjiang China 80 F3
Baidoa Somalia see Baydhabo
Baidoi Co l. China 83 F2
Baidu China 77 H3
Baie-aux-Feuilles Canada see Tasiujaq
Baie-Comeau Canada 123 H4
Baie-du-Poste Canada see Mistissini
Baie-St-Paul Canada 123 H5
Baie-Trinite Canada 123 I4
Baie Verte Canada 123 K4
Baiguan China see Shangyu
Baiguo Hubei China 77 G2
Baiguo Hunan China 77 G3
Baihanchang China 76 C3
Baihar India 82 E5
Baihe Jilin China 74 C4
Baihe Shaanxi China 77 F1
Baiji Iraq see Bayjī
▶Baikal, Lake Rus. Fed. 72 J2
Deepest lake in the world and in Asia. 3rd largest lake in Asia.
Baikunthpur India 83 E5
Baile Átha Cliath Rep. of Ireland see Dublin
Baile Átha Luain Rep. of Ireland see Athlone
Baile Mhartainn U.K. 50 B3
Băileşti Romania 59 J2
Bailey Range hills Australia 109 C7
Bailianhe Shuiku resr China 77 G2
Bailieborough Rep. of Ireland 51 F4
Bailleul France 52 C4
Baillie r. Canada 121 J1
Bailong China see Hadapu
Bailong Jiang r. China 76 E1
Baima Qinghai China 76 D1
Baima Xizang China see Baxoi
Baima Jian mt. China 77 H2
Baimuru P.N.G. 69 K8
Bain r. U.K. 48 G5
Bainang China 83 G3
Bainbridge GA U.S.A. 133 C6
Bainbridge IN U.S.A. 134 B4
Bainbridge NY U.S.A. 135 H2
Bainduru India 84 B3
Baingoin China 83 G3
Baini China see Yuqing
Baiona Spain 57 B2
Baiqên China 76 D1
Baiquan China 74 B3
Bā'ir Jordan 85 C4
Bā'ir, Wādī watercourse Jordan/Saudi Arabia 85 C4
Bairab Co l. China 83 E2
Bairat India 82 D4
Baird U.S.A. 131 D5
Baird Mountains U.S.A. 118 C3
▶Bairiki Kiribati 150 H5
Capital of Kiribati, on Tarawa atoll.
Bairin Youqi China see Daban
Bairnsdale Australia 112 C6
Baisha Chongqing China 76 E2
Baisha Hainan China 77 F5
Baisha Sichuan China 77 F2
Baishan Guangxi China see Mashan
Baishan Jilin China 74 B4
Baishan Jilin China see Baishanzhen
Baishanzhen China 74 B4
Baishi Shaanxi China 77 F1
Baishui Sichuan China 76 E1
Baishui Jiang r. China 76 E1
Baisogala Lith. 45 M9
Baitadi Nepal 82 E3
Baitang China 76 C1
Bai Thương Vietnam 70 D3
Baixi China see Yibin
Baiyashi China see Dong'an
Baiyin China 72 I5
Baiyü China 76 C2
Baiyuda Desert Sudan 86 D6
Baja Hungary 58 H1
Baja, Punta pt Mex. 127 E7
Baja California pen. Mex. 127 E7
Baja California state Mex. 127 E7
Baja California Norte state Mex. see Baja California
Baja California Sur state Mex. 127 E8
Bajan Mex. 131 C7
Bajau i. Indon. 71 D7
Bajaur reg. Pak. 89 H3
Bajawa Indon. 108 C2
Baj Baj India 83 G5
Bājgīrān Iran 88 E2
Bājil Yemen 86 F7
Bajo Caracoles Arg. 144 B7
Bajoga Nigeria 96 E3
Bajoi China 76 D2
Bajrakot India 83 F5
Bakala Cent. Afr. Rep. 97 F4
Bakanas Kazakh. 80 E3
Bakar Pak. 89 H5
Bakel Senegal 96 B3
Baker CA U.S.A. 128 E4
Baker ID U.S.A. 126 E3
Baker LA U.S.A. 131 F6
Baker MT U.S.A. 126 G3
Baker NV U.S.A. 129 F2
Baker OR U.S.A. 126 D3
Baker WV U.S.A. 135 F4
Baker, Mount vol. U.S.A. 126 C2
Baker Butte mt. U.S.A. 129 H4
▶Baker Island terr. N. Pacific Ocean 107 I1
United States Unincorporated Territory.
Baker Island U.S.A. 120 C4
Baker Lake salt flat Australia 109 D6
Baker Lake Canada 121 M1
Baker Lake l. Canada 121 M1
Baker's Dozen Islands Canada 122 F2
Bakersfield U.S.A. 128 D4
Bakersville U.S.A. 132 D4
Bâ Kêv Cambodia 71 D4
Bakhardok Turkm. 88 E2
Bākharz mts Iran 89 F3
Bakhasar India 82 B4
Bakhirevo Rus. Fed. 74 C2
Bakhmach Ukr. 43 G6
Bakhma Dam Iraq see Bēkma, Sadd
Bakhmut Ukr. see Artemivs'k
Bākhtarān Iran see Kermānshāh
Bakhtegan, Daryācheh-ye l. Iran 88 D4
Bakhtiari Country reg. Iran 88 C3
Bakı Azer. see Baku
Bakırköy Turkey 59 M4
Bakkejord Norway 44 K2
Bakloh India 82 C2
Bako Eth. 98 D3
Bakongan Indon. 71 B7
Bakouma Cent. Afr. Rep. 98 C3
Baksan Rus. Fed. 91 F2
▶Baku Azer. 91 H2
Capital of Azerbaijan.
Baku Dem. Rep. Congo 98 D3
Bakutis Coast Antarctica 152 J2
Baky Azer. see Baku
Balâ Turkey 90 D3
Bala U.K. 49 D6
Bala, Cerros de mts Bol. 142 E6
Balabac i. Phil. 68 F5
Balabac Strait Malaysia/Phil. 68 F5
Baladeh Māzandarān Iran 88 C2
Baladeh Māzandarān Iran 88 C2
Baladek Rus. Fed. 74 D1
Balaghat India 82 E5
Balaghat Range hills India 84 B2
Bālā Ḥowz Iran 88 E4
Balaka Malawi 99 D5
Balakān Azer. 91 G2
Balakhna Rus. Fed. 42 I4
Balakhta Rus. Fed. 72 G1
Balaklava Australia 111 B7
Balaklava Ukr. 90 D1
Balakleya Ukr. see Balakliya
Balakliya Ukr. 43 H6
Balakovo Rus. Fed. 43 J5
Bala Lake U.K. see Tegid, Llyn
Balaman India 82 E4
Balan India 82 B4
Balanda Rus. Fed. see Kalininsk
Balanda r. Rus. Fed. 43 J6
Balan Dağı hill Turkey 59 M6
Balanga Phil. 69 G4
Balangir India see Bolangir
Balaözen r. Kazakh./Rus. Fed. see Malyy Uzen'
Balarampur India see Balrampur
Balashov Rus. Fed. 43 I6
Balasore India see Baleshwar
Balaton, Lake Hungary 58 G1
Balatonboglár Hungary 58 G1
Balatonfüred Hungary 58 G1
Balbina Brazil 143 G4
Balbina, Represa de resr Brazil 143 G4
Balbriggan Rep. of Ireland 51 F4
Balchik Bulg. 59 M3
Balclutha N.Z. 113 B8
Balcones Escarpment U.S.A. 131 C6
Bald Knob U.S.A. 134 E5
Bald Mountain U.S.A. 129 F3
Baldock Lake Canada 121 L3
Baldwin Canada 134 F1
Baldwin FL U.S.A. 133 D6
Baldwin MI U.S.A. 134 C2
Baldwin PA U.S.A. 134 F3
Baldy Mount Canada 126 D2
Baldy Mountain hill Canada 121 K5
Baldy Peak U.S.A. 129 I5
Bale Indon. 68 C7
Bâle Switz. see Basel
Baléa Mali 96 B3
Baleares is Spain see Balearic Islands
Baleares, Islas is Spain see Balearic Islands
Baleares Insulae is Spain see Balearic Islands
Balearic Islands is Spain 57 G4
Balears is Spain see Balearic Islands
Balears, Illes is Spain see Balearic Islands
Baleia, Ponta da pt Brazil 145 D2
Bale Mountains National Park Eth. 98 D3
Baler Phil. 69 G3
Baleshwar India 83 F5
Balestrand Norway 45 E6
Baléyara Niger 96 D3
Balezino Rus. Fed. 41 Q4
Balfe's Creek Australia 110 D4
Balfour Downs Australia 108 C5
Balgo Australia 108 D5
Balguntay China 80 G3
Bali India 82 C4
Bali i. Indon. 108 A2
Bali, Laut sea Indon. 108 A1
Balia India see Ballia
Baliapal India 83 F5
Balige Indon. 71 B7
Baliguda India 84 D1
Balıkesir Turkey 59 L5
Balīkh r. Syria/Turkey 85 D2
Balikpapan Indon. 68 F7
Balimila Reservoir India 84 D2
Balimo P.N.G. 69 K8
Balin China 74 A2
Baling Malaysia 71 C6
Balingen Germany 47 L6
Balintore U.K. 50 F3
Bali Sea Indon. see Bali, Laut
Balk Neth. 52 F2
Balkan Mountains Bulg./Serb. and Mont. 59 J3
Balkassar Pak. 89 I3
Balkhash Kazakh. 80 D2
▶Balkhash, Lake Kazakh. 80 D2
4th largest lake in Asia.
Balkhash, Ozero l. Kazakh. see Balkhash, Lake
Balkuduk Kazakh. 43 J7
Ballachulish U.K. 50 D4
Balladonia Australia 109 C8
Balladoran Australia 112 D3
Ballaghaderreen Rep. of Ireland 51 D4
Ballan Australia 112 B6
Ballangen Norway 44 J2
Ballantine U.S.A. 126 F3
Ballantrae U.K. 50 E5
Ballarat Australia 112 A6
Ballard, Lake salt flat Australia 105 C7
Ballarpur India 84 C2
Ballater U.K. 50 F3
Ballé Mali 96 C3
Ballena, Punta pt Chile 144 B3
Balleny Islands Antarctica 152 H2
Ballia India 83 F4
Ballina Australia 112 F2
Ballina Rep. of Ireland 51 C3
Ballinafad Rep. of Ireland 51 D3
Ballinalack Rep. of Ireland 51 E4
Ballinamore Rep. of Ireland 51 E3
Ballinasloe Rep. of Ireland 51 D4
Ballindine Rep. of Ireland 51 D4
Ballinger U.S.A. 131 D6
Ballinluig U.K. 50 F4
Ballinrobe Rep. of Ireland 51 C4
Ballon d'Alsace mt. France 47 K7
Ballston Spa U.S.A. 135 I2
Ballybay Rep. of Ireland 51 F3
Ballybrack Rep. of Ireland 51 B6
Ballybunnion Rep. of Ireland 51 C5
Ballycanew Rep. of Ireland 51 F5
Ballycastle Rep. of Ireland 51 C3
Ballycastle U.K. 51 F2
Ballyclare U.K. 51 G3
Ballyconnell Rep. of Ireland 51 E3
Ballygar Rep. of Ireland 51 D4
Ballygawley U.K. 51 E3
Ballygorman Rep. of Ireland 51 E2
Ballyhaunis Rep. of Ireland 51 D4
Ballyheigue Rep. of Ireland 51 C5
Ballykelly U.K. 51 E2
Ballylynan Rep. of Ireland 51 E5
Ballymacmague Rep. of Ireland 51 E5
Ballymahon Rep. of Ireland 51 E4
Ballymena U.K. 51 F3
Ballymoney U.K. 51 F2
Ballymote Rep. of Ireland 51 D3
Ballynahinch U.K. 51 G3
Ballyshannon Rep. of Ireland 51 D3
Ballyteige Bay Rep. of Ireland 51 F5
Ballyvaughan Rep. of Ireland 51 C4
Ballyward U.K. 51 F3
Balmartin U.K. see Baile Mhartainn
Balmer India see Barmer
Balmertown Canada 121 M5
Balmorhea U.S.A. 131 C6
Balochistan prov. Pak. 89 G4
Balombo Angola 99 B5
Balonne r. Australia 112 D2
Balotra India 82 C4
Balqash Kazakh. see Balkhash
Balqash Köli l. Kazakh. see Balkhash, Lake
Balrampur India 83 E4
Balranald Australia 112 A5
Balş Romania 59 K2
Balsam Lake Canada 135 F1
Balsas Brazil 143 I5
Balta Ukr. 43 F7
Baltasound U.K. 50 [inset]
Baltay Rus. Fed. 43 J5
Bălţi Moldova 43 E7
Baltic U.S.A. 134 E3
Baltic Sea g. Europe 45 J9
Balṭīm Egypt see Balṭīm
Balṭīm Egypt 90 C5
Baltimore S. Africa 101 I2
Baltimore MD U.S.A. 135 G4
Baltimore OH U.S.A. 134 D4
Baltinglass Rep. of Ireland 51 F5
Baltistan reg. Jammu and Kashmir 82 C2
Baltiysk Rus. Fed. 45 K9
Balu India 76 B3
Baluarte, Arroyo watercourse U.S.A. 131 D7
Baluch Ab well Iran 88 E4
Balumundam Indon. 71 B7
Balurghat India 83 G4
Balve Germany 53 H3
Balvi Latvia 45 O8
Balya Turkey 59 L5
Balykchy Kyrg. 80 E3
Balykshi Kazakh. 78 E2
Balyqshy Kazakh. see Balykshi
Bam Iran 88 E4
Bām Iran 88 E2
Bama China 76 E3
▶Bamako Mali 96 C3
Capital of Mali.
Bamba Mali 96 C3
Bambari Cent. Afr. Rep. 98 C3
Bambel Indon. 71 B7
Bamberg Germany 53 K5
Bamberg U.S.A. 133 D5
Bambili Dem. Rep. Congo 98 C3
Bambio Cent. Afr. Rep. 98 B3
Bamboesberg mts S. Africa 101 H6
Bamboo Creek Australia 108 C5
Bambouti Cent. Afr. Rep. 98 C3
Bambuí Brazil 145 B3
Bamda China 76 C2
Bamenda Cameroon 96 E4
Bāmīān Afgh. 89 G3
Bamiantong China see Muling
Bamingui Cent. Afr. Rep. 98 C3
Bamingui-Bangoran, Parc National du nat. park Cent. Afr. Rep. 98 B3
Bâmnak Cambodia 71 D4
Bamnet Narong Thai. 70 C4
Bamor India 82 D4
Bamori India 84 C1
Bam Posht reg. Iran 89 F5
Bam Posht, Kūh-e mts Iran 89 F5
Bampton U.K. 49 D8
Bampūr Iran 89 F5
Bampūr watercourse Iran 89 E5
Bamrūd Iran 89 F3
Bam Tso l. China 83 G3
Bamyili Australia 108 F3
Banaba i. Kiribati 107 G2
Banabuiu, Açude resr Brazil 139 K5
Bañados del Izozog swamp Bol. 142 F7
Banagher Rep. of Ireland 51 E4
Banalia Dem. Rep. Congo 98 C3
Banamana, Lagoa l. Moz. 101 K2
Banamba Mali 96 C3
Banámichi Mex. 127 F7
Banana Australia 110 E5
Bananal, Ilha do i. Brazil 143 H6
Bananga India 71 A6
Banapur India 84 E2
Banas r. India 82 D4
Banaz Turkey 59 M5
Ban Ban Laos 70 C3
Banbar China 76 B2
Ban Bo Laos 70 C3
Banbridge U.K. 51 F3
Ban Bua Chum Thai. 70 C4
Ban Bua Yai Thai. 70 C4
Ban Bungxai Laos 70 D4
Banbury U.K. 49 F6
Ban Cang Vietnam 70 C2
Banc d'Arguin, Parc National du nat. park Mauritania 96 B2
Ban Channabot Thai. 70 C3
Banchory U.K. 50 G3
Bancroft Canada 135 G1
Bancroft Zambia see Chililabombwe
Banda Dem. Rep. Congo 98 C3
Banda India 82 E4
Banda, Kepulauan is Indon. 69 H7
Banda, Laut sea Indon. 69 H8
Banda Aceh Indon. 71 A6
Banda Banda, Mount Australia 112 F3
Banda Daud Shah Pak. 89 H3
Bandahara, Gunung mt. Indon. 71 B7
Bandama r. Côte d'Ivoire 96 C4
Bandān Kūh mts Iran 89 F4
Bandar India see Machilipatnam
Bandar Moz. 99 D5
Bandar Abbas Iran see Bandar-e 'Abbās
Bandarban Bangl. 83 H5
Bandar-e 'Abbās Iran 88 E5
Bandar-e Anzalī Iran 88 C2
Bandar-e Deylam Iran 88 C4
Bandar-e Emām Khomeynī Iran 88 C4
Bandar-e Lengeh Iran 88 D5
Bandar-e Ma'shur Iran 88 C4
Bandar-e Nakhīlū Iran 88 D5
Bandar-e Pahlavī Iran see Bandar-e Anzalī
Bandar-e Shāh Iran see Bandar-e Torkeman
Bandar-e Shāhpūr Iran see Bandar-e Emām Khomeynī
Bandar-e Shīū' Iran 88 D5
Bandar-e Torkeman Iran 88 D2
Bandar Labuan Malaysia see Labuan
Bandar Lampung Indon. 68 D8
Bandarpunch mt. India 82 D3
▶Bandar Seri Begawan Brunei 68 E6
Capital of Brunei.
Banda Sea sea Indon. see Banda, Laut
Band-e Amīr l. Afgh. 89 G3
Band-e Amīr, Daryā-ye r. Afgh. 89 G2
Band-e Bābā mts Afgh. 89 F3
Bandeira Brazil 145 C1
Bandeirante Brazil 145 A1
Bandeiras, Pico de mt. Brazil 145 C3
Bandelierkop S. Africa 101 I2
Banderas Mex. 131 B6
Banderas, Bahía de b. Mex. 136 C4
Band-e Sar Qom Iran 88 D3
Band-e Torkestān mts Afgh. 89 F3
Bandhi Pak. 89 H5
Bandhogarh India 82 E5
Bandi r. India 82 C4
Bandiagara Mali 96 C3
Bandikui India 82 D4
Bandipur National Park India 84 C4
Bandırma Turkey 59 L4
Bandjarmasin Indon. see Banjarmasin
Bandon Rep. of Ireland 51 D6
Bandon r. Rep. of Ireland 51 D6
Ban Don Thai. see Surat Thani
Bandon U.S.A. 126 B4
Band Qīr Iran 88 C4
Bandra India 84 B2
Bandundu Dem. Rep. Congo 98 B4
Bandung Indon. 68 D8
Bandya Australia 109 C6
Bāneh Iran 88 B3
Banera India 82 C4
Banes Cuba 137 I4
Banff Canada 120 H5
Banff U.K. 50 G3
Banff National Park Canada 120 G5
Banfora Burkina 96 C3
Banga Dem. Rep. Congo 99 C4
Bangalore India 84 C3
Bangalow Australia 112 F2
Bangaon India 83 G5
Bangar Brunei 68 F6
Bangassou Cent. Afr. Rep. 98 C3
Bangdag Co salt l. China 83 E2
Banggai Indon. 69 G7
Banggai, Kepulauan is Indon. 69 G7
Banggi i. Malaysia 68 F5
Banghāzī Libya see Benghazi
Banghiang, Xé r. Laos 70 D3
Bangka i. Indon. 68 D7
Bangka, Selat sea chan. Indon. 68 D7
Bangkalan Indon. 68 E8
Bangkaru i. Indon. 71 B7
Bangko Indon. 68 C7
▶Bangkok Thai. 71 C4
Capital of Thailand.
Bangkok, Bight of b. Thai. 71 C4
Bangkor China 83 F3
Bangla state India see West Bengal
▶Bangladesh country Asia 83 G4
Asia 6, 62–63
Bangma Shan mts China 76 C4
Bang Mun Nak Thai. 70 C3
Bangolo Côte d'Ivoire 96 C4
Bangong Co salt l. China/Jammu and Kashmir 82 D2
Bangor Northern Ireland U.K. 51 G3
Bangor Wales U.K. 48 C5
Bangor ME U.S.A. 132 G2
Bangor MI U.S.A. 134 B2
Bangor PA U.S.A. 135 H3
Bangor Erris Rep. of Ireland 51 C3
Bangs, Mount U.S.A. 129 G3
Bang Saphan Yai Thai. 71 B5
Bangsund Norway 44 G4
Bangued Phil. 69 G3
▶Bangui Cent. Afr. Rep. 98 B3
Capital of Central African Republic.
Bangweulu, Lake Zambia 99 C5
Banhā Egypt 90 C5
Banhine, Parque Nacional de nat. park Moz. 101 K2
Ban Hin Heup Laos 70 C3
Ban Houayxay Laos 70 C2
Ban Houei Sai Laos see Ban Houayxay
Ban Huai Khon Thai. 70 C3
Ban Huai Yang Thai. 71 B5
Bani, Jbel ridge Morocco 54 C6
Bania Cent. Afr. Rep. 98 B3
Bani-Bangou Niger 96 D3
Banifing r. Mali 96 C3
Banī Forūr, Jazīreh-ye i. Iran 88 D5

Banihal Pass and Tunnel Jammu and Kashmir 82 C2
Banister r. U.S.A. 134 F5
Banī Suwayf Egypt 90 C5
Banī Walīd Libya 97 E1
Banī Wuṭayfān well Saudi Arabia 88 C5
Bāniyās Al Qunayṭirah Syria 85 B3
Bāniyās Ṭarṭūs Syria 85 B2
Bani Yas reg. U.A.E. 88 D6
Banja Luka Bos.-Herz. 58 G2
Banjarmasin Indon. 68 E7
Banjes, Liqeni i resr Albania 59 I4

▶Banjul Gambia 96 B3
Capital of The Gambia.

Banka India 83 F4
Banka Banka Australia 108 F4
Bankapur India 84 B3
Bankass Mali 96 C3
Ban Kengkabao Laos 70 D3
Ban Khao Yoi Thai. 71 B4
Ban Khok Kloi Thai. 71 B5
Bankilaré Niger 96 D3
Banks Island B.C. Canada 120 D4
Banks Island N.W.T. Canada 118 F2
Banks Islands Vanuatu 107 G3
Banks Lake Canada 121 M2
Banks Lake U.S.A. 126 D3
Banks Peninsula N.Z. 113 D6
Banks Strait Australia 111 [inset]
Bankura India 83 F5
Ban Lamduan Thai. 71 C4
Banlan China 77 F3
Ban Mae La Luang Thai. 70 B3
Banmaw Myanmar see Bhamo
Banmo Myanmar see Bhamo
Bann r. Rep. of Ireland 51 F5
Bann r. U.K. 51 F2
Ban Nakham Laos 70 D3
Bannerman Town Bahamas 133 E7
Banning U.S.A. 128 E5
Banningville Dem. Rep. Congo see Bandundu
Ban Noi Myanmar 70 B3
Ban Nong Kung Thai. 70 D3
Bannu Pak. 89 H3
Bano India 83 F5
Bañolas Spain see Banyoles
Ban Phai Thai. 70 C3
Ban Phôn Laos see Ban Phon
Ban Phon Laos 70 D4
Banqiao Yunnan China 76 C3
Banqiao Yunnan China 76 E3
Bansi Bihar India 83 F4
Bansi Rajasthan India 82 C4
Bansi Uttar Pradesh India 82 D4
Bansi Uttar Pradesh India 83 E4
Bansihari India 83 G4
Banská Bystrica Slovakia 47 Q6
Banspani India 83 F5
Bansur India 82 D4
Ban Sut Ta Thai. 70 B3
Ban Suwan Wari Thai. 70 D4
Banswara India 82 C5
Banteer Rep. of Ireland 51 D5
Ban Tha Song Yang Thai. 70 B3
Banthat mts Cambodia/Thai. see Cardamom Range
Ban Tha Tum Thai. 70 C4
Ban Tôp Laos 70 D3
Bantry Rep. of Ireland 51 C6
Bantry Bay Rep. of Ireland 51 C6
Bantval India 84 B3
Ban Wang Chao Thai. 70 B3
Ban Woen Laos 70 C3
Ban Xepian Laos 70 D4
Banyak, Pulau-pulau is Indon. 71 B7
Ban Yang Yong Thai. 71 B4
Banyo Cameroon 96 E4
Banyoles Spain 57 H2
Banyuwangi Indon. 108 A2
Banzare Coast Antarctica 152 G2
Banzare Seamount sea feature Indian Ocean 149 N9
Banzart Tunisia see Bizerte
Banzkow Germany 53 L1
Banzyville Dem. Rep. Congo see Mobayi-Mbongo
Bao'an China see Shenzhen
Baochang China 73 L4
Baocheng China 76 E1
Baoding China 73 L5
Baofeng China 77 G1
Bao Ha Vietnam 70 D2
Baohe China see Weixi
Baoji Shaanxi China 76 E1
Baoji Shaanxi China 76 E1
Baokang Hubei China 77 F2
Baokang Nei Mongol China 74 A3
Baolin China 74 C3
Bao Lôc Vietnam 71 D5
Baoqing China 74 D3
Baoro Cent. Afr. Rep. 98 B3
Baoshan China 76 C3
Baotou China 73 K4
Baotou Shan mt. China/N. Korea 74 C4
Baoulé r. Mali 96 C3
Baoxing China 76 D2
Baoying China 77 H1
Baoyou China see Ledong
Bap India 82 C4
Bapatla India 84 D3
Bapaume France 52 C4
Baptiste Lake Canada 135 F1
Bapu China see Meigu
Baq'ā' oasis Saudi Arabia 91 F6
Baqbaq Egypt see Buqbuq
Baqên Xizang China 76 B1
Baqên Xizang China 76 B2
Baqiu China 77 G3
Ba'qūbah Iraq 91 G4
Bar Serb. and Mont. 59 H3
Bara Sudan 86 D7
Baraawe Somalia 98 E3
Bara Banki India see Barabanki
Barabanki India 82 E4
Baraboo U.S.A. 130 F3
Baracaju r. Brazil 145 A1
Baracaldo Spain see Barakaldo
Baracoa Cuba 137 J4
Baradá, Nahr r. Syria 85 C3
Baradine Australia 112 D3
Baradine r. Australia 112 D3
Baragarh India see Bargarh
Barahona Dom. Rep. 137 J5
Barail Range mts India 83 H4
Baraka watercourse Eritrea/Sudan 97 G3
Barakaldo Spain 57 E2
Barakī Barak Afgh. 89 H3
Baralaba Australia 110 E5
Bara Lacha Pass India 82 D2
Baralzon Lake Canada 121 L3
Baram India 83 F5
Baram r. Malaysia 68 E6
Baramati India 84 B2
Baramula India see Baramulla
Baramulla India 82 C2
Baran India 82 D4
Baran r. Pak. 89 H5
Bārān, Kūh-e mts Iran 89 F3
Baranavichy Belarus 45 O10
Barang, Dasht-i des. Afgh. 89 F3
Baranikha Rus. Fed. 65 R3
Baranīs Egypt 86 E5
Baranīs Egypt see Baranīs
Barannda India 82 E4
Baranof Island U.S.A. 120 C3
Baranovichi Belarus see Baranavichy
Baranowicze Belarus see Baranavichy
Baraouéli Mali 96 C3
Baraque de Fraiture hill Belgium 52 F4
Barasat India 83 G5
Barat Daya, Kepulauan is Indon. 108 D1
Baraut India 82 D3
Barbacena Brazil 145 C3
▶Barbados country West Indies 137 M6
North America 9, 116–117
Barbar, Gebel el mt. Egypt see Barbar, Jabal
Barbar, Jabal mt. Egypt 85 A5
Barbara Lake Canada 122 D4
Barbastro Spain 57 G2
Barbate de Franco Spain 57 D5
Barberton S. Africa 101 J3
Barberton U.S.A. 134 E3
Barbezieux-St-Hilaire France 56 D4
Barbour Bay Canada 121 M2
Barbourville U.S.A. 134 D5
Barboza Phil. 69 G4
Barbuda i. Antigua and Barbuda 137 L5
Barby (Elbe) Germany 53 L3
Barcaldine Australia 110 D4
Barce Libya see Al Marj
Barcelona Spain 57 H3
Barcelona Venez. 142 F1
Barcelonnette France 56 H4
Barcelos Brazil 142 F4
Barchfeld Germany 53 K4
Barcino Spain see Barcelona
Barclay de Tolly atoll Fr. Polynesia see Raroia
Barclayville Liberia 96 C4
Barcoo watercourse Australia 110 C5
Barcoo Creek watercourse Australia see Cooper Creek
Barcoo National Park Australia see Welford National Park
Barcs Hungary 58 G2
Bärdä Azer. 91 G2
Bárðarbunga mt. Iceland 44 [inset]
Bardaskan Iran 88 E3
Bardawīl, Khabrat al salt pan Saudi Arabia 85 D4
Bardawīl, Sabkhat al lag. Egypt 85 A4
Barddhaman India 83 F5
Bardejov Slovakia 43 D6
Bardera Somalia see Baardheere
Bardhaman India see Barddhaman
Bar Đôn Vietnam 71 D4
Bardsey Island U.K. 49 C6
Bardsīr Iran 88 E4
Barðsneshorn pt Iceland 40 D2
Bardstown U.S.A. 134 C5
Barduli Italy see Barletta
Bardwell U.S.A. 131 F4
Bareilly India 82 D3
Barellan Australia 112 C5
Barentin France 49 H9
Barentsburg Svalbard 64 C2
Barents Sea Arctic Ocean 42 I1
Barentu Eritrea 86 E6
Barfleur, Pointe de pt France 49 F9
Bārgāh Iran 88 E5
Bargarh India 83 E5
Barghamad Iran 88 E2
Bargrennan U.K. 50 E5
Bargteheide Germany 53 K1
Barguna Bangl. 83 G5
Barhaj India 83 E4
Barham Australia 112 B5
Bari Italy 58 G4
Bari Doab lowland Pak. 89 I4
Barika Alg. 54 F4
Barinas Venez. 142 D2
Baripada India 83 F5
Bariri Brazil 145 A3
Bari Sadri India 82 C4
Barisal Bangl. 83 G5
Barisan, Pegunungan mts Indon. 68 C7
Barito r. Indon. 68 E7
Barium Italy see Bari
Barkal Bangl. 83 H5
Barkam China 76 D2
Barkan, Ra's-e pt Iran 88 C4
Barkava Latvia 45 O8
Bark Lake Canada 135 G1
Barkly East S. Africa 101 H6
Barkly Homestead Australia 110 A3
Barkly-Oos S. Africa see Barkly East
Barkly Tableland reg. Australia 110 A3
Barkly-Wes S. Africa see Barkly West
Barkly West S. Africa 100 G5
Barkol China 80 H3
Barla Turkey 59 N5
Bârlad Romania 59 L1
Bar-le-Duc France 52 F6
Barlee, Lake salt flat Australia 109 B7
Barlee Range hills Australia 109 A5
Barletta Italy 58 G4
Barlow Canada 120 B2
Barlow Lake Canada 121 K2
Barmah Forest Australia 112 B5
Barmedman Australia 112 C5
Barmen-Elberfeld Germany see Wuppertal
Barmer India 82 B4
Barm Fīrūz, Kūh-e mt. Iran 88 C4
Barmouth U.K. 49 C6
Barnala India 82 C3
Barnard Castle U.K. 48 F4
Barnato Australia 112 B3
Barnaul Rus. Fed. 72 E2
Barnegat Bay U.S.A. 135 H4
Barnes Icecap Canada 119 K2
Barnesville GA U.S.A. 133 D5
Barnesville MN U.S.A. 130 D2
Barneveld Neth. 52 F2
Barneville-Carteret France 49 F9
Barneys Lake imp. l. Australia 112 B4
Barney Top mt. U.S.A. 129 H3
Barnsley U.K. 48 F5
Barnstable U.S.A. 135 J3
Barnstaple U.K. 49 C7
Barnstaple Bay U.K. see Bideford Bay
Barnstorf Germany 53 I2
Baro Nigeria 96 D4
Baroda Gujarat India see Vadodara
Baroda Madhya Pradesh India 82 D4
Baroghil Pass Afgh. 89 I2
Barong China 76 C2
Barons Range hills Australia 109 D6
Barpathar India 76 B3
Barpeta India 83 G4
Bar Pla Soi Thai. see Chon Buri
Barques, Point Aux U.S.A. 134 D1
Barquisimeto Venez. 142 E1
Barra Brazil 143 J6
Barra i. U.K. 50 B4
Barra, Ponta da pt Moz. 101 L2
Barra, Sound of sea chan. U.K. 50 B3
Barraba Australia 112 E3
Barra Bonita Brazil 145 A3
Barracão do Barreto Brazil 143 G5
Barra do Bugres Brazil 143 G7
Barra do Corda Brazil 143 I5
Barra do Cuieté Brazil 145 C2
Barra do Garças Brazil 143 H7
Barra do Piraí Brazil 145 C3
Barra do São Manuel Brazil 143 G5
Barra do Turvo Brazil 145 A4
Barra Falsa, Ponta da pt Moz. 101 L2
Barraigh i. U.K. see Barra
Barra Mansa Brazil 145 B3
Barrana Pak. 89 I4
Barranca Peru 142 C4
Barranqueras Arg. 144 E3
Barranquilla Col. 142 D1
Barre MA U.S.A. 135 I2
Barre VT U.S.A. 135 I1
Barre des Ecrins mt. France 56 H4
Barreiras Brazil 143 J6
Barreirinha Brazil 143 G4
Barreirinhas Brazil 143 J4
Barreiro Port. 57 B4
Barreiros Brazil 143 K5
Barren Island India 71 A4
Barren Island Kiribati see Starbuck Island
Barren River Lake U.S.A. 134 B5
Barretos Brazil 145 A3
Barrett, Mount hill Australia 108 D4
Barrhead Canada 120 H4
Barrhead U.K. 50 E5
Barrie Canada 134 F1
Barrier Bay Antarctica 152 E2
Barrière Canada 120 F5
Barrier Range hills Australia 111 C6
Barrington Canada 123 I6
Barrington, Mount Australia 112 E4
Barrington Tops National Park Australia 112 E4
Barringun Australia 112 B2
Barro Alto Brazil 145 A1
Barrocão Brazil 145 C2
Barron U.S.A. 130 F2
Barrow r. Rep. of Ireland 51 F5
Barrow U.S.A. 118 C2
Barrow, Point U.S.A. 118 C2
Barrow Creek Australia 108 F5
Barrow-in-Furness U.K. 48 D4
Barrow Island Australia 108 A5
Barrow Range hills Australia 105 D6
Barrow Strait Canada 119 I2
Barr Smith Range hills Australia 109 C6
Barry U.K. 49 D7
Barrydale S. Africa 100 E7
Barry Mountains Australia 112 C6
Barrys Bay Canada 135 G1
Barryville U.S.A. 135 H3
Barsa-Kel'mes, Shor salt marsh Uzbek. 91 J2
Barsalpur India 82 C3
Barshatas Kazakh. 80 E2
Barshi India see Barsi
Barsi India 84 B2
Barsinghausen Germany 53 J2
Barstow U.S.A. 128 E4
Barsur India 84 D2
Bar-sur-Aube France 56 G2
Bartang Tajik. 89 H2
Barth Germany 47 N3
Bartica Guyana 143 G2
Bartın Turkey 90 D2
Bartle Frere, Mount Australia 110 D3
Bartlett U.S.A. 130 D3
Bartlett Reservoir U.S.A. 129 H5
Barton U.S.A. 135 I1
Barton-upon-Humber U.K. 48 G5
Bartoszyce Poland 47 R3
Bartow U.S.A. 133 D7
Barú, Volcán vol. Panama 137 H7
Barung i. Indon. 68 E8
Barunga Australia see Bamyili
Barun-Torey, Ozero l. Rus. Fed. 73 L2
Barus Indon. 71 B7
Baruunturuun Mongolia 80 H2
Baruun-Urt Mongolia 73 K3
Baruva India 84 E2
Barwani India 82 C5
Barwéli Mali see Baraouéli
Barwon r. Australia 112 C3
Barygaza India see Bharuch
Barysaw Belarus 45 P9
Barysh Rus. Fed. 43 J5
Basaga Turkm. 89 G2
Basăk, Tônlé r. Cambodia 71 D5
Basalt r. Australia 110 D3
Basalt Island Hong Kong China 77 [inset]
Basankusu Dem. Rep. Congo 98 B3
Basar India 84 C2
Basarabi Romania 59 M2
Basargechar Armenia see Vardenis
Bascuñán, Cabo c. Chile 144 B3
Basel Switz. 56 H3
Bashäkerd, Kūhhā-ye mts Iran 88 E5
Bashanta Rus. Fed. see Gorodovikovsk
Bashaw Canada 120 H4
Bashee r. S. Africa 101 I7
Bāshī Iran 88 C4
Bashi Channel Phil./Taiwan 69 G2
Bashmakovo Rus. Fed. 43 I5
Bāsht Iran 88 C4
Bashtanka Ukr. 43 G7
Basi Punjab India 82 D3
Basi Rajasthan India 82 D4
Basia India 83 F5
Basilan i. Phil. 69 G5
Basildon U.K. 49 H7
Basile, Pico mt. Equat. Guinea 92 D4
Basin U.S.A. 126 F3
Basingstoke U.K. 49 F7
Basin Lake Canada 121 J4
Basirhat India 83 G5
Basīṭ, Ra's al pt Syria 85 B2
Başkale Turkey 91 G3
Baskatong, Réservoir resr Canada 122 G5
Baskerville, Cape Australia 108 C4
Başkomutan Tarıhı Milli Parkı nat. park Turkey 59 N5
Başköy Turkey 85 A1
Baskunchak, Ozero l. Rus. Fed. 43 J6
Basle Switz. see Basel
Basmat India 84 C2
Basoko Dem. Rep. Congo 98 C3
Basra Iraq 91 G5
Bassano Canada 121 H5
Bassano del Grappa Italy 58 D2
Bassar Togo 96 D4
Bassas da India reef Indian Ocean 99 D6
Bassas de Pedro Padua Bank sea feature India 84 B3
Bassein Myanmar 70 A3
Bassein r. Myanmar 70 A3
Basse-Normandie admin. reg. France 49 F9
Bassenthwaite Lake U.K. 48 D4
Basse Santa Su Gambia 96 B3

▶Basse-Terre Guadeloupe 137 L5
Capital of Guadeloupe.

▶Basseterre St Kitts and Nevis 137 L5
Capital of St Kitts and Nevis.

Bassett NE U.S.A. 130 D3
Bassett VA U.S.A. 134 F5
Bassikounou Mauritania 96 C3
Bass Rock i. U.K. 50 G4
Bass Strait Australia 111 D8
Bassum Germany 53 I2
Basswood Lake Canada 122 C4
Båstad Sweden 45 H8
Bastānābād Iran 88 B2
Bastheim Germany 53 K4
Basti India 83 E4
Bastia Corsica France 56 I5
Bastioes r. Brazil 143 K5
Bastogne Belgium 52 F4
Bastrop LA U.S.A. 131 F5
Bastrop TX U.S.A. 131 D6
Basul r. Pak. 89 G5
Basuo China see Dongfang
Basutoland country Africa see Lesotho
Başyayla Turkey 85 A1
Bata Equat. Guinea 96 D4
Batabanó, Golfo de b. Cuba 133 H4
Batagay Rus. Fed. 65 O3
Batala India 82 C3
Batalha Port. 57 B4
Batam i. Indon. 71 D7
Batamay Rus. Fed. 65 N3
Batamshinskiy Kazakh. 80 A1
Batamshy Kazakh. see Batamshinskiy
Batan Jiangsu China 77 I1
Batan Qinghai China 76 D1
Batan i. Phil. 69 G2
Batang China 76 C2
Batangafo Cent. Afr. Rep. 98 B3
Batangas Phil. 69 G4
Batangtoru Indon. 71 B7
Batan Islands Phil. 69 G2
Batavia Indon. see Jakarta
Batavia NY U.S.A. 135 F2
Batavia OH U.S.A. 134 C4
Bataysk Rus. Fed. 43 H7
Batchawana Mountain hill Canada 122 D5
Bătdâmbâng Cambodia 71 C4
Bateemeucica, Gunung mt. Indon. 71 A6
Batéké, Plateaux Congo 98 B4
Batemans Bay Australia 112 E5
Bates Range hills Australia 109 C6
Batesville AR U.S.A. 131 F5
Batesville IN U.S.A. 134 C4
Batesville MS U.S.A. 131 F5
Batetskiy Rus. Fed. 42 F4
Bath N.B. Canada 123 I5
Bath Ont. Canada 135 G1
Bath U.K. 49 E7
Bath ME U.S.A. 135 K2
Bath NY U.S.A. 135 G2
Bath PA U.S.A. 135 H3
Batha watercourse Chad 97 E3
Bathgate U.K. 50 F5
Bathinda India 82 C3
Bathurst Australia 112 D4
Bathurst Canada 123 I5
Bathurst Gambia see Banjul
Bathurst S. Africa 101 H7
Bathurst, Cape Canada 118 F2
Bathurst, Lake Australia 112 D5
Bathurst Inlet Canada 118 H3
Bathurst Inlet inlet Canada 118 H3
Bathurst Island Australia 108 E2
Bathurst Island Canada 119 I2
Batié Burkina 96 C4
Batı Menteşe Dağları mts Turkey 59 L6
Batı Toroslar mts Turkey 59 N6
Batken Kyrg. 80 D4
Batkes Indon. 108 E1
Bāṭlāq-e Gavkhūnī marsh Iran 88 D3
Batley U.K. 48 F5
Batlow Australia 112 D5
Batman Turkey 91 F3
Batna Alg. 54 F4
Batok, Bukit hill Sing. 71 [inset]

▶Baton Rouge U.S.A. 131 F6
State capital of Louisiana.

Batopilas Mex. 127 G8
Batouri Cameroon 97 E4
Batrā' tourist site Jordan see Petra
Batrā', Jabal al mt. Jordan 85 B5
Batroûn Lebanon 85 B2
Båtsfjord Norway 44 P1
Battambang Cambodia see Bătdâmbâng
Batticaloa Sri Lanka 84 D5
Batti Malv i. India 71 A5
Battipaglia Italy 58 F4
Battle r. Canada 121 I4
Battle Creek U.S.A. 134 C2
Battleford Canada 121 I4
Battle Mountain U.S.A. 128 E1
Battle Mountain mt. U.S.A. 128 E1
Battura Glacier Jammu and Kashmir 82 C1
Batu mt. Eth. 98 D3
Batu, Pulau-pulau is Indon. 68 B7
Batudaka i. Indon. 69 G7
Batu Gajah Malaysia 71 C6
Batum Georgia see Bat'umi
Bat'umi Georgia 91 F2
Batu Pahat Malaysia 71 C7
Batu Putih, Gunung mt. Malaysia 71 C6
Baturaja Indon. 68 C7
Baturité Brazil 143 K4
Batyrevo Rus. Fed. 43 J5
Batys Qazaqstan admin. div. Kazakh. see Zapadnyy Kazakhstan
Bau Sarawak Malaysia 68 E6
Baubau Indon. 69 G8
Baucau East Timor 108 D2
Bauchi Nigeria 96 D3
Bauda India see Boudh
Baudette U.S.A. 130 E1
Baudh India see Boudh
Baugé France 56 D3
Bauhinia Australia 110 E5
Baukau East Timor see Baucau
Bauld, Cape Canada 123 L4
Baume-les-Dames France 56 H3
Baunach r. Germany 53 K5
Baundal India 82 C2
Baura Bangl. 83 G4
Bauru Brazil 145 A3
Bausendorf Germany 52 G4
Bauska Latvia 45 N8
Bautino Kazakh. 91 H1
Bautzen Germany 47 O5
Bavaria land Germany see Bayern
Bavaria reg. Germany 53 L6
Bavda India 84 B2
Baviaanskloofberge mts S. Africa 100 F7
Bavispe r. Mex. 127 F7
Bavla India 82 C5
Bavly Rus. Fed. 41 Q5
Baw Myanmar 70 A2
Bawal India 82 D3
Baw Baw National Park Australia 112 C6
Bawdeswell U.K. 49 I6
Bawdwin Myanmar 70 B2
Bawean i. Indon. 68 E8
Bawinkel Germany 53 H2
Bawlake Myanmar 70 B3
Bawolung China 76 D2
Baxi China 76 D1
Baxley U.S.A. 133 D6
Baxoi China 76 C2
Baxter Mountain U.S.A. 129 J2
Bay China see Baicheng
Bayamo Cuba 137 I4
Bayan Heilong. China 74 B3
Bayan Qinghai China 76 C1
Bayan Mongolia 73 K3
Bayana India 82 D4
Bayanaul Kazakh. 80 E1
Bayanbulag Mongolia 80 I2
Bayanbulak China 80 F3
Bayanday Rus. Fed. 72 J2
Bayan Gol China see Dengkou
Bayan Har Shan mts China 76 B1
Bayan Har Shankou pass China 76 C1
Bayanhongor Mongolia 80 J2
Bayan Hot China 72 J5
Bayan Mod China 72 I4
Bayan Obo China 73 J4
Bayan-Ovoo Mongolia 80 H3
Bayan Ul Hot China 73 L4
Bayard U.S.A. 129 I5
Bayasgalant Mongolia 73 K3
Bayat Turkey 59 N5
Bayāẓ Iran 88 E4
Baybay Phil. 69 G4
Bayboro U.S.A. 133 E5
Bayburt Turkey 91 F2
Bay City MI U.S.A. 134 D2
Bay City TX U.S.A. 131 D6
Baydaratskaya Guba Rus. Fed. 64 H3
Baydhabo Somalia 98 E3
Bayerischer Wald mts Germany 53 M5
Bayerischer Wald nat. park Germany 53 M5
Bayern land Germany 53 L6
Bayer Wald, Nationalpark nat. park Germany 47 N6
Bayeux France 49 G9
Bayfield Canada 134 E2
Bayındır Turkey 59 L5
Bay Islands is Hond. see La Bahía, Islas de
Bayizhen China 76 B2
Bayjī Iraq 91 F4
Baykal, Ozero l. Rus. Fed. see Baikal, Lake
Baykal-Amur Magistral Rus. Fed. 74 C1
Baykal Range mts Rus. Fed. see Baykal'skiy Khrebet
Baykal'skiy Khrebet mts Rus. Fed. 73 J2
Baykan Turkey 91 F3
Bay-Khaak Rus. Fed. 80 H1
Baykibashevo Rus. Fed. 41 R4
Baykonur Kazakh. see Baykonyr
Baykonyr Kazakh. 80 B2
Baymak Rus. Fed. 64 G4
Bay Minette U.S.A. 133 C6
Baynūna'h reg. U.A.E. 88 D6
Bayombong Phil. 69 G3
Bayona Spain see Baiona
Bayonne France 56 D5
Bayonne U.S.A. 135 H3
Bay Port U.S.A. 134 D2
Bayqongyr Kazakh. see Baykonyr
Bayram-Ali Turkm. see Bayramaly
Bayramaly Turkm. 89 F2
Bayramiç Turkey 59 L5
Bayreuth Germany 53 L5
Bayrūt Lebanon see Beirut
Bays, Lake of Canada 134 F1
Bayshore U.S.A. 134 C1
Bay Shore U.S.A. 135 I3
Bay Springs U.S.A. 131 F6
Bayston Hill U.K. 49 E6
Baysun Uzbek. 89 G2
Bayt Lahm West Bank see Bethlehem
Baytown U.S.A. 131 E6
Bay View N.Z. 113 F4
Bayy al Kabīr, Wādī watercourse Libya 97 E1
Baza Spain 57 E5
Baza, Sierra de mts Spain 57 E5
Bazardüzü Dağı mt. Azer./Rus. Fed. see Bazardyuzyu, Gora
Bazardyuzyu, Gora mt. Azer./Rus. Fed. 91 G2
Bāzār-e Māsāl Iran 88 C2
Bazarnyy Karabulak Rus. Fed. 43 J5
Bazaruto, Ilha do i. Moz. 99 D6
Bazdar Pak. 89 G5
Bazhong China 76 E2
Bazhou China see Bazhong
Bazin r. Canada 122 G5
Bazmān Iran 89 F5
Bazmān, Kūh-e mt. Iran 89 F4
Bcharré Lebanon 85 C2
Be r. Vietnam 71 D5
Beach U.S.A. 130 C2
Beachy Head hd U.K. 49 H8
Beacon U.S.A. 135 I3
Beacon Bay S. Africa 101 H7
Beaconsfield U.K. 49 G7
Beagle, Canal sea chan. Arg. 144 C8
Beagle Bank reef Australia 108 C3
Beagle Bay Australia 108 C4
Beagle Gulf Australia 108 E3
Bealanana Madag. 99 E5
Béal an Átha Rep. of Ireland see Ballina
Béal Átha na Sluaighe Rep. of Ireland see Ballinasloe
Beale, Lake India 84 B2
Beaminster U.K. 49 E8
Bear r. U.S.A. 126 E4
Bearalváhki Norway see Berlevåg
Bear Cove Point Canada 121 O2
Beardmore Canada 122 D4
Beardmore Glacier Antarctica 152 H1
Beardmore Reservoir Australia 112 D1
Bear Island Arctic Ocean see Bjørnøya
Bear Island Canada 122 E3
Bear Island Rep. of Ireland 51 C6
Bear Lake l. Canada 122 A3
Bear Lake U.S.A. 134 B1
Bear Lake l. U.S.A. 126 F4
Bearma r. India 82 D4
Bear Mountain U.S.A. 130 C3
Bearnaraigh i. U.K. see Berneray
Bear Paw Mountain U.S.A. 126 F2
Bearpaw Mountains U.S.A. 126 F2
Bearskin Lake Canada 121 N4
Beas Dam India 82 C3
Beata, Cabo c. Dom. Rep. 137 J5
Beatrice U.S.A. 130 D3
Beatrice, Cape Australia 110 B2
Beatton r. Canada 120 F3
Beatton River Canada 120 F3
Beatty U.S.A. 128 E3
Beattyville Canada 122 F4
Beattyville U.S.A. 134 D5
Beaucaire France 56 G5
Beauchene Island Falkland Is 144 E8
Beaufort Australia 112 A6
Beaufort NC U.S.A. 133 E5
Beaufort SC U.S.A. 133 D5
Beaufort Island Hong Kong China 77 [inset]
Beaufort Sea Canada/U.S.A. 118 D2
Beaufort West S. Africa 100 F7
Beaulieu r. Canada 121 H2
Beauly U.K. 50 E3
Beauly r. U.K. 50 E3
Beaumaris U.K. 48 C5
Beaumont Belgium 52 E4
Beaumont N.Z. 113 B7
Beaumont MS U.S.A. 131 F6
Beaumont TX U.S.A. 131 E6
Beaune France 56 G3
Beaupréau France 56 D3
Beauquesne France 52 C4
Beauraing Belgium 52 E4
Beauséjour Canada 121 L5
Beauvais France 52 C5
Beauval France 52 C4
Beaver r. Alberta/Saskatchewan Canada 121 J4
Beaver r. Ont. Canada 122 D3
Beaver r. Y.T. Canada 120 E3
Beaver OK U.S.A. 131 C4
Beaver PA U.S.A. 134 E3
Beaver UT U.S.A. 129 G2
Beaver r. U.S.A. 129 G2
Beaver Creek Canada 153 A2
Beavercreek U.S.A. 134 C4
Beaver Creek r. MT U.S.A. 130 B1
Beaver Creek r. ND U.S.A. 130 C2
Beaver Dam KY U.S.A. 134 B5
Beaver Dam WI U.S.A. 130 F3
Beaver Falls U.S.A. 134 E3
Beaverhead Mountains U.S.A. 126 E3
Beaverhill Lake Alta Canada 121 H4
Beaver Hill Lake Canada 121 M4
Beaverhill Lake N.W.T. Canada 121 J2
Beaver Island U.S.A. 132 C2
Beaverlodge Canada 120 G4

Beaverton Canada 134 F1
Beaverton MI U.S.A. 134 C2
Beaverton OR U.S.A. 126 C3
Beawar India 82 C4
Beazley Arg. 144 C4
Bebedouro Brazil 145 A3
Bebington U.K. 48 D5
Bebra Germany 53 J4
Bêca China 76 C2
Bécard, Lac l. Canada 123 G1
Beccles U.K. 49 I6
Bečej Serb. and Mont. 59 I2
Becerreá Spain 57 C2
Béchar Alg. 54 D5
Bechhofen Germany 53 K5
Bechuanaland country Africa see Botswana
Beckley U.S.A. 134 E5
Beckum Germany 53 I3
Becky Peak U.S.A. 129 F2
Bečov nad Teplou Czech Rep. 53 M4
Bedale U.K. 48 F4
Bedburg Germany 52 G4
Bedelē Eth. 98 D3
Bederkesa Germany 53 I1
Bedford N.S. Canada 123 J5
Bedford Que. Canada 135 I1
Bedford E. Cape S. Africa 101 H7
Bedford Kwazulu-Natal S. Africa 101 J5
Bedford U.K. 49 G6
Bedford IN U.S.A. 134 B4
Bedford KY U.S.A. 134 C4
Bedford PA U.S.A. 135 F3
Bedford VA U.S.A. 134 F5
Bedford, Cape Australia 110 D2
Bedford Downs Australia 108 D4
Bedgerebong Australia 112 C4
Bedi India 82 B5
Bedla India 82 C4
Bedlington U.K. 48 F3
Bedok Sing. 71 [inset]
Bedok Jetty Sing. 71 [inset]
Bedok Reservoir Sing. 71 [inset]
Bedou China 77 F3
Bedourie Australia 110 B5
Bedum Neth. 52 G1
Bedworth U.K. 49 F6
Beechworth Australia 112 C6
Beechy Canada 121 J5
Beecroft Peninsula Australia 112 E5
Beed India see Bid
Beelitz Germany 53 M2
Beenleigh Australia 112 F1
Beernem Belgium 52 D3
Beersheba Israel 85 B4
Be'ér Sheva' Israel see Beersheba
Be'ér Sheva' watercourse Israel 85 B4
Beervlei Dam S. Africa 100 F7
Beerwah Australia 112 F1
Beetaloo Australia 108 F4
Beethoven Peninsula Antarctica 152 L2
Beeville U.S.A. 131 D6
Befori Dem. Rep. Congo 98 C3
Beg, Lough l. U.K. 51 F3
Bega Australia 112 D6
Begari r. Pak. 89 H4
Begicheva, Ostrov i. Rus. Fed. see Bol'shoy Begichev, Ostrov
Begur, Cap de c. Spain 57 H3
Begusarai India 83 F4
Béhague, Pointe pt Fr. Guiana 143 H3
Behbehān Iran 88 C4
Behrendt Mountains Antarctica 152 L2
Behrūsī Iran 88 D4
Behshahr Iran 88 D2
Behsūd Afgh. 89 G3
Bei'an China 74 B2
Bei'ao China see Dongtou
Beibei China 76 E2
Beichuan China 76 E2
Beida Libya see Al Bayḍā'
Beigang Taiwan see Peikang
Beiguan China see Anyang
Beihai China 77 F4
Bei Hulsan Hu salt l. China 83 H1

▶Beijing China 73 L5
Capital of China.

Beijing municipality China 73 L4
Beik Myanmar see Mergui
Beilen Neth. 52 G2
Beiliu China 77 F4
Beilngries Germany 53 L5
Beiluheyan China 76 B1
Beinn an Oir hill U.K. 50 D5
Beinn an Tuirc hill U.K. 50 D5
Beinn Bheigeir hill U.K. 50 C5
Beinn Bhreac hill U.K. 50 D4
Beinn Dearg mt. U.K. 50 E3
Beinn Heasgarnich mt. U.K. 50 E4
Beinn Mholach hill U.K. 50 C2
Beinn Mhòr hill U.K. 50 B3
Beinn na Faoghlia i. U.K. see Benbecula
Beipan Jiang r. China 76 E3
Beipiao China 73 M4
Beira Moz. 99 D5

▶Beirut Lebanon 85 B3
Capital of Lebanon.

Bei Shan mts China 80 I3
Beitbridge Zimbabwe 99 C6
Beith U.K. 50 E5
Beit Jālā West Bank 85 B4
Beja Port. 57 C4
Béja Tunisia 58 C6
Bejaïa Alg. 57 I5
Béjar Spain 57 D3
Beji r. Pak. 80 C6
Bekaa valley Lebanon see El Béqaa
Bekdash Turkm. 91 I2
Békés Hungary 59 I1
Békéscsaba Hungary 59 I1
Bekily Madag. 99 E6
Bekkai Japan 74 G4
Bēkma, Sadd dam Iraq 91 G3
Bekovo Rus. Fed. 43 I5
Bekwai Ghana 96 C4
Bela India 83 E4
Bela Pak. 89 G5
Belab r. Pak. 89 H4
Bela-Bela S. Africa 101 I3
Bélabo Cameroon 96 E4
Bela Crkva Serb. and Mont. 59 I2
Bel Air U.S.A. 135 G4
Belalcázar Spain 57 D4
Bělá nad Radbuzou Czech Rep. 53 M5
Belapur India 84 B2
Belaraboon Australia 112 B4
▶Belarus country Europe 43 E5
Europe 5, 38–39
Belau country N. Pacific Ocean see Palau
Bela Vista Brazil 144 E2
Bela Vista Moz. 101 K4
Bela Vista de Goiás Brazil 145 A2
Belawan Indon. 71 B7
Belaya r. Rus. Fed. 65 S3
also known as Bila
Belaya Glina Rus. Fed. 43 I7
Belaya Kalitva Rus. Fed. 43 I6
Belaya Kholunitsa Rus. Fed. 42 K4
Belaya Tserkva Ukr. see Bila Tserkva
Belbédji Niger 96 D3
Bełchatów Poland 47 Q5
Belcher U.S.A. 134 D5
Belcher Islands Canada 122 F2
Belchiragh Afgh. 89 G3
Belcoo U.K. 51 E3
Belden U.S.A. 128 C1
Belding U.S.A. 134 C2
Beleapani reef India see Cherbaniani Reef
Belebey Rus. Fed. 41 Q5
Beledweyne Somalia 98 E3
Belém Brazil 143 I4
Belém Novo Brazil 145 A5
Belén Arg. 144 C3
Belen Antalya Turkey 85 A1
Belen Hatay Turkey 85 C1
Belen U.S.A. 127 G6
Belep, Îles is New Caledonia 107 G3
Belev Rus. Fed. 43 H5
Belfast S. Africa 101 J3

▶Belfast U.K. 51 G3
Capital of Northern Ireland.

Belfast U.S.A. 132 G2
Belfast Lough inlet U.K. 51 G3
Bēlfodiyo Eth. 98 D2
Belford U.K. 48 F3
Belfort France 56 H3
Belgaum India 84 B3
Belgern Germany 53 N3
Belgian Congo country Africa see Congo, Democratic Republic of
België country Europe see Belgium
Belgique country Europe see Belgium
▶Belgium country Europe 52 E4
Europe 5, 38–39
Belgorod Rus. Fed. 43 H6
Belgorod-Dnestrovskyy Ukr. see Bilhorod-Dnistrovs'kyy
Belgrade ME U.S.A. 135 K1
Belgrade MT U.S.A. 126 F3

▶Belgrade Serb. and Mont. 59 I2
Capital of Serbia and Montenegro.

Belgrano II research station Antarctica 152 A1
Belice r. Sicily Italy 58 E6
Belinskiy Rus. Fed. 43 I5
Belinyu Indon. 68 D7
Belitung i. Indon. 68 D7
Belize Angola 99 B4

▶Belize Belize 136 G5
Former capital of Belize.

▶Belize country Central America 136 G5
North America 9, 116–117
Beljak Austria see Villach
Belkina, Mys pt Rus. Fed. 74 E3
Bel'kovskiy, Ostrov i. Rus. Fed. 65 O2
Bell Australia 112 E1
Bell r. Australia 112 D4
Bell r. Canada 122 F4
Bella Bella Canada 120 D4
Bellac France 56 E3
Bella Coola Canada 120 E4
Bellaire U.S.A. 134 C1
Bellary India 84 C3
Bellata Australia 112 D2
Bella Unión Uruguay 144 E4
Bella Vista U.S.A. 128 B1
Bellbrook Australia 112 F3
Bell Cay reef Australia 110 E4
Belledonne mts France 56 G4
Bellefontaine U.S.A. 134 D3
Bellefonte U.S.A. 135 G3
Belle Fourche U.S.A. 130 C2
Belle Fourche r. U.S.A. 130 C2
Belle Glade U.S.A. 133 D7
Belle-Île i. France 56 C3
Belle Isle i. Canada 123 L4
Belle Isle, Strait of Canada 123 K4
Belleville Canada 135 G1
Belleville IL U.S.A. 130 F4
Belleville KS U.S.A. 130 D4
Bellevue IA U.S.A. 130 F3
Bellevue MI U.S.A. 134 C2
Bellevue OH U.S.A. 134 D3
Bellevue WA U.S.A. 126 C3
Bellin Canada see Kangirsuk
Bellingham U.K. 48 E3
Bellingham U.S.A. 126 C2
Bellingshausen research station Antarctica 152 A2
Bellingshausen Sea Antarctica 152 L2
Bellinzona Switz. 56 I3
Bellows Falls U.S.A. 135 I2
Bellpat Pak. 89 H4
Belluno Italy 58 E1
Belluru India 84 C3
Bell Ville Arg. 144 D4
Bellville S. Africa 100 D7
Belm Germany 53 I2
Belmont Australia 112 E4
Belmont U.K. 50 [inset]
Belmont U.S.A. 135 F2
Belmonte Brazil 145 D1

▶Belmopan Belize 136 G5
Capital of Belize.

Belmore, Mount hill Australia 112 F2
Belmullet Rep. of Ireland 51 C3
Belo Madag. 99 E6
Belo Campo Brazil 145 C1
Belœil Belgium 52 D4
Belogorsk Rus. Fed. 74 C2
Belogorsk Ukr. see Bilohirs'k
Beloha Madag. 99 E6
Belo Horizonte Brazil 145 C2
Beloit KS U.S.A. 130 D4
Beloit WI U.S.A. 130 F3
Belokurikha Rus. Fed. 80 F1
Belo Monte Brazil 143 H4
Belomorsk Rus. Fed. 42 G2
Belonia India 83 G5
Belorechensk Rus. Fed. 91 E1
Belorechenskaya Rus. Fed. see Belorechensk
Belören Turkey 90 D3
Beloretsk Rus. Fed. 64 G4
Belorussia country Europe see Belarus
Belorusskaya S.S.R. country Europe see Belarus
Belostok Poland see Białystok
Belot, Lac l. Canada 118 F3
Belo Tsiribihina Madag. 99 E5
Belovo Rus. Fed. 72 F2
Beloyarskiy Rus. Fed. 41 T3
Beloye, Ozero l. Rus. Fed. 42 H3
Beloye More sea Rus. Fed. see White Sea
Belozersk Rus. Fed. 42 H3
Belpre U.S.A. 134 E4
Beltana Australia 111 B6
Belted Range mts U.S.A. 128 E3
Belton U.S.A. 131 D6
Bel'ts' Moldova see Bălţi
Bel'tsy Moldova see Bălţi
Belukha, Gora mt. Kazakh./Rus. Fed. 80 G2
Belush'ye Rus. Fed. 42 J2
Belvidere IL U.S.A. 130 F3
Belvidere NJ U.S.A. 135 H3
Belyando r. Australia 110 D4
Belyayevka Ukr. see Bilyayivka
Belyy Rus. Fed. 42 G5
Belyy, Ostrov i. Rus. Fed. 64 I2
Belzig Germany 53 M2
Belzoni U.S.A. 131 F5
Bemaraha, Plateau du Madag. 99 E5
Bembe Angola 99 B4
Bemidji U.S.A. 130 E2
Béna Burkina 96 C3
Bena Dibele Dem. Rep. Congo 98 C4
Ben Alder mt. U.K. 50 E4
Benalla Australia 112 B6
Benares India see Varanasi
Ben Arous Tunisia 58 D6
Benavente Spain 57 D2
Ben Avon mt. U.K. 50 F3
Benbane Head hd U.K. 51 F2
Benbecula i. U.K. 50 B3
Ben Boyd National Park Australia 112 E6
Benburb U.K. 51 F3
Bên Cat Vietnam 71 D5
Bencha China 77 I1
Ben Chonzie hill U.K. 50 F4
Ben Cleuch hill U.K. 50 F4
Ben Cruachan mt. U.K. 50 D4
Bend U.S.A. 126 C3
Bendearg mt. S. Africa 101 H6
Bender Moldova see Tighina
Bender-Bayla Somalia 98 F3
Bendery Moldova see Tighina
Bendigo Australia 112 B6
Bendoc Australia 112 D6
Bene Moz. 99 D5
Benedict, Mount hill Canada 123 K3
Benenitra Madag. 99 E6
Benešov Czech Rep. 47 O6
Bénestroff France 52 G6
Benevento Italy 58 F4
Beneventum Italy see Benevento
Benezette U.S.A. 135 F3
Beng, Nam r. Laos 70 C3
Bengal, Bay of sea Indian Ocean 81 G8
Bengamisa Dem. Rep. Congo 98 C3
Bengbu China 77 H1
Benghazi Libya 97 F1
Bengkalis Indon. 71 C7
Bengkalis i. Indon. 71 C7
Bengkulu Indon. 68 C7
Bengtsfors Sweden 45 H7
Benguela Angola 99 B5
Benha Egypt see Banhā
Ben Hiant hill U.K. 50 C4
Ben Hope hill U.K. 50 E2
Ben Horn hill U.K. 50 E2
Beni r. Bol. 142 E6
Beni Dem. Rep. Congo 98 C3
Beni Nepal 83 E3
Beni-Abbès Alg. 54 D5
Beniah Lake Canada 121 H2
Benidorm Spain 57 F4
Beni Mellal Morocco 54 C5
▶Benin country Africa 96 D4
Africa 7, 94–95
Benin, Bight of g. Africa 96 D4
Benin City Nigeria 96 D4
Beni-Saf Alg. 57 F6
Beni Snassen, Monts des mts Morocco 57 E6
Beni Suef Egypt see Banī Suwayf
Benito, Islas is Mex. 127 E7
Benito Juárez Arg. 144 E5
Benito Juárez Mex. 129 F5
Benjamim Constant Brazil 142 E4
Benjamin U.S.A. 131 D5
Benjamín Hill Mex. 127 F7
Benjina Indon. 69 I8
Benkelman U.S.A. 130 C3
Ben Klibreck hill U.K. 50 E2
Ben Lavin Nature Reserve S. Africa 101 I2
Ben Lawers mt. U.K. 50 E4
Ben Lomond mt. Australia 112 E3
Ben Lomond hill U.K. 50 E4
Ben Lomond National Park Australia 111 [inset]
Ben Macdui mt. U.K. 50 F3
Benmara Australia 110 B3
Ben More hill U.K. 50 C4
Ben More mt. U.K. 50 E4
Benmore, Lake N.Z. 113 C7
Ben More Assynt hill U.K. 50 E2
Bennetta, Ostrov i. Rus. Fed. 65 P2
Bennett Island Rus. Fed. see Bennetta, Ostrov
Bennett Lake Canada 120 C3
Bennettsville U.S.A. 133 E5
Ben Nevis mt. U.K. 50 D4
Bennington NH U.S.A. 135 J2
Bennington VT U.S.A. 135 I2
Benoni S. Africa 101 I4
Ben Rinnes hill U.K. 50 F3
Bensheim Germany 53 I5
Benson AZ U.S.A. 129 H6
Benson MN U.S.A. 130 E2
Benta Seberang Malaysia 71 C6
Benteng Indon. 69 G8
Bentinck Island Myanmar 71 B5
Bentiu Sudan 86 C8
Bent Jbaïl Lebanon 85 B3
Bentley U.K. 48 F5
Bento Gonçalves Brazil 145 A5
Benton AR U.S.A. 131 E5
Benton CA U.S.A. 128 D3
Benton IL U.S.A. 130 F4
Benton KY U.S.A. 131 F4
Benton LA U.S.A. 131 E5
Benton MO U.S.A. 131 F4
Benton PA U.S.A. 135 G3
Bentong Malaysia see Bentung
Benton Harbor U.S.A. 134 B2
Bentonville U.S.A. 131 E4
Bên Tre Vietnam 71 D5
Bentuang Karimun National Park Indon. 68 E6
Bentung Malaysia 71 C7
Benue r. Nigeria 96 D4
Benum, Gunung mt. Malaysia 71 C7
Ben Vorlich hill U.K. 50 E4
Benwee Head hd Rep. of Ireland 51 C3
Benwood U.S.A. 134 E3
Ben Wyvis mt. U.K. 50 E3
Benxi Liaoning China 74 A4
Benxi Liaoning China 74 B4
Beograd Serb. and Mont. see Belgrade
Béoumi Côte d'Ivoire 96 C4
Beppu Japan 75 C6
Béqaa valley Lebanon see El Béqaa
Berach r. India 82 C4
Beraketa Madag. 99 E6
Bérard, Lac l. Canada 123 H2
Berasia India 82 D5
Berat Albania 59 H4
Beravina Madag. 99 E5
Berbak National Park Indon. 68 C7
Berber Sudan 86 D6
Berbera Somalia 98 E2
Berbérati Cent. Afr. Rep. 98 B3
Berchtesgaden, Nationalpark nat. park Germany 47 N7
Berck France 52 B4
Berdichev Ukr. see Berdychiv
Berdigestyakh Rus. Fed. 65 N3
Berdyans'k Ukr. 43 H7
Berdychiv Ukr. 43 F6
Berea KY U.S.A. 134 C5
Berea OH U.S.A. 134 E3
Beregovo Ukr. see Berehove
Beregovoy Rus. Fed. 74 B1
Berehove Ukr. 43 D6
Bereina P.N.G. 69 L8
Bereket Turkm. see Gazandzhyk
Berekum Ghana 96 C4
Berenice Egypt see Baranīs
Berenice Libya see Benghazi
Berens r. Canada 121 L4
Berens Island Canada 121 L4
Berens River Canada 121 L4
Beresford U.S.A. 130 D3
Bereza Belarus see Byaroza
Berezino Belarus see Byerazino
Berezivka Ukr. 43 F7
Berezne Ukr. 43 E6
Bereznik Rus. Fed. 42 I3
Berezniki Rus. Fed. 41 R4
Berezov Rus. Fed. see Berezovo
Berezovka Rus. Fed. 74 B2
Berezovka Ukr. see Berezivka
Berezovo Rus. Fed. 41 T3
Berezovyy Rus. Fed. 74 D2
Berga Germany 53 L3
Berga Spain 57 G2
Bergama Turkey 59 L5
Bergamo Italy 58 C2
Bergby Sweden 45 J6
Bergen Mecklenburg-Vorpommern Germany 47 N3
Bergen Niedersachsen Germany 49 J2
Bergen Norway 45 D6
Bergen U.S.A. 135 G2
Bergen op Zoom Neth. 52 E3
Bergerac France 56 E4
Bergères-lès-Vertus France 52 E6
Bergheim (Erft) Germany 52 G4
Bergisches Land reg. Germany 53 H4
Bergisch Gladbach Germany 52 H4
Bergland Namibia 100 C2
Bergomum Italy see Bergamo
Bergoo U.S.A. 134 E4
Bergsjö Sweden 45 J6
Bergsviken Sweden 44 L4
Bergtheim Germany 53 K5
Bergues France 52 C4
Bergum Neth. 52 G1
Bergville S. Africa 101 I5
Berhampur India see Baharampur
Beringa, Ostrov i. Rus. Fed. 65 R4
Beringen Belgium 52 F3
Beringovskiy Rus. Fed. 65 S3
Bering Sea N. Pacific Ocean 65 S4
Bering Strait Rus. Fed./U.S.A. 65 U3
Berīs, Ra's pt Iran 89 F5
Berislav Ukr. see Beryslav
Berkåk Norway 44 G5
Berkane Morocco 57 E6
Berkel r. Neth. 52 G2
Berkeley U.S.A. 128 B3
Berkeley Springs U.S.A. 135 F4
Berkhout Neth. 52 F2
Berkner Island Antarctica 152 A1
Berkovitsa Bulg. 59 J3
Berkshire Downs hills U.K. 49 F7
Berkshire Hills U.S.A. 135 I2
Berland r. Canada 120 G4
Berlare Belgium 52 E3
Berlevåg Norway 44 P1

▶Berlin Germany 53 N2
Capital of Germany.

Berlin land Germany 53 N2
Berlin MD U.S.A. 135 H4
Berlin NH U.S.A. 135 J1
Berlin PA U.S.A. 135 F4
Berlin Lake U.S.A. 134 E3
Bermagui Australia 112 E6
Bermejo r. Arg./Bol. 144 E3
Bermejo Bol. 142 F8
Bermen, Lac l. Canada 123 H3

▶Bermuda terr. N. Atlantic Ocean 137 L2
United Kingdom Overseas Territory.
North America 9, 116–117

Bermuda Rise sea feature N. Atlantic Ocean 148 D4

▶Bern Switz. 56 H3
Capital of Switzerland.

Bernalillo U.S.A. 127 G6
Bernardino de Campos Brazil 145 A3
Bernardo O'Higgins, Parque Nacional nat. park Chile 144 B7
Bernasconi Arg. 144 D5
Bernau Germany 53 N2
Bernburg (Saale) Germany 53 L3
Berne Germany 53 I1
Berne Switz. see Bern
Berne U.S.A. 134 C3
Berner Alpen mts Switz. 56 H3
Berneray i. Scotland U.K. 50 B3
Berneray i. Scotland U.K. 50 B4
Bernier Island Australia 109 A6
Bernina Pass Switz. 56 J3
Bernkastel-Kues Germany 52 H5
Beroea Greece see Veroia
Beroea Syria see Aleppo
Beroroha Madag. 99 E6
Beroun Czech Rep. 47 O6
Berounka r. Czech Rep. 47 O6
Berovina Madag. see Beravina
Berri Australia 111 C7
Berriane Alg. 54 E5
Berridale Australia 112 D6
Berriedale U.K. 50 F2
Berrigan Australia 112 B5
Berrima Australia 112 E5
Berrouaghia Alg. 57 H5
Berry Australia 112 E5
Berry U.S.A. 134 C4
Berryessa, Lake U.S.A. 128 B2
Berry Head hd U.K. 49 D8
Berry Islands Bahamas 133 E7
Berryville U.S.A. 135 G4
Berseba Namibia 100 C4
Bersenbrück Germany 53 H2
Bertam Malaysia 71 C6
Berté, Lac l. Canada 123 H4
Berthoud Pass U.S.A. 126 G5
Bertolínia Brazil 143 J5
Bertoua Cameroon 96 E4
Bertraghboy Bay Rep. of Ireland 51 C4
Beru atoll Kiribati 107 H2
Beruri Brazil 142 F4
Beruwala Sri Lanka 84 C5
Berwick Australia 112 B7
Berwick U.S.A. 135 G3
Berwick-upon-Tweed U.K. 48 E3
Berwyn hills U.K. 49 D6
Beryslav Ukr. 59 O1
Berytus Lebanon see Beirut
Besalampy Madag. 99 E5
Besançon France 56 H3
Besar, Gunung mt. Malaysia 71 C7
Besbay Kazakh. 80 A2
Beserah Malaysia 71 C7
Beshkent Uzbek. 89 G2
Beshneh Iran 88 D4
Besikama Indon. 108 D2
Besitang Indon. 71 B6
Beskra Alg. see Biskra
Beslan Rus. Fed. 91 G2
Besnard Lake Canada 121 J4
Besni Turkey 90 E3
Besor watercourse Israel 85 B4
Beşparmak Dağları mts Cyprus see Pentadaktylos Range
Bessbrook U.K. 51 F3
Bessemer U.S.A. 133 C5
Besshoky, Gora hill Kazakh. 91 I1
Besskorbnaya Rus. Fed. 43 I7
Bessonovka Rus. Fed. 43 J5
Betanzos Spain 57 B2
Bethal S. Africa 101 I4
Bethanie Namibia 100 C4
Bethany U.S.A. 130 E3
Bethel U.S.A. 123 H5
Bethel Park U.S.A. 134 E3
Bethesda U.K. 48 C5
Bethesda MD U.S.A. 135 G4
Bethesda OH U.S.A. 134 E3
Bethlehem S. Africa 101 I5
Bethlehem U.S.A. 135 H3
Bethlehem West Bank 85 B4
Bethulie S. Africa 101 G6
Béthune France 52 C4
Beti Pak. 89 H4
Betim Brazil 145 B2
Bet Lehem West Bank see Bethlehem
Betma India 82 C5
Betong Thai. 71 C6
Betoota Australia 110 C5
Betpak-Dala plain Kazakh. 80 D2
Betroka Madag. 99 E6
Bet She'an Israel 85 B3
Betsiamites Canada 123 H4
Betsiamites r. Canada 123 H4
Bettiah India 83 F4
Bettyhill U.K. 50 E2
Bettystown Rep. of Ireland 51 F4
Betul India 82 D5
Betwa r. India 82 D4
Betws-y-coed U.K. 49 D5
Betzdorf Germany 53 H4
Beulah Australia 111 C7
Beulah MI U.S.A. 134 B1
Beulah ND U.S.A. 130 C2
Beult r. U.K. 49 H7
Beuthen Poland see Bytom
Bever r. Germany 53 H2
Beverley U.K. 48 G5
Beverly MA U.S.A. 135 J2
Beverly OH U.S.A. 134 E4
Beverly Hills U.S.A. 128 D4
Beverly Lake Canada 121 K1
Beverstedt Germany 53 I1
Beverungen Germany 53 J3
Beverwijk Neth. 52 E2
Bewani P.N.G. 69 K7
Bexbach Germany 53 H5
Bexhill U.K. 49 H8
Bexley, Cape Canada 118 G3
Beyānlū Iran 88 B3
Beyce Turkey see Orhaneli
Bey Dağları mts Turkey 59 N6
Beykoz Turkey 59 M4
Beyla Guinea 96 C4
Beylagan Azer. see Beyläqan
Beyläqan Azer. 91 G3
Beyneu Kazakh. 78 E2
Beypazarı Turkey 59 N4
Beypınarı Turkey 90 E3
Beypore India 84 B4
Beyrouth Lebanon see Beirut
Beyşehir Turkey 90 C3
Beyşehir Gölü l. Turkey 90 C3
Beytonovo Rus. Fed. 74 B1
Beytüşşebap Turkey 91 F3
Bezameh Iran 88 E3
Bezbozhnik Rus. Fed. 42 K4
Bezhanitsy Rus. Fed. 42 F4
Bezhetsk Rus. Fed. 42 H4
Béziers France 56 F5
Bezmein Turkm. see Byuzmeyin
Bezwada India see Vijayawada
Bhabha India see Bhabhua
Bhabhar India 82 B4
Bhabhua India 83 E4
Bhabua India see Bhabhua
Bhachau India 82 B5
Bhachbhar India 82 B4
Bhadgaon Nepal see Bhaktapur
Bhadohi India 83 E4
Bhadra India 82 C3
Bhadrachalam Road Station India see Kottagudem
Bhadrak India 83 F5
Bhadrakh India see Bhadrak
Bhadravati India 84 B3
Bhag Pak. 89 G4
Bhagalpur India 83 F4
Bhainsa India 84 C2
Bhainsdehi India 82 D5
Bhairab Bazar Bangl. 83 G4
Bhairi Hol mt. Pak. 89 G5
Bhaktapur Nepal 83 F4
Bhalki India 84 C2
Bhamo Myanmar 70 B1
Bhamragarh India 84 D2
Bhandara India 82 D5
Bhanjanagar India 84 E2
Bhanrer Range hills India 82 D5
Bhaptiahi India 83 F4
Bharat country Asia see India
Bharatpur India 82 D4
Bhareli r. India 83 H4
Bharuch India 82 C5
Bhatapara India 83 E5
Bhatarsaigh i. U.K. see Vatersay
Bhatghar Lake India 84 B2
Bhatinda India see Bathinda
Bhatnair India see Hanumangarh
Bhatpara India 83 G5
Bhaunagar India see Bhavnagar
Bhavani r. India 84 C4
Bhavani Sagar l. India 84 C4
Bhavnagar India 82 C5
Bhawana Pak. 89 I4
Bhawanipatna India 84 D2
Bheanaraigh, Eilean i. U.K. see Berneray
Bheemavaram India see Bhimavaram
Bhekuzulu S. Africa 101 J4
Bhera Pak. 89 I3
Bhikhna Thori Nepal 83 F4
Bhilai India 82 E5
Bhildi India 82 C4
Bhilwara India 82 C4
Bhima r. India 84 C2
Bhimar India 82 B4
Bhimavaram India 84 D2
Bhimlath India 82 E5
Bhind India 82 D4
Bhinga India 83 E4
Bhiwandi India 84 B2
Bhiwani India 82 D3
Bhogaipur India 82 D4
Bhojpur Nepal 83 F4
Bhola Bangl. 83 G5
Bhongweni S. Africa 101 I6
Bhopal India 82 D5
Bhopalpatnam India 84 D2
Bhrigukaccha India see Bharuch
Bhuban India 84 E1
Bhubaneshwar India 84 E1
Bhubaneswar India see Bhubaneshwar
Bhuj India 82 B5
Bhumiphol Dam Thai. 70 B3
Bhusawal India 82 C5
▶Bhutan country Asia 83 G4
Asia 6, 62–63
Bhuttewala India 82 B4
Bia r. Ghana 96 C4
Bia, Phou mt. Laos 70 C3
Bīabān mts Iran 88 E5
Biafo Glacier Jammu and Kashmir 82 C2
Biafra, Bight of g. Africa see Benin, Bight of
Biak Indon. 69 J7
Biak i. Indon. 69 J7
Biała Podlaska Poland 43 D5
Białogard Poland 47 O4
Białystok Poland 43 D5

Bianco, Monte mt. France/Italy see Blanc, Mont
Biandangang Kou r. mouth China 77 I1
Bianzhao China 74 A3
Bianzhuang China see Cangshan
Biaora India 82 D5
Biarritz France 56 D5
Bi'ār Tabrāk well Saudi Arabia 88 B5
Bibai Japan 74 F4
Bibbenluke Australia 112 D6
Bibbiena Italy 58 D3
Bibby Island Canada 121 M2
Biberach an der Riß Germany 47 L6
Bibile Sri Lanka 84 D5
Biblis Germany 53 I5
Biblos Lebanon see Jbail
Bicas Brazil 145 C3
Biçer Turkey 59 N5
Bicester U.K. 49 F7
Bichabhera India 82 C4
Bicheng China see Bishan
Bichevaya Rus. Fed. 74 D3
Bichi r. Rus. Fed. 74 E1
Bickerton Island Australia 110 B2
Bickleigh U.K. 49 D8
Bicknell U.S.A. 134 B4
Bicuari, Parque Nacional do nat. park Angola 99 B5
Bid India 84 B2
Bida Nigeria 96 D4
Bidar India 84 C2
Biddeford U.S.A. 135 J2
Biddinghuizen Neth. 52 F2
Bidean nam Bian mt. U.K. 50 D4
Bideford U.K. 49 C7
Bideford Bay U.K. 49 C7
Bidokht Iran 88 E3
Bidzhan Rus. Fed. 74 C3
Bié Angola see Kuito
Biedenkopf Germany 53 I4
Biel Switz. 56 H3
Bielawa Poland 47 P5
Bielefeld Germany 53 I2
Bielitz Poland see Bielsko-Biała
Biella Italy 58 C2
Bielsko-Biała Poland 47 Q6
Bielstein hill Germany 53 J3
Bienenbüttel Germany 53 K1
Biên Hoa Vietnam 71 D5
Bienne Switz. see Biel
Bienville, Lac l. Canada 123 G3
Bié Plateau Angola 99 B5
Bierbank Australia 112 B1
Biesiesvlei S. Africa 101 G4
Bietigheim-Bissingen Germany 53 J6
Bièvre Belgium 52 F5
Bifoun Gabon 98 B4
Big r. Canada 123 K3
Biga Turkey 59 L4
Bigadiç Turkey 59 M5
Biga Yarımadası pen. Turkey 59 L5
Big Baldy Mountain U.S.A. 126 F3
Big Bar Creek Canada 120 F5
Big Bear Lake U.S.A. 128 E4
Big Belt Mountains U.S.A. 126 F3
Big Bend Swaziland 101 J4
Big Bend National Park U.S.A. 131 C6
Bigbury-on-Sea U.K. 49 D8
Big Canyon watercourse U.S.A. 131 C6
Biger Nuur salt l. Mongolia 80 I2
Big Falls U.S.A. 130 E1
Big Fork r. U.S.A. 130 E1
Biggar Canada 121 J4
Biggar U.K. 50 F5
Biggar, Lac l. Canada 122 G4
Bigge Island Australia 108 D3
Biggenden Australia 111 F5
Bigger, Mount Canada 120 B3
Biggesee l. Germany 53 H3
Biggleswade U.K. 49 G6
Biggs CA U.S.A. 128 C2
Biggs OR U.S.A. 126 C3
Big Hole r. U.S.A. 126 E3
Bighorn r. U.S.A. 126 G3
Bighorn Mountains U.S.A. 126 G3
Big Island Nunavut Canada 119 K3
Big Island N.W.T. Canada 120 G2
Big Island Ont. Canada 121 M5
Big Kalzas Lake Canada 120 C2
Big Lake l. Canada 121 H1
Big Lake U.S.A. 131 C6
Bignona Senegal 96 B3
Big Pine U.S.A. 128 D3
Big Pine Peak U.S.A. 128 D4
Big Raccoon r. U.S.A. 134 B4
Big Rapids U.S.A. 134 C2
Big River Canada 121 J4
Big Sable Point U.S.A. 134 B1
Big Salmon r. Canada 120 C2
Big Sand Lake Canada 121 L3
Big Sandy r. U.S.A. 126 F4
Big Sandy Lake Canada 121 J4
Big Smokey Valley U.S.A. 128 E2
Big South Fork National River and Recreation Area park U.S.A. 134 C5
Big Spring U.S.A. 131 C5
Big Stone Canada 121 I5
Big Stone Gap U.S.A. 134 D5
Bigstone Lake Canada 121 M4
Big Timber U.S.A. 126 F3
Big Trout Lake Canada 121 N4
Big Trout Lake l. Canada 121 N4
Big Valley Canada 121 H4
Big Water U.S.A. 129 H3
Bihać Bos.-Herz. 58 F2
Bihar state India 83 F4
Bihariganj India 83 F4
Bihar Sharif India 83 F4
Bihor, Vârful mt. Romania 59 J1
Bihoro Japan 74 G4
Bijagós, Arquipélago dos is Guinea-Bissau 96 B3
Bijaipur India 82 D4
Bijapur India 84 B2
Bījār Iran 88 B3
Bijbehara Jammu and Kashmir 82 C2
Bijeljina Bos.-Herz. 59 H2
Bijelo Polje Serb. and Mont. 59 H3
Bijeraghogarh India 82 E5
Bijiang China see Zhiziluo
Bijie China 76 E3
Bijji India 84 D2
Bijnor India 82 D3
Bijnore India see Bijnor
Bijnot Pak. 89 H4
Bijrān well Saudi Arabia 88 C5
Bijrān, Khashm hill Saudi Arabia 88 C5
Bikampur India 82 C4
Bikaner India 82 C3
Bīkhūyeh Iran 88 D5
Bikin Rus. Fed. 74 D3
Bikin r. Rus. Fed. 74 D3
Bikini atoll Marshall Is 150 H5
Bikori Sudan 86 D7
Bikoro Dem. Rep. Congo 98 B4
Bikou China 76 E1
Bikramganj India 83 F4
Bilād Banī Bū 'Alī Oman 87 I5
Bilaigarh India 84 D1
Bilara India 82 C4
Bilaspur Chhattisgarh India 83 E5
Bilaspur Himachal Pradesh India 82 D3
Biläsuvar Azer. 91 H3
Bila Tserkva Ukr. 43 F6
Bilauktaung Range mts Myanmar/Thai. 71 B4
Bilbao Spain 57 E2
Bilbays Egypt 90 C5
Bilbeis Egypt see Bilbays
Bilbo Spain see Bilbao
Bilecik Turkey 59 M4
Biłgoraj Poland 43 D6
Bilharamulo Tanz. 98 D4
Bilhaur India 82 E4
Bilhorod-Dnistrovs'kyy Ukr. 59 N1
Bili Dem. Rep. Congo 98 C3
Bilibino Rus. Fed. 65 R3
Bilin Myanmar 70 B3
Bill U.S.A. 126 G4
Billabalong Australia 109 A6
Billabong Creek r. Australia see Moulamein Creek
Billericay U.K. 49 H7
Billiluna Australia 108 D4
Billingham U.K. 48 F4
Billings U.S.A. 126 F3
Billiton i. Indon. see Belitung
Bill of Portland hd U.K. 49 E8
Bill Williams r. U.S.A. 129 F4
Bill Williams Mountain U.S.A. 129 G4
Bilma Niger 96 E3
Bilo r. Rus. Fed. see Belaya
Biloela Australia 110 E5
Bilohirs'k Ukr. 90 D1
Bilohir"ya Ukr. 43 E6
Biloku Guyana 143 G3
Biloli India 84 C2
Bilovods'k Ukr. 43 H6
Biloxi U.S.A. 131 F6
Bilpa Morea Claypan salt flat Australia 110 B5
Bilston U.K. 50 F5
Biltine Chad 97 F3
Bilto Norway 44 L2
Bilugyun Island Myanmar 70 B3
Bilyayivka Ukr. 59 N1
Bilzen Belgium 52 F4
Bima Indon. 108 B2
Bimberi, Mount Australia 112 D5
Bimini Islands Bahamas 133 E7
Bimlipatam India 84 D2
Bināb Iran 88 C2
Bina-Etawa India 82 D4
Binaija, Gunung mt. Indon. 67 E8
Bīnālūd, Kūh-e mts Iran 88 E2
Binboğa Daği mt. Turkey 90 E3
Bincheng China see Binzhou
Binchuan China 76 D3
Bindebango Australia 112 C1
Bindle Australia 112 D1
Bindu Dem. Rep. Congo 99 B4
Bindura Zimbabwe 99 D5
Binefar Spain 57 G3
Binga Zimbabwe 99 C5
Binga, Monte mt. Moz. 99 D5
Bingara Australia 112 B2
Bingaram i. India 84 B4
Bing Bong Australia 110 B2
Bingen am Rhein Germany 53 H5
Bingham U.S.A. 135 K1
Binghamton U.S.A. 135 H2
Bingmei China see Congjiang
Bingöl Turkey 91 F3
Bingol Dağı mt. Turkey 91 F3
Bingxi China see Yushan
Bingzhongluo China 76 C2
Binh Gia Vietnam 70 D2
Binika India 83 E5
Binjai Indon. 71 B7
Bin Mürkhan well U.A.E. 88 D5
Binnaway Australia 112 D3
Binpur India 83 F5
Bintan i. Indon. 71 D7
Bint Jbeil Lebanon see Bent Jbaïl
Bintulu Sarawak Malaysia 68 E6
Binxian Heilong. China 74 B3
Binxian Shaanxi China 77 F1
Binya Australia 112 C5
Binyang China 77 F4
Bin-Yauri Nigeria 96 D3
Binzhou Guangxi China see Binyang
Binzhou Heilong. China see Binxian
Binzhou Shandong China 73 L5
Bioco i. Equat. Guinea 96 D4
Biograd na Moru Croatia 58 F3
Bioko i. Equat. Guinea see Bioco
Biokovo mts Croatia 58 G3
Biquinhas Brazil 145 B2
Bir India see Bid
Bira Rus. Fed. 74 D2
Bi'r Abū Jady oasis Syria 85 D1
Bīrag, Kūh-e mts Iran 89 F5
Birāk Libya 97 E2
Birakan Rus. Fed. 74 C2
Bi'r al 'Abd Egypt 85 A4
Bi'r al Halbā well Syria 85 D2
Bi'r al Jifjāfah well Egypt 85 A4
Bi'r al Khamsah well Egypt 90 B5
Bi'r al Mālihah well Egypt 85 A5
Bi'r al Mulūsi Iraq 91 F4
Bi'r al Munbatiḥ well Syria 85 D2
Bi'r al Qaṭrānī well Egypt 90 B5
Bi'r al Ubbayiḍ well Egypt 90 B6
Birandozero Rus. Fed. 42 H3
Bi'r an Nuṣf well Egypt see Bi'r an Nuṣṣ
Bi'r an Nuṣṣ well Egypt 90 B5
Bir Anzarane W. Sahara 96 B2
Birao Cent. Afr. Rep. 98 C3
Bi'r ar Rābiyah well Egypt 90 B5
Biratnagar Nepal 83 F4
Bi'r aṭ Ṭarfāwī well Libya 90 B5
Bi'r Başīrī well Syria 85 C2
Bi'r Bayḍā' well Egypt 85 B4
Bi'r Baylī well Egypt 90 B5
Bîr Beida well Egypt see Bi'r Bayḍā'
Bi'r Buṭaymān Syria 91 E3
Birch r. Canada 121 H3
Birch Hills Canada 121 J4
Birch Island Canada 120 G5
Birch Lake N.W.T. Canada 120 G2
Birch Lake Ont. Canada 121 M5
Birch Lake Sask. Canada 121 I4
Birch Mountains Canada 120 H3
Birch River U.S.A. 134 E4
Birch Run U.S.A. 134 D2
Bircot Eth. 98 E3
Birdaard Neth. 52 F1
Bîr Dignâsh well Egypt see Bi'r Diqnāsh
Bi'r Diqnāsh well Egypt 90 B5
Bird Island N. Mariana Is see Farallon de Medinilla
Birdseye U.S.A. 129 H2
Birdsville Australia 111 B5
Birecik Turkey 90 E3
Bîr el 'Abd Egypt see Bi'r al 'Abd
Bir el Arbi well Alg. 57 I6
Bîr el Istabl well Egypt see Bi'r Istabl
Bîr el Khamsa well Egypt see Bi'r al Khamsah
Bîr el Nuṣṣ well Egypt see Bi'r an Nuṣṣ
Bîr el Obeiyiḍ well Egypt see Bi'r al Ubbayiḍ
Bîr el Qaṭrâni well Egypt see Bi'r al Qaṭrānī
Bîr el Râbia well Egypt see Bi'r ar Rābiyah
Birendranagar Nepal see Surkhet
Bir en Natrûn well Sudan 86 C6
Bireun Indon. 71 B6
Bi'r Fāḍil well Saudi Arabia 88 C6
Bi'r Fajr well Saudi Arabia 90 E5
Bi'r Fu'ād well Egypt 90 B5
Bîr Gifgâfa well Egypt see Bi'r al Jifjāfah
Bi'r Ḥajal well Syria 85 D2
Birhan mt. Eth. 98 D2
Bi'r Ḥasanah well Egypt 85 A4
Bi'r Ḥayzān well Saudi Arabia 90 E6
Bi'r Ibn Hirmās Saudi Arabia see Al Bi'r
Bir Ibn Juhayyim Saudi Arabia 88 C6
Birigüi Brazil 145 A3
Bīrīn Syria 85 C2
Bi'r Istabl well Egypt 90 B5
Bīrjand Iran 88 E3
Bi'r Jubnī well Libya 90 B5
Birkát Hamad well Iraq 91 G5
Birkenfeld Germany 53 H5
Birkenhead U.K. 48 D5
Birkirkara Malta 58 F7
Birksgate Range hills Australia 109 E6
Bîrlad Romania see Bârlad
Bi'r Lahfān well Egypt 85 A4
Birlik Kazakh. see Brlik
Birmal reg. Afgh. 89 H3
Birmingham U.K. 49 F6
Birmingham U.S.A. 133 C5
Bîr Mogreïn Mauritania 96 B2
Bi'r Muhaymid al Wazwaz well Syria 85 D2
Bi'r Nāḥid oasis Egypt 90 C5
Birnin-Gwari Nigeria 96 D3
Birnin-Kebbi Nigeria 96 D3
Birnin Konni Niger 96 D3
Birobidzhan Rus. Fed. 74 D2
Bi'r Qaşīr as Sirr well Egypt 90 B5
Birr Rep. of Ireland 51 E4
Bi'r Rawḍ Sālim well Egypt 85 A4
Birrie r. Australia 112 C2
Birrindudu Australia 108 E4
Bîr Rôd Sâlim well Egypt see Bi'r Rawḍ Sālim
Birsay U.K. 50 F1
Bi'r Shalatayn Egypt 86 E5
Bîr Shalatein Egypt see Bi'r Shalatayn
Birsk Rus. Fed. 41 R4
Birstall U.K. 49 F6
Birstein Germany 53 J4
Bir Ṭalḥah well Saudi Arabia 88 B6
Birthday Mountain hill Australia 110 C2
Birtle Canada 121 K5
Biru China 76 B2
Birur India 84 B3
Bi'r Usaylīlah well Saudi Arabia 88 B6
Biruxiong China see Biru
Biržai Lith. 45 N8
Bisa India 70 A1
Bisa i. Indon. 69 H7
Bisalpur India 82 D3
Bisau India 82 C3
Bisbee U.S.A. 127 F7
Biscay, Bay of sea France/Spain 56 B4
Biscay Abyssal Plain sea feature N. Atlantic Ocean 148 H3
Biscayne National Park U.S.A. 133 D7
Biscoe Islands Antarctica 152 L2
Biscotasi Lake Canada 122 E5
Biscotasing Canada 122 E5
Bisezhai China 76 D4
Bishan China 76 E2
Bishbek Kyrg. see Bishkek
Bishenpur India see Bishnupur
▶Bishkek Kyrg. 80 D3
Capital of Kyrgyzstan.
Bishnath India 76 B3
Bishnupur Manipur India 83 H4
Bishnupur W. Bengal India 83 F5
Bisho S. Africa 101 H7
Bishop U.S.A. 128 D3
Bishop Auckland U.K. 48 F4
Bishop Lake Canada 120 G1
Bishop's Stortford U.K. 49 H7
Bishopville U.S.A. 133 D5
Bishrī, Jabal hills Syria 85 D2
Bishui Heilong. China 74 A1
Bishui Henan China see Biyang
Biskra Alg. 54 F5
Bislig Phil. 69 H5
▶Bismarck U.S.A. 130 C2
State capital of North Dakota.
Bismarck Archipelago is P.N.G. 69 L7
Bismarck Range mts P.N.G. 69 K7
Bismarck Sea P.N.G. 69 L7
Bismark (Altmark) Germany 53 L2
Bismil Turkey 91 F3
Bismo Norway 44 F6
Bison U.S.A. 130 C2
Bispgården Sweden 44 J5
Bispingen Germany 53 K1
Bissa, Djebel mt. Alg. 57 G5
Bissamcuttak India 84 D2
▶Bissau Guinea-Bissau 96 B3
Capital of Guinea-Bissau.
Bissaula Nigeria 96 E4
Bissett Canada 121 M5
Bistcho Lake Canada 120 G3
Bistriṭa Romania 59 K1
Bistriṭa r. Romania 59 L1
Bitburg Germany 52 G5
Bitche France 53 H5
Bithur India 82 E4
Bithynia reg. Turkey 59 M4
Bitkine Chad 97 E3
Bitlis Turkey 91 F3
Bitola Macedonia 59 I4
Bitolj Macedonia see Bitola
Bitonto Italy 58 G4
Bitrān, Jabal hill Saudi Arabia 84 B6
Bitra Par reef India 84 B4
Bitter Creek r. U.S.A. 129 I2
Bitterfeld Germany 53 M3
Bitterfontein S. Africa 100 D6
Bitter Lakes Egypt 90 D5
Bitterroot r. U.S.A. 126 E3
Bitterroot Range mts U.S.A. 126 E3
Bitterwater U.S.A. 128 C3
Bittkau Germany 53 L2
Bitung Indon. 69 H6
Biu Nigeria 96 E3
Biwa-ko l. Japan 75 D6
Biwmaris U.K. see Beaumaris
Biyang China 77 G1
Bīye K'obē Eth. 98 E2
Biysk Rus. Fed. 72 F2
Bizana S. Africa 101 I6
Bizerta Tunisia see Bizerte
Bizerte Tunisia 58 C6
Bīzhanābād Iran 88 E5
▶Bjargtangar hd Iceland 44 [inset]
Most westerly point of Europe.
Bjästa Sweden 44 K5
Bjelovar Croatia 58 G2
Bjerkvik Norway 44 J2
Bjerringbro Denmark 45 F8
Bjørgan Norway 44 G5
Björkliden Sweden 44 K2
Björklinge Sweden 45 J6
Bjorli Norway 44 F5
Björna Sweden 44 K5
Björneborg Fin. see Pori
▶Bjørnøya i. Arctic Ocean 64 C2
Part of Norway.
Bjurholm Sweden 44 K5
Bla Mali 96 C3
Black r. Man. Canada 121 L5
Black r. Ont. Canada 122 E4
Black r. AR U.S.A. 131 F5
Black r. AR U.S.A. 131 F5
Black r. AZ U.S.A. 129 H5
Black r. Vietnam 70 D2
Blackadder Water r. U.K. 50 G5
Blackall Australia 110 D5
Blackbear r. Canada 121 N4
Black Birch Lake Canada 121 J3
Black Bourton U.K. 49 F7
Blackbull Australia 110 C3
Blackburn U.K. 48 E5
Blackbutt Australia 112 F1
Black Butte mt. U.S.A. 128 B2
Black Butte Lake U.S.A. 128 B2
Black Canyon gorge U.S.A. 129 F4
Black Canyon of the Gunnison National Park U.S.A. 129 J2
Black Combe hill U.K. 48 D4
Black Creek watercourse U.S.A. 129 I4
Black Donald Lake Canada 135 G1
Blackdown Tableland National Park Australia 110 E4
Blackduck U.S.A. 130 E2
Blackfalds Canada 120 H4
Blackfoot U.S.A. 126 E4
Black Foot r. U.S.A. 126 E3
Black Forest mts Germany 47 L7
Black Hill hill U.K. 48 F5
Black Hills SD U.S.A. 124 G3
Black Hills SD U.S.A. 126 G3
Black Island Canada 121 L5
Black Lake Canada 121 J3
Black Lake l. Canada 121 J3
Black Lake l. U.S.A. 134 C1
Black Mesa mt. U.S.A. 129 I5
Black Mesa ridge U.S.A. 129 H3
Black Mountain Pak. 89 I3
Black Mountain hill U.K. 49 D7
Black Mountain AK U.S.A. 118 B3
Black Mountain CA U.S.A. 128 E4
Black Mountain KY U.S.A. 134 D5
Black Mountain NM U.S.A. 129 I5
Black Mountains hills U.K. 49 D7
Black Mountains U.S.A. 129 F4
Black Nossob watercourse Namibia 100 D2
Black Pagoda India see Konarka
Blackpool U.K. 48 D5
Black Range mts U.S.A. 129 I5
Black River MI U.S.A. 134 D1
Black River NY U.S.A. 135 H1
Black River Falls U.S.A. 130 F2
Black Rock hill Jordan see 'Unāb, Jabal al
Black Rock Desert U.S.A. 126 D4
Blacksburg U.S.A. 134 E5
Black Sea Asia/Europe 43 H8
Blacks Fork r. U.S.A. 126 F4
Blackshear U.S.A. 133 D6
Blacksod Bay Rep. of Ireland 51 B3
Black Springs U.S.A. 128 D2
Blackstairs Mountains hills Rep. of Ireland 51 F5
Blackstone U.S.A. 135 F5
Black Sugarloaf mt. Australia 112 E3
Black Tickle Canada 123 L3
Blackville Australia 112 E3
Blackwater Australia 110 E4
Blackwater Rep. of Ireland 51 F5
Blackwater r. Rep. of Ireland 51 E5
Blackwater r. Rep. of Ireland/U.K. 51 F3
Blackwater watercourse U.S.A. 131 C5
Blackwater Lake Canada 120 F2
Blackwater Reservoir U.K. 50 E4
Blackwood r. Australia 109 A8
Blackwood National Park Australia 110 D4
Bladensburg National Park Australia 110 C4
Blaenavon U.K. 49 D7
Blagodarnyy Rus. Fed. 91 F1
Blagoevgrad Bulg. 59 J3
Blagoveshchensk Amurskaya Oblast' Rus. Fed. 74 B2
Blagoveshchensk Respublika Bashkortostan Rus. Fed. 41 R4
Blaikiston, Mount Canada 120 H5
Blaine Lake Canada 121 J4
Blair U.S.A. 130 D3
Blair Athol Australia 110 D4
Blair Atholl U.K. 50 F4
Blairgowrie U.K. 50 F4
Blairsden U.S.A. 128 C2
Blairsville U.S.A. 133 D5
Blakang Mati, Pulau i. Sing. see Sentosa
Blakely U.S.A. 133 C6
Blakeney U.K. 49 I6
▶Blanc, Mont mt. France/Italy 56 H4
5th highest mountain in Europe.
Blanca, Bahía b. Arg. 144 D5
Blanca, Sierra mt. U.S.A. 127 G6
Blanca Peak U.S.A. 127 G5
Blanche, Lake salt flat S.A. Australia 111 B6
Blanche, Lake salt flat W.A. Australia 108 C5
Blanchester U.S.A. 134 D4
Blanc Nez, Cap c. France 52 B4
Blanco r. Bol. 142 F6
Blanco U.S.A. 129 J3
Blanco, Cape U.S.A. 126 B4
Blanc-Sablon Canada 123 K4
Bland r. Australia 112 C4
Bland U.S.A. 134 E5
Blanda r. Iceland 44 [inset]
Blandford Forum U.K. 49 E8
Blanding U.S.A. 129 I3
Blanes Spain 57 H3
Blangah, Telok Sing. 71 [inset]
Blangkejeren Indon. 71 B7
Blangpidie Indon. 71 B7
Blankenberge Belgium 52 D3
Blankenheim Germany 52 G4
Blanquilla, Isla i. Venez. 142 F1
Blansko Czech Rep. 47 P6
Blantyre Malawi 99 D5
Blarney Rep. of Ireland 51 D6
Blaufelden Germany 53 J5
Blåviksjön Sweden 44 K4
Blaye France 56 D4
Blayney Australia 112 D4
Blaze, Point Australia 108 E3
Bleckede Germany 53 K1
Bleilochtalsperre resr Germany 53 L4
Blenheim Canada 134 E2
Blenheim N.Z. 113 D5
Blenheim Palace tourist site U.K. 49 F7
Blerick Neth. 52 G3
Blessington Lakes Rep. of Ireland 51 F4
Bletchley U.K. 49 G6
Blida Alg. 57 H5
Blies r. Germany 53 H5
Bligh Water b. Fiji 107 H3
Blind River Canada 122 E5
Bliss U.S.A. 126 E4
Blissfield U.S.A. 134 D3
Blitta Togo 96 D4
Blocher U.S.A. 134 C4
Block Island U.S.A. 135 J3
Block Island Sound sea chan. U.S.A. 135 J3
Bloemfontein S. Africa 101 H5
Bloemhof S. Africa 101 G4
Bloemhof Dam S. Africa 101 G4
Bloemhof Dam Nature Reserve S. Africa 101 G4
Blomberg Germany 53 J3
Blönduós Iceland 44 [inset]
Blongas Indon. 108 B2
Bloods Range mts Australia 109 E6
Bloodsworth Island U.S.A. 135 G4
Bloodvein r. Canada 121 L5
Bloody Foreland pt Rep. of Ireland 51 D2
Bloomer U.S.A. 130 F2
Bloomfield Canada 135 G2
Bloomfield IA U.S.A. 130 E3
Bloomfield IN U.S.A. 134 B4
Bloomfield MO U.S.A. 131 F4
Bloomfield NM U.S.A. 129 J3
Blooming Prairie U.S.A. 130 E3
Bloomington IL U.S.A. 130 F3
Bloomington IN U.S.A. 134 B4
Bloomington MN U.S.A. 130 E2
Bloomsburg U.S.A. 135 G3
Blossburg U.S.A. 135 G3
Blosseville Kyst coastal area Greenland 119 P3
Blouberg S. Africa 101 I2
Blouberg Nature Reserve S. Africa 101 I2
Blountstown U.S.A. 133 C6
Blountville U.S.A. 134 D5
Bloxham U.K. 49 F6
Blue r. Canada 120 D3
Blue watercourse U.S.A. 129 I5
Blue Bell Knoll mt. U.S.A. 129 H2
Blueberry r. Canada 120 F3
Blue Diamond U.S.A. 129 F3
Blue Earth U.S.A. 130 E3
Bluefield VA U.S.A. 132 D4
Bluefield WV U.S.A. 134 E5
Bluefields Nicaragua 137 H6
Blue Hills Turks and Caicos Is 129 F8
Blue Knob hill U.S.A. 135 F3
Blue Mesa Reservoir U.S.A. 129 J2
Blue Mountain hill Canada 123 K4
Blue Mountain India 83 H5
Blue Mountain Lake U.S.A. 135 H2
Blue Mountain Pass Lesotho 101 H5
Blue Mountains Australia 112 D4
Blue Mountains U.S.A. 126 D3
Blue Mountains National Park Australia 112 E4
Blue Nile r. Eth./Sudan 86 D6
also known as Ābay Wenz (Ethiopia), Bahr el Azraq (Sudan)
Bluenose Lake Canada 118 G3
Blue Ridge GA U.S.A. 133 C5
Blue Ridge VA U.S.A. 134 F5
Blue Ridge mts U.S.A. 134 E5
Blue Stack hill Rep. of Ireland 51 D3
Blue Stack Mts hills Rep. of Ireland 51 D3
Bluestone Lake U.S.A. 134 E5
Bluewater U.S.A. 129 J4
Bluff N.Z. 113 B8
Bluff U.S.A. 129 I3
Bluffdale U.S.A. 129 H1
Bluff Island Hong Kong China 73 [inset]
Bluff Knoll mt. Australia 109 B8
Bluffton IN U.S.A. 134 C3
Bluffton OH U.S.A. 134 D3
Blumenau Brazil 145 A4
Blustry Mountain Canada 126 C2
Blyde River Canyon Nature Reserve S. Africa 101 J3
Blyth Canada 134 E2
Blyth England U.K. 48 F3
Blyth England U.K. 48 F5
Blythe U.S.A. 129 F5
Blytheville U.S.A. 131 F5
Bø Norway 45 F7
Bo Sierra Leone 96 B4
Boa Esperança Brazil 145 B3
Bo'ai Henan China 77 G1
Bo'ai Yunnan China 76 E4
Boali Cent. Afr. Rep. 98 B3
Boalsert Neth. see Bolsward
Boane Moz. 101 K4
Boa Nova Brazil 145 C1
Boardman U.S.A. 134 E3
Boatlaname Botswana 101 G2
Boa Viagem Brazil 143 K5
Boa Vista Brazil 142 F3
Boa Vista i. Cape Verde 96 [inset]
Bobadah Australia 112 C4
Bobai China 77 F4
Bobaomby, Tanjona c. Madag. 99 E5
Bobbili India 84 D2
Bobcaygeon Canada 135 F1
Bobo-Dioulasso Burkina 96 C3
Bobotov Kuk mt. Serb. and Mont. see Durmitor
Bobriki Rus. Fed. see Novomoskovsk
Bobrinets Ukr. see Bobrynets'
Bobrov Rus. Fed. 43 I6
Bobrovitsa Ukr. see Bobrovytsya
Bobrovytsya Ukr. 43 F6
Bobruysk Belarus see Babruysk
Bobrynets' Ukr. 43 G6
Bobs Lake Canada 135 G1
Bobuk Sudan 86 D7
Bobures Venez. 142 D2
Boby mt. Madag. 99 E6
Boca de Macareo Venez. 142 F2
Boca do Acre Brazil 142 E5
Boca do Jari Brazil 143 H4
Bocaiúva Brazil 145 C2
Bocaranga Cent. Afr. Rep. 98 B3
Boca Raton U.S.A. 133 D7
Bocas del Toro Panama 137 H7
Bochnia Poland 47 R6
Bocholt Germany 52 G3
Bochum Germany 53 H3
Bochum S. Africa 101 I2
Bockenem Germany 53 K2
Bocoio Angola 99 B5
Bocoyna Mex. 127 G8
Boda Cent. Afr. Rep. 98 B3
Bodalla Australia 112 E6
Bodallin Australia 109 B7
Bodaybo Rus. Fed. 65 M4
Boddam U.K. 50 H3
Bode r. Germany 53 L3
Bodega Head hd U.S.A. 128 B2
Bodélé reg. Chad 97 E3
Boden Sweden 44 L4
Bodenham U.K. 49 E6
Bodensee l. Germany/Switz. see Constance, Lake
Bodenteich Germany 53 K2
Bodenwerder Germany 53 J3
Bodie U.S.A. 128 D2
Bodinayakkanur India 84 C4
Bodmin U.K. 49 C8
Bodmin Moor moorland U.K. 49 C8
Bodø Norway 44 I3
Bodoquena Brazil 143 G7
Bodoquena, Serra da hills Brazil 144 E2
Bodrum Turkey 59 L6
Bodträskfors Sweden 44 L3
Boechout Belgium 52 E3
Boende Dem. Rep. Congo 97 F5
Boerne U.S.A. 131 D6
Boeuf r. U.S.A. 131 F6
Boffa Guinea 96 B3
Bogalay Myanmar see Bogale
Bogale Myanmar 70 A3
Bogale r. Myanmar 70 A4
Bogalusa U.S.A. 131 F6
Bogan r. Australia 112 C2
Bogandé Burkina 96 C3
Bogan Gate Australia 112 C4
Bogani Nani Wartabone National Park Indon. 69 G6
Boğazlıyan Turkey 90 D3
Bogcang Zangbo r. China 83 F3
Bogda Shan mts China 80 G3
Boggabilla Australia 112 E2
Boggabri Australia 112 E3
Boggeragh Mts hills Rep. of Ireland 51 C5
Boghar Alg. 57 H6
Boghari Alg. see Ksar el Boukhari

Bognor Regis U.K. 49 G8
Bogodukhov Ukr. see Bohodukhiv
Bog of Allen reg. Rep. of Ireland 51 E4
Bogong, Mount Australia 112 C6
Bogopol' Rus. Fed. 74 D3
Bogor Indon. 68 D8
Bogoroditsk Rus. Fed. 43 H5
Bogorodsk Rus. Fed. 42 I4
Bogorodskoye Khabarovskiy Kray Rus. Fed. 74 F1
Bogorodskoye Kirovskaya Oblast' Rus. Fed. 42 K4
▶Bogotá Col. 142 D3
Capital of Colombia and 5th most populous city in South America.
Bogotol Rus. Fed. 64 J4
Bogoyavlenskoye Rus. Fed. see Pervomayskiy
Bogra Bangl. 83 G4
Boguchany Rus. Fed. 65 K4
Boguchar Rus. Fed. 43 I6
Bogué Mauritania 96 B3
Bo Hai g. China 73 L5
Bohain-en-Vermandois France 52 D5
Bohai Wan b. China 66 D4
Bohemia reg. Czech Rep. 47 N6
Bohemian Forest mts Germany see Böhmer Wald
Böhlen Germany 53 M3
Bohlokong S. Africa 101 I5
Böhme r. Germany 53 J2
Böhmer Wald mts Germany 53 M5
Bohmte Germany 53 I2
Bohodukhiv Ukr. 43 G6
Bohol i. Phil. 69 G5
Bohol Sea Phil. 69 G5
Böhöt Mongolia 73 J3
Bohu China 80 G3
Boiaçu Brazil 142 F4
Boichoko S. Africa 100 F5
Boigu Island Australia 69 K8
Boikhutso S. Africa 101 H4
Boileau, Cape Australia 108 C4
Boim Brazil 143 G4
Boipeba, Ilha i. Brazil 145 D1
Bois r. Brazil 145 A2
Bois Blanc Island U.S.A. 132 C2
▶Boise U.S.A. 126 D4
State capital of Idaho.
Boise City U.S.A. 131 C4
Boissevain Canada 121 K5
Boitumelong S. Africa 101 G4
Boizenburg Germany 53 K1
Bojd Iran 88 E3
Bojnūrd Iran 88 E2
Bokaak atoll Marshall Is see Taongi
Bokajan India 83 H4
Bokaro India 83 F5
Bokaro Reservoir India 83 F5
Bokatola Dem. Rep. Congo 98 B4
Boké Guinea 96 B3
Bokele Dem. Rep. Congo 98 C4
Bokhara r. Australia 112 C2
Bo Kheo Cambodia see Bâ Kêv
Boknafjorden sea chan. Norway 45 D7
Bokoko Dem. Rep. Congo 98 C3
Bokoro Chad 97 E3
Bokovskaya Rus. Fed. 43 I6
Bokspits S. Africa 100 E4
Boktor Rus. Fed. 74 E2
Bokurdak Turkm. see Bakhardok
Bol Chad 97 E3
Bolaiti Dem. Rep. Congo 97 F5
Bolama Guinea-Bissau 96 B3
Bolangir India 84 D1
Bolan Pass Pak. 89 G4
Bolbec France 52 E2
Bole China 80 F3
Bole Ghana 96 C4
Boleko Dem. Rep. Congo 98 B4
Bolen Rus. Fed. 74 D2
Bolgar Rus. Fed. 43 K5
Bolgatanga Ghana 96 C3
Bolgrad Ukr. see Bolhrad
Bolhrad Ukr. 59 M2
Boli China 74 C3
Bolia Dem. Rep. Congo 98 B4
Boliden Sweden 44 L4
Bolingbrook U.S.A. 134 A3
Bolintin-Vale Romania 59 K2
Bolívar Peru 142 C5
Bolivar NY U.S.A. 135 F2
Bolivar TN U.S.A. 131 F5
Bolívar, Pico mt. Venez. 142 D2
Bolivia Cuba 133 E8
▶Bolivia country S. America 142 E7
5th largest country in South America.
South America 9, 140–141
Bolkhov Rus. Fed. 43 H5
Bollène France 56 G4
Bollnäs Sweden 45 J6
Bollon Australia 112 C2
Bollstabruk Sweden 44 J5
Bolmen l. Sweden 45 H8
Bolobo Dem. Rep. Congo 98 B4
Bologna Italy 58 D2
Bolognesi Peru 142 D5
Bologoye Rus. Fed. 42 G4
Bolokanang S. Africa 101 G5
Bolomba Dem. Rep. Congo 98 B3
Bolon' Rus. Fed. see Achan
Bolovens, Phouphieng plat. Laos 70 D4
Bolpur India 83 F5
Bolsena, Lago di l. Italy 58 D3
Bol'shakovo Rus. Fed. 45 L9
Bol'shaya Chernigovka Rus. Fed. 41 Q5
Bol'shaya Glushitsa Rus. Fed. 43 K5
Bol'shaya Imandra, Ozero l. Rus. Fed. 44 R3
Bol'shaya Martinovka Rus. Fed. 39 I7
Bol'shaya Tsarevshchina Rus. Fed. see Volzhskiy
Bol'shenarymskoye Kazakh. 80 F2
Bol'shevik, Ostrov i. Rus. Fed. 65 L2
Bol'shezemel'skaya Tundra lowland Rus. Fed. 42 L2
Bol'shiye Barsuki, Peski des. Kazakh. 80 A2
Bol'shiye Chirki Rus. Fed. 42 J3
Bol'shiye Kozly Rus. Fed. 42 H2
Bol'shoy Aluy r. Rus. Fed. 65 Q3
Bol'shoy Begichev, Ostrov i. Rus. Fed. 153 E2
Bol'shoye Murashkino Rus. Fed. 42 J5
Bol'shoy Irgiz r. Rus. Fed. 43 J6
Bol'shoy Kamen' Rus. Fed. 74 D4
Bol'shoy Kavkaz mts Asia/Europe see Caucasus
Bol'shoy Kundysh r. Rus. Fed. 42 J4
Bol'shoy Lyakhovskiy, Ostrov i. Rus. Fed. 65 P2
Bol'shoy Tokmak Kyrg. see Tokmok
Bol'shoy Tokmak Ukr. see Tokmak
Bolsward Neth. 52 F1
Bolton Canada 134 F2
Bolton U.K. 48 E5
Bolu Turkey 59 N4
Boluntay China 83 H1
Boluo China 77 G4
Bolus Head hd Rep. of Ireland 51 B6
Bolvadin Turkey 59 N5
Bolzano Italy 58 D1
Boma Dem. Rep. Congo 99 B4
Bomaderry Australia 112 E5
Bombala Australia 112 D6
Bombay India see Mumbai
Bombay Beach U.S.A. 129 F5
Bomberai, Semenanjung pen. Indon. 69 I7
Bomboma Dem. Rep. Congo 98 B3
Bom Comércio Brazil 142 E5
Bomdila India 83 H4
Bomi China 76 B2
Bomili Dem. Rep. Congo 98 C3
Bom Jardim Brazil 145 D1
Bom Jardim de Goiás Brazil 145 A2
Bom Jesus Brazil 145 A5
Bom Jesus da Gurgueia, Serra do hills Brazil 143 J5
Bom Jesus da Lapa Brazil 145 C1
Bom Jesus do Norte Brazil 145 C3
Bømlo i. Norway 45 D7
Bomokandi r. Dem. Rep. Congo 98 C3
Bom Retiro Brazil 145 A4
Bom Sucesso Brazil 145 B3
Bon, Cap c. Tunisia 58 D6
Bon, Ko i. Thai. 71 B5
Bona Alg. see Annaba
Bona, Mount U.S.A. 120 A2
Bonāb Iran 88 B2
Bon Air U.S.A. 135 G5
Bonaire i. Neth. Antilles 137 K6
Bonanza Peak U.S.A. 126 C2
Bonaparte Archipelago is Australia 108 D3
Bonaparte Lake Canada 120 F5
Bonar Bridge U.K. 50 E3
Bonavista Canada 123 L4
Bonavista Bay Canada 123 L4
Bonchester Bridge U.K. 50 G5
Bondo Dem. Rep. Congo 98 C3
Bondokodi Indon. 68 F8
Bondoukou Côte d'Ivoire 96 C4
Bonduel U.S.A. 134 A1
Bondyuzhskiy Rus. Fed. see Mendeleyevsk
Bône Alg. see Annaba
Bone, Teluk b. Indon. 69 G8
Bönen Germany 53 H3
Bonerate, Kepulauan is Indon. 108 C1
Bo'ness U.K. 50 F4
▶Bonete, Cerro mt. Arg. 144 C3
3rd highest mountain in South America.
Bonga Eth. 98 D3
Bongaigaon India 83 G4
Bongandanga Dem. Rep. Congo 98 C3
Bongani S. Africa 100 F5
Bongao Phil. 68 F5
Bongba China 82 E2
Bong Co l. China 83 G3
Bongo, Massif des mts Cent. Afr. Rep. 98 C3
Bongo, Serra do mts Angola 99 B4
Bongolava mts Madag. 99 E5
Bongor Chad 97 E3
Bông Sơn Vietnam 71 E4
Bonham U.S.A. 131 D5
Bonheiden Belgium 52 E3
Boni Mali 96 C3
Bonifacio Corsica France 56 I6
Bonifacio, Bocche di strait France/Italy see Bonifacio, Strait of
Bonifacio, Bouches de strait France/Italy see Bonifacio, Strait of
Bonifacio, Strait of France/Italy 56 I6
▶Bonin Islands Japan 75 F8
Part of Japan.
▶Bonn Germany 52 H4
Former capital of Germany.
Bonna Germany see Bonn
Bonnåsjøen Norway 44 I3
Bonners Ferry U.S.A. 126 D2
Bonnet, Lac du resr Canada 117 M5
Bonneville France 56 H3
Bonneville Salt Flats U.S.A. 129 G1
Bonnières-sur-Seine France 52 B5
Bonnie Rock Australia 109 B7
Bonnieville U.S.A. 134 C5
Bonnyrigg U.K. 50 F5
Bonnyville Canada 121 I4
Bonobono Phil. 68 F5
Bonom Mhai mt. Vietnam 71 D5
Bononia Italy see Bologna
Bonorva Sardinia Italy 58 C4
Bonshaw Australia 112 E2
Bontebok National Park S. Africa 100 E8
Bonthe Sierra Leone 96 B4
Bontoc Phil. 77 I5
Bontosunggu Indon. 68 F8
Bontrug S. Africa 101 G7
Bonvouloir Islands P.N.G. 110 E1
Bonwapitse Botswana 101 H2
Boo, Kepulauan is Indon. 69 H7
Book Cliffs ridge U.S.A. 129 I2
Booker U.S.A. 131 C4
Boolba Australia 112 D2
Booligal Australia 112 B4
Boomer U.S.A. 134 E4
Boomi Australia 112 D2
Boon U.S.A. 134 C1
Boonah Australia 112 F1
Boone CO U.S.A. 127 G5
Boone IA U.S.A. 130 E3
Boone NC U.S.A. 132 D4
Boone Lake U.S.A. 134 D5
Boones Mill U.S.A. 134 F5
Booneville AR U.S.A. 131 E5
Booneville KY U.S.A. 134 D5
Booneville MS U.S.A. 131 F5
Böön Tsagaan Nuur salt l. Mongolia 80 I2
Boonville CA U.S.A. 128 B2
Boonville IN U.S.A. 134 B4
Boonville MO U.S.A. 130 E4
Boonville NY U.S.A. 135 H2
Boorabin National Park Australia 109 C7
Boorama Somalia 98 E3
Booroorban Australia 112 B5
Boorowa Australia 112 D5
Boort Australia 112 A6
Boothby, Cape Antarctica 152 D2
Boothia, Gulf of Canada 119 J3
Boothia Peninsula Canada 119 I2
Bootle U.K. 48 E5
Booué Gabon 98 B4
Boppard Germany 53 H4
Boqê China 83 G3
Boqueirão, Serra do hills Brazil 143 J6
Bor Czech Rep. 53 M5
Bor Rus. Fed. 42 J4
Bor Sudan 97 G4
Bor Turkey 90 D3
Bor Serb. and Mont. 59 J2
Boraha, Nosy i. Madag. 99 F5
Borah Peak U.S.A. 126 E3
Borai India 84 D1
Borakalalo Nature Reserve S. Africa 101 H3
Boran Kazakh. see Buran
Boraphet, Bung l. Thai. 70 C4
Boraphet, Nong l. Thai. see Boraphet, Bung
Borås Sweden 45 H8
Borasambar India 84 D1
Borāzjān Iran 88 C4
Borba Brazil 143 G4
Borba China 76 C1
Borborema, Planalto da plat. Brazil 143 K5
Borchen Germany 53 I3
Borçka Turkey 91 F2
Bor Dağı mt. Turkey 59 M6
Bordeaux France 56 D4
Borden Island Canada 119 G2
Borden Peninsula Canada 119 J2
Border Ranges National Park Australia 112 F2
Borðeyri Iceland 44 [inset]
Bordj Bou Arréridj Alg. 57 I5
Bordj Bounaama Alg. 57 G6
Bordj Flye Ste-Marie Alg. 96 C2
Bordj Messaouda Alg. 54 F5
Bordj Mokhtar Alg. 96 D2
Bordj Omar Driss Alg. see Bordj Omer Driss
Bordj Omer Driss Alg. 96 D2
Boreas Abyssal Plain sea feature Arctic Ocean 153 H1
Borel r. Canada 123 H2
Borgå Fin. see Porvoo
Borgarfjörður Iceland 44 [inset]
Borgarnes Iceland 44 [inset]
Børgefjell Nasjonalpark nat. park Norway 44 H4
Borger U.S.A. 131 C5
Borgholm Sweden 45 J8
Borgne, Lake b. U.S.A. 131 F6
Borgo San Lorenzo Italy 58 D3
Bori India 84 C1
Bori r. India 82 C5
Borikhan Laos 70 C3
Borislav Ukr. see Boryslav
Borisoglebsk Rus. Fed. 43 I6
Borisov Belarus see Barysaw
Borisovka Rus. Fed. 43 H6
Borispol' Ukr. see Boryspil'
Bo River Post Sudan 97 F4
Borja Peru 142 C4
Borken Germany 52 G3
Borkenes Norway 44 J2
Borkovskaya Rus. Fed. 42 K2
Borkum Germany 52 G1
Borkum i. Germany 52 G1
Borlänge Sweden 45 I6
Borlaug Norway 45 E6
Borlu Turkey 59 M5
Borna Germany 53 M3
Born-Berge hill Germany 53 K3
Borndiep sea chan. Neth. 52 F1
Borne Neth. 52 G2
▶Borneo i. Asia 68 E6
Largest island in Asia and 3rd in the world.
Asia 60–61
World 12–13
Bornholm county Denmark 153 H3
Bornholm i. Denmark 45 I9
Bornova Turkey 59 L5
Borodino Rus. Fed. 64 J3
Borodinskoye Rus. Fed. 45 P6
Borogontsy Rus. Fed. 65 O3
Borohoro Shan mts China 80 F3
Borok-Sulezhskiy Rus. Fed. 42 H4
Boromo Burkina 96 C3
Boron U.S.A. 128 E4
Borondi India 84 D2
Boroughbridge U.K. 48 F4
Borovichi Rus. Fed. 42 G4
Borovoy Kirovskaya Oblast' Rus. Fed. 42 K4
Borovoy Respublika Kareliya Rus. Fed. 44 R4
Borovoy Respublika Komi Rus. Fed. 42 L3
Borpeta India see Barpeta
Borrisokane Rep. of Ireland 51 D5
Borroloola Australia 110 B3
Børsa Norway 44 G5
Borşa Romania 43 E7
Borshchiv Ukr. 43 E6
Borshchovochnyy Khrebet mts Rus. Fed. 73 J3
Bortala China see Bole
Borton U.S.A. 134 B4
Borūjen Iran 88 C4
Borūjerd Iran 88 C3
Borun Iran 88 E3
Borve U.K. 50 C3
Boryslav Ukr. 43 D6
Boryspil' Ukr. 43 F6
Borzna Ukr. 43 G6
Borzya Rus. Fed. 73 L2
Bosanska Dubica Bos.-Herz. 58 G2
Bosanska Gradiška Bos.-Herz. 58 G2
Bosanska Krupa Bos.-Herz. 58 G2
Bosanski Novi Bos.-Herz. 58 G2
Bosansko Grahovo Bos.-Herz. 58 G2
Boscawen Island Tonga see Niuatoputopu
Bose China 76 E4
Boshof S. Africa 101 G5
Boshruyeh Iran 88 E3
Bosna i Hercegovina country Europe see Bosnia-Herzegovina
Bosna Saray Bos.-Herz. see Sarajevo
▶Bosnia-Herzegovina country Europe 58 G2
Europe 5, 38–39
Bosobogolo Pan salt pan Botswana 100 F3
Bosobolo Dem. Rep. Congo 98 B3
Bōsō-hantō pen. Japan 75 F6
Bosporus strait Turkey 59 M4
Bossaga Turkm. see Basaga
Bossangoa Cent. Afr. Rep. 98 B3
Bossembélé Cent. Afr. Rep. 98 B3
Bossier City U.S.A. 131 E5
Bossiesvlei Namibia 100 C3
Bossut, Cape Australia 108 C4
Bostan China 83 F1
Bostān Iran 88 B4
Bostan Pak. 89 G4
Bostāneh, Ra's-e pt Iran 88 D5
Bosten Hu l. China 80 G3
Boston U.K. 49 G6
▶Boston U.S.A. 135 J2
State capital of Massachusetts.
Boston Mountains U.S.A. 131 E5
Boston Spa U.K. 48 F5
Boswell U.S.A. 134 B3
Botad India 82 B5
Botany Bay Australia 112 E4
Botev mt. Bulg. 59 K3
Botevgrad Bulg. 59 J3
Bothaville S. Africa 101 H4
Bothnia, Gulf of Fin./Sweden 45 K6
Bothwell Canada 134 E2
Botkins U.S.A. 134 C3
Botlikh Rus. Fed. 91 G2
Botoşani Romania 43 E7
Botou China 73 L5
Bô Trach Vietnam 70 D3
Botshabelo S. Africa 101 H5
▶Botswana country Africa 99 C6
Africa 7, 94–95
Botte Donato, Monte mt. Italy 58 G5
Bottenviken g. Fin./Sweden see Bothnia, Gulf of
Bottesford U.K. 48 G5
Bottrop Germany 52 G3
Botucatu Brazil 145 A3
Botuporã Brazil 145 C1
Botwood Canada 123 L4
Bouaflé Côte d'Ivoire 96 C4
Bouaké Côte d'Ivoire 96 C4
Bouar Cent. Afr. Rep. 98 B3
Bouârfa Morocco 54 D5
Bouba Ndjida, Parc National de nat. park Cameroon 97 E4
Bouca Cent. Afr. Rep. 98 B3
Boucaut Bay Australia 108 F3
Bouchain France 52 D4
Bouctouche Canada 123 I5
Boudh India 84 E1
Bougaa Alg. 57 I5
Bougainville, Cape Australia 104 D3
Bougainville Island P.N.G. 106 F2
Bougainville Reef Australia 110 D2
Boughessa Mali 96 D3
Bougie Alg. see Bejaïa
Bougouni Mali 96 C3
Bougtob Alg. 54 E5
Bouillon Belgium 52 F5
Bouira Alg. 57 H5
Bou Izakarn Morocco 96 C2
Boujdour W. Sahara 96 B2
Boulder Australia 109 C7
Boulder CO U.S.A. 126 G4
Boulder MT U.S.A. 126 E3
Boulder UT U.S.A. 129 H3
Boulder Canyon gorge U.S.A. 129 F3
Boulder City U.S.A. 129 F4
Boulevard U.S.A. 128 E5
Boulia Australia 110 B4
Boulogne France see Boulogne-sur-Mer
Boulogne-Billancourt France 52 C6
Boulogne-sur-Mer France 52 B4
Boumerdes Alg. 57 H5
Bouna Côte d'Ivoire 96 C4
Bou Naceur, Jbel mt. Morocco 54 D5
Boû Nâga Mauritania 96 B3
Boundary Mountains U.S.A. 135 J1
Boundary Peak U.S.A. 128 D3
Boundiali Côte d'Ivoire 96 C4
Boundji Congo 98 B4
Boun Nua Laos 70 C2
Bountiful U.S.A. 129 H1
Bounty Islands N.Z. 107 H6
Bounty Trough sea feature S. Pacific Ocean 150 H9
Bourail New Caledonia 107 G4
Bourbon reg. France see Bourbonnais
Bourbon terr. Indian Ocean see Réunion
Bourbon U.S.A. 134 B3
Bourbonnais reg. France 56 F3
Bourem Mali 96 C3
Bouressa Mali see Boughessa
Bourg-Achard France 49 H9
Bourganeuf France 56 E4
Bourg-en-Bresse France 56 G3
Bourges France 56 F3
Bourget Canada 135 H1
Bourgogne reg. France see Burgundy
Bourgogne, Canal de France 52 G3
Bourke Australia 112 B3
Bourne U.K. 49 G6
Bournemouth U.K. 49 F8
Bourtoutou Chad 97 F3
Bou Saâda Alg. 57 I6
Bou Salem Tunisia 58 C6
Bouse U.S.A. 129 F5
Bouse Wash watercourse U.S.A. 129 F4
Boussu Belgium 52 D4
Boutilimit Mauritania 96 B3
Bouvet Island terr. S. Atlantic Ocean see Bouvetøya
▶Bouvetøya terr. S. Atlantic Ocean 148 I9
Dependency of Norway.
Bouy France 52 E5
Bova Marina Italy 58 F6
Bovenden Germany 53 J3
Bow r. Alta Canada 121 I5
Bowa China see Muli
Bowbells U.S.A. 130 C1
Bowden U.S.A. 134 F4
Bowditch atoll Tokelau see Fakaofo
Bowen Australia 110 E4
Bowen, Mount Australia 112 D6
Bowenville Australia 112 E1
Bowers Ridge sea feature Bering Sea 150 H2
Bowie Australia 110 D4
Bowie AZ U.S.A. 129 I5
Bowie TX U.S.A. 131 D5
Bow Island Canada 121 I5
Bowkan Iran 88 B2
Bowling Green KY U.S.A. 134 B5
Bowling Green MO U.S.A. 130 F4
Bowling Green OH U.S.A. 134 D3
Bowling Green VA U.S.A. 135 G4
Bowling Green Bay National Park Australia 110 D3
Bowman U.S.A. 130 C2
Bowman, Mount Canada 126 C2
Bowman Island Antarctica 152 F2
Bowman Peninsula Antarctica 152 L2
Bowmore U.K. 50 C5
Bowo China see Bomi
Bowral Australia 112 E5
Bowser Lake Canada 120 D3
Boxberg Germany 53 J5
Box Elder U.S.A. 130 C2
Box Elder r. U.S.A. 130 C2
Boxtel Neth. 52 F3
Boyabat Turkey 90 D2
Boyana tourist site Bulg. 59 J3
Boyang China 77 H2
Boyd r. Australia 112 F2
Boyd Lagoon salt flat Australia 109 D6
Boyd Lake Canada 121 K2
Boydton U.S.A. 135 F5
Boyers U.S.A. 134 F3
Boykins U.S.A. 135 G5
Boyle Canada 121 H4
Boyle Rep. of Ireland 51 D4
Boyne r. Rep. of Ireland 51 F4
Boyne City U.S.A. 134 C1
Boysen Reservoir U.S.A. 126 F4
Boysun Uzbek. see Baysun
Boyuibe Bol. 142 F8
Böyük Qafqaz mts Asia/Europe see Caucasus
▶Bozcaada i. Turkey 59 L5
Most westerly point of Asia.
Bozdağ mt. Turkey 59 L5
Bozdağ mt. Turkey 85 C1
Boz Dağları mts Turkey 59 L5
Bozdoğan Turkey 59 M6
Bozeat U.K. 49 G6
Bozeman U.S.A. 126 F3
Bozen Italy see Bolzano
Bozhou China 77 G1
Bozoum Cent. Afr. Rep. 98 B3
Bozova Turkey 90 E3
Bozqūsh, Kūh-e mts Iran 88 B2
Bozüyük Turkey 59 N5
Bozyazı Turkey 85 A1
Bra Italy 58 B2
Brač i. Croatia 58 G3
Bracadale U.K. 50 C3
Bracadale, Loch b. U.K. 50 C3
Bracara Port. see Braga
Bracciano, Lago di l. Italy 58 E3
Bracebridge Canada 134 F1
Brachet, Lac au l. Canada 123 H4
Bräcke Sweden 44 I5
Brackenheim Germany 53 J5
Brackettville U.S.A. 131 C6
Bracknell U.K. 49 G7
Bradano r. Italy 58 G4
Bradenton U.S.A. 133 D7
Bradford Canada 134 F1
Bradford U.K. 48 F5
Bradford OH U.S.A. 134 C3
Bradford PA U.S.A. 135 F3
Bradley U.S.A. 134 B3
Brady U.S.A. 131 D6
Brady Glacier U.S.A. 120 B3
Brae U.K. 50 [inset]
Braemar U.K. 50 F3
Braga Port. 57 B3
Bragado Arg. 144 D5
Bragança Brazil 143 I4
Bragança Port. 57 C3
Bragança Paulista Brazil 145 B3
Brahin Belarus 43 F6
Brahlstorf Germany 53 K1
Brahmanbaria Bangl. 83 G5
Brahmapur India 84 E2
Brahmaputra r. Asia 83 H4
also known as Dihang (India) or Jamuna (Bangladesh) or Siang (India) or Yarlung Zangbo (China)
Brahmaur India 82 D2
Brăila Romania 59 L2
Braine France 52 D5
Braine-le-Comte Belgium 52 E4
Brainerd U.S.A. 130 E2
Braintree U.K. 49 H7
Braithwaite Point Australia 108 F2
Brak r. S. Africa 101 I2
Brake (Unterweser) Germany 53 I1
Brakel Belgium 52 D4
Brakel Germany 53 J3
Brakwater Namibia 100 C2
Bramfield Australia 109 F8
Bramming Denmark 45 F9
Brämön i. Sweden 44 J5
Brampton Canada 134 F2
Brampton England U.K. 48 E4
Brampton England U.K. 49 I6
Bramsche Germany 53 I2
Bramwell Australia 110 C2
Brancaster U.K. 49 H6
Branch Canada 123 L5
Branco r. Brazil 142 F4
Brandberg mt. Namibia 99 B6
Brandbu Norway 45 G6
Brande Denmark 45 F9
Brandenburg Germany 53 M2
Brandenburg land Germany 53 N2
Brandenburg U.S.A. 134 B5
Brandfort S. Africa 101 H5
Brandis Germany 53 N3
Brandon Canada 121 L5
Brandon U.K. 49 H6
Brandon MS U.S.A. 131 F5
Brandon VT U.S.A. 135 I2
Brandon Head hd Rep. of Ireland 51 B5
Brandon Mountain hill Rep. of Ireland 51 B5
Brandvlei S. Africa 100 E6
Braniewo Poland 47 Q3
Bransfield Strait Antarctica 152 L2
Branson U.S.A. 131 C4
Brantford Canada 134 E2
Branxton Australia 112 E4
Bras d'Or Lake Canada 123 J5
Brasil country S. America see Brazil
Brasil, Planalto do plat. Brazil 143 J7
Brasileia Brazil 142 E6
▶Brasília Brazil 145 B1
Capital of Brazil.
Brasília de Minas Brazil 145 B2
Braslav Belarus see Braslaw
Braslaw Belarus 45 O9
Braşov Romania 59 K2
Brassey, Mount Australia 109 F5
Brassey Range hills Australia 109 C6
Brasstown Bald mt. U.S.A. 133 D5
▶Bratislava Slovakia 47 P6
Capital of Slovakia.
Bratsk Rus. Fed. 72 I1
Bratskoye Vodokhranilishche resr Rus. Fed. 72 I1
Brattleboro U.S.A. 135 I2
Braunau am Inn Austria 47 N6
Braunfels Germany 53 I4
Braunlage Germany 53 K3
Braunsbedra Germany 53 L3
Braunschweig Germany 53 K2
Brava i. Cape Verde 96 [inset]
Brave U.S.A. 134 E4
Bråviken inlet Sweden 45 J7
Bravo, Cerro mt. Bol. 142 F7
Bravo del Norte, Río r. Mex./U.S.A. 127 G7 see Rio Grande
Brawley U.S.A. 129 F5
Bray Rep. of Ireland 51 F4
Bray Island Canada 119 K3
Brazeau r. Canada 120 H4
Brazeau, Mount Canada 120 G4
▶Brazil country S. America 143 G5
Largest country in South America and 5th in the world. Most populous country in South America and 5th in the world.
South America 9, 140–141
Brazil U.S.A. 134 B4
Brazil Basin sea feature S. Atlantic Ocean 148 G7
Brazos r. U.S.A. 131 E6
▶Brazzaville Congo 99 B4
Capital of Congo.
Brčko Bos.-Herz. 58 H2
Bré Rep. of Ireland see Bray
Breadalbane Australia 110 B4
Breaksea Sound inlet N.Z. 113 A7
Bream Bay N.Z. 113 E2
Brechfa U.K. 49 C7
Brechin U.K. 50 G4
Brecht Belgium 52 E3
Breckenridge MI U.S.A. 134 C2
Breckenridge MN U.S.A. 130 D2
Breckenridge TX U.S.A. 131 D5
Břeclav Czech Rep. 47 P6
Brecon U.K. 49 D7
Brecon Beacons reg. U.K. 49 D7
Brecon Beacons National Park U.K. 49 D7
Breda Neth. 52 E3
Bredasdorp S. Africa 100 E8
Bredbo Australia 112 D5
Breddin Germany 53 M2
Bredevoort Neth. 52 G3
Bredviken Sweden 44 I3
Bree Belgium 52 F3
Breed U.S.A. 134 A1
Bregenz Austria 47 L7
Breiðafjörður b. Iceland 44 [inset]
Breiðdalsvík Iceland 44 [inset]
Breidenbach Germany 53 I4
Breien U.S.A. 130 C2
Breitenfelde Germany 53 K1
Breitengüßbach Germany 53 K5
Breiter Luzinsee l. Germany 53 N1
Breivikbotn Norway 44 M1
Breizh reg. France see Brittany
Brejo Velho Brazil 145 C1
Brekstad Norway 44 F5
Bremen Germany 53 I1

Bremen land Germany 53 I1
Bremen IN U.S.A. 134 B3
Bremen OH U.S.A. 134 D4
Bremer Bay Australia 109 B8
Bremerhaven Germany 53 I1
Bremer Range hills Australia 105 C8
Bremersdorp Swaziland see Manzini
Bremervörde Germany 53 J1
Bremm Germany 52 H4
Brenham U.S.A. 131 D6
Brenna Norway 44 H4
Brennero, Passo di pass Austria/Italy see Brenner Pass
Brennerpaß pass Austria/Italy see Brenner Pass
Brenner Pass Austria/Italy 58 D1
Brentwood U.K. 49 H7
Brescia Italy 58 D2
Breslau Poland see Wrocław
Bresle r. France 52 B4
Brésolles, Lac l. Canada 123 H3
Bressanone Italy 58 D1
Bressay i. U.K. 50 [inset]
Bressuire France 56 D3
Brest Belarus 45 M10
Brest France 56 B2
Brest-Litovsk Belarus see Brest
Bretagne reg. France see Brittany
Breteuil France 52 C5
Brétigny-sur-Orge France 52 C6
Breton Canada 120 H4
Breton Sound b. U.S.A. 131 F6
Brett, Cape N.Z. 113 E2
Bretten Germany 53 I5
Bretton U.K. 48 E5
Breueh, Pulau i. Indon. 71 A6
Brevard U.S.A. 133 D5
Breves Brazil 143 H4
Brewarrina Australia 112 C2
Brewer U.S.A. 132 G2
Brewster NE U.S.A. 130 D3
Brewster OH U.S.A. 134 E3
Brewster, Kap c. Greenland see Kangikajik
Brewster, Lake imp. l. Australia 112 B4
Brewton U.S.A. 133 C6
Breyten S. Africa 101 I4
Breytovo Rus. Fed. 42 H4
Brezhnev Rus. Fed. see Naberezhnyye Chelny
Brezno Slovakia 47 Q6
Brezovo Bulg. 59 K3
Brezovo Polje hill Croatia 58 G2
Bria Cent. Afr. Rep. 98 C3
Briançon France 56 H4
Brian Head mt. U.S.A. 129 G3
Bribbaree Australia 112 C5
Bribie Island Australia 112 F1
Briceni Moldova 43 E6
Brichany Moldova see Briceni
Brichen' Moldova see Briceni
Bridgend U.K. 49 D7
Bridge of Orchy U.K. 50 E4
Bridgeport CA U.S.A. 128 D2
Bridgeport CT U.S.A. 135 I3
Bridgeport IL U.S.A. 134 B4
Bridgeport NE U.S.A. 130 C3
Bridger Peak U.S.A. 126 G4
Bridgeton U.S.A. 135 H4
Bridgetown Australia 109 B8

►Bridgetown Barbados 137 M6
Capital of Barbados.

Bridgetown Canada 123 I5
Bridgeville U.S.A. 135 H4
Bridgewater Canada 123 I5
Bridgewater U.S.A. 135 H2
Bridgnorth U.K. 49 E6
Bridgton U.S.A. 135 J1
Bridgwater U.K. 49 D7
Bridgwater Bay U.K. 49 D7
Bridlington U.K. 48 G4
Bridlington Bay U.K. 48 G4
Bridport Australia 111 [inset]
Bridport U.K. 49 E8
Brie reg. France 56 F2
Brie-Comte-Robert France 52 C6
Brieg Poland see Brzeg
Briery Knob mt. U.S.A. 134 E4
Brig Switz. 56 H3
Brigg U.K. 48 G5
Brigham City U.S.A. 126 E4
Brightlingsea U.K. 49 I7
Brighton Canada 135 G1
Brighton U.K. 49 G8
Brighton CO U.S.A. 126 G5
Brighton MI U.S.A. 134 D2
Brighton NY U.S.A. 135 G2
Brighton WV U.S.A. 134 D4
Brignoles France 56 H5
Brikama Gambia 96 B3
Brilon Germany 53 I3
Brindisi Italy 58 G4
Brinkley U.S.A. 131 F5
Brion, Île i. Canada 123 J5
Brioude France 56 F4
Brisay Canada 123 H3

►Brisbane Australia 112 F1
State capital of Queensland and 3rd most populous city in Oceania.

Brisbane Ranges National Park Australia 112 B6
Bristol U.K. 49 E7
Bristol CT U.S.A. 135 I3
Bristol FL U.S.A. 133 C6
Bristol NH U.S.A. 135 J2
Bristol RI U.S.A. 135 J3
Bristol TN U.S.A. 134 D5
Bristol VT U.S.A. 135 I1
Bristol Bay U.S.A. 118 B4
Bristol Channel est. U.K. 49 C7
Bristol Lake U.S.A. 129 F4
Britannia Island New Caledonia see Maré
British Antarctic Territory reg. Antarctica 152 L2
British Columbia prov. Canada 120 F5
British Empire Range mts Canada 119 J1
British Guiana country S. America see Guyana
British Honduras country Central America see Belize

►British Indian Ocean Territory terr. Indian Ocean 149 M6
United Kingdom Overseas Territory.

British Solomon Islands country S. Pacific Ocean see Solomon Islands
Brito Godins Angola see Kiwaba N'zogi
Brits S. Africa 101 H3
Britstown S. Africa 100 F6
Brittany reg. France 56 C2
Britton U.S.A. 130 D2
Brive-la-Gaillarde France 56 E4
Briviesca Spain 57 E2
Brixham U.K. 49 D8
Brixia Italy see Brescia
Brlik Kazakh. 80 D3
Brno Czech Rep. 47 P6
Broach India see Bharuch
Broad r. U.S.A. 133 D5
Broadalbin U.S.A. 135 H2
Broad Arrow Australia 109 C7
Broadback r. Canada 122 F4
Broad Bay U.K. see Tuath, Loch a'
Broadford Australia 112 B6
Broadford Rep. of Ireland 51 D5
Broadford U.K. 50 D3
Broad Law hill U.K. 50 F5
Broadmere Australia 110 A3
Broad Peak China/Jammu and Kashmir 89 J3
Broad Sound sea chan. Australia 110 E4
Broadstairs U.K. 49 I7
Broadus U.S.A. 126 G3
Broadview Canada 121 K5
Broadway U.S.A. 135 F4
Broadwood N.Z. 113 D2
Brochet Canada 121 K3
Brochet, Lac l. Canada 121 K3
Brocken mt. Germany 53 K3
Brockman, Mount Australia 108 B5
Brockport NY U.S.A. 135 G2
Brockport PA U.S.A. 135 F3
Brockton U.S.A. 135 J2
Brockville Canada 135 H1
Brockway U.S.A. 135 F3
Brodeur Peninsula Canada 119 J2
Brodhead U.S.A. 134 C5
Brodick U.K. 50 D5
Brodnica Poland 47 Q4
Brody Ukr. 43 E6
Broken Arrow U.S.A. 131 E4
Broken Bay Australia 112 E4
Broken Bow NE U.S.A. 130 D3
Broken Bow OK U.S.A. 131 E5
Brokenhead r. Canada 121 L5
Broken Hill Australia 111 C6
Broken Hill Zambia see Kabwe
Broken Plateau sea feature Indian Ocean 149 O8
Brokopondo Suriname 143 G2
Brokopondo Stuwmeer resr Suriname see Professor van Blommestein Meer
Bromberg Poland see Bydgoszcz
Brome Germany 53 K2
Bromsgrove U.K. 49 E6
Brønderslev Denmark 45 F8
Brønnøysund Norway 44 H4
Bronson FL U.S.A. 133 D6
Bronson MI U.S.A. 134 C3
Brooke U.K. 49 I6
Brookfield U.S.A. 134 A2
Brookhaven U.S.A. 131 F6
Brookings OR U.S.A. 126 B4
Brookings SD U.S.A. 130 D2
Brookline U.S.A. 135 J2
Brooklyn U.S.A. 134 C2
Brooklyn Park U.S.A. 130 E2
Brookneal U.S.A. 135 F5
Brooks Canada 121 I5
Brooks Brook Canada 120 C2
Brooks Range mts U.S.A. 118 D3
Brookston U.S.A. 134 B3
Brooksville FL U.S.A. 133 D6
Brooksville KY U.S.A. 134 C4
Brookton Australia 109 B8
Brookville IN U.S.A. 134 C4
Brookville PA U.S.A. 134 F3
Brookville Lake U.S.A. 134 C4
Broom, Loch inlet U.K. 50 D3
Broome Australia 108 C4
Brora U.K. 50 F2
Brora r. U.K. 50 F2
Brösarp Sweden 45 I9
Brosna r. Rep. of Ireland 51 E4
Brosville U.S.A. 134 F5
Brothers is India 71 A5
Brough U.K. 48 E4
Brough Ness pt U.K. 50 G2
Broughshane U.K. 51 F3
Broughton Island Canada see Qikiqtarjuaq
Broughton Islands Australia 112 F4
Brovary Ukr. 43 F6
Brovinia Australia 111 E5
Brovst Denmark 45 F8
Brown City U.S.A. 134 D2
Brown Deer U.S.A. 134 B2
Browne Range hills Australia 109 D6
Brownfield U.S.A. 131 C5
Browning U.S.A. 126 E2
Brown Mountain U.S.A. 128 E4
Brownstown U.S.A. 134 B4
Brownsville KY U.S.A. 134 B5
Brownsville PA U.S.A. 134 F3
Brownsville TN U.S.A. 131 F5
Brownsville TX U.S.A. 131 D7
Brownwood U.S.A. 131 D6
Browse Island Australia 108 C3
Bruay-la-Bussière France 52 C4
Bruce Peninsula Canada 134 E1
Bruce Peninsula National Park Canada 134 E1
Bruce Rock Australia 109 B7
Bruchsal Germany 53 I5
Brück Germany 53 M2
Bruck an der Mur Austria 47 O7
Brue r. U.K. 49 E7
Bruges Belgium see Brugge
Brugge Belgium 52 D3
Brühl Baden-Württemberg Germany 53 I5
Brühl Nordrhein-Westfalen Germany 52 G4
Bruin KY U.S.A. 134 D4
Bruin PA U.S.A. 134 F3
Bruin Point mt. U.S.A. 129 H2
Bruint India 83 I3
Brûk, Wâdi el watercourse Egypt see Burūk, Wādī al
Brukkaros Namibia 100 D3
Brûlé Canada 120 G4
Brûlé, Lac l. Canada 123 J3
Brûly Belgium 52 E5
Brumado Brazil 145 C1
Brumath France 53 H6
Brumunddal Norway 45 G6
Brunau Germany 53 L2
Brundisium Italy see Brindisi
Bruneau U.S.A. 126 E4
►Brunei country Asia 68 E6
Asia 6, 62–63
Brunei Brunei see Bandar Seri Begawan
Brunette Downs Australia 110 A3
Brunflo Sweden 44 I5
Brunico Italy 58 D1
Brünn Czech Rep. see Brno
Brunner, Lake N.Z. 113 C6
Bruno Canada 121 J4
Brunswick Germany see Braunschweig
Brunswick GA U.S.A. 133 D6
Brunswick MD U.S.A. 135 G4
Brunswick ME U.S.A. 135 K2
Brunswick, Península de pen. Chile 144 B8
Brunswick Bay Australia 108 D3
Brunswick Lake Canada 122 E4
Bruntál Czech Rep. 47 P6
Brunt Ice Shelf Antarctica 152 B2
Bruntville S. Africa 101 J5
Bruny Island Australia 111 [inset]
Brusa Turkey see Bursa
Brusenets Rus. Fed. 42 I3
Brushton U.S.A. 135 H1
Brusque Brazil 145 A4
Brussel Belgium see Brussels

►Brussels Belgium 52 E4
Capital of Belgium.

Bruthen Australia 112 C6
Bruxelles Belgium see Brussels
Bruzual Venez. 142 E2
Bryan OH U.S.A. 134 C3
Bryan TX U.S.A. 131 D6
Bryan, Mount hill Australia 111 B7
Bryan Coast Antarctica 152 L2
Bryansk Rus. Fed. 43 G5
Bryanskoye Rus. Fed. 91 G1
Bryant Pond U.S.A. 135 J1
Bryantsburg U.S.A. 134 C4
Bryce Canyon National Park U.S.A. 129 G3
Bryce Mountain U.S.A. 129 I5
Brynbuga U.K. see Usk
Bryne Norway 45 D7
Bryukhovetskaya Rus. Fed. 43 H7
Brzeg Poland 47 P5
Brześć nad Bugiem Belarus see Brest
Bua r. Malawi 99 D5
Bu'aale Somalia 98 E3
Buala Solomon Is 107 F2
Bu'ayj well Saudi Arabia 88 C5
Būbīyān Island Kuwait 88 C4
Bucak Turkey 59 N6
Bucaramanga Col. 142 D2
Buccaneer Archipelago is Australia 108 C4
Buchanan Liberia 96 B4
Buchanan MI U.S.A. 134 B3
Buchanan VA U.S.A. 134 F5
Buchanan, Lake salt flat Australia 110 D4
Buchan Gulf Canada 119 K2

►Bucharest Romania 59 L2
Capital of Romania.

Büchen Germany 53 K1
Buchen (Odenwald) Germany 53 J5
Buchholz Germany 53 M1
Bucholz in der Nordheide Germany 53 J1
Buchon, Point U.S.A. 128 C4
Buchy France 52 B5
Bucin, Pasul pass Romania 59 K1
Buckambool Mountain hill Australia 112 B3
Bückeburg Germany 53 J2
Bücken Germany 53 J2
Buckeye U.S.A. 129 G5
Buckhannon U.S.A. 134 E4
Buckhaven U.K. 50 F4
Buckhorn Lake Canada 135 F1
Buckie U.K. 50 G3
Buckingham U.K. 49 G6
Buckingham U.S.A. 135 F5
Buckingham Bay Australia 67 F9
Buckland Tableland reg. Australia 110 E5
Buckleboo Australia 109 G8
Buckle Island Antarctica 152 H2
Buckley watercourse Australia 110 B4
Buckley Bay Antarctica 152 G2
Bucklin U.S.A. 130 D4
Buckskin Mountains U.S.A. 129 G4
Bucks Mountain U.S.A. 128 C2
Bucksport U.S.A. 123 H5
Bückwitz Germany 53 M2
Bucureşti Romania see Bucharest
Bucyrus U.S.A. 134 D3
Buda-Kashalyova Belarus 43 F5
Budalin Myanmar 70 A2

►Budapest Hungary 59 H1
Capital of Hungary.

Budaun India 82 D3
Budawang National Park Australia 112 E5
Budda Australia 112 B3
Budd Coast Antarctica 152 F2
Budduso Sardinia Italy 58 C4
Bude U.K. 49 C8
Bude U.S.A. 131 F6
Budennovsk Rus. Fed. 91 G1
Buderim Australia 112 F1
Büding Iran 88 E5
Büdingen Germany 53 J4
Budiyah, Jabal hills Egypt 85 A5
Budongquan China 83 H2
Budoni Sardinia Italy 58 C4
Budū', Sabkhat al salt pan Saudi Arabia 88 C6
Budweis Czech Rep. see České Budějovice
Buenaventura Col. 142 C3
Buena Vista i. N. Mariana Is see Tinian
Buena Vista CO U.S.A. 126 G5
Buena Vista VA U.S.A. 134 F5
Buendia, Embalse de resr Spain 57 E3

►Buenos Aires Arg. 144 E4
Capital of Argentina. 2nd most populous city in South America.

Buenos Aires, Lago l. Arg./Chile 144 B7
Buerarema Brazil 145 D1
Buet r. Canada 123 H1
Búfalo Mex. 131 B7
Buffalo r. Canada 120 H2
Buffalo KY U.S.A. 134 C5
Buffalo MO U.S.A. 130 E4
Buffalo NY U.S.A. 135 F2
Buffalo OK U.S.A. 131 D4
Buffalo SD U.S.A. 130 C2
Buffalo TX U.S.A. 131 D6
Buffalo WY U.S.A. 126 G3
Buffalo Head Hills Canada 120 G3
Buffalo Head Prairie Canada 120 G3
Buffalo Hump mt. U.S.A. 126 E3
Buffalo Lake Alta Canada 121 H4
Buffalo Lake N.W.T. Canada 120 H2
Buffalo Narrows Canada 121 I4
Buffels watercourse S. Africa 100 C5
Buffels Drift S. Africa 101 H2
Buftea Romania 59 K2
Bug r. Poland 47 S5
Buga Col. 142 C3
Bugaldie Australia 112 D3
Bugdayli Turkm. 88 D2
Buggenhout Belgium 52 E3
Bugojno Bos.-Herz. 58 G2
Bugrino Rus. Fed. 42 K1
Bugsuk i. Phil. 68 F5
Bugt China 74 A2
Bugul'ma Rus. Fed. 41 Q5
Bugun' Kazakh. 80 B2
Bügür China see Luntai
Buguruslan Rus. Fed. 41 Q5
Būhābād Iran 88 D4
Buhera Zimbabwe 99 D5
Bühl Germany 53 I6
Buhuşi Romania 59 L1
Buick Canada 120 F3
Builth Wells U.K. 49 D6
Bui National Park Ghana 96 C4
Buinsk Rus. Fed. 43 K5
Bu'in Zahrā Iran 88 C3
Buir Nur l. Mongolia 73 L3
Buitepos Namibia 100 D2
Bujanovac Serb. and Mont. 59 I3

►Bujumbura Burundi 98 C4
Capital of Burundi.

Bukachacha Rus. Fed. 73 L2
Buka Daban mt. China 83 G1
Buka Island P.N.G. 106 F2
Būkand Iran 88 D4
Bukavu Dem. Rep. Congo 98 C4
Bukhara Uzbek. 89 G2
Bukhoro Uzbek. see Bukhara
Bukit Baka - Bukit Raya National Park Indon. 68 E7
Bukit Timah Sing. 71 [inset]
Bukittinggi Indon. 68 C7
Bukkapatnam India 84 C3
Bukoba Tanz. 98 D4
Bükreş Romania see Bucharest
Būl, Kūh-e mt. Iran 88 D4
Bula P.N.G. 69 K8
Bülach Switz. 56 I3
Bulan i. Indon. 71 C7
Bulancak Turkey 90 E2
Bulandshahr India 82 D3
Bulanık Turkey 91 F3
Bulava Rus. Fed. 74 F2
Bulawayo Zimbabwe 99 C6
Buldan Turkey 59 M5
Buldana India see Buldhana
Buldhana India 84 C1
Buleda reg. Pak. 89 F5
Bulembu Swaziland 101 J3
Bulgan Bulgan Mongolia 80 J2
Bulgan Hovd Mongolia see Bürenhayrhan
Bulgar Rus. Fed. see Bolgar
►Bulgaria country Europe 59 K3
Europe 5, 38–39
Bŭlgariya country Europe see Bulgaria
Bulkley Ranges mts Canada 120 D4
Bullawarra, Lake salt flat Australia 112 A1
Bullen r. Canada 121 K1
Buller r. N.Z. 113 C5
Buller, Mount Australia 112 C6
Bulleringa National Park Australia 110 C3
Bullfinch Australia 109 B7
Bullhead City U.S.A. 129 F4
Bulli Australia 112 E5
Bullion Mountains U.S.A. 128 E4
Bullo r. Australia 108 E3
Bulloo Downs Australia 111 C6
Bulloo Lake salt flat Australia 111 C6
Büllsport Namibia 100 C3
Bully Choop Mountain U.S.A. 128 B1
Bulman Australia 108 F3
Bulman Gorge Australia 108 F3
Bulmer Lake Canada 120 F2
Buloh, Pulau i. Sing. 71 [inset]
Buloke, Lake dry lake Australia 112 A6
Bulolo P.N.G. 69 L8
Bulsar India see Valsad
Bultfontein S. Africa 101 H5
Bulukumba Indon. 69 G8
Bulun Rus. Fed. 65 N2
Bulungu Dem. Rep. Congo 99 C4
Bulungur Uzbek. 89 G2
Bumba Dem. Rep. Congo 98 C3
Būmbah Libya 90 A4
Bumbah, Khalīj b. Libya 90 A4
Bumhkang Myanmar 70 B1
Bumpha Bum mt. Myanmar 70 B1
Buna Dem. Rep. Congo 98 B4
Buna Kenya 98 D3
Bunayyān well Saudi Arabia 88 C6
Bunazi Tanz. 98 D4
Bunbeg Rep. of Ireland 51 D2
Bunbury Australia 109 A8
Bunclody Rep. of Ireland 51 F5
Buncrana Rep. of Ireland 51 E2
Bunda Tanz. 98 D4
Bundaberg Australia 110 F5
Bundaleer Australia 112 C2
Bundarra Australia 112 E3
Bundi India 82 C4
Bundjalung National Park Australia 112 F2
Bundoran Rep. of Ireland 51 D3
Bunduqiya Sudan 97 G4
Buner reg. Pak. 89 I3
Bungalaut, Selat sea chan. Indon. 68 B7
Bungay U.K. 49 I6
Bungendore Australia 112 D5
Bunger Hills Antarctica 152 F2
Bungle Bungle National Park Australia see Purnululu National Park
Bungo-suidō sea chan. Japan 71 D6
Bunguran, Kepulauan is Indon. see Natuna, Kepulauan
Bunguran, Pulau i. Indon. see Natuna Besar
Bunia Dem. Rep. Congo 98 D3
Bunianga Dem. Rep. Congo 98 C4
Buningonia well Australia 109 C7
Bunji Jammu and Kashmir 82 C2
Bunker Group atolls Australia 110 F4
Bunkeya Dem. Rep. Congo 99 C5
Bunnell U.S.A. 133 D6
Bünsum China 83 E3
Bunya Mountains National Park Australia 112 E1
Bünyan Turkey 90 D3
Bunyu i. Indon. 68 F6
Buôn Mê Thuôt Vietnam 71 E4
Buorkhaya, Guba b. Rus. Fed. 65 O2
Bup r. China 83 F3
Buqayq Saudi Arabia see Abqaiq
Buqbuq Egypt 90 B5
Bura Kenya 98 D4
Buraan Somalia 98 E2
Buram Sudan 97 F3
Buran Kazakh. 80 G2
Buranhaém Brazil 145 C2
Buranhaém r. Brazil 145 D2
Burao Somalia 98 E3
Burāq Syria 85 C3
Buray r. India 82 C5
Buraydah Saudi Arabia 86 F4
Burbach Germany 53 I4
Burbank U.S.A. 128 D4
Burcher Australia 112 C4
Burdaard Neth. see Birdaard
Burdalyk Turkm. 89 G2
Burdigala France see Bordeaux
Burdur Turkey 59 N6
Burdur Gölü l. Turkey 59 N6
Burdwan India see Barddhaman
Burē Eth. 98 D2
Bure r. U.K. 49 I6
Bureå Sweden 44 L4
Bureinskiy Khrebet mts Rus. Fed. 74 D2
Bürenhayrhan Mongolia 80 H2
Bureya r. Rus. Fed. 74 C2
Bureya Range mts Rus. Fed. see Bureinskiy Khrebet
Bureyinski Zapovednik nature res. Rus. Fed. 74 D2
Burford Canada 134 E2
Burgas Bulg. 59 L3
Burgaw U.S.A. 133 E5
Burg bei Magdeburg Germany 53 L2
Burgbernheim Germany 53 K5
Burgdorf Germany 53 K2
Burgeo Canada 123 K5
Burgersdorp S. Africa 101 H6
Burgersfort S. Africa 101 J3
Burges, Mount hill Australia 109 C7
Burgess Hill U.K. 49 G8
Burghaun Germany 53 J4
Burghausen Germany 47 N6
Burghead U.K. 50 F3
Burgh-Haamstede Neth. 52 D3
Burgio, Serra di hill Sicily Italy 58 F6
Burglengenfeld Germany 53 M5
Burgos Mex. 131 D7
Burgos Spain 57 E2
Burgstädt Germany 53 M4
Burgsvik Sweden 45 K8
Burgum Neth. see Bergum
Burgundy reg. France 56 G3
Burhan Budai Shan mts China 80 H4
Burhaniye Turkey 59 L5
Burhanpur India 82 D5
Burhar-Dhanpuri India 83 E5
Buri Brazil 145 A3
Burias i. Phil. 69 G4
Burin Canada 123 L5
Burin Peninsula Canada 123 L5
Buriram Thai. 70 C4
Buritama Brazil 145 A3
Buriti Alegre Brazil 145 A2
Buriti Bravo Brazil 143 J5
Buritirama Brazil 143 J6
Buritis Brazil 145 B1
Burj Pak. 89 G4
Burke U.S.A. 130 D3
Burke Island Antarctica 152 K2
Burke Pass N.Z. see Burkes Pass
Burkes Pass N.Z. 113 C7
Burkesville U.S.A. 134 C5
Burketown Australia 110 B3
Burkeville U.S.A. 135 F5
►Burkina country Africa 96 C3
Africa 7, 94–95
Burkina Faso country Africa see Burkina
Burk's Falls Canada 122 F5
Burley U.S.A. 126 E4
Burlington Canada 134 F2
Burlington CO U.S.A. 130 C4
Burlington IA U.S.A. 130 F3
Burlington KS U.S.A. 130 E4
Burlington KY U.S.A. 134 C4
Burlington VT U.S.A. 135 I1
Burlington WI U.S.A. 134 A2
Burmantovo Rus. Fed. 41 S3
Burnaby Canada 120 F5
Burnet U.S.A. 131 D6
Burney U.S.A. 128 C1
Burney, Monte vol. Chile 144 B8
Burnham U.S.A. 135 G3
Burnie Australia 111 [inset]
Burniston U.K. 48 G4
Burnley U.K. 48 E5
Burns U.S.A. 126 D4
Burnside r. Canada 118 H3
Burnside U.S.A. 134 C5
Burnside, Lake salt flat Australia 109 C6
Burns Junction U.S.A. 126 D4
Burns Lake Canada 120 E4
Burntisland U.K. 50 F4
Burnt Lake Canada see Brûlé, Lac
Burntwood r. Canada 121 L4
Burog Co l. China 83 F2
Buron r. Canada 123 H2
Burovoy Uzbek. 89 F1
Burqin China 80 G2
Burqu' Jordan 85 D3
Burra Australia 111 B7
Burravoe U.K. 50 [inset]
Burrel Albania 59 I4
Burrel U.S.A. 128 D3
Burren reg. Rep. of Ireland 51 C4
Burrendong Reservoir Australia 112 D4
Burren Junction Australia 112 D3
Burrewarra Point Australia 112 E5
Burrinjuck Australia 112 D5
Burrinjuck Reservoir Australia 112 D5
Burro, Serranías del mts Mex. 131 C6
Burr Oak Reservoir U.S.A. 134 D4
Burro Creek watercourse U.S.A. 129 G4
Burro Peak U.S.A. 129 I5
Burrowa Pine Mountain National Park Australia 112 C6
Burrow Head hd U.K. 50 E6
Burrows U.S.A. 134 B3
Burrundie Australia 108 E3
Bursa Turkey 59 M4
Bûr Safâga Egypt see Būr Safājah
Būr Safājah Egypt 86 D4
Bûr Sa'îd Egypt see Port Said
Bûr Sa'îd Egypt see Port Said
Būr Sa'īd governorate Egypt see Būr Sa'īd
Būr Sa'īd governorate Egypt 85 A4
Bursinskoye Vodokhranilishche resr Rus. Fed. 74 C2
Bürstadt Germany 53 I5
Būr Sudan Sudan see Port Sudan
Burt Lake U.S.A. 132 C2
Burton U.S.A. 134 D2
Burton, Lac l. Canada 122 F3
Burtonport Rep. of Ireland 51 D3
Burton upon Trent U.K. 49 F6
Burträsk Sweden 44 L4
Burt Well Australia 109 F5
Buru i. Indon. 69 H7
Burūk, Wādī al watercourse Egypt 85 A4
Burullus, Bahra el lag. Egypt see Burullus, Lake
Burullus, Buḥayrat al lag. Egypt see Burullus, Lake
Burullus, Lake lag. Egypt 90 C5
Burultokay China see Fuhai
Burūn, Ra's pt Egypt 85 A4
►Burundi country Africa 98 C4
Africa 7, 94–95
Burunniy Rus. Fed. see Tsagan Aman
Bururi Burundi 98 C4
Burwash Landing Canada 120 B2
Burwick U.K. 50 G2
Buryn' Ukr. 43 G6
Bury St Edmunds U.K. 49 H6
Burzil Pass Jammu and Kashmir 82 C2
Busan S. Korea see Pusan
Busanga Dem. Rep. Congo 98 C4
Busby U.S.A. 126 G3
Buseire Syria see Al Buşayrah
Bush r. U.K. 51 F2
Būshehr Iran 88 C4
Bushêngcaka China 83 E2
Bushenyi Uganda 98 D4
Bushire Iran see Būshehr
Bushmills U.K. 51 F2
Bushnell U.S.A. 133 D6
Businga Dem. Rep. Congo 98 C3
Buşrá ash Shām Syria 85 C3
Busse Rus. Fed. 74 B2
Busselton Australia 109 A8
Bussum Neth. 52 F2
Bustillos, Lago l. Mex. 127 G7
Busto Arsizio Italy 58 C2
Buta Dem. Rep. Congo 98 C3
Butare Rwanda 98 C4
Butaritari atoll Kiribati 150 H5
Bute Australia 111 B7
Bute i. U.K. 50 D5
Butedale Canada 120 D4
Butha Buthe Lesotho 101 I5
Butha Qi China see Zalantun
Buthidaung Myanmar 70 A2
Butler AL U.S.A. 131 F5
Butler GA U.S.A. 133 C5
Butler IN U.S.A. 134 C3
Butler KY U.S.A. 134 C4
Butler MO U.S.A. 130 E4
Butler PA U.S.A. 134 F3
Butlers Bridge Rep. of Ireland 51 E3
Buton i. Indon. 69 G7
Bütow Germany 53 M1
Butte MT U.S.A. 126 E3
Butte NE U.S.A. 130 D3
Buttelstedt Germany 53 L3
Butterworth Malaysia 71 C6
Butterworth S. Africa 101 I7
Buttes, Sierra mt. U.S.A. 128 C2
Buttevant Rep. of Ireland 51 D5
Butt of Lewis hd U.K. 50 C2
Button Bay Canada 121 M3
Butuan Phil. 69 H5
Butuo China 76 D3
Buturlinovka Rus. Fed. 43 I6
Butwal Nepal 83 E4
Butzbach Germany 53 I4
Buulobarde Somalia 98 E3
Buur Gaabo Somalia 98 E4
Buurhabaka Somalia 98 E3
Buxar India 83 F4
Buxtehude Germany 53 J1
Buxton U.K. 48 F5

C

Changbai Shan mts China/N. Korea 74 B4
Chang Cheng research station Antarctica see Great Wall
Changcheng China 77 F5
Changchow Fujian China see Zhangzhou
Changchow Jiangsu China see Changzhou
Changchun China 74 B4
Changchunling China 74 B3
Changde China 77 F2
Changgang China 77 G3
Changge China 77 G1
Changgi-ap pt S. Korea 75 C5
Changgo China 83 F3
Chang Hu l. China 77 G2
Changhua Taiwan 77 I3
Changhŭng S. Korea 75 B6
Changhwa Taiwan see Changhua
Changi Sing. 71 [inset]
Changji China 80 G3
Changjiang China 77 F5
Chang Jiang r. China 77 I2 see Yangtze
Changjiang Kou China see Mouth of the Yangtze
Changjin-ho resr N. Korea 75 B4
Changkiang China see Zhanjiang
Changlang India 83 H4
Changleng China see Xinjian
Changling China 74 A3
Changlung Jammu and Kashmir 87 M3
Changma China 80 I4
Changning Jiangxi China see Xunwu
Changning Sichuan China 76 E2
Changnyŏn N. Korea 75 B5
Ch'ang-pai Shan mts China/N. Korea see Changbai Shan
Changpu China see Suining
Changp'yŏng S. Korea 75 C5
Changsan-got pt N. Korea 75 B5
Changsha China 77 G2
Changshan China 77 H2
Changshi China 76 E3
Changshoujie China 77 G2
Changshu China 77 I2
Changtai China 77 H3
Changteh China see Changde
Changting Fujian China 77 H3
Changting Heilong. China 74 C3
Ch'angwŏn S. Korea 75 C6
Changxing China 77 H2
Changyang China 77 F2
Changyŏn N. Korea 75 B5
Changyuan China 77 G1
Changzhi China 73 K5
Changzhou China 77 H2
Chañi, Nevado de mt. Arg. 144 C2
Chania Greece 59 K7
Chanion, Kolpos b. Greece 59 J7
Chankou China 76 E1
Channahon U.S.A. 134 A3
Channapatna India 84 C3
Channel Islands English Chan. 49 E9
Channel Islands U.S.A. 128 D5
Channel Islands National Park U.S.A. 128 D4
Channel-Port-aux-Basques Canada 123 K5
Channel Rock i. Bahamas 133 E8
Channel Tunnel France/U.K. 49 I7
Channing U.S.A. 131 C5
Chantada Spain 57 C2
Chanthaburi Thai. 71 C4
Chantilly France 52 C5
Chanumla India 71 A5
Chanute U.S.A. 130 E4
Chanuwala Pak. 89 I3
Chany, Ozero salt l. Rus. Fed. 64 I4
Chaohu China 77 H2
Chao Hu l. China 77 H2
Chaor He r. China see Qulin Gol
Chaouèn Morocco 57 D6
Chaowula Shan mt. China 76 C1
Chaoyang Guangdong China 77 H4
Chaoyang Heilong. China see Jiayin
Chaoyang Liaoning China 73 M4
Chaoyangcun China 74 B2
Chaozhong China 74 A2
Chaozhou China 77 H4
Chapada Diamantina, Parque Nacional nat. park Brazil 145 C1
Chapada dos Veadeiros, Parque Nacional da nat. park Brazil 145 B1
Chapais Canada 122 G4
Chapak Guzar Afgh. 89 G2
Chapala, Laguna de l. Mex. 136 D4
Chapayev Kazakh. 78 E1
Chapayevo Kazakh. see Chapayev
Chapayevsk Rus. Fed. 43 K5
Chapecó Brazil 144 F3
Chapecó r. Brazil 144 F3
Chapel-en-le-Frith U.K. 48 F5
Chapelle-lez-Herlaimont Belgium 52 E4
Chapeltown U.K. 48 F5
Chapleau Canada 122 E5
Chaplin Canada 121 J5
Chaplin Lake Canada 121 J5
Chaplygin Rus. Fed. 43 H5
Chapman, Mount Canada 120 G5
Chapmanville U.S.A. 134 D5
Chappell U.S.A. 130 C3
Chappell Islands Australia 111 [inset]
Chapra Bihar India see Chhapra
Chapra Jharkhand India see Chatra
Chapri Pass Afgh. 89 G3
Charagua Bol. 142 F7
Charay Mex. 127 F8
Charcas Mex. 136 D4
Charcot Island Antarctica 152 L2
Chard Canada 121 I4
Chard U.K. 49 E8
Chardara Kazakh. see Shardara
Chardara, Step' plain Kazakh. 80 C3
Chardon U.S.A. 134 E3
Chardzhev Turkm. see Turkmenabat
Chardzhou Turkm. see Turkmenabat
Charef Alg. 57 H6
Charef, Oued watercourse Morocco 54 D5
Charente r. France 56 D4
Chari r. Cameroon/Chad 97 E3
Chārī Iran 88 E4
Chārīkār Afgh. 89 H3
Chariton U.S.A. 130 E3
Chärjew Turkm. see Turkmenabat
Charkayuvom Rus. Fed. 42 L2
Chār Kent Afgh. 89 G2
Charkhlik China see Ruoqiang
Charleroi Belgium 52 E4
Charles, Cape U.S.A. 135 H5
Charlesbourg Canada 123 H5
Charles City IA U.S.A. 130 E3
Charles City VA U.S.A. 135 G5
Charles de Gaulle airport France 52 C5
Charles Hill Botswana 100 E2
Charles Island Galápagos Ecuador see Santa María, Isla
Charles Lake Canada 121 I3
Charles Point Australia 108 E3
Charleston N.Z. 113 C5
Charleston IL U.S.A. 130 F4
Charleston MO U.S.A. 131 F4
Charleston SC U.S.A. 133 E5

▶Charleston WV U.S.A. 134 E4
State capital of West Virginia.

Charleston Peak U.S.A. 129 F3
Charlestown Rep. of Ireland 51 D4
Charlestown IN U.S.A. 134 C4
Charlestown NH U.S.A. 135 I2
Charlestown RI U.S.A. 135 J3
Charles Town U.S.A. 135 G4
Charleville Australia 111 D5
Charleville Rep. of Ireland see Rathluirc
Charleville-Mézières France 52 E5
Charlevoix U.S.A. 134 C1
Charlie Lake Canada 120 F3
Charlotte MI U.S.A. 134 C2
Charlotte NC U.S.A. 133 D5
Charlotte TN U.S.A. 134 B5

▶Charlotte Amalie Virgin Is (U.S.A.) 137 L5
Capital of the U.S. Virgin Islands.

Charlotte Harbor b. U.S.A. 133 D7
Charlotte Lake Canada 120 E4
Charlottesville U.S.A. 135 F4

▶Charlottetown Canada 123 J5
Provincial capital of Prince Edward Island.

Charlton Australia 112 A6
Charlton Island Canada 122 F3
Charron Lake Canada 121 M4
Charsadda Pak. 89 H3
Charshanga Turkm. 89 G2
Charshangngy Turkm. see Charshanga
Charters Towers Australia 110 D4
Chartres France 56 E2
Chas India 83 F5
Chase Canada 120 G5
Chase U.S.A. 134 C2
Chase City U.S.A. 135 F5
Chashmeh Nūrī Iran 88 E3
Chashmeh-ye Ab-e Garm spring Iran 88 E3
Chashmeh-ye Garm Ab spring Iran 88 E3
Chashmeh-ye Magu well Iran 88 E3
Chashmeh-ye Mūkīk spring Iran 88 E3
Chashmeh-ye Palasi Iran 88 D3
Chashmeh-ye Safid spring Iran 88 E3
Chashmeh-ye Shotoran well Iran 88 D3
Chashniki Belarus 43 F5
Chaska U.S.A. 130 E2
Chaslands Mistake c. N.Z. 113 B8
Chasŏng N. Korea 74 B4
Chasseral mt. Switz. 47 K7
Chassiron, Pointe de pt France 56 D3
Chastab, Kūh-e mts Iran 88 D3
Chāt Iran 88 D2
Chatanika U.S.A. 118 D3
Châteaubriant France 56 D3
Château-du-Loir France 56 E3
Châteaudun France 56 E2
Chateaugay U.S.A. 135 H1
Châteauguay Canada 135 I1
Châteauguay r. Canada 123 H2
Châteauguay, Lac l. Canada 123 H2
Châteaulin France 56 B2
Châteaumeillant France 56 F3
Châteauneuf-en-Thymerais France 52 B6
Châteauneuf-sur-Loire France 56 F3
Chateau Pond l. Canada 123 K3
Châteauroux France 56 E3
Château-Salins France 52 G6
Château-Thierry France 52 D5
Chateh Canada 120 G3
Châtelet Belgium 52 E4
Châtellerault France 56 E3
Chatfield U.S.A. 122 B6
Chatham Canada 134 D2
Chatham U.K. 49 H7
Chatham MA U.S.A. 135 K3
Chatham NY U.S.A. 135 I2
Chatham PA U.S.A. 135 H4
Chatham VA U.S.A. 134 F5
Chatham, Isla i. Chile 144 B8
Chatham Island Galápagos Ecuador see San Cristóbal, Isla
Chatham Island N.Z. 107 I6
Chatham Island Samoa see Savai'i
Chatham Islands N.Z. 107 I6
Chatham Rise sea feature S. Pacific Ocean 150 I8
Chatham Strait U.S.A. 120 C3
Châtillon-sur-Seine France 56 G3
Chatkal Range mts Kyrg./Uzbek. 80 D3
Chatom U.S.A. 131 F6
Chatra India 83 F4
Chatra Nepal 83 F4
Chatsworth Canada 134 E1
Chatsworth U.S.A. 135 H4
Chattagam Bangl. see Chittagong
Chattanooga U.S.A. 133 C5
Chattarpur India see Chhatarpur
Chatteris U.K. 49 H6
Chattisgarh state India see Chhattisgarh
Chatturat Thai. 70 C4
Chatyr-Tash Kyrg. 80 E3
Châu Đốc Vietnam 71 D5
Chauhtan India 82 B4
Chauk Myanmar 70 A2
Chaumont France 56 G2
Chauncey U.S.A. 134 D4
Chaungzon Myanmar 70 B3
Chaunskaya Guba b. Rus. Fed. 65 R3
Chauny France 52 D5
Chau Phu Vietnam see Châu Đốc
Chausy Belarus see Chavusy
Chautauqua, Lake U.S.A. 134 F2
Chauter Pak. 89 G4
Chauvin Canada 121 I4
Chavakachcheri Sri Lanka 84 D4
Chaves Port. 57 C3
Chavigny, Lac l. Canada 122 G2
Chavusy Belarus 43 F5
Chawal r. Pak. 89 G4
Chây r. Vietnam 70 D2
Chayatyn, Khrebet ridge Rus. Fed. 74 E1
Chayevo Rus. Fed. 42 H4
Chaykovskiy Rus. Fed. 41 Q4
Chazhegovo Rus. Fed. 42 L3
Chazy U.S.A. 135 I1
Cheadle U.K. 49 F6
Cheaha Mountain hill U.S.A. 133 C5
Cheat r. U.S.A. 134 F4
Cheatham Lake U.S.A. 134 B5
Cheb Czech Rep. 53 M4
Chebba Tunisia 58 D7
Cheboksarskoye Vodokhranilishche resr Rus. Fed. 42 J5
Cheboksary Rus. Fed. 42 J4
Cheboygan U.S.A. 132 C2
Chechen', Ostrov i. Rus. Fed. 91 G2
Chech'ŏn S. Korea 75 C5
Chedabucto Bay Canada 123 J5
Cheddar U.K. 49 E7
Cheduba Myanmar 70 A3
Cheduba Island Myanmar 70 A3
Chée r. France 52 E6
Cheektowaga U.S.A. 135 F2
Cheepie Australia 112 B1
Cheetham, Cape Antarctica 152 H2
Chefoo China see Yantai
Chefornak U.S.A. 118 B3
Chefu Moz. 101 K2
Chegdomyn Rus. Fed. 74 D2
Chegga Mauritania 96 C2
Chegutu Zimbabwe 99 D5
Chehalis U.S.A. 126 C3
Chehar Burj Iran 88 E2
Chehardeh Iran 88 E3
Chehel Chashmeh, Kūh-e hill Iran 88 B3
Chehel Dokhtarān, Kūh-e mt. Iran 89 F4
Chehell'āyeh Iran 88 E4
Cheju S. Korea 75 B6
Cheju-do i. S. Korea 75 B6
Cheju-haehyŏp sea chan. S. Korea 75 B6
Chek Chue Hong Kong China see Stanley
Chekhov Moskovskaya Oblast' Rus. Fed. 43 H5
Chekhov Sakhalinskaya Oblast' Rus. Fed. 74 F3
Chekiang prov. China see Zhejiang
Chekichler Turkm. see Chekishlyar
Chekishlyar Turkm. 88 D2
Chek Lap Kok reg. Hong Kong China 77 [inset]
Chek Mun Hoi Hap Hong Kong China see Tolo Channel
Chekunda Rus. Fed. 74 D2
Chela, Serra da mts Angola 99 B5
Chelan, Lake U.S.A. 126 C2
Cheleken Turkm. 88 D2
Chélif, Oued r. Alg. 57 G5
Cheline Moz. 101 L2
Chelkar Kazakh. see Shalkar
Chełm Poland 43 D6
Chelmer r. U.K. 49 H7
Chełmno Poland 47 Q4
Chelmsford U.K. 49 H7
Chelsea MI U.S.A. 134 C2
Chelsea VT U.S.A. 135 I2
Cheltenham U.K. 49 E7
Chelva Spain 57 F4
Chelyabinsk Rus. Fed. 64 H4
Chelyuskin Rus. Fed. 153 E1
Chemba Moz. 99 D5
Chêm Co l. China 82 D2
Chemenibit Turkm. 89 F3
Chemnitz Germany 53 M4
Chemulpo S. Korea see Inch'ŏn
Chenab r. India/Pak. 82 B3
Chenachane, Oued watercourse Alg. 96 C2
Chendir r. Turkm. see Chandyr
Cheney U.S.A. 126 D3
Cheney Reservoir U.S.A. 130 D4
Chengalpattu India 84 D3
Chengbu China 77 F3
Chengchow China see Zhengzhou
Chengde China 73 L4
Chengdu China 76 E2
Chengele India 76 C2
Chenggong China 76 D3
Chenghai China 77 H4
Cheng Hai l. China 76 D3
Chengjiang China see Taihe
Chengmai China 77 F5
Chengtu China see Chengdu
Chengwu China 77 G1
Chengxian China 76 E1
Chengxiang Chongqing China see Wuxi
Chengxiang Jiangxi China see Quannan
Chengzhong China see Ningming
Cheniu Shan i. China 77 H1
Chenkaladi Sri Lanka 84 D5
Chennai India 84 D3
Chenqian Shan i. China 77 I2
Chenqing China 74 B2
Chenqingqiao China see Chenqing
Chenstokhov Poland see Częstochowa
Chentejn Nuruu mts Mongolia 73 J3
Chenxi China 77 F3
Chenyang China see Chenxi
Chenying China see Wannian
Chenzhou China 77 G3
Cheo Reo Vietnam 71 E4
Chepén Peru 142 C5
Chepes Arg. 144 C4
Chepo Panama 137 I7
Chepstow U.K. 49 E7
Cheptsa r. Rus. Fed. 42 K4
Chequamegon Bay U.S.A. 130 F2
Cher r. France 56 E3
Chera state India see Kerala
Cheraw U.S.A. 133 E5
Cherbaniani Reef India 84 A3
Cherbourg France 56 D2
Cherchell Alg. 57 H5
Cherchen China see Qiemo
Cherdakly Rus. Fed. 43 K5
Cherdyn' Rus. Fed. 41 R3
Chereapani reef India see Byramgore Reef
Cheremkhovo Rus. Fed. 72 I2
Cheremshany Rus. Fed. 74 D3
Cheremukhovka Rus. Fed. 42 K4
Cherepanovo Rus. Fed. 72 E2
Cherepovets Rus. Fed. 42 H4
Cherevkovo Rus. Fed. 42 J3
Chergui, Chott ech imp. l. Alg. 54 D5
Chéria Alg. 58 B7
Cheriton U.S.A. 135 H5
Cheriyam atoll India 84 B4
Cherkassy Ukr. see Cherkasy
Cherkasy Ukr. 43 G6
Cherkessk Rus. Fed. 91 F1
Cherla India 84 D2
Chernaya Rus. Fed. 42 M1
Chernaya r. Rus. Fed. 42 M1
Chernigov Ukr. see Chernihiv
Chernigovka Rus. Fed. 74 D3
Chernihiv Ukr. 43 F6
Cherninivka Ukr. 43 H7
Chernivtsi Ukr. 43 E6
Chernobyl' Ukr. see Chornobyl'
Chernogorsk Rus. Fed. 72 G2
Chernovtsy Ukr. see Chernivtsi
Chernoye More sea Asia/Europe see Black Sea
Chernushka Rus. Fed. 41 R4
Chernyakhiv Ukr. 43 F6
Chernyakhovsk Rus. Fed. 45 L9
Chernyanka Rus. Fed. 43 H6
Chernyayevo Rus. Fed. 74 B1
Chernyshevsk Rus. Fed. 73 L2
Chernyshevskiy Rus. Fed. 65 M3
Chernyshkovskiy Rus. Fed. 43 I6
Chernyye Zemli reg. Rus. Fed. 43 J7
Chernyy Irtysh r. China/Kazakh. see Ertix He
Chernyy Porog Rus. Fed. 42 G3
Chernyy Yar Rus. Fed. 43 J6
Cherokee U.S.A. 130 E3
Cherokee Sound Bahamas 133 E7

▶Cherrapunji India 83 G4
Highest recorded annual rainfall in the world.

Cherry Creek r. U.S.A. 130 C2
Cherry Creek Mountains U.S.A. 129 F1
Cherry Hill U.S.A. 135 H4
Cherry Island Solomon Is 107 G3
Cherry Lake U.S.A. 128 D2
Cherskiy Rus. Fed. 153 C2
Cherskiy Range mts Rus. Fed. see Cherskogo, Khrebet
Cherskogo, Khrebet mts Rus. Fed. 65 P3
Cherskogo, Khrebet mts Rus. Fed. 73 K2
Chertkov Ukr. see Chortkiv
Chertkovo Rus. Fed. 43 I6
Cherven Bryag Bulg. 59 K3
Chervonoarmeyskoye Ukr. see Vil'nyans'k
Chervonoarmiys'k Donets'ka Oblast' Ukr. see Krasnoarmiys'k
Chervonoarmiys'k Rivnens'ka Oblast' Ukr. see Radyvyliv
Chervonograd Ukr. see Chervonohrad
Chervonohrad Ukr. 43 E6
Chervyen' Belarus 43 F5
Cherwell r. U.K. 49 F7
Cherykaw Belarus 43 F5
Chesapeake U.S.A. 135 G5
Chesapeake Bay U.S.A. 135 G4
Chesham U.K. 49 G7
Cheshire Plain U.K. 48 E5
Cheshme 2-y Turkm. 89 F2
Cheshskaya Guba b. Rus. Fed. 42 J2
Cheshtebe Tajik. 89 I2
Cheshunt U.K. 49 G7
Chesnokovka Rus. Fed. see Novoaltaysk
Chester Canada 123 I5
Chester U.K. 48 E5
Chester CA U.S.A. 128 C1
Chester IL U.S.A. 130 F4
Chester MT U.S.A. 126 F2
Chester OH U.S.A. 134 E4
Chester SC U.S.A. 133 D5
Chester r. U.S.A. 135 G4
Chesterfield U.K. 48 F5
Chesterfield U.S.A. 135 G5
Chesterfield, Îles is New Caledonia 107 F3
Chesterfield Inlet Canada 121 N2
Chesterfield Inlet inlet Canada 121 M2
Chester-le-Street U.K. 48 F4
Chestertown MD U.S.A. 135 G4
Chestertown NY U.S.A. 135 I2
Chesterville Canada 135 H1
Chestnut Ridge U.S.A. 134 F3
Chesuncook Lake U.S.A. 132 G2
Chetaïbi Alg. 58 B6
Chéticamp Canada 123 J5
Chetlat i. India 84 B4
Chetumal Mex. 136 G5
Chetwynd Canada 120 F4
Cheung Chau Hong Kong China 77 [inset]
Chevelon Creek r. U.S.A. 129 H4
Cheviot N.Z. 113 D6
Cheviot Hills U.K. 48 E3
Cheviot Range hills Australia 110 C5
Chevreulx r. Canada 122 G3
Cheyenne OK U.S.A. 131 D5

▶Cheyenne WY U.S.A. 126 G4
State capital of Wyoming.

Cheyenne r. U.S.A. 130 C2
Cheyenne Wells U.S.A. 130 C4
Cheyne Bay Australia 109 B8
Cheyur India 84 D3
Chezacut Canada 120 E4
Chhapra India 83 F4
Chhata India 82 D4
Chhatak Bangl. 83 G4
Chhatarpur Jharkhand India 83 F4
Chhatarpur Madhya Pradesh India 82 D4
Chhatr Pak. 89 H4
Chhatrapur India 84 E2
Chhattisgarh state India 83 E5
Chhay Arêng, Stœ̆ng r. Cambodia 71 C5
Chhindwara India 82 D5
Chhitkul India 82 D3
Chhukha Bhutan 83 G4
Chi, Lam r. Thai. 71 C4
Chi, Mae Nam r. Thai. 70 D4
Chiai Taiwan 77 I4
Chiamboni Somalia 98 E4
Chiange Angola 99 B5
Chiang Kham Thai. 70 C3
Chiang Khan Thai. 70 C3
Chiang Mai Thai. 70 B3
Chiang Rai Thai. 70 B3
Chiang Saen Thai. 70 C2
Chiari Italy 58 C2
Chiautla Mex. 136 E5
Chiavenno Italy 58 C1
Chiayi Taiwan see Chiai
Chiba Japan 75 F6
Chibi China 77 G2
Chibia Angola 99 B5
Chibizovka Rus. Fed. see Zherdevka
Chiboma Moz. 99 D6
Chibougamau Canada 122 G4
Chibougamau, Lac l. Canada 122 G4
Chibu-Sangaku National Park Japan 75 E5
Chibuto Moz. 101 K3
Chibuzhang Hu l. China 83 G2
Chicacole India see Srikakulam

▶Chicago U.S.A. 134 B3
4th most populous city in North America.

Chic-Chocs, Monts mts Canada 123 I4
Chichagof U.S.A. 120 B3
Chichagof Island U.S.A. 120 C3
Chichak r. Pak. 89 G5
Chichaoua Morocco 54 C5
Chichatka Rus. Fed. 74 A1
Chicheng China see Pengxi
Chichester U.K. 49 G8
Chichester Range mts Australia 108 B5
Chichgarh India 84 D1
Chichibu Japan 75 E6
Chichibu-Tama National Park Japan 75 E6
Chichijima-rettō is Japan 75 F8
Chickasha U.S.A. 131 D5
Chiclana de la Frontera Spain 57 C5
Chiclayo Peru 142 C5
Chico r. Arg. 144 C6
Chico U.S.A. 128 C2
Chicomo Moz. 101 L3
Chicopee U.S.A. 135 I2
Chicoutimi Canada 123 H4
Chicualacuala Moz. 101 J2
Chidambaram India 84 C4
Chidenguele Moz. 101 L3
Chidley, Cape Canada 119 L3
Chido China see Sêndo
Chido S. Korea 75 B6
Chiducuane Moz. 101 L3
Chiefland U.S.A. 133 D6
Chiêm Hoa Vietnam 70 D2
Chiemsee l. Germany 47 N7
Chiengmai Thai. see Chiang Mai
Chiers r. France 52 F5
Chieti Italy 58 F3
Chifeng China 73 L4
Chifre, Serra do mts Brazil 145 C2
Chiganak Kazakh. 80 D2
Chiginagak Volcano, Mount U.S.A. 118 C4
Chigu China 83 G3
Chigubo Moz. 101 K2
Chigu Co l. China 83 G3
Chihli, Gulf of China see Bo Hai
Chihuahua Mex. 127 G7
Chihuahua state Mex. 127 G7
Chiili Kazakh. 80 C3
Chikalda India 82 D5
Chikan China 77 F4
Chikaskia r. U.S.A. 131 D4
Chikhali Kalan Parasia India 82 D5
Chikhli India 84 C1
Chikishlyar Turkm. see Chekishlyar
Chikmagalur India 84 B3
Chikodi India 84 B2
Chilanko r. Canada 120 F4
Chilas Jammu and Kashmir 82 C2
Chilaw Sri Lanka 84 C5
Chilcotin r. Canada 120 F5
Childers Australia 110 F5
Childress U.S.A. 131 C5
▶Chile country S. America 144 B4
South America 9, 140–141
Chile Basin sea feature S. Pacific Ocean 151 O8
Chile Chico Chile 144 B7
Chile Rise sea feature S. Pacific Ocean 151 O8
Chilgir Rus. Fed. 43 J7
Chilhowie U.S.A. 134 E5
Chilia-Nouă Ukr. see Kiliya
Chilik Kazakh. 80 E3
Chilika Lake India 84 E2
Chililabombwe Zambia 99 C5
Chilko r. Canada 120 F4
Chilko Lake Canada 120 E5
Chilkoot Pass Canada/U.S.A. 120 C3
Chilkoot Trail National Historic Site nat. park Canada 120 C3
Chillán Chile 144 B5
Chillicothe MO U.S.A. 130 E4
Chillicothe OH U.S.A. 134 D4
Chilliwack Canada 120 F5
Chil'mamedkum, Peski des. Turkm. 88 D1
Chilo India 82 C4
Chiloé, Isla de i. Chile 144 B6
Chiloé, Isla Grande de i. Chile see Chiloé, Isla de
Chilpancingo Mex. 136 E5
Chilpancingo de los Bravos Mex. see Chilpancingo
Chilpi Jammu and Kashmir 82 C1
Chiltern Hills U.K. 49 G7
Chilton U.S.A. 134 A1
Chiluage Angola 99 C4
Chilubi Zambia 99 C5
Chilung Taiwan 77 I3
Chilwa, Lake Malawi 99 D5
Chimala Tanz. 99 D4
Chimaltenango Guat. 136 F6
Chi Ma Wan Hong Kong China 77 [inset]
Chimay Belgium 52 E4
Chimbas Arg. 144 C4
Chimbay Uzbek. 80 A3
Chimborazo mt. Ecuador 142 C4
Chimbote Peru 142 C5
Chimboy Uzbek. see Chimbay
Chimian Pak. 89 I4
Chimishliya Moldova see Cimişlia
Chimkent Kazakh. see Shymkent
Chimney Rock U.S.A. 129 J3
Chimoio Moz. 99 D5
Chimtargha, Qullai mt. Tajik. 89 H2
Chimtorga, Gora mt. Tajik. see Chimtargha, Qullai

▶China country Asia 72 H5
Most populous country in the world and in Asia. 2nd largest country in Asia and 4th largest in the world.
Asia 6, 62–63

China Mex. 131 D7
China, Republic of country Asia see Taiwan
China Bakir r. Myanmar see To
China Lake CA U.S.A. 128 E4
China Lake ME U.S.A. 135 K1
Chinandega Nicaragua 136 G6
China Point U.S.A. 128 D5
Chinati Peak U.S.A. 131 B6
Chincha Alta Peru 142 C6
Chinchaga r. Canada 120 G3
Chinchilla Australia 112 E1
Chincholi India 84 C2
Chinchorro, Banco sea feature Mex. 137 G5
Chincoteague Bay U.S.A. 135 H5
Chinde Moz. 99 D5
Chindo S. Korea 75 B6
Chin-do i. S. Korea 75 B6
Chindwin r. Myanmar 70 A2
Chinese Turkestan aut. reg. China see Xinjiang Uygur Zizhiqu
Chinghai prov. China see Qinghai
Chingiz-Tau, Khrebet mts Kazakh. 80 E2
Chingleput India see Chengalpattu
Chingola Zambia 99 C5
Chinguar Angola 99 B5
Chinguețti Mauritania 96 B2
Chinhae S. Korea 75 C6
Chinhoyi Zimbabwe 99 D5
Chini India see Kalpa
Chining China see Jining
Chiniot Pak. 89 I4
Chinipas Mex. 127 F8
Chinit, Stœ̆ng r. Cambodia 71 D4
Chinju S. Korea 75 C6
Chinle U.S.A. 129 I3
Chinmen Taiwan 77 H3
Chinmen Tao i. Taiwan 77 H3
Chinnamp'o N. Korea see Namp'o
Chinnur India 84 C2
Chino Creek watercourse U.S.A. 129 G4
Chinon France 56 E3
Chinook U.S.A. 126 F2
Chinook Trough sea feature N. Pacific Ocean 150 I3
Chino Valley U.S.A. 129 G4
Chintamani India 84 C3
Chioggia Italy 58 E2
Chios Greece 59 L5
Chios i. Greece 59 K5
Chipata Zambia 99 D5
Chipchihua, Sierra de mts Arg. 144 C6
Chiphu Cambodia 71 D5
Chipindo Angola 99 B5
Chipinga Zimbabwe see Chipinge
Chipinge Zimbabwe 99 D6
Chipley U.S.A. 133 C6
Chipman Canada 123 I5
Chippenham U.K. 49 E7
Chippewa, Lake U.S.A. 130 F2
Chippewa Falls U.S.A. 130 F2
Chipping Norton U.K. 49 F7
Chipping Sodbury U.K. 49 E7
Chipurupalle Andhra Pradesh India 84 D2
Chipurupalle Andhra Pradesh India 84 D2
Chiquilá Mex. 133 C8
Chiquinquira Col. 142 D2
Chir r. Rus. Fed. 43 I6
Chirada India 84 D3
Chirala India 84 D3
Chiras Afgh. 89 G3
Chirchik Uzbek. 80 C3
Chiredzi Zimbabwe 99 D6
Chirfa Niger 96 E2
Chiricahua National Monument nat. park U.S.A. 129 I5
Chiricahua Peak U.S.A. 129 I6
Chirikof Island U.S.A. 118 C4
Chiriquí, Golfo de b. Panama 137 H7
Chiriquí, Volcán de vol. Panama see Barú, Volcán
Chiri-san mt. S. Korea 75 B6
Chirk U.K. 49 D6
Chirnside U.K. 50 G5
Chirripo mt. Costa Rica 137 H7
Chisamba Zambia 99 C5
Chisana r. U.S.A. 120 A2
Chisasibi Canada 122 F3
Chishima-retto is Rus. Fed. see Kuril Islands
Chisholm Canada 120 H4
Chishtian Mandi Pak. 89 I4
Chishui China 76 E2
Chishuihe China 76 E3
Chisimaio Somalia see Kismaayo

▶Chişinău Moldova 59 M1
Capital of Moldova.

Chistopol' Rus. Fed. 42 K5
Chita Rus. Fed. 73 K2
Chitado Angola 99 B5
Chitaldrug India see Chitradurga
Chitalwana India 82 B4
Chitambo Zambia 99 D5
Chita Oblast admin. div. Rus. Fed. see Chitinskaya Oblast'
Chitato Angola 99 C4
Chitek Lake Canada 121 J4
Chitek Lake l. Canada 121 L4
Chitembo Angola 99 B5
Chitina U.S.A. 118 D3

Chitinskaya Oblast' admin. div. Rus. Fed. 74 A1
Chitipa Malawi 99 D4
Chitkul India see Chhitkul
Chitobe Moz. 99 D6
Chitoor India see Chittoor
Chitor India see Chittaurgarh
Chitose Japan 74 F4
Chitradurga India 84 C3
Chitrakoot India 82 E4
Chitrakut India see Chitrakoot
Chitral Pak. 89 H3
Chitral r. Pak. 89 H3
Chitravati r. India 84 C3
Chitré Panama 137 H7
Chitrod India 82 B5
Chittagong Bangl. 83 G5
Chittaurgarh India 82 C4
Chittoor India 84 C3
Chittor India see Chittoor
Chittorgarh India see Chittaurgarh
Chittur India 84 C4
Chitungwiza Zimbabwe 99 D5
Chiu Lung Hong Kong China see Kowloon
Chiume Angola 99 C5
Chivasso Italy 58 B2
Chívato, Punta pt Mex. 127 F8
Chivhu Zimbabwe 99 D5
Chixi China 77 G4
Chizarira National Park Zimbabwe 99 C5
Chizha Vtoraya Kazakh. 43 K6
Chizhou China 77 H2
Chizu Japan 75 D6
Chkalov Rus. Fed. see Orenburg
Chkalovsk Rus. Fed. 42 I4
Chkalovskoye Rus. Fed. 74 D3
Chlef Alg. see Ech Chélif
Chloride U.S.A. 129 F4
Chlya, Ozero l. Rus. Fed. 74 F1
Choa Chu Kang Sing. 71 [inset]
Choa Chu Kang hill Sing. 71 [inset]
Chobe National Park Botswana 99 C5
Chodov Czech Rep. 53 M4
Choele Choel Arg. 144 C5
Chogar r. Rus. Fed. 74 D1
Chogori Feng mt. China/Jammu and Kashmir see K2
Chograyskoye Vodokhranilishche resr Rus. Fed. 43 J7
Choiseul i. Solomon Is 107 F2
Choix Mex. 127 F8
Chojnice Poland 47 P4
Chōkai-san vol. Japan 75 F5
Ch'ok'ē mts Eth. 98 D2
Ch'ok'ē Mountains Eth. see Ch'ok'ē
Chokola mt. China 82 E3
Choksum China 83 F3
Chokue Moz. see Chókwé
Chokurdakh Rus. Fed. 65 P2
Chókwé Moz. 101 K3
Cho La pass China 76 C2
Cholame U.S.A. 128 C4
Chola Shan mts China 76 C1
Cholet France 56 D3
Cholpon-Ata Kyrg. 80 E3
Choluteca Hond. 137 G6
Choma Zambia 99 C5
Chomo Ganggar mt. China 83 G3
Chơ Moi Vietnam 70 D2
Chomo Lhari mt. China/Bhutan 83 G4
Chom Thong Thai. 70 B3
Chomutov Czech Rep. 47 N5
Ch'ŏnan S. Korea 75 B5
Chon Buri Thai. 71 C4
Ch'ŏnch'ŏn N. Korea 74 B4
Chone Ecuador 142 B4
Ch'ŏngch'ŏn-gang r. N. Korea 75 B5
Ch'ongdo S. Korea 75 C6
Chonggye China see Qonggyai
Ch'ŏngjin N. Korea 74 C4
Ch'ŏngju S. Korea 75 B5
Chông Kal Cambodia 71 C4
Chongkü China 76 C2
Chonglong China see Zizhong
Chongming Dao i. China 77 I2
Chongoroi Angola 99 B5
Chŏngp'yŏng N. Korea 75 B5
Chongqing China 76 E2
Chongqing municipality China 76 E2
Chonguene Moz. 101 K3
Chŏngŭp S. Korea 75 B6
Chongyang China 77 G2
Chongyi China 77 G3
Chongzuo China 76 E4
Chŏnju S. Korea 75 B6
Chonogol Mongolia 73 L3
Cho Oyu mt. China/Nepal 83 F3
Chopda India 82 C5
Chơ Phươc Hai Vietnam 71 D5
Chor Pak. 89 H5
Chorley U.K. 48 E5
Chornobyl' Ukr. 43 F6
Chornomors'ke Ukr. 59 O2
Chortkiv Ukr. 43 E6
Ch'osan N. Korea 74 B4
Chōshi Japan 75 F6
Chosŏn country Asia see South Korea
Chosŏn-minjujuŭi-inmin-konghwaguk country Asia see North Korea
Choszczno Poland 47 O4
Chota Peru 142 C5
Chota Sinchula hill India 83 G4
Choteau U.S.A. 126 E3
Choti Pak. 89 H4
Choûm Mauritania 96 B2
Chowchilla U.S.A. 128 C3
Chowghat India 84 B4
Chown, Mount Canada 120 G4
Choybalsan Mongolia 73 K3
Choyr Mongolia 73 J3
Chrétiens, Île aux i. Canada see Christian Island
Chřiby hills Czech Rep. 47 P6
Chrisman U.S.A. 134 B4
Chrissiesmeer S. Africa 101 J4
Christchurch N.Z. 113 D6
Christchurch U.K. 49 F8
Christian, Cape Canada 119 L2
Christiana S. Africa 101 G4
Christiania Norway see Oslo
Christian Island Canada 134 E1
Christiansburg U.S.A. 134 E5
Christianshåb Greenland see Qasigiannguit
Christie Bay Canada 121 I2
Christie Island Myanmar 71 B5
Christina r. Canada 121 I3
Christina, Mount N.Z. 113 B7

▶Christmas Island terr. Indian Ocean 68 D9
Australian External Territory.
Asia 6

Christopher, Lake salt flat Australia 109 D6
Chrudim Czech Rep. 47 O6
Chrysi i. Greece 59 K7
Chrysochou Bay Cyprus 85 A2
Chrysochous, Kolpos b. Cyprus see Chrysochou Bay
Chu Kazakh. see Shu
Chu r. Kazakh./Kyrg. 80 C3
Chuadanga Bangl. 83 G5
Chuali, Lago l. Moz. 101 K3
Chuanhui China see Zhoukou
Chuansha China 77 I2
Chubalung China 76 C2
Chubarovka Ukr. see Polohy
Chubartau Kazakh. see Barshatas
Chuchkovo Rus. Fed. 43 I5
Chuckwalla Mountains U.S.A. 129 F5
Chudniv Ukr. 43 F6
Chudovo Rus. Fed. 42 F4
Chudskoye, Ozero l. Estonia/Rus. Fed. see Peipus, Lake
Chugach Mountains U.S.A. 118 D3
Chūgoku-sanchi mts Japan 75 D6
Chugqênsumdo China see Jigzhi
Chuguchak China see Tacheng
Chuguyev Ukr. see Chuhuyiv
Chuguyevka Rus. Fed. 74 D3
Chugwater U.S.A. 126 G4
Chuhai China see Zhuhai
Chuhuyiv Ukr. 43 H6
Chu-Iliyskiye Gory mts Kazakh. 80 D3
Chujiang China see Shimen
Chukai Malaysia see Cukai
Chukchagirskoye, Ozero l. Rus. Fed. 74 E1
Chukchi Abyssal Plain sea feature Arctic Ocean 153 B1
Chukchi Peninsula Rus. Fed. see Chukotskiy Poluostrov
Chukchi Plateau sea feature Arctic Ocean 153 B1
Chukchi Sea Rus. Fed./U.S.A. 65 T3
Chukhloma Rus. Fed. 42 I4
Chukotskiy, Mys c. Rus. Fed. 118 A3
Chukotskiy Poluostrov pen. Rus. Fed. 65 T3
Chu Lai Vietnam 70 E4
Chulakkurgan Kazakh. see Sholakkorgan
Chulaktau Kazakh. see Karatau
Chulasa Rus. Fed. 42 J2
Chula Vista U.S.A. 128 E5
Chulucanas Peru 142 B5
Chulung Pass Pak. 82 D2
Chulym Rus. Fed. 64 J4
Chumar Jammu and Kashmir 78 D2
Chumbicha Arg. 144 C3
Chumda China 76 C1
Chumikan Rus. Fed. 65 O4
Chum Phae Thai. 70 C3
Chumphon Thai. 71 B5
Chum Saeng Thai. 70 C4
Chunar India 83 E4
Ch'unch'ŏn S. Korea 75 B5
Chunchura India 83 G5
Chundzha Kazakh. 80 E3
Chunga Zambia 99 C5
Chung-hua Jen-min Kung-ho-kuo country Asia see China
Chung-hua Min-kuo country Asia see Taiwan
Ch'ungju S. Korea 75 B5
Chungking China see Chongqing
Ch'ungmu S. Korea see T'ongyŏng
Chŭngsan N. Korea 75 B5
Chungyang Shanmo mts Taiwan 77 I4
Chunskiy Rus. Fed. 72 H1
Chunya r. Rus. Fed. 65 K3
Chuôi, Hon i. Vietnam 71 D5
Chuosijia China see Guanyinqiao
Chupa Rus. Fed. 44 R3
Chūplū Iran 88 B2
Chuquicamata Chile 144 C2
Chur Switz. 56 I3
Churachandpur India 83 H4
Chūrān Iran 88 D4
Churapcha Rus. Fed. 65 O3
Churchill Canada 121 M3
Churchill r. Man. Canada 121 M3
Churchill r. Nfld. and Lab. Canada 123 J3
Churchill, Cape Canada 121 M3
Churchill Falls Canada 123 J3
Churchill Lake Canada 121 I4
Churchill Mountains Antarctica 152 H1
Churchill Sound sea chan. Canada 122 F2
Churchs Ferry U.S.A. 130 D1
Churchville U.S.A. 134 F4
Churia Ghati Hills Nepal 83 F4
Churu India 82 C3
Churubusco U.S.A. 134 C3
Churún-Merú waterfall Venez. see Angel Falls
Chushul Jammu and Kashmir 82 D2
Chuska Mountains U.S.A. 129 I3
Chusovaya r. Rus. Fed. 41 R4
Chusovoy Rus. Fed. 41 R4
Chust Ukr. see Khust
Chute-des-Passes Canada 123 H4
Chutia Assam India 83 H4
Chutia Jharkhand India 83 F5
Chutung Taiwan 77 I3
Chuuk is Micronesia 150 G5
Chuxiong China 76 D3
Chüy r. Kazakh./Kyrg. see Chu
Chư Yang Sin mt. Vietnam 71 E4
Chuzhou Anhui China 77 H1
Chuzhou Jiangsu China 77 H1
Chymyshliya Moldova see Cimişlia
Chyulu Hills National Park Kenya 98 D4
Ciadâr-Lunga Moldova see Ciadîr-Lunga
Ciadîr-Lunga Moldova 59 M1
Ciamis Indon. 68 D8
Cianjur Indon. 68 D8
Cianorte Brazil 144 F2
Cibecue U.S.A. 129 H4
Cibolo Creek r. U.S.A. 131 D6
Cíbuta, Sierra mt. Mex. 127 F7
Čičarija mts Croatia 58 E2
Cicero U.S.A. 134 B3
Cide Turkey 90 D2
Ciechanów Poland 47 R4
Ciego de Ávila Cuba 137 I4
Ciénaga Col. 142 D1
Ciénega Mex. 131 C7
Ciénega de Flores Mex. 131 C7
Cienfuegos Cuba 137 H4
Cieza Spain 57 F4
Çiftlik Turkey see Kelkit
Cifuentes Spain 57 E3
Cigüela r. Spain 57 E4
Cihanbeyli Turkey 90 D3
Cijara, Embalse de resr Spain 57 D4
Cilacap Indon. 68 D8
Çıldır Turkey 91 F2
Çıldır Gölü l. Turkey 91 F2
Çildiroba Turkey 85 C1
Cilento e del Vallo di Diano, Parco Nazionale del nat. park Italy 58 F4
Cili China 77 F2
Cilician Gates pass Turkey see Gülek Boğazı
Cill Airne Rep. of Ireland see Killarney
Cill Chainnigh Rep. of Ireland see Kilkenny
Cill Mhantáin Rep. of Ireland see Wicklow
Cilo Dağı mt. Turkey 91 G3
Çiloy Adası i. Azer. 91 H2
Cimarron CO U.S.A. 129 J2
Cimarron KS U.S.A. 130 C4
Cimarron NM U.S.A. 127 G5
Cimarron r. U.S.A. 131 D4
Cimişlia Moldova 59 M1
Cimone, Monte mt. Italy 58 D2
Cîmpina Romania see Câmpina
Cîmpulung Romania see Câmpulung
Cîmpulung Moldovenesc Romania see Câmpulung Moldovenesc
Cina, Tanjung c. Indon. 68 C8
Çınar Turkey 91 F3
Cinaruco-Capanaparo, Parque Nacional nat. park Venez. 142 E2
Cinca r. Spain 57 G3
Cincinnati U.S.A. 134 C4
Cinco de Outubro Angola see Xá-Muteba
Cinderford U.K. 49 E7
Çine Turkey 59 M6
Ciney Belgium 52 F4
Cintalapa Mex. 136 F5
Cinto, Monte mt. France 56 I5
Ciping China see Jinggangshan
Circeo, Parco Nazionale del nat. park Italy 58 E4
Circle AK U.S.A. 118 D3
Circle MT U.S.A. 126 G3
Circleville OH U.S.A. 134 D4
Circleville UT U.S.A. 129 G2
Cirebon Indon. 68 D8
Cirencester U.K. 49 F7
Cirò Marina Italy 58 G5
Cirta Alg. see Constantine
Cisco U.S.A. 129 I2
Citlaltépetl vol. Mex. see Orizaba, Pico de
Čitluk Bos.-Herz. 58 G3
Citronelle U.S.A. 131 F6
Citrus Heights U.S.A. 128 C2
Città di Castello Italy 58 E3
Ciucaş, Vârful mt. Romania 59 K2
Ciudad Acuña Mex. 131 C6
Ciudad Altamirano Mex. 136 D5
Ciudad Bolívar Venez. 142 F2
Ciudad Camargo Mex. 131 B7
Ciudad Constitución Mex. 136 B3
Ciudad del Carmen Mex. 136 F5
Ciudad Delicias Mex. 131 B6
Ciudad de Panamá Panama see Panama City
Ciudad de Valles Mex. 136 E4
Ciudad Flores Guat. see Flores
Ciudad Guayana Venez. 142 F2
Ciudad Guerrero Mex. 127 G7
Ciudad Guzmán Mex. 136 D5
Ciudad Juárez Mex. 127 G7
Ciudad Lerdo Mex. 131 C7
Ciudad Mante Mex. 136 E4
Ciudad Obregón Mex. 127 F8
Ciudad Real Spain 57 E4
Ciudad Río Bravo Mex. 131 D7
Ciudad Rodrigo Spain 57 C3
Ciudad Trujillo Dom. Rep. see Santo Domingo
Ciudad Victoria Mex. 131 D8
Ciutadella de Menorca Spain 57 H3
Cıva Burnu pt Turkey 90 E2
Cividale del Friuli Italy 58 E1
Civitanova Marche Italy 58 E3
Civitavecchia Italy 58 D3
Çivril Turkey 59 M5
Cixi China 77 I2
Cizre Turkey 91 F3
Clacton-on-Sea U.K. 49 I7
Clady U.K. 51 E3
Claire, Lake Canada 121 H3
Clairfontaine Alg. see El Aouinet
Clamecy France 56 F3
Clane Rep. of Ireland 51 F4
Clanton U.S.A. 133 C5
Clanwilliam Dam S. Africa 100 D7
Clara Rep. of Ireland 51 E4
Clara Island Myanmar 71 B5
Claraville Australia 110 C3
Clare N.S.W. Australia 112 A4
Clare S.A. Australia 111 B7
Clare r. Rep. of Ireland 51 C4
Clare U.S.A. 134 C2
Clarecastle Rep. of Ireland 51 D5
Clare Island Rep. of Ireland 51 B4
Claremont U.S.A. 135 I2
Claremore U.S.A. 131 E4
Claremorris Rep. of Ireland 51 D4
Clarence r. Australia 112 F2
Clarence N.Z. 113 D6
Clarence Island Antarctica 152 A2
Clarence Strait Iran see Khūran
Clarence Strait U.S.A. 120 C3
Clarence Town Bahamas 133 F8
Clarendon AR U.S.A. 131 F5
Clarendon PA U.S.A. 134 F3
Clarendon TX U.S.A. 131 C5
Clarenville Canada 123 L4
Claresholm Canada 120 H5
Clarie Coast Antarctica see Wilkes Coast
Clarinda U.S.A. 130 E3
Clarington U.S.A. 134 E4
Clarion IA U.S.A. 130 E3
Clarion PA U.S.A. 134 F3
Clarion r. U.S.A. 134 F3
Clarión, Isla i. Mex. 136 B5
Clark U.S.A. 130 D2
Clark, Mount Canada 120 F1
Clarkdale U.S.A. 129 G4
Clarkebury S. Africa 101 I6
Clarke Range mts Australia 110 D4
Clarke River Australia 110 D3
Clarke's Head Canada 123 L4
Clark Mountain U.S.A. 129 F4
Clark Point Canada 134 E1
Clarksburg U.S.A. 134 E4
Clarksdale U.S.A. 131 F5
Clarks Hill U.S.A. 134 B3
Clarksville AR U.S.A. 131 E5
Clarksville IN U.S.A. 134 B4
Clarksville TN U.S.A. 134 B5
Clarksville TX U.S.A. 131 E5
Clarksville VA U.S.A. 135 F5
Claro r. Goiás Brazil 145 A2
Claro r. Mato Grosso Brazil 145 A1
Clashmore Rep. of Ireland 51 E5
Claude U.S.A. 131 C5
Claudy U.K. 51 E3
Clavier Belgium 52 F4
Claxton U.S.A. 133 D5
Clay U.S.A. 134 E4
Clayburg U.S.A. 135 I1
Clay Center KS U.S.A. 130 D4
Clay Center NE U.S.A. 130 D3
Clay City IN U.S.A. 134 B4
Clay City KY U.S.A. 134 D5
Clayhole Wash watercourse U.S.A. 129 G3
Claypool U.S.A. 129 H5
Clay Springs U.S.A. 129 H4
Clayton DE U.S.A. 135 H4
Clayton GA U.S.A. 133 D5
Clayton MI U.S.A. 134 C3
Clayton MO U.S.A. 130 F4
Clayton NM U.S.A. 131 C4
Clayton NY U.S.A. 135 G1
Claytor Lake U.S.A. 134 E5
Clay Village U.S.A. 134 C4
Clear, Cape Rep. of Ireland 51 C6
Clearco U.S.A. 134 E4
Clear Creek Canada 134 E2
Clear Creek r. U.S.A. 129 H4
Cleare, Cape U.S.A. 118 D4
Clearfield PA U.S.A. 135 F3
Clearfield UT U.S.A. 126 E4
Clear Fork Brazos r. U.S.A. 131 D5
Clear Hills Canada 120 G3
Clear Island Rep. of Ireland 51 C6
Clear Lake IA U.S.A. 130 E3
Clear Lake SD U.S.A. 130 D2
Clear Lake l. CA U.S.A. 128 B2
Clear Lake l. UT U.S.A. 129 G2
Clearmont U.S.A. 126 G3
Clearwater Canada 120 G5
Clearwater r. Alberta/Saskatchewan Canada 121 I3
Clearwater r. Alta Canada 120 H4
Clearwater U.S.A. 133 D7
Clearwater Lake Canada 121 K4
Clearwater Mountains U.S.A. 126 E3
Cleaton U.S.A. 134 B5
Cleburne U.S.A. 131 D5
Cleethorpes U.K. 48 G5
Clementi Sing. 71 [inset]
Clendenin U.S.A. 134 E4
Clendening Lake U.S.A. 134 E3
Clères France 52 B5
Clerf Lux. see Clervaux
Clerke Reef Australia 108 B4
Clermont Australia 110 D4
Clermont France 52 C5
Clermont-en-Argonne France 52 F5
Clermont-Ferrand France 56 F4
Clervaux Lux. 52 G4
Cles Italy 58 D1
Clevedon U.K. 49 E7
Cleveland MS U.S.A. 131 F5
Cleveland OH U.S.A. 134 E3
Cleveland TN U.S.A. 133 C5
Cleveland UT U.S.A. 129 H2
Cleveland WI U.S.A. 134 B2
Cleveland, Cape Australia 110 D3
Cleveland, Mount U.S.A. 126 E2
Cleveland Heights U.S.A. 134 E3
Cleveland Hills U.K. 48 F4
Cleveleys U.K. 48 D5
Cleves Germany see Kleve
Clew Bay Rep. of Ireland 51 C4
Clifden Rep. of Ireland 51 B4
Cliff U.S.A. 129 I5
Cliffoney Rep. of Ireland 51 D3
Clifton Australia 112 E1
Clifton U.S.A. 129 I5
Clifton Beach Australia 110 D3
Clifton Forge U.S.A. 134 F5
Clifton Park U.S.A. 135 I2
Climax Canada 121 I5
Climax U.S.A. 134 C2
Clinch Mountain mts U.S.A. 134 D5
Cline River Canada 120 G4
Clinton B.C. Canada 120 F5
Clinton Ont. Canada 134 E2
Clinton IA U.S.A. 130 F3
Clinton IL U.S.A. 130 F3
Clinton IN U.S.A. 134 B4
Clinton KY U.S.A. 131 F4
Clinton MI U.S.A. 134 D2
Clinton MO U.S.A. 130 E4
Clinton MS U.S.A. 131 F5
Clinton NC U.S.A. 133 E5
Clinton OK U.S.A. 131 D5
Clinton-Colden Lake Canada 121 J1
Clintwood U.S.A. 134 D5

▶Clipperton, Île terr. N. Pacific Ocean 151 M5
French Overseas Territory.

Clishham hill U.K. 50 C3
Clitheroe U.K. 48 E5
Clive Lake Canada 120 G2
Cliza Bol. 142 E7
Clocolan S. Africa 101 H5
Cloghan Rep. of Ireland 51 E4
Clonakilty Rep. of Ireland 51 D6
Clonbern Rep. of Ireland 51 D4
Cloncurry Australia 110 C4
Cloncurry r. Australia 110 C3
Clones Rep. of Ireland 51 E3
Clonmel Rep. of Ireland 51 E5
Clonygowan Rep. of Ireland 51 E4
Cloonbannin Rep. of Ireland 51 C5
Clooneagh Rep. of Ireland 51 E4
Cloppenburg Germany 53 I2
Cloquet U.S.A. 130 E2
Cloquet r. U.S.A. 130 E2
Cloud Peak WY U.S.A. 124 F3
Cloud Peak WY U.S.A. 126 G3
Clova Canada 122 G4
Clover U.S.A. 129 G1
Cloverdale CA U.S.A. 128 B2
Cloverdale IN U.S.A. 134 B4
Cloverport U.S.A. 134 B5
Clovis CA U.S.A. 128 D3
Clovis NM U.S.A. 131 C5
Cloyne Canada 135 G1
Cluain Meala Rep. of Ireland see Clonmel
Cluanie, Loch l. U.K. 50 D3
Cluff Lake Mine Canada 121 I3
Cluj-Napoca Romania 59 J1
Clun U.K. 49 D6
Clunes Australia 112 A6
Cluny Australia 110 B5
Cluses France 56 H3
Cluster Springs U.S.A. 135 F5
Clut Lake Canada 120 G1
Clutterbuck Head hd Canada 123 H1
Clutterbuck Hills hill Australia 109 D6
Clwydian Range hills U.K. 48 D5
Clyde Canada 120 H4
Clyde r. U.K. 50 E5
Clyde NY U.S.A. 135 G2
Clyde OH U.S.A. 134 D3
Clyde, Firth of est. U.K. 50 E5
Clydebank U.K. 50 E5
Clyde River Canada 119 L2
Côa r. Port. 57 C3
Coachella U.S.A. 128 E5
Coahuila state Mex. 131 C7
Coahuila de Zaragoza state Mex. see Coahuila
Coal r. Canada 120 E3
Coal City U.S.A. 134 A3
Coaldale U.S.A. 128 E2
Coalgate U.S.A. 131 D5
Coal Harbour Canada 120 E5
Coalinga U.S.A. 128 C3
Coalport U.S.A. 135 F3
Coal River Canada 120 E3
Coal Valley U.S.A. 129 F3
Coalville U.K. 49 F6
Coalville U.S.A. 129 H1
Coari Brazil 142 F4
Coari r. Brazil 142 F4
Coarsegold U.S.A. 128 D3
Coastal Plain U.S.A. 131 E6
Coast Mountains Canada 120 E4
Coast Range hills Australia 111 E5
Coast Ranges mts U.S.A. 128 B1
Coatbridge U.K. 50 E5
Coatesville U.S.A. 135 H4
Coaticook Canada 135 J1
Coats Island Canada 119 J3
Coats Land reg. Antarctica 152 A1
Coatzacoalcos Mex. 136 F5
Cobar Australia 112 B3
Cobargo Australia 112 D6
Cobden Australia 112 A7
Cóbh Rep. of Ireland 51 D6
Cobham r. Canada 121 M4
Cobija Bol. 142 E6
Coblenz Germany see Koblenz
Cobleskill U.S.A. 135 H2
Cobourg Peninsula Australia 108 F2
Cobra Australia 109 B6
Cobram Australia 112 B5
Coburg Germany 53 K4
Coburg Island Canada 119 K2
Coca Ecuador 142 C4
Coca Spain 57 D3
Cocalinho Brazil 145 A1
Cocanada India see Kakinada
Cochabamba Bol. 142 E7
Cochem Germany 53 H4
Cochin India 84 C4
Cochin reg. Vietnam 71 D5
Cochinos, Bahía de b. Cuba see Pigs, Bay of
Cochise U.S.A. 129 I5
Cochise Head mt. U.S.A. 129 I5
Cochrane Alta Canada 120 H5
Cochrane Ont. Canada 122 E4
Cochrane r. Canada 121 K3
Cockburn Australia 111 C7
Cockburnspath U.K. 50 G5
Cockburn Town Bahamas 133 F7
Cockburn Town Turks and Caicos Is see Grand Turk
Cockermouth U.K. 48 D4
Cocklebiddy Australia 109 D8
Cockscomb mt. S. Africa 100 G7
Coco r. Hond./Nicaragua 137 H6
Coco, Cayo i. Cuba 133 E8
Coco, Isla de i. N. Pacific Ocean 137 G7
Cocobeach Gabon 98 A3
Coco Channel India 71 A4
Cocomórachic Mex. 127 G7
Coconino Plateau U.S.A. 129 G4
Cocopara National Park Australia 112 C5
Cocos Brazil 145 B1
Cocos Basin sea feature Indian Ocean 149 O5

▶Cocos Islands terr. Indian Ocean 68 B9
Australian External Territory.
Asia 6

Cocos Ridge sea feature N. Pacific Ocean 151 O5
Cocuy, Sierra Nevada del mt. Col. 142 D2
Cod, Cape U.S.A. 135 J3
Codajás Brazil 142 F4
Coderre Canada 121 J5
Codfish Island N.Z. 113 A8
Codigoro Italy 58 E2
Cod Island Canada 123 J2
Codlea Romania 59 K2
Codó Brazil 143 J4
Codsall U.K. 49 E6
Cod's Head hd Rep. of Ireland 47 B6
Cody U.S.A. 126 F3
Coeburn U.S.A. 134 D5
Coen Australia 110 C2
Coesfeld Germany 53 H3
Coeur d'Alene U.S.A. 126 D3
Coeur d'Alene Lake U.S.A. 126 D3
Coevorden Neth. 52 G2
Coffee Bay S. Africa 101 I6
Coffeyville U.S.A. 131 E4
Coffin Bay Australia 111 A7
Coffin Bay National Park Australia 111 A7
Coffs Harbour Australia 112 F3
Cofimvaba S. Africa 101 H7
Cognac France 56 D4
Cogo Equat. Guinea 96 D4
Coguno Moz. 101 L3
Cohoes U.S.A. 135 I2
Cohuna Australia 112 B5
Coiba, Isla de i. Panama 137 H7
Coigeach, Rubha pt U.K. 50 D2
Coihaique Chile 144 B7
Coimbatore India 84 C4
Coimbra Port. 57 B3
Coipasa, Salar de salt flat Bol. 142 E7
Coire Switz. see Chur
Colac Australia 112 A7
Colair Lake India see Kolleru Lake
Colatina Brazil 145 C2
Colbitz Germany 53 L2
Colborne Canada 135 G2
Colby U.S.A. 130 C4
Colchester U.K. 49 H7
Colchester U.S.A. 135 I3
Cold Bay U.S.A. 118 B4
Coldingham U.K. 50 G5
Colditz Germany 53 M3
Cold Lake Canada 121 I4
Cold Lake l. Canada 121 I4
Coldspring U.S.A. 131 E6
Coldstream Canada 120 G5
Coldstream U.K. 50 G5
Coldwater Canada 134 F1
Coldwater KS U.S.A. 131 D4
Coldwater MI U.S.A. 134 C3
Coldwater r. U.S.A. 131 F5
Coleambally Australia 112 B5
Colebrook U.S.A. 135 J1
Coleman r. Australia 110 C2
Coleman U.S.A. 131 D6
Çölemerik Turkey see Hakkâri
Colenso S. Africa 101 I5
Cole Peninsula Antarctica 152 L2
Coleraine Australia 111 C8
Coleraine U.K. 51 F2
Coles, Punta de pt Peru 142 D7
Coles Bay Australia 111 [inset]
Colesberg S. Africa 101 G6
Coleville Canada 121 I5
Colfax CA U.S.A. 128 C2
Colfax LA U.S.A. 131 E6
Colfax WA U.S.A. 126 D3
Colhué Huapí, Lago l. Arg. 144 C7
Coligny S. Africa 101 H4
Colima Mex. 136 D5
Colima, Nevado de vol. Mex. 136 D5
Coll i. U.K. 50 C4
Collado Villalba Spain 57 E3
Collarenebri Australia 112 D2
College Station U.S.A. 131 D6
Collerina Australia 112 C2
Collie N.S.W. Australia 112 D3
Collie W.A. Australia 109 B8
Collier Bay Australia 108 D4
Collier Range National Park Australia 109 B6
Collingwood Canada 134 E1
Collingwood N.Z. 113 D5
Collins U.S.A. 131 F6
Collins Glacier Antarctica 152 E2
Collinson Peninsula Canada 115 H2
Collipulli Chile 144 B5
Collmberg hill Germany 53 N3
Collooney Rep. of Ireland 51 D3
Colmar France 56 H2
Colmenar Viejo Spain 57 E3
Colmonell U.K. 50 E5
Colne r. U.K. 49 H7
Cologne Germany 52 G4
Coloma U.S.A. 134 B2
Colomb-Béchar Alg. see Béchar
Colômbia Brazil 145 A3
Colombia Mex. 131 D7

▶Colombia country S. America 142 D3
2nd most populous and 4th largest country in South America.
South America 9, 140–141

Colombian Basin sea feature S. Atlantic Ocean 148 C5

▶Colombo Sri Lanka 84 C5
Former capital of Sri Lanka.

Colomiers France 56 E5
Colón Buenos Aires Arg. 144 D4
Colón Entre Ríos Arg. 144 E4
Colón Cuba 133 D8
Colón Panama 137 I7
Colon U.S.A. 134 C3
Colón, Archipiélago de is Ecuador see Galapagos Islands
Colona Australia 109 F7
Colonelganj India 83 E4

El Dátil Mex. 127 E7
El Desemboque Mex. 127 E7
El Diamante Mex. 131 C6
El'dikan Rus. Fed. 65 O3
El Djezair *country* Africa *see* Algeria
El Djezair Alg. *see* Algiers
El Doctor Mex. 129 F6
Eldon U.S.A. 130 E4
Eldorado Arg. 144 F3
Eldorado Brazil 145 A4
El Dorado Col. 142 D3
El Dorado Mex. 124 F7
El Dorado *AR* U.S.A. 131 E5
El Dorado *KS* U.S.A. 130 D4
Eldorado U.S.A. 131 C6
El Dorado Venez. 142 F2
Eldorado Mountains U.S.A. 129 F4
Eldoret Kenya 98 D3
Elea, Cape Cyprus *see* Elaia, Cape
Eleanor U.S.A. 134 E4
Electric Peak U.S.A. 126 F3
Elefantes *r.* Moz. *see* Olifants
El Eglab *plat.* Alg. 96 C2
El Ejido Spain 57 E5

▶Elemi Triangle *terr.* Africa 98 D3
Disputed territory (Ethiopia/Kenya/Sudan) administered by Kenya.

El Encanto Col. 142 D4
Elend Germany 53 K3
Elephanta Caves *tourist site* India 84 B2
Elephant Butte Reservoir U.S.A. 127 G6
Elephant Island Antarctica 152 A2
Elephant Pass Sri Lanka 84 D4
Elephant Point Bangl. 83 H5
Eleşkirt Turkey 91 F3
El Eulma Alg. 54 F4
Eleuthera *i.* Bahamas 133 E7
Eleven Point *r.* U.S.A. 131 F4
El Fahs Tunisia 58 C6
El Faiyûm Egypt *see* Al Fayyūm
El Fasher Sudan 97 F3
El Ferrol Spain *see* Ferrol
El Ferrol del Caudillo Spain *see* Ferrol
Elfershausen Germany 53 J4
El Fud Eth. 98 E3
El Fuerte Mex. 127 F8
El Gara Egypt *see* Qārah
El Geneina Sudan 97 F3
El Geteina Sudan 86 D7
El Ghardaqa Egypt *see* Al Ghurdaqah
El Ghor *plain* Jordan/West Bank *see* Al Ghawr
Elgin U.K. 50 F3
Elgin *IL* U.S.A. 130 F3
Elgin *ND* U.S.A. 130 C2
Elgin *NV* U.S.A. 129 F3
Elgin *TX* U.S.A. 131 D6
El'ginskiy Rus. Fed. 65 P3
El Gîza Egypt *see* Giza
El Goléa Alg. 54 E5
El Golfo de Santa Clara Mex. 127 E7
Elgon, Mount Kenya/Uganda 78 C6
El Hadjar Alg. 58 B6
El Ḥammâm Egypt *see* Al Ḥammām
El Hammâmi *reg.* Mauritania 96 B2
El Hank *esc.* Mali/Mauritania 96 C2
El Ḥarra Egypt *see* Al Ḥarrah
El Hazim Jordan *see* Al Hazīm
El Heiz Egypt *see* Al Ḥayz
El Hierro *i.* Canary Is 96 B2
El Homr Alg. 54 E6
El Homra Sudan 86 D7
Eliase Indon. 108 E2
Elías Piña Dom. Rep. 137 J5
Elichpur India *see* Achalpur
Elida U.S.A. 134 C3
Elie U.K. 50 G4
Elila *r.* Dem. Rep. Congo 98 C4
Elim U.S.A. 118 B3
Elimberrum France *see* Auch
Eling China *see* Yinjiang
Elingampangu Dem. Rep. Congo 98 C4
Eliot, Mount Canada 123 J2
Élisabethville Dem. Rep. Congo *see* Lubumbashi
Eliseu Martins Brazil 143 J5
El Iskandarîya Egypt *see* Alexandria
Elista Rus. Fed. 43 J7
Elizabeth *NJ* U.S.A. 135 H3
Elizabeth *WV* U.S.A. 134 E4
Elizabeth, Mount *hill* Australia 108 D4
Elizabeth Bay Namibia 100 B4
Elizabeth City U.S.A. 132 E4
Elizabeth Island Pitcairn Is *see* Henderson Island
Elizabeth Point Namibia 100 B4
Elizabethton U.S.A. 132 D4
Elizabethtown *IL* U.S.A. 130 F4
Elizabethtown *KY* U.S.A. 134 C5
Elizabethtown *NC* U.S.A. 133 E5
Elizabethtown *NY* U.S.A. 135 I1
El Jadida Morocco 54 C5
El Jaralito Mex. 131 B7
El Jem Tunisia 58 D7
Elk *r.* Canada 120 H5
Ełk Poland 47 S4
Elk *r.* U.S.A. 135 H4
El Kaa Lebanon *see* Qaa
El Kab Sudan 86 D6
Elkader U.S.A. 130 F3
El Kala Alg. 58 C6
Elk City U.S.A. 131 D5
Elkedra Australia 110 A4
Elkedra *watercourse* Australia 110 B4
El Kef Tunisia *see* Le Kef
El Kelaâ des Srarhna Morocco 54 C5
Elkford Canada 120 H5
Elk Grove U.S.A. 128 C2
El Khalil West Bank *see* Hebron
El Khandaq Sudan 86 D6
El Khârga Egypt *see* Al Khārijah
El Kharrûba Egypt *see* Al Kharrūbah
Elkhart *IN* U.S.A. 134 C3
Elkhart *KS* U.S.A. 131 C4
El Khartûm Sudan *see* Khartoum
El Khenachich *esc.* Mali *see* El Khnâchîch
El Khnâchîch *esc.* Mali 96 C2
Elkhorn U.S.A. 130 F3
Elkhorn City U.S.A. 134 D5
Elkhovo Bulg. 59 L3
Elki Turkey *see* Beytüşşebap
Elkin U.S.A. 132 D4
Elkins U.S.A. 134 F4
Elk Island National Park Canada 121 H4
Elk Lake Canada 122 E5
Elk Lake *l.* U.S.A. 134 C1
Elkland U.S.A. 135 G3
Elk Mountain U.S.A. 126 G4
Elk Mountains U.S.A. 129 J2
Elko Canada 120 H5
Elko U.S.A. 129 F1
Elk Point Canada 121 I4
Elk Point U.S.A. 130 D3
Elk Springs U.S.A. 129 I1
Elkton *MD* U.S.A. 135 H4
Elkton *VA* U.S.A. 135 F4
El Kûbri Egypt *see* Al Kūbrī
El Kuntilla Egypt *see* Al Kuntillah
Elkview U.S.A. 134 E4
Ellas *country* Europe *see* Greece
Ellaville U.S.A. 133 C5
Ell Bay Canada 121 O1
Ellef Ringnes Island Canada 119 H2
Ellen, Mount U.S.A. 129 H2
Ellenburg Depot U.S.A. 135 I1
Ellendale U.S.A. 130 D2
Ellensburg U.S.A. 126 C3
Ellenville U.S.A. 135 H3
El León, Cerro *mt.* Mex. 131 B7
Ellesmere, Lake N.Z. 113 D6

▶Ellesmere Island Canada 119 J2
4th largest island in North America.

Ellesmere Island National Park Reserve Canada *see* Quttinirpaaq National Park
Ellesmere Port U.K. 48 E5
Ellettsville U.S.A. 134 B4
Ellice *r.* Canada 121 K1
Ellice Island *atoll* Tuvalu *see* Funafuti
Ellice Islands *country* S. Pacific Ocean *see* Tuvalu
Ellicott City U.S.A. 135 G4
Ellijay U.S.A. 133 C5
Ellingen Germany 53 K5
Elliot Australia 108 F4
Elliot S. Africa 101 H6
Elliot, Mount Australia 110 D3
Elliotdale S. Africa 101 I6
Elliot Knob *mt.* U.S.A. 134 F4
Elliot Lake Canada 122 E5
Ellisras S. Africa 101 H2
Elliston U.S.A. 134 E5
Ellon U.K. 50 G3
Ellora Caves *tourist site* India 84 B1
Ellsworth *KS* U.S.A. 130 D4
Ellsworth *ME* U.S.A. 132 G2
Ellsworth *NE* U.S.A. 130 C3
Ellsworth *WI* U.S.A. 130 E2
Ellsworth Land *reg.* Antarctica 152 K1
Ellsworth Mountains Antarctica 152 L1
Ellwangen (Jagst) Germany 53 K6
El Maghreb *country* Africa *see* Morocco
Elmakuz Dağı *mt.* Turkey 85 A1
Elmalı Turkey 59 M6
El Malpais National Monument *nat. park* U.S.A. 129 J4
El Manşûra Egypt *see* Al Manşūrah
El Maţarîya Egypt *see* Al Maţarīyah
El Mazâr Egypt *see* Al Mazār
El Meghaïer Alg. 54 F5
El Milia Alg. 54 F4
El Minya Egypt *see* Al Minyā
Elmira *Ont.* Canada 134 E2
Elmira *P.E.I.* Canada 123 J5
Elmira *MI* U.S.A. 134 C1
Elmira *NY* U.S.A. 135 G2
El Mirage U.S.A. 129 G5
El Moral Spain 57 E5
Elmore Australia 112 B6
El Mreyyé *reg.* Mauritania 96 C3
Elmshorn Germany 53 J1
El Muglad Sudan 86 C7
Elmvale Canada 134 F1
Elnesvågen Norway 44 E5
El Nevado, Cerro *mt.* Col. 142 D3
El Oasis Mex. 129 F5
El Obeid Sudan 86 D7
El Odaiya Sudan 86 C7
El Oro Mex. 131 C7
Elorza Venez. 142 E2
El Oued Alg. 54 F5
Eloy U.S.A. 129 H5
El Palmito Mex. 131 B7
El Paso *IL* U.S.A. 130 F3
El Paso *KS* U.S.A. *see* Derby
El Paso *TX* U.S.A. 127 G7
Elphin U.K. 50 D2
Elphinstone *i.* Myanmar *see* Thayawthadangyi Kyun
El Portal U.S.A. 128 D3
El Porvenir Mex. 131 B6
El Porvenir Panama 137 I7
El Prat de Llobregat Spain 57 H3
El Progreso Hond. 136 G5
El Puerto de Santa María Spain 57 C5
El Qâhira Egypt *see* Cairo
El Qasimiye *r.* Lebanon 85 B3
El Quds Israel/West Bank *see* Jerusalem
El Quşeima Egypt *see* Al Quşaymah
El Quşeir Egypt *see* Al Quşayr
El Qûşîya Egypt *see* Al Qūşīyah
El Regocijo Mex. 131 B8
El Reno U.S.A. 131 D5
Elrose Canada 121 I5
Elsa Canada 120 C2
El Şaff Egypt *see* Aş Şaff
El Sahuaro Mex. 127 E7
El Salado Mex. 131 C7
El Salto Mex. 131 B8
▶El Salvador *country* Central America 136 G6
North America 9, 116–117
El Salvador Chile 144 C3
El Salvador Mex. 131 C7
Elsass *reg.* France *see* Alsace
El Sauz Mex. 127 G7
Else *r.* Germany 53 I2
El Sellûm Egypt *see* As Sallūm
Elsen Nur *l.* China 83 H2
Elsey Australia 108 F3
El Shallûfa Egypt *see* Ash Shallūfah
El Sharana Australia 108 F3
El Shaţţ Egypt *see* Ash Shaţţ
Elsie U.S.A. 134 C2
Elsinore Denmark *see* Helsingør
Elsinore *CA* U.S.A. 128 E5
Elsinore *UT* U.S.A. 129 G2
Elsinore Lake U.S.A. 128 E5
El Sueco Mex. 127 G7
El Suweis Egypt *see* Suez
El Suweis *governorate* Egypt *see* As Suways
El Tama, Parque Nacional *nat. park* Venez. 142 D2
El Tarf Alg. 58 C6
El Teleno *mt.* Spain 57 C2
El Temascal Mex. 131 D7
El Ter *r.* Spain 57 H2
El Thamad Egypt *see* Ath Thamad
El Tigre Venez. 142 F2
Eltmann Germany 53 K5
El'ton Rus. Fed. 43 J6
El'ton, Ozero *l.* Rus. Fed. 43 J6
El Tren Mex. 127 E7
El Tuparro, Parque Nacional *nat. park* Col. 142 E2
El Ţûr Egypt *see* Aţ Ţūr
El Turbio Chile 144 B8
El Uqşur Egypt *see* Luxor
Eluru India 84 D2
Elva Estonia 45 O7
Elvanfoot U.K. 50 F5
Elvas Port. 57 C4
Elverum Norway 45 G6
Elvira Brazil 142 D5
El Wak Kenya 98 E3
El Wâţya *well* Egypt *see* Al Wāţiyah
Elwood *IN* U.S.A. 134 C3
Elwood *NE* U.S.A. 130 D3
El Wuz Sudan 86 D7
Elx Spain *see* Elche-Elx
Elxleben Germany 53 K3
Ely U.K. 49 H6
Ely *MN* U.S.A. 130 F2
Ely *NV* U.S.A. 129 F2
Elyria U.S.A. 134 D3
Elz Germany 53 I4
El Zagâzîg Egypt *see* Az Zaqāzīq
Elze Germany 53 J2
Émaé *i.* Vanuatu 107 G3
Emāmrūd Iran 88 D2
Emām Şaḩeb Afgh. 89 H2
Emām Taqī Iran 88 E2
Emån *r.* Sweden 45 J8
Emas, Parque Nacional das *nat. park* Brazil 143 H7
Emba Kazakh. 80 A2
Emba *r.* Kazakh. 80 A2
Embalenhle S. Africa 101 I4
Embarcación Arg. 144 D2
Embarras Portage Canada 121 I3
Embi Kazakh. *see* Emba
Embira *r.* Brazil *see* Envira
Emborcação, Represa de *resr* Brazil 145 B2
Embrun Canada 135 H1
Embu Kenya 98 D4
Emden Germany 53 H1
Emden Deep *sea feature* N. Pacific Ocean *see* Cape Johnson Depth
Emei China *see* Emeishan
Emeishan China 76 D2
Emei Shan *mt.* China 76 D2
Emerald Australia 110 E4
Emeril Canada 123 I3
Emerita Augusta Spain *see* Mérida
Emerson Canada 121 L5
Emerson U.S.A. 134 D4
Emery U.S.A. 129 H2
Emesa Syria *see* Homs
Emet Turkey 59 M5
eMgwenya S. Africa 101 J3
Emigrant Pass U.S.A. 128 E1
Emigrant Valley U.S.A. 129 F3
eMijindini S. Africa 101 J3
Emi Koussi *mt.* Chad 97 E3
Emile *r.* Canada 120 G2
Emiliano Zapata Mex. 136 F5
Emin China 80 F2
Emine, Nos *pt* Bulg. 59 L3
Eminence U.S.A. 134 C4
Eminska Planina *hills* Bulg. 59 L3
Emirdağ Turkey 59 N5
Emir Dağı *mt.* Turkey 59 N5
Emir Dağları *mts* Turkey 59 N5
Emmaboda Sweden 45 I8
Emmaste Estonia 45 M7
Emmaville Australia 112 E2
Emmeloord Neth. 52 F2
Emmelshausen Germany 53 H4
Emmen Neth. 52 G2
Emmen Switz. 56 I3
Emmerich Germany 52 G3
Emmet Australia 110 D5
Emmetsburg U.S.A. 130 E3
Emmett U.S.A. 126 D4
Emmiganuru India 84 C3
Emo Canada 121 M5
Emona Slovenia *see* Ljubljana
Emory Peak U.S.A. 131 C6
Empalme Mex. 127 F8
Empangeni S. Africa 101 J5
Emperor Seamount Chain *sea feature* N. Pacific Ocean 150 H2
Emperor Trough *sea feature* N. Pacific Ocean 150 H2
Empingham Reservoir U.K. *see* Rutland Water
Emplawas Indon. 108 E2
Empoli Italy 58 D3
Emporia *KS* U.S.A. 130 D4
Emporia *VA* U.S.A. 135 G5
Emporium U.S.A. 135 F3
Empress Canada 121 I5
Empty Quarter *des.* Saudi Arabia *see* Rub' al Khālī
Ems *r.* Germany 53 H1
Emsdale Canada 134 F1
Emsdetten Germany 53 H2
Ems-Jade-Kanal *canal* Germany 53 H1
Emzinoni S. Africa 101 I4
Enafors Sweden 44 H5
Encantadas, Serra das *hills* Brazil 144 F4
Encarnación Para. 144 E3
Enchi Ghana 96 C4
Encinal U.S.A. 131 D6
Encinitas U.S.A. 128 E5
Encino U.S.A. 127 G6
Encruzilhada Brazil 145 C1
Endako Canada 120 E4
Endau-Rompin *nat. park* Malaysia 71 C7
Ende Indon. 108 C2
Endeavour Strait Australia 110 C1
Endeh Indon. *see* Ende
Enderby Canada 120 G5
Enderby *atoll* Micronesia *see* Puluwat
Enderby Land *reg.* Antarctica 152 D2
Endicott U.S.A. 135 G2
Endicott Mountains U.S.A. 118 C3
EnenKio *terr.* N. Pacific Ocean *see* Wake Island
Energodar Ukr. *see* Enerhodar
Enerhodar Ukr. 43 G7
Enewetak *atoll* Marshall Is 150 G5
Enez Turkey 59 L4
Enfe Lebanon 85 B2
Enfião, Ponta do *pt* Angola 99 B5
Enfidaville Tunisia 58 D6
Enfield U.S.A. 132 E4
Engan Norway 44 F5
Engaru Japan 74 F3
Engcobo S. Africa 101 H6
En Gedi Israel 85 B4
Engelhard U.S.A. 132 F5
Engel's Rus. Fed. 43 J6
Engelschmangat *sea chan.* Neth. 52 E1
Enggano *i.* Indon. 68 C8
Enghien Belgium 52 E4
England *admin. div.* U.K. 49 E6
Englee Canada 123 L4
Englehart Canada 122 F5
Englewood *FL* U.S.A. 133 D7
Englewood *OH* U.S.A. 134 C4
English *r.* Canada 121 M5
English U.S.A. 134 B4
English Bazar India *see* Ingraj Bazar
English Channel France/U.K. 49 F9
English Coast Antarctica 152 L2
Engozero Rus. Fed. 42 G2
Enhlalakahle S. Africa 101 J5
Enid U.S.A. 131 D4
Eniwa Japan 74 F4
Eniwetok *atoll* Marshall Is *see* Enewetak
Enjiang China *see* Yongfeng
Enkeldoorn Zimbabwe *see* Chivhu
Enkhuizen Neth. 52 F2
Enköping Sweden 45 J7
Enna *Sicily* Italy 58 F6
Ennadai Lake Canada 121 K2
En Nahud Sudan 86 C7
Ennedi, Massif *mts* Chad 97 F3
Ennell, Lough *l.* Rep. of Ireland 51 E4
Enngonia Australia 112 B2
Enning U.S.A. 130 C2
Ennis Rep. of Ireland 51 D5
Ennis *MT* U.S.A. 126 F3
Ennis *TX* U.S.A. 131 D5
Enniscorthy Rep. of Ireland 51 F5
Enniskillen U.K. 51 E3
Ennistymon Rep. of Ireland 51 C5
En Nâqoûra Lebanon 85 B3
Enns *r.* Austria 47 O6
Eno Fin. 44 Q5
Enoch U.S.A. 129 G3
Enontekiö Fin. 44 M2
Enosburg Falls U.S.A. 135 I1
Enosville U.S.A. 134 B4
Enping China 77 G4
Ens Neth. 52 F2
Ensay Australia 112 C6
Enschede Neth. 52 G2
Ense Germany 53 I3
Ensenada Mex. 127 D7
Enshi China 77 F2
Ensley U.S.A. 133 C6
Entebbe Uganda 98 D3
Enterprise Canada 120 G2
Enterprise *AL* U.S.A. 133 C6
Enterprise *OR* U.S.A. 126 D3
Enterprise *UT* U.S.A. 129 G3
Entre Ríos Bol. 142 F8
Entre Rios Brazil 143 H5
Entre Rios de Minas Brazil 145 B3
Entroncamento Port. 57 B4
Enugu Nigeria 96 D4
Enurmino Rus. Fed. 65 T3
Envira Brazil 142 D5
Envira *r.* Brazil 142 D5
Enyamba Dem. Rep. Congo 98 C4
Eochaill Rep. of Ireland *see* Youghal
Epe Neth. 52 F2
Epéna Congo 98 B3
Épernay France 52 D5
Ephraim U.S.A. 129 H2
Ephrata U.S.A. 135 G3
Epi *i.* Vanuatu 107 G3
Epidamnus Albania *see* Durrës
Épinal France 56 H2
Episkopi Bay Cyprus 85 A2
Episkopis, Kolpos *b.* Cyprus *see* Episkopi Bay
ePitoli S. Africa *see* Pretoria
Epomeo, Monte *hill* Italy 58 E4
Epping U.K. 49 H7
Epping Forest National Park Australia 110 D4
Eppstein Germany 53 I4
Eppynt, Mynydd *hills* U.K. 49 D6
Epsom U.K. 49 G7
Epte *r.* France 52 B5
Eqlīd Iran 88 D4
▶Equatorial Guinea *country* Africa 96 D4
Africa 7, 94–95
Équerdreville-Hainneville France 49 F9
Erac Creek *watercourse* Australia 112 B1
Erandol India 84 B1
Erawadi *r.* Myanmar *see* Irrawaddy
Erawan National Park Thai. 71 B4
Erbaa Turkey 90 E2
Erbendorf Germany 53 M5
Erbeskopf *hill* Germany 52 H5
Ercan *airport* Cyprus 85 A2
Erciş Turkey 91 F3
Erciyes Dağı *mt.* Turkey 90 D3
Érd Hungary 58 H1
Erdaobaihe China *see* Baihe
Erdaogou China 76 B1
Erdao Jiang *r.* China 74 B4
Erdek Turkey 59 L4
Erdemli Turkey 85 B1
Erdenet Mongolia 80 J2
Erdi *reg.* Chad 97 F3
Erdniyevskiy Rus. Fed. 43 J7
Erebus, Mount *vol.* Antarctica 152 H1
Erechim Brazil 144 F3
Ereentsav Mongolia 73 L3
Ereğli *Konya* Turkey 90 D3
Ereğli *Zonguldak* Turkey 59 N4
Erego Moz. *see* Errego
Erei, Monti *mts Sicily* Italy 58 F6
Erementaŭ Kazakh. *see* Yereymentau
Erenhot China 73 K4
Erepucu, Lago de *l.* Brazil 143 G4
Erevan Armenia *see* Yerevan
Erfurt Germany 53 L4
Erfurt *airport* Germany 53 K4
Ergani Turkey 91 E3
'Erg Chech *des.* Alg./Mali 96 C2
Ergel Mongolia 73 J4
Ergene *r.* Turkey 59 L4
Ērgļi Latvia 45 N8
Ergu China 74 C3
Ergun China 73 M2
Ergun He *r.* China/Rus. Fed. *see* Argun'
Ergun Youqi China *see* Ergun
Ergun Zuoqi China *see* Genhe
Er Hai *l.* China 76 D3
Erhulai China 74 B4
Eriboll, Loch *inlet* U.K. 50 E2
Ericht *r.* U.K. 50 F4
Ericht, Loch *l.* U.K. 50 E4
Erickson Canada 121 L5
Erie *KS* U.S.A. 131 E4
Erie *PA* U.S.A. 134 E2
Erie, Lake Canada/U.S.A. 134 E2
'Erîgât *des.* Mali 96 C3
Erik Eriksenstretet *sea chan.* Svalbard 64 D2
Eriksdale Canada 121 L5
Erimo-misaki *c.* Japan 74 F4
Erin Canada 134 E2
Erinpura Road India 82 C4
Eriskay *i.* U.K. 50 B3
▶Eritrea *country* Africa 86 E6
Africa 7, 94–95
Erlangen Germany 53 L5
Erlangping China 77 F1
Erldunda Australia 109 F6
Erlistoun *watercourse* Australia 109 C6
Erlong Shan *mt.* China 74 C4
Erlongshan Shuiku *resr* China 74 B4
Ermak Kazakh. *see* Aksu
Ermelo Neth. 52 F2
Ermelo S. Africa 101 I4
Ermenek Turkey 85 A1
Ermenek *r.* Turkey 85 A1
Ermont Egypt *see* Armant
Ermoupoli Greece 59 K6
Ernakulam India 84 C4
Erne *r.* Rep. of Ireland/U.K. 51 D3
Ernest Giles Range *hills* Australia 109 C6
Erode India 84 C4
Eromanga Australia 111 C5
Erongo *admin. reg.* Namibia 100 B1
Erp Neth. 52 F3
Erqu China *see* Zhouzhi
Errabiddy Hills Australia 109 A6
Er Rachidia Morocco 54 D5
Er Raoui *des.* Alg. 54 D6
Errego Moz. 99 D5
Er Remla Tunisia 58 D7
Er Renk Sudan 86 D7
Errigal *hill* Rep. of Ireland 51 D2
Errinundra National Park Australia 112 D6
Erris Head *hd* Rep. of Ireland 51 B3
Errol U.S.A. 135 J1
Erromango *i.* Vanuatu 107 G3
Erronan *i.* Vanuatu *see* Futuna
Erseka Albania *see* Ersekë
Ersekë Albania 59 I4
Erskine U.S.A. 130 D2
Ersmark Sweden 44 L5
Ertai China 80 H2
Ertil' Rus. Fed. 43 I6
Ertis *r.* Kazakh./Rus. Fed. *see* Irtysh
Ertix He *r.* China/Kazakh. 80 G2
Ērtra *country* Africa *see* Eritrea
Eruh Turkey 91 F3
Erwin U.S.A. 132 D4
Erwitte Germany 53 I3
Erxleben *Sachsen-Anhalt* Germany 53 L2
Erxleben *Sachsen-Anhalt* Germany 53 L2
Eryuan China 76 C3
Erzerum Turkey *see* Erzurum
Erzgebirge *mts* Czech Rep./Germany 53 N4
Erzhan China 74 B2
Erzin Turkey 85 C1
Erzincan Turkey 91 E3
Erzurum Turkey 91 F3
Esa-ala P.N.G. 110 E1
Esan-misaki *pt* Japan 74 F4
Esashi Japan 74 F3
Esbjerg Denmark 45 F9
Esbo Fin. *see* Espoo
Escalante U.S.A. 129 H3
Escalante *r.* U.S.A. 129 H3
Escalante Desert U.S.A. 129 G3
Escalón Mex. 131 B7
Escambia *r.* U.S.A. 133 C6
Escanaba U.S.A. 132 C2
Escárcega Mex. 136 F5
Escatrón Spain 57 F3
Escaut *r.* Belgium 52 D4
Esch Neth. 52 F3
Eschede Germany 53 K2
Eschscholtz *atoll* Marshall Is *see* Bikini
Esch-sur-Alzette Lux. 52 F5
Eschwege Germany 53 K3
Eschweiler Germany 52 G4
Escondido *r.* Mex. 131 C6
Escondido U.S.A. 128 E5
Escudilla *mt.* U.S.A. 129 I5
Escuinapa Mex. 136 C4
Escuintla Guat. 136 F6
Eséka Cameroon 96 E4
Eşen Turkey 59 M6
Esenguly Turkm. 88 D2
Esens Germany 53 H1
Eşfahān Iran 88 C3
Esfarayen, Reshteh-ye *mts* Iran 88 E2
Esfideh Iran 89 E3
Eshan China 76 D3
Eshāqābād Iran 88 E3
Eshkamesh Afgh. 89 H2
Eshkanān Iran 88 D5
Eshowe S. Africa 101 J5
Esikhawini S. Africa 101 K5
Esil Kazakh. *see* Yesil'
Esil *r.* Kazakh./Rus. Fed. *see* Ishim
Esk Australia 112 F1
Esk *r.* Australia 111 [inset]
Esk *r.* U.K. 48 D4
Eskdalemuir U.K. 50 F5
Esker Canada 123 I3
Eskifjörður Iceland 44 [inset]
Eski Gediz Turkey 59 M5
Eskilstuna Sweden 45 J7
Eskimo Lakes Canada 118 E3
Eskimo Point Canada *see* Arviat
Eski Mosul Iraq 91 F3
Eskipazar Turkey 90 D2
Eskişehir Turkey 59 N5
Eski-Yakkabag Uzbek. 89 G2
Esla *r.* Spain 57 C3
Eslāmābād-e Gharb Iran 88 B3
Esler Dağı *mt.* Turkey 59 M6
Eslohe (Sauerland) Germany 53 I3
Eslöv Sweden 45 H9
Esmā'īlī-ye Soflá Iran 88 E4
Eşme Turkey 59 M5
Esmeraldas Ecuador 142 C3
Esmont U.S.A. 135 F5
Esnagami Lake Canada 122 D4
Esnes France 52 D4
Espakeh Iran 89 F5
Espalion France 56 F4
España *country* Europe *see* Spain
Espanola Canada 122 E5
Espanola U.S.A. 131 B4
Espelkamp Germany 53 I2
Esperance Australia 109 C8
Esperance Bay Australia 109 C8
Esperanza *research station* Antarctica 152 A2
Esperanza Arg. 144 B8
Esperanza Mex. 127 F8
Espichel, Cabo *c.* Port. 57 B4
Espigão, Serra do *mts* Brazil 141 A4
Espigüete *mt.* Spain 57 D2
Espinazo Mex. 131 C7
Espinhaço, Serra do *mts* Brazil 145 C2
Espinosa Brazil 145 C1
Espírito Santo Brazil *see* Vila Velha
Espírito Santo *state* Brazil 145 C2
Espíritu Santo *i.* Vanuatu 107 G3
Espíritu Santo, Isla *i.* Mex. 124 E7
Espoo Fin. 45 N6
Espuña *mt.* Spain 57 F5
Esqueda Mex. 127 F7
Esquel Arg. 144 B6
Esquimalt Canada 120 F5
Essaouira Morocco 96 C1
Es Semara W. Sahara 96 B2
Essen Belgium 52 E3

▶Essen Germany 52 H3
5th most populous city in Europe.

Essen (Oldenburg) Germany 53 H2
Essequibo *r.* Guyana 143 G2
Essex Canada 134 D2
Essex *CA* U.S.A. 129 F4
Essex *MD* U.S.A. 135 G4
Essex *NY* U.S.A. 135 I1
Essexville U.S.A. 134 D2
Esslingen am Neckar Germany 53 J6
Esso Rus. Fed. 65 Q4
Essoyla Rus. Fed. 42 G3
Eşţahbān Iran 88 D4
Estância Brazil 143 K6
Estancia U.S.A. 127 G6
Estand, Kūh-e *mt.* Iran 89 F4
Estats, Pic d' *mt.* France/Spain 56 E5
Estcourt S. Africa 101 I5
Este *r.* Germany 53 J1
Estelí Nicaragua 137 G6
Estella Spain 57 E2
Estepa Spain 57 D5
Estepona Spain 57 D5
Esteras de Medinaceli Spain 57 E3
Esterhazy Canada 121 K5
Estero Bay U.S.A. 128 C4
Esteros Para. 144 D2
Estevan Canada 121 K5
Estevan Group *is* Canada 120 D4
Estherville U.S.A. 130 E3
Estill U.S.A. 133 D5
Eston Canada 121 I5
▶Estonia *country* Europe 45 N7
Europe 5, 38–39
Estonskaya S.S.R. *country* Europe *see* Estonia
Estrées-St-Denis France 52 C5
Estrela Brazil 145 A5
Estrela, Serra da *mts* Port. 57 C3
Estrela do Sul Brazil 145 B2
Estrella *mt.* Spain 57 E4
Estrella, Punta *pt* Mex. 127 E7
Estremoz Port. 57 C4
Estrondo, Serra *hills* Brazil 143 I5
Etadunna Australia 111 B6
Etah India 82 D4
Étain France 52 F5
Etamamiou Canada 123 K4
Étampes France 56 F2
Étaples France 52 B4
Etawah *Rajasthan* India 82 D4
Etawah *Uttar Pradesh* India 82 D4
eThandakukhanya S. Africa 101 J4
Ethelbert Canada 121 K5
Ethel Creek Australia 109 C5
E'Thembini S. Africa 100 F5

▶Ethiopia *country* Africa 98 D3
3rd most populous country in Africa.
Africa 7, 94–95

Etimesğut Turkey 90 D3

Etive, Loch inlet U.K. 50 D4
Etna, Mount vol. Sicily Italy 58 F6
Etne Norway 45 D7
Etobicoke Canada 134 F2
Etolin Strait U.S.A. 118 B3
Etorofu-tō i. Rus. Fed. see Iturup, Ostrov
Etosha National Park Namibia 99 B5
Etosha Pan salt pan Namibia 99 B5
Etoumbi Congo 98 B3
Etrek r. Iran/Turkm. see Atrek
Étrépagny France 52 B5
Étretat France 49 H9
Ettelbruck Lux. 52 G5
Etten-Leur Neth. 52 E3
Ettlingen Germany 53 I6
Ettrick Water r. U.K. 50 F5
Euabalong Australia 112 C4
Euboea i. Greece see Evvoia
Eucla Australia 109 E7
Euclid U.S.A. 134 E3
Euclides da Cunha Brazil 143 K6
Eucumbene, Lake Australia 112 D6
Eudistes, Lac des l. Canada 123 I4
Eudora U.S.A. 131 F5
Eudunda Australia 111 B7
Eufaula AL U.S.A. 133 C6
Eufaula OK U.S.A. 131 E5
Eufaula Lake resr U.S.A. 131 E5
Eugene U.S.A. 126 C3
Eugenia, Punta pt Mex. 127 E8
Eugowra Australia 112 D4
Eulo Australia 112 B2
Eumungerie Australia 112 D3
Eungella Australia 110 E4
Eungella National Park Australia 110 E4
Eunice LA U.S.A. 131 E6
Eunice NM U.S.A. 131 C5
Eupen Belgium 52 G4

▶Euphrates r. Asia 91 G5
Longest river in western Asia. Also known as Al Furāt (Iraq/Syria) or Fırat (Turkey).

Eura Fin. 45 M6
Eure r. France 52 B5
Eureka CA U.S.A. 126 B4
Eureka KS U.S.A. 130 D4
Eureka MT U.S.A. 126 E2
Eureka NV U.S.A. 129 F2
Eureka OH U.S.A. 134 D4
Eureka SD U.S.A. 130 D2
Eureka UT U.S.A. 129 G2
Eureka Sound sea chan. Canada 119 J2
Eureka Springs U.S.A. 131 E4
Eureka Valley U.S.A. 128 E3
Euriowie Australia 111 C6
Euroa Australia 112 B6
Eurombah Australia 111 E5
Eurombah Creek r. Australia 111 E5
Europa, Île i. Indian Ocean 99 E6
Europa, Punta de pt Gibraltar see Europa Point
Europa Point Gibraltar 57 D5
Euskirchen Germany 52 G4
Eutaw U.S.A. 133 C5
Eutsuk Lake Canada 120 E4
Eutzsch Germany 53 M3
Eva Downs Australia 108 F4
Evans, Lac l. Canada 122 F4
Evans, Mount U.S.A. 126 G5
Evansburg Canada 120 H4
Evans City U.S.A. 134 E3
Evans Head Australia 112 F2
Evans Head hd Australia 112 F2
Evans Ice Stream Antarctica 152 L1
Evans Strait Canada 121 P2
Evanston IL U.S.A. 134 B2
Evanston WY U.S.A. 126 F4
Evansville Canada 122 E5
Evansville IN U.S.A. 134 B5
Evansville WY U.S.A. 126 G4
Evant U.S.A. 131 D6
Eva Perón Arg. see La Plata
Evart U.S.A. 134 C2
Evaton S. Africa 101 H4
Evaz Iran 88 D5
Evening Shade U.S.A. 131 F4
Evensk Rus. Fed. 65 Q3
Everard, Cape Australia 112 D6
Everard, Lake salt flat Australia 111 A6
Everard, Mount Australia 109 F5
Everard Range hills Australia 109 F6
Everdingen Neth. 52 F3
Everek Turkey see Develi

▶Everest, Mount China/Nepal 83 F4
Highest mountain in the world and in Asia.
Asia 60–61
World 12–13

Everett PA U.S.A. 135 F3
Everett WA U.S.A. 126 C3
Evergem Belgium 52 D3
Everglades swamp U.S.A. 133 D7
Everglades National Park U.S.A. 133 D7
Evergreen U.S.A. 133 C6
Evesham Australia 110 C4
Evesham U.K. 49 F6
Evesham, Vale of valley U.K. 49 F6
Evijärvi Fin. 44 M5
Evje Norway 45 E7
Évora Port. 57 C4
Evoron, Ozero l. Rus. Fed. 74 E2
Évreux France 52 B5
Evros r. Bulgaria see Maritsa
Evros r. Turkey see Meriç
Evrotas r. Greece 59 J6
Évry France 52 C6
Evrychou Cyprus 85 A2
Evrykhou Cyprus see Evrychou
Evvoia i. Greece 59 K5
Ewan Australia 110 D3
Ewaso Ngiro r. Kenya 98 E3
Ewe, Loch b. U.K. 50 D3
Ewing U.S.A. 134 D5
Ewo Congo 98 B4
Exaltación Bol. 142 E6
Excelsior S. Africa 101 H5
Excelsior Mountain U.S.A. 128 D2
Excelsior Mountains U.S.A. 128 D2
Exe r. U.K. 49 D8
Exeter Australia 112 E5
Exeter Canada 134 E2
Exeter U.K. 49 D8
Exeter CA U.S.A. 128 D3
Exeter NH U.S.A. 135 J2
Exeter Lake Canada 121 I1
Exloo Neth. 52 G2
Exminster U.K. 49 D8
Exmoor hills U.K. 49 D7
Exmoor National Park U.K. 49 D7
Exmore U.S.A. 135 H5
Exmouth Australia 108 A5
Exmouth U.K. 49 D8
Exmouth, Mount Australia 112 D3
Exmouth Gulf Australia 108 A5
Exmouth Lake Canada 120 H1
Exmouth Plateau sea feature Indian Ocean 149 P7
Expedition National Park Australia 110 E5
Expedition Range mts Australia 110 E5
Exploits r. Canada 123 L4
Exton U.S.A. 135 H3
Extremadura aut. comm. Spain 57 D4
Exuma Cays is Bahamas 133 E7
Exuma Sound sea chan. Bahamas 133 F7
Eyasi, Lake salt l. Tanz. 98 D4
Eyawadi r. Myanmar see Irrawaddy
Eye U.K. 49 I6
Eyeberry Lake Canada 121 J2
Eyelenoborsk Rus. Fed. 41 S3
Eyemouth U.K. 50 G5
Eyjafjörður inlet Iceland 44 [inset]
Eyl Somalia 98 E3
Eylau Rus. Fed. see Bagrationovsk
Eynsham U.K. 49 F7

▶Eyre, Lake salt lake Australia 111 B6
Largest lake in Oceania and lowest point.
Oceania 102–103

Eyre (North), Lake salt lake Australia 111 B6
Eyre (South), Lake salt lake Australia 111 B6
Eyre Creek watercourse Australia 110 B5
Eyre Mountains N.Z. 113 B7
Eyre Peninsula Australia 111 A7
Eystrup Germany 53 J2
Eysturoy i. Faroe Is 44 [inset]
Ezakheni S. Africa 101 J5
Ezel U.S.A. 134 D5
Ezenzeleni S. Africa 101 I4
Ezequiel Ramos Mexía, Embalse resr Arg. 144 C5
Ezhou China 77 G2
Ezhva Rus. Fed. 42 K3
Ezine Turkey 59 L5
Ezo i. Japan see Hokkaidō
Ezousa r. Cyprus 85 A2

F

Faaborg Denmark see Fåborg
Faadhippolhu Atoll Maldives 84 B5
Faafxadhuun Somalia 98 E3
Fabens U.S.A. 127 G7
Faber, Mount hill Sing. 71 [inset]
Faber Lake Canada 120 G2
Fåborg Denmark 45 G9
Fabriano Italy 58 E3
Faches-Thumesnil France 52 D4
Fachi Niger 96 E3
Fada Chad 97 F3
Fada-N'Gourma Burkina 96 D3
Fadghāmī Syria 91 F4
Fadiffolu Atoll Maldives see Faadhippolhu Atoll
Fadippolu Atoll Maldives see Faadhippolhu Atoll
Faenza Italy 58 D2
Færoerne terr. N. Atlantic Ocean see Faroe Islands
Faeroes terr. N. Atlantic Ocean see Faroe Islands
Făgăraş Romania 59 K2

▶Fagatogo American Samoa 107 I3
Capital of American Samoa.

Fagersta Sweden 45 I7
Fagne reg. Belgium 52 E4
Fagurhólsmýri Iceland 44 [inset]
Fagwir Sudan 86 D8
Fahraj Iran 88 D4
Fā'id Egypt 90 D5
Fairbanks U.S.A. 118 D3
Fairborn U.S.A. 134 C4
Fairbury U.S.A. 130 D3
Fairchance U.S.A. 134 F4
Fairfax U.S.A. 135 G4
Fairfield CA U.S.A. 128 B2
Fairfield IA U.S.A. 130 F3
Fairfield ID U.S.A. 126 E4
Fairfield IL U.S.A. 130 F4
Fairfield OH U.S.A. 134 C4
Fairfield TX U.S.A. 131 D6
Fair Haven U.S.A. 135 I2
Fair Head hd U.K. 51 F2
Fair Isle i. U.K. 50 H1
Fairlee U.S.A. 135 I2
Fairmont MN U.S.A. 130 E3
Fairmont WV U.S.A. 134 E4
Fair Oaks U.S.A. 134 B3
Fairview Australia 110 D2
Fairview Canada 120 G3
Fairview MI U.S.A. 134 C1
Fairview OK U.S.A. 131 D4
Fairview PA U.S.A. 134 E2
Fairview UT U.S.A. 129 H2
Fairview Park Hong Kong China 77 [inset]
Fairweather, Cape U.S.A. 120 B3
Fairweather, Mount Canada/U.S.A. 120 B3
Fais i. Micronesia 69 K5
Faisalabad Pak. 89 I4
Faissault France 52 E5
Faith U.S.A. 130 C2
Faizabad Afgh. see Feyzābād
Faizabad India 83 E4
Fakaofo atoll Tokelau 107 I2
Fakaofu atoll Tokelau see Fakaofo
Fakenham U.K. 49 H6
Fåker Sweden 44 I5
Fakfak Indon. 69 I7
Fakhrabad Iran 88 D4
Fakiragram India 83 G4
Fako vol. Cameroon see Cameroun, Mont
Fal r. U.K. 49 C8
Falaba Sierra Leone 96 B4
Falaise Lake Canada 120 G2
Falam Myanmar 70 A2
Falavarjan Iran 88 C3
Falcon Lake Canada 121 M5
Falcon Lake l. Mex./U.S.A. 131 D7
Falenki Rus. Fed. 42 K4
Falfurrias U.S.A. 131 D7
Falher Canada 120 G4
Falkenberg Germany 53 N3
Falkenberg Sweden 45 H8
Falkenhagen Germany 53 M1
Falkenhain Germany 53 M3
Falkensee Germany 53 N2
Falkenstein Germany 53 M5
Falkirk U.K. 50 F5
Falkland U.K. 50 F4
Falkland Escarpment sea feature S. Atlantic Ocean 148 E9

▶Falkland Islands terr. S. Atlantic Ocean 144 E8
United Kingdom Overseas Territory.
South America 9, 140–141

Falkland Plateau sea feature S. Atlantic Ocean 148 E9
Falkland Sound sea chan. Falkland Is 144 D8
Falköping Sweden 45 H7
Fallbrook U.S.A. 128 E5
Fallieres Coast Antarctica 152 L2
Fallingbostel Germany 53 J2
Fallon U.S.A. 128 D2
Fall River U.S.A. 135 J3
Fall River Pass U.S.A. 126 G4
Falls City U.S.A. 130 E3
Falmouth U.K. 49 B8
Falmouth KY U.S.A. 134 C4
Falmouth VA U.S.A. 135 G4
False r. Canada 123 H2
False Bay S. Africa 100 D8
False Point India 83 F5
Falster i. Denmark 45 G9
Fălticeni Romania 43 E7
Falun Sweden 45 I6
Famagusta Cyprus 85 A2
Famagusta Bay Cyprus see Ammochostos Bay
Fameck France 52 G5
Famenin Iran 88 C3
Fame Range hills Australia 109 C6
Family Lake Canada 121 M5
Family Well Australia 108 D5
Fāmūr, Daryācheh-ye l. Iran 88 C4
Fana Mali 96 C3
Fanad Head hd Rep. of Ireland 47 E2
Fandriana Madag. 99 E6
Fane r. Rep. of Ireland 51 F4
Fang Thai. 70 B3
Fangcheng Guangxi China see Fangchenggang
Fangcheng Henan China 77 G1
Fangchenggang China 77 F4
Fangdou Shan mts China 77 F2
Fangliao Taiwan 77 I4
Fangshan Taiwan 77 I4
Fangxian China 77 F1
Fangzheng China 74 C3
Fankuai China 77 F2
Fankuaidian China see Fankuai
Fanling Hong Kong China 77 [inset]
Fannich, Loch l. U.K. 50 D3
Fannūj Iran 89 E5
Fano Italy 58 E3
Fanshan Anhui China 77 H2
Fanshan Zhejiang China 77 I3
Fan Si Pan mt. Vietnam 70 C2
Fanum Fortunae Italy see Fano
Faqīh Aḥmadān Iran 88 C4
Farab Turkm. see Farap
Faraba Mali 96 B3
Faradofay Madag. see Tôlañaro
Farafangana Madag. 99 E6
Farāfirah, Wāḥāt al oasis Egypt 86 C4
Farafra Oasis oasis Egypt see Farāfirah, Wāḥāt al
Farāh Afgh. 89 F3
Faraḥābād Iran see Khezerābād
Farallon de Medinilla i. N. Mariana Is 69 L3
Farallon de Pajaros vol. N. Mariana Is 69 K2
Farallones de Cali, Parque Nacional nat. park Col. 142 C3
Faranah Guinea 96 B3
Farap Turkm. 89 F2
Fararah Oman 87 I6
Farasān, Jazā'ir is Saudi Arabia 86 F6
Faraulep atoll Micronesia 69 K5
Fareham U.K. 49 F8
Farewell, Cape Greenland 119 N3
Farewell, Cape N.Z. 113 D5
Farewell Spit N.Z. 113 D5
Färgelanda Sweden 45 H7
Farghona Uzbek. see Fergana
Fargo U.S.A. 130 D2
Faribault U.S.A. 130 E2
Faribault, Lac l. Canada 123 H2
Faridabad India 82 D3
Faridkot India 82 C3
Faridpur Bangl. 83 G5
Farīmān Iran 89 E3
Farkhar Afgh. see Farkhato
Farkhato Afgh. 89 H2
Farkhor Tajik. 89 H2
Farmahin Iran 88 C3
Farmer Island Canada 122 E2
Farmerville U.S.A. 131 E5
Farmington Canada 120 F4
Farmington ME U.S.A. 135 J1
Farmington MO U.S.A. 130 F4
Farmington NH U.S.A. 135 J2
Farmington NM U.S.A. 129 I3
Farmington Hills U.S.A. 134 D2
Far Mountain Canada 120 E4
Farmville U.S.A. 135 F5
Farnborough U.K. 49 G7
Farne Islands U.K. 48 F3
Farnham U.K. 49 G7
Farnham, Lake salt flat Australia 109 D6
Farnham, Mount Canada 120 G5
Faro Brazil 143 G4
Faro Canada 120 C2
Faro Port. 57 C5
Fårö i. Sweden 45 K8
Faroe - Iceland Ridge sea feature Arctic Ocean 153 I2

▶Faroe Islands terr. N. Atlantic Ocean 44 [inset]
Self-governing Danish Territory.
Europe 5, 38–39

Fårösund Sweden 45 K8
Farquhar Group is Seychelles 99 F5
Farquharson Tableland hills Australia 109 C6
Farrāshband Iran 88 D4
Farr Bay Antarctica 152 F2
Farristown U.S.A. 134 C5
Farrukhabad India see Fatehgarh
Fārsī Afgh. 89 F3
Farsund Norway 45 E7
Fārūj Iran 88 E2
Farwell MI U.S.A. 134 C2
Farwell TX U.S.A. 131 C5
Fasā Iran 88 D4
Fasano Italy 58 G4
Faşikan Geçidi pass Turkey 85 A1
Faßberg Germany 53 K2
Fastiv Ukr. 43 F6
Fastov Ukr. see Fastiv
Fatehabad India 82 C3
Fatehgarh India 82 D4
Fatehpur Rajasthan India 82 C4
Fatehpur Uttar Pradesh India 82 E4
Fatick Senegal 96 B3
Fattoilep atoll Micronesia see Faraulep
Faughan r. U.K. 51 E2
Faulkton U.S.A. 130 D2
Faulquemont France 52 G5
Fauresmith S. Africa 101 G5
Fauske Norway 44 I3
Faust Canada 120 H4
Fawcett Canada 120 H4
Fawley U.K. 49 F8
Fawn r. Canada 121 N4
Faxaflói b. Iceland 44 [inset]
Faxälven r. Sweden 44 J5
Faya Chad 97 E3
Fayette AL U.S.A. 133 C5
Fayette MO U.S.A. 130 E4
Fayette MS U.S.A. 131 F6
Fayette OH U.S.A. 134 C3
Fayetteville AR U.S.A. 131 E4
Fayetteville NC U.S.A. 133 E5
Fayetteville TN U.S.A. 133 C5
Fayetteville WV U.S.A. 134 E4
Fâyid Egypt see Fā'id
Faylakah i. Kuwait 88 C4
Fazao Malfakassa, Parc National de nat. park Togo 96 D4
Fazilka India 82 C3
Fazrān, Jabal hill Saudi Arabia 88 C5
Fdérik Mauritania 96 B2
Fead Group is P.N.G. see Nuguria Islands
Feale r. Rep. of Ireland 51 C5
Fear, Cape U.S.A. 133 E5
Featherston N.Z. 113 E5
Feathertop, Mount Australia 112 C6
Fécamp France 56 E2
Federal District admin. dist. Brazil see Distrito Federal
Federalsburg U.S.A. 135 H4
Federated Malay States country Asia see Malaysia
Fedusar India 82 C4
Fehet Lake Canada 121 M1
Fehmarn i. Germany 47 M3
Fehrbellin Germany 53 M2
Feia, Lagoa lag. Brazil 145 C3
Feicheng China see Feixian
Feijó Brazil 142 D5
Feilding N.Z. 113 E5
Fei Ngo Shan hill Hong Kong China see Kowloon Peak
Feio r. Brazil see Aguapeí
Feira de Santana Brazil 145 D1
Feixi China 77 H2
Feixian China 77 H1
Fejd-el-Abiod pass Alg. 58 B6
Feke Turkey 90 D3
Felanitx Spain 57 H4
Feldberg Germany 53 N1
Feldberg mt. Germany 47 L7
Feldkirch Austria 47 L7
Feldkirchen in Kärnten Austria 47 O7
Felidhu Atoll Maldives 81 D11
Felidu Atoll Maldives see Felidhu Atoll
Felipe C. Puerto Mex. 136 G5
Felixlândia Brazil 145 B2
Felixstowe U.K. 49 I7
Felixton S. Africa 101 J5
Fellowsville U.S.A. 134 F4
Felsina Italy see Bologna
Felton U.S.A. 135 H4
Feltre Italy 58 D1
Femunden l. Norway 44 G5
Femundsmarka Nasjonalpark nat. park Norway 44 H5
Fenaio, Punta del pt Italy 58 D3
Fence Lake U.S.A. 129 I4
Fener Burnu hd Turkey 85 B1
Fénérive Madag. see Fenoarivo Atsinanana
Fengari mt. Greece 59 K4
Fengcheng Fujian China see Lianjiang
Fengcheng Fujian China see Anxi
Fengcheng Fujian China see Yongding
Fengcheng Guangdong China see Xinfeng
Fengcheng Guangxi China see Fengshan
Fengcheng Guizhou China see Tianzhu
Fengcheng Jiangxi China 77 G2
Fenggang Fujian China see Shaxian
Fenggang Guizhou China 76 E3
Fenggang Jiangxi China see Yihuang
Fengguang China 74 B3
Fenghuang China 77 F3
Fengjiaba China see Wangcang
Fengjie China 77 F2
Fengkai China 77 F4
Fenglin Taiwan 77 I4
Fengming Shaanxi China see Qishan
Fengming Sichuan China see Pengshan
Fengqing China 76 C3
Fengshan Fujian China see Luoyuan
Fengshan Guangxi China 76 E3
Fengshan Hubei China see Luotian
Fengshan Yunnan China see Fengqing
Fengshuba Shuiku resr China 77 G3
Fengshui Shan mt. China 74 A1
Fengtongzai Giant Panda Reserve nature res. China 76 D2
Fengxian China 76 E1
Fengxiang Heilong. China see Luobei
Fengxiang Yunnan China see Lincang
Fengyang China 77 H1
Fengyüan Taiwan 77 I3
Fengzhen China 73 K4
Feni Bangl. 83 G5
Feni Islands P.N.G. 106 F2
Fennville U.S.A. 134 B2
Feno, Capo di c. Corsica France 56 I6
Fenoarivo Atsinanana Madag. 99 E5
Fenshui Guan pass China 77 H3
Fenton U.S.A. 134 D2
Fenua Ura atoll Fr. Polynesia see Manuae
Fenyi China 77 G3
Feodosiya Ukr. 90 D1
Fer, Cap de c. Alg. 58 B6
Férai Greece see Feres
Ferdows Iran 88 E3
Fère-Champenoise France 52 D6
Feres Greece 59 L4
Fergana Uzbek. 87 L1
Fergus Canada 134 E2
Fergus Falls U.S.A. 130 D2
Ferguson Lake Canada 121 L2
Fergusson Island P.N.G. 106 F2
Fériana Tunisia 58 C7
Ferijaz Serb. and Mont. see Uroševac
Ferkessédougou Côte d'Ivoire 96 C4
Fermo Italy 58 E3
Fermont Canada 123 I3
Fermoselle Spain 57 C3
Fermoy Rep. of Ireland 51 D5
Fernandina, Isla i. Galápagos Ecuador 142 [inset]
Fernandina Beach U.S.A. 133 D6
Fernando de Magallanes, Parque Nacional nat. park Chile 144 B8
Fernando de Noronha i. Brazil 148 F6
Fernandópolis Brazil 145 A3
Fernando Poó i. Equat. Guinea see Bioco
Fernão Dias Brazil 145 B2
Ferndale U.S.A. 128 A1
Ferndown U.K. 49 F8
Fernlee Australia 112 C2
Fernley U.S.A. 128 D2
Ferns Rep. of Ireland 51 F5
Ferozepore India see Firozpur
Ferrara Italy 58 D2
Ferreira-Gomes Brazil 143 H3
Ferro, Capo c. Sardinia Italy 58 C4
Ferrol Spain 57 B2
Ferron U.S.A. 129 H2
Ferros Brazil 145 C2
Ferryland Canada 123 L5
Ferryville Tunisia see Menzel Bourguiba
Fertő-tavi nat. park Hungary 58 G1
Ferwerd Neth. 52 F1
Ferwert Neth. see Ferwerd
Fès Morocco 54 D5
Feshi Dem. Rep. Congo 99 B4
Fessenden U.S.A. 130 D2
Festus U.S.A. 130 F4
Fété Bowé Senegal 96 B3
Fethard Rep. of Ireland 51 E5
Fethiye Malatya Turkey see Yazıhan
Fethiye Muğla Turkey 59 M6
Fethiye Körfezi b. Turkey 59 M6
Fetisovo Kazakh. 91 I2
Fetlar i. U.K. 50 [inset]
Fettercairn U.K. 50 G4
Feucht Germany 53 L5
Feuchtwangen Germany 53 K5
Feuilles, Rivière aux r. Canada 123 H2
Fevral'sk Rus. Fed. 74 C1
Fevzipaşa Turkey 90 E3
Feyzābād Afgh. 89 H2
Feyzābād Kermān Iran 88 D4
Feyzābād Khorāsān Iran 88 E3
Fez Morocco see Fès
Ffestiniog U.K. 49 D6
Fianarantsoa Madag. 99 E6
Fichē Eth. 98 D3
Fichtelgebirge hills Germany 53 M4
Field U.S.A. 134 D5
Fier Albania 59 H4
Fiery Creek r. Australia 110 B3
Fife Lake U.S.A. 134 C1
Fife Ness pt U.K. 50 G4
Fifield Australia 112 C4
Fifth Meridian Canada 120 H3
Figeac France 56 F4
Figueira da Foz Port. 57 B3
Figueras Spain see Figueres
Figueres Spain 57 H2
Figuig Morocco 54 D5
Figuil Cameroon 97 E4

▶Fiji country S. Pacific Ocean 107 H3
4th most populous and 5th largest country in Oceania.
Oceania 8, 104–105

Fīk' Eth. 98 E3
Filadelfia Para. 144 D2
Filchner Ice Shelf Antarctica 152 A1
Filey U.K. 48 G4
Filibe Bulg. see Plovdiv
Filingué Niger 96 D3
Filipinas country Asia see Philippines
Filippiada Greece 59 I5
Filipstad Sweden 45 I7
Fillan Norway 44 F5
Fillmore CA U.S.A. 128 D4
Fillmore UT U.S.A. 129 G2
Fils r. Germany 53 J6
Filtu Eth. 98 E3
Fimbull Ice Shelf Antarctica 152 C2
Fin Iran 88 C3
Finch Canada 135 H1
Findhorn r. U.K. 50 F3
Fındık Turkey 88 A2
Findlay U.S.A. 134 D3
Fine U.S.A. 135 H1
Finger Lake Canada 121 M4
Finger Lakes U.S.A. 135 G2
Finike Turkey 59 N6
Finike Körfezi b. Turkey 59 N6
Finisterre Spain see Fisterra
Finisterre, Cabo c. Spain see Finisterre, Cape
Finisterre, Cape Spain 57 B2
Finke watercourse Australia 110 A5
Finke, Mount hill Australia 109 F7
Finke Bay Australia 108 E3
Finke Gorge National Park Australia 109 F6

▶Finland country Europe 44 O5
Europe 5, 38–39

Finland, Gulf of Europe 45 M7
Finlay r. Canada 120 E3
Finlay, Mount Canada 120 E3
Finlay Forks Canada 120 F4
Finley U.S.A. 130 D2
Finn r. Rep. of Ireland 51 E3
Finne ridge Germany 53 L3
Finnigan, Mount Australia 110 D2
Finniss, Cape Australia 109 F8
Finnmarksvidda reg. Norway 44 H2
Finnsnes Norway 44 J2
Fins Oman 88 E6
Finschhafen P.N.G. 69 L8
Finspång Sweden 45 I7
Fintona U.K. 51 E3
Fintown Rep. of Ireland 51 D3
Finucane Range hills Australia 110 C4
Fionn Loch l. U.K. 50 D3
Fionnphort U.K. 50 C4
Fiordland National Park N.Z. 113 A7
Fir reg. Saudi Arabia 88 B4
Firat r. Turkey 90 E3 see Euphrates
Firebaugh U.S.A. 128 C3
Firedrake Lake Canada 121 J2
Firenze Italy see Florence
Fireside Canada 120 E3
Firk, Sha'īb watercourse Iraq 91 G5
Firmat Arg. 144 D4
Firminy France 56 G4
Firmum Italy see Fermo
Firmum Picenum Italy see Fermo
Firovo Rus. Fed. 42 G4
Firozabad India 82 D4
Firozkoh reg. Afgh. 89 G3
Firozpur India 82 C3
First Three Mile Opening sea chan. Australia 110 D2
Fīrūzābād Iran 88 D4
Fīrūzkūh Iran 88 D3
Firyuza Turkm. 88 E2
Fischbach Germany 53 H5
Fischersbrunn Namibia 100 B3
Fish watercourse Namibia 100 C5
Fisher Australia 109 E7
Fisher Bay Antarctica 152 G2
Fisher Glacier Antarctica 152 E2
Fisher River Canada 121 L5
Fishers U.S.A. 134 B4
Fishers Island U.S.A. 135 J3
Fisher Strait Canada 119 J3
Fishguard U.K. 49 C7
Fishing Creek U.S.A. 135 G4
Fishing Lake Canada 121 M4
Fish Lake Canada 120 F2
Fish Point U.S.A. 134 D2
Fish Ponds Hong Kong China 77 [inset]
Fiske, Cape Antarctica 152 L2
Fiskenæsset Greenland see Qeqertarsuatsiaat
Fismes France 52 D5
Fisterra Spain 57 B2
Fisterra, Cabo c. Spain see Finisterre, Cape
Fitchburg U.S.A. 130 F3
Fitri, Lac l. Chad 97 E3
Fitzgerald Canada 121 I3
Fitzgerald U.S.A. 133 D6
Fitzgerald River National Park Australia 109 B8
Fitz Hugh Sound sea chan. Canada 120 D5
Fitz Roy Arg. 144 C7
Fitzroy r. Australia 108 C4
Fitzroy, Cerro mt. Arg. 144 B7
Fitzroy Crossing Australia 108 D4
Fitzwilliam Island Canada 134 E1
Fiume Croatia see Rijeka
Fivemiletown U.K. 51 E3
Five Points U.S.A. 128 C3
Fizi Dem. Rep. Congo 99 C4
Fizuli Azer. see Füzuli
Flå Norway 45 F6
Flagstaff S. Africa 101 I6
Flagstaff U.S.A. 129 H4
Flagstaff Lake U.S.A. 132 G2
Flaherty Island Canada 122 F2
Flambeau r. U.S.A. 130 F2
Flamborough Head hd U.K. 48 G4
Fläming hills Germany 53 M2
Flaming Gorge Reservoir U.S.A. 126 F4
Flaminksvlei salt pan S. Africa 100 E6
Flanagan r. Canada 121 M4
Flandre reg. France 52 C4
Flannagan Lake U.S.A. 134 D5
Flannan Isles U.K. 50 B2
Flåsjön l. Sweden 44 I4
Flat r. Canada 120 E2
Flat r. U.S.A. 134 C2
Flat Creek Canada 120 B2
Flathead r. U.S.A. 124 E2
Flathead Lake U.S.A. 126 E3
Flatiron mt. U.S.A. 126 E3
Flat Island S. China Sea 68 F4
Flat Lick U.S.A. 134 D5
Flattery, Cape Australia 110 D2
Flattery, Cape U.S.A. 126 B2
Flat Top mt. Canada 120 B2
Flatwillow Creek r. U.S.A. 126 G3

Flatwoods U.S.A. 134 E4
Fleetmark Germany 53 L2
Fleetwood Australia 110 D4
Fleetwood U.K. 48 D5
Fleetwood U.S.A. 135 H3
Flekkefjord Norway 45 E7
Flemingsburg U.S.A. 134 D4
Flemington U.S.A. 135 H3
Flen Sweden 45 J7
Flensburg Germany 47 L3
Flers France 56 D2
Flesherton Canada 134 E1
Fletcher Lake Canada 121 I2
Fletcher Peninsula Antarctica 152 L2
Fleur de Lys Canada 123 K4
Fleur-de-May, Lac l. Canada 123 I4
Flinders r. Australia 110 C3
Flinders Chase National Park Australia 111 B7
Flinders Group National Park Australia 110 D2
Flinders Island Australia 111 [inset]
Flinders Passage Australia 110 E3
Flinders Ranges mts Australia 111 B7
Flinders Ranges National Park Australia 111 B6
Flinders Reefs Australia 110 E3
Flin Flon Canada 121 K4
Flint U.K. 48 D5
Flint U.S.A. 134 D2
Flint r. U.S.A. 133 C6
Flint Island Kiribati 151 J6
Flinton Australia 112 D1
Flisa Norway 45 H6

▶Flissingskiy, Mys c. Rus. Fed. 64 H2
Most easterly point of Europe.

Flixecourt France 52 C4
Flodden U.K. 48 E3
Flöha Germany 53 N4
Flood Range mts Antarctica 152 J1
Flora r. Australia 108 E3
Flora U.S.A. 134 B3
Florac France 56 F4
Florala U.S.A. 133 C6
Florange France 52 G5
Flora Reef Australia 110 D3
Florence Italy 58 D3
Florence AL U.S.A. 133 C5
Florence AZ U.S.A. 129 H5
Florence CO U.S.A. 127 G5
Florence OR U.S.A. 126 B4
Florence SC U.S.A. 133 E5
Florence WI U.S.A. 130 F2
Florence Junction U.S.A. 129 H5
Florencia Col. 142 C3
Florennes Belgium 52 E4
Florentia Italy see Florence
Florentino Ameghino, Embalse resr Arg. 144 C6
Flores r. Arg. 144 E5
Flores Guat. 136 G5
Flores i. Indon. 108 C2
Flores, Laut sea Indon. 108 B1
Flores Island Canada 120 E5
Flores Sea Indon. see Flores, Laut
Floresta Brazil 143 K5
Floresville U.S.A. 131 D6
Floriano Brazil 143 J5
Florianópolis Brazil 145 A4
Florida Uruguay 144 E4
Florida state U.S.A. 133 D6
Florida, Straits of Bahamas/U.S.A. 133 D8
Florida Bay U.S.A. 133 D7
Florida City U.S.A. 133 D7
Florida Islands Solomon Is 107 G2
Florida Keys is U.S.A. 133 D7
Florin U.S.A. 128 C2
Florina Greece 59 I4
Florissant U.S.A. 130 F4
Florø Norway 45 D6
Flour Lake Canada 123 I3
Floyd U.S.A. 134 E5
Floyd, Mount U.S.A. 129 G4
Floydada U.S.A. 131 C5
Fluessen l. Neth. 52 F2
Flushing Neth. see Vlissingen
Fly r. P.N.G. 69 K8
Flying Fish, Cape Antarctica 152 K2
Flying Mountain U.S.A. 129 I6
Flylân i. Neth. see Vlieland
Foam Lake Canada 121 K5
Foča Bos.-Herz. 58 H3
Foça Turkey 59 L5
Fochabers U.K. 50 F3
Focșani Romania 59 L2
Fogang China 77 G4
Foggia Italy 58 F4
Fogi Indon. 69 H7
Fogo i. Cape Verde 96 [inset]
Fogo Island Canada 123 L4
Foinaven hill U.K. 50 E2
Foix France 56 E5
Folda sea chan. Norway 44 I3
Foldereid Norway 44 H4
Foldfjorden sea chan. Norway 44 G4
Folegandros i. Greece 59 K6
Foleyet Canada 122 E4
Foley Island Canada 119 K3
Foligno Italy 58 E3
Folkestone U.K. 49 I7
Folkingham U.K. 49 G6
Folkston U.S.A. 133 D6
Folldal Norway 44 G5
Follonica Italy 58 D3
Folsom Lake U.S.A. 128 C2
Fomboni Comoros 99 E5
Fomento Cuba 133 E8
Fomin Rus. Fed. 43 I7
Fominskaya Rus. Fed. 42 K2
Fominskoye Rus. Fed. 42 I4
Fonda U.S.A. 135 H2
Fond-du-Lac Canada 121 J3
Fond du Lac r. Canada 121 J3
Fond du Lac U.S.A. 134 A2
Fondevila Spain 57 B3
Fondi Italy 58 E4
Fonni Sardinia Italy 58 C4
Fonsagrada Spain see A Fonsagrada
Fonseca, Golfo do b. Central America 136 G6
Fontaine Lake Canada 121 J3
Fontanges Canada 123 H3
Fontas Canada 120 F3
Fontas r. Canada 120 F3
Fonte Boa Brazil 142 E4
Fonteneau, Lac l. Canada 123 J4
Fontur pt Iceland 44 [inset]
Foochow China see Fuzhou
Foot's Bay Canada 134 F1
Foping China 77 F1
Foraker, Mount U.S.A. 118 C3
Foraulep atoll Micronesia see Faraulep
Forbes Australia 112 D4
Forbes, Mount Canada 120 G4
Forchheim Germany 53 L5
Ford r. U.S.A. 132 C2
Ford City U.S.A. 128 D4
Førde Norway 45 D6
Forde Lake Canada 121 L2
Fordham U.K. 49 H6
Fordingbridge U.K. 49 F8
Ford Range mts Antarctica 152 J1
Fords Bridge Australia 112 B2
Fordsville U.S.A. 134 B5
Fordyce U.S.A. 131 E5
Forécariah Guinea 96 B4
Forel, Mont mt. Greenland 119 O3
Foreland hd U.K. 49 F8
Foreland Point U.K. 49 D7
Foremost Canada 126 F2
Foresight Mountain Canada 116 E4
Forest Canada 134 E2
Forest MS U.S.A. 131 F5
Forest OH U.S.A. 134 D3
Forestburg Canada 121 H4
Forest Creek r. Australia 110 C3
Forest Hill Australia 112 C5
Forest Ranch U.S.A. 128 C2
Forestville Canada 123 H4
Forestville CA U.S.A. 128 B2
Forestville MI U.S.A. 134 D2
Forfar U.K. 50 G4
Forgan U.S.A. 131 C4
Forges-les-Eaux France 52 B5
Forillon, Parc National de nat. park Canada 123 I4
Forked River U.S.A. 135 H4
Forks U.S.A. 126 B3
Fork Union U.S.A. 135 F5
Forlì Italy 58 E2
Forman U.S.A. 130 D2
Formby U.K. 48 D5
Formentera i. Spain 57 G4
Formentor, Cap de c. Spain 57 H4
Formerie France 52 B5
Former Yugoslav Republic of Macedonia country Europe see Macedonia
Formiga Brazil 145 B3
Formosa Arg. 144 E3
Formosa country Asia see Taiwan
Formosa Brazil 145 B1
Formosa, Serra hills Brazil 143 G6
Formosa Bay Kenya see Ungwana Bay
Formosa Strait China/Taiwan see Taiwan Strait
Formoso r. Bahia Brazil 145 B1
Formoso r. Tocantins Brazil 145 A1
Fornos Moz. 101 L2
Forres U.K. 50 F3
Forrest Vic. Australia 112 A7
Forrest W.A. Australia 109 E7
Forrestal Range mts Antarctica 152 A1
Forrest City U.S.A. 131 F5
Forrest Lake Canada 121 I3
Forrest Lakes salt flat Australia 109 E7
Fors Sweden 44 J5
Forsayth Australia 110 C3
Forsnäs Sweden 44 M3
Forssa Fin. 45 M6
Forster Australia 112 F4
Forsyth GA U.S.A. 133 D5
Forsyth MT U.S.A. 126 G3
Forsyth Range hills Australia 110 C4
Fort Abbas Pak. 89 I4
Fort Albany Canada 122 E3
Fortaleza Brazil 143 K4
Fort Amsterdam U.S.A. see New York
Fort Archambault Chad see Sarh
Fort Ashby U.S.A. 135 F4
Fort Assiniboine Canada 120 H4
Fort Augustus U.K. 50 E3
Fort Beaufort S. Africa 101 H7
Fort Benton U.S.A. 126 F3
Fort Brabant Canada see Tuktoyaktuk
Fort Bragg U.S.A. 128 B2
Fort Branch U.S.A. 134 B4
Fort Carillon U.S.A. see Ticonderoga
Fort Charlet Alg. see Djanet
Fort Chimo Canada see Kuujjuaq
Fort Chipewyan Canada 121 I3
Fort Collins U.S.A. 126 G4
Fort-Coulonge Canada 122 F5
Fort Crampel Cent. Afr. Rep. see Kaga Bandoro
Fort-Dauphin Madag. see Tôlañaro
Fort Davis U.S.A. 131 C6

▶Fort-de-France Martinique 137 L6
Capital of Martinique.

Fort de Kock Indon. see Bukittinggi
Fort de Polignac Alg. see Illizi
Fort Dodge U.S.A. 130 E3
Fort Duchesne U.S.A. 129 I1
Fort Edward U.S.A. 135 I2
Fortescue r. Australia 108 B5
Forte Veneza Brazil 143 H5
Fort Flatters Alg. see Bordj Omer Driss
Fort Foureau Cameroon see Kousséri
Fort Franklin Canada see Déline
Fort Gardel Alg. see Zaouatallaz
Fort Gay U.S.A. 134 D4
Fort George Canada see Chisasibi
Fort Good Hope Canada 118 F3
Fort Gouraud Mauritania see Fdérik
Forth r. U.K. 50 F4
Forth, Firth of est. U.K. 50 F4
Fort Hertz Myanmar see Putao
Fortification Range mts U.S.A. 129 F2
Fortín General Mendoza Para. 144 D2
Fortín Leonida Escobar Para. 144 D2
Fortín Madrejón Para. 144 E2
Fortín Pilcomayo Arg. 144 D2
Fortín Ravelo Bol. 142 F7
Fortín Sargento Primero Leyes Arg. 144 E2
Fortín Suárez Arana Bol. 142 F7
Fortín Teniente Juan Echauri López Para. 144 D2
Fort Jameson Zambia see Chipata
Fort Johnston Malawi see Mangochi
Fort Kent U.S.A. 132 G2
Fort Lamy Chad see Ndjamena
Fort Laperrine Alg. see Tamanrasset
Fort Laramie U.S.A. 126 G4
Fort Lauderdale U.S.A. 133 D7
Fort Liard Canada 120 F2
Fort Mackay Canada 121 I3
Fort Macleod Canada 120 H5
Fort Madison U.S.A. 130 F3
Fort Manning Malawi see Mchinji
Fort McMurray Canada 121 I3
Fort McPherson Canada 118 E3
Fort Meyers Beach U.S.A. 133 D7
Fort Morgan U.S.A. 130 C3
Fort Munro Pak. 89 H4
Fort Myers U.S.A. 133 D7
Fort Nelson Canada 120 F3
Fort Nelson r. Canada 120 F3
Fort Norman Canada see Tulita
Fort Orange U.S.A. see Albany
Fort Payne U.S.A. 133 C5
Fort Peck U.S.A. 126 G2
Fort Peck Reservoir U.S.A. 126 G3
Fort Pierce U.S.A. 133 D7
Fort Portal Uganda 98 D3
Fort Providence Canada 120 G2
Fort Randall U.S.A. see Cold Bay
Fort Resolution Canada 120 H2
Fortrose N.Z. 113 B8
Fortrose U.K. 50 E3
Fort Rosebery Zambia see Mansa
Fort Rousset Congo see Owando
Fort Rupert Canada see Waskaganish
Fort Sandeman Pak. see Zhob
Fort Saskatchewan Canada 120 H4
Fort Scott U.S.A. 130 E4
Fort Severn Canada 122 D2
Fort-Shevchenko Kazakh. 78 E2
Fort Simpson Canada 120 F2
Fort Smith Canada 121 H2
Fort Smith U.S.A. 131 E5
Fort St James Canada 120 E4
Fort St John Canada 120 F3
Fort Stockton U.S.A. 131 C6
Fort Sumner U.S.A. 127 G6
Fort Supply U.S.A. 131 D4
Fort Thomas U.S.A. 129 I5
Fort Trinquet Mauritania see Bîr Mogreïn
Fortuna U.S.A. 130 C1
Fortune Bay Canada 123 L5
Fort Valley U.S.A. 133 D5
Fort Vermilion Canada 120 G3
Fort Victoria Zimbabwe see Masvingo
Fort Ware Canada see Ware
Fort Wayne U.S.A. 134 C3
Fort William U.K. 50 D4
Fort Worth U.S.A. 131 D5
Fort Yates U.S.A. 130 C2
Fort Yukon U.S.A. 118 D3
Forum Iulii France see Fréjus
Forūr, Jazīreh-ye i. Iran 88 D5
Forvik Norway 44 H4
Foshan China 77 G4
Fo Shek Chau Hong Kong China see Basalt Island
Fossano Italy 58 B2
Fossil U.S.A. 126 C3
Fossil Downs Australia 108 D4
Foster Australia 112 C7
Foster U.S.A. 134 C4
Foster, Mount Canada/U.S.A. 120 C3
Foster Lakes Canada 121 J3
Fostoria U.S.A. 134 D3
Fotadrevo Madag. 99 E6
Fotherby U.K. 48 G5
Fotokol Cameroon 97 E3
Fotuna i. Vanuatu see Futuna
Fougères France 56 D2
Foula i. U.K. 50 [inset]
Foul Island Myanmar 70 A3
Foulness Point U.K. 49 H7
Foul Point Sri Lanka 84 D4
Foumban Cameroon 96 E4
Foundation Ice Stream glacier Antarctica 152 L1
Fount U.S.A. 134 D5
Fountains Abbey (NT) tourist site U.K. 48 F4
Fourches, Mont des hill France 56 G2
Four Corners U.S.A. 128 E4
Fouriesburg S. Africa 101 I5
Fourmies France 52 E4
Fournier, Lac l. Canada 123 I4
Fournoi i. Greece 59 L6
Fourpeaked Mountain U.S.A. 118 C4
Fouta Djallon reg. Guinea 96 B3
Foveaux Strait N.Z. 113 A8
Fowey r. U.K. 49 C8
Fowler CO U.S.A. 127 G5
Fowler IN U.S.A. 134 B3
Fowler Ice Rise Antarctica 152 L1
Fowlers Bay Australia 106 D5
Fowlers Bay b. Australia 109 F8
Fowlerville U.S.A. 134 C2
Fox r. B.C. Canada 120 E3
Fox r. Man. Canada 121 M3
Fox r. U.S.A. 130 F3
Fox Creek Canada 120 G4
Fox Creek U.S.A. 134 C5
Foxdale Isle of Man 48 C4
Foxe Basin g. Canada 119 K3
Foxe Channel Canada 119 J3
Foxe Peninsula Canada 119 K3
Fox Glacier N.Z. 113 C6
Fox Islands U.S.A. 118 B4
Fox Lake Canada 120 H3
Fox Mountain Canada 120 C2
Fox Valley Canada 121 I5
Foyers U.K. 50 E3
Foyle r. Rep. of Ireland/U.K. 51 E3
Foyle, Lough b. Rep. of Ireland/U.K. 51 E2
Foynes Rep. of Ireland 51 C5
Foz de Areia, Represa de resr Brazil 145 A4
Foz do Cunene Angola 99 B5
Foz do Iguaçu Brazil 144 F3
Fraga Spain 57 G3
Frakes, Mount Antarctica 152 K1
Framingham U.S.A. 135 J2
Framnes Mountains Antarctica 152 E2
Franca Brazil 145 B3
Français, Récif des reef New Caledonia 107 G3
Francavilla Fontana Italy 58 G4

▶France country Europe 56 F3
3rd largest and 4th most populous country in Europe.
Europe 5, 38–39

Frances Australia 111 C8
Frances Lake Canada 120 D2
Frances Lake l. Canada 120 D2
Franceville Gabon 98 B4
Francis Canada 121 K5
Francis atoll Kiribati see Beru
Francis, Lake U.S.A. 135 J1
Francisco de Orellana Ecuador see Puerto Francisco de Orellana
Francisco I. Madero Coahuila Mex. 131 C7
Francisco I. Madero Durango Mex. 131 B7
Francisco Zarco Mex. 128 E5
Francistown Botswana 99 C6
Francois Canada 123 K5
François Lake Canada 120 E4
Francois Peron National Park Australia 109 A6
Francs Peak U.S.A. 126 F4
Franeker Neth. 52 F1
Frankenberg Germany 53 N4
Frankenberg (Eder) Germany 53 I3
Frankenhöhe hills Germany 47 M6
Frankenmuth U.S.A. 134 D2
Frankenthal (Pfalz) Germany 53 I5
Frankenwald mts Germany 53 L4
Frankford Canada 135 G1
Frankfort IN U.S.A. 134 B3

▶Frankfort KY U.S.A. 134 C4
State capital of Kentucky.

Frankfort MI U.S.A. 134 B1
Frankfort OH U.S.A. 134 D4
Frankfurt Germany see Frankfurt am Main
Frankfurt am Main Germany 53 I4
Frankfurt an der Oder Germany 47 O4
Frank Hann National Park Australia 109 C8
Frankin Lake U.S.A. 129 F1
Fränkische Alb hills Germany 53 K6
Fränkische Schweiz reg. Germany 53 L5
Frankland, Cape Australia 111 [inset]
Franklin AZ U.S.A. 129 I5
Franklin GA U.S.A. 133 C5
Franklin IN U.S.A. 134 B4
Franklin KY U.S.A. 134 B5
Franklin LA U.S.A. 131 F6
Franklin MA U.S.A. 135 J2
Franklin NC U.S.A. 133 D5
Franklin NE U.S.A. 130 D3
Franklin NH U.S.A. 135 J2
Franklin PA U.S.A. 134 F3
Franklin TN U.S.A. 132 C5
Franklin TX U.S.A. 131 D6
Franklin VA U.S.A. 135 G5
Franklin WV U.S.A. 134 F4
Franklin Bay Canada 153 A2
Franklin D. Roosevelt Lake resr U.S.A. 126 D2
Franklin Furnace U.S.A. 134 D4
Franklin-Gordon National Park Australia 111 [inset]
Franklin Island Antarctica 152 H1
Franklin Mountains Canada 120 F2
Franklin Strait Canada 119 I2
Franklinton U.S.A. 131 F6
Franklinville U.S.A. 135 F2
Frankston Australia 112 B7
Fränsta Sweden 44 J5
Frantsa-Iosifa, Zemlya is Rus. Fed. 64 G2
Franz Canada 122 D4
Franz Josef Glacier N.Z. 113 C6
Frasca, Capo della c. Sardinia Italy 58 C5
Frascati Italy 58 E4
Fraser r. Australia 108 C4
Fraser r. B.C. Canada 120 F5
Fraser r. Nfld. and Lab. Canada 123 J2
Fraser, Mount hill Australia 109 B6
Fraserburg S. Africa 100 E6
Fraserburgh U.K. 50 G3
Fraserdale Canada 122 E4
Fraser Island Australia 110 F5
Fraser Island National Park Australia 110 F5
Fraser Lake Canada 120 E4
Fraser National Park Australia 112 B6
Fraser Plateau Canada 120 E4
Fraser Range hills Australia 109 C8
Frauenfeld Switz. 56 I3
Fray Bentos Uruguay 144 E4
Frazeysburg U.S.A. 134 D3
Frechen Germany 52 G4
Freckleton U.K. 48 E5
Frederic U.S.A. 134 C1
Frederica U.S.A. 135 H4
Fredericia Denmark 45 F9
Frederick MD U.S.A. 135 G4
Frederick OK U.S.A. 131 D5
Frederick Reef Australia 110 F4
Fredericksburg TX U.S.A. 131 D6
Fredericksburg VA U.S.A. 135 G4
Fredericktown U.S.A. 130 F4

▶Fredericton Canada 123 I5
Provincial capital of New Brunswick.

Frederikshåb Greenland see Paamiut
Frederikshavn Denmark 45 G8
Frederiksværk Denmark 45 H9
Fredonia AZ U.S.A. 129 G3
Fredonia KS U.S.A. 131 E4
Fredonia NY U.S.A. 134 F2
Fredonia WI U.S.A. 134 B2
Fredrika Sweden 44 K4
Fredrikshamn Fin. see Hamina
Fredrikstad Norway 45 G7
Freedonyer Peak U.S.A. 128 C1
Freehold U.S.A. 135 H3
Freeland U.S.A. 135 H3
Freeling Heights hill Australia 111 B6
Freel Peak U.S.A. 128 D2
Freels, Cape Canada 123 L4
Freeman U.S.A. 130 D3
Freeman, Lake U.S.A. 134 B3
Freeport FL U.S.A. 133 C6
Freeport IL U.S.A. 130 F3
Freeport TX U.S.A. 131 E6
Freeport City Bahamas 133 E7
Freer U.S.A. 131 D7
Freesoil U.S.A. 134 B1
Free State prov. S. Africa 101 H5

▶Freetown Sierra Leone 96 B4
Capital of Sierra Leone.

Fregenal de la Sierra Spain 57 C4
Fregon Australia 109 F6
Fréhel, Cap c. France 56 C2
Freiberg Germany 53 N4
Freiburg Switz. see Fribourg
Freiburg im Breisgau Germany 47 K6
Freisen Germany 53 H5
Freising Germany 47 M6
Freistadt Austria 47 O6
Fréjus France 56 H5
Fremantle Australia 109 A8
Fremont CA U.S.A. 128 C3
Fremont IN U.S.A. 134 C3
Fremont MI U.S.A. 134 C2
Fremont NE U.S.A. 130 D3
Fremont OH U.S.A. 134 D3
Fremont r. U.S.A. 129 H2
Fremont Junction U.S.A. 129 H2
Frenchburg U.S.A. 134 D5
French Cay i. Turks and Caicos Is 133 F8
French Congo country Africa see Congo

▶French Guiana terr. S. America 143 H3
French Overseas Department.
South America 9, 140–141

French Guinea country Africa see Guinea
French Island Australia 112 B7
French Lick U.S.A. 134 B4
Frenchman r. U.S.A. 126 G2
Frenchman Lake CA U.S.A. 128 C2
Frenchman Lake NV U.S.A. 129 F3
Frenchpark Rep. of Ireland 51 D4
French Pass N.Z. 113 D5

▶French Polynesia terr. S. Pacific Ocean 151 K7
French Overseas Territory.
Oceania 8, 104–105

French Somaliland country Africa see Djibouti

▶French Southern and Antarctic Lands terr. Indian Ocean 149 M8
French Overseas Territory.

French Sudan country Africa see Mali
French Territory of the Afars and Issas country Africa see Djibouti
Frenda Alg. 57 G6
Frentsjer Neth. see Franeker
Freren Germany 53 H2
Fresco r. Brazil 143 H5
Freshford Rep. of Ireland 51 E5
Fresnillo Mex. 136 D4
Fresno U.S.A. 128 D3
Fresno r. U.S.A. 128 C3
Fresno Reservoir U.S.A. 126 F2
Fressel, Lac l. Canada 122 G3
Freu, Cap des c. Spain 57 H4
Freudenberg Germany 53 H4
Freudenstadt Germany 47 L6
Frévent France 52 C4
Frew watercourse Australia 110 A4
Frewena Australia 110 A3
Freycinet Estuary inlet Australia 109 A6
Freycinet Peninsula Australia 111 [inset]
Freyenstein Germany 53 M1
Freyming-Merlebach France 52 G5
Fria Guinea 96 B3
Fria, Cape Namibia 99 B5
Friant U.S.A. 128 D3
Frias Arg. 144 C3
Fribourg Switz. 56 H3
Friday Harbor U.S.A. 126 C2
Friedeburg Germany 53 H1
Friedens U.S.A. 135 F3
Friedland Rus. Fed. see Pravdinsk
Friedrichshafen Germany 47 L7
Friedrichskanal canal Germany 53 L2
Friend U.S.A. 130 D3
Friendly Islands country S. Pacific Ocean see Tonga
Friendship U.S.A. 130 F3
Friesack Germany 53 M2
Friese Wad tidal flat Neth. 52 F1
Friesoythe Germany 53 H1
Frinton-on-Sea U.K. 49 I7
Frio r. U.S.A. 131 D6
Frio watercourse U.S.A. 131 C5
Frisco Mountain U.S.A. 129 G2
Frissell, Mount hill U.S.A. 135 I2
Fritzlar Germany 53 J3
Frjentsjer Neth. see Franeker
Frobisher Bay Canada see Iqaluit
Frobisher Bay b. Canada 119 L3
Frobisher Lake Canada 121 I3
Frohavet b. Norway 44 F5
Frohburg Germany 53 M3
Froissy France 52 C5
Frolovo Rus. Fed. 43 I6
Frome watercourse Australia 111 B6
Frome U.K. 49 E7
Frome r. U.K. 49 E8
Frome, Lake salt flat Australia 111 B6
Frome Downs Australia 111 B6
Fröndenberg Germany 53 H3
Frontera Coahuila Mex. 131 C7
Frontera Tabasco Mex. 136 F5
Fronteras Mex. 127 F7
Front Royal U.S.A. 135 F4
Frosinone Italy 58 E4
Frostburg U.S.A. 135 F4
Frøya i. Norway 44 F5
Fruges France 52 C4
Fruita U.S.A. 129 I2
Fruitland U.S.A. 129 H1
Fruitvale U.S.A. 129 I2
Frunze Kyrg. see Bishkek
Frusino Italy see Frosinone
Fruska Gora nat. park Serb. and Mont. 59 H2
Frýdek-Místek Czech Rep. 47 Q6
Fu'an China 77 H3
Fucheng Anhui China see Fengyang
Fucheng Shaanxi China see Fuxian
Fuchuan China 77 F3
Fuchun Jiang r. China 77 I2
Fude China 77 H3
Fuding China 77 I3
Fudul reg. Saudi Arabia 88 B6
Fuenlabrada Spain 57 E3
Fuerte r. Mex. 127 F8
Fuerte Olimpo Para. 144 E2
Fuerteventura i. Canary Is 96 B2
Fufeng China 76 E1
Fuga i. Phil. 69 G3
Fugong China 76 C3
Fugou China 77 G1
Fuhai China 80 G2
Fuḩaymī Iraq 91 F4
Fujairah U.A.E. 88 E5
Fujeira U.A.E. see Fujairah
Fuji Japan 75 E6
Fujian prov. China 77 H3
Fuji-Hakone-Izu National Park Japan 75 E6
Fujin China 74 C3
Fujinomiya Japan 75 E6
Fuji-san vol. Japan 75 E6
Fujiyoshida Japan 75 E6
Fûka Egypt see Fūkah
Fūkah Egypt 90 B5
Fukien prov. China see Fujian
Fukuchiyama Japan 75 D6
Fukue-jima i. Japan 75 C6
Fukui Japan 75 E5
Fukuoka Japan 75 C6
Fukushima Japan 75 F5
Fukuyama Japan 75 C7
Fûl, Gebel hill Egypt see Fūl, Jabal
Fūl, Jabal hill Egypt 85 A5
Fulchhari Bangl. 83 G4
Fulda Germany 53 J4
Fulda r. Germany 53 J3
Fulham U.K. 49 G7
Fuli China see Jixian
Fuliji China 77 H1
Fuling China 76 E2
Fulitun China see Jixian
Fullerton CA U.S.A. 128 E5
Fullerton NE U.S.A. 130 D3
Fullerton, Cape Canada 121 N2
Fulton IN U.S.A. 134 B3
Fulton MO U.S.A. 130 F4
Fulton MS U.S.A. 131 F5
Fulton NY U.S.A. 135 G2
Fumane Moz. 101 K3
Fumay France 52 E5
Fumin China 76 D3
Funabashi Japan 75 E6
Funafuti atoll Tuvalu 107 H2
Funan China 77 G1

▶Funchal Madeira 96 B1
Capital of Madeira.

Fundão Brazil 145 C2
Fundão Port. 57 C3
Fundi Italy see Fondi
Fundición Mex. 127 F8
Fundy, Bay of g. Canada 123 I5
Fundy National Park Canada 119 I5
Fünen i. Denmark see Fyn
Funeral Peak U.S.A. 128 E3
Fünfkirchen Hungary see Pécs
Fung Wong Shan hill Hong Kong China see Lantau Peak
Funhalouro Moz. 101 L2
Funing Jiangsu China 77 H1
Funing Yunnan China 76 E4
Funiu Shan mts China 77 F1
Funtua Nigeria 96 D3
Funzie U.K. 50 [inset]
Fuqing China 77 H3
Fürgun, Kūh-e mt. Iran 88 E5
Furmanov Rus. Fed. 42 I4
Furmanovka Kazakh. see Moyynkum
Furmanovo Kazakh. see Zhalpaktal
Furnas, Represa resr Brazil 145 B3
Furneaux Group is Australia 111 [inset]
Furnes Belgium see Veurne
Furong China see Wan'an
Fürstenau Germany 53 H2
Fürstenberg Germany 53 N1
Fürstenwalde Germany 47 O4
Fürth Germany 53 K5
Furth im Wald Germany 53 M5
Furukawa Japan 75 F5
Fury and Hecla Strait Canada 119 J3
Fusan S. Korea see Pusan
Fushun China 74 A4
Fushuncheng China see Shuncheng
Fusong China 74 B4
Fu Tau Pun Chau i. Hong Kong China 77 [inset]
Futuna i. Vanuatu 107 H3
Futuna Islands Wallis and Futuna Is see Hoorn, Îles de
Fuxian Liaoning China see Wafangdian
Fuxian Shaanxi China 73 J5
Fuxian Hu l. China 76 D3
Fuxin China 73 M4
Fuxing China see Wangmo
Fuxinzhen China see Fuxin
Fuyang Anhui China 77 G1
Fuyang Guangxi China see Fuchuan
Fuyang Zhejiang China 77 H2
Fuying Dao i. China 77 I3
Fuyu Anhui China see Susong
Fuyu Heilong. China 74 B3

Fuyu Jilin China 74 B3
Fuyu Jilin China see Songyuan
Fuyuan Heilong. China 74 D2
Fuyuan Yunnan China 76 E3
Fuyun China 80 G2
Fuzhou Fujian China 77 H3
Fuzhou Jiangxi China 77 H3
Füzuli Azer. 91 G3
Fyn i. Denmark 45 G9
Fyne, Loch inlet U.K. 50 D5

G

Gaaf Atoll Maldives see Huvadhu Atoll
Gaâfour Tunisia 58 C6
Gaalkacyo Somalia 98 E3
Gabakly Turkm. see Kabakly
Gabasumdo China see Tongde
Gabbs U.S.A. 128 E2
Gabbs Valley Range mts U.S.A. 128 D2
Gabd Pak. 89 F5
Gabela Angola 99 B5
Gaberones Botswana see Gaborone
Gabès Tunisia 54 G5
Gabès, Golfe de g. Tunisia 54 G5
Gabo Island Australia 112 D6
▶Gabon country Africa 98 B4
Africa 7, 94–95

▶Gaborone Botswana 101 G3
Capital of Botswana.

Gābrīk Iran 88 E5
Gabrovo Bulg. 59 K3
Gabú Guinea-Bissau 96 B3
Gadag India 84 B3
Gadaisu P.N.G. 110 E1
Gadchiroli India 84 D1
Gäddede Sweden 44 I4
Gadê China 76 C1
Gades Spain see Cádiz
Gadhap Pak. 89 G5
Gadhka India 89 H6
Gadhra India 82 B5
Gadra Pak. 89 H5
Gadsden U.S.A. 133 C5
Gadwal India 84 C2
Gadyach Ukr. see Hadyach
Gæi'dnuvuop'pi Norway 44 M2
Gaer U.K. 49 D7
Găeşti Romania 59 K2
Gaeta Italy 58 E4
Gaeta, Golfo di g. Italy 58 E4
Gaferut i. Micronesia 69 L5
Gaffney U.S.A. 133 D5
Gafsa Tunisia 58 C7
Gagarin Rus. Fed. 43 G5
Gagnoa Côte d'Ivoire 96 C4
Gagnon Canada 123 H4
Gago Coutinho Angola see
Lumbala N'guimbo
Gagra Georgia 43 I8
Gaiab watercourse Namibia 100 D5
Gaibanda Bangl. see Gaibandha
Gaibandha Bangl. 83 G4
Gaifi, Wâdi el watercourse Egypt see
Jayfī, Wādī al
Gail U.S.A. 131 C5
Gaildorf Germany 53 J6
Gaillac France 56 E5
Gaillimh Rep. of Ireland see Galway
Gaillon France 52 B5
Gaindainqoinkor China see Lhünzhub
Gainesboro U.S.A. 134 C5
Gainesville FL U.S.A. 133 D6
Gainesville GA U.S.A. 133 D5
Gainesville MO U.S.A. 131 E4
Gainesville TX U.S.A. 131 D5
Gainsborough U.K. 48 G5
Gairdner, Lake salt flat Australia 111 A6
Gairloch U.K. 50 D3
Gair Loch b. U.K. 50 D3
Gajah Hutan, Bukit hill Malaysia/Thai.
71 C6
Gajipur India see Ghazipur
Gajol India 83 G4
Gakarosa mt. S. Africa 100 F4
Gala China 83 G3
Galaasiya Uzbek. 89 G2
Gala Co l. China 83 G3
Galâla el Baharîya, Gebel el plat. Egypt
see Jalālah al Baḩrīyah, Jabal
Galana r. Kenya 98 E4
Galanta Slovakia 47 P6
Galaosiyo Uzbek. see Galaasiya

▶Galapagos Islands is Ecuador 151 O6
Part of Ecuador. Most westerly point of
South America.

Galapagos Rise sea feature Pacific Ocean
151 N6
Galashiels U.K. 50 G5
Galaţi Romania 59 M2
Galatina Italy 58 H4
Gala Water r. U.K. 50 G5
Galax U.S.A. 134 E5
Galaymor Turkm. see Kala-I-Mor
Galbally Rep. of Ireland 51 D5
Galdhøpiggen mt. Norway 45 F6
Galeana Chihuahua Mex. 127 G7
Galeana Nuevo León Mex. 131 C7
Galena AK U.S.A. 118 C3
Galena IL U.S.A. 130 F3
Galena MD U.S.A. 135 H4
Galena MO U.S.A. 131 E4
Galera, Punta pt Chile 144 B6
Galesburg IL U.S.A. 130 F3
Galesburg MI U.S.A. 134 C2
Galeshewe S. Africa 100 G5
Galeton U.S.A. 135 G3
Galey r. Rep. of Ireland 51 C5
Galheirão r. Brazil 145 B1
Galiano Island Canada 120 F5
Galich Rus. Fed. 42 I4
Galichskaya Vozvyshennost' hills
Rus. Fed. 42 I4
Galicia aut. comm. Spain 57 C2
Galičica nat. park Macedonia 59 I4
Galilee, Lake salt flat Australia 110 D4
Galilee, Sea of l. Israel 85 B3
Galion U.S.A. 134 D3
Galiuro Mountains U.S.A. 129 H5
Galizia aut. comm. Spain see Galicia
Gallabat Sudan 86 E7
Gallatin MO U.S.A. 130 E4
Gallatin TN U.S.A. 134 B5
Galle Sri Lanka 84 D5
Gallego Rise sea feature Pacific Ocean
151 M6
Gallegos r. Arg. 144 C8
Gallia country Europe see France

▶Gallinas, Punta pt Col. 142 D1
Most northerly point of South America.

Gallipoli Italy 58 H4
Gallipoli Turkey 59 L4
Gallipolis U.S.A. 134 D4
Gällivare Sweden 44 L3
Gällö Sweden 44 I5
Gallo Island U.S.A. 135 G2
Gallo Mountains U.S.A. 129 I4
Gallup U.S.A. 129 I4
Gallyaaral Uzbek. 89 G1
Galmisdale U.K. 50 C4
Galong Australia 112 D5
Galoya Sri Lanka 84 D4
Gal Oya National Park Sri Lanka 84 D5
Galston U.K. 50 E5
Galt U.S.A. 128 C2
Galtat Zemmour W. Sahara 96 B2
Galtee Mountains hills Rep. of Ireland
51 D5
Galtymore hill Rep. of Ireland 46 C4
Galūgāh, Kūh-e mts Iran 88 D4
Galveston IN U.S.A. 134 B3
Galveston TX U.S.A. 131 E6
Galveston Bay U.S.A. 131 E6
Galwa Nepal 83 E3
Galway Rep. of Ireland 51 C4
Galway Bay Rep. of Ireland 51 C4
Gâm r. Vietnam 70 D2
Gamalakhe S. Africa 101 J6
Gamba China 83 G3
Gamba Gabon 98 A4
Gambēla Eth. 98 D3
Gambēla National Park Eth. 98 D3
Gambell U.S.A. 118 A3
Gambella Eth. see Gambēla
▶Gambia, The country Africa 96 B3
Africa 7, 94–95
Gambier, Îles is Fr. Polynesia 147 L7
Gambier Islands Australia 111 B7
Gambier Islands Fr. Polynesia see
Gambier, Îles
Gambo Canada 123 L4
Gamboma Congo 98 B4
Gamboola Australia 110 C3
Gamboula Cent. Afr. Rep. 98 B3
Gamda China see Zamtang
Gamlakarleby Fin. see Kokkola
Gamleby Sweden 45 J8
Gammelstaden Sweden 44 M4
Gammon Ranges National Park Australia
111 B6
Gamova, Mys pt Rus. Fed. 74 C4
Gamshadzai Kūh mts Iran 89 F4
Gamtog China 76 C2
Gamud mt. Eth. 98 D3
Gana China 76 D1
Ganado U.S.A. 129 I4
Gananoque Canada 135 G1
Ganāveh Iran 88 C4
Gäncä Azer. 91 G2
Gancheng China 77 F5
Ganda Angola 99 B5
Gandaingoin China 83 G3
Gandajika Dem. Rep. Congo 99 C4
Gandak Dam Nepal 83 E4
Gandari Mountain Pak. 89 H4
Gandava Pak. 89 G4
Gander Canada 123 L4
Ganderkesee Germany 53 I1
Gandesa Spain 57 G3
Gandhidham India 82 B5
Gandhinagar India 82 C5
Gandhi Sagar resr India 82 C4
Gandía Spain 57 F4
Gandzha Azer. see Gäncä
Ganga r. Bangl./India 83 G5 see Ganges
Ganga Cone sea feature Indian Ocean see
Ganges Cone
Gangán Arg. 144 C6
Ganganagar India 82 C3
Gangapur India 82 D4
Ganga Sera India 82 B4
Gangaw Myanmar 70 A2
Gangawati India 84 C3
Gangaw Range mts Myanmar 70 B2
Gangca China 80 J4
Gangdisê Shan mts China 83 E3
Ganges r. Bangl./India 83 G5
also known as Ganga
Ganges France 56 F5
Ganges, Mouths of the Bangl./India
83 G5
Ganges Cone sea feature Indian Ocean
149 N4
Gangouyi China 72 J5
Gangra Turkey see Çankırı
Gangtok India 83 G4
Gangu China 76 E1
Gani Indon. 69 H7
Gan Jiang r. China 77 H2
Ganjig China 73 M4
Ganluo China 76 D2
Ganmain Australia 112 C5
Gannan China 74 A3
Gannat France 56 F3
Gannett Peak U.S.A. 126 F4
Gänq China 80 H4
Ganshui China 76 E2
Gansu prov. China 76 D1
Gantheaume Point Australia 108 C4
Gantsevichi Belarus see Hantsavichy
Ganxian China 77 G3
Ganye Nigeria 96 E4
Ganyu China 77 H1
Ganyushkino Kazakh. 41 P6
Ganzhou China 77 G3
Ganzi Sudan 97 G4
Gao Mali 96 C3
Gaocheng China see Litang
Gaocun China see Mayang
Gaohe China see Huaining
Gaohebu China see Huaining
Gaoleshan China see Xianfeng
Gaoliangjian China see Hongze
Gaomutang China 77 F3
Gaoping China 77 G1
Gaotai China 80 I4
Gaoting China see Daishan
Gaotingzhen China see Daishan
Gaoua Burkina 96 C3
Gaoual Guinea 96 B3
Gaoxiong Taiwan see Kaohsiung
Gaoyao China see Zhaoqing
Gaoyou China 77 H1
Gaoyou Hu l. China 77 H1
Gap France 56 H4
Gap Carbon hd Alg. 57 F6
Gapuwiyak Australia 110 A2
Gaqoi China 83 E3
Gar China 82 E2
Gar Pak. 89 F5
Gar' r. Rus. Fed. 74 C1
Gara, Lough l. Rep. of Ireland 51 D4
Garabekevyul Turkm. 89 G2
Garabekewül Turkm. see Garabekevyul
Garabil Belentligi hills Turkm. see
Karabil', Vozvyshennost'
Garabogaz Aylagy b. Turkm. see
Kara-Bogaz-Gol, Zaliv
Garabogazköl Aylagy b. Turkm. see
Kara-Bogaz-Gol, Zaliv
Garabogazköl Bogazy sea chan. Turkm.
see Kara-Bogaz-Gol, Proliv
Garāgheh Iran 89 F4
Garagum des. Turkm. see Kara Kumy
Garagum des. Turkm. see Karakum Desert
Garagum Kanaly canal Turkm. see
Karakumskiy Kanal
Garah Australia 112 D2
Garalo Mali 96 C3
Garamätnyýaz Turkm. see Karamet-Niyaz
Garamba r. Dem. Rep. Congo 98 C3
Garanhuns Brazil 143 K5
Ga-Rankuwa S. Africa 101 H3
Garapuava Brazil 145 B2
Gárasavvon Sweden see Karesuando
Garautha India 82 D4
Garba China see Jiulong
Garbahaarey Somalia 98 E3
Garba Tula Kenya 98 D3
Garberville U.S.A. 128 B1
Garbo China see Lhozhag
Garbsen Germany 53 J2
Garça Brazil 145 A3
Garco China 83 G2
Garda, Lago di Italy see Garda, Lake
Garda, Lake Italy 58 D2
Garde, Cap de c. Alg. 58 B6
Gardelegen Germany 53 L2
Garden City U.S.A. 130 C4
Garden Hill Canada 121 M4
Garden Mountain U.S.A. 134 E5
Gardeyz Afgh. see Gardēz
Gardēz Afgh. 89 H3
Gardinas Belarus see Hrodna
Gardiner U.S.A. 135 K1
Gardiner, Mount Australia 108 F5
Gardiner Range hills Australia 108 E4
Gardiners Island U.S.A. 135 I3
Gardīz Afgh. see Gardēz
Gardner atoll Micronesia see Faraulep
Gardner U.S.A. 135 J2
Gardner Inlet Antarctica 152 L1
Gardner Island atoll Kiribati see
Nikumaroro
Gardner Pinnacles is U.S.A. 150 I4
Gáregasnjárga Fin. see Karigasniemi
Garelochhead U.K. 50 E4
Garet El Djenoun mt. Alg. 96 D2
Gargano, Parco Nazionale del nat. park
Italy 58 F4
Gargantua, Cape Canada 122 D5
Gargunsa China see Gar
Gargždai Lith. 45 L9
Garhchiroli India see Gadchiroli
Garhi Madhya Pradesh India 84 C1
Garhi Rajasthan India 82 C5
Garhi Ikhtiar Khan Pak. 89 H4
Garhi Khairo Pak. 89 G4
Garhwa India 83 E4
Gari Rus. Fed. 41 S4
Gariau Indon. 69 I7
Garibaldi, Mount Canada 120 F5
Gariep Dam resr S. Africa 101 G6
Garies S. Africa 100 C6
Garigliano r. Italy 58 E4
Garissa Kenya 98 D4
Garkalne Latvia 45 N8
Garkung Caka l. China 83 F2
Garland U.S.A. 131 D5
Garm Tajik. see Gharm
Garm Āb Iran 89 E3
Garmab Iran 88 E3
Garmī Iran 88 C2
Garmsar Iran 88 D3
Garmsel reg. Afgh. 89 F4
Garner IA U.S.A. 130 E3
Garner KY U.S.A. 134 D5
Garnett U.S.A. 130 E4
Garnpung Lake imp. l. Australia 112 A4
Garo Hills India 83 G4
Garonne r. France 56 D4
Garoowe Somalia 98 E3
Garopaba Brazil 145 A5
Garoua Cameroon 96 E4
Garoua Boulai Cameroon 97 E4
Garqêntang China see Sog
Garré Arg. 144 D5
Garrett U.S.A. 134 C3
Garrison U.S.A. 130 E2
Garruk Pak. 89 G4
Garry r. U.K. 50 E3
Garrychyrla Turkm. see
imeni Kerbabayeva
Garry Lake Canada 121 K1
Garrynahine U.K. 50 C2
Garsen Kenya 98 E4
Garshy Turkm. see Karshi
Garsila Sudan 97 F3
Gartar China see Qianning
Garth U.K. 49 D6
Gartog China see Markam
Gartok China see Garyarsa
Gartow Germany 53 L1
Garub Namibia 100 C4
Garvagh U.K. 51 F3
Garve U.K. 50 E3
Garwa India see Garhwa
Garwha India see Garhwa
Gar Xincun China 82 E2
Gary IN U.S.A. 134 B3
Gary WV U.S.A. 134 E5
Garyarsa China 82 E3
Garyi China 76 C2
Garyū-zan mt. Japan 75 D6
Garza García Mex. 131 C7
Garzê China 76 C2
Gasan-Kuli Turkm. see Esenguly
Gasan-Kuliyskiy Zapovednik nature res.
Turkm. 88 D2
Gas City U.S.A. 134 C3
Gascogne reg. France see Gascony
Gascogne, Golfe de g. France see
Gascony, Gulf of
Gascony reg. France 56 D5
Gascony, Gulf of France 56 C5
Gascoyne r. Australia 109 A6
Gascoyne Junction Australia 109 A6
Gasherbrum I mt.
China/Jammu and Kashmir 82 D2
Gashua Nigeria 96 E3
Gask Iran 89 E3
Gaspar Cuba 133 E8
Gaspar, Selat sea chan. Indon. 68 D7
Gaspé Canada 123 I4
Gaspé, Cap c. Canada 123 I4
Gaspé, Péninsule de pen. Canada 123 I4
Gassan vol. Japan 75 F5
Gassaway U.S.A. 134 E4
Gasselte Neth. 52 G2
Gasteiz Spain see Vitoria-Gasteiz
Gastello Rus. Fed. 74 F2
Gaston U.S.A. 135 G5
Gaston, Lake U.S.A. 135 G5
Gastonia U.S.A. 133 D5
Gata, Cabo de c. Spain 57 E5
Gata, Cape Cyprus 85 A2
Gata, Sierra de mts Spain 57 C3
Gataga r. Canada 120 E3
Gatas, Akra c. Cyprus see Gata, Cape
Gatchina Rus. Fed. 45 Q7
Gate City U.S.A. 134 D5
Gatehouse of Fleet U.K. 50 E6
Gatentiri Indon. 69 K8
Gateshead U.K. 48 F4
Gates of the Arctic National Park and
Preserve U.S.A. 118 C3
Gatesville U.S.A. 131 D6
Gateway U.S.A. 129 I2
Gatineau Canada 135 H1
Gatineau r. Canada 122 G5
Gatong China see Jomda
Gatooma Zimbabwe see Kadoma
Gatton Australia 112 F1
Gatvand Iran 88 C3
Gatyana S. Africa see Willowvale
Gau i. Fiji 107 H3
Gauer Lake Canada 121 L3
Gauhati India see Guwahati
Gaujas nacionālais parks nat. park Latvia
45 N8
Gaul country Europe see France
Gaula r. Norway 44 G5
Gaume reg. Belgium 52 F5
Gaurama Brazil 145 A4
Gauribidanur India 84 C3
Gauteng prov. S. Africa 101 I4
Gavarr Armenia see Kamo
Gāvbandī Iran 88 D5
Gāvbūs, Kūh-e mts Iran 88 D5

▶Gavdos i. Greece 59 K7
Most southerly point of Europe.

Gavião r. Brazil 145 C1
Gavīleh Iran 88 B3
Gav Khūnī Iran 88 D3
Gävle Sweden 45 J6
Gavrilovka Vtoraya Rus. Fed. 43 I5
Gavrilov-Yam Rus. Fed. 42 H4
Gawachab Namibia 100 C4
Gawai Myanmar 76 C3
Gawan India 83 F4
Gawilgarh Hills India 82 D5
Gawler Australia 111 B7
Gawler Ranges hills Australia 111 A7
Gaxun Nur salt l. China 80 J3
Gaya India 83 F4
Gaya Niger 96 D3
Gaya He r. China 74 C4
Gayéri Burkina 96 D3
Gaylord U.S.A. 134 C1
Gayndah Australia 111 E5
Gayny Rus. Fed. 42 L3
Gaysin Ukr. see Haysyn
Gayutino Rus. Fed. 42 H4
Gaz Iran 88 C3

▶Gaza terr. Asia 85 B4
Semi-autonomous region.
Asia 6

▶Gaza Gaza 85 B4
Capital of Gaza.

Gaza prov. Moz. 101 K2
Gazan Pak. 89 G4
Gazandzhyk Turkm. 88 D2
Gazanjyk Turkm. see Gazandzhyk
Gaza Strip terr. Asia see Gaza
Gaziantep Turkey 90 E3
Gaziantep prov. Turkey 85 C1
Gazibenli Turkey see Yahyalı
Gazīk Iran 89 F3
Gazimağusa Cyprus see Famagusta
Gazimurskiy Khrebet mts Rus. Fed. 73 L2
Gazimurskiy Zavod Rus. Fed. 73 L2
Gazipaşa Turkey 85 A1
Gazli Uzbek. 89 F1
Gaz Māhū Iran 88 E5
Gbarnga Liberia 96 C4
Gboko Nigeria 96 D4
Gcuwa S. Africa see Butterworth
Gdańsk Poland 47 Q3
Gdańsk, Gulf of Poland/Rus. Fed. 47 Q3
Gdańska, Zatoka g. Poland/Rus. Fed. see
Gdańsk, Gulf of
Gdingen Poland see Gdynia
Gdov Rus. Fed. 45 O7
Gdynia Poland 47 Q3
Gearhart Mountain U.S.A. 126 C4
Gearraidh na h-Aibhne U.K. see
Garrynahine
Gebe i. Indon. 69 H6
Gebesee Germany 53 K3
Geçitkale Cyprus see Lefkonikon
Gedaref Sudan 86 E7
Gedern Germany 53 J4
Gedinne Belgium 52 E5
Gediz r. Turkey 59 L5
Gedney Drove End U.K. 49 H6
Gedong, Tanjong pt Sing. 71 [inset]
Gedser Denmark 45 G9
Geel Belgium 52 F3
Geelong Australia 112 B7
Geelvink Channel Australia 109 A7
Geel Vloer salt pan S. Africa 100 E5
Gees Gwardafuy c. Somalia see
Gwardafuy, Gees
Geeste Germany 53 H2
Geesthacht Germany 53 K1
Ge Hu l. China 77 H2
Geidam Nigeria 96 E3
Geiersberg hill Germany 53 J5
Geikie r. Canada 121 K3
Geilenkirchen Germany 52 G4
Geilo Norway 45 F6
Geiranger Norway 44 E5
Geislingen an der Steige Germany 53 J6
Geisûm, Gezâ'ir is Egypt see
Qaysūm, Juzur
Geita Tanz. 98 D4
Geithain Germany 53 M3
Gejiu China 76 D4
Gekdepe Turkm. 88 E2
Gela Sicily Italy 58 F6
Gêladaindong mt. China 83 G2
Geladī Eth. 98 E3
Gelang, Tanjung pt Malaysia 71 C7
Geldern Germany 52 G3
Gelendzhik Rus. Fed. 90 E1
Gelephu Bhutan 83 G4
Gelibolu Turkey see Gallipoli
Gelidonya Burnu pt Turkey see
Yardımcı Burnu
Gelincik Dağı mt. Turkey 59 N5
Gelmord Iran 88 E3
Gelnhausen Germany 53 J4
Gelsenkirchen Germany 52 H3
Gemas Malaysia 71 C7
Gemena Dem. Rep. Congo 98 B3
Geminokağı Cyprus see
Karavostasi
Gemlik Turkey 59 M4
Gemona del Friuli Italy 58 E1
Gemsa Egypt see Jamsah
Gemsbok National Park Botswana 100 E3
Gemsbokplein well S. Africa 100 E4
Genalē Wenz r. Eth. 98 E3
Genappe Belgium 52 E4
General Acha Arg. 144 D5
General Alvear Arg. 144 C5
General Belgrano II research station
Antarctica see Belgrano II
General Bernardo O'Higgins
research station Antarctica 152 A2
General Bravo Mex. 131 D7

▶General Carrera, Lago l. Arg./Chile
144 B7
Deepest lake in South America.

General Conesa Arg. 144 D6
General Freire Angola see Muxaluando
General Juan Madariaga Arg. 144 E5
General La Madrid Arg. 144 D5
General Machado Angola see Camacupa
General Pico Arg. 144 D5
General Pinedo Arg. 144 D3
General Roca Arg. 144 C5
General Salgado Brazil 145 A3
General San Martín research station
Antarctica see San Martín
General Santos Phil. 69 H5
General Simón Bolívar Mex. 131 C7
General Trías Mex. 127 G7
General Villegas Arg. 144 D5
Genesee U.S.A. 135 G3
Geneseo U.S.A. 135 G2
Geneva S. Africa 101 H4
Geneva Switz. 56 H3
Geneva AL U.S.A. 133 C6
Geneva IL U.S.A. 134 A3
Geneva NE U.S.A. 130 D3
Geneva NY U.S.A. 135 G2
Geneva OH U.S.A. 134 E3
Geneva, Lake France/Switz. 56 H3
Genève Switz. see Geneva
Genf Switz. see Geneva
Gengda China see Gana
Gengma China 76 C4
Gengxuan China see Gengma
Genhe China 74 A2
Genichesk Ukr. see Heniches'k
Genji India 82 C5
Genk Belgium 52 F4
Gennep Neth. 52 F3
Genoa Australia 112 D6
Genoa Italy 58 C2
Genoa, Gulf of Italy 58 C2
Genova Italy see Genoa
Genova, Golfo di Italy see Genoa, Gulf of
Gent Belgium see Ghent
Genthin Germany 53 M2
Gentioux, Plateau de France 56 F4
Genua Italy see Genoa
Geographe Bay Australia 109 A8
Geographical Society Ø i. Greenland
119 P2
Geok-Tepe Turkm. see Gekdepe
Georga, Zemlya i. Rus. Fed. 64 F1
George r. Canada 123 I2
George S. Africa 100 F7
George, Lake Australia 112 D5
George, Lake FL U.S.A. 133 D6
George, Lake NY U.S.A. 135 I2
George Land i. Rus. Fed. see
Georga, Zemlya
Georges Mills U.S.A. 135 I2
George Sound inlet N.Z. 113 A7
Georgetown Australia 110 C3

▶George Town Cayman Is 137 H5
Capital of the Cayman Islands.

Georgetown Gambia 96 B3

▶Georgetown Guyana 143 G2
Capital of Guyana.

George Town Malaysia 71 C6
Georgetown DE U.S.A. 135 H4
Georgetown GA U.S.A. 133 C6
Georgetown IL U.S.A. 134 B4
Georgetown KY U.S.A. 134 C4
Georgetown OH U.S.A. 134 D4
Georgetown SC U.S.A. 133 E5
Georgetown TX U.S.A. 131 D6
George VI Sound sea chan. Antarctica
152 L2
George V Land reg. Antarctica 152 G2
George West U.S.A. 131 D6
▶Georgia country Asia 91 F2
Asia 6, 62–63
Georgia state U.S.A. 133 D5
Georgia, Strait of Canada 120 E5
Georgiana U.S.A. 131 G6
Georgian Bay Canada 134 E1
Georgian Bay Islands National Park
Canada 134 F1
Georgienne, Baie b. Canada see
Georgian Bay
Georgina watercourse Australia 110 B5
Georgiu-Dezh Rus. Fed. see Liski
Georgiyevka Vostochnyy Kazakhstan
Kazakh. 80 F2
Georgiyevka Zhambylskaya Oblast'
Kazakh. see Korday
Georgiyevsk Rus. Fed. 91 F1
Georgiyevskoye Rus. Fed. 42 J4
Georg von Neumayer research station
Antarctica see Neumayer
Gera Germany 53 M4
Geraardsbergen Belgium 52 D4
Geral, Serra mts Brazil 145 A4
Geral de Goiás, Serra hills Brazil 145 B1
Geraldine N.Z. 113 C7
Geral do Paraná, Serra hills Brazil 145 B1
Geraldton Australia 109 A7
Gerar watercourse Israel 85 B4
Gerber U.S.A. 128 B1
Gercüş Turkey 91 F3
Gerede Turkey 90 D2
Gereshk Afgh. 89 G4
Gerik Malaysia 71 C6
Gerlach U.S.A. 128 D1
Gerlachovský štít mt. Slovakia 47 R6
Germaine, Lac l. Canada 123 I3
Germania country Europe see Germany
Germanicea Turkey see Kahramanmaraş
Germansen Landing Canada 120 E4
German South-West Africa country Africa
see Namibia
Germantown OH U.S.A. 134 C4
Germantown WI U.S.A. 134 A2

▶Germany country Europe 47 L5
2nd most populous country in Europe.
Europe 5, 38–39

Germersheim Germany 53 I5
Gernsheim Germany 53 I5
Gerolstein Germany 52 G4
Gerolzhofen Germany 53 K5
Gerona Spain see Girona
Gerrit Denys is P.N.G. see Lihir Group
Gers r. France 56 E4
Gersfeld (Rhön) Germany 53 J4
Gersoppa India 84 B3
Gerstungen Germany 53 K4
Gerwisch Germany 53 L2
Géryville Alg. see El Bayadh
Gêrzê China 83 F2
Gerze Turkey 90 D2
Gescher Germany 52 H3
Gesoriacum France see
Boulogne-sur-Mer
Gessie U.S.A. 134 B3
Gete r. Belgium 52 F4
Gettysburg PA U.S.A. 135 G4
Gettysburg SD U.S.A. 130 D2
Gettysburg National Military Park
nat. park U.S.A. 135 G4
Getz Ice Shelf Antarctica 152 J2
Geumpang Indon. 71 B6
Geureudong, Gunung vol. Indon. 71 B6
Geurie Australia 112 D4
Gevaş Turkey 91 F3
Gevgelija Macedonia 59 J4
Gexto Spain see Algorta
Gey Iran see Nīkshahr
Geyikli Turkey 59 L5
Geysdorp S. Africa 101 G4
Geyserville U.S.A. 128 B2
Geyve Turkey 59 N4
Gezīr Iran 88 D5
Ghaap Plateau S. Africa 100 F4
Ghāb, Wādī al r. Syria 85 C2
Ghabāghib Syria 85 C3
Ghabeish Sudan 86 C7
Ghadaf, Wādī al watercourse Jordan 85 C4
Ghadamés Libya see Ghadāmis
Ghadāmis Libya 96 D1
Ghaem Shahr Iran 88 D2
Ghaghara r. India 83 F4
Ghaibi Dero Pak. 89 G5
Ghalend Iran 89 F4
Ghalkarteniz, Solonchak salt marsh
Kazakh. 80 B2
Ghallaorol Uzbek. see Gallyaaral
▶Ghana country Africa 96 C4
Africa 7, 94–95
Ghanādah, Rās pt U.A.E. 88 D5

Ghantila India 82 B5
Ghanwā Saudi Arabia 86 G4
Ghanzi Botswana 99 C6
Ghanzi admin. dist. Botswana 100 F2
Ghap'an Armenia see Kapan
Ghardaïa Alg. 54 E5
Gharghoda India 84 D1
Ghârib, Gebel mt. Egypt see Ghārib, Jabal
Ghārib, Jabal mt. Egypt 90 D5
Gharm Tajik. 89 H2
Gharq Ābād Iran 88 C3
Gharwa India see Garhwa
Gharyān Libya 97 E1
Ghāt Libya 96 E2
Ghatgan India 83 F5
Ghatol India 82 C5
Ghawdex i. Malta see Gozo
Ghazal, Bahr el watercourse Chad 97 E3
Ghazaouet Alg. 57 F6
Ghaziabad India 82 D3
Ghazi Ghat Pak. 89 H4
Ghazipur India 83 E4
Ghazna Afgh. see Ghaznī
Ghaznī Afgh. 89 H3
Ghazni r. Afgh. 89 G3
Ghazoor Afgh. 89 G3
Ghazzah Gaza see Gaza
Ghebar Gumbad Iran 88 E3
Ghent Belgium 52 D3
Gheorghe Gheorghiu-Dej Romania see Onești
Gheorgheni Romania 59 K1
Gherla Romania 59 J1
Ghijduwon Uzbek. see Gizhduvan
Ghilzai reg. Afgh. 89 G4
Ghīnah, Wādī al watercourse Saudi Arabia 85 D4
Ghisonaccia Corsica France 56 I5
Ghorak Afgh. 89 G3
Ghost Lake Canada 120 H2
Ghotaru India 82 B4
Ghotki Pak. 89 H5
Ghuari r. India 83 F4
Ghudamis Libya see Ghadāmis
Ghurayfah hill Saudi Arabia 85 C4
Ghūrī Iran 88 D4
Ghurian Afgh. 89 F3
Ghurrab, Jabal hill Saudi Arabia 88 B5
Ghuzor Uzbek. see Guzar
Ghyvelde France 52 C3
Gia Đinh Vietnam 71 D5
Giaginskaya Rus. Fed. 91 F1
Gialias r. Cyprus 85 A2
Gia Nghia Vietnam 71 D4
Giannitsa Greece 59 J4
Giant's Castle mt. S. Africa 101 I5
Giant's Causeway lava field U.K. 51 F2
Gianysada i. Greece 59 L7
Gia Rai Vietnam 71 D5
Giarre Sicily Italy 58 F6
Gibb r. Australia 108 D3
Gibbonsville U.S.A. 126 E3
Gibeon Namibia 100 C3
Gibraltar terr. Europe 57 D5

▶**Gibraltar** Gibraltar 148 H3
United Kingdom Overseas Territory.
Europe 5, 38–39

Gibraltar, Strait of Morocco/Spain 57 C6
Gibraltar Range National Park Australia 112 F2
Gibson Australia 109 C8
Gibson City U.S.A. 134 A3
Gibson Desert Australia 109 C6
Gichgeniyn Nuruu mts Mongolia 80 H2
Gidar Pak. 89 G4
Giddalur India 84 C3
Gîddi, Gebel el hill Egypt see Jiddī, Jabal al
Giddings U.S.A. 131 D6
Gīdolē Eth. 97 G4
Gien France 56 F3
Gießen Germany 53 I4
Gīfan Iran 88 E2
Gifford r. Canada 119 J2
Gifhorn Germany 53 K2
Gift Lake Canada 120 H4
Gifu Japan 75 E6
Giganta, Cerro mt. Mex. 127 F8
Gigha i. U.K. 50 D5
Gīgīga Eth. see Jijiga
Gijón Spain see Gijón-Xixón
Gijón-Xixón Spain 57 D2
Gila r. U.S.A. 129 F5
Gila Bend U.S.A. 129 G5
Gila Bend Mountains U.S.A. 129 G5
Gīlān-e Gharb Iran 88 B3
Gilbert r. Australia 110 C3
Gilbert AZ U.S.A. 129 H5
Gilbert WV U.S.A. 134 E5
Gilbert Islands Kiribati 150 H5
Gilbert Islands country Pacific Ocean see Kiribati
Gilbert Peak U.S.A. 129 H1
Gilbert Ridge sea feature Pacific Ocean 150 H6
Gilbert River Australia 110 C3
Gilbués Brazil 143 I5
Gil Chashmeh Iran 88 E3
Gilé Moz. 99 D5
Giles Creek r. Australia 108 E4
Gilford Island Canada 120 E5
Gilgai Australia 112 E2
Gilgandra Australia 112 D3
Gil Gil Creek r. Australia 112 D2
Gilgit Jammu and Kashmir 82 C2
Gilgit r. Jammu and Kashmir 87 L2
Gilgunnia Australia 112 C4
Gilındire Turkey see Aydıncık
Gillam Canada 121 M3
Gillen, Lake salt flat Australia 109 D6
Gilles, Lake salt flat Australia 111 B7
Gillett U.S.A. 135 G3
Gillette U.S.A. 126 G3
Gilliat Australia 110 C4
Gillingham England U.K. 49 E7
Gillingham England U.K. 49 H7
Gilling West U.K. 48 F4
Gilman U.S.A. 134 B3
Gilmer U.S.A. 131 E5
Gilmour Island Canada 122 F2
Gilroy U.S.A. 128 C3
Gīmbī Eth. 98 D3
Gimhae S. Korea see Kimhae
Gimli Canada 121 L5
Gimol'skoye, Ozero l. Rus. Fed. 42 G3
Ginebra, Laguna l. Bol. 142 E6
Gineifa Egypt see Junayfah
Gin Gin Australia 110 E5
Gingin Australia 109 A7
Gīnīr Eth. 98 E3
Ginosa Italy 58 G4
Ginzo de Limia Spain see Xinzo de Limia
Gioia del Colle Italy 58 G4
Gipouloux r. Canada 122 G3
Gippsland reg. Australia 112 B7
Girâ, Wâdi watercourse Egypt see Jirā', Wādī
Gīrān Rīg mt. Iran 88 E4
Girard U.S.A. 134 E2
Girardin, Lac l. Canada 123 I2
Girdab Iran 88 E3
Giresun Turkey 90 E2
Girgenti Sicily Italy see Agrigento
Giridh India see Giridih
Giridih India 83 F4
Girilambone Australia 112 C3
Girna r. India 82 C5
Gir National Park India 82 B5
Girne Cyprus see Kyrenia
Girón Ecuador 142 C4
Giron Sweden see Kiruna
Girona Spain 57 H3
Gironde est. France 56 D4
Girot Pak. 89 I3
Girral Australia 112 C4
Girraween National Park Australia 112 E2
Girvan U.K. 50 E5
Girvas Rus. Fed. 42 G3
Gisborne N.Z. 113 G4
Giscome Canada 120 F4
Gislaved Sweden 45 H8
Gisors France 52 B5
Gissar Tajik. see Hisor
Gissar Range mts Tajik./Uzbek. 89 G2
Gissarskiy Khrebet mts Tajik./Uzbek. see Gissar Range
Gitarama Rwanda 98 C4
Gitega Burundi 98 C4
Giuba r. Somalia see Jubba
Giulianova Italy 58 E3
Giurgiu Romania 59 K3
Giuvala, Pasul pass Romania 59 K2
Givar Iran 88 E2
Givet France 52 E4
Givors France 56 G4
Givry-en-Argonne France 52 E6
Giyani S. Africa 101 J2
Giza Egypt 90 C5
Gizhduvan Uzbek. 89 G1
Gizhiga Rus. Fed. 65 R3
Gjakovë Serb. and Mont. see Đakovica
Gjilan Serb. and Mont. see Gnjilane
Gjirokastër Albania 59 I4
Gjirokastra Albania see Gjirokastër
Gjoa Haven Canada 119 I3
Gjøra Norway 44 F5
Gjøvik Norway 45 G6
Glace Bay Canada 123 K5
Glacier Bay National Park and Preserve U.S.A. 120 B3
Glacier National Park Canada 120 G5
Glacier National Park U.S.A. 126 E2
Glacier Peak vol. U.S.A. 126 C2
Gladstad Norway 44 G4
Gladstone Australia 110 E4
Gladstone Canada 121 L5
Gladwin U.S.A. 134 C2
Gladys U.S.A. 134 F5
Gladys Lake Canada 120 C3
Glamis U.K. 50 F4
Glamis U.S.A. 129 F5
Glamoč Bos.-Herz. 58 G2
Glan r. Germany 53 H5
Glandorf Germany 53 I2
Glanton U.K. 48 F3
Glasgow U.K. 50 E5
Glasgow KY U.S.A. 134 C5
Glasgow MT U.S.A. 126 G2
Glasgow VA U.S.A. 134 F5
Glaslyn Canada 121 I4
Glass, Loch l. U.K. 50 E3
Glass Mountain U.S.A. 128 D3
Glastonbury U.K. 49 E7
Glauchau Germany 53 M4
Glazov Rus. Fed. 42 L4
Gleiwitz Poland see Gliwice
Glen U.S.A. 135 J1
Glen Allen U.S.A. 135 G5
Glen Alpine Dam S. Africa 101 I2
Glenamaddy Rep. of Ireland 51 D4
Glenamoy r. Rep. of Ireland 51 C3
Glen Arbor U.S.A. 134 C1
Glenbawn Reservoir Australia 112 E4
Glenboro Canada 121 L5
Glen Canyon gorge U.S.A. 129 H3
Glen Canyon Dam U.S.A. 129 H3
Glencoe Canada 134 E2
Glencoe S. Africa 101 J5
Glencoe U.S.A. 130 E2
Glendale AZ U.S.A. 129 G5
Glendale CA U.S.A. 128 D4
Glendale UT U.S.A. 129 G3
Glendale Lake U.S.A. 135 F3
Glen Davis Australia 112 E4
Glenden Australia 110 E4
Glendive U.S.A. 126 G3
Glendon Canada 121 I4
Glendo Reservoir U.S.A. 126 G4
Glenfield U.S.A. 135 H2
Glengavlen Rep. of Ireland 51 E3
Glengyle Australia 110 B5
Glen Innes Australia 112 E2
Glenluce U.K. 50 E6
Glen Lyon U.S.A. 135 G3
Glenlyon Peak Canada 120 C2
Glen More valley U.K. 50 E3
Glenmorgan Australia 112 D1
Glenn U.S.A. 128 B2
Glennallen U.S.A. 118 D3
Glennie U.S.A. 134 D1
Glenns Ferry U.S.A. 126 E4
Glenora Canada 120 D3
Glenore Australia 110 C3
Glenormiston Australia 110 B4
Glenreagh Australia 112 F3
Glen Rose U.S.A. 131 D5
Glenrothes U.K. 50 F4
Glens Falls U.S.A. 135 I2
Glen Shee valley U.K. 50 F4
Glenties Rep. of Ireland 51 D3
Glenveagh National Park Rep. of Ireland 51 E2
Glenville U.S.A. 134 E4
Glenwood AR U.S.A. 131 E5
Glenwood IA U.S.A. 130 E3
Glenwood MN U.S.A. 130 E2
Glenwood NM U.S.A. 129 I5
Glenwood Springs U.S.A. 129 J2
Glevum U.K. see Gloucester
Glinde Germany 53 K1
Glittertinden mt. Norway 45 F6
Gliwice Poland 47 Q5
Globe U.S.A. 129 H5
Glogau Poland see Głogów
Głogów Poland 47 P5
Glomfjord Norway 44 H3
Glomma r. Norway 44 G7
Glommersträsk Sweden 44 K4
Glorieuses, Îles is Indian Ocean 99 E5
Glorioso Islands Indian Ocean see Glorieuses, Îles
Gloster U.S.A. 131 F6
Gloucester Australia 112 E3
Gloucester U.K. 49 E7
Gloucester MA U.S.A. 135 J2
Gloucester VA U.S.A. 135 G5
Gloversville U.S.A. 135 H2
Glovertown Canada 123 L4
Glöwen Germany 53 M2
Glubinnoye Rus. Fed. 74 D3
Glubokiy Krasnoyarskiy Kray Rus. Fed. 72 H2
Glubokiy Rostovskaya Oblast' Rus. Fed. 43 I6
Glubokoye Belarus see Hlybokaye
Glubokoye Kazakh. 80 F1
Gluggarnir hill Faroe Is 44 [inset]
Glukhov Ukr. see Hlukhiv
Glusburn U.K. 48 F5
Glynebwy U.K. see Ebbw Vale
Gmelinka Rus. Fed. 43 J6
Gmünd Austria 47 O6
Gmunden Austria 47 N7
Gnarp Sweden 45 J5
Gnarrenburg Germany 53 J1
Gnesen Poland see Gniezno
Gniezno Poland 47 P4
Gnjilane Serb. and Mont. 59 I3
Gnowangerup Australia 109 B8
Gnows Nest Range hills Australia 109 B7
Goa India 84 B3
Goa state India 84 B3
Goageb Namibia 100 C4
Goalen Head hd Australia 112 E6
Goalpara India 83 G4
Goat Fell hill U.K. 50 D5
Goba Eth. 98 E3
Gobabis Namibia 100 D2
Gobannium U.K. see Abergavenny
Gobas Namibia 100 D4
Gobi des. China/Mongolia 72 J4
Gobindpur India 83 F5
Gobles U.S.A. 134 C2
Gobō Japan 75 D6
Goch Germany 52 G3
Gochas Namibia 100 D3
Go Công Vietnam 71 D5
Godalming U.K. 49 G7
Godavari r. India 84 D2
Godavari, Cape India 84 D2
Godda India 83 F4
Godē Eth. 98 E3
Godere Eth. 98 E3
Goderich Canada 134 E2
Goderville France 49 H9
Godhavn Greenland see Qeqertarsuaq
Godhra India 82 C5
Godia Creek b. India 89 H6
Gods r. Canada 121 M3
Gods Lake Canada 121 M4
God's Mercy, Bay of Canada 121 O2
Godthåb Greenland see Nuuk
Godwin-Austen, Mount China/Jammu and Kashmir see K2
Goedereede Neth. 52 D3
Goedgegun Swaziland see Nhlangano
Goegap Nature Reserve S. Africa 100 D5
Goélands, Lac aux l. Canada 123 J3
Goes Neth. 52 D3
Gogama Canada 122 E5
Gogebic Range hills U.S.A. 130 F2
Gogra r. India see Ghaghara
Goiana Brazil 143 L5
Goiandira Brazil 145 A2
Goianésia Brazil 145 A1
Goiânia Brazil 145 A2
Goiás Brazil 145 A1
Goiás state Brazil 145 A2
Goinsargoin China 76 C2
Goio-Erê Brazil 144 F2
Gojra Pak. 89 I4
Gokak India 84 B2
Gokarn India 84 B3
Gök Çay r. Turkey 85 A1
Gökçeada i. Turkey 59 K4
Gökdepe Turkm. see Gekdepe
Gökdere r. Turkey 85 A1
Goklenkuy, Solonchak salt l. Turkm. 88 E1
Gökova Körfezi b. Turkey 59 L6
Gokprosh Hills Pak. 89 F5
Göksun Turkey 90 E3
Goksu Parkı Turkey 85 A1
Gokteik Myanmar 70 B2
Gokwe Zimbabwe 99 C5
Gol Norway 45 F6
Golaghat India 83 H4
Golbāf Iran 88 E4
Gölbaşı Turkey 90 E3
Golconda U.S.A. 128 E1
Gölcük Turkey 59 M4
Gold U.S.A. 135 G3
Gołdap Poland 47 S3
Gold Beach U.S.A. 126 B4
Goldberg Germany 53 M1
Gold Coast country Africa see Ghana
Gold Coast Australia 112 F2
Golden U.S.A. 126 G5
Golden Bay N.Z. 113 D5
Goldendale U.S.A. 126 C3
Goldene Aue reg. Germany 53 K3
Golden Gate Highlands National Park S. Africa 101 I5
Golden Hinde mt. Canada 120 E5
Golden Lake Canada 135 G1
Golden Prairie Canada 121 I5
Goldenstedt Germany 53 I2
Goldfield U.S.A. 128 E3
Goldsand Lake Canada 121 K3
Goldsboro U.S.A. 133 E5
Goldstone Lake U.S.A. 128 E4
Goldsworthy Australia 108 B5
Goldthwaite U.S.A. 131 D6
Goldvein U.S.A. 135 G4
Göle Turkey 91 F2
Golestān Afgh. 89 F3
Goleta U.S.A. 128 D4
Golets-Davydov, Gora mt. Rus. Fed. 73 J2
Golfo di Orosei Gennargentu e Asinara, Parco Nazionale del nat. park Sardinia Italy 58 C4
Gölgeli Dağları mts Turkey 59 M6
Goliad U.S.A. 131 D6
Golingka China see Gongbo'gyamda
Gölköy Turkey 90 E2
Gollel Swaziland see Lavumisa
Golm Germany 53 M2
Golmberg hill Germany 53 N2
Golmud China 80 H4
Golovnino Rus. Fed. 74 G4
Golpāyegān Iran 88 C3
Gölpazarı Turkey 59 N4
Golspie U.K. 50 F3
Gol Vardeh Iran 89 F3
Golyama Syutkya mt. Bulg. 59 K4
Golyam Persenk mt. Bulg. 59 K4
Golyshi Rus. Fed. see Vetluzhskiy
Golzow Germany 53 M2
Goma Dem. Rep. Congo 98 C4
Gomang Co salt l. China 83 G3
Gomati r. India 87 N4
Gombak, Bukit hill Sing. 71 [inset]
Gombe Nigeria 96 E3
Gombe r. Tanz. 99 D4
Gombi Nigeria 96 E3
Gombroon Iran see Bandar-e 'Abbās
Gomel' Belarus see Homyel'
Gómez Palacio Mex. 131 C7
Gomīshān Iran 88 D2
Gommern Germany 53 L2
Gomo Co salt l. China 83 F2
Gonābād Iran 88 E2
Gonaïves Haiti 137 J5
Gonarezhou National Park Zimbabwe 99 D6
Gonbad-e Kavus Iran 88 D2
Gonda India 83 E4
Gondal India 82 B5
Gondar Eth. see Gonder
Gonder Eth. 98 D2
Gondia India 82 E5
Gondiya India see Gondia
Gönen Turkey 59 L4
Gonfreville-l'Orcher France 49 H9
Gong'an China 77 G2
Gongbalou China see Gamba
Gongbo'gyamda China 76 B2
Gongchang China see Longxi
Gongcheng China 77 F3
Gongga Shan mt. China 76 D2
Gonghe Qinghai China 80 J4
Gonghe Yunnan China see Mouding
Gongjiang China see Yudu
Gongogi r. Brazil 145 D1
Gongolgon Australia 112 C3
Gongpoquan China 80 I3
Gongquan China see Gongxian
Gongtang China see Damxung
Gongwang Shan mts China 76 D3
Gongxian China 76 E2
Gonjo China 76 C2
Gonjog China see Coqên
Gonzales CA U.S.A. 128 C3
Gonzales TX U.S.A. 131 D6
Gonzha Rus. Fed. 74 B1
Goochland U.S.A. 135 G5
Goodenough, Cape Antarctica 152 G2
Goodenough Island P.N.G. 106 F2
Gooderham Canada 135 F1
Good Hope, Cape of S. Africa 100 D8
Good Hope Mountain Canada 126 B2
Gooding U.S.A. 126 E4
Goodland IN U.S.A. 134 B3
Goodland KS U.S.A. 130 C4
Goodlettsville U.S.A. 134 B5
Goodooga Australia 112 C2
Goodspeed Nunataks Antarctica 152 E2
Goole U.K. 48 G5
Goolgowi Australia 112 B5
Goolma Australia 112 D4
Gooloogong Australia 112 D4
Goomalling Australia 109 B7
Goombalie Australia 112 B2
Goondiwindi Australia 112 E2
Goongarrie, Lake salt flat Australia 109 C7
Goongarrie National Park Australia 109 C7
Goonyella Australia 110 D4
Goorly, Lake salt flat Australia 109 B7
Goose Bay Canada see Happy Valley - Goose Bay
Goose Creek U.S.A. 133 D5
Goose Lake U.S.A. 126 C4
Gooty India 84 C3
Gopalganj Bangl. 83 G5
Gopalganj India 83 F4
Gopeshwar India 82 D3
Göppingen Germany 53 J6
Gorakhpur India 83 E4
Goražde Bos.-Herz. 58 H3
Gorbernador U.S.A. 129 J3
Gorczański Park Narodowy nat. park Poland 47 R6
Gorda, Punta pt U.S.A. 128 A1
Gördes Turkey 59 M5
Gordil Cent. Afr. Rep. 98 C3
Gordon r. Canada 121 O1
Gordon U.K. 50 G5
Gordon U.S.A. 130 C3
Gordon, Lake Australia 111 [inset]
Gordon Downs Australia 108 E4
Gordon Lake Canada 121 I3
Gordon Lake U.S.A. 135 F4
Gordonsville U.S.A. 135 F4
Goré Chad 97 E4
Gorē Eth. 98 D3
Gore N.Z. 113 B8
Gore U.S.A. 135 F4
Gorebridge U.K. 50 F5
Gore Point U.S.A. 118 C4
Gorey Rep. of Ireland 51 F5
Gorg Iran 89 E4
Gorgān Iran 88 D2
Gorgan Bay Iran 88 D2
Gorge Range hills Australia 108 B5
Gorgona, Isla i. Col. 142 C3
Gorham U.S.A. 135 J1
Gori Georgia 86 F1
Gorinchem Neth. 52 E3
Goris Armenia 91 G3
Gorizia Italy 58 E2
Gorki Belarus see Horki
Gor'kiy Rus. Fed. see Nizhniy Novgorod
Gor'kovskoye Vodokhranilishche resr Rus. Fed. 42 I4
Gorlice Poland 43 D6
Görlitz Germany 47 O5
Gorlovka Ukr. see Horlivka
Gorna Dzhumaya Bulg. see Blagoevgrad
Gorna Oryakhovitsa Bulg. 59 K3
Gornji Milanovac Serb. and Mont. 59 I2
Gornji Vakuf Bos.-Herz. 58 G3
Gorno-Altaysk Rus. Fed. 80 G1
Gornotrakiyska Nizina lowland Bulg. 59 K3
Gornozavodsk Permskaya Oblast' Rus. Fed. 41 R4
Gornozavodsk Sakhalinskaya Oblast' Rus. Fed. 74 F3
Gornyak Rus. Fed. 80 F1
Gornye Klyuchi Rus. Fed. 74 D3
Gornyy Rus. Fed. 43 K6
Goro i. Fiji see Koro
Gorodenka Ukr. see Horodenka
Gorodets Rus. Fed. 42 I4
Gorodishche Penzenskaya Oblast' Rus. Fed. 43 J5
Gorodishche Volgogradskaya Oblast' Rus. Fed. 43 J6
Gorodok Belarus see Haradok
Gorodok Rus. Fed. see Zakamensk
Gorodok Khmel'nyts'ka Oblast' Ukr. see Horodok
Gorodok L'vivs'ka Oblast' Ukr. see Horodok
Gorodovikovsk Rus. Fed. 43 I7
Goroka P.N.G. 69 L8
Gorokhovets Rus. Fed. 42 I4
Gorom Gorom Burkina 96 C3
Gorong, Kepulauan is Indon. 69 I7
Gorongosa mt. Moz. 99 D5
Gorongosa, Parque Nacional de nat. park Moz. 99 D5
Gorontalo Indon. 69 G6
Gorshechnoye Rus. Fed. 43 H6
Gort Rep. of Ireland 51 D4
Gortahork Rep. of Ireland 51 D2
Gorutuba r. Brazil 145 C1
Gorveh Iran 88 E4
Goryachiy Klyuch Rus. Fed. 91 E1
Görzke Germany 53 M2
Gorzów Wielkopolski Poland 47 O4
Gosainthan mt. China see Xixabangma Feng
Gosforth U.K. 48 F3
Goshen CA U.S.A. 128 D3
Goshen IN U.S.A. 134 C3
Goshen NH U.S.A. 135 I2
Goshen NY U.S.A. 135 H3
Goshen VA U.S.A. 134 F5
Goshoba Turkm. see Koshoba
Goslar Germany 53 K3
Gospić Croatia 58 F2
Gosport U.K. 49 F8
Gossi Mali 96 C3
Gostivar Macedonia 59 I4
Gosu China 76 C1
Göteborg Sweden see Gothenburg
Götene Sweden 45 H7
Gotenhafen Poland see Gdynia
Gotha Germany 53 K4
Gothenburg Sweden 45 G8
Gothenburg U.S.A. 130 C3
Gotland i. Sweden 45 K8
Gotō-rettō is Japan 75 C6
Gotse Delchev Bulg. 59 J4
Gotska Sandön i. Sweden 45 K7
Gōtsu Japan 75 D6
Göttingen Germany 53 J3
Gott Peak Canada 120 F5
Gottwaldow Czech Rep. see Zlín
Gouda Neth. 52 E2
Goudiri Senegal 96 B3
Goudoumaria Niger 96 E3
Goûgaram Niger 96 D3

▶**Gough Island** S. Atlantic Ocean 148 H8
Dependency of St Helena.

Gouin, Réservoir resr Canada 122 G4
Goulburn Australia 112 D5
Goulburn r. N.S.W. Australia 112 E4
Goulburn r. Vic. Australia 112 B6
Goulburn Islands Australia 108 F2
Goulburn River National Park Australia 112 E4
Gould Coast Antarctica 152 J1
Goulou atoll Micronesia see Ngulu
Goundam Mali 96 C3
Goundi Chad 97 E4
Goupil, Lac l. Canada 123 H3
Gouraya Alg. 57 G5
Gourcy Burkina 96 C3
Gourdon France 56 E4
Gouré Niger 96 E3
Gouripur Bangl. 83 G4
Gourits r. S. Africa 100 E8
Gourma-Rharous Mali 96 C3
Gournay-en-Bray France 52 B5
Goussainville France 52 C5
Gouverneur U.S.A. 135 H1
Governador Valadares Brazil 145 C2
Governor's Harbour Bahamas 133 E7
Govĭ Altayn Nuruu mts Mongolia 80 I3
Govind Ballash Pant Sagar resr India 83 E4
Gowal Pak. 89 H4
Gowanda U.S.A. 135 F2
Gowan Range hills Australia 110 D5
Gowārān Afgh. 89 G4
Gowd-e Mokh l. Iran 88 D4
Gowd-e Zereh plain Afgh. 89 F4
Gowmal Kalay Afgh. 89 H3
Gowna, Lough l. Rep. of Ireland 51 E4
Goya Arg. 144 E3
Göyçay Azer. 91 G2
Goyder watercourse Australia 109 F6
Goymatdag hills Turkm. see Koymatdag, Gory
Göynük Turkey 59 N4
Goyoum Cameroon 96 E4
Gozareh Afgh. 89 F3
Goz-Beïda Chad 97 F3
Gozha Co salt l. China 82 E2
Gözkaya Turkey 85 C1
Gozo i. Malta 58 F6
Graaf-Reinet S. Africa 100 G7
Grabfeld plain Germany 53 K4
Grabo Côte d'Ivoire 96 C4
Grabouw S. Africa 100 D8
Grabow Germany 53 L1
Gračac Croatia 58 F2
Gracefield Canada 122 F5
Gracey U.S.A. 134 B5
Gradaús, Serra dos hills Brazil 143 H5
Gradiška Bos.-Herz. see Bosanska Gradiška
Grady U.S.A. 131 C5
Gräfenhainichen Germany 53 M3
Grafenwöhr Germany 53 L5
Grafton Australia 112 F2
Grafton ND U.S.A. 130 D1
Grafton WI U.S.A. 134 B2
Grafton WV U.S.A. 134 E4
Grafton, Cape Australia 110 D3
Grafton, Mount U.S.A. 129 F2
Grafton Passage Australia 110 D3
Graham NC U.S.A. 132 E4
Graham TX U.S.A. 131 D5
Graham, Mount U.S.A. 129 I5
Graham Bell Island Rus. Fed. see Greem-Bell, Ostrov
Graham Island B.C. Canada 120 C4
Graham Island Nunavut Canada 119 I2
Graham Land reg. Antarctica 152 L2
Grahamstown S. Africa 101 H7
Grahovo Bos.-Herz. see Bosansko Grahovo
Graigue Rep. of Ireland 51 F5
Grajaú Brazil 143 I5
Grajaú r. Brazil 143 J4
Grammont Belgium see Geraardsbergen
Grammos mt. Greece 59 I4
Grampian Mountains U.K. 50 E4
Grampians National Park Australia 111 C8
Granada Nicaragua 137 G6
Granada Spain 57 E5
Granada U.S.A. 130 C4
Granard Rep. of Ireland 51 E4
Granbury U.S.A. 131 D5
Granby Canada 123 G5
Gran Canaria i. Canary Is 96 B2
Gran Chaco reg. Arg./Para. 144 D3
Grand r. MO U.S.A. 134 B2
Grand r. SD U.S.A. 130 C2
Grand Atlas mts Morocco see Haut Atlas
Grand Bahama i. Bahamas 133 E7
Grand Ballon mt. France 47 K7
Grand Bank Canada 123 L5
Grand Banks of Newfoundland sea feature N. Atlantic Ocean 148 E3
Grand-Bassam Côte d'Ivoire 96 C4
Grand Bay Canada 123 I5
Grand Bend Canada 134 E2
Grand Blanc U.S.A. 134 D2
Grand Canal Rep. of Ireland 51 E4
Grand Canary i. Canary Is see Gran Canaria
Grand Canyon U.S.A. 129 G3
Grand Canyon gorge U.S.A. 129 G3
Grand Canyon National Park U.S.A. 129 G3
Grand Canyon - Parashant National Monument nat. park U.S.A. 129 G3
Grand Cayman i. Cayman Is 137 H5
Grande r. Bahia Brazil 145 B1
Grande r. São Paulo Brazil 145 A3
Grande r. Nicaragua 137 H6
Grande, Bahía b. Arg. 144 C8
Grande, Ilha i. Brazil 145 B3
Grande Cache Canada 120 G4
Grande Comore i. Comoros see Njazidja
Grande Prairie Canada 120 G4
Grand Erg de Bilma des. Niger 96 E3
Grand Erg Occidental des. Alg. 54 D5
Grand Erg Oriental des. Alg. 54 F6
Grande-Rivière Canada 123 I4
Grandes, Salinas salt marsh Arg. 144 C4
Grande-Vallée Canada 123 I4
Grand Falls N.B. Canada 123 I5
Grand Falls Nfld. and Lab. Canada 123 L4
Grand Forks Canada 120 G5
Grand Forks U.S.A. 130 D2
Grand Gorge U.S.A. 135 H2
Grand Haven U.S.A. 134 B2
Grandin, Lac l. Canada 120 G1
Grandioznyy, Pik mt. Rus. Fed. 72 H2
Grand Island U.S.A. 130 D3
Grand Isle U.S.A. 131 F6
Grand Junction U.S.A. 129 I2
Grand Lac Germain l. Canada 123 I4
Grand-Lahou Côte d'Ivoire 96 C4
Grand Lake N.B. Canada 123 I5
Grand Lake Nfld. and Lab. Canada 123 J3
Grand Lake Nfld. and Lab. Canada 123 K4
Grand Lake LA U.S.A. 131 E6
Grand Lake MI U.S.A. 134 D1
Grand Lake St Marys U.S.A. 130 C3
Grand Ledge U.S.A. 134 C2
Grand Manan Island Canada 123 I5
Grand Marais MI U.S.A. 132 C2
Grand Marais MN U.S.A. 130 F2

Grand-Mère Canada 123 G5
Grand Mesa U.S.A. 129 J2
Grândola Port. 57 B4
Grand Passage New Caledonia 107 G3
Grand Rapids Canada 121 L4
Grand Rapids *MI* U.S.A. 134 C2
Grand Rapids *MN* U.S.A. 130 E2
Grand-Sault Canada *see* Grand Falls
Grand St-Bernard, Col du *pass* Italy/Switz. *see* Great St Bernard Pass
Grand Teton *mt.* U.S.A. 126 F4
Grand Teton National Park U.S.A. 126 F4
Grand Traverse Bay U.S.A. 134 C1

▶Grand Turk Turks and Caicos Is 137 J4
Capital of the Turks and Caicos Islands.

Grandville U.S.A. 134 C2
Grandvilliers France 52 B5
Grand Wash Cliffs *mts* U.S.A. 129 F4
Grange Rep. of Ireland 51 E6
Grängesberg Sweden 45 I6
Grangeville U.S.A. 126 D3
Granisle Canada 120 E4
Granite Falls U.S.A. 130 E2
Granite Mountain U.S.A. 128 E1
Granite Mountains *CA* U.S.A. 129 F4
Granite Mountains *CA* U.S.A. 129 F5
Granite Peak *MT* U.S.A. 126 F3
Granite Peak *UT* U.S.A. 129 G1
Granite Range *mts AK* U.S.A. 120 A3
Granite Range *mts NV* U.S.A. 128 D1
Granitola, Capo *c. Sicily* Italy 58 E6
Granja Brazil 143 J4
Gran Laguna Salada *l.* Arg. 144 C6
Gränna Sweden 45 I7
Gran Paradiso *mt.* Italy 58 B2
Gran Paradiso, Parco Nazionale del *nat. park* Italy 58 B2
Gran Pilastro *mt.* Austria/Italy 47 M7
Gran San Bernardo, Colle del *pass* Italy/Switz. *see* Great St Bernard Pass
Gran Sasso e Monti della Laga, Parco Nazionale del *nat. park* Italy 58 E3
Granschütz Germany 53 M3
Gransee Germany 53 N1
Grant U.S.A. 130 C3
Grant, Mount U.S.A. 128 E2
Grantham U.K. 49 G6
Grant Island Antarctica 152 J2
Grant Lake Canada 120 G1
Grantown-on-Spey U.K. 50 F3
Grant Range *mts* U.S.A. 129 F2
Grants U.S.A. 129 J4
Grants Pass U.S.A. 126 C4
Grantsville *UT* U.S.A. 129 G1
Grantsville *WV* U.S.A. 134 E4
Granville Canada 120 B2
Granville France 56 D2
Granville *AZ* U.S.A. 129 I5
Granville *NY* U.S.A. 135 I2
Granville *TN* U.S.A. 134 C5
Granville Lake Canada 121 K3
Grão Mogol Brazil 145 C2
Grapevine Mountains U.S.A. 128 E3
Gras, Lac de *l.* Canada 121 I1
Graskop S. Africa 101 J3
Grasplatz Namibia 100 B4
Grass *r.* Canada 121 L3
Grass *r.* U.S.A. 135 H1
Grasse France 56 H5
Grassflat U.S.A. 135 F3
Grassington U.K. 48 F4
Grasslands National Park Canada 121 J5
Grassrange U.S.A. 126 F3
Grass Valley U.S.A. 128 C2
Grassy Butte U.S.A. 130 C2
Grästorp Sweden 45 H7
Gratz U.S.A. 134 C4
Graudenz Poland *see* Grudziądz
Graus Spain 57 G2
Gravatai Brazil 145 A5
Grave, Pointe de *pt* France 56 D4
Gravelbourg Canada 121 J5
Gravel Hill Lake Canada 121 K2
Gravelines France 52 C4
Gravelotte S. Africa 101 J2
Gravenhurst Canada 134 F1
Grave Peak U.S.A. 126 E3
Gravesend Australia 112 E2
Gravesend U.K. 49 H7
Gravina in Puglia Italy 58 G4
Grawn U.S.A. 134 C1
Gray France 56 G3
Gray *GA* U.S.A. 133 D5
Gray *KY* U.S.A. 134 C5
Gray *ME* U.S.A. 135 J2
Grayback Mountain U.S.A. 126 C4
Gray Lake Canada 121 I2
Grayling *r.* Canada 120 E3
Grayling U.S.A. 134 C1
Grays U.K. 49 H7
Grays Harbor *inlet* U.S.A. 126 B3
Grays Lake U.S.A. 126 F4
Grayson U.S.A. 134 D4
Graz Austria 47 O7
Greasy Lake Canada 120 F2
Great Abaco *i.* Bahamas 133 E7
Great Australian Bight *g.* Australia 109 E8
Great Baddow U.K. 49 H7
Great Bahama Bank *sea feature* Bahamas 133 E7
Great Barrier Island N.Z. 113 E3
Great Barrier Reef Australia 110 D1
Great Barrier Reef Marine Park (Cairns Section) Australia 110 D3
Great Barrier Reef Marine Park (Capricorn Section) Australia 110 E4
Great Barrier Reef Marine Park (Central Section) Australia 110 E3
Great Barrier Reef Marine Park (Far North Section) Australia 110 D2
Great Barrington U.S.A. 135 I2
Great Basalt Wall National Park Australia 110 D3
Great Basin U.S.A. 128 E2
Great Basin National Park U.S.A. 129 F2
Great Bear *r.* Canada 120 E1

▶Great Bear Lake Canada 120 G1
4th largest lake in North America.

Great Belt *sea chan.* Denmark 45 G9
Great Bend U.S.A. 130 D4
Great Bitter Lake Egypt 85 A4
Great Blasket Island Rep. of Ireland 51 B5

▶Great Britain *i.* U.K. 46 G4
Largest island in Europe.
Europe 36–37

Great Clifton U.K. 48 D4
Great Coco Island Cocos Is 68 A4
Great Cumbrae *i.* U.K. 50 E5
Great Dismal Swamp National Wildlife Refuge *nature res.* U.S.A. 135 G5
Great Dividing Range *mts* Australia 112 B6
Great Eastern Erg *des.* Alg. *see* Grand Erg Oriental
Greater Antarctica *reg.* Antarctica *see* East Antarctica
Greater Antilles *is* Caribbean Sea 137 H4
Greater Khingan Mountains China *see* Da Hinggan Ling
Greater St Lucia Wetland Park *nature res.* S. Africa 101 K4
Greater Tunb *i.* The Gulf 88 D5
Great Exuma *i.* Bahamas 133 F8
Great Falls U.S.A. 126 F3
Great Fish *r.* S. Africa 101 H7
Great Fish Point S. Africa 101 H7
Great Fish River Reserve Complex *nature res.* S. Africa 101 H7
Great Gandak *r.* India 83 F4
Great Ganges *atoll* Cook Is *see* Manihiki
Great Guana Cay *i.* Bahamas 133 E7
Great Inagua *i.* Bahamas 137 J4
Great Karoo *plat.* S. Africa 100 F7
Great Kei *r.* S. Africa 101 I7
Great Lake Australia 111 [inset]
Great Malvern U.K. 49 E6
Great Meteor Tablemount *sea feature* N. Atlantic Ocean 148 G4
Great Namaqualand *reg.* Namibia 100 C4
Great Nicobar *i.* India 71 A6
Great Ormes Head *hd* U.K. 48 D5
Great Ouse *r.* U.K. 49 H6
Great Oyster Bay Australia 111 [inset]
Great Palm Islands Australia 106 D3
Great Plain of the Koukdjuak Canada 119 K3
Great Plains U.S.A. 130 C3
Great Point U.S.A. 135 J3
Great Rift Valley Africa 98 D4
Great Ruaha *r.* Tanz. 99 D4
Great Sacandaga Lake U.S.A. 135 H2
Great Salt Lake U.S.A. 129 G1
Great Salt Lake Desert U.S.A. 129 G1
Great Sand Hills Canada 121 I5
Great Sand Sea *des.* Egypt/Libya 90 B5
Great Sandy Desert Australia 108 C5
Great Sandy Island Australia *see* Fraser Island
Great Sea Reef Fiji 107 H3

▶Great Slave Lake Canada 120 H2
Deepest and 5th largest lake in North America.

Great Smoky Mountains U.S.A. 133 C5
Great Smoky Mountains National Park U.S.A. 132 D5
Great Snow Mountain Canada 120 E3
Great St Bernard Pass Italy/Switz. 58 B2
Greatstone-on-Sea U.K. 49 H8
Great Stour *r.* U.K. 49 I7
Great Torrington U.K. 49 C8
Great Victoria Desert Australia 109 E7
Great Wall *research station* Antarctica 152 A2
Great Wall *tourist site* China 73 L4
Great Waltham U.K. 49 H7
Great Western Erg *des.* Alg. *see* Grand Erg Occidental
Great West Torres Islands Myanmar 71 B5
Great Whernside *hill* U.K. 48 F4
Great Yarmouth U.K. 49 I6
Grebenkovskiy Ukr. *see* Hrebinka
Grebyonka Ukr. *see* Hrebinka
Greco, Cape Cyprus *see* Greko, Cape
Gredos, Sierra de *mts* Spain 57 D3
▶Greece *country* Europe 59 I5
Europe 5, 38–39
Greece U.S.A. 135 G2
Greeley U.S.A. 126 G4
Greely Center U.S.A. 130 D3
Greem-Bell, Ostrov *i.* Rus. Fed. 64 H1
Green *r. KY* U.S.A. 134 B5
Green *r. WY* U.S.A. 129 I2
Green Bay U.S.A. 134 A1
Green Bay *b.* U.S.A. 134 B1
Greenbrier U.S.A. 134 B5
Greenbrier *r.* U.S.A. 134 E5
Green Cape Australia 112 E6
Greencastle Bahamas 133 E7
Greencastle U.K. 51 F3
Greencastle U.S.A. 134 B4
Green Cove Springs U.S.A. 133 D6
Greene *ME* U.S.A. 135 J1
Greene *NY* U.S.A. 135 H2
Greeneville U.S.A. 132 D4
Greenfield *CA* U.S.A. 128 C3
Greenfield *IN* U.S.A. 134 C4
Greenfield *MA* U.S.A. 135 I2
Greenfield *OH* U.S.A. 134 D4
Green Head *hd* Australia 109 A7
Greenhill Island Australia 108 F2
Green Island Taiwan *see* Lü Tao
Green Lake Canada 121 J4

▶Greenland *terr.* N. America 119 N3
Self-governing Danish Territory. Largest island in the world and in North America.
North America 9, 114–115, 116–117
World 12–13

Greenland Basin *sea feature* Arctic Ocean 153 I2
Greenland Fracture Zone *sea feature* Arctic Ocean 153 I1
Greenland Sea Greenland/Svalbard 64 A2
Greenlaw U.K. 50 G5
Green Mountains U.S.A. 135 I1
Greenock U.K. 50 E5
Greenore Rep. of Ireland 51 F3
Greenport U.S.A. 135 I3
Green River P.N.G. 69 K7
Green River *UT* U.S.A. 129 H2
Green River *WY* U.S.A. 126 F4
Green River Lake U.S.A. 134 C5
Greensboro U.S.A. 133 D5
Greensburg *IN* U.S.A. 134 C4
Greensburg *KS* U.S.A. 130 D4
Greensburg *KY* U.S.A. 134 C5
Greensburg *LA* U.S.A. 131 F6
Greensburg *PA* U.S.A. 134 F3
Greens Peak U.S.A. 129 I4
Greenstone Point U.K. 50 D3
Green Swamp U.S.A. 133 E5
Greentown U.S.A. 134 C3
Greenup *IL* U.S.A. 130 F4
Greenup *KY* U.S.A. 134 D4
Green Valley Canada 135 H1
Greenville Canada 120 D4
Greenville Liberia 96 C4
Greenville *AL* U.S.A. 133 C6
Greenville *IL* U.S.A. 130 F4
Greenville *KY* U.S.A. 134 B5
Greenville *ME* U.S.A. 132 G2
Greenville *MI* U.S.A. 134 C2
Greenville *MS* U.S.A. 131 F5
Greenville *NC* U.S.A. 132 E5
Greenville *NH* U.S.A. 135 J2
Greenville *OH* U.S.A. 134 C3
Greenville *PA* U.S.A. 134 E3
Greenville *SC* U.S.A. 133 D5
Greenville *TX* U.S.A. 131 D5
Greenwich *atoll* Micronesia *see* Kapingamarangi
Greenwich *CT* U.S.A. 135 I3
Greenwich *OH* U.S.A. 134 D3
Greenwood *AR* U.S.A. 131 E5
Greenwood *IN* U.S.A. 134 B4
Greenwood *MS* U.S.A. 131 F5
Greenwood *SC* U.S.A. 133 D5
Gregory *r.* Australia 110 B3
Gregory, Lake *salt flat S.A.* Australia 111 B6
Gregory, Lake *salt flat W.A.* Australia 108 D5
Gregory, Lake *salt flat W.A.* Australia 109 B6
Gregory Downs Australia 110 B3
Gregory National Park Australia 108 E4
Gregory Range *hills Qld* Australia 110 C3
Gregory Range *hills W.A.* Australia 108 C5
Greifswald Germany 47 N3
Greiz Germany 53 M4
Greko, Cape Cyprus 85 B2
Gremikha Rus. Fed. 153 G2
Gremyachinsk Rus. Fed. 41 R4
Grenå Denmark 45 G8
Grenaa Denmark *see* Grenå
Grenada U.S.A. 131 F5
▶Grenada *country* West Indies 137 L6
North America 9, 116–117
Grenade France 56 E5
Grenen *spit* Denmark 45 G8
Grenfell Australia 112 D4
Grenfell Canada 121 K5
Grenoble France 56 G4
Grense-Jakobselv Norway 44 Q2
Grenville, Cape Australia 110 C1
Grenville Island Fiji *see* Rotuma
Greshak Pak. 89 G5
Gresham U.S.A. 126 C3
Gressåmoen Nasjonalpark *nat. park* Norway 44 H4
Greta *r.* U.K. 48 E4
Gretna U.K. 50 F6
Gretna *LA* U.S.A. 131 F6
Gretna *VA* U.S.A. 134 F5
Greußen Germany 53 K3
Grevelingen *sea chan.* Neth. 52 D3
Greven Germany 53 H2
Grevena Greece 59 I4
Grevenbicht Neth. 52 F3
Grevenbroich Germany 52 G3
Grevenmacher Lux. 52 G5
Grevesmühlen Germany 47 M4
Grey, Cape Australia 110 B2
Greybull U.S.A. 126 F3
Greybull *r.* U.S.A. 126 F3
Grey Hunter Peak Canada 120 C2
Grey Islands Canada 123 L4
Greylock, Mount U.S.A. 135 I2
Greymouth N.Z. 113 C6
Grey Range *hills* Australia 112 A2
Grey's Plains Australia 109 A6
Greytown S. Africa 101 J5
Grez-Doiceau Belgium 52 E4
Gribanovskiy Rus. Fed. 43 I6
Gridley U.S.A. 128 C2
Griffin U.S.A. 133 C5
Griffith Australia 112 C5
Grigan *i.* N. Mariana Is *see* Agrihan
Grik Malaysia *see* Gerik
Grim, Cape Australia 111 [inset]
Grimari Cent. Afr. Rep. 98 C3
Grimma Germany 53 M3
Grimmen Germany 47 N3
Grimnitzsee *l.* Germany 53 N2
Grimsby U.K. 48 G5
Grímsey *i.* Iceland 44 [inset]
Grimshaw Canada 120 G3
Grímsstaðir Iceland 44 [inset]
Grimstad Norway 45 F7
Grindavík Iceland 44 [inset]
Grindsted Denmark 45 F9
Grind Stone City U.S.A. 134 D1
Grindul Chituc *spit* Romania 59 M2
Grinnell Peninsula Canada 119 I2
Griqualand East *reg.* S. Africa 101 I6
Griqualand West *reg.* S. Africa 100 F5
Griquatown S. Africa 100 F5
Grise Fiord Canada 119 J2
Grishino Ukr. *see* Krasnoarmiys'k
Gris Nez, Cap *c.* France 52 B4
Gritley U.K. 50 G2
Grizzly Bear Mountain *hill* Canada 120 F1
Grmeč *mts* Bos.-Herz. 58 G2
Grobbendonk Belgium 52 E3
Groblersdal S. Africa 101 I3
Groblershoop S. Africa 100 F5
Grodekovo Rus. Fed. 74 C3
Grodno Belarus *see* Hrodna
Groen *watercourse* S. Africa 100 F6
Groen *watercourse* S. Africa 100 C6
Groix, Île de *i.* France 56 C3
Grombalia Tunisia 58 D6
Gronau (Westfalen) Germany 52 H2
Grong Norway 44 H4
Groningen Neth. 52 G1
Groninger Wad *tidal flat* Neth. 52 G1
Grønland *terr.* N. America *see* Greenland
Groom Lake U.S.A. 129 F3
Groot-Aar Pan *salt pan* S. Africa 100 E4
Groot Berg *r.* S. Africa 100 D7
Groot Brakrivier S. Africa 100 F8
Grootdraaidam *dam* S. Africa 101 I4
Grootdrink S. Africa 100 E5
Groote Eylandt *i.* Australia 110 B2
Grootfontein Namibia 99 B5
Groot Karas Berg *plat.* Namibia 100 D4
Groot Letaba *r.* S. Africa 101 J2
Groot Marico S. Africa 101 H3
Groot Swartberge *mts* S. Africa 100 E7
Grootvloer *salt pan* S. Africa 100 E5
Groot Winterberg *mt.* S. Africa 101 H7
Gros Morne National Park Canada 123 K4
Gross Barmen Namibia 100 C2
Große Aue *r.* Germany 53 J2
Große Laaber *r.* Germany 53 M6
Großengottern Germany 53 K3
Großenkneten Germany 53 I2
Großenlüder Germany 53 J4
Großer Arber *mt.* Germany 53 N5
Großer Beerberg *hill* Germany 53 K4
Großer Eyberg *hill* Germany 53 H5
Großer Gleichberg *hill* Germany 53 K4
Großer Kornberg *hill* Germany 53 M4
Großer Osser *mt.* Czech Rep./Germany 53 N5
Großer Rachel *mt.* Germany 47 N6
Grosser Speikkogel *mt.* Austria 47 O7
Grosseto Italy 58 D3
Grossevichi Rus. Fed. 74 E3
Groß-Gerau Germany 53 I5
Großglockner *mt.* Austria 47 N7
Groß Oesingen Germany 53 K2
Großrudestedt Germany 53 L3
Groß Schönebeck Germany 53 N2
Gross Ums Namibia 100 D2
Großvenediger *mt.* Austria 47 N7
Gros Ventre Range *mts* U.S.A. 126 F4
Groswater Bay Canada 123 K3
Groton U.S.A. 130 D2
Grottoes U.S.A. 135 F4
Grou Neth. *see* Grouw
Groundhog *r.* Canada 122 E4
Grouw Neth. 52 F1
Grove U.S.A. 131 E4
Grove City U.S.A. 134 D4
Grove Hill U.S.A. 133 C6
Grove Mountains Antarctica 152 E2
Grover Beach U.S.A. 128 C4
Grovertown U.S.A. 134 B3
Groveton *NH* U.S.A. 135 J1
Groveton *TX* U.S.A. 131 E6
Growler Mountains U.S.A. 129 G5
Groznyy Rus. Fed. 91 G2
Grubišno Polje Croatia 58 G2
Grudovo Bulg. *see* Sredets
Grudziądz Poland 47 Q4
Grünau Namibia 100 D4
Grünberg Poland *see* Zielona Góra
Grundarfjörður Iceland 44 [inset]
Grundy U.S.A. 134 D5
Gruñidora Mex. 131 C7
Grünstadt Germany 53 I5
Gruver U.S.A. 131 C4
Gruzinskaya S.S.R. *country* Asia *see* Georgia
Gryazi Rus. Fed. 43 H5
Gryazovets Rus. Fed. 42 I4
Gryfice Poland 47 O4
Gryfino Poland 47 O4
Gryfów Śląski Poland 47 O5
Gryllefjord Norway 44 J2
Grytviken S. Georgia 144 I8
Gua India 83 F5
Guacanayabo, Golfo de *b.* Cuba 137 I4
Guachochi Mex. 127 G8
Guadajoz *r.* Spain 57 D5
Guadalajara Mex. 136 D4
Guadalajara Spain 57 E3
Guadalcanal *i.* Solomon Is 107 G2
Guadalete *r.* Spain 57 C5
Guadalope *r.* Spain 57 F3
Guadalquivir *r.* Spain 57 C5
Guadalupe Mex. 131 C7
Guadalupe *i.* Mex. 127 D7
Guadalupe *watercourse* Mex. 128 E5
Guadalupe U.S.A. 128 C4
Guadalupe, Sierra de *mts* Spain 57 D4
Guadalupe Aguilera Mex. 131 B7
Guadalupe Bravos Mex. 127 G7
Guadalupe Mountains National Park U.S.A. 127 G7
Guadalupe Peak U.S.A. 127 G7
Guadalupe Victoria *Baja California* Mex. 129 F5
Guadalupe Victoria *Durango* Mex. 131 B7
Guadarrama, Sierra de *mts* Spain 57 D3

▶Guadeloupe *terr.* West Indies 137 L5
French Overseas Department.
North America 9, 116–117

Guadeloupe Passage Caribbean Sea 137 L5
Guadiana *r.* Port./Spain 57 C5
Guadix Spain 57 E5
Guafo, Isla *i.* Chile 144 B6
Guaíba Brazil 145 A5
Guaiçuí Brazil 145 B2
Guaíra Brazil 144 F2
Guajaba, Cayo *i.* Cuba 133 E8
Guaje, Llano de *plain* Mex. 131 C7
Gualala U.S.A. 128 B2
Gualeguay Arg. 144 E4
Gualeguaychu Arg. 144 E4
Gualicho, Salina *salt flat* Arg. 144 C6

▶Guam *terr.* N. Pacific Ocean 69 K4
United States Unincorporated Territory.
Oceania 8, 104–105

Guamblin, Isla *i.* Chile 144 A6
Guampí, Sierra de *mts* Venez. 142 E2
Guamúchil Mex. 127 F8
Guanabacoa Cuba 133 D8
Guanacevi Mex. 131 B7
Guanahacabibes, Península de *pen.* Cuba 133 C8
Guanajay Cuba 133 D8
Guanajuato Mex. 136 D4
Guanambi Brazil 145 C1
Guanare Venez. 142 E2
Guandu China 77 G3
Guane Cuba 137 H4
Guang'an China 76 E2
Guangchang China 77 H3
Guangdong *prov.* China 77 [inset]
Guanghai China 77 G4
Guanghan China 76 E2
Guanghua China *see* Laohekou
Guangming China *see* Xide
Guangming Ding *mt.* China 77 H2
Guangnan China 76 E3
Guangshan China 77 G2
Guangxi *aut. reg.* China *see* Guangxi Zhuangzu Zizhiqu
Guangxi Zhuangzu Zizhiqu *aut. reg.* China 76 F4
Guangyuan China 76 E1
Guangze China 77 H3
Guangzhou China 77 G4
Guanhães Brazil 145 C2
Guanhe Kou *r. mouth* China 77 H1
Guanipa *r.* Venez. 142 F2
Guanling China 76 E3
Guanmian Shan *mts* China 77 F2
Guannan China 77 H1
Guanpo China 77 F1
Guanshui China 74 B4
Guansuo China *see* Guanling
Guantánamo Cuba 137 I4
Guanxian China *see* Dujiangyan
Guanyang China 77 F3
Guanyinqiao China 76 D2
Guanyun China 77 H1
Guapé Brazil 145 B3
Guapí Col. 142 C3
Guaporé *r.* Bol./Brazil 142 E6
Guaporé Brazil 145 A5
Guaqui Bol. 142 E7
Guará *r.* Brazil 145 B1
Guarabira Brazil 143 K5
Guaranda Ecuador 142 C4
Guarapari Brazil 145 C3
Guarapuava Brazil 145 A4
Guararapes Brazil 145 A3
Guaratinguetá Brazil 145 B3
Guaratuba Brazil 145 A4
Guaratuba, Baía de *b.* Brazil 145 A4
Guarda Port. 57 C3
Guardafui, Cape Somalia *see* Gwardafuy, Gees
Guardiagrele Italy 58 F3
Guardo Spain 57 D2
Guárico, del Embalse *resr* Venez. 142 E2
Guarujá Brazil 145 B3
Guasave Mex. 127 F8
Guasdualito Venez. 142 D2

▶Guatemala *country* Central America 136 F5
4th most populous country in Central and North America.
North America 9, 116–117

Guatemala Guat. *see* Guatemala City

▶Guatemala City Guat. 136 F6
Capital of Guatemala.

Guaviare *r.* Col. 142 E3
Guaxupé Brazil 145 B3
Guayaquil Ecuador 142 C4
Guayaquil, Golfo de *g.* Ecuador 142 B4
Guaymas Mex. 127 F8
Guba Eth. 98 D2
Gubakha Rus. Fed. 41 R4
Gubbi India 84 C3
Gubio Nigeria 96 E3
Gubkin Rus. Fed. 43 H6
Gucheng China 77 F1
Gudari India 84 D2
Gudbrandsdalen *valley* Norway 45 F6
Gudermes Rus. Fed. 91 G2
Gudivada India 84 D2
Gudiyattam India 84 C3
Gudur *Andhra Pradesh* India 84 C3
Gudur *Andhra Pradesh* India 84 C3
Gudvangen Norway 45 E6
Gudzhal *r.* Rus. Fed. 74 D2
Guè, Rivière du *r.* Canada 123 H2
Guecho Spain *see* Algorta
Guéckédou Guinea 96 B4
Guelma Alg. 58 B6
Guelmine Morocco 96 B2
Guelph Canada 134 E2
Guémez Mex. 131 D8
Guénange France 52 G5
Guerara Alg. 54 E5
Guérard, Lac *l.* Canada 123 I2
Guercif Morocco 54 D5
Guéret France 56 E3

▶Guernsey *terr.* Channel Is 49 E9
United Kingdom Crown Dependency.
Europe 5, 38–39

Guernsey U.S.A. 126 G4
Guérou Mauritania 96 B3
Guerrah Et-Tarf *salt pan* Alg. 58 B7
Guerrero Negro Mex. 127 E8
Guers, Lac *l.* Canada 123 I2
Gueugnon France 56 G3
Gufeng China *see* Pingnan
Gufu China *see* Xingshan
Gugē *mt.* Eth. 98 D3
Gügerd, Küh-e *mts* Iran 88 D3
Guguan *i.* N. Mariana Is 69 L3
Guhakolak, Tanjung *pt* Indon. 68 D8
Guhe China 77 H2
Güh Küh *mt.* Iran 88 E5
Guhuai China *see* Pingyu
Guiana Basin *sea feature* N. Atlantic Ocean 148 E5
Guiana Highlands *mts* S. America 142 E2
Guichi China *see* Chizhou
Guidan-Roumji Niger 96 D3
Guider Cameroon 97 E4
Guiding China 76 E3
Guidong China 77 G3
Guidonia-Montecelio Italy 58 E4
Guigang China 77 F4
Guiglo Côte d'Ivoire 96 C4
Guignicourt France 52 D5
Guija Moz. 101 K3
Guiji Shan *mts* China 77 I2
Guildford U.K. 49 G7
Guilford U.S.A. 132 G2
Guilherme Capelo Angola *see* Cacongo
Guilin China 77 F3
Guillaume-Delisle, Lac *l.* Canada 122 F2
Guimarães Brazil 143 J4
Guimarães Port. 57 B3
Guinan China 76 D1
▶Guinea *country* Africa 96 B3
Africa 7, 94–95
Guinea, Gulf of Africa 96 D4
Guinea Basin *sea feature* N. Atlantic Ocean 148 H5
▶Guinea-Bissau *country* Africa 96 B3
africa 7, 94–95
Guinea-Conakry *country* Africa *see* Guinea
Guinea Ecuatorial *country* Africa *see* Equatorial Guinea
Guiné-Bissau *country* Africa *see* Guinea-Bissau
Guinée *country* Africa *see* Guinea
Güines Cuba 137 H4
Guînes France 52 B4
Guines, Lac *l.* Canada 123 J3
Guingamp France 56 C2
Guipavas France 56 B2
Guiping China 77 F4
Güira de Melena Cuba 133 D8
Guiratinga Brazil 143 H7
Guiscard France 52 D5
Guise France 52 D5
Guishan China *see* Xinping
Guishun China 76 E3
Guixi *Chongqing* China *see* Dianjiang
Guixi *Jiangxi* China 77 H2
Guiyang *Guizhou* China 76 E3
Guiyang *Hunan* China 77 G3
Guizhou *prov.* China 76 E3
Guizi China 77 F4
Gujarat *state* India 82 C5
Gujar Khan Pak. 89 I3
Gujerat *state* India *see* Gujarat
Gujranwala Pak. 89 I3
Gujrat Pak. 89 I3
Gukovo Rus. Fed. 43 H6
Gulabgarh Jammu and Kashmir 82 D2
Gulbarga India 84 C2
Gulbene Latvia 45 O8
Gul'cha Kyrg. *see* Gülchö
Gülchö Kyrg. 80 D3
Gülcihan Turkey 85 B1
Gülek Boğazı *pass* Turkey 90 D3
Gulfport U.S.A. 131 F6
Gulian China 74 A1
Gulin China 76 E3
Gulistan Uzbek. 80 C3
Guliston Uzbek. *see* Gulistan
Gülitz Germany 53 L1
Guliya Shan *mt.* China 74 A2
Gulja China *see* Yining
Gul Kach Pak. 89 H4
Gul'kevichi Rus. Fed. 91 F1
Gull Lake Canada 121 I5
Gullrock Lake Canada 121 M5
Gullträsk Sweden 44 L3
Güllük Körfezi *b.* Turkey 59 L6
Gülnar Turkey 85 A1
Gulü China *see* Xincai
Gulu Uganda 98 D3
Guluwuru Island Australia 110 B1
Gulyayevskiye Koshki, Ostrova *is* Rus. Fed. 42 L1
Guma China *see* Pishan
Gumal *r.* Pak. 89 H4
Gumare Botswana 99 C5
Gumbaz Pak. 89 H4
Gumbinnen Rus. Fed. *see* Gusev
Gumdag Turkm. 88 D2
Gumel Nigeria 96 D3
Gümgüm Turkey *see* Varto
Gumla India 83 F5
Gummersbach Germany 53 H3
Gümüşhacıköy Turkey 90 D2
Gümüşhane Turkey 91 E2
Guna India 82 D4
Gunan China *see* Qijiang
Guna Terara *mt.* Eth. 86 E7
Gunbar Australia 112 B5
Gunbower Australia 112 B5
Güncang China 76 B2
Gund *r.* Tajik. *see* Gunt
Gundagai Australia 112 D5
Gundelsheim Germany 53 J5
Güney Turkey 59 M5
Güneydoğu Toroslar *plat.* Turkey 90 F3
Gunglilap Myanmar 70 B1
Gungu Dem. Rep. Congo 99 B4
Gunib Rus. Fed. 91 G2
Gunisao *r.* Canada 121 L4
Gunisao Lake Canada 121 L4
Gunnaur India 82 D3
Gunnbjørn Fjeld *nunatak* Greenland 119 P3
Gunnedah Australia 112 E3
Gunning Australia 112 D5
Gunnison U.S.A. 127 G5
Gunnison *r.* U.S.A. 129 I2
Güns Hungary *see* Kőszeg
Gunt *r.* Tajik. 89 H2
Guntakal India 84 C3
Güntersberge Germany 53 K3
Guntur India 84 D2
Gunung Gading National Park Malaysia 71 E7
Gunung Leuser National Park Indon. 71 B7
Gunung Lorentz National Park Indon. 69 J7

Harry S. Truman Reservoir U.S.A. 130 E4
Har Sai Shan mt. China 76 C1
Harsefeld Germany 53 J1
Harsīn Iran 88 B3
Harşit r. Turkey 90 E2
Hârşova Romania 59 L2
Harstad Norway 44 J2
Harsud India 82 D5
Harsum Germany 53 J2
Hart r. Canada 118 E3
Hart U.S.A. 134 B2
Hartbees watercourse S. Africa 100 E5
Hartberg Austria 47 O7
Harteigan mt. Norway 45 E6
Harter Fell hill U.K. 48 E4
▶Hartford CT U.S.A. 135 I3
State capital of Connecticut.
Hartford KY U.S.A. 134 B5
Hartford MI U.S.A. 134 B2
Hartford City U.S.A. 134 C3
Hartland U.K. 49 C8
Hartland U.S.A. 135 K1
Hartland Point U.K. 49 C7
Hartlepool U.K. 48 F4
Hartley U.S.A. 131 C5
Hartley Zimbabwe see Chegutu
Hartley Bay Canada 120 D4
Hartola Fin. 45 O6
Harts r. S. Africa 101 G5
Härtsfeld hills Germany 53 K6
Harts Range mts Australia 109 F5
Hartsville U.S.A. 134 B5
Hartswater S. Africa 100 G4
Hartville U.S.A. 131 E4
Hartwell U.S.A. 133 D5
Har Us Nuur l. Mongolia 80 H2
Harūz-e Bālā Iran 88 E4
Harvard, Mount U.S.A. 126 G5
Harvey Australia 109 A8
Harvey U.S.A. 130 C2
Harvey Mountain U.S.A. 128 C1
Harwich U.K. 49 I7
Haryana state India 82 D3
Harz hills Germany 47 M5
Har Zin Israel 85 B4
Ḩaşāh, Wādī al watercourse Jordan 85 B4
Ḩaşāh, Wādī al watercourse Jordan/Saudi Arabia 85 C4
Hasalbag China 89 J2
Ḩasanah, Wādī watercourse Egypt 85 A4
Hasan Dağı mts Turkey 90 D3
Hasan Guli Turkm. see Esenguly
Hasankeyf Turkey 91 F3
Hasan Küleh Afgh. 89 F3
Hasanur India 84 C4
Hasbaïya Lebanon 85 B3
Hasbaya Lebanon see Hasbaïya
Hase r. Germany 53 H2
Haselünne Germany 53 H2
Hashak Iran 89 F5
HaSharon plain Israel 85 B3
Hashtgerd Iran 88 C3
Hashtpar Iran 88 C2
Hashtrud Iran 88 B2
Haskell U.S.A. 131 D5
Haslemere U.K. 49 G7
Hăşmaşul Mare mt. Romania 55 K1
Ḩaşş, Jabal al hills Syria 85 C1
Hassan India 84 C3
Hassayampa watercourse U.S.A. 129 G5
Haßberge hills Germany 53 K4
Hasselt Belgium 52 F4
Hasselt Neth. 52 G2
Hassi Bel Guebbour Alg. 96 D2
Hassi Messaoud Alg. 54 F5
Hässleholm Sweden 45 H8
Hastings Australia 112 B7
Hastings r. Australia 112 F3
Hastings Canada 135 G1
Hastings N.Z. 113 F4
Hastings U.K. 49 H8
Hastings MI U.S.A. 134 C2
Hastings MN U.S.A. 130 E2
Hastings NE U.S.A. 130 D3
Hata India 83 E4
Hatay Turkey see Antakya
Hatay prov. Turkey 85 C1
Hatch U.S.A. 129 G3
Hatches Creek Australia 110 A4
Hatchet Lake Canada 121 K3
Hatfield Australia 112 A4
Hatfield U.K. 48 G5
Hatgal Mongolia 80 J1
Hath India 84 D1
Hat Head National Park Australia 112 F3
Hathras India 82 D4
Ha Tiên Vietnam 71 D5
Ha Tinh Vietnam 70 D3
Hatisar Bhutan see Gelephu
Hatod India 82 C5
Hato Hud East Timor see Hatudo
Hatra Iraq 91 F4
Hattah Australia 111 C7
Hatteras, Cape U.S.A. 133 F5
Hatteras Abyssal Plain sea feature S. Atlantic Ocean 148 D4
Hattfjelldal Norway 44 H4
Hattiesburg U.S.A. 131 F6
Hattingen Germany 53 H3
Hattras Passage Myanmar 71 B4
Hatudo East Timor 108 D2
Hat Yai Thai. 71 C6
Hau Bon Vietnam see Cheo Reo
Haubstadt U.S.A. 134 B4
Haud reg. Eth. 98 E3
Hauge Norway 45 E7
Haugesund Norway 45 D7
Haukeligrend Norway 45 E7
Haukipudas Fin. 44 N4
Haukivesi l. Fin. 44 P5
Haultain r. Canada 121 J4
Hauraki Gulf N.Z. 113 E3
Haut Atlas mts Morocco 54 C5
Haute-Normandie admin. reg. France 52 B5
Haute-Volta country Africa see Burkina
Haut-Folin hill France 56 G3
Hauts Plateaux Alg. 54 D5
▶Havana Cuba 137 H4
Capital of Cuba.
Havana U.S.A. 130 F3
Havant U.K. 49 G8
Havasu, Lake U.S.A. 129 F4
Havel r. Germany 53 L2
Havelange Belgium 52 F4
Havelberg Germany 53 M2
Havelock Canada 135 G1
Havelock N.Z. 113 D5
Havelock Swaziland see Bulembu
Havelock U.S.A. 133 E5
Havelock Falls Australia 108 F3
Havelock Island India 71 A5
Havelock North N.Z. 113 F4
Haverfordwest U.K. 49 C7
Haverhill U.S.A. 135 J2
Haveri India 84 B3
Haversin Belgium 52 F4
Havixbeck Germany 53 H3
Havlíčkův Brod Czech Rep. 47 O6
Havøysund Norway 44 N1
Havran Turkey 59 L5
Havre U.S.A. 126 F2
Havre Aubert, Île du i. Canada 123 J5
Havre Rock i. Kermadec Is 107 I5
Havre-St-Pierre Canada 123 J4
Havza Turkey 90 D2
Hawaii i. HI U.S.A. 127 [inset]
Hawaiian Islands N. Pacific Ocean 150 I4
Hawaiian Ridge sea feature N. Pacific Ocean 150 I4
Hawaii Volcanoes National Park HI U.S.A. 127 [inset]
Ḩawallī Kuwait 88 C4
Hawar i. Bahrain see Huwār
Hawarden U.K. 48 D5
Hawea, Lake N.Z. 113 B7
Hawera N.Z. 113 E4
Hawes U.K. 48 E4
Hawesville U.S.A. 134 B5
Hawi HI U.S.A. 127 [inset]
Hawick U.K. 50 G5
Ḩawīzah, Hawr al imp. l. Iraq 87 G5
Hawkdun Range mts N.Z. 113 B7
Hawke Bay N.Z. 113 F4
Hawkes Bay Canada 123 K4
Hawkins Peak U.S.A. 129 G3
Hawlēr Iraq see Arbīl
Hawley U.S.A. 135 H3
Hawng Luk Myanmar 70 B2
Ḩawrān, Wādī watercourse Iraq 91 F4
Ḩawshah, Jibāl al mts Saudi Arabia 88 B6
Hawston S. Africa 100 D8
Hawthorne U.S.A. 128 D2
Haxat China 74 B3
Haxby U.K. 48 F4
Hay Australia 112 B5
Hay watercourse Australia 110 B5
Hay r. Canada 120 H2
Haya China 72 I4
Hayachine-san mt. Japan 75 F5
Hayastan country Asia see Armenia
Haydān, Wādī al r. Jordan 85 B4
Haydarābad Iran 88 B2
Hayden AZ U.S.A. 129 H5
Hayden CO U.S.A. 129 J1
Hayden IN U.S.A. 134 C4
Hayes r. Man. Canada 121 M3
Hayes r. Nunavut Canada 119 I3
Hayes Halvø pen. Greenland 119 L2
Hayfield Reservoir U.S.A. 129 F5
Hayfork U.S.A. 128 B1
Hayl, Wādī watercourse Syria 85 C3
Hayl, Wādī al watercourse Syria 85 D2
Hayle U.K. 49 B8
Haymā' Oman 87 I6
Haymana Turkey 90 D3
Haymarket U.S.A. 135 G4
Hay-on-Wye U.K. 49 D6
Hayrabolu Turkey 59 L4
Hay River Canada 118 G3
Hay River Reserve Canada 120 H2
Hays KS U.S.A. 130 D4
Hays MT U.S.A. 126 F2
Ḩays Yemen 86 F7
Haysville U.S.A. 131 D4
Haysyn Ukr. 43 F6
Ḩayţān, Jabal hill Egypt 85 A4
Hayward CA U.S.A. 128 B3
Hayward WI U.S.A. 130 F2
Haywards Heath U.K. 49 G8
Hazar Turkm. see Cheleken
Hazarajat reg. Afgh. 89 G3
Hazard U.S.A. 134 D5
Hazaribag India see Hazaribagh
Hazaribagh India 83 F5
Hazaribagh Range mts India 83 E5
Hazār Masjed, Kūh-e mts Iran 88 E2
Hazebrouck France 52 C4
Hazelton Canada 120 E4
Hazen Strait Canada 119 G2
Hazerswoude-Rijndijk Neth. 52 E2
Hazhdanahr reg. Afgh. 89 G2
Hazleton IN U.S.A. 134 B4
Hazleton PA U.S.A. 135 H3
Hazlett, Lake salt flat Australia 108 E5
Hazrat Sultan Afgh. 89 G2
H. Bouchard Arg. 144 D4
Headford Rep. of Ireland 51 C4
Headingly Australia 110 B4
Head of Bight b. Australia 109 E7
Healdsburg U.S.A. 128 B2
Healesville Australia 112 B6
Healy U.S.A. 118 D3
Heanor U.K. 49 F5
▶Heard and McDonald Islands terr. Indian Ocean 149 M9
Australian External Territory.
Heard Island Indian Ocean 149 M9
Hearne U.S.A. 131 D6
Hearne Lake Canada 121 H2
Hearrenfean Neth. see Heerenveen
Hearst Canada 122 E4
Hearst Island Antarctica 152 L2
Heart r. U.S.A. 130 C2
Heart of Neolithic Orkney tourist site U.K. 50 F1
Heathcote Australia 112 B6
Heathfield U.K. 49 H8
Heathsville U.S.A. 135 G5
Hebbardsville U.S.A. 134 B5
Hebbronville U.S.A. 131 D7
Hebei prov. China 73 L5
Hebel Australia 112 C2
Heber U.S.A. 129 H4
Heber City U.S.A. 129 H1
Heber Springs U.S.A. 131 E5
Hebi China 73 K5
Hebron Canada 123 J2
Hebron U.S.A. 130 D3
Hebron West Bank 85 B4
Hecate Strait Canada 120 D4
Hecheng Jiangxi China see Zixi
Hecheng Zhejiang China see Qingtian
Hechi China 77 F3
Hechuan Chongqing China 76 E2
Hechuan Jiangxi China see Yongxing
Hecla Island Canada 121 L5
Hede China see Sheyang
Hede Sweden 44 H5
Hedemora Sweden 45 I6
He Devil Mountain U.S.A. 126 D3
Hedi Shuiku resr China 77 F4
Heech Neth. see Heeg
Heeg Neth. 52 F2
Heek Germany 52 H2
Heer Belgium 52 E4
Heerde Neth. 52 G2
Heerenveen Neth. 52 F2
Heerhugowaard Neth. 52 E2
Heerlen Neth. 52 F4
Ḩefa Israel see Haifa
Ḩefa, Mifraz Israel see Haifa, Bay of
Hefei China 77 H2
Hefeng China 77 F2
Heflin U.S.A. 133 C5
Hegang China 74 C3
Heho Myanmar 70 B2
Heidan r. Jordan see Haydān, Wādī al
Heidberg hill Germany 53 L3
Heide Germany 47 L3
Heide Namibia 100 C2
Heidelberg Germany 53 I5
Heidelberg S. Africa 101 I4
Heidenheim an der Brenz Germany 53 K6
Heihe China 74 B2
Heilbron S. Africa 101 H4
Heilbronn Germany 53 J5
Heiligenhafen Germany 47 M3
Hei Ling Chau i. Hong Kong China 77 [inset]
Heilongjiang prov. China 74 C3
Heilong Jiang r. China 74 D2
also known as Amur (Rus. Fed.)
Heilong Jiang r. Rus. Fed. see Amur
Heilsbronn Germany 53 K5
Heilungkiang prov. China see Heilongjiang
Heinola Fin. 45 O6
Heinze Islands Myanmar 71 B4
Heirnkut Myanmar 70 A1
Heishi Beihu l. China 83 E2
Heishui China 76 D1
Heisker Islands U.K. see Monach Islands
Heist-op-den-Berg Belgium 52 E3
Ḩeiţân, Gebel hill Egypt see Ḩayţān, Jabal
Ḩejaz reg. Saudi Arabia see Hijaz
Hejiang China 76 E2
He Jiang r. China 77 F4
Hejing China 80 G3
Hekimhan Turkey 90 E3
Hekla vol. Iceland 44 [inset]
Hekou Gansu China 72 I5
Hekou Hubei China 77 G2
Hekou Jiangxi China see Yanshan
Hekou Sichuan China see Yajiang
Hekou Yunnan China 76 D4
Helagsfjället mt. Sweden 44 H5
Helam India 76 B3
Helan Shan mts China 72 J5
Helbra Germany 53 L3
Helen atoll Palau 69 I6
Helena AR U.S.A. 131 F5
▶Helena MT U.S.A. 126 E3
State capital of Montana.
Helen Reef Palau 69 I6
Helensburgh U.K. 50 E4
Helen Springs Australia 108 F4
Ḩelez Israel 85 B4
Helgoland i. Germany 47 K3
Helgoländer Bucht g. Germany 47 L3
Heligoland i. Germany see Helgoland
Heligoland Bight g. Germany see Helgoländer Bucht
Heliopolis Lebanon see Ba'albek
Helixi China see Ningguo
Hella Iceland 44 [inset]
Helland Norway 44 J2
Hellas country Europe see Greece
Helleh r. Iran 88 C4
Hellespont strait Turkey see Dardanelles
Hellevoetsluis Neth. 52 E3
Hellhole Gorge National Park Australia 110 D5
Hellín Spain 57 F4
Hellinikon tourist site Greece 86 A3
Hells Canyon gorge U.S.A. 126 D3
Hell-Ville Madag. see Andoany
Helmand r. Afgh. 89 F4
Helmantica Spain see Salamanca
Helmbrechts Germany 53 L4
Helme r. Germany 53 L3
Helmeringhausen Namibia 100 C3
Helmond Neth. 52 F3
Helmsdale U.K. 50 F2
Helmsdale r. U.K. 50 F2
Helmstedt Germany 53 L2
Helong China 74 C4
Helper U.S.A. 129 H2
Helpter Berge hills Germany 53 N1
Helsingborg Sweden 45 H8
Helsingfors Fin. see Helsinki
Helsingør Denmark 45 H8
▶Helsinki Fin. 45 N6
Capital of Finland.
Helston U.K. 49 B8
Helvécia Brazil 145 D2
Helvetic Republic country Europe see Switzerland
Ḩelwân Egypt see Ḩulwān
Hemel Hempstead U.K. 49 G7
Hemet U.S.A. 128 E5
Hemingford U.S.A. 130 C3
Hemlock Lake U.S.A. 135 G2
Hemmingen Germany 53 J2
Hemmingford Canada 135 I1
Hemmoor Germany 53 J1
Hempstead U.S.A. 131 D6
Hemsby U.K. 49 I6
Hemse Sweden 45 K8
Henan China 76 D1
Henan prov. China 77 G1
Henares r. Spain 57 E3
Henashi-zaki pt Japan 75 E4
Henbury Australia 109 F6
Hendek Turkey 59 N4
Henderson KY U.S.A. 134 B5
Henderson NC U.S.A. 132 E4
Henderson NV U.S.A. 129 F3
Henderson NY U.S.A. 135 G2
Henderson TN U.S.A. 131 F5
Henderson TX U.S.A. 131 E5
Henderson Island Pitcairn Is 151 L7
Hendersonville NC U.S.A. 133 D5
Hendersonville TN U.S.A. 134 B5
Henderville atoll Kiribati see Aranuka
Hendon U.K. 49 G7
Hendorābī i. Iran 88 D5
Hendy-Gwyn U.K. see Whitland
Hengām Iran 89 E5
Hengduan Shan mts China 76 C2
Hengelo Neth. 52 G2
Hengfeng China 77 H2
Hengnan China see Hengyang
Hengshan China 74 C3
Heng Shan mt. China 77 G3
Hengshui Hebei China 73 L5
Hengshui Jiangxi China see Chongyi
Hengxian China 77 F4
Hengyang Hunan China 77 G3
Hengyang Hunan China 77 G3
Hengzhou China see Hengxian
Heniches'k Ukr. 43 G7
Henley N.Z. 113 C7
Henley-on-Thames U.K. 49 G7
Henlopen, Cape U.S.A. 135 H4
Hennef (Sieg) Germany 53 H4
Hennenman S. Africa 101 H4
Hennepin U.S.A. 130 F3
Hennessey U.S.A. 131 D4
Hennigsdorf Berlin Germany 53 N2
Henniker U.S.A. 135 J2
Henning U.S.A. 134 B3
Henrietta U.S.A. 131 D5
Henrietta Maria, Cape Canada 122 E3
Henrieville U.S.A. 129 H3
Henrique de Carvalho Angola see Saurimo
Henry, Cape U.S.A. 135 G5
Henry Ice Rise Antarctica 152 A1
Henryk Arctowski research station Antarctica see Arctowski
Henry Kater, Cape Canada 119 L3
Henry Mountains U.S.A. 129 H2
Hensall Canada 134 E2
Henshaw, Lake U.S.A. 128 E5
Hentiesbaai Namibia 100 B2
Henty Australia 112 C5
Henzada Myanmar 70 A3
Heping Guangdong China 77 G3
Heping Guizhou China see Huishui
Heping Guizhou China see Yanhe
Hepo China see Jiexi
Heppner U.S.A. 126 D3
Heptanesus is Greece see Ionian Islands
Hepu China 77 F4
Heqing China 76 D3
Heraclea Turkey see Ereğli
Heraclea Pontica Turkey see Ereğli
Heraklion Greece see Iraklion
Herald Cays atolls Australia 110 E3
Herāt Afgh. 89 F3
Hérault r. France 56 F5
Herbertabad India 71 A5
Herbert Downs Australia 110 B4
Herbert River Falls National Park Australia 110 D3
Herbert Wash salt flat Australia 109 D6
Herborn Germany 53 I4
Herbstein Germany 53 J4
Hercules Dome ice feature Antarctica 152 K1
Herdecke Germany 53 H3
Herdorf Germany 53 H4
Hereford U.K. 49 E6
Hereford U.S.A. 131 C5
Héréhérétué atoll Fr. Polynesia 151 K7
Herent Belgium 52 E4
Herford Germany 53 I2
Heringen (Werra) Germany 53 K4
Herington U.S.A. 130 D4
Herīs Iran 88 B2
Herisau Switz. 56 I3
Herkimer U.S.A. 135 H2
Herlen Gol r. China/Mongolia 73 L3
Herlen He r. China/Mongolia see Herlen Gol
Herleshausen Germany 53 K3
Herlong U.S.A. 128 C1
Herm i. Channel Is 49 E9
Hermanas Mex. 131 C7
Herma Ness hd U.K. 50 [inset]
Hermann U.S.A. 130 F4
Hermannsburg Germany 53 K2
Hermanus S. Africa 100 D8
Hermel Lebanon 85 C2
Hermes, Cape S. Africa 101 I6
Hermidale Australia 112 C3
Hermiston U.S.A. 126 D3
Hermitage MO U.S.A. 130 E4
Hermitage PA U.S.A. 134 E3
Hermitage Bay Canada 123 K5
Hermite, Islas is Chile 144 C9
Hermit Islands P.N.G. 69 L7
Hermon, Mount Lebanon/Syria 85 B3
Hermonthis Egypt see Armant
Hermopolis Magna Egypt see Al Ashmūnayn
Hermosa U.S.A. 129 J3
Hermosillo Mex. 127 F7
Hernandarias Para. 144 F3
Hernando U.S.A. 131 F5
Herndon CA U.S.A. 128 D3
Herndon PA U.S.A. 135 G3
Herndon WV U.S.A. 134 E5
Herne Germany 53 H3
Herne Bay U.K. 49 I7
Herning Denmark 45 F8
Heroica Nogales Mex. see Nogales
Heroica Puebla de Zaragoza Mex. see Puebla
Hérouville-St-Clair France 49 G9
Herowābād Iran see Khalkhāl
Herrera del Duque Spain 57 D4
Herrieden Germany 53 K5
Hershey U.S.A. 135 G3
Hertford U.K. 49 G7
Hertzogville S. Africa 101 G5
Herve Belgium 52 F4
Hervé, Lac l. Canada 123 H3
Hervey Islands Cook Is 151 J7
Herzberg Brandenburg Germany 53 M2
Herzberg Brandenburg Germany 53 N3
Herzlake Germany 53 H2
Herzliyya Israel 85 B3
Herzogenaurach Germany 53 K5
Herzsprung Germany 53 M1
Ḩesār Iran 88 C4
Ḩeşār Iran 88 E5
Hesdin France 52 C4
Hesel Germany 53 H1
Heshan China 77 F4
Heshengqiao China 77 G2
Hesperia U.S.A. 128 E4
Hesperus U.S.A. 129 I3
Hesperus Peak U.S.A. 129 I3
Hesquiat Canada 120 E5
Hess r. Canada 120 C2
Heßdorf Germany 53 K5
Hesse land Germany see Hessen
Hesselberg hill Germany 53 K5
Hessen land Germany 53 J4
Hessisch Lichtenau Germany 53 J3
Hess Mountains Canada 120 C2
Het r. Laos 70 D2
Heteren Neth. 52 F3
Hetou China 77 F4
Hettinger U.S.A. 130 C2
Hetton U.K. 48 E4
Hettstedt Germany 53 L3
Heung Kong Tsai Hong Kong China see Aberdeen
Ḩevron West Bank see Hebron
Hexham U.K. 48 E4
Hexian Anhui China 77 H2
Hexian Guangxi China see Hezhou
Heyang China 77 F1
Ḩeydarābād Iran 89 F4
Heydebreck Poland see Kędzierzyn-Koźle
Heysham U.K. 48 E4
Heyshope Dam S. Africa 101 J4
Heyuan China 77 G4
Heywood U.K. 48 E5
Heze China 77 G1
Hezhang China 76 E3
Hezheng China 76 D1
Hezhou China 77 F3
Hezuo China 76 D1
Hezuozhen China see Hezuo
Hialeah U.S.A. 133 D7
Hiawassee U.S.A. 133 D5
Hiawatha U.S.A. 130 E4
Hibbing U.S.A. 130 E2
Hibbs, Point Australia 111 [inset]
Hibernia Reef Australia 108 C3
Hīchān Iran 89 F5
Hicks Bay N.Z. 113 G3
Hicks Lake Canada 121 K2
Hicksville U.S.A. 134 C3
Hico U.S.A. 131 D5
Hidaka-sanmyaku mts Japan 74 F4
Hidalgo Mex. 131 D7
Hidalgo del Parral Mex. 131 B7
Hidrolândia Brazil 145 A2
Hierosolyma Israel/West Bank see Jerusalem
Higashi-suidō sea chan. Japan 75 C6
Higgins U.S.A. 131 C4
Higgins Bay U.S.A. 135 H2
Higgins Lake U.S.A. 134 C1
High Atlas mts Morocco see Haut Atlas
High Desert U.S.A. 126 C4
High Island i. Hong Kong China 77 [inset]
High Island U.S.A. 131 E6
High Island Reservoir Hong Kong China 77 [inset]
Highland Peak CA U.S.A. 128 D2
Highland Peak NV U.S.A. 129 F3
Highlands U.S.A. 135 I3
Highland Springs U.S.A. 135 G5
High Level Canada 120 G3
Highmore U.S.A. 130 D2
High Point U.S.A. 132 E5
High Point hill U.S.A. 135 H3
High Prairie Canada 120 G4
High River Canada 120 H5
Highrock Lake Man. Canada 121 K4
Highrock Lake Sask. Canada 121 J3
High Springs U.S.A. 133 D6
High Tatras mts Poland/Slovakia see Tatra Mountains
High Wycombe U.K. 49 G7
Higuera de Zaragoza Mex. 127 F8
Higüey Dom. Rep. 137 K5
Hiiumaa i. Estonia 45 M7
Hijānah, Buḩayrat al imp. l. Syria 85 C3
Hijaz reg. Saudi Arabia 86 E4
Ḩikmah, Ra's al pt Egypt 90 B5
Hiko U.S.A. 129 F3
Hikone Japan 75 E6
Hikurangi mt. N.Z. 113 G3
Hila Indon. 108 D1
Hilāl, Jabal hill Egypt 85 A4
Hilāl, Ra's al pt Libya 86 B3
Hilary Coast Antarctica 152 H1
Hildale U.S.A. 129 G3
Hildburghausen Germany 53 K4
Hilders Germany 53 K4
Hildesheim Germany 53 J2
Hillah Iraq 91 G4
Hill City U.S.A. 130 D4
Hillegom Neth. 52 E2
Hill End Australia 112 D4
Hillerød Denmark 45 H9
Hillgrove Australia 110 D3
Hill Island Lake Canada 121 I2
Hillman U.S.A. 134 D1
Hillsboro ND U.S.A. 130 D2
Hillsboro NM U.S.A. 127 G6
Hillsboro OH U.S.A. 134 D4
Hillsboro OR U.S.A. 126 C3
Hillsboro TX U.S.A. 131 D5
Hillsdale IN U.S.A. 134 B4
Hillsdale MI U.S.A. 134 C3
Hillside Australia 108 B5
Hillston Australia 112 B4
Hillsville U.S.A. 134 E5
Hilo HI U.S.A. 127 [inset]
Hilton Australia 110 B4
Hilton S. Africa 101 J5
Hilton U.S.A. 135 G2
Hilton Head Island U.S.A. 133 D5
Hilvan Turkey 90 E3
Hilversum Neth. 52 F2
Himachal Pradesh state India 82 D3
Himalaya mts Asia 82 D2
Himalchul mt. Nepal 83 F3
Himanka Fin. 44 M4
Ḩimār, Wādī al watercourse Syria/Turkey 85 D1
Himarë Albania 59 H4
Himatnagar India 82 C5
Himeji Japan 75 D6
Ḩimş Syria see Homs
Ḩimş, Baḩrat resr Syria see Qaţţīnah, Buḩayrat
Hinchinbrook Island Australia 110 D3
Hinckley U.K. 49 F6
Hinckley MN U.S.A. 130 E2
Hinckley UT U.S.A. 129 G2
Hinckley Reservoir U.S.A. 135 H2
Hindaun India 82 D4
Hinderwell U.K. 48 G4
Hindley U.K. 48 E5
Hindman U.S.A. 134 D5
Hindmarsh, Lake dry lake Australia 111 C8
Hindu Kush mts Afgh./Pak. 89 G3
Hindupur India 84 C3
Hines Creek Canada 120 G3
Hinesville U.S.A. 133 D6
Hinganghat India 84 C1
Hingoli India 84 C2
Hınıs Turkey 91 F3
Hinnøya i. Norway 44 I2
Hinojosa del Duque Spain 57 D4
Hinsdale U.S.A. 135 I2
Hinte Germany 53 H1
Hinthada Myanmar see Henzada
Hinton Canada 120 G4
Hinton U.S.A. 134 E5
Hiort i. U.K. see St Kilda
Hippolytushoef Neth. 52 E2
Hipponium Italy see Vibo Valentia
Hippo Regius Alg. see Annaba
Hippo Zarytus Tunisia see Bizerte
Hirabit Dağ mt. Turkey 91 G3
Hirakud Dam India 83 E5
Hirakud Reservoir India 83 E5
Hirapur India 82 D4
Hiriyur India 84 C3
Hirosaki Japan 74 F4
Hiroshima Japan 75 D6
Hirschaid Germany 53 L5
Hirschberg Germany 53 L4
Hirschberg mt. Germany 47 M7
Hirschberg Poland see Jelenia Góra
Hirschenstn mt. Germany 53 M6
Hirson France 52 E5
Hîrşova Romania see Hârşova
Hirta is U.K. see St Kilda
Hirtshals Denmark 45 F8
Hisar India 82 C3
Hisar Iran 88 C2
Hisarköy Turkey see Domaniç
Hisarönü Turkey 59 O4
Hisb, Sha'ib watercourse Iraq 91 G5
Ḩisbān Jordan 85 B4
Hisiu P.N.G. 69 L8
Hisor Tajik. 89 H2
Hisor Tizmasi mts Tajik./Uzbek. see Gissar Range
Hispalis Spain see Seville
Hispania country Europe see Spain
▶Hispaniola i. Caribbean Sea 137 J4
Consists of the Dominican Republic and Haiti.
Hispur Glacier Jammu and Kashmir 82 C1
Hissar India see Hisar
Hisua India 83 F4
Ḩisyah Syria 85 C2
Hīt Iraq 91 F4
Hitachi Japan 75 F5
Hitachinaka Japan 75 F5
Hitra i. Norway 44 F5
Hitzacker Germany 53 L1
Hiva Oa i. Fr. Polynesia 151 K6
Hixon Canada 120 F4
Hixson Cay reef Australia 110 F4
Hiyon watercourse Israel 85 B4
Hizan Turkey 91 F3
Hjälmaren l. Sweden 45 I7
Hjerkinn Norway 44 F5
Hjo Sweden 45 I7
Hjørring Denmark 45 G8
Hkakabo Razi mt. China/Myanmar 76 C2
Hlaingdet Myanmar 70 B2
Hlako Kangri mt. China see Lhagoi Kangri
Hlane Royal National Park Swaziland 101 J4
Hlatikulu Swaziland 101 J4
Hlegu Myanmar 70 B3
Hlohlowane S. Africa 101 H5
Hlotse Lesotho 101 I5
Hluhluwe-Umfolozi Park nature res. S. Africa 101 J5
Hlukhiv Ukr. 43 G6
Hlung-Tan Myanmar 70 B2
Hlusha Belarus 43 F5
Hlybokaye Belarus 45 O9
Ho Ghana 96 D4

Huzhou China 77 I2
Hvannadalshnúkur *vol.* Iceland 44 [inset]
Hvar *i.* Croatia 58 G3
Hvide Sande Denmark 45 F8
Hvíta *r.* Iceland 44 [inset]
Hwange Zimbabwe 99 C5
Hwange National Park Zimbabwe 99 C5
Hwang Ho *r.* China *see* Yellow River
Hwedza Zimbabwe 99 D5
Hwlffordd U.K. *see* Haverfordwest
Hyannis *MA* U.S.A. 135 J3
Hyannis *NE* U.S.A. 130 C3
Hyargas Nuur *salt l.* Mongolia 80 H2
Hyco Lake U.S.A. 134 F5
Hyde N.Z. 113 C7
Hyden Australia 109 B8
Hyden U.S.A. 134 D5
Hyde Park U.S.A. 135 I1
Hyderabad India 84 C2
Hyderabad Pak. 89 H5
Hydra *i.* Greece *see* Ydra
Hyères France 56 H5
Hyères, Îles d' *is* France 56 H5
Hyesan N. Korea 74 C4
Hyland, Mount Australia 112 F3
Hyland Post Canada 120 D3
Hyllestad Norway 45 D6
Hyltebruk Sweden 45 H8
Hyndman Peak U.S.A. 126 E4
Hyōno-sen *mt.* Japan 75 D6
Hyrcania Iran *see* Gorgān
Hyrynsalmi Fin. 44 P4
Hysham U.S.A. 126 G3
Hythe Canada 120 G4
Hythe U.K. 49 I7
Hyūga Japan 75 C6
Hyvinkää Fin. 45 N6

I

Iaciara Brazil 145 B1
Iaco *r.* Brazil 142 E5
Iaçu Brazil 145 C1
Iadera Croatia *see* Zadar
Iaeger U.S.A. 134 E5
Iakora Madag. 99 E6
Ialomița *r.* Romania 59 L2
Ianca Romania 59 L2
Iași Romania 59 L1
Iba Phil. 69 F3
Ibadan Nigeria 96 D4
Ibagué Col. 142 C3
Ibaiti Brazil 145 A3
Ibapah U.S.A. 129 G1
Ibarra Ecuador 142 C3
Ibb Yemen 86 F7
Ibbenbüren Germany 53 H2
Iberá, Esteros del *marsh* Arg. 144 E3
Iberia Peru 142 E6

▶Iberian Peninsula Europe 57
Consists of Portugal, Spain and Gibraltar.

Iberville, Lac d' *l.* Canada 123 G3
Ibeto Nigeria 96 D3
iBhayi S. Africa *see* Port Elizabeth
Ibi Indon. 71 B6
Ibi Nigeria 96 D4
Ibiá Brazil 145 B2
Ibiaí Brazil 145 B2
Ibiapaba, Serra da *hills* Brazil 143 J4
Ibiassucê Brazil 145 C1
Ibicaraí Brazil 145 D1
Ibiquera Brazil 145 C1
Ibirama Brazil 145 A4
Ibiranhém Brazil 145 C2
Ibitinga Brazil 145 A3
Ibiza Spain 57 G4
Ibiza *i.* Spain 57 G4
Iblei, Monti *mts Sicily* Italy 58 F6
Ibn Buşayyiş *well* Saudi Arabia 88 B5
Ibotirama Brazil 143 J6
Iboundji, Mont *hill* Gabon 98 B4
Ibrā' Oman 88 E6
İbradı Turkey 90 C3
Ibrī Oman 88 E6
Ica Peru 142 C6
Ica *r.* Peru *see* Putumayo
Içana Brazil 142 E3
Içana *r.* Brazil 142 E3
Icaria *i.* Greece *see* Ikaria
Icatu Brazil 143 J4
Iceberg Canyon *gorge* U.S.A. 129 F3
İçel Turkey 85 B1
İçel *prov.* Turkey 85 A1

▶Iceland *country* Europe 44 [inset]
2nd largest island in Europe.
Europe 5, 38–39

Iceland Basin *sea feature*
N. Atlantic Ocean 148 G2
Icelandic Plateau *sea feature*
N. Atlantic Ocean 153 I2
Ichalkaranji India 84 B2
Ichinomiya Japan 75 E6
Ichinoseki Japan 75 F5
Ichinskiy, Vulkan *vol.* Rus. Fed. 65 Q4
Ichkeul National Park Tunisia 58 C6
Ichnya Ukr. 43 G6
Ichtegem Belgium 52 D3
Ichtershausen Germany 53 K4
Icó Brazil 143 K5
Iconha Brazil 145 C3
Iconium Turkey *see* Konya
Icosium Alg. *see* Algiers
Iculisma France *see* Angoulême
Icy Cape U.S.A. 118 B2
İd Turkey *see* Narman
Idabel U.S.A. 131 E5
Ida Grove U.S.A. 130 E3
Idah Nigeria 96 D4
Idaho *state* U.S.A. 126 E3
Idaho City U.S.A. 126 E4
Idaho Falls U.S.A. 126 E4
Idalia National Park Australia 110 D5
Idar India 82 C5
Idar-Oberstein Germany 53 H5
Ideriyn Gol *r.* Mongolia 80 J2
Idfū Egypt 86 D5
Idhān Awbārī *des.* Libya 96 E2
Idhān Murzūq *des.* Libya 96 E2
Idhra *i.* Greece *see* Ydra
Idi Amin Dada, Lake
Dem. Rep. Congo/Uganda *see* Edward, Lake
Idiofa Dem. Rep. Congo 99 B4
Idivuoma Sweden 44 M2
Idkū Egypt 90 C5
Idle *r.* U.K. 48 G5
Idlewild *airport* U.S.A. *see* John F. Kennedy
Idlib Syria 85 C2
Idra *i.* Greece *see* Ydra
Idre Sweden 45 H6
Idstein Germany 53 I4
Idutywa S. Africa 101 I7
Idzhevan Armenia *see* Ijevan
Iecava Latvia 45 N8
Iepê Brazil 145 A3
Ieper Belgium 52 C4
Ierapetra Greece 59 K7
Ierissou, Kolpos *b.* Greece 59 J4
Ifakara Tanz. 99 D4
Ifalik *atoll* Micronesia 69 K5
Ifaluk *atoll* Micronesia *see* Ifalik
Ifanadiana Madag. 99 E6
Ife Nigeria 96 D4
Ifenat Chad 97 E3
Iferouâne Niger 96 D3
Iffley Australia 110 C3
Ifjord Norway 44 O1
Ifôghas, Adrar des *hills* Mali 92 D3
Iforas, Adrar des *hills* Mali *see* Ifôghas, Adrar des
Igan *Sarawak* Malaysia 68 E6
Iganga Uganda 97 G4
Igarapava Brazil 145 B3
Igarka Rus. Fed. 64 J3
Igatpuri India 84 B2
Igbeti Nigeria *see* Igbetti
Igbetti Nigeria 96 D4
Igdir Iran 88 B2
Iğdır Turkey 91 G3
Iggesund Sweden 45 J6
Igikpak, Mount U.S.A. 118 C3
Igizyar China 89 J2
Iglesias *Sardinia* Italy 58 C5
Iglesiente *reg. Sardinia* Italy 58 C5
Igloolik Canada 119 J3
Igluligaarjuk Canada *see* Chesterfield Inlet
Ignace Canada 121 N5
Ignacio Zaragosa Mex. 127 G7
Ignacio Zaragoza Mex. 131 C8
Ignalina Lith. 45 O9
İğneada Turkey 59 L4
İğneada Burnu *pt* Turkey 59 M4
Ignoitijala India 71 A5
iGoli S. Africa *see* Johannesburg
Igoumenitsa Greece 59 I5
Igra Rus. Fed. 41 Q4
Igrim Rus. Fed. 41 S3
Iguaçu *r.* Brazil 145 A4
Iguaçu, Saltos do *waterfall* Arg./Brazil *see* Iguaçu Falls
Iguaçu Falls Arg./Brazil 144 F3
Iguaí Brazil 145 C1
Iguala Mex. 136 E5
Igualada Spain 57 G3
Iguape Brazil 145 B4
Iguaraçu Brazil 145 A3
Iguatama Brazil 145 B3
Iguatemi Brazil 144 F2
Iguatu Brazil 143 K5
Iguazú, Cataratas do *waterfall* Arg./Brazil *see* Iguaçu Falls
Iguéla Gabon 98 A4
Iguidi, Erg *des.* Alg./Mauritania 96 C2
Igunga Tanz. 99 D4
Iharaña Madag. 99 E5
Ihavandhippolhu Atoll Maldives 84 B5
Ihavandiffulu Atoll Maldives *see* Ihavandhippolhu Atoll
Ih Bogd Uul *mt.* Mongolia 80 J3
Ihosy Madag. 99 E6
Iide-san *mt.* Japan 75 E5
Iijärvi *l.* Fin. 44 O2
Iijoki *r.* Fin. 44 N4
Iisalmi Fin. 44 O5
Iizuka Japan 75 C6
Ijebu-Ode Nigeria 96 D4
Ijevan Armenia 91 G2
IJmuiden Neth. 52 E2
IJssel *r.* Neth. 52 F2
IJsselmeer *l.* Neth. 52 F2
IJzer *r.* Belgium *see* Yser
Ikaahuk Canada *see* Sachs Harbour
Ikaalinen Fin. 45 M6
Ikageleng S. Africa 101 H3
Ikageng S. Africa 101 H4
iKapa S. Africa *see* Cape Town
Ikare Nigeria 96 D4
Ikaria *i.* Greece 59 L6
Ikast Denmark 45 F8
Ikeda Japan 74 F4
Ikela Dem. Rep. Congo 98 C4
Ikhtiman Bulg. 59 J3
Ikhutseng S. Africa 100 G5
Iki-Burul Rus. Fed. 43 J7
Ikom Nigeria 96 D4
Iksan S. Korea 75 B6
Ikungu Tanz. 99 D4
Ilagan Phil. 77 I5
Ilaisamis Kenya 98 D3
Īlām Iran 88 B3
Ilam Nepal 83 F4
Ilan Taiwan 77 I3
Ilave Peru 142 E7
Iława Poland 47 Q4
Ilazārān, Kūh-e *mt.* Iran 88 E4
Île-à-la-Crosse Canada 121 J4
Île-à-la-Crosse, Lac *l.* Canada 121 J4
Ilebo Dem. Rep. Congo 99 C4
Île-de-France *admin. reg.* France 52 C6
Île Europa *i.* Indian Ocean *see* Europa, Île
Ilek Kazakh. 41 Q5
Ilen *r.* Rep. of Ireland 51 C6
Ileret Kenya 98 D3
Ileza Rus. Fed. 42 I3
Ilfeld Germany 53 K3
Ilford Canada 121 M3
Ilford U.K. 49 H7
Ilfracombe Australia 110 D4
Ilfracombe U.K. 49 C7
Ilgaz Turkey 90 D2
Ilgın Turkey 90 C3
Ilha Grande, Represa *resr* Brazil 144 F2
Ilha Solteíra, Represa *resr* Brazil 145 A3
Ílhavo Port. 57 B3
Ilhéus Brazil 145 D1
Ili Kazakh. *see* Kapchagay
Iliamna Lake U.S.A. 118 C4
İliç Turkey 90 E3
Il'ichevsk Azer. *see* Şärur
Il'ichevsk Ukr. *see* Illichivs'k
Ilici Spain *see* Elche-Elx
Iligan Phil. 69 G5
Ilimananngip Nunaa *i.* Greenland 119 P2
Il'inka Rus. Fed. 43 J7
Il'inskiy *Permskaya Oblast'* Rus. Fed. 41 R4
Il'inskiy *Sakhalinskaya Oblast'* Rus. Fed. 74 F3
Il'insko-Podomskoye Rus. Fed. 42 J3
Ilion U.S.A. 135 H2
Ilium *tourist site* Turkey *see* Troy
Iliysk Kazakh. *see* Kapchagay
Ilkal India 84 C3
Ilkeston U.K. 49 F6
Ilkley U.K. 48 F5
Illapel Chile 144 B4
Illéla Niger 96 D3
Iller *r.* Germany 47 L6
Illichivs'k Ukr. 59 N1
Illimani, Nevado de *mt.* Bol. 142 E7
Illinois *r.* U.S.A. 130 F4
Illinois *state* U.S.A. 134 A3
Illizi Alg. 96 D2
Illogwa *watercourse* Australia 106 A5
Ilm *r.* Germany 53 L3
Ilmajoki Fin. 44 M5
Il'men', Ozero *l.* Rus. Fed. 42 F4
Ilmenau Germany 53 K4
Ilmenau *r.* Germany 53 K1
Ilminster U.K. 49 E8
Ilo Peru 142 D7
Iloilo Phil. 69 G4
Ilomantsi Fin. 44 Q5
Ilong India 76 B3
Ilorin Nigeria 96 D4
Ilovlya Rus. Fed. 43 I6
Ilsede Germany 53 K2
Iluka Australia 112 F2
Ilulissat Greenland 119 M3
Iluppur India 84 C4
Ilva *i.* Italy *see* Elba, Isola d'
Imabari Japan 75 D6
Imaichi Japan 75 E5
Imala Moz. 99 D5
Imam-baba Turkm. 89 F2
İmamoğlu Turkey 90 D3
Iman Rus. Fed. *see* Dal'nerechensk
Iman *r.* Rus. Fed. 74 D3
Imari Japan 75 C6
Imaruí Brazil 145 A5
Imataca, Serranía de *mts* Venez. 142 F2
Imatra Fin. 45 P6
Imbituva Brazil 145 A4
imeni Babushkina Rus. Fed. 38 I4
imeni 26 Bakinskikh Komissarov Azer. *see* 26 Bakı Komissarı
imeni 26 Bakinskikh Komissarov Turkm. 88 D2
imeni C. A. Niyazova Turkm. 89 F2
imeni Chapayevka Turkm. *see* imeni C. A. Niyazova
imeni Kalinina Tajik. *see* Cheshtebe
imeni Kerbabayeva Turkm. 89 F2
imeni Kirova Kazakh. *see* Kopbirlik
imeni Petra Stuchki Latvia *see* Aizkraukle
imeni Poliny Osipenko Rus. Fed. 74 E1
imeni Tel'mana Rus. Fed. 74 D2
Īmī Eth. 98 E3
Imishli Azer. *see* İmişli
İmişli Azer. 91 H3
Imit Jammu and Kashmir 82 C1
Imja-do *i.* S. Korea 75 B6
Imlay U.S.A. 128 D1
Imlay City U.S.A. 134 D2
Imola Italy 58 D2
iMonti S. Africa *see* East London
Impendle S. Africa 101 I5
Imperatriz Brazil 143 I5
Imperia Italy 58 C3
Imperial *CA* U.S.A. 129 F5
Imperial *NE* U.S.A. 130 C3
Imperial Beach U.S.A. 128 E5
Imperial Dam U.S.A. 129 F5
Imperial Valley *plain* U.S.A. 129 F5
Imperieuse Reef Australia 108 B4
Impfondo Congo 98 B3
Imphal India 83 H4
İmralı Adası *i.* Turkey 59 M4
İmroz Turkey 59 K4
İmroz *i.* Turkey *see* Gökçeada
Imtān Syria 85 C3
Imuris Mex. 127 F7
In *r.* Rus. Fed. 74 D2
Ina Japan 75 E6
Inambari *r.* Peru 142 E6
Inari Fin. 44 O2
Inarijärvi *l.* Fin. 44 O2
Inarijoki *r.* Fin./Norway 44 N2
Inca Spain 57 H4
İnce Burnu *pt* Turkey 59 L4
İnce Burun *pt* Turkey 55 L3
Inch Rep. of Ireland 51 F5
Inchard, Loch *b.* U.K. 50 D2
Incheon S. Korea *see* Inch'ŏn
Inchicronan Lough *l.* Rep. of Ireland 51 D5
Inch'ŏn S. Korea 75 B5
Incirli Turkey *see* Karasu
Indaal, Loch *b.* U.K. 50 C5
Indalsälven *r.* Sweden 44 J5
Indalstø Norway 45 D6
Inda Silasē Eth. 98 D2
Indaw Myanmar 70 A2
Indawgyi, Lake Myanmar 76 C3
Indé Mex. 131 B7
Indefatigable Island *Galápagos* Ecuador *see* Santa Cruz, Isla
Independence *CA* U.S.A. 128 D3
Independence *IA* U.S.A. 130 F3
Independence *KS* U.S.A. 131 E4
Independence *KY* U.S.A. 134 C4
Independence *MO* U.S.A. 130 E4
Independence *VA* U.S.A. 134 E5
Independence Mountains U.S.A. 126 D4
Inder China 74 A3
Inderborskiy Kazakh. 78 E2
Indi India 84 C2

▶India *country* Asia 81 E7
2nd most populous country in the world and in Asia. 3rd largest country in Asia.
Asia 6, 62–63

Indian *r.* Canada 120 B2
Indiana U.S.A. 134 F3
Indiana *state* U.S.A. 134 B3
Indian-Antarctic Ridge *sea feature*
Southern Ocean 150 D9

▶Indianapolis U.S.A. 134 B4
State capital of Indiana.

Indian Cabins Canada 120 G3
Indian Desert India/Pak. *see* Thar Desert
Indian Harbour Canada 123 K3
Indian Head Canada 121 K5
Indian Lake U.S.A. 135 H2
Indian Lake *l. NY* U.S.A. 135 H2
Indian Lake *l. OH* U.S.A. 134 D3
Indian Lake *l. PA* U.S.A. 135 F3

▶Indian Ocean 149
3rd largest ocean in the world.

Indianola *IA* U.S.A. 130 E3
Indianola *MS* U.S.A. 131 F5
Indian Peak U.S.A. 129 G2
Indian Springs *IN* U.S.A. 134 B4
Indian Springs *NV* U.S.A. 129 F3
Indian Wells U.S.A. 129 H4
Indiga Rus. Fed. 42 K2
Indigirka *r.* Rus. Fed. 65 P2
Indigskaya Guba *b.* Rus. Fed. 38 K2
Inđija Serb. and Mont. 59 I2
Indin Lake Canada 120 H1
Indio U.S.A. 128 E5
Indira Point India *see* Pygmalion Point
Indispensable Reefs Solomon Is 107 G3
Indjija Serb. and Mont. *see* Inđija
Indo-China *reg.* Asia 70 D3

▶Indonesia *country* Asia 68 E7
4th most populous country in the world and 3rd in Asia.
Asia 6, 62–63

Indore India 82 C5
Indrapura, Gunung *vol.* Indon. *see* Kerinci, Gunung
Indravati *r.* India 84 D2
Indre *r.* France 56 E3
Indulkana Australia 109 F6
Indur India *see* Nizamabad
Indus *r.* China/Pak. 89 G6
also known as Sênggê Zangbo *or* Shiquan He
Indus, Mouths of the Pak. 89 G5
Indus Cone *sea feature* Indian Ocean 149 M4
Indwe S. Africa 101 H6
İnebolu Turkey 90 D2
İnegöl Turkey 59 M4
Inevi Turkey *see* Cihanbeyli
Inez U.S.A. 134 D5
Infantes Spain *see* Villanueva de los Infantes
Infiernillo, Presa *resr* Mex. 136 D5
Ing, Nam Mae *r.* Thai. 70 C2
Inga Rus. Fed. 44 S3
Ingalls, Mount U.S.A. 128 C2
Ingelmunster Belgium 52 D4
Ingenika *r.* Canada 120 E3
Ingersoll Canada 134 E2
Ingham Australia 110 D3
Ingichka Uzbek. 89 G2
Ingleborough *hill* U.K. 48 E4
Inglefield Land *reg.* Greenland 119 K2
Ingleton U.K. 48 E4
Inglewood *Qld* Australia 112 E2
Inglewood *Vic.* Australia 112 A6
Inglewood U.S.A. 128 D5
Ingoka Pum *mt.* Myanmar 70 B1
Ingoldmells U.K. 48 H5
Ingolstadt Germany 53 L6
Ingomar Australia 109 F7
Ingomar U.S.A. 126 G3
Ingonish Canada 123 J5
Ingraj Bazar India 83 G4
Ingram U.S.A. 134 F5
Ingray Lake Canada 120 G1
Ingrid Christensen Coast Antarctica 152 E2
Ingwavuma S. Africa 101 K4
Ingwavuma *r.* S. Africa/Swaziland *see* Ngwavuma
Ingwiller France 53 H6
Inhaca Moz. 101 K3
Inhaca, Península *pen.* Moz. 101 K4
Inhambane Moz. 101 L2
Inhambane *prov.* Moz. 101 L2
Inhaminga Moz. 99 D5
Inharrime Moz. 101 L3
Inhassoro Moz. 99 D6
Inhaúmas Brazil 145 B1
Inhobim Brazil 145 C1
Inhumas Brazil 145 A2
Inis Rep. of Ireland *see* Ennis
Inis Córthaidh Rep. of Ireland *see* Enniscorthy
Inishark *i.* Rep. of Ireland 51 B4
Inishbofin *i.* Rep. of Ireland 51 B4
Inisheer *i.* Rep. of Ireland 51 C4
Inishkea North *i.* Rep. of Ireland 51 B3
Inishkea South *i.* Rep. of Ireland 51 B3
Inishmaan *i.* Rep. of Ireland 51 C4
Inishmore *i.* Rep. of Ireland 51 C4
Inishmurray *i.* Rep. of Ireland 51 D3
Inishowen *pen.* Rep. of Ireland 51 E2
Inishowen Head *hd* Rep. of Ireland 51 F2
Inishtrahull *i.* Rep. of Ireland 51 E2
Inishturk *i.* Rep. of Ireland 51 B4
Injune Australia 111 E5
Inkerman Australia 110 C3
Inklin Canada 120 C3
Inklin *r.* Canada 120 C3
Inkylap Turkm. 89 F2
Inland Kaikoura Range *mts* N.Z. 113 D6
Inland Sea Japan *see* Seto-naikai
Inlet U.S.A. 135 H2
Inn *r.* Europe 47 M7
Innaanganeq *c.* Greenland 119 L2
Innamincka Australia 111 C5
Innamincka Regional Reserve *nature res.* Australia 111 C5
Inndyr Norway 44 I3
Inner Sound *sea chan.* U.K. 50 D3
Innes National Park Australia 111 B7
Innisfail Australia 110 D3
Innisfail Canada 120 H4
Innokent'yevka Rus. Fed. 74 C2
Innoko *r.* U.S.A. 118 C3
Innsbruck Austria 47 M7
Innuksuak *r.* Canada 122 F2
Inny *r.* Rep. of Ireland 51 E4
Inocência Brazil 145 A2
Inongo Dem. Rep. Congo 98 B4
İnönü Turkey 59 N5
Inoucdjouac Canada *see* Inukjuak
Inowrocław Poland 47 Q4
In Salah Alg. 96 D2
Insch U.K. 50 G3

▶Inscription, Cape Austr. 110 B3
Most westerly point of Oceania.

Insein Myanmar 70 B3
Insterburg Rus. Fed. *see* Chernyakhovsk
Inta Rus. Fed. 41 S2
Interamna Italy *see* Teramo
Interlaken Switz. 56 H3
International Falls U.S.A. 130 E1
Interview Island India 71 A4
Intracoastal Waterway *canal* U.S.A. 131 E6
Intutu Peru 142 D4
Inubō-zaki *pt* Japan 75 F6
Inukjuak Canada 122 F2
Inuvik Canada 118 E3
Inveraray U.K. 50 D4
Inverbervie U.K. 50 G4
Invercargill N.Z. 113 B8
Inverell Australia 112 E2
Invergordon U.K. 50 E3
Inverkeithing U.K. 50 F4
Inverleigh Australia 110 C3
Invermay Canada 121 K5
Inverness Canada 123 J5
Inverness U.K. 50 E3
Inverness *CA* U.S.A. 128 B2
Inverness *FL* U.S.A. 133 D6
Inverurie U.K. 50 G3
Investigator Channel Myanmar 71 B4
Investigator Group *is* Australia 109 F8
Investigator Ridge *sea feature*
Indian Ocean 149 O6
Investigator Strait Australia 111 B7
Inwood U.S.A. 135 F4
Inya Rus. Fed. 80 G1
Inyanga Zimbabwe *see* Nyanga
Inyangani *mt.* Zimbabwe 99 D5
Inyokern U.S.A. 128 E4
Inyo Mountains U.S.A. 128 D3
Inyonga Tanz. 99 D4
Inza Rus. Fed. 43 J5
Inzhavino Rus. Fed. 43 I5
Ioannina Greece 59 I5
Iokanga *r.* Rus. Fed. 42 H2
Iola U.S.A. 130 E4
Iolgo, Khrebet *mts* Rus. Fed. 80 G1
Iolotan' Turkm. *see* Yeloten
Iona Canada 123 J5
Iona *i.* U.K. 50 C4
Iona, Parque Nacional do *nat. park* Angola 99 B5
Ione U.S.A. 128 E2
Iongo Angola 99 B4
Ionia U.S.A. 134 C2
Ionian Islands Greece 59 H5
Ionian Sea Greece/Italy 58 H5
Ionioi Nisoi *is* Greece *see* Ionian Islands
Ios *i.* Greece 59 K6
Iowa *state* U.S.A. 130 E3
Iowa City U.S.A. 130 F3
Iowa Falls U.S.A. 130 E3
Ipameri Brazil 145 A2
Ipanema Brazil 145 C2
Iparía Peru 142 D5
Ipatinga Brazil 145 C2
Ipatovo Rus. Fed. 43 I7
Ipelegeng S. Africa 101 G4
Ipiales Col. 142 C3
Ipiaú Brazil 145 D1
Ipirá Brazil 145 D1
Ipiranga Brazil 145 A4
iPitoli S. Africa *see* Pretoria
Ipixuna *r.* Brazil 142 F5
Ipoh Malaysia 71 C6
Iporá Brazil 145 A2
Ippy Cent. Afr. Rep. 98 C3
İpsala Turkey 59 L4
Ipswich Australia 112 F1
Ipswich U.K. 49 I6
Ipswich U.S.A. 130 D2
Ipu Brazil 143 J4

▶Iqaluit Canada 119 L3
Territorial capital of Nunavut.

Iquique Chile 144 B2
Iquiri *r.* Brazil *see* Ituxi
Iquitos Peru 142 D4
Īrafshān *reg.* Iran 89 F5
Irai Brazil 144 F3
Irakleio Greece *see* Iraklion
Iraklion Greece 59 K7
Iramaia Brazil 145 C1
▶Iran *country* Asia 88 D3
Asia 6, 62–63
Iran, Pegunungan *mts* Indon. 68 E6
Īrānshahr Iran 89 F5
Irapuato Mex. 136 D4
▶Iraq *country* Asia 91 F4
Asia 6, 62–63
Irara Brazil 145 D1
Irati Brazil 145 A4
Irayel' Rus. Fed. 42 L2
Irazú, Volcán *vol.* Costa Rica 133 H7
Irbid Jordan 85 B3
Irbil Iraq *see* Arbīl
Irbit Rus. Fed. 64 H4
Irecê Brazil 143 J6

▶Ireland *i.* Rep. of Ireland/U.K. 51
4th largest island in Europe.

▶Ireland, Republic of *country* Europe 51 E4
Europe 5, 38–39
Irema Dem. Rep. Congo 98 C4
Irgiz Kazakh. 80 B2
Irgiz *r.* Kazakh. 80 B2
Iri S. Korea *see* Iksan
Irian, Teluk *b.* Indon. *see* Cenderawasih, Teluk
Iriba Chad 97 F3
Īrī Dāgh *mt.* Iran 88 B2
Iriga Phil. 69 G4
Irîgui *reg.* Mali/Mauritania 96 C3
Iringa Tanz. 99 D4
Iriri *r.* Brazil 143 H4
Irish Free State *country* Europe *see* Ireland, Republic of
Irish Sea Rep. of Ireland/U.K. 51 G4
Irituia Brazil 143 I4
'Irj *well* Saudi Arabia 88 C5
Irkutsk Rus. Fed. 72 I2
Irma Canada 121 I4
Irmak Turkey 90 D3
Irminger Basin *sea feature*
N. Atlantic Ocean 148 F2
Iron Baron Australia 111 B7
Irondequoit U.S.A. 135 G2
Iron Mountain U.S.A. 130 F2
Iron Mountain *mt.* U.S.A. 129 G3
Iron Range National Park Australia 110 C2
Iron River U.S.A. 130 F2
Ironton *MO* U.S.A. 130 F4
Ironton *OH* U.S.A. 134 D4
Ironwood Forest National Monument *nat. park* U.S.A. 129 H5
Iroquois *r.* U.S.A. 134 B3
Iroquois Falls Canada 122 E4
Irosin Phil. 69 G4
Irpen' Ukr. *see* Irpin'
Irpin' Ukr. 43 F6
'Irq al Ḩarūrī *des.* Saudi Arabia 88 B5
'Irq al Maẓhūr *des.* Saudi Arabia 88 A5
'Irq Banbān *des.* Saudi Arabia 88 B5
'Irq Jahām *des.* Saudi Arabia 88 B5
Irrawaddy *r.* Myanmar 70 A4
Irrawaddy, Mouths of the Myanmar 70 A4
Irshad Pass Afgh./Jammu and Kashmir 89 I2
Irta Rus. Fed. 42 K3
Irthing *r.* U.K. 48 E4

▶Irtysh *r.* Kazakh./Rus. Fed. 80 E1
5th longest river in Asia. Part of the 2nd longest river in Asia (Ob'-Irtysh).

Irún Spain 57 F2
Iruña Spain *see* Pamplona
Iruñea Spain *see* Pamplona
Irvine U.K. 50 E5
Irvine *CA* U.S.A. 128 E5
Irvine *KY* U.S.A. 134 D5
Irvine Glacier Antarctica 152 L2
Irving U.S.A. 131 D5
Irvington U.S.A. 134 B5
Irwin *r.* Australia 109 A7
Irwinton U.S.A. 133 D5
Isa Nigeria 96 D3
Isaac *r.* Australia 110 E4
Isabel U.S.A. 130 C2
Isabela Phil. 69 G5
Isabela, Isla *i. Galápagos* Ecuador 142 [inset]
Isabelia, Cordillera *mts* Nicaragua 137 G6
Isabella Lake U.S.A. 128 D4
Isachsen, Cape Canada 119 H2
Ísafjarðardjúp *est.* Iceland 44 [inset]
Ísafjörður Iceland 44 [inset]
Isa Khel Pak. 89 H3
Isar *r.* Germany 53 M6
Isbister U.K. 50 [inset]
Ischia, Isola d' *i.* Italy 58 E4
Ise Japan 75 E6
Isère *r.* France 56 G4
Isère, Pointe *pt* Fr. Guiana 143 H2
Iserlohn Germany 53 H3
Isernhagen Germany 53 J2
Isernia Italy 58 F4
Ise-shima National Park Japan 75 E6
Ise-wan *b.* Japan 75 E6
Iseyin Nigeria 96 D4
Isfahan Iran *see* Eşfahān
Isfana Kyrg. 89 H2
Isheyevka Rus. Fed. 43 K5
Ishigaki Japan 73 M8
Ishikari-wan *b.* Japan 74 F4
Ishim *r.* Kazakh./Rus. Fed. 80 D1
Ishinomaki Japan 75 F5
Ishinomaki-wan *b.* Japan 73 Q5
Ishioka Japan 75 F5
Ishkoshim Tajik. 89 H2
Ishpeming U.S.A. 132 C2
Ishtikhon Uzbek. *see* Ishtykhan
Ishtragh Afgh. 89 H2
Ishtykhan Uzbek. 89 G2
Ishurdi Bangl. 83 G4
Ishwardi Bangl. *see* Ishurdi
Isiboro Sécure, Parque Nacional *nat. park* Bol. 142 E7
Isigny-sur-Mer France 49 F9
Işıklar Dağı *mts* Turkey 59 L4
Işıklı Turkey 59 M5
Isil'kul' Rus. Fed. 64 I4
Isipingo S. Africa 101 J5
Isiro Dem. Rep. Congo 98 C3
Isisford Australia 110 D5
Iskateley Rus. Fed. 42 L2
İskenderun Turkey 85 C1
İskenderun Körfezi *b.* Turkey 81 B1
İskilip Turkey 90 D2

Iskitim Rus. Fed. **64** J4
Iskŭr *r.* Bulg. **59** K3
Iskushuban Somalia **98** F2
Isla *r. Scotland* U.K. **50** F4
Isla *r. Scotland* U.K. **50** G3
Isla Gorge National Park Australia **110** E5
İslahiye Turkey **90** E3
Islamabad India *see* **Anantnag**

▶**Islamabad** Pak. **89** I3
Capital of Pakistan.

Islamgarh Pak. **89** H5
Islamkot Pak. **89** H5
Island *r.* Canada **120** F2
Ísland *country* Europe *see* **Iceland**
Island U.S.A. **134** B5
Island Falls U.S.A. **132** G2
Island Lagoon *salt flat* Australia **111** B6
Island Lake Canada **121** M4
Island Lake *l.* Canada **121** M4
Island Magee *pen.* U.K. **51** G3
Island Pond U.S.A. **135** J1
Islands, Bay of N.Z. **113** E2
Islay *i.* U.K. **50** C5

▶**Isle of Man** *terr.* Irish Sea **48** C4
United Kingdom Crown Dependency.
Europe 5

Isle of Wight U.S.A. **135** G5
Isle Royale National Park U.S.A. **130** F2
Ismail Ukr. *see* **Izmayil**
Ismâ'ilîya Egypt *see* **Al Ismā'īlīyah**
Ismâ'ilîya *governorate* Egypt *see* **Ismā'īlīyah**
Ismā'īlīyah *governorate* Egypt **85** A4
Ismailly Azer. *see* **İsmayıllı**
İsmayıllı Azer. **91** H2
Isojoki Fin. **44** L5
Isoka Zambia **99** D5
Isokylä Fin. **44** O3
Isokyrö Fin. **44** M5
Isola di Capo Rizzuto Italy **58** G5
Ispahan Iran *see* **Eşfahān**
Isparta Turkey **59** N6
Isperikh Bulg. **59** L3
Ispikan Pak. **89** F5
İspir Turkey **91** F2
Ispisar Tajik. *see* **Khŭjand**
Isplinji Pak. **89** G4
▶**Israel** *country* Asia **85** B4
Asia 6, 62–63
Israelite Bay Australia **109** C8
Isra'īl *country* Asia *see* **Israel**
Isselburg Germany **52** G3
Issia Côte d'Ivoire **96** C4
Issoire France **56** F4
Issyk-Kul' Kyrg. *see* **Balykchy**
Issyk-Kul', Ozero *salt l.* Kyrg. *see* **Ysyk-Köl**
Istalif Afgh. **89** H3

▶**İstanbul** Turkey **59** M4
2nd most populous city in Europe.

İstanbul Boğazı *strait* Turkey *see* **Bosporus**
Īstgāh-e Eznā Iran **88** C3
Istiaia Greece **59** J5
Istik *r.* Tajik. **89** I2
Istra *pen.* Croatia *see* **Istria**
Istres France **56** G5
Istria *pen.* Croatia **58** E2
Iswardi Bangl. *see* **Ishurdi**
Itabapoana *r.* Brazil **145** C3
Itaberá Brazil **145** A3
Itaberaba Brazil **145** C1
Itaberaí Brazil **145** A2
Itabira Brazil **145** C2
Itabirito Brazil **145** C3
Itabuna Brazil **145** D1
Itacajá Brazil **143** I5
Itacarambi Brazil **145** B1
Itacoatiara Brazil **143** G4
Itaetê Brazil **145** C1
Itagmatana Iran *see* **Hamadān**
Itaguaçu Brazil **145** C2
Itaí Brazil **145** A3
Itaiópolis Brazil **145** A4
Itäisen Suomenlahden kansallispuisto *nat. park* Fin. **45** O6
Itaituba Brazil **143** G4
Itajaí Brazil **145** A4
Itajubá Brazil **145** B3
Itajuipe Brazil **145** D1
Italia *country* Europe *see* **Italy**
Italia, Laguna *l.* Bol. **142** F6

▶**Italy** *country* Europe **58** E3
5th most populous country in Europe.
Europe 5, 38–39

Itamarandiba Brazil **145** C2
Itambé Brazil **145** C1
Itambé, Pico de *mt.* Brazil **145** C2
It Amelân *i.* Neth. *see* **Ameland**
Itampolo Madag. **99** E6
Itanagar India **83** H4
Itanguari *r.* Brazil **145** B1
Itanhaém Brazil **145** B4
Itanhém Brazil **145** C2
Itanhém *r.* Brazil **145** D2
Itaobím Brazil **145** C2
Itapaci Brazil **145** A1
Itapajipe Brazil **145** A2
Itapebi Brazil **145** D1
Itapecerica Brazil **145** B3
Itapemirim Brazil **145** C3
Itaperuna Brazil **145** C3
Itapetinga Brazil **145** C1
Itapetininga Brazil **145** A3
Itapeva Brazil **145** A3
Itapeva, Lago *l.* Brazil **145** A5
Itapicuru Brazil **143** J6
Itapicuru, Serra de *hills* Brazil **143** I5
Itapicuru Mirim Brazil **143** J4
Itapipoca Brazil **143** K4
Itapira Brazil **145** B3
Itaporanga Brazil **145** A3
Itapuã Brazil **145** A5
Itaqui Brazil **144** E3
Itararé Brazil **145** A4
Itarsi India **82** D5
Itarumã Brazil **145** A2
Itatiba Brazil **145** B3
Itatuba Brazil **142** F5
Itaúna Brazil **145** B3
Itaúnas Brazil **145** D2
Itbayat *i.* Phil. **69** G2
Itchen Lake Canada **121** H1
Itea Greece **59** J5
Ithaca *MI* U.S.A. **134** C2
Ithaca *NY* U.S.A. **135** G2
It Hearrenfean Neth. *see* **Heerenveen**
iThekweni S. Africa *see* **Durban**
Ith Hils *ridge* Germany **53** J2
Ithrah Saudi Arabia **85** C4
Itihusa-yama *mt.* Japan **75** C6
Itilleq Greenland **119** M3
Itimbiri *r.* Dem. Rep. Congo **98** C3
Itinga Brazil **145** C2
Itiquira Brazil **143** H7
Itiruçu Brazil **145** C1
Itiúba, Serra de *hills* Brazil **143** K6
Itō Japan **75** E6
iTswane S. Africa *see* **Pretoria**
Ittiri *Sardinia* Italy **58** C4
Ittoqqortoormiit Greenland **119** P2
Itu Brazil **145** B3
Itu Abu Island Spratly Is **68** E4
Ituaçu Brazil **145** C1
Ituberá Brazil **145** D1
Ituí *r.* Brazil **142** D4
Ituiutaba Brazil **145** A2
Itumbiara Brazil **145** A2
Itumbiara, Barragem *resr* Brazil **145** A2
Ituni Guyana **143** G2
Itupiranga Brazil **143** I5
Ituporanga Brazil **145** A4
Iturama Brazil **145** A2
Iturbide Mex. **131** D7
Ituri *r.* Dem. Rep. Congo **98** C3
Iturup, Ostrov *i.* Rus. Fed. **74** G3
Itutinga Brazil **145** B3
Ituxi *r.* Brazil **142** F5
Ītyop'ia *country* Africa *see* **Ethiopia**
Itz *r.* Germany **53** K5
Itzehoe Germany **47** L4
Iuka U.S.A. **131** F5
Iul'tin Rus. Fed. **65** T3
Ivalo Fin. **44** O2
Ivalojoki *r.* Fin. **44** O2
Ivanava Belarus **45** N10
Ivanhoe Australia **112** B4
Ivanhoe U.S.A. **130** D2
Ivanhoe Lake Canada **121** J2
Ivankiv Ukr. **43** F6
Ivankovtsy Rus. Fed. **74** D2
Ivano-Frankivs'k Ukr. **43** E6
Ivano-Frankovsk Ukr. *see* **Ivano-Frankivs'k**
Ivanovka Rus. Fed. **74** B2
Ivanovo Belarus *see* **Ivanava**
Ivanovo *tourist site* Bulg. **59** K3
Ivanovo Rus. Fed. **42** I4
Ivanteyevka Rus. Fed. **43** K5
Ivantsevichi Belarus *see* **Ivatsevichy**
Ivatsevichy Belarus **45** N10
Ivaylovgrad Bulg. **59** L4
Ivdel' Rus. Fed. **41** S3
Ivittuut Greenland **119** N3
Iviza *i.* Spain *see* **Ibiza**
Ivory Coast *country* Africa *see* **Côte d'Ivoire**
Ivrea Italy **58** B2
İvrindi Turkey **59** L5
Ivris Ugheltekhili *pass* Georgia **91** G2
Ivry-la-Bataille France **52** B6
Ivugivik Canada *see* **Ivujivik**
Ivujivik Canada **119** K3
Ivyanyets Belarus **45** O10
Ivydale U.S.A. **134** E4
Iwaki Japan **75** F5
Iwaki-san *vol.* Japan **74** F4
Iwakuni Japan **75** D6
Iwamizawa Japan **74** F4
Iwo Nigeria **96** D4
Iwye Belarus **45** N10
Ixelles Belgium **52** E4
Ixiamas Bol. **142** E6
Ixmiquilpán Mex. **136** E4
Ixopo S. Africa **101** J6
Ixtlán Mex. **136** D4
Ixworth U.K. **49** H6
İyirmi Altı Bakı Komissarı Azer. *see* **26 Bakı Komissarı**
Izabal, Lago de *l.* Guat. **136** G5
Izberbash Rus. Fed. **91** G2
Izegem Belgium **52** D4
Īzeh Iran **88** C4
Izgal Pak. **89** I3
Izhevsk Rus. Fed. **41** Q4
Izhma *Respublika Komi* Rus. Fed. **42** L2
Izhma *Respublika Komi* Rus. Fed. *see* **Sosnogorsk**
Izhma *r.* Rus. Fed. **42** L2
Izmail Ukr. *see* **Izmayil**
Izmayil Ukr. **59** M2
İzmir Turkey **59** L5
İzmir Körfezi *g.* Turkey **59** L5
İzmit Turkey *see* **Kocaeli**
İzmit Körfezi *b.* Turkey **59** M4
Izozog Bol. **142** F7
Izra' Syria **85** C3
Iztochni Rodopi *mts* Bulg. **59** K4
Izu-hantō *pen.* Japan **75** E6
Izuhara Japan **75** C6
Izumo Japan **75** D6

▶**Izu-Ogasawara Trench** *sea feature* N. Pacific Ocean **150** F3
5th deepest trench in the world.

Izu-shotō *is* Japan **75** E6
Izyaslav Ukr. **43** E6
Iz"yayu Rus. Fed. **42** M2
Izyum Ukr. **43** H6

J

Jabal Dab Saudi Arabia **88** C6
Jabalón *r.* Spain **57** D4
Jabalpur India **82** D5
Jabbūl, Sabkhat al *salt flat* Syria **85** C2
Jabir *reg.* Oman **88** E6
Jabiru Australia **108** F3
Jablah Syria **85** B2
Jablanica Bos.-Herz. **58** G3
Jaboatão Brazil **143** L5
Jaboticabal Brazil **145** A3
Jabung, Tanjung *pt* Indon. **68** C7
Jacaraci Brazil **145** C1
Jacareacanga Brazil **143** G5
Jacareí Brazil **145** B3
Jacarézinho Brazil **145** A3
Jáchymov Czech Rep. **53** M4
Jacinto Brazil **145** C2
Jack *r.* Australia **110** D2
Jack Lake Canada **135** F1
Jackman U.S.A. **132** G2
Jacksboro U.S.A. **131** D5
Jackson Australia **112** D1
Jackson *AL* U.S.A. **133** C6
Jackson *CA* U.S.A. **128** C2
Jackson *GA* U.S.A. **133** D5
Jackson *KY* U.S.A. **134** D5
Jackson *MI* U.S.A. **134** C2
Jackson *MN* U.S.A. **130** E3

▶**Jackson** *MS* U.S.A. **131** F5
State capital of Mississippi.

Jackson *NC* U.S.A. **132** E4
Jackson *OH* U.S.A. **134** D4
Jackson *TN* U.S.A. **131** F5
Jackson *WY* U.S.A. **126** F4
Jackson, Mount Antarctica **152** L2
Jackson Head *hd* N.Z. **113** B6
Jacksonville *AR* U.S.A. **131** E5
Jacksonville *FL* U.S.A. **133** D6
Jacksonville *IL* U.S.A. **130** F4
Jacksonville *NC* U.S.A. **133** E5
Jacksonville *OH* U.S.A. **134** D4
Jacksonville *TX* U.S.A. **131** E6
Jacksonville Beach U.S.A. **133** D6
Jack Wade U.S.A. **118** D3
Jacmel Haiti **137** J5
Jacobabad Pak. **89** H4
Jacobina Brazil **143** J6
Jacob Lake U.S.A. **129** G3
Jacobsdal S. Africa **100** G5
Jacques-Cartier, Détroit de *sea chan.* Canada **123** I4
Jacques Cartier, Mont *mt.* Canada **123** I4
Jacques Cartier Passage Canada *see* **Jacques-Cartier, Détroit de**
Jacuí Brazil **145** B3
Jacuípe *r.* Brazil **143** K6
Jacunda Brazil **143** I4
Jaddangi India **84** D2
Jaddi, Ras *pt* Pak. **89** F5
Jadebusen *b.* Germany **53** I1
J. A. D. Jensen Nunatakker *nunataks* Greenland **119** N3
Jadotville Dem. Rep. Congo *see* **Likasi**
Jādū Libya **96** E1
Jaén Spain **57** E5
Ja'farābād Iran **88** E2
Jaffa, Cape Australia **111** B8
Jaffna Sri Lanka **84** C4
Jafr, Qa' al *imp. l.* Jordan **85** C4
Jagadhri India **82** D3
Jagalur India **84** C3
Jagatsingapur India *see* **Jagatsinghpur**
Jagatsinghpur India **83** F5
Jagdalpur India **84** D2
Jagdaqi China **74** B2
Jagersfontein S. Africa **101** G5
Jaggang China **82** D2
Jaggayyapeta India **84** D2
Jaghīn Iran **88** E5
Jagok Tso *salt l.* China *see* **Urru Co**
Jagsamka China *see* **Luding**
Jagst *r.* Germany **53** J5
Jagtial India **84** C2
Jaguariaíva Brazil **145** A4
Jaguaripe Brazil **145** D1
Jagüey Grande Cuba **133** D8
Jahanabad India *see* **Jehanabad**
Jahmah *well* Iraq **91** G5
Jahrom Iran **88** D4
Jaicós Brazil **143** J5
Jaigarh India **84** B2
Jailolo Gilolo *i.* Indon. *see* **Halmahera**
Jaintapur Bangl. *see* **Jaintiapur**
Jaintiapur Bangl. **83** H4
Jaipur India **82** C4
Jaipurhat Bangl. *see* **Joypurhat**
Jais India **83** E4
Jaisalmer India **82** B4
Jaisamand Lake India **82** C4
Jaitaran India **82** C4
Jaitgarh *hill* India **84** C1
Jajapur India *see* **Jajpur**
Jajarkot Nepal **87** N4
Jajce Bos.-Herz. **58** G2
Jajnagar *state* India *see* **Orissa**
Jajpur India **83** F5
Jakar Bhutan **83** G4

▶**Jakarta** Indon. **68** D8
Capital of Indonesia.

Jakes Corner Canada **120** C2
Jakhan India **82** B5
Jakin *mt.* Afgh. **89** G4
Jakkī Kowr Iran **89** F5
Jäkkvik Sweden **44** J3
Jakliat India **82** C3
Jakobshavn Greenland *see* **Ilulissat**
Jakobstad Fin. **44** M5
Jal U.S.A. **131** C5
Jalaid China *see* **Inder**
Jalājil Saudi Arabia **88** B5
Jalālābād Afgh. **89** H3
Jalal-Abad Kyrg. **80** D3
Jalālah al Baḥrīyah, Jabal *plat.* Egypt **90** C5
Jalāmid, Ḥazm al *ridge* Saudi Arabia **91** E5
Jalandhar India **82** C3
Jalapa Mex. **136** E5
Jalapa Enríquez Mex. *see* **Jalapa**
Jalapur Pirwala Pak. **89** H4
Jalasjärvi Fin. **44** M5
Jalaun India **82** D4
Jalawlā' Iraq **91** G4
Jaldak Afgh. **89** G4
Jaldrug India **84** C2
Jales Brazil **145** A3
Jalesar India **82** D4
Jalgaon India **82** C5
Jalībah Iraq **91** G5
Jalingo Nigeria **96** E4
Jallābī Iran **88** E5
Jalna India **84** B2
Jālo Iran **89** F5
Jalón *r.* Spain **57** F3
Jalor India *see* **Jalore**
Jalore India **82** C4
Jalpa Mex. **136** D4
Jalpaiguri India **83** G4
Jālū Libya **97** F2
Jalūlā Iraq *see* **Jalawlā'**
Jām *reg.* Iran **89** F3
▶**Jamaica** *country* West Indies **137** I5
North America 9, 116–117
Jamaica Channel Haiti/Jamaica **137** I5
Jamalpur Bangl. **83** G4
Jamalpur India **83** F4
Jamanxim *r.* Brazil **143** G4
Jambi Indon. **68** C7
Jambin Australia **110** E5
Jambo India **82** C4
Jambuair, Tanjung *pt* Indon. **67** B6
Jamda India **83** F5
Jamekunte India **84** C2
James *r. N. Dakota/S. Dakota* U.S.A. **130** D3
James *r. VA* U.S.A. **135** G5
James, Baie *b.* Canada *see* **James Bay**
Jamesabad Pak. **89** H5
James Bay Canada **122** E3
Jamesburg U.S.A. **135** H3
James Island *Galápagos* Ecuador *see* **San Salvador, Isla**
Jameson Land *reg.* Greenland **119** P2
James Peak N.Z. **113** B7
James Ranges *mts* Australia **109** F6
James Ross Island Antarctica **152** A2
James Ross Strait Canada **119** I3
Jamestown Australia **111** B7
Jamestown Canada *see* **Wawa**
Jamestown S. Africa **101** H6

▶**Jamestown** St Helena **148** H7
Capital of St Helena and Dependencies.

Jamestown *ND* U.S.A. **130** D2
Jamestown *NY* U.S.A. **134** F2
Jamestown *TN* U.S.A. **134** C5
Jamkhed India **84** B2
Jammu India **82** C2

▶**Jammu and Kashmir** *terr.* Asia **82** D2
Disputed territory (India/Pakistan).
Asia 6, 62–63

Jamnagar India **82** B5
Jampur Pak. **89** H4
Jamrud Pak. **89** H3
Jämsä Fin. **45** N6
Jamsah Egypt **90** D6
Jämsänkoski Fin. **44** N6
Jamshedpur India **83** F5
Jamtari Nigeria **96** E4
Jamui India **83** F4
Jamuna *r.* Bangl. *see* **Raimangal**
Jamuna *r.* India *see* **Yamuna**
Janā *i.* Saudi Arabia **88** C5
Janāb, Wādī al *watercourse* Jordan **85** C4
Janakpur India **83** E5
Janaúba Brazil **145** C1
Jand Pak. **89** I3
Jandaia Brazil **145** A2
Jandaq Iran **88** D3
Jandola Pak. **89** H3
Jandowae Australia **112** E1
Janesville *CA* U.S.A. **128** C1
Janesville *WI* U.S.A. **130** F3
Jangada Brazil **145** A4
Jangal Iran **88** E3
Jangamo Moz. **101** L3
Jangaon India **84** C2
Jangipur India **83** G4
Jangnga Turkm. *see* **Dzhanga**
Jangngai Ri *mts* China **83** F2
Jänickendorf Germany **53** N2
Jani Khel Pak. **89** H3

▶**Jan Mayen** *terr.* Arctic Ocean **153** I2
Part of Norway.

Jan Mayen Fracture Zone *sea feature* Arctic Ocean **153** I2
Janos Mex. **127** F7
Jans Bay Canada **121** I4
Jansenville S. Africa **100** G7
Januária Brazil **145** B1
Janūb Sīnā' *governorate* Egypt **85** A5
Janûb Sînâ' *governorate* Egypt *see* **Janūb Sīnā'**
Janzar *mt.* Pak. **89** F5
Jaodar Pak. **89** F5
▶**Japan** *country* Asia **75** D5
Asia 6, 62–63
Japan, Sea of N. Pacific Ocean **75** D5
Japan Alps National Park Japan *see* **Chibu-Sangaku National Park**
Japan Trench *sea feature* N. Pacific Ocean **150** F3
Japiim Brazil **142** D5
Japurá *r.* Brazil **142** F4
Japvo Mount India **83** H4
Jarābulus Syria **85** D1
Jaraguá Brazil **145** A1
Jaraguá, Serra *mts* Brazil **145** A4
Jaraguá do Sul Brazil **145** A4
Jarash Jordan **85** B3
Jarboesville U.S.A. *see* **Lexington Park**
Jardine River National Park Australia **110** C1
Jardinésia Brazil **145** A2
Jardinópolis Brazil **145** B3
Jargalang China **74** A4
Jargalant *Bayanhongor* Mongolia **80** I2
Jargalant *Dornod* Mongolia **73** L3
Jargalant *Hovd* Mongolia *see* **Hovd**
Jari *r.* Brazil **143** H4
Järna Sweden **45** J7
Jarocin Poland **47** P5
Jarosław Poland **43** D6
Järpen Sweden **44** H5
Jarqŭrghon Uzbek. *see* **Dzharkurgan**
Jarrettsville U.S.A. **135** G4
Jarú Brazil **142** F6
Jarud China *see* **Lubei**
Järvakandi Estonia **45** N7
Järvenpää Fin. **45** N6

▶**Jarvis Island** *terr.* S. Pacific Ocean **150** J6
United States Unincorporated Territory.

Jarwa India **83** E4
Jashpurnagar India **83** F5
Jāsk Iran **88** E5
Jāsk-e Kohneh Iran **88** E5
Jasliq Uzbek. *see* **Zhaslyk**
Jasło Poland **43** D6
Jasol India **82** C4
Jason Islands Falkland Is **144** D8
Jason Peninsula Antarctica **152** L2
Jasonville U.S.A. **134** B4
Jasper Canada **118** G4
Jasper *AL* U.S.A. **133** C5
Jasper *FL* U.S.A. **133** D6
Jasper *GA* U.S.A. **133** C5
Jasper *IN* U.S.A. **134** B4
Jasper *NY* U.S.A. **135** G2
Jasper *TN* U.S.A. **133** C5
Jasper *TX* U.S.A. **131** E6
Jasper National Park Canada **120** G4
Jasrasar India **82** C4
Jaşşān Iraq **91** G4
Jassy Romania *see* **Iaşi**
Jastrzębie-Zdrój Poland **47** Q6
Jaswantpura India **82** C4
Jászberény Hungary **59** H1
Jataí Brazil **145** A2
Jatapu *r.* Brazil **143** G4
Jath India **84** B2
Jati Pak. **89** H5
Jatibonico Cuba **133** E8
Játiva Spain *see* **Xátiva**
Jatoi Pak. **89** H4
Jat Poti Afgh. **89** G4
Jaú Brazil **145** A3
Jaú *r.* Brazil **142** F4
Jaú, Parque Nacional do *nat. park* Brazil **142** F4
Jaua Sarisariñama, Parque Nacional *nat. park* Venez. **142** F3
Jauja Peru **142** C6
Jaunlutriņi Latvia **45** M8
Jaunpiebalga Latvia **45** O8
Jaunpur India **83** E4
Jauri Iran **89** F4
Java Georgia **91** F2

▶**Java** *i.* Indon. **108** A1
5th largest island in Asia.

Javaés *r.* Brazil *see* **Formoso**
Javand Afgh. **89** G3
Javari *r.* Brazil/Peru *see* **Yavari**
Java Ridge *sea feature* Indian Ocean **149** P6
Javarthushuu Mongolia **73** K3
Java Sea Indon. *see* **Jawa, Laut**

▶**Java Trench** *sea feature* Indian Ocean **149** O6
Deepest point in the Indian Ocean.

Java Trench *sea feature* Indian Ocean **149** P6
Jävenitz Germany **53** L2
Jävre Sweden **44** L4
Jawa *i.* Indon. *see* **Java**
Jawa, Laut *sea* Indon. **68** E7
Jawhar India **84** B2
Jawhar Somalia **98** E3
Jawor Poland **47** P5
Jay U.S.A. **131** E4

▶**Jaya, Puncak** *mt.* Indon. **69** J7
Highest mountain in Oceania.
Oceania 102–103

Jayakusumu *mt.* Indon. *see* **Jaya, Puncak**
Jayakwadi Sagar *l.* India **84** B2
Jayantiapur Bangl. *see* **Jaintiapur**
Jayapura Indon. **69** K7
Jayawijaya, Pegunungan *mts* Indon. **69** J7
Jayb, Wādī al *watercourse* Israel/Jordan **85** B4
Jayfī, Wādī al *watercourse* Egypt **85** B4
Jaypur India **84** D2
Jayrūd Syria **85** C3
Jayton U.S.A. **131** C5
Jazīreh-ye Shīf Iran **88** C4
Jazminal Mex. **131** C7
Jbail Lebanon **85** B2
J. C. Murphey Lake U.S.A. **134** B3
Jean U.S.A. **129** F4
Jean Marie River Canada **120** F2
Jeannin, Lac *l.* Canada **123** I2
Jebāl Bārez, Kūh-e *mts* Iran **88** E4
Jebel, Bahr el *r.* Sudan/Uganda *see* **White Nile**
Jebel Abyad Plateau Sudan **86** C6
Jech Doab *lowland* Pak. **89** I4
Jedburgh U.K. **50** G5
Jeddah Saudi Arabia **86** E5
Jedeida Tunisia **58** C6
Jeetze *r.* Germany **53** L1
Jefferson *IA* U.S.A. **130** E3
Jefferson *NC* U.S.A. **132** D4
Jefferson *OH* U.S.A. **134** E3
Jefferson *TX* U.S.A. **131** E5
Jefferson, Mount U.S.A. **128** E2
Jefferson, Mount *vol.* U.S.A. **126** C3

▶**Jefferson City** U.S.A. **130** E4
State capital of Missouri.

Jeffersonville *GA* U.S.A. **133** D5
Jeffersonville *IN* U.S.A. **134** C4
Jeffersonville *OH* U.S.A. **134** D4
Jeffrey's Bay S. Africa **100** G8
Jehanabad India **83** F4
Jeju S. Korea *see* **Cheju**
Jejuí Guazú *r.* Para. **144** E2
Jēkabpils Latvia **45** N8
Jelbart Ice Shelf Antarctica **152** B2
Jelenia Góra Poland **47** O5
Jelep La *pass* China/India **83** G4
Jelgava Latvia **45** M8
Jellico U.S.A. **134** C5
Jellicoe Canada **122** D4
Jelloway U.S.A. **134** D3
Jemaja *i.* Indon. **71** D7
Jember Indon. **68** E8
Jempang, Danau *l.* Indon. **68** F7
Jena Germany **53** L4
Jena U.S.A. **131** E6
Jendouba Tunisia **58** C6
Jengish Chokusu *mt.* China/Kyrg. *see* **Pobeda Peak**
Jenīn West Bank **85** B3
Jenkins U.S.A. **134** D5
Jenne Mali *see* **Djenné**
Jenner Canada **121** I5
Jennings *r.* Canada **120** C3
Jennings U.S.A. **131** E6
Jenolan Caves Australia **112** E4
Jenpeg Canada **121** L4
Jensen U.S.A. **129** I1
Jens Munk Island Canada **119** K3
Jeparit Australia **111** C8
Jequié Brazil **145** C1
Jequitaí *r.* Brazil **145** B2
Jequitinhonha Brazil **145** C2
Jequitinhonha *r.* Brazil **145** D1
Jerba, Île de *i.* Tunisia **54** G5
Jerbar Sudan **97** G4
Jereh Iran **88** C4
Jérémie Haiti **137** J5
Jerez Mex. **136** D4
Jerez de la Frontera Spain **57** C5
Jerggul Norway **44** N2
Jergucat Albania **59** I5
Jericho Australia **110** D4
Jericho West Bank **85** B4
Jerichow Germany **53** M2
Jerid, Chott el *salt l.* Tunisia **54** F5
Jerilderie Australia **112** B5
Jerimoth Hill *hill* U.S.A. **135** J3
Jeroaquara Brazil **145** A1
Jerome U.S.A. **126** E4
Jerruck Pak. **89** H5

▶**Jersey** *terr.* Channel Is **49** E9
United Kingdom Crown Dependency.
Europe 5, 38–39

Jersey City U.S.A. **135** H3
Jersey Shore U.S.A. **135** G3
Jerseyville U.S.A. **130** F4
Jerumenha Brazil **143** J5

▶**Jerusalem** Israel/West Bank **85** B4
Capital of Israel (De facto capital. Disputed).

Jervis Bay Australia **112** E5
Jervis Bay *b.* Australia **112** E5
Jervis Bay Territory *admin. div.* Australia **112** E5
Jesenice Slovenia **58** F1
Jesenice, Vodní nádrž *resr* Czech Rep. **53** M4
Jesi Italy **58** E3
Jesselton *Sabah* Malaysia *see* **Kota Kinabalu**
Jessen Germany **53** M3
Jessheim Norway **45** G6
Jessore Bangl. **83** G5
Jesteburg Germany **53** J1
Jesu Maria Island P.N.G. *see* **Rambutyo Island**
Jesup U.S.A. **133** D6
Jesús María, Barra *spit* Mex. **131** D7
Jetmore U.S.A. **130** D4
Jever Germany **53** H1
Jewell Ridge U.S.A. **134** E5
Jewish Autonomous Oblast *admin. div.* Rus. Fed. *see* **Yevreyskaya Avtonomnaya Oblast'**
Jeypur India *see* **Jaypur**
Jezzine Lebanon **85** B3
Jhabua India **82** C5
Jhajhar India *see* **Jhajjar**
Jhajjar India **82** D3
Jhal Pak. **89** G4
Jhalawar India **82** D4
Jhal Jhao Pak. **89** G5
Jhang Pak. **89** I4
Jhansi India **82** D4
Jhanzi *r.* India **70** A1
Jhapa Nepal **83** F4
Jharia India **83** F5
Jharkhand *state* India **83** F5
Jharsuguda India **83** F5
Jhawani Nepal **83** F4
Jhelum *r.* India/Pak. **89** I4
Jhelum Pak. **89** I3
Jhenaidah Bangl. **83** G5
Jhenaidaha Bangl. *see* **Jhenaidah**
Jhenida Bangl. *see* **Jhenaidah**
Jhimpir Pak. **89** H5
Jhudo Pak. **89** H5
Jhumritilaiya India **83** F4
Jhund India **82** B5
Jhunjhunun India **82** C3
Jiachuan China **76** E1
Jiachuanzhen China *see* **Jiachuan**
Jiading *Jiangxi* China *see* **Xinfeng**
Jiading *Shanghai* China **77** I2
Jiahe China **77** G3
Jiajiang China **76** D2
Jiamusi China **74** C3
Ji'an *Jiangxi* China **77** G3
Ji'an *Jilin* China **74** B4
Jianchuan China **76** C3
Jiande China **77** H2
Jiangbei China *see* **Yubei**
Jiangbiancun China **77** G3
Jiangcheng China **76** D4

Jiangcun China 77 F3
Jiangdu China 77 H1
Jiange China see Pu'an
Jianghong China 77 F4
Jiangjin China 76 E2
Jiangjunmiao China 80 G3
Jiangkou Guangdong China see Fengkai
Jiangkou Guizhou China 77 F3
Jiangkou Shaanxi China 76 E1
Jiangling China see Jingzhou
Jiangluozhen China 76 E1
Jiangmen China 77 G4
Jiangna China see Yanshan
Jiangshan China 77 H2
Jiangsi China see Dejiang
Jiangsu prov. China 77 H1
Jiangxi prov. China 77 G3
Jiangxia China 77 G2
Jiangyan China 77 I1
Jiangyin China 77 I2
Jiangyou China 76 E2
Jiangzhesongrong China 83 F3
Jianjun China see Yongshou
Jiankang China 76 D3
Jianli China 77 G2
Jian'ou China 77 H3
Jianping China see Langxi
Jianpur India 83 E4
Jianshe China see Baiyü
Jianshi China 77 F2
Jianshui China 76 D4
Jianshui Hu l. China 83 E2
Jianxing China 76 E2
Jianyang Fujian China 77 H3
Jianyang Sichuan China 76 E2
Jiaochang China 76 D1
Jiaochangba China see Jiaochang
Jiaocheng China see Jiaoling
Jiaohe China 74 B4
Jiaojiang China see Taizhou
Jiaokui China see Yiliang
Jiaoling China 77 H3
Jiaopingdu China 76 D3
Jiaowei China 77 H3
Jiaozuo China 77 G1
Jiasa China 76 D3
Jiashan China see Mingguang
Jia Tsuo La pass China 83 F3
Jiawang China 77 H1
Jiaxian China 77 G1
Jiaxing China 77 I2
Jiayi Taiwan see Chiai
Jiayin China 74 C2
Jiayuguan China 80 I4
Jiazi China 77 H4
Jībūtī country Africa see Djibouti
Jibuti Djibouti see Djibouti
Jiddah Saudi Arabia see Jeddah
Jiddī, Jabal al hill Egypt 85 A4
Jidong China 74 C3
Jiehkkevarri mt. Norway 44 K2
Jieshi China 77 G4
Jieshipu China 76 E1
Jieshi Wan b. China 77 G4
Iešjávri l. Norway 44 N2
Jiexi China 77 G4
Jiexiu China 73 K5
Jieyang China 77 H4
Jieznas Lith. 45 N9
Jigzhi China 76 D1
Jiḥār, Wādī al watercourse Syria 85 C2
Jihlava Czech Rep. 47 O6
Jija Sarai Afgh. 89 F3
Jijel Alg. 54 F4
Jijiga Eth. 98 E3
Jījīrud Iran 88 C3
Jijü China 76 D2
Jil'ād reg. Jordan 85 B3
Jilf al Kabīr, Haḍabat al plat. Egypt 86 C5
Jilh al 'Ishār plain Saudi Arabia 88 B5
Jilib Somalia 98 E3
Jilin China 74 B4
Jilin prov. China 74 B4
Jilin Hada Ling mts China 74 B4
Jiliu He r. China 74 A2
Jiloi India 82 C4
Jilong Taiwan see Chilung
Jīma Eth. 98 D3
Jimda China see Zindo
Jiménez Chihuahua Mex. 131 B7
Jiménez Coahuila Mex. 131 C6
Jiménez Tamaulipas Mex. 131 D7
Jimía, Cerro mt. Hond. 136 G5
Jimsar China 80 G3
Jim Thorpe U.S.A. 135 H3
Jinan China 73 L5
Jin'an China see Songpan
Jinbi China see Dayao
Jinchang China 72 I5
Jincheng Shanxi China 77 G1
Jincheng Sichuan China see Yilong
Jincheng Yunnan China see Wuding
Jinchengjiang China see Hechi
Jinchuan Gansu China see Jinchang
Jinchuan Jiangxi China see Xingan
Jind India 82 D3
Jinding China see Lanping
Jindřichův Hradec Czech Rep. 47 O6
Jin'e China see Longchang
Jingbian China 73 J5
Jingchuan China 76 E1
Jingde China 77 H2
Jingdezhen China 77 H2
Jingellic Australia 112 C5
Jinggangshan China 77 G3
Jinggang Shan hill China 77 G3
Jinggongqiao China 77 H2
Jinggu China 76 D4
Jing He r. China 77 F1
Jinghong China 76 D4
Jingle China 73 K5
Jingmen China 77 G2
Jingpo China 74 C4
Jingpo Hu resr China 74 C4
Jingsha China see Jingzhou
Jingtai China 72 I5
Jingtieshan China 80 I4
Jingxi China 76 E4
Jingxian Anhui China 77 H2
Jingxian Hunan China see Jingzhou
Jingyang China see Jingde
Jingyu China 74 B4
Jingyuan China 72 I5
Jingzhou Hubei China 77 G2
Jingzhou Hubei China 77 G2
Jingzhou Hunan China 77 F3
Jinhe Nei Mongol China 74 A2
Jinhe Yunnan China see Jinping
Jinhu China 77 H1
Jinhua Yunnan China see Jianchuan
Jinhua Zhejiang China 77 H2
Jining Nei Mongol China 73 K4
Jining Shandong China 77 H1
Jinja Uganda 98 D3
Jinjiang Hainan China see Chengmai
Jinjiang Yunnan China 76 D3
Jin Jiang r. China 77 G2
Jinka Eth. 98 D3
Jinmen Taiwan see Chinmen
Jinmen Dao i. Taiwan see Chinmen Tao
Jinmu Jiao pt China 77 F5
Jinning China 76 D3
Jinotepe Nicaragua 137 G6
Jinping Guizhou China 77 F3
Jinping Yunnan China 76 D4
Jinping Yunnan China see Qiubei
Jinping Shan mts China 76 D3
Jinsen S. Korea see Inch'ŏn
Jinsha China 76 E3
Jinsha Jiang r. China 76 E2 see Yangtze
Jinshan Nei Mongol China see Guyang
Jinshan Shanghai China 77 I2
Jinshan Yunnan China see Lufeng
Jinshi Hunan China 77 F2
Jinshi Hunan China see Xinning
Jintur India 84 C2
Jinxi Anhui China see Taihu
Jinxi Jiangxi China 77 H3
Jinxi Liaoning China see Lianshan
Jin Xi r. China 77 H3
Jinxian China 77 H2
Jinxiang China 77 H1
Jinyun China 77 I2
Jinz, Qā' al salt flat Jordan 85 C4
Jinzhai China 77 G2
Jinzhong China 73 K5
Jinzhou China 73 M4
Jinzhu China see Daocheng
Ji-Paraná Brazil 142 F6
Jipijapa Ecuador 142 B4
Ji Qu r. China 76 C2
Jiquiriçá Brazil 145 D1
Jiquitaia Brazil 145 D2
Jirā', Wādī watercourse Egypt 85 A5
Jirānīyāt, Shi'bān al watercourse Saudi Arabia 85 D4
Jirgatol Tajik. 89 H2
Jiri r. India 83 H4
Jīroft Iran 88 E4
Jirriiban Somalia 98 E3
Jirwān Saudi Arabia 88 C6
Jirwan well Saudi Arabia 88 C6
Jishou China 77 F2
Jisr ash Shughūr Syria 85 C2
Jitian China see Lianshan
Jitra Malaysia 71 C6
Jiu r. Romania 59 J3
Jiuding Shan mt. China 76 D2
Jiujiang Jiangxi China 77 G2
Jiujiang Jiangxi China 77 H2
Jiulian China see Mojiang
Jiuling Shan mts China 77 G2
Jiulong Hong Kong China see Kowloon
Jiulong Sichuan China 76 D2
Jiuqian China 77 F3
Jiuquan China 80 I4
Jiuxu China 76 E3
Jiuzhou Jiang r. China 77 F4
Jiwani Pak. 89 F5
Jiwen China 74 A2
Jixi Anhui China 77 H2
Jixi Heilong. China 74 C3
Jixian China 74 C3
Jiyuan China 77 G1
Jīzah, Ahrāmāt al tourist site Egypt see Pyramids of Giza
Jīzān Saudi Arabia 86 F6
Jizzakh Uzbek. see Dzhizak
Joaçaba Brazil 145 A4
Joaíma Brazil 145 C2
João Belo Moz. see Xai-Xai
João de Almeida Angola see Chibia
João Pessoa Brazil 143 L5
João Pinheiro Brazil 145 B2
Joaquin V. González Arg. 144 D3
Job Peak U.S.A. 128 D2
Jocketa Germany 53 M4
Joda India 83 F5
Jodhpur India 82 C4
Jodiya India 82 B5
Joensuu Fin. 44 P5
Jōetsu Japan 75 E5
Jofane Moz. 99 D6
Joffre, Mount Canada 120 H5
Jogbura Nepal 82 E3
Jõgeva Estonia 45 O7
Jogjakarta Indon. see Yogyakarta
Jõgua Estonia 45 O7
Johannesburg S. Africa 101 H4
Johannesburg U.S.A. 128 E4
Johan Peninsula Canada 119 K2
Johi Pak. 89 G5
John Day U.S.A. 126 D3
John Day r. U.S.A. 126 C3
John D'Or Prairie Canada 120 H3
John F. Kennedy airport U.S.A. 135 I3
John H. Kerr Reservoir U.S.A. 135 F5
John Jay, Mount Canada/U.S.A. 120 D3
John o'Groats U.K. 50 F2
Johnson U.S.A. 130 C4
Johnsonburg U.S.A. 135 F3
Johnson City NY U.S.A. 135 H2
Johnson City TN U.S.A. 132 D4
Johnson City TX U.S.A. 131 D6
Johnsondale U.S.A. 128 D4
Johnson Draw watercourse U.S.A. 131 C6
Johnson's Crossing Canada 120 C2
Johnston, Lake salt flat Australia 109 C8
Johnston and Sand Islands terr. N. Pacific Ocean see Johnston Atoll
▶Johnston Atoll terr. N. Pacific Ocean 150 I4
United States Unincorporated Territory.
Johnstone U.K. 50 E5
Johnstone Lake Canada see Old Wives Lake
Johnston Range hills Australia 109 B7
Johnstown Rep. of Ireland 51 E5
Johnstown NY U.S.A. 135 H2
Johnstown PA U.S.A. 135 F3
Johor, Selat strait Malaysia/Sing. 71 [inset]
Johor, Sungai r. Malaysia 71 [inset]
Johor Bahru Malaysia 71 [inset]
Johore Bahru Malaysia see Johor Bahru
Jōhvi Estonia 45 O7
Joinville Brazil 145 A4
Joinville France 56 G2
Joinville Island Antarctica 152 A2
Jokkmokk Sweden 44 K3
Jökulsá r. Iceland 44 [inset]
Jökulsá á Fjöllum r. Iceland 44 [inset]
Jökulsá í Fljótsdal r. Iceland 44 [inset]
Jolfa Iran 88 B2
Joliet U.S.A. 134 A3
Joliet, Lac l. Canada 122 F4
Joliette Canada 123 G5
Jolly Lake Canada 121 H1
Jolo Phil. 69 G5
Jolo i. Phil. 69 G5
Jomda China 76 C2
Jonancy U.S.A. 134 D5
Jonava Lith. 45 N9
Jonê China 76 D1
Jonesboro AR U.S.A. 131 F5
Jonesboro LA U.S.A. 131 E5
Jones Sound sea chan. Canada 119 J2
Jonesville MI U.S.A. 134 C3
Jonesville VA U.S.A. 134 D5
Jonglei Canal Sudan 86 D8
Jönköping Sweden 45 I8
Jonquière Canada 123 H4
Joplin U.S.A. 131 E4
Joppa Israel see Tel Aviv-Yafo
Jora India 82 D4
▶Jordan country Asia 85 C4
Asia 6, 62–63
Jordan r. Asia 85 B4
Jordan U.S.A. 126 G3
Jordan r. U.S.A. 126 D4
Jordânia Brazil 145 C1
Jordet Norway 45 H6
Jorhat India 83 H4
Jork Germany 53 J1
Jorm Afgh. 89 H2
Jörn Sweden 44 L4
Joroinen Fin. 44 O5
Jørpeland Norway 45 E7
Jos Nigeria 96 D4
José de San Martín Arg. 144 B6
Joseph, Lac l. Canada 123 I3
Joseph Bonaparte Gulf Australia 108 E3
Joseph City U.S.A. 129 H4
Joshimath India 82 D3
Joshipur India 84 E1
Joshua Tree National Park U.S.A. 129 F5
Jos Plateau Nigeria 96 D4
Jostedalsbreen Nasjonalpark nat. park Norway 45 E6
Jotunheimen Nasjonalpark nat. park Norway 45 F6
Jouaiya Lebanon 85 B3
Joubertina S. Africa 100 F7
Jouberton S. Africa 101 H4
Joûnié Lebanon 85 B3
Joure Neth. 52 F2
Joutsa Fin. 45 O6
Joutseno Fin. 45 P6
Jouy-aux-Arches France 52 G5
Jovellanos Cuba 133 D8
Jowai India 83 H4
Jowr Deh Iran 88 C2
Jowzak Iran 89 F4
Joy, Mount Canada 120 C2
Joyce's Country reg. Rep. of Ireland 51 C4
Joypurhat Bangl. 83 G4
Juan Aldama Mex. 131 C7
Juancheng China 77 G1
Juan de Fuca Strait Canada/U.S.A. 124 C2
Juan Fernández, Archipiélago is S. Pacific Ocean 151 O8
Juan Fernández Islands S. Pacific Ocean see Juan Fernández, Archipiélago
Juanjuí Peru 142 C5
Juankoski Fin. 44 P5
Juan Mata Ortíz Mex. 127 F7
Juaréz Mex. 131 C7
Juárez, Sierra de mts Mex. 123 D6
Juàzeiro Brazil 143 J5
Juàzeiro do Norte Brazil 143 K5
Juba r. Somalia see Jubba
Juba Sudan 97 G4
Jubany research station Antarctica 152 A2
Jubba r. Somalia 98 E4
Jubbah Saudi Arabia 91 F5
Jubbulpore India see Jabalpur
Jubilee Lake salt flat Australia 109 D7
Juby, Cap c. Morocco 96 B2
Júcar r. Spain 57 F4
Juçara Brazil 145 A1
Juchitán Mex. 136 F5
Jucuruçu Brazil 145 D2
Jucuruçu r. Brazil 145 D2
Judaberg Norway 45 D7
Judaidat al Hamir Iraq 91 F5
Judayyidat 'Ar'ar well Iraq 91 F5
Judenburg Austria 47 O7
Judian China 76 C3
Judith Gap U.S.A. 126 F3
Juegang China see Rudong
Juelsminde Denmark 45 G9
Juerana Brazil 145 D2
Jugar China see Sêrxü
Juigalpa Nicaragua 137 G6
Juillet, Lac l. Canada 123 J3
Juína Brazil 143 G6
Juist i. Germany 52 H1
Juiz de Fora Brazil 145 C3
Julaca Bol. 142 E8
Julesburg U.S.A. 130 C3
Julia Brazil 142 E4
Juliaca Peru 142 D7
Julia Creek Australia 110 C4
Julian U.S.A. 128 E5
Julian, Lac l. Canada 122 F3
Julianadorp Neth. 52 E2
Julian Alps mts Slovenia see Julijske Alpe
Julianatop mt. Indon. see Mandala, Puncak
Juliana Top mt. Suriname 143 G3
Julianehåb Greenland see Qaqortoq
Jülich Germany 52 G4
Julijske Alpe mts Slovenia 58 E1
Julimes Mex. 131 B6
Juliomagus France see Angers
Julius, Lake Australia 110 B4
Jullundur India see Jalandhar
Juma Uzbek. see Dzhuma
Jumbilla Peru 142 C5
Jumilla Spain 57 F4
Jumla Nepal 83 E3
Jümme r. Germany 53 H1
Jumna r. India see Yamuna
Jump r. U.S.A. 130 F2
Junagadh India 82 B5
Junagarh India 84 D2
Junan China 77 H1
Junayfah Egypt 85 A4
Junbuk Iran 88 E3
Junction TX U.S.A. 131 D6
Junction UT U.S.A. 129 G2
Junction City KS U.S.A. 130 D4
Junction City KY U.S.A. 134 C5
Junction City OR U.S.A. 126 C3
Jundiaí Brazil 145 B3
Jundian China 77 F1
▶Juneau AK U.S.A. 120 C3
State capital of Alaska.
Juneau WI U.S.A. 130 F3
Juneau Icefield Canada 120 C3
Junee Australia 112 C5
Jûn el Khudr b. Lebanon 85 B3
Jungar Qi China see Shagedu
Jungfrau mt. Switz. 56 H3
Junggar Pendi basin China 80 G2
Juniata r. U.S.A. 135 G3
Junín Arg. 144 D4
Junín Peru 142 C6
Junior U.S.A. 134 F4
Juniper Mountain U.S.A. 129 I1
Juniper Mountains U.S.A. 129 G4
Junipero Serro Peak U.S.A. 124 C3
Junlian China 76 E2
Junmenling China 77 G3
Juno U.S.A. 131 C6
Junsele Sweden 44 J5
Junshan Hu l. China 77 H2
Junxi China see Datian
Junxian China see Danjiangkou
Ju'nyung China 76 C1
Ju'nyunggoin China see Ju'nyung
Juodupė Lith. 45 N8
Jupiá Brazil 145 A3
Jupiá, Represa resr Brazil 145 A3
Jupiter U.S.A. 133 D7
Juquiá r. Brazil 145 B4
Jur r. Sudan 86 C8
Jura mts France/Switz. 56 G4
Jura i. U.K. 50 D4
Jura, Sound of sea chan. U.K. 50 D5
Juraci Brazil 145 C1
Jurbarkas Lith. 45 M9
Jurf ad Darāwīsh Jordan 85 B4
Jürgenstorf Germany 53 M1
Jurhen Ul mts China 83 G2
Jūrmala Latvia 45 M8
Jurmu Fin. 44 O4
Jurong Sing. 71 [inset]
Jurong, Sungai r. Sing. 71 [inset]
Jurong Island reg. Sing. 71 [inset]
Juruá r. Brazil 142 E4
Juruena r. Brazil 143 G5
Juruti Brazil 143 G4
Jurva Fin. 44 L5
Jūshqān Iran 88 E2
Jūsīyah Syria 85 C2
Justice U.S.A. 134 E5
Jutaí Brazil 142 E5
Jutaí r. Brazil 142 E4
Jüterbog Germany 53 N3
Jutiapa Guat. 136 G6
Juticalpa Hond. 137 G6
Jutis Sweden 44 J3
Jutland pen. Denmark 45 F8
Juuka Fin. 44 P5
Juva Fin. 44 O6
Juwain Afgh. 89 F4
Juye China 77 H1
Jūyom Iran 88 D4
Južnoukrajinsk Ukr. see Yuzhnoukrayinsk
Jwaneng Botswana 100 G3
Jylland pen. Denmark see Jutland
Jyväskylä Fin. 44 N5

K

▶K2 mt. China/Jammu and Kashmir 82 D2
2nd highest mountain in the world and in Asia.
World 12–13
Ka r. Nigeria 96 D3
Kaafu Atoll Maldives see Male Atoll
Kaa-Iya, Parque Nacional nat. park Bol. 142 F7
Kaakhka Turkm. see Kaka
Kaala mt. HI U.S.A. 127 [inset]
Kaapstad S. Africa see Cape Town
Kaarina Fin. 45 M6
Kaarßen Germany 53 L1
Kaarst Germany 52 G3
Kaavi Fin. 44 P5
Kaba China see Habahe
Kabakly Turkm. 89 F2
Kabala Sierra Leone 96 B4
Kabale Uganda 98 C4
Kabalega Falls National Park Uganda see Murchison Falls National Park
Kabalo Dem. Rep. Congo 99 C4
Kabambare Dem. Rep. Congo 99 C4
Kabangu Dem. Rep. Congo 99 C5
Kabanjahe Indon. 71 B7
Kabara i. Fiji 107 I3
Kabarega National Park Uganda see Murchison Falls National Park
Kabaw Valley Myanmar 70 A2
Kabbani r. India 84 C3
Kåbdalis Sweden 44 L3
Kabinakagami r. Canada 122 D4
Kabinakagami Lake Canada 122 D4
Kabinda Dem. Rep. Congo 99 C4
Kabīr r. Syria 85 B2
Kabīrkūh mts Iran 88 B3
Kabo Cent. Afr. Rep. 98 B3
Kābol Afgh. see Kābul
Kabompo r. Zambia 99 C5
Kabongo Dem. Rep. Congo 99 C4
Kabūdeh Iran 89 F3
Kabūd Gonbad Iran 89 E2
Kabūd Rāhang Iran 88 C3
▶Kābul Afgh. 89 H3
Capital of Afghanistan.
Kābul r. Afgh. 89 I3
Kabuli P.N.G. 69 L7
Kabunda Dem. Rep. Congo 99 C5
Kabunduk Indon. 108 B2
Kaburuang i. Indon. 69 H6
Kabūtar Khān Iran 88 E4
Kabwe Zambia 99 C5
Kacha Kuh mts Iran/Pak. 89 F4
Kachalinskaya Rus. Fed. 43 J6
Kachchh, Great Rann of marsh India see Kachchh, Rann of
Kachchh, Gulf of India 82 B5
Kachchh, Rann of marsh India 82 B4
Kachia Nigeria 96 D4
Kachiry Kazakh. 72 D2
Kachkanar Rus. Fed. 41 R4
Kachret'i Georgia 91 G2
Kachug Rus. Fed. 72 J2
Kaçkar Dağı mt. Turkey 91 F2
Kadaingti Myanmar 70 B3
Kadaiyanallur India 84 C4
Kadanai r. Afgh./Pak. 89 G4
Kadan Kyun i. Myanmar 71 B4
Kadavu i. Fiji 107 H3
Kadavu Passage Fiji 107 H3
Kaddam l. India 84 C2
Kade Ghana 96 C4
Kādhimain Iraq see Al Kāẓimīyah
Kadi India 82 C5
Kadıköy Turkey 59 M4
Kadınhanı Turkey 90 D3
Kadiolo Mali 96 C3
Kadiri India 84 C3
Kadirli Turkey 90 E3
Kadirpur Pak. 89 I4
Kadiyevka Ukr. see Stakhanov
Kadmat atoll India 84 B4
Ka-do i. N. Korea 75 B5
Kadok Malaysia 71 C6
Kadoka U.S.A. 130 C3
Kadoma Zimbabwe 99 C5
Kadonkani Myanmar 70 A4
Kadu Myanmar 70 B1
Kadugli Sudan 86 C7
Kaduna Nigeria 96 D3
Kaduna r. Nigeria 96 D4
Kadusam mt. China/India 83 I3
Kaduy Rus. Fed. 42 H4
Kadyy Rus. Fed. 42 I4
Kadzherom Rus. Fed. 42 L2
Kaédi Mauritania 96 B3
Kaélé Cameroon 97 E3
Kaeng Krachan National Park Thai. 71 B4
Kaesŏng N. Korea 75 B5
Kāf Saudi Arabia 85 C4
Kafa Ukr. see Feodosiya
Kafakumba Dem. Rep. Congo 99 C4
Kafan Armenia see Kapan
Kafanchan Nigeria 96 D4
Kafireas, Akra pt Greece 59 K5
Kafiristan reg. Pak. 89 H3
Kafr ash Shaykh Egypt 90 C5
Kafr el Sheikh Egypt see Kafr ash Shaykh
Kafue Zambia 99 C5
Kafue r. Zambia 99 C5
Kafue National Park Zambia 99 C5
Kaga Japan 75 E5
Kaga Bandoro Cent. Afr. Rep. 98 B3
Kagan Pak. 89 I3
Kagan Uzbek. 89 G2
Kagang China 76 D1
Kaganovichabad Tajik. see Kolkhozobod
Kaganovichi Pervyye Ukr. see Polis'ke
Kagarlyk Ukr. see Kaharlyk
Kåge Sweden 44 L4
Kağızman Turkey 91 F2
Kagmar Sudan 86 D7
Kagoshima Japan 75 C7
Kagoshima pref. Japan 75 C7
Kagul Moldova see Cahul
Kahama Tanz. 98 D4
Kaharlyk Ukr. 43 F6
Kaherekoau Mountains N.Z. 113 A7
Kahla Germany 53 L4
Kahnūj Iran 88 E4
Kahoka U.S.A. 130 F3
Kahoolawe i. HI U.S.A. 127 [inset]
Kahperusvaarat mts Fin. 44 L2
Kahramanmaraş Turkey 90 E3
Kahror Pak. 89 H4
Kâhta Turkey 90 E3
Kahuku HI U.S.A. 127 [inset]
Kahuku Point HI U.S.A. 127 [inset]
Kahului i. U.S.A. see Kahoolawe
Kahurangi National Park N.Z. 113 D5
Kahurangi Point N.Z. 113 D5
Kahuta Pak. 89 I3
Kahuzi-Biega, Parc National du nat. park Dem. Rep. Congo 98 C4
Kai, Kepulauan is Indon. 69 I8
Kaiapoi N.Z. 113 D6
Kaibab U.S.A. 129 G3
Kaibab Plateau U.S.A. 129 G3
Kai Besar i. Indon. 69 I8
Kaibito Plateau U.S.A. 129 H3
Kaifeng Henan China 77 G1
Kaifeng Henan China 77 G1
Kaihua Yunnan China see Wenshan
Kaihua Zhejiang China 77 H2
Kaiingveld reg. S. Africa 100 E5
Kaijiang China 76 E2
Kai Kecil i. Indon. 69 I8
Kai Keung Leng Hong Kong China 77 [inset]
Kaikoura N.Z. 113 D6
Kailas mt. China see Kangrinboqê Feng
Kailasahar India see Kailashahar
Kailashahar India 83 H4
Kailas Range mts China see Gangdisê Shan
Kaili China 76 E3
Kailu China 73 M4
Kailua HI U.S.A. 127 [inset]
Kailua Kona HI U.S.A. 127 [inset]
Kaimana Indon. 69 I7
Kaimanawa Mountains N.Z. 113 E4
Kaimar China 76 B1
Kaimur Range hills India 82 E4
Käina Estonia 45 M7
Kainan Japan 75 D6
Kainda Kyrg. see Kayyngdy
Kaindy Kyrg. see Kayyngdy
Kainji Lake National Park Nigeria 96 D4
Kaipara Harbour N.Z. 113 E3
Kaiparowits Plateau U.S.A. 129 H3
Kaiping China 77 G4
Kaipokok Bay Canada 123 K3
Kairana India 82 D3
Kairiru Island P.N.G. 69 K7
Kaironi Indon. 69 I7
Kairouan Tunisia 58 D7
Kaiserslautern Germany 53 H5
Kaiser Wilhelm II Land reg. Antarctica 152 E2
Kaitaia N.Z. 113 D2
Kaitangata N.Z. 113 B8
Kaitawa N.Z. 113 F4
Kaithal India 82 D3
Kaitum Sweden 44 L3
Kaiwatu Indon. 108 D2
Kaiwi Channel HI U.S.A. 127 [inset]
Kaixian China 77 F2
Kaiyang China 76 E3
Kaiyuan Liaoning China 74 B4
Kaiyuan Yunnan China 76 D4
Kajaani Fin. 44 O4
Kajabbi Australia 110 C4
Kajaki Afgh. 89 G3
Kajrān Afgh. 89 G3
Kaka Turkm. 89 E2
Kakabeka Falls Canada 122 C4
Kakadu National Park Australia 108 F3
Kakagi Lake Canada 121 M5
Kakamas S. Africa 100 E5
Kakamega Kenya 98 D3
Kakana India 71 A5
Kakar Pak. 89 G5
Kakata Liberia 96 B4
Kake U.S.A. 120 C3
Kakenge Dem. Rep. Congo 99 C4
Kakerbeck Germany 53 L2
Kakhi Azer. see Qax
Kakhovka Ukr. 59 O1
Kakhovs'ke Vodoskhovyshche resr Ukr. 43 G7
Kakhul Moldova see Cahul
Kākī Iran 88 C4
Kakinada India 84 D2
Kakisa Canada 120 G2
Kakisa r. Canada 120 G2
Kakisa Lake Canada 120 G2
Kakogawa Japan 75 D6
Kakori India 82 E4
Kakshaal-Too mts China/Kyrg. 80 E3
Kaktovik U.S.A. 118 D2
Kakul Pak. 89 I3
Kakwa r. Canada 120 G4
Kala Pak. 89 H4
Kala Tanz. 99 D4
Kalaâ Kebira Tunisia 58 D7
Kalaallit Nunaat terr. N. America see Greenland
Kalabahi Indon. 108 D2
Kalabáka Greece see Kalampaka
Kalabgur India 84 C2
Kalabo Zambia 99 C5
Kalach Rus. Fed. 43 I6
Kalacha Dida Kenya 98 D3
Kalach-na-Donu Rus. Fed. 43 I6
Kaladan r. India/Myanmar 70 A2
Kaladar Canada 135 G1
Ka Lae pt HI U.S.A. 127 [inset]
Kalagwe Myanmar 70 B2
Kalahari Desert Africa 100 F2
Kalahari Gemsbok National Park S. Africa 100 E3
Kalaikhum Tajik. see Qal'aikhum
Kalai-Khumb Tajik. see Qal'aikhum
Kala-I-Mor Turkm. 89 F3
Kalajoki Fin. 44 M4
Kalalé Benin 96 D3
Kalam India 84 C1
Kalam Pak. 89 I3
Kalámai Greece see Kalamata
Kalamare Botswana 101 H2
Kalamaria Greece 59 J4
Kalamata Greece 59 J6
Kalamazoo U.S.A. 134 C2
Kalampaka Greece 59 I5
Kalanchak Ukr. 59 O1
Kalandi Pak. 89 F4
Kalandula Angola see Calandula
Kalannie Australia 109 B7
Kalān Zīād Iran 89 E5
Kalapana HI U.S.A. 127 [inset]
Kalār Iraq 91 G4
Kalasin Thai. 70 C3
Kalāt Afgh. 89 G3
Kalāt Khorāsān Iran see Kabūd Gonbad
Kalāt Sīstān va Balūchestān Iran 89 E5
Kalat Balochistan Pak. 89 G4

Kalat Balochistan Pak. 89 G5
Kalat, Kūh-e mt. Iran 88 E3
Kalaupapa U.S.A. 127 [inset]
Kalaus r. Rus. Fed. 43 J7
Kalaw Myanmar 70 B2
Kälbäcär Azer. 91 G2
Kalbarri Australia 109 A6
Kalbarri National Park Australia 109 A6
Kalbe (Milde) Germany 53 L2
Kale Turkey 59 M6
Kalecik Turkey 90 D2
Kalefeld Germany 53 K3
Kaleindaung inlet Myanmar 70 A3
Kalemie Dem. Rep. Congo 99 C4
Kalemyo Myanmar 70 A2
Kāl-e Namak Iran 88 D3
Kalevala Rus. Fed. 44 Q4
Kalewa Myanmar 70 A2
Kaleybar Iran 88 B2
Kalgan China see Zhangjiakou
Kalghatgi India 84 B3
Kalgoorlie Australia 109 C7
Kāl Gūsheh Iran 88 E4
Kali Croatia 58 F2
Kali r. India/Nepal 82 E3
Kaliakra, Nos pt Bulg. 59 M3
Kali Gandaki r. Nepal 83 F4
Kaligiri India 84 C3
Kalikata India see Kolkata
Kalima Dem. Rep. Congo 98 C4
Kalimantan reg. Indon. 68 E7
Kálimnos i. Greece see Kalymnos
Kalinin Rus. Fed. see Tver'
Kalinin Adyndaky Tajik. see Cheshtebe
Kaliningrad Rus. Fed. 45 L9
Kalinino Armenia see Tashir
Kalinino Rus. Fed. 42 I4
Kalininsk Rus. Fed. 43 J6
Kalininskaya Rus. Fed. 43 H7
Kalinjara India 82 C5
Kalinkavichy Belarus 43 F5
Kalinkovichi Belarus see Kalinkavichy
Kalisch Poland see Kalisz
Kalispell U.S.A. 126 E2
Kalisz Poland 47 Q5
Kalitva r. Rus. Fed. 43 I6
Kaliua Tanz. 99 D4
Kaliujar India 82 E4
Kalix Sweden 44 M4
Kalkalighat India 83 H4
Kalkalpen, Nationalpark nat. park Austria 47 O7
Kalkan Turkey 59 M6
Kalkaska U.S.A. 134 C1
Kalkfeld Namibia 99 B6
Kalkfonteindam dam S. Africa 97 G5
Kalkudah Sri Lanka 84 D5
Kall Germany 52 G4
Kallang r. Sing. 71 [inset]
Kallaste Estonia 45 O7
Kallavesi l. Fin. 44 O5
Kallsedet Sweden 44 H5
Kallsjön l. Sweden 44 H5
Kallur India 84 C2
Kalmar Sweden 45 J8
Kalmarsund sea chan. Sweden 45 J8
Kalmit hill Germany 53 I5
Kalmūkh Qal'eh Iran 88 E2
Kalmunai Sri Lanka 84 D5
Kalmykia aut. rep. Rus. Fed. see Kalmykiya-Khalm'g-Tangch, Respublika
Kalmykiya-Khalm'g-Tangch, Respublika aut. rep. Rus. Fed. 91 G1
Kalmykovo Kazakh. see Taypak
Kalmytskaya Avtonomnaya Oblast' aut. rep. Rus. Fed. see Kalmykiya-khalm'g-Tangch, Respublika
Kalnai India 83 E5
Kalodnaye Belarus 45 O11
Kalol India 82 C5
Kalomo Zambia 99 C5
Kalone Peak Canada 120 E4
Kalpa India 82 D3
Kalpeni atoll India 84 B4
Kalpetta India 84 C4
Kalpi India 82 D4
Kaltag U.S.A. 118 C3
Kaltensundheim Germany 53 K4
Kaltukatjara Australia 109 E6
Kalu India 89 I4
Kaluga Rus. Fed. 43 H5
Kalukalukuang i. Indon. 68 F8
Kalundborg Denmark 45 G9
Kalush Ukr. 43 E6
Kalvakol India 84 C2
Kälviä Fin. 44 M5
Kal'ya Rus. Fed. 41 R3
Kalyan India 84 B2
Kalyandurg India 87 M7
Kalyansingapuram India 84 D2
Kalyazin Rus. Fed. 42 H4
Kalymnos i. Greece 59 L6
Kama Dem. Rep. Congo 98 C4
Kama Myanmar 70 A3

▶Kama r. Rus. Fed. 42 L4
4th longest river in Europe.

Kamaishi Japan 75 F5
Kamalia Pak. 89 I4
Kaman Turkey 90 D3
Kamaniskeg Lake Canada 135 G1
Kamanjab Namibia 99 B5
Kamarān i. Yemen 86 F6
Kamaran Island Yemen see Kamarān
Kamard reg. Afgh. 89 G3
Kamarod Pak. 89 F5
Kamaron Sierra Leone 96 B4
Kamashi Uzbek. 89 G2
Kamasin India 82 E4
Kambaiti Myanmar 70 B1
Kambalda Australia 109 C7
Kambam India 84 C4
Kambara i. Fiji see Kabara
Kambia Sierra Leone 96 B4
Kambing, Pulau i. East Timor see Ataúro, Ilha de
Kambo-san mt. N. Korea see Kwanmo-bong
Kambove Dem. Rep. Congo 99 C5
Kambūt Libya 90 B5
Kamchatka, Poluostrov pen. Rus. Fed. see Kamchatka Peninsula
Kamchatka Basin sea feature Bering Sea 150 H2
Kamchatka Peninsula Rus. Fed. 65 Q4
Kamchiya r. Bulg. 59 L3
Kameia, Parque Nacional de nat. park Angola see Cameia, Parque Nacional da
Kamelik r. Rus. Fed. 43 K5
Kamen Germany 53 H3
Kamen', Gory mt. Rus. Fed. 64 K3
Kamenets-Podol'skiy Ukr. see Kam"yanets'-Podil's'kyy
Kamenitsa mt. Bulg. 59 J4
Kamenjak, Rt pt Croatia 58 E2
Kamenka Kazakh. 41 Q5
Kamenka Arkhangel'skaya Oblast' Rus. Fed. 42 J2
Kamenka Penzenskaya Oblast' Rus. Fed. 43 J5
Kamenka Primorskiy Kray Rus. Fed. 74 E3
Kamenka-Bugskaya Ukr. see Kam"yanka-Buz'ka
Kamenka-Strumilovskaya Ukr. see Kam"yanka-Buz'ka
Kamen'-na-Obi Rus. Fed. 72 E2
Kamennogorsk Rus. Fed. 45 P6
Kamennomostskiy Rus. Fed. 91 F1
Kamenolomni Rus. Fed. 43 I7
Kamenongue Angola see Camanongue
Kamen'-Rybolov Rus. Fed. 74 D3
Kamenskoye Rus. Fed. 65 R3
Kamenskoye Ukr. see Dniprodzerzhyns'k
Kamensk-Shakhtinskiy Rus. Fed. 43 I6
Kamensk-Ural'skiy Rus. Fed. 64 H4
Kamet mt. China 82 D3
Kamiesberge mts S. Africa 100 D6
Kamieskroon S. Africa 100 C6
Kamileroi Australia 110 C3
Kamilukuak Lake Canada 121 K2
Kamina Dem. Rep. Congo 99 C4
Kaminak Lake Canada 121 M2
Kaminuriak Lake Canada see Qamanirjuaq Lake
Kamishihoro Japan 74 F4
Kamloops Canada 120 F5
Kamo Armenia 91 G2
Kamoke Pak. 89 I4
Kamonia Dem. Rep. Congo 99 C4

▶Kampala Uganda 98 D3
Capital of Uganda.

Kampar r. Indon. 68 C6
Kampar Malaysia 71 C6
Kampara India 84 D1
Kampen Neth. 52 F2
Kampene Dem. Rep. Congo 98 C4
Kamphaeng Phet Thai. 70 B3
Kampinoski Park Narodowy nat. park Poland 47 R4
Kâmpóng Cham Cambodia 71 D5
Kâmpóng Chhnăng Cambodia 71 D4
Kâmpóng Khleăng Cambodia 71 D4
Kâmpóng Saôm Cambodia see Sihanoukville
Kâmpóng Spœ Cambodia 71 D5
Kâmpóng Thum Cambodia 71 D4
Kâmpóng Trâbêk Cambodia 71 D5
Kâmpôt Cambodia 71 D5
Kampuchea country Asia see Cambodia
Kamrau, Teluk b. Indon. 69 I7
Kamsack Canada 121 K5
Kamskoye Vodokhranilishche resr Rus. Fed. 41 R4
Kamsuuma Somalia 98 E3
Kamuchawie Lake Canada 121 K3
Kamuli Uganda 98 D3
Kam"yanets'-Podil's'kyy Ukr. 43 E6
Kam"yanka-Buz'ka Ukr. 43 E6
Kamyanyets Belarus 45 M10
Kāmyārān Iran 88 B3
Kamyshin Rus. Fed. 43 J6
Kamyslybas, Ozero l. Kazakh. 80 B2
Kamyzyak Rus. Fed. 43 K7
Kamzar Oman 88 E5
Kanaaupscow r. Canada 122 F3
Kanab U.S.A. 129 G3
Kanab Creek r. U.S.A. 129 G3
Kanairiktok r. Canada 123 K3
Kanak Pak. 89 G4
Kananga Dem. Rep. Congo 99 C4
Kanangio, Mount vol. P.N.G. 69 L7
Kanangra-Boyd National Park Australia 112 E4
Kanarak India see Konarka
Kanarraville U.S.A. 129 G3
Kanas watercourse Namibia 100 C4
Kanash Rus. Fed. 42 J5
Kanauj India see Kannauj
Kanazawa Japan 75 E5
Kanbalu Myanmar 70 A2
Kanchanaburi Thai. 71 B4
Kanchanjanga mt. India/Nepal see Kangchenjunga
Kanchipuram India 84 C3
Kand mt. Pak. 89 G4
Kanda Pak. 89 G4
Kandahār Afgh. 89 G4
Kandalaksha Rus. Fed. 44 R3
Kandalakshskiy Zaliv g. Rus. Fed. 44 R3
Kandang Indon. 71 B7
Kandar Indon. 108 E2
Kandavu i. Fiji see Kadavu
Kandavu Passage Fiji see Kadavu Passage
Kandé Togo 96 D4
Kandhkot Pak. 89 H4
Kandi Benin 96 D3
Kandi India 84 C2
Kandiaro Pak. 89 H5
Kandıra Turkey 59 N4
Kandos Australia 112 D4
Kandreho Madag. 99 E5
Kandrian P.N.G. 69 L8
Kandukur India 84 C3
Kandy Sri Lanka 84 D5
Kandyagash Kazakh. 80 A2
Kane U.S.A. 135 F3
Kane Bassin b. Greenland 153 K1
Kaneh watercourse Iran 88 D5
Kaneohe HI U.S.A. 127 [inset]
Kaneti Pak. 89 G4
Kanevskaya Rus. Fed. 43 H7
Kang Afgh. 89 F4
Kang Botswana 100 F2
Kangaamiut Greenland 119 M3
Kangaarsussuaq c. Greenland 119 K2
Kangaba Mali 96 C3
Kangal Turkey 90 E3
Kangān Būshehr Iran 88 D5
Kangān Hormozgan Iran 88 E5
Kangandala, Parque Nacional de nat. park Angola see Cangandala, Parque Nacional de
Kangar Malaysia 71 C6
Kangaroo Island Australia 111 B7
Kangaroo Point Australia 110 B3
Kangaslampi Fin. 44 P5
Kangasniemi Fin. 44 O6
Kangāvar Iran 88 B3

▶Kangchenjunga mt. India/Nepal 83 G4
3rd highest mountain in the world and in Asia.
World 12–13

Kangding China 76 D2
Kangean, Kepulauan is Indon. 68 F8
Kangen r. Sudan 97 G4
Kangerlussuaq Greenland 119 M3
Kangerlussuaq inlet Greenland 119 M3
Kangerlussuaq inlet Greenland 153 J2
Kangersuatsiaq Greenland 119 M2
Kangertittivaq sea chan. Greenland 119 P2
Kanggye N. Korea 74 B4
Kanghwa S. Korea 75 B5
Kangikajik c. Greenland 119 P2
Kangiqsualujjuaq Canada 123 I2
Kangirsuk Canada 123 H1
Kang Krung National Park Thai. 71 B5
Kangle Gansu China 76 D1
Kangle Jiangxi China see Wanzai
Kanglong China 76 C1
Kangmar China 83 F3
Kangnŭng S. Korea 75 C5
Kango Gabon 98 B3
Kangping China 74 A4
Kangri Karpo Pass China/India 83 I3
Kangrinboqê Feng mt. China 82 E3
Kangto mt. China/India 83 H4
Kangtog China 83 F2
Kangxian China 76 E1
Kanibongan Sabah Malaysia 68 F5
Kanifing Gambia 96 B3
Kanigiri India 84 C3
Kanimekh Uzbek. 89 G1
Kanin, Poluostrov pen. Rus. Fed. 42 J2
Kanin Nos Rus. Fed. 153 G2
Kanin Nos, Mys c. Rus. Fed. 42 I1
Kaninskiy Bereg coastal area Rus. Fed. 42 I2
Kanjiroba mt. Nepal 83 E3
Kankaanpää Fin. 45 M6
Kankakee U.S.A. 134 B3
Kankan Guinea 96 C3
Kanker India 84 D1
Kankesanturai Sri Lanka 84 D4
Kankossa Mauritania 96 B3
Kanmaw Kyun i. Myanmar 71 B5
Kannauj India 82 D4
Kanniya Kumari c. India see Comorin, Cape
Kannonkoski Fin. 44 N5
Kannur India see Cannanore
Kannus Fin. 44 M5
Kano Nigeria 96 D3
Kanonpunt pt S. Africa 100 E8
Kanosh U.S.A. 129 G2
Kanovlei Namibia 99 B5
Kanoya Japan 75 C7
Kanpur Orissa India 84 E1
Kanpur Uttar Pradesh India 82 E4
Kanpur Pak. 89 H4
Kanrach reg. Pak. 89 G5
Kansai airport Japan 75 D6
Kansas U.S.A. 134 B4
Kansas r. U.S.A. 130 E4
Kansas state U.S.A. 130 D4
Kansas City KS U.S.A. 130 E4
Kansas City MO U.S.A. 130 E4
Kansk Rus. Fed. 65 K4
Kansu prov. China see Gansu
Kantang Thai. 71 B6
Kantara hill Cyprus 85 A2
Kantaralak Thai. 71 D4
Kantavu i. Fiji see Kadavu
Kantchari Burkina 96 D3
Kantemirovka Rus. Fed. 43 H6
Kanthi India 83 F5
Kantishna r. U.S.A. 118 C3
Kanton atoll Kiribati 107 I2
Kantulong Myanmar 70 B3
Kanturk Rep. of Ireland 51 D5
Kanuku Mountains Guyana 143 G3
Kanur India 84 C3
Kanus Namibia 100 D4
Kanyakubja India see Kannauj
KaNyamazane S. Africa 101 J3
Kanye Botswana 101 G3
Kaôh Pring i. Cambodia 71 C5
Kaohsiung Taiwan 77 I4
Kaôh Smăch i. Cambodia 71 C5
Kaôh Tang i. Cambodia 71 C5
Kaokoveld plat. Namibia 99 B5
Kaolack Senegal 96 B3
Kaoma Zambia 99 C5
Kaouadja Cent. Afr. Rep. 98 C3
Kapa S. Africa see Cape Town
Kapaa HI U.S.A. 127 [inset]
Kapaau HI U.S.A. 127 [inset]
Kapan Armenia 91 G3
Kapanga Dem. Rep. Congo 99 C4
Kaparhā Iran 88 C4
Kapatu Zambia 99 D4
Kapchagay Kazakh. 80 E3
Kapchagayskoye Vodokhranilishche resr Kazakh. 80 E3
Kap Dan Greenland see Kulusuk
Kapellen Belgium 52 E3
Kapello, Akra pt Greece 59 J6
Kapellskär Sweden 45 K7
Kapelskär Sweden see Kapellskär
Kapili r. India 83 G4
Kapingamarangi atoll Micronesia 150 G5
Kapingamarangi Rise sea feature N. Pacific Ocean 150 G5
Kapıorman Dağları mts Turkey 59 N4
Kapip Pak. 89 H4
Kapiri Mposhi Zambia 99 C5
Kapisillit Greenland 119 M3
Kapiskau r. Canada 122 E3
Kapit Sarawak Malaysia 68 E6
Kapiti Island N.Z. 113 E5
Kaplankyr, Chink hills Asia 91 I2
Kaplankyrskiy Gosudarstvennyy Zapovednik nature res. Turkm. 88 E1
Kapoeta Sudan 97 G4
Kapondai, Tanjung pt Indon. 69 G8
Kaposvár Hungary 58 G1
Kappel Germany 53 H5
Kappeln Germany 47 L3
Kapsukas Lith. see Marijampolė
Kaptai Bangl. 83 H5
Kapuas r. Indon. 68 D7
Kapuriya India 82 C4
Kapurthala India 82 C3
Kapuskasing Canada 122 E4
Kapustin Yar Rus. Fed. 43 J6
Kaputar mt. Australia 112 E3
Kaputir Kenya 98 D3
Kapuvár Hungary 58 G1
Kapydzhik, Gora mt. Armenia/Azer. see Qazangödağ
Kapyl' Belarus 45 O10
Kaqung China 89 J2
Kara India 82 E4
Kara Togo 96 D4
Kara r. Turkey 91 F3
Kara Art Pass China/Tajik. 89 I2
Kara-Balta Kyrg. 80 D3
Karabalyk Kazakh. 78 F1
Karabekaul' Turkm. see Garabekevyul
Karabiga Turkey 59 L4
Karabil', Vozvyshennost' hills Turkm. 89 F2
Kara-Bogaz-Gol, Proliv sea chan. Turkm. 91 I2
Kara-Bogaz-Gol, Zaliv b. Turkm. 91 I2
Kara-Bogaz-Gol'skiy Zaliv b. Turkm. see Kara-Bogaz-Gol, Zaliv
Karabük Turkey 90 D2
Karaburun Turkey 59 L5
Karabutak Kazakh. 80 B2
Karacabey Turkey 59 M4
Karacaköy Turkey 59 M4
Karacalı Dağ mt. Turkey 91 E3
Karaçal Tepe mt. Turkey 85 A1
Karacasu Turkey 59 M6
Karaca Yarımadası pen. Turkey 59 N6
Karachayevsk Rus. Fed. 91 F2
Karachev Rus. Fed. 43 G5
Karachi Pak. 89 G5
Karacurun Turkey see Hilvan
Karad India 84 B2
Kara Dağ hill Turkey 85 D1
Kara Dağ mt. Turkey 90 D3
Kara-Dar'ya Uzbek. see Payshanba
Kara Deniz sea Asia/Europe see Black Sea
Karagan Rus. Fed. 74 A1
Karaganda Kazakh. 80 D2
Karagayly Kazakh. 80 E2
Karaginskiy Zaliv b. Rus. Fed. 65 R4
Karagiye, Vpadina depr. Kazakh. 91 H2
Karagola India 83 F4
Karahallı Turkey 59 M5
Karahasanlı Turkey 90 D3
Karaikal India 84 C4
Karaikkudi India 84 C4
Karaisalı Turkey 90 D3
Karaj Iran 88 C3
Karak Jordan see Al Karak
Karakalli Turkey see Özalp
Karakax China see Moyu
Karakax He r. China 82 E1
Karakax Shan mts China 82 E2
Karakelong i. Indon. 69 H6
Karaki China 82 E1
Karaklis Armenia see Vanadzor
Karakoçan Turkey 91 F3
Kara-Köl Kyrg. 79 G2
Karakol Kyrg. 80 E3
Karakoram Pass China/Jammu and Kashmir 82 D2
Karakoram Range mts Asia 89 I2
Kara K'orē Eth. 98 D2
Karakorum Range mts Asia see Karakoram Range
Karaköse Turkey see Ağrı
Kara Kul' Kyrg. see Kara-Köl
Karakul' Uzbek. 89 F2
Karakul', Ozero l. Tajik. see Qarokŭl
Kara Kum des. Turkm. see Kara Kumy
Kara Kum des. Turkm. see Karakum Desert
Karakum, Peski Kazakh. see Karakum Desert
Karakum Desert Kazakh. 78 E2
Karakum Desert Turkm. see Kara Kumy
Karakum Desert Turkm. 88 F2
Karakumskiy Kanal canal Turkm. 89 F2
Kara Kumy des. Turkm. 88 E2
Karakurt Turkey 91 F2
Karakuş Dağı ridge Turkey 59 N5
Karal Chad 97 E3
Karala Estonia 45 L7
Karalundi Australia 109 B6
Karama r. Indon. 68 F7
Karaman Turkey 90 D3
Karaman prov. Turkey 85 A1
Karamanlı Turkey 59 M6
Karamay China 80 F2
Karambar Pass Afgh./Pak. 89 I2
Karamea N.Z. 113 D5
Karamea Bight b. N.Z. 113 C5
Karamendy Kazakh. 80 B1
Karamet-Niyaz Turkm. 89 G2
Karamiran China 83 F1
Karamiran Shankou pass China 83 F1
Karamürsel Turkey 59 M4
Karamyshevo Rus. Fed. 45 P8
Karān i. Saudi Arabia 88 C5
Karangasem Indon. 108 A2
Karanja India 84 C1
Karanjia India 82 E5
Karapınar Gaziantep Turkey 85 C1
Karapınar Konya Turkey 90 D3
Karas admin. reg. Namibia 100 C4
Karasay China 83 E1
Karasburg Namibia 100 D5
Kara Sea Rus. Fed. 64 I2
Kárášjohka Norway 44 N2
Karasjok Norway see Kárášjohka
Kara Strait Rus. Fed. see Karskiye Vorota, Proliv
Karasu r. Syria/Turkey 85 C1
Karasu Bitlis Turkey see Hizan
Karasu Sakarya Turkey 59 N4
Karasu r. Turkey 91 F3
Karasubazar Ukr. see Bilohirs'k
Karasuk Rus. Fed. 64 I4
Karāt Iran 89 F3
Karataş Turkey 85 B1
Karataş Burnu hd Turkey see Fener Burnu
Karatau Kazakh. 80 D3
Karatau, Khrebet mts Kazakh. 80 C3
Karatepe Turkey 85 A1
Karathuri Myanmar 71 B5
Karativu i. Sri Lanka 84 C4
Karatsu Japan 75 C6
Karaudanawa Guyana 143 G3
Karaulbazar Uzbek. 89 G2
Karauli India 82 D4
Karavan Kyrg. see Kerben
Karavostasi Cyprus 85 A2
Karawang Indon. 68 D8
Karayılan Turkey 85 C1
Karayulgan China 80 F3
Karazhal Kazakh. 80 D2
Karbalā' Iraq 91 G4
Karben Germany 53 I4
Karcag Hungary 59 I1
Karden Germany 53 H4
Kardhítsa Greece see Karditsa
Karditsa Greece 59 I5
Kärdla Estonia 45 M7
Karee S. Africa 101 H5
Kareeberge mts S. Africa 100 E6
Kareima Sudan 86 D6
Kareli India 82 D5
Karelia aut. rep. Rus. Fed. see Kareliya, Respublika
Kareliya, Respublika aut. rep. Rus. Fed. 44 R5
Karel'skaya A.S.S.R. aut. rep. Rus. Fed. see Kareliya, Respublika
Karel'skiy Bereg coastal area Rus. Fed. 44 R3
Karema Tanz. 99 D4
Karera India 82 D4
Karesuando Sweden 44 M2
Kārevāndar Iran 89 F5
Kargalinskaya Rus. Fed. 91 G2
Kargalinski Rus. Fed. see Kargalinskaya
Kargapazarı Dağları mts Turkey 91 F3
Karghalik China see Yecheng
Kargı Turkey 90 D2
Kargil India 82 D2
Kargilik China see Yecheng
Kargıpınarı Turkey 85 B1
Kargopol' Rus. Fed. 42 H3
Karholmsbruk Sweden 45 J6
Kari Nigeria 96 E3
Karīān Iran 88 E5
Kariba Zimbabwe 99 C5
Kariba, Lake resr Zambia/Zimbabwe 99 C5
Kariba Dam Zambia/Zimbabwe 99 C5
Kariba-yama vol. Japan 74 E4
Karibib Namibia 100 B1
Karigasniemi Fin. 44 N2
Karijini National Park Australia 109 B5
Karijoki Fin. 44 L5
Karikachi-tōge pass Japan 74 F4
Karikari, Cape N.Z. 113 D2
Karimata, Pulau-pulau is Indon. 68 D7
Karimata, Selat strait Indon. 68 D7
Karimganj India 83 H4
Karimnagar India 84 C2
Karimun Besar i. Indon. 71 C7
Karimunjawa, Pulau-pulau is Indon. 68 E8
Káristos Greece see Karystos
Karjat Maharashtra India 84 B2
Karjat Maharashtra India 84 B2
Karkaralinsk Kazakh. 80 E2
Karkar Island P.N.G. 69 L7
Karkh Pak. 89 G5
Karkinits'ka Zatoka g. Ukr. 59 O2
Kärkölä Fin. 45 N6
Karkonoski Park Narodowy nat. park Czech Rep./Poland see Krkonošský narodní park
Karksi-Nuia Estonia 45 N7
Karkūk Iraq see Kirkūk
Karlachi Pak. 89 H3
Karlik Shan mts China 80 H3
Karlıova Turkey 91 F3
Karlivka Ukr. 43 G6
Karl Marks, Qullai mt. Tajik. 89 I2
Karl-Marx-Stadt Germany see Chemnitz
Karlovac Croatia 58 F2
Karlovka Ukr. see Karlivka
Karlovo Bulg. 59 K3
Karlovy Vary Czech Rep. 53 M4
Karlsbad Germany 53 I6
Karlsborg Sweden 45 I7
Karlsburg Romania see Alba Iulia
Karlshamn Sweden 45 I8
Karlskoga Sweden 45 I7
Karlskrona Sweden 45 I8
Karlsruhe Germany 53 I5
Karlstad Sweden 45 H7
Karlstad U.S.A. 130 D1
Karlstadt Germany 53 J5
Karluk U.S.A. 118 C4
Karlyuk Turkm. 89 G2
Karmala India 84 B2
Karmel, Har hill Israel see Carmel, Mount
Karmona Spain see Córdoba
Karmøy i. Norway 45 D7
Karmpur Pak. 89 I4
Karnabchul', Step' plain Uzbek. 89 G2
Karnafuli Reservoir Bangl. 83 H5
Karnal India 82 D3
Karnataka state India 84 B3
Karnavati India see Ahmadabad
Karnes City U.S.A. 131 D6
Karnobat Bulg. 59 L3
Karodi Pak. 89 G5
Karoi Zimbabwe 99 C5
Karokpi Myanmar 70 B4
Karo La pass China 83 G3
Karong India 83 H4
Karonga Malawi 99 D4
Karonie Australia 109 C7
Karoo National Park S. Africa 100 F7
Karoo Nature Reserve S. Africa 100 G7
Karoonda Australia 111 B7
Karora Eritrea 86 E6
Káros i. Greece see Keros
Karossa Indon. 68 F7
Karossa, Tanjung pt Indon. 108 B2
Karow Germany 53 M1
Karpasia pen. Cyprus 85 B2
Karpas Peninsula Cyprus see Karpasia
Karpathos i. Greece 59 L7
Karpathou, Steno sea chan. Greece 59 L6
Karpaty mts Europe see Carpathian Mountains
Karpenisi Greece 59 I5
Karpilovka Belarus see Aktsyabrski
Karpinsk Rus. Fed. 41 S4
Karpogory Rus. Fed. 42 J2
Karpuz r. Turkey 85 A1
Karratha Australia 108 B5
Karroo plat. S. Africa see Great Karoo
Karrychirla Turkm. see imeni Kerbabayeva
Kars Turkey 91 F2
Kärsämäki Fin. 44 N5
Kārsava Latvia 45 O8
Karshi Turkm. 91 I2
Karshi Uzbek. 89 G2
Karshinskaya Step' plain Uzbek. 89 G2
Karskiye Vorota, Proliv strait Rus. Fed. 64 G3
Karskoye More sea Rus. Fed. see Kara Sea
Karstädt Germany 53 L1
Karstula Fin. 44 N5
Karsu Turkey 85 C1
Karsun Rus. Fed. 43 J5
Kartal Turkey 59 M4
Kartaly Rus. Fed. 64 H4
Kartayel' Rus. Fed. 42 L2
Karttula Fin. 44 O5
Karumba Australia 110 C3
Karumbhar Island India 82 B5
Karun, Kūh-e hill Iran 88 C4
Kārūn, Rūd-e r. Iran 88 C4
Karuni Indon. 108 B2
Karur India 84 C4
Karvia Fin. 44 M5
Karviná Czech Rep. 47 Q6
Karwar India 84 B3
Karyagino Azer. see Füzuli
Karymskoye Rus. Fed. 73 K2
Karynzharyk, Peski des. Kazakh. 91 I2
Karystos Greece 59 K5
Kaş Turkey 59 M6
Kasa India 84 B2
Kasaba Turkey see Turgutlu
Kasabonika Canada 122 C3
Kasabonika Lake Canada 122 C3
Kasaï r. Dem. Rep. Congo 98 B4
also known as Kwa
Kasaï, Plateau du Dem. Rep. Congo 99 C4
Kasaji Dem. Rep. Congo 99 C5
Kasama Zambia 99 D5
Kasan Uzbek. 89 G2
Kasane Botswana 99 C5
Kasaragod India 84 B3
Kasargod India see Kasaragod
Kasargode India see Kasaragod
Kasatkino Rus. Fed. 74 C2
Kasba Lake Canada 121 K2
Kasba Tadla Morocco 54 C5
Kasenga Dem. Rep. Congo 99 C5
Kasengu Dem. Rep. Congo 99 C4
Kasese Dem. Rep. Congo 98 C4
Kasese Uganda 98 D3
Kasevo Rus. Fed. see Neftekamsk
Kasganj India 82 D4
Kasha China see Gonjo
Kashabowie Canada 122 C4
Kāshān Iran 88 C3
Kashary Rus. Fed. 43 I6
Kashechewan Canada 122 E3
Kashgar China see Kashi
Kashi China 80 E4
Kashihara Japan 75 D6
Kashima-nada b. Japan 75 F5
Kashin Rus. Fed. 42 H4
Kashipur India 82 D3
Kashira Rus. Fed. 43 H5
Kashiwazaki Japan 75 E5
Kashkarantsy Rus. Fed. 42 H2
Kashku'iyeh Iran 88 D4
Kāshmar Iran 88 E3
Kashmir terr. Asia see Jammu and Kashmir
Kashmir, Vale of reg. India 82 C2
Kashyukulu Dem. Rep. Congo 99 C4
Kasi India see Varanasi
Kasigar Afgh. 89 H3
Kasimov Rus. Fed. 43 I5
Kaskattama r. Canada 121 N3
Kaskinen Fin. 44 L5
Kas Klong i. Cambodia see Kŏng, Kaôh
Kaskö Fin. see Kaskinen
Kaslo Canada 120 G5
Kasmere Lake Canada 121 K3
Kasongo Dem. Rep. Congo 99 C4
Kasongo-Lunda Dem. Rep. Congo 99 B4
Kasos i. Greece 59 L7
Kaspiy Mangy Oypaty lowland Kazakh./Rus. Fed. see Caspian Lowland
Kaspiysk Rus. Fed. 91 G2
Kaspiyskiy Rus. Fed. see Lagan'
Kaspiyskoye More l. Asia/Europe see Caspian Sea
Kassa Slovakia see Košice
Kassala Sudan 86 E6
Kassandras, Akra pt Greece 59 J5
Kassandras, Kolpos b. Greece 59 J4
Kassel Germany 53 J3
Kasserine Tunisia 58 C7
Kastag Pak. 89 F5
Kastamonu Turkey 90 D2
Kastellaun Germany 53 H4

Kastelli Greece 59 J7
Kastéllion Greece see Kastelli
Kastellorizon i. Greece see Megisti
Kasterlee Belgium 52 E3
Kastoria Greece 59 I4
Kastornoye Rus. Fed. 43 H6
Kastsyukovichy Belarus 43 G5
Kasulu Tanz. 99 D4
Kasumkent Rus. Fed. 91 H2
Kasungu Malawi 99 D5
Kasungu National Park Malawi 99 D5
Kasur Pak. 89 I4
Katâdtlit Nunât terr. N. America see Greenland
Katahdin, Mount U.S.A. 132 G2
Kataklik Jammu and Kashmir 82 D2
Katako-Kombe Dem. Rep. Congo 98 C4
Katakwi Uganda 98 D3
Katana India 82 C5
Katangi India 82 D5
Katanning Australia 109 B8
Katavi National Park Tanz. 99 D4
Katawaz reg. Afgh. 89 G3
Katchall i. India 71 A6
Katea Dem. Rep. Congo 99 C4
Katerini Greece 59 J4
Katesh Tanz. 99 D4
Kate's Needle mt. Canada/U.S.A. 120 C3
Katete Zambia 99 D5
Katherîna, Gebel mt. Egypt see Kātrīnā, Jabal
Katherine Australia 108 F3
Katherine Gorge National Park Australia see Nitmiluk National Park
Kathi India 89 I6
Kathiawar pen. India 82 B5
Kathihar India see Katihar
Kathiraveli Sri Lanka 84 D4
Kathiwara India 82 C5
Kathleen Falls Australia 108 E3
Kathlehong S. Africa 101 I4

▶Kathmandu Nepal 83 F4
Capital of Nepal.

Kathu S. Africa 100 F4
Kathua India 82 C2
Kati Mali 96 C3
Katihar India 83 F4
Kati-Kati S. Africa 101 H7
Katima Mulilo Namibia 99 C5
Katimik Lake Canada 121 L4
Katiola Côte d'Ivoire 96 C4
Kā Tiritiri o te Moana mts N.Z. see Southern Alps
Katkop Hills S. Africa 100 E6
Katmai National Park and Preserve U.S.A. 118 C4
Katmandu Nepal see Kathmandu
Kato Achaïa Greece 59 I5
Kat O Chau Hong Kong China see Crooked Island
Kat O Hoi b. Hong Kong China see Crooked Harbour
Katoomba Australia 112 E4
Katowice Poland 47 Q5
Katoya India 83 G5
Katrancık Dağı mts Turkey 59 M6
Kātrīnā, Jabal mt. Egypt 90 D5
Katrine, Loch l. U.K. 50 E4
Katrineholm Sweden 45 J7
Katse Dam Lesotho 101 I5
Katsina Nigeria 96 D3
Katsina-Ala Nigeria 96 D4
Katsuura Japan 75 F6
Kattaktoc, Cap c. Canada 123 I2
Kattakurgan Uzbek. 89 G2
Kattamudda Well Australia 108 D5
Kattaqŭrghon Uzbek. see Kattakurgan
Kattasang Hills Afgh. 89 G3
Kattegat strait Denmark/Sweden 45 G8
Kattowitz Poland see Katowice
Katumbar India 82 D4
Katunino Rus. Fed. 42 J4
Katuri Pak. 89 H4
Katwa India see Katoya
Katwijk aan Zee Neth. 52 E2
Katzenbuckel hill Germany 53 J5
Kauai i. U.S.A. 127 [inset]
Kauai Channel U.S.A. 127 [inset]
Kaub Germany 53 H4
Kaufungen Germany 53 J3
Kauhajoki Fin. 44 M5
Kauhava Fin. 44 M5
Kaukauna U.S.A. 134 A1
Kaukkwè Hills Myanmar 70 B1
Kaukonen Fin. 44 N3
Kaula i. HI U.S.A. 127 [inset]
Kaulakahi Channel HI U.S.A. 127 [inset]
Kaumajet Mountains Canada 123 J2
Kaunakakai HI U.S.A. 127 [inset]
Kaunas Lith. 45 M9
Kaunata Latvia 45 O8
Kaundy, Vpadina depr. Kazakh. 91 I2
Kaunia Bangl. 83 G4
Kaura-Namoda Nigeria 96 D3
Kau Sai Chau i. Hong Kong China 77 [inset]
Kaustinen Fin. 44 M5
Kautokeino Norway 44 M2
Kau-ye Kyun i. Myanmar 71 B5
Kavadarci Macedonia 59 J4
Kavak Turkey 90 E2
Kavaklıdere Turkey 59 M6
Kavala Greece 59 K4
Kavalas, Kolpos b. Greece 59 K4
Kavalerovo Rus. Fed. 74 D3
Kavali India 84 D3
Kavār Iran 88 D4
Kavaratti India 84 B4
Kavaratti atoll India 84 B4
Kavarna Bulg. 59 M3
Kavendou, Mont mt. Guinea 96 B3
Kaveri r. India 84 C4
Kavīr Iran 88 C3
Kavīr salt flat Iran 88 D3
Kavīr, Dasht-e des. Iran 88 D3
Kavīr Kūshk well Iran 88 E3
Kavkasioni mts Asia/Europe see Caucasus
Kawa Myanmar 70 B3
Kawagama Lake Canada 135 F1
Kawagoe Japan 75 E6
Kawaguchi Japan 75 E6
Kawaihae HI U.S.A. 127 [inset]
Kawaikini, Mount HI U.S.A. 127 [inset]
Kawakawa N.Z. 113 E2
Kawambwa Zambia 99 C4
Kawana Zambia 99 C5
Kawardha India 82 E5
Kawartha Lakes Canada 135 F1
Kawasaki Japan 75 E6
Kawau Island N.Z. 113 E3
Kawawachikamach Canada 123 I3
Kawdut Myanmar 70 B4
Kawerau N.Z. 113 F4
Kawhia N.Z. 113 E4
Kawhia Harbour N.Z. 113 E4
Kawich Peak U.S.A. 128 E3
Kawich Range mts U.S.A. 128 E3
Kawinaw Lake Canada 121 L4
Kaw Lake U.S.A. 131 D4
Kawlin Myanmar 70 A2
Kawm Umbū Egypt 86 D5
Kawngmeum Myanmar 70 B2
Kawthaung Myanmar 71 B5
Kaxgar China see Kashi
Kaxgar He r. China 80 E4
Kax He r. China 80 F3
Kaxtax Shan mts China 83 E1
Kaya Burkina 96 C3
Kayadibi Turkey 90 E3
Kayan r. Indon. 68 F6
Kayankulam India 84 C4
Kayar India 84 C2
Kaycee U.S.A. 126 G4
Kaydak, Sor dry lake Kazakh. 91 I1
Kaydanovo Belarus see Dzyarzhynsk
Kayembe-Mukulu Dem. Rep. Congo 99 C4
Kayenta U.S.A. 129 H3
Kayes Mali 96 B3
Kaymaz Turkey 59 N5
Kaynar Kazakh. 80 E2
Kaynar Turkey 90 E3
Kayseri Turkey 90 D3
Kayuyu Dem. Rep. Congo 98 C4
Kayyngdy Kyrg. 80 D3
Kazach'ye Rus. Fed. 65 O2
Kazakh Azer. see Qazax
Kazakhskaya S.S.R. country Asia see Kazakhstan
Kazakhskiy Melkosopochnik plain Kazakh. 80 D1
Kazakhskiy Zaliv b. Kazakh. 91 I2

▶Kazakhstan country Asia 78 F2
4th largest country in Asia.
Asia 6, 62–63

Kazakhstan Kazakh. see Aksay
Kazakstan country Asia see Kazakhstan
Kazan r. Canada 121 M2
Kazan' Rus. Fed. 42 K5
Kazandzhik Turkm. see Gazandzhyk
Kazanka r. Rus. Fed. 42 K5
Kazanlı Turkey 85 B1
Kazanlŭk Bulg. 59 K3
Kazan-rettō is Japan see Volcano Islands
Kazatin Ukr. see Kozyatyn

▶Kazbek mt. Georgia/Rus. Fed. 43 J8
4th highest mountain in Europe.

Kaz Dağı mts Turkey 59 L5
Kāzerūn Iran 88 C4
Kazhim Rus. Fed. 42 K3
Kazidi Tajik. see Qozideh
Kazi Magomed Azer. see Qazımämmäd
Kazincbarcika Hungary 43 D6
Kaziranga National Park India 83 H4
Kazret'i Georgia 91 G2
Kaztalovka Kazakh. 41 P6
Kazy Turkm. 88 E2
Kazym r. Rus. Fed. 41 T3
Kazymskiy Mys Rus. Fed. 41 T3
Kea i. Greece 59 K6
Keady U.K. 51 F3
Keams Canyon U.S.A. 129 H4
Kéamu i. Vanuatu see Anatom
Kearney U.S.A. 130 D3
Kearny U.S.A. 129 H5
Keban Turkey 90 E3
Keban Barajı resr Turkey 90 E3
Kébémèr Senegal 96 B3
Kebili Tunisia 54 F5
Kebīr, Nahr al r. Lebanon/Syria 85 B2
Kebkabiya Sudan 97 F3
Kebnekaise mt. Sweden 44 K3
Kebock Head hd U.K. 50 C2
K'ebrī Dehar Eth. 98 E3
Kech reg. Pak. 89 F5
Kechika r. Canada 120 E3
Keçiborlu Turkey 59 N6
Kecskemét Hungary 59 H1
K'eda Georgia 91 F2
Kėdainiai Lith. 45 M9
Kedairu Passage Fiji see Kadavu Passage
Kedgwick Canada 123 I5
Kedian China 77 G2
Kedong China 74 B3
Kedva r. Rus. Fed. 42 L2
Kędzierzyn-Koźle Poland 47 Q5
Keele r. Canada 120 E1
Keele Peak Canada 120 D2
Keeler U.S.A. 128 E3
Keeley Lake Canada 121 I4
Keeling Islands terr. Indian Ocean see Cocos Islands
Keen, Mount hill U.K. 50 G4
Keene CA U.S.A. 128 D4
Keene KY U.S.A. 134 C5
Keene NH U.S.A. 135 I2
Keene OH U.S.A. 134 E3
Keepit, Lake resr Australia 112 E3
Keep River National Park Australia 108 E3
Keerbergen Belgium 52 E3
Keer-weer, Cape Australia 110 C2
Keetmanshoop Namibia 100 D4
Keewatin Canada 121 M5
Kefallinía i. Greece see Cephalonia
Kefallonia i. Greece see Cephalonia
Kefamenanu Indon. 108 D2
Kefe Ukr. see Feodosiya
Keffi Nigeria 96 D4
Keflavík Iceland 44 [inset]
Kegalla Sri Lanka 84 D5
Kegen Kazakh. 80 E3
Keglo, Baie de b. Canada 123 I2
Keg River Canada 120 G3
Kegul'ta Rus. Fed. 43 J7
Kehra Estonia 45 N7
Kehsi Mansam Myanmar 70 B2
Keighley U.K. 48 F5
Keila Estonia 45 N7
Keimoes S. Africa 100 E5
Keitele Fin. 44 O5
Keitele l. Fin. 44 O5
Keith Australia 111 C8
Keith U.K. 50 G3
Keith Arm b. Canada 120 F1
Kejimkujik National Park Canada 123 I5
Kekaha HI U.S.A. 127 [inset]
Kékes mt. Hungary 47 R7
Kekri India 82 C4
K'elafo Eth. 98 E3
Kelai i. Maldives 84 B5
Kelang Malaysia 71 C7
Kelberg Germany 52 G4
Kelheim Germany 53 L6
Kelibia Tunisia 58 D6
Kelifskiy Uzboy marsh Turkm. 89 F2
Kelīrī Iran 88 E5
Kelkheim (Taunus) Germany 53 I4
Kelkit Turkey 91 E2
Kelkit r. Turkey 90 E2
Kéllé Congo 98 B4
Keller Lake Canada 120 F2
Kellett, Cape Canada 118 F2
Kelleys Island U.S.A. 134 D3
Kelliher Canada 121 K5
Kelloselkä Fin. 44 P3
Kells Rep. of Ireland 51 F4
Kells r. U.K. 51 F3
Kelly U.S.A. 134 B5
Kelly Lake Canada 120 E1
Kelly Range hills Australia 109 C6
Kelmė Lith. 45 M9
Kelmis Belgium 52 G4
Kelo Chad 97 E4
Kelowna Canada 120 G5
Kelp Head hd Canada 120 E5
Kelseyville U.S.A. 128 B2
Kelso U.K. 50 G5
Kelso CA U.S.A. 129 F4
Kelso WA U.S.A. 126 C3
Keluang Malaysia 71 C7
Kelvington Canada 121 K4
Kem' Rus. Fed. 42 G2
Kem' r. Rus. Fed. 42 G2
Ke Macina Mali see Massina
Kemah Turkey 90 E3
Kemaliye Turkey 90 E3
Kemalpaşa Turkey 59 L5
Kemano Canada 120 E4
Kembé Cent. Afr. Rep. 98 C3
Kemeneshát hills Hungary 58 G1
Kemer Antalya Turkey 59 N6
Kemer Muğla Turkey 59 M6
Kemer Barajı resr Turkey 59 M6
Kemerovo Rus. Fed. 64 J4
Kemi Fin. 44 N4
Kemijärvi Fin. 44 O3
Kemijärvi l. Fin. 44 O3
Kemijoki r. Fin. 44 N4
Kemiö Fin. see Kimito
Kemir Turkm. 88 D2
Kemmerer U.S.A. 126 F4
Kemnath Germany 53 L5
Kemnay U.K. 50 G3
Kemp Coast reg. Antarctica see Kemp Land
Kempele Fin. 44 N4
Kempen Germany 52 G3
Kempisch Kanaal canal Belgium 52 F3
Kemp Land reg. Antarctica 152 D2
Kemp Peninsula Antarctica 152 A2
Kemp's Bay Bahamas 133 E7
Kempsey Australia 112 F3
Kempt, Lac l. Canada 122 G5
Kempten (Allgäu) Germany 47 M7
Kempton U.S.A. 134 B3
Kempton Park S. Africa 101 I4
Kemptville Canada 135 H1
Kemujan i. Indon. 68 E8
Ken r. India 82 E4
Kenai U.S.A. 118 C3
Kenai Fiords National Park U.S.A. 118 C4
Kenai Mountains U.S.A. 118 C4
Kenamu r. Canada 123 K3
Kenansville U.S.A. 133 E5
Kenâyis, Râs el pt Egypt see Ḥikmah, Ra's al
Kenbridge U.S.A. 135 F5
Kendal U.K. 48 E4
Kendall Australia 112 F3
Kendall, Cape Canada 119 J3
Kendallville U.S.A. 134 C3
Kendari Indon. 69 G7
Kendawangan Indon. 68 E7
Kendégué Chad 97 E3
Kendrapara India 83 F5
Kendraparha India see Kendrapara
Kendrick Peak U.S.A. 129 H4
Kendujhar India see Keonjhar
Kendujhargarh India see Keonjhar
Kendyrli-Kayasanskoye, Plato plat. Kazakh. 91 I2
Kendyrlisor, Solonchak salt l. Kazakh. 91 I2
Kenebri Australia 112 D3
Kenedy U.S.A. 131 D6
Kenema Sierra Leone 96 B4
Keneurgench Turkm. 87 I1
Kenge Dem. Rep. Congo 99 B4
Keng Lap Myanmar 70 C2
Kengtung Myanmar 70 B2
Kenhardt S. Africa 100 E5
Kéniéba Mali 96 B3
Kénitra Morocco 54 C5
Kenmare Rep. of Ireland 51 C6
Kenmare U.S.A. 130 C1
Kenmare River inlet Rep. of Ireland 51 B6
Kenmore U.S.A. 135 F2
Kenn Germany 52 G5
Kenna U.S.A. 131 C5
Kennebec U.S.A. 130 D3
Kennebec r. U.S.A. 132 G2
Kennebunkport U.S.A. 135 J2
Kennedy, Cape U.S.A. see Canaveral, Cape
Kennedy Range National Park Australia 109 A6
Kennedy Town Hong Kong China 77 [inset]
Kenner U.S.A. 131 F6
Kennet r. U.K. 49 G7
Kenneth Range hills Australia 109 B5
Kennett U.S.A. 131 F4
Kennewick U.S.A. 126 D3
Kenn Reef Australia 110 F4
Kenogami r. Canada 122 D4
Keno Hill Canada 120 C2
Kenora Canada 121 M5
Kenosha U.S.A. 134 B2
Kenozero, Ozero l. Rus. Fed. 42 H3
Kent r. U.K. 48 E4
Kent OH U.S.A. 134 E3
Kent TX U.S.A. 131 B6
Kent VA U.S.A. 134 E5
Kent WA U.S.A. 126 C3
Kentani S. Africa 101 I7
Kent Group is Australia 111 [inset]
Kentland U.S.A. 134 B3
Kenton U.S.A. 134 D3
Kent Peninsula Canada 118 H3
Kentucky state U.S.A. 134 C5
Kentucky Lake U.S.A. 131 F4
▶Kenya country Africa 98 D3
Africa 7, 94–95

▶Kenya, Mount Kenya 98 D4
2nd highest mountain in Africa.

Kenyir, Tasik resr Malaysia 71 C6
Keokuk U.S.A. 130 F3
Keoladao National Park India 82 D4
Keonjhar India 83 F5
Keonjhargarh India see Keonjhar
Keosauqua U.S.A. 130 F3
Keowee, Lake resr U.S.A. 133 D5
Kepina r. Rus. Fed. 42 I2
Keppel Bay Australia 110 E4
Kepsut Turkey 59 M5
Kera India 83 F5
Kerāh Iran 88 E4
Kerala state India 84 B4
Kerang Australia 112 A5
Kerava Fin. 45 N6
Kerba Alg. 57 G5
Kerbela Iraq see Karbalā'
Kerben Kyrg. 80 D3
Kerbi r. Rus. Fed. 74 E1
Kerbodot, Lac l. Canada 123 I3
Kerch Ukr. 90 E1
Kerchem'ya Rus. Fed. 42 L3
Kerema P.N.G. 69 L8
Keremeos Canada 120 G5
Kerempe Burun pt Turkey 90 D2
Keren Eritrea 86 E6
Kerewan Gambia 96 B3
Kergeli Turkm. 88 E2
Kerguélen, Îles is Indian Ocean 149 M9
Kerguelen Islands Indian Ocean see Kerguélen, Îles
Kerguelen Plateau sea feature Indian Ocean 149 M9
Kericho Kenya 98 D4
Kerikeri N.Z. 113 D2
Kerimäki Fin. 44 P6
Kerinci, Gunung vol. Indon. 68 C7
Kerinci Seblat National Park Indon. 68 C7
Kerintji vol. Indon. see Kerinci, Gunung
Keriya He watercourse China 72 E5
Keriya Shankou pass China 83 E2
Kerken Germany 52 G3
Kerkenah, Îles is Tunisia 58 D7
Kerki Turkm. 89 G2
Kerkichi Turkm. 89 G2
Kerkinitis, Limni l. Greece 59 J4
Kérkira i. Greece see Corfu
Kerkouane tourist site Tunisia 58 D6
Kerkyra Greece 59 H5
Kerkyra i. Greece see Corfu
Kerma Sudan 86 D6
Kermadec Islands S. Pacific Ocean 107 I5

▶Kermadec Trench sea feature S. Pacific Ocean 150 I8
4th deepest trench in the world.

Kermān Iran 88 E4
Kerman U.S.A. 128 C3
Kermān Desert Iran 88 E4
Kermānshāh Iran 88 B3
Kermānshāhān Iran 88 D4
Kermine Uzbek. see Navoi
Kermit U.S.A. 131 C6
Kern r. U.S.A. 128 D4
Kernertut, Cap c. Canada 123 I2
Keros i. Greece 59 K6
Keros Rus. Fed. 42 L3
Kérouané Guinea 96 C4
Kerpen Germany 52 G4
Kerr, Cape Antarctica 152 H1
Kerrobert Canada 121 I5
Kerrville U.S.A. 131 D6
Kerry Head hd Rep. of Ireland 51 C5
Kerteminde Denmark 45 G9
Kerulen r. China/Mongolia see Herlen Gol
Kerur India 84 B2
Keryneia Cyprus see Kyrenia
Kerzaz Alg. 96 C2
Kerzhenets r. Rus. Fed. 42 J4
Kesagami Lake Canada 122 E4
Kesälahti Fin. 44 P6
Keşan Turkey 59 L4
Keşap Turkey 43 H8
Kesariya India 83 F4
Kesennuma Japan 75 F5
Keshan China 74 B2
Keshem Afgh. 89 H2
Keshena U.S.A. 134 A1
Keshendeh-ye Bala Afgh. 89 G2
Keshod India 82 B5
Keshvar Iran 88 C3
Keskin Turkey 90 D3
Keskozero Rus. Fed. 42 G3
Kesova Gora Rus. Fed. 42 H4
Kessel Neth. 52 G3
Kestell S. Africa 101 I5
Kesten'ga Rus. Fed. 44 Q4
Kestilä Fin. 44 O4
Keswick Canada 134 F1
Keswick U.K. 48 D4
Keszthely Hungary 58 G1
Ketapang Indon. 68 E7
Ketchikan U.S.A. 120 D4
Keti Bandar Pak. 89 G5
Ketmen', Khrebet mts China/Kazakh. 80 F3
Kettering U.K. 49 G6
Kettering U.S.A. 134 C4
Kettle r. Canada 120 G5
Kettle Creek r. U.S.A. 135 G3
Kettle Falls U.S.A. 126 D2
Kettleman City U.S.A. 128 D3
Kettle River Range mts U.S.A. 126 D2
Keuka U.S.A. 135 G2
Keuka Lake U.S.A. 135 G2
Keumgang, Mount N. Korea see Kumgang-san
Keumsang, Mount N. Korea see Kumgang-san
Keuruu Fin. 44 N5
Kew Turks and Caicos Is 133 F8
Kewanee U.S.A. 130 F3
Kewaunee U.S.A. 134 B1
Keweenaw Bay U.S.A. 130 F2
Keweenaw Peninsula U.S.A. 130 F2
Keweenaw Point U.S.A. 132 C2
Key, Lough l. Rep. of Ireland 51 D3
Keyala Sudan 97 G4
Keyano Canada 123 G3
Keya Paha r. U.S.A. 130 D3
Key Harbour Canada 122 E5
Keyihe China 74 A2
Key Largo U.S.A. 133 D7
Keymir Turkm. see Kemir
Keynsham U.K. 49 E7
Keyser U.S.A. 135 F4
Keystone Lake U.S.A. 131 D4
Keystone Peak U.S.A. 129 H6
Keysville U.S.A. 135 F5
Keytesville U.S.A. 130 E4
Keyvy, Vozvyshennost' hills Rus. Fed. 42 H2
Key West U.S.A. 133 D7
Kez Rus. Fed. 41 Q4
Kezi Zimbabwe 99 C6
Kgalagadi admin. dist. Botswana 100 E3
Kgalazadi admin. dist. Botswana see Kgalagadi
Kgatlen admin. dist. Botswana see Kgatleng
Kgatleng admin. dist. Botswana 101 H3
Kgomofatshe Pan salt pan Botswana 100 E2
Kgoro Pan salt pan Botswana 100 G3
Kgotsong S. Africa 101 H4
Khabab Syria 85 C3
Khabar Iran 88 D4
Khabarikha Rus. Fed. 42 L2
Khabarovsk Rus. Fed. 74 D2
Khabarovskiy Kray admin. div. Rus. Fed. 74 D2
Khabarovsk Kray admin. div. Rus. Fed. see Khabarovskiy Kray
Khabary Rus. Fed. 72 D2
Khabis Iran see Shahdād
Khabody Pass Afgh. 89 F3
Khachmas Azer. see Xaçmaz
Khadar, Jabal mt. Oman 88 E6
Khadro Pak. 89 H5
Khafs Banbān well Saudi Arabia 88 B5
Khagaria India 83 F4
Khagrachari Bangl. 83 G5
Khagrachhari Bangl. see Khagrachari
Khairgarh Pak. 89 H4
Khairpur Punjab Pak. 89 I4
Khairpur Sindh Pak. 89 H5
Khāīz, Kūh-e mt. Iran 88 C4
Khaja Du Koh hill Afgh. 89 G2
Khajuha India 82 E4
Khāk-e Jabbar Afgh. 89 H3
Khakhea Botswana 100 F3
Khakīr Afgh. 89 G3
Khak-rēz Afgh. 89 G4
Khakriz reg. Afgh. 89 G4
Khalach Turkm. 89 G2
Khalajestan reg. Iran 88 C3
Khalatse Jammu and Kashmir 82 D2
Khalifat mt. Pak. 89 G4
Khalīj Surt g. Libya see Sirte, Gulf of
Khalilabad India 83 E4
Khalīlī Iran 88 D5
Khalkabad Turkm. 89 F1
Khalkhāl Iran 88 C2
Khálki i. Greece see Chalki
Khalkís Greece see Chalkida
Khallikot India 84 E2
Khalturin Rus. Fed. see Orlov
Khamar-Daban, Khrebet mts Rus. Fed. 72 I2
Khamaria India 84 D1
Khambhat India 82 C5
Khambhat, Gulf of India 84 A2
Khamgaon India 84 C1
Khamir Yemen 86 F6
Khamis Mushayṭ Saudi Arabia 86 F6
Khamkkeut Laos 70 D3
Khamma well Saudi Arabia 88 B5
Khammam India 84 D2
Khammouan Laos see Muang Khammouan
Khamra Rus. Fed. 65 M3
Khamseh reg. Iran 88 C3
Khan Afgh. 89 H3
Khan, Nam r. Laos 70 C3
Khānābād Afgh. 89 H2
Khān al Baghdādī Iraq 91 F4
Khān al Mashāhidah Iraq 91 G4
Khān al Muşallá Iraq 91 G4
Khanapur India 84 B2
Khān ar Raḥbah Iraq 91 G5
Khanasur Pass Iran/Turkey 91 G3
Khanbalik China see Beijing
Khānch Iran 88 B2
Khandu India 89 I6
Khandwa India 82 D5
Khandyga Rus. Fed. 65 O3
Khanewal Pak. 89 H4
Khanh Dương Vietnam 71 E4
Khan Hung Vietnam see Soc Trăng
Khaniá Greece see Chania
Khānī Yek Iran 88 D4
Khanka, Lake China/Rus. Fed. 74 D3
Khanka, Ozero l. China/Rus. Fed. see Khanka, Lake
Khankendi Azer. see Xankändi
Khanna India 82 D3
Khannā, Qā' salt pan Jordan 85 C3
Khanpur Pak. 89 H4
Khān Ruḥābah Iraq see Khān ar Raḥbah
Khansar Pak. 89 H4
Khān Shaykhūn Syria 85 C2
Khantayskoye, Ozero l. Rus. Fed. 64 K3
Khanthabouli Laos see Savannakhét
Khanty-Mansiysk Rus. Fed. 64 H3
Khān Yūnis Gaza 85 B4
Khanzi admin. dist. Botswana see Ghanzi
Khao Ang Rua Nai Wildlife Reserve nature res. Thai. 71 C4
Khao Banthat Wildlife Reserve nature res. Thai. 71 B6
Khao Chum Thong Thai. 71 B5
Khaoen Si Nakarin National Park Thai. 71 B4
Khao Laem National Park Thai. 70 B4
Khao Laem Reservoir Thai. 70 B4
Khao Luang National Park Thai. 71 B5
Khao Pu-Khao Ya National Park Thai. 71 B6
Khao Soi Dao Wildlife Reserve nature res. Thai. 71 C4
Khao Sok National Park Thai. 67 B5
Khao Yai National Park Thai. 71 C4
Khapalu Jammu and Kashmir 80 E4
Khaptad National Park Nepal 82 E3
Kharabali Rus. Fed. 43 J7
Kharagpur Bihar India 83 F4
Kharagpur W. Bengal India 83 F5
Khārān r. Iran 87 I4
Kharari India see Abu Road
Kharda India 84 B2
Khardi India 82 C6
Khardong La pass Jammu and Kashmir see Khardung La
Khardung La pass Jammu and Kashmir 82 D2
Kharez Ilias Afgh. 89 F3
Kharfiyah Iraq 91 G5
Kharga Egypt see Al Khārijah
Kharga r. Rus. Fed. 74 D1
Khârga, El Wâḥât el oasis Egypt see Khārijah, Wāḥāt al
Kharga Oasis Egypt see Khārijah, Wāḥāt al
Khārg Islands Iran 88 C4
Khargon India 82 C5
Khari r. Rajasthan India 82 C4
Khari r. Rajasthan India 82 C4
Kharian Pak. 89 I3
Khariar India 84 D1
Khārijah, Wāḥāt al oasis Egypt 86 D5
Kharîm, Gebel hill Egypt see Kharīm, Jabal
Kharīm, Jabal hill Egypt 85 A4
Kharkhara r. India 82 E5
Kharkiv Ukr. 43 H6
Khar'kov Ukr. see Kharkiv
Khār Kūh mt. Iran 88 D4
Kharlovka Rus. Fed. 42 H1
Kharlu Rus. Fed. 44 Q6
Kharmanli Bulg. 59 K4
Kharoti reg. Afgh. 89 H3
Kharovsk Rus. Fed. 42 I4
Kharsia India 83 E5

▶Khartoum Sudan 86 D6
Capital of Sudan.

Kharwar reg. Afgh. 89 H3
Khasardag, Gora mt. Turkm. 88 E2
Khasav'yurt Rus. Fed. 91 G2
Khash Afgh. 89 F4
Khāsh Iran 89 F4
Khash Desert Afgh. 89 F4
Khashgort Rus. Fed. 41 T2
Khashm el Girba Sudan 86 E7
Khashm Şana' Saudi Arabia 90 E6
Khash Rūd r. Afgh. 89 F4
Khashuri Georgia 91 F2
Khasi Hills India 83 G4
Khaskovo Bulg. 59 K4
Khatanga Rus. Fed. 65 L2
Khatanga, Gulf of Rus. Fed. see Khatangskiy Zaliv
Khatangskiy Zaliv b. Rus. Fed. 65 L2
Khatayakha Rus. Fed. 42 M2
Khatinza Pass Pak. 89 H2
Khatmat al Malāha Oman 88 E5
Khatyrka Rus. Fed. 65 S3
Khavda India 82 B5
Khawak Pass Afgh. 89 H3
Khayamnandi S. Africa 101 G6
Khaybar Saudi Arabia 86 E4
Khayelitsha S. Africa 100 D8
Khayrān, Ra's al pt Oman 88 E6
Khê Bo Vietnam 70 D3
Khedrī Iran 88 E3
Khefa Israel see Haifa
Khehuene, Ponta pt Moz. 101 L2
Khemis Miliana Alg. 57 H5
Khemmarat Thai. 70 D3
Khenchela Alg. 58 B7
Khenifra Morocco 54 C5
Kherāmeh Iran 88 D4
Kherrata Alg. 57 I5
Kherreh Iran 88 D5
Khersan r. Iran 88 C4
Kherson Ukr. 59 O1
Kheta r. Rus. Fed. 65 L2
Kheyrābād Iran 88 D4
Khezerābād Iran 88 D2
Khiching India 83 F5
Khilok Rus. Fed. 73 K2
Khilok r. Rus. Fed. 73 J2
Khinganskiy Zapovednik nature res. Rus. Fed. 74 C2
Khinsar Pak. 89 H5
Khíos i. Greece see Chios
Khirbat Isrīyah Syria 85 C2

Kualasimpang Indon. 71 B6
Kuala Terengganu Malaysia 71 C6
Kualatungal Indon. 68 C7
Kuamut *Sabah* Malaysia 68 F5
Kuandian China 74 B4
Kuantan Malaysia 71 C7
Kuba Azer. *see* **Quba**
Kuban' *r.* Rus. Fed. 43 H7
Kubār Syria 91 E4
Kubaybāt Syria 85 C2
Kubaysah Iraq 91 F4
Kubenskoye, Ozero *l.* Rus. Fed. 42 H4
Kubrat Bulg. 59 L3
Kubuang Indon. 68 F6
Kuchaman Road India 89 I5
Kuchema Rus. Fed. 42 I2
Kuching *Sarawak* Malaysia 68 E6
Kucing *Sarawak* Malaysia *see* **Kuching**
Kuçovë Albania 59 H4
Kuda India 82 B5
Kudal India 84 B3
Kudap Indon. 71 C7
Kudat *Sabah* Malaysia 68 F5
Kudligi India 84 C3
Kudremukh *mt.* India 84 B3
Kudus Indon. 68 E8
Kudymkar Rus. Fed. 41 Q4
Kueishan Tao *i.* Taiwan 77 I3
Kufstein Austria 47 N7
Kugaaruk Canada 119 J3
Kugesi Rus. Fed. 42 J4
Kugka Lhai China 83 G3
Kugluktuk Canada 118 G3
Kugmallit Bay Canada 153 A2
Kūh, Ra's-al- *pt* Iran 88 E5
Kūhak Iran 89 F5
Kuhanbokano *mt.* China 83 E3
Kuhbier Germany 53 M1
Kūhdasht Iran 88 B3
Kūhīn Iran 88 C2
Kūhīrī Iran 89 F5
Kuhmo Fin. 44 P4
Kuhmoinen Fin. 45 N6
Kūhpāyeh *mt.* Iran 88 E4
Kūhrān, Kūh-e *mt.* Iran 88 E5
Kühren Germany 53 M3
Kui Buri Thai. 71 B4
Kuis Namibia 100 C3
Kuiseb *watercourse* Namibia 100 B2
Kuitan China 77 G4
Kuito Angola 99 B5
Kuitun China *see* **Kuytun**
Kuiu Island U.S.A. 120 C3
Kuivaniemi Fin. 44 N4
Kujang N. Korea 75 B5
Kuji Japan 75 F4
Kujū-san *vol.* Japan 75 C6
Kukālār, Kūh-e *hill* Iran 88 C4
Kukan Rus. Fed. 74 D2
Kukës Albania 59 I3
Kukesi Albania *see* **Kukës**
Kukmor Rus. Fed. 42 K4
Kukshi India 82 C5
Kukunuru India 84 D2
Kukurtli Turkm. 88 E2
Kūl *r.* Iran 88 D5
Kula Turkey 59 M5
Kulaisila India 83 F5
Kula Kangri *mt.* China/Bhutan 79 G3
Kulandy Kazakh. 80 A2
Kulaneh *reg.* Pak. 89 F5
Kular Rus. Fed. 65 O2
Kuldīga Latvia 45 L8
Kuldja China *see* **Yining**
Kul'dur Rus. Fed. 74 C2
Kule Botswana 100 E2
Kulebaki Rus. Fed. 43 I5
Kulen Cambodia 71 D4
Kulgera Australia 109 F6
Kulikovo Rus. Fed. 42 J3
Kulim Malaysia 71 C6
Kulin Australia 109 B8
Kulja Australia 109 B7
Kulkyne *watercourse* Australia 112 B3
Kullu India 82 D3
Kulmbach Germany 53 L4
Kŭlob Tajik. 89 H2
Kuloy Rus. Fed. 42 I3
Kuloy *r.* Rus. Fed. 42 I2
Kulp Turkey 91 F3
Kul'sary Kazakh. 78 E2
Külsheim Germany 53 J5
Kulu India *see* **Kullu**
Kulu Turkey 90 D3
Kulunda Rus. Fed. 72 D2
Kulundinskaya Step' *plain* Kazakh./Rus. Fed. 72 D2
Kulundinskoye, Ozero *salt l.* Rus. Fed. 72 D2
Kulusuk Greenland 119 O3
Kulwin Australia 111 C7
Kulyab Tajik. *see* **Kŭlob**
Kuma *r.* Rus. Fed. 43 J7
Kumagaya Japan 75 E5
Kumai, Teluk *b.* Indon. 68 E7
Kumalar Dağı *mts* Turkey 59 N5
Kumamoto Japan 75 C6
Kumano Japan 75 E6
Kumanovo Macedonia 59 I3
Kumara Rus. Fed. 74 B2
Kumasi Ghana 96 C4
Kumayri Armenia *see* **Gyumri**
Kumba Cameroon 96 D4
Kumbakonam India 84 C4
Kumbe Indon. 69 K8
Kümbet Turkey 59 N5
Kumbharli Ghat *mt.* India 84 B2
Kumbla India 84 B3
Kumchuru Botswana 100 F2
Kum-Dag Turkm. *see* **Gumdag**
Kumdah Saudi Arabia 86 G5
Kumel *well* Iran 88 D3
Kumeny Rus. Fed. 42 K4
Kumertau Rus. Fed. 64 G4
Kumgang-san *mt.* N. Korea 71 C5
Kumguri India 83 G4
Kumhwa S. Korea 75 B5
Kumi S. Korea 75 C5
Kumi Uganda 97 G4
Kumkurgan Uzbek. 89 G2
Kumla Sweden 45 I7
Kumlu Turkey 85 C1
Kummersdorf-Alexanderdorf Germany 53 N2
Kumo Nigeria 96 E3
Kŭmŏ-do *i.* S. Korea 75 B6
Kumon Range *mts* Myanmar 70 B1
Kumphawapi Thai. 70 C3
Kums Namibia 100 D5
Kumta India 84 B3
Kumu Dem. Rep. Congo 98 C3
Kumukh Rus. Fed. 91 G2
Kumul China *see* **Hami**
Kumund India 84 D1
Kumylzhenskaya Rus. Fed. *see* **Kumylzhenskiy**
Kumylzhenskiy Rus. Fed. 43 I6
Kun *r.* Myanmar 70 B3
Kunar *r.* Afgh. 89 H3
Kunashir, Ostrov *i.* Rus. Fed. 70 G3
Kunashirskiy Proliv *sea chan.* Japan/Rus. Fed. *see* **Nemuro-kaikyō**
Kunchaung Myanmar 70 B2
Kunchuk Tso *salt l.* China 83 E2
Kunda Estonia 45 O7
Kunda India 83 E4
Kundapura India 84 B3
Kundelungu, Parc National de *nat. park* Dem. Rep. Congo 99 C5
Kundelungu Ouest, Parc National de *nat. park* Dem. Rep. Congo 99 C5
Kundia India 82 C4
Kundur *i.* Indon. 68 C6
Kunduz Afgh. 89 H2
Kunene *r.* Angola *see* **Cunene**
Kuneneng *admin. dist.* Botswana *see* **Kweneng**
Künes China *see* **Xinyuan**
Kungälv Sweden 45 G8
Kunghit Island Canada 120 D4
Kungrad Uzbek. 80 A3
Kungsbacka Sweden 45 H8
Kungshamn Sweden 45 G7
Kungu Dem. Rep. Congo 98 B3
Kungur *mt.* China *see* **Kongur Shan**
Kungur Rus. Fed. 41 R4
Kunhing Myanmar 70 B2
Kuni *r.* India 84 C2
Kūnīch Iran 88 E5
Kunié *i.* New Caledonia *see* **Pins, Île des**
Kunigai India 84 C3
Kunimi-dake *mt.* Japan 75 C6
Kunlavav India 82 B5
Kunlong Myanmar 70 B2
Kunlun Shan *mts* China 82 D1
Kunlun Shankou *pass* China 79 H2
Kunming China 76 D3
Kunsan S. Korea 75 B6
Kunshan China 77 I2
Kununurra Australia 108 E3
Kunwak *r.* Canada 121 L2
Kun'ya Rus. Fed. 42 F4
Kunyang *Yunnan* China *see* **Jinning**
Kunyang *Zhejiang* China *see* **Pingyang**
Kunya-Urgench Turkm. *see* **Keneurgench**
Künzelsau Germany 53 J5
Künzels-Berg *hill* Germany 53 L3
Kuocang Shan *mts* China 77 I2
Kuohijärvi *l.* Fin. 45 N6
Kuolayarvi Rus. Fed. 44 P3
Kuopio Fin. 44 O5
Kuortane Fin. 44 M5
Kupa *r.* Croatia/Slovenia 58 G2
Kupang Indon. 108 C2
Kupari India 83 F5
Kupiškis Lith. 45 N9
Kupreanof Island U.S.A. 120 C3
Kupwara India 82 C2
Kup''yans'k Ukr. 43 H6
Kuqa China 80 F3
Kür *r.* Georgia 91 G2
also known as Kur (Russian Federation), Kura
Kur *r.* Rus. Fed. 74 D2
also known as Kür (Georgia), Kura
Kuragino Rus. Fed. 72 G2
Kurakh Rus. Fed. 43 J8
Kurama Range *mts* Asia 87 K1
Kuraminskiy Khrebet *mts* Asia *see* **Kurama Range**
Kūrān Dap Iran 89 E5
Kurashiki Japan 75 D6
Kurasia India 83 E5
Kurayn *i.* Saudi Arabia 88 C5
Kurayoshi Japan 75 D6
Kurchatov Rus. Fed. 43 G6
Kurchum Kazakh. 80 F2
Kürdämir Azer. 91 H2
Kŭrdzhali Bulg. 59 K4
Kure Japan 75 D6
Küre Turkey 90 D2
Kure Atoll U.S.A. 150 I4
Kuressaare Estonia 45 M7
Kurgal'dzhino Kazakh. *see* **Korgalzhyn**
Kurgal'dzhinskiy Kazakh. *see* **Korgalzhyn**
Kurgan Rus. Fed. 64 H4
Kurganinsk Rus. Fed. 91 F1
Kurgannaya Rus. Fed. *see* **Kurganinsk**
Kurgantyube Tajik. *see* **Qŭrghonteppa**
Kuri Afgh. 89 H2
Kuri India 82 B4
Kuria Muria Islands Oman *see* **Ḥalāniyāt, Juzur al**
Kuridala Australia 110 C4
Kurigram Bangl. 83 G4
Kurikka Fin. 44 M5
Kuril Basin *sea feature* Sea of Okhotsk 150 F2
Kuril Islands Rus. Fed. 74 H3
Kurilovka Rus. Fed. 43 K6
Kuril'sk Rus. Fed. 74 G3
Kuril'skiye Ostrova *is* Rus. Fed. *see* **Kuril Islands**
Kuril Trench *sea feature* N. Pacific Ocean 150 F3
Kurkino Rus. Fed. 43 H5
Kurmashkino Kazakh. *see* **Kurchum**
Kurmuk Sudan 86 D7
Kurnool India 84 C3
Kuroiso Japan 75 F5
Kurort Schmalkalden Germany 53 K4
Kurovskiy Rus. Fed. 74 B1
Kurow N.Z. 113 C7
Kurram Pak. 89 H3
Kurri Kurri Australia 112 E4
Kursavka Rus. Fed. 91 F1
Kürshim Kazakh. *see* **Kurchum**
Kurshskiy Zaliv *b.* Lith./Rus. Fed. *see* **Courland Lagoon**
Kuršiu marios *b.* Lith./Rus. Fed. *see* **Courland Lagoon**
Kursk Rus. Fed. 43 H6
Kurskaya Rus. Fed. 91 G1
Kurskiy Zaliv *b.* Lith./Rus. Fed. *see* **Courland Lagoon**
Kurşunlu Turkey 90 D2
Kurtalan Turkey 91 F3
Kurtoğlu Burnu *pt* Turkey 59 M6
Kurtpınar Turkey 85 B1
Kurucaşile Turkey 90 D2
Kuruçay Turkey 90 E3
Kurukshetra India 82 D3
Kuruktag *mts* China 80 G3
Kuruman S. Africa 100 F4
Kuruman *watercourse* S. Africa 100 E4
Kurume Japan 75 C6
Kurumkan Rus. Fed. 73 K2
Kurunegala Sri Lanka 84 D5
Kurupam India 84 D2
Kurush, Jebel *hills* Sudan 86 D5
Kur'ya Rus. Fed. 41 R3
Kuryk Kazakh. 91 H2
Kuşadası Turkey 59 L6
Kuşadası Körfezi *b.* Turkey 59 L6
Kusaie *atoll* Micronesia *see* **Kosrae**
Kusary Azer. *see* **Qusar**
Kuşcenneti *nature res.* Turkey 85 B1
Kuschke Nature Reserve S. Africa 101 I3
Kusel Germany 53 H5
Kuş Gölü *l.* Turkey 59 L4
Kushalgarh India 82 C5
Kushchevskaya Rus. Fed. 43 H7
Kushimoto Japan 75 D6
Kushiro Japan 74 G4
Kushka Turkm. *see* **Gushgy**
Kushkopola Rus. Fed. 42 J3
Kushmurun Kazakh. 78 F1
Kushtagi India 84 C3
Kushtia Bangl. 83 G5
Kushtih Iran 89 E4
Kuskan Turkey 85 A1
Kuskokwim *r.* U.S.A. 118 B3
Kuskokwim Bay U.S.A. 118 B4
Kuskokwim Mountains U.S.A. 118 C3
Kuşluyan Turkey *see* **Gölköy**
Kusŏng N. Korea 75 B5
Kustanay Kazakh. *see* **Kostanay**
Küstence Romania *see* **Constanța**
Küstenkanal *canal* Germany 53 H1
Kustia Bangl. *see* **Kushtia**
Kut Iran 88 C4
Kut, Ko *i.* Thai. 71 C5
Kūt 'Abdollāh Iran 88 C4
Kutacane Indon. 71 B7
Kütahya Turkey 59 M5
K'ut'aisi Georgia 91 F2
Kut-al-Imara Iraq *see* **Al Kūt**
Kutan Rus. Fed. 91 G1
Kutanibong Indon. 71 B7
Kutaraja Indon. *see* **Banda Aceh**
Kutayfat Ţurayf *vol.* Saudi Arabia 85 D4
Kutch, Gulf of India *see* **Kachchh, Gulf of**
Kutch, Rann of *marsh* India *see* **Kachchh, Rann of**
Kutchan Japan 74 F4
Kutina Croatia 58 G2
Kutjevo Croatia 58 G2
Kutkai Myanmar 70 B2
Kutno Poland 47 Q4
Kutru India 84 D2
Kutu Dem. Rep. Congo 98 B4
Kutubdia Island Bangl. 83 G5
Kutum Sudan 97 F3
Kutztown U.S.A. 135 H3
Kuujjua *r.* Canada 118 G2
Kuujjuaq Canada 123 H2
Kuujjuarapik Canada 122 F3
Kuuli-Mayak Turkm. 88 D1
Kuusamo Fin. 44 P4
Kuusankoski Fin. 45 O6
Kuvango Angola 99 B5
Kuvshinovo Rus. Fed. 42 G4
▶**Kuwait** *country* Asia 88 B4
Asia 6, 62–63

▶**Kuwait** Kuwait 88 B4
Capital of Kuwait.

Kuwajleen *atoll* Marshall Is *see* **Kwajalein**
Kuybyshev *Novosibirskaya Oblast'* Rus. Fed. 64 I4
Kuybyshev *Respublika Tatarstan* Rus. Fed. *see* **Bolgar**
Kuybyshev *Samarskaya Oblast'* Rus. Fed. *see* **Samara**
Kuybysheve Ukr. 43 H7
Kuybyshevka-Vostochnaya Rus. Fed. *see* **Belogorsk**
Kuybyshevskoye Vodokhranilishche *resr* Rus. Fed. 43 K5
Kuyeda Rus. Fed. 41 R4
Kuygan Kazakh. 80 D2
Kuytun China 80 F3
Kuytun Rus. Fed. 72 I2
Kuyucak Turkey 59 M6
Kuzino Rus. Fed. 41 R4
Kuznechnoye Rus. Fed. 45 P6
Kuznetsk Rus. Fed. 43 J5
Kuznetsovo Rus. Fed. 74 E3
Kuznetsovs'k Ukr. 43 E6
Kuzovatovo Rus. Fed. 43 J5
Kvænangen *sea chan.* Norway 44 L1
Kvaløya *i.* Norway 44 K2
Kvalsund Norway 44 M1
Kvarnerić *sea chan.* Croatia 58 F2
Kvitøya *ice feature* Svalbard 64 E2
Kwa *r.* Dem. Rep. Congo *see* **Kasaï**
Kwabhaca S. Africa *see* **Mount Frere**
Kwadelen *atoll* Marshall Is *see* **Kwajalein**
Kwajalein *atoll* Marshall Is 150 H5
Kwale Nigeria 96 D4
KwaMashu S. Africa 101 J5
KwaMhlanga S. Africa 101 I3
Kwa Mtoro Tanz. 99 D4
Kwangch'ŏn S. Korea 75 B5
Kwangchow China *see* **Guangzhou**
Kwangju S. Korea 75 B6
Kwangsi Chuang Autonomous Region *aut. reg.* China *see* **Guangxi Zhuangzu Zizhiqu**
Kwangtung *prov.* China *see* **Guangdong**
Kwanmo-bong *mt.* N. Korea 74 C4
Kwanobuhle S. Africa 101 G7
KwaNojoli S. Africa 101 G7
Kwanonqubela S. Africa 101 H7
Kwanonzame S. Africa 100 G6
Kwanza *r.* Angola *see* **Cuanza**
Kwatinidubu S. Africa 101 H7
KwaZamokhule S. Africa 101 I4
Kwazamukucinga S. Africa 100 G7
Kwazamuxolo S. Africa 100 G6
KwaZanele S. Africa 101 I4
Kwazulu-Natal *prov.* S. Africa 97 J5
Kweichow *prov.* China *see* **Guizhou**
Kweiyang China *see* **Guiyang**
Kwekwe Zimbabwe 99 C5
Kweneng *admin. dist.* Botswana 100 G2
Kwenge *r.* Dem. Rep. Congo 99 B4
Kwetabohigan *r.* Canada 122 E4
Kwezi-Naledi S. Africa 101 H6
Kwidzyn Poland 47 Q4
Kwikila P.N.G. 69 L8
Kwilu *r.* Angola/Dem. Rep. Congo 99 B4
Kwo Chau Kwan To *is Hong Kong* China *see* **Ninepin Group**
Kwoka *mt.* Indon. 69 I7
Kyabra Australia 111 C5
Kyabram Australia 112 B6
Kyadet Myanmar 70 A2
Kyaikkami Myanmar 70 B3
Kyaiklat Myanmar 70 A3
Kyaikto Myanmar 70 B3
Kyakhta Rus. Fed. 72 J2
Kyalite Australia 112 A5
Kyancutta Australia 109 F8
Kyangin Myanmar 70 B3
Kyangngoin China 76 B2
Kyaukhnyat Myanmar 70 B3
Kyaukkyi Myanmar 70 B3
Kyaukme Myanmar 70 B2
Kyaukpadaung Myanmar 70 A2
Kyaukpyu Myanmar 70 A3
Kyaukse Myanmar 70 B2
Kyauktaw Myanmar 70 A2
Kyaunggon Myanmar 70 A3
Kybartai Lith. 45 M9
Kyebogyi Myanmar 70 B3
Kyêbxang Co *l.* China 83 G2
Kyeikdon Myanmar 70 B3
Kyeikywa Myanmar 70 B3
Kyeintali Myanmar 70 A3
Kyela Tanz. 99 D4
Kyelang India 82 D2
Kyidaunggan Myanmar 70 B3
Kyiv Ukr. *see* **Kiev**
Kyklades *is* Greece *see* **Cyclades**
Kyle Canada 121 I5
Kyle of Lochalsh U.K. 50 D3
Kyll *r.* Germany 52 G5
Kyllini *mt.* Greece 59 J6
Kymi Greece 59 K5
Kymis, Akra *pt* Greece 59 K5
Kyneton Australia 112 B6
Kynuna Australia 110 C4
Kyoga, Lake Uganda 98 D3
Kyōga-misaki *pt* Japan 75 D6
Kyogle Australia 112 F2
Kyong Myanmar 70 B2
Kyŏngju S. Korea 75 C6
Kyonpyaw Myanmar 70 A3
Kyōto Japan 75 D6
Kyparissia Greece 59 I6
Kypros *country* Asia *see* **Cyprus**
Kypshak, Ozero *salt l.* Kazakh. 79 F1
Kyra Rus. Fed. 73 K3
Kyra Panagia *i.* Greece 59 K5
Kyrenia Cyprus 85 A2
Kyrenia Mountains Cyprus *see* **Pentadaktylos Range**
Kyrgyz Ala-Too *mts* Kazakh./Kyrg. *see* **Kirghiz Range**
▶**Kyrgyzstan** *country* Asia 80 D3
Asia 6, 62–63
Kyritz Germany 53 M2
Kyrksæterøra Norway 44 F5
Kyrta Rus. Fed. 41 R3
Kyssa Rus. Fed. 42 J2
Kytalyktakh Rus. Fed. 65 O3
Kythira *i.* Greece 59 J6
Kythnos *i.* Greece 59 K6
Kyunglung China 82 E3
Kyunhla Myanmar 70 A2
Kyun Pila *i.* Myanmar 71 B5
Kyuquot Canada 120 E5
Kyurdamir Azer. *see* **Kürdämir**
Kyūshū *i.* Japan 75 C7
Kyushu-Palau Ridge *sea feature* N. Pacific Ocean 150 F4
Kyustendil Bulg. 59 J3
Kywebwe Myanmar 70 B3
Kywong Australia 112 C5
Kyyev Ukr. *see* **Kiev**
Kyyiv Ukr. *see* **Kiev**
Kyyivs'ke Vodoskhovyshche *resr* Ukr. 43 F6
Kyyjärvi Fin. 44 N5
Kyzyl Rus. Fed. 80 H1
Kyzyl-Art, Pereval *pass* Kyrg./Tajik. *see* **Kyzylart Pass**
Kyzylart Pass Kyrg./Tajik. 89 I2
Kyzyl-Burun Azer. *see* **Siyäzän**
Kyzyl-Kiya Kyrg. *see* **Kyzyl-Kyya**
Kyzylkum, Peski *des.* Kazakh./Uzbek. *see* **Kyzylkum Desert**
Kyzylkum Desert Kazakh./Uzbek. 80 B3
Kyzyl-Kyya Kyrg. 80 D3
Kyzyl-Mazhalyk Rus. Fed. 80 H1
Kyzylorda Kazakh. 80 C3
Kyzylrabot Tajik. *see* **Qizilrabot**
Kyzylsay Kazakh. 91 I2
Kyzylysor Kazakh. 91 H1
Kyzylzhar Kazakh. 80 C2
Kzyl-Dzhar Kazakh. *see* **Kyzylzhar**
Kzyl-Orda Kazakh. *see* **Kyzylorda**
Kzyltu Kazakh. *see* **Kishkenekol'**

L

Laagri Estonia 45 N7
Laam Atoll Maldives *see* **Hadhdhunmathi Atoll**
La Angostura, Presa de *resr* Mex. 136 F5
Laanila Fin. 44 O2
Laascaanood Somalia 98 E3
La Ascensión, Bahía de *b.* Mex. 137 G5
Laasgoray Somalia 98 E2

▶**Laâyoune** W. Sahara 96 B2
Capital of Western Sahara.

La Babia Mex. 131 C6
La Bahía, Islas de *is* Hond. 137 G5
La Baie Canada 123 H4
La Baleine, Grande Rivière de *r.* Canada 122 F3
La Baleine, Petite Rivière de *r.* Canada 122 F3
La Baleine, Rivière à *r.* Canada 123 I2
La Banda Arg. 144 D3
La Barge U.S.A. 126 F4
Labasa Fiji 107 H3
La Baule-Escoublac France 56 C3
Labazhskoye Rus. Fed. 42 L2
Labe *r.* Czech Rep. *see* **Elbe**
Labé Guinea 96 B3
La Belle U.S.A. 133 D7
La Bénoué, Parc National de *nat. park* Cameroon 97 E4
Laberge, Lake Canada 120 C2
Labian, Tanjung *pt* Malaysia 68 F5
La Biche, Lac *l.* Canada 121 H4
Labinsk Rus. Fed. 91 F1
Labis Malaysia 71 C7
La Boquilla Mex. 131 B7
La Boucle du Baoulé, Parc National de *nat. park* Mali 96 C3
Labouheyre France 56 D4
Laboulaye Arg. 144 D4
Labrador *reg.* Canada 123 J3
Labrador City Canada 123 I3
Labrador Sea Canada/Greenland 119 M3
Labrang China *see* **Xiahe**
Lábrea Brazil 142 F5
Labuan Malaysia 68 F5
Labudalin China *see* **Ergun**
Labuhanbilik Indon. 71 C7
Labuhanruku Indon. 71 B7
Labuna Indon. 69 H7
Labutta Myanmar 70 A3
Labyrinth, Lake *salt flat* Australia 111 A6
Labytnangi Rus. Fed. 64 H3
Laç Albania 59 H4
La Cabrera, Sierra de *mts* Spain 57 C2
La Cadena Mex. 131 B7
Lac Allard Canada 123 J4
La Calle Alg. *see* **El Kala**
La Cañiza Spain *see* **A Cañiza**
La Capelle France 52 D5
La Carlota Arg. 144 D4
La Carolina Spain 57 E4
Lăcăuți, Vârful *mt.* Romania 59 L2
Laccadive, Minicoy and Amindivi Islands *union terr.* India *see* **Lakshadweep**
Laccadive Islands India 84 B4
Lac du Bonnet Canada 121 L5
Lacedaemon Greece *see* **Sparti**
La Ceiba Hond. 137 G5
Lacepede Bay Australia 111 B8
Lacepede Islands Australia 108 C4
Lacha, Ozero *l.* Rus. Fed. 42 H3
Lachendorf Germany 53 K2
Lachine U.S.A. 134 D1

▶**Lachlan** *r.* Australia 112 A5
5th longest river in Oceania.

La Chorrera Panama 137 I7
Lachute Canada 122 G5
Laçın Azer. 91 G3
La Ciotat France 56 G5
Lac La Biche Canada 121 I4
Lac la Martre Canada *see* **Wha Ti**
Lacolle Canada 135 I1
La Colorada *Sonora* Mex. 127 F7
La Colorada *Zacatecas* Mex. 131 C8
Lacombe Canada 120 H4
La Comoé, Parc National de *nat. park* Côte d'Ivoire 96 C4
Laconi *Sardinia* Italy 58 C5
Laconia U.S.A. 135 J2
La Corey Canada 121 I4
La Coruña Spain *see* **A Coruña**
La Corvette, Lac de *l.* Canada 122 G3
La Coubre, Pointe de *pt* France 56 D4
La Crete Canada 120 G3
La Crosse *KS* U.S.A. 130 D4
La Crosse *VA* U.S.A. 135 F5
La Crosse *WI* U.S.A. 130 F3
La Cruz Mex. 136 C4
Lac Thiên Vietnam 71 E4
La Cuesta Mex. 131 C6
La Culebra, Sierra de *mts* Spain 57 C3
La Cygne U.S.A. 130 E4
Ladainha Brazil 145 C2
Ladakh *reg.* Jammu and Kashmir 82 D2
Ladakh Range *mts* India 82 D2
Ladang, Ko *i.* Thai. 71 B6
La Demajagua Cuba 133 D8
La Demanda, Sierra de *mts* Spain 57 E2
La Déroute, Passage de *strait* Channel Is/France 49 E9
Ladik Turkey 90 D2
Lādīz Iran 89 F4
Ladnun India 82 C4

▶**Ladoga, Lake** Rus. Fed. 45 Q6
2nd largest lake in Europe.

Ladong China 77 F3
Ladozhskoye Ozero *l.* Rus. Fed. *see* **Ladoga, Lake**
Ladrones *terr.* N. Pacific Ocean *see* **Northern Mariana Islands**
Ladu *mt.* India 83 H4
Ladue *r.* Canada/U.S.A. 120 A2
Ladva-Vetka Rus. Fed. 42 G3
Ladybank U.K. 50 F4
Ladybrand S. Africa 101 H5
Lady Frere S. Africa 101 H6
Lady Grey S. Africa 101 H6
Ladysmith S. Africa 101 I5
Ladysmith U.S.A. 130 F2
Ladzhanurges Georgia *see* **Lajanurpekhi**
Lae P.N.G. 69 L8
Laem Ngop Thai. 71 C4
Lærdalsøyri Norway 45 E6
La Esmeralda Bol. 142 F8
Læsø *i.* Denmark 45 G8
Lafayette Alg. *see* **Bougaa**
Lafayette *AL* U.S.A. 133 C5
Lafayette *IN* U.S.A. 134 B3
Lafayette *LA* U.S.A. 131 E6
Lafayette *TN* U.S.A. 134 B5
Lafé Cuba 133 C8
La Fère France 52 D5
Laferte *r.* Canada 120 G2
La Ferté-Gaucher France 52 D6
La-Ferté-Milon France 52 D5
La Ferté-sous-Jouarre France 52 D6
Lafia Nigeria 96 D4
Lafiagi Nigeria 96 D4
Laflamme *r.* Canada 122 F4
Lafleche Canada 121 J5
La Flèche France 56 D3
La Follette U.S.A. 134 C5
La Forest, Lac *l.* Canada 123 H3
Laforge Canada 123 G3
Laforge *r.* Canada 123 G3
La Frégate, Lac de *l.* Canada 122 G3
Lāft Iran 88 D5
Laful India 71 A6
La Galissonnière, Lac *l.* Canada 123 J4

▶**La Galite** *i.* Tunisia 58 C6
Most northerly point of Africa.

La Galite, Canal de *sea chan.* Tunisia 58 C6
La Gallega Mex. 131 B7
Lagan' Rus. Fed. 43 J7
Lagan *r.* U.K. 51 G3
La Garamba, Parc National de *nat. park* Dem. Rep. Congo 98 C3
Lagarto Brazil 143 K6
Lage Germany 53 I3
Lågen *r.* Norway 45 G7
Lage Vaart *canal* Neth. 52 F2
Lagg U.K. 50 D5
Laggan U.K. 50 E3
Lagh Bor *watercourse* Kenya/Somalia 98 E3
Laghouat Alg. 54 E5
Lagkor Co *salt l.* China 83 F2
La Gloria Mex. 131 D7
Lago Agrio Ecuador *see* **Nueva Loja**
Lagoa Santa Brazil 145 C2
Lagoa Vermelha Brazil 145 A5
Lagodekhi Georgia 91 G2
Lagolândia Brazil 145 A1
La Gomera *i.* Canary Is 96 B2
La Gonâve, Île de *i.* Haiti 137 J5
Lagong *i.* Indon. 71 E7

▶**Lagos** Nigeria 96 D4
Former capital of Nigeria. 2nd most populous city in Africa.

Lagos Port. 57 B5
Lagosa Tanz. 99 C4
La Grande *r.* Canada 122 F3
La Grande U.S.A. 126 D3
La Grande 2, Réservoir *resr* Canada 122 F3
La Grande 3, Réservoir *resr* Canada 122 G3
La Grande 4, Réservoir *resr* *Que.* Canada 123 G3
Lagrange Australia 108 C4
La Grange *CA* U.S.A. 128 C3
La Grange *GA* U.S.A. 133 C5
Lagrange U.S.A. 134 C3
La Grange *KY* U.S.A. 132 C4
La Grange *TX* U.S.A. 131 D6
La Gran Sabana *plat.* Venez. 138 F2
La Grita Venez. 142 D2
La Guajira, Península de *pen.* Col. 142 D1
Laguna Brazil 145 A5
Laguna Dam U.S.A. 129 F5
Laguna Mountains U.S.A. 128 E5
Lagunas Chile 144 C2
Laguna San Rafael, Parque Nacional *nat. park* Chile 144 B7
Laha China 74 B2
La Habana Cuba *see* **Havana**
La Habra U.S.A. 128 E5
Lahad Datu *Sabah* Malaysia 68 F5
La Hague, Cap de *c.* France 56 D2
Laharpur India 82 E4
Lahat Indon. 68 C7
Lahe Myanmar 70 A1
Lahemaa rahvuspark *nat. park* Estonia 45 N7
La Hève, Cap de *c.* France 49 H9
Lahewa Indon. 71 B7
Laḥij Yemen 86 F7
Lāhījān Iran 88 C2
Lahn *r.* Germany 53 H4
Lahnstein Germany 53 H4
Laholm Sweden 45 H8
Lahontan Reservoir U.S.A. 128 D2
Lahore Pak. 89 I4
Lahri Pak. 89 H4
Lahti Fin. 45 N6
Laï Chad 97 E4
Lai'an China 77 H1
Laibach Slovenia *see* **Ljubljana**
Laibin China 77 F4
Laidley Australia 112 F1
Laifeng China 77 F2
L'Aigle France 56 E2
Laihia Fin. 44 M5
Lai-hka Myanmar 70 B2
Lai-Hsak Myanmar 70 B2
Laimakuri India 83 H4
Laingsburg S. Africa 100 E7
Laingsburg U.S.A. 134 C2

Loyalty Islands New Caledonia see Loyauté, Îles
Loyang China see Luoyang
Loyauté, Îles is New Caledonia 107 G4
Loyev Belarus see Loyew
Loyew Belarus 43 F6
Lozère, Mont mt. France 56 F4
Loznica Serb. and Mont. 59 H2
Lozova Ukr. 43 H6
Lozovaya Ukr. see Lozova
Lua r. Dem. Rep. Congo 98 B3
Luacano Angola 99 C5
Lu'an China 77 H2
Luân Châu Vietnam 70 C2
Luanchuan China 77 F1

▶Luanda Angola 99 B4
Capital of Angola.

Luang, Khao mt. Thai. 71 B5
Luang, Thale lag. Thai. 71 C6
Luang Namtha Laos see Louang Namtha
Luang Phrabang, Thiu Khao mts Laos/Thai. 70 C3
Luang Prabang Laos see Louangphrabang
Luanhaizi China 76 B1
Luanshya Zambia 99 C5
Luanza Dem. Rep. Congo 99 C4
Luao Angola see Luau
Luarca Spain 57 C2
Luashi Dem. Rep. Congo 99 C5
Luau Angola 99 C5
Luba Equat. Guinea 96 D4
Lubaczów Poland 43 D6
Lubalo Angola 99 B4
Lubānas ezers l. Latvia 45 O8
Lubang Islands Phil. 68 F4
Lubango Angola 99 B5
Lubao Dem. Rep. Congo 99 C4
Lubartów Poland 43 D6
Lübbecke Germany 53 I2
Lubbeskolk salt pan S. Africa 100 D5
Lubbock U.S.A. 131 C5
Lübbow Germany 53 L2
Lübeck Germany 47 M4
Lubeck U.S.A. 134 E4
Lubefu Dem. Rep. Congo 99 C4
Lubei China 73 M4
Lüben Poland see Lubin
Lubersac France 56 E4
Lubin Poland 47 P5
Lublin Poland 43 D6
Lubnān country Asia see Lebanon
Lubnān, Jabal mts Lebanon see Liban, Jebel
Lubny Ukr. 43 G6
Lubok Antu Sarawak Malaysia 64 E6
Lübtheen Germany 53 L1
Lubudi Dem. Rep. Congo 99 C4
Lubuklinggau Indon. 68 C7
Lubukpakam Indon. 71 B7
Lubuksikaping Indon. 68 C6
Lubumbashi Dem. Rep. Congo 99 C5
Lubutu Dem. Rep. Congo 98 C4
Lübz Germany 53 M1
Lucala Angola 99 B4
Lucan Canada 134 E2
Lucan Rep. of Ireland 51 F4
Lucania, Mount Canada 120 A2
Lucapa Angola 99 C4
Lucas U.S.A. 134 B5
Lucasville U.S.A. 134 D4
Lucca Italy 58 D3
Luce Bay U.K. 50 E6
Lucedale U.S.A. 131 F6
Lucélia Brazil 145 A3
Lucena Phil. 69 G4
Lucena Spain 57 D5
Lučenec Slovakia 47 Q6
Lucera Italy 58 F4
Lucerne Switz. 56 I3
Lucerne Valley U.S.A. 128 E4
Lucero Mex. 127 G7
Luchegorsk Rus. Fed. 74 D3
Lucheng Guangxi China see Luchuan
Lucheng Sichuan China see Kangding
Luchuan China 77 F4
Lüchun China 76 D4
Lucipara, Kepulauan is Indon. 69 H8
Łuck Ukr. see Luts'k
Luckeesarai India see Lakhisarai
Luckenwalde Germany 53 N2
Luckhoff S. Africa 100 G5
Lucknow Canada 134 E2
Lucknow India 82 E4
Lücongpo China 77 F2
Lucrecia, Cabo c. Cuba 137 I4
Lucusse Angola 99 C5
Lucy Creek Australia 110 B4
Lüda China see Dalian
Lüdenscheid Germany 53 H3
Lüderitz Namibia 100 B4
Ludewa Tanz. 99 D5
Ludhiana India 82 C3
Ludian China 76 D3
Luding China 76 D2
Ludington U.S.A. 134 B2
Ludlow U.K. 49 E6
Ludlow U.S.A. 128 E4
Ludogorie reg. Bulg. 59 L3
Ludowici U.S.A. 133 D6
Ludvika Sweden 45 I6
Ludwigsburg Germany 53 J6
Ludwigsfelde Germany 53 N2
Ludwigshafen am Rhein Germany 53 I5
Ludwigslust Germany 53 L1
Ludza Latvia 45 O8
Luebo Dem. Rep. Congo 99 C4
Luena Angola 99 B5
Luena Flats plain Zambia 99 C5
Lüeyang China 76 E1
Lufeng Guangdong China 77 G4
Lufeng Yunnan China 76 D3
Lufkin U.S.A. 131 E6
Lufu China see Shilin
Luga Rus. Fed. 45 P7
Luga r. Rus. Fed. 45 P7
Lugano Switz. 56 I3
Lugansk Ukr. see Luhans'k
Lugau Germany 53 M4
Lügde Germany 53 J3
Lugdunum France see Lyon
Lugg r. U.K. 49 E6
Luggudontsen mt. China 83 G3
Lugo Italy 58 D2
Lugo Spain 57 C2
Lugoj Romania 59 I2
Luhans'k Ukr. 43 H6
Luhe China 77 H1
Luhe r. Germany 53 K1
Luḩfī, Wādī watercourse Jordan 85 C3
Luhit r. China/India see Zayü Qu
Luhit r. India 83 H4
Luhua China see Heishui
Luhuo China 76 D2
Luhyny Ukr. 43 F6
Luia Angola 99 C4
Luiana Angola 99 C5
Luichow Peninsula China see Leizhou Bandao
Luik Belgium see Liège
Luimneach Rep. of Ireland see Limerick
Luiro r. Fin. 44 O3
Luis Echeverría Álvarez Mex. 128 E5
Luitpold Coast Antarctica 152 A1
Luiza Dem. Rep. Congo 99 C4
Lujiang China 77 H2
Lüjing China 76 E1
Lukackek Rus. Fed. 74 D1
Lukapa Angola see Lucapa
Lukavac Bos.-Herz. 58 H2
Lukenga, Lac l. Dem. Rep. Congo 99 C4
Lukenie r. Dem. Rep. Congo 98 B4
Lukh r. Rus. Fed. 42 I4
Lukhovitsy Rus. Fed. 43 H5
Luk Keng Hong Kong China 77 [inset]
Lukou China see Zhuzhou
Lukovit Bulg. 59 K3
Łuków Poland 43 D6
Lukoyanov Rus. Fed. 43 J5
Lukusuzi National Park Zambia 99 D5
Luleå Sweden 44 M4
Luleälven r. Sweden 44 M4
Lüleburgaz Turkey 59 L4
Luliang China 76 D3
Lüliang Shan mts China 73 K5
Lulimba Dem. Rep. Congo 99 C4
Luling U.S.A. 131 D6
Lulonga r. Dem. Rep. Congo 98 B3
Luluabourg Dem. Rep. Congo see Kananga
Lülung China 83 F3
Lumachomo China 83 F3
Lumajang Indon. 68 E8
Lumajangdong Co salt l. China 82 E2
Lumbala Moxico Angola see Lumbala Kaquengue
Lumbala Moxico Angola see Lumbala N'guimbo
Lumbala Kaquengue Angola 99 C5
Lumbala N'guimbo Angola 99 C5
Lumberton U.S.A. 133 E5
Lumbini Nepal 83 E4
Lumbis Indon. 68 F6
Lumbrales Spain 57 C3
Lumezzane Italy 58 D2
Lumi P.N.G. 69 K7
Lumphăt Cambodia 71 D4
Lumpkin U.S.A. 133 C5
Lumsden Canada 121 J5
Lumsden N.Z. 113 B7
Lumut Malaysia 71 C6
Lumut, Tanjung pt Indon. 68 D7
Luna U.S.A. 129 I5
Lunan China see Shilin
Lunan Bay U.K. 50 G4
Lunan Lake Canada 121 M1
Lunan Shan mts China 76 D3
Luna Pier U.S.A. 134 D3
Lund Pak. 89 H5
Lund Sweden 45 H9
Lund NV U.S.A. 129 F2
Lund UT U.S.A. 129 G2
Lundar Canada 121 L5
Lundy Island U.K. 49 C7
Lüneburg Germany 53 K1
Lune r. Germany 53 I1
Lune r. U.K. 48 E4
Lüneburg Germany 53 K1
Lüneburger Heide reg. Germany 53 K1
Lünen Germany 53 H3
Lunenburg U.S.A. 135 F5
Lunéville France 56 H2
Lunga r. Zambia 99 C5
Lungdo China 83 E2
Lunggar China 83 E3
Lung Kwu Chau i. Hong Kong China 77 [inset]
Lungleh India see Lunglei
Lunglei India 83 H5
Lungmari mt. China 83 F3
Lungmu Co salt l. China 82 E2
Lungnaquilla Mountain hill Rep. of Ireland 51 F5
Lungwebungu r. Zambia 99 C5
Lunh Nepal 83 E3
Luni India 82 C4
Luni r. India 82 B4
Luni r. Pak. 89 H4
Luninets Belarus see Luninyets
Luning U.S.A. 128 D2
Luninyets Belarus 45 O10
Lunkaransar India 82 C3
Lunkha India 82 C3
Lünne Germany 53 H2
Lunsar Sierra Leone 96 B4
Lunsklip S. Africa 101 I3
Luntai China 80 F3
Luobei China 74 C3
Luobuzhuang China 80 G4
Luocheng Fujian China see Hui'an
Luocheng Guangxi China 77 F3
Luodian China 76 E3
Luoding China 77 F4
Luodou Sha i. China 77 F4
Luohe China 77 G1
Luo He r. China 77 G1
Luonan China 77 F1
Luoning China 77 F1
Luoping China 76 E3
Luotian China 77 G2
Luoto Fin. 44 M5
Luoxiao Shan mts China 77 G3
Luoxiong China see Luoping
Luoyang Guangdong China see Boluo
Luoyang Henan China 77 G1
Luoyang Zhejiang China see Taishun
Luoyuan China 77 H3
Luozigou China 74 C4
Lupane Zimbabwe 99 C5
Lupanshui China 76 E3
L'Upemba, Parc National de nat. park Dem. Rep. Congo 95 C4
Lupeni Romania 59 J2
Lupilichi Moz. 99 D5
Lupton U.S.A. 129 I4
Luqiao China see Luding
Luqu China 76 D1
Lu Qu r. China see Tao He
Luquan China 76 C1
Luray U.S.A. 135 F4
Luremo Angola 99 B4
Lurgan U.K. 51 F3
Luring China see Oma
Lúrio Moz. 99 E5
Lurio r. Moz. 99 E5

▶Lusaka Zambia 99 C5
Capital of Zambia.

Lusambo Dem. Rep. Congo 99 C4
Lusancay Islands and Reefs P.N.G. 106 F2
Lusangi Dem. Rep. Congo 99 C4
Luseland Canada 121 I4
Lush, Mount hill Australia 108 D4
Lushi China 77 F1
Lushnja Albania see Lushnjë
Lushnjë Albania 59 H4
Lushui China 76 C3
Lushuihe China 74 B4
Lüsi China 77 I1
Lusikisiki S. Africa 101 I6
Lusk U.S.A. 126 G4
Luso Angola see Luena
Lussvale Australia 112 C1
Lut, Bahrat salt l. Asia see Dead Sea
Lut, Dasht-e des. Iran 88 E4
Lü Tao i. Taiwan 77 I4
Lutetia France see Paris
Lūt-e Zangī Aḥmad des. Iran 88 E4
Luther U.S.A. 134 C1
Luther Lake Canada 134 E2
Lutherstadt Wittenberg Germany 53 M3
Luton U.K. 49 G7
Łutselk'e Canada 121 I2
Luts'k Ukr. 43 E6
Luttelgeest Neth. 52 F2
Luttenberg Neth. 52 G2
Lutto r. Fin./Rus. Fed. see Lotta
Lutz U.S.A. 133 D6
Lützelbach Germany 53 J5
Lützow-Holm Bay Antarctica 152 D2
Lutzputs S. Africa 100 E5
Lutzville S. Africa 100 D6
Luumäki Fin. 45 O6
Luuq Somalia 98 E3
Luverne AL U.S.A. 133 C6
Luverne MN U.S.A. 130 D3
Luvuei Angola 99 C5
Luvuvhu r. S. Africa 101 J2
Luwero Uganda 98 D3
Luwingu Zambia 99 C5
Luwuk Indon. 69 G7
▶Luxembourg country Europe 52 G5
Europe 5, 38–39

▶Luxembourg Lux. 52 G5
Capital of Luxembourg.

Luxemburg country Europe see Luxembourg
Luxeuil-les-Bains France 56 H3
Luxi Hunan China 77 F2
Luxi Yunnan China 76 C3
Luxi Yunnan China 76 D3
Luxolweni S. Africa 101 G6
Luxor Egypt 86 D4
Luyi China 77 G1
Luykgestel Neth. 52 F3
Luza Rus. Fed. 42 J3
Luza r. Rus. Fed. 42 J3
Luza r. Rus. Fed. 42 M2
Luzern Switz. see Lucerne
Luzhai China 77 F3
Luzhang China see Lushui
Luzhi China 76 E3
Luzhou China 76 E2
Luziânia Brazil 145 B2
Luzon i. Phil. 69 G3
Luzon Strait Phil. 69 G2
Luzy France 56 F3
L'viv Ukr. 43 E6
L'vov Ukr. see L'viv
Lwów Ukr. see L'viv
Lyady Rus. Fed. 45 P7
Lyakhavichy Belarus 45 O10
Lyakhovichi Belarus see Lyakhavichy
Lyallpur Pak. see Faisalabad
Lyamtsa Rus. Fed. 42 H2
Lycia reg. Turkey 59 M6
Lyck Poland see Ełk
Lycksele Sweden 44 K4
Lycopolis Egypt see Asyūţ
Lydd U.K. 49 H8
Lydda Israel see Lod
Lyddan Island Antarctica 152 B2
Lydenburg S. Africa 101 J3
Lydia reg. Turkey 59 L5
Lydney U.K. 49 E7
Lyel'chytsy Belarus 43 F6
Lyell, Mount U.S.A. 128 D3
Lyell Brown, Mount hill Australia 109 E5
Lyell Island Canada 120 D4
Lyepyel' Belarus 45 P9
Lykens U.S.A. 135 G3
Lyman U.S.A. 126 F4
Lyme Bay U.K. 49 E8
Lyme Regis U.K. 49 E8
Lymington U.K. 49 F8
Lynchburg OH U.S.A. 134 D4
Lynchburg TN U.S.A. 132 C5
Lynchburg VA U.S.A. 134 F5
Lynchville U.S.A. 135 J1
Lyndhurst N.S.W. Australia 112 D4
Lyndhurst Qld Australia 110 D3
Lyndhurst S.A. Australia 111 B6
Lyndon Australia 109 A5
Lyndon r. Australia 109 A5
Lyndonville U.S.A. 135 I1
Lyne r. U.K. 48 D4
Lyness U.K. 50 F2
Lyngdal Norway 45 E7
Lynn U.K. see King's Lynn
Lynn IN U.S.A. 134 C3
Lynn MA U.S.A. 135 J2
Lynndyl U.S.A. 129 G2
Lynn Lake Canada 121 K3
Lynton U.K. 49 D7
Lynx Lake Canada 121 J2
Lyon France 56 G4
Lyon r. U.K. 50 F4
Lyon Mountain U.S.A. 135 I1
Lyons Australia 109 F7
Lyons France see Lyon
Lyons GA U.S.A. 133 D5
Lyons NY U.S.A. 135 G2
Lyons Falls U.S.A. 135 H2
Lyozna Belarus 43 F5
Lyra Reef P.N.G. 106 F2
Lys r. France 52 D4
Lysekil Sweden 45 G7
Lyskovo Rus. Fed. 42 J4
Lys'va Rus. Fed. 41 R4
Lysychans'k Ukr. 43 H6
Lysyye Gory Rus. Fed. 43 J6
Lytham St Anne's U.K. 48 D5
Lytton Canada 120 F5
Lyuban' Belarus 45 P10
Lyubertsy Rus. Fed. 41 N4
Lyubeshiv Ukr. 43 E6
Lyubim Rus. Fed. 42 I4
Lyubytino Rus. Fed. 42 G4
Lyudinovo Rus. Fed. 43 G5
Lyunda r. Rus. Fed. 42 J4
Lyzha r. Rus. Fed. 42 M2

M

Ma r. Myanmar 70 B2
Ma, Nam r. Laos 70 C2
Ma'agan Israel 85 B3
Maale Maldives see Male
Maale Atholhu atoll Maldives see Male Atoll
Maalhosmadulu Atholhu Uthuruburi atoll Maldives see North Maalhosmadulu Atoll
Maalhosmadulu Atoll Maldives 84 B5
Ma'ān Jordan 85 B4
Maan Turkey see Nusratiye
Maaninka Fin. 44 O5
Maaninkavaara Fin. 44 P3
Ma'anshan China 77 H2
Maardu Estonia 45 N7
Maarianhamina Fin. see Mariehamn
Ma'arrat an Nu'mān Syria 85 C2
Maarssen Neth. 52 F2
Maas r. Neth. 52 E3
also known as Meuse (Belgium/France)
Maaseik Belgium 52 F3
Maasin Phil. 69 G4
Maasmechelen Belgium 52 F4
Maas-Schwalm-Nette nat. park Germany/Neth. 52 F3
Maastricht Neth. 52 F4
Maaza Plateau Egypt 90 C6
Maba Guangdong China see Qujiang
Maba Jiangsu China 77 H1
Mabai China see Maguan
Mabalane Moz. 101 K2
Mabana Dem. Rep. Congo 98 C3
Mabaruma Guyana 142 G2
Mabein Myanmar 70 B2
Mabel Creek Australia 109 F7
Mabel Downs Australia 108 D4
Mabella Canada 122 C4
Mabel Lake Canada 120 G5
Maberly Canada 135 G1
Mabian China 76 D2
Mablethorpe U.K. 48 H5
Mabopane S. Africa 101 I3
Mabote Moz. 101 L2
Mabou Canada 123 J5
Mabrak, Jabal mt. Jordan 85 B4
Mabuasehube Game Reserve nature res. Botswana 100 F3
Mabule Botswana 100 G3
Mabutsane Botswana 100 F3
Macá, Monte mt. Chile 144 B7
Macadam Plains Australia 109 B6
Macaé Brazil 145 C3
Macajuba Brazil 145 C1
Macaloge Moz. 99 D5
MacAlpine Lake Canada 119 H3
Macamic Canada 122 F4
Macandze Moz. 101 K2
Macao China see Macau
Macao aut. reg. China see Macau
Macapá Brazil 143 H3
Macará Ecuador 142 C4
Macarani Brazil 145 C1
Macas Ecuador 142 C4
Macassar Indon. see Makassar
Macau Brazil 143 K5
Macau China 77 G4
Macau aut. reg. China 77 G4
Macaúba Brazil 143 H6
Macauley Island N.Z. 107 I5
Macau Special Administrative Region aut. reg. China see Macau
Maccaretane Moz. 101 K3
Macclenny U.S.A. 133 D6
Macclesfield U.K. 48 E5
Macdiarmid Canada 122 C4
Macdonald, Lake salt flat Australia 109 E5
Macdonald Range hills Australia 108 D3
Macdonnell Ranges mts Australia 109 E5
MacDowell Lake Canada 121 M4
Macduff U.K. 50 G3
Macedo de Cavaleiros Port. 57 C3
Macedon mt. Australia 112 B6
Macedon country Europe see Macedonia
▶Macedonia country Europe 59 I4
Europe 5, 38–39
Maceió Brazil 143 K5
Macenta Guinea 96 C4
Macerata Italy 58 E3
Macfarlane, Lake salt flat Australia 111 B7
Macgillycuddy's Reeks mts Rep. of Ireland 51 C6
Machachi Ecuador 142 C4
Machaila Moz. 101 K2
Machakos Kenya 98 D4
Machala Ecuador 142 C4
Machali China see Madoi
Machanga Moz. 99 D6
Machar Marshes Sudan 86 D8
Machattie, Lake salt flat Australia 110 B5
Machatuine Moz. 101 K3
Machault France 52 E5
Machaze Moz. see Chitobe
Macheng China 77 G2
Macherla India 84 C2
Machhagan India 83 F5
Machias ME U.S.A. 132 H2
Machias NY U.S.A. 135 F2
Machilipatnam India 84 D2
Machiques Venez. 142 D1
Māch Kowr Iran 89 F5
Machrihanish U.K. 50 D5
Machu Picchu tourist site Peru 142 D6
Machynlleth U.K. 49 D6
Macia Moz. 101 K3
Macías Nguema i. Equat. Guinea see Bioco
Măcin Romania 59 M2
Macintyre r. Australia 112 E2
Macintyre Brook r. Australia 112 E2
Mack U.S.A. 129 I2
Maçka Turkey 91 E2
Mackay Australia 110 E4
MacKay r. Canada 121 I3
Mackay U.S.A. 126 E3
Mackay, Lake salt flat Australia 108 E5
MacKay Lake Canada 121 I2
Mackenzie r. Australia 110 E4
Mackenzie Canada 120 F4
Mackenzie r. Canada 120 F2
Mackenzie Guyana see Linden
Mackenzie atoll Micronesia see Ulithi
Mackenzie Bay Antarctica 152 E2
Mackenzie Bay Canada 118 E3
Mackenzie Highway Canada 120 G2
Mackenzie King Island Canada 119 G2
Mackenzie Mountains Canada 120 C1

▶Mackenzie-Peace-Finlay r. Canada 118 E3
2nd longest river in North America.

Mackillop, Lake salt flat Australia see Yamma Yamma, Lake
Mackintosh Range hills Australia 109 D6
Macklin Canada 121 I4
Macksville Australia 112 F3
Maclean Australia 112 F2
Maclear S. Africa 101 I6
MacLeod Canada see Fort Macleod
MacLeod, Lake imp. l. Australia 109 A6
Macmillan r. Canada 120 C2
Macmillan Pass Canada 120 D2
Macomb U.S.A. 130 F3
Macomer Sardinia Italy 58 C4
Mâcon France 56 G3
Macon GA U.S.A. 133 D5
Macon MO U.S.A. 130 E4
Macon MS U.S.A. 131 F5
Macon OH U.S.A. 134 D4
Macondo Angola 99 C5
Macoun Lake Canada 121 K3
Macpherson Robertson Land reg. Antarctica see Mac. Robertson Land
Macpherson's Strait India 71 A5
Macquarie r. Australia 112 C3
Macquarie, Lake b. Australia 112 E4

▶Macquarie Island S. Pacific Ocean 150 G9
Part of Australia. Most southerly point of Oceania.

Macquarie Marshes Australia 112 C3
Macquarie Mountain Australia 112 D4
Macquarie Ridge sea feature S. Pacific Ocean 150 G9
MacRitchie Reservoir Sing. 71 [inset]
Mac. Robertson Land reg. Antarctica 152 E2
Macroom Rep. of Ireland 51 D6
Macumba Australia 111 A5
Macumba watercourse Australia 111 B5
Macuzari, Presa resr Mex. 127 F8
Mādabā Jordan 85 B4
Madadeni S. Africa 101 J4

▶Madagascar country Africa 99 E6
Largest island in Africa and 4th in the world.
Africa 7, 92–93, 94–95
World 12–13

Madagascar Basin sea feature Indian Ocean 149 L7
Madagascar Ridge sea feature Indian Ocean 149 K8
Madagasikara country Africa see Madagascar
Madakasira India 84 C3
Madama Niger 97 E2
Madan Bulg. 59 K4
Madanapalle India 84 C3
Madang P.N.G. 69 L8
Madaoua Niger 96 D3
Madaripur Bangl. 83 G5
Madau Turkm. 88 D2
Madaw Turkm. see Madau
Madawaska Canada 135 G1
Madawaska r. Canada 135 G1
Madaya Myanmar 70 B2
Madded India 84 D2

▶Madeira r. Brazil 142 G4
4th longest river in South America.

▶Madeira terr. N. Atlantic Ocean 96 B1
Autonomous Region of Portugal.
Africa 7, 94–95

Madeira, Arquipélago da terr. N. Atlantic Ocean see Madeira
Maden Turkey 91 E3
Madera Mex. 127 F7
Madera U.S.A. 128 C3
Madgaon India 84 B3
Madha India 84 B2
Madhavpur India 82 B5
Madhepura India 83 F4
Madhipura India see Madhepura
Madhubani India 83 F4
Madhya Pradesh state India 82 D5
Madibogo S. Africa 101 G4
Madidi r. Bol. 142 E6
Madikeri India 84 B3
Madikwe Game Reserve nature res. S. Africa 101 H3
Madill U.S.A. 131 D5
Madīnat ath Thawrah Syria 85 D2
Madingo-Kayes Congo 99 B4
Madingou Congo 99 B4
Madison FL U.S.A. 133 D6
Madison GA U.S.A. 133 D5
Madison IN U.S.A. 134 C4
Madison ME U.S.A. 135 K1
Madison NE U.S.A. 130 D3
Madison SD U.S.A. 130 D2
Madison VA U.S.A. 135 F4

▶Madison WI U.S.A. 130 F3
State capital of Wisconsin.

Madison WV U.S.A. 134 E4
Madison r. U.S.A. 126 F3
Madison Heights U.S.A. 134 F5
Madisonville KY U.S.A. 134 B5
Madisonville TX U.S.A. 131 E6
Madiun Indon. 68 E8
Madley, Mount hill Australia 109 C6
Madoc Canada 135 G1
Mado Gashi Kenya 98 D3
Madoi China 76 C1
Madona Latvia 45 O8
Madpura India 82 B4
Madra Dağı mts Turkey 59 L5
Madrakah Saudi Arabia 86 E5
Madrakah, Ra's c. Oman 87 I6
Madras India see Chennai
Madras state India see Tamil Nadu
Madras U.S.A. 126 C3
Madre, Laguna lag. Mex. 131 D7
Madre, Laguna lag. U.S.A. 131 D7
Madre de Dios r. Peru 142 E6
Madre de Dios, Isla i. Chile 144 A8
Madre del Sur, Sierra mts Mex. 136 D5
Madre Mountain U.S.A. 129 J4
Madre Occidental, Sierra mts Mex. 127 F7
Madre Oriental, Sierra mts Mex. 131 C7

▶Madrid Spain 57 E3
Capital of Spain.

Madridejos Spain 57 E4
Madruga Cuba 133 D8
Madugula India 84 D2
Madura i. Indon. 68 E8
Madura, Selat sea chan. Indon. 68 E8
Madurai India 84 C4
Madurantakam India 84 C3
Madvār, Kūh-e mt. Iran 88 D4
Madvezh'ya vol. Rus. Fed. 74 H3
Madwas India 83 E4
Maé i. Vanuatu see Émaé
Maebashi Japan 75 E5
Mae Hong Son Thai. 70 B3
Mae Ping National Park Thai. 70 B3
Mae Ramat Thai. 70 B3
Mae Sai Thai. 70 B2
Mae Sariang Thai. 70 B3
Mae Sot Thai. 70 B3
Mae Suai Thai. 70 B3
Mae Tuen Wildlife Reserve nature res. Thai. 70 B3
Maevatanana Madag. 99 E5
Maéwo i. Vanuatu 107 G3
Mae Wong National Park Thai. 70 B4
Mae Yom National Park Thai. 70 C3
Mafeking Canada 121 K4
Mafeking S. Africa see Mafikeng
Mafeteng Lesotho 101 H5
Maffra Australia 112 C6
Mafia Island Tanz. 99 D4
Mafikeng S. Africa 101 G3
Mafinga Tanz. 99 D4
Mafra Brazil 145 A4
Mafraq Jordan see Al Mafraq
Magabeni S. Africa 101 J6
Magadan Rus. Fed. 65 Q4
Magadi Kenya 98 D4
Magaiza Moz. 101 K2
Magallanes Chile see Punta Arenas
Magallanes, Estrecho de Chile see Magellan, Strait of
Magangue Col. 142 D2
Mağara Dağı mt. Turkey 85 A1
Magaramkent Rus. Fed. 91 H2
Magaria Niger 96 D3
Magarida P.N.G. 110 E1
Magas Rus. Fed. 91 G2
Magazine Mountain hill U.S.A. 131 E5
Magdagachi Rus. Fed. 74 B1
Magdalena Bol. 142 F6
Magdalena r. Col. 142 D1
Magdalena Baja California Sur Mex. 127 E8
Magdalena Sonora Mex. 127 F7
Magdalena r. Mex. 127 F7
Magdalena, Bahía b. Mex. 136 B4
Magdalena, Isla i. Chile 144 B6
Magdeburg Germany 53 L2
Magdelaine Cays atoll Australia 110 E3

Magellan, Strait of Chile 144 B8
Magellan Seamounts *sea feature* N. Pacific Ocean 150 F4
Magenta, Lake *salt flat* Australia 109 B8
Magerøya *i.* Norway 44 N1
Maggiorasca, Monte *mt.* Italy 58 C2
Maggiore, Lago Italy *see* Maggiore, Lake
Maggiore, Lake Italy 58 C2
Maghâgha Egypt *see* Maghāghah
Maghāghah Egypt 90 C5
Maghama Mauritania 96 B3
Maghâra, Gebel *hill* Egypt *see* Magharah, Jabal
Magharah, Jabal *hill* Egypt 85 A4
Maghera U.K. 51 F3
Magherafelt U.K. 51 F3
Maghnia Alg. 57 F6
Maghor Afgh. 89 F3
Maghull U.K. 48 E5
Magilligan Point U.K. 51 F2
Magma U.S.A. 129 H5
Magna Grande *mt. Sicily* Italy 58 F6
Magnetic Island Australia 110 D3
Magnetic Passage Australia 110 D3
Magnetity Rus. Fed. 44 R2
Magnitogorsk Rus. Fed. 64 G4
Magnolia *AR* U.S.A. 131 E5
Magnolia *MS* U.S.A. 131 F6
Magny-en-Vexin France 52 B5
Mago Rus. Fed. 74 F1
Màgoé Moz. 99 D5
Magog Canada 135 I1
Mago National Park Eth. 98 D3
Magosa Cyprus *see* Famagusta
Magpie *r.* Canada 123 I4
Magpie, Lac *l.* Canada 123 I4
Magta' Lahjar Mauritania 96 B3
Magu Tanz. 98 D4
Magu, Khrebet *mts* Rus. Fed. 74 E1
Maguan China 76 E4
Magude Moz. 101 K3
Magueyal Mex. 131 C7
Magura Bangl. 83 G5
Maguse Lake Canada 121 M2
Magway Myanmar *see* Magwe
Magwe Myanmar 70 A2
Magyar Köztársaság *country* Europe *see* Hungary
Magyichaung Myanmar 70 A2
Mahābād Iran 88 B2
Mahabharat Range *mts* Nepal 83 F4
Mahaboobnagar India *see* Mahbubnagar
Mahad India 84 B2
Mahadeo Hills India 82 D5
Mahaffey U.S.A. 135 F3
Mahajan India 82 C3
Mahajanga Madag. 99 E5
Mahakam *r.* Indon. 68 F7
Mahalapye Botswana 101 H2
Mahale Mountains National Park Tanz. 99 C4
Mahalevona Madag. 99 E5
Mahallāt Iran 88 C3
Māhān Iran 88 E4
Mahanadi *r.* India 84 E1
Mahanoro Madag. 99 E5
Maha Oya Sri Lanka 84 D5
Maharashtra *state* India 84 B2
Maha Sarakham Thai. 70 C3
Mahasham, Wâdi el *watercourse* Egypt *see* Muhashsham, Wādī al
Mahaxai Laos 70 D3
Mahbubabad India 84 D2
Mahbubnagar India 84 C2
Mahd adh Dhahab Saudi Arabia 86 F5
Mahdia Alg. 57 G6
Mahdia Guyana 143 G2
Mahdia Tunisia 58 D7
Mahe China 76 E1
Mahé *i.* Seychelles 149 L6
Mahendragiri *mt.* India 84 E2
Mahenge Tanz. 99 D4
Mahesana India 82 C5
Mahi *r.* India 82 C5
Mahia Peninsula N.Z. 113 F4
Mahilyow Belarus 43 F5
Mahim India 84 B2
Mah Jān Iran 88 D4
Mahlabatini S. Africa 101 J5
Mahlsdorf Germany 53 L2
Mahmudabad Iran 88 D2
Maḩmūd-e 'Erāqī Afgh. *see* Maḩmūd-e Rāqī
Maḩmūd-e Rāqī Afgh. 89 H3
Mahnomen U.S.A. 130 D2
Maho Sri Lanka 84 D5
Mahoba India 82 D4
Maholi India 82 E4
Mahón Spain 57 I4
Mahony Lake Canada 120 E1
Mahrauni India 82 D4
Mahrès Tunisia 58 D7
Māhrūd Iran 89 F3
Mahsana India *see* Mahesana
Mahudaung *mts* Myanmar 70 A2
Mahukona *HI* U.S.A. 127 [inset]
Mahur India 84 C2
Mahuva India 82 B5
Mahwa India 82 D4
Mahya Dağı *mt.* Turkey 59 L4
Mai *i.* Vanuatu *see* Émaé
Maiaia Moz. *see* Nacala
Maibang India 70 A1
Maicao Col. 142 D1
Maicasagi *r.* Canada 122 F4
Maicasagi, Lac *l.* Canada 122 F4
Maichen China 77 F4
Maidenhead U.K. 49 G7
Maidstone Canada 121 I4
Maidstone U.K. 49 H7
Maiduguri Nigeria 96 E3
Maiella, Parco Nazionale della *nat. park* Italy 58 F3
Mai Gudo *mt.* Eth. 98 D3
Maigue *r.* Rep. of Ireland 51 D5
Maihar India 82 E4
Maiji Shan *mt.* China 76 E1
Maikala Range *hills* India 82 E5
Maiko *r.* Dem. Rep. Congo 98 C3
Mailan Hill *mt.* India 83 E5
Mailly-le-Camp France 52 E6
Mailsi Pak. 89 I4
Main *r.* Germany 53 I4
Main *r.* U.K. 51 F3
Main Brook Canada 123 L4
Mainburg Germany 53 L6
Main Channel *lake channel* Canada 134 E1
Maindargi India 84 C2
Mai-Ndombe, Lac *l.* Dem. Rep. Congo 98 B4
Main-Donau-Kanal *canal* Germany 53 K5
Maindong China 83 F3
Main Duck Island Canada 135 G2
Maine *state* U.S.A. 135 K1
Maine, Gulf of Canada/U.S.A. 135 K2
Mainé Hanari, Cerro *hill* Col. 142 D4
Maïné-Soroa Niger 96 E3
Maingkaing Myanmar 70 A1
Maingkwan Myanmar 70 B1
Maingy Island Myanmar 71 B4
Mainhardt Germany 53 J5
Mainkung China 76 C2
Mainland *i. Scotland* U.K. 50 F1
Mainland *i. Scotland* U.K. 50 [inset]
Mainleus Germany 53 L4
Mainoru Australia 108 F3
Mainpat *reg.* India 83 E5
Mainpuri India 82 D4
Main Range National Park Australia 112 F2
Maintenon France 52 B6
Maintirano Madag. 99 E5
Mainz Germany 53 I4
Maio *i.* Cape Verde 96 [inset]
Maipú Arg. 144 E5
Maiskhal Island Bangl. 83 G5
Maisons-Laffitte France 52 C6
Maitengwe Botswana 99 C6
Maitland *N.S.W.* Australia 112 E4
Maitland *S.A.* Australia 111 B7
Maitland *r.* Australia 108 B5
Maitri *research station* Antarctica 152 C2
Maiwo *i.* Vanuatu *see* Maéwo
Maiyu, Mount *hill* Australia 108 E4
Maíz, Islas del *is* Nicaragua 137 H6
Maizar Pak. 89 H3
Maizuru Japan 75 D6
Maja Jezercë *mt.* Albania 59 H3
Majene Indon. 68 F7
Majestic U.S.A. 134 D5
Majḩūd *well* Saudi Arabia 88 C6
Majī Eth. 98 D3
Majiang *Guangxi* China 77 F4
Majiang *Guizhou* China 76 E3
Majiazi China 74 B2
Majōl *country* N. Pacific Ocean *see* Marshall Islands
Major, Puig *mt.* Spain 57 H4
Majorca *i.* Spain 57 H4
Mājro *atoll* Marshall Is *see* Majuro
Majunga Madag. *see* Mahajanga
Majuro *atoll* Marshall Is 150 H5
Majwemasweu S. Africa 101 H5
Makabana Congo 98 B4
Makale Indon. 69 F7

▶Makalu *mt.* China/Nepal 83 F4
5th highest mountain in the world and in Asia.
World 12–13

Makalu Barun National Park Nepal 83 F4
Makanchi Kazakh. 80 F2
Makanpur India 82 E4
Makari Mountain National Park Tanz. *see* Mahale Mountains National Park
Makarov Rus. Fed. 74 F2
Makarov Basin *sea feature* Arctic Ocean 153 B1
Makarska Croatia 58 G3
Makarwal Pak. 89 H3
Makar'ye Rus. Fed. 42 K4
Makar'yev Rus. Fed. 42 I4
Makasar, Selat *strait* Indon. *see* Makassar, Selat
Makassar Indon. 68 F8
Makassar, Selat *strait* Indon. 68 F7
Makassar Strait Indon. *see* Makassar, Selat
Makat Kazakh. 78 E2
Makatini Flats *lowland* S. Africa 101 K4
Makedonija *country* Europe *see* Macedonia
Makeni Sierra Leone 96 B4
Makete Tanz. 99 D4
Makeyevka Ukr. *see* Makiyivka
Makgadikgadi *depr.* Botswana 99 C6
Makgadikgadi Pans National Park Botswana 99 C6
Makhachkala Rus. Fed. 91 G2
Makhad Pak. 89 H3
Makhado S. Africa *see* Louis Trichardt
Makhâzin, Kathîb el *des.* Egypt 85 A4
Makhâzin, Kathîb el *des.* Egypt *see* Makhāzin, Kathīb al
Makhazine, Barrage El *dam* Morocco 57 D6
Makhmūr Iraq 91 F4
Makhtal India 84 C2
Makin *atoll* Kiribati *see* Butaritari
Makindu Kenya 98 D4
Makinsk Kazakh. 79 G1
Makira *i.* Solomon Is *see* San Cristobal
Makiyivka Ukr. 43 H6
Makkah Saudi Arabia *see* Mecca
Makkovik Canada 123 K3
Makkovik, Cape Canada 123 K3
Makkum Neth. 52 F1
Makó Hungary 59 I1
Makokou Gabon 98 B3
Makopong Botswana 100 F3
Makotipoko Congo 97 E5
Makran *reg.* Iran/Pak. 89 F5
Makrana India 82 C4
Makran Coast Range *mts* Pak. 89 F5
Makri India 84 D2
Maksatikha Rus. Fed. 42 G4
Maksi India 82 D5
Maksimovka Rus. Fed. 74 E3
Maksotag Iran 89 F4
Maksudangarh India 82 D5
Mākū Iran 88 B2
Makunguwiro Tanz. 99 D5
Makurdi Nigeria 96 D4
Makwassie S. Africa 101 G4
Mal India 83 G4
Mala Rep. of Ireland *see* Mallow
Mala *i.* Solomon Is *see* Malaita
Malå Sweden 44 K4
Mala, Punta *pt* Panama 137 H7
Malabar Coast India 84 B3

▶Malabo Equat. Guinea 96 D4
Capital of Equatorial Guinea.

Malaca Spain *see* Málaga
Malacca Malaysia *see* Melaka
Malacca, Strait of Indon./Malaysia 71 B6
Malad City U.S.A. 126 E4
Maladzyechna Belarus 45 O9
Malá Fatra *nat. park* Slovakia 47 Q6
Málaga Spain 57 D5
Malaga U.S.A. 131 B5
Malagasy Republic *country* Africa *see* Madagascar
Malaita *i.* Solomon Is 107 G2
Malakal Sudan 86 D8
Malakanagiri India *see* Malkangiri
Malakheti Nepal 82 E3
Malakula *i.* Vanuatu 107 G3
Malan, Ras *pt* Pak. 89 G5
Malang Indon. 68 E8
Malangana Nepal *see* Malangwa
Malange Angola *see* Malanje
Malangwa Nepal 83 F4
Malanje Angola 99 B4
Malappuram India 84 C4
Mälaren *l.* Sweden 45 J7
Malargüe Arg. 144 C5
Malartic Canada 122 F4
Malaspina Glacier U.S.A. 120 A3
Malatya Turkey 90 E3
Malavalli India 84 C3
▶Malawi *country* Africa 99 D5
Africa 7, 94–95
Malawi, Lake Africa *see* Nyasa, Lake
Malawi National Park Zambia *see* Nyika National Park
Malaya *pen.* Malaysia *see* Peninsular Malaysia
Malaya Pera Rus. Fed. 42 L2
Malaya Vishera Rus. Fed. 42 G4
Malaybalay Phil. 69 H5
Malāyer Iran 88 C3
Malay Peninsula Asia 71 B4
Malay Reef Australia 110 E3
▶Malaysia *country* Asia 68 D5
Asia 6, 62–63
Malaysia, Semenanjung *pen.* Malaysia *see* Peninsular Malaysia
Malazgirt Turkey 91 F3
Malbon Australia 110 C4
Malbork Poland 47 Q3
Malborn Germany 52 G5
Malchin Germany 47 N4
Malcolm Australia 109 C7
Malcolm, Point Australia 109 C8
Malcolm Island Myanmar 71 B5
Maldegem Belgium 52 D3
Malden U.S.A. 131 F4
Malden Island Kiribati 151 J6
▶Maldives *country* Indian Ocean 81 D10
Asia 6, 62–63
Maldon Australia 112 B6
Maldon U.K. 49 H7
Maldonado Uruguay 144 F4

▶Male Maldives 81 D11
Capital of the Maldives.

Maleas, Akra *pt* Greece 59 J6
Male Atoll Maldives 81 D11
Malebogo S. Africa 101 G5
Malegaon *Maharashtra* India 84 B1
Malegaon *Maharashtra* India 84 C2
Malé Karpaty *hills* Slovakia 47 P6
Malek Sīāh, Kūh-e *mt.* Afgh. 89 F4
Malele Dem. Rep. Congo 99 B4
Maler Kotla India 82 C3
Maleševske Planine *mts* Bulg./Macedonia 59 J4
Malgobek Rus. Fed. 91 G2
Malgomaj *l.* Sweden 44 J4
Malha, Naqb *mt.* Egypt *see* Māliḩah, Naqb
Malhada Brazil 145 C1
Malheur *r.* U.S.A. 126 D3
Malheur Lake U.S.A. 126 D4
▶Mali *country* Africa 96 C3
Africa 7, 94–95
Mali Dem. Rep. Congo 98 C4
Mali Guinea 96 B3
Maliana East Timor 108 D2
Malianjing China 80 I3
Māliḩah, Naqb *mt.* Egypt 85 A5
Malik Naro *mt.* Pak. 89 F4
Mali Kyun *i.* Myanmar 71 B4
Malili Indon. 69 G7
Malin Ukr. *see* Malyn
Malindi Kenya 98 E4
Malines Belgium *see* Mechelen
Malin Head *hd* Rep. of Ireland 51 E2
Malin More Rep. of Ireland 51 D3
Malipo China 76 E4
Mali Raginac *mt.* Croatia 58 F2
Malita Phil. 69 H5
Malka *r.* Rus. Fed. 91 G2
Malkangiri India 84 D2
Malkapur India 84 B2
Malkara Turkey 59 L4
Mal'kavichy Belarus 45 O10
Malko Tŭrnovo Bulg. 59 L4
Mallacoota Australia 112 D6
Mallacoota Inlet *b.* Australia 112 D6
Mallaig U.K. 50 D4
Mallani *reg.* India 89 H5
Mallawī Egypt 90 C6
Mallee Cliffs National Park Australia 111 C7
Mallery Lake Canada 121 L1
Mallét Brazil 145 A4
Mallorca *i.* Spain *see* Majorca
Mallow Rep. of Ireland 51 D5
Mallowa Well Australia 108 D5
Mallwyd U.K. 49 D6
Malm Norway 44 G4
Malmberget Sweden 44 L3
Malmédy Belgium 52 G4
Malmesbury S. Africa 100 D7
Malmesbury U.K. 49 E7
Malmö Sweden 45 H9
Malmyzh Rus. Fed. 42 K4
Maloca Brazil 143 G3
Malone U.S.A. 135 H1
Malonje *mt.* Tanz. 99 D4
Maloshuyka Rus. Fed. 42 H3
Malosmadulu Atoll Maldives *see* Maalhosmadulu Atoll
Måløy Norway 44 D6
Maloyaroslavets Rus. Fed. 43 H5
Malozemel'skaya Tundra *lowland* Rus. Fed. 42 K2
Malpelo, Isla de *i.* N. Pacific Ocean 137 H8
Malprabha *r.* India 84 C2
▶Malta *country* Europe 58 F7
Europe 5, 38–39
Malta Latvia 45 O8
Malta *ID* U.S.A. 126 E4
Malta *MT* U.S.A. 126 G2
Malta Channel Italy/Malta 58 F6
Maltahöhe Namibia 100 C3
Maltby U.K. 48 F5
Maltby le Marsh U.K. 48 H5
Malton U.K. 48 G4
Malukken *is* Indon. *see* Moluccas
Maluku *is* Indon. *see* Moluccas
Maluku, Laut *sea* Indon. 69 H6
Ma'lūlā, Jabal *mts* Syria 85 C3
Malung Sweden 45 H6
Maluti Mountains Lesotho 101 I5
Malu'u Solomon Is 107 G2
Malvan India 84 B2
Malvasia Greece *see* Monemvasia
Malvern U.K. *see* Great Malvern
Malvern U.S.A. 131 E5
Malvérnia Moz. *see* Chicualacuala
Malvinas, Islas *terr.* S. Atlantic Ocean *see* Falkland Islands
Malyn Ukr. 43 F6
Malyy Anyuy *r.* Rus. Fed. 65 R3
Malyye Derbety Rus. Fed. 43 J7
Malyy Kavkaz *mts* Asia *see* Lesser Caucasus
Malyy Lyakhovskiy, Ostrov *i.* Rus. Fed. 65 P2
Malyy Uzen' *r.* Kazakh./Rus. Fed. 43 K6
Mama *r.* Rus. Fed. 65 P3
Mamadysh Rus. Fed. 42 K5
Mamafubedu S. Africa 101 I4
Mamatān Nāvar *l.* Afgh. 89 G4
Mamba China 76 B2
Mambai Brazil 145 B1
Mambasa Dem. Rep. Congo 98 C3
Mamburao Phil. 69 G4
Mamelodi S. Africa 101 I3
Mamfe Cameroon 96 D4
Mamison Pass Georgia/Rus. Fed. 91 F2
Mamit India 83 H5
Mammoth U.S.A. 129 H5
Mammoth Cave National Park U.S.A. 134 B5
Mammoth Reservoir U.S.A. 128 D3
Mamonas Brazil 145 C1
Mamoré *r.* Bol./Brazil 142 E6
Mamou Guinea 96 B3
Mampikony Madag. 99 E5
Mampong Ghana 96 C4
Mamuju Indon. 68 F7
Mamuno Botswana 100 E2
Man Côte d'Ivoire 96 C4
Man India 84 B2
Man *r.* India 84 B2
Man U.S.A. 134 E5

▶Man, Isle of *terr.* Irish Sea 48 C4
United Kingdom Crown Dependency.
Europe 5

Manacapuru Brazil 142 F4
Manacor Spain 57 H4
Manado Indon. 69 G6

▶Managua Nicaragua 137 G6
Capital of Nicaragua.

Manakara Madag. 99 E6
Manakau *mt.* N.Z. 113 D6
Manākhah Yemen 86 F6

▶Manama Bahrain 88 C5
Capital of Bahrain.

Manamadurai India 84 C4
Mana Maroka National Park S. Africa 101 H5
Manamelkudi India 84 C4
Manam Island P.N.G. 69 L7
Mananara Avaratra Madag. 99 E5
Manangoora Australia 110 B3
Mananjary Madag. 99 E6
Manantali, Lac de *l.* Mali 96 B3
Manantenina Madag. 99 E6
Mana Pass China/India 82 D3
Mana Pools National Park Zimbabwe 99 C5

▶Manapouri, Lake N.Z. 113 A7
Deepest lake in Oceania.

Manasa India 82 C4
Manas He *r.* China 80 G2
Manas Hu *l.* China 80 G2
Manāşīr *reg.* U.A.E. 88 D6
Manaslu *mt.* Nepal 83 F3
Manassas U.S.A. 135 G4
Manastir Macedonia *see* Bitola
Manas Wildlife Sanctuary *nature res.* Bhutan 83 G4
Man-aung Myanmar *see* Cheduba
Man-aung Kyun *i.* Myanmar *see* Cheduba Island
Manaus Brazil 142 F4
Manavgat Turkey 90 C3
Manbazar India 83 F5
Manbij Syria 85 C1
Manby U.K. 48 H5
Mancelona U.S.A. 134 C1
Manchar India 84 B2
Manchester U.K. 48 E5
Manchester *CT* U.S.A. 135 I3
Manchester *IA* U.S.A. 130 F3
Manchester *KY* U.S.A. 134 D5
Manchester *MD* U.S.A. 135 G4
Manchester *MI* U.S.A. 134 C2
Manchester *NH* U.S.A. 135 J2
Manchester *OH* U.S.A. 134 D4
Manchester *TN* U.S.A. 132 C5
Manchester *VT* U.S.A. 135 I2
Mancılık Turkey 90 E3
Mand Pak. 89 F5
Mand, Rūd-e *r.* Iran 88 C4
Manda Tanz. 99 D4
Manda, Jebel *mt.* Sudan 97 F4
Manda, Parc National de *nat. park* Chad 97 E4
Mandabe Madag. 99 E6
Mandai Sing. 71 [inset]
Mandal Afgh. 89 F3
Mandal Norway 45 E7

▶Mandala, Puncak *mt.* Indon. 69 K7
3rd highest mountain in Oceania.

Mandalay Myanmar 70 B2
Mandale Myanmar *see* Mandalay
Mandalgovĭ Mongolia 72 J3
Mandalī Iraq 91 G4
Mandalt China 73 K4
Mandan U.S.A. 130 C2
Mandas *Sardinia* Italy 58 C5
Mandasa India 84 E2
Mandasor India *see* Mandsaur
Mandav Hills India 82 B5
Mandera Kenya 98 E3
Manderfield U.S.A. 129 G2
Manderscheid Germany 52 G4
Mandeville Jamaica 137 I5
Mandeville N.Z. 113 B7
Mandha India 82 B4
Mandhoúdhíon Greece *see* Mantoudi
Mandi India 82 D3
Mandiana Guinea 96 C3
Mandi Burewala Pak. 89 I4
Mandié Moz. 99 D5
Mandini S. Africa 101 J5
Mandira Dam India 83 F5
Mandla India 82 E5
Mandleshwar India 82 C5
Mandrael India 82 D4
Mandritsara Madag. 99 E5
Mandsaur India 82 C4
Mandurah Australia 109 A8
Manduria Italy 58 G4
Mandvi India 82 B5
Mandya India 84 C3
Manerbio Italy 58 D2
Manevychi Ukr. 43 E6
Manfalūţ Egypt 90 C6
Manfredonia Italy 58 F4
Manfredonia, Golfo di *g.* Italy 58 G4
Manga Brazil 145 C1
Manga Burkina 96 C3
Mangabeiras, Serra das *hills* Brazil 143 I6
Mangai Dem. Rep. Congo 98 B4
Mangaia *i.* Cook Is 151 J7
Mangakino N.Z. 113 E4
Mangalagiri India 84 D2
Mangaldai India 70 A1
Mangaldoi India *see* Mangaldai
Mangalia Romania 59 M3
Mangalmé Chad 97 E3
Mangalore India 84 B3
Mangaon India 84 B2
Mangareva Islands Fr. Polynesia *see* Gambier, Îles
Mangaung *Free State* S. Africa 97 H5
Mangaung *Free State* S. Africa *see* Bloemfontein
Mangawan India 83 E4
Ma'ngê China *see* Luqu
Mangea *i.* Cook Is *see* Mangaia
Mangghyshlaq Kazakh. *see* Mangystau
Mangghystaū Kazakh. *see* Mangystau
Mangghystaū *admin. div.* Kazakh. *see* Mangistauskaya Oblast'
Mangghyt Uzbek. *see* Mangit
Manghit Uzbek. *see* Mangit
Mangin Range *mts* Myanmar *see* Mingin Range
Mangistau Kazakh. *see* Mangystau
Mangistauskaya Oblast' *admin. div.* Kazakh. 91 I2
Mangit Uzbek. 80 B3
Mangla Bangl. *see* Mongla
Mangla China *see* Guinan
Mangla Pak. 89 I3
Manglaqiongtuo China *see* Guinan
Mangnai China 80 H4
Mangnai Zhen China 80 H4
Mangochi Malawi 99 D5
Mangoky *r.* Madag. 99 E6
Mangole *i.* Indon. 69 H7
Mangoli India 84 B2
Mangotsfield U.K. 49 E7
Mangqystaū Shyghanaghy *b.* Kazakh. *see* Mangyshlakskiy Zaliv
Mangra China *see* Guinan
Mangral India 82 B5
Mangrul India 84 C1
Mangshi China *see* Luxi
Mangualde Port. 57 C3
Manguéni, Plateau du Niger 96 E2
Mangui China 74 A2
Mangula Zimbabwe *see* Mhangura
Mangum U.S.A. 131 D5
Mangyshlak Kazakh. *see* Mangystau
Mangyshlak, Poluostrov *pen.* Kazakh. 91 H1
Mangyshlak Oblast *admin. div.* Kazakh. *see* Mangistauskaya Oblast'
Mangyshlakskaya Oblast' *admin. div.* Kazakh. *see* Mangistauskaya Oblast'
Mangyshlakskiy Zaliv *b.* Kazakh. 91 H1
Mangystau Kazakh. 91 H2
Manhã Brazil 145 B1
Manhattan U.S.A. 130 D4
Manhica Moz. 101 K3
Manhoca Moz. 101 K4
Manhuaçu Brazil 145 C3
Manhuaçu *r.* Brazil 145 C2
Mani China 83 F2
Mania *r.* Madag. 99 E5
Maniago Italy 58 E1
Manicouagan Canada 123 H4
Manicouagan *r.* Canada 123 H4
Manicouagan, Réservoir *resr* Canada 123 H4
Manic Trois, Réservoir *resr* Canada 123 H4
Manīfah Saudi Arabia 88 C5
Maniganggo China 76 C2
Manigotagan Canada 121 L5
Manihiki *atoll* Cook Is 150 J6
Maniitsoq Greenland 119 M3
Manikchhari Bangl. 83 H5
Manikgarh India *see* Rajura

▶Manila Phil. 69 G4
Capital of the Philippines.

Manila U.S.A. 126 F4
Manildra Australia 112 D4
Manilla Australia 112 E3
Maningrida Australia 108 F3
Manipur India *see* Imphal
Manipur *state* India 83 H4
Manisa Turkey 59 L5
Manistee U.S.A. 134 B1
Manistee *r.* U.S.A. 134 B1
Manistique U.S.A. 132 C2
Manitoba *prov.* Canada 121 L4
Manitoba, Lake Canada 121 L5
Manito Lake Canada 121 I4
Manitou Canada 121 L5
Manitou, Lake U.S.A. 134 B3
Manitou Beach U.S.A. 135 G2
Manitou Falls Canada 121 M5
Manitou Islands U.S.A. 134 B1
Manitoulin Island Canada 122 E5
Manitouwadge Canada 122 D4
Manitowoc U.S.A. 134 B1
Maniwaki Canada 122 G5
Manizales Col. 142 C2
Manja Madag. 99 E6
Manjarabad India 84 B3
Manjeri India 84 C4
Manjhand Pak. 89 H5
Manjhi India 83 F4
Manjra *r.* India 84 C2
Man Kabat Myanmar 70 B1
Mankaiana Swaziland *see* Mankayane
Mankato *KS* U.S.A. 130 D4
Mankato *MN* U.S.A. 130 E2
Mankayane Swaziland 101 J4
Mankera Pak. 89 H4
Mankono Côte d'Ivoire 96 C4
Mankota Canada 121 J5
Manley Hot Springs U.S.A. 118 C3
Manmad India 84 B1
Mann *r.* Australia 108 F3
Mann, Mount Australia 109 E6
Manna Indon. 68 C7
Man Na Myanmar 70 B2
Mannahill Australia 111 B7
Mannar Sri Lanka 84 C4
Mannar, Gulf of India/Sri Lanka 84 C4
Manneru *r.* India 84 D3
Mannessier, Lac *l.* Canada 123 H3
Mannheim Germany 53 I5
Mannicolo Islands Solomon Is *see* Vanikoro Islands
Manning *r.* Australia 112 F3
Manning Canada 120 G3
Manning U.S.A. 133 D5
Mannington U.S.A. 134 E4
Manningtree U.K. 49 I7
Mann Ranges *mts* Australia 109 E6
Mannsville *KY* U.S.A. 134 C5
Mannsville *NY* U.S.A. 135 G2
Mannu, Capo *c. Sardinia* Italy 58 C4
Mannville Canada 121 I4
Man-of-War Rocks *is* U.S.A. *see* Gardner Pinnacles
Manoharpur India 82 D4
Manohar Thana India 82 D4
Manokotak U.S.A. 118 C4
Manokwari Indon. 69 I7
Manoron Myanmar 71 B5
Manosque France 56 G5
Manouane *r.* Canada 123 H4
Manouane, Lac *l.* Canada 123 H4
Man Pan Myanmar 70 B2
Manp'o N. Korea 74 B4
Manra *i.* Kiribati 107 I2
Manresa Spain 57 G3
Mansa *Gujarat* India 82 C5
Mansa *Punjab* India 82 C3
Mansa Zambia 99 C5
Mansa Konko Gambia 96 B3
Man Sam Myanmar 70 B2
Mansehra Pak. 87 L3
Mansel Island Canada 119 K3
Mansfield Australia 112 C6
Mansfield U.K. 49 F5
Mansfield *LA* U.S.A. 131 E5
Mansfield *OH* U.S.A. 134 D3
Mansfield *PA* U.S.A. 135 G3
Mansfield, Mount U.S.A. 135 I1
Man Si Myanmar 70 B1
Mansi Myanmar 70 A1
Manso *r.* Brazil *see* Mortes, Rio das
Manta Ecuador 142 B4
Mantaro *r.* Peru 142 D6
Manteca U.S.A. 128 C3
Mantena Brazil 145 C2
Manteo U.S.A. 132 F5
Mantes-la-Jolie France 52 B6
Mantiqueira, Serra da *mts* Brazil 145 B3
Manton U.S.A. 134 C1
Mantoudi Greece 59 J5
Mantova Italy *see* Mantua
Mäntsälä Fin. 45 N6
Mänttä Fin. 44 N5
Mantua Cuba 133 C8
Mantua Italy 58 D2
Mantuan Downs Australia 110 D5
Manturovo Rus. Fed. 42 J4

Mäntyharju Fin. 45 O6
Mäntyjärvi Fin. 44 O3
Manú Peru 142 D6
Manu, Parque Nacional nat. park Peru 142 D6
Manuae atoll Fr. Polynesia 151 J7
Manua Islands American Samoa 107 I3
Manuel Ribas Brazil 145 A4
Manuel Vitorino Brazil 145 C1
Manuelzinho Brazil 143 H5
Manui i. Indon. 69 G7
Manukau N.Z. 113 E3
Manukau Harbour N.Z. 113 E3
Manunda watercourse Australia 111 B7
Manusela National Park Indon. 69 H7
Manus Island P.N.G. 69 L7
Manvi India 84 C3
Many U.S.A. 131 E6
Manyana Botswana 101 G3
Manyas Turkey 59 L4
Manyas Gölü l. Turkey see Kuş Gölü
Manych-Gudilo, Ozero l. Rus. Fed. 43 I7
Many Island Lake Canada 121 I5
Manyoni Tanz. 99 D4
Manzai Pak. 89 H3
Manzanares Spain 57 E4
Manzanillo Cuba 137 I4
Manzanillo Mex. 136 D5
Manzhouli China 73 L3
Manzini Swaziland 101 J4
Mao Chad 97 E3
Maó Spain see Mahón
Maoba Guizhou China 76 E3
Maoba Hubei China 77 F2
Maocifan China 77 G2
Mao'ergai China 76 D1
Maoke, Pegunungan mts Indon. 69 J7
Maokeng S. Africa 101 H4
Maokui Shan mt. China 74 A4
Maolin China 74 A4
Maoming China 77 F4
Ma On Shan hill Hong Kong China 77 [inset]
Maopi T'ou c. Taiwan 77 I4
Maopora i. Indon. 108 D1
Maotou Shan mt. China 76 D3
Mapai Moz. 101 J2
Mapam Yumco l. China 83 E3
Mapanza Zambia 99 C5
Maphodi S. Africa 101 G6
Mapimí Mex. 131 C7
Mapimí, Bolsón de des. Mex. 131 B7
Mapin i. Phil. 68 F5
Mapinhane Moz. 101 L2
Mapiri Bol. 142 E7
Maple r. MI U.S.A. 134 C2
Maple r. ND U.S.A. 130 D2
Maple Creek Canada 121 I5
Maple Heights U.S.A. 134 E3
Maple Peak U.S.A. 129 I5
Mapmakers Seamounts sea feature N. Pacific Ocean 150 H4
Mapoon Australia 110 C1
Mapor i. Indon. 71 D7
Mapoteng Lesotho 101 H5
Maprik P.N.G. 69 K7
Mapuera r. Brazil 143 G4
Mapulanguene Moz. 101 K3

▶Maputo Moz. 101 K3
Capital of Mozambique.

Maputo prov. Moz. 101 K3
Maputo r. Moz./S. Africa 101 K4
Maputo, Baía de b. Moz. 101 K4
Maputsoe Lesotho 101 H5
Maqanshy Kazakh. see Makanchi
Maqar an Na'am well Iraq 91 F5
Maqat Kazakh. see Makat
Maqên China 76 D1
Maqên Kangri mt. China 76 C1
Maqnā Saudi Arabia 90 D5
Maqteïr reg. Mauritania 96 B2
Maqu China 76 D1
Ma Qu r. China see Yellow River
Maquan He r. China 83 F3
Maquela do Zombo Angola 99 B4
Maquinchao Arg. 144 C6
Mar r. Pak. 89 G5
Mar, Serra do mts Rio de Janeiro/São Paulo Brazil 145 B3
Mar, Serra do mts Rio Grande do Sul/Santa Catarina Brazil 145 A5
Mara r. Canada 121 I1
Mara India 83 E5
Mara S. Africa 101 I2
Maraã Brazil 142 E4
Maraba Brazil 143 I5
Maraboon, Lake resr Australia 110 E4
Maracá, Ilha de i. Brazil 143 H3
Maracaibo Venez. 142 D1
Maracaibo, Lago de Venez. see Maracaibo, Lake
Maracaibo, Lake Venez. 142 D2
Maracaju Brazil 144 E2
Maracaju, Serra de hills Brazil 144 E2
Maracanda Uzbek. see Samarkand
Maracás Brazil 145 C1
Maracás, Chapada de hills Brazil 145 C1
Maracay Venez. 142 E1
Marādah Libya 97 E2
Maradi Niger 96 D3
Marāgheh Iran 88 B2
Marahuaca, Cerro mt. Venez. 142 E3
Marajó, Baía de est. Brazil 143 I4
Marajó, Ilha de i. Brazil 143 H4
Marakele National Park S. Africa 101 H3
Maralal Kenya 98 D3
Maralbashi China see Bachu
Maralinga Australia 109 E7
Maralwexi China see Bachu
Maramasike i. Solomon Is 107 G2
Maramba Zambia see Livingstone
Marambio research station Antarctica 152 A2
Maran Malaysia 71 C7
Maran mt. Pak. 89 G4
Marana U.S.A. 129 H5
Marand Iran 88 B2
Marandellas Zimbabwe see Marondera
Marang Malaysia 71 C6
Marang Myanmar 71 B5
Maranhão r. Brazil 145 A1
Maranoa r. Australia 112 D1
Marañón r. Peru 142 D4
Marão Moz. 101 L3
Marão mt. Port. 57 C3
Mara Rosa Brazil 145 A1
Maraş Turkey see Kahramanmaraş
Marathon Canada 122 D4
Marathon FL U.S.A. 133 D7
Marathon NY U.S.A. 135 G2
Marathon TX U.S.A. 131 C6
Maratua i. Indon. 68 F6
Maraú Brazil 145 D1
Maravillas Creek watercourse U.S.A. 131 C6
Mārāzā Azer. 91 H2
Marbella Spain 57 D5
Marble Bar Australia 108 B5
Marble Canyon U.S.A. 129 H3
Marble Canyon gorge U.S.A. 129 H3
Marble Hall S. Africa 101 I3
Marble Hill U.S.A. 131 F4
Marble Island Canada 121 N2
Marbul Pass Jammu and Kashmir 82 C2
Marburg S. Africa 101 J6
Marburg Slovenia see Maribor
Marburg an der Lahn Germany 53 I4
Marca, Ponta do pt Angola 99 B5
Marcali Hungary 58 G1
Marcelino Ramos Brazil 145 A4
March U.K. 49 H6
Marche reg. France 56 E3
Marche-en-Famenne Belgium 52 F4
Marchena Spain 57 D5
Marchinbar Island Australia 110 B1
Mar Chiquita, Lago l. Arg. 144 D4
Marchtrenk Austria 47 O6
Marco U.S.A. 133 D7
Marcoing France 52 D4
Marcona Peru 142 C7
Marcopeet Islands Canada 122 F2
Marcus Baker, Mount U.S.A. 118 D3
Marcy, Mount U.S.A. 135 I1
Mardan Pak. 89 I3
Mar del Plata Arg. 144 E5
Mardīan Afgh. 89 G2
Mardin Turkey 91 F3
Maré i. New Caledonia 107 G4
Maree, Loch l. U.K. 50 D3
Mareh Iran 89 E5
Marengo IA U.S.A. 130 E3
Marengo IN U.S.A. 134 B4
Marevo Rus. Fed. 42 G4
Marfa U.S.A. 131 B6
Marganets Ukr. see Marhanets'
Margao India see Madgaon
Margaret r. Australia 108 D4
Margaret watercourse Australia 111 B6
Margaret, Mount hill Australia 108 B5
Margaret Lake Alta Canada 120 H3
Margaret Lake N.W.T. Canada 120 G1
Margaret River Australia 109 A8
Margaretville U.S.A. 135 H2
Margarita, Isla de i. Venez. 142 F1
Margaritovo Rus. Fed. 74 D4
Margate U.K. 49 I7
Margherita, Lake Eth. see Abaya, Lake

▶Margherita Peak Dem. Rep. Congo/Uganda 98 C3
3rd highest mountain in Africa.

Marghilon Uzbek. see Margilan
Margilan Uzbek. 80 D3
Mārgo, Dasht-i des. Afgh. see Mārgow, Dasht-e
Margog Caka l. China 83 F2
Mārgow, Dasht-e des. Afgh. 89 F4
Margraten Neth. 52 F4
Marguerite Canada 120 F4
Marguerite, Pic mt. Dem. Rep. Congo/Uganda see Margherita Peak
Marguerite Bay Antarctica 152 L2
Margyang China 83 G3
Marhaj Khalīl Iraq 91 G4
Marhanets' Ukr. 43 G7
Marhoum Alg. 54 D5
Mari Myanmar 70 B1
Maria atoll Fr. Polynesia 151 J7
María Elena Chile 144 C2
Maria Island Australia 110 A2
Maria Island Myanmar 71 B5
Maria Island National Park Australia 111 [inset]
Mariala National Park Australia 111 D5
Mariana Brazil 145 C3
Marianao Cuba 133 D8
Mariana Ridge sea feature N. Pacific Ocean 150 F4

▶Mariana Trench sea feature N. Pacific Ocean 150 F5
Deepest trench in the world.

Mariani India 83 H4
Mariánica, Cordillera mts Spain see Morena, Sierra
Marian Lake Canada 120 G2
Marianna AR U.S.A. 131 F5
Marianna FL U.S.A. 133 C6
Mariano Machado Angola see Ganda
Mariánské Lázně Czech Rep. 53 M5
Marias r. U.S.A. 126 F3
Marías, Islas is Mex. 136 C4

▶Mariato, Punta pt Panama 137 H7
Most southerly point of North America.

Maria van Diemen, Cape N.Z. 113 D2
Ma'rib Yemen 86 G6
Maribor Slovenia 58 F1
Marica r. Bulg. see Maritsa
Maricopa AZ U.S.A. 129 G5
Maricopa CA U.S.A. 128 D4
Maricopa Mountains U.S.A. 129 G5
Maridi Sudan 97 F4
Marie Byrd Land reg. Antarctica 152 J1
Marie-Galante i. Guadeloupe 133 L5
Mariehamn Fin. 45 K6
Mariembero r. Brazil 145 A1
Marienbad Czech Rep. see Mariánské Lázně
Marienberg Germany 53 N4
Marienburg Poland see Malbork
Marienhafe Germany 53 H1
Mariental Namibia 100 C3
Marienwerder Poland see Kwidzyn
Mariestad Sweden 45 H7
Mariet r. Canada 122 F2
Marietta GA U.S.A. 133 C5
Marietta OH U.S.A. 134 E4
Marietta OK U.S.A. 131 D5
Marignane France 56 G5
Marii, Mys pt Rus. Fed. 66 G2
Mariinsk Rus. Fed. 64 J4
Mariinskiy Posad Rus. Fed. 42 J4
Marijampolė Lith. 45 M9
Marília Brazil 145 A3
Marillana Australia 108 B5
Marimba Angola 99 B4
Marín Spain 57 B2
Marina U.S.A. 128 C3
Marina di Gioiosa Ionica Italy 58 G5
Mar'ina Gorka Belarus see Mar"ina Horka
Mar"ina Horka Belarus 45 P10
Marinduque i. Phil. 69 G4
Marinette U.S.A. 134 B1
Maringá Brazil 145 A3
Maringa r. Dem. Rep. Congo 98 B3
Maringo U.S.A. 134 D3
Marinha Grande Port. 57 B4
Marion AL U.S.A. 133 C5
Marion AR U.S.A. 131 F5
Marion IL U.S.A. 130 F4
Marion IN U.S.A. 134 C3
Marion KS U.S.A. 130 D4
Marion MI U.S.A. 134 C1
Marion NY U.S.A. 135 G2
Marion OH U.S.A. 134 D3
Marion SC U.S.A. 133 E5
Marion VA U.S.A. 134 E5
Marion, Lake U.S.A. 133 D5
Marion Reef Australia 110 F3
Maripa Venez. 142 E2
Mariposa U.S.A. 128 D3
Marisa Indon. 69 G6
Mariscal Estigarribia Para. 144 D2
Maritime Alps mts France/Italy 56 H4
Maritime Kray admin. div. Rus. Fed. see Primorskiy Kray
Maritimes, Alpes mts France/Italy see Maritime Alps
Maritsa r. Bulg. 59 L4
also known as Evros (Greece), Marica (Bulgaria), Meriç (Turkey)
Marittime, Alpi mts France/Italy see Maritime Alps
Mariupol' Ukr. 43 H7
Mariusa nat. park Venez. 142 F2
Marīvān Iran 88 B3
Marjan Afgh. see Wazi Khwa
Marjayoûn Lebanon 85 B3
Marka Somalia 98 E3
Markala Mali 96 C3
Markam China 76 C2
Markaryd Sweden 45 H8
Markdale Canada 134 E1
Marken S. Africa 101 I2
Markermeer l. Neth. 52 F2
Market Deeping U.K. 49 G6
Market Drayton U.K. 49 E6
Market Harborough U.K. 49 G6
Markethill U.K. 51 F3
Market Weighton U.K. 48 G5
Markha r. Rus. Fed. 65 M3
Markham Canada 134 F2
Markit China 80 E4
Markkleeberg Germany 53 M3
Markleeville U.S.A. 128 D2
Marklohe Germany 53 J2
Markog Qu r. China 76 D1
Markounda Cent. Afr. Rep. 98 B3
Markovo Rus. Fed. 65 S3
Markranstädt Germany 53 M3
Marks Rus. Fed. 43 J6
Marks U.S.A. 131 F5
Marksville U.S.A. 131 E6
Marktheidenfeld Germany 53 J5
Marktredwitz Germany 53 M4
Marl Germany 52 H3
Marla Australia 109 F6
Marlborough Downs hills U.K. 49 F7
Marle France 52 D5
Marlette U.S.A. 134 D2
Marlin U.S.A. 131 D6
Marlinton U.S.A. 134 E4
Marlo Australia 112 D6
Marmagao India 84 B3
Marmande France 56 E4
Marmara, Sea of g. Turkey 59 M4
Marmara Denizi g. Turkey see Marmara, Sea of
Marmara Gölü l. Turkey 59 M5
Marmarica reg. Libya 90 B5
Marmaris Turkey 59 M6
Marmarth U.S.A. 130 C2
Marmet U.S.A. 134 E4
Marmion, Lake salt l. Australia 109 C7
Marmion Lake Canada 121 N5
Marmolada mt. Italy 58 D1
Marne r. France 52 C6
Marne-la-Vallée France 52 C6
Marnitz Germany 53 L1
Maroantsetra Madag. 99 E5
Maroc country Africa see Morocco
Marol Jammu and Kashmir 82 D2
Marol Pak. 89 I4
Maroldsweisach Germany 53 K4
Maromokotro mt. Madag. 99 E5
Marondera Zimbabwe 99 D5
Maroochydore Australia 112 F1
Maroonah Australia 109 A5
Maroon Peak U.S.A. 126 G5
Marosvás>o1a>rhely Romania see Târgu Mureş
Maroua Cameroon 97 E3
Marovoay Madag. 99 E5
Marqādah Syria 91 F4
Mar Qu r. China see Markog Qu
Marquard S. Africa 101 H5
Marquesas Islands Fr. Polynesia 151 K6
Marquesas Keys is U.S.A. 133 D7
Marquês de Valença Brazil 145 C3
Marquette U.S.A. 132 C2
Marquez U.S.A. 131 D6
Marquion France 52 D4
Marquise France 52 B4
Marquises, Îles is Fr. Polynesia see Marquesas Islands
Marra Australia 112 A3
Marra r. Australia 112 C3
Marra, Jebel mt. Sudan 97 F3
Marracuene Moz. 101 K3
Marrakech Morocco 54 C5
Marrakesh Morocco see Marrakech
Marrangua, Lagoa l. Moz. 101 L3
Marra Plateau Sudan 97 F3
Marrar Australia 112 C5
Marrawah Australia 111 [inset]
Marree Australia 111 B6
Marrowbone U.S.A. 134 C5
Marruecos country Africa see Morocco
Marrupa Moz. 99 D5
Marryat Australia 109 F6
Marsá al 'Alam Egypt 86 D4
Marsa 'Alam Egypt see Marsá al 'Alam
Marsa al Burayqah Libya 97 E1
Marsabit Kenya 98 D3
Marsala Sicily Italy 58 E6
Marsá Maṭrūḥ Egypt 90 B5
Marsberg Germany 53 I3
Marsciano Italy 58 E3
Marsden Australia 112 C4
Marsden Canada 121 I4
Marsdiep sea chan. Neth. 52 E2
Marseille France 56 G5
Marseilles France see Marseille
Marsfjället mt. Sweden 44 I4
Marshall watercourse Australia 110 B4
Marshall AR U.S.A. 131 E5
Marshall IL U.S.A. 134 B4
Marshall MI U.S.A. 134 C2
Marshall MN U.S.A. 130 E2
Marshall MO U.S.A. 130 E4
Marshall TX U.S.A. 131 E5
▶Marshall Islands country N. Pacific Ocean 150 H5
Oceania 8, 104–105
Marshalltown U.S.A. 130 E3
Marshfield MO U.S.A. 131 E4
Marshfield WI U.S.A. 130 F2
Marsh Harbour Bahamas 133 E7
Mars Hill U.S.A. 132 H2
Marsh Island U.S.A. 131 F6
Marsh Peak U.S.A. 129 I1
Marsh Point Canada 121 M3
Marsing U.S.A. 126 D4
Märsta Sweden 45 J7
Marsyaty Rus. Fed. 41 S3
Martaban Myanmar 70 B3
Martaban, Gulf of Myanmar 70 B3
Martapura Indon. 68 E7
Marten River Canada 122 F5
Marte R. Gómez, Presa resr Mex. 131 D7
Martha's Vineyard i. U.S.A. 135 J3
Martigny Switz. 56 H3
Martim Vaz, Ilhas is S. Atlantic Ocean see Martin Vas, Ilhas
Martin r. Canada 120 F2
Martin Slovakia 47 Q6
Martin MI U.S.A. 134 C2
Martin SD U.S.A. 130 C3
Martinez Lake U.S.A. 129 F5
Martinho Campos Brazil 145 B2

▶Martinique terr. West Indies 137 L6
French Overseas Department.
North America 9, 116–117

Martinique Passage Dominica/Martinique 137 L5
Martin Peninsula Antarctica 152 K2
Martinsburg U.S.A. 135 G4
Martins Ferry U.S.A. 134 E3
Martinsville IL U.S.A. 134 B4
Martinsville IN U.S.A. 134 B4
Martinsville VA U.S.A. 134 F5

▶Martin Vas, Ilhas is S. Atlantic Ocean 148 G7
Most easterly point of South America.

Martin Vaz Islands S. Atlantic Ocean see Martin Vas, Ilhas
Martök Kazakh. see Martuk
Marton N.Z. 113 E5
Martorell Spain 57 G3
Martos Spain 57 E5
Martuk Kazakh. 78 E1
Martuni Armenia 91 G2
Maruf Afgh. 89 G4
Maruim Brazil 143 K6
Marukhis Ugheltekhili pass Georgia/Rus. Fed. 91 F2
Marulan Australia 112 D5
Marusthali reg. India 89 H5
Marvast Iran 88 D4
Marv Dasht Iran 88 D4
Marvejols France 56 F4
Marvine, Mount U.S.A. 129 H2
Marwayne Canada 121 I4
Mary r. Australia 108 E3
Mary Turkm. 89 F2
Maryborough Qld Australia 111 F5
Maryborough Vic. Australia 112 A6
Marydale S. Africa 100 F5
Mary Frances Lake Canada 121 J2
Mary Lake Canada 121 K2
Maryland state U.S.A. 135 G4
Maryport U.K. 48 D4
Mary's Harbour Canada 123 L3
Marysvale U.S.A. 129 G2
Marysville CA U.S.A. 128 C2
Marysville KS U.S.A. 130 D4
Marysville OH U.S.A. 134 D3
Maryvale N.T. Australia 109 F6
Maryvale Qld Australia 110 D3
Maryville MO U.S.A. 130 E3
Maryville TN U.S.A. 132 D5
Marzagão Brazil 145 A2
Marzahna Germany 53 M2
Masada tourist site Israel 85 B4
Masāhūn, Kūh-e mt. Iran 88 D4
Masai Steppe plain Tanz. 99 D4
Masaka Uganda 98 D4
Masakhane S. Africa 101 H6
Masalembu Besar i. Indon. 68 E8
Masallı Azer. 91 H3
Masan S. Korea 75 C6
Masasi Tanz. 99 D5
Masavi Bol. 142 F7
Masbate Phil. 69 G4
Masbate i. Phil. 69 G4
Mascara Alg. 57 G6
Mascarene Basin sea feature Indian Ocean 149 L7
Mascarene Plain sea feature Indian Ocean 149 L7
Mascarene Ridge sea feature Indian Ocean 149 L6
Mascote Brazil 145 D1
Masein Myanmar 70 A2
Masela Indon. 108 E2
Masela i. Indon. 108 E2

▶Maseru Lesotho 101 H5
Capital of Lesotho.

Mashai Lesotho 101 I5
Mashan China 77 F4
Masherbrum mt. Jammu and Kashmir 82 D2
Mashhad Iran 89 E2
Mashket r. Pak. 89 F5
Mashki Chah Pak. 89 F4
Masi Norway 44 M2
Masiáca Mex. 127 F8
Masibambane S. Africa 101 H6
Masīlah, Wādī al watercourse Yemen 86 H6
Masilo S. Africa 101 H5
Masi-Manimba Dem. Rep. Congo 99 B4
Masindi Uganda 98 D3
Masinyusane S. Africa 100 F6
Masira, Gulf of Oman see Maṣīrah, Khalīj
Maṣīrah, Jazīrat i. Oman 87 I5
Maṣīrah, Khalīj b. Oman 87 I6
Masira Island Oman see Maṣīrah, Jazīrat
Masjed Soleymān Iran 88 C4
Mask, Lough l. Rep. of Ireland 51 C4
Maskūtān Iran 89 E5
Maslovo Rus. Fed. 41 S3
Masoala, Tanjona c. Madag. 99 F5
Mason MI U.S.A. 134 C2
Mason OH U.S.A. 134 C4
Mason TX U.S.A. 131 D6
Mason, Lake salt flat Australia 109 B6
Mason Bay N.Z. 113 A8
Mason City U.S.A. 130 E3
Masontown U.S.A. 134 F4
Masqaṭ Oman see Muscat
Masqaṭ reg. Oman see Muscat
'Masrūg well Oman 88 D6
Massa Italy 58 D2
Massachusetts state U.S.A. 135 I2
Massachusetts Bay U.S.A. 135 J2
Massadona U.S.A. 129 I1
Massafra Italy 58 G4
Massakory Chad 97 E3
Massa Marittimo Italy 58 D3
Massangena Moz. 99 D6
Massango Angola 99 B4
Massawa Eritrea 86 E6
Massawippi, Lac l. Canada 135 I1
Massena U.S.A. 135 H1
Massenya Chad 97 E3
Masset Canada 120 C4
Massieville U.S.A. 134 D4
Massif Central mts France 56 F4
Massilia France see Marseille
Massillon U.S.A. 134 E3
Massina Mali 96 C3
Massinga Moz. 101 L2
Massingir Moz. 101 K2
Massingir, Barragem de resr Moz. 101 K2
Masson Island Antarctica 152 F2
Mastchoh Tajik. 89 H2
Masterton N.Z. 113 E5
Masticho, Akra pt Greece 59 L5
Mastung Pak. 78 F4
Mastūrah Saudi Arabia 86 E5
Masty Belarus 45 N10
Masuda Japan 75 C6
Masuku Gabon see Franceville
Masulipatam India see Machilipatnam
Masulipatnam India see Machilipatnam
Masuna i. American Samoa see Tutuila
Masvingo Zimbabwe 99 D6
Masvingo prov. Zimbabwe 101 J1
Maswa Tanz. 98 D4
Maswaar i. Indon. 69 I7
Maṣyāf Syria 85 C2
Mat, Hon i. Vietnam 70 D3
Mat, Nam r. Laos 70 D3
Mata Myanmar 70 B1
Matabeleland South prov. Zimbabwe 101 I1
Matachewan Canada 122 E5
Matadi Dem. Rep. Congo 99 B4
Matador U.S.A. 131 C5
Matagalpa Nicaragua 137 G6
Matagami Canada 122 F4
Matagami, Lac l. Canada 122 F4
Matagorda Island U.S.A. 131 D6
Matak i. Indon. 71 D7
Matakana Island N.Z. 113 F3
Matala Angola 99 B5
Maṭāli', Jabal hill Saudi Arabia 91 F6
Matam Senegal 96 B3
Matamey Niger 96 D3
Matamoros U.S.A. 135 H3
Matamoros Coahuila Mex. 131 C7
Matamoros Tamaulipas Mex. 131 D7
Matandu r. Tanz. 99 D4
Matane Canada 123 I4
Matanzas Cuba 137 H4
Matapan, Cape pt Greece see Tainaro, Akra
Matapédia, Lac l. Canada 123 I4
Maṭār well Saudi Arabia 88 B5
Matara Sri Lanka 84 D5
Mataram Indon. 108 B2
Matarani Peru 142 D7
Mataranka Australia 108 F3
Mataripe Brazil 145 D1
Mataró Spain 57 H3
Matasiri i. Indon. 68 F7
Matatiele S. Africa 101 I6
Matatila Dam India 82 D4
Mataura N.Z. 113 B8

▶Matā'utu Wallis and Futuna Is 107 I3
Capital of Wallis and Futuna.

Mata-Utu Wallis and Futuna Is see Matā'utu
Matawai N.Z. 113 F4
Matay Kazakh. 80 E2
Matcha Tajik. see Mastchoh
Mategua Bol. 142 F6
Matehuala Mex. 131 C8
Matemanga Tanz. 99 D5
Matera Italy 58 G4
Mateur Tunisia 58 C6
Mathaji India 82 B4
Matheson Canada 122 E4
Mathews U.S.A. 135 G5
Mathis U.S.A. 131 D6
Mathoura Australia 112 B5
Mathura India 82 D4
Mati Phil. 69 H5
Matiali India 83 G4
Matias Cardoso Brazil 145 C1
Matías Romero Mex. 136 E5
Matimekosh Canada 123 I3
Matin India 83 E5
Matinenda Lake Canada 122 E5
Matizi China 76 D1
Matla r. India 83 G5
Matlabas r. S. Africa 101 H2
Matli Pak. 89 H5
Matlock U.K. 49 F5
Mato, Cerro mt. Venez. 142 E2
Matobo Hills Zimbabwe 99 C6
Mato Grosso Brazil 142 G7
Mato Grosso state Brazil 145 A1
Mato Grosso, Planalto do plat. Brazil 143 H7
Matopo Hills Zimbabwe see Matobo Hills
Matos Costa Brazil 145 A4
Matosinhos Port. 57 B3
Mato Verde Brazil 145 C1
Maṭraḥ Oman 88 E6
Matroosberg mt. S. Africa 100 D7
Matsesta Rus. Fed. 91 E2
Matsue Japan 75 D6
Matsumoto Japan 75 E5
Matsu Tao i. Taiwan 77 I3
Matsuyama Japan 75 D6
Mattagami r. Canada 122 E4
Mattamuskeet, Lake U.S.A. 132 E5
Mattawa Canada 122 F5
Matterhorn mt. Italy/Switz. 58 B2
Matterhorn mt. U.S.A. 126 E4
Matthew Town Bahamas 137 J4
Maṭṭī, Sabkhat salt pan Saudi Arabia 88 D6
Mattoon U.S.A. 130 F4
Matturai Sri Lanka see Matara
Matuku i. Fiji 107 H3
Matumbo Angola 99 B5
Maturín Venez. 142 F2
Matusadona National Park Zimbabwe 99 C5
Matwabeng S. Africa 101 H5
Maty Island P.N.G. see Wuvulu Island
Mau India see Maunath Bhanjan
Maúa Moz. 99 D5
Maubeuge France 52 D4
Maubin Myanmar 70 A3
Ma-ubin Myanmar 70 B1
Maubourguet France 56 E5
Mauchline U.K. 50 E5
Maudaha India 82 E4
Maude Australia 111 D7
Maud Seamount sea feature S. Atlantic Ocean 148 I10
Mau-é-ele Moz. see Marão
Maués Brazil 143 G4
Maughold Head hd Isle of Man 48 C4
Maug Islands N. Mariana Is 69 L2
Maui i. HI U.S.A. 127 [inset]
Maukkadaw Myanmar 70 A2
Maulbronn Germany 53 I6
Maule r. Chile 144 B5
Maulvi Bazar Bangl. see Moulvibazar
Maumee U.S.A. 134 D3
Maumee Bay U.S.A. 134 D3
Maumere Indon. 108 C2
Maumturk Mts hills Rep. of Ireland 51 C4
Maun Botswana 99 C5
Mauna Kea vol. HI U.S.A. 127 [inset]
Mauna Loa vol. HI U.S.A. 127 [inset]
Maunath Bhanjan India 83 E4
Maunatlala Botswana 101 H2
Maungaturoto N.Z. 113 E3
Maungdaw Myanmar 70 A2
Maungmagan Islands Myanmar 71 B4
Maurepas, Lake U.S.A. 131 F6
Mauriac France 56 F4
Maurice country Indian Ocean see Mauritius
Maurice, Lake salt flat Australia 109 E7
Maurik Neth. 52 F3
▶Mauritania country Africa 96 B3
Africa 7, 94–95
Mauritanie country Africa see Mauritania
▶Mauritius country Indian Ocean 149 L7
Africa 7, 94–95
Maurs France 56 F4
Mauston U.S.A. 130 F3
Mava Dem. Rep. Congo 98 C3
Mavago Moz. 99 D5
Mavan, Kūh-e hill Iran 88 E3
Mavanza Moz. 101 L2
Mavinga Angola 99 C5
Mavrovo nat. park Macedonia 59 I4
Mavume Moz. 101 L2
Mavuya S. Africa 101 H6
Ma Wan i. Hong Kong China 77 [inset]
Māwān, Khashm hill Saudi Arabia 88 B6
Mawana India 82 D3
Mawanga Dem. Rep. Congo 99 B4
Ma Wang Dui tourist site China 77 G2
Mawei China 77 H3

Mawjib, Wādī al r. Jordan 85 B4
Mawkmai Myanmar 70 B2
Mawlaik Myanmar 70 A2
Mawlamyaing Myanmar see Moulmein
Mawlamyine Myanmar see Moulmein
Mawqaq Saudi Arabia 91 F6
Mawson research station Antarctica 152 E2
Mawson Coast Antarctica 152 E2
Mawson Escarpment Antarctica 152 E2
Mawson Peninsula Antarctica 152 H2
Maw Taung mt. Myanmar 71 B5
Mawza Yemen 86 F7
Maxán Arg. 144 C3
Maxhamish Lake Canada 120 F3
Maxia, Punta mt. Sardinia Italy 58 C5
Maxixe Moz. 101 L2
Maxmo Fin. 44 M5
May, Isle of i. U.K. 50 G4
Maya r. Rus. Fed. 65 O3
Mayaguana i. Bahamas 133 F8
Mayaguana Passage Bahamas 133 F8
Mayagüez Puerto Rico 137 K5
Mayahi Niger 96 D3
Mayakovskiy, Qullai mt. Tajik. 89 H2
Mayakovskogo, Pik mt. Tajik. see Mayakovskiy, Qullai
Mayama Congo 98 B4
Maya Mountains Belize/Guat. 136 G5
Mayan China see Mayanhe
Mayang China 77 F3
Mayanhe China 76 E1
Mayar hill U.K. 50 F4
Maybeury U.S.A. 134 E5
Maybole U.K. 50 E5
Maych'ew Eth. 98 D2
Maydān Shahr Afgh. see Meydān Shahr
Maydh Somalia 86 G7
Maydos Turkey see Eceabat
Mayen Germany 53 H4
Mayenne France 56 D2
Mayenne r. France 56 D3
Mayer U.S.A. 129 G4
Mayêr Kangri mt. China 83 F2
Mayersville U.S.A. 131 F5
Mayerthorpe Canada 120 H4
Mayfield N.Z. 113 C6
Mayi He r. China 74 C3
Maykop Rus. Fed. 91 F1
Maymyo Myanmar 70 B2
Mayna Respublika Khakasiya Rus. Fed. 64 K4
Mayna Ul'yanovskaya Oblast' Rus. Fed. 43 J5
Mayni India 84 B2
Maynooth Canada 135 G1
Mayo Canada 120 C2
Mayo U.S.A. 133 D6
Mayo Alim Cameroon 96 E4
Mayoko Congo 98 B4
Mayo Lake Canada 120 C2
Mayo Landing Canada see Mayo
Mayor, Puig mt. Spain see Major, Puig
Mayor Island N.Z. 113 F3
Mayor Pablo Lagerenza Para. 144 D1

▶Mayotte terr. Africa 99 E5
French Territorial Collectivity.
Africa 7, 94–95

Mayskiy Amurskaya Oblast' Rus. Fed. 74 C1
Mayskiy Kabardino-Balkarskaya Respublika Rus. Fed. 91 G2
Mays Landing U.S.A. 135 H4
Mayson Lake Canada 121 J3
Maysville U.S.A. 134 D4
Mayumba Gabon 98 B4
Mayum La pass China 83 E3
Mayuram India 84 C4
Mayville MI U.S.A. 134 D2
Mayville ND U.S.A. 130 D2
Mayville NY U.S.A. 134 F2
Mayville WI U.S.A. 134 A2
Mazabuka Zambia 99 C5
Mazaca Turkey see Kayseri
Mazagan Morocco see El Jadida
Mazar China 82 D1
Mazar, Koh-i- mt. Afgh. 89 G3
Mazara, Val di valley Sicily Italy 58 E6
Mazara del Vallo Sicily Italy 58 E6
Mazār-e Sharīf Afgh. 89 G2
Mazārī' reg. U.A.E. 88 D6
Mazatán Mex. 127 F7
Mazatlán Mex. 136 C4
Mazatzal Peak U.S.A. 129 H4
Mazdaj Iran 91 H4
Mažeikiai Lith. 45 M8
Mazīm Oman 88 E6
Mazocahui Mex. 127 F7
Mazocruz Peru 142 E7
Mazomora Tanz. 99 D4
Mazu Dao i. Taiwan see Matsu Tao
Mazunga Zimbabwe 99 C6
Mazyr Belarus 43 F5
Mazzouna Tunisia 58 C7

▶Mbabane Swaziland 101 J4
Capital of Swaziland.

Mbahiakro Côte d'Ivoire 96 C4
Mbaïki Cent. Afr. Rep. 98 B3
Mbakaou, Lac de l. Cameroon 96 E4
Mbala Zambia 99 D4
Mbale Uganda 98 D3
Mbalmayo Cameroon 96 E4
Mbam r. Cameroon 96 E4
Mbandaka Dem. Rep. Congo 98 B4
M'banza Congo Angola 99 B4
Mbarara Uganda 97 G5
Mbari r. Cent. Afr. Rep. 98 C3
Mbaswana S. Africa 101 K4
Mbemkuru r. Tanz. 99 D4
Mbeya Tanz. 99 D4
Mbinga Tanz. 99 D5
Mbini Equat. Guinea 96 D4
Mbizi Zimbabwe 99 D6
Mboki Cent. Afr. Rep. 98 C3
Mbomo Congo 98 B3
Mbouda Cameroon 96 E4
Mbour Senegal 96 B3
Mbout Mauritania 96 B3
Mbozi Tanz. 99 D4
Mbrès Cent. Afr. Rep. 98 B3
Mbuji-Mayi Dem. Rep. Congo 99 C4
Mbulu Tanz. 98 D4
Mburucuyá Arg. 144 E3
McAdam Canada 123 I5
McAlester U.S.A. 131 E5
McAlister mt. Australia 112 D5
McAllen U.S.A. 131 D7
McArthur r. Australia 110 B2
McArthur U.S.A. 134 D4
McArthur Mills Canada 135 G1
McBain U.S.A. 134 C1
McBride Canada 120 F4
McCall U.S.A. 126 D3
McCamey U.S.A. 131 C6
McCammon U.S.A. 126 E4
McCauley Island Canada 120 D4
McClintock, Mount Antarctica 152 H1
McClintock Channel Canada 119 H2
McClintock Range hills Australia 108 D4
McClure, Lake U.S.A. 128 C3
McClure Strait Canada 118 G2
McClusky U.S.A. 130 C2
McComb U.S.A. 131 F6
McConaughy, Lake U.S.A. 130 C3
McConnellsburg U.S.A. 135 G4
McConnelsville U.S.A. 134 E4
McCook U.S.A. 130 C3
McCormick U.S.A. 133 D5
McCrea r. Canada 120 H2
McCreary Canada 121 L5
McDame Canada 120 D3
McDermitt U.S.A. 126 D4
McDonald Islands Indian Ocean 149 M9
McDonald Peak U.S.A. 126 E3
McDonough U.S.A. 133 C5
McDougall's Bay S. Africa 100 C5
McDowell Peak U.S.A. 129 H5
McFarland U.S.A. 128 D4
McGill U.S.A. 129 F2
McGivney Canada 123 I5
McGrath AK U.S.A. 118 C3
McGrath MN U.S.A. 130 E2
McGraw U.S.A. 135 G2
McGregor r. Canada 120 F4
McGregor S. Africa 100 D7
McGregor, Lake Canada 120 H5
McGregor Range hills Australia 111 C5
McGuire, Mount U.S.A. 126 E3
Mchinga Tanz. 99 D4
Mchinji Malawi 99 D5
McIlwraith Range hills Australia 110 C2
McInnes Lake Canada 121 M4
McIntosh U.S.A. 130 C2
McKay Range hills Australia 108 C5
McKean i. Kiribati 107 I2
McKee U.S.A. 134 C5
McKenzie r. U.S.A. 126 C3
McKinlay r. Australia 110 C4

▶McKinley, Mount U.S.A. 118 C3
Highest mountain in North America.
North America 114–115

McKinney U.S.A. 131 D5
McKittrick U.S.A. 128 D4
McLaughlin U.S.A. 130 C2
McLeansboro U.S.A. 130 F4
McLennan Canada 120 G4
McLeod r. Canada 120 H4
McLeod Bay Canada 121 I2
McLeod Lake Canada 120 F4
McLoughlin, Mount U.S.A. 126 C4
McMillan, Lake U.S.A. 131 B5
McMinnville OR U.S.A. 126 C3
McMinnville TN U.S.A. 132 C5
McMurdo research station Antarctica 152 H1
McMurdo Sound b. Antarctica 152 H1
McNary U.S.A. 129 I4
McNaughton Lake Canada see Kinbasket Lake
McPherson U.S.A. 130 D4
McQuesten r. Canada 120 B2
McRae U.S.A. 133 D5
McTavish Arm b. Canada 120 G1
McVeytown U.S.A. 135 G3
McVicar Arm b. Canada 120 F1
Mdantsane S. Africa 101 H7
M'Daourouch Alg. 58 B6
Mê, Hon i. Vietnam 70 D3
Mead, Lake resr U.S.A. 129 F3
Meade U.S.A. 131 C4
Meade r. U.S.A. 118 C2
Meadow Australia 109 A6
Meadow SD U.S.A. 130 C2
Meadow UT U.S.A. 129 G2
Meadow Lake Canada 121 I4
Meadville MS U.S.A. 131 F6
Meadville PA U.S.A. 134 E3
Meaford Canada 134 E1
Meaken-dake vol. Japan 74 G4
Mealhada Port. 57 B3
Mealy Mountains Canada 123 K3
Meandarra Australia 112 D1
Meander River Canada 120 G3
Meaux France 52 C6
Mecca Saudi Arabia 86 E5
Mecca CA U.S.A. 128 E5
Mecca OH U.S.A. 134 E3
Mechanic Falls U.S.A. 135 J1
Mechanicsville U.S.A. 135 G5
Mechelen Belgium 52 E3
Mechelen Neth. 52 F4
Mecherchar i. Palau see Eil Malk
Mecheria Alg. 54 D5
Mechernich Germany 52 G4
Mecitözü Turkey 90 D2
Meckenheim Germany 52 H4
Mecklenburger Bucht b. Germany 47 M3
Mecklenburg-Vorpommern land Germany 53 M1
Mecklenburg - West Pomerania land Germany see Mecklenburg-Vorpommern
Meda r. Australia 108 C4
Meda Port. 57 C3
Medak India 84 C2
Medan Indon. 71 B7
Medanosa, Punta pt Arg. 144 C7
Médanos de Coro, Parque Nacional nat. park Venez. 142 E1
Medawachchiya Sri Lanka 84 D4
Médéa Alg. 57 H5
Medebach Germany 53 I3
Medellín Col. 142 C2
Meden r. U.K. 48 G5
Medenine Tunisia 54 G5
Mederdra Mauritania 96 B3
Medford NY U.S.A. 135 I3
Medford OK U.S.A. 131 D4
Medford OR U.S.A. 126 C4
Medford WI U.S.A. 130 F2
Medgidia Romania 59 M2
Media U.S.A. 135 H4
Mediaș Romania 59 K1
Medicine Bow r. U.S.A. 126 G4
Medicine Bow Mountains U.S.A. 126 G4
Medicine Bow Peak U.S.A. 126 G4
Medicine Hat Canada 121 I5
Medicine Lake U.S.A. 126 G2
Medicine Lodge U.S.A. 131 D4
Medina Brazil 145 C2
Medina Saudi Arabia 86 E5
Medina ND U.S.A. 130 D2
Medina NY U.S.A. 135 F2
Medina OH U.S.A. 134 E3
Medinaceli Spain 57 E3
Medina del Campo Spain 57 D3
Medina de Rioseco Spain 57 D3
Medina Lake U.S.A. 131 D6
Medinipur India 83 F5
Mediolanum Italy see Milan
Mediterranean Sea 54 K5
Mednyy, Ostrov i. Rus. Fed. 150 H2
Médoc reg. France 56 D4
Mêdog China 76 B2
Medora U.S.A. 130 C2
Medstead Canada 121 I4
Meduro atoll Marshall Is see Majuro
Medvedevo Rus. Fed. 42 J4
Medveditsa r. Rus. Fed. 43 I6
Medvednica mts Croatia 58 F2
Medvezh'i, Ostrova is Rus. Fed. 65 R2
Medvezh'ya, Gora mt. Rus. Fed. 74 E3
Medvezh'yegorsk Rus. Fed. 42 G3
Medway r. U.K. 49 H7
Meekatharra Australia 109 B6
Meeker CO U.S.A. 129 J1
Meeker OH U.S.A. 134 D3
Meelpaeg Reservoir Canada 123 K4
Meemu Atoll Maldives see Mulaku Atoll
Meerane Germany 53 M4
Meerlo Neth. 52 G3
Meerut India 82 D3
Mega Escarpment Eth./Kenya 98 D3
Megalopoli Greece 59 J6
Megamo Indon. 69 I7
Mégantic, Lac l. Canada 123 H5
Megara Greece 59 J5
Megezez mt. Eth. 98 D3

▶Meghalaya state India 83 G4
Highest mean annual rainfall in the world.

Meghasani mt. India 83 F5
Meghri Armenia 91 G3
Megin Turkm. 88 E2
Megisti i. Greece 59 M6
Megri Armenia see Meghri
Mehamn Norway 44 O1
Mehar Pak. 89 G5
Meharry, Mount Australia 109 B5
Mehbubnagar India see Mahbubnagar
Mehdia Tunisia see Mahdia
Meherpur Bangl. 83 G5
Meherrin U.S.A. 135 F5
Meherrin r. U.S.A. 135 G5
Mehlville U.S.A. 130 F4
Mehrakān salt marsh Iran 88 D5
Mehrān Hormozgan Iran 88 D5
Mehrān Īlām Iran 88 B3
Mehren Germany 52 G4
Mehriz Iran 88 D4
Mehsana India see Mahesana
Mehtar Lām Afgh. 89 H3
Meia Ponte r. Brazil 145 A2
Meicheng China see Minqing
Meiganga Cameroon 97 E4
Meighen Island Canada 119 I2
Meigu China 76 D2
Meihekou China 74 B4
Meikeng China 77 G3
Meikle r. Canada 120 G3
Meikle Says Law hill U.K. 50 G5
Meiktila Myanmar 70 A2
Meilin China see Ganxian
Meilleur r. Canada 120 E2
Meilu China 77 F4
Meine Germany 53 K2
Meinersen Germany 53 K2
Meiningen Germany 53 K4
Meishan Anhui China see Jinzhai
Meishan Sichuan China 76 D2
Meishan Shuiku resr China 77 G2
Meißen Germany 47 N5
Meister r. Canada 120 D2
Meitan China 76 E3
Meixi China 74 C3
Meixian China see Meizhou
Meixing China see Xiaojin
Meizhou China 77 H3
Mej r. India 82 D4
Mejicana mt. Arg. 144 C3
Mejillones Chile 144 B2
Mékambo Gabon 98 B3
Mek'elē Eth. 98 D2
Mekelle Eth. see Mek'elē
Mékhé Senegal 96 B3
Mekhtar Pak. 89 H4
Meknassy Tunisia 58 C7
Meknès Morocco 54 C5
Mekong r. Xizang/Yunnan China 72 C2
Mekong r. Laos/Thai. 70 D4
also known as Mae Nam Khong (Laos/Thailand)
Mekong, Mouths of the Vietnam 71 D5
Mekoryuk U.S.A. 118 B3
Melaka Malaysia 71 C7
Melanau, Gunung hill Indon. 71 E7
Melanesia is Pacific Ocean 150 G6
Melanesian Basin sea feature Pacific Ocean 150 G5

▶Melbourne Australia 112 B6
State capital of Victoria. 2nd most populous city in Oceania.

Melbourne U.S.A. 133 D6
Melby U.K. 50 [inset]
Meldorf Germany 47 L3
Melekess Rus. Fed. see Dimitrovgrad
Melenki Rus. Fed. 43 I5
Melet Turkey see Mesudiye
Mélèzes, Rivière aux r. Canada 123 H2
Melfa U.S.A. 135 H5
Mélfi Chad 97 E3
Melfi Italy 58 F4
Melfort Canada 121 J4
Melhus Norway 44 G5
Meliadine Lake Canada 121 M2
Melide Spain 57 C2

▶Melilla N. Africa 57 E6
Spanish Territory.

Melimoyu, Monte mt. Chile 144 B6
Meliskerke Neth. 52 D3
Melita Canada 121 K5
Melitene Turkey see Malatya
Melitopol' Ukr. 43 G7
Melk Austria 47 O6
Melka Guba Eth. 98 D3
Melksham U.K. 49 E7
Mellakoski Fin. 44 N3
Mellansel Sweden 44 K5
Melle Germany 53 I2
Mellerud Sweden 45 H7
Mellette U.S.A. 130 D2
Mellid Spain see Melide
Mellilia N. Africa see Melilla
Mellor Glacier Antarctica 152 E2
Mellrichstadt Germany 53 K4
Mellum i. Germany 53 I1
Melmoth S. Africa 101 J5
Mel'nichoye Rus. Fed. 74 D3
Melo Uruguay 144 F4
Meloco Moz. 99 D5
Melolo Indon. 108 C2
Melozitna r. U.S.A. 118 C3
Melrhir, Chott salt l. Alg. 54 F5
Melrose Australia 109 C6
Melrose U.K. 50 G5
Melrose U.S.A. 130 E2
Melsungen Germany 53 J3
Melton Australia 112 B6
Melton Mowbray U.K. 49 G6
Melun France 56 F2
Melville Canada 121 K5
Melville, Cape Australia 110 D2
Melville, Lake Canada 123 K3
Melville Bugt b. Greenland see Qimusseriarsuaq
Melville Island Australia 108 E2
Melville Island Canada 119 H2
Melville Peninsula Canada 119 J3
Melvin U.S.A. 134 A3
Melvin, Lough l. Rep. of Ireland/U.K. 51 D3
Mêmar Co salt l. China 83 E2
Memba Moz. 99 E5
Memberamo r. Indon. 69 J7
Memel Lith. see Klaipėda
Memel S. Africa 101 I4
Memmelsdorf Germany 53 K5
Memmingen Germany 47 M7
Mempawah Indon. 68 D6
Memphis tourist site Egypt 90 C5
Memphis MI U.S.A. 134 D2
Memphis TN U.S.A. 131 F5
Memphis TX U.S.A. 131 C5
Memphrémagog, Lac l. Canada 135 I1
Mena Ukr. 43 G6
Mena U.S.A. 131 E5
Menado Indon. see Manado
Ménaka Mali 96 D3
Menard U.S.A. 131 D6
Menasha U.S.A. 134 A1
Mendanha Brazil 145 C2
Mendarik i. Indon. 71 D7
Mende France 56 F4
Mendefera Eritrea 86 E7
Mendeleyev Ridge sea feature Arctic Ocean 153 B1
Mendeleyevsk Rus. Fed. 42 L5
Mendenhall U.S.A. 131 F6
Mendenhall, Cape U.S.A. 118 B4
Mendenhall Glacier U.S.A. 120 C3
Méndez Mex. 131 D7
Mendī Eth. 98 D3
Mendi P.N.G. 69 K8
Mendip Hills U.K. 49 E7
Mendocino U.S.A. 128 B2
Mendocino, Cape U.S.A. 128 A1
Mendocino, Lake U.S.A. 128 B2
Mendooran Australia 112 D3
Mendota CA U.S.A. 128 C3
Mendota IL U.S.A. 130 F3
Mendoza Arg. 144 C4
Menemen Turkey 59 L5
Ménerville Alg. see Thenia
Mengban China 76 D4
Mengcheng China 77 H1
Menghai China 76 D4
Mengjin China 77 G1
Mengla China 76 D4
Menglang China see Lancang
Menglie China see Jiangcheng
Mengyang China see Mingshan
Mengzi China 76 D4
Menihek Canada 123 I3
Menihek Lakes Canada 123 I3
Menindee Australia 111 C7
Menindee Lake Australia 111 C7
Ménistouc, Lac l. Canada 123 I3
Menkere Rus. Fed. 65 N3
Mennecy France 52 C6
Menominee U.S.A. 134 B1
Menomonee Falls U.S.A. 134 A2
Menomonie U.S.A. 130 F2
Menongue Angola 99 B5
Menorca i. Spain see Minorca
Mentawai, Kepulauan is Indon. 68 B7
Mentawai, Selat sea chan. Indon. 68 C7
Menteroda Germany 53 K3
Mentmore U.S.A. 129 I4
Menton France 56 H5
Mentone U.S.A. 131 C6
Menuf Egypt see Minūf
Menzel Bourguiba Tunisia 58 C6
Menzelet Barajı resr Turkey 90 E3
Menzelinsk Rus. Fed. 41 Q4
Menzel Temime Tunisia 58 D6
Menzies Australia 109 C7
Menzies, Mount Antarctica 148 E2
Meobbaai b. Namibia 100 B3
Meoqui Mex. 131 B6
Meppel Neth. 52 G2
Meppen Germany 53 H2
Mepuze Moz. 101 K2
Meqheleng S. Africa 101 H5
Mequon U.S.A. 134 B2
Merak Indon. 68 D8
Meråker Norway 44 G5
Merano Italy 58 D1
Meratswe r. Botswana 100 G2
Merauke Indon. 69 K8
Merca Somalia see Marka
Mercantour, Parc National du nat. park France 56 H4
Merced U.S.A. 128 C3
Merced r. U.S.A. 128 C3
Mercedes Arg. 144 E3
Mercedes Uruguay 144 E4
Mercer ME U.S.A. 135 K1
Mercer PA U.S.A. 134 E3
Mercer WI U.S.A. 130 F2
Mercês Brazil 145 C3
Mercury Islands N.Z. 113 E3
Mercy, Cape Canada 119 L3
Merdenik Turkey see Göle
Mere Belgium 52 D4
Mere U.K. 49 E7
Meredith U.S.A. 135 J2
Meredith, Lake U.S.A. 131 C5
Merefa Ukr. 43 H6
Merga Oasis Sudan 86 C6
Mergui Myanmar 71 B4
Mergui Archipelago is Myanmar 71 B5
Meriç r. Turkey 59 L4
also known as Evros (Greece), Marica, Maritsa (Bulgaria)
Mérida Mex. 136 G4
Mérida Spain 57 C4
Mérida Venez. 142 D2
Mérida, Cordillera de mts Venez. 142 D2
Meriden U.S.A. 135 I3
Meridian MS U.S.A. 131 F5
Meridian TX U.S.A. 131 D6
Mérignac France 56 D4
Merijärvi Fin. 44 N4
Merikarvia Fin. 45 L6
Merimbula Australia 112 D6
Merín, Laguna l. Brazil/Uruguay see Mirim, Lagoa
Meringur Australia 111 C7
Merir i. Palau 69 I6
Merjayoun Lebanon see Marjayoûn
Merkel U.S.A. 131 C5
Merluna Australia 110 C2
Mermaid Reef Australia 108 B4
Meron, Har mt. Israel 85 B3
Merowe Sudan 86 D6
Mêrqung Co l. China 83 F3
Merredin Australia 109 B7
Merrick hill U.K. 50 E5
Merrickville Canada 135 H1
Merrill MI U.S.A. 134 C2
Merrill WI U.S.A. 130 F2
Merrill, Mount Canada 120 E2
Merrillville U.S.A. 134 B3
Merriman U.S.A. 130 C3
Merritt Canada 120 F5
Merritt Island U.S.A. 133 D6
Merriwa Australia 112 E4
Merrygoen Australia 112 D3
Mersa Fatma Eritrea 86 F7
Mersa Maṭrûḥ Egypt see Marsá Maṭrūḥ
Mersch Lux. 52 G5
Merseburg (Saale) Germany 53 L3
Mersey est. U.K. 48 E5
Mersin Turkey see İçel
Mersing Malaysia 71 C7
Mērsrags Latvia 45 M8
Merta India 82 C4
Merthyr Tydfil U.K. 49 D7
Mértola Port. 57 C5
Mertz Glacier Antarctica 152 G2
Mertz Glacier Tongue Antarctica 152 G2
Mertzon U.S.A. 131 C6
Méru France 52 C5

▶Meru vol. Tanz. 98 D4
4th highest mountain in Africa.

Merui Pak. 89 F4
Merv Turkm. see Mary
Merweville S. Africa 100 E7
Merzifon Turkey 90 D2
Merzig Germany 52 G5
Merz Peninsula Antarctica 152 L2
Mesa AZ U.S.A. 129 H5
Mesa NM U.S.A. 127 G6
Mesabi Range hills U.S.A. 130 E2
Mesagne Italy 58 G4
Mesa Negra mt. U.S.A. 129 J4
Mesara, Ormos b. Greece 59 K7
Mesa Verde National Park U.S.A. 129 I3
Meschede Germany 53 I3
Mese Myanmar 70 B3
Meselefors Sweden 44 J4
Mesgouez Lake Canada 122 G4
Meshed Iran see Mashhad
Meshkān Iran 88 E2
Meshra'er Req Sudan 86 C8
Mesick U.S.A. 134 C1
Mesimeri Greece 59 J4
Mesolongi Greece 59 I5
Mesolóngion Greece see Mesolongi
Mesopotamia reg. Iraq 91 F4
Mesquita Brazil 145 C2
Mesquite NV U.S.A. 129 F3
Mesquite TX U.S.A. 131 D5
Mesquite Lake U.S.A. 129 F4
Messaad Alg. 54 E5
Messana Sicily Italy see Messina
Messina Sicily Italy 58 F5
Messina S. Africa 101 J2
Messina, Strait of Italy 58 F5
Messina, Stretta di Italy see Messina, Strait of
Messini Greece 59 J6
Messiniakos Kolpos b. Greece 59 J6
Mesta r. Bulg. 59 K4
Mesta r. Greece see Nestos
Mestghanem Alg. see Mostaganem
Mestlin Germany 53 L1
Meston, Akra pt Greece 59 K5
Mestre Italy 58 E2
Mesudiye Turkey 90 E2
Meta r. Col./Venez. 142 E2
Métabetchouan Canada 123 H4
Meta Incognita Peninsula Canada 119 L3
Metairie U.S.A. 131 F6
Metallifere, Colline mts Italy 58 D3
Metán Arg. 144 C3
Meteghan Canada 123 I5
Meteor Depth sea feature S. Atlantic Ocean 148 G9
Methoni Greece 59 I6
Methuen U.S.A. 135 J2
Methven U.K. 50 F4
Metionga Lake Canada 122 C4
Metković Croatia 58 G3
Metlaoui Tunisia 54 F5
Metoro Moz. 99 D5
Metro Indon. 68 D8
Metropolis U.S.A. 131 F4
Metsada tourist site Israel see Masada
Metter U.S.A. 133 D5
Mettet Belgium 52 E4
Mettingen Germany 53 H2
Mettler U.S.A. 128 D4
Mettur India 84 C4
Metu Eth. 98 D3
Metz France 52 G5
Metz U.S.A. 134 C3
Meulaboh Indon. 71 B6
Meureudu Indon. 71 B6
Meuse r. Belgium/France 52 F3
also known as Maas (Netherlands)
Meuselwitz Germany 53 M3
Mevagissey U.K. 49 C8
Mêwa China 76 D1
Mexia U.S.A. 131 D6
Mexiana, Ilha i. Brazil 143 I3
Mexicali Mex. 129 F5
Mexican Hat U.S.A. 129 I3
Mexican Water U.S.A. 129 I3

▶Mexico country Central America 136 D4
2nd most populous and 3rd largest country in Central and North America.
North America 9, 116–117

México Mex. see Mexico City
Mexico ME U.S.A. 135 J1
Mexico MO U.S.A. 130 F4
Mexico NY U.S.A. 135 G2
Mexico, Gulf of Mex./U.S.A. 125 H6

▶Mexico City Mex. 136 E5
Capital of Mexico. Most populous city in North America and 2nd in the world.

Meybod Iran 88 D3
Meydanī, Ra's-e pt Iran 88 E5
Meydān Shahr Afgh. 89 H3
Meyenburg Germany 53 M1
Meyersdale U.S.A. 134 F4
Meymaneh Afgh. 89 G3
Meymeh Iran 88 C3
Meynypil'gyno Rus. Fed. 153 C2
Mezada tourist site Israel see Masada
Mezdra Bulg. 59 J3
Mezen' Rus. Fed. 42 J2
Mezen' r. Rus. Fed. 42 J2
Mézenc, Mont mt. France 56 G4
Mezenskaya Guba b. Rus. Fed. 42 I2
Mezhdurechensk Kemerovskaya Oblast' Rus. Fed. 72 F2
Mezhdurechensk Respublika Komi Rus. Fed. 42 K3
Mezhdurechnye Rus. Fed. see Shali
Mezhdusharskiy, Ostrov i. Rus. Fed. 64 G2
Mezitli Turkey 85 B1
Mezőtúr Hungary 59 I1
Mežvidi Latvia 45 O8
Mhàil, Rubh' a' pt U.K. 50 C5
Mhangura Zimbabwe 99 D5
Mhlume Swaziland 101 J4
Mhow India 82 C5
Mi r. Myanmar 83 H5
Miahuatlán Mex. 136 E5
Miajadas Spain 57 D4
Miaméré Cent. Afr. Rep. 98 B3
Miami AZ U.S.A. 129 H5
Miami FL U.S.A. 133 D7
Miami OK U.S.A. 131 E4
Miami Beach U.S.A. 133 D7
Miancaowan China 76 C1
Mīāndehī Iran 88 E3
Miandowāb Iran 88 B2
Miandrivazo Madag. 99 E5
Mīāneh Iran 88 B2
Miang, Phu mt. Thai. 70 C3
Miani India 89 I4
Miani Hor b. Pak. 89 G5
Mianjoi Afgh. 89 G3
Mianning China 76 D2
Mianwali Pak. 89 H3
Mianxian China 76 E1
Mianyang Hubei China see Xiantao
Mianyang Shaanxi China see Mianxian
Mianyang Sichuan China 76 E2
Mianzhu China 76 E2
Miaoli Taiwan 77 I3
Miarinarivo Madag. 99 E5
Miarritze France see Biarritz
Miass Rus. Fed. 64 H4
Mica Creek Canada 120 G4
Mica Mountain U.S.A. 129 H5
Micang Shan mts China 76 E1
Michalovce Slovakia 43 D6

Michel Canada 121 I4
Michelau in Oberfranken Germany 53 L4
Michelson, Mount U.S.A. 118 D3
Michelstadt Germany 53 J5
Michendorf Germany 53 N2
Micheng China see Midu
Michigan state U.S.A. 134 C2

▶Michigan, Lake U.S.A. 134 B2
3rd largest lake in North America and 5th in the world.
World 12–13

Michigan City U.S.A. 134 B3
Michinberi India 84 D2
Michipicoten Bay Canada 122 D5
Michipicoten Island Canada 122 D5
Michipicoten River Canada 122 D5
Michurin Bulg. see Tsarevo
Michurinsk Rus. Fed. 43 I5
Micronesia country N. Pacific Ocean see Micronesia, Federated States of
Micronesia is Pacific Ocean 150 F5
▶Micronesia, Federated States of country N. Pacific Ocean 150 G5
Oceania 8, 104–105
Midai i. Indon. 71 D7
Mid-Atlantic Ridge sea feature Atlantic Ocean 148 E4
Mid-Atlantic Ridge sea feature Atlantic Ocean 148 G8
Middelburg Neth. 52 D3
Middelburg E. Cape S. Africa 101 G6
Middelburg Mpumalanga S. Africa 101 I3
Middelfart Denmark 45 F9
Middelharnis Neth. 52 E3
Middelwit S. Africa 101 H3
Middle Alkali Lake U.S.A. 126 C4
Middle America Trench sea feature N. Pacific Ocean 151 N5
Middle Andaman i. India 71 A4
Middle Atlas mts Morocco see Moyen Atlas
Middle Bay Canada 123 K4
Middlebourne U.S.A. 134 E4
Middleburg U.S.A. 135 G3
Middleburgh U.S.A. 135 H2
Middlebury IN U.S.A. 134 C3
Middlebury VT U.S.A. 135 I1
Middle Caicos i. Turks and Caicos Is 133 G8
Middle Concho r. U.S.A. 131 C6
Middle Congo country Africa see Congo
Middle Island Thai. see Tasai, Ko
Middle Loup r. U.S.A. 130 D3
Middlemarch N.Z. 113 C7
Middlemount Australia 110 E4
Middle River U.S.A. 135 G4
Middlesbrough U.K. 48 F4
Middle Strait India see Andaman Strait
Middleton Australia 110 C4
Middleton Canada 123 I5
Middleton Island atoll American Samoa see Rose Island
Middletown CA U.S.A. 128 B2
Middletown CT U.S.A. 135 I3
Middletown NY U.S.A. 135 H3
Middletown VA U.S.A. 135 F4
Midelt Morocco 54 D5
Midhurst U.K. 49 G8
Midi, Canal du France 56 F5
Mid-Indian Basin sea feature Indian Ocean 149 N6
Mid-Indian Ridge sea feature Indian Ocean 149 M7
Midland Canada 135 F1
Midland CA U.S.A. 129 F5
Midland IN U.S.A. 134 B4
Midland MI U.S.A. 134 C2
Midland SD U.S.A. 130 C2
Midland TX U.S.A. 131 C5
Midleton Rep. of Ireland 51 D6
Midnapore India see Medinipur
Midnapur India see Medinipur
Midongy Atsimo Madag. 99 E6
Mid-Pacific Mountains sea feature N. Pacific Ocean 150 G4
Midu China 76 D3
Miðvágur Faroe Is 44 [inset]
Midway Oman see Thamarīt

▶Midway Islands terr. N. Pacific Ocean 150 I4
United States Unincorporated Territory.

Midway Well Australia 109 C5
Midwest U.S.A. 126 G4
Midwest City U.S.A. 131 D5
Midwoud Neth. 52 F2
Midyat Turkey 91 F3
Midye Turkey see Kıyıköy
Mid Yell U.K. 50 [inset]
Midzhur mt. Bulg./Serb. and Mont. 90 A2
Miehikkälä Fin. 45 O6
Miekojärvi l. Fin. 44 N3
Mielec Poland 43 D6
Mienhua Yü i. Taiwan 77 I3
Mieraslompolo Fin. 44 O2
Mierašluoppal Fin. see Mieraslompolo
Miercurea-Ciuc Romania 59 K1
Mieres Spain 57 D2
Mieres del Camín Spain see Mieres
Mī'ēso Eth. 98 E3
Mieste Germany 53 L2
Mifflinburg U.S.A. 135 G3
Mifflintown U.S.A. 135 G3
Migang Shan mt. China 76 E1
Migdol S. Africa 101 G4
Miging India 76 B2
Miguel Auza Mex. 131 C7
Miguel Hidalgo, Presa resr Mex. 127 F8
Mihalıççık Turkey 59 N5
Mihara Japan 75 D6
Mihintale Sri Lanka 84 D4
Mihmandar Turkey 85 B1
Mijares r. Spain see Millárs
Mijdrecht Neth. 52 E2
Mikhaylov Rus. Fed. 43 H5
Mikhaylovgrad Bulg. see Montana
Mikhaylovka Amurskaya Oblast' Rus. Fed. 74 C2
Mikhaylovka Primorskiy Kray Rus. Fed. 74 D4
Mikhaylovka Tul'skaya Oblast' Rus. Fed. see Kimovsk
Mikhaylovka Volgogradskaya Oblast' Rus. Fed. 43 I6
Mikhaylovskiy Rus. Fed. 80 E1
Mikhaylovskoye Rus. Fed. see Shpakovskoye
Mikhaytov Island Antarctica 152 E2
Mikhrot Timna Israel 85 B5
Mikir Hills India 83 H4
Mikkeli Fin. 45 O6
Mikkelin mlk Fin. 45 O6
Mikkwa r. Canada 120 H3
Mikonos i. Greece see Mykonos
Mikoyan Armenia see Yeghegnadzor
Mikulkin, Mys c. Rus. Fed. 42 J2
Mikumi National Park Tanz. 99 D4
Mikun' Rus. Fed. 42 K3
Mikuni-sanmyaku mts Japan 75 E5
Mikura-jima i. Japan 75 E6
Milaca U.S.A. 130 E2
Miladhunmadulu Atoll Maldives 84 B5
Miladummadulu Atoll Maldives see Miladhunmadulu Atoll
Milan Italy 58 C2
Milan MI U.S.A. 134 D2
Milan MO U.S.A. 130 E3
Milan OH U.S.A. 134 D3
Milange Moz. 99 D5
Milano Italy see Milan
Milas Turkey 59 L6
Milazzo Sicily Italy 58 F5
Milazzo, Capo di c. Sicily Italy 58 F5
Milbank U.S.A. 130 D2
Milbridge U.S.A. 132 H2
Milde r. Germany 53 L2
Mildenhall U.K. 49 H6
Mildura Australia 111 C7
Mile China 76 D3
Mileiz, Wâdi el watercourse Egypt see Mulayz, Wādī al
Miles Australia 112 E1
Miles City U.S.A. 126 G3
Milestone Rep. of Ireland 51 D5
Miletto, Monte mt. Italy 58 F4
Mileura Australia 109 B6
Milford Rep. of Ireland 51 E2
Milford DE U.S.A. 135 H4
Milford IL U.S.A. 134 B3
Milford MA U.S.A. 135 J2
Milford MI U.S.A. 134 D2
Milford NE U.S.A. 130 D3
Milford NH U.S.A. 135 J2
Milford PA U.S.A. 135 H3
Milford UT U.S.A. 129 G2
Milford VA U.S.A. 135 G4
Milford Haven U.K. 49 B7
Milford Sound N.Z. 113 A7
Milford Sound inlet N.Z. 113 A7
Milgarra Australia 110 C3
Milḩ, Baḩr al l. Iraq see Razāzah, Buḩayrat ar
Miliana Alg. 57 H5
Milid Turkey see Malatya
Milikapiti Australia 108 E2
Miling Australia 109 B7
Milk r. U.S.A. 126 G2
Milk, Wadi el watercourse Sudan 86 D6
Mil'kovo Rus. Fed. 65 Q4
Millaa Millaa Australia 110 D3
Millárs r. Spain 57 F4
Millau France 56 F4
Millbrook Canada 135 F1
Mill Creek r. U.S.A. 128 B1
Milledgeville U.S.A. 133 D5
Mille Lacs lakes U.S.A. 130 E2
Mille Lacs, Lac des l. Canada 119 I5
Millen U.S.A. 133 D5
Millennium Island atoll Kiribati see Caroline Island
Miller U.S.A. 130 D2
Miller Lake Canada 134 E1
Millerovo Rus. Fed. 43 I6
Millersburg OH U.S.A. 134 E3
Millersburg PA U.S.A. 135 G3
Millers Creek U.S.A. 134 D5
Millersville U.S.A. 135 G4
Millerton Lake U.S.A. 128 D3
Millet Canada 120 H4
Milleur Point U.K. 50 D5
Mill Hall U.S.A. 135 G3
Millicent Australia 111 C8
Millington MI U.S.A. 134 D2
Millington TN U.S.A. 131 F5
Millinocket U.S.A. 132 G2
Mill Island Canada 119 K3
Millmerran Australia 112 E1
Millom U.K. 48 D4
Millport U.K. 50 E5
Millsboro U.S.A. 135 H4
Mills Creek watercourse Australia 110 C4
Mills Lake Canada 120 G2
Millstone KY U.S.A. 134 D5
Millstone WV U.S.A. 134 E4
Millstream-Chichester National Park Australia 108 B5
Millthorpe Australia 112 D4
Milltown Canada 123 I5
Milltown U.S.A. 126 E3
Milltown Malbay Rep. of Ireland 51 C5
Millungera Australia 110 C3
Millville U.S.A. 135 H4
Millwood U.S.A. 134 B5
Millwood Lake U.S.A. 131 E5
Milly Milly Australia 109 B6
Milne Land i. Greenland see Ilimananngip Nunaa
Milner U.S.A. 129 J1
Milo r. Guinea 96 C3
Milogradovo Rus. Fed. 74 D4
Miloli'i HI U.S.A. 127 [inset]
Milos i. Greece 59 K6
Milparinka Australia 111 C6
Milpitas U.S.A. 128 C3
Milroy U.S.A. 135 G3
Milton N.Z. 113 B8
Milton DE U.S.A. 135 H4
Milton NH U.S.A. 135 J2
Milton WV U.S.A. 134 D4
Milton Keynes U.K. 49 G6
Miluo China 77 G2
Milverton Canada 134 E2
Milwaukee U.S.A. 134 B2

▶Milwaukee Deep sea feature Caribbean Sea 148 D4
Deepest point in the Atlantic Ocean (Puerto Rico Trench).

Mimbres watercourse U.S.A. 129 J5
Mimili Australia 109 F6
Mimisal India 84 C4
Mimizan France 56 D4
Mimongo Gabon 98 B4
Mimosa Rocks National Park Australia 112 E6
Mina Mex. 131 C7
Mina U.S.A. 128 D2
Mīnāb Iran 88 E5
Minaçu Brazil 145 A1
Minahasa, Semenanjung pen. Indon. 69 G6
Minahassa Peninsula Indon. see Minahasa, Semenanjung
Minaker Canada see Prophet River
Mīnākh Syria 85 C1
Minaki Canada 121 M5
Minamia Australia 108 F3
Minami-Daitō-jima i. Japan 73 O7
Minami-Iō-jima vol. Japan 69 K2
Min'an China see Longshan
Minaret of Jam tourist site Afgh. 89 G3
Minas Indon. 71 C7
Minas Uruguay 144 E4
Minas de Matahambre Cuba 133 D8
Minas Gerais state Brazil 145 B2
Minas Novas Brazil 145 C2
Minatitlán Mex. 136 F5
Minbu Myanmar 70 A2
Minbya Myanmar 70 A2
Minchinmávida vol. Chile 144 B6
Mindanao i. Phil. 69 H5
Mindanao Trench sea feature N. Pacific Ocean see Philippine Trench
Mindelo Cape Verde 96 [inset]
Minden Canada 135 F1
Minden Germany 53 I2
Minden LA U.S.A. 131 E5
Minden NE U.S.A. 124 H3
Minden NV U.S.A. 128 D2
Mindon Myanmar 70 A3
Mindoro i. Phil. 69 G4
Mindoro Strait Phil. 69 F4
Mindouli Congo 98 B4
Mine Head hd Rep. of Ireland 51 E6
Minehead U.K. 49 D7
Mineola U.S.A. 135 I3
Mineral U.S.A. 135 G4
Mineral'nyye Vody Rus. Fed. 91 F1
Mineral Wells U.S.A. 131 D5
Mineralwells U.S.A. 134 E4
Minersville PA U.S.A. 135 G3
Minersville UT U.S.A. 129 G2
Minerva U.S.A. 134 E3
Minerva Reefs Fiji 107 I4
Minfeng China 83 E1
Minga Dem. Rep. Congo 99 C5
Mingäçevir Azer. 91 G2
Mingäçevir Su Anbarı resr Azer. 91 G2
Mingala Cent. Afr. Rep. 98 C3
Mingan, Îles de is Canada 123 J4
Mingan Archipelago National Park Reserve Canada see L'Archipélago de Mingan, Réserve du Parc National de
Mingbulak Uzbek. 80 B3
Mingechaur Azer. see Mingäçevir
Mingechaurskoye Vodokhranilishche resr Azer. see Mingäçevir Su Anbarı
Mingenew Australia 109 A7
Mingfeng China see Yuan'an
Minggang China 77 G1
Mingguang China 77 H1
Mingin Range mts Myanmar 70 A2
Minglanilla Spain 57 F4
Mingoyo Tanz. 99 D5
Mingshan China 76 D2
Mingshui Gansu China 80 I3
Mingshui Heilong. China 74 B3
Mingteke China 82 C1
Mingulay i. U.K. 50 B4
Mingxi China 77 H3
Mingzhou China see Suide
Minhe China see Jinxian
Minhla Magwe Myanmar 70 A3
Minhla Pegu Myanmar 70 A3
Minho r. Port./Spain see Miño
Minicoy atoll India 84 B4
Minigwal, Lake salt flat Australia 109 C7
Minilya Australia 109 A5
Minilya r. Australia 109 A5
Minipi Lake Canada 123 J3
Miniss Lake Canada 121 N5
Minitonas Canada 121 K4
Minjian China see Mabian
Min Jiang r. Sichuan China 76 E2
Min Jiang r. China 77 H3
Minna Nigeria 96 D4
Minna Bluff pt Antarctica 152 H1
Minne Sweden 44 I5
Minneapolis KS U.S.A. 130 D4
Minneapolis MN U.S.A. 130 E2
Minnedosa Canada 121 L5
Minnehaha Springs U.S.A. 134 F4
Minneola U.S.A. 131 C4
Minnesota r. U.S.A. 130 E2
Minnesota state U.S.A. 130 E2
Minnewaukan U.S.A. 130 D1
Minnitaki Lake Canada 121 N5
Miño r. Port./Spain 57 B3
also known as Minho
Minorca i. Spain 57 H3
Minot U.S.A. 130 C1
Minqār, Ghadīr imp. l. Syria 85 C3
Minqing China 77 H3
Minquan China 77 G1
Min Shan mts China 76 D1
Minsin Myanmar 70 A1

▶Minsk Belarus 45 O10
Capital of Belarus.

Mińsk Mazowiecki Poland 47 R4
Minsterley U.K. 49 E6
Mintaka Pass China/Jammu and Kashmir 82 C1
Minto, Lac l. Canada 122 G2
Minto, Mount Antarctica 152 H2
Minto Inlet Canada 118 G2
Minton Canada 121 J5
Mīnudasht Iran 88 D2
Minūf Egypt 90 C5
Minusinsk Rus. Fed. 72 G2
Minvoul Gabon 98 B3
Minxian China 76 E1
Minya Konka mt. China see Gongga Shan
Minywa Myanmar 70 A2
Minzong India 83 I4
Mio U.S.A. 134 C1
Miquelon Canada 122 F4
Miquelon i. St Pierre and Miquelon 123 K5
Mirabad Afgh. 89 F4
Mirabel airport Canada 122 G5
Mirabela Brazil 145 B2
Mirador, Parque Nacional de nat. park Brazil 143 I5
Mīrah, Wādī al watercourse Iraq/Saudi Arabia 91 F4
Miraí Brazil 145 C3
Miraj India 84 B2
Miramar Arg. 144 E5
Miramichi Canada 123 I5
Miramichi Bay Canada 123 I5
Mirampelou, Kolpos b. Greece 59 K7
Miranda Brazil 144 E2
Miranda Moz. see Macaloge
Miranda U.S.A. 128 B1
Miranda, Lake salt flat Australia 109 C6
Miranda de Ebro Spain 57 E2
Mirandela Port. 57 C3
Mirandola Italy 58 D2
Mirante Brazil 145 C1
Mirante, Serra do hills Brazil 145 A3
Mirassol Brazil 145 A3
Mir-Bashir Azer. see Tärtär
Mirbāṭ Oman 87 H6
Mirboo North Australia 112 C7
Mirepoix France 56 E5
Mirgarh Pak. 89 I4
Mirgorod Ukr. see Myrhorod
Miri Sarawak Malaysia 68 E6
Miri mt. Pak. 89 F4
Mirialguda India 84 C2
Miri Hills India 83 H4
Mirim, Lagoa l. Brazil/Uruguay 144 F4
Mirim, Lagoa do l. Brazil 145 A5
Mirintu watercourse Australia 112 A2
Mirjan India 84 B3
Mirny research station Antarctica 152 F2
Mirnyy Arkhangel'skaya Oblast' Rus. Fed. 42 I3
Mirnyy Respublika Sakha (Yakutiya) Rus. Fed. 65 M3
Mirond Lake Canada 121 K4
Mironovka Ukr. see Myronivka
Mirow Germany 53 M1
Mirpur Khas Pak. 89 H5
Mirpur Sakro Pak. 89 G5
Mirs Bay Hong Kong China 77 [inset]
Mirtoan Sea Greece see Mirtoö Pelagos
Mirtoö Pelagos sea Greece 59 J6
Miryalaguda India see Mirialguda
Miryang S. Korea 75 C6
Mirzachirla Turkm. see Murzechirla
Mirzachul Uzbek. see Gulistan
Mirzapur India 83 E4
Mirzawal India 82 C3
Misaw Lake Canada 121 K3
Miscou Island Canada 123 I5
Misehkow r. Canada 122 C4
Mīsh, Kūh-e hill Iran 88 E3
Misha India 71 A6
Mishāsh al Ashāwī well Saudi Arabia 88 C5
Mishāsh az Ẓuayyinī well Saudi Arabia 88 C5
Mishawaka U.S.A. 134 B3
Mishicot U.S.A. 134 B1
Mi-shima i. Japan 75 C6
Mishmi Hills India 83 H3
Mishvan' Rus. Fed. 42 L2
Misima Island P.N.G. 110 F1
Misis Dağ hills Turkey 85 B1
Miskin Oman 88 E6
Miskitos, Cayos is Nicaragua 137 H6
Miskolc Hungary 43 D6
Mismā, Tall al hill Jordan 85 C3
Misoöl i. Indon. 69 I7
Misquah Hills U.S.A. 130 F2
Misr country Africa see Egypt
Misraç Turkey see Kurtalan
Miṣrātah Libya 97 E1
Missinaibi r. Canada 122 E4
Mission Beach Australia 110 D3
Mission Viejo U.S.A. 128 E5
Missisa r. Canada 122 D3
Missisa Lake Canada 122 D3
Missisicabi r. Canada 122 F4
Mississauga Canada 134 F2
Mississinewa Lake U.S.A. 134 C3

▶Mississippi r. U.S.A. 131 F6
4th longest river in North America. Part of the longest (Mississippi-Missouri).

Mississippi state U.S.A. 131 F5
Mississippi Delta U.S.A. 131 F6
Mississippi Lake Canada 135 G1

▶Mississippi-Missouri r. U.S.A. 125 I4
Longest river and largest drainage basin in North America and 4th longest river in the world.
North America 114–115
World 12–13

Mississippi Sound sea chan. U.S.A. 131 F6
Missolonghi Greece see Mesolongi
Missoula U.S.A. 126 E3

▶Missouri r. U.S.A. 130 F4
3rd longest river in North America. Part of the longest (Mississippi-Missouri).

Missouri state U.S.A. 130 E4
Mistanipisipou r. Canada 123 J4
Mistassibi r. Canada 119 K5
Mistassini Canada 123 G4
Mistassini r. Canada 123 G4
Mistassini, Lac l. Canada 122 G4
Mistastin Lake Canada 123 J3
Mistelbach Austria 47 P6
Mistinibi, Lac l. Canada 123 J2
Mistissini Canada 122 G4
Misty Fiords National Monument Wilderness nat. park U.S.A. 120 D4
Misumba Dem. Rep. Congo 99 C4
Misuratah Libya see Miṣrātah
Mitchell Australia 111 D5
Mitchell r. N.S.W. Australia 112 F2
Mitchell r. Qld Australia 110 C2
Mitchell r. Vic. Australia 112 C6
Mitchell Canada 134 E2
Mitchell IN U.S.A. 134 B4
Mitchell OR U.S.A. 126 C3
Mitchell SD U.S.A. 130 D3
Mitchell, Lake Australia 110 D3
Mitchell, Mount U.S.A. 132 D5
Mitchell and Alice Rivers National Park Australia 110 C2
Mitchell Island Cook Is see Nassau
Mitchell Island atoll Tuvalu see Nukulaelae
Mitchell Point Australia 108 E2
Mitchelstown Rep. of Ireland 51 D5
Mīt Ghamr Egypt see Mīt Ghamr
Mīt Ghamr Egypt 90 C5
Mithi Pak. 89 H5
Mithrau Pak. 89 H5
Mitilíni Greece see Mytilini
Mitkof Island U.S.A. 120 C3
Mito Japan 75 F5
Mitole Tanz. 99 D4
Mitre mt. N.Z. 113 E5
Mitre Island Solomon Is 107 H3
Mitrofanovka Rus. Fed. 43 H6
Mitrovica Serb. and Mont. see Kosovska Mitrovica
Mitrovicë Serb. and Mont. see Kosovska Mitrovica
Mitsinjo Madag. 99 E5
Mits'iwa Eritrea see Massawa
Mitta Mitta Australia 112 C6
Mittellandkanal canal Germany 53 I2
Mitterteich Germany 53 M5
Mittimatalik Canada see Pond Inlet
Mittweida Germany 53 M4
Mitú Col. 142 D3
Mitumba, Chaîne des mts Dem. Rep. Congo 99 C5
Mitzic Gabon 98 B3
Miughalaigh i. U.K. see Mingulay
Miura Japan 75 E6
Mixian China see Xinmi
Miyake-jima i. Japan 75 E6
Miyako Japan 75 F5
Miyakonojō Japan 75 C7
Miyang China see Mile
Miyani India 82 B5
Miyazaki Japan 75 C7
Miyazu Japan 75 D6
Miyi China 76 D3
Miyoshi Japan 75 D6
Mīzāni Afgh. 89 G3
Mīzan Teferī Eth. 98 D3
Mizdah Libya 97 E1
Mizen Head hd Rep. of Ireland 51 C6
Mizhhir"ya Ukr. 43 D6
Mizo Hills state India see Mizoram
Mizoram state India 83 H5
Mizpe Ramon Israel 85 B4
Mizusawa Japan 75 F5
Mjölby Sweden 45 I7
Mkata Tanz. 99 D4
Mkushi Zambia 99 C5
Mladá Boleslav Czech Rep. 47 O5
Mladenovac Serb. and Mont. 59 I2
Mława Poland 47 R4
Mlilwane Nature Reserve Swaziland 101 J4
Mljet i. Croatia 58 G3
Mlungisi S. Africa 101 H6
Mmabatho S. Africa 101 G3
Mmamabula Botswana 101 H2
Mmathethe Botswana 101 G3
Mo Norway 45 D6
Moa i. Indon. 108 E2
Moab reg. Jordan 85 B4
Moab U.S.A. 129 I2
Moa Island Australia 110 C1
Moala i. Fiji 107 H3
Mo'alla Iran 88 D3
Moamba Moz. 101 K3
Moanda Gabon 98 B4
Moapa U.S.A. 129 F3
Moate Rep. of Ireland 51 E4
Mobārakeh Iran 88 C3
Mobayembongo Dem. Rep. Congo see Mobayi-Mbongo
Mobayi-Mbongo Dem. Rep. Congo 98 C3
Moberly U.S.A. 130 E4
Moberly Lake Canada 120 F4
Mobha India 82 C5
Mobile AL U.S.A. 131 F6
Mobile AZ U.S.A. 129 G5
Mobile Bay U.S.A. 131 F6
Moble watercourse Australia 112 B1
Mobridge U.S.A. 130 C2
Mobutu, Lake Dem. Rep. Congo/Uganda see Albert, Lake
Mobutu Sese Seko, Lake Dem. Rep. Congo/Uganda see Albert, Lake
Moca Geçidi pass Turkey 85 A1
Moçambique country Africa see Mozambique
Moçambique Moz. 99 E5
Moçâmedes Angola see Namibe
Môc Châu Vietnam 70 D2
Mocha Yemen 86 F7
Mocha, Isla i. Chile 144 B5
Mochirma, Parque Nacional nat. park Venez. 142 F1
Mochudi Botswana 101 H3
Mochudi admin. dist. Botswana see Kgatleng
Mocimboa da Praia Moz. 99 E5
Möckern Germany 53 L2
Möckmühl Germany 53 J5
Mockträsk Sweden 44 L4
Mocoa Col. 142 C3
Mococa Brazil 145 B3
Mocoduene Moz. 101 L2
Mocorito Mex. 127 G8
Moctezuma Chihuahua Mex. 127 G7
Moctezuma San Luis Potosí Mex. 136 D4
Moctezuma Sonora Mex. 127 F7
Mocuba Moz. 99 D5
Mocun China 77 G4
Modan Indon. 69 I7
Modane France 56 H4
Modder r. S. Africa 101 G5
Modena Italy 58 D2
Modena U.S.A. 129 G3
Modesto U.S.A. 128 C3
Modesto Lake U.S.A. 128 C3
Modot Mongolia 73 J3
Modung China 76 C2
Moe Australia 112 C7
Moel Sych hill U.K. 49 D6
Moelv Norway 45 G6
Moen Norway 44 K2
Moenjodaro tourist site Pak. 89 H5
Moenkopi U.S.A. 129 H3
Moenkopi Wash r. U.S.A. 129 H4
Moeraki Point N.Z. 113 C7
Moero, Lake Dem. Rep. Congo/Zambia see Mweru, Lake
Moers Germany 52 G3
Moffat U.K. 50 F5
Moga India 82 C3

▶Mogadishu Somalia 98 E3
Capital of Somalia.

Mogador Morocco see Essaouira
Mogadore Reservoir U.S.A. 134 E3
Moganyaka S. Africa 101 I3
Mogaung Myanmar 70 B1
Mogdy Rus. Fed. 74 D2
Mögelin Germany 53 M2
Mogilev Belarus see Mahilyow
Mogilev Podol'skiy Ukr. see Mohyliv Podil's'kyy
Mogi-Mirim Brazil 145 B3
Mogiquiçaba Brazil 145 D2
Mogocha Rus. Fed. 73 L2
Mogod mts Tunisia 58 C6
Mogoditshane Botswana 101 G3
Mogollon Mountains U.S.A. 125 I5
Mogollon Plateau U.S.A. 129 H4
Mogontiacum Germany see Mainz
Mogroum Chad 97 E3
Moguqi China 74 A3
Mogwadi S. Africa see Dendron
Mogwase S. Africa 101 H3
Mogzon Rus. Fed. 73 K2
Mohács Hungary 58 H2
Mohaka r. N.Z. 113 F4
Mohala India 84 D1
Mohale Dam Lesotho 101 I5
Mohale's Hoek Lesotho 101 H6
Mohall U.S.A. 130 C1
Mohammad Iran 88 E3
Mohammadia Alg. 57 G6
Mohan r. India/Nepal 82 E3
Mohana India 82 D4
Mohave, Lake U.S.A. 129 F4
Mohawk r. U.S.A. 135 I2
Mohawk Mountains U.S.A. 129 G5
Moher, Cliffs of Rep. of Ireland 51 C5
Mohill Rep. of Ireland 51 E4
Möhne r. Germany 53 H3
Möhnetalsperre resr Germany 53 I3
Mohon Peak U.S.A. 129 G4
Mohoro Tanz. 99 D4
Mohyliv Podil's'kyy Ukr. 43 E6
Moi Norway 45 E7
Moijabana Botswana 101 H2
Moincêr China 82 E3
Moinda China 83 G3
Moine Moz. 101 K3
Moinești Romania 59 L1
Mointy Kazakh. see Moyynty
Mo i Rana Norway 44 I3
Moirang India 76 B3
Mõisaküla Estonia 45 N7
Moisie Canada 123 I4
Moisie r. Canada 123 I4
Moissac France 56 E4
Mojave U.S.A. 128 D4
Mojave r. U.S.A. 128 E4
Mojave Desert U.S.A. 128 E4
Mojiang China 76 D4
Moji das Cruzes Brazil 145 B3
Mojos, Llanos de plain Bol. 142 E6
Moju r. Brazil 143 I4
Mokama India 83 F4
Mokau N.Z. 113 E4
Mokau r. N.Z. 113 E4
Mokelumne r. U.S.A. 128 C2
Mokelumne Aqueduct canal U.S.A. 128 C2
Mokhoabong Pass Lesotho 101 I5
Mokhotlong Lesotho 101 I5
Mokhtārān Iran 88 E3
Moknine Tunisia 58 D7
Mokohinau Islands N.Z. 113 E2
Mokokchung India 83 H4
Mokolo Cameroon 97 E3
Mokolo r. S. Africa 101 H2
Mokp'o S. Korea 75 B6
Mokrous Rus. Fed. 43 J6
Moksha r. Rus. Fed. 43 I5
Mokshan Rus. Fed. 43 J5
Möksy Fin. 44 N5
Môktama Myanmar see Martaban
Môktama, Gulf of Myanmar see Martaban, Gulf of
Mokundurra India see Mukandwara
Mokwa Nigeria 96 D4
Molatón mt. Spain 57 F4
Moldavia country Europe see Moldova
Moldavskaya S.S.R. country Europe see Moldova
Molde Norway 44 E5
Moldjord Norway 44 I3
▶Moldova country Europe 43 F7
Europe 5, 38–39

Moldoveanu, Vârful mt. Romania 59 K2
Moldovei de Sud, Cîmpia plain Moldova 59 M1
Molega Lake Canada 123 I5
Molen r. S. Africa 101 I4
Mole National Park Ghana 96 C4
Molepolole Botswana 101 G3
Molėtai Lith. 45 N9
Molfetta Italy 58 G4
Molière Alg. see Bordj Bounaama
Molihong Shan mt. China see Morihong Shan
Molina de Aragón Spain 57 F3
Moline U.S.A. 131 D4
Molkom Sweden 45 H7
Mollagara Turkm. see Mollakara
Mollakara Turkm. 88 D2
Mol Len mt. India 83 H4
Möllenbeck Germany 53 N1
Mollendo Peru 142 D7
Mölln Germany 53 K1
Mölnlycke Sweden 45 H8
Molochnyy Rus. Fed. 44 R2
Molodechno Belarus see Maladzyechna
Molodezhnaya research station Antarctica 152 D2
Molokai i. HI U.S.A. 127 [inset]
Moloma r. Rus. Fed. 42 K4
Molong Australia 112 D4
Molopo watercourse Botswana/S. Africa 100 E5
Molotov Rus. Fed. see Perm'
Molotovsk Kyrg. see Kayyngdy
Molotovsk Arkhangel'skaya Oblast' Rus. Fed. see Severodvinsk
Molotovsk Kirovskaya Oblast' Rus. Fed. see Nolinsk
Moloundou Cameroon 97 E4
Molson Lake Canada 121 L4
Molu i. Indon. 69 I8
Moluccas is Indon. 69 H7
Molucca Sea sea Indon. see Maluku, Laut
Moma Moz. 99 D5
Momba Australia 112 A3
Mombaça Brazil 143 K5
Mombasa Kenya 98 D4
Mombetsu Hokkaidō Japan see Monbetsu
Mombetsu Hokkaidō Japan see Monbetsu
Mombi New India 83 H4
Mombum Indon. 69 J8
Momchilgrad Bulg. 59 K4
Momence U.S.A. 134 B3
Momi, Ra's pt Yemen 87 H7
Mompós Col. 142 D2
Møn i. Denmark 45 H9
Mon India 83 H4
Mona terr. Irish Sea see Isle of Man
Mona U.S.A. 129 H2
Monaca U.S.A. 134 E3
Monach, Sound of sea chan. U.K. 50 B3
Monach Islands U.K. 50 B3
▶Monaco country Europe 56 H5
Europe 5, 38–39
Monaco Basin sea feature N. Atlantic Ocean 148 G4
Monadhliath Mountains U.K. 50 E3
Monaghan Rep. of Ireland 51 F3
Monahans U.S.A. 131 C6
Mona Passage Dom. Rep./Puerto Rico 137 K5
Monapo Moz. 99 E5
Monar, Loch l. U.K. 50 D3
Monarch Mountain Canada 120 E5
Monarch Pass U.S.A. 127 G5
Mona Reservoir U.S.A. 129 H2
Monashee Mountains Canada 120 G5
Monastir Macedonia see Bitola
Monastir Tunisia 58 D7
Monastyrishche Ukr. see Monastyryshche
Monastyryshche Ukr. 43 F6
Monbetsu Hokkaidō Japan 74 F3
Monbetsu Hokkaidō Japan 74 F4
Moncalieri Italy 58 B2
Monchegorsk Rus. Fed. 44 R3
Mönchengladbach Germany 52 G3
Monchique Port. 57 B5
Moncks Corner U.S.A. 133 D5
Monclova Mex. 131 C7
Moncouche, Lac l. Canada 123 H4
Moncton Canada 123 I5
Mondego r. Port. 57 B3
Mondlo S. Africa 101 J4
Mondo Chad 97 E3
Mondovì Italy 58 B2
Mondragone Italy 58 E4
Mondy Rus. Fed. 72 I2
Monemvasia Greece 59 J6
Monessen U.S.A. 134 F3
Moneta U.S.A. 126 G4
Moneygall Rep. of Ireland 51 E5
Moneymore U.K. 51 F3
Monfalcone Italy 58 E2
Monfalut Egypt see Manfalūṭ
Monforte Spain 57 C2
Monga Dem. Rep. Congo 98 C3
Mongala r. Dem. Rep. Congo 98 B3
Mongar Bhutan 83 G4
Mongbwalu Dem. Rep. Congo 98 D3
Mông Cai Vietnam 70 D2
Mongers Lake salt flat Australia 109 B7
Mong Hang Myanmar 70 B2
Mong Hkan Myanmar 70 C2
Mong Hpayak Myanmar 70 B2
Mong Hsat Myanmar 70 B2
Mong Hsawk Myanmar 70 B2
Mong Hsu Myanmar 70 B2
Monghyr India see Munger
Mong Kung Myanmar 70 B2
Mong Kyawt Myanmar 70 B3
Mongla Bangl. 83 G5
Mong Lin Myanmar 70 C2
Mong Loi Myanmar 70 C2
Mong Long Myanmar 70 B2
Mong Nai Myanmar 70 B2
Mong Nawng Myanmar 70 B2
Mongo Chad 97 E3
▶Mongolia country Asia 72 I3
Asia 6, 62–63
Mongol Uls country Asia see Mongolia
Mongonu Nigeria 96 E3
Mongora Pak. 89 I3
Mongour hill U.K. 50 G4
Mong Pan Myanmar 70 B2
Mong Ping Myanmar 70 B2
Mong Pu Myanmar 70 B2
Mong Pu-awn Myanmar 70 B2
Mong Si Myanmar 70 B2
Mongu Zambia 99 C5
Mong Un Myanmar 70 C2
Mong Yai Myanmar 70 B2
Mong Yang Myanmar 70 B2
Mong Yawn Myanmar 70 B2
Mong Yawng Myanmar 70 C2
Mönh Hayrhan Uul mt. Mongolia 80 H2
Moniaive U.K. 50 F5
Monitor Mountain U.S.A. 128 E2
Monitor Range mts U.S.A. 128 E2
Monivea Rep. of Ireland 51 D4
Monkey Bay Malawi 99 D5
Monkira Australia 110 C5
Monkton Canada 134 E2
Monmouth U.K. 49 E7
Monmouth U.S.A. 130 F3
Monmouth Mountain Canada 120 F5
Monnow r. U.K. 49 E7
Mono, Punta del pt Nicaragua 137 H6
Mono Lake U.S.A. 128 D2
Monolithos Greece 59 L6
Monomoy Point U.S.A. 135 J3
Monon U.S.A. 134 B3
Monopoli Italy 58 G4
Monreal del Campo Spain 57 F3
Monreale Sicily Italy 58 E5
Monroe IN U.S.A. 134 C3
Monroe LA U.S.A. 131 E5
Monroe MI U.S.A. 134 D3
Monroe NC U.S.A. 133 D5
Monroe WI U.S.A. 130 F3
Monroe Center U.S.A. 130 F2
Monroe Lake U.S.A. 134 B4
Monroeton U.S.A. 135 G3

▶Monrovia Liberia 96 B4
Capital of Liberia.

Mons Belgium 52 D4
Monschau Germany 52 G4
Monselice Italy 58 D2
Montabaur Germany 53 H4
Montagu S. Africa 100 E7
Montague Canada 123 J5
Montague MI U.S.A. 134 B2
Montague TX U.S.A. 131 D5
Montague Range hills Australia 109 B6
Montalto mt. Italy 58 F5
Montalto Uffugo Italy 58 G5
Montana Bulg. 59 J3
Montana state U.S.A. 126 F3
Montargis France 56 F3
Montauban France 56 E4
Montauk U.S.A. 135 J3
Montauk Point U.S.A. 135 J3
Mont-aux-Sources mt. Lesotho 101 I5
Montbard France 56 G3
Montblanc Spain 57 G3
Montblanch Spain see Montblanc
Montbrison France 56 G4
Montceau-les-Mines France 56 G3
Montcornet France 52 E5
Mont-de-Marsan France 56 D5
Montdidier France 52 C5
Monte Alegre Brazil 143 H4
Monte Alegre de Goiás Brazil 145 B1
Monte Alegre de Minas Brazil 145 A2
Monte Azul Brazil 145 C1
Monte Azul Paulista Brazil 145 A3
Montebello Canada 122 G5
Montebello Islands Australia 104 A5
Montebelluna Italy 58 E2
Monte-Carlo Monaco 56 H5
Monte Christo S. Africa 101 H2
Monte Cristi Dom. Rep. 137 J5
Monte Dourado Brazil 143 H4
Monte Falterona, Campigna e delle Foreste Casentinesi, Parco Nazionale del nat. park Italy 58 D3
Montego Bay Jamaica 137 I5
Montélimar France 56 G4
Monte Lindo r. Para. 144 E2
Montello U.S.A. 130 F3
Montemorelos Mex. 131 D7
Montemor-o-Novo Port. 57 B4
Montenegro aut. rep. Serb. and Mont. see Crna Gora
Montepulciano Italy 58 D3
Monte Quemado Arg. 144 D3
Montereau-faut-Yonne France 56 F2
Monterey Mex. see Monterrey
Monterey CA U.S.A. 128 C3
Monterey VA U.S.A. 134 F4
Monterey Bay U.S.A. 128 B3
Montería Col. 142 C2
Monteros Arg. 144 C3
Monterrey Baja California Mex. 129 F5
Monterrey Nuevo León Mex. 131 C7
Montervary hd Rep. of Ireland 51 C6
Montesano U.S.A. 126 C3
Montesano sulla Marcellana Italy 58 F4
Monte Santo Brazil 143 K6
Monte Santu, Capo di c. Sardinia Italy 58 C4
Montes Claros Brazil 145 C2
Montesilvano Italy 58 F3
Montevarchi Italy 58 D3

▶Montevideo Uruguay 144 E4
Capital of Uruguay.

Montevideo U.S.A. 130 E2
Montezuma U.S.A. 130 E3
Montezuma Creek U.S.A. 129 I3
Montezuma Peak U.S.A. 128 E3
Montfort Neth. 52 F3
Montgomery U.K. 49 D6

▶Montgomery AL U.S.A. 133 C5
State capital of Alabama.

Montgomery WV U.S.A. 134 E4
Montgomery Islands Australia 108 C3
Monthey Switz. 56 H3
Monticello AR U.S.A. 131 F5
Monticello FL U.S.A. 133 D6
Monticello IN U.S.A. 134 B3
Monticello KY U.S.A. 134 C5
Monticello MO U.S.A. 130 F3
Monticello NY U.S.A. 135 H3
Monticello UT U.S.A. 129 I3
Montignac France 56 E4
Montignies-le-Tilleul Belgium 52 E4
Montigny-lès-Metz France 52 G5
Montilla Spain 57 D5
Monti Sibillini, Parco Nazionale dei nat. park Italy 58 E3
Montividiu Brazil 145 A2
Montivilliers France 49 H9
Mont-Joli Canada 123 H4
Mont-Laurier Canada 122 G5
Montluçon France 56 F3
Montmagny Canada 123 H5
Montmédy France 52 F5
Montmirail France 52 D6
Montmorillon France 56 E3
Montmort-Lucy France 52 D6
Monto Australia 110 E5
Montour Falls U.S.A. 135 G2
Montoursville U.S.A. 135 G3
Montpelier ID U.S.A. 126 F4

▶Montpelier VT U.S.A. 135 I1
State capital of Vermont.

Montpellier France 56 F5
Montréal Canada 122 G5
Montreal r. Ont. Canada 122 D5
Montreal r. Ont. Canada 122 F5
Montreal Lake Canada 121 J4
Montreal Lake l. Canada 121 J4
Montreal River Canada 122 D5
Montreuil France 52 B4
Montreux Switz. 56 H3
Montrose well S. Africa 100 E4
Montrose U.K. 50 G4
Montrose CO U.S.A. 129 J2
Montrose PA U.S.A. 135 H3
Montross U.S.A. 135 G4
Monts, Pointe des pt Canada 123 I4

▶Montserrat terr. West Indies 137 L5
United Kingdom Overseas Territory.
North America 9, 116–117

Mont-St-Aignan France 49 I9
Montviel, Lac l. Canada 123 H3
Monument Valley reg. U.S.A. 129 H3
Monywa Myanmar 70 A2
Monza Italy 58 C2
Monze, Cape pt Pak. see Muari, Ras
Monzón Spain 57 G3
Mooi r. S. Africa 101 J5
Mooifontein Namibia 100 C4
Mookane Botswana 101 H2
Mookgopong S. Africa see Naboomspruit
Moolawatana Australia 111 B6
Moomba Australia 111 C6
Moomin Creek r. Australia 112 D2
Moonaree Australia 111 A6
Moonbi Range mts Australia 112 E3
Moonda Lake salt flat Australia 111 C5
Moonie Australia 112 E1
Moonie r. Australia 112 D2
Moora Australia 109 B7
Mooraberree Australia 110 C5
Moorcroft U.S.A. 126 G3
Moore r. Australia 109 A7
Moore U.S.A. 126 F3
Moore, Lake salt flat Australia 109 B7
Moore Embayment b. Antarctica 152 H1
Moorefield U.S.A. 135 F4
Moore Haven U.S.A. 133 D7
Moore Reef Australia 110 E3
Moore Reservoir U.S.A. 135 J1
Moore River National Park Australia 109 A7
Moores Island Bahamas 133 E7
Moorfoot Hills U.K. 50 F5
Moorhead U.S.A. 130 D2
Moorman U.S.A. 134 B5
Moornanyah Lake imp. l. Australia 112 A4
Mooroopna Australia 112 B6
Moorreesburg S. Africa 100 D7
Moorrinya National Park Australia 110 D4
Moose r. Canada 122 E4
Moose Factory Canada 122 E4
Moosehead Lake U.S.A. 132 G2
Moose Jaw Canada 121 J5
Moose Jaw r. Canada 121 J5
Moose Lake U.S.A. 130 E2
Mooselookmeguntic Lake U.S.A. 135 J1
Moose Mountain Creek r. Canada 121 K5
Moosilauke, Mount U.S.A. 135 J1
Moosomin Canada 121 K5
Moosonee Canada 122 E4
Mootwingee National Park Australia 111 C6
Mopane S. Africa 101 I2
Mopeia Moz. 99 D5
Mopipi Botswana 99 C6
Mopti Mali 96 C3
Moqor Afgh. 89 G3
Moquegua Peru 142 D7
Mora Cameroon 97 E3
Mora Spain 57 E4
Mora Sweden 45 I6
Mora MN U.S.A. 130 E2
Mora NM U.S.A. 127 G6
Mora r. U.S.A. 127 G6
Moradabad India 82 D3
Morada Nova Brazil 143 K5
Moraine Lake Canada 121 J1
Moraleda, Canal sea chan. Chile 144 B6
Moram India 84 C2
Moramanga Madag. 99 E5
Moran U.S.A. 126 F4
Moranbah Australia 110 E4
Morang Nepal see Biratnagar
Morar, Loch l. U.K. 50 D4
Morari, Tso l. Jammu and Kashmir 82 D2
Moratuwa Sri Lanka 84 C5
Moravia reg. Czech Rep. 47 P6
Moravia U.S.A. 135 G2
Morawa Australia 109 A7
Moray Firth b. U.K. 50 E3
Moray Range hills Australia 108 E3
Morbach Germany 52 H5
Morbeng S. Africa see Soekmekaar
Morbi India 82 B5
Morcenx France 56 D4
Morcillo Mex. 131 B7
Mordaga China 73 M2
Mor Dağı mt. Turkey 91 G3
Morden Canada 121 L5
Mordovo Rus. Fed. 43 I5
Moreau r. U.S.A. 130 C2
Moreau, South Fork r. U.S.A. 130 C2
Morecambe U.K. 48 E4
Morecambe Bay U.K. 48 D4
Moree Australia 112 D2
Morehead P.N.G. 69 K8
Morehead U.S.A. 134 D4
Morehead City U.S.A. 137 I2
Moreland U.S.A. 134 C5
More Laptevykh sea Rus. Fed. see Laptev Sea
Morelia Mex. 136 D5
Morella Australia 110 C4
Morella Spain 57 F3
Morelos Mex. 127 G8
Morena India 82 D4
Morena, Sierra mts Spain 57 C5
Morenci AZ U.S.A. 129 I5
Morenci MI U.S.A. 134 C3
Moreni Romania 59 K2
Moreno Mex. 127 F7
Moreno Valley U.S.A. 128 E5
Moresby, Mount Canada 120 C4
Moresby Island Canada 120 C4
Moreswe Pan salt pan Botswana 100 G2
Moreton Bay Australia 112 F1
Moreton-in-Marsh U.K. 49 F7
Moreton Island Australia 112 F1
Moreton Island National Park Australia 112 F1
Moreuil France 52 C5
Morez France 56 H3
Morfou Cyprus 85 A2
Morfou Bay Cyprus 85 A2
Morgan U.S.A. 126 F4
Morgan City U.S.A. 131 F6
Morgan Hill U.S.A. 128 C3
Morganton U.S.A. 132 D5
Morgantown KY U.S.A. 134 B5
Morgantown WV U.S.A. 134 F4
Morgenzon S. Africa 101 I4
Morges Switz. 56 H3
Morhar r. India 83 F4
Mori China 80 H3
Mori Japan 74 F4
Moriah, Mount U.S.A. 129 F2
Moriarty's Range hills Australia 112 B2
Morice Lake Canada 120 E4
Morichal Col. 142 D3
Morihong Shan mt. China 74 B4
Morija Lesotho 101 H5
Morin Dawa China see Nirji
Moringen Germany 53 J3
Morioka Japan 75 F5
Moris Mex. 127 F7
Morisset Australia 112 E4
Moriyoshi-zan vol. Japan 75 F5
Morjärv Sweden 44 M3
Morjen r. Pak. 89 F4
Morki Rus. Fed. 42 K4
Morlaix France 56 C2
Morley U.K. 48 F5
Mormam Flat Dam U.S.A. 129 H5
Mormant France 52 C6
Mormon Lake U.S.A. 129 H4
Mormugao India see Marmagao
Morne Diablotins vol. Dominica 137 L5
Morney watercourse Australia 110 C5
Mornington, Isla i. Chile 144 A7
Mornington Abyssal Plain sea feature S. Atlantic Ocean 148 C9
Mornington Island Australia 110 B3
Mornington Peninsula National Park Australia 112 B7
Moro Pak. 89 G5
Moro U.S.A. 126 C3
Morobe P.N.G. 69 L8
▶Morocco country Africa 96 C1
Africa 7, 94–95
Morocco U.S.A. 134 B3
Morococala mt. Bol. 142 E7
Morogoro Tanz. 99 D4
Moro Gulf Phil. 69 G5
Morojaneng S. Africa 101 H5
Morokweng S. Africa 100 F4
Morombe Madag. 99 E6
Morón Cuba 133 E8
Mörön Mongolia 80 J2
Morondava Madag. 99 E6
Morón de la Frontera Spain 57 D5

▶Moroni Comoros 99 E5
Capital of the Comoros.

Moroni U.S.A. 129 H2
Moron Us He r. China see Tongtian He
Morotai i. Indon. 69 H6
Moroto Uganda 98 D3
Morozovsk Rus. Fed. 43 I6
Morpeth Canada 134 E2
Morpeth U.K. 48 F3
Morphou Cyprus see Morfou
Morrill U.S.A. 134 C5
Morrilton U.S.A. 131 E5
Morrin Canada 121 H5
Morrinhos Brazil 145 A2
Morris Canada 121 L5
Morris IL U.S.A. 130 F3
Morris MN U.S.A. 130 E2
Morris PA U.S.A. 135 G3

▶Morris Jesup, Kap c. Greenland 153 I1
Most northerly point of North America.

Morrison U.S.A. 130 F3
Morristown AZ U.S.A. 129 G5
Morristown NJ U.S.A. 135 H3
Morristown NY U.S.A. 135 H1
Morristown TN U.S.A. 132 D4
Morrisville U.S.A. 135 H2
Morro Brazil 145 B2
Morro Bay U.S.A. 128 C4
Morro d'Anta Brazil 145 D2
Morro do Chapéu Brazil 143 J6
Morro Grande hill Brazil 143 H4
Morrosquillo, Golfo de b. Col. 142 C2
Morrumbene Moz. 101 L2
Morschen Germany 53 J3
Morse Canada 121 J5
Morse U.S.A. 131 C4
Morse, Cape Antarctica 152 G2
Morse Reservoir U.S.A. 134 B3
Morshanka Rus. Fed. 43 I5
Morshansk Rus. Fed. see Morshanka
Morsott Alg. 58 C7
Mort watercourse Australia 110 C4
Mortagne-au-Perche France 56 E2
Mortagne-sur-Sèvre France 56 D3
Mortara Italy 58 C2
Mortehoe U.K. 49 C7
Morteros Arg. 144 D4
Mortes, Rio das r. Brazil 145 A1
Mortimer's Bahamas 133 F8
Mortlake Australia 112 A7
Mortlock Islands Micronesia 150 G5
Mortlock Islands P.N.G. see Tauu Islands
Morton U.K. 49 G6
Morton TX U.S.A. 131 C5
Morton WA U.S.A. 126 C3
Morton National Park Australia 112 E5
Morundah Australia 112 C5
Morupule Botswana 101 H2
Moruroa atoll Fr. Polynesia see Mururoa
Moruya Australia 112 E5
Morven Australia 111 D5
Morven hill U.K. 50 F2
Morvern reg. U.K. 50 D4
Morvi India see Morbi
Morwara India 82 B4
Morwell Australia 112 C7
Morzhovets, Ostrov i. Rus. Fed. 42 I2
Mosbach Germany 53 J5
Mosborough U.K. 48 F5
Mosby U.S.A. 126 G3

▶Moscow Rus. Fed. 42 H5
Capital of the Russian Federation and 3rd most populous city in Europe.

Moscow ID U.S.A. 126 D3
Moscow PA U.S.A. 135 H3
Moscow University Ice Shelf Antarctica 152 G2
Mosel r. Germany 53 H4
Moselebe watercourse Botswana 100 F3
Moselle r. France 52 G5
Möser Germany 53 L2
Moses, Mount U.S.A. 128 E1
Moses Lake U.S.A. 126 D3
Mosgiel N.Z. 113 C7
Moshaweng watercourse S. Africa 100 F4
Moshchnyy, Ostrov i. Rus. Fed. 45 O7
Moshi Tanz. 98 D4
Mosh'yuga Rus. Fed. 42 L2
Mosi-oa-Tunya waterfall Zambia/Zimbabwe see Victoria Falls
Mosjøen Norway 44 H4
Moskal'vo Rus. Fed. 74 F1
Moskenesøy i. Norway 44 H3
Moskva Rus. Fed. see Moscow
Moskva Tajik. 89 H2
Mosonmagyaróvár Hungary 47 P7
Mosquera Col. 142 C3
Mosquero U.S.A. 127 G6
Mosquito r. Brazil 145 C1
Mosquito Creek Lake U.S.A. 134 E3
Mosquito Lake Canada 121 K2
Moss Norway 45 G7
Mossâmedes Angola see Namibe
Mossat U.K. 50 G3
Mossburn N.Z. 113 B7
Mosselbaai S. Africa see Mossel Bay
Mossel Bay S. Africa 100 F8
Mossel Bay b. S. Africa 100 F8
Mossgiel Australia 112 B4
Mossman Australia 110 D3
Mossoró Brazil 143 K5
Moss Vale Australia 112 E5
Mossy r. Canada 121 K4
Most Czech Rep. 47 N5
Mostaganem Alg. 57 G6
Mostar Bos.-Herz. 58 G3
Mostoos Hills Canada 121 I4
Mostovskoy Rus. Fed. 91 F1
Mosty Belarus see Masty
Mosul Iraq 91 F3
Møsvatnet l. Norway 45 F7
Motala Sweden 45 I7
Motaze Moz. 101 K3
Motetema S. Africa 101 I3
Moth India 82 D4
Motherwell U.K. 50 F5
Motian Ling hill China 74 A4
Motihari India 83 F4
Motilla del Palancar Spain 57 F4
Motiti Island N.Z. 113 F3
Motokwe Botswana 100 F3
Motril Spain 57 E5
Motru Romania 59 J2
Mott U.S.A. 130 C2
Motu Ihupuku i. N.Z. see Campbell Island
Motul Mex. 136 G4
Mouaskar Alg. see Mascara
Mouding China 76 D3
Moudjéria Mauritania 96 B3
Moudros Greece 59 K5
Mouhijärvi Fin. 45 M6
Mouila Gabon 98 B4
Moulamein Australia 112 B5
Moulamein Creek r. Australia 112 A5
Moulavibazar Bangl. see Moulvibazar
Mould Bay Canada 118 G2
Moulèngui Binza Gabon 98 B4
Moulins France 56 F3
Moulmein Myanmar 70 B3
Moulouya, Oued r. Morocco 54 D4
Moultrie U.S.A. 133 D6
Moultrie, Lake U.S.A. 133 E5
Moulvibazar Bangl. 83 G4
Mound City KS U.S.A. 130 E4
Mound City SD U.S.A. 130 C2
Moundou Chad 97 E4
Moundsville U.S.A. 134 E4
Moŭng Roessei Cambodia 71 C4
Mount Abu India 82 C4
Mountain r. Canada 120 D1
Mountainair U.S.A. 127 G6
Mountain Brook U.S.A. 133 C5
Mountain City U.S.A. 134 E5
Mountain Home AR U.S.A. 131 E4
Mountain Home ID U.S.A. 126 E4
Mountain Home UT U.S.A. 129 H1
Mountain Lake Park U.S.A. 134 F4
Mountain View U.S.A. 131 E5
Mountain Zebra National Park S. Africa 101 G7
Mount Airy U.S.A. 134 E5
Mount Aspiring National Park N.Z. 113 B7
Mount Assiniboine Provincial Park Canada 120 H5
Mount Ayliff S. Africa 101 I6
Mount Ayr U.S.A. 130 E3
Mount Bellew Rep. of Ireland 51 D4
Mount Buffalo National Park Australia 112 C6
Mount Carmel U.S.A. 134 B4
Mount Carmel Junction U.S.A. 129 G3
Mount Cook National Park N.Z. 113 C6
Mount Coolon Australia 110 D4
Mount Darwin Zimbabwe 99 D5
Mount Denison Australia 108 F5
Mount Desert Island U.S.A. 132 G2
Mount Dutton Australia 111 A5
Mount Eba Australia 111 A6
Mount Elgon National Park Uganda 98 D3
Mount Fletcher S. Africa 101 I6
Mount Forest Canada 134 E2
Mount Frankland National Park Australia 109 B8
Mount Frere S. Africa 101 I6
Mount Gambier Australia 111 C8
Mount Gilead U.S.A. 134 D3
Mount Hagen P.N.G. 69 K8
Mount Holly U.S.A. 135 H4
Mount Hope Australia 112 B4
Mount Hope U.S.A. 134 E5
Mount Howitt Australia 111 C5
Mount Isa Australia 110 B4
Mount Jackson U.S.A. 135 F4
Mount Jewett U.S.A. 135 F3
Mount Joy U.S.A. 135 G3
Mount Kaputar National Park Australia 112 E3
Mount Keith Australia 109 C6
Mount Lofty Range mts Australia 111 B7
Mount Magnet Australia 109 B7
Mount Manara Australia 112 A4
Mount McKinley National Park U.S.A. see Denali National Park and Preserve
Mount Meadows Reservoir U.S.A. 128 C1
Mountmellick Rep. of Ireland 51 E4
Mount Moorosi Lesotho 101 H6
Mount Morgan Australia 110 E4
Mount Morris MI U.S.A. 134 D2
Mount Morris NY U.S.A. 135 G2
Mount Murchison Australia 112 A3
Mount Nebo U.S.A. 134 E4
Mount Olivet U.S.A. 134 C4
Mount Pearl Canada 123 L5
Mount Pleasant Canada 123 I5
Mount Pleasant IA U.S.A. 130 F3
Mount Pleasant MI U.S.A. 134 C2
Mount Pleasant TX U.S.A. 131 E5
Mount Pleasant UT U.S.A. 129 H2
Mount Rainier National Park U.S.A. 126 C3
Mount Remarkable National Park Australia 111 B7
Mount Revelstoke National Park Canada 120 G5
Mount Robson Provincial Park Canada 120 G4
Mount Rogers National Recreation Area park U.S.A. 134 E5
Mount Sanford Australia 108 E4
Mount's Bay U.K. 49 B8
Mount Shasta U.S.A. 126 C4
Mountsorrel U.K. 49 F6
Mount Sterling U.S.A. 134 D4
Mount St Helens National Volcanic Monument nat. park U.S.A. 126 C3
Mount Swan Australia 110 A4
Mount Union U.S.A. 135 G3
Mount Vernon Australia 109 B6
Mount Vernon IL U.S.A. 130 F4
Mount Vernon IN U.S.A. 132 C4
Mount Vernon KY U.S.A. 134 C5
Mount Vernon MO U.S.A. 131 E4
Mount Vernon OH U.S.A. 134 D3
Mount Vernon TX U.S.A. 131 E5
Mount Vernon WA U.S.A. 126 C2
Mount William National Park Australia 111 [inset]
Mount Willoughby Australia 109 F6
Moura Australia 110 E5
Moura Brazil 142 F4
Moura Port. 57 C4
Mourdi, Dépression du depr. Chad 97 F3
Mourdiah Mali 96 C3
Mourne r. U.K. 51 E3
Mourne Mountains hills U.K. 51 F3
Mousa i. U.K. 50 [inset]
Mouscron Belgium 52 D4
Mousgougou Chad 98 B2
Moussafoyo Chad 97 E4
Moussoro Chad 97 E3
Moutamba Congo 98 B4
Mouth of the Yangtze China 77 I2
Moutong Indon. 69 G6
Mouy France 52 C5
Mouydir, Monts du plat. Alg. 96 D2
Mouzon France 52 F5
Movas Mex. 127 F7
Mowbullan, Mount Australia 112 E1
Moxey Town Bahamas 133 E7
Moy r. Rep. of Ireland 51 C3
Moyale Eth. 98 D3
Moyen Atlas mts Morocco 54 C5
Moyen Congo country Africa see Congo
Moyeni Lesotho 101 H6
Moynalyk Rus. Fed. 80 I1
Moynaq Uzbek. see Muynak
Moyo i. Indon. 108 B2
Moyobamba Peru 142 C5
Moyock U.S.A. 135 G5

Moyola r. U.K. 51 F3
Moyu China 82 D1
Moyynkum Kazakh. 80 D3
Moyynkum, Peski des. Kazakh. 80 C3
Moyynty Kazakh. 80 D2
▶Mozambique country Africa 99 D6
Africa 7, 94–95
Mozambique Channel Africa 99 E6
Mozambique Ridge sea feature Indian Ocean 149 K7
Mozdok Rus. Fed. 91 G2
Mozdūrān Iran 89 F2
Mozhaysk Rus. Fed. 43 H5
Mozhga Rus. Fed. 42 L4
Mozhnābād Iran 89 F3
Mozo Myanmar 76 B4
Mozyr' Belarus see Mazyr
Mpaathutlwa Pan salt pan Botswana 100 E3
Mpanda Tanz. 99 D4
Mpen India 83 I4
Mpika Zambia 99 D5
Mpolweni S. Africa 101 J5
Mporokoso Zambia 99 D4
Mpulungu Zambia 99 D4
Mpumalanga prov. S. Africa 101 I4
Mpunde mt. Tanz. 99 D4
Mpwapwa Tanz. 99 D4
Mqanduli S. Africa 101 I6
Mqinvartsveri mt. Georgia/Rus. Fed. see Kazbek
Mrewa Zimbabwe see Murehwa
Mrkonjić-Grad Bos.-Herz. 58 G2
M'Saken Tunisia 58 D7
Mshinskaya Rus. Fed. 45 P7
M'Sila Alg. 57 I6
Msta r. Rus. Fed. 42 F4
Mstislavl' Belarus see Mstsislaw
Mstsislaw Belarus 43 F5
Mtelo Kenya 98 D3
Mtoko Zimbabwe see Mutoko
Mtorwi Tanz. 99 D4
Mtsensk Rus. Fed. 43 H5
Mts'ire Kavkasioni Asia see Lesser Caucasus
Mtubatuba S. Africa 101 K5
Mtunzini S. Africa 101 J5
Mtwara Tanz. 99 E5
Mu r. Myanmar 70 A2
Mu'āb, Jibāl reg. Jordan see Moab
Muanda Dem. Rep. Congo 99 B4
Muang Ham Laos 70 D2
Muang Hiam Laos 70 C2
Muang Hinboun Laos 70 D3
Muang Hôngsa Laos 70 C3
Muang Khammouan Laos 70 D3
Muang Khi Laos 70 C3
Muang Không Laos 71 D4
Muang Khoua Laos 70 C2
Muang Lamam Laos see Ban Phon
Muang Mok Laos 70 D3
Muang Ngoy Laos 70 C2
Muang Ou Nua Laos 70 C2
Muang Pakbeng Laos 70 C3
Muang Paktha Laos 70 C2
Muang Pakxan Laos see Muang Xaignabouri
Muang Phalan Laos 68 D3
Muang Phin Laos 70 D3
Muang Phôn-Hông Laos 70 C3
Muang Sam Sip Thai. 70 D4
Muang Sing Laos 70 C2
Muang Soum Laos 70 C3
Muang Souy Laos 70 C3
Muang Thadua Laos 70 C3
Muang Thai country Asia see Thailand
Muang Va Laos 70 C2
Muang Vangviang Laos 70 C3
Muang Xaignabouri Laos 70 C3
Muang Xaignabouri Laos 70 C3
Muang Xay Laos 70 C2
Muang Xon Laos 70 C2
Muar Malaysia 71 C7
Muarabungo Indon. 68 C7
Muarateweh Indon. 68 E7
Muari, Ras pt Pak. 89 G5
Mu'ayqil, Khashm al hill Saudi Arabia 88 C5
Mubarek Uzbek. 89 G2
Mubarraz well Saudi Arabia 91 F5
Mubende Uganda 98 D3
Mubi Nigeria 96 E3
Muborak Uzbek. see Mubarek
Mubur i. Indon. 71 D7
Mucajaí, Serra do mts Brazil 138 F3
Mucalic r. Canada 123 I2
Muccan Australia 108 C5
Much Germany 53 H4
Muchinga Escarpment Zambia 99 D5
Muchuan China 76 D2
Muck i. U.K. 50 C4
Mucojo Moz. 99 E5
Muconda Angola 99 C5
Mucubela Moz. 99 D5
Mucugê Brazil 145 C1
Mucur Turkey 90 D3
Mucuri Brazil 145 D2
Mucuri r. Brazil 145 D2
Mudabidri India 84 B3
Mudan China see Heze
Mudanjiang China 74 C3
Mudan Jiang r. China 74 C3
Mudan Ling mts China 74 B4
Mudanya Turkey 59 M4
Mudaybī Oman 88 E6
Mudaysīsāt, Jabal al hill Jordan 85 C4
Muddus nationalpark nat. park Sweden 44 K3
Muddy r. U.S.A. 129 F3
Muddy Gap Pass U.S.A. 126 G4
Muddy Peak U.S.A. 129 F3
Mūd-e Dahanāb Iran 88 E3
Mudersbach Germany 53 H4
Mudgal India 84 C3
Mudgee Australia 112 D4
Mudhol India 84 B2
Mudigere India 84 B3
Mudjatik r. Canada 121 J3
Mud Lake U.S.A. 128 E3
Mudraya country Africa see Egypt
Mudurnu Turkey 59 N4
Mud'yuga Rus. Fed. 42 H3
Mueda Moz. 99 D5
Mueller Range hills Australia 108 D4
Muertos Cays is Bahamas 133 D7
Muftyuga Rus. Fed. 42 J2
Mufulira Zambia 99 C5
Mufumbwe Zambia 99 C5
Mufu Shan mts China 77 G2
Muğan Düzü lowland Azer. 91 H3
Mugarripug China 83 F2
Mughalbhin Pak. see Jati
Mughal Kot Pak. 89 H4
Mughal Sarai India 83 E4
Mūghār Iran 88 D3
Mughayrā' Saudi Arabia 85 C5
Mughayrā' well Saudi Arabia 88 B5
Muğla Turkey 59 M6
Mugodzhary, Gory mts Kazakh. 80 A2
Mugxung China 76 B1
Mūḩ, Sabkhat imp. l. Syria 85 D2
Muhammad Ashraf Pak. 89 H5
Muhammad Qol Sudan 86 E5
Muhammarah Iran see Khorramshahr
Muhashsham, Wādī al watercourse Egypt 85 B4
Muḩaysh, Wādī al watercourse Jordan 85 C5
Muhaysin Syria 85 D1
Mühlanger Germany 53 M3
Mühlberg Germany 53 N3
Mühlhausen (Thüringen) Germany 53 K3
Mühlig-Hofmann Mountains Antarctica 152 C2
Muhos Fin. 44 N4
Muḩradah Syria 85 C2
Muhri Pak. 89 G4
Mui Bai Bung c. Vietnam see Mui Ca Mau
Mui Ba Lang An pt Vietnam 70 E4
Mui Ca Mau c. Vietnam 71 D5
Mui Dinh hd Vietnam 71 E5
Mui Độc pt Vietnam 70 D3
Muié Angola 99 C5
Mui Kê pt Vietnam 71 E5
Mui Nây pt Vietnam 71 E4
Muineachán Rep. of Ireland see Monaghan
Muine Bheag Rep. of Ireland 51 F5
Muir U.S.A. 134 C2
Muirkirk U.K. 50 E5
Muir of Ord U.K. 50 E3
Mui Ron hd Vietnam 70 D3
Muite Moz. 99 D5
Muji China 82 D1
Muju S. Korea 75 B5
Mukacheve Ukr. 43 D6
Mukachevo Ukr. see Mukacheve
Mukah Sarawak Malaysia 68 E6
Mukalla Yemen 86 G7
Mukandwara India 82 D4
Mukdahan Thai. 70 D3
Mukden China see Shenyang
Muketei r. Canada 122 D3
Mukhen Rus. Fed. 74 E2
Mukhino Rus. Fed. 74 B1
Mukhtuya Rus. Fed. see Lensk
Mukinbudin Australia 109 B7
Mu Ko Chang Marine National Park Thai. 71 C5
Mukojima-rettō is Japan 75 F8
Mukry Turkm. 89 G2
Muktsar India 82 C3
Mukutawa r. Canada 121 L4
Mukwonago U.S.A. 134 A2
Mula r. India 84 B2
Mulakatholhu atoll Maldives see Mulaku Atoll
Mulaku Atoll Maldives 81 D11
Mulan China 74 C3
Mulanje, Mount Malawi 99 D5
Mulapula, Lake salt flat Australia 111 B6
Mulatos Mex. 127 F7
Mulayḩ Saudi Arabia 88 B5
Mulayḩah, Jabal hill U.A.E. 88 D5
Mulayz, Wādī al watercourse Egypt 85 A4
Mulchatna r. U.S.A. 118 C3
Mulde r. Germany 53 M3
Mule Creek NM U.S.A. 129 I5
Mule Creek WY U.S.A. 126 G4
Mulegé Mex. 127 E8
Mules i. Indon. 108 C2
Muleshoe U.S.A. 131 C5
Mulga Park Australia 109 E6
Mulgathing Australia 109 F7
Mulhacén mt. Spain 57 E5
Mülhausen France see Mulhouse
Mülheim an der Ruhr Germany 52 G3
Mulhouse France 56 H3
Muli China 76 D3
Muli Rus. Fed. see Vysokogorniy
Mulia Indon. 69 J7
Muling Heilong. China 74 C3
Muling Heilong. China 74 C3
Muling He r. China 74 D3
Mull i. U.K. 50 D4
Mull, Sound of sea chan. U.K. 50 C4
Mullaghcleevaun hill Rep. of Ireland 51 F4
Mullaittivu Sri Lanka 84 D4
Mullaley Australia 112 D3
Mullengudgery Australia 112 C3
Mullens U.S.A. 134 E5
Muller watercourse Australia 108 F5
Muller, Pegunungan mts Indon. 68 E6
Mullett Lake U.S.A. 134 C1
Mullewa Australia 109 A7
Mullica r. U.S.A. 135 H4
Mullingar Rep. of Ireland 51 E4
Mullion Creek Australia 112 D4
Mull of Galloway c. U.K. 50 E6
Mull of Kintyre hd U.K. 50 D5
Mull of Oa hd U.K. 50 C5
Mullumbimby Australia 112 F2
Mulobezi Zambia 99 C5
Mulshi Lake India 84 B2
Multai India 82 D5
Multan Pak. 89 H4
Multia Fin. 44 N5
Multien reg. France 52 C6
Mulug India 84 C2
▶Mumbai India 84 B2
2nd most populous city in Asia and 5th in the world.
Mumbil Australia 112 D4
Mumbwa Zambia 99 C5
Muminabad Tajik. see Leningrad
Mŭ'minobod Tajik. see Leningrad
Mun, Mae Nam r. Thai. 70 D4
Muna i. Indon. 69 G8
Muna Mex. 136 G4
Muna r. Rus. Fed. 65 N3
Munabao Pak. 89 H5
Munaðarnes Iceland 44 [inset]
Münchberg Germany 53 L4
München Germany see Munich
München-Gladbach Germany see Mönchengladbach
Münchhausen Germany 53 I4
Muncho Lake Canada 120 E3
Muncie U.S.A. 134 C3
Muncoonie West, Lake salt flat Australia 110 B5
Muncy U.S.A. 135 G3
Munda Pak. 89 H4
Mundel Lake Sri Lanka 84 C5
Mundesley U.K. 49 I6
Mundford U.K. 49 H6
Mundiwindi Australia 109 C5
Mundra India 82 B5
Munds Park U.S.A. 129 H4
Mundubbera Australia 111 E5
Mundwa India 82 C4
Munfordville U.S.A. 134 C5
Mungallala Australia 111 D5
Mungana Australia 110 D3
Mungári Moz. 99 D5
Mungbere Dem. Rep. Congo 98 C3
Mungeli India 83 E5
Munger India 83 F4
Mu Nggava i. Solomon Is see Rennell
Mungindi Australia 112 D2
Mungla Bangl. see Mongla
Mungo Angola 99 B5
Mungo, Lake Australia 112 A4
Mungo National Park Australia 112 A4
Munich Germany 47 M6
Munising U.S.A. 132 C2
Munjpur India 82 B5
Munkács Ukr. see Mukacheve
Munkedal Sweden 45 G7
Munkelva Norway 44 P2
Munkfors Sweden 45 H7
Munkhafaḑ al Qaţţārah depr. Egypt see Qattara Depression
Munku-Sardyk, Gora mt. Mongolia/Rus. Fed. 72 I2
Münnerstadt Germany 53 K4
Munnik S. Africa 101 I2
Munroe Lake Canada 121 L3
Munsan S. Korea 75 B5
Münster Hessen Germany 53 I5
Münster Niedersachsen Germany 53 K2
Münster Nordrhein-Westfalen Germany 53 H3
Munster reg. Rep. of Ireland 51 D5
Münsterland reg. Germany 53 H3
Muntadgin Australia 109 B7
Munyal-Par sea feature India see Bassas de Pedro Padua Bank
Munzur Vadisi Milli Parkı nat. park Turkey 55 L4
Muojärvi l. Fin. 44 P4
Mương Lam Vietnam 70 D3
Mương Nhie Vietnam 70 C2
Muong Sai Laos see Muang Xay
Muonio Fin. 44 M3
Muonioälven r. Fin./Sweden 44 M3
Muonionjoki r. Fin./Sweden see Muonioälven
Mupa, Parque Nacional da nat. park Angola 99 B5
Muping China see Baoxing
Muqaynimah well Saudi Arabia 88 C6
Muqdisho Somalia see Mogadishu
Muquem Brazil 145 A1
Muqui Brazil 145 C3
Mur r. Austria 47 P7
also known as Mura (Croatia/Slovenia)
Mura r. Croatia/Slovenia see Mur
Murai, Tanjong pt Sing. 71 [inset]
Murai Reservoir Sing. 71 [inset]
Murakami Japan 75 E5
Murallón, Cerro mt. Chile 144 B7
Muramvya Burundi 98 C4
Murashi Rus. Fed. 42 K4
Murat r. Turkey 91 E3
Muratlı Turkey 59 L4
Muraysah, Ra's al pt Libya 90 B5
Murchison watercourse Australia 109 A6
Murchison, Mount Antarctica 152 H2
Murchison, Mount hill Australia 109 B6
Murchison Falls National Park Uganda 98 D3
Murcia Spain 57 F5
Murcia aut. comm. Spain 57 F5
Murdo U.S.A. 130 C3
Murehwa Zimbabwe 99 D5
Mureşul r. Romania 59 I1
Muret France 56 E5
Murewa Zimbabwe see Murehwa
Murfreesboro AR U.S.A. 131 E5
Murfreesboro TN U.S.A. 132 C5
Murg r. Germany 53 I6
Murgab Tajik. see Murghob
Murgab Turkm. see Murgap
Murgab r. Turkm. see Murgap
Murgap Turkm. 89 F2
Murgap r. Turkm. 87 J2
Murghab r. Afgh. 89 F3
Murghab reg. Afgh. 89 F3
Murgha Kibzai Pak. 89 H4
Murghob Tajik. 89 I2
Murgh Pass Afgh. 89 H3
Murgon Australia 111 E5
Murgoo Australia 109 B6
Muri India 83 F5
Muriaé Brazil 145 C3
Murid Pak. 89 G4
Muriege Angola 99 C4
Müritz l. Germany 53 M1
Müritz, Nationalpark nat. park Germany 53 N1
Murmansk Rus. Fed. 44 R2
Murmanskaya Oblast' admin. div. Rus. Fed. 44 S2
Murmanskiy Bereg coastal area Rus. Fed. 42 G1
Murmansk Oblast admin. div. Rus. Fed. see Murmanskaya Oblast'
Muro, Capo di c. Corsica France 56 I6
Murom Rus. Fed. 42 I5
Muroran Japan 74 F4
Muros Spain 57 B2
Muroto Japan 75 D6
Muroto-zaki pt Japan 75 D6
Murphy ID U.S.A. 126 D4
Murphy NC U.S.A. 133 D5
Murphysboro U.S.A. 130 F4
Murrah reg. Saudi Arabia 88 C6
Murrah al Kubrá, Al Buḩayrah al l. Egypt see Great Bitter Lake
Murrah aş Şughrá, Al Buḩayrah al l. Egypt see Little Bitter Lake
Murra Murra Australia 112 C2
Murrat el Kubra, Buheirat l. Egypt see Great Bitter Lake
Murrat el Sughra, Buheirat l. Egypt see Little Bitter Lake
▶Murray r. S.A. Australia 111 B7
3rd longest river in Oceania. Part of the longest (Murray-Darling).
Murray r. W.A. Australia 109 A8
Murray KY U.S.A. 131 F4
Murray UT U.S.A. 129 H1
Murray, Lake P.N.G. 69 K8
Murray, Lake U.S.A. 133 D5
Murray, Mount Canada 120 D2
Murray Bridge Australia 111 B7
▶Murray-Darling r. Austr. 106 E5
Longest river and largest drainage basin in Oceania.
Oceania 102–103
Murray Downs Australia 108 F5
Murray Range hills Australia 109 E6
Murraysburg S. Africa 100 F6
Murray Sunset National Park Australia 111 C7
Murrhardt Germany 53 J6
Murrieta U.S.A. 128 E5
Murringo Australia 112 D5
Murrisk reg. Rep. of Ireland 51 C4
Murrough Rep. of Ireland 51 C4
▶Murrumbidgee r. Australia 112 A5
4th longest river in Oceania.
Murrumburrah Australia 112 D5
Murrurundi Australia 112 E3
Mursan India 82 D4
Murshidabad India 83 G4
Murska Sobota Slovenia 58 G1
Mürt Iran 89 F5
Murtoa Australia 111 C8
Murua i. P.N.G. see Woodlark Island
Murud India 84 B2
Murud, Gunung mt. Indon. 68 F6
Murunkan Sri Lanka 84 D4
Murupara N.Z. 113 F4
Mururoa atoll Fr. Polynesia 151 K7
Murviedro Spain see Sagunto
Murwara India 82 E5
Murwillumbah Australia 112 F2
Murzechirla Turkm. 89 F2
Murzūq Libya 97 E2
Mürzzuschlag Austria 47 O7
Muş Turkey 91 F3
Mūsā, Khowr-e b. Iran 88 C4
Musa Khel Bazar Pak. 89 H4
Musala mt. Bulg. 59 J3
Musala i. Indon. 71 B7
Musan N. Korea 74 C4
Musandam Peninsula Oman/U.A.E. 88 E5
Mūsá Qal'eh, Rūd-e r. Afgh. 89 G3
Musay'īd Qatar see Umm Sa'id
▶Muscat Oman 88 E6
Capital of Oman.
Muscat reg. Oman 88 E5
Muscat and Oman country Asia see Oman
Muscatine U.S.A. 130 F3
Musgrave Australia 110 C2
Musgrave Harbour Canada 123 L4
Musgrave Ranges mts Australia 109 E6
Mushāsh al Kabid well Jordan 85 C5
Mushayyish, Wādī al watercourse Jordan 85 C4
Mushie Dem. Rep. Congo 98 B4
Mushkaf Pak. 89 G4
Music Mountain U.S.A. 129 G4
Musinia Peak U.S.A. 129 H2
Muskeg r. Canada 120 F2
Muskeget Channel U.S.A. 135 J3
Muskegon MI U.S.A. 132 C3
Muskegon MI U.S.A. 134 B2
Muskegon r. U.S.A. 134 B2
Muskegon Heights U.S.A. 134 B2
Muskeg River Canada 120 G4
Muskogee U.S.A. 131 E5
Muskoka, Lake Canada 134 F1
Muskrat Dam Lake Canada 121 N4
Musmar Sudan 86 E6
Musoma Tanz. 98 D4
Musquanousse, Lac l. Canada 123 J4
Musquaro, Lac l. Canada 123 J4
Mussau Island P.N.G. 69 L7
Musselburgh U.K. 50 F5
Musselkanaal Neth. 52 H2
Musselshell r. U.S.A. 126 G3
Mussende Angola 99 B5
Mustafakemalpaşa Turkey 59 M4
Mustjala Estonia 45 M7
Mustvee Estonia 45 O7
Musu-dan pt N. Korea 74 C4
Muswellbrook Australia 112 E4
Mūţ Egypt 86 C4
Mut Turkey 85 A1
Mutá, Ponta do pt Brazil 145 D1
Mutare Zimbabwe 99 D5
Mutayr reg. Saudi Arabia 88 B5
Mutina Italy see Modena
Muting Indon. 69 K8
Mutis Col. 142 B2
Mutnyy Materik Rus. Fed. 42 L2
Mutoko Zimbabwe 99 D5
Mutsamudu Comoros 99 E5
Mutsu Japan 74 F4
Muttaburra Australia 110 D4
Muttonbird Islands N.Z. 113 A8
Mutton Island Rep. of Ireland 51 C5
Muttukuru India 84 D3
Muttupet India 84 C4
Mutum Brazil 145 C2
Mutunópolis Brazil 145 A1
Mutur Sri Lanka 84 D4
Mutusjärvi r. Fin. 44 O2
Muurola Fin. 44 N3
Mu Us Shamo des. China 73 J5
Muxaluando Angola 99 B4
Muxi China see Muchuan
Muxima Angola 99 B4
Muyezerskiy Rus. Fed. 44 R5
Muyinga Burundi 98 D4
Muynak Uzbek. 80 A3
Mŭynoq Uzbek. see Muynak
Muyumba Dem. Rep. Congo 99 C4
Muyunkum, Peski des. Kazakh. see Moyynkum, Peski
Muyuping China 77 F2
Muzaffarabad Pak. 89 I3
Muzaffargarh Pak. 89 H4
Muzaffarnagar India 82 D3
Muzaffarpur India 83 F4
Muzamane Moz. 101 K2
Muzhi Rus. Fed. 41 S2
Mūzīn Iran 89 F5
Muzon, Cape U.S.A. 120 C4
Múzquiz Mex. 131 C7
Muztag mt. China 82 E2
Muz Tag mt. China 83 F1
Muztagata mt. China 89 I2
Muztor Kyrg. see Toktogul
Mvadi Gabon 98 B3
Mvolo Sudan 97 F4
Mvuma Zimbabwe 99 D5
Mwanza Malawi 99 D5
Mwanza Tanz. 98 D4
Mweelrea hill Rep. of Ireland 51 C4
Mweka Dem. Rep. Congo 99 C4
Mwene-Ditu Dem. Rep. Congo 99 C4
Mwenezi Zimbabwe 99 D6
Mwenga Dem. Rep. Congo 98 C4
Mweru, Lake Dem. Rep. Congo/Zambia 99 C4
Mweru Wantipa National Park Zambia 99 C4
Mwimba Dem. Rep. Congo 99 C4
Mwinilunga Zambia 99 C5
Myadaung Myanmar 70 B2
Myadzyel Belarus 45 O9
Myajlar India 82 B4
Myall Lakes National Park Australia 112 F4
Myanaung Myanmar 70 A3
▶Myanmar country Asia 70 A2
Asia 6, 62–63
Myauk-U Myanmar see Myohaung
Myaungmya Myanmar 70 A3
Myawadi Thai. 70 B3
Mybster U.K. 50 F2
Myebon Myanmar 70 A2
Myede Myanmar 70 A3
Myeik Myanmar see Mergui
Myingyan Myanmar 70 A2
Myinkyado Myanmar 70 B2
Myinmoletkat mt. Myanmar 71 B4
Myitkyina Myanmar 70 B1
Myitson Myanmar 70 B2
Myitta Myanmar 71 B4
Myittha Myanmar 70 B2
Mykolayiv Ukr. 59 O1
Mykonos i. Greece 59 K6
Myla Rus. Fed. 42 K2
Myla r. Rus. Fed. 42 K2
Mylae Sicily Italy see Milazzo
Mylasa Turkey see Milas
Mymensing Bangl. see Mymensingh
Mymensingh Bangl. 83 G4
Mynämäki Fin. 45 M6
Myohaung Myanmar 70 A2
Myŏnggan N. Korea 74 C4
Myory Belarus 45 O9
Mýrdalsjökull ice cap Iceland 44 [inset]
Myre Norway 44 I2
Myrheden Sweden 44 L4
Myrhorod Ukr. 43 G6
Myrnam Canada 121 I4
Myronivka Ukr. 43 F6
Myrtle Beach U.S.A. 133 E5
Myrtleford Australia 112 C6
Myrtle Point U.S.A. 126 B4
Mys Articheskiy c. Rus. Fed. 153 E1
Mysia reg. Turkey 59 L5
Mys Lazareva Rus. Fed. see Lazarev
Myślibórz Poland 47 O4
My Son Sanctuary tourist site Vietnam 70 E4
Mysore India 84 C3
Mysore state India see Karnataka
Mys Shmidta Rus. Fed. 65 T3
Mysy Rus. Fed. 42 L3
My Tho Vietnam 71 D5
Mytilene i. Greece see Lesbos
Mytilini Greece 59 L5
Mytilini Strait Greece/Turkey 59 L5
Mytishchi Rus. Fed. 42 H5
Myton U.S.A. 129 H1
Myyeldino Rus. Fed. 42 L3
Mzamomhle S. Africa 101 H6
Mže r. Czech Rep. 53 M5
Mzimba Malawi 99 D5
Mzuzu Malawi 99 D5

N

Naab r. Germany 53 M5
Naalehu HI U.S.A. 127 [inset]
Naantali Fin. 45 M6
Naas Rep. of Ireland 51 F4
Naba Myanmar 70 B1
Nababeep S. Africa 100 C5
Nababganj Bangl. see Nawabganj
Nabadwip India see Navadwip
Nabarangapur India 84 D2
Nabarangpur India see Nabarangapur
Nabari Japan 75 E6
Nabatîyé et Tahta Lebanon 85 B3
Nabatiyet et Tahta Lebanon see Nabatîyé et Tahta
Nabberu, Lake salt flat Australia 109 C6
Nabburg Germany 53 M5
Naberera Tanz. 99 D4
Naberezhnyye Chelny Rus. Fed. 41 Q4
Nabesna U.S.A. 120 A2
Nabeul Tunisia 58 D6
Nabha India 82 D3
Nabil'skiy Zaliv lag. Rus. Fed. 74 F2
Nabire Indon. 69 J7
Nabi Younés, Ras en pt Lebanon 85 B3
Nāblus West Bank 85 B3
Naboomspruit S. Africa 101 I3
Nabq Reserve nature res. Egypt 90 D5
Nābulus West Bank see Nāblus
Nacala Moz. 99 E5
Nachalovo Rus. Fed. 43 K7
Nachicapau, Lac l. Canada 123 I2
Nachingwea Tanz. 99 D5
Nachna India 82 B4
Nachuge India 71 A5
Nacimiento Reservoir U.S.A. 128 C4
Naco U.S.A. 127 F7
Nacogdoches U.S.A. 131 E6
Nada China see Danzhou
Nadaleen r. Canada 120 C2
Nådendal Fin. see Naantali
Nadezhdinskoye Rus. Fed. 74 D2
Nadiad India 82 C5
Nadol India 82 C4
Nador Morocco 57 E6
Nadqān, Qalamat well Saudi Arabia 88 C6
Nadūshan Iran 88 D3
Nadvirna Ukr. 43 E6
Nadvoitsy Rus. Fed. 42 G3
Nadvornaya Ukr. see Nadvirna
Nadym Rus. Fed. 64 I3
Næstved Denmark 45 G9
Nafarroa aut. comm. Spain see Navarra
Nafas, Ra's an mt. Egypt 85 B5
Nafha, Har hill Israel 85 B4
Nafpaktos Greece 59 I5
Nafplio Greece 59 J6
Naftalan Azer. 91 G2
Naft-e Safīd Iran 88 C4
Naft-e Shāh Iran see Naft Shahr
Naft Shahr Iran 88 B3
Nafūd ad Daḩl des. Saudi Arabia 88 B6
Nafūd al Ghuwayţah des. Saudi Arabia 85 D5
Nafūd al Jur'ā des. Saudi Arabia 88 B5
Nafūd as Sirr des. Saudi Arabia 88 B5
Nafūd as Surrah des. Saudi Arabia 88 A6
Nafūd Qunayfidhah des. Saudi Arabia 88 B5
Nafūsah, Jabal hills Libya 96 E1
Nafy Saudi Arabia 86 F4
Nag, Co l. China 83 G2
Naga Phil. 69 G4
Nagagami r. Canada 122 D4
Nagagami Lake Canada 122 D4
Nagahama Japan 75 D6
Naga Hills India 83 H4
Naga Hills state India see Nagaland
Nagaland state India 83 H4
Nagamangala India 84 C3
Nagambie Australia 112 B6
Nagano Japan 75 E5
Nagaoka Japan 75 E5
Nagaon India 83 H4
Nagapatam India see Nagapattinam
Nagapattinam India 84 C4
Nagar Himachal Pradesh India 87 M3
Nagar Karnataka India 84 B3
Nagaram India 84 D2
Nagari Hills India 84 C3
Nagarjuna Sagar Reservoir India 84 C2
Nagar Parkar Pak. 89 H5
Nagasaki Japan 75 C6
Nagato Japan 75 C6
Nagaur India 82 C4
Nagbhir India 84 C1
Nagda India 82 C5
Nageezi U.S.A. 129 J3
Nagercoil India 84 C4
Nagha Kalat Pak. 89 G5
Nag' Hammâdi Egypt see Naj' Ḩammādī
Nagina India 82 D3
Nagold r. Germany 53 I6
Nagong Chu r. China see Parlung Zangbo
Nagorno-Karabakh aut. reg. Azer. see Dağlıq Qarabağ
Nagornyy Karabakh aut. reg. Azer. see Dağlıq Qarabağ
Nagorsk Rus. Fed. 42 K4
Nagoya Japan 75 E6
Nagpur India 82 D5
Nagqu China 76 B2
Nag Qu r. China 76 B2
Nagurskoye Rus. Fed. 64 F1
Nagyatád Hungary 58 G1
Nagybecskerek Serb. and Mont. see Zrenjanin
Nagyenyed Romania see Aiud
Nagykanizsa Hungary 58 G1
Nagyvárad Romania see Oradea
Naha Japan 73 N7
Nahan India 82 D3
Nahanni Butte Canada 120 F2
Nahanni National Park Canada 120 E2
Nahanni Range mts Canada 120 F2
Naharāyim Jordan 85 B3
Nahariyya Israel 85 B3
Nahāvand Iran 88 C3
Nahr Dijlah r. Iraq/Syria 91 G5 see Tigris
Nahuel Huapi, Parque Nacional nat. park Arg. 144 B6
Nahunta U.S.A. 133 D6
Naica Mex. 131 B7
Nai Ga Myanmar 76 C3
Naij Tal China 83 H2

Naikliu Indon. 108 C2
Nain Canada 123 J2
Nā'īn Iran 88 D3
Nainital India 82 D3
Naini Tal India see Nainital
Nairn U.K. 50 F3
Nairn r. U.K. 50 F3

▶Nairobi Kenya 98 D4
Capital of Kenya.

Naissus Serb. and Mont. see Niš
Naivasha Kenya 98 D4
Najafābād Iran 88 C3
Na'jān Saudi Arabia 88 B5
Najd reg. Saudi Arabia 86 F4
Nájera Spain 57 E2
Naj' Ḥammādī Egypt 86 D4
Naji China 74 A2
Najibabad India 82 D3
Najin N. Korea 74 C4
Najitun China see Naji
Najrān Saudi Arabia 86 F6
Nakadōri-shima i. Japan 75 C6
Na Kae Thai. 70 D3
Nakambé r. Burkina/Ghana see White Volta
Nakanbe r. Burkina/Ghana see White Volta
Nakanno Rus. Fed. 65 L3
Nakano-shima i. Japan 75 D5
Nakasongola Uganda 97 G4
Nakatsu Japan 75 C6
Nakatsugawa Japan 75 E6
Nakfa Eritrea 86 E6
Nakhichevan' Azer. see Naxçıvan
Nakhl Egypt 85 A5
Nakhodka Rus. Fed. 74 D4
Nakhola India 83 H4
Nakhon Nayok Thai. 71 C4
Nakhon Pathom Thai. 71 C4
Nakhon Phanom Thai. 70 D3
Nakhon Ratchasima Thai. 70 C4
Nakhon Sawan Thai. 70 C4
Nakhon Si Thammarat Thai. 71 B5
Nakhtarana India 82 B5
Nakina Canada 122 D4
Nakina r. Canada 120 C3
Naknek U.S.A. 118 C4
Nakonde Zambia 99 D4
Nakskov Denmark 45 G9
Naktong-gang r. S. Korea 75 C6
Nakuru Kenya 98 D4
Nakusp Canada 120 G5
Nal Pak. 89 G5
Nal r. Pak. 89 G5
Na-lang Myanmar 70 B2
Nalázi Moz. 101 K3
Nalbari India 83 G4
Nal'chik Rus. Fed. 91 F2
Naldurg India 84 C2
Nalgonda India 84 C2
Naliya India 82 B5
Nallamala Hills India 84 C3
Nallıhan Turkey 59 N4
Nālūt Libya 96 E1
Namaacha Moz. 101 K3
Namacurra Moz. 99 D5
Namadgi National Park Australia 112 D5
Namahadi S. Africa 101 I4
Namak, Daryācheh-ye salt flat Iran 88 C3
Namak, Kavīr-e salt flat Iran 88 E3
Namakkal India 84 C4
Namakwaland reg. Namibia see Great Namaqualand
Namakzar-e Shadad salt flat Iran 88 E4
Namaland reg. Namibia see Great Namaqualand
Namangan Uzbek. 80 D3
Namaqualand reg. Namibia see Great Namaqualand
Namaqualand reg. S. Africa 100 C5
Namaqua National Park S. Africa 100 C6
Namas Indon. 69 K8
Namatanai P.N.G. 106 F2
Nambour Australia 112 F1
Nambucca Heads Australia 112 F3
Nambung National Park Australia 109 A7
Năm Căn Vietnam 71 D5
Namcha Barwa mt. China see Namjagbarwa Feng
Namche Bazar Nepal 83 F4
Nam Co salt l. China 83 G3
Namdalen valley Norway 44 H4
Namdalseid Norway 44 G4
Nam Đinh Vietnam 70 D2
Namen Belgium see Namur
Nam-gang r. N. Korea 75 B5
Namhae-do i. S. Korea 75 B6
Namhsan Myanmar 70 B2
Namib Desert Namibia 100 B3
Namibe Angola 99 B5
▶Namibia country Africa 99 B6
Africa 7, 94–95
Namibia Abyssal Plain sea feature N. Atlantic Ocean 148 I8
Namib-Naukluft Game Park nature res. Namibia 100 B3
Namie Japan 75 F5
Namīn Iran 91 H3
Namjagbarwa Feng mt. China 76 B2
Namlan Myanmar 70 B2
Namlang r. Myanmar 70 B2
Nam Loi r. Myanmar see Nanlei He
Nam Nao National Park Thai. 70 C3
Nam Ngum Reservoir Laos 70 C3
Namoi r. Australia 112 D3
Namonuito atoll Micronesia 69 L5
Nampa mt. Nepal 82 E3
Nampa U.S.A. 126 D4
Nampala Mali 96 C3
Nam Phong Thai. 70 C3
Namp'o N. Korea 75 B5
Nampula Moz. 99 D5
Namsai Myanmar 70 B1
Namsang Myanmar 70 B2
Namsen r. Norway 44 G4
Nam She Tsim hill Hong Kong China see Sharp Peak
Namsos Norway 44 G4
Namti Myanmar 70 B1
Namtok Myanmar 70 B3
Namtok Chattakan National Park Thai. 70 C3
Namton Myanmar 70 B2
Namtsy Rus. Fed. 65 N3
Namtu Myanmar 70 B2
Namu Canada 120 E5
Namuli, Monte mt. Moz. 99 D5
Namuno Moz. 99 D5
Namur Belgium 52 E4
Namutoni Namibia 99 B5
Namwŏn S. Korea 75 B6
Namya Ra Myanmar 70 B1
Namyit Island S. China Sea 68 E4
Nan Thai. 70 C3
Nana Bakassa Cent. Afr. Rep. 98 B3
Nanaimo Canada 120 F5
Nanam N. Korea 74 C4
Nan'an China 77 H3
Nanango Australia 112 F1
Nananib Plateau Namibia 100 C3
Nanao Japan 75 E5
Nanatsu-shima i. Japan 75 E5
Nanbai China see Zunyi
Nanbin China see Shizhu
Nanbu China 76 E2
Nancha China 74 C3
Nanchang Jiangxi China 77 G2
Nanchang Jiangxi China 77 G2
Nanchong China 76 E2
Nanchuan China 76 E2
Nancowry i. India 71 A6
Nancun China 77 G1
Nancy France 52 G6
Nancy (Essey) airport France 52 G6
Nanda Devi mt. India 82 E3
Nanda Kot mt. India 82 E3
Nandan China 76 E3
Nandapur India 84 D2
Nanded India 84 C2
Nander India see Nanded
Nandewar Range mts Australia 112 E3
Nandod India 84 B1
Nandurbar India 82 C5
Nandyal India 84 C3
Nanfeng Guangdong China 77 F4
Nanfeng Jiangxi China 77 H3
Nang China 76 B2
Nanga Eboko Cameroon 96 E4
Nanga Parbat mt. Jammu and Kashmir 82 C2
Nangar National Park Australia 112 D4
Nangatayap Indon. 68 E7
Nangin Myanmar 71 B5
Nangnim-sanmaek mts N. Korea 75 B4
Nangqên China 76 C1
Nangulangwa Tanz. 99 D4
Nanguneri India 84 C4
Nanhua China 76 D3
Nanhui China 77 I2
Nanjian China 76 D3
Nanjiang China 76 E1
Nanjing China 77 H1
Nanji Shan i. China 77 I3
Nanka Jiang r. China 76 C4
Nankang China 77 G3
Nanking China see Nanjing
Nankova Angola 99 B5
Nanlei He r. China 76 C4
also known as Nam Loi (Myanmar)
Nanling China 77 H2
Nan Ling mts China 77 F3
Nanliu Jiang r. China 77 F4
Nanlong China see Nanbu
Nannilam India 84 C4
Nannine Australia 109 B6
Nanning China 77 F4
Nannup Australia 109 A8
Na Noi Thai. 70 C3
Nanortalik Greenland 119 N3
Nanouki atoll Kiribati see Nonouti
Nanouti atoll Kiribati see Nonouti
Nanpan Jiang r. China 76 E3
Nanping China 77 H3
Nanpu China see Pucheng
Nanri Dao i. China 77 H3
Nansei-shotō is Japan see Ryukyu Islands
Nansen Basin sea feature Arctic Ocean 153 H1
Nansen Sound sea chan. Canada 119 I1
Nan-sha Ch'ün-tao is S. China Sea see Spratly Islands
Nanshan Island S. China Sea 68 F4
Nansha Qundao is S. China Sea see Spratly Islands
Nansio Tanz. 98 D4
Nantes France 56 D3
Nantes à Brest, Canal de France 56 C3
Nanteuil-le-Haudouin France 52 C5
Nanthi Kadal lag. Sri Lanka 84 D4
Nanticoke Canada 134 E2
Nanticoke U.S.A. 135 H4
Nantong China 77 I2
Nantou China 77 [inset]
Nant'ou Taiwan 77 I4
Nantucket U.S.A. 135 J3
Nantucket Island U.S.A. 135 K3
Nantucket Sound g. U.S.A. 135 J3
Nantwich U.K. 49 E5
Nanumaga i. Tuvalu see Nanumanga
Nanumanga i. Tuvalu 107 H2
Nanumea atoll Tuvalu 107 H2
Nanuque Brazil 145 C2
Nanusa, Kepulauan is Indon. 69 H6
Nanxi China 76 E2
Nanxian China 77 G2
Nanxiong China 77 G3
Nanyang China 77 G1
Nanyuki Kenya 98 D4
Nanzhang China 77 F2
Nanzhao China see Zhao'an
Nanzhou China see Nanxian
Naococane, Lac l. Canada 123 H3
Naoero country S. Pacific Ocean see Nauru
Naogaon Bangl. 83 G4
Naokot Pak. 89 H5
Naoli He r. China 74 D3
Naomid, Dasht-e des. Afgh./Iran 89 F3
Naoshera Jammu and Kashmir 82 C2
Napa U.S.A. 128 B2
Napaktulik Lake Canada 121 H1
Napanee Canada 135 G1
Napasoq Greenland 119 M3
Naperville U.S.A. 134 A3
Napier N.Z. 113 F4
Napier Range hills Australia 108 D4
Napierville Canada 135 I1
Naples Italy 58 F4
Naples FL U.S.A. 133 D7
Naples ME U.S.A. 135 J2
Naples TX U.S.A. 131 E5
Naples UT U.S.A. 129 I1
Napo China 76 E4
Napoleon IN U.S.A. 134 C4
Napoleon ND U.S.A. 130 D2
Napoleon OH U.S.A. 134 C3
Napoli Italy see Naples
Naqadeh Iran 88 B2
Nara India 82 B5
Nara Japan 75 D6
Nara Mali 96 C3
Narach Belarus 45 O9
Naracoorte Australia 111 C8
Naradhan Australia 112 C4
Narainpur India 84 D2
Naralua India 83 F4
Naranjal Ecuador 142 C4
Naranjo Mex. 127 F8
Narasapur India 84 D2
Narasaraopet India 84 D2
Narasinghapur India 84 E1
Narathiwat Thai. 71 C6
Nara Visa U.S.A. 131 C5
Narayanganj Bangl. 83 G5
Narayanganj India 82 E5
Narayangarh India 82 C4
Narbada r. India see Narmada
Narberth U.K. 49 C7
Narbo France see Narbonne
Narbonne France 56 F5
Narborough Island Galápagos Ecuador see Fernandina, Isla
Narcea r. Spain 57 C2
Narcondam Island India 71 A4
Nardò Italy 58 H4
Narechi r. Pak. 89 H4
Narembeen Australia 109 B8
Nares Abyssal Plain sea feature S. Atlantic Ocean 148 D4
Nares Deep sea feature N. Atlantic Ocean 148 D4
Nares Strait Canada/Greenland 119 K2
Naretha Australia 109 D7
Narew r. Poland 47 R4
Narib Namibia 100 C3
Narikel Jinjira i. Bangl. see St Martin's Island
Narimanov Rus. Fed. 43 J7
Narimskiy Khrebet mts Kazakh. see Narymskiy Khrebet
Narin Afgh. 89 H2
Narin reg. Afgh. 89 H2
Narince Turkey 90 E3
Narin Gol watercourse China 83 H1
Narizon, Punta pt Mex. 127 F8
Narkher India 82 D5
Narmada r. India 82 C5
Narman Turkey 91 F2
Narnaul India 82 D3
Narni Italy 58 E3
Narnia Italy see Narni
Narodnaya, Gora mt. Rus. Fed. 41 S3
Naro-Fominsk Rus. Fed. 43 H5
Narok Kenya 98 D4
Narooma Australia 112 E6
Narovchat Rus. Fed. 43 I5
Narowlya Belarus 43 F6
Närpes Fin. 44 L5
Narrabri Australia 112 D3
Narragansett Bay U.S.A. 135 J3
Narran r. Australia 112 C2
Narrandera Australia 112 C5
Narran Lake Australia 112 C2
Narrogin Australia 109 B8
Narromine Australia 112 D4
Narrows U.S.A. 134 E5
Narrowsburg U.S.A. 135 H3
Narsapur India 84 C2
Narsaq Greenland 119 N3
Narshingdi Bangl. see Narsingdi
Narsimhapur India see Narsinghpur
Narsingdi Bangl. 83 G5
Narsinghpur India 82 D5
Narsipatnam India 84 D2
Nartkala Rus. Fed. 91 F2
Naruto Japan 75 D6
Narva Estonia 45 P7
Narva Bay Estonia/Rus. Fed. 45 O7
Narva laht b. Estonia/Rus. Fed. see Narva Bay
Narva Reservoir resr Estonia/Rus. Fed. see Narvskoye Vodokhranilishche
Narva veehoidla resr Estonia/Rus. Fed. see Narvskoye Vodokhranilishche
Narvik Norway 44 J2
Narvskiy Zaliv b. Estonia/Rus. Fed. see Narva Bay
Narvskoye Vodokhranilishche resr Estonia/Rus. Fed. 45 P7
Narwana India 82 D3
Nar'yan-Mar Rus. Fed. 42 L2
Narymskiy Khrebet mts Kazakh. 80 F2
Naryn Kyrg. 80 E3
Näsåker Sweden 44 J5
Nashik India 84 B1
Nashua U.S.A. 135 J2
Nashville AR U.S.A. 131 E5
Nashville GA U.S.A. 133 D6
Nashville IN U.S.A. 134 B4
Nashville NC U.S.A. 132 E5
Nashville OH U.S.A. 134 D3

▶Nashville TN U.S.A. 132 C4
State capital of Tennessee.

Naşīb Syria 85 C3
Näsijärvi l. Fin. 45 M6
Nasik India see Nashik
Nasir Pak. 89 H4
Nasir Sudan 86 D8
Nasirabad Bangl. see Mymensingh
Nasirabad India 82 C4
Naskaupi r. Canada 123 J3
Naşr Egypt 90 C5
Nasratabad Iran see Zābol
Naşrīān-e Pā'īn Iran 88 B3
Nass r. Canada 120 D4
Nassau r. Australia 110 C2

▶Nassau Bahamas 133 E7
Capital of The Bahamas.

Nassau i. Cook Is 107 J3
Nassau U.S.A. 135 I2
Nassawadox U.S.A. 135 H5
Nasser, Lake resr Egypt 86 D5
Nässjö Sweden 45 I8
Nassuttooq inlet Greenland 119 M3
Nastapoca r. Canada 122 F2
Nastapoka Islands Canada 122 F2
Nasugbu Phil. 69 G4
Nasva Rus. Fed. 42 F4
Nata Botswana 99 C6
Natal Brazil 143 K5
Natal Indon. 68 B6
Natal prov. S. Africa see Kwazulu-Natal
Natal Basin sea feature Indian Ocean 149 K8
Natal Drakensberg Park nat. park S. Africa 101 I5
Naţanz Iran 88 C3
Natashquan Canada 123 J4
Natashquan r. Canada 123 J4
Natchez U.S.A. 131 F6
Natchitoches U.S.A. 131 E6
Nathalia Australia 112 B6
Nathia Gali Pak. 89 I3
Nati, Punta pt Spain 57 H3
Natillas Mex. 131 C7
National City U.S.A. 128 E5
National West Coast Tourist Recreation Area park Namibia 100 B2
Natitingou Benin 96 D3
Natividad, Isla i. Mex. 127 E8
Natividade Brazil 143 I6
Natkyizin Myanmar 70 B4
Natla r. Canada 120 D2
Natmauk Myanmar 70 A2
Nator Bangl. see Natore
Nátora Mex. 127 F7
Natore Bangl. 83 G4
Natori Japan 75 F5
Natron, Lake salt l. Tanz. 98 D4
Nattai National Park Australia 112 E5
Nattalin Myanmar 70 A3
Nattaung mt. Myanmar 70 B3
Na'tū Iran 89 F3
Natuna, Kepulauan is Indon. 71 D6
Natuna Besar i. Indon. 71 E6
Natural Bridges National Monument nat. park U.S.A. 129 H3
Naturaliste, Cape Australia 109 A8
Naturaliste Plateau sea feature Indian Ocean 149 P8
Naturita U.S.A. 129 I2
Nauchas Namibia 100 C2
Nau Co l. China 83 E2
Nauen Germany 53 M2
Naufragados, Ponta dos pt Brazil 145 A4
Naujoji Akmenė Lith. 45 M8
Naukh India 82 C4
Naumburg (Hessen) Germany 53 J3
Naumburg (Saale) Germany 53 L3
Naunglon Myanmar 70 B3
Naungpale Myanmar 70 B3
Naupada India 84 E2
Na'ūr Jordan 85 B4
Nauroz Kalat Pak. 89 G4
Naurskaya Rus. Fed. 91 G2
Nauru i. Nauru 107 G2
▶Nauru country S. Pacific Ocean 107 G2
Oceania 8, 104–105
Naustdal Norway 45 D6
Nauta Peru 142 D4
Nautaca Uzbek. see Karshi
Naute Dam Namibia 100 C4
Nauzad Afgh. 89 G3
Nava Mex. 131 C6
Navadwip India 83 G5
Navahrudak Belarus 45 N10
Navajo Lake U.S.A. 129 J3
Navajo Mountain U.S.A. 129 H3
Navalmoral de la Mata Spain 57 D4
Navalvillar de Pela Spain 57 D4
Navan Rep. of Ireland 51 F4
Navangar India see Jamnagar
Navapolatsk Belarus 45 P9
Nāvar, Dasht-e depr. Afgh. 89 G3
Navarin, Mys c. Rus. Fed. 65 S3
Navarra aut. comm. Spain 57 F2
Navarra, Comunidad Foral de aut. comm. Spain see Navarra
Navarre Australia 112 A6
Navarre aut. comm. Spain see Navarra
Navarro r. U.S.A. 128 B2
Navashino Rus. Fed. 42 I5
Navasota U.S.A. 131 D6

▶Navassa Island terr. West Indies 137 I5
United States Unincorporated Territory.

Naver r. U.K. 50 E2
Näverede Sweden 44 I5
Navlakhi India 82 B5
Navlya Rus. Fed. 43 G5
Năvodari Romania 59 M2
Navoi Uzbek. 89 G1
Navoiy Uzbek. see Navoi
Navojoa Mex. 127 F8
Navolato Mex. 136 C4
Návpaktos Greece see Nafpaktos
Návplion Greece see Nafplio
Navşar Turkey see Şemdinli
Navsari India 84 B1
Nawá Syria 85 C3
Nawabganj Bangl. 83 G4
Nawabshah Pak. 89 H5
Nawada India 83 F4
Nāwah Afgh. 89 G3
Nawalgarh India 82 C4
Nawanshahr India 82 D3
Nawan Shehar India see Nawanshahr
Nawar, Dasht-i depr. Afgh. see Nāvar, Dasht-e
Nawarangpur India see Nabarangapur
Nawngcho Myanmar see Nawnghkio
Nawnghkio Myanmar 70 B2
Nawng Hpa Myanmar 70 B2
Nawngleng Myanmar 70 B2
Nawoiy Uzbek. see Navoi
Naxçıvan Azer. 91 G3
Naxos i. Greece 59 K6
Nayagarh India 84 E1
Nayak Afgh. 89 G3
Nayar Mex. 136 D4
Nāy Band, Kūh-e mt. Iran 88 E3
Nayong China 76 E3
Nayoro Japan 74 F3
Nazaré Brazil 145 D1
Nazareno Mex. 131 C7
Nazareth Israel 85 B3
Nazário Brazil 145 A2
Nazas Mex. 131 B7
Nazas r. Mex. 131 B7
Nazca Peru 142 D6
Nazca Ridge sea feature S. Pacific Ocean 151 O7
Nāzīl Iran 89 F4
Nazilli Turkey 59 M6
Nazimabad Pak. 89 G5
Nazımiye Turkey 91 E3
Nazir Hat Bangl. 83 G5
Nazko Canada 120 F4
Nazran' Rus. Fed. 91 G2
Nazrēt Eth. 98 D3
Nazwá Oman 88 E6
Ncojane Botswana 100 E2
N'dalatando Angola 99 B4
Ndélé Cent. Afr. Rep. 98 C3
Ndendé Gabon 98 B4
Ndende i. Solomon Is see Ndeni
Ndeni i. Solomon Is 107 G3

▶Ndjamena Chad 97 E3
Capital of Chad.

N'Djamena Chad see Ndjamena
Ndjouani i. Comoros see Nzwani
Ndoi i. Fiji see Doi
Ndola Zambia 99 C5
Nduke i. Solomon Is see Kolombangara
Ndwedwe S. Africa 101 J5
Ne, Hon i. Vietnam 70 D3
Neabul Creek r. Australia 112 C1
Neagh, Lough l. U.K. 51 F3
Neah Bay U.S.A. 126 B2
Neale, Lake salt flat Australia 109 E6
Nea Liosia Greece 59 J5
Neapoli Greece 59 J6
Neapolis Italy see Naples
Nea Roda Greece 59 J4
Neath U.K. 49 D7
Neath r. U.K. 49 D7
Nebbi Uganda 98 D3
Nebine Creek r. Australia 112 C2
Nebitdag Turkm. 88 D2
Neblina, Pico da mt. Brazil 142 E3
Nebo Australia 110 E4
Nebo, Mount U.S.A. 129 H2
Nebolchi Rus. Fed. 42 G4
Nebraska state U.S.A. 130 C3
Nebraska City U.S.A. 130 E3
Nebrodi, Monti mts Sicily Italy 58 F6
Neches r. U.S.A. 131 E6
Nechisar National Park Eth. 98 D3
Nechranice, Vodní nádrž resr Czech Rep. 53 N4
Neckar r. Germany 53 I5
Neckarsulm Germany 53 J5
Necker Island U.S.A. 150 J4
Necochea Arg. 144 E5
Nederland country Europe see Netherlands
Nederlandse Antillen terr. West Indies see Netherlands Antilles
Neder Rijn r. Neth. 52 F3
Nedlouc, Lac l. Canada 123 G2
Nedluk Lake Canada see Nedlouc, Lac
Nêdong China 83 G3
Nedre Soppero Sweden 44 L2
Nédroma Alg. 57 F6
Needle Mountain U.S.A. 126 F3
Needles U.S.A. 129 F4
Neemach India see Neemuch
Neemuch India 82 C4
Neenah U.S.A. 134 A1
Neepawa Canada 121 L5
Neergaard Lake Canada 119 J2
Neerijnen Neth. 52 F3
Neerpelt Belgium 52 F3
Neftçala Azer. 91 H3
Neftechala Azer. see 26 Bakı Komissarı
Neftechala Azer. see Neftçala
Neftegorsk Sakhalinskaya Oblast' Rus. Fed. 74 F1
Neftegorsk Samarskaya Oblast' Rus. Fed. 43 K5
Neftekamsk Rus. Fed. 41 Q4
Neftekumsk Rus. Fed. 91 G1
Nefteyugansk Rus. Fed. 64 I3
Neftezavodsk Turkm. see Seydi
Neftezavodsk Turkm. see Seydi
Nefyn U.K. 49 C6
Nefza Tunisia 58 C6
Negage Angola 99 B4
Negār Iran 88 E4
Negara Indon. 108 A2
Negēlē Eth. 98 D3
Negev des. Israel 85 B4
Negomane Moz. 99 D5
Negombo Sri Lanka 84 C5
Negotino Macedonia 59 J4
Negra, Cordillera mts Peru 142 C5
Negra, Punta pt Peru 142 B5
Negra, Serra mts Brazil 145 C2
Negrais, Cape Myanmar 70 A4
Négrine Alg. 58 B7
Negro r. Arg. 144 D6
Negro r. Brazil 143 G7
Negro r. Brazil 145 A4
Negro r. S. America 142 G4
Negro, Cabo c. Morocco 57 D6
Negroponte i. Greece see Evvoia
Negros i. Phil. 69 G5
Negru Vodă, Podişul plat. Romania 59 M3
Nehbandān Iran 89 F4
Nehe China 74 B2
Neijiang China 76 E2
Neilburg Canada 121 I4
Neimenggu aut. reg. China see Nei Mongol Zizhiqu
Nei Mongol Zizhiqu aut. reg. China 74 A2
Neinstedt Germany 53 L3
Neiva Col. 142 C3
Neixiang China 77 F1
Nejanilini Lake Canada 121 L3
Nejd reg. Saudi Arabia see Najd
Neka Iran 88 D2
Nek'emtē Eth. 98 D3
Nekrasovskoye Rus. Fed. 42 I4
Neksø Denmark 45 I9
Nelang India 82 D3
Nelia Australia 110 C4
Nelidovo Rus. Fed. 42 G4
Neligh U.S.A. 130 D3
Nel'kan Rus. Fed. 65 P3
Nellore India 84 C3
Nelluz watercourse Turkey 85 D1
Nel'ma Rus. Fed. 74 E3
Nelson Canada 120 G5
Nelson r. Canada 121 M3
Nelson N.Z. 113 D5
Nelson U.K. 48 E5
Nelson U.S.A. 129 G4
Nelson, Cape Australia 111 C8
Nelson, Cape P.N.G. 69 L8
Nelson, Estrecho strait Chile 144 A8
Nelson Bay Australia 112 F4
Nelson Forks Canada 120 F3
Nelsonia U.S.A. 135 H5
Nelson Lakes National Park N.Z. 113 D6
Nelson Reservoir U.S.A. 126 G2
Nelspruit S. Africa 101 J3
Néma Mauritania 96 C3
Nema Rus. Fed. 42 K4
Neman r. Belarus/Lith. see Nyoman
Neman Rus. Fed. 45 M9
Nemausus France see Nîmes
Nemawar India 82 D5
Nemed Rus. Fed. 42 L3
Nementcha, Monts des mts Alg. 58 B7
Nemetocenna France see Arras
Nemetskiy, Mys c. Rus. Fed. 44 Q2
Nemirov Ukr. see Nemyriv
Némiscau r. Canada 122 F4
Nemiscau, Lac l. Canada 122 F4
Nemor He r. China 74 B2
Nemours Alg. see Ghazaouet
Nemours France 56 F2
Nemrut Dağı mt. Turkey 91 F3
Nemunas r. Lith. see Nyoman
Nemuro Japan 74 G4
Nemuro-kaikyō sea chan. Japan/Rus. Fed. 74 G4
Nemyriv Ukr. 43 F6
Nenagh Rep. of Ireland 51 D5
Nenana U.S.A. 118 D3
Nene r. U.K. 49 H6
Nenjiang China 74 B2
Nen Jiang r. China 74 B3
Neosho U.S.A. 131 E4
▶Nepal country Asia 83 E3
Asia 6, 62–63
Nepalganj Nepal 83 E3
Nepean Canada 135 H1
Nepean, Point Australia 112 B7
Nephi U.S.A. 129 H2
Nephin hill Rep. of Ireland 51 C3
Nephin Beg Range hills Rep. of Ireland 51 C3
Nepisiguit r. Canada 123 I5
Nepoko r. Dem. Rep. Congo 98 C3
Nérac France 56 E4
Nerang Australia 112 F1
Nera Tso l. China 83 H3
Nerchinsk Rus. Fed. 73 L2
Nerekhta Rus. Fed. 42 I4
Néret, Lac l. Canada 123 H3
Neretva r. Bos.-Herz./Croatia 58 G3
Nêri Pünco l. China 83 G3
Neriquinha Angola 99 C5
Neris r. Lith. 45 M9
also known as Viliya (Belarus/Lithuania)
Nerl' r. Rus. Fed. 42 H4
Nerópolis Brazil 145 A2
Neryungri Rus. Fed. 65 N4
Nes Neth. 52 F1
Nes Norway 45 F6
Nes' Rus. Fed. 42 J2
Nesbyen Norway 45 F6
Neskaupstaður Iceland 44 [inset]
Nesle France 52 C5
Nesna Norway 44 H3
Nesri India 84 B2
Ness r. U.K. 50 E3
Ness, Loch l. U.K. 50 E3
Ness City U.S.A. 130 D4
Nesse r. Germany 53 K4
Nesselrode, Mount Canada/U.S.A. 120 C3
Nestor Falls Canada 121 M5
Nestos r. Greece 59 K4
also known as Mesta
Nesvizh Belarus see Nyasvizh
Netanya Israel 85 B3
▶Netherlands country Europe 52 F2
Europe 5, 38–39

▶Netherlands Antilles terr. West Indies 137 K6
Self-governing Netherlands Territory.
North America 9, 116–117

Netphen Germany 53 I4
Netrakona Bangl. 83 G4
Netrokona Bangl. see Netrakona
Nettilling Lake Canada 119 K3
Neubrandenburg Germany 53 N1
Neuburg an der Donau Germany 53 L6
Neuchâtel Switz. 56 H3
Neuchâtel, Lac de l. Switz. 56 H3
Neuendettelsau Germany 53 K5
Neuenhaus Germany 52 G2
Neuenkirchen Germany 53 J1
Neuenkirchen (Oldenburg) Germany 53 I2
Neufchâteau Belgium 52 F5
Neufchâteau France 56 G2
Neufchâtel-en-Bray France 52 B5
Neufchâtel-Hardelot France 52 B4
Neuharlingersiel Germany 53 H1

Norderney Germany 53 H1
Norderstedt Germany 53 K1
Nordfjordeid Norway 44 D6
Nordfold Norway 44 I3
Nordfriesische Inseln Germany see North Frisian Islands
Nordhausen Germany 53 K3
Nordholz Germany 53 I1
Nordhorn Germany 52 H2
Nordkapp c. Norway see North Cape
Nordkjosbotn Norway 44 K2
Nordkynhalvøya i. Norway 44 O1
Nordli Norway 44 H4
Nördlingen Germany 53 K6
Nordmaling Sweden 44 K5
Nord- og Østgrønland, Nationalparken i nat. park Greenland 119 O2

▶Nordøstrundingen c. Greenland 153 I1
Most easterly point of North America.

Nord-Ostsee-Kanal Germany see Kiel Canal
Norðoyar i. Faroe Is 40 E3
Nord - Pas-de-Calais admin. reg. France 52 C4
Nordpfälzer Bergland reg. Germany 53 H5
Nordre Strømfjord inlet Greenland see Nassuttooq
Nordrhein-Westfalen land Germany 53 H3
Nordvik Rus. Fed. 65 M2
Nore r. Rep. of Ireland 51 F5
Nore, Pic de mt. France 56 F5
Noreg country Europe see Norway
Norfolk NE U.S.A. 130 D3
Norfolk NY U.S.A. 135 H1
Norfolk VA U.S.A. 135 G5

▶Norfolk Island terr. S. Pacific Ocean 107 G4
Australian External Territory.
Oceania 8, 104–105

Norfolk Island Ridge sea feature Tasman Sea 150 H7
Norfork Lake U.S.A. 131 E4
Norg Neth. 52 G1
Norge country Europe see Norway
Norheimsund Norway 45 E6
Noril'sk Rus. Fed. 64 J3
Norkyung China see Bainang
Norland Canada 135 F1
Norma Co l. China 83 G2
Norman U.S.A. 131 D5
Norman, Lake resr U.S.A. 132 D5
Normanby Island P.N.G. 110 E1
Normandes, Îles is English Chan. see Channel Islands
Normandia Brazil 143 G3
Normandie reg. France see Normandy
Normandie, Collines de hills France 56 D2
Normandy reg. France 56 D2
Normanton Australia 110 C3
Norquay Canada 121 K5
Ñorquinco Arg. 144 B6
Norra Kvarken strait Fin./Sweden 44 L5
Norra Storfjället mts Sweden 44 I4
Norrent-Fontes France 52 C4
Norris Lake U.S.A. 134 D5
Norristown U.S.A. 135 H3
Norrköping Sweden 45 J7
Norrtälje Sweden 45 K7
Norseman Australia 109 C8
Norsjö Sweden 44 K4
Norsk Rus. Fed. 74 C1
Norsup Vanuatu 107 G3
Norte, Punta pt Arg. 144 E5
Norte, Serra do hills Brazil 143 G6
Nortelândia Brazil 143 G6
Nörten-Hardenberg Germany 53 J3
North, Cape Antarctica 152 H2
North, Cape Canada 123 J5
Northallerton U.K. 48 F4
Northam Australia 109 B7
Northampton Australia 106 B4
Northampton U.K. 49 G6
Northampton MA U.S.A. 135 I2
Northampton PA U.S.A. 135 H3
North Andaman i. India 71 A4
North Anna r. U.S.A. 135 G5
North Arm b. Canada 120 H2
North Atlantic Ocean Atlantic Ocean 125 O4
North Augusta U.S.A. 133 D5
North Aulatsivik Island Canada 123 J2
North Australian Basin sea feature Indian Ocean 149 P6
North Baltimore U.S.A. 134 D3
North Battleford Canada 121 I4
North Bay Canada 122 F5
North Belcher Islands Canada 122 F2
North Berwick U.K. 50 G4
North Berwick U.S.A. 135 J2
North Bourke Australia 112 B3
North Branch U.S.A. 130 E2
North Caicos i. Turks and Caicos Is 133 G8
North Canton U.S.A. 134 E3
North Cape Canada 123 I5
North Cape Norway 44 N1
North Cape N.Z. 113 D2
North Cape U.S.A. 118 A4
North Caribou Lake Canada 117 N4
North Carolina state U.S.A. 132 E4
North Cascades National Park U.S.A. 126 C2
North Channel lake channel Canada 122 E5
North Channel U.K. 51 G2
North Charleston U.S.A. 133 E5
North Chicago U.S.A. 134 B2
Northcliffe Glacier Antarctica 152 F2
North Collins U.S.A. 135 F2
North Concho r. U.S.A. 131 C6
North Conway U.S.A. 135 J1
North Dakota state U.S.A. 130 C2
North Downs hills U.K. 49 G7
North East U.S.A. 134 F2
Northeast Foreland c. Greenland see Nordøstrundingen
North-East Frontier Agency state India see Arunachal Pradesh
Northeast Pacific Basin sea feature N. Pacific Ocean 151 J4
Northeast Point Bahamas 133 F8
Northeast Providence Channel Bahamas 133 E7
North Edwards U.S.A. 128 E4
Northeim Germany 53 J3
Northern prov. S. Africa see Limpopo
Northern Areas admin. div. Pak. 89 I2
Northern Cape prov. S. Africa 96 D5
Northern Donets r. Rus. Fed./Ukr. see Severskiy Donets
Northern Dvina r. Rus. Fed. see Severnaya Dvina
Northern Indian Lake Canada 121 L3
Northern Ireland prov. U.K. 51 F3
Northern Lau Group is Fiji 107 I3
Northern Light Lake Canada 122 C4

▶Northern Mariana Islands terr. N. Pacific Ocean 69 K3
United States Commonwealth.
Oceania 8, 104–105

Northern Rhodesia country Africa see Zambia
Northern Sporades is Greece see Voreioi Sporades
Northern Territory admin. div. Australia 106 D3
Northern Transvaal prov. S. Africa see Limpopo
North Esk r. U.K. 50 G4
Northfield MN U.S.A. 130 E2
Northfield VT U.S.A. 135 I1
North Foreland c. U.K. 49 I7
North Fork U.S.A. 128 D3
North Fork Pass Canada 118 E3
North French r. Canada 122 E4
North Frisian Islands Germany 47 L3
North Geomagnetic Pole (2004) Arctic Ocean 119 K2
North Grimston U.K. 48 G4
North Haven U.S.A. 135 I3
North Head hd N.Z. 113 E3
North Henik Lake Canada 121 L2
North Hero U.S.A. 135 I1
North Horr Kenya 98 D3
North Island India 84 B4

▶North Island N.Z. 113 D4
3rd largest island in Oceania.

North Jadito Canyon gorge U.S.A. 129 H4
North Judson U.S.A. 134 B3
North Kingsville U.S.A. 134 E3
North Knife r. Canada 121 M3
North Knife Lake Canada 121 L3
▶North Korea country Asia 75 B5
Asia 6, 62–63
North Lakhimpur India 83 H4
North Las Vegas U.S.A. 129 F3
North Little Rock U.S.A. 131 E5
North Loup r. U.S.A. 130 D3
North Luangwa National Park Zambia 99 D5
North Maalhosmadulu Atoll Maldives 84 B5
North Magnetic Pole (2004) Canada 119 G1
North Malosmadulu Atoll Maldives see North Maalhosmadulu Atoll
North Mam Peak U.S.A. 129 J2
North Muskegon U.S.A. 134 B2
North Palisade mt. U.S.A. 128 D3
North Perry U.S.A. 134 E3
North Platte U.S.A. 130 C3
North Platte r. U.S.A. 130 C3
North Pole Arctic Ocean 153 I1
North Port U.S.A. 133 D7
North Reef Island India 71 A4
North Rhine - Westphalia land Germany see Nordrhein-Westfalen
North Rim U.S.A. 129 G3
North Rona i. U.K. see Rona
North Ronaldsay i. U.K. 50 G1
North Ronaldsay Firth sea chan. U.K. 50 G1
North Saskatchewan r. Canada 121 J4
North Schell Peak U.S.A. 129 F2
North Sea Europe 46 H2
North Seal r. Canada 121 L3
North Sentinel Island India 71 A5
North Shields U.K. 48 F3
North Shoal Lake Canada 121 L5
North Shoshone Peak U.S.A. 128 E2
North Siberian Lowland Rus. Fed. 64 L2
North Siberian Lowland Rus. Fed. 153 E2
North Simlipal National Park India 83 F5
North Sinai governorate Egypt see Shamāl Sīnā'
North Slope plain U.S.A. 118 D3
North Somercotes U.K. 48 H5
North Spirit Lake Canada 121 M4
North Stradbroke Island Australia 112 F1
North Sunderland U.K. 48 F3
North Syracuse U.S.A. 135 G2
North Taranaki Bight b. N.Z. 109 E4
North Terre Haute U.S.A. 134 B4
Northton U.K. 50 B3
North Tonawanda U.S.A. 135 F2
North Trap reef N.Z. 113 A8
North Troy U.S.A. 135 I1
North Tyne r. U.K. 48 E4
North Uist i. U.K. 50 B3
Northumberland National Park U.K. 48 E3
Northumberland Strait Canada 123 I5
North Vancouver Canada 120 F5
North Vernon U.S.A. 134 C4
Northville U.S.A. 135 H2
North Wabasca Lake Canada 120 H3
North Walsham U.K. 49 I6
Northway Junction U.S.A. 120 A2
North West prov. S. Africa 100 G4
Northwest Atlantic Mid-Ocean Channel N. Atlantic Ocean 148 E1
North West Cape Australia 108 A5
North West Frontier prov. Pak. 89 H3
North West Nelson Forest Park nat. park N.Z. see Kahurangi National Park
Northwest Pacific Basin sea feature N. Pacific Ocean 150 G3
Northwest Providence Channel Bahamas 133 E7
North West River Canada 119 K3
Northwest Territories admin. div. Canada 120 J2
Northwich U.K. 48 E5
North Wildwood U.S.A. 135 H4
North Windham U.S.A. 135 J2
Northwind Ridge sea feature Arctic Ocean 153 B1
Northwood U.S.A. 135 J2
North York Canada 134 F2
North York Moors moorland U.K. 48 G4
North York Moors National Park U.K. 48 G4
Norton U.K. 48 G4
Norton KS U.S.A. 130 D4
Norton VA U.S.A. 134 D5
Norton VT U.S.A. 135 J1
Norton de Matos Angola see Balombo
Norton Shores U.S.A. 134 B2
Norton Sound sea chan. U.S.A. 118 B3
Nortonville U.S.A. 134 B5
Norvegia, Cape Antarctica 152 B2
Norwalk CT U.S.A. 135 I3
Norwalk OH U.S.A. 134 D3
▶Norway country Europe 44 E6
Europe 5, 38–39
Norway U.S.A. 135 J1
Norway House Canada 121 L4
Norwegian Basin sea feature N. Atlantic Ocean 148 H1
Norwegian Bay Canada 119 I2
Norwegian Sea N. Atlantic Ocean 153 H2
Norwich Canada 134 E2
Norwich U.K. 49 I6
Norwich CT U.S.A. 135 I3
Norwich NY U.S.A. 135 H2
Norwood CO U.S.A. 129 I2
Norwood NY U.S.A. 135 H1
Norwood OH U.S.A. 134 C4
Nose Lake Canada 121 I1
Noshiro Japan 75 F4
Nosop watercourse Africa 100 D2
also known as Nossob
Nosovaya Rus. Fed. 42 L1
Noşratābād Iran 89 E4
Noss, Isle of i. U.K. 50 [inset]
Nossebro Sweden 45 H7
Nossen Germany 53 N3
Nossob watercourse Africa 100 D2
also known as Nosop
Notakwanon r. Canada 123 J2
Notch Peak U.S.A. 129 G2
Noteć r. Poland 47 O4
Notikewin r. Canada 120 G3
Noto, Golfo di g. Sicily Italy 58 F6
Notodden Norway 45 F7
Noto-hantō pen. Japan 75 E5
Notre Dame, Monts mts Canada 123 H5
Notre Dame Bay Canada 123 L4
Notre-Dame-de-Koartac Canada see Quaqtaq
Nottawasaga Bay Canada 134 E1
Nottaway r. Canada 122 F4
Nottingham U.K. 49 F6
Nottingham Island Canada 119 K3
Nottoway r. U.S.A. 135 G5
Nottuln Germany 53 H3
Notukeu Creek r. Canada 121 J5
Nouabalé-Ndoki, Parc National nat. park Congo 98 B3
Nouâdhibou Mauritania 96 B2
Nouâdhibou, Râs c. Mauritania 96 B2

▶Nouakchott Mauritania 96 B3
Capital of Mauritania.

Nouâmghâr Mauritania 96 B3
Nouei Vietnam 70 D4

▶Nouméa New Caledonia 107 G4
Capital of New Caledonia.

Nouna Burkina 96 C3
Noupoort S. Africa 100 G6
Nousu Fin. 44 P3
Nouveau-Brunswick prov. Canada see New Brunswick
Nouveau-Comptoir Canada see Wemindji
Nouvelle Calédonie i. S. Pacific Ocean 107 G4
Nouvelle Calédonie terr. S. Pacific Ocean see New Caledonia
Nouvelle-France, Cap de c. Canada 119 K3
Nouvelles Hébrides country S. Pacific Ocean see Vanuatu
Nova América Brazil 145 A1
Nova Chaves Angola see Muconda
Nova Freixa Moz. see Cuamba
Nova Friburgo Brazil 145 C3
Nova Gaia Angola see Cambundi-Catembo
Nova Goa India see Panaji
Nova Gradiška Croatia 58 G2
Nova Iguaçu Brazil 145 C3
Nova Kakhovka Ukr. 59 O1
Nova Lima Brazil 145 C2
Nova Lisboa Angola see Huambo
Novalukoml' Belarus 43 F5
Nova Mambone Moz. 99 D6
Nova Nabúri Moz. 99 D5
Nova Odesa Ukr. 43 F7
Nova Paraiso Brazil 142 F3
Nova Pilão Arcado Brazil 143 J5
Nova Ponte Brazil 145 B2
Nova Ponte, Represa resr Brazil 145 B2
Novara Italy 58 C2
Nova Roma Brazil 145 B1
Nova Scotia prov. Canada 123 I6
Nova Sento Sé Brazil 143 J5
Novato U.S.A. 128 B2
Nova Trento Brazil 145 A4
Nova Venécia Brazil 145 C2
Nova Xavantino Brazil 143 H6
Novaya Kakhovka Ukr. see Nova Kakhovka
Novaya Kazanka Kazakh. 41 P6
Novaya Ladoga Rus. Fed. 42 G3
Novaya Lyalya Rus. Fed. 41 S4
Novaya Odessa Ukr. see Nova Odesa
Novaya Sibir', Ostrov i. Rus. Fed. 65 P2
Novaya Ussura Rus. Fed. 74 E2

▶Novaya Zemlya is Rus. Fed. 64 G2
3rd largest island in Europe.

Nova Zagora Bulg. 59 L3
Novelda Spain 57 F4
Nové Zámky Slovakia 47 Q7
Novgorod Rus. Fed. see Velikiy Novgorod
Novgorod-Severskiy Ukr. see Novhorod-Sivers'kyy
Novgorod-Volynskiy Ukr. see Novohrad-Volyns'kyy
Novhorod-Sivers'kyy Ukr. 43 G6
Novi Grad Bos.-Herz. see Bosanski Novi
Novi Iskŭr Bulg. 59 J3
Novikovo Rus. Fed. 74 F3
Novi Kritsim Bulg. see Stamboliyski
Novi Ligure Italy 58 C2
Novi Pazar Bulg. 59 L3
Novi Pazar Serb. and Mont. 59 I3
Novi Sad Serb. and Mont. 59 H2
Novo Acre Brazil 145 C1
Novoalekseyevka Kazakh. see Khobda
Novoaltaysk Rus. Fed. 72 E2
Novoanninskiy Rus. Fed. 43 I6
Novo Aripuanã Brazil 142 F5
Novoazovs'k Ukr. 43 H7
Novocheboksarsk Rus. Fed. 42 J4
Novocherkassk Rus. Fed. 43 I7
Novo Cruzeiro Brazil 145 C2
Novodugino Rus. Fed. 42 G5
Novodvinsk Rus. Fed. 42 I2
Novoekonomicheskoye Ukr. see Dymytrov
Novogeorgiyevka Rus. Fed. 74 B2
Novogrudok Belarus see Navahrudak
Novo Hamburgo Brazil 145 A5
Novohradské Hory mts Czech Rep. 47 O6
Novohrad-Volyns'kyy Ukr. 43 E6
Novokhopersk Rus. Fed. 43 I6
Novokiyevskiy Uval Rus. Fed. 74 C2
Novokubansk Rus. Fed. 91 F1
Novokubanskiy Rus. Fed. see Novokubansk
Novokuybyshevsk Rus. Fed. 43 K5
Novokuznetsk Rus. Fed. 72 F2
Novolazarevskaya research station Antarctica 152 C2
Novolukoml' Belarus see Novalukoml'
Novo Mesto Slovenia 58 F2
Novomikhaylovskiy Rus. Fed. 90 E1
Novomoskovsk Rus. Fed. 43 H5
Novomoskovs'k Ukr. 43 G6
Novonikolayevsk Rus. Fed. see Novosibirsk
Novonikolayevskiy Rus. Fed. 43 I6
Novooleksiyivka Ukr. 43 G7
Novopashiyskiy Rus. Fed. see Gornozavodsk
Novopokrovka Rus. Fed. 74 D3
Novopokrovskaya Rus. Fed. 43 I7
Novopolotsk Belarus see Navapolatsk
Novopskov Ukr. 43 H6
Novo Redondo Angola see Sumbe
Novorossiyka Rus. Fed. 74 C1
Novorossiysk Rus. Fed. 90 E1
Novorybnaya Rus. Fed. 65 L2
Novorzhev Rus. Fed. 42 F4
Novoselovo Rus. Fed. 72 G1
Novoselskoye Rus. Fed. see Achkhoy-Martan
Novosel'ye Rus. Fed. 45 P7
Novosergiyevka Rus. Fed. 41 Q5
Novoshakhtinsk Rus. Fed. 43 H7
Novosheshminsk Rus. Fed. 42 K5
Novosibirsk Rus. Fed. 64 J4
Novosibirskiye Ostrova is Rus. Fed. see New Siberia Islands
Novosil' Rus. Fed. 43 H5
Novosokol'niki Rus. Fed. 42 F4
Novospasskoye Rus. Fed. 43 J5
Novotroyits'ke Ukr. 43 G7
Novoukrainka Ukr. see Novoukrayinka
Novoukrayinka Ukr. 43 F6
Novouzensk Rus. Fed. 43 K6
Novovolyns'k Ukr. 43 E6
Novovoronezh Rus. Fed. 43 H6
Novovoronezhskiy Rus. Fed. see Novovoronezh
Novo-Voskresenovka Rus. Fed. 74 B1
Novozybkov Rus. Fed. 43 F5
Nový Jičín Czech Rep. 47 P6
Novyy Afon Georgia see Akhali Ap'oni
Novyy Bor Rus. Fed. 42 L2
Novyy Donbass Ukr. see Dymytrov
Novyye Petushki Rus. Fed. see Petushki
Novyy Kholmogory Rus. Fed. see Archangel
Novyy Margelan Uzbek. see Fergana
Novyy Nekouz Rus. Fed. 42 H4
Novyy Oskol Rus. Fed. 43 H6
Novyy Port Rus. Fed. 64 I3
Novyy Urengoy Rus. Fed. 64 I3
Novyy Urgal Rus. Fed. 74 D2
Novyy Uzen' Kazakh. see Zhanaozen
Novyy Zay Rus. Fed. 42 L5
Now Iran 88 D4
Nowabganj Bangl. see Nawabganj
Nowata U.S.A. 131 E4
Nowdī Iran 88 C2
Nowgong India see Nagaon
Now Kharegan Iran 88 D2
Nowleye Lake Canada 121 K2
Nowogard Poland 47 O4
Noworadomsk Poland see Radomsko
Nowra Australia 112 E5
Nowrangapur India see Nabarangapur
Nowshera Pak. 89 I3
Nowyak Lake Canada 121 L2
Nowy Sącz Poland 47 R6
Nowy Targ Poland 47 R6
Noxen U.S.A. 135 G3
Noy, Xé r. Laos 70 D3
Noyabr'sk Rus. Fed. 64 I3
Noyes Island U.S.A. 120 C4
Noyon France 52 C5
Nozizwe S. Africa 101 G6
Nqamakwe S. Africa 101 H7
Nqutu S. Africa 101 J5
Nsanje Malawi 99 D5
Nsombo Zambia 99 C5
Nsukka Nigeria 96 D4
Nsumbu National Park Zambia see Sumbu National Park
Ntambu Zambia 99 C5
Ntha S. Africa 101 H4
Ntoum Gabon 98 A3
Ntungamo Uganda 98 D4
Nuanetsi Zimbabwe see Mwenezi
Nu'aym reg. Oman 88 D6
Nuba Mountains Sudan 86 D7
Nubian Desert Sudan 86 D5
Nudo Coropuna mt. Peru 142 D7
Nueces r. U.S.A. 131 D7
Nueltin Lake Canada 121 L2
Nueva Ciudad Guerrero Mex. 131 D7
Nueva Gerona Cuba 137 H4
Nueva Harberton Arg. 144 C8
Nueva Imperial Chile 144 B5
Nueva Loja Ecuador 142 C3
Nueva Rosita Mex. 131 C7
Nueva San Salvador El Salvador 136 G6
Nueva Villa de Padilla Mex. 131 D7
Nueve de Julio Arg. see 9 de Julio
Nuevitas Cuba 137 I4
Nuevo, Golfo g. Arg. 144 D6
Nuevo Casas Grandes Mex. 127 G7
Nuevo Ideal Mex. 131 B7
Nuevo Laredo Mex. 131 D7
Nuevo León Mex. 129 F5
Nuevo León state Mex. 131 D7
Nuevo Rocatuerte Ecuador 142 C4
Nugaal watercourse Somalia 98 E3
Nugget Point N.Z. 113 B8
Nugur India 84 D2
Nuguria Islands P.N.G. 106 F2
Nuh, Ras pt Pak. 89 F5
Nuhaka N.Z. 113 F4
Nui atoll Tuvalu 107 H2
Nui Con Voi r. Vietnam see Red River
Nuiqsut U.S.A. 118 C2
Nui Ti On mt. Vietnam 70 D4
Nujiang China 76 C2
Nu Jiang r. China/Myanmar see Salween
Nu Jiang r. China/Myanmar see Salween
Nukey Bluff hill Australia 111 A7
Nukha Azer. see Şäki

▶Nuku'alofa Tonga 107 I4
Capital of Tonga.

Nukufetau atoll Tuvalu 107 H2
Nukuhiva i. Fr. Polynesia see Nuku Hiva
Nuku Hiva i. Fr. Polynesia 151 K6
Nukuhu P.N.G. 69 L8
Nukulaelae atoll Tuvalu 107 H2
Nukulailai atoll Tuvalu see Nukulaelae
Nukumanu Islands P.N.G. 107 F2
Nukunau i. Kiribati see Nikunau
Nukunono atoll Tokelau 107 I2
Nukunonu atoll Tokelau see Nukunono
Nukus Uzbek. 80 A3
Nulato U.S.A. 118 C3
Nullagine Australia 108 C5
Nullarbor Australia 109 E7
Nullarbor National Park Australia 109 E7
Nullarbor Plain Australia 109 E7
Nullarbor Regional Reserve park Australia 109 E7
Nuluarniavik, Lac l. Canada 122 F2
Nulu'erhu Shan mts China 73 L4
Num i. Indon. 69 J7
Numalla, Lake salt flat Australia 112 B2
Numan Nigeria 98 B3
Numanuma P.N.G. 110 E1
Numazu Japan 75 E6
Numbulwar Australia 110 A2
Numedal valley Norway 45 F6
Numfoor i. Indon. 69 I7
Numin He r. China 74 B3
Numurkah Australia 112 B6
Nunaksaluk Island Canada 123 J3
Nunakuluut i. Greenland 119 N3
Nunap Isua c. Greenland see Farewell, Cape
Nunarsuit i. Greenland see Nunakuluut
Nunavik reg. Canada 122 G1
Nunavut admin. div. Canada 121 L2
Nunda U.S.A. 135 G2
Nundle Australia 112 E3
Nuneaton U.K. 49 F6
Nungba India 83 H4
Nungesser Lake Canada 121 M5
Nungnain Sum China 73 L3
Nunivak Island U.S.A. 118 B4
Nunkapasi India 84 E1
Nunkun mt. Jammu and Kashmir 82 D2
Nunligran Rus. Fed. 65 T3
Nuñomoral Spain 57 C3
Nunspeet Neth. 52 F2
Nuojiang China see Tongjiang
Nuoro Sardinia Italy 58 C4
Nupani i. Solomon Is 107 G3
Nuqrah Saudi Arabia 86 F4
Nur r. Iran 88 D2
Nūrābād Iran 88 C4
Nurakita i. Tuvalu see Niulakita
Nurata Uzbek. 80 C3
Nur Dağları mts Turkey 85 B1
Nurek Tajik. see Norak
Nurek Reservoir Tajik. see Norak, Obanbori
Nurekskoye Vodokhranilishche resr Tajik. see Norak, Obanbori
Nuremberg Germany 53 L5
Nuri Mex. 127 F7
Nuristan reg. Afgh. 89 H3
Nurla Jammu and Kashmir 82 D2
Nurlat Rus. Fed. 43 K5
Nurmes Fin. 44 P5
Nurmo Fin. 44 M5
Nürnberg Germany see Nuremberg
Nurota Uzbek. see Nurata
Nurri, Mount hill Australia 112 C3
Nusawulan Indon. 69 I7
Nusaybin Turkey 91 F3
Nu Shan mts China 76 C3
Nushki Pak. 89 G4
Nusratiye Turkey 85 D1
Nutak Canada 123 J2
Nutarawit Lake Canada 121 L2
Nutrioso U.S.A. 129 I5
Nuttal Pak. 89 H4
Nutwood Downs Australia 108 F3
Nutzotin Mountains U.S.A. 120 A2

▶Nuuk Greenland 119 M3
Capital of Greenland.

Nuupas Fin. 44 O3
Nuussuaq Greenland 119 M2
Nuussuaq pen. Greenland 119 M2
Nuwaybi' al Muzayyinah Egypt 90 D5
Nuweiba el Muzeina Egypt see Nuwaybi' al Muzayyinah
Nuwerus S. Africa 100 D6
Nuweveldberge mts S. Africa 100 E7
Nuyts, Point Australia 109 B8
Nuyts Archipelago is Australia 109 F8
Nuzvid India 84 D2
Nwanedi Nature Reserve S. Africa 101 J2
Nxai Pan National Park Botswana 99 C5
Nyagan' Rus. Fed. 41 T3
Nyagquka China see Yajiang
Nyagrong China see Xinlong
Nyahururu Kenya 98 D3
Nyah West Australia 112 A5
Nyainqêntanglha Feng mt. China 83 G3
Nyainqêntanglha Shan mts China 83 G3
Nyainrong China 76 B1
Nyainronglung China see Nyainrong
Nyåker Sweden 44 K5
Nyakh Rus. Fed. see Nyagan'
Nyaksimvol' Rus. Fed. 41 S3
Nyala Sudan 97 F3
Nyalam China 83 F3
Nyalikungu Tanz. see Maswa
Nyamandhiovu Zimbabwe 99 C5
Nyamtumbo Tanz. 99 D5
Nyande Zimbabwe see Masvingo
Nyandoma Rus. Fed. 42 I3
Nyandomskiy Vozvyshennost' hills Rus. Fed. 42 H3
Nyanga Congo 98 B4
Nyanga Zimbabwe 99 D5
Nyangbo China 76 B2
Nyarling r. Canada 120 H2

▶Nyasa, Lake Africa 99 D4
3rd largest lake in Africa.

Nyasaland country Africa see Malawi
Nyashabozh Rus. Fed. 42 L2
Nyasvizh Belarus 45 O10
Nyaungdon Myanmar see Yandoon
Nyaunglebin Myanmar 70 B3
Nyborg Denmark 45 G9
Nyborg Norway 44 P1
Nybro Sweden 45 I8
Nyeboe Land reg. Greenland 119 M1
Nyêmo China 83 G3
Nyenchen Tanglha Range mts China see Nyainqêntanglha Shan
Nyeri Kenya 98 D4
Nyi, Co l. China 83 F2
Nyika National Park Zambia 99 D5
Nyima China 83 F3
Nyimba Zambia 99 D5
Nyingchi China 76 B2
Nyinma China see Maqu
Nyíregyháza Hungary 43 D7
Nyiru, Mount Kenya 98 D3
Nykarleby Fin. 44 M5
Nykøbing Denmark 45 G9
Nykøbing Sjælland Denmark 45 G9
Nyköping Sweden 45 J7
Nyland Sweden 44 J5
Nylstroom S. Africa 101 I3
Nylsvley nature res. S. Africa 101 I3
Nymagee Australia 112 C4
Nymboida National Park Australia 112 F2
Nynäshamn Sweden 45 J7
Nyngan Australia 112 C3
Nyogzê China 83 E3
Nyoman r. Belarus/Lith. 45 M10
also known as Neman or Nemunas
Nyon Switz. 56 H3
Nyons France 56 G4
Nýřany Czech Rep. 53 N5
Nyrob Rus. Fed. 41 R3
Nysa Poland 47 P5
Nysh Rus. Fed. 74 F2
Nyssa U.S.A. 126 D4
Nystad Fin. see Uusikaupunki
Nytva Rus. Fed. 41 R4
Nyuksenitsa Rus. Fed. 42 J3
Nyunzu Dem. Rep. Congo 99 C4
Nyurba Rus. Fed. 65 M3
Nyyskiy Zaliv lag. Rus. Fed. 74 F1
Nzambi Congo 98 B4
Nzega Tanz. 99 D4
Nzérékoré Guinea 96 C4
N'zeto Angola 99 B4
Nzwani i. Comoros 99 E5

O

Oahe, Lake U.S.A. 130 C2
Oahu i. HI U.S.A. 127 [inset]
Oaitupu i. Tuvalu see Vaitupu
Oak Bluffs U.S.A. 135 J3
Oak City U.S.A. 129 G2
Oak Creek U.S.A. 129 J1
Oakdale U.S.A. 131 E6
Oakes U.S.A. 130 D2
Oakey Australia 112 E1
Oak Grove KY U.S.A. 134 B5
Oak Grove LA U.S.A. 131 F5
Oak Grove MI U.S.A. 134 C1
Oakham U.K. 49 G6
Oak Harbor U.S.A. 134 D3
Oak Hill OH U.S.A. 134 D4
Oak Hill WV U.S.A. 134 E5
Oakhurst U.S.A. 128 D3
Oak Lake Canada 121 K5

Oakland CA U.S.A. 128 B3
Oakland MD U.S.A. 134 F4
Oakland ME U.S.A. 135 K1
Oakland NE U.S.A. 130 D3
Oakland OR U.S.A. 126 C4
Oakland airport U.S.A. 128 B3
Oakland City U.S.A. 134 B4
Oaklands Australia 112 C5
Oak Lawn U.S.A. 134 B3
Oakley U.S.A. 130 C4
Oakover r. Australia 108 C5
Oak Park IL U.S.A. 134 B3
Oak Park MI U.S.A. 134 C2
Oak Park Reservoir U.S.A. 129 I1
Oakridge U.S.A. 126 C4
Oak Ridge U.S.A. 132 C4
Oakvale Australia 111 C7
Oak View U.S.A. 128 D4
Oakville Canada 134 F2
Oakwood OH U.S.A. 134 C3
Oakwood TN U.S.A. 134 B5
Oamaru N.Z. 113 C7
Oaro N.Z. 113 D6
Oasis CA U.S.A. 128 E3
Oasis NV U.S.A. 126 E4
Oates Coast reg. Antarctica see Oates Land
Oates Land reg. Antarctica 152 H2
Oaxaca Mex. 136 E5
Oaxaca de Juárez Mex. see Oaxaca
Ob' r. Rus. Fed. 72 E2
Ob, Gulf of sea chan. Rus. Fed. see Obskaya Guba
Oba Canada 122 D4
Oba i. Vanuatu see Aoba
Obala Cameroon 96 E4
Obama Japan 75 D6
Oban U.K. 50 D4
O Barco Spain 57 C2
Obbia Somalia see Hobyo
Obdorsk Rus. Fed. see Salekhard
Óbecse Serb. and Mont. see Bečej
Obed Canada 120 G4
Oberaula Germany 53 J4
Oberdorla Germany 53 K3
Oberhausen Germany 52 G3
Oberlin KS U.S.A. 130 C4
Oberlin LA U.S.A. 131 E6
Oberlin OH U.S.A. 134 D3
Obermoschel Germany 53 H5
Oberon Australia 112 D4
Oberpfälzer Wald mts Germany 53 M5
Obersinn Germany 53 J4
Oberthulba Germany 53 J4
Obertshausen Germany 53 I4
Oberwälder Land reg. Germany 53 J3
Obi i. Indon. 69 H7
Óbidos Brazil 143 G4
Obihiro Japan 74 F4
Obil'noye Rus. Fed. 43 J7

▶Ob'-Irtysh r. Rus. Fed. 64 H3
2nd longest river and largest drainage basin in Asia and 5th longest river in the world.
Asia 60–61
World 12–13

Obluch'ye Rus. Fed. 74 C2
Obninsk Rus. Fed. 43 H5
Obo Cent. Afr. Rep. 98 C3
Obock Djibouti 86 F7
Ŏbŏk N. Korea 74 C4
Obokote Dem. Rep. Congo 98 C4
Obo Liang China 80 H4
Obouya Congo 98 B4
Oboyan' Rus. Fed. 43 H6
Obozerskiy Rus. Fed. 42 I3
Obregón, Presa resr Mex. 127 F8
Obrenovac Serb. and Mont. 59 I2
Obruk Turkey 90 D3
Observatory Hill hill Australia 109 F7
Obshchiy Syrt hills Rus. Fed. 41 Q5
Obskaya Guba sea chan. Rus. Fed. 64 I3
Obuasi Ghana 96 C4
Ob"yachevo Rus. Fed. 42 K3
Ocala U.S.A. 133 D6
Ocampo Mex. 131 C7
Ocaña Col. 142 D2
Ocaña Spain 57 E4
Occidental, Cordillera mts Chile 142 E7
Occidental, Cordillera mts Col. 142 C3
Occidental, Cordillera mts Peru 142 D7
Oceana U.S.A. 134 E5
Ocean Cay i. Bahamas 133 E7
Ocean City MD U.S.A. 135 H4
Ocean City NJ U.S.A. 135 H4
Ocean Falls Canada 120 E4
Ocean Island Kiribati see Banaba
Ocean Island atoll U.S.A. see Kure Atoll
Oceanside U.S.A. 128 E5
Ocean Springs U.S.A. 131 F6
Ochakiv Ukr. 59 N1
Och'amch'ire Georgia 91 F2
Ocher Rus. Fed. 41 Q4
Ochiishi-misaki pt Japan 74 G4
Ochil Hills U.K. 50 F4
Ochrida, Lake Albania/Macedonia see Ohrid, Lake
Ochsenfurt Germany 53 K5
Ochtrup Germany 53 H2
Ocilla U.S.A. 133 D6
Ockelbo Sweden 45 J6
Ocolaşul Mare, Vârful mt. Romania 59 K1
Oconomowoc U.S.A. 134 A2
Oconto U.S.A. 134 B1
Octeville-sur-Mer France 49 H9
October Revolution Island Rus. Fed. see Oktyabr'skoy Revolyutsii, Ostrov
Ocussi enclave East Timor 108 D2
Ocussi-Ambeno enclave East Timor see Ocussi
Oda, Jebel mt. Sudan 86 E5
Ódáðahraun lava field Iceland 44 [inset]
Ŏdaejin N. Korea 74 C4
Odae-san National Park S. Korea 75 C5
Ōdate Japan 75 F4
Odawara Japan 75 E6
Odda Norway 45 E6
Odei r. Canada 121 L3
Odell U.S.A. 134 B3
Odem U.S.A. 131 D7
Odemira Port. 57 B5
Ödemiş Turkey 59 L5
Ödenburg Hungary see Sopron
Odense Denmark 45 G9
Odenwald reg. Germany 53 I5
Oder r. Germany 53 J3
also known as Odra (Poland)
Oderbucht b. Germany 47 O3
Oder-Havel-Kanal canal Germany 53 N2
Odesa Ukr. 59 N1
Ödeshog Sweden 45 I7
Odessa Ukr. see Odesa
Odessa TX U.S.A. 131 C6
Odessa WA U.S.A. 126 D3
Odessus Bulg. see Varna
Odiel r. Spain 57 C5
Odienné Côte d'Ivoire 96 C4
Odintsovo Rus. Fed. 42 H5
Ôdôngk Cambodia 71 D5
Odra r. Germany/Pol. 47 Q6
also known as Oder (Germany)
Odzala, Parc National d' nat. park Congo 98 B3
Oea Libya see Tripoli
Oé-Cusse enclave East Timor see Ocussi
Oecussi enclave East Timor see Ocussi
Oeiras Brazil 143 J5
Oekussi enclave East Timor see Ocussi
Oelsnitz Germany 53 M4
Oenkerk Neth. 52 F1
Oenpelli Australia 108 F3
Oesel i. Estonia see Hiiumaa
Oeufs, Lac des l. Canada 123 G3
Of Turkey 91 F2
O'Fallon r. U.S.A. 126 G3
Ofanto r. Italy 58 G4
Ofaqim Israel 85 B4
Offa Nigeria 96 D4
Offenbach am Main Germany 53 I4
Offenburg Germany 47 K6
Oga Japan 75 E5
Ogadēn reg. Eth. 98 E3
Oga-hantō pen. Japan 75 E5
Ōgaki Japan 75 E6
Ogallala U.S.A. 130 C3
Ogasawara-shotō is Japan see Bonin Islands
Ogbomosho Nigeria 96 D4
Ogbomoso Nigeria see Ogbomosho
Ogden IA U.S.A. 130 E3
Ogden UT U.S.A. 126 F4
Ogden, Mount Canada 120 C3
Ogdensburg U.S.A. 135 H1
Ogidaki Canada 122 D5
Ogilvie r. Canada 118 E3
Ogilvie Mountains Canada 118 D3
Oglethorpe, Mount U.S.A. 133 C5
Oglio r. Italy 58 D2
Oglongi Rus. Fed. 74 E1
Ogmore Australia 110 E4
Ogoamas, Gunung mt. Indon. 69 G6
Ogodzha Rus. Fed. 74 D1
Ogoja Nigeria 96 D4
Ogoki r. Canada 122 D4
Ogoki Lake Canada 130 G1
Ogoki Reservoir Canada 122 C4
Ogoron Rus. Fed. 74 C1
Ogosta r. Bulg. 59 J3
Ogre Latvia 45 N8
Ogulin Croatia 58 F2
Ogurchinskiy, Ostrov i. Turkm. 88 D2
Ogurjaly Adasy i. Turkm. see Ogurchinskiy, Ostrov
Oğuzeli Turkey 85 C1
Ohai N.Z. 113 A7
Ohakune N.Z. 113 E4
Ohanet Alg. 96 D2
Ōhata Japan 74 F4
Ohcejohka Fin. see Utsjoki
O'Higgins, Lago l. Chile 144 B7
Ohio r. U.S.A. 134 A5
Ohio state U.S.A. 134 D3
Ohm r. Germany 53 I4
Ohrdruf Germany 53 K4
Ohře r. Czech Rep. 53 N4
Ohre r. Germany 53 L2
Ohrid Macedonia 59 I4
Ohrid, Lake Albania/Macedonia 59 I4
Ohridsko Ezero l. Albania/Macedonia see Ohrid, Lake
Ohrigstad S. Africa 101 J3
Öhringen Germany 53 J5
Ohrit, Liqeni i l. Albania/Macedonia see Ohrid, Lake
Ohura N.Z. 113 E4
Oiapoque r. Brazil/Fr. Guiana 143 H3
Oich r. U.K. 50 E3
Oiga China 76 B2
Oignies France 52 C4
Oil City U.S.A. 134 F3
Oise r. France 52 C6
Ōita Japan 75 C6
Oiti mt. Greece 59 J5
Ojai U.S.A. 128 D4
Ojalava i. Samoa see Upolu
Ojinaga Mex. 131 B6
Ojiya Japan 75 E5
Ojo Caliente U.S.A. 127 G5
Ojo de Laguna Mex. 127 G7

▶Ojos del Salado, Nevado mt. Arg./Chile 144 C3
2nd highest mountain in South America.

Oka r. Rus. Fed. 43 I4
Oka r. Rus. Fed. 72 I1
Okahandja Namibia 100 C1
Okahukura N.Z. 113 E4
Okakarara Namibia 99 B6
Okak Islands Canada 123 J2
Okanagan Lake Canada 120 G5
Okanda Sri Lanka 84 D5
Okano r. Gabon 98 B4
Okanogan U.S.A. 126 D2
Okanogan r. U.S.A. 126 D2
Okara Pak. 89 I4
Okarem Turkm. 88 D2
Okataina vol. N.Z. see Tarawera, Mount
Okaukuejo Namibia 99 B5
Okavango r. Africa 99 C5

▶Okavango Delta swamp Botswana 99 C5
Largest oasis in the world.

Okavango Swamps Botswana see Okavango Delta
Okaya Japan 75 E5
Okayama Japan 75 D6
Okazaki Japan 75 E6
Okeechobee U.S.A. 133 D7
Okeechobee, Lake U.S.A. 133 D7
Okeene U.S.A. 131 D4
Okefenokee Swamp U.S.A. 133 D6
Okehampton U.K. 49 C8
Okemah U.S.A. 131 D5
Oker r. Germany 53 K2
Okha India 82 B5
Okha Rus. Fed. 74 F1
Okha Rann marsh India 82 B5
Okhotsk Rus. Fed. 65 P4
Okhotsk, Sea of Japan/Rus. Fed. 74 G3
Okhotskoye More sea Japan/Rus. Fed. see Okhotsk, Sea of
Okhtyrka Ukr. 43 G6
Okinawa i. Japan 75 B8
Okinawa-guntō is Japan see Okinawa-shotō
Okinawa-shotō is Japan 75 B8
Okino-Daitō-jima i. Japan 73 O8
Okino-Tori-shima i. Japan 73 P8
Oki-shotō is Japan 73 O5
Oki-shotō is Japan 75 D5
Okkan Myanmar 70 A3
Oklahoma state U.S.A. 131 D5

▶Oklahoma City U.S.A. 131 D5
State capital of Oklahoma.

Okmulgee U.S.A. 131 D5
Okolona KY U.S.A. 134 C4
Okolona MS U.S.A. 131 F5
Okondja Gabon 98 B4
Okovskiy Les for. Rus. Fed. 42 G5
Okoyo Congo 98 B4
Øksfjord Norway 44 M1
Oktemberyan Armenia see Hoktemberyan
Oktwin Myanmar 70 B3
Oktyabr' Kazakh. see Kandyagash
Oktyabr'sk Kazakh. see Kandyagash
Oktyabr'skiy Belarus see Aktsyabrski
Oktyabr'skiy Amurskaya Oblast' Rus. Fed. 74 C1
Oktyabr'skiy Arkhangel'skaya Oblast' Rus. Fed. 42 I3
Oktyabr'skiy Kamchatskaya Oblast' Rus. Fed. 65 Q4
Oktyabr'skiy Respublika Bashkortostan Rus. Fed. 41 Q5
Oktyabr'skiy Volgogradskaya Oblast' Rus. Fed. 43 I7
Oktyabr'skoye Rus. Fed. 41 T3
Oktyabr'skoy Revolyutsii, Ostrov i. Rus. Fed. 65 K2
Okulovka Rus. Fed. 42 G4
Okushiri-tō i. Japan 74 E4
Okusi enclave East Timor see Ocussi
Okuta Nigeria 96 D4
Okwa watercourse Botswana 100 G1
Ólafsvík Iceland 44 [inset]
Olakkur India 84 C3
Olancha U.S.A. 128 D3
Olancha Peak U.S.A. 128 D3
Öland i. Sweden 45 J8
Olary Australia 111 C7
Olathe CO U.S.A. 129 J2
Olathe KS U.S.A. 130 E4
Olavarría Arg. 144 D5
Oława Poland 47 P5
Olbernhau Germany 53 N4
Olbia Sardinia Italy 58 C4
Old Bahama Channel Bahamas/Cuba 133 E8
Old Bastar India 84 D2
Oldcastle Rep. of Ireland 51 E4
Old Cork Australia 110 C4
Old Crow Canada 118 E3
Oldeboorn Neth. 52 F1
Oldenburg Germany 53 I1
Oldenburg in Holstein Germany 47 M3
Oldenzaal Neth. 52 G2
Olderdalen Norway 44 L2
Old Forge U.S.A. 135 H2
Old Gidgee Australia 109 B6
Oldham U.K. 48 E5
Old Harbor U.S.A. 118 C4
Old Head of Kinsale hd Rep. of Ireland 51 D6
Oldman r. Canada 120 I5
Oldmeldrum U.K. 50 G3
Old Perlican Canada 123 L5
Old River U.S.A. 128 D4
Olds Canada 120 H5
Old Speck Mountain U.S.A. 135 J1
Old Station U.S.A. 128 C1
Old Wives Lake Canada 121 J5
Olean U.S.A. 135 F2
Olecko Poland 47 S3
Olekma r. Rus. Fed. 65 N3
Olekminsk Rus. Fed. 65 N3
Olekminskiy-Stanovik mts Rus. Fed. 73 M2
Oleksandrivs'k Ukr. see Zaporizhzhya
Oleksandriya Ukr. 43 G6
Ølen Norway 45 D7
Olenegorsk Rus. Fed. 44 R2
Olenek Rus. Fed. 65 M3
Olenek r. Rus. Fed. 65 M2
Olenek Bay Rus. Fed. see Olenekskiy Zaliv
Olenekskiy Zaliv b. Rus. Fed. 65 N2
Olenino Rus. Fed. 42 G4
Olenitsa Rus. Fed. 42 G2
Olenivs'ki Kar"yery Ukr. see Dokuchayevs'k
Olenya Rus. Fed. see Olenegorsk
Oleshky Ukr. see Tsyurupyns'k
Olevs'k Ukr. 43 E6
Ol'ga Rus. Fed. 74 D4
Olga, Lac l. Canada 122 F4
Olga, Mount Australia 109 E6
Ol'ginsk Rus. Fed. 74 D1
Olginskoye Rus. Fed. see Kochubeyevskoye
Ölgiy Mongolia 80 G2
Olhão Port. 57 C5
Olia Chain mts Australia 109 E6
Olifants r. Moz./S. Africa 101 J3
also known as Elefantes
Olifants watercourse Namibia 100 D3
Olifants S. Africa 101 J2
Olifants r. W. Cape S. Africa 100 D6
Olifants r. W. Cape S. Africa 100 E7
Olifantshoek S. Africa 100 F4
Olifantsrivierberge mts S. Africa 100 D7
Olimarao atoll Micronesia 69 L5
Olimbos hill Cyprus see Olympos
Olimbos mt. Greece see Olympus, Mount
Olimpos Beydağları Milli Parkı nat. park Turkey 59 N6
Olinda Brazil 143 L5
Olinga Moz. 99 D5
Olio Australia 110 C4
Oliphants Drift S. Africa 101 H3
Olisipo Port. see Lisbon
Oliva Spain 57 F4
Oliva, Cordillera de mts Arg./Chile 144 C3
Olivares, Cerro de mt. Arg./Chile 144 C4
Olive Hill U.S.A. 134 D4
Olivehurst U.S.A. 128 C2
Oliveira dos Brejinhos Brazil 145 C1
Olivença Moz. see Lupilichi
Olivenza Spain 57 C4
Oliver Lake Canada 121 K3
Olivet MI U.S.A. 134 C2
Olivet SD U.S.A. 130 D3
Olivia U.S.A. 130 E2
Ol'khovka Rus. Fed. 43 J6
Ollagüe Chile 144 C2
Ollombo Congo 98 B4
Olmaliq Uzbek. see Almalyk
Olmos Peru 142 C5
Olmütz Czech Rep. see Olomouc
Olney U.K. 49 G6
Olney IL U.S.A. 130 F4
Olney MD U.S.A. 135 G4
Olney TX U.S.A. 131 D5
Olofström Sweden 45 I8
Olomane r. Canada 123 J4
Olomouc Czech Rep. 47 P6
Olonets Rus. Fed. 42 G3
Olongapo Phil. 69 G4
Oloron-Ste-Marie France 56 D5
Olosenga atoll American Samoa see Swains Island
Olot Spain 57 H2
Olot Uzbek. see Alat
Olovyannaya Rus. Fed. 73 L2
Oloy, Qatorkŭhi mts Asia see Alai Range
Olpe Germany 53 H3
Olsztyn Poland 47 R4
Olt r. Romania 59 K3
Olten Switz. 56 H3
Olteniţa Romania 59 L2
Oltu Turkey 91 F2
Oluan Pi c. Taiwan 77 I4
Ol'viopol' Ukr. see Pervomays'k
Olymbos hill Cyprus see Olympos

▶Olympia U.S.A. 126 C3
State capital of Washington.

Olympic National Park U.S.A. 126 C3
Olympos hill Cyprus 85 A2
Olympos Greece see Olympus, Mount
Olympos nat. park Greece 59 J4
Olympus, Mount Greece 59 J4
Olympus, Mount U.S.A. 126 C3
Olyutorskiy Rus. Fed. 65 R3
Olyutorskiy, Mys c. Rus. Fed. 65 S4
Olyutorskiy Zaliv b. Rus. Fed. 65 R4
Olzheras Rus. Fed. see Mezhdurechensk
Oma China 83 E2
Oma r. Rus. Fed. 42 J2
Omagh U.K. 51 E3
Omaha U.S.A. 130 E3
Omaheke admin. reg. Namibia 100 D2
Omal'skiy Khrebet mts Rus. Fed. 74 E1
▶Oman country Asia 87 I6
Asia 6, 62–63
Oman, Gulf of Asia 88 E5
Omarkot Pak. 89 H4
Omaruru Namibia 99 B6
Omate Peru 142 D7
Omaweneno Botswana 100 F3
Omba i. Vanuatu see Aoba
Ombai, Selat sea chan. East Timor/Indon. 108 D2
Ombalantu Namibia see Uutapi
Omboué Gabon 98 A4
Ombu China 83 F3
Omdraaisvlei S. Africa 100 F6
Omdurman Sudan 86 D6
Omeo Australia 112 C6
Omer U.S.A. 134 D1
Ometepec Mex. 136 E5
Omgoy Wildlife Reserve nature res. Thai. 70 B3
Om Hajēr Eritrea 86 E7
Omīdīyeh Iran 88 C4
Omineca Mountains Canada 116 E3
Omitara Namibia 100 C2
Ōmiya Japan 75 E6
Ommaney, Cape U.S.A. 120 C3
Ommen Neth. 52 G2
Omolon Rus. Fed. 65 R3
Omo National Park Eth. 98 D3
Omsk Rus. Fed. 64 I4
Omsukchan Rus. Fed. 65 Q3
Ōmū Japan 74 F3
O-mu Myanmar 70 B2
Omu, Vârful mt. Romania 59 K2
Ōmura Japan 75 C6
Omutninsk Rus. Fed. 42 L4
Onaman Lake Canada 122 D4
Onamia U.S.A. 130 E2
Onancock U.S.A. 135 H5
Onangué, Lac l. Gabon 98 B4
Onaping Lake Canada 122 E5
Onatchiway, Lac l. Canada 123 H4
Onavas Mex. 127 F7
Onawa U.S.A. 130 D3
Onaway U.S.A. 134 C1
Onbingwin Myanmar 71 B4
Oncativo Arg. 144 D4
Onchan Isle of Man 48 C4
Oncócua Angola 99 B5
Öncül Turkey 85 D1
Ondal India see Andal
Ondangwa Namibia 99 B5
Onderstedorings S. Africa 100 E6
Ondjiva Angola 99 B5
Ondo Nigeria 96 D4
Öndörhaan Mongolia 73 K3
Ondozero Rus. Fed. 42 G3
One Botswana 100 E2
One and a Half Degree Channel Maldives 81 D11
Onega Rus. Fed. 42 H3
Onega r. Rus. Fed. 42 H3
Onega, Lake Rus. Fed. 41 N3

▶Onega, Lake Rus. Fed. 42 G3
3rd largest lake in Europe.

Onega Bay g. Rus. Fed. see Onezhskaya Guba
One Hundred and Fifty Mile House Canada see 150 Mile House
One Hundred Mile House Canada see 100 Mile House
Oneida NY U.S.A. 135 H2
Oneida TN U.S.A. 134 C5
Oneida Lake U.S.A. 135 H2
O'Neill U.S.A. 130 D3
Onekama U.S.A. 134 B1
Onekotan, Ostrov i. Rus. Fed. 65 Q5
Oneonta AL U.S.A. 133 C5
Oneonta NY U.S.A. 135 H2
Oneşti Romania 59 L1
Onezhskaya Guba g. Rus. Fed. 42 G2
Onezhskoye Ozero l. Rus. Fed. see Onega, Lake
Onezhskoye Ozero l. Rus. Fed. see Onega, Lake
Ong r. India 84 D1
Onga Gabon 98 B4
Ongers watercourse S. Africa 100 F5
Ongi Mongolia 72 I3
Ongiyn Gol r. Mongolia 80 J3
Ongjin N. Korea 75 B5
Ongole India 84 D3
Onida U.S.A. 130 C2
Onilahy r. Madag. 99 E6
Onistagane, Lac l. Canada 123 H4
Onitsha Nigeria 96 D4
Onjati Mountain Namibia 100 C2
Onjiva Angola see Ondjiva
Ono-i-Lau i. Fiji 107 I4
Onomichi Japan 75 D6
Onon atoll Micronesia see Namonuito
Onor, Gora mt. Rus. Fed. 74 F2
Onotoa atoll Kiribati 107 H2
Onseepkans S. Africa 100 D5
Onslow Australia 108 A5
Onslow Bay U.S.A. 133 E5
Onstwedde Neth. 52 H1
Ontake-san vol. Japan 75 E6
Ontario prov. Canada 134 E1
Ontario U.S.A. 128 E4
Ontario, Lake Canada/U.S.A. 135 G2
Ontong Java Atoll Solomon Is 107 F2
Onutu atoll Kiribati see Onotoa
Onverwacht Suriname 143 G2
Onyx U.S.A. 128 D4
Oodnadatta Australia 111 A5
Oodweyne Somalia 98 E3
Ooldea Australia 109 E7
Ooldea Range hills Australia 109 E7
Oologah Lake resr U.S.A. 131 E4
Ooratippra r. Australia 110 B4
Oos-Londen S. Africa see East London
Oostburg Neth. 52 D3
Oostende Belgium see Ostend
Oostendorp Neth. 52 F2
Oosterhout Neth. 52 E3
Oosterschelde est. Neth. 52 D3
Oosterwolde Neth. 52 G2
Oostvleteren Belgium 52 C4
Oost-Vlieland Neth. 52 F1
Ootacamund India see Udagamandalam
Ootsa Lake Canada 120 E4
Ootsa Lake l. Canada 120 E4
Opal Mex. 131 C7
Opala Dem. Rep. Congo 98 C4
Oparino Rus. Fed. 42 K4
Oparo i. Fr. Polynesia see Rapa
Opasatika r. Canada 122 E4
Opasatika Lake Canada 122 E4
Opasquia Canada 121 M4
Opataca, Lac l. Canada 122 G4
Opava Czech Rep. 47 P6
Opel hill Germany 53 H5
Opelika U.S.A. 133 C5
Opelousas U.S.A. 131 E6
Opeongo Lake Canada 122 F5
Opheim U.S.A. 126 G2
Opienge Dem. Rep. Congo 98 C3
Opinaca r. Canada 122 F3
Opinaca, Réservoir resr Canada 122 F3
Opinnagau r. Canada 122 E3
Opiscotéo, Lac l. Canada 123 H3
Op Luang National Park Thai. 70 B3
Opmeer Neth. 52 E2
Opochka Rus. Fed. 45 P8
Opocopa, Lac l. Canada 123 I3
Opodepe Mex. 136 B3
Opole Poland 47 P5
Oporto Port. 57 B3
Opotiki N.Z. 113 F4
Opp U.S.A. 133 C6
Oppdal Norway 44 F5
Oppeln Poland see Opole
Opportunity U.S.A. 126 D3
Opunake N.Z. 113 D4
Opuwo Namibia 99 B5
Oqsu r. Tajik. 89 I2
Oracle U.S.A. 129 H5
Oradea Romania 59 I1
Orahovac Serb. and Mont. 59 I3
Orai India 82 D4
Oraibi U.S.A. 129 H4
Oraibi Wash watercourse U.S.A. 129 H4
Oral Kazakh. see Ural'sk
Oran Alg. 57 F6
Orán Arg. 144 D2
O Rang Cambodia 71 D4
Orang India 83 H4
Ŏrang N. Korea 74 C4
Orange Australia 112 D4
Orange France 56 G4
Orange r. Namibia/S. Africa 100 C5
Orange CA U.S.A. 128 E5
Orange MA U.S.A. 135 I2
Orange TX U.S.A. 131 E6
Orange VA U.S.A. 135 F4
Orange, Cabo c. Brazil 143 H3
Orangeburg U.S.A. 133 D5
Orange City U.S.A. 130 D3
Orange Cone sea feature S. Atlantic Ocean 148 I8
Orange Free State prov. S. Africa see Free State
Orangeville Canada 134 E2
Orange Walk Belize 136 G5
Oranienburg Germany 53 N2
Oranje r. Namibia/S. Africa see Orange
Oranje Gebergte hills Suriname 143 G3
Oranjemund Namibia 100 C5

▶Oranjestad Aruba 137 J6
Capital of Aruba.

Oranmore Rep. of Ireland 51 D4
Orapa Botswana 99 C6
Orăştie Romania 59 J2
Oraşul Stalin Romania see Braşov
Oravais Fin. 44 M5
Orba Co l. China 82 E2
Orbetello Italy 58 D3
Orbost Australia 112 D6
Orcadas research station S. Atlantic Ocean 152 A2
Orchard City U.S.A. 129 J2
Orchha India 82 D4
Orchila, Isla i. Venez. 142 E1
Orchy r. U.K. 50 D4
Orcutt U.S.A. 128 C4
Ord r. Australia 108 E3
Ord U.S.A. 130 D3
Ord, Mount hill Australia 108 D4
Ordenes Spain see Ordes
Orderville U.S.A. 129 G3
Ordes Spain 57 B2
Ordesa - Monte Perdido, Parque Nacional nat. park Spain 57 G2
Ord Mountain U.S.A. 128 E4
Ord River Dam Australia 108 E4
Ordu Hatay Turkey see Yayladağı
Ordu Ordu Turkey 90 E2
Ordubad Azer. 91 G3
Ordway U.S.A. 130 C4
Ordzhonikidze Rus. Fed. see Vladikavkaz
Ore Nigeria 96 D4
Oreana U.S.A. 128 D1
Örebro Sweden 45 I7
Oregon IL U.S.A. 130 F3
Oregon OH U.S.A. 134 D3
Oregon state U.S.A. 126 C4
Oregon City U.S.A. 126 C3
Orekhov Ukr. see Orikhiv
Orekhovo-Zuyevo Rus. Fed. 42 H5
Orel Rus. Fed. 43 H5
Orel, Gora mt. Rus. Fed. 74 E1
Orel', Ozero l. Rus. Fed. 74 E1
Orem U.S.A. 129 H1
Ore Mountains Czech Rep./Germany see Erzgebirge
Orenburg Rus. Fed. 64 G4
Orense Spain see Ourense
Oreor Palau see Koror
Orepuki N.Z. 113 A8
Öresund strait Denmark/Sweden 45 H9
Oretana, Cordillera mts Spain see Toledo, Montes de
Orewa N.Z. 113 E3
Oreye Belgium 52 F4
Orfanou, Kolpos b. Greece 59 J4
Orford Australia 111 [inset]
Orford U.K. 49 I6
Orford Ness hd U.K. 49 I6
Organabo Fr. Guiana 143 H2
Organ Pipe Cactus National Monument nat. park U.S.A. 129 G5
Orge r. France 52 C6
Orgün Afgh. 89 H3
Orhaneli Turkey 59 M5
Orhangazi Turkey 59 M4
Orhon Gol r. Mongolia 80 J2
Orichi Rus. Fed. 42 K4
Oriental, Cordillera mts Bol. 142 E7
Oriental, Cordillera mts Col. 142 D2
Oriental, Cordillera mts Peru 142 E6
Orihuela Spain 57 F4
Orikhiv Ukr. 43 G7
Orillia Canada 134 F1
Orimattila Fin. 45 N6
Orin U.S.A. 126 G4
Orinoco r. Col./Venez. 142 F2
Orinoco Delta Venez. 142 F2
Orissa state India 84 E1
Orissaare Estonia 45 M7
Oristano Sardinia Italy 58 C5
Orivesi Fin. 45 N6
Orivesi l. Fin. 44 P5
Oriximiná Brazil 143 G4
Orizaba Mex. 136 E5

▶Orizaba, Pico de vol. Mex. 136 E5
3rd highest mountain in North America.

Orizona Brazil 145 A2
Orkanger Norway 44 F5
Örkelljunga Sweden 45 H8
Orkla r. Norway 44 F5
Orkney S. Africa 101 H4
Orkney is U.K. 50 F1
Orla U.S.A. 131 C6
Orland U.S.A. 128 B2
Orlândia Brazil 145 B3
Orlando U.S.A. 133 D6
Orland Park U.S.A. 134 B3
Orleaes Brazil 145 A5
Orléans France 56 E3
Orleans IN U.S.A. 134 B4
Orleans VT U.S.A. 135 I1
Orléans, Île d' i. Canada 123 H5
Orléansville Alg. see Ech Chélif

Orlik Rus. Fed. 72 H2
Orlov Rus. Fed. 42 K4
Orlov Gay Rus. Fed. 43 K6
Orlovskiy Rus. Fed. 43 I7
Orly *airport* France 52 C6
Ormara Pak. 89 G5
Ormara, Ras *hd* Pak. 89 G5
Ormiston Canada 121 J5
Ormoc Phil. 69 G4
Ormskirk U.K. 48 E5
Ormstown Canada 135 I1
Ornach Pak. 89 G5
Ornain *r.* France 52 E6
Orne *r.* France 56 D2
Ørnes Norway 44 H3
Örnsköldsvik Sweden 44 K5
Orobie, Alpi *mts* Italy 58 C1
Orobo, Serra do *hills* Brazil 145 C1
Orodara Burkina 96 C3
Orofino U.S.A. 126 D3
Oro Grande U.S.A. 128 E4
Orogrande U.S.A. 127 G6
Orol Dengizi *salt l.* Kazakh./Uzbek. *see* Aral Sea
Oromocto Canada 123 I5
Oromocto Lake Canada 123 I5
Oron Israel 85 B4
Orona *atoll* Kiribati 107 I2
Orono U.S.A. 132 G2
Orontes *r.* Asia 90 E3 *see* 'Āṣī, Nahr al
Orontes *r.* Lebanon/Syria 85 C2
Oroqen Zizhiqi China *see* Alihe
Oroquieta Phil. 69 G5
Orós, Açude *resr* Brazil 143 K5
Orosei, Golfo di *b.* *Sardinia* Italy 58 C4
Orosháza Hungary 59 I1
Oroville U.S.A. 128 C2
Oroville, Lake U.S.A. 128 C2
Orqohan China 74 A2
Orr U.S.A. 130 E1
Orsa Sweden 45 I6
Orsha Belarus 43 F5
Orshanka Rus. Fed. 42 J4
Orsk Rus. Fed. 64 G4
Ørsta Norway 44 E5
Orta Toroslar *plat.* Turkey 85 A1
Ortegal, Cabo *c.* Spain 57 C2
Orthez France 56 D5
Ortigueira Spain 57 C2
Ortiz Mex. 127 F7
Ortles *mt.* Italy 58 D1
Orton U.K. 48 E4
Ortona Italy 58 F3
Ortonville U.S.A. 130 D2
Ortospana Afgh. *see* Kābul
Orulgan, Khrebet *mts* Rus. Fed. 65 N3
Orumbo Namibia 100 C2
Orūmīyeh Iran *see* Urmia
Oruro Bol. 142 E7
Orūzgān Afgh. 89 G3
Orvieto Italy 58 E3
Orville Coast Antarctica 152 L1
Orwell *OH* U.S.A. 134 E3
Orwell *VT* U.S.A. 135 I2
Oryol Rus. Fed. *see* Orel
Os Norway 44 G5
Osa Rus. Fed. 41 R4
Osa, Península de *pen.* Costa Rica 137 H7
Osage *IA* U.S.A. 130 E3
Osage *WV* U.S.A. 134 E4
Osage *WY* U.S.A. 126 G3
Ōsaka Japan 75 D6
Osakarovka Kazakh. 80 D1
Osawatomie U.S.A. 130 E4
Osborne U.S.A. 130 D4
Osby Sweden 45 H8
Osceola *IA* U.S.A. 130 E3
Osceola *MO* U.S.A. 130 E4
Osceola *NE* U.S.A. 130 D3
Oschatz Germany 53 N3
Oschersleben (Bode) Germany 53 L2
Oschiri *Sardinia* Italy 58 C4
Ösel *i.* Estonia *see* Hiiumaa
Osetr *r.* Rus. Fed. 43 H5
Ōse-zaki *pt* Japan 75 C6
Osgoode Canada 135 H1
Osgood Mountains U.S.A. 126 D4
Osh Kyrg. 80 D3
Oshakati Namibia 99 B5
Oshawa Canada 135 F2
Oshika-hantō *pen.* Japan 75 F5
Ō-shima *i.* Japan 74 E4
Ō-shima *i.* Japan 75 E6
Oshkosh *NE* U.S.A. 130 C3
Oshkosh *WI* U.S.A. 134 A1
Oshmyany Belarus *see* Ashmyany
Oshnovīyeh Iran 88 B2
Oshogbo Nigeria 96 D4
Oshtorān Kūh *mt.* Iran 88 C3
Oshwe Dem. Rep. Congo 98 B4
Osijek Croatia 58 H2
Osilinka *r.* Canada 120 E3
Osimo Italy 58 E3
Osipenko Ukr. *see* Berdyans'k
Osipovichi Belarus *see* Asipovichy
Osiyan India 82 C4
Osizweni S. Africa 101 J4
Osječenica *mts* Bos.-Herz. 58 G2
Ösjön *l.* Sweden 44 I5
Oskaloosa U.S.A. 130 E3
Oskarshamn Sweden 45 J8
Öskemen Kazakh. *see* Ust'-Kamenogorsk

▶Oslo Norway 45 G7
Capital of Norway.

Oslofjorden *sea chan.* Norway 41 G7
Osmanabad India 84 C2
Osmancık Turkey 90 D2
Osmaneli Turkey 59 M4
Osmaniye Turkey 90 E3
Osmannagar India 84 C2
Os'mino Rus. Fed. 45 P7
Osnabrück Germany 53 I2
Osnaburg *atoll* Fr. Polynesia *see* Mururoa
Osogbo Nigeria *see* Oshogbo
Osogovska Planina *mts* Bulg./Macedonia 59 J3
Osogovske Planine *mts* Bulg./Macedonia *see* Osogovska Planina
Osogovski Planini *mts* Bulg./Macedonia *see* Osogovska Planina
Osorno Chile 144 B6
Osorno Spain 57 D2
Osoyoos Canada 120 G5
Osøyri Norway 45 D6
Osprey Reef Australia 110 D2
Oss Neth. 52 F3
Ossa, Mount Australia 111 [inset]
Osseo U.S.A. 122 C5
Ossineke U.S.A. 134 D1
Ossining U.S.A. 135 I3
Ossipee U.S.A. 135 J2
Ossipee Lake U.S.A. 135 J2
Oßmannstedt Germany 53 L3
Ossokmanuan Lake Canada 123 I3
Ossora Rus. Fed. 65 R4
Ostashkov Rus. Fed. 42 G4
Ostbevern Germany 53 H2
Oste *r.* Germany 53 J1
Ostend Belgium 52 C3
Ostende Belgium *see* Ostend
Osterburg (Altmark) Germany 53 L2
Österbymo Sweden 45 I8
Österdalälven *l.* Sweden 45 H6
Østerdalen *valley* Norway 45 G5
Osterfeld Germany 53 L3
Osterholz-Scharmbeck Germany 53 I1
Osterode am Harz Germany 53 K3
Österreich *country* Europe *see* Austria
Östersund Sweden 44 I5
Osterwieck Germany 53 K3
Ostfriesische Inseln Germany *see* East Frisian Islands
Ostfriesland *reg.* Germany 53 H1
Östhammar Sweden 45 K6
Ostrava Czech Rep. 47 Q6
Ostróda Poland 47 Q4
Ostrogozhsk Rus. Fed. 43 H6
Ostrov Czech Rep. 53 M4
Ostrov Rus. Fed. 45 P8
Ostrovets Poland *see* Ostrowiec Świętokrzyski
Ostrovskoye Rus. Fed. 42 I4
Ostrov Vrangelya *i.* Rus. Fed. *see* Wrangel Island
Ostrów Poland *see* Ostrów Wielkopolski
Ostrowiec Poland *see* Ostrowiec Świętokrzyski
Ostrowiec Świętokrzyski Poland 43 D6
Ostrów Mazowiecka Poland 47 R4
Ostrowo Poland *see* Ostrów Wielkopolski
Ostrów Wielkopolski Poland 47 P5
O'Sullivan Lake Canada 122 D4
Osŭm *r.* Bulg. 59 K3
Ōsumi-shotō *is* Japan 75 C7
Osuna Spain 57 D5
Oswego *KS* U.S.A. 131 E4
Oswego *NY* U.S.A. 135 G2
Oswestry U.K. 49 D6
Otago Peninsula N.Z. 113 C7
Otahiti *i.* Fr. Polynesia *see* Tahiti
Otaki N.Z. 113 E5
Otanmäki Fin. 44 O4
Otaru Japan 74 F4
Otavi Namibia 99 B5
Ōtawara Japan 75 F5
Otdia *atoll* Marshall Is *see* Wotje
Otelnuc, Lac *l.* Canada 123 H2
Otematata N.Z. 113 C7
Otepää Estonia 45 O7
Otgon Tenger Uul *mt.* Mongolia 80 I2
Otinapa Mex. 131 B7
Otira N.Z. 113 C6
Otis U.S.A. 130 C3
Otish, Monts *hills* Canada 123 H4
Otjinene Namibia 99 B6
Otjiwarongo Namibia 99 B6
Otjozondjupa *admin. reg.* Namibia 100 C1
Otley U.K. 48 F5
Otorohanga N.Z. 113 E4
Otoskwin *r.* Canada 121 N5
Otpan, Gora *hill* Kazakh. 91 H1
Otpor Rus. Fed. *see* Zabaykal'sk
Otradnoye Rus. Fed. *see* Otradnyy
Otradnyy Rus. Fed. 43 K5
Otranto Italy 58 H4
Otranto, Strait of Albania/Italy 58 H4
Otrogovo Rus. Fed. *see* Stepnoye
Otrozhnyy Rus. Fed. 65 S3
Otsego Lake U.S.A. 135 H2
Ōtsu Japan 75 D6
Otta Norway 45 F6

▶Ottawa Canada 135 H1
Capital of Canada.

Ottawa *r.* Canada 122 G5
also known as Rivière des Outaouais
Ottawa *IL* U.S.A. 130 F3
Ottawa *KS* U.S.A. 130 E4
Ottawa *OH* U.S.A. 134 C3
Ottawa Islands Canada 122 E2
Otter *r.* U.K. 49 D8
Otterbein U.S.A. 134 B3
Otterburn U.K. 48 E3
Otter Rapids Canada 122 E4
Ottersberg Germany 53 J1
Ottignies Belgium 52 E4
Ottumwa U.S.A. 130 E3
Ottweiler Germany 53 H5
Otukpo Nigeria 96 D4
Oturkpo Nigeria *see* Otukpo
Otuzco Peru 142 C5
Otway, Cape Australia 112 A7
Otway National Park Australia 112 A7
Ouachita *r.* U.S.A. 131 F6
Ouachita, Lake U.S.A. 131 E5
Ouachita Mountains *Arkansas/Oklahoma* U.S.A. 125 I5
Ouachita Mountains *Arkansas/Oklahoma* U.S.A. 131 E5
Ouadda Cent. Afr. Rep. 98 C3
Ouaddaï *reg.* Chad 97 F3

▶Ouagadougou Burkina 96 C3
Capital of Burkina.

Ouahigouya Burkina 96 C3
Ouahran Alg. *see* Oran
Ouaka *r.* Cent. Afr. Rep. 98 B3
Oualâta Mauritania 96 C3
Ouallam Niger 96 D3
Ouanda-Djailé Cent. Afr. Rep. 94 C3
Ouando Cent. Afr. Rep. 98 C3
Ouango Cent. Afr. Rep. 98 C3
Ouara *r.* Cent. Afr. Rep. 98 C3
Ouarâne *reg.* Mauritania 96 C2
Ouargaye Burkina 96 D3
Ouargla Alg. 54 F5
Ouarogou Burkina *see* Ouargaye
Ouarzazate Morocco 54 C5
Oubangui *r.* Cent. Afr. Rep./Dem. Rep. Congo *see* Ubangi
Oubergpas *pass* S. Africa 100 G7
Oudenaarde Belgium 52 D4
Oudtshoorn S. Africa 100 F7
Oud-Turnhout Belgium 52 E3
Oued Tlélat Alg. 57 F6
Oued Zem Morocco 54 C5
Oued Zénati Alg. 58 B6
Ouessant, Île d' *i.* France 56 B2
Ouesso Congo 98 B3
Ouezzane Morocco 57 D6
Oughter, Lough *l.* Rep. of Ireland 51 E3
Ouguati Namibia 100 B1
Ouistreham France 49 G9
Oujda Morocco 57 F6
Oujeft Mauritania 96 B3
Oulainen Fin. 44 N4
Oulangan kansallispuisto *nat. park* Fin. 44 P3
Ouled Djellal Alg. 57 I6
Ouled Farès Alg. 57 G5
Ouled Naïl, Monts des *mts* Alg. 57 H6
Oulu Fin. 44 N4
Oulujärvi *l.* Fin. 44 O4
Oulujoki *r.* Fin. 44 N4
Oulunsalo Fin. 44 N4
Oulx Italy 58 B2
Oum-Chalouba Chad 97 F3
Oum el Bouaghi Alg. 58 B7
Oum-Hadjer Chad 97 E3
Ounasjoki *r.* Fin. 44 N3
Oundle U.K. 49 G6
Oungre Canada 121 K5
Ounianga Kébir Chad 97 F3
Oupeye Belgium 52 F4
Our *r.* Lux. 52 G5
Ouray *CO* U.S.A. 129 J2
Ouray *UT* U.S.A. 129 I1
Ourcq *r.* France 52 D5
Ourense Spain 57 C2
Ouricurí Brazil 143 J5
Ourinhos Brazil 145 A3
Ouro *r.* Brazil 145 A1
Ouro Preto Brazil 145 C3
Ourthe *r.* Belgium 52 F4
Ous Rus. Fed. 41 S3
Ouse *r.* *England* U.K. 48 G5
Ouse *r.* *England* U.K. 49 H8
Outaouais, Rivière des *r.* Canada 122 G5 *see* Ottawa
Outardes *r.* Canada 123 H4
Outardes Quatre, Réservoir *resr* Canada 123 H4
Outer Hebrides *is* U.K. 50 B3
Outer Mongolia *country* Asia *see* Mongolia
Outer Santa Barbara Channel U.S.A. 128 D5
Outjo Namibia 99 B6
Outlook Canada 121 J5
Outokumpu Fin. 44 P5
Out Skerries *is* U.K. 50 [inset]
Ouvéa *atoll* New Caledonia 107 G4
Ouyanghai Shuiku *resr* China 77 G3
Ouyen Australia 111 C7
Ouzel *r.* U.K. 49 G6
Ovace, Punta d' *mt.* *Corsica* France 56 I6
Ovacık Turkey 85 A1
Ovada Italy 58 C2
Ovalle Chile 144 B4
Ovamboland *reg.* Namibia 99 B5
Ovan Gabon 98 B3
Ovar Port. 57 B3
Overath Germany 53 H4
Överkalix Sweden 44 M3
Overlander Roadhouse Australia 109 A6
Overland Park U.S.A. 130 E4
Overton U.S.A. 129 F3
Övertorneå Sweden 44 M3
Överum Sweden 45 J8
Overveen Neth. 52 E2
Ovid *CO* U.S.A. 130 C3
Ovid *NY* U.S.A. 135 G2
Oviedo Spain 57 D2
Ovoot Mongolia 73 K3
Øvre Anarjokka Nasjonalpark *nat. park* Norway 44 N2
Øvre Dividal Nasjonalpark *nat. park* Norway 44 K2
Øvre Rendal Norway 45 G6
Ovruch Ukr. 43 F6
Ovsyanka Rus. Fed. 74 B1
Owando Congo 98 B4
Owa Rafa *i.* Solomon Is *see* Santa Ana
Owasco Lake U.S.A. 135 G2
Owase Japan 75 E6
Owatonna U.S.A. 130 E2
Owbeh Afgh. 89 F3
Owego U.S.A. 135 G2
Owel, Lough *l.* Rep. of Ireland 51 E4
Owen Island Myanmar 71 B5
Owenmore *r.* Rep. of Ireland 51 C3
Owenmore *r.* Rep. of Ireland 51 D3
Owenreagh *r.* U.K. 51 E3
Owen River N.Z. 113 D5
Owens *r.* U.S.A. 128 E3
Owensboro U.S.A. 134 B5
Owen Sound Canada 134 E1
Owen Sound *inlet* Canada 134 E1
Owen Stanley Range *mts* P.N.G. 69 L8
Owenton U.S.A. 134 C4
Owerri Nigeria 96 D4
Owikeno Lake Canada 120 E5
Owingsville U.S.A. 134 D4
Owl *r.* Canada 121 M3
Owl Creek Mountains U.S.A. 126 F4
Owo Nigeria 96 D4
Owosso U.S.A. 134 C2
Owyhee U.S.A. 126 D4
Owyhee *r.* U.S.A. 126 D4
Owyhee Mountains U.S.A. 126 D4
Öxarfjörður *b.* Iceland 44 [inset]
Oxbow Canada 121 K5
Ox Creek *r.* U.S.A. 130 C1
Oxelösund Sweden 45 J7
Oxford N.Z. 113 D6
Oxford U.K. 49 F7
Oxford *IN* U.S.A. 134 B3
Oxford *MA* U.S.A. 135 J2
Oxford *MD* U.S.A. 135 G4
Oxford *MS* U.S.A. 131 F5
Oxford *NC* U.S.A. 132 E4
Oxford *NY* U.S.A. 135 H2
Oxford *OH* U.S.A. 134 C4
Oxford House Canada 121 M4
Oxford Lake Canada 121 M4
Oxley Australia 112 B5
Oxleys Peak Australia 112 E3
Oxley Wild Rivers National Park Australia 112 F3
Ox Mountains *hills* Rep. of Ireland *see* Slieve Gamph
Oxnard U.S.A. 128 D4
Oxtongue Lake Canada 135 F1
Oxus *r.* Asia *see* Amudar'ya
Øya Norway 44 H3
Oyama Japan 75 E5
Oyem Gabon 98 B3
Oyen Canada 121 I5
Oygon Mongolia 80 I2
Oykel *r.* U.K. 50 E3
Oyo Nigeria 96 D4
Oyonnax France 56 G3
Oyster Rocks *is* India 84 B3
Oyten Germany 53 J1
Oytograk China 83 E1
Oyukludağı *mt.* Turkey 85 A1
Özalp Turkey 91 G3
Ozamiz Phil. 69 G5
Ozark *AL* U.S.A. 133 C6
Ozark *AR* U.S.A. 131 E5
Ozark *MO* U.S.A. 131 E4
Ozark Plateau U.S.A. 131 E4
Ozarks, Lake of the U.S.A. 130 E4
O'zbekiston *country* Asia *see* Uzbekistan
Özen Kazakh. *see* Kyzylsay
Ozernovskiy Rus. Fed. 65 Q4
Ozernyy Rus. Fed. 43 G5
Ozerpakh Rus. Fed. 74 F1
Ozersk Rus. Fed. 45 M9
Ozerskiy Rus. Fed. 74 F3
Ozery Rus. Fed. 43 H5
Ozeryane Rus. Fed. 74 C2
Ozieri *Sardinia* Italy 58 C4
Ozinki Rus. Fed. 43 K6
Oznachennoye Rus. Fed. *see* Sayanogorsk
Ozona U.S.A. 131 C6
Ozuki Japan 75 C6

P

Paamiut Greenland 119 N3
Pa-an Myanmar 70 B3
Paanopa *i.* Kiribati *see* Banaba
Paarl S. Africa 100 D7
Paatsjoki *r.* Europe *see* Patsoyoki
Paballelo S. Africa 100 E5
P'abal-li N. Korea 74 C4
Pabbay *i.* U.K. 50 B3
Pabianice Poland 47 Q5
Pabianitz Poland *see* Pabianice
Pabna Bangl. 83 G4
Pabradė Lith. 45 N9
Pab Range *mts* Pak. 89 G5
Pacaás Novos, Parque Nacional *nat. park* Brazil 142 F6
Pacaraimã, Serra *mts* S. America *see* Pakaraima Mountains
Pacasmayo Peru 142 C5
Pachagarh Bangl. *see* Panchagarh
Pacheco *Chihuahua* Mex. 127 F7
Pacheco *Zacatecas* Mex. 131 C7
Pachikha Rus. Fed. 42 J3
Pachino *Sicily* Italy 58 F6
Pachmarhi India 82 D5
Pachor India 82 D5
Pachora India 84 B1
Pachpadra India 82 C4
Pachuca Mex. 136 E4
Pachuca de Soto Mex. *see* Pachuca
Pacific-Antarctic Ridge *sea feature* S. Pacific Ocean 151 J9
Pacific Grove U.S.A. 128 C3

▶Pacific Ocean 150–151
Largest ocean in the world.

Pacific Rim National Park Canada 120 E5
Pacitan Indon. 68 E8
Packsaddle Australia 111 C6
Pacoval Brazil 143 H4
Pacuí *r.* Brazil 145 B2
Paczków Poland 47 P5
Padali Rus. Fed. *see* Amursk
Padampur India 82 C3
Padang Indon. 68 C7
Padang *i.* Indon. 71 C7
Padang Endau Malaysia 71 C7
Padangpanjang Indon. 68 C7
Padangsidimpuan Indon. 71 B7
Padany Rus. Fed. 42 G3
Padatha, Kūh-e *mt.* Iran 88 C3
Padaung Myanmar 70 A3
Padcaya Bol. 142 F8
Padderborn-Lippstadt *airport* Germany 53 I3
Paden City U.S.A. 134 E4
Paderborn Germany 53 I3
Padeșu, Vârful *mt.* Romania 59 J2
Padibyu Myanmar 70 B2
Padilla Bol. 142 F7
Padjelanta nationalpark *nat. park* Sweden 44 J3
Padova Italy *see* Padua
Padrão, Ponta do *pt* Angola 99 B4
Padrauna India 83 F4
Padre Island U.S.A. 131 D7
Padstow U.K. 49 C8
Padsvillye Belarus 45 O9
Padua India 84 D2
Padua Italy 58 D2
Paducah *KY* U.S.A. 131 F4
Paducah *TX* U.S.A. 131 C5
Padum Jammu and Kashmir 82 D2
Paegam N. Korea 74 C4
Paektu-san *mt.* China/N. Korea *see* Baotou Shan
Paengnyŏng-do *i.* S. Korea 75 B5
Pafos Cyprus *see* Paphos
Pafuri Moz. 101 J2
Pag Croatia 58 F2
Pag *i.* Croatia 58 F2
Paga Indon. 108 C2
Pagadian Phil. 69 G5
Pagai Selatan *i.* Indon. 68 C7
Pagalu *i.* Equat. Guinea *see* Annobón
Pagan *i.* N. Mariana Is 69 L3
Pagasitikos Kolpos *b.* Greece 59 J5
Pagatan Indon. 68 F7
Page U.S.A. 129 H3
Paget, Mount S. Georgia 144 I8
Paget Cay *reef* Australia 110 F3
Pagon *i.* N. Mariana Is *see* Pagan
Pagosa Springs U.S.A. 127 G5
Pagqên China *see* Gadê
Pagwa River Canada 122 D4
Pagwi P.N.G. 69 K7
Pahala *HI* U.S.A. 127 [inset]
Pahang *r.* Malaysia 71 C7
Pahlgam Jammu and Kashmir 82 C2
Pahoa *HI* U.S.A. 127 [inset]
Pahokee U.S.A. 133 D7
Pahra Kariz Afgh. 89 F3
Pahranagat Range *mts* U.S.A. 129 F3
Pahrump U.S.A. 129 F3
Pahuj *r.* India 82 D4
Pahute Mesa *plat.* U.S.A. 128 E3
Pai Thai. 70 B3
Paicines U.S.A. 128 C3
Paide Estonia 45 N7
Paignton U.K. 49 D8
Päijänne *l.* Fin. 45 N6
Paikü Co *l.* China 83 F3
Pailin Cambodia 71 C4
Pailolo Channel *HI* U.S.A. 127 [inset]
Paimio Fin. 45 M6
Painel Brazil 145 A4
Painesville U.S.A. 134 E3
Pains Brazil 145 B3
Painted Desert U.S.A. 129 H3
Painted Rock Dam U.S.A. 129 G5
Paint Hills Canada *see* Wemindji
Paint Rock U.S.A. 131 D6
Paintsville U.S.A. 134 D5
Paisley U.K. 50 E5
Paita Peru 142 B5
Paitou China 77 I2
Paiva Couceiro Angola *see* Quipungo
Paizhou China 77 G2
Pajala Sweden 44 M3
Paka Malaysia 71 C6
Pakala India 84 C3
Pakanbaru Indon. *see* Pekanbaru
Pakangyi Myanmar 70 A2
Pakaraima Mountains Guyana 142 G3
Pakaraima Mountains S. America 142 F3
Pakaur India 83 F4
Pakesley Canada 122 E5
Pakhachi Rus. Fed. 65 R3
Pakhoi China *see* Beihai
Paki Nigeria 96 D3

▶Pakistan *country* Asia 89 H4
4th most populous country in Asia.
Asia 6, 62–63

Pakkat Indon. 71 B7
Paknampho Thai. *see* Nakhon Sawan
Pakokku Myanmar 70 A2
Pakowki Lake *imp. l.* Canada 121 I5
Pakpattan Pak. 89 I4
Pak Phanang Thai. 71 C5
Pak Phayun Thai. 71 C6
Pakruojis Lith. 45 M9
Paks Hungary 58 H1
Pakse Laos *see* Pakxé
Pak Tam Chung *Hong Kong* China 77 [inset]
Pak Thong Chai Thai. 70 C4
Pakur India *see* Pakaur
Pakxé Laos 70 D4
Pakxeng Laos 70 C2
Pala Chad 97 E4
Pala Myanmar 71 B4
Palaestinia *reg.* Asia *see* Palestine
Palaiochora Greece 59 J7
Palaiseau France 52 C6
Palakkad India *see* Palghat
Palakkat India *see* Palghat
Palamakoloi Botswana 100 F2
Palamau India *see* Palamu
Palamós Spain 57 H3
Palamu India 83 F5
Palana Rus. Fed. 65 Q4
Palandur India 84 D1
Palangān, Kūh-e *mts* Iran 89 F4
Palangkaraya Indon. 68 E7
Palani India 84 C4
Palanpur India 82 C4
Palantak Pak. 89 G5
Palapye Botswana 101 H2
Palatka Rus. Fed. 65 Q3
Palatka U.S.A. 133 D6
▶Palau *country* N. Pacific Ocean 69 I5
Asia 6, 62–63
Palau Islands Palau 69 I5
Palauk Myanmar 71 B4
Palaw Myanmar 71 B4
Palawan *i.* Phil. 68 F5
Palawan Passage *strait* Phil. 68 F5
Palawan Trough *sea feature* N. Pacific Ocean 150 D5
Palayankottai India 84 C4
Palchal Lake India 84 D2
Paldiski Estonia 45 N7
Palekh Rus. Fed. 42 I4
Palembang Indon. 68 C7
Palena Chile 144 B6
Palencia Spain 57 D2
Palermo *Sicily* Italy 58 E5
Palestine *reg.* Asia 85 B3
Palestine U.S.A. 131 E6
Paletwa Myanmar 70 A2
Palezgir Pak. 89 H4
Palghat India 84 C4
Palgrave, Mount *hill* Australia 109 A5
Palhoca Brazil 145 A4
Pali *Chhattisgarh* India 84 D1
Pali *Maharashtra* India 84 B2
Pali *Rajasthan* India 82 C4

▶Palikir Micronesia 150 G5
Capital of Micronesia.

Palinuro, Capo *c.* Italy 58 F4
Paliouri, Akra *pt* Greece 59 J5
Palisade U.S.A. 129 I2
Paliseul Belgium 52 F5
Palitana India 82 B5
Palivere Estonia 45 M7
Palk Bay Sri Lanka 84 C4
Palkino Rus. Fed. 45 P8
Palkonda Range *mts* India 84 C3
Palk Strait India/Sri Lanka 84 C4
Palla Bianca *mt.* Austria/Italy *see* Weißkugel
Pallamallawa Australia 112 E2
Pallas Green Rep. of Ireland 51 D5
Pallas ja Ounastunturin kansallispuisto *nat. park* Fin. 44 M2
Pallasovka Rus. Fed. 43 J6
Pallavaram India 84 D3
Palliser, Cape N.Z. 113 E5
Palliser, Îles *is* Fr. Polynesia 151 K7
Palliser Bay N.Z. 113 E5
Pallu India 82 C3
Palma *r.* Brazil 145 B1
Palma del Río Spain 57 D5
Palma de Mallorca Spain 57 H4
Palmaner India 84 C3
Palmares Brazil 143 K5
Palmares do Sul Brazil 145 A5
Palmas *Paraná* Brazil 145 A4
Palmas *Tocantins* Brazil 143 I6
Palmas, Cape Liberia 96 C4
Palm Bay U.S.A. 133 D7
Palmdale U.S.A. 128 D4
Palmeira Brazil 145 A4
Palmeira das Missões Brazil 144 F3
Palmeira dos Índios Brazil 143 K5
Palmeirais Brazil 143 J5
Palmeiras Brazil 145 C1
Palmeirinhas, Ponta das *pt* Angola 99 B4
Palmer *research station* Antarctica 152 L2
Palmer *r.* Australia 110 C3
Palmer *watercourse* Australia 109 F6
Palmer U.S.A. 118 D3
Palmer Land *reg.* Antarctica 152 L2
Palmerston *N.T.* Australia 108 E3
Palmerston *N.T.* Australia *see* Darwin
Palmerston Canada 134 E2
Palmerston *atoll* Cook Is 107 J3
Palmerston N.Z. 113 C7
Palmerston North N.Z. 113 E5
Palmerton U.S.A. 135 H3
Palmerville Australia 110 D2
Palmetto Point Bahamas 133 E7
Palmi Italy 58 F5
Palmira Col. 142 C3
Palmira Cuba 133 D8
Palm Springs U.S.A. 128 E5
Palmyra Syria *see* Tadmur
Palmyra *MO* U.S.A. 130 F4
Palmyra *PA* U.S.A. 135 G3
Palmyra *VA* U.S.A. 135 F5

▶Palmyra Atoll *terr.* N. Pacific Ocean 150 J5
United States Unincorporated Territory.

Palmyras Point India 83 F5
Palni Hills India 84 C4
Palo Alto U.S.A. 128 B3
Palo Blanco Mex. 131 C7
Palo Chino *watercourse* Mex. 127 E7
Palo Duro *watercourse* U.S.A. 131 C5
Paloich Sudan 86 D7
Palojärvi Fin. 44 M2
Palojoensuu Fin. 44 M2
Palomaa Fin. 44 O2
Palomar Mountain U.S.A. 128 E5
Paloncha India 84 D2
Palo Pinto U.S.A. 131 D5
Palopo Indon. 69 G7
Palos, Cabo de *c.* Spain 57 F5
Palo Verde U.S.A. 129 F5
Paltamo Fin. 44 O4
Palu Indon. 68 F7
Palu *i.* Indon. 108 C2
Palu Turkey 91 E3
Pal'vart Turkm. 89 G2
Palwal India 82 D3
Palwancha India *see* Paloncha
Palyeskaya Nizina *marsh* Belarus/Ukr. *see* Pripet Marshes
Pambarra Moz. 101 L1
Pambula Australia 112 D6
Pamidi India 84 C3
Pamiers France 56 E5
Pamir *mts* Asia 89 I2
Pamlico Sound *sea chan.* U.S.A. 133 E5
Pamouscachiou, Lac *l.* Canada 123 H4
Pampa U.S.A. 131 C5
Pampa de Infierno Arg. 144 D3
Pampas *reg.* Arg. 144 D5
Pampeluna Spain *see* Pamplona
Pamphylia *reg.* Turkey 59 N6
Pamplin U.S.A. 135 F5
Pamplona Col. 142 D2
Pamplona Spain 57 F2
Pampow Germany 53 L1
Pamukova Turkey 59 N4
Pamzal Jammu and Kashmir 82 D2
Pana U.S.A. 130 F4
Panaca U.S.A. 129 F3
Panache, Lake Canada 122 E5
Panagyurishte Bulg. 59 K3
Panaitan *i.* Indon. 68 D8
Panaji India 84 B3
▶Panama *country* Central America 137 H7
North America 9, 116–117

▶Panama *i.* Indon. 108 C2
Most southerly point of Asia.

Panamá Panama *see* Panama City

Pequeña, Punta *pt* Mex. 127 E8
Pequop Mountains U.S.A. 129 F1
Peradeniya Sri Lanka 84 D5
Pera Head *hd* Australia 110 C2
Perak *i.* Malaysia 71 B6
Perales del Alfambra Spain 57 F3
Perambalur India 84 C4
Pérämeren kansallispuisto *nat. park* Fin.
44 N4
Peräseinäjoki Fin. 44 M5
Percé Canada 123 I4
Percival Lakes *salt flat* Australia 108 D5
Percy U.S.A. 135 J1
Percy Isles Australia 110 E4
Percy Reach *l.* Canada 135 G1
Perdizes Brazil 145 B2
Perdu, Lac *l.* Canada 123 H4
Peregrebnoye Rus. Fed. 41 T3
Pereira Col. 142 C3
Pereira Barreto Brazil 145 A3
Pereira de Eça Angola *see* Ondjiva
Pere Marquette *r.* U.S.A. 134 B2
Peremul Par *reef* India 84 B4
Peremyshlyany Ukr. 43 E6
Perenjori Australia 109 B7
Pereslavl'-Zalesskiy Rus. Fed. 42 H4
Pereslavskiy Natsional'nyy Park *nat. park*
Rus. Fed. 42 H4
Pereyaslavka Rus. Fed. 74 D3
Pereval Klukhorskiy *pass* Rus. Fed. 91 F2
Pereyaslav-Khmel'nitskiy Ukr. *see*
Pereyaslav-Khmel'nyts'kyy
Pereyaslav-Khmel'nyts'kyy Ukr. 43 F6
Perforated Island Thai. *see* Bon, Ko
Pergamino Arg. 144 D4
Perhentian Besar, Pulau *i.* Malaysia 71 C6
Perho Fin. 44 N5
Péribonca, Lac *l.* Canada 123 H4
Perico Arg. 144 C2
Pericos Mex. 127 G8
Peridot U.S.A. 129 H5
Périgueux France 56 E4
Perijá, Parque Nacional *nat. park* Venez.
142 D2
Perija, Sierra de *mts* Venez. 138 D2
Periyar India *see* Erode
Perkasie U.S.A. 135 H3
Perlas, Punta de *pt* Nicaragua 137 H6
Perleberg Germany 53 L1
Perm' Rus. Fed. 41 R4
Permas Rus. Fed. 42 J4
Pernambuco Brazil *see* Recife
Pernambuco Abyssal Plain *sea feature*
S. Atlantic Ocean 148 G6
Pernatty Lagoon *salt flat* Australia 111 B6
Pernem India 84 B3
Pernik Bulg. 59 J3
Pernov Estonia *see* Pärnu
Perojpur Bangl. *see* Pirojpur
Peron Islands Australia 108 E3
Péronne France 52 C5
Perpignan France 56 F5
Perranporth U.K. 49 B8
Perrégaux Alg. *see* Mohammadia
Perris U.S.A. 128 E5
Perros-Guirec France 56 C2
Perrot, Île *i.* Canada 135 I1
Perry *FL* U.S.A. 133 D6
Perry *GA* U.S.A. 133 D5
Perry *MI* U.S.A. 134 C2
Perry *OK* U.S.A. 131 D4
Perry Lake U.S.A. 130 D4
Perryton U.S.A. 131 C4
Perryville *AK* U.S.A. 118 C4
Perryville *MO* U.S.A. 130 F4
Perseverancia Bol. 142 F6
Pershore U.K. 49 E6
Persia *country* Asia *see* Iran
Persian Gulf Asia *see* The Gulf
Pertek Turkey 91 E3

▶ Perth Australia 109 A7
State capital of Western Australia. 4th
most populous city in Oceania.

Perth Canada 135 G1
Perth U.K. 50 F4
Perth Amboy U.S.A. 135 H3
Perth-Andover Canada 123 I5
Perth Basin *sea feature* Indian Ocean
149 P7
Pertominsk Rus. Fed. 42 H2
Pertunmaa Fin. 45 O6
Pertusato, Capo *c.* Corsica France 56 I6
Peru *atoll* Kiribati *see* Beru

▶ Peru *country* S. America 142 D6
3rd largest and 4th most populous country
in South America.
South America 9, 140–141

Peru *IL* U.S.A. 130 F3
Peru *IN* U.S.A. 134 B3
Peru *NY* U.S.A. 135 I1
Peru-Chile Trench *sea feature*
S. Pacific Ocean 151 O6
Perugia Italy 58 E3
Peruru India 84 C3
Perusia Italy *see* Perugia
Péruwelz Belgium 52 D4
Pervomaysk Rus. Fed. 43 I5
Pervomays'k Ukr. 43 F6
Pervomayskiy Kazakh. 80 F1
Pervomayskiy *Arkhangel'skaya Oblast'*
Rus. Fed. *see* Novodvinsk
Pervomayskiy *Tambovskaya Oblast'*
Rus. Fed. 43 I5
Pervomays'kyy Ukr. 43 H6
Pervorechenskiy Rus. Fed. 65 R3
Pesaro Italy 58 E3
Pescadores *is* Taiwan *see*
P'enghu Ch'üntao
Pescara Italy 58 F3
Pescara *r.* Italy 58 F3
Peschanokopskoye Rus. Fed. 39 I7
Peschanoye Rus. Fed. *see* Yashkul'
Peschanyy, Mys *pt* Kazakh.
87 H2
Pesha *r.* Rus. Fed. 42 J2
Peshanjan Afgh. 89 F3
Peshawar Pak. 89 H3
Peshkopi Albania 59 I4

Peshtera Bulg. 59 K3
Peski Turkm. 89 F2
Peski Karakumy *des.* Turkm. *see*
Karakum Desert
Peskovka Rus. Fed. 42 L4
Pesnica Slovenia 58 F1
Pessac France 56 D4
Pessin Germany 53 M2
Pestovo Rus. Fed. 42 G4
Pestravka Rus. Fed. 43 K5
Petah Tiqwa Israel 85 B3
Petaling Jaya Malaysia 71 C7
Petalion, Kolpos *sea chan.* Greece 59 K5
Petaluma U.S.A. 128 B2
Pétange Lux. 52 F5
Petatlán Mex. 136 D5
Petauke Zambia 99 D5
Petenwell Lake U.S.A. 130 F2
Peterbell Canada 122 E4
Peterborough Australia 111 B7
Peterborough Canada 135 F1
Peterborough U.K. 49 G6
Peterborough U.S.A. 135 J2
Peterculter U.K. 50 G3
Peterhead U.K. 50 H3
Peter I Island Antarctica 152 K2
Peter I Øy *i.* Antarctica *see* Peter I Island
Peter Lake Canada 121 M2
Peterlee U.K. 48 F4
Petermann Bjerg *nunatak* Greenland
119 P2
Petermann Ranges *mts* Australia 109 E6
Peter Pond Lake Canada 121 I4
Peters, Lac *l.* Canada 123 H2
Petersberg Germany 53 J4
Petersburg *AK* U.S.A. 120 C3
Petersburg *IL* U.S.A. 130 F4
Petersburg *IN* U.S.A. 134 B4
Petersburg *NY* U.S.A. 135 I2
Petersburg *VA* U.S.A. 135 G5
Petersburg *WV* U.S.A. 134 F4
Petersfield U.K. 49 G7
Petershagen Germany 53 I2
Petersville U.S.A. 118 C3
Peter the Great Bay Rus. Fed. *see*
Petra Velikogo, Zaliv
Petetil India 84 B2
Petilia Policastro Italy 58 G5
Petit Atlas *mts* Morocco *see* Anti Atlas
Petitcodiac Canada 123 I5
Petitjean Morocco *see* Sidi Kacem
Petit Lac Manicouagan *l.* Canada 123 I3
Petit Mécatina *r.* Nfld. and Lab./Que.
Canada 123 K4
Petit Mécatina, Île du *i.* Canada 123 K4
Petit Morin *r.* France 52 D6
Petitot *r.* Canada 120 F2
Petit Saut Dam *resr* Fr. Guiana 143 H3
Petit St-Bernard, Col du *pass* France
56 H4
Peto Mex. 136 G4
Petoskey U.S.A. 132 C2
Petra *tourist site* Jordan 85 B4
Petra Velikogo, Zaliv *b.* Rus. Fed. 74 C4
Petre, Point Canada 135 G2
Petrich Bulg. 59 J4
Petrified Forest National Park U.S.A.
129 I4
Petrikau Poland *see* Piotrków Trybunalski
Petrikov Belarus *see* Pyetrykaw
Petrinja Croatia 58 G2
Petroaleksandrovsk Uzbek. *see* Turtkul'
Petrograd Rus. Fed. *see* St Petersburg
Petrokhanski Prokhod *pass* Bulg. 59 J3
Petrokov Poland *see* Piotrków Trybunalski
Petrolia Canada 134 D2
Petrolia U.S.A. 128 A1
Petrolina Brazil 143 J5
Petrolina de Goiás Brazil 145 A2
Petropavl Kazakh. *see* Petropavlovsk
Petropavlovsk Kazakh. 79 G1
Petropavlovsk Rus. Fed. *see*
Petropavlovsk-Kamchatskiy
Petropavlovsk-Kamchatskiy Rus. Fed.
65 Q4
Petrópolis Brazil 145 C3
Petroşani Romania 59 J2
Petrovsk Rus. Fed. 43 J5
Petrovskoye Rus. Fed. *see* Svetlograd
Petrovsk-Zabaykal'skiy Rus. Fed. 73 J2
Petrozavodsk Rus. Fed. 42 G3
Petrus Steyn S. Africa 101 I4
Petrusville S. Africa 100 G6
Petsamo Rus. Fed. *see* Pechenga
Pettau Slovenia *see* Ptuj
Petten Neth. 52 E2
Pettigo U.K. 51 E3
Petukhovo Rus. Fed. 64 H4
Petushki Rus. Fed. 42 H5
Petzeck *mt.* Austria 47 N7
Peuetsagu, Gunung *vol.* Indon. 71 B6
Peureula Indon. 71 B6
Pevek Rus. Fed. 65 S3
Pêxung China 76 B1
Pey Ostān Iran 88 E3
Peza *r.* Rus. Fed. 42 J2
Pezinok Slovakia 47 P6
Pezu Pak. 89 H3
Pfälzer Wald *hills* Germany 49 H5
Pforzheim Germany 53 I6
Pfungstadt Germany 53 I5
Phagwara India 82 C3
Phahameng *Free State* S. Africa 101 H5
Phahameng *Limpopo* S. Africa 101 I3
Phalaborwa S. Africa 101 J2
Phalodi India 82 C4
Phalsund India 82 B4
Phalta India 83 G5
Phaluai, Ko *i.* Thai. 71 B5
Phalut Peak India/Nepal 83 G4
Phan Thai. 70 B3
Phanat Nikhom Thai. 71 C4
Phangan, Ko *i.* Thai. 71 C5
Phang Hoei, San Khao *mts* Thai. 70 C3
Phangnga Thai. 71 B5
Phanom Dong Rak, Thiu Khao *mts*
Cambodia/Thai. 71 C4
Phan Rang Vietnam 71 E5
Phan Thiêt Vietnam 71 E5
Phapon Myanmar *see* Pyapon
Phat Diêm Vietnam 70 D2

Phatthalung Thai. 71 C6
Phayam, Ko *i.* Thai. 71 B5
Phayao Thai. 70 B3
Phayuhakhiri Thai. 70 C4
Phek India 83 H4
Phelps Lake Canada 121 K3
Phen Thai. 70 C3
Phenix U.S.A. 135 F5
Phenix City U.S.A. 133 C5
Phet Buri Thai. 71 B4
Phetchabun Thai. 70 C3
Phiafai Laos 70 D4
Phichai Thai. 70 C3
Phichit Thai. 70 C3
Philadelphia Jordan *see* 'Ammān
Philadelphia Turkey *see* Alaşehir
Philadelphia *MS* U.S.A. 131 F5
Philadelphia *NY* U.S.A. 135 H1
Philadelphia *PA* U.S.A. 135 H3
Philip U.S.A. 130 C2
Philip Atoll Micronesia *see* Sorol
Philippeville Alg. *see* Skikda
Philippeville Belgium 52 E4
Philippi U.S.A. 134 E4
Philippi, Lake *salt flat* Australia 110 B5
Philippine Neth. 52 D3
Philippine Basin *sea feature*
N. Pacific Ocean 150 E4

▶ Philippines *country* Asia 69 G4
Asia 6, 62–63

Philippine Sea N. Pacific Ocean 69 G3

▶ Philippine Trench *sea feature*
N. Pacific Ocean 150 E4
3rd deepest trench in the world.

Philippolis S. Africa 101 G6
Philippopolis Bulg. *see* Plovdiv
Philippsburg Germany 53 I5
Philipsburg *MT* U.S.A. 126 E3
Philipsburg *PA* U.S.A. 135 F3
Philipstown S. Africa *see* Douglas
Philip Island Australia 110 U6
Phillip Island Australia 112 B7
Phillips *ME* U.S.A. 135 J1
Phillips *WI* U.S.A. 130 F2
Phillipsburg U.S.A. 130 D4
Phillips Range *hills* Australia 108 D4
Philmont U.S.A. 135 I2
Philomelium Turkey *see* Akşehir
Phiritona S. Africa 101 H4
Phitsanulok Thai. 70 C3

▶ Phnom Penh Cambodia 71 D5
Capital of Cambodia.

Phnum Pénh Cambodia *see* Phnom Penh
Pho, Laem *pt* Thai. 71 C6
Phoenicia U.S.A. 135 H2

▶ Phoenix U.S.A. 127 E6
State capital of Arizona.

Phoenix Island Kiribati *see* Rawaki
Phoenix Islands Kiribati 107 I2
Phon Thai. 70 C4
Phong Nha Vietnam 70 D3
Phôngsali Laos 70 C2
Phong Saly Laos *see* Phôngsali
Phong Thô Vietnam 70 C2
Phon Phisai Thai. 70 C3
Phon Thong Thai. 70 C3
Phrae Thai. 70 C3
Phra Nakhon Si Ayutthaya Thai. *see*
Ayutthaya
Phrao Thai. 70 B3
Phra Saeng Thai. 71 B5
Phrom Phiram Thai. 70 C3
Phsar Ream Cambodia 71 C5
Phuchong-Nayoi National Park Thai.
71 D4
Phu Cuong Vietnam *see* Thu Dâu Môt
Phu Hôi Vietnam 71 E4
Phuket Thai. 71 B6
Phuket, Ko *i.* Thai. 71 B6
Phu-khieo Wildlife Reserve *nature res.*
Thai. 70 C3
Phulabani India *see* Phulbani
Phulbani India 84 D1
Phulchhari Ghat Bangl. *see* Fulchhari
Phulji Pak. 89 G5
Phu Luang National Park Thai. 70 C3
Phu Ly Vietnam 70 D2
Phumĭ Bŏeng Mealea Cambodia 71 D4
Phumĭ Chhlong Cambodia 71 D4
Phumĭ Kaôh Kŏng Cambodia 71 C5
Phumĭ Kon Kriel Cambodia 71 C4
Phumĭ Mlu Prey Cambodia 71 D4
Phumĭ Moŭng Cambodia 71 C4
Phumĭ Prêk Kak Cambodia 71 D4
Phumĭ Sâmraông Cambodia 71 C4
Phumĭ Trâm Kak Cambodia 71 D5
Phumĭ Veal Renh Cambodia 71 C5
Phu My Vietnam 71 E4
Phung Hiêp Vietnam 71 D5
Phu Phac Mo *mt.* Vietnam 70 C2
Phu Phan National Park Thai. 70 C3
Phu Quôc, Đao *i.* Vietnam 71 C5
Phu Tho Vietnam 70 D2
Phu Vinh Vietnam *see* Tra Vinh
Piaca Brazil 143 I5
Piacenza Italy 58 C2
Piacouadie, Lac *l.* Canada 123 H4
Piagochioui *r.* Canada 122 F3
Piai, Tanjung *pt* Malaysia 71 C7
Pian *r.* Australia 112 D3
Pianosa, Isola *i.* Italy 58 D3
Piatra Neamţ Romania 59 L1
Piave *r.* Italy 58 E2
Piazza Armerina Italy 58 F6
Pibor Post Sudan 97 G4
Pic *r.* Canada 122 D4
Picacho U.S.A. 129 H5
Picachos, Cerro dos *mt.* Mex. 127 E7
Picardie *admin. reg.* France 52 C5
Picardie *reg.* France *see* Picardy
Picardy *admin. reg.* France *see* Picardie
Picardy *reg.* France 52 B5
Picauville France 49 F9
Picayune U.S.A. 131 F6
Piceance Creek *r.* U.S.A. 129 I1

Pichanal Arg. 144 D2
Pichhor India 82 D4
Pichilemu Chile 144 B4
Pichilingue Mex. 136 B4
Pickens U.S.A. 134 E4
Pickering Canada 134 F2
Pickering U.K. 48 G4
Pickering, Vale of *valley* U.K. 48 G4
Pickle Lake Canada 119 I4
Pico da Neblina, Parque Nacional do
nat. park Brazil 142 E3
Picos Brazil 143 J5
Pico Truncado Arg. 144 C7
Picton Australia 112 E5
Picton Canada 135 G2
Picton N.Z. 113 E5
Pictou Canada 123 J5
Picture Butte Canada 121 H5
Pidarak Pak. 89 F5
Piday India 82 C5
Pidurutalagala *mt.* Sri Lanka 84 D5
Piedade Brazil 145 B3
Piedra de Águila Arg. 144 B6
Piedras, Punta *pt* Arg. 144 E5
Piedras Blancas Point U.S.A. 128 C4
Piedras Negras Mex. 131 C6
Pie Island Canada 122 C4
Pieksämäki Fin. 44 O5
Pielavesi Fin. 44 O5
Pielinen *l.* Fin. 44 P5
Pieljekaise nationalpark *nat. park* Sweden
44 J3
Pienaarsrivier S. Africa 101 I3
Pieniński Park Narodowy *nat. park*
Poland 47 R6
Pieninský *nat. park* Slovakia 47 R6
Pierce U.S.A. 130 D3
Pierce Lake Canada 121 M4
Pierceland Canada 121 I4
Pierceton U.S.A. 134 C3
Pieria *mts* Greece 59 J4
Pierowall U.K. 50 G1
Pierpont U.S.A. 134 E3

▶ Pierre U.S.A. 130 C2
State capital of South Dakota.

Pierrelatte France 56 G4
Pierre Lake Canada 121 M4
Pie Town U.S.A. 129 I4
Pietra Spada, Passo di *pass* Italy 58 G5
Piet Retief S. Africa 101 J4
Pietrosa *mt.* Romania 59 K1
Pietrosa *mt.* Romania 59 K1
Pieve di Cadore Italy 58 E1
Pigeon Bay Canada 134 D3
Pigeon Lake Canada 120 H4
Piggott U.S.A. 131 F4
Pigg's Peak Swaziland 101 J3
Pigs, Bay of Cuba 133 D8
Pihij India 82 C5
Pihkva järv *l.* Estonia/Rus. Fed. *see*
Pskov, Lake
Pihlajavesi *l.* Fin. 44 P6
Pihlava Fin. 45 L6
Pihtipudas Fin. 44 N5
Piippola Fin. 44 N4
Piispajärvi Fin. 44 P4
Pikalevo Rus. Fed. 42 G4
Pike U.S.A. 134 E4
Pike Bay Canada 134 E1
Pikelot *i.* Micronesia 69 L5
Pikes Peak U.S.A. 126 G5
Piketon U.S.A. 134 D4
Pikeville *KY* U.S.A. 134 D5
Pikeville *TN* U.S.A. 132 C5
Pikinni *atoll* Marshall Is *see* Bikini
Piła Poland 47 P4
Pilanesberg National Park S. Africa
101 H3
Pilar Arg. 144 E4
Pilar Para. 144 E3
Pilar de Goiás Brazil 145 A1
Pilaya *r.* Bol. 142 F8
Pilcomayo *r.* Bol./Para. 142 F8
Piler India 84 C3
Pili, Cerro *mt.* Chile 144 C2
Pilibangan India 82 C3
Pilibhit India 82 D3
Pilipinas *country* Asia *see*
Philippines
Pillau Rus. Fed. *see* Baltiysk
Pillcopata Peru 142 D6
Pilliga Australia 112 D3
Pillsbury, Lake U.S.A. 128 B2
Pil'na Rus. Fed. 42 J5
Pil'nya, Ozero *l.* Rus. Fed. 42 M1
Pilões, Serra dos *mts* Brazil 145 B2
Pílos Greece *see* Pylos
Pilot Knob *mt.* U.S.A. 126 D4
Pilot Peak U.S.A. 128 E2
Pilot Station U.S.A. 118 B3
Pilsen Czech Rep. *see* Plzeň
Piltene Latvia 45 L8
Pil'tun, Zaliv *lag.* Rus. Fed. 74 F1
Pilu Pak. 89 H5
Pima U.S.A. 129 I5
Pimenta Bueno Brazil 142 F6
Pimento U.S.A. 134 B4
Pimpalner India 84 B1
Pin *r.* India 82 D2
Pin *r.* Myanmar 70 A2
Pinahat India 82 D4
Pinaleno Mountains U.S.A. 129 H5
Pinamar Arg. 144 E5
Pinang Malaysia *see* George Town
Pinang *i.* Malaysia 71 C6
Pinar del Río Cuba 137 H4
Pinarhisar Turkey 59 L4
Piñas Ecuador 142 C4
Pincher Creek Canada 120 H5
Pinckneyville U.S.A. 130 F4
Pinconning U.S.A. 134 D2
Pindaí Brazil 145 C1
Pindamonhangaba Brazil 145 B3
Pindar Australia 109 A7
Pindaré *r.* Brazil 143 J4
Pindi Road India 82 C4
Pindos *mts* Greece *see*
Pindus Mountains
Pindos *mts* Greece *see* Pindus Mountains

Pindrei India 82 E5
Pindus Mountains Greece 59 I5
Pine *watercourse* Australia 111 C7
Pine *r.* MI U.S.A. 134 C1
Pine *r.* WI U.S.A. 134 A1
Pine Bluff U.S.A. 131 E5
Pine Bluffs U.S.A. 126 G4
Pine Creek Australia 108 E3
Pine Creek *r.* U.S.A. 135 G3
Pinecrest U.S.A. 128 C2
Pinedale *NM* U.S.A. 129 I4
Pinedale *WY* U.S.A. 126 F4
Pine Dock Canada 121 L5
Pine Falls Canada 121 L5
Pine Flat Lake U.S.A. 128 D3
Pinega Rus. Fed. 42 I2
Pinega *r.* Rus. Fed. 42 I2
Pinehouse Lake Canada 121 J4
Pinehouse Lake *l.* Canada 121 J4
Pineimuta *r.* Canada 121 N4
Pineios *r.* Greece 59 J5
Pine Island Bay Antarctica 151 N10
Pine Island Glacier Antarctica 152 K1
Pine Islands *FL* U.S.A. 133 D7
Pine Islands *FL* U.S.A. 133 D7
Pine Knot U.S.A. 134 C5
Pineland U.S.A. 131 E6
Pine Mountain U.S.A. 128 C4
Pine Peak U.S.A. 129 G4
Pine Point Canada 120 I2
Pine Point *pt* Canada 120 H2
Pineridge U.S.A. 128 D3
Pine Ridge U.S.A. 130 C3
Pinerolo Italy 58 B2
Pines, Isle of *i.* Cuba *see*
La Juventud, Isla de
Pines, Île des *i.* New Caledonia *see*
Pins, Île des
Pinetop U.S.A. 129 I4
Pinetown S. Africa 101 J5
Pine Valley U.S.A. 135 G2
Pineville *KY* U.S.A. 134 D5
Pineville *MO* U.S.A. 131 E4
Pineville *WV* U.S.A. 134 E5
Ping, Mae Nam *r.* Thai. 70 C4
Ping'an China 76 D1
Pingba China 76 D3
Pingbian China 76 D4
Ping Dao *i.* China 77 H1
Pingdingbu China *see* Guyuan
Pingdingshan China 77 G1
Pingdong Taiwan *see* P'ingtung
Pingdu *Jiangxi* China *see* Anfu
Pingdu *Shandong* China 73 L5
Pingguo China 76 E4
Pinghe China 77 H3
Pinghu China *see* Pingtang
Pingjiang China 77 G2
Pingjinpu China 76 E2
Pingle China 77 F3
Pingli China 77 F1
Pingliang China 76 E1
Pinglu China 77 F3
Pingma China *see* Tiandong
Pingnan China 77 H3
Pingqiao China 77 G1
Pingshan *Sichuan* China 76 E2
Pingshan *Yunnan* China *see* Luquan
Pingshi China 77 G3
Pingtan China 77 H3
Pingtan Dao *i.* China *see* Haitan Dao
Pingtang China 76 E3
P'ingtung Taiwan 77 I4
Pingxi China *see* Yuping
Pingxiang *Guangxi* China 76 E4
Pingxiang *Jiangxi* China 77 G3
Pingyang *Heilong.* China 74 B2
Pingyang *Zhejiang* China 77 I3
Pingyi China 77 H1
Pingyu China 77 G1
Pingyuanjie China 76 D4
Pingzhai China 77 F3
Pinhal Brazil 145 B3
Pinheiro Brazil 143 I4
Pinhoe U.K. 49 D8
Pini *i.* Indon. 68 B6
Piniós *r.* Greece *see* Pineios
Pinjin Australia 109 C7
Pink Mountain Canada 120 F3
Pinlaung Myanmar 70 B2
Pinlebu Myanmar 70 A1
Pinnacle *hill* U.S.A. 135 F4
Pinnacles National Monument *nat. park*
U.S.A. 128 C3
Pinnau *r.* Germany 53 J1
Pinneberg Germany 53 J1
Pinnes, Akra *pt* Greece 59 K4
Pinos, Isla de *i.* Cuba *see*
La Juventud, Isla de
Pinos, Mount U.S.A. 128 D4
Pinotepa Nacional Mex. 136 E5
Pins, Île des *i.* New Caledonia 107 G4
Pins, Pointe aux *pt* Canada 134 E2
Pinsk Belarus 45 O10
Pinta, Sierra *hill* U.S.A. 129 G5
Pintada Creek *watercourse* U.S.A. 127 G6
Pintados Chile 144 C2
Pintura U.S.A. 129 G3
Pioche U.S.A. 129 F3
Piodi Dem. Rep. Congo 99 C4
Pioneer Mountains U.S.A. 126 E3
Pioner, Ostrov *i.* Rus. Fed. 64 K2
Pionerskiy *Kaliningradskaya Oblast'*
Rus. Fed. 45 L9
Pionerskiy *Khanty-Mansiyskiy Avtonomnyy
Okrug* Rus. Fed. 41 S3
Pionki Poland 47 R5
Piopio N.Z. 113 E4
Piopiotahi *inlet* N.Z. *see* Milford Sound
Piorini, Lago *l.* Brazil 142 F4
Piotrków Trybunalski Poland 47 Q5
Pipa Dingzi *mt.* China 74 C4
Pipar India 82 C4
Pipar Road India 82 C4
Piper Peak U.S.A. 128 E3
Pipestone Canada 121 K5

Pipestone *r.* Canada 121 N4
Pipestone U.S.A. 130 D3
Pipli India 82 C3
Pipmuacan, Réservoir *resr* Canada 123 H4
Piqua U.S.A. 134 C3
Piquiri *r.* Brazil 145 A4
Pira Benin 96 D4
Piracanjuba Brazil 145 A2
Piracicaba Brazil 145 B3
Piracicaba *r.* Brazil 145 B3
Piraçununga Brazil 145 B3
Piracuruca Brazil 143 J4
Piraeus Greece 59 J5
Piraí do Sul Brazil 145 A4
Pirílevs Greece *see* Piraeus
Piraju Brazil 145 A3
Pirajuí Brazil 145 A3
Pirallahı Adası Azer. 91 H2
Piranhas *Bahia* Brazil 145 C1
Piranhas *Goiás* Brazil 145 A2
Piranhas *r. Rio Grande do Norte* Brazil
143 K5
Piranhas *r.* Brazil 145 A2
Pirapora Brazil 145 B2
Piraube, Lac *l.* Canada 123 H4
Pirawa India 82 D4
Pirenópolis Brazil 145 A1
Pires do Rio Brazil 145 A2
Pírgos Greece *see* Pyrgos
Pirin *nat. park* Bulg. 59 J4
Pirineos *mts* Europe *see* Pyrenees
Piripiri Brazil 143 J4
Pirlerkondu Turkey *see* Taşkent
Pirmasens Germany 53 H5
Pirojpur Bangl. 83 G5
Pir Panjal Pass Jammu and Kashmir 82 C2
Pir Panjal Range *mts* India/Pak. 89 I3
Piryatin Ukr. *see* Pyryatyn
Pirzada Afgh. 89 G4
Pisa Italy 58 D3
Pisae Italy *see* Pisa
Pisagua Chile 142 D7
Pisang, Kepulauan *is* Indon. 69 I7
Pisaurum Italy *see* Pesaro
Pisco Peru 142 C6
Písek Czech Rep. 47 O6
Pisha China *see* Ningnan
Pishan China 82 D1
Pishin Iran 80 B6
Pishin Pak. 89 G4
Pishin Lora *r.* Pak. 89 G4
Pishpek Kyrg. *see* Bishkek
Pisidia *reg.* Turkey 90 C3

▶ Pissis, Cerro Arg. 144 C3
4th highest mountain in South America.

Pisté Mex. 136 G4
Pisticci Italy 58 G4
Pistoia Italy 58 D3
Pistoriae Italy *see* Pistoia
Pisuerga *r.* Spain 57 D3
Pita Guinea 96 B3
Pitaga Canada 123 I3
Pitanga Brazil 145 A4
Pitangui Brazil 145 B2
Pitar India 82 B5
Pitarpunga Lake *imp. l.* Australia 112 A5
Pitcairn, Henderson, Ducie and Oeno
Islands *terr.* S. Pacific Ocean *see*
Pitcairn Islands
Pitcairn Island Pitcairn Is 151 L7

▶ Pitcairn Islands *terr.* S. Pacific Ocean
151 L7
United Kingdom Overseas Territory.
Oceania 8, 104–105

Piteå Sweden 44 L4
Piteälven *r.* Sweden 44 L4
Pitelino Rus. Fed. 43 I5
Piterka Rus. Fed. 43 J6
Piteşti Romania 59 K2
Pithoragarh India 82 E3
Pithiviers France 52 C6
Pitiquito Mex. 127 E7
Pitkyaranta Rus. Fed. 42 F3
Pitlochry U.K. 50 F4
Pitong China *see* Pixian
Pitsane Siding Botswana 101 G3
Pitt Island Canada 120 D4
Pitt Island N.Z. 107 I6
Pitt Islands Solomon Is *see*
Vanikoro Islands
Pittsboro U.S.A. 131 F5
Pittsburg *KS* U.S.A. 131 E4
Pittsburg *TX* U.S.A. 131 E5
Pittsburgh U.S.A. 134 F3
Pittsfield *MA* U.S.A. 135 I2
Pittsfield *ME* U.S.A. 135 K1
Pittsfield *VT* U.S.A. 135 I2
Pittston U.S.A. 135 H3
Pittsworth Australia 112 E1
Pitz Lake Canada 121 L2
Piumhi Brazil 145 B3
Piura Peru 142 B5
Piute Mountains U.S.A. 129 F4
Piute Peak U.S.A. 128 D4
Piute Reservoir U.S.A. 129 G2
Piuthan Nepal 83 E3
Pivabiska *r.* Canada 122 E4
Pivka Slovenia 58 F2
Pixaria *mt.* Greece *see* Pyxaria
Pixian China 76 D2
Pixley U.S.A. 128 D4
Piz Bernina *mt.* Italy/Switz. 58 C1
Piz Buin *mt.* Austria/Switz. 47 M7
Pizhanka Rus. Fed. 42 K4
Pizhi Nigeria 96 D4
Pizhma Rus. Fed. 42 J4
Pizhma *r.* Rus. Fed. 42 L2
Pizhou China 77 H1
Placentia Canada 123 L5
Placentia Italy *see* Piacenza
Placentia Bay Canada 123 L5
Placerville *CA* U.S.A. 128 C2
Placerville *CO* U.S.A. 129 I2
Placetas Cuba 133 E8
Plácido de Castro Brazil 142 E6
Plain Dealing U.S.A. 131 E5

Plainfield CT U.S.A. 135 J3
Plainfield IN U.S.A. 134 B4
Plainfield VT U.S.A. 135 I1
Plains KS U.S.A. 131 C4
Plains TX U.S.A. 131 C5
Plainview U.S.A. 131 C5
Plainville IN U.S.A. 134 B4
Plainville KS U.S.A. 130 D4
Plainwell U.S.A. 134 C2
Plaka, Akra pt Greece 59 L7
Plakoti, Cape Cyprus 85 B2
Plamondon Canada 121 H4
Planá Czech Rep. 53 M5
Plana Cays is Bahamas 133 F8
Planada U.S.A. 128 C3
Planaltina Brazil 145 B1
Plane r. Germany 53 M2
Plankinton U.S.A. 130 D3
Plano U.S.A. 131 D5
Planura Brazil 145 A3
Plaquemine U.S.A. 131 F6
Plasencia Spain 57 C3
Plaster City U.S.A. 129 F5
Plaster Rock Canada 123 I5
Plastun Rus. Fed. 74 E3
Platani r. Sicily Italy 58 E6
Platberg mt. S. Africa 101 I5

▶Plateau Antarctica
Lowest recorded annual mean temperature in the world.
World 16-17

Plateau of Tibet China 83 F2
Platina U.S.A. 128 B1
Platinum U.S.A. 153 B3
Plato Col. 142 D2
Platte r. U.S.A. 130 E3
Platte City U.S.A. 130 E4
Plattling Germany 53 M6
Plattsburgh U.S.A. 135 I1
Plattsmouth U.S.A. 130 E3
Plau Germany 53 M1
Plauen Germany 53 M4
Plauer See l. Germany 53 M1
Plavsk Rus. Fed. 43 H5
Playa Noriega, Lago l. Mex. 127 F7
Playas Ecuador 142 B4
Playas Lake U.S.A. 129 I6
Plây Cu Vietnam 71 E4
Pleasant, Lake U.S.A. 129 G5
Pleasant Bay U.S.A. 135 K3
Pleasant Grove U.S.A. 129 H1
Pleasant Hill Lake U.S.A. 134 D3
Pleasanton U.S.A. 131 D6
Pleasant Point N.Z. 113 C7
Pleasantville U.S.A. 135 H4
Pleasure Ridge Park U.S.A. 134 C4
Pleaux France 56 F4
Pledger Lake Canada 122 E4
Plei Doch Vietnam 71 D4
Pleinfeld Germany 53 K5
Pleiße r. Germany 53 M3
Plenty watercourse Australia 110 B5
Plenty, Bay of g. N.Z. 113 F3
Plentywood U.S.A. 126 G2
Plesetsk Rus. Fed. 42 I3
Pleshchentsy Belarus see Plyeshchanitsy
Pletipi, Lac l. Canada 123 H4
Plettenberg Germany 53 H3
Plettenberg Bay S. Africa 100 F8
Pleven Bulg. 59 K3
Plevna Bulg. see Pleven
Pljevlja Serb. and Mont. 59 H3
Płock Poland 47 Q4
Pločno mt. Bos.-Herz. 58 G3
Plodovoye Rus. Fed. 42 F3
Ploemeur France 56 C3
Ploești Romania see Ploiești
Ploiești Romania 59 L2
Plomb du Cantal mt. France 56 F4
Ploskoye Rus. Fed. see Stanovoye
Płoty Poland 47 O4
Ploudalmézeau France 56 B2
Plouzané France 56 B2
Plovdiv Bulg. 59 K3
Plover Cove Reservoir Hong Kong China 77 [inset]
Plozk Poland see Płock
Plum U.S.A. 134 F3
Plumridge Lakes salt flat Australia 109 D7
Plungė Lith. 45 L9
Plutarco Elías Calles, Presa resr Mex. 127 F7
Pluto, Lac l. Canada 123 H3
Plyeshchanitsy Belarus 45 O9
Ply Huey Wati, Khao mt. Myanmar/Thai. 70 B3

▶Plymouth Montserrat 137 L5
Capital of Montserrat, largely abandoned in 1997 owing to volcanic activity.

Plymouth U.K. 49 C8
Plymouth CA U.S.A. 128 C2
Plymouth IN U.S.A. 134 B3
Plymouth MA U.S.A. 135 J3
Plymouth NC U.S.A. 132 E5
Plymouth NH U.S.A. 135 J2
Plymouth WI U.S.A. 134 B2
Plymouth Bay U.S.A. 135 J3
Plynlimon hill U.K. 49 D6
Plyussa Rus. Fed. 45 P7
Plzeň Czech Rep. 47 N6
Pô Burkina 96 C3
Po r. Italy 58 E2
Pô, Parc National de nat. park Burkina 96 C3
Pobeda Peak China/Kyrg. 80 F3
Pobedy, Pik mt. China/Kyrg. see Pobeda Peak
Pocahontas U.S.A. 131 F4
Pocatello U.S.A. 126 E4
Pochala Sudan 97 G4
Pochayiv Ukr. 43 E6
Pochep Rus. Fed. 43 G5
Pochinki Rus. Fed. 43 J5
Pochinok Rus. Fed. 43 G5
Pochutla Mex. 136 E5
Pocking Germany 47 N6
Pocklington U.K. 48 G5
Poções Brazil 145 C1
Pocomoke City U.S.A. 135 H4
Pocomoke Sound b. U.S.A. 135 H5
Poconé Brazil 143 G7
Pocono Mountains hills U.S.A. 135 H3
Pocono Summit U.S.A. 135 H3
Poços de Caldas Brazil 145 B3
Podanur India 84 C4
Poddor'ye Rus. Fed. 42 F4
Podgorenskiy Rus. Fed. 43 H6
Podgorica Serb. and Mont. 59 H3
Podgornoye Rus. Fed. 64 J4
Podile India 84 C3
Podișul Transilvaniei plat. Romania see Transylvanian Basin
Podkamennaya Tunguska r. Rus. Fed. 65 K3
Podocarpus, Parque Nacional nat. park Ecuador 142 C4
Podol'sk Rus. Fed. 43 H5
Podporozh'ye Rus. Fed. 42 G3
Podujevë Serb. and Mont. see Podujevo
Podujevo Serb. and Mont. 59 I3
Podz' Rus. Fed. 42 K3
Poelela, Lagoa l. Moz. 101 L3
Poeppel Corner salt flat Australia 111 B5
Poetovio Slovenia see Ptuj
Pofadder S. Africa 100 D5
Pogar Rus. Fed. 43 G5
Poggibonsi Italy 58 D3
Poggio di Montieri mt. Italy 58 D3
Pogradec Albania 59 I4
Pogranichnik Afgh. 89 F3
Po Hai g. China see Bo Hai
P'ohang S. Korea 75 C5
Pohnpei atoll Micronesia 150 G5
Pohri India 82 D4
Poi India 83 H4
Poiana Mare Romania 59 J3
Poinsett, Cape Antarctica 152 F2
Point Arena U.S.A. 128 B2
Point au Fer Island U.S.A. 131 F6
Pointe a la Hache U.S.A. 131 F6
Pointe-à-Pitre Guadeloupe 137 L5
Pointe-Noire Congo 99 B4
Point Hope U.S.A. 118 B3
Point Lake Canada 120 H1
Point of Rocks U.S.A. 126 F4
Point Pelee National Park Canada 134 D3
Point Pleasant NJ U.S.A. 135 H3
Point Pleasant WV U.S.A. 134 D4
Poitiers France 56 E3
Poitou reg. France 56 E3
Poix-de-Picardie France 52 B5
Pojuca r. Brazil 145 D1
Pokaran India 82 B4
Pokataroo Australia 112 D2
Pokcha Rus. Fed. 41 R3
Pokhara Nepal 83 E3
Pokhvistnevo Rus. Fed. 41 Q5
Pok Liu Chau i. Hong Kong China see Lamma Island
Poko Dem. Rep. Congo 98 C3
Pokosnoye Rus. Fed. 72 I1
Pokran Pak. 89 G5
P'ok'r Kovkas mts Asia see Lesser Caucasus
Pokrovka Chitinskaya Oblast' Rus. Fed. 74 A1
Pokrovka Primorskiy Kray Rus. Fed. 74 C4
Pokrovsk Respublika Sakha (Yakutiya) Rus. Fed. 65 N3
Pokrovsk Saratovskaya Oblast' Rus. Fed. see Engel's
Pokrovskoye Rus. Fed. 43 H7
Pokshen'ga r. Rus. Fed. 42 J3
Pol India 82 C5
Pola Croatia see Pula
Polacca Wash watercourse U.S.A. 129 H4
Pola de Lena Spain 57 D2
Pola de Siero Spain 57 D2
▶Poland country Europe 40 J5
Europe 5, 38–39
Poland NY U.S.A. 135 H2
Poland OH U.S.A. 134 E3
Polar Plateau Antarctica 152 A1
Polatlı Turkey 90 D3
Polatsk Belarus 45 P9
Polavaram India 84 D2
Polcirkeln Sweden 44 L3
Pol-e Fāsā Iran 88 D4
Pole-Khatum Iran 89 F2
Pol-e Khomrī Afgh. 89 H3
Pol-e Safid Iran 88 D2
Polessk Rus. Fed. 45 L9
Poles'ye marsh Belarus/Ukr. see Pripet Marshes
Polgahawela Sri Lanka 84 D5
Poli Cyprus see Polis
Políaigos i. Greece see Polyaigos
Police Poland 47 O4
Policoro Italy 58 G4
Poligny France 56 G3
Políkastron Greece see Polykastro
Polillo Islands Phil. 69 G3
Polis Cyprus 85 A2
Polis'ke Ukr. 43 F6
Polis'kyy Zapovidnyk nature res. Ukr. 43 F6
Politovo Rus. Fed. 42 K2
Políyiros Greece see Polygyros
Polkowice Poland 47 P5
Pollachi India 84 C4
Pollard Islands U.S.A. see Gardner Pinnacles
Polle Germany 53 J3
Pollino, Monte mt. Italy 58 G5
Pollino, Parco Nazionale del nat. park Italy 58 G5
Pollock Pines U.S.A. 128 C2
Pollock Reef Australia 109 C8
Polmak Norway 44 O1
Polnovat Rus. Fed. 41 T3
Polo Fin. 44 P4
Poloat atoll Micronesia see Puluwat
Pologi Ukr. see Polohy
Polohy Ukr. 43 H7
Polonne Ukr. 43 E6
Polonnoye Ukr. see Polonne
Polotsk Belarus see Polatsk
Polperro U.K. 49 C8
Polska country Europe see Poland
Polson U.S.A. 126 E3
Polta r. Rus. Fed. 42 I2
Poltava Ukr. 43 G6
Poltoratsk Turkm. see Ashgabat
Põltsamaa Estonia 45 N7
Polunochnoye Rus. Fed. 41 S3
Põlva Estonia 45 O7
Polvadera U.S.A. 127 G6
Polvijärvi Fin. 44 P5
Polyaigos i. Greece 59 K6
Polyanovgrad Bulg. see Karnobat
Polyarnyy Chukotskiy Avtonomnyy Okrug Rus. Fed. 65 S3
Polyarnyy Murmanskaya Oblast' Rus. Fed. 44 R2
Polyarnyye Zori Rus. Fed. 44 R3
Polyarnyy Ural mts Rus. Fed. 41 S2
Polygyros Greece 59 J4
Polykastro Greece 59 J4
Polynesia is Pacific Ocean 150 I6
Polynésie Française terr. S. Pacific Ocean see French Polynesia
Pom Indon. 69 J7
Pomarkku Fin. 45 M6
Pombal Pará Brazil 143 H4
Pombal Paraíba Brazil 143 K5
Pombal Port. 57 B4
Pomene Moz. 101 L2
Pomeroy S. Africa 101 J5
Pomeroy U.K. 51 F3
Pomeroy OH U.S.A. 134 D4
Pomeroy WA U.S.A. 126 D3
Pomezia Italy 58 E4
Pomfret S. Africa 100 F3
Pomona Namibia 100 B4
Pomona U.S.A. 128 E4
Pomorie Bulg. 59 L3
Pomorska, Zatoka b. Poland 47 O3
Pomorskie, Pojezierze reg. Poland 47 O4
Pomorskiy Bereg coastal area Rus. Fed. 42 G2
Pomorskiy Proliv sea chan. Rus. Fed. 42 K1
Pomos Point Cyprus 85 A2
Pomo Tso l. China see Puma Yumco
Pomou, Akra pt Cyprus see Pomos Point
Pomozdino Rus. Fed. 42 L3
Pompain China 76 B2
Pompano Beach U.S.A. 133 D7
Pompei Italy 58 F4
Pompéia Brazil 145 A3
Pompey France 52 G6
Pompeyevka Rus. Fed. 74 C2
Ponape atoll Micronesia see Pohnpei
Ponask Lake Canada 121 M4
Ponazyrevo Rus. Fed. 42 J4
Ponca City U.S.A. 131 D4
Ponce Puerto Rico 137 K5
Ponce de Leon Bay U.S.A. 133 D7
Poncheville, Lac l. Canada 122 F4
Pondicherry India 84 C4
Pondicherry union terr. India 84 C4
Pondichéry India see Pondicherry
Pond Inlet Canada 153 K2
Ponds Bay Canada see Pond Inlet
Ponente, Riviera di coastal area Italy 58 B3
Poneto U.S.A. 134 C3
Ponferrada Spain 57 C2
Pongara, Pointe pt Gabon 98 A3
Pongaroa N.Z. 113 F5
Pongo watercourse Sudan 97 F4
Pongola r. S. Africa 101 K4
Pongolapoort Dam l. S. Africa 101 J4
Ponnagyun Myanmar 70 A2
Ponnaivar r. India 84 C4
Ponnampet India 84 B3
Ponnani India 84 B4
Ponnyadaung Range mts Myanmar 70 A2
Pono Indon. 69 I8
Ponoka Canada 120 H4
Ponoy r. Rus. Fed. 42 I2
Pons r. Canada 123 H2

▶Ponta Delgada Arquipélago dos Açores 148 G3
Capital of the Azores.

Ponta Grossa Brazil 145 A4
Pontal Brazil 145 A3
Pontalina Brazil 145 A2
Pont-à-Mousson France 52 G6
Ponta Porã Brazil 144 E2
Pontarfynach U.K. see Devil's Bridge
Pont-Audemer France 49 H9
Pontault-Combault France 52 C6
Pontax r. Canada 122 F4
Pontchartrain, Lake U.S.A. 131 F6
Pont-de-Loup Belgium 52 E4
Ponte Alta do Norte Brazil 143 I6
Ponte de Sor Port. 57 B4
Ponte Firme Brazil 145 B2
Pontefract U.K. 48 F5
Ponteix Canada 121 J5
Ponteland U.K. 48 F3
Ponte Nova Brazil 145 C3
Pontes-e-Lacerda Brazil 143 G7
Pontevedra Spain 57 B2
Ponthierville Dem. Rep. Congo see Ubundu
Pontiac IL U.S.A. 130 F3
Pontiac MI U.S.A. 134 D2
Pontiae is Italy see Ponziane, Isole
Pontianak Indon. 68 D7
Pontine Islands is Italy see Ponziane, Isole
Pont-l'Abbé France 56 B3
Pontoise France 52 C5
Ponton watercourse Australia 105 C7
Ponton Canada 121 L4
Pontotoc U.S.A. 131 F5
Pont-Ste-Maxence France 52 C5
Pontypool U.K. 49 D7
Pontypridd U.K. 49 D7
Ponza, Isola di i. Italy 58 E4
Ponziane, Isole is Italy 58 E4
Poochera Australia 109 F8
Poole U.K. 49 F8
Poole U.S.A. 134 B5
Poolowanna Lake salt flat Australia 111 B5
Poona India see Pune
Pooncarie Australia 111 C7
Poonch India see Punch
Poopelloe, Lake salt l. Australia 112 B3
Poopó, Lago de l. Bol. 142 E7
Poor Knights Islands N.Z. 113 E2
Popayán Col. 142 C3
Poperinge Belgium 52 C4
Popigay r. Rus. Fed. 65 L2
Popiltah Australia 111 C7
Popilta Lake imp. l. Australia 111 C7
Poplar r. Canada 121 L4
Poplar U.S.A. 126 G2
Poplar Bluff U.S.A. 131 F4
Poplar Camp U.S.A. 134 E5
Poplarville U.S.A. 131 F6

▶Popocatépetl, Volcán vol. Mex. 136 E5
5th highest mountain in North America.

Popokabaka Dem. Rep. Congo 99 B4
Popondetta P.N.G. 69 L8
Popovichskaya Rus. Fed. see Kalininskaya
Popovo Bulg. 59 L3
Popovo Polje plain Bos.-Herz. 58 G3
Poppberg hill Germany 53 L5
Poppenberg hill Germany 53 K3
Poprad Slovakia 47 R6
Poquoson U.S.A. 135 G5
Porali r. Pak. 89 G5
Porangahau N.Z. 113 F5
Porangatu Brazil 145 A1
Porbandar India 82 B5
Porcher Island Canada 120 D4
Porcos r. Brazil 145 B1
Porcupine, Cape Canada 123 K3
Porcupine Abyssal Plain sea feature N. Atlantic Ocean 148 G2
Porcupine Gorge National Park Australia 110 D4
Porcupine Hills Canada 121 K4
Porcupine Mountains U.S.A. 130 F2
Poreč Croatia 58 E2
Porecatu Brazil 145 A3
Poretskoye Rus. Fed. 43 J5
Pori Fin. 45 L6
Porirua N.Z. 113 E5
Porkhov Rus. Fed. 45 P8
Porlamar Venez. 142 F1
Pormpuraaw Australia 110 C2
Pornic France 56 C3
Poronaysk Rus. Fed. 74 F2
Porong China see Baingoin
Poros Greece 59 J6
Porosozero Rus. Fed. 42 G3
Porpoise Bay Antarctica 152 G2
Porsangen sea chan. Norway 44 N1
Porsangerhalvøya pen. Norway 44 N1
Porsgrunn Norway 45 F7
Porsuk r. Turkey 59 N5
Portadown U.K. 51 F3
Portaferry U.K. 51 G3
Portage MI U.S.A. 134 C2
Portage PA U.S.A. 135 F3
Portage WI U.S.A. 130 F3
Portage Lakes U.S.A. 134 E3
Portage la Prairie Canada 121 L5
Portal U.S.A. 130 C1
Port Alberni Canada 120 E5
Port Albert Australia 112 C7
Portalegre Port. 57 C4
Portales U.S.A. 131 C5
Port-Alfred Canada see La Baie
Port Alfred S. Africa 101 H7
Port Alice Canada 120 E5
Port Allegany U.S.A. 135 F3
Port Allen U.S.A. 131 F6
Port Alma Australia 110 E4
Port Angeles U.S.A. 126 C2
Port Antonio Jamaica 137 I5
Portarlington Rep. of Ireland 51 E4
Port Arthur Australia 111 [inset]
Port Arthur U.S.A. 131 E6
Port Askaig U.K. 50 C5
Port Augusta Australia 111 B7

▶Port-au-Prince Haiti 137 J5
Capital of Haiti.

Port Austin U.S.A. 134 D1
Port aux Choix Canada 123 K4
Portavogie U.K. 51 G3
Port Beaufort S. Africa 100 E8
Port Blair India 71 A5
Port Bolster Canada 134 F1
Portbou Spain 57 H2
Port Burwell Canada 134 E2
Port Campbell Australia 112 A7
Port Campbell National Park Australia 112 A7
Port Carling Canada 134 F1
Port-Cartier Canada 123 I4
Port Chalmers N.Z. 113 C7
Port Charlotte U.S.A. 133 D7
Port Clements Canada 120 C4
Port Clinton U.S.A. 134 D3
Port Credit Canada 134 F2
Port-de-Paix Haiti 137 J5
Port Dickson Malaysia 71 C7
Port Douglas Australia 110 D3
Port Edward Canada 120 D4
Port Edward S. Africa 101 J6
Porteira Brazil 143 G4
Porteirinha Brazil 145 C1
Portel Brazil 143 H4
Port Elgin Canada 134 E1
Port Elizabeth S. Africa 101 G7
Port Ellen U.K. 50 C5
Port Erin Isle of Man 48 C4
Porter Lake N.W.T. Canada 121 J2
Porter Lake Sask. Canada 121 J3
Porter Landing Canada 120 D3
Porterville S. Africa 100 D7
Porterville U.S.A. 128 D3
Port Étienne Mauritania see Nouâdhibou
Port Everglades U.S.A. see Fort Lauderdale
Port Fitzroy N.Z. 113 E3
Port Francqui Dem. Rep. Congo see Ilebo
Port-Gentil Gabon 98 A4
Port Glasgow U.K. 50 E5
Port Harcourt Nigeria 96 D4
Port Harrison Canada see Inukjuak
Porthcawl U.K. 49 D7
Port Hedland Australia 108 B5
Port Henry U.S.A. 135 I1
Port Herald Malawi see Nsanje
Porthleven U.K. 49 B8
Porthmadog U.K. 49 C6
Port Hope Canada 135 F2
Port Hope Simpson Canada 123 L3
Port Hueneme U.S.A. 128 D4
Port Huron U.S.A. 134 D2
Portimão Port. 57 B5
Port Jackson Australia see Sydney
Port Jackson inlet Australia 112 E4
Port Keats Australia see Wadeye
Port Klang Malaysia see Pelabuhan Kelang
Port Láirge Rep. of Ireland see Waterford
Portland N.S.W. Australia 112 D4
Portland Vic. Australia 111 C8
Portland IN U.S.A. 134 C3
Portland ME U.S.A. 135 J2
Portland MI U.S.A. 134 C2
Portland OR U.S.A. 126 C3
Portland TN U.S.A. 134 B5
Portland, Isle of pen. U.K. 49 E8
Portland Bill hd U.K. see Bill of Portland
Portland Creek Pond l. Canada 123 K4
Portland Roads Australia 110 C2
Port-la-Nouvelle France 56 F5
Portlaoise Rep. of Ireland 51 E4
Port Lavaca U.S.A. 131 D6
Portlaw Rep. of Ireland 51 E5
Portlethen U.K. 50 G3
Port Lincoln Australia 111 A7
Port Loko Sierra Leone 96 B4

▶Port Louis Mauritius 149 L7
Capital of Mauritius.

Port-Lyautrey Morocco see Kénitra
Port Macquarie Australia 112 F3
Portmadoc U.K. see Porthmadog
Port McNeill Canada 120 E5
Port-Menier Canada 123 I4

▶Port Moresby P.N.G. 69 L8
Capital of Papua New Guinea.

Portnaguran U.K. 50 C2
Portnahaven U.K. 50 C5
Port nan Giúran U.K. see Portnaguran
Port Neill Australia 111 B7
Port Ness U.K. 50 C2
Portneuf r. Canada 123 H4
Port Nis U.K. see Port Ness
Port Noarlunga Australia 111 B7
Port Nolloth S. Africa 100 C5
Port Norris U.S.A. 135 H4
Port-Nouveau-Québec Canada see Kangiqsualujjuaq
Porto Port. see Oporto
Porto Acre Brazil 142 E5
Porto Alegre Brazil 145 A5
Porto Alexandre Angola see Tombua
Porto Amboim Angola 99 B5
Porto Amélia Moz. see Pemba
Porto Artur Brazil 143 G6
Porto Belo Brazil 145 A4
Porto de Moz Brazil 143 H4
Porto de Santa Cruz Brazil 145 C1
Porto dos Gaúchos Óbidos Brazil 143 G6
Porto Esperança Brazil 143 G7
Porto Esperidião Brazil 143 G7
Portoferraio Italy 58 D3
Porto Franco Brazil 143 I5

▶Port of Spain Trin. and Tob. 137 L6
Capital of Trinidad and Tobago.

Porto Grande Brazil 143 H3
Portogruaro Italy 58 E2
Porto Jofre Brazil 143 G7
Portola U.S.A. 128 C2
Portomaggiore Italy 58 D2
Porto Mendes Brazil 144 F2
Porto Murtinho Brazil 144 E2
Porto Nacional Brazil 143 I6

▶Porto-Novo Benin 96 D4
Capital of Benin.

Porto Novo Cape Verde 96 [inset]
Porto Primavera, Represa resr Brazil 144 F2
Port Orchard U.S.A. 126 C3
Port Orford U.S.A. 126 B4
Porto Rico Angola 99 B4
Porto Santo, Ilha de i. Madeira 96 B1
Porto Seguro Brazil 145 D2
Porto Tolle Italy 58 E2
Porto Torres Sardinia Italy 58 C4
Porto União Brazil 145 A4
Porto-Vecchio Corsica France 56 I6
Porto Velho Brazil 142 F5
Portoviejo Ecuador 142 B4
Porto Wálter Brazil 142 D5
Portpatrick U.K. 50 D6
Port Perry Canada 135 F1
Port Phillip Bay Australia 112 B7
Port Pirie Australia 111 B7
Port Radium Canada see Echo Bay
Portreath U.K. 49 B8
Portree U.K. 50 C3
Port Rexton Canada 123 L4
Port Royal U.S.A. 135 G4
Port Royal Sound inlet U.S.A. 133 D5
Portrush U.K. 51 F2
Port Safaga Egypt see Būr Safājah
Port Said Egypt 85 A4
Portsalon Rep. of Ireland 51 E2
Port Sanilac U.S.A. 134 D2
Port Severn Canada 134 F1
Port Shepstone S. Africa 101 J6
Port Simpson Canada see Lax Kw'alaams
Portsmouth U.K. 49 F8
Portsmouth NH U.S.A. 135 J2
Portsmouth OH U.S.A. 134 D4
Portsmouth VA U.S.A. 135 G5
Portsoy U.K. 50 G3
Port Stanley Falkland Is see Stanley
Port Stephens b. Australia 112 F4
Portstewart U.K. 51 F2
Port St Joe U.S.A. 133 C6
Port St Lucie City U.S.A. 133 D7
Port St Mary Isle of Man 48 C4
Port Sudan Sudan 86 E6
Port Swettenham Malaysia see Pelabuhan Kelang
Port Talbot U.K. 49 D7
Porttipahdan tekojärvi l. Fin. 44 O2
Port Townsend U.S.A. 126 C2
▶Portugal country Europe 57 C4
Europe 5, 38–39
Portugália Angola see Chitato
Portuguese East Africa country Africa see Mozambique
Portuguese Guinea country Africa see Guinea-Bissau
Portuguese Timor country Asia see East Timor
Portuguese West Africa country Africa see Angola
Portumna Rep. of Ireland 51 D4
Portus Herculis Monoeci country Europe see Monaco
Port-Vendres France 56 F5

▶Port Vila Vanuatu 107 G3
Capital of Vanuatu.

Portville U.S.A. 135 F2
Port Vladimir Rus. Fed. 44 R2
Port Waikato N.Z. 113 E3
Port Washington U.S.A. 134 B2
Port William U.K. 50 E6
Porvenir Bol. 142 E6
Porvenir Chile 144 B8
Porvoo Fin. 45 N6
Posada Spain 57 D2
Posada de Llanera Spain see Posada
Posadas Arg. 144 E3
Posen Poland see Poznań
Posen U.S.A. 134 D1
Poseyville U.S.A. 134 B4
Poshekhon'ye Rus. Fed. 42 H4
Poshekon'ye-Volodarsk Rus. Fed. see Poshekhon'ye
Posht-e Badam Iran 88 D3
Poshteh-ye Chaqvīr hill Iran 88 E4
Posht-e Kūh mts Iran 88 B3
Posht-e Rūd-e Zamindavar reg. Afgh. see Zamīndāvar
Posht Kūh hill Iran 88 C2
Posio Fin. 44 P3
Poso Indon. 69 G7
Posof Turkey 91 F2
Posŏng S. Korea 75 B6
Possession Island Namibia 100 B4
Pößneck Germany 53 L4
Post U.S.A. 131 C5
Postavy Belarus see Pastavy
Poste-de-la-Baleine Canada see Kuujjuarapik
Postmasburg S. Africa 100 F5
Poston U.S.A. 129 F4
Postville Canada 123 K3
Postville U.S.A. 122 C6
Post Weygand Alg. 96 D2
Postysheve Ukr. see Krasnoarmiys'k
Pota Indon. 108 C2
Pótam Mex. 127 F8
Poté Brazil 145 C2
Poteau U.S.A. 131 E5
Potegaon India 84 D2
Potentia Italy see Potenza
Potenza Italy 58 F4
Potgietersrus S. Africa 101 I3
Poth U.S.A. 131 D6
P'ot'i Georgia 91 F2
Potikal India 84 D2
Potiraguá Brazil 145 D1
Potiskum Nigeria 96 E3
Potlatch U.S.A. 126 D3
Pot Mountain U.S.A. 126 E3
Po Toi i. Hong Kong China 77 [inset]
Potomac r. U.S.A. 135 G4
Potosí Bol. 142 E7
Potosi U.S.A. 130 F4
Potosi Mountain U.S.A. 129 F4
Potrerillos Chile 144 C3
Potrero del Llano Mex. 131 B6
Potsdam Germany 53 N2
Potsdam U.S.A. 135 H1
Potter U.S.A. 130 C3
Potterne U.K. 49 E7
Potters Bar U.K. 49 G7
Potter Valley U.S.A. 128 B2
Pottstown U.S.A. 135 H3
Pottsville U.S.A. 135 G3
Pottuvil Sri Lanka 84 D5
Potwar reg. Pak. 89 I3
Pouch Cove Canada 123 L5
Poughkeepsie U.S.A. 135 I3
Poulin de Courval, Lac l. Canada 123 H4
Poulton-le-Fylde U.K. 48 E5
Pouso Alegre Brazil 145 B3
Poŭthĭsăt Cambodia 71 C4
Poŭthĭsăt, Stœ̆ng r. Cambodia 71 D4
Považská Bystrica Slovakia 47 Q6
Povenets Rus. Fed. 42 G3
Poverty Bay N.Z. 113 F4
Povlen mt. Serb. and Mont. 59 H2
Póvoa de Varzim Port. 57 B3
Povorino Rus. Fed. 43 I6
Povorotnyy, Mys hd Rus. Fed. 74 D4
Poway U.S.A. 128 E5
Powder r. U.S.A. 126 G3
Powder, South Fork r. U.S.A. 126 G4
Powder River U.S.A. 126 G4
Powell r. U.S.A. 134 D5
Powell, Lake resr U.S.A. 129 H3
Powell Lake Canada 120 E5
Powell Mountain U.S.A. 128 D2
Powell Point Bahamas 133 E7
Powell River Canada 120 E5
Powhatan AR U.S.A. 131 F4
Powhatan VA U.S.A. 135 G5
Powo China 76 C1
Pōwrize Turkm. see Firyuza
Poxoréu Brazil 143 H7
Poyang China see Boyang
Poyang Hu l. China 77 H2
Poyan Reservoir Sing. 71 [inset]
Poyarkovo Rus. Fed. 74 C2
Pozantı Turkey 90 D3

Požarevac Serb. and Mont. 59 I2
Poza Rica Mex. 136 E4
Pozdeyevka Rus. Fed. 74 C2
Požega Croatia 58 G2
Požega Serb. and Mont. 59 I3
Pozharskoye Rus. Fed. 74 D3
Poznań Poland 47 P4
Pozoblanco Spain 57 D4
Pozo Colorado Para. 144 E2
Pozsony Slovakia *see* Bratislava
Pozzuoli Italy 58 F4
Prabumulih Indon. 68 C7
Prachatice Czech Rep. 47 O6
Prachi *r.* India 83 F6
Prachin Buri Thai. 71 C4
Prachuap Khiri Khan Thai. 71 B5
Prades France 56 F5
Prado Brazil 145 D2

▶Prague Czech Rep. 47 O5
Capital of the Czech Republic.

Praha Czech Rep. *see* Prague

▶Praia Cape Verde 96 [inset]
Capital of Cape Verde.

Praia do Bilene Moz. 101 K3
Prainha Brazil 143 H4
Prairie Australia 110 D4
Prairie *r.* U.S.A. 130 E2
Prairie Dog Town Fork *r.* U.S.A. 131 C5
Prairie du Chien U.S.A. 130 F3
Prairie River Canada 121 K4
Pram, Khao *mt.* Thai. 71 B5
Pran *r.* Thai. 71 C4
Pran Buri Thai. 71 B4
Prapat Indon. 71 B7
Prasonisi, Akra *pt* Greece 59 L7
Prata Brazil 145 A2
Prata *r.* Brazil 145 A2
Prat de Llobregat Spain *see* El Prat de Llobregat
Prathes Thai *country* Asia *see* Thailand
Prato Italy 58 D3
Pratt U.S.A. 130 D4
Prattville U.S.A. 133 C5
Pravdinsk Rus. Fed. 45 L9
Praya Indon. 108 B2
Preah, Prêk *r.* Cambodia 71 D4
Preăh Vihear Cambodia 71 D4
Preble U.S.A. 135 G2
Prechistoye *Smolenskaya Oblast'* Rus. Fed. 43 G5
Prechistoye *Yaroslavskaya Oblast'* Rus. Fed. 42 I4
Precipice National Park Australia 110 E5
Preeceville Canada 121 K5
Pregolya *r.* Rus. Fed. 45 L9
Preiļi Latvia 45 O8
Prelate Canada 121 I5
Premer Australia 112 D3
Prémery France 56 F3
Premnitz Germany 53 M2
Prentiss U.S.A. 131 F6
Prenzlau Germany 47 N4
Preparis Island Cocos Is 68 A4
Preparis North Channel Cocos Is 68 A4
Preparis South Channel Cocos Is 68 A4
Přerov Czech Rep. 47 P6
Presa San Antonio Mex. 131 C7
Prescelly Mts *hills* U.K. *see* Preseli, Mynydd
Prescott Canada 135 H1
Prescott *AR* U.S.A. 131 E5
Prescott *AZ* U.S.A. 129 G4
Prescott Valley U.S.A. 129 G4
Preseli, Mynydd *hills* U.K. 49 C7
Preševo Serb. and Mont. 59 I3
Presidencia Roque Sáenz Peña Arg. 144 D3
Presidente Dutra Brazil 143 J5
Presidente Eduardo Frei *research station* Antarctica 152 A2
Presidente Hermes Brazil 142 F6
Presidente Olegário Brazil 145 B2
Presidente Prudente Brazil 145 A3
Presidente Venceslau Brazil 145 A3
Presidio U.S.A. 131 B6
Preslav Bulg. *see* Veliki Preslav
Prešov Slovakia 43 D6
Prespa, Lake Europe 59 I4
Prespansko Ezero *l.* Europe *see* Prespa, Lake
Prespes *nat. park* Greece 59 I4
Prespës, Liqeni i *l.* Europe *see* Prespa, Lake
Presque Isle *ME* U.S.A. 132 G2
Presque Isle *MI* U.S.A. 134 D1
Pressburg Slovakia *see* Bratislava
Presteigne U.K. 49 D6
Preston U.K. 48 E5
Preston *ID* U.S.A. 126 F4
Preston *MN* U.S.A. 130 E3
Preston *MO* U.S.A. 130 E4
Preston, Cape Australia 108 B5
Prestonpans U.K. 50 G5
Prestonsburg U.S.A. 134 D5
Prestwick U.K. 50 E5
Preto *r. Bahia* Brazil 143 J6
Preto *r. Minas Gerais* Brazil 145 B2
Preto *r.* Brazil 145 D1

▶Pretoria S. Africa 101 I3
Official capital of South Africa.

Pretoria-Witwatersrand-Vereeniging *prov.* S. Africa *see* Gauteng
Pretzsch Germany 53 M3
Preussisch-Eylau Rus. Fed. *see* Bagrationovsk
Preußisch Stargard Poland *see* Starogard Gdański
Preveza Greece 59 I5
Prewitt U.S.A. 129 I4
Prey Vêng Cambodia 71 D5
Priaral'skiye Karakumy, Peski *des.* Kazakh. 80 B2
Priargunsk Rus. Fed. 73 L2
Pribilof Islands U.S.A. 118 A4
Priboj Serb. and Mont. 59 H3
Price *r.* Australia 108 E3
Price *NC* U.S.A. 134 F5
Price *UT* U.S.A. 129 H2
Price *r.* U.S.A. 129 H2
Price Island Canada 120 D4
Prichard *AL* U.S.A. 131 F6
Prichard *WV* U.S.A. 134 D4
Pridorozhnoye Rus. Fed. *see* Khulkhuta
Priekule Latvia 45 L8
Priekuļi Latvia 45 N8
Prienai Lith. 45 M9
Prieska S. Africa 100 F5
Prievidza Slovakia 47 Q6
Prignitz *reg.* Germany 53 M1
Prijedor Bos.-Herz. 58 G2
Prijepolje Serb. and Mont. 59 H3
Prikaspiyskaya Nizmennost' *lowland* Kazakh./Rus. Fed. *see* Caspian Lowland
Prilep Macedonia 59 I4
Priluki Ukr. *see* Pryluky
Přimda Czech Rep. 53 M5
Primero de Enero Cuba 133 E8
Primorsk Rus. Fed. 45 P6
Primorsk Ukr. *see* Prymors'k
Primorskiy Kray *admin. div.* Rus. Fed. 74 D3
Primorsko-Akhtarsk Rus. Fed. 43 H7
Primo Tapia Mex. 128 E5
Primrose Lake Canada 121 I4
Prims *r.* Germany 52 G5
Prince Albert Canada 121 J4
Prince Albert S. Africa 100 F7
Prince Albert Mountains Antarctica 152 H1
Prince Albert National Park Canada 121 J4
Prince Albert Peninsula Canada 118 G2
Prince Albert Road S. Africa 100 E7
Prince Alfred, Cape Canada 118 F2
Prince Alfred Hamlet S. Africa 100 D7
Prince Charles Island Canada 119 K3
Prince Charles Mountains Antarctica 152 E2
Prince Edward Island *prov.* Canada 123 J5

▶Prince Edward Islands Indian Ocean 149 K9
Part of South Africa.

Prince Edward Point Canada 135 G2
Prince Frederick U.S.A. 135 G4
Prince George Canada 120 F4
Prince Harald Coast Antarctica 152 D2
Prince of Wales, Cape U.S.A. 118 B3
Prince of Wales Island Australia 110 C1
Prince of Wales Island Canada 119 I2
Prince of Wales Island U.S.A. 120 C4
Prince of Wales Strait Canada 118 G2
Prince Patrick Island Canada 118 G2
Prince Regent Inlet *sea chan.* Canada 119 I2
Prince Rupert Canada 120 D4
Princess Anne U.S.A. 135 H4
Princess Astrid Coast Antarctica 152 C2
Princess Charlotte Bay Australia 110 C2
Princess Elizabeth Land *reg.* Antarctica 152 E2
Princess Mary Lake Canada 121 L1
Princess Ragnhild Coast Antarctica 152 C2
Princess Royal Island Canada 120 D4
Princeton Canada 120 F5
Princeton *CA* U.S.A. 128 B2
Princeton *IL* U.S.A. 130 F3
Princeton *IN* U.S.A. 134 B4
Princeton *MO* U.S.A. 130 E3
Princeton *NJ* U.S.A. 135 H3
Princeton *WV* U.S.A. 134 E5
Prince William Sound *b.* U.S.A. 118 D3
Príncipe *i.* São Tomé and Príncipe 96 D4
Prineville U.S.A. 126 C3
Prins Harald Kyst *coastal area* Antarctica *see* Prince Harald Coast
Prinzapolca Nicaragua 137 H6
Priozersk Rus. Fed. 45 Q6
Priozyorsk Rus. Fed. *see* Priozersk
Pripet *r.* Belarus/Ukr. 43 F6 *also spelt* Pryp"yat' (Ukraine) *or* Prypyats' (Belarus)
Pripet Marshes Belarus/Ukr. 43 E6
Prirechnyy Rus. Fed. 44 Q2
Prishtinë Serb. and Mont. *see* Priština
Priština Serb. and Mont. 59 I3
Pritzier Germany 53 L1
Pritzwalk Germany 53 M1
Privas France 56 G4
Privlaka Croatia 58 F2
Privolzhsk Rus. Fed. 42 I4
Privolzhskaya Vozvyshennost' *hills* Rus. Fed. 43 J6
Privolzhskiy Rus. Fed. 43 J6
Privolzh'ye Rus. Fed. 43 K5
Priyutnoye Rus. Fed. 43 I7
Prizren Serb. and Mont. 59 I3
Probolinggo Indon. 68 E8
Probstzella Germany 53 L4
Probus U.K. 49 C8
Proddatur India 84 C3
Professor van Blommestein Meer *resr* Suriname 143 G3
Progreso Hond. *see* El Progreso
Progreso Mex. 131 C7
Progress Rus. Fed. 74 C2
Project City U.S.A. 126 C4
Prokhladnyy Rus. Fed. 91 G2
Prokop'yevsk Rus. Fed. 72 F2
Prokuplje Serb. and Mont. 59 I3
Proletarsk Rus. Fed. 43 I7
Proletarskaya Rus. Fed. *see* Proletarsk
Prome Myanmar *see* Pyè
Promissão Brazil 145 A3
Promissão, Represa *resr* Brazil 145 A3
Prophet *r.* Canada 120 F3
Prophet River Canada 120 F3
Propriá Brazil 143 K6
Proskurov Ukr. *see* Khmel'nyts'kyy
Prosser U.S.A. 126 D3
Protem S. Africa 100 E8
Provadiya Bulg. 59 L3
Prøven Greenland *see* Kangersuatsiaq
Provence *reg.* France 56 G5
Providence *KY* U.S.A. 134 B5
Providence *MD* U.S.A. *see* Annapolis

▶Providence *RI* U.S.A. 135 J3
State capital of Rhode Island.

Providence, Cape N.Z. 113 A8
Providencia, Isla de *i.* Caribbean Sea 137 H6
Provideniya Rus. Fed. 65 T3
Provincetown U.S.A. 135 J2
Provo U.S.A. 129 H1
Provost Canada 121 I4
Prudentópolis Brazil 145 A4
Prudhoe Bay U.S.A. 118 D2
Prüm Germany 52 G4
Prüm *r.* Germany 52 G5
Prunelli-di-Fiumorbo *Corsica* France 56 I5
Pruntytown U.S.A. 134 E4
Prusa Turkey *see* Bursa
Prushkov Poland *see* Pruszków
Pruszków Poland 47 R4
Prut *r.* Europe 43 F7
Prydz Bay Antarctica 152 E2
Pryelbrusskiy Natsional'nyy Park *nat. park* Rus. Fed. 43 I8
Pryluky Ukr. 43 G6
Prymors'k Ukr. 43 H7
Prymors'ke Ukr. *see* Sartana
Pryp"yat' *r.* Ukr. 43 F6 *see* Pripet
Prypyats' *r.* Belarus 41 L5 *see* Pripet
Przemyśl Poland 43 D6
Przheval'sk Kyrg. *see* Karakol
Psara *i.* Greece 59 K5
Pskov Rus. Fed. 45 P8
Pskov, Lake Estonia/Rus. Fed. 45 O7
Pskov Oblast *admin. div.* Rus. Fed. *see* Pskovskaya Oblast'
Pskovskaya Oblast' *admin. div.* Rus. Fed. 45 P8
Pskovskoye Ozero *l.* Estonia/Rus. Fed. *see* Pskov, Lake
Ptolemaïda Greece 59 I4
Ptolemais Israel *see* 'Akko
Ptuj Slovenia 58 F1
Pua Thai. 70 C3
Puaka *hill* Sing. 71 [inset]
Pu'an *Guizhou* China 76 E3
Pu'an *Sichuan* China 76 E2
Puan S. Korea 75 B6
Pucallpa Peru 142 D5
Pucheng *Fujian* China 77 H3
Pucheng *Shaanxi* China 77 F1
Puchezh Rus. Fed. 42 I4
Puch'ŏn S. Korea 75 B5
Puck Poland 47 Q3
Pudai *watercourse* Afgh. *see* Dor
Pūdanū Iran 88 D3
Pudasjärvi Fin. 44 O4
Pudimoe S. Africa 100 G4
Pudozh Rus. Fed. 42 H3
Pudsey U.K. 48 F5
Pudu China *see* Suizhou
Puduchcheri India *see* Pondicherry
Pudukkottai India 84 C4
Puebla *Baja California* Mex. 129 F5
Puebla *Puebla* Mex. 136 E5
Puebla de Sanabria Spain 57 C2
Puebla de Zaragoza Mex. *see* Puebla
Pueblo U.S.A. 127 G5
Pueblo Yaqui Mex. 127 F8
Puelches Arg. 144 C5
Puelén Arg. 144 C5
Puente-Genil Spain 57 D5
Pu'er China 76 D4
Puerco *watercourse* U.S.A. 129 H4
Puerto Acosta Bol. 142 E7
Puerto Alegre Bol. 142 F6
Puerto Ángel Mex. 136 E5
Puerto Armuelles Panama 137 H7
Puerto Ayacucho Venez. 142 E2
Puerto Bahía Negra Para. *see* Bahía Negra
Puerto Baquerizo Moreno *Galápagos* Ecuador 142 [inset]
Puerto Barrios Guat. 136 G5
Puerto Cabello Venez. 142 E1
Puerto Cabezas Nicaragua 137 H6
Puerto Carreño Col. 142 E2
Puerto Casado Para. 144 E2
Puerto Cavinas Bol. 142 E6
Puerto Coig Arg. 144 C8
Puerto Cortés Mex. 136 B4
Puerto de Lobos Mex. 127 E7
Puerto Escondido Mex. 136 E5
Puerto Francisco de Orellana Ecuador *see* Coca
Puerto Frey Bol. 142 F6
Puerto Génova Bol. 142 E6
Puerto Guarani Para. 144 E2
Puerto Heath Bol. 142 E6
Puerto Huitoto Col. 142 D3
Puerto Inírida Col. 142 E3
Puerto Isabel Bol. 143 G7
Puerto Leguízamo Col. 142 D4
Puerto Lempira Hond. 137 H5
Puerto Libertad Mex. 127 E7
Puerto Limón Costa Rica 137 H6
Puertollano Spain 57 D4
Puerto Lobos Arg. 144 C6
Puerto Madryn Arg. 144 C6
Puerto Maldonado Peru 142 E6
Puerto Máncora Peru 142 B4
Puerto México Mex. *see* Coatzacoalcos
Puerto Montt Chile 144 B6
Puerto Natales Chile 144 B8
Puerto Nuevo Col. 142 E2
Puerto Peñasco Mex. 127 E7
Puerto Pirámides Arg. 144 D6
Puerto Plata Dom. Rep. 137 J5
Puerto Portillo Peru 142 D5
Puerto Prado Peru 142 D6
Puerto Princesa Phil. 68 F5
Puerto Rico Arg. 144 E3
Puerto Rico Bol. 142 E6

▶Puerto Rico *terr.* West Indies 137 K5
United States Commonwealth.
North America 9, 116–117

▶Puerto Rico Trench *sea feature* Caribbean Sea 148 D4
Deepest trench in the Atlantic Ocean.

Puerto Santa Cruz Arg. 144 C8
Puerto Sastre Para. 144 E2
Puerto Saucedo Bol. 142 F6
Puerto Suárez Bol. 143 G7
Puerto Supe Peru 142 C6
Puerto Vallarta Mex. 136 C4
Puerto Victoria Peru 142 D5
Puerto Visser Arg. 144 C7
Puerto Yartou Chile 144 B8
Puerto Ybapobó Para. 144 E2
Pugachev Rus. Fed. 43 K5
Pugal India 82 C3
Puge China 76 D3
Pūhāl-e Khamīr, Kūh-e *mts* Iran 88 D5
Puhiwaero *c.* N.Z. *see* South West Cape
Puigmal *mt.* France/Spain 56 F5
Pui O Wan *b. Hong Kong* China 77 [inset]
Puji China *see* Puge
Pukaki, Lake N.Z. 113 C7
Pukapuka *atoll* Cook Is 107 J3
Pukaskwa National Park Canada 122 D4
Pukatawagan Canada 121 K4
Pukchin N. Korea 75 B4
Pukch'ŏng N. Korea 75 C4
Pukekohe N.Z. 113 E3
Puketeraki Range *mts* N.Z. 113 D6
Pukeuri Junction N.Z. 113 C7
Puksubaek-san *mt.* N. Korea 74 B4
Pula China *see* Nyingchi
Pula Croatia 58 E2
Pula *Sardinia* Italy 58 C5
Pulap *atoll* Micronesia 69 L5
Pulaski *NY* U.S.A. 135 G2
Pulaski *VA* U.S.A. 134 E5
Pulaski *WI* U.S.A. 134 A1
Pulheim Germany 52 G3
Pulicat Lake *inlet* India 84 D3
Pulivendla India 84 C3
Pulkkila Fin. 44 N4
Pullman U.S.A. 126 D3
Pulo Anna *i.* Palau 69 I6
Pulozero Rus. Fed. 44 R2
Púlpito, Punta *pt* Mex. 127 F8
Pulu China 82 E1
Pülümür Turkey 91 E3
Pulusuk *atoll* Micronesia 69 L5
Puluwat *atoll* Micronesia 69 L5
Pulwama India 89 I3
Pumasillo, Cerro *mt.* Peru 142 D6
Puma Yumco *l.* China 83 G3
Pumiao China *see* Yongning
Puná, Isla *i.* Ecuador 142 B4
Punakha Bhutan 83 G4
Punch India 82 C2
Punchaw Canada 120 F4
Punda Maria S. Africa 101 J2
Pundri India 82 D3
Pune India 84 B2
P'ungsan N. Korea 74 C4
Puning China 77 H4
Punjab *state* India 82 C3
Punjab *prov.* Pak. 89 H4
Punmah Glacier China/Jammu and Kashmir 82 D2
Puno Peru 142 D7
Punta, Cerro de *mt.* Puerto Rico 137 K5
Punta Abreojos Mex. 127 E8
Punta Alta Arg. 144 D5
Punta Arenas Chile 144 B8
Punta Balestrieri *mt.* Italy 58 C4
Punta del Este Uruguay 144 F5
Punta Delgada Arg. 144 D6
Punta Gorda Belize 136 G5
Punta Gorda U.S.A. 133 D7
Punta Norte Arg. 144 D6
Punta Prieta Mex. 127 E7
Puntarenas Costa Rica 137 H6
Punxsutawney U.S.A. 135 F3
Puokio Fin. 44 O4
Puolanka Fin. 44 O4
Puqi China *see* Chibi
Pur *r.* Rus. Fed. 64 I3
Puracé, Volcán de *vol.* Col. 142 C3
Purcell U.S.A. 131 D5
Purcell Mountains Canada 120 G5
Purgatoire *r.* U.S.A. 130 C4
Puri India 84 E2
Purmerend Neth. 52 E2
Purna *r. Maharashtra* India 82 D5
Purna *r. Maharashtra* India 84 C2
Purnea India *see* Purnia
Purnia India 83 F4
Purnululu National Park Australia 108 E4
Pursat Cambodia *see* Poŭthĭsăt
Puruliya India 83 F5

▶Purus *r.* Peru 142 F4
3rd longest river in South America.

Puruvesi *l.* Fin. 44 P6
Purwodadi Indon. 68 E8
Puryŏng N. Korea 74 C4
Pusad India 84 C2
Pusan S. Korea 75 C6
Pusatlı Dağı *mt.* Turkey 85 A1
Pushchino Rus. Fed. 43 H5
Pushemskiy Rus. Fed. 42 J3
Pushkin Rus. Fed. 45 Q7
Pushkino Azer. *see* Biläsuvar
Pushkinskaya, Gora *mt.* Rus. Fed. 74 F3
Pushkinskiye Gory Rus. Fed. 45 P8
Pusht-i-Rud *reg.* Afgh. *see* Zamīndāvar
Pustoshka Rus. Fed. 42 F4
Pusur *r.* Bangl. 83 G5
Putahow Lake Canada 121 K3
Putain Indon. 108 D2
Putao Myanmar 70 B1
Puteoli Italy *see* Pozzuoli
Puthein Myanmar *see* Bassein
Putian China 77 H3
Puting China *see* De'an
Puting, Tanjung *pt* Indon. 68 E7
Putlitz Germany 53 M1
Putna *r.* Romania 59 L2
Putney U.S.A. 135 I2
Putoi *i. Hong Kong* China *see* Po Toi
Putorana, Gory *mts* Rus. Fed. 153 E2

▶Putrajaya Malaysia 71 C7
Joint capital of Malaysia, with Kuala Lumpur.

Putre Chile 142 E7
Putsonderwater S. Africa 100 E5
Puttalam Sri Lanka 84 C4
Puttalam Lagoon Sri Lanka 84 C4
Puttelange-aux-Lacs France 52 G5
Putten Neth. 52 F2
Puttershoek Neth. 52 E3
Puttgarden Germany 47 M3
Putumayo *r.* Col. 142 D4 *also known as* Iça (Peru)
Putuo China *see* Shenjiamen
Puumala Fin. 45 P6
Puuwai *HI* U.S.A. 127 [inset]
Puvurnituq Canada 122 F1
Puyallup U.S.A. 126 C3
Puyang China 77 G1
Puy de Sancy *mt.* France 56 F4
Puyehue, Parque Nacional *nat. park* Chile 144 B6
Puysegur Point N.Z. 113 A8
Puzla Rus. Fed. 42 L3
Pweto Dem. Rep. Congo 99 C4
Pwinbyu Myanmar 70 A2
Pwllheli U.K. 49 C6
Pyal'ma Rus. Fed. 42 G3
Pyalo Myanmar 70 A3
Pyamalaw *r.* Myanmar 70 A4
Pyandzh Tajik. *see* Panj
Pyaozero, Ozero *l.* Rus. Fed. 44 Q3
Pyaozerskiy Rus. Fed. 44 Q4
Pyapali India 84 C3
Pyapon Myanmar 70 A3
Pyasina *r.* Rus. Fed. 64 J2
Pyatigorsk Rus. Fed. 91 F1
Pyatikhatki Ukr. *see* P"yatykhatky
P"yatykhatky Ukr. 43 G6
Pyay Myanmar *see* Pyè
Pychas Rus. Fed. 42 L4
Pyè Myanmar 70 A3
Pye, Mount *hill* N.Z. 113 B8
Pyetrykaw Belarus 43 F5
Pygmalion Point India 71 A6
Pyhäjoki Fin. 44 N4
Pyhäjoki *r.* Fin. 44 N4
Pyhäntä Fin. 44 O4
Pyhäsalmi Fin. 44 N5
Pyhäselkä *l.* Fin. 44 P5
Pyi Myanmar *see* Pyè
Pyin Myanmar *see* Pyè
Pyingaing Myanmar 70 A2
Pyinmana Myanmar 70 B3
Pyle U.K. 49 D7
Pyl'karamo Rus. Fed. 64 J3
Pylos Greece 59 I6
Pymatuning Reservoir U.S.A. 134 E3
Pyŏktong N. Korea 74 B4
P'yŏnggang N. Korea 75 B5
P'yŏnghae S. Korea 75 C5
P'yŏngsong N. Korea 75 B5
P'yŏngt'aek S. Korea 75 B5

▶P'yŏngyang N. Korea 75 B5
Capital of North Korea.

Pyramid Hill Australia 112 B6
Pyramid Lake U.S.A. 128 D1
Pyramid Peak U.S.A. 129 J1
Pyramid Range *mts* U.S.A. 128 D2
Pyramids of Giza *tourist site* Egypt 90 C5
Pyrénées *mts* Europe *see* Pyrenees
Pyrenees *mts* Europe 57 H2
Pyrénées Occidentales, Parc National des *nat. park* France/Spain 56 D5
Pyrgos Greece 59 I6
Pyryatyn Ukr. 43 G6
Pyrzyce Poland 47 O4
Pyshchug Rus. Fed. 42 J4
Pytalovo Rus. Fed. 45 O8
Pyu Myanmar 70 B3
Pyxaria *mt.* Greece 59 J5

Q

Qaa Lebanon 85 C2
Qaanaaq Greenland *see* Thule
Qabātiya West Bank 85 B3
Qabnag China 76 B2
Qabqa China *see* Gonghe
Qacentina Alg. *see* Constantine
Qacha's Nek Lesotho 101 I6
Qādes Afgh. 89 F3
Qādisīyah, Sadd *dam* Iraq 91 F4
Qadisiyah Dam Iraq *see* Qādisīyah, Sadd
Qa'emabad Iran 89 F4
Qagan China 73 L3
Qagan Nur China 73 K4
Qagan Nur *l.* China 74 B3
Qagan Us *Nei Mongol* China 73 K4
Qagan Us *Qinghai* China *see* Dulan
Qagbasêrag China 76 B2
Qagca China 76 C1
Qagcaka China 83 E2
Qagchêng China *see* Xiangcheng
Qahremānshahr Iran *see* Kermānshāh
Qaidam He *r.* China 83 H1
Qaidam Pendi *basin* China 80 H4
Qainaqangma China 83 G2
Qaisar Afgh. 89 G3
Qaisar, Koh-i- *mt.* Afgh. *see* Qeyşār, Kūh-e
Qakar China 82 E1
Qal'a Beni Hammad *tourist site* Alg. 57 I6
Qalā Diza Iraq 91 G3
Qalagai Afgh. 89 H3
Qala-i-Kang Afgh. *see* Kang
Qal'aikhum Tajik. 89 H2
Qala Jamal Afgh. 89 F3
Qalansīyah Yemen 87 H7
Qala Shinia Takht Afgh. 89 G3
Qalāt Afgh. *see* Kalāt
Qal'at al Ḥiṣn Syria 85 C2
Qal'at al Mu'aẓẓam Saudi Arabia 90 E6
Qal'at Bīshah Saudi Arabia 86 F5
Qal'at Muqaybirah, Jabal *mt.* Syria 85 D2
Qal'eh Dāgh *mt.* Iran 88 B2
Qal'eh Tirpul Afgh. 89 F3
Qal'eh-ye Bost Afgh. 89 G4
Qal'eh-ye Now Afgh. 89 F3
Qal'eh-ye Shūrak *well* Iran 88 E3
Qalhāt Oman 88 E6
Qalīb Bāqūr *well* Iraq 91 G5
Qalluviartuuq, Lac *l.* Canada 122 G2
Qalyūb Egypt 90 C5
Qalyûb Egypt *see* Qalyūb
Qamalung China 76 C1
Qamanirjuaq Lake Canada 121 M2
Qamanittuaq Canada *see* Baker Lake
Qamashi Uzbek. *see* Kamashi
Qamata S. Africa 101 H6
Qamdo China 76 C2
Qanāt as Suways *canal* Egypt *see* Suez Canal
Qandahar Afgh. *see* Kandahār
Qandarānbāshī, Kūh-e *mt.* Iran 88 B2
Qandyaghash Kazakh. *see* Kandyagash
Qangzê China 82 D3
Qapan Iran 88 D2
Qapshagay Kazakh. *see* Kapchagay
Qapshagay Bögeni *resr* Kazakh. *see* Kapchagayskoye Vodokhranilishche
Qapugtang China *see* Zadoi
Qaqortoq Greenland 119 N3
Qara Āghach *r.* Iran *see* Mand, Rūd-e
Qarabutaq Kazakh. *see* Karabutak
Qaraçala Azer. 88 C2
Qara Ertis *r.* China/Kazakh. *see* Ertix He
Qaraghandy Kazakh. *see* Karaganda
Qaraghayly Kazakh. *see* Karagayly
Qārah Egypt 90 B5
Qārah Saudi Arabia 91 F5
Qarah Bāgh Afgh. 89 H3
Qarak China 89 J2
Qaraqum *des.* Turkm. *see* Kara Kumy
Qaraqum *des.* Turkm. *see* Karakum Desert
Qara Quzi Iran 88 D2
Qarasu Azer. 91 H2
Qara Şū Chāy *r.* Syria/Turkey *see* Karasu
Qara Tarai *mt.* Afgh. 89 G3
Qarataū Kazakh. *see* Karatau
Qarataū Zhotasy *mts* Kazakh. *see* Karatau, Khrebet
Qara Tikan Iran 88 C2
Qarazhal Kazakh. *see* Karazhal
Qardho Somalia 98 E3
Qareh Chāy *r.* Iran 88 C3
Qareh Sū *r.* Iran 88 B2
Qareh Tekān Iran 89 F2
Qarhan China 83 H1
Qarkilik China *see* Ruoqiang
Qarn al Kabsh, Jabal *mt.* Egypt 90 D5
Qarnayn *i.* U.A.E. 88 D5
Qarnein *i.* U.A.E. *see* Qarnayn
Qarn el Kabsh, Gebel *mt.* Egypt *see* Qarn al Kabsh, Jabal
Qarokŭl *l.* Tajik. 89 I2
Qarqan China *see* Qiemo
Qarqan He *r.* China 80 G4
Qarqaraly Kazakh. *see* Karkaralinsk
Qarshi Uzbek. *see* Karshi
Qarshi Chŭli *plain* Uzbek. *see* Karshinskaya Step'
Qartaba Lebanon 85 B2
Qārūh, Jazīrat *i.* Kuwait 88 C4
Qārūn, Birkat *l.* Egypt 90 C5
Qârûn, Birket *l.* Egypt *see* Qārūn, Birkat
Qaryat al Gharab Iraq 91 G5
Qaryat al Ulyā Saudi Arabia 88 B5
Qasa Murg *mts* Afgh. 89 F3
Qāsemābād Iran 88 E3
Qash Qai *reg.* Iran 88 C4
Qasigiannguit Greenland 119 M3
Qaşr al Azraq Jordan 85 C4
Qaşr al Farāfirah Egypt 90 B6
Qaşr al Kharānah Jordan 85 C4
Qaşr al Khubbāz Iraq 91 F4
Qaşr 'Amrah *tourist site* Jordan 85 C4
Qaşr Burqu' *tourist site* Jordan 85 C3
Qaşr-e Shīrīn Iran 88 B3
Qaşr Farâfra Egypt *see* Qaşr al Farāfirah
Qassimiut Greenland 119 N3
Qaţanā Syria 85 C3
▶Qatar *country* Asia 88 C5
Asia 6, 62–63
Qaţmah Syria 85 C1
Qaţrūyeh Iran 88 D4
Qaţţāfī, Wādī al *watercourse* Jordan 85 C4
Qaţţâra, Râs *esc.* Egypt *see* Qaţţārah, Ra's
Qattara Depression Egypt 90 B5
Qaţţārah, Ra's *esc.* Egypt 90 B5
Qaţţīnah, Buḩayrat *resr* Syria 81 C2
Qax Azer. 91 G2
Qāyen Iran 88 E3
Qaynar Kazakh. *see* Kaynar
Qaysīyah, Qa' al *imp. l.* Jordan 85 C4
Qaysūm, Juzur *is* Egypt 90 D6
Qayyārah Iraq 91 F4
Qazangödağ *mt.* Armenia/Azer. 91 G3
Qazaq Shyghanaghy *b.* Kazakh. *see* Kazakhskiy Zaliv
Qazaqstan *country* Asia *see* Kazakhstan
Qazax Azer. 86 G1
Qazi Ahmad Pak. 89 H5
Qazımämmäd Azer. 91 H2
Qazvīn Iran 88 C2
Qeisûm, Gezâ'ir *is* Egypt *see* Qaysūm, Juzur
Qeisum Islands Egypt *see* Qaysūm, Juzur
Qena Egypt *see* Qinā
Qeqertarsuaq Greenland 119 M3
Qeqertarsuaq *i.* Greenland 119 M3
Qeqertarsuatsiaat Greenland 119 M3
Qeqertarsuup Tunua *b.* Greenland 119 M3
Qeshm Iran 88 E5
Qeydār Iran 88 C2
Qeydū Iran 88 C3
Qeys *i.* Iran 88 D5
Qeyşār, Kūh-e *mt.* Afgh. 89 G3
Qezel Owzan, Rūdkhāneh-ye *r.* Iran 88 C2
Qeẓi'ot Israel 85 B4
Qian'an China 74 B3
Qian Gorlos China *see* Qianguozhen
Qianguozhen China 74 B3

Qianjiang Chongqing China 77 F2
Qianjiang Hubei China 77 G2
Qianjin Heilong. China 74 D3
Qianjin Jilin China 74 C3
Qianning China 76 D2
Qianqihao China 74 A3
Qian Shan mts China 74 A4
Qianxi China 76 E3
Qiaocheng China see Bozhou
Qiaojia China 76 D3
Qiaoshan China see Huangling
Qiaowa China see Muli
Qiaowan China 80 I3
Qiaozhuang China see Qingchuan
Qibā' Saudi Arabia 91 G6
Qibing S. Africa 101 H5
Qichun China 77 G2
Qidong China 77 G3
Qidukou China 76 B1
Qiemo China 80 G4
Qijiang China 76 E2
Qijiaojing China 80 H3
Qikiqtarjuaq Canada 119 L3
Qila Ladgasht Pak. 89 F5
Qila Saifullah Pak. 89 H4
Qilian China 80 J4
Qilian Shan mts China 80 I4
Qillak i. Greenland 119 O3
Qiman Tag mts China 83 G1
Qimusseriarsuaq b. Greenland 119 L2
Qinā Egypt 86 D4
Qin'an China 76 E1
Qincheng China see Nanfeng
Qing'an China 74 B3
Qingchuan China 76 E1
Qingdao China 73 M5
Qinggang China 74 B3
Qinggil China see Qinghe
Qinghai prov. China 76 B1
Qinghai Hu salt l. China 80 J4
Qinghai Nanshan mts China 80 I4
Qinghe Heilong. China 74 C3
Qinghe Xinjiang China 80 H2
Qinghecheng China 74 B4
Qinghua China see Bo'ai
Qingjiang Jiangsu China see Huai'an
Qingjiang Jiangxi China see Zhangshu
Qing Jiang r. China 77 F2
Qingkou China see Ganyu
Qinglan China 77 F5
Qingliu China 77 H3
Qinglong China 83 G3
Qingpu China 77 I2
Qingquan China see Xishui
Qingshan China see Wudalianchi
Qingshui China 76 E1
Qingshuihe Nei Mongol China 73 K5
Qingshuihe Qinghai China 76 C1
Qingtian China 77 I2
Qingyang Anhui China 77 H2
Qingyang Jiangsu China see Sihong
Qingyuan Gansu China see Weiyuan
Qingyuan Guangdong China 77 G4
Qingyuan Guangxi China see Yizhou
Qingyuan Liaoning China 74 B4
Qingyuan Zhejiang China 77 H3
Qingzang Gaoyuan plat. China see Plateau of Tibet
Qingzhen China 76 E3
Qinhuangdao China 73 L5
Qinjiang China see Shicheng
Qin Ling mts China 76 E1
Qinshui China 77 G1
Qinting China see Lianhua
Qinzhou China 77 F4
Qionghai China 77 F5
Qiongjiexue China see Qonggyai
Qionglai China 76 D2
Qionglai Shan mts China 76 D2
Qiongxi China see Hongyuan
Qiongzhong China 77 F5
Qiongzhou Haixia strait China see Hainan Strait
Qiqian China 74 A1
Qiqihar China 74 A3
Qīr Iran 88 D4
Qira China 82 E1
Qîraîya, Wâdi watercourse Egypt see Qurayyah, Wādī
Qiryat Israel 85 B3
Qiryat Shemona Israel 85 B3
Qishan China 76 E1
Qishon r. Israel 85 B3
Qitab ash Shāmah vol. crater Saudi Arabia 85 C4
Qitaihe China 74 C3
Qiubei China 76 E3
Qiujin China 77 G2
Qixing He r. China 74 D3
Qiyang China 77 F3
Qizhou Liedao i. China 77 F5
Qızılağac Körfäzi b. Azer. 88 C2
Qizil-Art, Aghbai pass Kyrg./Tajik. see Kyzylart Pass
Qizilqum des. Kazakh./Uzbek. see Kyzylkum Desert
Qizilrabot Tajik. 89 I2
Qogir Feng mt. China/Jammu and Kashmir see K2
Qog Qi China see Sain Us
Qom Iran 88 C3
Qomdo China see Qumdo
Qomisheh Iran see Shahrezā
Qomolangma Feng mt. China/Nepal see Everest, Mount
Qomsheh Iran see Shahrezā
Qonāq, Kūh-e hill Iran 88 C3
Qondūz Afgh. see Kunduz
Qonggyai China 83 G3
Qong Muztag mt. China 83 E2
Qongrat Uzbek. see Kungrad
Qoornoq Greenland 119 M3
Qoqek China see Tacheng
Qorghalzhyn Kazakh. see Korgalzhyn
Qornet es Saouda mt. Lebanon 85 C2
Qorowulbozor Uzbek. see Karaulbazar
Qorveh Iran 88 B3
Qosh Tepe Iraq 91 F3
Qostanay Kazakh. see Kostanay
Qoubaiyat Lebanon 85 C2
Qowowuyag mt. China/Nepal see Cho Oyu
Qozideh Tajik. 89 H2
Quabbin Reservoir U.S.A. 135 I2
Quadra Island Canada 120 E5
Quadros, Lago dos l. Brazil 145 A5
Quaidabad Pak. 89 H3
Quail Mountains U.S.A. 128 E4
Quairading Australia 109 B8
Quakenbrück Germany 53 H2
Quakertown U.S.A. 135 H3
Quambatook Australia 112 A5
Quambone Australia 112 C3
Quamby Australia 110 C4
Quanah U.S.A. 131 D5
Quanbao Shan mt. China 77 F1
Quan Dao Hoang Sa is S. China Sea see Paracel Islands
Quân Đao Nam Du i. Vietnam 71 D5
Quan Dao Truong Sa is S. China Sea see Spratly Islands
Quang Ngai Vietnam 70 E4
Quang Tri Vietnam 70 D3
Quan Long Vietnam see Ca Mau
Quannan China 77 G3
Quan Phu Quoc i. Vietnam see Phu Quôc, Đao
Quantock Hills U.K. 49 D7
Quanwan Hong Kong China see Tsuen Wan
Quanzhou Fujian China 77 H3
Quanzhou Guangxi China 77 F3
Qu'Appelle r. Canada 121 K5
Quaqtaq Canada 119 L3
Quarry Bay Hong Kong China 77 [inset]
Quartu Sant'Elena Sardinia Italy 58 C5
Quartzite Mountain U.S.A. 128 E3
Quartzsite U.S.A. 129 F5
Quba Azer. 91 H2
Quchan Iran 88 E2
Qudaym Syria 85 D2
Queanbeyan Australia 112 D5

▶Québec Canada 123 H5
Provincial capital of Québec.

Québec prov. Canada 135 I1
Quebra Anzol r. Brazil 145 B2
Quedlinburg Germany 53 L3
Queen Adelaide Islands Chile see La Reina Adelaida, Archipiélago de
Queen Anne U.S.A. 135 H4
Queen Bess, Mount Canada 122 B2
Queen Charlotte Canada 120 C4
Queen Charlotte Islands Canada 120 C4
Queen Charlotte Sound sea chan. Canada 120 D5
Queen Charlotte Strait Canada 120 E5
Queen Creek U.S.A. 129 H5
Queen Elizabeth Islands Canada 119 H2
Queen Elizabeth National Park Uganda 98 C4
Queen Mary Land reg. Antarctica 152 F2
Queen Maud Gulf Canada 115 H3
Queen Maud Land reg. Antarctica 152 C2
Queen Maud Mountains Antarctica 152 J1
Queenscliff Australia 112 B7
Queensland state Australia 112 B1
Queenstown Australia 111 [inset]
Queenstown N.Z. 113 B7
Queenstown Rep. of Ireland see Cóbh
Queenstown S. Africa 101 H6
Queenstown Sing. 71 [inset]
Queets U.S.A. 126 B3
Queimada, Ilha i. Brazil 143 H4
Quelimane Moz. 99 D5
Quellón Chile 144 B6
Quelpart Island S. Korea see Cheju-do
Quemado U.S.A. 129 I4
Quemoy i. Taiwan see Chinmen Tao
Que Que Zimbabwe see Kwekwe
Querétaro Mex. 136 D4
Querétaro de Arteaga Mex. see Querétaro
Querfurt Germany 53 L3
Querobabi Mex. 127 F7
Quesnel Canada 120 F4
Quesnel Lake Canada 120 F4
Quetta Pak. 89 G4
Quetzaltenango Guat. 136 F6
Queuco Chile 144 B5
Quezaltenango Guat. see Quetzaltenango

▶Quezon City Phil. 69 G4
Former capital of the Philippines.

Qufu China 77 H1
Quibala Angola 99 B5
Quibaxe Angola 99 B4
Quibdó Col. 142 C2
Quiberon France 56 C3
Quiçama, Parque Nacional do nat. park Angola 99 B4
Qui Châu Vietnam 70 D3
Quiet Lake Canada 120 C2
Quilengues Angola 99 B5
Quillabamba Peru 142 D6
Quillacollo Bol. 142 E7
Quillan France 56 F5
Quill Lakes Canada 121 J5
Quilmes Arg. 144 E4
Quilon India 84 C4
Quilpie Australia 112 B1
Quilpué Chile 144 B4
Quimbele Angola 99 B4
Quimilí Arg. 144 D3
Quimper France 56 B3
Quimperlé France 56 C3
Quinag hill U.K. 50 D2
Quincy CA U.S.A. 128 C2
Quincy FL U.S.A. 133 C6
Quincy IL U.S.A. 130 F4
Quincy IN U.S.A. 134 B4
Quincy MA U.S.A. 135 J2
Quincy MI U.S.A. 134 C3
Quincy OH U.S.A. 134 D3
Quines Arg. 144 C4
Quinga Moz. 99 E5
Qui Nhơn Vietnam 71 E4
Quinn Canyon Range mts U.S.A. 129 F3
Quinto Spain 57 F3
Quionga Moz. 99 E5
Quipungo Angola 99 B5
Quirima Angola 99 B5
Quirindi Australia 112 E3
Quirinópolis Brazil 145 A2
Quissanga Moz. 99 E5
Quissico Moz. 101 L3
Quitapa Angola 99 B5
Quitilipi Arg. 144 D3
Quitman GA U.S.A. 133 D6
Quitman MS U.S.A. 131 F5

▶Quito Ecuador 142 C4
Capital of Ecuador.

Quitovac Mex. 127 E7
Quixadá Brazil 143 K4
Quixeramobim Brazil 143 K5
Qujiang Guangdong China 77 G3
Qujiang Sichuan China see Quxian
Qujie China 77 F4
Qujing China 76 D3
Qulandy Kazakh. see Kulandy
Qulbān Layyah well Iraq 88 B4
Qulin Gol r. China 74 A3
Qulsary Kazakh. see Kul'sary
Qulyndy Zhazyghy plain Kazakh./Rus. Fed. see Kulundinskaya Step'
Qulzum, Bahr al Egypt see Suez Bay
Qumar He r. China 72 G6
Qumarheyan China 80 H4
Qumarlêb China see Sêrwolungwa
Qumarrabdün China 76 B1
Qumbu S. Africa 101 I6
Qumdo China 76 B2
Qumqŭrghon Uzbek. see Kumkurgan
Qumrha S. Africa 101 H7
Qumulangma mt. China/Nepal see Everest, Mount
Qunayy well Saudi Arabia 88 B6
Qundūz Afgh. see Kunduz
Qŭnghirot Uzbek. see Kungrad
Quntamari China 83 G2
Qu'nyido China 76 C2
Quoich r. Canada 121 M1
Quoich, Loch l. U.K. 50 D3
Quoile r. U.K. 51 G3
Quoin Point S. Africa 100 D8
Quoxo r. Botswana 100 G2
Qŭqon Uzbek. see Kokand
Qurama, Qatorkŭhi mts Asia see Kurama Range
Qurama Tizmasi mts Asia see Kurama Range
Qurayyah, Wādī watercourse Egypt 85 B4
Qurayyat al Milḥ l. Jordan 85 C4
Qŭrghonteppa Tajik. 89 H2
Qusar Azer. 91 H2
Qushan China see Beichuan
Qŭshrabot Uzbek. see Koshrabad
Qusmuryn Kazakh. see Kushmurun
Qusum China 82 D2
Quthing Lesotho see Moyeni
Quttinirpaaq National Park Canada 119 K1
Quwayq, Nahr r. Syria/Turkey 85 C2
Quxar China see Lhazê
Quxian Sichuan China 76 E2
Quxian Zhejiang China see Quzhou
Quyang China see Jingzhou
Quyghan Kazakh. see Kuygan
Quynh Lưu Vietnam 70 D3
Quyon Canada 135 G1
Qūyūn Eshek i. Iran 88 B2
Quzhou China 77 H2
Qypshaq Köli salt l. Kazakh. see Kypshak, Ozero
Qyrghyz Zhotasy mts Kazakh./Kyrg. see Kirghiz Range
Qyteti Stalin Albania see Kuçovë
Qyzylorda Kazakh. see Kyzylorda
Qyzylqum des. Kazakh./Uzbek. see Kyzylkum Desert
Qyzyltū Kazakh. see Kishkenekol'
Qyzylzhar Kazakh. see Kyzylzhar

R

Raa Atoll Maldives see North Maalhosmadulu Atoll
Raab r. Austria 47 P7
Raab Hungary see Győr
Raahe Fin. 44 N4
Rääkkylä Fin. 44 P5
Raalte Neth. 52 G2
Raanujärvi Fin. 44 N3
Raasay i. U.K. 50 C3
Raasay, Sound of sea chan. U.K. 50 C3
Raba Indon. 108 B2
Rabang China 82 E2
Rabat Gozo Malta see Victoria
Rabat Malta 58 F7

▶Rabat Morocco 54 C5
Capital of Morocco.

Rabaul P.N.G. 106 F2
Rabbath Ammon Jordan see 'Ammān
Rabbit r. Canada 120 E3
Rabbit Flat Australia 108 E5
Rabbitskin r. Canada 120 F2
Rābigh Saudi Arabia 86 E5
Rabnabad Islands Bangl. 83 G5
Râbniţa Moldova see Rîbniţa
Rabocheostrovsk Rus. Fed. 42 G2
Racaka China see Riwoqê
Raccoon Cay i. Bahamas 133 F8
Race, Cape Canada 123 L5
Race Point U.S.A. 135 J2
Rachaïya Lebanon 85 B3
Rachal U.S.A. 131 D7
Rachaya Lebanon see Rachaïya
Rachel U.S.A. 129 F3
Rach Gia Vietnam 71 D5
Rach Gia, Vinh b. Vietnam 71 D5
Racibórz Poland 47 Q5
Racine WI U.S.A. 134 B2
Racine WV U.S.A. 134 E4
Rădăuţi Romania 43 E7
Radcliff U.S.A. 134 C5
Radde Rus. Fed. 74 C2
Radford U.S.A. 134 E5
Radisson Que. Canada 122 F3
Radisson Sask. Canada 121 J4
Radlinski, Mount Antarctica 152 K1
Radnevo Bulg. 59 K3
Radom Poland 47 R5
Radom Sudan 97 F4
Radomir Bulg. 59 J3
Radom National Park Sudan 97 F4
Radomsko Poland 47 Q5
Radoviš Macedonia 90 A2
Radstock U.K. 49 E7
Radstock, Cape Australia 109 F8
Radun' Belarus 45 N9
Radviliškis Lith. 45 M9
Radyvyliv Ukr. 43 E6
Rae Bareli India 82 E4
Rae-Edzo Canada 120 G2
Rae Lakes Canada 120 G1
Raeside, Lake salt flat Australia 109 C7
Raetihi N.Z. 113 E4
Rāf hill Saudi Arabia 91 E5
Rafaela Arg. 144 D4
Rafah Gaza see Rafiah
Rafaï Cent. Afr. Rep. 98 C3
Rafḥā' Saudi Arabia 91 F5
Rafiah Gaza 85 B4
Rafsanjān Iran 88 D4
Raft r. U.S.A. 126 E4
Raga Sudan 97 F4
Rägelin Germany 53 M1
Ragged, Mount hill Australia 109 C8
Ragged Island Bahamas 133 F8
Rāgh Afgh. 89 H2
Rago Nasjonalpark nat. park Norway 44 J3
Ragösen Germany 53 M2
Ragueneau Canada 123 H4
Raguhn Germany 53 M3
Ragusa Croatia see Dubrovnik
Ragusa Sicily Italy 58 F6
Ra'gyagoinba China 76 D1
Raha Indon. 69 G7
Rahachow Belarus 43 F5
Rahad r. Sudan 86 D7
Rahaeng Thai. see Tak
Rahden Germany 53 I2
Rahimyar Khan Pak. 89 H4
Rahovec Serb. and Mont. see Orahovac
Rahuri India 84 B2
Rai, Hon i. Vietnam 71 D5
Raiatea i. Fr. Polynesia 151 J7
Raibu i. Indon. see Air
Raichur India 84 C2
Raiganj India 83 G4
Raigarh Chhattisgarh India 83 E5
Raigarh Orissa India 84 D2
Raijua i. Indon. 108 C2
Railroad Pass U.S.A. 128 E2
Railroad Valley U.S.A. 129 F2
Raimangal r. Bangl. 83 G5
Raimbault, Lac l. Canada 123 H3
Rainbow Lake Canada 120 G3
Raine Island Australia 110 D1
Rainelle U.S.A. 134 E5
Raini r. Pak. 89 H4
Rainier, Mount vol. U.S.A. 126 C3
Rainy r. Canada/U.S.A. 121 M5
Rainy Lake Canada/U.S.A. 125 I2
Rainy River Canada 121 M5
Raipur Chhattisgarh India 83 E5
Raipur W. Bengal India 83 F5
Raisen India 82 D5
Raisio Fin. 45 M6
Raismes France 52 D4
Raitalai India 82 D5
Raivavae i. Fr. Polynesia 151 K7
Raiwind Pak. 89 I4
Raja, Ujung pt Indon. 71 B7
Rajaampat, Kepulauan is Indon. 69 H7
Rajahmundry India 84 D2
Raja-Jooseppi Fin. 44 P2
Rajanpur Pak. 89 H4
Rajapalaiyam India 84 C4
Rajapur India 84 B2
Rajasthan state India 82 C4
Rajasthan Canal India 82 C3
Rajauri India see Rajouri
Rajevadi India 84 B2
Rajgarh India 82 D4
Rājījovsset Fin. see Raja-Jooseppi
Rajkot India 82 B5
Raj Mahal India 82 C4
Rajmahal Hills India 83 F4
Rajnandgaon India 82 E5
Rajouri India 82 C2
Rajpipla India 82 C5
Rajpur India 82 C5
Rajpura India 82 D3
Rajputana Agency state India see Rajasthan
Rajsamand India 82 C4
Rajshahi Bangl. 83 G4
Rājū Syria 85 C1
Rajula India 84 A1
Rajur India 84 C1
Rajura India 84 C2
Raka China 83 F3
Rakan, Ra's pt Qatar 88 C5
Rakaposhi mt. Jammu and Kashmir 82 C1
Raka Zangbo r. China see Dogxung Zangbo
Rakhiv Ukr. 43 E6
Rakhni Pak. 89 H4
Rakhshan r. Pak. 89 F5
Rakitnoye Belgorodskaya Oblast' Rus. Fed. 43 G6
Rakitnoye Primorskiy Kray Rus. Fed. 74 D3
Rakiura i. N.Z. see Stewart Island
Rakke Estonia 45 O7
Rakkestad Norway 45 G7
Rakni r. Pak. 89 H4
Rakovski Bulg. 59 K3
Rakushechnyy, Mys pt Kazakh. 91 H2
Rakvere Estonia 45 O7

▶Raleigh U.S.A. 132 E5
State capital of North Carolina.

Ralston U.S.A. 135 G3
Ram r. Canada 120 F2
Ramagiri India 84 E2
Ramah U.S.A. 129 I4
Ramalho, Serra do hills Brazil 145 B1
Ramallah West Bank 85 B4
Ramanagaram India 84 C3
Ramanathapuram India 84 C4
Ramapo Deep sea feature N. Pacific Ocean 150 F3
Ramapur India 84 D1
Ramas, Cape India 84 B3
Ramatlabama S. Africa 101 G3
Rambhapur India 82 C5
Rambouillet France 52 B6
Rambutyo Island P.N.G. 69 L7
Rame Head hd Australia 112 D6
Rame Head hd U.K. 49 C8
Rameshki Rus. Fed. 42 H4
Ramezān Kalak Iran 89 F5
Ramgarh Jharkhand India 83 F5
Ramgarh Madhya Pradesh India 82 E5
Ramgarh Rajasthan India 82 B4
Ramgarh Rajasthan India 82 C3
Ramgul reg. Afgh. 89 H3
Rāmhormoz Iran 88 C4
Ramingining Australia 108 F3
Ramitan Uzbek. see Romitan
Ramla Israel 85 B4
Ramlat Rabyānah des. Libya see Rebiana Sand Sea
Ramm, Jabal mts Jordan 85 B5
Ramnad India see Ramanathapuram
Râmnicu Sărat Romania 59 L2
Râmnicu Vâlcea Romania 59 K2
Ramon' Rus. Fed. 43 H6
Ramona U.S.A. 128 E5
Ramos r. Mex. 131 B7
Ramotswa Botswana 101 G3
Rampart of Genghis Khan tourist site Asia 73 K3
Rampur India 82 D3
Rampur Boalia Bangl. see Rajshahi
Ramree Myanmar 70 A3
Ramree Island Myanmar 70 A3
Ramsele Sweden 44 J5
Ramsey Isle of Man 48 C4
Ramsey U.K. 49 G6
Ramsey U.S.A. 135 H3
Ramsey Bay Isle of Man 48 C4
Ramsey Island U.K. 49 B7
Ramsey Lake Canada 122 E5
Ramsgate U.K. 49 I7
Rāmshir Iran 88 C4
Ramsing mt. India 83 H3
Ramu Bangl. 83 H5
Ramusio, Lac l. Canada 123 J3
Ramygala Lith. 45 N9
Ranaghat India 83 G5
Ranai i. U.S.A. see Lanai
Rana Pratap Sagar resr India 78 C4
Ranapur India 82 C5
Ranasar India 82 B4
Rancagua Chile 144 B4
Rancharia Brazil 145 A3
Rancheria Canada 120 D2
Rancheria r. Canada 120 D2
Ranchi India 83 F5
Ranco, Lago l. Chile 144 B6
Rand Australia 112 C5
Randalstown U.K. 51 F3
Randers Denmark 45 G8
Randijaure l. Sweden 44 K3
Randolph ME U.S.A. 135 K1
Randolph UT U.S.A. 126 F4
Randolph VT U.S.A. 135 I2
Randsjö Sweden 44 H5
Råneå Sweden 44 M4
Ranérou Senegal 96 B3
Ranfurly N.Z. 113 C7
Rangae Thai. 71 C6
Rangamati Bangl. 83 H5
Rangapara North India 83 H4
Rangeley Lake U.S.A. 135 J1
Rangely U.S.A. 129 I1
Ranger Lake Canada 122 E5
Rangiora N.Z. 113 D6
Rangitata r. N.Z. 113 C7
Rangitikei r. N.Z. 113 E5
Rangke China see Zamtang
Rangkŭl Tajik. 89 I2
Rangôn Myanmar see Rangoon

▶Rangoon Myanmar 70 B3
Capital of Myanmar.

Rangoon r. Myanmar 70 B3
Rangpur Bangl. 83 G4
Rangsang i. Indon. 71 C7
Rangse Myanmar 70 A1
Ranibennur India 84 B3
Raniganj India 83 F5
Ranipur Pak. 89 H5
Raniwara India 82 C4
Rankin U.S.A. 131 C6
Rankin Inlet Canada 121 M2
Rankin's Springs Australia 112 C4
Ranna Estonia 45 O7
Rannes Australia 110 E5
Rannoch, L. U.K. 50 E4
Ranong Thai. 71 B5
Ranot Thai. 71 C6
Ranpur India 82 B5
Ranrkan Pak. 89 H4
Rānsa Iran 88 C3
Ransby Sweden 45 H6
Rantasalmi Fin. 44 P5
Rantau i. Indon. 71 C7
Rantauprapat Indon. 71 B7
Rantoul U.S.A. 134 A3
Rantsila Fin. 44 N4
Ranua Fin. 44 O4
Rānya Iraq 91 G3
Ranyah, Wādī watercourse Saudi Arabia 86 F5
Rao Go mt. Laos/Vietnam 70 D3
Raohe China 74 D3
Raoul Island Kermadec Is 107 I4
Rapa i. Fr. Polynesia 151 K7
Rapa-iti i. Fr. Polynesia see Rapa
Rapallo Italy 58 C2
Rapar India 82 B5
Raphoe Rep. of Ireland 51 E3
Rapidan r. U.S.A. 135 G4
Rapid City U.S.A. 130 C2
Rapid River U.S.A. 132 C2
Rapla Estonia 45 N7
Rapur Andhra Pradesh India 84 C3
Rapur Gujarat India 82 B5
Raqqa Syria see Ar Raqqah
Raquette Lake U.S.A. 135 H2
Rara National Park Nepal 83 E3
Raritan Bay U.S.A. 135 H3
Raroia atoll Fr. Polynesia 151 K7
Rarotonga i. Cook Is 151 J7
Ras India 82 C4
Rasa, Punta pt Arg. 144 D6
Ra's ad Daqm Oman 87 I6
Ra's al Ḥikmah Egypt 90 B5
Ras al Khaimah U.A.E. see Ra's al Khaymah
Ra's al Khaymah U.A.E. 88 D5
Ra's an Naqb Jordan 85 B4
Ras Dashen mt. Eth. see Ras Dejen

▶Ras Dejen mt. Eth. 98 D2
5th highest mountain in Africa.

Raseiniai Lith. 45 M9
Râs el Hikma Egypt see Ra's al Ḥikmah
Ra's Ghārib Egypt 90 D5
Rashad Sudan 86 D7
Rashîd Egypt see Rashīd
Rashīd Egypt 90 C5
Rashid Qala Afgh. 89 G4
Rashm Iran 88 D3
Rasht Iran 88 C2
Raskam mts China 82 C1
Ras Koh mt. Pak. 89 G4
Raskoh mts Pak. 89 G4
Raso, Cabo c. Arg. 144 C6
Raso da Catarina hills Brazil 143 K5
Rason Lake salt flat Australia 109 D7
Rasony Belarus 45 P9
Rasra India 83 E4
Rasshua, Ostrov i. Rus. Fed. 73 S3
Rass Jebel Tunisia 58 D6
Rasskazovo Rus. Fed. 43 I5
Rastatt Germany 53 I6
Rastede Germany 53 I1
Rastow Germany 53 L1
Rasūl watercourse Iran 88 D5
Rasul Pak. 89 I3
Ratae U.K. see Leicester
Rätan Sweden 44 I5
Ratanda S. Africa 101 I4
Ratangarh India 82 C3
Rätansbyn Sweden 44 I5
Rat Buri Thai. 71 B4
Rathangan Rep. of Ireland 51 F4
Rathbun Lake U.S.A. 130 E3
Rathdowney Rep. of Ireland 51 E5
Rathdrum Rep. of Ireland 51 F5
Rathedaung Myanmar 70 A2
Rathenow Germany 53 M2
Rathfriland U.K. 51 F3
Rathkeale Rep. of Ireland 51 D5
Rathlin Island U.K. 51 F2
Rathluirc Rep. of Ireland 51 D5
Ratibor Poland see Racibórz
Ratingen Germany 52 G3
Ratisbon Germany see Regensburg
Ratiya India 82 C3
Rat Lake Canada 121 L3
Ratlam India 82 C5
Ratnagiri India 84 B2
Ratnapura Sri Lanka 84 D5
Ratne Ukr. 43 E6
Ratno Ukr. see Ratne
Raton U.S.A. 127 G5
Rattray Head hd U.K. 50 H3
Rättvik Sweden 45 I6
Ratz, Mount Canada 120 C3
Ratzeburg Germany 53 K1
Raub Malaysia 71 C7
Rauðamýri Iceland 44 [inset]
Raudhatain Kuwait 88 B4
Rauenstein Germany 53 L4
Raufarhöfn Iceland 44 [inset]
Raukumara Range mts N.Z. 113 F4
Raul Soares Brazil 145 C3
Rauma Fin. 45 L6
Raurkela India 83 F5
Rauschen Rus. Fed. see Svetlogorsk
Rausu Japan 74 G3
Rautavaara Fin. 44 P5
Rautjärvi Fin. 45 P6
Ravānsar Iran 88 B3
Rāvar Iran 88 E4
Ravat Kyrg. 89 H2
Ravels Belgium 52 E3
Ravena U.S.A. 135 I2
Ravenglass U.K. 48 D4
Ravenna Italy 58 E2
Ravenna NE U.S.A. 130 D3
Ravenna OH U.S.A. 134 E3
Ravensburg Germany 47 L7
Ravenshoe Australia 110 D3
Ravenswood Australia 110 D4
Ravi r. Pak. 89 H4
Ravnina Maryyskaya Oblast' Turkm. 89 F2
Ravnina Maryyskaya Oblast' Turkm. 89 F2
Rāwah Iraq 91 F4
Rawaki i. Kiribati 107 I2
Rawalpindi Pak. 89 I3
Rawalpindi Lake Canada 120 H1
Rawāndiz Iraq 91 G3
Rawi, Ko i. Thai. 71 B6
Rawicz Poland 47 P5
Rawlinna Australia 109 D7
Rawlins U.S.A. 126 G4
Rawlinson Range hills Australia 109 E6
Rawnina Turkm. see Ravnina
Rawson Arg. 144 C6
Rawu China 76 C2
Raxón, Cerro mt. Guat. 136 G5
Ray, Cape Canada 123 K5
Raya, Bukit mt. Indon. 68 E7
Rayachoti India 84 C3
Rayadurg India 84 C3
Rayagada India 84 D2
Rayagarha India see Rayagada
Rayak Lebanon 85 C3
Raychikhinsk Rus. Fed. 74 C2
Raydah Yemen 86 F6

Rayes Peak U.S.A. **128** D4
Rayevskiy Rus. Fed. **41** Q5
Rayleigh U.K. **49** H7
Raymond U.S.A. **135** J2
Raymond Terrace Australia **112** E4
Raymondville U.S.A. **131** D7
Raymore Canada **121** J5
Rayner Glacier Antarctica **152** D2
Rayong Thai. **71** C4
Raystown Lake U.S.A. **135** F3
Raz, Pointe du pt France **56** B2
Razan Iran **88** C3
Răzān Iran **88** C3
Razani Pak. **89** H3
Razāzah, Buḩayrat ar l. Iraq **91** F4
Razdan Armenia see Hrazdan
Razdel'naya Ukr. see Rozdil'na
Razdol'noye Rus. Fed. **74** C4
Razeh Iran **88** C3
Razgrad Bulg. **59** L3
Razim, Lacul lag. Romania **59** M2
Razisi China **76** D1
Razlog Bulg. **59** J4
Razmak Pak. **89** H3
Raz''yezd 3km Rus. Fed. see Novyy Urgal
Ré, Île de i. France **56** D3
Reading U.K. **49** G7
Reading MI U.S.A. **134** C3
Reading OH U.S.A. **134** C4
Reading PA U.S.A. **135** H3
Reagile S. Africa **101** H3
Realicó Arg. **144** D5
Réalmont France **56** F5
Reăng Kesei Cambodia **71** C4
Reate Italy see Rieti
Rebais France **52** D6
Rebecca, Lake salt flat Australia **109** C7
Rebiana Sand Sea des. Libya **97** F2
Reboly Rus. Fed. **44** Q5
Rebrikha Rus. Fed. **72** E2
Rebun-tō i. Japan **74** F3
Recherche, Archipelago of the is Australia **109** C8
Rechitsa Belarus see Rechytsa
Rechna Doab lowland Pak. **89** I4
Rechytsa Belarus **43** F5
Recife Brazil **143** L5
Recife, Cape S. Africa **101** G8
Recklinghausen Germany **53** H3
Reconquista Arg. **144** E3
Recreo Arg. **144** C3
Rectorville U.S.A. **134** D4
Red r. Australia **110** C3
Red r. Canada **120** E3
Red r. Canada/U.S.A. **130** D1
Red r. TN U.S.A. **134** B5
Red r. U.S.A. **131** F6
Red r. Vietnam **70** D2
Redang i. Malaysia **71** C6
Red Bank NJ U.S.A. **135** H3
Red Bank TN U.S.A. **134** C5
Red Basin China see Sichuan Pendi
Red Bay Canada **123** K4
Redberry Lake Canada **121** J4
Red Bluff U.S.A. **128** B1
Red Bluff Lake U.S.A. **131** C6
Red Butte mt. U.S.A. **129** G4
Redcar U.K. **48** F4
Redcliff Canada **126** F2
Redcliffe, Mount hill Australia **109** C7
Red Cliffs Australia **111** C7
Red Cloud U.S.A. **130** D3
Red Deer Canada **120** H4
Red Deer r. Alberta/Saskatchewan Canada **121** I5
Red Deer r. Man./Sask. Canada **121** K4
Red Deer Lake Canada **121** K4
Reddersburg S. Africa **101** H5
Redding U.S.A. **128** B1
Redditch U.K. **49** F6
Rede r. U.K. **48** E3
Redenção Brazil **143** H5
Redfield U.S.A. **130** D2
Red Granite Mountain Canada **120** B2
Red Hills U.S.A. **131** D4
Red Hook U.S.A. **135** I3
Red Indian Lake Canada **123** K4
Redkey U.S.A. **134** C3
Redkino Rus. Fed. **42** H4
Redknife r. Canada **120** G2
Red Lake Canada **121** M5
Red Lake U.S.A. **129** G4
Red Lake r. U.S.A. **130** D2
Red Lake Falls U.S.A. **121** I5
Red Lakes U.S.A. **130** E1
Redlands U.S.A. **128** E4
Red Lion U.S.A. **135** G4
Red Lodge U.S.A. **126** F3
Redmesa U.S.A. **129** I3
Redmond OR U.S.A. **126** C3
Redmond UT U.S.A. **129** H2
Red Oak U.S.A. **130** E3
Redonda Island Canada **120** E5
Redondo Port. **57** C4
Redondo Beach U.S.A. **128** D5
Red Peak U.S.A. **126** E3
Red River, Mouths of the Vietnam **70** D2
Red Rock Canada **122** C4
Red Rock AZ U.S.A. **129** H5
Redrock U.S.A. **129** I5
Red Rock PA U.S.A. **135** G3
Redrock Lake Canada **120** H1
Redstone r. Canada **120** E1
Red Sucker Lake Canada **121** M4
Reduzum Neth. see Roordahuizum
Redwater Canada **120** H4
Redway U.S.A. **128** B1
Red Wing U.S.A. **130** E2
Redwood City U.S.A. **128** B3
Redwood Falls U.S.A. **130** E2
Redwood National Park U.S.A. **126** B4
Redwood Valley U.S.A. **128** B2
Ree, Lough l. Rep. of Ireland **51** E4
Reed U.S.A. **134** B5
Reed City U.S.A. **134** C2
Reedley U.S.A. **128** D3
Reedsport U.S.A. **126** B4
Reedsville U.S.A. **134** E4
Reedville U.S.A. **135** G5
Reedy U.S.A. **134** E4

Reedy Glacier Antarctica **152** J1
Reefton N.Z. **113** C6
Rees Germany **52** G3
Reese r. U.S.A. **128** E1
Refahiye Turkey **90** E3
Refugio U.S.A. **131** D6
Regen Germany **53** N6
Regen r. Germany **53** M5
Regência Brazil **145** D2
Regensburg Germany **53** M5
Regenstauf Germany **53** M5
Reggane Alg. **96** D2
Reggio Calabria Italy see **Reggio di Calabria**
Reggio Emilia-Romagna Italy see **Reggio nell'Emilia**
Reggio di Calabria Italy **58** F5
Reggio Emilia Italy see **Reggio nell'Emilia**
Reggio nell'Emilia Italy **58** D2
Reghin Romania **59** K1
Regi Afgh. **89** G3

▶Regina Canada **121** J5
Provincial capital of Saskatchewan.

Régina Fr. Guiana **143** H3
Registän reg. Afgh. **89** G4
Registro Brazil **144** G2
Registro do Araguaia Brazil **145** A1
Regium Lepidum Italy see **Reggio nell'Emilia**
Regozero Rus. Fed. **44** Q4
Rehau Germany **53** M4
Rehburg (Rehburg-Loccum) Germany **53** J2
Rehli India **82** D5
Rehoboth Namibia **100** C2
Rehoboth Bay U.S.A. **135** H4
Rehovot Israel **85** B4
Reibell Alg. see **Ksar Chellala**
Reibitz Germany **53** M3
Reichenbach Germany **53** M4
Reichshoffen France **53** H6
Reid Australia **109** E7
Reidh, Rubha pt U.K. **50** D3
Reidsville U.S.A. **132** E4
Reigate U.K. **49** G7
Reiley Peak U.S.A. **129** H5
Reims France **52** E5
Reinbek Germany **53** K1
Reindeer r. Canada **121** K4
Reindeer Island Canada **121** L4
Reindeer Lake Canada **121** K3
Reine Norway **44** H3
Reinosa Spain **57** D2
Reinsfeld Germany **52** G5
Reiphólsfjöll hill Iceland **44** [inset]
Reisaelva r. Norway **44** L2
Reisa Nasjonalpark nat. park Norway **44** M2
Reisjärvi Fin. **44** N5
Reitz S. Africa **101** I4
Rekapalle India **84** D2
Reken Germany **52** H3
Reliance Canada **121** I2
Rellano Mex. **131** B7
Rellingen Germany **53** J1
Remagen Germany **53** H4
Remarkable, Mount hill Australia **111** B7
Remedios Cuba **133** E8
Remeshk Iran **88** E5
Remhoogte Pass Namibia **100** C2
Remi France see **Reims**
Remmel Mountain U.S.A. **126** C2
Remscheid Germany **53** H3
Rena Norway **45** G6
Renaix Belgium see **Ronse**
Renam Myanmar **76** C3
Renapur India **84** C2
Rendsburg Germany **47** L3
René-Levasseur, Île i. Canada **123** H4
Renews Canada **123** L5
Renfrew Canada **135** G1
Renfrew U.K. **50** E5
Rengali Reservoir India **83** F5
Rengat Indon. **68** C7
Rengo Chile **144** B4
Ren He r. China **77** F1
Renheji China **77** G2
Renhua China **77** G3
Reni Ukr. **59** M2
Renick U.S.A. **134** E5
Renland reg. Greenland see **Tuttut Nunaat**
Rennell i. Solomon Is **107** G3
Renner Springs Australia **108** F4
Rennerod Germany **53** I4
Rennes France **56** D2
Rennick Glacier Antarctica **152** H2
Rennie Canada **121** M5
Reno r. Italy **58** E2
Reno U.S.A. **128** D2
Renovo U.S.A. **135** G3
Rensselaer U.S.A. **134** B3
Renswoude Neth. **52** F2
Renton U.S.A. **126** C3
Réo Burkina **96** C3
Reo Indon. **108** C2
Repalle India **84** D2
Repetek Turkm. **89** F2
Repetekskiy Zapovednik nature res. Turkm. **89** F2
Repolka Rus. Fed. **45** P7
Reppublic U.S.A. **126** D2
Republican r. U.S.A. **130** D4
▶Republic of Ireland country Europe **51** E4
Europe 5, 38–39

▶Republic of South Africa country Africa **100** F5
5th most populous country in Africa.
Africa 7, 94–95

Repulse Bay b. Australia **110** E4
Repulse Bay Canada **119** J3
Requena Peru **142** D5
Requena Spain **57** F4
Reşadiye Turkey **90** E2
Reserva Brazil **145** A4
Reserve U.S.A. **129** I5
Reshi China **77** F2

Reshteh-ye Alborz mts Iran see **Elburz Mountains**
Resistencia Arg. **144** E3
Reşiţa Romania **59** I2
Resolute Bay Canada **119** I2
Resolution Island Canada **119** L3
Resolution Island N.Z. **113** A7
Resplendor Brazil **145** C2
Restigouche r. Canada **123** I5
Resülayn Turkey see **Ceylanpınar**
Retalhuleu Guat. **136** F6
Retezat, Parcul Naţional nat. park Romania **59** J2
Retford U.K. **48** G5
Rethel France **52** E5
Rethem (Aller) Germany **53** J2
Réthimnon Greece see **Rethymno**
Rethymno Greece **59** K7
Retreat Australia **110** C5
Reuden Germany **53** M2
Reus Spain **57** G3
Reusam, Pulau i. Indon. **71** B7
Reutlingen Germany **47** L6
Reval Estonia see **Tallinn**
Revda Rus. Fed. **44** S3
Revel Estonia see **Tallinn**
Revel France **56** F5
Revelstoke Canada **120** G5
Revillagigedo, Islas is Mex. **136** B5
Revillagigedo Island U.S.A. **120** D4
Revin France **52** E5
Revivim Israel **85** B4
Revolyutsii, Pik mt. Tajik. see **Revolyutsiya, Qullai**
Revolyutsiya, Qullai mt. Tajik. **89** I2
Rewa India **82** E4
Rewari India **82** D3
Rexburg U.S.A. **126** F4
Rexton Canada **123** I5
Reyes, Point U.S.A. **128** B2
Reyhanlı Turkey **85** C1
Reykir Iceland **44** [inset]
Reykjanes Ridge sea feature N. Atlantic Ocean **148** F2
Reykjanestá pt Iceland **44** [inset]

▶Reykjavík Iceland **44** [inset]
Capital of Iceland.

Reyneke, Ostrov i. Rus. Fed. **74** E1
Reynoldsburg U.S.A. **134** D4
Reynolds Range mts Australia **108** F5
Reynosa Mex. **131** D7
Rezā Iran **88** D3
Rezā'īyeh Iran see **Urmia**
Rezā'īyeh, Daryācheh-ye salt l. Iran see **Urmia, Lake**
Rēzekne Latvia **45** O8
Rezvān Iran **89** F4
Rezvāndeh Iran see **Rezvānshahr**
Rezvānshahr Iran **88** C2
Rhaeader Gwy U.K. see **Rhayader**
Rhayader U.K. **49** D6
Rheda-Wiedenbrück Germany **53** I3
Rhede Germany **53** G3
Rhegium Italy see **Reggio di Calabria**
Rheims France see **Reims**
Rhein r. Germany **53** G3 see **Rhine**
Rheine Germany **53** H2
Rheinland-Pfalz land Germany **53** H5
Rheinsberg Germany **53** M1
Rheinstetten Germany **53** I6
Rhemilès well Alg. **96** C2
Rhin r. France **53** I6 see **Rhine**
Rhine r. Germany **53** G3
also spelt Rhein (Germany) or Rhin (France)
Rhinebeck U.S.A. **135** I3
Rhinelander U.S.A. **130** F2
Rhineland-Palatinate land Germany see **Rheinland-Pfalz**
Rhinkanal canal Germany **53** M2
Rhinow Germany **53** M2
Rhiwabon U.K. see **Ruabon**
Rho Italy **58** C2
Rhode Island state U.S.A. **135** J3
Rhodes Greece **59** M6
Rhodes i. Greece **59** M6
Rhodesia country Africa see **Zimbabwe**
Rhodes Peak U.S.A. **126** E3
Rhodope Mountains Bulg./Greece **59** J4
Rhodus i. Greece see **Rhodes**
Rhône r. France/Switz. **56** G5
Rhum i. U.K. see **Rum**
Rhuthun U.K. see **Ruthin**
Rhydaman U.K. see **Ammanford**
Rhyl U.K. **48** D5
Riachão Brazil **143** I5
Riacho Brazil **145** C2
Riacho de Santana Brazil **145** C1
Riacho dos Machados Brazil **145** C1
Rialma Brazil **145** A1
Rialto U.S.A. **128** E4
Riang Jammu and Kashmir **82** C2
Riau, Kepulauan is Indon. **68** C6
Ribadeo Spain **57** C2
Ribadesella Spain **57** D2
Ribas do Rio Pardo Brazil **144** F2
Ribat Afgh. **89** H2
Ribat-i-Shur waterhole Iran **88** E3
Ribáuè Moz. **99** D5
Ribble r. U.K. **48** E5
Ribblesdale valley U.K. **48** E4
Ribe Denmark **45** F9
Ribécourt-Dreslincourt France **52** C5
Ribeira r. Brazil **145** B4
Ribeirão Preto Brazil **145** B3
Ribemont France **52** D5
Ribérac France **56** E4
Riberalta Bol. **142** E6
Ribeiro Moldova **43** F7
Ribnitz-Damgarten Germany **47** N3
Říčany Czech Rep. **47** O6
Rice U.S.A. **135** F5
Rice Lake Canada **135** F1
Richards Bay S. Africa **101** K5

Richards Inlet Antarctica **152** H1
Richards Island Canada **118** E3
Richardson r. Canada **121** I3
Richardson U.S.A. **131** D5
Richardson Island Canada **120** G1
Richardson Lakes U.S.A. **135** J1
Richardson Mountains Canada **118** E3
Richardson Mountains N.Z. **113** B7
Richfield U.S.A. **129** G2
Richfield Springs U.S.A. **135** H2
Richford NY U.S.A. **135** G2
Richford VT U.S.A. **135** I1
Richgrove U.S.A. **128** D4
Richland U.S.A. **126** D3
Richland Center U.S.A. **130** F3
Richmond N.S.W. Australia **112** E4
Richmond Qld Australia **110** C4
Richmond Canada **135** H1
Richmond N.Z. **113** D5
Richmond Kwazulu-Natal S. Africa **101** J5
Richmond N. Cape S. Africa **100** F6
Richmond U.K. **48** F4
Richmond CA U.S.A. **128** B3
Richmond IN U.S.A. **134** C4
Richmond KY U.S.A. **134** C5
Richmond MI U.S.A. **134** D2
Richmond MO U.S.A. **130** E4
Richmond TX U.S.A. **131** E6

▶Richmond VA U.S.A. **135** G5
State capital of Virginia.

Richmond Dale U.S.A. **134** D4
Richmond Hill U.S.A. **133** D6
Richmond Range hills Australia **112** F2
Richtersveld National Park S. Africa **100** C5
Richvale U.S.A. **128** C2
Richwood U.S.A. **134** E4
Rico U.S.A. **129** I3
Ricomagus France see **Riom**
Riddell Nunataks Antarctica **152** E2
Rideau Lakes Canada **135** G1
Ridge r. Canada **122** D4
Ridgecrest U.S.A. **128** E4
Ridge Farm U.S.A. **134** B4
Ridgeland MS U.S.A. **131** F5
Ridgeland SC U.S.A. **133** D5
Ridgetop U.S.A. **134** B5
Ridgetown Canada **134** E2
Ridgeway OH U.S.A. **134** D3
Ridgeway VA U.S.A. **134** F5
Ridgway CO U.S.A. **129** J2
Ridgway PA U.S.A. **135** F3
Riding Mountain National Park Canada **121** K5
Riecito Venez. **142** E1
Riemst Belgium **52** F4
Riesa Germany **53** N3
Riesco, Isla i. Chile **144** B8
Riet watercourse S. Africa **100** E6
Rietavas Lith. **45** L9
Rietfontein S. Africa **100** E4
Rieti Italy **58** E3
Rifā'ī, Tall mt. Jordan/Syria **85** C3
Rifeng China see **Lichuan**
Rifle U.S.A. **129** J2
Riftstangi pt Iceland **44** [inset]
Rift Valley Lakes National Park Eth. see **Abijatta-Shalla National Park**

▶Rīga Latvia **45** N8
Capital of Latvia.

Riga, Gulf of Estonia/Latvia **45** M8
Rigain Púnco l. China **83** F2
Rīgān Iran **88** E4
Rīgas jūras līcis b. Estonia/Latvia see **Riga, Gulf of**
Rigby U.S.A. **126** F4
Rīgestān reg. Afgh. see **Registän**
Rigolet Canada **123** K3
Rigside U.K. **50** F5
Riihimäki Fin. **45** N6
Riia laht b. Estonia/Latvia see **Riga, Gulf of**
Riihimäki Fin. **45** N6
Ritchie's Archipelago is India **71** A4
Riiser-Larsen Ice Shelf Antarctica **152** B2
Riito Mex. **129** F5
Rijau Nigeria **96** D3
Rijeka Croatia **58** F2
Rikā, Wādī ar watercourse Saudi Arabia **88** B6
Rikitgaib Indon. **71** B6
Rikor India **76** B2
Rikuchū-kaigan National Park Japan **75** F5
Rikuzen-takata Japan **75** F5
Rila mts Bulg. **59** J3
Rila China **83** F3
Riley U.S.A. **126** D4
Rileyville U.S.A. **135** F4
Rillieux-la-Pape France **56** G4
Rillito U.S.A. **129** H5
Rimah, Wādī al watercourse Saudi Arabia **86** F4
Rimavská Sobota Slovakia **47** R6
Rimbey Canada **120** H4
Rimini Italy **58** E2
Rîmnicu Sărat Romania see **Râmnicu Sărat**
Rîmnicu Vîlcea Romania see **Râmnicu Vâlcea**
Rimouski Canada **123** H4
Rimpar Germany **53** J5
Rimsdale, Loch l. U.K. **50** E2
Rinbung China **83** G3
Rincão Brazil **145** A3
Rindal Norway **44** F5
Ringarooma Bay Australia **111** [inset]
Ringas India **82** C4
Ringe Germany **52** G2
Ringebu Norway **45** G6
Ringkhung Myanmar **70** B1
Ringkøbing Denmark **45** F8
Ringsend U.K. **51** F2
Ringsted Denmark **45** G9
Ringtor China **83** E3
Ringvassøy i. Norway **44** K2
Ringwood Australia **112** B6
Ringwood U.K. **49** F8
Rinjani, Gunung vol. Indon. **68** F8
Rinns Point U.K. **50** C5
Rinqênzê China **83** G3

Richards Inlet Antarctica **152** H1
Rio Azul Brazil **145** A4
Riobamba Ecuador **142** C4
Rio Blanco U.S.A. **129** J2
Rio Bonito Brazil **145** C3
Rio Branco Brazil **142** E6
Rio Branco, Parque Nacional do nat. park Brazil **142** F3
Río Bravo, Parque Internacional del nat. park Mex. **131** C6
Rio Brilhante Brazil **144** F2
Rio Casca Brazil **145** C3
Río Claro Brazil **145** B3
Río Colorado Arg. **144** D5
Río Cuarto Arg. **144** D4
Rio das Pedras Moz. **101** L2
Rio de Contas Brazil **145** C1

▶Rio de Janeiro Brazil **145** C3
3rd most populous city in South America. Former capital of Brazil.

Rio de Janeiro state Brazil **145** C3

▶Río de la Plata-Paraná r. S. America **144** E4
2nd longest river in South America.

Rio Dell U.S.A. **128** A1
Rio do Sul Brazil **145** A4
Río Gallegos Arg. **144** C8
Río Grande Arg. **144** C8
Rio Grande Brazil **144** F4
Río Grande Mex. **136** D4
Rio Grande r. Mex./U.S.A. **127** G5
also known as Río Bravo del Norte
Rio Grande City U.S.A. **131** D7
Rio Grande do Sul state Brazil **145** A5
Rio Grande Rise sea feature S. Atlantic Ocean **148** F8
Ríohacha Col. **142** D1
Río Hondo, Embalse resr Arg. **144** C3
Rioja Peru **142** C5
Río Lagartos Mex. **133** B8
Río Largo Brazil **143** K5
Río Muni reg. Equat. Guinea **96** E4
Río Negro, Embalse del resr Uruguay **144** E4
Rioni r. Georgia **91** F2
Rio Novo Brazil **145** C3
Rio Pardo de Minas Brazil **145** C1
Rio Preto Brazil **145** C3
Rio Preto, Serra do hills Brazil **145** B2
Rio Rancho U.S.A. **127** G6
Río Tigre Ecuador **142** C4
Rio Verde Brazil **145** A2
Río Verde Mex. **136** E4
Rio Verde de Mato Grosso Brazil **143** H7
Rio Vista U.S.A. **128** C2
Ripky Ukr. **43** F6
Ripley England U.K. **48** F4
Ripley England U.K. **49** F5
Ripley NY U.S.A. **134** F2
Ripley OH U.S.A. **134** D4
Ripley WV U.S.A. **134** E4
Ripoll Spain **57** H2
Ripon U.K. **48** F4
Ripon U.S.A. **128** C3
Ripu India **83** G4
Risca U.K. **49** D7
Rise Pish Iran **89** F5
Rising Sun IN U.S.A. **134** C4
Rising Sun MD U.S.A. **135** G4
Risle r. France **49** H9
Risør Norway **45** F7
Rissa Norway **44** F5
Ristiina Fin. **45** O6
Ristijärvi Fin. **44** P4
Ristikent Rus. Fed. **44** Q2
Risum Germany **47** K3
Ritchie S. Africa **100** G5
Ritscher Upland mts Antarctica **152** B2
Ritsem Sweden **44** J3
Ritter, Mount U.S.A. **128** D3
Ritterhude Germany **53** I1
Ritzville U.S.A. **126** D3
Riu, Laem pt Thai. **71** B5
Riva del Garda Italy **58** D2
Rivas Nicaragua **137** G6
Rivera Arg. **144** D5
Rivera Uruguay **144** E4
River Cess Liberia **96** C4
Riverhead U.S.A. **135** I3
Riverhurst Canada **121** J5
Riverina Australia **109** C7
Riverina reg. Australia **112** B5
Riversdale S. Africa **100** E8
Riverside S. Africa **101** I6
Riverside U.S.A. **128** E5
Rivers Inlet Canada **120** E5
Riversleigh Australia **110** B3
Riverton N.Z. **113** B8
Riverton VA U.S.A. **135** F4
Riverton WY U.S.A. **126** F4
Riverview Canada **123** I5
Rivesaltes France **56** F5
Riviera Beach U.S.A. **133** D7
Rivière-du-Loup Canada **123** H5
Rivière-Pentecote Canada **123** I4
Riviere-Pigou Canada **123** I4
Rivne Ukr. **43** E6
Rivungo Angola **99** C5
Riwaka N.Z. **113** D5
Riwoqê China **76** C2

▶Riyadh Saudi Arabia **86** G5
Capital of Saudi Arabia.

Riyan India **89** I5
Riza well Iran **88** D3
Rize Turkey **91** F2
Rizhao Shandong China **77** H1
Rizhao Shandong China **77** H1
Rizokarpaso Cyprus see **Rizokarpason**
Rizokarpason Cyprus **85** B2
Rīzū well Iran **88** D4
Rīzū'īyeh Iran **88** E4

Rjukan Norway **45** F7
Rjuvbrokkene mt. Norway **45** E7
Rkîz Mauritania **96** B3
Roa Norway **45** G6
Roachdale U.S.A. **134** B4
Roach Lake U.S.A. **129** F4
Roade U.K. **49** G6
Roads U.S.A. **134** D4

▶Road Town Virgin Is (U.K.) **137** L5
Capital of the British Virgin Islands.

Roan Norway **44** G4
Roan Fell hill U.K. **50** G5
Roan High Knob mt. U.S.A. **132** D4
Roanne France **56** G3
Roanoke IN U.S.A. **134** C3
Roanoke VA U.S.A. **134** F5
Roanoke r. U.S.A. **132** E4
Roanoke Rapids U.S.A. **132** E4
Roan Plateau U.S.A. **129** I2
Roaring Spring U.S.A. **135** F3
Roaringwater Bay Rep. of Ireland **51** C6
Roatán Hond. **137** G5
Röbäck Sweden **44** L5
Robat r. Afgh. **89** F4
Robāţe Tork Iran **88** C3
Robāţ Karīm Iran **88** C3
Robāt-Sang Iran **88** E3
Robb Canada **120** G4
Robbins Island Australia **111** [inset]
Robbinsville U.S.A. **133** D5
Robe Australia **111** B8
Robe r. Australia **108** A5
Robe r. Rep. of Ireland **51** C4
Röbel Germany **53** M1
Robert Glacier Antarctica **152** D2
Robert Lee U.S.A. **131** C6
Roberts U.S.A. **126** E4
Roberts, Mount Australia **112** F2
Robertsburg U.S.A. **134** E4
Roberts Butte mt. Antarctica **152** H2
Roberts Creek Mountain U.S.A. **128** E2
Robertsfors Sweden **44** L4
Robertson S. Africa **100** D7
Robertson Bay Antarctica **152** H2
Robertson Island Antarctica **152** A2
Robertson Range hills Australia **109** C5
Robertsport Liberia **96** B4
Roberval Canada **123** G4
Robhanais, Rubha hd U.K. see **Butt of Lewis**
Robin Hood's Bay U.K. **48** G4
Robin's Nest hill Hong Kong China **77** [inset]
Robinson Canada **120** C2
Robinson U.S.A. **134** B4
Robinson Range hills Australia **109** B6
Robinson River Australia **110** B3
Robles Pass U.S.A. **129** H5
Roblin Canada **121** K5
Robsart Canada **121** I5
Robson, Mount Canada **120** G4
Robstown U.S.A. **131** D7
Roby U.S.A. **131** C5
Roçadas Angola see **Xangongo**
Rocca Busambra mt. Sicily Italy **58** E6
Rocha Uruguay **144** F4
Rochdale U.K. **48** E5
Rochechouart France **56** E4
Rochefort Belgium **52** F4
Rochefort France **56** D4
Rochefort, Lac l. Canada **123** G2
Rochegda Rus. Fed. **42** I3
Rochester U.K. **49** H7
Rochester IN U.S.A. **134** B3
Rochester MI U.S.A. **134** D2
Rochester MN U.S.A. **130** E2
Rochester NH U.S.A. **135** J2
Rochester NY U.S.A. **135** G2
Rochford U.K. **49** H7
Rochlitz Germany **53** M3
Roc'h Trévezel hill France **56** C2
Rock r. Canada **120** E2
Rockall i. N. Atlantic Ocean **40** D4
Rockall Bank sea feature N. Atlantic Ocean **148** G2
Rock Creek Canada **120** B1
Rock Creek U.S.A. **134** E3
Rock Creek r. U.S.A. **126** G2
Rockdale U.S.A. **131** D6
Rockefeller Plateau Antarctica **152** J1
Rockford AL U.S.A. **133** C5
Rockford IL U.S.A. **130** F3
Rockford MI U.S.A. **134** C2
Rockglen Canada **121** J5
Rockhampton Australia **110** E4
Rockhampton Downs Australia [cut off]
Rock Hill U.S.A. **133** D5
Rockingham Australia **109** A8
Rockingham U.S.A. **133** E5
Rockingham Bay Australia **1** [cut off]
Rockinghorse Lake Canada [cut off]
Rock Island Canada **135** I1
Rock Island U.S.A. **130** F3
Rocklake U.S.A. **130** D1
Rockland MA U.S.A. **135** J2
Rockland ME U.S.A. **132** G [cut off]
Rockland Canada **12** [cut off]
▶R[cut off]
Rocknest Lake Canada **12** [cut off]
Rockport IN U.S.A. **134** B [cut off]
Rockport TX U.S.A. **131** [cut off]
Rock Rapids U.S.A. **130** [cut off]
Rock River U.S.A. **126** G [cut off]
Rock Sound Bahamas [cut off]
Rock Springs MT U.S. [cut off]
Rocksprings U.S.A. **13** [cut off]
Rock Springs WY U.S [cut off]
Rockstone Guyana **1** [cut off]
Rockville CT U.S.A. **1** [cut off]
Rockville IN U.S.A. **1** [cut off]
Rockville MD U.S.A [cut off]
Rockwell City U.S.A [cut off]
Rockwood U.S.A. [cut off]
Rockwood PA U.S [cut off]
Rockyford Canad [cut off]
Rocky Harbour C [cut off]
Rocky Hill U.S.A. [cut off]
Rocky Island La [cut off]
Rocky Lane Car [cut off]
Rocky Mount [cut off]

Rocky Mountain House Canada **120** H4
Rocky Mountain National Park U.S.A. **126** G4
Rocky Mountains Canada/U.S.A. **124** F3
Rocourt-St-Martin France **52** D5
Rocroi France **52** E5
Rodberg Norway **45** F6
Rødbyhavn Denmark **45** G9
Roddickton Canada **123** L4
Rodeio Brazil **145** A4
Rodel U.K. **50** C3
Roden Neth. **52** G1
Rödental Germany **53** L4
Rodeo Arg. **144** C4
Rodeo Mex. **131** B7
Rodeo U.S.A. **127** F7
Rodez France **56** F4
Ródhos *i.* Greece *see* **Rhodes**
Rodi *i.* Greece *see* **Rhodes**
Roding Germany **53** M5
Rodney, Cape U.S.A. **118** B3
Rodniki Rus. Fed. **42** I4
Rodolfo Sanchez Toboada Mex. **127** D7
Rodopi Planina *mts* Bulg./Greece *see* **Rhodope Mountains**
Rodos Greece *see* **Rhodes**
Rodos *i.* Greece *see* **Rhodes**
Rodosto Turkey *see* **Tekirdağ**
Rodrigues Island Mauritius **149** M7
Roe *r.* U.K. **51** F2
Roebourne Australia **108** B5
Roebuck Bay Australia **108** C4
Roedtan S. Africa **101** I3
Roe Plains Australia **109** D7
Roermond Neth. **52** F3
Roeselare Belgium **52** D4
Roes Welcome Sound *sea chan.* Canada **119** J3
Rogachev Belarus *see* **Rahachow**
Rogätz Germany **53** L2
Rogers U.S.A. **131** E4
Rogers, Mount U.S.A. **134** E5
Rogers City U.S.A. **134** D1
Rogers Lake U.S.A. **128** E4
Rogerson U.S.A. **126** E4
Rogersville U.S.A. **134** D5
Roggan *r.* Canada **122** F3
Roggan, Lac *l.* Canada **122** F3
Roggeveen Basin *sea feature* S. Pacific Ocean **151** O8
Roggeveld *plat.* S. Africa **100** E7
Roggeveldberge *esc.* S. Africa **100** E7
Roghadal U.K. *see* **Rodel**
Rognan Norway **44** I3
Rögnitz *r.* Germany **53** K1
Rogue *r.* U.S.A. **126** B4
Roha India **84** B2
Rohnert Park U.S.A. **128** B2
Rohrbach in Oberösterreich Austria **47** N6
Rohrbach-lès-Bitche France **53** H5
Rohri Pak. **89** H5
Rohtak India **82** D3
Roi Et Thai. **70** C3
Roi Georges, Îles du *is* Fr. Polynesia **151** K6
Rois-Bheinn *hill* U.K. **50** D4
Roisel France **52** D5
Roja Latvia **45** M8
Rojas Arg. **144** D4
Rokeby Australia **110** C2
Rokeby National Park Australia **110** C2
Rokiškis Lith. **45** N9
Roknäs Sweden **44** L4
Rokytne Ukr. **43** E6
Rolagang China **83** G2
Rola Kangri *mt.* China **83** G2
Rolândia Brazil **145** A3
Rolim de Moura Brazil **142** F6
Roll *AZ* U.S.A. **129** G5
Roll *IN* U.S.A. **134** C3
Rolla *MO* U.S.A. **130** F4
Rolla *ND* U.S.A. **130** D1
Rollag Norway **45** F6
Rolleston Australia **110** E5
Rolleville Bahamas **133** F8
Rolling Fork U.S.A. **131** F5
Rollins U.S.A. **126** E3
Roma Australia **111** E5
Roma *i.* Indon. **108** D1
Roma Italy *see* **Rome**
Roma Lesotho **101** H5
Roma Sweden **45** K8
Romain, Cape U.S.A. **133** E5
Romaine *r.* Canada **123** J4
Roman Romania **59** L1
Românâ, Câmpia *plain* Romania **59** J2
…omanche Gap *sea feature* S. Atlantic Ocean **148** G6
…omanet, Lac *l.* Canada **123** I2
▶**…Romania** *country* Europe **59** K2
Europe 5, 38–39
…man-Kosh *mt.* Ukr. **90** D1
…mano, Cape U.S.A. **133** D7
…manovka Rus. Fed. **73** K2
…mans-sur-Isère France **56** G4
…manzof, Cape U.S.A. **118** B3
…mbas France **52** G5
…mblon Phil. **69** G4

▶**…ome** Italy **58** E4
…apital of Italy.

…e *GA* U.S.A. **133** C5
…e *ME* U.S.A. **135** K1
…e *NY* U.S.A. **135** H2
…e *TN* U.S.A. **134** B5
… City U.S.A. **134** C3
…o U.S.A. **134** D2
…ord U.K. **49** H7
…y-sur-Seine France **56** F2
…an Uzbek. **89** G2
…ey U.S.A. **135** F4
…y Marsh *reg.* U.K. **49** H7
… Ukr. **43** G6
… Denmark **45** F9
…novo Rus. Fed. **43** J5
…ntin-Lanthenay France **56** E3
… *r.* Malaysia **71** C7
… U.K. **49** F8
… U.S.A. **134** D2
… **84** B3
…K. **50** D1

Ronas Hill *hill* U.K. **50** [inset]
Roncador, Serra do *hills* Brazil **143** H6
Roncador Reef Solomon Is **107** F2
Ronda Spain **57** D5
Ronda, Serranía de *mts* Spain **57** D5
Rondane Nasjonalpark *nat. park* Norway **45** F6
Rondon Brazil **144** F2
Rondonópolis Brazil **143** H7
Rondout Reservoir U.S.A. **135** H3
Rongcheng *Anhui* China *see* **Qingyang**
Rongcheng *Guangxi* China *see* **Rongxian**
Rongcheng *Hubei* China *see* **Jianli**
Rong Chu *r.* China **83** G3
Rongelap *atoll* Marshall Is **150** H5
Rongjiang *Guizhou* China **77** F3
Rongjiang *Jiangxi* China *see* **Nankang**
Rongjiawan China *see* **Yueyang**
Rongklang Range *mts* Myanmar **70** A2
Rongmei China *see* **Hefeng**
Rongshui China **77** F3
Rongwo China *see* **Tongren**
Rongxian China **77** F4
Rongyul China **76** C2
Rongzhag China *see* **Danba**
Rönlap *atoll* Marshall Is *see* **Rongelap**
Rønne Denmark **45** I9
Ronneby Sweden **45** I8
Ronne Entrance *strait* Antarctica **152** L2
Ronne Ice Shelf Antarctica **152** L1
Ronnenberg Germany **53** J2
Ronse Belgium **52** D4
Roodeschool Neth. **52** G1
Rooke Island P.N.G. *see* **Umboi**
Roordahuizum Neth. **52** F1
Roorkee India **82** D3
Roosendaal Neth. **52** E3
Roosevelt *AZ* U.S.A. **129** H5
Roosevelt *UT* U.S.A. **129** I1
Roosevelt, Mount Canada **120** E3
Roosevelt Island Antarctica **152** I1
Root *r.* Canada **120** F2
Root *r.* U.S.A. **130** F3
Ropar India *see* **Rupnagar**
Roper *r.* Australia **110** A2
Roper Bar Australia **108** F3
Roquefort France **56** D4
Roraima, Mount Guyana **142** F2
Rori India **82** C3
Rori Indon. **69** J7
Røros Norway **44** G5
Rørvik Norway **44** G4
Rosa, Punta *pt* Mex. **127** F8
Rosalia U.S.A. **126** D3
Rosamond U.S.A. **128** D4
Rosamond Lake U.S.A. **128** D4
Rosario Arg. **144** D4
Rosário Brazil **143** J4
Rosario *Baja California* Mex. **127** E7
Rosario *Coahuila* Mex. **131** C7
Rosario *Sinaloa* Mex. **136** C4
Rosario *Sonora* Mex. **124** F6
Rosario *Zacatecas* Mex. **131** C7
Rosario Venez. **142** D1
Rosário do Sul Brazil **144** F4
Rosário Oeste Brazil **143** G6
Rosarito *Baja California* Mex. **127** E7
Rosarito *Baja California* Mex. **128** E5
Rosarito *Baja California Sur* Mex. **127** F8
Rosarno Italy **58** F5
Roscoff France **56** C2
Roscommon Rep. of Ireland **51** D4
Roscommon U.S.A. **134** C1
Roscrea Rep. of Ireland **51** E5
Rose *r.* Australia **110** A2
Rose, Mount U.S.A. **128** D2
Rose Atoll American Samoa *see* **Rose Island**

▶**Roseau** Dominica **137** L5
Capital of Dominica.

Roseau U.S.A. **130** E1
Roseau *r.* U.S.A. **130** D1
Roseberth Australia **111** B5
Rose Blanche Canada **123** K5
Rosebud *r.* Canada **120** H5
Rosebud U.S.A. **126** G3
Roseburg U.S.A. **126** C4
Rose City U.S.A. **134** C1
Rosedale U.S.A. **131** F5
Rosedale Abbey U.K. **48** G4
Roseires Reservoir Sudan **86** D7
Rose Island *atoll* American Samoa **107** J3
Rosenberg U.S.A. **131** E6
Rosendal Norway **45** E7
Rosendal S. Africa **101** H5
Rosenheim Germany **47** N7
Rose Peak U.S.A. **129** I5
Rose Point Canada **120** D4
Roseto degli Abruzzi Italy **58** F3
Rosetown Canada **121** J5
Rosetta Egypt *see* **Rashīd**
Rose Valley Canada **121** K4
Roseville *CA* U.S.A. **128** C2
Roseville *MI* U.S.A. **134** D2
Roseville *OH* U.S.A. **134** D4
Rosewood Australia **112** F1
Roshchino Rus. Fed. **45** P6
Rosh Pinah Namibia **100** C4
Roshtkala Tajik. *see* **Roshtqal'a**
Roshtqal'a Tajik. **89** H2
Rosignano Marittimo Italy **58** D3
Roşiori de Vede Romania **59** K2
Roskilde Denmark **45** H9
Roskruge Mountains U.S.A. **129** H5
Roslavl' Rus. Fed. **43** G5
Roslyakovo Rus. Fed. **44** R2
Roslyatino Rus. Fed. **42** J4
Ross N.Z. **113** C6
Ross, Mount *hill* N.Z. **113** E5
Rossano Italy **58** G5
Rossan Point Rep. of Ireland **51** D3
Ross Barnett Reservoir U.S.A. **131** F5
Ross Bay Junction Canada **123** I3
Ross Carbery Rep. of Ireland **51** C6
Ross Dependency *reg.* Antarctica **152** I2
Rosseau, Lake Canada **134** F1
Rossel Island P.N.G. **110** F1
Ross Ice Shelf Antarctica **152** I1
Rossignol, Lac *l.* Canada **122** G3
Rössing Namibia **100** B2
Ross Island Antarctica **152** H1
Rossiyskaya Sovetskaya Federativnaya Sotsialisticheskaya Respublika *country* Asia/Europe *see* **Russian Federation**
Rossland Canada **120** G5
Rosslare Rep. of Ireland **51** F5
Rosslare Harbour Rep. of Ireland **51** F5
Roßlau Germany **53** M3
Rosso Mauritania **96** B3
Ross-on-Wye U.K. **49** E7
Rossony Belarus *see* **Rasony**
Rossosh' Rus. Fed. **43** H6
Ross River Canada **120** C2
Ross Sea Antarctica **152** H1
Roßtal Germany **53** K5
Røssvatnet *l.* Norway **44** I4
Rossville U.S.A. **134** B3
Roßwein Germany **53** N3
Rosswood Canada **120** D4
Rostāq Afgh. **89** H2
Rostāq Iran **88** D5
Rosthern Canada **121** J4
Rostock Germany **47** N3
Rostov Rus. Fed. **42** H4
Rostov-na-Donu Rus. Fed. **43** H7
Rostov-on-Don Rus. Fed. *see* **Rostov-na-Donu**
Rosvik Sweden **44** L4
Roswell U.S.A. **127** G6
Rota *i.* N. Mariana Is **69** L4
Rot am See Germany **53** K5
Rotch Island Kiribati *see* **Tamana**
Rote *i.* Indon. **108** C2
Rotenburg (Wümme) Germany **53** J1
Roth Germany **53** L5
Rothaargebirge *hills* Germany **53** I4
Rothbury U.K. **48** F3
Rothenburg ob der Tauber Germany **53** K5
Rother *r.* U.K. **49** G8
Rothera *research station* Antarctica **152** L2
Rotherham U.K. **48** F5
Rothes U.K. **50** F3
Rothesay U.K. **50** D5
Rothwell U.K. **49** G6
Roti Indon. **108** C2
Roti *i.* Indon. *see* **Rote**
Roto Australia **112** B4
Rotomagus France *see* **Rouen**
Rotomanu N.Z. **113** C6
Rotondo, Monte *mt. Corsica* France **56** I5
Rotorua N.Z. **113** F4
Rotorua, Lake N.Z. **113** F4
Röttenbach Germany **53** L5
Rottendorf Germany **53** K5
Rottenmann Austria **47** O7
Rotterdam Neth. **52** E3
Rottleberode Germany **53** K3
Rottnest Island Australia **109** A8
Rottweil Germany **47** L6
Rotuma *i.* Fiji **107** H3
Rotumeroog *i.* Neth. **52** G1
Rotung India **76** B2
Rötviken Sweden **44** I5
Rötz Germany **53** M5
Roubaix France **52** D4
Rouen France **52** B5
Rough River Lake U.S.A. **134** B5
Roulers Belgium *see* **Roeselare**
Roumania *country* Europe *see* **Romania**
Roundeyed Lake Canada **123** H3
Round Hill *hill* U.K. **48** F4
Round Mountain Australia **112** F3
Round Rock *AZ* U.S.A. **129** I3
Round Rock *TX* U.S.A. **131** D6
Roundup U.S.A. **126** F3
Rousay *i.* U.K. **50** F1
Rouses Point U.S.A. **135** I1
Rouxville S. Africa **101** H6
Rouyn Canada **122** F4
Rovaniemi Fin. **44** N3
Roven'ki Rus. Fed. **43** H6
Rovereto Italy **58** D2
Rôviěng Tbong Cambodia **71** D4
Rovigo Italy **58** D2
Rovinj Croatia **58** E2
Rovno Ukr. *see* **Rivne**
Rovnoye Rus. Fed. **43** J6
Rovuma *r.* Moz./Tanz. *see* **Ruvuma**
Rowena Australia **112** D2
Rowley Island Canada **119** K3
Rowley Shoals *sea feature* Australia **108** B4
Równe Ukr. *see* **Rivne**
Roxas *Mindoro* Phil. **69** G4
Roxas *Palawan* Phil. **68** F4
Roxas *Panay* Phil. **69** G4
Roxboro U.S.A. **132** E4
Roxburgh N.Z. **113** B7
Roxburgh Island Cook Is *see* **Rarotonga**
Roxby Downs Australia **111** B6
Roxo, Cabo *c.* Senegal **96** B3
Roy *MT* U.S.A. **126** F3
Roy *NM* U.S.A. **127** G5
Royal Canal Rep. of Ireland **51** E4
Royal Chitwan National Park Nepal **83** F4
Royale, Île *i.* Canada *see* **Cape Breton Island**
Royale, Isle *i.* U.S.A. **130** F1
Royal Natal National Park S. Africa **101** I5
Royal National Park Australia **112** E5
Royal Oak U.S.A. **134** D2
Royal Suklaphanta National Park Nepal **82** E3
Royan France **56** D4
Roye France **52** C5
Roy Hill Australia **108** B5
Royston U.K. **49** G6
Rozdil'na Ukr. **59** N1
Rozivka Ukr. **43** H7
Rtishchevo Rus. Fed. **43** I5
Ruabon U.K. **49** D6
Ruaha National Park Tanz. **99** D4
Ruahine Range *mts* N.Z. **113** F5
Ruanda *country* Africa *see* **Rwanda**
Ruapehu, Mount *vol.* N.Z. **113** E4
Ruapuke Island N.Z. **113** B8
Ruatoria N.Z. **113** G3
Ruba Belarus **43** F5

▶**Rub' al Khālī** *des.* Saudi Arabia **86** G6
Largest uninterrupted stretch of sand in the world.

Rubaydā *reg.* Saudi Arabia **88** C5
Rubtsovsk Rus. Fed. **80** F1
Ruby U.S.A. **118** C3
Ruby Dome *mt.* U.S.A. **129** F1
Ruby Mountains U.S.A. **129** F1
Rubys Inn U.S.A. **129** G3
Ruby Valley U.S.A. **129** F1
Rucheng China **77** G3
Ruckersville U.S.A. **135** F4
Rudall River National Park Australia **108** C5
Rudarpur India **83** E4
Ruda Śląska Poland **47** Q5
Rudauli India **83** E4
Rūdbār Iran **88** C2
Rudkøbing Denmark **45** G9
Rudnaya Pristan' Rus. Fed. **74** D3
Rudnichnyy Rus. Fed. **42** L4
Rudnik Ingichka Uzbek. *see* **Ingichka**
Rudnya *Smolenskaya Oblast'* Rus. Fed. **43** F5
Rudnya *Volgogradskaya Oblast'* Rus. Fed. **43** J6
Rudnyy Kazakh. **78** F1
Rudolf, Lake *salt l.* Eth./Kenya *see* **Turkana, Lake**

▶**Rudol'fa, Ostrov** *i.* Rus. Fed. **64** G1
Most northerly point of Europe.

Rudolph Island Rus. Fed. *see* **Rudol'fa, Ostrov**
Rudolstadt Germany **53** L4
Rudong China **77** I1
Rūdsar Iran **88** C2
Rue France **52** B4
Rufiji *r.* Tanz. **99** D4
Rufino Arg. **144** D4
Rufisque Senegal **96** B3
Rufrufua Indon. **69** I7
Rufunsa Zambia **99** C5
Rugao China **77** I1
Rugby U.K. **49** F6
Rugby U.S.A. **130** C1
Rugeley U.K. **49** F6
Rügen *i.* Germany **47** N3
Rugged Mountain Canada **120** E5
Rügland Germany **53** K5
Ruḥayyat al Ḥamr'ā' *waterhole* Saudi Arabia **88** B5
Ruhengeri Rwanda **98** C4
Ruhnu *i.* Estonia **45** M8
Ruhr *r.* Germany **53** G3
Ruhuna National Park Sri Lanka **84** D5
Rui'an China **77** I3
Rui Barbosa Brazil **145** C1
Ruicheng China **77** F1
Ruijin China **77** G3
Ruili China **76** C3
Ruin Point Canada **121** P2
Ruipa Tanz. **99** D4
Ruiz Mex. **136** C4
Ruiz, Nevado del *vol.* Col. **142** C3
Rujaylah, Ḥarrat ar *lava field* Jordan **85** C3
Rūjiena Latvia **45** N8
Ruk *is* Micronesia *see* **Chuuk**
Rukanpur Pak. **89** I4
Rukumkot Nepal **83** E3
Rukwa, Lake Tanz. **99** D4
Rulin China *see* **Chengbu**
Rulong China *see* **Xinlong**
Rum *i.* U.K. **50** C4
Rum, Jebel *mts* Jordan *see* **Ramm, Jabal**
Ruma Serb. and Mont. **59** H2
Rumāh Saudi Arabia **86** G4
Rumania *country* Europe *see* **Romania**
Rumbek Sudan **97** F4
Rumberpon *i.* Indon. **69** I7
Rum Cay *i.* Bahamas **133** F8
Rum Jungle Australia **108** E3
Rummānā *hill* Syria **85** D3
Rumphi Malawi **99** D5
Runan China **77** G1
Runaway, Cape N.Z. **113** F3
Runcorn U.K. **48** E5
Rundu Namibia **99** B5
Rundvik Sweden **44** K5
Rŭng, Kaôh *i.* Cambodia **71** C5
Rungwa Tanz. **99** D4
Rungwa *r.* Tanz. **99** D4
Runheji China **77** H1
Runing China *see* **Runan**
Runton Range *hills* Australia **109** C5
Ruokolahti Fin. **45** P6
Ruoqiang China **80** G4
Rupa India **83** H4
Rupat *i.* Indon. **71** C7
Rupert *r.* Canada **122** F4
Rupert *ID* U.S.A. **126** E4
Rupert *WV* U.S.A. **134** E5
Rupert Bay Canada **122** F4
Rupert Coast Antarctica **152** J1
Rupert House Canada *see* **Waskaganish**
Rupnagar India **82** D3
Rupshu *reg.* Jammu and Kashmir **82** D2
Ruqqād, Wādī ar *watercourse* Israel **85** B3
Rural Retreat U.S.A. **134** E5
Rusaddir N. Africa *see* **Melilla**
Rusape Zimbabwe **99** D5
Ruschuk Bulg. *see* **Ruse**
Ruse Bulg. **59** K3
Rusera India **83** F4
Rush U.S.A. **134** D4
Rush Creek *r.* U.S.A. **130** C4
Rushden U.K. **49** G6
Rushinga Zimbabwe **99** D5
Rushville *IL* U.S.A. **130** F3
Rushville *IN* U.S.A. **134** C4
Rushville *NE* U.S.A. **130** C3
Rushworth Australia **112** B6
Rusk U.S.A. **131** E6
Russell *Man.* Canada **121** K5
Russell *Ont.* Canada **135** H1
Russell N.Z. **113** E2
Russell *KS* U.S.A. **130** D4
Russell *PA* U.S.A. **134** F3
Russell Bay Antarctica **152** J2
Russell Lake *Man.* Canada **121** K3
Russell Lake *N.W.T.* Canada **120** H2
Russell Lake *Sask.* Canada **121** J3
Russell Range *hills* Australia **109** C8
Russell Springs U.S.A. **134** C5
Russellville *AR* U.S.A. **131** E5
Russellville *KY* U.S.A. **134** B5
Rüsselsheim Germany **53** I4
Russia *country* Asia/Europe *see* **Russian Federation**
Russian *r.* U.S.A. **128** B2

▶**Russian Federation** *country* Asia/Europe **64** I3
Largest country in the world, Europe and Asia. Most populous country in Europe and 5th in Asia.
Asia 6, 62–63
Europe 5, 38–39

Russian Soviet Federal Socialist Republic *country* Asia/Europe *see* **Russian Federation**
Russkiy, Ostrov *i.* Rus. Fed. **74** C4
Russkiy Kameshkir Rus. Fed. **43** J5
Rust'avi Georgia **91** G2
Rustburg U.S.A. **134** F5
Rustenburg S. Africa **101** H3
Ruston U.S.A. **131** E5
Rutanzige, Lake Dem. Rep. Congo/Uganda *see* **Edward, Lake**
Ruteng Indon. **108** C2
Ruth U.S.A. **129** F2
Rüthen Germany **53** I3
Rutherglen Australia **112** C6
Ruther Glen U.S.A. **135** G5
Ruthin U.K. **49** D5
Ruthiyai India **82** D4
Ruth Reservoir U.S.A. **128** B1
Rutka *r.* Rus. Fed. **42** J4
Rutland U.S.A. **135** I2
Rutland Water *resr* U.K. **49** G6
Rutledge Lake Canada **121** I2
Rutog *Xizang* China **76** B2
Rutög China **82** D2
Rutog *Xizang* China **83** F3
Rutul Rus. Fed. **91** G2
Ruukki Fin. **44** N4
Ruvuma *r.* Moz./Tanz. **99** E5
also known as Rovuma
Ruwayshid, Wādī *watercourse* Jordan **85** C3
Ruwayṭah, Wādī *watercourse* Jordan **85** C5
Ruweis U.A.E. **88** D5
Ruwenzori National Park Uganda *see* **Queen Elizabeth National Park**
Ruza Rus. Fed. **42** H5
Ruzayevka Kazakh. **78** F1
Ruzayevka Rus. Fed. **43** J5
Ruzhou China **77** G1
Ružomberok Slovakia **47** Q6
▶**Rwanda** *country* Africa **98** C4
Africa 7, 94–95
Ryābād Iran **88** D2
Ryan, Loch *b.* U.K. **50** D5
Ryazan' Rus. Fed. **43** H5
Ryazhsk Rus. Fed. **43** I5
Rybachiy, Poluostrov *pen.* Rus. Fed. **44** R2
Rybach'ye Kyrg. *see* **Balykchy**
Rybinsk Rus. Fed. **42** H4
Rybinskoye Vodokhranilishche *resr* Rus. Fed. **42** H4
Rybnik Poland **47** Q5
Rybnitsa Moldova *see* **Rîbniţa**
Rybnoye Rus. Fed. **43** H5
Rybreka Rus. Fed. **42** G3
Ryd Sweden **45** I8
Rydberg Peninsula Antarctica **152** L2
Ryde U.K. **49** F8
Rye U.K. **49** H8
Rye *r.* U.K. **48** G4
Rye Bay U.K. **49** H8
Ryegate U.S.A. **126** F3
Rye Patch Reservoir U.S.A. **128** D1
Rykovo Ukr. *see* **Yenakiyeve**
Ryl'sk Rus. Fed. **43** G6
Rylstone Australia **112** D4
Ryn-Peski *des.* Kazakh. **41** P6
Ryukyu Islands Japan **75** B8
Ryūkyū-rettō *is* Japan *see* **Ryukyu Islands**
Ryukyu Trench *sea feature* N. Pacific Ocean **150** E4
Rzeszów Poland **43** D6
Rzhaksa Rus. Fed. **43** I5
Rzhev Rus. Fed. **42** G4

S

Sa'ādah al Barşā' *pass* Saudi Arabia **85** C5
Sa'ādatābād Iran **88** D4
Saal an der Donau Germany **53** L6
Saale *r.* Germany **53** L3
Saalfeld Germany **53** L4
Saanich Canada **120** F5
Saar *land* Germany *see* **Saarland**
Saar *r.* Germany **52** G5
Saarbrücken Germany **52** G5
Saaremaa *i.* Estonia **45** M7
Saarenkylä Fin. **44** N3
Saargau *reg.* Germany **52** G5
Saarijärvi Fin. **44** N5
Saari-Kämä Fin. **44** O3
Saarikoski Fin. **44** L2
Saaristomeren kansallispuisto *nat. park* Fin. *see* **Skärgårdshavets nationalpark**
Saarland *land* Germany **52** G5
Saarlouis Germany **52** G5
Saatlı Azer. **91** H3
Saatly Azer. *see* **Saatlı**
Sab'a Egypt *see* **Saba'ah**
Saba'ah Egypt **85** A4
Sab' Ābār Syria **85** C3
Šabac Serb. and Mont. **59** H2
Sabadell Spain **57** H3
Sabae Japan **75** E6
Sabak Malaysia **71** C7
Sabalana *i.* Indon. **68** F8
Sabalana, Kepulauan *is* Indon. **68** F8
Sabana, Archipiélago de *is* Cuba **137** H4
Sabang Indon. **71** A6
Şabanözü Turkey **90** D2
Sabará Brazil **145** C2
Sabastiya West Bank **85** B3
Sab'atayn, Ramlat as *des.* Yemen **86** G6
Sabaudia Italy **58** E4
Sabaya Bol. **142** E7
Sabdê China **76** D2
Sabelo S. Africa **100** F6
Şabḩā Jordan **85** C3
Sabhā Libya **97** E2
Şabḩā' Saudi Arabia **88** B6
Sabhrai India **82** B5
Sabi *r.* India **82** D3
Sabi *r.* Moz./Zimbabwe *see* **Save**
Sabie Moz. **101** K3
Sabie *r.* Moz./S. Africa **101** K3
Sabie S. Africa **101** J3
Sabina U.S.A. **134** D4
Sabinal Mex. **127** G7
Sabinal, Cayo *i.* Cuba **133** E8
Sabinas Mex. **131** C7
Sabinas *r.* Mex. **131** C7
Sabinas Hidalgo Mex. **131** C7
Sabine *r.* U.S.A. **131** E6
Sabine Lake U.S.A. **131** E6
Sabine Pass U.S.A. **131** E6
Sabini, Monti *mts* Italy **58** E3
Sabirabad Azer. **91** H2
Sabkhat al Bardawīl Reserve *nature res.* Egypt *see* **Lake Bardawil Reserve**
Sable, Cape Canada **123** I6
Sable, Cape U.S.A. **133** D7
Sable, Lac du *l.* Canada **123** I3
Sable Island Canada **123** K6
Sabon Kafi Niger **96** D3
Sabrina Coast Antarctica **152** F2
Sabugal Port. **57** C3
Sabzawar Afgh. *see* **Shīndand**
Sabzevār Iran **88** E2
Sabzvārān Iran *see* **Jīroft**
Sacalinul Mare, Insula *i.* Romania **59** M2
Sacaton U.S.A. **129** H5
Sac City U.S.A. **130** E3
Săcele Romania **59** K2
Sachigo *r.* Canada **121** N4
Sachigo Lake Canada **121** M4
Sachin India **82** C5
Sach'on S. Korea **75** C6
Sach Pass India **82** D2
Sachsen *land* Germany **53** N3
Sachsen-Anhalt *land* Germany **53** L2
Sachsenheim Germany **53** J6
Sachs Harbour Canada **118** F2
Sacirsuyu *r.* Syria/Turkey *see* **Sājūr, Nahr**
Sackpfeife *hill* Germany **53** I4
Sackville Canada **123** I5
Saco *ME* U.S.A. **135** J2
Saco *MT* U.S.A. **126** G2
Sacramento Brazil **145** B2

▶**Sacramento** U.S.A. **128** C2
State capital of California.

Sacramento *r.* U.S.A. **128** C2
Sacramento Mountains U.S.A. **127** G6
Sacramento Valley U.S.A. **128** B1
Sada S. Africa **101** H7
Sádaba Spain **57** F2
Sá da Bandeira Angola *see* **Lubango**
Şadad Syria **85** C2
Şa'dah Yemen **86** F6
Sadao Thai. **71** C6
Saddat al Hindīyah Iraq **91** G4
Saddleback Mesa *mt.* U.S.A. **131** C5
Saddle Hill *hill* Australia **110** D2
Saddle Peak *hill* India **71** A4
Sa Đec Vietnam **71** D5
Sadêng China **76** B2
Sadieville U.S.A. **134** C4
Sadīj *watercourse* Iran **88** E5
Sadiola Mali **96** B3
Sadiqabad Pak. **89** H4
Sad Istragh *mt.* Afgh./Pak. **89** I2
Sa'dīyah, Hawr as *imp. l.* Iraq **91** G4
Sa'dīyyat *i.* U.A.E. **88** D5
Sado *r.* Port. **57** B4
Sadoga-shima *i.* Japan **75** E5
Sadot Egypt *see* **Sadūt**
Sadovoye Rus. Fed. **43** J7
Sa Dragonera *i.* Spain **57** H4
Sadras India **84** D3
Sadūt Egypt **85** B4
Sadût Egypt *see* **Sadūt**
Sæby Denmark **45** G8
Saena Julia Italy *see* **Siena**
Safad Israel *see* **Ẕefat**
Safayal Maqūf *well* Iraq **91** G5
Safed Khirs *mts* Afgh. **89** H2
Safed Koh *mts* Afgh. **89** G3
Safed Koh *mts* Afgh./Pak. **89** H3
Saffānīyah, Ra's as *pt* Saudi Arabia **88** C4
Säffle Sweden **45** H7
Safford U.S.A. **129** I5
Saffron Walden U.K. **49** H6
Safi Morocco **54** C5
Safīdār, Kūh-e *mt.* Iran **88** D4
Safid Kūh *mts* Afgh. *see* **Paropamisus**
Safid Sagak Iran **89** F3
Safiras, Serra das *mts* Brazil **145** C2
Şāfītā Syria **85** C2
Safonovo *Arkhangel'skaya Oblast'* Rus. Fed. **42** K2
Safonovo *Smolenskaya Oblast'* Rus. Fed. **43** G5
Safrā' al Asyāḩ *esc.* Saudi Arabia **88** A5
Safrā' as Sark *esc.* Saudi Arabia **86** F4
Safranbolu Turkey **90** D2
Saga China **83** F3
Saga Japan **75** C6
Saga Kazakh. **80** B1
Sagaing Myanmar **70** A2
Sagami-nada *g.* Japan **75** E6
Sagamore U.S.A. **134** F3
Saganthit Kyun *i.* Myanmar **71** B4
Sagar *Karnataka* India **84** B3
Sagar *Karnataka* India **84** C2
Sagar *Madhya Pradesh* India **82** D5
Sagaredzho Georgia *see* **Sagarejo**
Sagarejo Georgia **91** G2
Sagar Island India **83** G5

Sagarmatha National Park Nepal **83** F4
Sagastyr Rus. Fed. **65** N2
Sagavanirktok *r.* U.S.A. **118** D2
Sage U.S.A. **126** F4
Saggi, Har *mt.* Israel **85** B4
Saghand Iran **88** D3
Saginaw U.S.A. **134** D2
Saginaw Bay U.S.A. **134** D2
Saglek Bay Canada **123** J2
Saglouc Canada *see* **Salluit**
Sagone, Golfe de *b. Corsica* France **56** I5
Sagres Port. **57** B5
Sagthale India **82** C5
Saguache U.S.A. **127** G5
Sagua la Grande Cuba **137** H4
Saguaro Lake U.S.A. **129** H5
Saguaro National Park U.S.A. **129** H5
Saguenay *r.* Canada **123** H4
Sagunt Spain *see* **Sagunto**
Sagunto Spain **57** F4
Saguntum Spain *see* **Sagunto**
Sahagún Spain **57** D2
Sahand, Kūh-e *mt.* Iran **88** B2

▶**Sahara** *des.* Africa **96** D3
Largest desert in the world.

Şaḩara el Gharbîya *des.* Egypt *see* **Western Desert**
Şaḩara el Sharqîya *des.* Egypt *see* **Eastern Desert**
Saharan Atlas *mts* Alg. *see* **Atlas Saharien**
Saharanpur India **82** D3
Sahara Well Australia **108** C5
Saharsa India **83** F4
Sahaswan India **82** D3
Sahat, Kūh-e *hill* Iran **88** D3
Sahatwar India **83** F4
Şahbuz Azer. **91** G3
Sahdol India *see* **Shahdol**
Sahebganj India *see* **Sahibganj**
Sahebgunj India *see* **Sahibganj**
Saheira, Wâdi el *watercourse* Egypt *see* **Suhaymī, Wādī as**
Sahel *reg.* Africa **96** C3
Sahibganj India **83** F4
Sahiwal Pak. **89** I4
Sahlābād Iran **89** E3
Şaḩm Oman **88** E5
Şaḩneh Iran **88** B3
Şaḩrā al Ḩijārah *reg.* Iraq **91** G5
Sahuaripa Mex. **127** F7
Sahuayo Mex. **136** D4
Sahuteng China *see* **Zadoi**
Sa Huynh Vietnam **71** E4
Sahyadri *mts* India *see* **Western Ghats**
Sahyadriparvat Range *hills* India **84** B1
Sai *r.* India **83** E4
Sai Buri Thai. **71** C6
Saïda Alg. **57** G6
Saïda Lebanon *see* **Sidon**
Sai Dao Tai, Khao *mt.* Thai. **71** C4
Saïdia Morocco **57** E6
Sa'īdīyeh Iran *see* **Solṭānīyeh**
Saidpur Bangl. **83** G4
Saiha India **83** H5
Saihan Tal China **73** K4
Saijō Japan **75** D6
Saikai National Park Japan **75** C6
Saiki Japan **75** C6
Sai Kung *Hong Kong* China **77** [inset]
Sailana India **82** C5
Saimaa *l.* Fin. **45** P6
Saimbeyli Turkey **90** E3
Saindak Pak. **89** F4
Sa'īndezh Iran **88** B2
Sa'īn Qal'eh Iran *see* **Sa'īndezh**
St Abb's Head *hd* U.K. **50** G5
St Agnes U.K. **49** B8
St Agnes *i.* U.K. **49** A9
St Alban's Canada **123** L5
St Albans U.K. **49** G7
St Albans *VT* U.S.A. **135** I1
St Albans *WV* U.S.A. **134** E4
St Alban's Head *hd* U.K. **49** E8
St Albert Canada **120** H4
St Aldhelm's Head *hd* U.K. *see* **St Alban's Head**
St-Amand-les-Eaux France **52** D4
St-Amand-Montrond France **56** F3
St-Amour France **56** G3
St-André, Cap *pt* Madag. *see* **Vilanandro, Tanjona**
St Andrews U.K. **50** G4
St Andrew Sound *inlet* U.S.A. **133** D6
St Anne U.S.A. **134** B3
St Ann's Bay Jamaica **137** I5
St Anthony Canada **123** L4
St Anthony U.S.A. **126** F4
St-Arnaud Alg. *see* **El Eulma**
St Arnaud Australia **112** A6
St Arnaud Range *mts* N.Z. **113** D6
St-Arnoult-en-Yvelines France **52** B6
St-Augustin Canada **123** K4
St Augustin *r.* Canada **123** K4
St Augustine U.S.A. **133** D6
St Austell U.K. **49** C8
St-Avertin France **56** E3
St-Avold France **52** G5
St Barbe Canada **123** K4
St-Barthélemy *i.* West Indies **137** L5
St Bees U.K. **48** D4
St Bees Head *hd* U.K. **48** D4
St Bride's Bay U.K. **49** B7
St-Brieuc France **56** C2
St Catharines Canada **134** F2
St Catherines Island U.S.A. **133** D6
St Catherine's Point U.K. **49** F8
St-Céré France **56** E4
St-Chamond France **56** G4
St Charles *ID* U.S.A. **126** F4
St Charles *MD* U.S.A. **135** G4
St Charles *MI* U.S.A. **134** C2
St Charles *MO* U.S.A. **130** F4
St-Chély-d'Apcher France **56** F4
St Christopher and Nevis *country* West Indies *see* **St Kitts and Nevis**
St Clair *r.* Canada/U.S.A. **134** D2
St Clair, Lake Canada/U.S.A. **134** D2
St-Claude France **56** G3
St Clears U.K. **49** C7
St Cloud U.S.A. **130** E2
St Croix *r.* U.S.A. **122** B5
St Croix Falls U.S.A. **130** E2
St David U.S.A. **129** H6
St David's Head *hd* U.K. **49** B7
St-Denis France **52** C6

▶**St-Denis** Réunion **149** L7
Capital of Réunion.

St-Denis-du-Sig Alg. *see* **Sig**
St-Dié France **56** H2
St-Dizier France **52** E6
St-Domingue *country* West Indies *see* **Haiti**
Sainte Anne Canada **121** L5
Ste-Anne, Lac *l.* Canada **123** I4
St Elias, Cape U.S.A. **118** D4

▶**St Elias, Mount** U.S.A. **120** A2
4th highest mountain in North America.

St Elias Mountains Canada **120** A2
Ste-Marguerite *r.* Canada **123** I4
Ste-Marie, Cap *c.* Madag. *see* **Vohimena, Tanjona**
Sainte-Marie, Île *i.* Madag. *see* **Boraha, Nosy**
Ste-Maxime France **56** H5
Sainte Rose du Lac Canada **121** L5
Saintes France **56** D4
Sainte Thérèse, Lac *l.* Canada **120** F1
St-Étienne France **56** G4
St-Étienne-du-Rouvray France **52** B5
St-Fabien Canada **123** H4
St-Félicien Canada **123** G4
Saintfield U.K. **51** G3
St-Florent *Corsica* France **56** I5
St-Florent-sur-Cher France **56** F3
St Floris, Parc National *nat. park* Cent. Afr. Rep. **98** C3
St-Flour France **56** F4
St Francesville U.S.A. **131** F6
St Francis U.S.A. **130** C4
St Francis *r.* U.S.A. **131** F5
St Francis Isles Australia **109** F8
St-François *r.* Canada **123** G5
St-François, Lac *l.* Canada **123** H5
St-Gaudens France **56** E5
St George Australia **112** D2
St George *r.* Australia **110** D3
St George *AK* U.S.A. **118** B4
St George *SC* U.S.A. **133** D5
St George *UT* U.S.A. **129** G3
St George, Point U.S.A. **126** B4
St George Head *hd* Australia **112** E5
St George Island U.S.A. **118** B4
St George Ranges *hills* Australia **108** D4
St-Georges Canada **123** H5

▶**St George's** Grenada **137** L6
Capital of Grenada.

St George's Bay *Nfld. and Lab.* Canada **123** K4
St George's Bay *N.S.* Canada **123** J5
St George's Channel P. N.G. **106** F2
St George's Channel Rep. of Ireland/U.K. **51** F6
St Gotthard Hungary *see* **Szentgotthárd**
St Gotthard Pass Switz. **56** I3
St Govan's Head *hd* U.K. **49** C7
St Helen U.S.A. **134** C1
St Helena U.S.A. **128** B2
St Helena *i.* S. Atlantic Ocean **148** H7

▶**St Helena and Dependencies** *terr.* S. Atlantic Ocean **148** H7
United Kingdom Overseas territory. Consists of St Helena, Ascension, Tristan da Cunha and Gough Island.
Africa 7

St Helena Bay S. Africa **100** D7
St Helens Australia **111** [inset]
St Helens U.K. **48** E5
St Helens U.S.A. **126** C3
St Helens, Mount *vol.* U.S.A. **126** C3
St Helens Point Australia **111** [inset]

▶**St Helier** Channel Is **49** E9
Capital of Jersey.

Sainthiya India **83** F5
St-Hubert Belgium **52** F4
St-Hyacinthe Canada **123** G5
St Ignace U.S.A. **132** C2
St Ignace Island Canada **122** D4
St Ishmael U.K. **49** C7
St Ives *England* U.K. **49** B8
St Ives *England* U.K. **49** G6
St-Jacques, Cap Vietnam *see* **Vung Tau**
St-Jacques-de-Dupuy Canada **122** F4
St James *MN* U.S.A. **130** E3
St James *MO* U.S.A. **130** F4
St James, Cape Canada **120** D5
St-Jean *r.* Canada **123** I4
St-Jean, Lac *l.* Canada **123** G4
St-Jean-d'Acre Israel *see* **'Akko**
St-Jean-d'Angély France **56** D4
St-Jean-de-Monts France **56** C3
St-Jean-sur-Richelieu Canada **135** I1
St-Jérôme Canada **122** G5
St Joe *r.* U.S.A. **126** D3
Saint John Canada **123** I5
St John U.S.A. **130** D4
St John *r.* U.S.A. **132** H2
St John, Cape Canada **123** L4
St John Bay Canada **123** K4
St John Island Canada **123** K4

▶**St John's** Antigua and Barbuda **137** L5
Capital of Antigua and Barbuda.

▶**St John's** Canada **123** L5
Provincial capital of Newfoundland and Labrador.

St Johns *AZ* U.S.A. **129** I4
St Johns *MI* U.S.A. **134** C2
St Johns *OH* U.S.A. **134** C3
St Johns *r.* U.S.A. **133** D6
St Johnsbury U.S.A. **135** I1
St John's Chapel U.K. **48** E4
St Joseph *IL* U.S.A. **134** A3
St Joseph *LA* U.S.A. **131** F6
St Joseph *MI* U.S.A. **134** B2
St Joseph *MO* U.S.A. **130** E4
St Joseph *r.* U.S.A. **134** C3
St Joseph, Lake Canada **121** N5
St-Joseph-d'Alma Canada *see* **Alma**
St Joseph Island Canada **122** E5
St-Junien France **56** E4
St Just U.K. **49** B8
St-Just-en-Chaussée France **52** C5
St Keverne U.K. **49** B8
St Kilda *i.* U.K. **40** E4
St Kilda *is* U.K. **46** C2
▶**St Kitts and Nevis** *country* West Indies **137** L5
North America 9, 116–117
St-Laurent *inlet* Canada *see* **St Lawrence**
St-Laurent, Golfe du *g.* Canada *see* **St Lawrence, Gulf of**
St-Laurent-du-Maroni Fr. Guiana **143** H2
St Lawrence Canada **123** L5
St Lawrence *inlet* Canada **123** H4
St Lawrence, Cape Canada **123** J5
St Lawrence, Gulf of Canada **123** J4
St Lawrence Island U.S.A. **118** B3
St Lawrence Islands National Park Canada **135** H1
St Lawrence Seaway *sea chan.* Canada/U.S.A. **135** H1
St-Léonard Canada **123** G5
St Leonard U.S.A. **135** G4
St Lewis *r.* Canada **123** K3
St-Lô France **56** D2
St-Louis Senegal **96** B3
St Louis *MI* U.S.A. **134** C2
St Louis *MO* U.S.A. **130** F4
St Louis *r.* U.S.A. **122** B5
▶**St Lucia** *country* West Indies **137** L6
North America 9, 116–117
St Lucia, Lake S. Africa **101** K5
St Lucia Estuary S. Africa **101** K5
St Luke's Island Myanmar *see* **Zadetkale Kyun**
St Magnus Bay U.K. **50** [inset]
St-Maixent-l'École France **56** D3
St-Malo France **56** C2
St-Malo, Golfe de *g.* France **56** C2
St-Marc Haiti **137** J5
St Maries U.S.A. **126** D3
St Marks S. Africa **101** H7
St Mark's S. Africa *see* **Cofimvaba**

▶**St-Martin** *i.* West Indies **137** L5
Dependency of Guadeloupe (France). The southern part of the island is the Dutch territory of Sint Maarten.

St Martin, Cape S. Africa **100** C7
St Martin, Lake Canada **121** L5
St Martin's *i.* U.K. **49** A9
St Martin's Island Bangl. **70** A2
St Mary Peak Australia **111** B6
St Mary Reservoir Canada **120** H5
St Mary's Canada **134** E2
St Mary's U.K. **50** G2
St Mary's *i.* U.K. **49** A9
St Marys *PA* U.S.A. **135** F3
St Marys *WV* U.S.A. **134** E4
St Marys *r.* U.S.A. **134** C3
St Mary's, Cape Canada **123** L5
St Mary's Bay Canada **123** L5
St Marys City U.S.A. **135** G4
St Matthew Island U.S.A. **118** A3
St Matthews U.S.A. **134** C4
St Matthew's Island Myanmar *see* **Zadetkyi Kyun**
St Matthias Group *is* P. N.G. **69** L7
St Maurice *r.* Canada **123** G5
St Mawes U.K. **49** B8
St-Médard-en-Jalles France **56** D4
St Meinrad U.S.A. **134** B4
St Michaels U.S.A. **135** G4
St Michael's Bay Canada **123** L3
St-Mihiel France **52** F6
St-Nazaire France **56** C3
St Neots U.K. **49** G6
St-Nicolas Belgium *see* **Sint-Niklaas**
St-Nicolas, Mont *hill* Lux. **52** G5
St-Nicolas-de-Port France **56** H2
St-Omer France **52** C4
Saintonge *reg.* France **56** D4
St-Pacôme Canada **123** H5
St-Palais France **56** D5
St Paris U.S.A. **134** D3
St Pascal Canada **123** H5
St Paul *r.* Canada **123** K4
St-Paul *atoll* Fr. Polynesia *see* **Héréhérétué**
St Paul *AK* U.S.A. **118** A4

▶**St Paul** *MN* U.S.A. **130** E2
State capital of Minnesota.

St Paul *NE* U.S.A. **130** D3
St-Paul, Île *i.* Indian Ocean **149** N8
St Paul Island U.S.A. **118** A4
St Peter and St Paul Rocks *is* N. Atlantic Ocean *see* **São Pedro e São Paulo**

▶**St Peter Port** Channel Is **49** E9
Capital of Guernsey.

St Peter's *Nova Scotia* Canada **123** J5
St Peters *P.E.I.* Canada **123** J5
St Petersburg Rus. Fed. **45** Q7
St Petersburg U.S.A. **133** D7
St-Pierre *mt.* France **56** G5

▶**St-Pierre** St Pierre and Miquelon **123** L5
Capital of St Pierre and Miquelon.

▶**St Pierre and Miquelon** *terr.* N. America **123** K5
French Territorial Collectivity.
North America 9, 116–117

St-Pierre-d'Oléron France **56** D4
St-Pierre-le-Moûtier France **56** F3
St-Pol-sur-Ternoise France **52** C4
St-Pourçain-sur-Sioule France **56** F3
St-Quentin France **52** D5
St Regis U.S.A. **126** E3
St Regis Falls U.S.A. **135** H1
St-Rémi Canada **135** I1
St-Saëns France **52** B5
St Sebastian Bay S. Africa **100** E8
St Siméon Canada **123** H5
St Simons Island U.S.A. **133** D6
St Theresa Point Canada **121** M4
St Thomas Canada **134** E2
St-Trond Belgium *see* **Sint-Truiden**
St-Tropez France **56** H5
St-Tropez, Cap de *c.* France **56** H5
St-Vaast-la-Hougue France **49** F9
St-Valery-en-Caux France **49** H9
St-Véran France **56** H4
St Vincent U.S.A. **130** D1
St Vincent *country* West Indies *see* **St Vincent and the Grenadines**
St Vincent, Cape Australia **111** [inset]
St Vincent, Cape Port. *see* **São Vicente, Cabo de**
St Vincent, Gulf Australia **111** B7
▶**St Vincent and the Grenadines** *country* West Indies **137** L6
North America 9, 116–117
St Vincent Passage St Lucia/St Vincent **137** L6
St-Vith Belgium **52** G4
St Walburg Canada **121** I4
St Williams Canada **134** E2
St-Yrieix-la-Perche France **56** E4
Sain Us China **72** J4
Saioa *mt.* Spain **57** F2
Saipal *mt.* Nepal **82** E3
Saipan *i.* N. Mariana Is **69** L3
Sai Pok Liu Hoi Hap *Hong Kong* China *see* **West Lamma Channel**
Saiteli Turkey *see* **Kadınhanı**
Saitlai Myanmar **70** A2
Saittanulkki *hill* Fin. **44** N3
Sai Yok National Park Thai. **71** B4
Sajam Indon. **69** I7
Sajama, Nevado *mt.* Bol. **142** E7
Sājir Saudi Arabia **88** B5
Sājūr, Nahr *r.* Syria/Turkey **85** D1
Sajzī Iran **88** D3
Sak *watercourse* S. Africa **100** E5
Sakaide Japan **75** D6
Sakākah Saudi Arabia **91** F5
Sakakawea, Lake U.S.A. **130** C2
Sakami Canada **122** G3
Sakami *r.* Canada **122** F3
Sakami Lake Canada **122** F3
Sakar *mts* Bulg. **59** L4
Sakaraha Madag. **99** E6
Sak'art'velo *country* Asia *see* **Georgia**
Sakarya Turkey **59** N4
Sakarya *r.* Turkey **59** N4
Sakassou Côte d'Ivoire **96** C4
Sakata Japan **75** E5
Sakchu N. Korea **75** B4
Sakesar Pak. **89** I3
Sakhalin *i.* Rus. Fed. **74** F2
Sakhalin Oblast *admin. div.* Rus. Fed. *see* **Sakhalinskaya Oblast'**
Sakhalinskaya Oblast' *admin. div.* Rus. Fed. **74** F2
Sakhalinskiy Zaliv *b.* Rus. Fed. **74** F1
Sakhi India **82** C3
Sakhile S. Africa **101** I4
Sakht-Sar Iran **88** C2
Şäki Azer. **91** G2
Şaki Nigeria *see* **Shaki**
Saki Ukr. *see* **Saky**
Šakiai Lith. **45** M9
Sakir *mt.* Pak. **89** G4
Sakishima-shotō *is* Japan **73** M8
Sakoli India **82** D5
Sakon Nakhon Thai. **70** D3
Sakrivier S. Africa **100** E6
Sakura Japan **75** F6
Saky Ukr. **90** D1
Säkylä Fin. **45** M6
Sal *i.* Cape Verde **96** [inset]
Sal *r.* Rus. Fed. **43** I7
Sala Sweden **45** J7
Salaberry-de-Valleyfield Canada **135** H1
Salacgrīva Latvia **45** N8
Sala Consilina Italy **58** F4
Salada, Laguna *salt l.* Mex. **129** F5
Saladas Arg. **144** E3
Salado *r. Buenos Aires* Arg. **144** E5
Salado *r. Santa Fé* Arg. **144** D4
Salado *r.* Mex. **131** D7
Salaga Ghana **96** C4
Salairskiy Kryazh *ridge* Rus. Fed. **72** E2
Salajwe Botswana **100** G2
Şalālah Oman **87** H6
Salamanca Mex. **136** D4
Salamanca Spain **57** D3
Salamanca U.S.A. **135** F2
Salamanga Moz. **101** K4
Salamantica Spain *see* **Salamanca**
Salamat, Bahr *r.* Chad **97** E4
Salāmī Iran **89** E3
Salamina *i.* Greece **59** J6
Salamis *tourist site* Cyprus **85** A2
Salamís *i.* Greece *see* **Salamina**
Salamīyah Syria **85** C2
Salamonie *r.* U.S.A. **134** C3
Salamonie Lake U.S.A. **134** C3
Salang Tunnel Afgh. **89** H3
Salantai Lith. **45** L8
Salar de Pocitos Arg. **144** C2
Salari Pak. **89** G5
Salas Spain **57** C2
Salaspils Latvia **45** N8
Salawati *i.* Indon. **69** I7
Salawin, Mae Nam *r.* China/Myanmar *see* **Salween**
Salaya India **82** B5
Salayar *i.* Indon. **69** G8

▶**Sala y Gómez, Isla** *i.* S. Pacific Ocean **151** M7
Most easterly point of Oceania

Salazar Angola *see* **N'dalatando**
Salbris France **56** F3
Šalčininkai Lith. **45** N9
Salcombe U.K. **49** D8
Saldae Alg. *see* **Bejaïa**
Saldaña Spain **57** D2
Saldanha S. Africa **100** C7
Saldanha Bay S. Africa **100** C7
Saldus Latvia **45** M8
Sale Australia **112** C7
Saleh, Teluk *b.* Indon. **68** F8
Şāleḩābād Iran **88** C3
Salekhard Rus. Fed. **64** H3
Salem India **84** C4
Salem *AR* U.S.A. **131** F4
Salem *IL* U.S.A. **130** F4
Salem *IN* U.S.A. **134** B4
Salem *MA* U.S.A. **135** J2
Salem *MO* U.S.A. **130** F4
Salem *NJ* U.S.A. **135** H4
Salem *NY* U.S.A. **135** I2
Salem *OH* U.S.A. **134** E3

▶**Salem** *OR* U.S.A. **126** C3
State capital of Oregon.

Salem *SD* U.S.A. **130** D3
Salem *VA* U.S.A. **134** E5
Salen *Scotland* U.K. **50** D4
Salen *Scotland* U.K. **50** D4
Salerno Italy **58** F4
Salerno, Golfo di *g.* Italy **58** F4
Salernum Italy *see* **Salerno**
Salford U.K. **48** E5
Salgótarján Hungary **47** Q6
Salgueiro Brazil **143** K5
Salian Afgh. **89** F4
Salibabu *i.* Indon. **69** H6
Salida U.S.A. **127** G5
Salies-de-Béarn France **56** D5
Salihli Turkey **59** M5
Salihorsk Belarus **45** O10
Salima Malawi **99** D5
Salina *KS* U.S.A. **130** D4
Salina *UT* U.S.A. **129** H2
Salina, Isola *i.* Italy **58** F5
Salina Cruz Mex. **136** E5
Salinas Brazil **145** C2
Salinas Ecuador **142** B4
Salinas Mex. **136** D4
Salinas *r.* Mex. **131** D7
Salinas U.S.A. **128** C3
Salinas *r.* U.S.A. **128** C3
Salinas, Cabo de *c.* Spain *see* **Ses Salines, Cap de**
Salinas, Ponta das *pt* Angola **99** B5
Salinas Peak U.S.A. **127** G6
Saline U.S.A. **134** D2
Saline *r.* U.S.A. **130** D4
Saline Valley *depr.* U.S.A. **128** E3
Salinópolis Brazil **143** I4
Salinosó Lachay, Punta *pt* Peru **142** C6
Salisbury U.K. **49** F7
Salisbury *MD* U.S.A. **135** H4
Salisbury *NC* U.S.A. **132** D5
Salisbury Zimbabwe *see* **Harare**
Salisbury Plain U.K. **49** E7
Şalkhad Syria **85** C3
Salla Fin. **44** P3
Sallisaw U.S.A. **131** E5
Salluit Canada **153** K2
Sallum, Khalīj as *b.* Egypt **90** B5
Sallyana Nepal **83** E3
Salmās Iran **88** B2
Salmi Rus. Fed. **42** F3
Salmo Canada **120** G5
Salmon U.S.A. **126** E3
Salmon *r.* U.S.A. **126** D3
Salmon Arm Canada **120** G5
Salmon Falls Creek *r.* U.S.A. **126** E4
Salmon Gums Australia **109** C8
Salmon Reservoir U.S.A. **135** H2
Salmon River Mountains U.S.A. **126** E3
Salmtal Germany **52** G5
Salo Fin. **45** M6
Salome U.S.A. **129** G5
Salon India **82** E4
Salon-de-Provence France **56** G5
Salonica Greece *see* **Thessaloniki**
Salonika Greece *see* **Thessaloniki**
Salpausselkä *reg.* Fin. **45** N6
Salqīn Syria **85** C1
Salses, Étang de *l.* France *see* **Leucate, Étang de**
Sal'sk Rus. Fed. **43** I7
Salsomaggiore Terme Italy **58** C2
Salt Jordan *see* **As Salṭ**
Salt *watercourse* S. Africa **100** F7
Salt *r.* U.S.A. **129** G5
Salta Arg. **144** C2
Saltaire U.K. **48** F5
Saltash U.K. **49** C8
Saltcoats U.K. **50** E5
Saltee Islands Rep. of Ireland **51** F5
Saltfjellet Svartisen Nasjonalpark *nat. park* Norway **44** I3
Saltfjorden *sea chan.* Norway **44** H3
Salt Fork Arkansas *r.* U.S.A. **131** D4
Salt Fork Lake U.S.A. **134** E3
Saltillo Mex. **131** C7
Salt Lake India **89** I5

▶**Salt Lake City** U.S.A. **129** H1
State capital of Utah.

Salt Lick U.S.A. **134** D4
Salto Brazil **145** B3
Salto Uruguay **144** E4
Salto da Divisa Brazil **145** D2
Salto Grande Brazil **145** A3
Salton Sea *salt l.* U.S.A. **129** F5
Salto Santiago, Represa de *resr* Brazil **144** F3
Salt Range *hills* Pak. **89** I3
Salt River Canada **121** H2
Saluda U.S.A. **135** G5
Salûm Egypt *see* **As Sallūm**
Salûm, Khalîg el *b.* Egypt *see* **Sallum, Khalīj as**
Saluq, Kūh-e *mt.* Iran **88** E2
Salur India **84** D2
Saluzzo Italy **58** B2
Salvador Brazil **145** D1
Salvador *country* Central America *see* **El Salvador**
Salvador, Lake U.S.A. **131** F6
Salvaleón de Higüey Dom. Rep. *see* **Higüey**
Salvation Creek *r.* U.S.A. **129** H2
Salwah Saudi Arabia **98** F1
Salwah, Dawḩat *b.* Qatar/Saudi Arabia **88** C5
Salween *r.* China/Myanmar **76** C5
also known as Mae Nam Khong *or* Mae Nam Salawin *or* Nu Jiang (China) *or* Thanlwin (Myanmar)
Salyan Azer. **91** H3
Salyan Nepal *see* **Sallyana**
Sal'yany Azer. *see* **Salyan**
Salyersville U.S.A. **134** D5
Salzbrunn Namibia **100** C3
Salzburg Austria **47** N7
Salzgitter Germany **53** K2
Salzhausen Germany **53** K1
Salzkotten Germany **53** I3
Salzmünde Germany **53** L3
Salzwedel Germany **53** L2
Sam India **82** B4
Samae San, Ko *i.* Thai. **71** C4
Samagaltay Rus. Fed. **80** H1
Samāh *well* Saudi Arabia **88** B4
Samaida Iran *see* **Someydeh**
Samaixung China **83** E2
Samakhixai Laos *see* **Attapu**
Samalanga Indon. **71** B6
Samalayuca Mex. **127** G7
Samalkot India **84** D2
Samālūṭ Egypt **90** C5
Samâlûṭ Egypt *see* **Samālūṭ**
Samana Cay *i.* Bahamas **133** F8
Samanala *mt.* Sri Lanka *see* **Adam's Peak**
Samandağı Turkey **85** B1
Samangān Afgh. *see* **Āybak**
Samangān Iran **89** F3
Samani Japan **74** F4
Samanlı Dağları *mts* Turkey **59** M4
Samar Kazakh. *see* **Samarskoye**
Samar *i.* Phil. **69** H4
Samara Rus. Fed. **43** K5
Samara *r.* Rus. Fed. **41** Q5
Samarga Rus. Fed. **74** E3
Samarinda Indon. **68** F7
Samarka Rus. Fed. **74** D3
Samarkand Uzbek. **89** G2
Samarkand, Pik *mt.* Tajik. *see* **Samarqand, Qullai**
Samarobriva France *see* **Amiens**
Samarqand Uzbek. *see* **Samarkand**
Samarqand, Qullai *mt.* Tajik. **89** H2
Sāmarrā' Iraq **91** F4
Samarskoye Kazakh. **80** F2
Samasata Pak. **89** H4
Samastipur India **83** F4
Şamaxı Azer. **91** H2
Samba Jammu and Kashmir **82** C2
Sambaliung *mts* Indon. **68** F6
Sambalpur India **83** E5
Sambar, Tanjung *pt* Indon. **68** E7
Sambas Indon. **71** E7
Sambat Ukr. *see* **Kiev**
Sambava Madag. **99** F5
Sambha India **83** G4
Sambhajinagar India *see* **Aurangabad**
Sambhal India **82** D3
Sambhar Lake India **82** C4
Sambir Ukr. **43** D6
Sambito *r.* Brazil **143** J5
Sâmbor Cambodia **71** D4
Sambor Ukr. *see* **Sambir**
Samborombón, Bahía *b.* Arg. **144** E5
Sambre *r.* Belgium/France **52** E4
Samch'ŏk S. Korea **75** C5
Samch'ŏnp'o S. Korea *see* **Sach'on**
Same Tanz. **98** D4
Samer France **52** B4
Sami India **82** B5
Samīrah Saudi Arabia **86** F4
Samirum Iran *see* **Yazd-e Khvāst**
Samjiyŏn N. Korea **74** C4
Şämkir Azer. **91** G2
Şamnan va Damghan *reg.* Iran **88** D3
Sam Neua Laos *see* **Xam Nua**
▶**Samoa** *country* S. Pacific Ocean **107** I3
Oceania 8, 104–105
Samoa Basin *sea feature* S. Pacific Ocea[n] **150** I7
Samoa i Sisifo *country* S. Pacific Ocean *see* **Samoa**
Samobor Croatia **58** F2
Samoded Rus. Fed. **42** I3
Samokov Bulg. **59** J3
Šamorín Slovakia **47** P6
Samos *i.* Greece **59** L6
Samosir *i.* Indon. **71** B7
Samothrace *i.* Greece *see* **Samoth[raki]**
Samothraki *i.* Greece **59** K4
Samoylovka Rus. Fed. **43** I6
Sampê China *see* **Xiangcheng**
Sampit Indon. **68** E7
Sampit, Teluk *b.* Indon. **68** E7
Sam Rayburn Reservoir U.S.A.
Samrong Cambodia *see* **Phum**
Samsang China **83** E3
Sam Sao, Phou *mts* Laos/Viet
Samson U.S.A. **133** C6
Sâm Sơn Vietnam **70** D3
Samsun Turkey **90** E2
Samti Afgh. **89** H2
Samui, Ko *i.* Thai. **71** C5
Samut Prakan Thai. **71** C4
Samut Sakhon Thai. **71** C
Samut Songkhram Thai.
Samyai China **83** G3
San Mali **96** C3
San, Phou *mt.* Laos **70**
San, Tônlé *r.* Cambodi

▶**Şan'ā'** Yemen **86** F6
Capital of Yemen.

Sanaa Yemen *see* **Ş**
Sanae *research stat*
San Agostín U.S.A
San Agustin, Cape
San Agustin, Plair

Shmidta, Ostrov i. Rus. Fed. 64 K1
Shmidta, Poluostrov pen. Rus. Fed. 74 F1
Shoal Lake Canada 121 K5
Shoals U.S.A. 134 B4
Shōbara Japan 75 D6
Shoh Tajik. 89 H2
Shohi Pass Pak. see Tal Pass
Shokanbetsu-dake mt. Japan 74 F4
Sholakkorgan Kazakh. 80 C3
Sholapur India see Solapur
Sholaqorghan Kazakh. see Sholakkorgan
Shomba r. Rus. Fed. 44 R4
Shomvukva Rus. Fed. 42 K3
Shona Ridge sea feature S. Atlantic Ocean 148 I9
Shonzha Kazakh. see Chundzha
Shor India 82 D2
Shorap Pak. 89 G5
Shorapur India 84 C2
Shorawak reg. Afgh. 89 G4
Shorewood IL U.S.A. 134 A3
Shorewood WI U.S.A. 134 B2
Shorkot Pak. 89 I4
Shorkozakhly, Solonchak salt flat Turkm. 91 J2
Shoshone CA U.S.A. 128 E4
Shoshone ID U.S.A. 126 E4
Shoshone r. U.S.A. 126 F3
Shoshone Mountains U.S.A. 128 E2
Shoshone Peak U.S.A. 128 E3
Shoshong Botswana 101 H2
Shoshoni U.S.A. 126 F4
Shostka Ukr. 43 G6
Shouyang Shan mt. China 77 F1
Showak Sudan 86 E7
Show Low U.S.A. 129 H4
Shoyna Rus. Fed. 42 J2
Shpakovskoye Rus. Fed. 91 F1
Shpola Ukr. 43 F6
Shqipëria country Europe see Albania
Shreve U.S.A. 134 D3
Shreveport U.S.A. 131 E5
Shrewsbury U.K. 49 E6
Shri Lanka country Asia see Sri Lanka
Shri Mohangarh India 82 B4
Shrirampur India 83 G5
Shu Kazakh. 80 D3
Shū r. Kazakh./Kyrg. see Chu
Shu'ab, Ra's pt Yemen 87 H7
Shuajingsi China 76 D1
Shuangbai China 76 D3
Shuangcheng Fujian China see Zherong
Shuangcheng Heilong. China 74 B3
Shuanghe China 77 G2
Shuanghechang China 76 E2
Shuanghedagang China 74 C2
Shuangjiang Guizhou China see Jiangkou
Shuangjiang Hunan China see Tongdao
Shuangjiang Yunnan China see Eshan
Shuangliao China 74 A4
Shuangliu China 76 D2
Shuangpai China 77 F3
Shuangshipu China see Fengxian
Shuangxi China see Shunchang
Shuangyang China 74 B4
Shuangyashan China 74 C3
Shubarkuduk Kazakh. 80 A2
Shubayḩ well Saudi Arabia 85 D4
Shugozero Rus. Fed. 42 G4
Shuicheng China see Lupanshui
Shuidong China see Dianbai
Shuijing China 76 E1
Shuikou China 77 F3
Shuikouguan China 76 E4
Shuikoushan China 77 G3
Shuiluocheng China see Zhuanglang
Shuizhai China see Wuhua
Shulan China 74 B3
Shumagin Islands U.S.A. 118 B4
Shumba Zimbabwe 99 C5
Shumen Bulg. 59 L3
Shumerlya Rus. Fed. 42 J5
Shumilina Belarus 43 F5
Shumyachi Rus. Fed. 43 G5
Shunchang China 77 H3
Shuncheng China 74 A4
Shunde China 77 G4
Shuoxian China see Shuozhou
Shuozhou China 73 K5
Shuqrah Yemen 86 G7
Shūr r. Iran 88 D4
Shūr r. Iran 89 F3
Shūr watercourse Iran 88 D5
Shur watercourse Iran 88 E3
Shūr, Rūd-e watercourse Iran 88 E4
Shūr Āb watercourse Iran 88 D4
Shurchi Uzbek. 89 G2
Shūrjestān Iran 88 D4
Shūrū Iran 89 F4
Shuryshkarskiy Sor, Ozero l. Rus. Fed. 41 T2
Shūsh Iran 88 C3
Shusha Azer. see Şuşa
Shushtar Iran 88 C3
Shutar Khun Pass Afgh. 89 G3
Shutfah, Qalamat well Saudi Arabia 88 D6
Shuwaysh, Tall ash hill Jordan 85 C4
Shuya Ivanovskaya Oblast' Rus. Fed. 42 I4
Shuya Respublika Kareliya Rus. Fed. 42 G3
Shuyskoye Rus. Fed. 42 I4
Shwebo Myanmar 70 A2
Shwedwin Myanmar 70 A1
Shwegun Myanmar 70 B3
Shwegyin Myanmar 70 B3
Shweudaung mt. Myanmar 70 B2
Shyghanaq Kazakh. see Chiganak
Shymkent Kazakh. 80 C3
Shyok Jammu and Kashmir 82 D2
Shypuvate Ukr. 43 H6
Shyroke Ukr. 43 G7
Sia Indon. 69 I8
Siabu Indon. 71 B7
Siahan Range mts Pak. 89 F5
Sīah Chashmeh Iran 88 B2
Siahgird Afgh. 89 G2
Siah Koh mts Afgh. 89 G3
Sialkot Pak. 89 I3
Siam country Asia see Thailand
Sian China see Xi'an
Sian Rus. Fed. 74 B1
Siang r. India see Brahmaputra
Siantan i. Indon. 71 D7
Siargao i. Phil. 69 H5
Siau i. Indon. 69 H6
Šiauliai Lith. 45 M9
Siazan' Azer. see Siyäzän
Si Bai, Lam r. Thai. 70 D4
Sibasa S. Africa 101 J2
Sibayi, Lake S. Africa 101 K4
Sibda China 76 C2
Šibenik Croatia 58 F3
Siberia reg. Rus. Fed. 65 M3
Siberut i. Indon. 68 B7
Siberut, Selat sea chan. Indon. 68 B7
Sibi Pak. 89 G4
Sibidiri P.N.G. 69 K8
Sibigo Indon. 71 A7
Sibiloi National Park Kenya 98 D3
Sibir' reg. Rus. Fed. see Siberia
Sibiti Congo 98 B4
Sibiu Romania 59 K2
Sibley U.S.A. 130 E3
Siboa Indon. 69 G6
Sibolga Indon. 71 B7
Siborongborong Indon. 71 B7
Sibsagar India 83 H4
Sibu Sarawak Malaysia 68 E6
Sibut Cent. Afr. Rep. 98 B3
Sibuyan i. Phil. 69 G4
Sibuyan Sea Phil. 69 G4
Sicamous Canada 120 G5
Sicca Veneria Tunisia see Le Kef
Siccus watercourse Australia 111 B6
Sicheng Anhui China see Sixian
Sicheng Guangxi China see Lingyun
Sichon Thai. 71 B5
Sichuan prov. China 76 D2
Sichuan Pendi basin China 76 E2
Sicié, Cap c. France 56 G5
Sicilia i. Italy see Sicily
Sicilian Channel Italy/Tunisia 58 E6
Sicily i. Italy 58 F5
Sicuani Peru 142 D6
Siddhapur India 82 C5
Siddipet India 84 C2
Sideros, Akra pt Greece 59 L7
Sidesaviwa S. Africa 100 F7
Sidhauli India 82 E4
Sidhi India 83 E4
Sidhpur India see Siddhapur
Sidi Aïssa Alg. 57 H6
Sidi Ali Alg. 57 G5
Sīdī Barrānī Egypt 90 B5
Sidi Bel Abbès Alg. 57 F6
Sidi Bennour Morocco 54 C5
Sidi Bou Sa'īd Tunisia see Sidi Bouzid
Sidi Bouzid Tunisia 58 C7
Sidi el Barráni Egypt see Sīdī Barrānī
Sidi El Hani, Sebkhet de salt pan Tunisia 58 D7
Sidi Ifni Morocco 96 B2
Sidi Kacem Morocco 54 C5
Sidikalang Indon. 71 B7
Sidi Khaled Alg. 54 E5
Sid Lake Canada 121 J2
Sidlaw Hills U.K. 50 F4
Sidley, Mount Antarctica 152 J1
Sidli India 83 G4
Sidmouth U.K. 49 D8
Sidney IA U.S.A. 130 E3
Sidney MT U.S.A. 126 G3
Sidney NE U.S.A. 130 C3
Sidney OH U.S.A. 134 C3
Sidney Lanier, Lake U.S.A. 133 D5
Sidoktaya Myanmar 70 A2
Sidon Lebanon 85 B3
Sidr Egypt see Sudr
Siedlce Poland 43 D5
Sieg r. Germany 53 H4
Siegen Germany 53 I4
Siĕmréab Cambodia 71 C4
Siem Reap Cambodia see Siĕmréab
Si'en China see Huanjiang
Siena Italy 58 D3
Sieradz Poland 47 Q5
Sierra Blanca U.S.A. 127 G7
Sierra Colorada Arg. 144 C6
Sierra Grande Arg. 144 C6
▶Sierra Leone country Africa 96 B4
Africa 7, 94–95
Sierra Leone Basin sea feature N. Atlantic Ocean 148 G5
Sierra Leone Rise sea feature N. Atlantic Ocean 148 G5
Sierra Madre Mountains U.S.A. 128 C4
Sierra Mojada Mex. 131 C7
Sierra Nevada, Parque Nacional nat. park Venez. 142 D2
Sierra Nevada de Santa Marta, Parque Nacional nat. park Col. 142 D1
Sierraville U.S.A. 128 C2
Sierra Vista U.S.A. 127 F7
Sierre Switz. 56 H3
Sievi Fin. 44 N5
Sifang Ling mts China 76 E4
Sifangtai China 74 B3
Sīfenī Eth. 98 E2
Sifnos i. Greece 59 K6
Sig Alg. 57 F6
Sigguup Nunaa pen. Greenland 119 M2
Sighetu Marmației Romania 43 D7
Sighișoara Romania 59 K1
Siglap Sing. 71 [inset]
Sigli Indon. 71 A6
Siglufjörður Iceland 44 [inset]
Signal de Botrange hill Belgium 52 G4
Signal de la Ste-Baume mt. France 56 G5
Signal Peak U.S.A. 129 F5
Signy-l'Abbaye France 52 E5
Sigourney U.S.A. 130 E3
Sigri, Akra pt Greece 59 K5
Sigsbee Deep sea feature G. of Mexico 151 N4
Sigüenza Spain 57 E3
Siguiri Guinea 96 C3
Sigulda Latvia 45 N8
Sigurd U.S.A. 129 H2
Sihanoukville Cambodia 71 C5
Sihaung Myauk Myanmar 70 A2
Sihawa India 84 D1
Sihong China 77 H1
Sihora India 82 E5
Sihui China 77 G4
Siikajoki Fin. 44 N4
Siilinjärvi Fin. 44 O5
Siirt Turkey 91 F3
Sijawal Pak. 82 B4
Sika India 82 B5
Sikaka Saudi Arabia see Sakākah
Sikandra Rao India 82 D4
Sikanni Chief Canada 120 F3
Sikanni Chief r. Canada 120 F3
Sikar India 82 C4
Sikaram mt. Afgh. 89 H3
Sikasso Mali 96 C3
Sikaw Myanmar 70 B2
Sikeston U.S.A. 131 F4
Sikhote-Alin' mts Rus. Fed. 74 D4
Sikhote-Alinskiy Zapovednik nature res. Rus. Fed. 74 E3
Sikinos i. Greece 59 K6
Sikkim state India 83 G4
Siksjö Sweden 44 J4
Sil r. Spain 57 C2
Šila' i. Saudi Arabia 90 D6
Šilalė Lith. 45 M9
Si Lanna National Park Thai. 70 B3
Silas U.S.A. 131 F6
Silavatturai Sri Lanka 84 C4
Silawaih Agam vol. Indon. 71 A6
Silberberg hill Germany 53 J1
Silchar India 83 H4
Şile Turkey 59 M4
Sileru r. India 84 D2
Silesia reg. Czech Rep./Poland 47 P5
Sileti r. Kazakh. 72 C2
Siletiteniz, Ozero salt l. Kazakh. 79 G1
Silgadi Nepal see Silgarhi
Silgarhi Nepal 82 E3
Silghat India 83 H4
Siliana Tunisia 58 C6
Silifke Turkey 85 A1
Siliguri India see Shiliguri
Siling Co salt l. China 83 G3
Silipur India 82 D4
Silistra Bulg. 59 L2
Silistria Bulg. see Silistra
Silivri Turkey 59 M4
Siljan l. Sweden 45 I6
Silkeborg Denmark 45 F8
Sillajhuay mt. Chile 142 E7
Sillamäe Estonia 45 O7
Sille Turkey 90 D3
Silli India 83 F5
Sillod India 84 B1
Silobela S. Africa 101 J4
Silsby Lake Canada 121 M4
Silt U.S.A. 129 J2
Siltaharju Fin. 44 O3
Sīlūp r. Iran 89 F5
Šilutė Lith. 45 L9
Silvan Turkey 91 F3
Silvânia Brazil 145 A2
Silvassa India 84 B1
Silver Bank Passage Turks and Caicos Is 137 J4
Silver Bay U.S.A. 130 F2
Silver City Canada 120 B2
Silver City NM U.S.A. 129 I5
Silver City NV U.S.A. 128 D2
Silver Creek r. U.S.A. 129 H4
Silver Lake U.S.A. 126 C4
Silver Lake l. U.S.A. 128 E4
Silvermine Mts hills Rep. of Ireland 51 D5
Silver Peak Range mts U.S.A. 128 E3
Silver Spring U.S.A. 135 G4
Silver Springs U.S.A. 128 D2
Silverthrone Mountain Canada 120 E5
Silvertip Mountain Canada 120 F5
Silverton U.K. 49 D8
Silverton CO U.S.A. 129 J3
Silverton TX U.S.A. 131 C5
Sima China 83 G3
Simanggang Sarawak Malaysia see Sri Aman
Simao China 76 D4
Simard, Lac l. Canada 122 F5
Simaria India 83 F4
Simav Turkey 59 M5
Simav Dağları mts Turkey 59 M5
Simba Dem. Rep. Congo 98 C3
Simbirsk Rus. Fed. see Ul'yanovsk
Simcoe Canada 134 E2
Simcoe, Lake Canada 134 F1
Simdega India 84 E1
Simēn mts Eth. 98 D2
Simēn Mountains Eth. see Simēn
Simeulue i. Indon. 71 B7
Simeulue Reserve nature res. Indon. 71 A7
Simferopol' Ukr. 90 D1
Simi i. Greece see Symi
Simikot Nepal 83 E3
Similan, Ko i. Thai. 71 B5
Simi Valley U.S.A. 128 D4
Simla India see Shimla
Simla U.S.A. 126 G5
Şimleu Silvaniei Romania 59 J1
Simmerath Germany 52 G4
Simmern (Hunsrück) Germany 53 H5
Simmesport U.S.A. 131 F6
Simms U.S.A. 126 F3
Simojärvi l. Fin. 44 O3
Simon Mex. 131 C7
Simonette r. Canada 120 G4
Simon Wash watercourse U.S.A. 129 I5
Simoom Sound Canada 120 E5
Simoon Sound Canada see Simoom Sound
Simpang Indon. 68 C7
Simpang Mangayau, Tanjung pt Malaysia 68 F5
Simplício Mendes Brazil 143 J5
Simplon Pass Switz. 56 I3
Simpson Canada 121 J5
Simpson U.S.A. 126 F2
Simpson Desert Australia 110 B5
Simpson Desert National Park Australia 110 B5
Simpson Desert Regional Reserve nature res. Australia 111 B5
Simpson Islands Canada 121 H2
Simpson Park Mountains U.S.A. 128 E2
Simpson Peninsula Canada 119 J3
Simrishamn Sweden 45 I9
Simushir, Ostrov i. Rus. Fed. 73 S3
Sina r. India 84 B2
Sinabang Indon. 71 B7
Sinabung vol. Indon. 71 B7
Sinai pen. Egypt 85 A5
Sinai, Mont hill France 52 E5
Sinai al Janûbîya governorate Egypt see Janūb Sīnā'
Sinai ash Shamâlîya governorate Egypt see Shamāl Sīnā'
Si Nakarin Reservoir Thai. 70 B4
Sinaloa state Mex. 127 F8
Sinalunga Italy 58 D3
Sinan China 77 F3
Sinancha Rus. Fed. see Cheremshany
Sinbo Myanmar 70 B1
Sinbyubyin Myanmar 71 B4
Sinbyugyun Myanmar 70 A2
Sincan Turkey 90 E3
Sincelejo Col. 142 C2
Sinchu Taiwan see T'aoyüan
Sinclair Mills Canada 120 F4
Sincora, Serra do hills Brazil 145 C1
Sind r. India 82 D4
Sind Pak. see Thul
Sind prov. Pak. see Sindh
Sinda Rus. Fed. 74 E2
Sindari India 82 B4
Sindelfingen Germany 53 I6
Sindh prov. Pak. 89 H5
Sindhuli Garhi Nepal 83 F4
Sindhulimadi Nepal see Sindhuli Garhi
Sındırgı Turkey 59 M5
Sindor Rus. Fed. 42 K3
Sindou Burkina 96 C3
Sindri India 83 F5
Sind Sagar Doab lowland Pak. 89 H4
Sinel'nikovo Ukr. see Synel'nykove
Sines Port. 57 B5
Sines, Cabo de c. Port. 57 B5
Sinettä Fin. 44 N3
Sinfra Côte d'Ivoire 96 C4
Sing Myanmar 70 B2
Singa Sudan 86 D7
Singanallur India 84 C4
▶Singapore country Asia 71 [inset]
Asia 6, 62–63

▶Singapore Sing. 71 [inset]
Capital of Singapore.

Singapore r. Sing. 71 [inset]
Singapore, Strait of Indon./Sing. 71 [inset]
Singapura country Asia see Singapore
Singapura Sing. see Singapore
Singapuru India 84 D2
Singaraja Indon. 108 A2
Sing Buri Thai. 70 C4
Singhampton Canada 134 E1
Singhana India 82 C3
Singida Tanz. 99 D4
Singidunum Serb. and Mont. see Belgrade
Singkaling Hkamti Myanmar 70 A1
Singkawang Indon. 68 D6
Singkep i. Indon. 68 C7
Singkil Indon. 71 B7
Singkuang Indon. 71 B7
Singleton Australia 112 E4
Singleton, Mount hill N.T. Australia 108 E5
Singleton, Mount hill W.A. Australia 109 B7
Singora Thai. see Songkhla
Sin'gosan N. Korea see Kosan
Singra India 83 G4
Singri India 83 H4
Singu Myanmar 76 B4
Singwara India 84 D1
Sin'gye N. Korea 75 B5
Sinhala country Asia see Sri Lanka
Sinhkung Myanmar 70 B1
Sining China see Xining
Siniscola Sardinia Italy 58 C4
Sinj Croatia 58 G3
Sinjai Indon. 69 G8
Sinjār, Jabal mt. Iraq 91 F3
Sinkat Sudan 86 E6
Sinkiang aut. reg. China see Xinjiang Uygur Zizhiqu
Sinkiang Uighur Autonomous Region aut. reg. China see Xinjiang Uygur Zizhiqu
Sinmi-do i. N. Korea 75 B5
Sinn Germany 53 I4
Sinnamary Fr. Guiana 143 H2
Sinn Bishr, Gebel hill Egypt see Sinn Bishr, Jabal
Sinn Bishr, Jabal hill Egypt 85 A5
Sinneh Iran see Sanandaj
Sinoia Zimbabwe see Chinhoyi
Sinop Brazil 143 G6
Sinop Turkey 90 D2
Sinope Turkey see Sinop
Sinp'a N. Korea 74 B4
Sinp'o N. Korea 75 C4
Sinsang N. Korea 75 B5
Sinsheim Germany 53 I5
Sintang Indon. 68 E6
Sint Eustatius i. Neth. Antilles 137 L5
Sint-Laureins Belgium 52 D3

▶Sint Maarten i. Neth. Antilles 137 L5
Part of the Netherlands Antilles. The northern part of the island is the French territory of St Martin.

Sint-Niklaas Belgium 52 E3
Sinton U.S.A. 131 D6
Sintra Port. 57 B4
Sint-Truiden Belgium 52 F4
Sinŭiju N. Korea 75 B4
Sinzig Germany 53 H4
Siófok Hungary 58 H1
Sioma Ngwezi National Park Zambia 99 C5
Sion Switz. 56 H3
Sion Mills U.K. 51 E3
Siorapaluk Greenland 119 K2
Sioux Center U.S.A. 125 H3
Sioux City U.S.A. 130 D3
Sioux Falls U.S.A. 130 D3
Sioux Lookout Canada 121 N5
Siphaqeni S. Africa see Flagstaff
Siping China 74 B4
Sipiwesk Canada 121 L4
Sipiwesk Lake Canada 121 L4
Siple, Mount Antarctica 152 J2
Siple Coast Antarctica 152 I1
Siple Island Antarctica 152 J2
Siponj Tajik. see Bartang
Sipsey r. U.S.A. 131 F5
Sipura i. Indon. 68 B7
Sīq, Wādī as watercourse Egypt 85 A5
Sir r. Pak. 89 H6
Sir, Dar"yoi r. Asia see Syrdar'ya
Sira India 84 C3
Sira r. Norway 45 E7
Şīr Abū Nu'āyr i. U.A.E. 88 D5
Siracusa Sicily Italy see Syracuse
Siraha Nepal see Sirha
Sirajganj Bangl. 83 G4
Sir Alexander, Mount Canada 120 F4
Şiran Turkey 91 E2
Sirbāl, Jabal mt. Egypt 90 D5
Şīr Banī Yās i. U.A.E. 88 D5
Sircilla India see Sirsilla
Sirdaryo r. Asia see Syrdar'ya
Sirdaryo Uzbek. see Syrdar'ya
Sirdingka China see Lhari
Sir Edward Pellew Group is Australia 110 B2
Sirha Nepal 83 F4
Sirḩān, Wādī as watercourse Jordan/Saudi Arabia 85 C4
Sirik, Tanjung pt Malaysia 68 E6
Siri Kit Dam Thai. 70 C3
Sirína i. Greece see Syrna
Sīrjā Iran 89 F5
Sir James MacBrien, Mount Canada 120 E2
Sīrjān Iran 88 D4
Sīrjān salt flat Iran 88 D4
Sirkazhi India 84 C4
Sirmilik National Park Canada 119 K2
Şırnak Turkey 91 F3
Sirohi India 82 C4
Sirombu Indon. 71 B7
Sironj India 82 D4
Síros i. Greece see Syros
Sirpur India 84 C2
Sirretta Peak U.S.A. 128 D4
Sīrrī, Jazīreh-ye i. Iran 88 D5
Sirsa India 82 C3
Sir Sandford, Mount Canada 120 G5
Sirsi Karnataka India 84 B3
Sirsi Madhya Pradesh India 82 D4
Sirsi Uttar Pradesh India 82 D3
Sirsilla India 84 C2
Sirte Libya 97 E1
Sirte, Gulf of Libya 97 E1
Sir Thomas, Mount hill Australia 109 E6
Siruguppa India 84 C3
Sirur India 84 B2
Şirvan Turkey 91 F3
Sirvel India 84 C3
Širvintai Lith. see Širvintos
Širvintos Lith. 45 N9
Sīrwān r. Iraq 91 G4
Sir Wilfrid Laurier, Mount Canada 120 G4
Sis Turkey see Kozan
Sisak Croatia 58 G2
Sisaket Thai. 70 D4
Siscia Croatia see Sisak
Sishen S. Africa 100 F4
Sishilipu China 76 E1
Sishuang Liedao is China 77 I3
Sisian Armenia 91 G3
Sisimiut Greenland 119 M3
Sisipuk Lake Canada 121 K4
Sisŏphŏn Cambodia 71 C4
Sissano P.N.G. 69 K7
Sisseton U.S.A. 130 D2
Sistān reg. Iran 89 F4
Sīstan, Daryācheh-ye marsh Afgh./Iran 89 F4
Sisteron France 56 G4
Sisters is India 71 A5
Sīt Iran 88 E5
Sitamarhi India 83 F4
Sitang China see Sinan
Sitapur India 82 E4
Siteia Greece 59 L7
Siteki Swaziland 101 J4
Sithonia pen. Greece 59 J4
Sitía Greece see Siteia
Sitidgi Lake Canada 118 E3
Sitila Moz. 101 L2
Siting China 76 E3
Sítio do Mato Brazil 145 C1
Sitka U.S.A. 120 C3
Sitka National Historical Park nat. park U.S.A. 120 C3
Sitra oasis Egypt see Sitrah
Sitrah oasis Egypt 90 B5
Sittang r. Myanmar 70 B3
Sittard Neth. 52 F4
Sittaung Myanmar 70 A1
Sittaung r. Myanmar see Sittang
Sittensen Germany 53 J1
Sittingbourne U.K. 49 H7
Sittoung r. Myanmar see Sittang
Sittwe Myanmar 70 A2
Situbondo Indon. 68 E8
Siumpu i. Indon. 69 G8
Siuri India 83 F5
Sivaganga India 84 C4
Sivakasi India 84 C4
Sivaki Rus. Fed. 74 B1
Sivan India see Siwan
Sivas Turkey 90 E3
Sivaslı Turkey 59 M5
Siverek Turkey 91 E3
Siverskiy Rus. Fed. 45 Q7
Sivers'kyy Donets' r. Rus. Fed./Ukr. see Severskiy Donets
Sivomaskinskiy Rus. Fed. 41 S2
Sivrice Turkey 91 E3
Sivrihisar Turkey 59 N5
Sivukile S. Africa 101 I4
Sīwa Egypt see Sīwah
Sīwah Egypt 90 B5
Sīwah, Wāḩāt oasis Egypt 90 B5
Siwalik Range mts India/Nepal 82 D3
Siwan India 83 F4
Siwana India 82 C4
Siwa Oasis oasis Egypt see Sīwah, Wāḩāt
Sixian China 77 H1
Sixmilecross U.K. 51 E3
Siyabuswa S. Africa 101 I3
Siyäzän Azer. 91 H2
Sīyunī Iran 88 D3
Sizhan China 74 B2
Siziwang Qi China see Ulan Hua
Sjælland i. Denmark see Zealand
Sjenica Serb. and Mont. 59 I3
Sjöbo Sweden 45 H9
Sjøvegan Norway 44 J2
Skadarsko Jezero nat. park Serb. and Mont. 59 H3
Skadovs'k Ukr. 59 O1
Skaftafell nat. park Iceland 40 [inset]
Skaftárós r. mouth Iceland 44 [inset]
Skagafjörður inlet Iceland 44 [inset]
Skagen Denmark 45 G8
Skagerrak strait Denmark/Norway 45 F8
Skagit r. U.S.A. 126 C2
Skagway U.S.A. 153 A3
Skaidi Norway 44 N1
Skaland Norway 44 J2
Skalmodal Sweden 44 I4
Skanderborg Denmark 45 F8
Skaneateles Lake U.S.A. 135 G2
Skara Sweden 45 H7
Skardarsko Jezero l. Albania/Serb. and Mont. see Scutari, Lake
Skardu Jammu and Kashmir 82 C2
Skärgårdshavets nationalpark nat. park Fin. 45 L7
Skarnes Norway 45 G6
Skarżysko-Kamienna Poland 47 R5
Skaulo Sweden 44 L3
Skawina Poland 47 Q6
Skeena r. Canada 120 D4
Skeena Mountains Canada 120 D3
Skegness U.K. 48 H5
Skellefteå Sweden 44 L4
Skellefteälven r. Sweden 44 L4
Skelleftehamn Sweden 44 L4
Skellig Rocks is Rep. of Ireland 51 B6
Skelmersdale U.K. 48 E5
Skerries Rep. of Ireland 51 F4
Ski Norway 45 G7
Skiathos i. Greece 59 J5
Skibbereen Rep. of Ireland 51 C6
Skibotn Norway 44 L2
Skiddaw hill U.K. 48 D4
Skien Norway 45 F7
Skiermûntseach Neth. see Schiermonnikoog
Skiermûntseach i. Neth. see Schiermonnikoog
Skierniewice Poland 47 R5
Skikda Alg. 58 B6
Skipsea U.K. 48 G5
Skipton Australia 112 A6
Skipton U.K. 48 E5
Skirlaugh U.K. 48 G5
Skíros i. Greece see Skyros
Skive Denmark 45 F8
Skjern Denmark 45 F9
Skjolden Norway 45 E6
Skobelev Uzbek. see Fergana
Skobeleva, Pik mt. Kyrg. 89 I2
Skodje Norway 44 E5
Skoganvarre Norway 44 N2
Skokie U.S.A. 134 B2
Skomer Island U.K. 49 B7
Skopelos i. Greece 59 J5
Skopin Rus. Fed. 43 H5

▶Skopje Macedonia 59 I4
Capital of Macedonia.

Skoplje Macedonia see Skopje
Skövde Sweden 45 H7
Skovorodino Rus. Fed. 74 A1
Skowhegan U.S.A. 135 K1
Skrunda Latvia 45 M8
Skukum, Mount Canada 120 C2
Skukuza S. Africa 101 J3
Skull Valley U.S.A. 129 G4
Skuodas Lith. 45 L8
Skurup Sweden 45 H9
Skutskär Sweden 45 J6
Skvyra Ukr. 43 F6
Skye i. U.K. 50 C3
Skylge i. Neth. see Terschelling
Skyring, Seno b. Chile 144 B8
Skyros Greece 59 K5
Skyros i. Greece 59 K5
Skytrain Ice Rise Antarctica 152 L1
Slættaratindur hill Faroe Is 44 [inset]
Slagelse Denmark 45 G9
Slagnäs Sweden 44 K4
Slane Rep. of Ireland 51 F4
Slaney r. Rep. of Ireland 51 F5
Slantsy Rus. Fed. 45 P7
Slapovi Krke nat. park Croatia 58 F3
Slashers Reefs Australia 110 D3
Slatina Croatia 58 G2
Slatina Romania 59 K2
Slaty Fork U.S.A. 134 E4
Slava Rus. Fed. 74 C1
Slave r. Canada 121 H2
Slave Coast Africa 96 D4
Slave Lake Canada 120 H4
Slave Point Canada 120 H2
Slavgorod Belarus see Slawharad
Slavgorod Rus. Fed. 72 D2
Slavkovichi Rus. Fed. 45 P8
Slavonska Požega Croatia see Požega
Slavonski Brod Croatia 58 H2
Slavuta Ukr. 43 E6
Slavutych Ukr. 43 F6
Slavyanka Rus. Fed. 74 C4
Slavyansk Ukr. see Slov"yans'k
Slavyanskaya Rus. Fed. see Slavyansk-na-Kubani
Slavyansk-na-Kubani Rus. Fed. 90 E1
Slawharad Belarus 43 F5
Sławno Poland 47 P3
Slayton U.S.A. 130 E3
Sleaford U.K. 49 G5
Slea Head hd Rep. of Ireland 51 B5
Sleat Neth. see Sloten
Sleat, Sound of sea chan. U.K. 50 D3
Sled Lake Canada 121 J4

Sleeper Islands Canada 122 F2
Sleeping Bear Dunes National Lakeshore nature res. U.S.A. 134 B1
Slessor Glacier Antarctica 152 B1
Slick Rock U.S.A. 129 I2
Slide Mountain U.S.A. 135 H3
Slieve Bloom Mts hills Rep. of Ireland 51 E5
Slieve Car hill Rep. of Ireland 51 C3
Slieve Donard hill U.K. 51 G3
Slieve Gamph hills Rep. of Ireland 51 C4
Slievekimalta hill Rep. of Ireland 51 D5
Slieve Mish Mts hills Rep. of Ireland 51 B5
Slieve Snaght hill Rep. of Ireland 51 E2
Sligachan U.K. 50 C3
Sligeach Rep. of Ireland see Sligo
Sligo Rep. of Ireland 51 D3
Sligo U.S.A. 134 F3
Sligo Bay Rep. of Ireland 51 D3
Slinger U.S.A. 134 A2
Slippery Rock U.S.A. 134 E3
Slite Sweden 45 K8
Sliven Bulg. 59 L3
Sloan U.S.A. 129 F4
Sloat U.S.A. 128 C2
Sloboda Rus. Fed. see Ezhva
Slobodchikovo Rus. Fed. 42 K3
Slobodskoy Rus. Fed. 42 K4
Slobozia Romania 59 L2
Slochteren Neth. 52 G1
Slonim Belarus 45 N10
Slootdorp Neth. 52 E2
Sloten Neth. 52 F2
Slough U.K. 49 G7
▶Slovakia country Europe 40 J6
Europe 5, 38–39
▶Slovenia country Europe 58 F2
Europe 5, 38–39
Slovenija country Europe see Slovenia
Slovenj Gradec Slovenia 58 F1
Slovensko country Europe see Slovakia
Slovenský raj nat. park Slovakia 47 R6
Slov"yans'k Ukr. 43 H6
Słowiński Park Narodowy nat. park Poland 47 P3
Sluch r. Ukr. 43 E6
Słupsk Poland 47 P3
Slussfors Sweden 44 J4
Slutsk Belarus 45 O10
Slyne Head hd Rep. of Ireland 51 B4
Slyudyanka Rus. Fed. 72 I2
Small Point U.S.A. 135 K2
Smallwood Reservoir Canada 119 I3
Smalyavichy Belarus 45 P9
Smalyenskaya Wzwyshsha hills Belarus/Rus. Fed. see Smolensko-Moskovskaya Vozvyshennost'
Smarhon' Belarus 45 O9
Smeaton Canada 121 J4
Smederevo Serb. and Mont. 59 I2
Smederevska Palanka Serb. and Mont. 59 I2
Smela Ukr. see Smila
Smethport U.S.A. 135 F3
Smidovich Rus. Fed. 74 D2
Smila Ukr. 43 F6
Smilde Neth. 52 G2
Smiltene Latvia 45 N8
Smirnykh Rus. Fed. 74 F2
Smith Canada 120 H4
Smith Center U.S.A. 130 D4
Smithfield S. Africa 101 H6
Smithfield NC U.S.A. 132 E5
Smithfield UT U.S.A. 126 F4
Smith Glacier Antarctica 152 K1
Smith Island India 71 A4
Smith Island MD U.S.A. 135 G4
Smith Island VA U.S.A. 135 H5
Smith Mountain Lake U.S.A. 134 F5
Smith River Canada 120 E3
Smiths Falls Canada 135 G1
Smithton Australia 111 [inset]
Smithtown Australia 112 F3
Smithville OK U.S.A. 131 E5
Smithville WV U.S.A. 134 E4
Smoke Creek Desert U.S.A. 128 D1
Smoky Bay Australia 109 F8
Smoky Cape Australia 112 F3
Smoky Falls Canada 122 E4
Smoky Hill r. U.S.A. 130 C4
Smoky Hills KS U.S.A. 124 H4
Smoky Hills KS U.S.A. 130 D4
Smoky Lake Canada 121 H4
Smoky Mountains U.S.A. 126 E4
Smøla i. Norway 44 E5
Smolenka Rus. Fed. 43 K6
Smolensk Rus. Fed. 43 G5
Smolensk-Moscow Upland hills Belarus/Rus. Fed. see Smolensko-Moskovskaya Vozvyshennost'
Smolensko-Moskovskaya Vozvyshennost' hills Belarus/Rus. Fed. 43 G5
Smolevichi Belarus see Smalyavichy
Smolyan Bulg. 59 K4
Smooth Rock Falls Canada 122 E4
Smoothrock Lake Canada 122 C4
Smoothstone Lake Canada 121 J4
Smørfjord Norway 44 N1
Smorgon' Belarus see Smarhon'
Smyley Island Antarctica 152 L2
Smyrna Turkey see İzmir
Smyrna U.S.A. 135 H4
Smyth Island atoll Marshall Is see Taongi
Snæfell mt. Iceland 44 [inset]
Snaefell hill Isle of Man 48 C4
Snag Canada 120 A2
Snake r. Canada 120 C1
Snake r. U.S.A. 126 D3
Snake Island Australia 112 C7
Snake Range mts U.S.A. 129 F2
Snake River Canada 120 F3
Snake River Plain U.S.A. 126 E4
Snare r. Canada 120 G2
Snare Lake Canada 121 J3
Snare Lakes Canada see Wekweti
Snares Islands N.Z. 107 G6
Snåsa Norway 44 H4
Sneedville U.S.A. 134 D5
Sneek Neth. 52 F1
Sneem Rep. of Ireland 51 C6
Sneeuberge mts S. Africa 100 G6
Snegamook Lake Canada 123 J3
Snegurovka Ukr. see Tetiyiv
Snelling U.S.A. 128 C3
Snettisham U.K. 49 H6
Snezhnogorsk Rus. Fed. 64 J3
Snežnik mt. Slovenia 58 F2
Sniečkus Lith. see Visaginas
Snihurivka Ukr. 43 G7
Snits Neth. see Sneek
Snizort, Loch b. U.K. 50 C3
Snoqualmie Pass U.S.A. 126 C3
Snøtinden mt. Norway 44 H3
Snoul Cambodia see Snuŏl
Snover U.S.A. 134 D2
Snovsk Ukr. see Shchors
Snowbird Lake Canada 121 K2
Snowcrest Mountain Canada 120 G5
Snowdon mt. U.K. 49 C5
Snowdonia National Park U.K. 49 D6
Snowdrift Canada see Łutselk'e
Snowdrift r. Canada 121 I2
Snowflake U.S.A. 129 H4
Snow Hill U.S.A. 135 H4
Snow Lake Canada 121 K4
Snowville U.S.A. 126 E4
Snow Water Lake U.S.A. 129 F1
Snowy r. Australia 112 D6
Snowy Mountain U.S.A. 135 H2
Snowy Mountains Australia 112 C6
Snowy River National Park Australia 112 D6
Snug Corner Bahamas 133 F8
Snug Harbour Nfld. and Lab. Canada 123 L3
Snug Harbour Ont. Canada 134 E1
Snuŏl Cambodia 71 D4
Snyder U.S.A. 131 C5
Soalala Madag. 99 E5
Soalara Madag. 99 E6
Soanierana-Ivongo Madag. 99 E5
Soan-kundo is S. Korea 75 B6
Soavinandriana Madag. 99 E5
Sobat r. Sudan 86 D8
Sobernheim Germany 53 H5
Sobger r. Indon. 69 K7
Sobinka Rus. Fed. 42 I5
Sobradinho, Barragem de resr Brazil 143 J6
Sobral Brazil 143 J4
Sochi Rus. Fed. 91 E2
Sŏch'ŏn S. Korea 75 B5
Society Islands Fr. Polynesia 151 J7
Socorro Brazil 145 B3
Socorro Col. 142 D2
Socorro U.S.A. 127 G6
Socorro, Isla i. Mex. 136 B5
Socotra i. Yemen 87 H7
Soc Trăng Vietnam 71 D5
Socuéllamos Spain 57 E4
Soda Lake CA U.S.A. 128 D4
Soda Lake CA U.S.A. 128 E4
Sodankylä Fin. 44 O3
Soda Plains Aksai Chin 82 D2
Soda Springs U.S.A. 126 F4
Söderhamn Sweden 45 J6
Söderköping Sweden 45 J7
Södertälje Sweden 45 J7
Sodiri Sudan 86 C7
Sodo Eth. 98 D3
Södra Kvarken strait Fin./Sweden 45 K6
Sodus U.S.A. 135 G2
Soë Indon. 69 G8
Soekarno, Puntjak mt. Indon. see Jaya, Puncak
Soekmekaar S. Africa 101 I2
Soerabaia Indon. see Surabaya
Soerendonk Neth. 52 F3
Soest Germany 53 I3
Soest Neth. 52 F2
Sofala Australia 112 D4

▶Sofia Bulg. 59 J3
Capital of Bulgaria.

Sofiya Bulg. see Sofia
Sofiyevka Ukr. see Vil'nyans'k
Sofiysk Khabarovskiy Kray Rus. Fed. 74 D1
Sofiysk Khabarovskiy Kray Rus. Fed. 74 E2
Sofporog Rus. Fed. 44 Q4
Softa Kalesi tourist site Turkey 85 A1
Sōfu-gan i. Japan 75 F7
Sog China 76 B2
Soğanlı Dağları mts Turkey 91 E2
Sogda Rus. Fed. 74 D2
Sögel Germany 53 H2
Sogma China 82 E2
Søgne Norway 45 E7
Sognefjorden inlet Norway 45 D6
Sogruma China 76 D1
Söğüt Turkey 59 N4
Söğüt Dağı mts Turkey 59 M6
Soh Iran 88 C3
Sohâg Egypt see Sawhāj
Sohagpur India 82 D5
Soham U.K. 49 H6
Sohan r. Pak. 89 H3
Sohano P.N.G. 106 F2
Sohar Oman see Şuḥār
Sohawal India 82 E4
Sohela India 83 E5
Sohng Gwe, Khao hill Myanmar/Thai. 71 B4
Sŏho-ri N. Korea 75 C4
Sohŭksan-do i. S. Korea 75 B6
Soignies Belgium 52 E4
Soila China 76 C2
Soini Fin. 44 N5
Soissons France 52 D5
Sojat India 82 C4
Sojat Road India 82 C4
Sok r. Rus. Fed. 43 K5
Sokal' Ukr. 43 E6
Sokch'o S. Korea 75 C5
Söke Turkey 59 L6
Sokh Tajik. 89 H2
Sokhor, Gora mt. Rus. Fed. 72 J2
Sokhumi Georgia 91 F2
Sokiryany Ukr. see Sokyryany
Sokodé Togo 96 D4
Soko Islands Hong Kong China 77 [inset]
Sokol Rus. Fed. 42 I4
Sokolo Mali 96 C3
Sokolov Czech Rep. 53 M4
Sokoto Nigeria 96 D3
Sokoto r. Nigeria 96 D3
Sokyryany Ukr. 43 E6
Sola Cuba 133 E8
Sola i. Tonga see Ata
Solan India 82 D3
Solana Beach U.S.A. 128 E5
Solander Island N.Z. 113 A8
Solapur India 84 B2
Soldotna U.S.A. 118 C3
Soledad U.S.A. 128 C3
Soledade Brazil 144 F3
Solenoye Rus. Fed. 43 I7
Solfjellsjøen Norway 44 H3
Solginskiy Rus. Fed. 42 I3
Solhan Turkey 91 F3
Soligalich Rus. Fed. 42 I4
Soligorsk Belarus see Salihorsk
Solihull U.K. 49 F6
Solikamsk Rus. Fed. 41 R4
Sol'-Iletsk Rus. Fed. 64 G4
Solimões r. S. America see Amazon
Solingen Germany 52 H3
Solitaire Namibia 100 B2
Sol-Karmala Rus. Fed. see Severnoye
Şollar Azer. 91 H2
Sollefteå Sweden 44 J5
Söllichau Germany 53 M3
Solling hills Germany 53 J3
Sollstedt Germany 53 K3
Sollum, Gulf of Egypt see Sallum, Khalīj as
Solms Germany 53 I4
Solnechnogorsk Rus. Fed. 42 H4
Solnechnyy Amurskaya Oblast' Rus. Fed. 74 A1
Solnechnyy Khabarovskiy Kray Rus. Fed. 74 E2
Solok Indon. 68 C7
Solomon U.S.A. 129 I5
Solomon, North Fork r. U.S.A. 130 D4

▶Solomon Islands country S. Pacific Ocean 107 G2
4th largest and 5th most populous country in Oceania.
Oceania 8, 104–105

Solomon Sea S. Pacific Ocean 106 F2
Solon U.S.A. 135 K1
Solon Springs U.S.A. 130 F2
Solor i. Indon. 108 C2
Solor, Kepulauan is Indon. 108 C2
Solothurn Switz. 56 H3
Solovetskiye Ostrova is Rus. Fed. 42 G2
Solov'yevsk Rus. Fed. 74 B1
Šolta i. Croatia 58 G3
Solṭānābād Kermān Iran 88 E4
Solṭānābād Khorāsān Iran 89 E3
Solṭānābād Iran 88 C3
Solṭānīyeh Iran 88 C2
Soltau Germany 53 J2
Sol'tsy Rus. Fed. 42 F4
Solvay U.S.A. 135 G2
Sölvesborg Sweden 45 I8
Solway Firth est. U.K. 50 F6
Solwezi Zambia 99 C5
Soma Turkey 59 L5
Somain France 52 D4
▶Somalia country Africa 98 E3
Africa 7, 94–95
Somali Basin sea feature Indian Ocean 149 L6
Somali Republic country Africa see Somalia
Sombo Angola 99 C4
Sombor Serb. and Mont. 59 H2
Sombrero Channel India 71 A6
Sombrio, Lago do l. Brazil 145 A5
Somero Fin. 45 M6
Somerset KY U.S.A. 134 C5
Somerset MI U.S.A. 134 C2
Somerset OH U.S.A. 134 D4
Somerset PA U.S.A. 134 F4
Somerset, Lake Australia 112 F1
Somerset East S. Africa 101 G7
Somerset Island Canada 119 I2
Somerset Reservoir U.S.A. 135 I2
Somerset West S. Africa 100 D8
Somersworth U.S.A. 135 J2
Somerton U.S.A. 129 F5
Somerville NJ U.S.A. 135 H3
Somerville TN U.S.A. 131 F5
Someydeh Iran 88 B3
Somme r. France 52 B4
Sommen l. Sweden 45 I7
Sömmerda Germany 53 L3
Sommet, Lac du l. Canada 123 H3
Somnath India 82 B5
Somutu Myanmar 70 B1
Son r. India 83 F4
Sonag China see Zêkog
Sonapur India 84 D1
Sonar r. India 82 D4
Sŏnch'ŏn N. Korea 75 B5
Sønderborg Denmark 45 F9
Sondershausen Germany 53 K3
Søndre Strømfjord Greenland see Kangerlussuaq
Søndre Strømfjord inlet Greenland see Kangerlussuaq
Sondrio Italy 58 C1
Sonepat India see Sonipat
Sonepur India see Sonapur
Songbai China see Shennongjia
Songbu China 77 G2
Sông Cau Vietnam 71 E4
Songcheng China see Xiapu
Sông Da, Hô resr Vietnam 70 D2
Songea Tanz. 99 D5
Songhua Hu resr China 74 B4
Songhua Jiang r. Heilongjiang/Jilin China 74 D3
Songhua Jiang r. Jilin China see Di'er Songhua Jiang
Songjiang China 77 I2
Songjianghe China 74 B4
Sŏngjin N. Korea see Kimch'aek
Songkan China 76 E2
Songkhla Thai. 71 C6
Songling China see Ta'erqi
Songlong Myanmar 70 B2
Sŏngnam S. Korea 75 B5
Songnim N. Korea 75 B5
Songo Angola 99 B4
Songo Moz. 99 D5
Songpan China 76 D1
Songshan China see Ziyun
Song Shan mt. China 77 G1
Songtao China 77 F2
Songxi China 77 H3
Songxian China 77 G1
Songyuan Fujian China see Songxi
Songyuan Jilin China 74 B3
Songzi China 77 F2
Sonid Youqi China see Saihan Tal
Sonid Zuoqi China see Mandalt
Sonipat India 82 D3
Sonkajärvi Fin. 44 O5
Sonkovo Rus. Fed. 42 H4
Sơn La Vietnam 70 C2
Sonmiani Pak. 89 G5
Sonmiani Bay Pak. 89 G5
Sonneberg Germany 53 L4
Sono r. Minas Gerais Brazil 145 B2
Sono r. Tocantins Brazil 143 I5
Sonoma U.S.A. 128 B2
Sonoma Peak U.S.A. 128 E1
Sonora r. Mex. 127 F7
Sonora state Mex. 127 F7
Sonora CA U.S.A. 128 C3
Sonora KY U.S.A. 134 C5
Sonora TX U.S.A. 131 C6
Sonoran Desert U.S.A. 129 G5
Sonoran Desert National Monument nat. park U.S.A. 127 E6
Sonqor Iran 88 B3
Sonsonate El Salvador 136 G6
Sonsorol Islands Palau 69 I5
Sơn Tây Vietnam 70 D2
Sonwabile S. Africa 101 I6
Soochow China see Suzhou
Soomaaliya country Africa see Somalia
Sopi, Tanjung pt Indon. 69 H6
Sopo watercourse Sudan 97 F4
Sopot Bulg. 59 K3
Sopot Poland 47 Q3
Sop Prap Thai. 70 B3
Sopron Hungary 58 G1
Sopur Jammu and Kashmir 82 C2
Sora Italy 58 E4
Sorab India 84 B3
Sorada India 84 E2
Söråker Sweden 44 J5
Sŏrak-san mt. S. Korea 75 C5
Sorak-san National Park S. Korea 75 C5
Sorel Canada 123 G5
Soreq r. Israel 85 B4
Sorgun Turkey 90 D3
Sorgun r. Turkey 85 B1
Soria Spain 57 E3
Sorkh, Kūh-e mts Iran 88 D3
Sorkhān Iran 88 E4
Sorkheh Iran 88 D3
Sørli Norway 44 H4
Soro India 83 F5
Soroca Moldova 43 F6
Sorocaba Brazil 145 B3
Soroki Moldova see Soroca
Sorol atoll Micronesia 69 K5
Sorong Indon. 69 I7
Soroti Uganda 98 D3
Sørøya i. Norway 44 M1
Sorraia r. Port. 57 B4
Sørreisa Norway 44 K2
Sorrento Italy 58 F4
Sorsele Sweden 44 J4
Sorsogon Phil. 69 G4
Sortavala Rus. Fed. 44 Q6
Sortland Norway 44 I2
Sortopolovskaya Rus. Fed. 42 K3
Sorvizhi Rus. Fed. 42 K4
Sŏsan S. Korea 75 B5
Sosenskiy Rus. Fed. 43 G5
Soshanguve S. Africa 101 I3
Sosna r. Rus. Fed. 43 H5
Sosneado mt. Arg. 144 C4
Sosnogorsk Rus. Fed. 42 L3
Sosnovka Arkhangel'skaya Oblast' Rus. Fed. 42 J3
Sosnovka Kaliningradskaya Oblast' Rus. Fed. 41 K5
Sosnovka Murmanskaya Oblast' Rus. Fed. 42 I2
Sosnovka Tambovskaya Oblast' Rus. Fed. 43 I5
Sosnovo Rus. Fed. 45 Q6
Sosnovo-Ozerskoye Rus. Fed. 73 K2
Sosnovyy Rus. Fed. 44 R4
Sosnovyy Bor Rus. Fed. 45 P7
Sosnowiec Poland 47 Q5
Sosnowitz Poland see Sosnowiec
Sos'va Khanty-Mansiyskiy Avtonomnyy Okrug Rus. Fed. 41 S3
Sos'va Sverdlovskaya Oblast' Rus. Fed. 41 S4
Sotang China 76 B2
Sotara, Volcán vol. Col. 142 C3
Sotkamo Fin. 44 P4
Sotteville-lès-Rouen France 52 B5
Souanké Congo 98 B3
Soubré Côte d'Ivoire 96 C4
Souderton U.S.A. 135 H3
Soufflenheim France 53 H6
Soufli Greece 59 L4
Soufrière St Lucia 137 L6
Soufrière vol. St Vincent 137 L6
Sougueur Alg. 57 G6
Souillac France 56 E4
Souilly France 52 F5
Souk Ahras Alg. 58 B6
Souk el Arbaâ du Rharb Morocco 54 C5
Sŏul S. Korea see Seoul
Soulac-sur-Mer France 56 D4
Soulom France 56 D5
Sounding Creek r. Canada 121 I4
Souni Cyprus 85 A2
Soûr Lebanon see Tyre
Soure Brazil 143 I4
Sour el Ghozlane Alg. 57 H5
Souris Canada 121 K5
Souris r. Canada 121 L5
Souriya country Asia see Syria
Sousa Brazil 143 K5
Sousa Lara Angola see Bocoio
Sousse Tunisia 58 D7
Soustons France 56 D5

▶South Africa, Republic of country Africa 100 F5
5th most populous country in Africa.
Africa 7, 94–95

Southampton Canada 134 E1
Southampton U.K. 49 F8
Southampton U.S.A. 135 I3
Southampton, Cape Canada 119 J3
Southampton Island Canada 119 J3
South Andaman i. India 71 A5
South Anna r. U.S.A. 135 G5
South Anston U.K. 48 F5
South Aulatsivik Island Canada 123 J2
South Australia state Australia 106 D5
South Australian Basin sea feature Indian Ocean 149 P8
Southaven U.S.A. 131 F5
South Baldy mt. U.S.A. 127 G6
South Bank U.K. 48 F4
South Bass Island U.S.A. 134 D3
South Bend IN U.S.A. 134 B3
South Bend WA U.S.A. 126 C3
South Bluff pt Bahamas 133 F8
South Boston U.S.A. 135 F5
South Brook Canada 123 K4
South Cape pt U.S.A. see Ka Lae
South Carolina state U.S.A. 133 D5
South Charleston OH U.S.A. 134 D4
South Charleston WV U.S.A. 134 E4
South China Sea N. Pacific Ocean 68 F4
South Coast Town Australia see Gold Coast
South Dakota state U.S.A. 130 C2
South Downs hills U.K. 49 G8
South-East admin. dist. Botswana 101 G3
South East Cape Australia 111 [inset]
Southeast Cape U.S.A. 118 B3
Southeast Indian Ridge sea feature Indian Ocean 149 N8
South East Isles Australia 109 C8
Southeast Pacific Basin sea feature S. Pacific Ocean 151 M10
South East Point Australia 112 C7
Southend Canada 121 K3
Southend U.K. 50 D5
Southend-on-Sea U.K. 49 H7
Southern admin. dist. Botswana 100 G3
Southern Alps mts N.Z. 113 C6
Southern Cross Australia 109 B7
Southern Indian Lake Canada 121 L3
Southern Lau Group is Fiji 107 I3
Southern National Park Sudan 97 F4
Southern Ocean 152 C2
Southern Pines U.S.A. 133 E5
Southern Rhodesia country Africa see Zimbabwe
Southern Uplands hills U.K. 50 E5
South Esk r. U.K. 50 F4
South Esk Tableland reg. Australia 108 D4
Southey Canada 121 J5
Southfield U.S.A. 134 D2
South Fiji Basin sea feature S. Pacific Ocean 150 H7
South Fork U.S.A. 128 B1
South Geomagnetic Pole (2004) Antarctica 152 F1
South Georgia i. S. Atlantic Ocean 144 I8

▶South Georgia and South Sandwich Islands terr. S. Atlantic Ocean 144 I8
United Kingdom Overseas Territory.

South Harris pen. U.K. 50 B3
South Haven U.S.A. 134 B2
South Henik Lake Canada 121 L2
South Hill U.S.A. 135 F5
South Honshu Ridge sea feature N. Pacific Ocean 150 F3
South Indian Lake Canada 121 L3
South Island India 84 B4

▶South Island N.Z. 113 D7
2nd largest island in Oceania.

South Junction Canada 121 M5
▶South Korea country Asia 75 B5
Asia 6, 62–63
South Lake Tahoe U.S.A. 128 C2
South Luangwa National Park Zambia 99 D5
South Magnetic Pole (2004) Antarctica 152 G2
South Mills U.S.A. 135 G5
Southminster U.K. 49 H7
South Mountains hills U.S.A. 135 G4
South New Berlin U.S.A. 135 H2
South Orkney Islands S. Atlantic Ocean 148 F10
South Paris U.S.A. 135 J1
South Platte r. U.S.A. 130 C3
South Point Bahamas 133 F8
South Pole Antarctica 152 C1
Southport Qld Australia 112 F1
Southport Tas. Australia 111 [inset]
Southport U.K. 48 D5
Southport U.S.A. 135 G2
South Portland U.S.A. 135 J2
South Ronaldsay i. U.K. 50 G2
South Royalton U.S.A. 135 I2
South Salt Lake U.S.A. 129 H1
South Sand Bluff pt S. Africa 101 J6
South Sandwich Islands S. Atlantic Ocean 148 G9
South Sandwich Trench sea feature S. Atlantic Ocean 148 G9
South San Francisco U.S.A. 128 B3
South Saskatchewan r. Canada 121 J4
South Seal r. Canada 121 L3
South Shetland Islands Antarctica 152 A2
South Shetland Trough sea feature S. Atlantic Ocean 152 L2
South Shields U.K. 48 F3
South Sinai governorate Egypt see Janūb Sīnā'
South Solomon Trench sea feature S. Pacific Ocean 150 G6
South Taranaki Bight b. N.Z. 113 E4
South Tasman Rise sea feature Southern Ocean 150 F9
South Tent mt. U.S.A. 129 H2
South Tons r. India 83 E4
South Twin Island Canada 122 F3
South Tyne r. U.K. 48 E4
South Uist i. U.K. 50 B3
South Wellesley Islands Australia 110 B3
South-West Africa country Africa see Namibia
South West Cape N.Z. 113 A8
South West Entrance sea chan. P.N.G. 110 E1
Southwest Indian Ridge sea feature Indian Ocean 149 K8
South West National Park Australia 111 [inset]
Southwest Pacific Basin sea feature S. Pacific Ocean 150 I8
Southwest Peru Ridge sea feature S. Pacific Ocean see Nazca Ridge
South West Rocks Australia 112 F3
South Whitley U.S.A. 134 C3
South Wichita r. U.S.A. 131 D5
South Windham U.S.A. 135 J2
Southwold U.K. 49 I6
Southwood National Park Australia 112 E1
Soutpansberg mts S. Africa 101 I2
Souttouf, Adrar mts W. Sahara 96 B2
Soverato Italy 58 G5
Sovetsk Kaliningradskaya Oblast' Rus. Fed. 45 L9
Sovetsk Kirovskaya Oblast' Rus. Fed. 42 K4
Sovetskaya Gavan' Rus. Fed. 74 F2
Sovetskiy Khanty-Mansiyskiy Avtonomnyy Okrug Rus. Fed. 41 S3
Sovetskiy Leningradskaya Oblast' Rus. Fed. 45 P6
Sovetskiy Respublika Mariy El Rus. Fed. 42 K4
Sovetskoye Chechenskaya Respublika Rus. Fed. see Shatoy
Sovetskoye Stavropol'skiy Kray Rus. Fed. see Zelenokumsk
Sovyets'kyy Ukr. 90 D1
Sowa China 76 C2
Soweto S. Africa 101 H4
Sōya-kaikyō strait Japan/Rus. Fed. see La Pérouse Strait
Sōya-misaki c. Japan 74 F3
Soyana r. Rus. Fed. 42 I2
Soyma r. Rus. Fed. 42 K2
Soyopa Mex. 127 F7
Sozh r. Europe 43 F6
Sozopol Bulg. 59 L3
Spa Belgium 52 F4

▶Spain country Europe 57 E3
4th largest country in Europe.
Europe 5, 38–39

Spalato Croatia see Split
Spalatum Croatia see Split
Spalding U.K. 49 G6
Spanish Canada 122 E5
Spanish Fork U.S.A. 129 H1
Spanish Guinea country Africa see Equatorial Guinea
Spanish Netherlands country Europe see Belgium
Spanish Sahara terr. Africa see Western Sahara
Spanish Town Jamaica 137 I5
Sparks U.S.A. 128 D2
Sparta Greece see Sparti
Sparta GA U.S.A. 133 D5
Sparta KY U.S.A. 134 C4
Sparta MI U.S.A. 134 C2
Sparta NC U.S.A. 134 E5
Sparta TN U.S.A. 132 C5
Spartanburg U.S.A. 133 D5
Sparti Greece 59 J6
Spartivento, Capo c. Italy 58 G6
Spas-Demensk Rus. Fed. 43 G5
Spas-Klepiki Rus. Fed. 43 I5
Spassk-Dal'niy Rus. Fed. 74 D3
Spassk-Ryazanskiy Rus. Fed. 43 I5
Spata (Eleftherios Venezielos) airport Greece 59 J6
Spatha, Akra pt Greece 59 J7
Spearman U.S.A. 131 C4
Speedway U.S.A. 134 B4
Spence Bay Canada see Taloyoak
Spencer IA U.S.A. 130 E3
Spencer ID U.S.A. 126 E3
Spencer IN U.S.A. 134 B4
Spencer NE U.S.A. 130 D3
Spencer WV U.S.A. 134 E4
Spencer, Cape U.S.A. 120 B3
Spencer Bay Namibia 100 B3
Spencer Gulf est. Australia 111 B7
Spencer Range hills Australia 108 E3
Spennymoor U.K. 48 F4
Sperrin Mountains hills U.K. 51 E3
Sperryville U.S.A. 135 F4
Spessart reg. Germany 53 J5
Spétsai i. Greece see Spetses
Spetses i. Greece 59 J6
Spey r. U.K. 50 F3
Speyer Germany 53 I5
Spezand Pak. 89 G4
Spice Islands Indon. see Moluccas
Spijk Neth. 52 G1
Spijkenisse Neth. 52 E3
Spilimbergo Italy 58 E1
Spilsby U.K. 48 H5
Spīn Būldak Afgh. 89 G4
Spintangi Pak. 89 H4
Spirit Lake U.S.A. 130 E3
Spirit River Canada 120 G4
Spirovo Rus. Fed. 42 G4
Spišská Nová Ves Slovakia 43 D6
Spiti r. India 82 D3

▶Spitsbergen i. Svalbard 64 C2
5th largest island in Europe.

Spittal an der Drau Austria 47 N7
Spitzbergen i. Svalbard see Spitsbergen
Split Croatia 58 G3
Split Lake Canada 121 L3

Split Lake *l.* Canada **121** L3
Spokane U.S.A. **126** D3
Spoletium Italy *see* **Spoleto**
Spoleto Italy **58** E3
Spóng Cambodia **71** D4
Spoon *r.* U.S.A. **130** F3
Spooner U.S.A. **130** F2
Spornitz Germany **53** L1
Spotsylvania U.S.A. **135** G4
Spotted Horse U.S.A. **126** G3
Spranger, Mount Canada **120** F4
Spratly Islands S. China Sea **68** E4
Spray U.S.A. **126** D3
Spree *r.* Germany **47** N4
Sprimont Belgium **52** F4
Springbok S. Africa **100** C5
Springdale Canada **123** L4
Springdale U.S.A. **134** C4
Springe Germany **53** J2
Springer U.S.A. **127** G5
Springerville U.S.A. **129** I4
Springfield *CO* U.S.A. **130** C4

▶**Springfield** *IL* U.S.A. **130** F4
State capital of Illinois.

Springfield *KY* U.S.A. **134** C5
Springfield *MA* U.S.A. **135** I2
Springfield *MO* U.S.A. **131** E4
Springfield *OH* U.S.A. **134** D4
Springfield *OR* U.S.A. **126** C3
Springfield *TN* U.S.A. **134** B5
Springfield *VT* U.S.A. **135** I2
Springfield *WV* U.S.A. **135** F4
Springfontein S. Africa **101** G6
Spring Glen U.S.A. **129** H2
Spring Grove U.S.A. **134** A2
Springhill Canada **123** I5
Spring Hill U.S.A. **133** D6
Springhouse Canada **120** F5
Spring Mountains U.S.A. **129** F3
Springs Junction N.Z. **113** D6
Springsure Australia **110** E5
Spring Valley *MN* U.S.A. **130** E3
Spring Valley *NY* U.S.A. **135** H3
Springview U.S.A. **130** D3
Springville *CA* U.S.A. **128** D3
Springville *NY* U.S.A. **135** F2
Springville *PA* U.S.A. **135** H3
Springville *UT* U.S.A. **129** H1
Sprowston U.K. **49** I6
Spruce Grove Canada **120** H4
Spruce Knob *mt.* U.S.A. **132** E4
Spruce Mountain *CO* U.S.A. **129** I2
Spruce Mountain *NV* U.S.A. **129** F1
Spurn Head *hd* U.K. **48** H5
Spuzzum Canada **120** F5
Squam Lake U.S.A. **135** J2
Square Lake U.S.A. **123** H5
Squillace, Golfo di *g.* Italy **58** G5
Squires, Mount *hill* Australia **109** D6
Srbija *aut. rep.* Serb. and Mont. **59** I3
Srbinje Bos.-Herz. *see* **Foča**
Srê Âmbĕl Cambodia **71** C5
Srebrenica Bos.-Herz. **58** H2
Sredets *Burgas* Bulg. **59** L3
Sredets *Sofiya-Grad* Bulg. *see* **Sofia**
Sredinnyy Khrebet *mts* Rus. Fed. **65** Q4
Sredna Gora *mts* Bulg. **59** J3
Srednekolymsk Rus. Fed. **65** Q3
Sredne-Russkaya Vozvyshennost' *hills* Rus. Fed. *see* **Central Russian Upland**
Sredne-Sibirskoye Ploskogor'ye *plat.* Rus. Fed. *see* **Central Siberian Plateau**
Sredneye Kuyto, Ozero *l.* Rus. Fed. **44** Q4
Sredniy Ural *mts* Rus. Fed. **41** R4
Srednogorie Bulg. **59** K3
Srednyaya Akhtuba Rus. Fed. **43** J6
Sreepur Bangl. *see* **Sripur**
Sre Khtum Cambodia **71** D4
Srê Noy Cambodia **71** D4
Sretensk Rus. Fed. **73** L2
Sri Aman *Sarawak* Malaysia **68** E6
Sriharikota Island India **84** D3

▶**Sri Jayewardenepura Kotte** Sri Lanka **84** C5
Capital of Sri Lanka.

Srikakulam India **84** E2
Sri Kalahasti India **84** C3
▶**Sri Lanka** *country* Asia **84** D5
Asia **6, 62–63**
Srinagar India **82** C2
Sri Pada *mt.* Sri Lanka *see* **Adam's Peak**
Sripur Bangl. **83** G4
Srirangam India **84** C4
Sri Thep *tourist site* Thai. **70** C3
Srivardhan India **84** B2
Staaten *r.* Australia **110** C3
Staaten River National Park Australia **110** C3
Stabroek Guyana *see* **Georgetown**
Stade Germany **53** J1
Staden Belgium **52** D4
Stadskanaal Neth. **52** G2
Stadtallendorf Germany **53** J4
Stadthagen Germany **53** J2
Stadtilm Germany **53** L4
Stadtlohn Germany **52** G3
Stadtoldendorf Germany **53** J3
Stadtroda Germany **53** L4
Staffa *i.* U.K. **50** C4
Staffelberg *hill* Germany **53** L4
Staffelstein Germany **53** K4
Stafford U.K. **49** E6
Stafford U.S.A. **135** G4
Stafford Creek Bahamas **133** E7
Stafford Springs U.S.A. **135** I3
Stagg Lake Canada **120** H2
Staicele Latvia **45** N8
Staines U.K. **49** G7
Stakhanov Ukr. **43** H6
Stakhanovo Rus. Fed. *see* **Zhukovskiy**
Stalbridge U.K. **49** E8
Stalham U.K. **49** I6
Stalin Bulg. *see* **Varna**
Stalinabad Tajik. *see* **Dushanbe**
Stalingrad Rus. Fed. *see* **Volgograd**
Staliniri Georgia *see* **Ts'khinvali**
Stalino Ukr. *see* **Donets'k**
Stalinogorsk Rus. Fed. *see* **Novomoskovsk**
Stalinogród Poland *see* **Katowice**
Stalinsk Rus. Fed. *see* **Novokuznetsk**
Stalowa Wola Poland **43** D6
Stamboliyski Bulg. **59** K3
Stamford Australia **110** C4
Stamford U.K. **49** G6
Stamford *CT* U.S.A. **135** I3
Stamford *NY* U.S.A. **135** H2
Stampalia *i.* Greece *see* **Astypalaia**
Stampriet Namibia **100** D3
Stamsund Norway **44** H2
Stanardsville U.S.A. **135** F4
Stanberry U.S.A. **130** E3
Stancomb-Wills Glacier Antarctica **152** B1
Standard Canada **120** H5
Standdaarbuiten Neth. **52** E3
Standerton S. Africa **101** I4
Standish U.S.A. **134** D2
Stanfield U.S.A. **129** H5
Stanford *KY* U.S.A. **134** C5
Stanford *MT* U.S.A. **126** F3
Stanger S. Africa **101** J5
Stanislaus *r.* U.S.A. **128** C3
Stanislav Ukr. *see* **Ivano-Frankivs'k**
Stanke Dimitrov Bulg. *see* **Dupnitsa**
Staňkov Czech Rep. **53** N5
Stanley Australia **111** [inset]
Stanley *Hong Kong* China **77** [inset]

▶**Stanley** Falkland Is **144** E8
Capital of the Falkland Islands.

Stanley U.K. **48** F4
Stanley *ID* U.S.A. **126** E3
Stanley *KY* U.S.A. **134** B5
Stanley *ND* U.S.A. **130** C1
Stanley *VA* U.S.A. **135** F4
Stanley, Mount *hill N.T.* Australia **108** E5
Stanley, Mount *hill Tas.* Australia **111** [inset]
Stanley, Mount Dem. Rep. Congo/Uganda *see* **Margherita Peak**
Stanleyville Dem. Rep. Congo *see* **Kisangani**
Stann Creek Belize *see* **Dangriga**
Stannington U.K. **48** F3
Stanovoye Rus. Fed. **43** H5
Stanovoye Nagor'ye *mts* Rus. Fed. **73** L1
Stanovoy Khrebet *mts* Rus. Fed. **65** N4
Stansmore Range *hills* Australia **108** E5
Stanthorpe Australia **112** E2
Stanton U.K. **49** H6
Stanton *KY* U.S.A. **134** D5
Stanton *MI* U.S.A. **134** C2
Stanton *ND* U.S.A. **130** C2
Stanton *TX* U.S.A. **131** C5
Stapleton U.S.A. **130** C3
Starachowice Poland **47** R5
Stara Planina *mts* Bulg./Serb. and Mont. *see* **Balkan Mountains**
Staraya Russa Rus. Fed. **42** F4
Stara Zagora Bulg. **59** K3
Starbuck Island Kiribati **151** J6
Star City U.S.A. **134** B3
Starcke National Park Australia **110** D2
Stargard in Pommern Poland *see* **Stargard Szczeciński**
Stargard Szczeciński Poland **47** O4
Staritsa Rus. Fed. **42** G4
Starke U.S.A. **133** D6
Starkville U.S.A. **131** F5
Star Lake U.S.A. **135** H1
Starnberger See *l.* Germany **47** M7
Starobel'sk Ukr. *see* **Starobil's'k**
Starobil's'k Ukr. **43** H6
Starogard Gdański Poland **47** Q4
Starokonstantinov Ukr. *see* **Starokostyantyniv**
Starokostyantyniv Ukr. **43** E6
Starominskaya Rus. Fed. **43** H7
Staroshcherbinovskaya Rus. Fed. **43** H7
Star Peak U.S.A. **128** D1
Start Point U.K. **49** D8
Starve Island Kiribati *see* **Starbuck Island**
Staryya Darohi Belarus **43** F5
Staryye Dorogi Belarus *see* **Staryya Darohi**
Staryy Kayak Rus. Fed. **65** L2
Staryy Oskol Rus. Fed. **43** H6
Staßfurt Germany **53** L3
State College U.S.A. **135** G3
State Line U.S.A. **131** F6
Staten Island Arg. *see* **Los Estados, Isla de**
Statenville U.S.A. **133** D6
Statesboro U.S.A. **133** D5
Statesville U.S.A. **132** D5
Statia *i.* Neth. Antilles *see* **Sint Eustatius**
Station U.S.A. **134** C4
Station Nord Greenland **153** I1
Stauchitz Germany **53** N3
Staufenberg Germany **53** I4
Staunton U.S.A. **134** F4
Stavanger Norway **45** D7
Staveley U.K. **48** F5
Stavropol' Rus. Fed. **91** F1
Stavropol' Kray *admin. div.* Rus. Fed. *see* **Stavropol'skiy Kray**
Stavropol'-na-Volge Rus. Fed. *see* **Tol'yatti**
Stavropol'skaya Vozvyshennost' *hills* Rus. Fed. **91** F1
Stavropol'skiy Kray *admin. div.* Rus. Fed. **91** F1
Stayner Canada **134** E1
Stayton U.S.A. **126** C3
Steadville S. Africa **101** I5
Steamboat Springs U.S.A. **126** G4
Stearns U.S.A. **134** C5
Stebbins U.S.A. **118** B3
Steele Island Antarctica **152** L2
Steelville U.S.A. **130** F4
Steen *r.* Canada **120** G3
Steenderen Neth. **52** G2
Steenkampsberge *mts* S. Africa **101** J3
Steen River Canada **120** G3
Steens Mountain U.S.A. **126** D4
Steenstrup Gletscher *glacier* Greenland *see* **Sermersuaq**
Steenvoorde France **52** C4
Steenwijk Neth. **52** G2
Stefansson Island Canada **119** H2
Stegi Swaziland *see* **Siteki**
Steigerwald *mts* Germany **53** K5
Stein Germany **53** L5
Steinach Germany **53** L4
Steinaker Reservoir U.S.A. **129** I1
Steinbach Canada **121** L5
Steinfeld (Oldenburg) Germany **53** I2
Steinfurt Germany **53** H2
Steinhausen Namibia **99** B6
Steinheim Germany **53** J3
Steinkjer Norway **44** G4
Steinkopf S. Africa **100** C5
Steinsdalen Norway **44** G4
Stella S. Africa **100** G4
Stella Maris Bahamas **133** F8
Stellenbosch S. Africa **100** D7
Stello, Monte *mt. Corsica* France **56** I5
Stelvio, Parco Nazionale dello *nat. park* Italy **58** D1
Stenay France **52** F5
Stendal Germany **53** L2
Stenhousemuir U.K. **50** F4
Stenungsund Sweden **45** G7
Steornabhagh U.K. *see* **Stornoway**
Stepanakert Azer. *see* **Xankändi**
Stephens, Cape N.Z. **113** D5
Stephens City U.S.A. **135** F4
Stephens Lake Canada **121** M3
Stephenville U.S.A. **131** D5
Stepnoy Rus. Fed. *see* **Elista**
Stepnoye Rus. Fed. **43** J6
Sterkfontein Dam *resr* S. Africa **101** I5
Sterkstroom S. Africa **101** H6
Sterlet Lake Canada **121** I1
Sterlibashevo Rus. Fed. **41** R5
Sterling S. Africa **100** E6
Sterling *CO* U.S.A. **130** C3
Sterling *IL* U.S.A. **130** F3
Sterling *MI* U.S.A. **134** C1
Sterling *UT* U.S.A. **129** H2
Sterling City U.S.A. **131** C6
Sterling Heights U.S.A. **134** D2
Sterlitamak Rus. Fed. **64** G4
Stettin Poland *see* **Szczecin**
Stettler Canada **121** H4
Steubenville *KY* U.S.A. **134** C5
Steubenville *OH* U.S.A. **134** E3
Stevenage U.K. **49** G7
Stevenson U.S.A. **126** C3
Stevenson Lake Canada **121** L4
Stevens Point U.S.A. **130** F2
Stevens Village U.S.A. **118** D3
Stevensville *MI* U.S.A. **134** B2
Stevensville *PA* U.S.A. **135** G3
Stewart Canada **120** D4
Stewart *r.* Canada **120** B2
Stewart, Isla *i.* Chile **144** B8
Stewart Crossing Canada **120** B2
Stewart Island N.Z. **113** A8
Stewart Islands Solomon Is **107** G2
Stewart Lake Canada **119** J3
Stewarton U.K. **50** E5
Stewarts Point U.S.A. **128** B2
Stewiacke Canada **123** J5
Steynsburg S. Africa **101** G6
Steyr Austria **47** O6
Steytlerville S. Africa **100** G7
Stiens Neth. **52** F1
Stif Alg. *see* **Sétif**
Stigler U.S.A. **131** E5
Stikine *r.* Canada **120** C3
Stikine Plateau Canada **120** D3
Stikine Strait U.S.A. **120** C3
Stilbaai S. Africa **100** E8
Stiles U.S.A. **134** A1
Stillwater *MN* U.S.A. **130** E2
Stillwater *OK* U.S.A. **131** D4
Stillwater Range *mts* U.S.A. **128** D2
Stillwell U.S.A. **134** B3
Stilton U.K. **49** G6
Stilwell U.S.A. **131** E5
Stinnett U.S.A. **131** C5
Štip Macedonia **59** J4
Stirling Australia **108** F5
Stirling Canada **135** G1
Stirling U.K. **50** F4
Stirling Creek *r.* Australia **108** E4
Stirling Range National Park Australia **109** B8
Stittsville Canada **135** H1
Stjørdalshalsen Norway **44** G5
Stockbridge U.S.A. **134** C2
Stockerau Austria **47** P6
Stockheim Germany **53** L4

▶**Stockholm** Sweden **45** K7
Capital of Sweden.

Stockinbingal Australia **112** C5
Stockport U.K. **48** E5
Stockton *CA* U.S.A. **128** C3
Stockton *KS* U.S.A. **130** D4
Stockton *MO* U.S.A. **130** E4
Stockton *UT* U.S.A. **129** G1
Stockton Lake U.S.A. **130** E4
Stockton-on-Tees U.K. **48** F4
Stockville U.S.A. **130** C3
Stod Czech Rep. **53** N5
Stœng Trêng Cambodia **71** D4
Stoer, Point of U.K. **50** D2
Stoke-on-Trent U.K. **49** E5
Stokesley U.K. **48** F4
Stokes Point Australia **111** [inset]
Stokes Range *hills* Australia **108** E4
Stokkseyri Iceland **44** [inset]
Stokkvågen Norway **44** H3
Stokmarknes Norway **44** I2
Stolac Bos.-Herz. **58** G3
Stolberg (Rheinland) Germany **52** G4
Stolbovoy Rus. Fed. **153** G2
Stolbtsy Belarus *see* **Stowbtsy**
Stolin Belarus **45** O11
Stollberg Germany **53** M4
Stolp Poland *see* **Słupsk**
Stolzenau Germany **53** J2
Stone U.K. **49** E6
Stoneboro U.S.A. **134** E3
Stonecliffe Canada **122** F5
Stonecutters' Island *pen. Hong Kong* China **77** [inset]
Stonehaven U.K. **50** G4
Stonehenge Australia **110** C5
Stonehenge *tourist site* U.K. **49** F7
Stoner U.S.A. **129** I3
Stonewall Canada **121** L5
Stonewall Jackson Lake U.S.A. **134** E4
Stony Creek U.S.A. **135** G5
Stony Lake Canada **121** L3
Stony Point U.S.A. **135** G2
Stony Rapids Canada **121** J3
Stony River U.S.A. **118** C3
Stooping *r.* Canada **122** E3
Stora Lulevatten *l.* Sweden **44** K3
Stora Sjöfallets nationalpark *nat. park* Sweden **44** J3
Storavan *l.* Sweden **44** K4
Store Bælt *sea chan.* Denmark *see* **Great Belt**
Støren Norway **44** G5
Storfjordbotn Norway **44** O1
Storforshei Norway **44** I3
Storjord Norway **44** I3
Storkerson Peninsula Canada **119** H2
Storm Bay Australia **111** [inset]
Stormberg S. Africa **101** H6
Storm Lake U.S.A. **130** E3
Stornosa *mt.* Norway **44** E6
Stornoway U.K. **50** C2
Storozhevsk Rus. Fed. **42** L3
Storozhynets' Ukr. **43** E6
Storrs U.S.A. **135** I3
Storseleby Sweden **44** J4
Storsjön *l.* Sweden **44** I5
Storskrymten *mt.* Norway **44** F5
Storslett Norway **44** L2
Stortemelk *sea chan.* Neth. **52** F1
Storuman Sweden **44** J4
Storuman *l.* Sweden **44** J4
Storvik Sweden **45** J6
Storvorde Denmark **45** G8
Storvreta Sweden **45** J7
Story U.S.A. **126** G3
Stotfold U.K. **49** G6
Stoughton Canada **121** K5
Stour *r. England* U.K. **49** F6
Stour *r. England* U.K. **49** F8
Stour *r. England* U.K. **49** I7
Stour *r. England* U.K. **49** I7
Stourbridge U.K. **49** E6
Stourport-on-Severn U.K. **49** E6
Stout Lake Canada **121** M4
Stowbtsy Belarus **45** O10
Stowe U.S.A. **135** I1
Stowmarket U.K. **49** H6
Stoyba Rus. Fed. **74** C1
Strabane U.K. **51** E3
Stradbally Rep. of Ireland **51** E4
Stradbroke U.K. **49** I6
Stradella Italy **58** C2
Strakonice Czech Rep. **47** N6
Stralsund Germany **47** N3
Strand S. Africa **100** D8
Stranda Norway **44** E5
Strangford U.K. **51** G3
Strangford Lough *inlet* U.K. **51** G3
Strangways *r.* Australia **108** F3
Stranraer U.K. **50** D6
Strasbourg France **56** H2
Strasburg Germany **53** N1
Strasburg U.S.A. **135** F4
Strassburg France *see* **Strasbourg**
Stratford Australia **112** C6
Stratford Canada **134** E2
Stratford *CA* U.S.A. **128** D3
Stratford *TX* U.S.A. **131** C4
Stratford-upon-Avon U.K. **49** F6
Strathaven U.K. **50** E5
Strathmore Canada **120** H5
Strathmore *r.* U.K. **50** E2
Strathnaver Canada **120** F4
Strathroy Canada **134** E2
Strathspey *valley* U.K. **50** F3
Strathy U.K. **50** F2
Stratton U.K. **49** C8
Stratton U.S.A. **135** J1
Stratton Mountain U.S.A. **135** I2
Straubing Germany **53** M6
Straumnes *pt* Iceland **44** [inset]
Strawberry U.S.A. **129** H4
Strawberry Mountain U.S.A. **126** D3
Strawberry Reservoir U.S.A. **129** H1
Streaky Bay Australia **109** F8
Streaky Bay *b.* Australia **109** F8
Streator U.S.A. **130** F3
Street U.K. **49** E7
Streetsboro U.S.A. **134** E3
Strehaia Romania **59** J2
Strehla Germany **53** N3
Streich Mound *hill* Australia **109** C7
Strelka Rus. Fed. **65** Q3
Strel'na *r.* Rus. Fed. **42** H2
Strenči Latvia **45** N8
Streymoy *i.* Faroe Is **44** [inset]
Stříbro Czech Rep. **53** M5
Strichen U.K. **50** G3
Strimonas *r.* Greece **59** J4
also known as Struma (Bulgaria)
Stroeder Arg. **144** D6
Strokestown Rep. of Ireland **51** D4
Stroma, Island of U.K. **50** F2
Stromboli, Isola *i.* Italy **58** F5
Stromness S. Georgia **144** I8
Stromness U.K. **50** F2
Strömstad Sweden **45** G7
Strömsund Sweden **44** I5
Strongsville U.S.A. **134** E3
Stronsay *i.* U.K. **50** G1
Stroud Australia **112** E4
Stroud U.K. **49** E7
Stroud Road Australia **112** E4
Stroudsburg U.S.A. **135** H3
Struer Denmark **45** F8
Struga Macedonia **59** I4
Strugi-Krasnyye Rus. Fed. **45** P7
Struis Bay S. Africa **100** E8
Strullendorf Germany **53** K5
Struma *r.* Bulg. **59** J4
also known as Strimonas (Greece)
Strumble Head *hd* U.K. **49** B6
Strumica Macedonia **59** J4
Struthers U.S.A. **134** E3
Stryama *r.* Bulg. **59** K3
Strydenburg S. Africa **100** F5
Stryn Norway **44** E6
Stryy Ukr. **43** D6
Strzelecki, Mount *hill* Australia **108** F5
Strzelecki Regional Reserve *nature res.* Australia **111** B6
Stuart *FL* U.S.A. **133** D7
Stuart *NE* U.S.A. **130** D3
Stuart *VA* U.S.A. **134** E5
Stuart Lake Canada **120** E4
Stuart Range *hills* Australia **111** A6
Stuarts Draft U.S.A. **134** F4
Stuart Town Australia **112** D4
Stuchka Latvia *see* **Aizkraukle**
Stučka Latvia *see* **Aizkraukle**
Studholme Junction N.Z. **113** C7
Studsviken Sweden **44** K5
Stukley, Lac *l.* Canada **135** I1
Stung Treng Cambodia *see* **Stœng Trêng**
Stupart *r.* Canada **121** M4
Stupino Rus. Fed. **43** H5
Sturge Island Antarctica **152** H2
Sturgeon *r. Ont.* Canada **122** F5
Sturgeon *r. Sask.* Canada **121** J4
Sturgeon Bay *b.* Canada **121** L4
Sturgeon Bay U.S.A. **134** B1
Sturgeon Bay Canal *lake channel* U.S.A. **134** B1
Sturgeon Falls Canada **122** F5
Sturgeon Lake *Ont.* Canada **121** N5
Sturgeon Lake *Ont.* Canada **135** F1
Sturgis *MI* U.S.A. **134** C3
Sturgis *SD* U.S.A. **130** C2
Sturt, Mount *hill* Australia **111** C6
Sturt Creek *watercourse* Australia **108** D4
Sturt National Park Australia **111** C6
Sturt Stony Desert Australia **111** C6
Stutterheim S. Africa **101** H7
Stuttgart Germany **53** J6
Stuttgart U.S.A. **131** F5
Stykkishólmur Iceland **44** [inset]
Styr *r.* Belarus/Ukr. **43** E5
Suaçuí Grande *r.* Brazil **145** C2
Suai East Timor **108** D2
Suakin Sudan **86** E6
Suao Taiwan **77** I3
Suaqui Grande Mex. **127** F7
Suau P.N.G. **110** E1
Subačius Lith. **45** N9
Subankhata India **83** G4
Subarnapur India *see* **Sonapur**
Sübāshī Iran **88** C3
Subay *reg.* Saudi Arabia **88** B5
Şubayḩah Saudi Arabia **85** D4
Subei China **80** H4
Subi Besar *i.* Indon. **71** E7
Subi Kecil *i.* Indon. **71** E7
Sublette U.S.A. **131** C4
Subotica Serb. and Mont. **59** H1
Success, Lake U.S.A. **128** D3
Succiso, Alpi di *mts* Italy **58** D2
Suceava Romania **43** E7
Suchan Rus. Fed. *see* **Partizansk**
Suck *r.* Rep. of Ireland **51** D4
Suckling, Mount P.N.G. **110** E1
Suckow Germany **53** L1

▶**Sucre** Bol. **142** E7
Legislative capital of Bolivia.

Suczawa Romania *see* **Suceava**
Sud, Grand Récif du *reef* New Caledonia **107** G4
Suda Rus. Fed. **42** H4
Sudak Ukr. **90** D1

▶**Sudan** *country* Africa **97** F3
Largest country in Africa.
Africa **7, 94–95**

Suday Rus. Fed. **42** I4
Sudayr *reg.* Saudi Arabia **88** B5
Sudbury Canada **122** E5
Sudbury U.K. **49** H6
Sudd *swamp* Sudan **86** C8
Sude *r.* Germany **53** K1
Sudest Island P.N.G. *see* **Tagula Island**
Sudetenland *mts* Czech Rep./Poland *see* **Sudety**
Sudety *mts* Czech Rep./Poland **47** O5
Sudislavl' Rus. Fed. **42** I4
Sudlersville U.S.A. **135** H4
Süd-Nord-Kanal *canal* Germany **52** H2
Sudogda Rus. Fed. **42** I5
Sudr Egypt **85** A5
Suðuroy *i.* Faroe Is **44** [inset]
Sue *watercourse* Sudan **97** F4
Sueca Spain **57** F4
Suez Egypt **85** A5
Suez, Gulf of Egypt **85** A5
Suez Bay Egypt **85** A5
Suez Canal Egypt **85** A4
Suffolk U.S.A. **135** G5
Sugarbush Hill *hill* U.S.A. **130** F2
Sugarloaf Mountain U.S.A. **135** J1
Sugarloaf Point Australia **112** F4
Sugun China **80** E4
Sūhāj Egypt *see* **Sawhāj**
Şuḩār Oman **88** E5
Suhaymī, Wādī as *watercourse* Egypt **85** A4
Sühbaatar Mongolia **72** J2
Suheli Par *i.* India **84** B4
Suhl Germany **53** K4
Suhlendorf Germany **53** K2
Suhul *reg.* Saudi Arabia **88** B6
Suhūl al Kidan *plain* Saudi Arabia **88** D6
Şuhut Turkey **59** N5
Sui Pak. **89** H4
Sui, Laem *pt* Thai. **71** B5
Suibin China **74** C3
Suid-Afrika *country* Africa *see* **Republic of South Africa**
Suide China **73** K5
Suidzhikurmsy Turkm. *see* **Madau**
Suifenhe China **74** C3
Suihua China **74** B3
Suileng China **74** B3
Suining *Hunan* China **77** F3
Suining *Jiangsu* China **77** H1
Suining *Sichuan* China **76** E2
Suippes France **52** E5
Suir *r.* Rep. of Ireland **51** E5
Suisse *country* Europe *see* **Switzerland**
Sui Vehar Pak. **89** H4
Suixi China **77** H1
Suixian *Henan* China **77** G1
Suixian *Hubei* China *see* **Suizhou**
Suiyang *Guizhou* China **76** E3
Suiyang *Henan* China **77** G1
Suiza *country* Europe *see* **Switzerland**
Suizhong China **73** M4
Suizhou China **77** G2
Sujangarh India **82** C4
Sujawal Pak. **89** H5
Suk *atoll* Micronesia *see* **Pulusuk**
Sukabumi Indon. **68** D8
Sukagawa Japan **75** F5
Sukarnapura Indon. *see* **Jayapura**
Sukarno, Puncak *mt.* Indon. *see* **Jaya, Puncak**
Sukchŏn N. Korea **75** B5
Sukhinichi Rus. Fed. **43** G5
Sukhona *r.* Rus. Fed. **42** J3
Sukhothai Thai. **70** B3
Sukhumi Georgia *see* **Sokhumi**
Sukhum-Kale Georgia *see* **Sokhumi**
Sukkertoppen Greenland *see* **Maniitsoq**
Sukkozero Rus. Fed. **42** G3
Sukkur Pak. **89** H5
Sukma India **84** D2
Sukpay Rus. Fed. **74** E3
Sukpay *r.* Rus. Fed. **74** E3
Sukri *r.* India **82** C4
Sukri *r.* India **82** C4
Suktel *r.* India **84** D1
Sukun *i.* Indon. **108** C2
Sula *i.* Norway **45** D6
Sula *r.* Rus. Fed. **42** K2
Sula, Kepulauan *is* Indon. **69** H7
Sulaiman Range *mts* Pak. **89** H4
Sulak Rus. Fed. **91** G2
Sūlār Iran **88** C4
Sula Sgeir *i.* U.K. **50** C1
Sulawesi *i.* Indon. *see* **Celebes**
Sulaymān Beg Iraq **91** G4
Sulayyimah Saudi Arabia **88** B6
Sulci *Sardinia* Italy *see* **Sant'Antioco**
Sulcis *Sardinia* Italy *see* **Sant'Antioco**
Suledeh Iran **88** C2
Sule Skerry *i.* U.K. **50** E1
Sule Stack *i.* U.K. **50** E1
Sulingen Germany **53** I2
Sulitjelma Norway **44** J3
Sulkava Fin. **44** P6
Sullana Peru **142** B4
Sullivan *IL* U.S.A. **130** F4
Sullivan *IN* U.S.A. **134** B4
Sullivan Bay Canada **120** E5
Sullivan Island Myanmar *see* **Lanbi Kyun**
Sullivan Lake Canada **121** I5
Sulmo Italy *see* **Sulmona**
Sulmona Italy **58** E3
Sulphur *LA* U.S.A. **131** E6
Sulphur *OK* U.S.A. **131** D5
Sulphur *r.* U.S.A. **131** E5
Sulphur Springs U.S.A. **131** E5
Sultan Canada **122** E5
Sultan, Koh-i- *mts* Pak. **89** F4
Sultanabad India *see* **Osmannagar**
Sultanabad Iran *see* **Arāk**
Sultan Dağları *mts* Turkey **59** N5
Sultanıye Turkey *see* **Karapınar**
Sultanpur India **83** E4
Sulu Archipelago *is* Phil. **69** G5
Sulu Basin *sea feature* N. Pacific Ocean **150** E5
Sülüklü Turkey **90** D3
Sülüktü Kyrg. **89** H2
Sulusaray Turkey **90** E3
Sulu Sea N. Pacific Ocean **68** F5
Suluvvaulik, Lac *l.* Canada **123** G2
Sulyukta Kyrg. *see* **Sülüktü**
Sulzbach-Rosenberg Germany **53** L5
Sulzberger Bay Antarctica **152** I1
Sumāil Oman **88** E6
Sumampa Arg. **144** D3
Sumapaz, Parque Nacional *nat. park* Col. **142** D3
Sūmār Iran **88** B3
Sumatera *i.* Indon. *see* **Sumatra**

▶**Sumatra** *i.* Indon. **71** B7
2nd largest island in Asia.

Šumava *nat. park* Czech Rep. **47** N6
Sumba *i.* Indon. **108** C2
Sumba, Selat *sea chan.* Indon. **108** B2
Sumbar *r.* Turkm. **88** D2
Sumbawa *i.* Indon. **108** B2
Sumbawabesar Indon. **108** B2
Sumbawanga Tanz. **99** D4
Sumbe Angola **99** B5
Sumbu National Park Zambia **99** D4
Sumburgh U.K. **50** [inset]
Sumburgh Head *hd* U.K. **50** [inset]
Sumdo China **76** D2
Sumdum, Mount U.S.A. **120** C3
Sume'eh Sarā Iran **88** C2
Sumeih Sudan **86** C8
Sumenep Indon. **68** E8
Sumgait Azer. *see* **Sumqayıt**
Sumisu-jima *i.* Japan **73** Q6
Summēl Iraq **91** F3
Summer Beaver Canada **122** C3
Summerford Canada **123** L4
Summer Island U.S.A. **132** C2
Summer Isles U.K. **50** D2
Summerland Canada **120** G5
Summersville U.S.A. **134** E4
Summit Lake Canada **120** F4
Summit Mountain U.S.A. **128** E2
Summit Peak U.S.A. **127** G5
Sumnal Aksai Chin **82** D2
Sumner N.Z. **113** D6
Sumner, Lake N.Z. **113** D6
Sumon-dake *mt.* Japan **75** E5
Šumperk Czech Rep. **47** P6
Sumpu Japan *see* **Shizuoka**
Sumqayıt Azer. **91** H2
Sumskiy Posad Rus. Fed. **42** G2
Sumter U.S.A. **133** D5
Sumur Jammu and Kashmir **82** D2
Sumy Ukr. **43** G6
Sumzom China **76** C2
Suna Rus. Fed. **42** K4
Sunaj India **82** D4

Sunam India 82 C3
Sunamganj Bangl. 83 G4
Sunart, Loch inlet U.K. 50 D4
Şunaynah Oman 88 D6
Sunburst U.S.A. 126 F2
Sunbury Australia 112 B6
Sunbury OH U.S.A. 134 D3
Sunbury PA U.S.A. 135 G3
Sunch'ŏn S. Korea 75 B6
Sun City S. Africa 101 H3
Sun City AZ U.S.A. 129 G5
Sun City CA U.S.A. 128 E5
Sunda, Selat strait Indon. 68 C8
Sunda Kalapa Indon. see Jakarta
Sundance U.S.A. 126 G3
Sundarbans coastal area Bangl./India 83 G5
Sundarbans National Park Bangl./India 83 G5
Sundargarh India 83 F5
Sunda Shelf sea feature Indian Ocean 149 P5
Sunda Strait Indon. see Sunda, Selat
Sunda Trench sea feature Indian Ocean see Java Trench
Sunda Trench sea feature Indian Ocean see Java Trench
Sunderland U.K. 48 F4
Sundern (Sauerland) Germany 53 I3
Sündiken Dağları mts Turkey 59 N5
Sundown National Park Australia 112 E2
Sundre Canada 120 H5
Sundridge Canada 122 F5
Sundsvall Sweden 44 J5
Sundukli, Peski des. Turkm. 89 F2
Sundumbili S. Africa 101 J5
Sungaipenuh Indon. 68 C7
Sungari r. China see Songhua Jiang
Sungei Petani Malaysia 71 C6
Sungei Seletar Reservoir Sing. 71 [inset]
Sungkiang China see Songjiang
Sung Kong i. Hong Kong China 77 [inset]
Sungqu China see Songpan
Sungsang Indon. 68 C7
Sungurlu Turkey 90 D2
Sun Kosi r. Nepal 83 F4
Sunman U.S.A. 134 C4
Sunndal Norway 45 E6
Sunndalsøra Norway 44 F5
Sunne Sweden 45 H7
Sunnyside U.S.A. 126 D3
Sunnyvale U.S.A. 128 B3
Sun Prairie U.S.A. 130 F3
Sunset House Canada 120 G4
Sunset Peak hill Hong Kong China 77 [inset]
Suntar Rus. Fed. 65 M3
Suntsar Pak. 89 F5
Sunwi-do i. N. Korea 75 B5
Sunwu China 74 B2
Sunyani Ghana 96 C4
Suolijärvet l. Fin. 44 P3
Suomi country Europe see Finland
Suomussalmi Fin. 44 P4
Suō-nada b. Japan 75 C6
Suonenjoki Fin. 44 O5
Suong r. Laos 70 C3
Suoyarvi Rus. Fed. 42 G3
Supa India 84 B3
Supaul India 83 F4
Superior AZ U.S.A. 129 H5
Superior MT U.S.A. 126 E3
Superior NE U.S.A. 130 D3
Superior WI U.S.A. 130 E2

▶Superior, Lake Canada/U.S.A. 125 J2
Largest lake in North America and 2nd in the world.
North America 114–115
World 12–13

Suphan Buri Thai. 71 C4
Süphan Dağı mt. Turkey 91 F3
Supiori i. Indon. 69 J7
Suponevo Rus. Fed. 43 G5
Support Force Glacier Antarctica 152 A1
Sūq ash Shuyūkh Iraq 91 G5
Suqian China 77 H1
Suquṭrá i. Yemen see Socotra
Ṣūr Oman 89 E6
Sur, Point U.S.A. 128 C3
Sur, Punta pt Arg. 144 E5
Sura r. Rus. Fed. 43 J4
Şuraabad Azer. 91 H2
Surabaya Indon. 68 E8
Sūrak Iran 88 E5
Surakarta Indon. 68 E8
Sūran Iran 89 F5
Şūrān Syria 85 C2
Surat Australia 112 D1
Surat India 82 C5
Suratgarh India 82 C3
Surat Thani Thai. 71 B5
Surazh Rus. Fed. 43 G5
Surbiton Australia 110 D4
Surdulica Serb. and Mont. 59 J3
Sûre r. Lux. 52 G5
Surendranagar India 82 B5
Surf U.S.A. 128 C4
Surgut Rus. Fed. 64 I3
Suri India see Siuri
Suriapet India 84 C2
Surigao Phil. 69 H5
Surin Thai. 70 C4
Surinam country S. America see Suriname
▶Suriname country S. America 143 G3
South America 9, 140–141
Surin Nua, Ko i. Thai. 71 B5
Suriyān Iran 88 D4
Surkhan Uzbek. 89 G2
Surkhduz Afgh. 89 G4
Surkhet Nepal 83 E3
Surkhon Uzbek. see Surkhan
Sürmene Turkey 91 F2
Surovikino Rus. Fed. 43 I6
Surpura India 82 C4
Surrey Canada 120 F5
Surry U.S.A. 135 G5
Surskoye Rus. Fed. 43 J5
Surt Libya see Sirte
Surtsey i. Iceland 44 [inset]
Sūrū Hormozgan Iran 88 E5
Sūrū Sīstān va Balūchestān Iran 88 E5
Suruç Turkey 85 D1
Surud, Raas pt Somalia 98 E2
Surud Ad mt. Somalia see Shimbiris
Suruga-wan b. Japan 75 E6
Surulangun Indon. 68 C7
Surwold Germany 53 H2
Suryapet India see Suriapet
Şuşa Azer. 91 G3
Susah Tunisia see Sousse
Susaki Japan 75 D6
Susan U.S.A. 135 G5
Sūsangerd Iran 88 C4
Susanino Rus. Fed. 74 F1
Susanville U.S.A. 128 C1
Suşehri Turkey 90 E2
Suso Thai. 71 B6
Susong China 77 H2
Susquehanna U.S.A. 135 H3
Susquehanna r. U.S.A. 135 G4
Susquehanna, West Branch r. U.S.A. 135 G3
Susques Arg. 144 C2
Sussex U.S.A. 135 G5
Susuman Rus. Fed. 65 P3
Susupu Indon. 69 H6
Susurluk Turkey 59 M5
Sutak Jammu and Kashmir 82 D2
Sutherland Australia 112 E5
Sutherland S. Africa 100 E7
Sutherland U.S.A. 130 C3
Sutherland Range hills Australia 109 D6
Sutjeska nat. park Bos.-Herz. 58 H3
Sutlej r. India/Pak. 82 B3
Sütlüce Turkey 85 A1
Sutter U.S.A. 128 C2
Sutterton U.K. 49 G6
Sutton Canada 135 I1
Sutton r. Canada 122 E3
Sutton U.K. 49 H6
Sutton NE U.S.A. 130 D3
Sutton WV U.S.A. 134 E4
Sutton Coldfield U.K. 49 F6
Sutton in Ashfield U.K. 49 F5
Sutton Lake Canada 122 D3
Sutton Lake U.S.A. 134 E4
Suttor r. Australia 110 D4
Suttsu Japan 74 F4
Sutwik Island U.S.A. 118 C4
Sutyr' r. Rus. Fed. 74 D2

▶Suva Fiji 107 H3
Capital of Fiji.

Suvadiva Atoll Maldives see Huvadhu Atoll
Suvalki Poland see Suwałki
Suvorov atoll Cook Is see Suwarrow
Suvorov Rus. Fed. 43 H5
Suwa Japan 75 E5
Suwałki Poland 43 D5
Suwannaphum Thai. 70 C4
Suwannee r. U.S.A. 133 D6
Suwanose-jima i. Japan 75 C7
Suwarrow atoll Cook Is 107 J3
Suwaylih Jordan 85 B3
Suwayr well Saudi Arabia 91 F5
Suways, Khalīj as g. Egypt see Suez, Gulf of
Suweilih Jordan see Suwaylih
Suweis, Khalîg el g. Egypt see Suez, Gulf of
Suweis, Qanâ el canal Egypt see Suez Canal
Suwŏn S. Korea 75 B5
Suz, Mys pt Kazakh. 91 I2
Suzaka Japan 75 E5
Suzdal' Rus. Fed. 42 I4
Suzhou Anhui China 77 H1
Suzhou Gansu China see Jiuquan
Suzhou Jiangsu China 77 I2
Suzi He r. China 74 B4
Suzuka Japan 75 E6
Suzu-misaki pt Japan 75 E5
Sværholthalvøya pen. Norway 44 O1

▶Svalbard terr. Arctic Ocean 64 C2
Part of Norway.

Svappavaara Sweden 44 L3
Svartenhuk Halvø pen. Greenland see Sigguup Nunaa
Svatove Ukr. 43 H6
Svay Chék Cambodia 71 C4
Svay Riĕng Cambodia 71 D5
Svecha Rus. Fed. 42 J4
Sveg Sweden 45 I5
Sveķi Latvia 45 O8
Svelgen Norway 44 D6
Svellingen Norway 44 F5
Švenčionėliai Lith. 45 N9
Švenčionys Lith. 45 O9
Svendborg Denmark 45 G9
Svensby Norway 44 K2
Svenstavik Sweden 44 I5
Sverdlovsk Rus. Fed. see Yekaterinburg
Sverdlovs'k Ukr. 43 H6
Sverdrup Islands Canada 119 I2
Sverige country Europe see Sweden
Sveti Nikole Macedonia 59 I4
Svetlaya Rus. Fed. 74 E3
Svetlogorsk Belarus see Svyetlahorsk
Svetlogorsk Kaliningradskaya Oblast' Rus. Fed. 45 L9
Svetlogorsk Krasnoyarskiy Kray Rus. Fed. 64 J3
Svetlograd Rus. Fed. 91 F1
Svetlovodsk Ukr. see Svitlovods'k
Svetlyy Kaliningradskaya Oblast' Rus. Fed. 45 L9
Svetlyy Orenburgskaya Oblast' Rus. Fed. 80 B1
Svetlyy Yar Rus. Fed. 43 J6
Svetogorsk Rus. Fed. 45 P6
Sviahnúkar vol. Iceland 44 [inset]
Svilaja mts Croatia 58 G3
Svilengrad Bulg. 59 L4
Svinecea Mare, Vârful mt. Romania 59 J2
Svintsovyy Rudnik Turkm. 89 G2
Svir Belarus 45 O9
Svir' r. Rus. Fed. 42 G3
Svishtov Bulg. 59 K3
Svitava r. Czech Rep. 47 P6
Svitavy Czech Rep. 47 P6
Svitlovods'k Ukr. 43 G6
Sviyaga r. Rus. Fed. 42 K5
Svizzera country Europe see Switzerland
Svobodnyy Rus. Fed. 74 C2
Svolvær Norway 44 I2
Svrljiške Planine mts Serb. and Mont. 59 J3
Svyatoy Nos, Mys c. Rus. Fed. 42 K2
Svyetlahorsk Belarus 43 F5
Swadlincote U.K. 49 F6
Swaffham U.K. 49 H6
Swain Reefs Australia 110 F4
Swainsboro U.S.A. 133 D5
Swains Island atoll American Samoa 107 I3
Swakop watercourse Namibia 100 B2
Swakopmund Namibia 100 B2
Swale r. U.K. 48 F4
Swallow Islands Solomon Is 107 G3
Swamihalli India 84 C3
Swampy r. Canada 123 H2
Swan r. Australia 109 A7
Swan r. Man./Sask. Canada 121 K4
Swan r. Ont. Canada 122 E3
Swanage U.K. 49 F8
Swandale U.S.A. 134 E4
Swan Hill Australia 112 A5
Swan Hills Canada 120 H4
Swan Islands is Caribbean Sea 137 H5
Swan Lake B.C. Canada 120 D4
Swan Lake Man. Canada 121 K4
Swanley U.K. 49 H7
Swanquarter U.S.A. 133 E5
Swan Reach Australia 111 B7
Swan River Canada 121 K4
Swansea U.K. 49 D7
Swansea Bay U.K. 49 D7
Swanton CA U.S.A. 128 B3
Swanton VT U.S.A. 135 I1
Swartbergpas pass S. Africa 100 F7
Swart Nossob watercourse Namibia see Black Nossob
Swartruggens S. Africa 101 H3
Swartz Creek U.S.A. 134 D2
Swasey Peak U.S.A. 129 G2
Swat Kohistan reg. Pak. 89 I3
Swatow China see Shantou
Swayzee U.S.A. 134 C3
▶Swaziland country Africa 101 J4
Africa 7, 94–95

▶Sweden country Europe 44 I5
5th largest country in Europe.
Europe 5, 38–39

Sweet Home U.S.A. 126 C3
Sweet Springs U.S.A. 134 E5
Sweetwater U.S.A. 131 C5
Sweetwater r. U.S.A. 126 G4
Swellendam S. Africa 100 E8
Świdnica Poland 47 P5
Świdwin Poland 47 O4
Świebodzin Poland 47 O4
Świecie Poland 47 Q4
Swift Current Canada 121 J5
Swiftcurrent Creek r. Canada 121 J5
Swilly r. Rep. of Ireland 51 E3
Swilly, Lough inlet Rep. of Ireland 51 E2
Swindon U.K. 49 F7
Swinford Rep. of Ireland 51 D4
Świnoujście Poland 47 O4
Swinton U.K. 50 G5
Swiss Confederation country Europe see Switzerland
Swiss National Park Switz. 58 D1
▶Switzerland country Europe 56 I3
Europe 5, 38–39
Swords Rep. of Ireland 51 F4
Swords Range hills Australia 110 C4
Syamozero, Ozero l. Rus. Fed. 42 G3
Syamzha Rus. Fed. 42 I3
Syang Nepal 83 E3
Syas'troy Rus. Fed. 42 G3
Sychevka Rus. Fed. 42 G5
Sydenham atoll Kiribati see Nonouti

▶Sydney Australia 112 E4
State capital of New South Wales. Most populous city in Oceania.

Sydney Canada 123 J5
Sydney Island Kiribati see Manra
Sydney Lake Canada 121 M5
Sydney Mines Canada 123 J5
Syedra tourist site Turkey 85 A1
Syeverodonets'k Ukr. 43 H6
Syke Germany 53 I2
Sykesville U.S.A. 135 F3
Syktyvkar Rus. Fed. 42 K3
Sylarna mt. Norway/Sweden 44 H5
Sylhet Bangl. 83 G4
Syloga Rus. Fed. 42 I3
Sylt i. Germany 47 L3
Sylva U.S.A. 133 D5
Sylvania GA U.S.A. 133 D5
Sylvania OH U.S.A. 134 D3
Sylvan Lake Canada 120 H4
Sylvester U.S.A. 133 D6
Sylvester, Lake salt flat Australia 110 A3
Sylvia, Mount Canada 120 E3
Symerton U.S.A. 134 A3
Symi i. Greece 59 L6
Synel'nykove Ukr. 43 G6
Syngyrli, Mys pt Kazakh. 91 I2
Synya Rus. Fed. 41 R2
Syowa research station Antarctica 152 D2
Syracusae Sicily Italy see Syracuse
Syracuse Sicily Italy 58 F6
Syracuse KS U.S.A. 130 C4
Syracuse NY U.S.A. 135 G2
Syrdar'ya r. Asia 80 C3
Syrdar'ya Uzbek. 80 C3
Syrdaryinskiy Uzbek. see Syrdar'ya
▶Syria country Asia 90 E4
Asia 6, 62–63
Syriam Myanmar 70 B3
Syrian Desert Asia 90 E4
Syrna i. Greece 59 L6
Syros i. Greece 59 K6
Syrskiy Rus. Fed. 43 H5
Sysmä Fin. 45 N6
Sysola r. Rus. Fed. 42 K3
Syumsi Rus. Fed. 42 K4
Syurkum Rus. Fed. 74 F2
Syurkum, Mys pt Rus. Fed. 74 F2
Syzran' Rus. Fed. 43 K5
Szabadka Serb. and Mont. see Subotica
Szczecin Poland 47 O4
Szczecinek Poland 47 P4
Szczytno Poland 47 R4
Szechwan prov. China see Sichuan
Szeged Hungary 59 I1
Székesfehérvár Hungary 58 H1
Szekszárd Hungary 58 H1
Szentes Hungary 59 I1
Szentgotthárd Hungary 58 G1
Szigetvár Hungary 58 G1
Szolnok Hungary 59 I1
Szombathely Hungary 58 G1
Sztálinváros Hungary see Dunaújváros

T

Taagga Duudka reg. Somalia 98 E3
Tābah Saudi Arabia 86 F4
Tabajara Brazil 142 F5
Tabakhmela Georgia see Kazret'i
Tabalo P.N.G. 69 L7
Tabanan Indon. 108 A2
Tabankulu S. Africa 101 I6
Ṭabaqah Ar Raqqah Syria see Madīnat ath Thawrah
Ṭabaqah Ar Raqqah Syria 85 D2
Tabar Islands P.N.G. 106 F2
Tabarka Tunisia 58 C6
Ṭabas Iran 89 E3
Tabāsin Iran 88 E4
Tābask, Kūh-e mt. Iran 88 C4
Tabatinga Amazonas Brazil 142 E4
Tabatinga São Paulo Brazil 145 A3
Tabatinga, Serra da hills Brazil 143 J6
Tabatsquri, Tba l. Georgia 91 F2
Tabayin Myanmar 70 A2
Tabbita Australia 112 B5
Tabelbala Alg. 54 D6
Taber Canada 121 H5
Tabet, Nam r. Myanmar 70 B1
Tabia Tsaka salt l. China 83 F3
Tabiteuea atoll Kiribati 107 H2
Tabivere Estonia 45 O7
Table Cape N.Z. 113 F4
Tabligbo Togo 96 D4
Tábor Czech Rep. 47 O6
Tabora Tanz. 99 D4
Tabou Côte d'Ivoire 96 C4
Tabrīz Iran 88 B2
Tabuaeran atoll Kiribati 151 J5
Tabūk Saudi Arabia 90 E5
Tabulam Australia 112 F2
Tabuyung Indon. 71 B7
Tabwémasana, Mount Vanuatu 107 G3
Täby Sweden 45 K7
Tacalé Brazil 143 H3
Tacheng China 80 F2
Tachie Canada 120 E4
Tachov Czech Rep. 53 M5
Tacloban Phil. 69 H4
Tacna Peru 142 D7
Tacoma U.S.A. 126 C3
Taco Pozo Arg. 144 D3
Tacuarembó Uruguay 144 E4
Tacupeto Mex. 127 F7
Tadcaster U.K. 48 F5
Tademaït, Plateau du Alg. 54 E6
Tadin New Caledonia 107 G4
Tadjikistan country Asia see Tajikistan
Tadjoura Djibouti 86 F7
Tadmur Syria 85 D2
Tadohae Haesang National Park S. Korea 75 B6
Tadoule Lake Canada 121 L3
Tadoussac Canada 123 H4
Tadpatri India 84 C3
Tadwale India 84 C2
Tadzhikskaya S.S.R. country Asia see Tajikistan
T'aean Haean National Park S. Korea 75 B5
Taech'ŏng-do i. S. Korea 75 B5
Taedasa-do N. Korea 75 B5
Taedong-man b. N. Korea 75 B5
Taegu S. Korea 75 C6
Taehan-min'guk country Asia see South Korea
Taehŭksan-kundo is S. Korea 75 B6
Taejŏn S. Korea 75 B5
Taejŏng S. Korea 75 B6
T'aepaek S. Korea 75 C5
Ta'erqi China 73 M3
Taf r. U.K. 49 C7
Tafahi i. Tonga 107 I3
Tafalla Spain 57 F2
Tafeng China see Lanshan
Tafila Jordan see Aṭ Ṭafilah
Tafi Viejo Arg. 144 C3
Tafresh Iran 88 C3
Taft Iran 88 D4
Taft U.S.A. 128 D4
Taftān, Kūh-e mt. Iran 89 F4
Taftanāz Syria 85 C2
Tafwap India 71 A6
Taganrog Rus. Fed. 43 H7
Taganrog, Gulf of Rus. Fed./Ukr. 43 H7
Taganrogskiy Zaliv b. Rus. Fed./Ukr. see Taganrog, Gulf of
Tagarev, Gora mt. Iran/Turkm. 88 E2
Tagarkaty, Pereval pass Tajik. 89 I2
Tagaung Myanmar 70 B2
Tagchagpu Ri mt. China 83 E2
Tagdempt Alg. see Tiaret
Taghmon Rep. of Ireland 51 F5
Tagish Canada 120 C2
Tagtabazar Turkm. 89 F3
Tagula P.N.G. 110 F1
Tagula Island P.N.G. 110 F1
Tagus r. Port. 57 B4
also known as Tajo (Portugal) or Tejo (Spain)
Taha China 74 B3
Tahaetkun Mountain Canada 120 G5
Tahan, Gunung mt. Malaysia 71 C6
Tahanroz'ka Zatoka b. Rus. Fed./Ukr. see Taganrog, Gulf of
Tahat, Mont mt. Alg. 96 D2
Tahaurawe i. U.S.A. see Kahoolawe
Tahe China 74 B1
Taheke N.Z. 113 D2
Tahiti i. Fr. Polynesia 151 K7
Tahlab r. Iran/Pak. 89 F4
Tahlab, Dasht-i- plain Pak. 89 F4
Tahlequah U.S.A. 131 E5
Tahltan Canada 120 D3
Tahoe, Lake U.S.A. 128 C2
Tahoe Lake Canada 119 H3
Tahoe Vista U.S.A. 128 C2
Tahoka U.S.A. 131 C5
Tahoua Niger 96 D3
Tahrūd Iran 88 E4
Tahrūd r. Iran 88 E4
Tahtsa Peak Canada 120 E4
Tahulandang i. Indon. 69 H6
Tahuna Indon. 69 H6
Taï, Parc National de nat. park Côte d'Ivoire 96 C4
Tai'an China 73 L5
Taibai China 76 E1
Taibai Shan mt. China 76 E1
Taibei Taiwan see T'aipei
Taibus Qi China see Baochang
T'aichung Taiwan 77 I3
Taidong Taiwan see T'aitung
Taigong China see Taijiang
Taihang Shan mts Hebei China 73 K5
Taihang Shan mts China 73 K5
Taihape N.Z. 113 E4
Taihe Jiangxi China 77 G3
Taihe Sichuan China see Shehong
Taihezhen China see Shehong
Tai Ho Wan Hong Kong China 77 [inset]
Taihu China 77 H2
Tai Hu l. China 77 I2
Taijiang China 77 F3
Taikang China 74 B3
Tailai China 74 A3
Tai Lam Chung Shui Tong resr Hong Kong China 77 [inset]
Tailem Bend Australia 111 B7
Tai Long Wan b. Hong Kong China 77 [inset]
Taimani reg. Afgh. 89 F3
Tai Mo Shan hill Hong Kong China 77 [inset]
Tain U.K. 50 F2
T'ainan Taiwan see Hsinying
T'ainan Taiwan 77 I4
Tainaro, Akra pt Greece 59 J6
Taining China 77 H3
Tai O Hong Kong China 77 [inset]
Taiobeiras Brazil 145 C1
Tai Pang Wan b. Hong Kong China see Mirs Bay

▶T'aipei Taiwan 77 I3
Capital of Taiwan.

Taiping Guangdong China see Shixing
Taiping Guangxi China see Chongzuo
Taiping Guangxi China 77 F4
Taiping Malaysia 71 C6
Taipingchuan China 74 A3
Tai Po Hong Kong China 77 [inset]
Tai Po Hoi b. Hong Kong China see Tolo Harbour
Tai Poutini National Park N.Z. see Westland National Park
Tairbeart U.K. see Tarbert
Tai Rom Yen National Park Thai. 71 B5
Tairuq Iran 88 B3
Tais P.N.G. 69 K8
Taishan China 77 G4
Taishun China 77 H3
Tai Siu Mo To is Hong Kong China see The Brothers
Taissy France 52 E5
Taitanu N.Z. 113 D6
Taitao, Península de pen. Chile 144 B7
Tai To Yan mt. Hong Kong China 77 [inset]
T'aitung Taiwan 77 I4
Tai Tung Shan hill Hong Kong China see Sunset Peak
Taivalkoski Fin. 44 P4
Taivaskero hill Fin. 44 N2
▶Taiwan country Asia 77 I4
Asia 6, 62–63
T'aiwan Haihsia strait China/Taiwan see Taiwan Strait
Taiwan Haixia strait China/Taiwan see Taiwan Strait
Taiwan Shan mts Taiwan see Chungyang Shanmo
Taiwan Strait China/Taiwan 77 H4
Taixian China see Jiangyan
Taixing China 77 I1
Taiyuan China 73 K5
Tai Yue Shan i. Hong Kong China see Lantau Island
Taizhao China 76 B2
Taizhong Taiwan see T'aichung
Taizhong Taiwan see Fengyüan
Taizhou Jiangsu China 77 H1
Taizhou Zhejiang China 77 I2
Taizhou Liedao i. China 77 I2
Taizhou Wan b. China 77 I2
Taizi He r. China 74 B4
Ta'izz Yemen 86 F7
Tājābād Iran 88 E4
Tajal Pak. 89 H5
Tajamulco, Volcán de vol. Guat. 136 F5
Tajerouine Tunisia 58 C7
▶Tajikistan country Asia 89 H2
Asia 6, 62–63
Tajitos Mex. 127 E7
Tajo r. Spain 57 C4 see Tagus
Tajrīsh Iran 88 C3
Tak Thai. 70 B3
Takāb Iran 88 B2
Takabba Kenya 98 E3
Takahashi Japan 75 D6
Takamatsu Japan 75 D6
Takaoka Japan 75 E5
Takapuna N.Z. 113 E3
Ta karpo China 83 G4
Takatokwane Botswana 100 G3
Takatshwaane Botswana 100 E2
Takatsuki-yama mt. Japan 75 D6
Takayama Japan 75 E5
Tak Bai Thai. 71 C6
Takefu Japan 75 E6
Takengon Indon. 71 B6
Takeo Cambodia see Takêv
Take-shima i. N. Pacific Ocean see Liancourt Rocks
Takestān Iran 88 C2
Takêv Cambodia 71 D5
Takhemaret Alg. 57 G6
Takhini Hotspring Canada 120 C2
Ta Khli Thai. 70 C4
Ta Khmau Cambodia 71 D5
Takhta-Bazar Turkm. see Tagtabazar
Takht Apān, Kūh-e mt. Iran 88 C3
Takhta Pul Post Afgh. 89 G4
Takhteh Iran 88 D4
Takht-e Soleymān mt. Iran 88 C2
Takht-i-Bakhti tourist site Pak. 89 H3
Takht-i-Sulaiman mt. Pak. 89 H4
Takijuq Lake Canada see Napaktulik Lake
Takingeun Indon. see Takengon
Takinoue Japan 74 F3
Takla Lake Canada 120 E4
Takla Landing Canada 120 E4
Takla Makan des. China see Taklimakan Desert
Taklimakan Desert China 82 E1
Taklimakan Shamo des. China see Taklimakan Desert
Takpa Shiri mt. China 76 B2
Taku Canada 120 C3
Takum Nigeria 96 D4
Talachyn Belarus 43 F5
Talaja India 82 C5
Talakan Amurskaya Oblast' Rus. Fed. 74 C2
Talakan Khabarovskiy Kray Rus. Fed. 74 D2
Talandzha Rus. Fed. 74 C2
Talangbatu Indon. 68 D7
Talara Peru 142 B4
Talar-i-Band mts Pak. see Makran Coast Range
Talas Kyrg. 80 D3
Talas Ala-Too mts Kyrg. 80 D3
Talas Range mts Kyrg. see Talas Ala-Too
Talasskiy Alatau, Khrebet mts Kyrg. see Talas Ala-Too
Ṭal'at Mūsá mt. Lebanon/Syria 85 C2
Talaud, Kepulauan is Indon. 69 H6
Talavera de la Reina Spain 57 D4
Talawgyi Myanmar 70 B1
Talaya Rus. Fed. 65 Q3
Talbehat India 82 D4
Talbīsah Syria 85 C2
Talbot, Mount hill Australia 109 D6
Talbotton U.S.A. 133 C5
Talbragar r. Australia 112 D4
Talca Chile 144 B5
Talcahuano Chile 144 B5
Taldan Rus. Fed. 74 B1
Taldom Rus. Fed. 42 H4
Taldykorgan Kazakh. 80 E3
Taldy-Kurgan Kazakh. see Taldykorgan
Taldyqorghan Kazakh. see Taldykorgan
Tālesh Iran see Hashtpar
Talgarth U.K. 49 D7
Talguppa India 84 B3
Talia Australia 111 A7
Taliabu i. Indon. 69 G7
Talikota India 84 C2
Talimardzhan Uzbek. 89 G2
Talin Hiag China 74 B3
Taliparamba India 84 B3
Talisay Phil. 69 G4
Talış Dağları mts Azer./Iran 88 C2
Talitsa Rus. Fed. 42 J4
Taliwang Indon. 108 B2
Talkeetna U.S.A. 118 C3
Talkeetna Mountains U.S.A. 118 D3
Talkh Āb Iran 88 E3
Tallacootra, Lake salt flat Australia 109 F7
Talladega U.S.A. 133 C5

▶Tallahassee U.S.A. 133 C6
State capital of Florida.

Tall al Aḥmar Syria 85 D1
Tall Baydar Syria 91 F3
Tall-e Ḥalāl Iran 88 D4

▶Tallinn Estonia 45 N7
Capital of Estonia.

Tall Kalakh Syria 85 C2
Tall Kayf Iraq 91 F3
Tall Kūjik Syria 91 F3
Tallow Rep. of Ireland 51 D5
Tallulah U.S.A. 131 F5
Tall 'Uwaynāt Iraq 91 F3
Tallymerjen Uzbek. see Talimardzhan
Talmont-St-Hilaire France 56 D3
Tal'ne Ukr. 43 F6
Tal'noye Ukr. see Tal'ne
Taloda India 82 C5
Talodi Sudan 86 D7
Taloga U.S.A. 131 D4
Talon, Lac l. Canada 123 I3
Ta-long Myanmar 70 B2
Tāloqān Afgh. 89 H2
Talos Dome ice feature Antarctica 152 H2
Ta Loung San mt. Laos 70 C2
Talovaya Rus. Fed. 43 I6
Taloyoak Canada 119 I3
Tal Pass Pak. 89 I3
Talsi Latvia 45 M8
Tal Sīyāh Iran 89 F4
Taltal Chile 144 B3
Taltson r. Canada 121 H2
Talu China 76 B2
Talvik Norway 44 M1
Talwood Australia 112 D2
Talyshskiye Gory mts Azer./Iran see Talış Dağları
Talyy Rus. Fed. 42 L2
Tamala Australia 109 A6
Tamala Rus. Fed. 43 I5
Tamale Ghana 96 C4
Tamana i. Kiribati 107 H2

Taman Negara National Park Malaysia 71 C6
Tamano Japan 75 D6
Tamanrasset Alg. 96 D2
Tamanthi Myanmar 70 A1
Tamaqua U.S.A. 135 H3
Tamar India 83 F5
Tamar Syria see Tadmur
Tamar r. U.K. 49 C8
Tamarugal, Pampa de plain Chile 142 E7
Tamasane Botswana 101 H2
Tamatave Madag. see Toamasina
Tamaulipas state Mex. 131 D7
Tambacounda Senegal 96 B3
Tambaqui Brazil 142 F5
Tambar Springs Australia 112 D3
Tambelan, Kepulauan is Indon. 71 D7
Tambelan Besar i. Indon. 71 D7
Tambo r. Australia 112 C6
Tambohorano Madag. 99 E5
Tambora, Gunung vol. Indon. 108 B2
Tamboritha mt. Australia 112 C6
Tambov Rus. Fed. 43 I5
Tambovka Rus. Fed. 74 C2
Tambura Sudan 97 F4
Tamburi Brazil 145 C1
Tâmchekkeţ Mauritania 96 B3
Tamdybulak Uzbek. 80 B3
Tâmega r. Port. 57 B3
Tamenghest Alg. see Tamanrasset
Tamenglong India 83 H4
Tamerza Tunisia 58 B7
Tamgak, Adrar mt. Niger 96 D3
Tamgué, Massif du mt. Guinea 96 B3
Tamiahua, Laguna de lag. Mex. 136 E4
Tamiang, Ujung pt Indon. 71 B6
Tamil Nadu state India 84 C4
Tamitsa Rus. Fed. 42 H2
Ţâmîya Egypt see Ţāmīyah
Ţāmīyah Egypt 90 C5
Tam Ky Vietnam 70 E4
Tammarvi r. Canada 121 K1
Tammerfors Fin. see Tampere
Tammisaari Fin. see Ekenäs
Tampa U.S.A. 133 D7
Tampa Bay U.S.A. 133 D7
Tampere Fin. 45 M6
Tampico Mex. 136 E4
Tampin Malaysia 71 C7
Tampines Sing. 71 [inset]
Tamsagbulag Mongolia 73 L3
Tamsweg Austria 47 N7
Tamu Myanmar 70 A1
Tamworth Australia 112 E3
Tamworth U.K. 49 F6
Tana r. Fin./Norway see Tenojoki
Tana r. Kenya 98 E4
Tana Madag. see Antananarivo
Tana i. Vanuatu see Tanna
Tana, Lake Eth. 98 D2
Tanabe Japan 75 D6
Tanabi Brazil 145 A3
Tana Bru Norway 44 P1
Tanada Lake U.S.A. 120 A2
Tanafjorden inlet Norway 44 P1
Tanah, Tanjung pt Indon. 68 D8
T'ana Hāyk' l. Eth. see Tana, Lake
Tanahgrogot Indon. 68 F7
Tanah Merah Malaysia 71 C6
Tanahputih Indon. 71 C7
Tanakeke i. Indon. 68 F8
Tanami Australia 108 E4
Tanami Desert Australia 108 E4
Tân An Vietnam 71 D5
Tanana r. U.S.A. 120 A2
Tananarive Madag. see Antananarivo
Tanandava Madag. 99 E6
Tancheng China see Pingtan
Tanch'ŏn N. Korea 75 C4
Tanda Côte d'Ivoire 96 C4
Tanda Uttar Pradesh India 82 D3
Tanda Uttar Pradesh India 83 E4
Tandag Phil. 69 H5
Ţăndărei Romania 59 L2
Tandaué Angola 99 B5
Tandi India 82 D2
Tandil Arg. 144 E5
Tando Adam Pak. 89 H5
Tando Alahyar Pak. 89 H5
Tando Bago Pak. 89 H5
Tandou Lake imp. l. Australia 111 C7
Tandragee U.K. 51 F3
Tandur India 84 C2
Tanduri Pak. 89 G4
Tanega-shima i. Japan 75 C7
Tanen Taunggyi mts Thai. 70 B3
Tanezrouft reg. Alg./Mali 96 C2
Ţanf, Jabal aţ hill Syria 85 D3
Tang, Ra's-e pt Iran 89 E5
Tanga Tanz. 99 D4
Tangail Bangl. 83 G4
Tanga Islands P.N.G. 106 F2
Tanganyika country Africa see Tanzania

▶Tanganyika, Lake Africa 99 C4
Deepest and 2nd largest lake in Africa.

Tangará Brazil 145 A4
Tangasseri India 84 C4
Tangdan China 76 D3
Tangeli Iran 88 D2
Tanger Morocco see Tangier
Tangerhütte Germany 53 L2
Tangermünde Germany 53 L2
Tang-e Sarkheh Iran 89 E5
Tanggor China 76 D1
Tanggulashan China 76 B1
Tanggula Shan mt. China 83 G2
Tanggula Shan mts China 83 G2
Tanggula Shankou pass China 83 G2
Tangguo China 83 F3
Tanghe China 77 G1
Tangier Morocco 57 D6
Tangiers Morocco see Tangier
Tang La pass China 83 G4
Tangla India 83 G4
Tanglag China 76 C1
Tanglin Sing. 71 [inset]
Tangmai China 76 B2
Tangnag China 76 D1
Tangorin Australia 110 D4
Tangra Yumco salt l. China 83 F3
Tangse Indon. 71 A6
Tangshan Guizhou China see Shiqian
Tangshan Hebei China 73 L5
Tangte mt. Myanmar 70 B2
Tangtse Jammu and Kashmir see Tanktse
Tangwan China 77 F3
Tangwanghe China 74 C2
Tangyuan China 74 C3
Tangyung Tso salt l. China 83 F3
Tanhaçu Brazil 145 C1
Tanhua Fin. 44 O3
Tani Cambodia 71 D5
Taniantaweng Shan mts China 76 B2
Tanimbar, Kepulauan is Indon. 108 E1
Taninthari Myanmar see Tenasserim
Tanintharyi Myanmar see Tenasserim
Taninthayi Myanmar see Tenasserim
Tanjah Morocco see Tangier
Tanjay Phil. 69 G5
Tanjore India see Thanjavur
Tanjung Indon. 68 F7
Tanjungbalai Indon. 71 B7
Tanjungkarang-Telukbetung Indon. see Bandar Lampung
Tanjungpandan Indon. 68 D7
Tanjungpinang Indon. 71 D7
Tanjungpura Indon. 71 B7
Tanjung Puting National Park Indon. 68 E7
Tanjungredeb Indon. 68 F6
Tanjungselor Indon. 68 F6
Tankse Jammu and Kashmir see Tanktse
Tanktse Jammu and Kashmir 82 D2
Tankuhi India 83 F4
Tankwa-Karoo National Park S. Africa 100 D7
Tanna i. Vanuatu 107 G3
Tannadice U.K. 50 G4
Tännäs Sweden 44 H5
Tanner, Mount Canada 120 G5
Tannu-Ola, Khrebet mts Rus. Fed. 80 H1
Tanot India 82 B4
Tanout Niger 96 D3
Tansen Nepal 83 E4
Tanshui Taiwan 77 I3
Ţanţā Egypt 90 C5
Ţanţa Egypt see Ţanţā
Tan-Tan Morocco 96 B2
Tantu China 74 A3
Tantura Israel 85 B3
Tanuku India 84 D2
Tanumbirini Australia 108 F4
Tanumshede Sweden 45 G7
▶Tanzania country Africa 99 D4
Africa 7, 94–95
Tanzilla r. Canada 120 D3
Tao, Ko i. Thai. 71 B5
Tao'an China see Taonan
Taobh Tuath U.K. see Northton
Taocheng China see Daxin
Tao He r. China 76 D1
Taohong China see Longhui
Taohuajiang China see Taojiang
Taohuaping China see Longhui
Taojiang China 77 G2
Taolanaro Madag. see Tôlañaro
Taonan China 74 A3
Taongi atoll Marshall Is 150 H5
Taos U.S.A. 127 G5
Taounate Morocco 54 D5
Taourirt Morocco 54 D5
Taoxi China 77 H3
Taoyang China see Lintao
Taoyuan China 77 F2
T'aoyüan Taiwan 77 I3
Tapa Estonia 45 N7
Tapachula Mex. 136 F6
Tapah Malaysia 71 C6
Tapajós r. Brazil 143 H4
Tapaktuan Indon. 71 B7
Tapauá Brazil 142 F5
Tapauá r. Brazil 142 F5
Taperoá Brazil 145 D1
Tapi r. India 82 C5
Tapiau Rus. Fed. see Gvardeysk
Tapis, Gunung mt. Malaysia 71 C6
Tapisuelas Mex. 127 F8
Taplejung Nepal 83 F4
Tap Mun Chau i. Hong Kong China 77 [inset]
Ta-pom Myanmar 70 B2
Tappahannock U.S.A. 135 G5
Tappeh, Kūh-e hill Iran 88 C3
Taprobane country Asia see Sri Lanka
Tapuaenuku mt. N.Z. 113 D5
Tapulonanjing mt. Indon. 71 B7
Tapurucuara Brazil 142 E4
Taputeouea atoll Kiribati see Tabiteuea
Ţaqţaq Iraq 91 G4
Taquara Brazil 145 A5
Taquari Mato Grosso Brazil 143 H7
Taquari Rio Grande do Sul Brazil 145 A5
Taquari r. Brazil 143 G7
Taquaritinga Brazil 145 A3
Tar r. Rep. of Ireland 51 E5
Tara Australia 112 E1
Ţarābulus Lebanon see Tripoli
Ţarābulus Libya see Tripoli
Tarahuwan India 82 E4
Tarai reg. India 83 G4
Tarakan Indon. 68 F6
Tarakan i. Indon. 68 F6
Tarakki reg. Afgh. 89 G3
Taraklı Turkey 59 N4
Taran, Mys pt Rus. Fed. 45 K9
Tarana Australia 112 D4
Taranagar India 82 C3
Taranaki, Mount vol. N.Z. 113 E4
Tarancón Spain 57 E3
Tarangambadi India 84 C4
Tarangire National Park Tanz. 98 D4
Taranto Italy 58 G4
Taranto, Golfo di g. Italy 58 G4
Taranto, Gulf of Italy see Taranto, Golfo di
Tarapoto Peru 142 C5
Tarapur India 84 B2
Tararua Range mts N.Z. 113 E5
Tarascon-sur-Ariège France 56 E5
Tarasovskiy Rus. Fed. 43 I6
Tarauacá Brazil 142 D5
Tarauacá r. Brazil 142 E5
Tarawera N.Z. 113 F4
Tarawera, Mount vol. N.Z. 113 F4
Taraz Kazakh. 80 D3
Tarazona Spain 57 F3
Tarazona de la Mancha Spain 57 F4
Tarbagatay, Khrebet mts Kazakh. 80 F2
Tarbat Ness pt U.K. 50 F3
Tarbert Rep. of Ireland 51 C5
Tarbert Scotland U.K. 50 C3
Tarbert Scotland U.K. 50 D5
Tarbes France 56 E5
Tarboro U.S.A. 132 E5
Tarcoola Australia 109 F7
Tarcoon Australia 112 C3
Tarcoonyinna watercourse Australia 109 F6
Tarcutta Australia 112 C5
Tardoki-Yani, Gora mt. Rus. Fed. 74 E2
Taree Australia 112 F3
Tarella Australia 111 C6
Tarentum Italy see Taranto
Ţarfā', Baţn aţ depr. Saudi Arabia 88 C6
Tarfaya Morocco 96 B2
Targa well Niger 96 D3
Targan China see Talin Hiag
Targhee Pass U.S.A. 126 F3
Târgovişte Romania 59 K2
Targuist Morocco 57 D6
Târgu Jiu Romania 59 J2
Târgu Mureş Romania 59 K1
Târgu Neamţ Romania 59 L1
Târgu Secuiesc Romania 59 L1
Targyailing China 83 F3
Tari P.N.G. 69 K8
Tarif U.A.E. 88 D5
Tarifa Spain 57 D5
Tarifa, Punta de pt Spain 57 D5
Tarija Bol. 142 F8
Tarikere India 84 B3
Tariku r. Indon. 69 J7
Tarīm Yemen 86 G6
Tarim Basin China 80 F4
Tarime Tanz. 98 D4
Tarim He r. China 80 G3
Tarim Pendi basin China see Tarim Basin
Tarīn Kowt Afgh. 89 G3
Taritatu r. Indon. 69 J7
Tarka r. S. Africa 101 G7
Tarkastad S. Africa 101 H7
Tarkio U.S.A. 130 E3
Tarko-Sale Rus. Fed. 64 I3
Tarkwa Ghana 96 C4
Tarlac Phil. 69 G3
Tarlo River National Park Australia 112 D5
Tarma Peru 142 C6
Tarmstedt Germany 53 J1
Tarn r. France 56 E4
Tärnaby Sweden 44 I4
Tarnak r. Afgh. 89 G4
Târnăveni Romania 59 K1
Tarnobrzeg Poland 43 D6
Tarnogskiy Gorodok Rus. Fed. 42 I3
Tarnopol Ukr. see Ternopil'
Tarnów Poland 43 D6
Tarnowitz Poland see Tarnowskie Góry
Tarnowskie Góry Poland 47 Q5
Taro Co salt l. China 83 E3
Ţārom Iran 88 D4
Taroom Australia 111 E5
Taroudannt Morocco 54 C5
Tarpaulin Swamp Australia 110 B3
Tarq Iran 88 C3
Tarquinia Italy 58 D3
Tarquinii Italy see Tarquinia
Tarrabool Lake salt flat Australia 110 A3
Tarraco Spain see Tarragona
Tarrafal Cape Verde 96 [inset]
Tarragona Spain 57 G3
Tårrajaur Sweden 44 K3
Tarran Hills hill Australia 112 C4
Tarrant Point Australia 110 B3
Tàrrega Spain 57 G3
Tarrong China see Nyêmo
Tarso Emissi mt. Chad 97 E2
Tarsus Turkey 85 B1
Tart China 83 H1
Tärtär Azer. 91 G2
Tartu Estonia 45 O7
Ţarţūs Syria 85 B2
Tarumovka Rus. Fed. 91 G1
Tarung Hka r. Myanmar 70 B1
Tarutao, Ko i. Thai. 71 B6
Tarutung Indon. 71 B7
Tarvisium Italy see Treviso
Tarz Iran 88 E4
Tasai, Ko i. Thai. 71 B5
Taschereau Canada 122 F4
Taseko Mountain Canada 120 F5
Tashauz Turkm. see Dashoguz
Tashi Chho Bhutan see Thimphu
Tashigang Bhutan see Trashigang
Tashino Rus. Fed. see Pervomaysk
Tashir Armenia 91 G2
Tashk, Daryācheh-ye l. Iran 88 D4

▶Tashkent Uzbek. 80 C3
Capital of Uzbekistan.

Tashkepri Turkm. 89 F2
Tāshqurghān Afgh. see Kholm
Tashtagol Rus. Fed. 72 F2
Tashtyp Rus. Fed. 72 F2
Tasialujjuaq, Lac l. Canada 123 G2
Tasiat, Lac l. Canada 122 G2
Tasiilap Karra c. Greenland 119 O3
Tasiilaq Greenland see Ammassalik
Tasīl Syria 85 B3
Tasiujaq Canada 123 H2
Tasiusaq Greenland 119 M2
Taşkent Turkey 85 A1
Tasker Niger 96 E3
Taskesken Kazakh. 80 F2
Taşköprü Turkey 90 D2
Tasman Abyssal Plain sea feature Tasman Sea 150 G8
Tasman Basin sea feature Tasman Sea 150 G8
Tasman Bay N.Z. 113 D5

▶Tasmania state Australia 111 [inset]
4th largest island in Oceania.

Tasman Islands P.N.G. see Nukumanu Islands
Tasman Mountains N.Z. 113 D5
Tasman Peninsula Australia 111 [inset]
Tasman Sea S. Pacific Ocean 106 H6
Taşova Turkey 90 E2
Tassara Niger 96 D3
Tassialouc, Lac l. Canada 122 G2
Tassili du Hoggar plat. Alg. 96 D2
Tassili n'Ajjer plat. Alg. 96 D2
Tasty Kazakh. 80 C3
Taşucu Turkey 85 A1
Tas-Yuryakh Rus. Fed. 65 M3
Tata Morocco 54 C6
Tatabánya Hungary 58 H1
Tata Mailau, Gunung mt. East Timor 108 D2
Tataouine Tunisia 54 G5
Tatarbunary Ukr. 59 M2
Tatarsk Rus. Fed. 64 I4
Tatarskiy Proliv strait Rus. Fed. 74 F2
Tatar Strait Rus. Fed. see Tatarskiy Proliv
Tate r. Australia 110 C3
Tateyama Japan 75 E6
Tathlina Lake Canada 120 G2
Tathlīth Saudi Arabia 86 F6
Tathlīth, Wādī watercourse Saudi Arabia 86 F5
Tathra Australia 112 D6
Tatinnai Lake Canada 121 L2
Tatishchevo Rus. Fed. 43 J6
Tatkon Myanmar 70 B2
Tatla Lake Canada 120 E5
Tatla Lake l. Canada 120 E5
Tatlayoko Lake Canada 120 E5
Tatnam, Cape Canada 121 N3
Tatra Mountains Poland/Slovakia 47 Q6
Tatry mts Poland/Slovakia see Tatra Mountains
Tatrzański Park Narodowy nat. park Poland 47 Q6
Tatshenshini-Alsek Provincial Wilderness Park Canada 120 B3
Tatsinskiy Rus. Fed. 43 I6
Tatta Pak. 89 G5
Tatuí Brazil 145 B3
Tatuk Mountain Canada 120 E4
Tatum U.S.A. 131 C5
Tatvan Turkey 91 F3
Tau Norway 45 D7
Taua Brazil 143 J5
Tauapeçaçu Brazil 142 F4
Taubaté Brazil 145 B3
Tauber r. Germany 53 J5
Tauberbischofsheim Germany 53 J5
Taucha Germany 53 M3
Taufstein hill Germany 53 J4
Taukum, Peski des. Kazakh. 80 D3
Taumarunui N.Z. 113 E4
Taumaturgo Brazil 142 D5
Taung S. Africa 100 G4
Taungdwingyi Myanmar 70 A2
Taunggyi Myanmar 70 B2
Taunglau Myanmar 70 B2
Taungnyo Range mts Myanmar 70 B3
Taungtha Myanmar 70 A2
Taungup Myanmar 76 B5
Taunton U.K. 49 D7
Taunton U.S.A. 135 J3
Taunus hills Germany 53 H4
Taupo N.Z. 113 F4
Taupo, Lake N.Z. 113 E4
Tauragė Lith. 45 M9
Tauranga N.Z. 113 F3
Taurasia Italy see Turin
Taureau, Réservoir resr Canada 122 G5
Taurianova Italy 58 G5
Tauroa Point N.Z. 113 D2
Taurus Mountains Turkey 85 A1
Taute r. France 49 F9
Tauu Islands P.N.G. 107 F2
Tauz Azer. see Tovuz
Tavas Turkey 59 M6
Tavastehus Fin. see Hämeenlinna
Taverham U.K. 49 I6
Taveuni i. Fiji 107 I3
Tavildara Tajik. 89 H2
Tavira Port. 57 C5
Tavistock Canada 134 E2
Tavistock U.K. 49 C8
Tavoy Myanmar 71 B4
Tavoy r. mouth Myanmar 71 B4
Tavoy Island Myanmar see Mali Kyun
Tavoy Point Myanmar 71 B4
Tavşanlı Turkey 59 M5
Taw r. U.K. 49 C7
Tawang India 83 G4
Tawas City U.S.A. 134 D1
Tawau Sabah Malaysia 68 F6
Tawè Myanmar see Tavoy
Tawe r. U.K. 49 D7
Ţawī Ḩafīr well U.A.E. 88 D5
Ţawī Murra well U.A.E. 88 D5
Tawmaw Myanmar 70 B1
Tawu Taiwan 77 I4
Taxkorgan China 80 E4
Tay r. Canada 120 C2
Tay r. U.K. 50 F4
Tay, Firth of est. U.K. 50 F4
Tay, Lake salt flat Australia 109 C8
Tay, Loch l. U.K. 50 E4
Tayandu, Kepulauan is Indon. 69 I8
Taybola Rus. Fed. 44 R2
Taycheedah U.S.A. 134 A2
Tayinloan U.K. 50 D5
Taylor Canada 120 F3
Taylor AK U.S.A. 118 B3
Taylor MI U.S.A. 134 D2
Taylor NE U.S.A. 130 D3
Taylor TX U.S.A. 131 D6
Taylor, Mount U.S.A. 129 J4
Taylorsville U.S.A. 134 C4
Taylorville U.S.A. 130 F4
Taymā' Saudi Arabia 90 E6
Taymura r. Rus. Fed. 65 K3
Taymyr, Ozero l. Rus. Fed. 65 L2
Taymyr, Poluostrov pen. Rus. Fed. see Taymyr Peninsula
Taymyr Peninsula Rus. Fed. 64 J2
Tây Ninh Vietnam 71 D5
Taypak Kazakh. 41 Q6
Taypaq Kazakh. see Taypak
Tayshet Rus. Fed. 72 H1
Taytay Phil. 68 F4
Tayuan China 74 B2
Tayyebād Iran 89 F3
Taz r. Rus. Fed. 64 I3
Taza Morocco 54 D5
Tāza Khurmātū Iraq 91 G4
Taze Myanmar 70 A2
Tazewell TN U.S.A. 134 D5
Tazewell VA U.S.A. 134 E5
Tazin r. Canada 121 I2
Tazin Lake Canada 121 I3
Tāzirbū Libya 97 F2
Tazmalt Alg. 57 I5
Tazovskaya Guba sea chan. Rus. Fed. 64 I3
Tbessa Alg. see Tébessa

▶T'bilisi Georgia 91 G2
Capital of Georgia.

Tbilisskaya Rus. Fed. 43 I7
Tchabal Mbabo mt. Cameroon 96 E4
Tchad country Africa see Chad
Tchamba Togo 96 D4
Tchibanga Gabon 98 B4
Tchigaï, Plateau du Niger 97 E2
Tchin-Tabaradene Niger 96 D3
Tcholliré Cameroon 97 E4
Tchula U.S.A. 131 F5
Tczew Poland 47 Q3
Te, Prêk r. Cambodia 71 D4
Teague, Lake salt flat Australia 109 C6
Te Anau N.Z. 113 A7
Te Anau, Lake N.Z. 113 A7
Teapa Mex. 136 F5
Te Araroa N.Z. 113 G3
Teate Italy see Chieti
Te Awamutu N.Z. 113 E4
Teba Indon. 69 J7
Tébarat Niger 96 D3
Tebas Indon. 71 E7
Tebay U.K. 48 E4
Tebesjuak Lake Canada 121 L2
Tébessa Alg. 58 C7
Tébessa, Monts de mts Alg. 58 C7
Tebingtinggi Indon. 71 B7
Téboursouk Tunisia 58 C6
Tébourba Tunisia 58 C6
Tebulos Mt'a Georgia/Rus. Fed. 91 G2
Tecate Mex. 128 E5
Tece Turkey 85 B1
Techiman Ghana 96 C4
Tecka Arg. 144 B6
Tecklenburger Land reg. Germany 53 H2
Tecoripa Mex. 127 F7
Técpan Mex. 136 D5
Tecuala Mex. 136 C4
Tecuci Romania 59 L2
Tecumseh MI U.S.A. 134 D3
Tecumseh NE U.S.A. 130 D3
Tedzhen Turkm. 89 F2
Teec Nos Pos U.S.A. 129 I3
Tees r. U.K. 48 F4
Teeswater Canada 134 E1
Tefé r. Brazil 142 F4
Tefenni Turkey 59 M6
Tegal Indon. 68 D8
Tegel airport Germany 53 N2
Tegid, Llyn l. U.K. 49 D6

▶Tegucigalpa Hond. 137 G6
Capital of Honduras.

Teguidda-n-Tessoumt Niger 96 D3
Tehachapi U.S.A. 128 D4
Tehachapi Mountains U.S.A. 128 D4
Tehachapi Pass U.S.A. 128 D4
Tehek Lake Canada 121 M1
Teheran Iran see Tehrān
Tehery Lake Canada 121 M1
Téhini Côte d'Ivoire 96 C4

▶Tehrān Iran 88 C3
Capital of Iran.

Tehri India see Tikamgarh
Tehuacán Mex. 136 E5
Tehuantepec, Golfo de Mex. see Tehuantepec, Gulf of
Tehuantepec, Gulf of Mex. 136 F5
Tehuantepec, Istmo de isthmus Mex. 136 F5
Teide, Pico del vol. Canary Is 96 B2
Teifi r. U.K. 49 C6
Teignmouth U.K. 49 D8
Teixeira de Sousa Angola see Luau
Teixeiras Brazil 145 C3
Teixeira Soares Brazil 145 A4
Tejakula Indon. 108 A2
Tejen Turkm. see Tedzhen
Tejo r. Port. 57 B4 see Tagus
Tejon Pass U.S.A. 128 D4
Tekapo, Lake N.Z. 113 C6
Tekax Mex. 136 G4
Tekeli Kazakh. 80 E3
Tekes China 80 F3
Tekiliktag mt. China 82 E1
Tekin Rus. Fed. 74 D2
Tekirdağ Turkey 59 L4
Tekka India 84 D2
Tekkali India 84 E2
Teknaf Bangl. 83 H5
Tekong Kechil, Pulau i. Sing. 71 [inset]
Te Kuiti N.Z. 113 E4
Tel r. India 84 D1
Télagh Alg. 57 F6
Telanaipura Indon. see Jambi
Tel Ashqelon tourist site Israel 81 B4
Télataï Mali 96 D3
Tel Aviv-Yafo Israel 85 B3
Telč Czech Rep. 47 O6
Telchac Puerto Mex. 136 G4
Telekhany Belarus see Tsyelyakhany
Telêmaco Borba Brazil 145 A4
Teleorman r. Romania 59 K3
Telerhteba, Djebel mt. Alg. 96 D2
Telescope Peak U.S.A. 128 E3
Teles Pires r. Brazil 143 G5
Telford U.K. 49 E6
Telgte Germany 53 H3
Télimélé Guinea 96 B3
Teljo, Jebel mt. Sudan 86 C7
Telkwa Canada 120 E4
Tell Atlas mts Alg. see Atlas Tellien
Tell City U.S.A. 134 B5
Teller U.S.A. 118 B3
Tell es Sultan West Bank see Jericho
Tellicherry India 84 B4
Tellin Belgium 52 F4
Telloh Iraq 91 G5
Telluride U.S.A. 129 J3
Tel'novskiy Rus. Fed. 74 F2
Telok Anson Malaysia see Teluk Intan
Telo Martius France see Toulon
Tel'pos-Iz, Gora mt. Rus. Fed. 41 R3
Telsen Arg. 144 C6
Telšiai Lith. 45 M9
Teltow Germany 53 N2
Teluk Anson Malaysia see Teluk Intan
Telukbetung Indon. see Bandar Lampung
Teluk Cenderawasih Marine National Park Indon. 69 I7
Teluk Intan Malaysia 71 C6
Temagami Lake Canada 122 F5
Temanggung Indon. 68 E8
Têmarxung China 83 G2
Temba S. Africa 101 I3
Tembagapura Indon. 69 J7
Tembenchi r. Rus. Fed. 65 K3
Tembilahan Indon. 68 C7
Tembisa S. Africa 101 I4
Tembo Aluma Angola 99 B4
Teme r. U.K. 49 E6
Temecula U.S.A. 128 E5
Temerluh Malaysia see Temerluh
Temerluh Malaysia 71 C7
Teminabuan Indon. 69 I7
Temirtau Kazakh. 80 D1
Témiscamie r. Canada 123 G4
Témiscamie, Lac l. Canada 123 G4
Temiscaming Canada 122 F5
Témiscamingue, Lac l. Canada 122 F5
Témiscouata, Lac l. Canada 123 H5
Temmes Fin. 44 N4
Temnikov Rus. Fed. 43 I5
Temora Australia 112 C5
Temósachic Mex. 127 G7
Tempe U.S.A. 129 H5
Tempe Downs Australia 109 F6
Tempelhof airport Germany 53 N2
Temple MI U.S.A. 134 C1
Temple TX U.S.A. 131 D6
Temple Bar U.K. 49 C6
Temple Dera Pak. 89 H4
Templemore Rep. of Ireland 51 E5
Temple Sowerby U.K. 48 E4
Templeton watercourse Australia 110 B4
Templin Germany 53 N1
Tempué Angola 99 B5
Temryuk Rus. Fed. 90 E1
Temryukskiy Zaliv b. Rus. Fed. 43 H7
Temuco Chile 144 B5
Temuka N.Z. 113 C7
Temuli China see Butuo
Tena Ecuador 142 C4
Tenabo Mex. 136 F4
Tenabo, Mount U.S.A. 128 E1
Tenali India 84 D2
Tenasserim Myanmar 71 B4
Tenasserim r. Myanmar 71 B4
Tenbury Wells U.K. 49 E6
Tenby U.K. 49 C7
Tendaho Eth. 98 E2
Tende, Col de pass France/Italy 56 H4
Ten Degree Channel India 71 A5
Tendō Japan 75 F5
Tenedos i. Turkey see Bozcaada
Ténenkou Mali 96 C3
Ténéré reg. Niger 96 D2
Ténéré du Tafassâsset des. Niger 96 E2
Tenerife i. Canary Is 96 B2
Ténès Alg. 57 G5
Teng, Nam r. Myanmar 70 B3
Tengah, Kepulauan is Indon. 68 F8
Tengah, Sungai r. Sing. 71 [inset]
Tengcheng China see Tengxian
Tengchong China 76 C3
Tengeh Reservoir Sing. 71 [inset]
Tengger Shamo des. China 72 I5
Tenggul i. Malaysia 71 C6
Tengiz, Ozero salt l. Kazakh. 80 C1
Tengqiao China 77 F5
Tengréla Côte d'Ivoire 96 C3
Ten'gushevo Rus. Fed. 43 I5
Tengxian China 77 F4
Teni India see Theni
Teniente Jubany research station Antarctica see Jubany
Tenille U.S.A. 133 D6
Tenke Dem. Rep. Congo 99 C5
Tenkeli Rus. Fed. 65 P2
Tenkodogo Burkina 96 C3
Ten Mile Lake salt flat Australia 109 C6
Ten Mile Lake Canada 123 K4
Tennant Creek Australia 108 F4
Tennessee r. U.S.A. 131 F4
Tennessee state U.S.A. 134 C5
Tennessee Pass U.S.A. 126 G5
Tennevoll Norway 44 J2
Tenojoki r. Fin./Norway 44 P1
Tenosique Mex. 136 F5
Tenteno Indon. 69 G7
Tenterden U.K. 49 H7
Tenterfield Australia 112 F2
Ten Thousand Islands U.S.A. 133 D7
Tentudia mt. Spain 57 C4
Tentulia Bangl. see Tetulia
Teodoro Sampaio Brazil 144 F2
Teófilo Otôni Brazil 145 C2
Tepa Indon. 108 E1
Tepache Mex. 127 F7
Te Paki N.Z. 113 D2
Tepatitlán Mex. 136 D4
Tepehuanes Mex. 131 B7
Tepeköy Turkey see Karakoçan
Tepelenë Albania 59 I4
Tepelská Vrchovina hills Czech Rep. 53 M5
Tepequem, Serra mts Brazil 137 L8
Tepic Mex. 136 D4
Te Pirita N.Z. 113 C6
Teplá r. Czech Rep. 53 M4
Teplice Czech Rep. 47 N5
Teplogorka Rus. Fed. 42 L3
Teploozersk Rus. Fed. 74 C2

Teploye Rus. Fed. 43 H5
Teploye Ozero Rus. Fed. see Teploozersk
Tepoca, Cabo c. Mex. 127 E7
Tepopa, Punta pt Mex. 127 E7
Tequila Mex. 136 D4
Téra Niger 96 D3
Teramo Italy 58 E3
Terang Australia 112 A7
Ter Apel Neth. 52 H2
Teratani r. Pak. 89 H4
Tercan Turkey 91 F3
Terebovlya Ukr. 43 E6
Terekty Kazakh. 80 G2
Teresa Cristina Brazil 145 A4
Tereshka r. Rus. Fed. 43 J6
Teresina Brazil 143 J5
Teresina de Goias Brazil 145 B1
Teresita Col. 142 E3
Teresópolis Brazil 145 C3
Teressa Island India 71 A5
Terezinha Brazil 143 H3
Tergeste Italy see Trieste
Tergnier France 52 D5
Teriberka Rus. Fed. 44 S2
Termez Uzbek. 89 G2
Termini Imerese Sicily Italy 58 E6
Términos, Laguna de lag. Mex. 136 F5
Termit-Kaoboul Niger 96 E3
Termiz Uzbek. see Termez
Termo U.S.A. 128 C1
Termoli Italy 58 F4
Termonde Belgium see Dendermonde
Tern r. U.K. 49 E6
Ternate Indon. 69 H6
Terneuzen Neth. 52 D3
Terney Rus. Fed. 74 E3
Terni Italy 58 E3
Ternopil' Ukr. 43 E6
Ternopol' Ukr. see Ternopil'
Terpeniya, Mys c. Rus. Fed. 74 G2
Terpeniya, Zaliv g. Rus. Fed. 74 F2
Terra Alta U.S.A. 134 F4
Terra Bella U.S.A. 128 D4
Terrace Canada 120 D4
Terrace Bay Canada 122 D4
Terra Firma S. Africa 100 F3
Terråk Norway 44 H4
Terralba Sardinia Italy 58 C5
Terra Nova Bay Antarctica 152 H1
Terra Nova National Park Canada 123 L4
Terre Adélie reg. Antarctica see Adélie Land
Terrebonne Bay U.S.A. 131 F6
Terre Haute U.S.A. 134 B4
Terre-Neuve prov. Canada see Newfoundland and Labrador
Terre-Neuve-et-Labrador prov. Canada see Newfoundland and Labrador
Terres Australes et Antarctiques Françaises terr. Indian Ocean see French Southern and Antarctic Lands
Terry U.S.A. 126 G3
Terschelling i. Neth. 52 F1
Terskiy Bereg coastal area Rus. Fed. 42 H2
Tertenia Sardinia Italy 58 C5
Terter Azer. see Tärtär
Teruel Spain 57 F3
Terutao National Park Thai. 71 B6
Tervola Fin. 44 N3
Tešanj Bos.-Herz. 58 G2
Teseney Eritrea 86 E6
Tesha r. Rus. Fed. 43 I5
Teshekpuk Lake U.S.A. 118 C2
Teshio Japan 74 F3
Teshio-gawa r. Japan 74 F3
Teslin Canada 120 C2
Teslin r. Canada 120 C2
Teslin Lake Canada 120 C2
Tesouras r. Brazil 145 A1
Tessalit Mali 96 D2
Tessaoua Niger 96 D3
Tessolo Moz. 101 L1
Test r. U.K. 49 F8
Testour Tunisia 58 C6
Tetachuck Lake Canada 120 E4
Tetas, Punta pt Chile 144 B2
Tete Moz. 99 D5
Te Teko N.Z. 113 F4
Teteriv r. Ukr. 43 F6
Teterow Germany 47 N4
Tetiyev Ukr. see Tetiyiv
Tetiyiv Ukr. 43 F6
Tetlin U.S.A. 120 A2
Tetlin Lake U.S.A. 120 A2
Tetney U.K. 48 G5
Teton r. U.S.A. 126 F3
Tétouan Morocco 57 D6
Tetovo Macedonia 59 I3
Tetpur India 82 B5
Tetuán Morocco see Tétouan
Tetulia Bangl. 83 G4
Tetulia sea chan. Bangl. 83 G5
Tetyukhe Rus. Fed. see Dal'negorsk
Tetyukhe-Pristan' Rus. Fed. see Rudnaya Pristan'
Tetyushi Rus. Fed. 43 K5
Teuco r. Arg. 144 D2
Teufelsbach Namibia 100 C2
Teunom Indon. 71 A6
Teunom r. Indon. 71 A6
Teutoburger Wald hills Germany 53 I2
Teuva Fin. 44 L5
Tevere r. Italy see Tiber
Teverya Israel see Tiberias
Teviot r. U.K. 50 G5
Te Waewae Bay N.Z. 113 A8
Te Waipounamu i. N.Z. see South Island
Tewane Botswana 101 H2
Tewantin Australia 111 F5
Tewkesbury U.K. 49 E7
Têwo China 76 D1
Texarkana AR U.S.A. 131 E5
Texarkana TX U.S.A. 131 E5
Texas Australia 112 E2
Texas state U.S.A. 131 D6
Texel i. Neth. 52 E1
Texhoma U.S.A. 131 C4
Texoma, Lake U.S.A. 131 D5
Teyateyaneng Lesotho 101 H5
Teykovo Rus. Fed. 42 I4
Teza r. Rus. Fed. 42 I4
Tezpur India 83 H4
Tezu India 83 I4
Tha, Nam r. Laos 70 C2
Thaa Atoll Maldives see Kolhumadulu Atoll
Tha-anne r. Canada 121 M2
Thabana-Ntlenyana mt. Lesotho 101 I5
Thaba Nchu S. Africa 101 H5
Thaba Putsoa mt. Lesotho 101 H5
Thaba-Tseka Lesotho 101 I5
Thabazimbi S. Africa 101 H3
Thab Lan National Park Thai. 71 C4
Tha Bo Laos 70 C3
Thabong S. Africa 101 H4
Thabyedaung Myanmar 76 C4
Thade r. Myanmar 70 A3
Thagyettaw Myanmar 71 B4
Tha Hin Thai. see Lop Buri
Thai Binh Vietnam 70 D2
▶Thailand country Asia 70 C4
Asia 6, 62–63
Thailand, Gulf of Asia 71 C5
Thai Muang Thai. 71 B5
Thai Nguyên Vietnam 70 D2
Thaj Saudi Arabia 88 C5
Thakurgaon Bangl. 83 G4
Thakurtola India 82 E5
Thal Germany 53 K4
Thala Tunisia 58 C7
Thalang Thai. 71 B5
Thalassery India see Tellicherry
Thal Desert Pak. 89 H4
Thale (Harz) Germany 53 L3
Thaliparamba India see Taliparamba
Thallon Australia 112 D2
Thalo Pak. 89 G4
Thamaga Botswana 101 G3
Thamar, Jabal mt. Yemen 86 G7
Thamarīt Oman 87 H6
Thame r. U.K. 49 F7
Thames r. Ont. Canada 125 K3
Thames r. Ont. Canada 134 D2
Thames N.Z. 113 E3
Thames est. U.K. 49 H7
Thames r. U.K. 49 H7
Thamesford Canada 134 E2
Thana India see Thane
Thanatpin Myanmar 70 B3
Thandwè Myanmar see Sandoway
Thane India 84 B2
Thanet, Isle of pen. U.K. 49 I7
Thăng Binh Vietnam 70 E4
Thangoo Australia 108 C4
Thangra Jammu and Kashmir 82 D2
Thanh Hoa Vietnam 70 D3
Thanh Tri Vietnam 71 D5
Thanjavur India 84 C4
Than Kyun i. Myanmar 71 B5
Thanlwin r. China/Myanmar see Salween
Thanlyin Myanmar see Syriam
Thaolintoa Lake Canada 121 L2
Tha Pla Thai. 70 C3
Thap Put Thai. 71 B5
Thapsacus Syria see Dibsī
Thap Sakae Thai. 71 B5
Tharabwin Myanmar 71 B4
Tharad India 82 B4
Thar Desert India/Pak. 89 H5
Thargomindah Australia 112 A1
Tharrawaw Myanmar 70 A3
Tharthār, Buḩayrat ath l. Iraq 91 F4
Tharwānīyyah U.A.E. 88 D6
Thasos i. Greece 59 K4
Thatcher U.S.A. 129 I5
Thât Khê Vietnam 70 D2
Thât Nôt Vietnam 71 D5
Thaton Myanmar 70 B3
Thaungdut Myanmar 70 A1
Tha Uthen Thai. 70 D3
Thayawthadangyi Kyun i. Myanmar 71 B4
Thayetmyo Myanmar 70 A3
Thazi Magwe Myanmar 70 A3
Thazi Mandalay Myanmar 83 I5
The Aldermen Islands N.Z. 113 F3
Theba U.S.A. 129 G5
▶The Bahamas country West Indies 133 E7
North America 9, 116–117
Thebes Greece see Thiva
The Bluff Bahamas 133 E7
The Broads nat. park U.K. 49 I6
The Brothers is Hong Kong China 77 [inset]
The Calvados Chain is P.N.G. 110 F1
The Cheviot hill U.K. 48 E3
The Dalles U.S.A. 126 C3
Thedford U.S.A. 130 C3
The Entrance Australia 112 E4
The Faither stack U.K. 50 [inset]
The Fens reg. U.K. 49 G6
▶The Gambia country Africa 96 B3
Africa 7, 94–95
Thegon Myanmar 70 A3
The Grampians mts Australia 111 C8
The Great Oasis oasis Egypt see Khārijah, Wāḩāt al
The Grenadines is St Vincent 137 L6
The Gulf Asia 88 C4

▶The Hague Neth. 52 E2
Seat of government of the Netherlands.

The Hunters Hills N.Z. 113 C7
Thekulthili Lake Canada 121 I2
The Lakes National Park Australia 112 C6
Thelon r. Canada 121 L1
The Lynd Junction Australia 110 D3
Themar Germany 53 K4
Thembalihle S. Africa 101 I4
The Minch sea chan. U.K. 50 C2
The Naze c. Norway see Lindesnes
The Needles stack U.K. 49 F8
Theni India 84 C4
Thenia Alg. 57 H5
Theniet El Had Alg. 57 H6
The North Sound sea chan. U.K. 50 G1
Theodore Australia 110 E5
Theodore Canada 121 K5
Theodore Roosevelt Lake U.S.A. 129 H5
Theodore Roosevelt National Park U.S.A. 130 C2
Theodosia Ukr. see Feodosiya
The Old Man of Coniston hill U.K. 48 D4
The Paps hill Rep. of Ireland 51 C5
The Pas Canada 121 K4
The Pilot mt. Australia 112 D6
Thera i. Greece see Thira
Thérain r. France 52 C5
Theresa U.S.A. 135 H1
Thermaïkos Kolpos g. Greece 59 J4
Thermopolis U.S.A. 126 F4
The Rock Australia 112 C5
Thérouanne France 52 C4
The Salt Lake salt flat Australia 111 C6

▶The Settlement Christmas I. 68 D9
Capital of Christmas Island.

The Skaw spit Denmark see Grenen
The Slot sea chan. Solomon Is see New Georgia Sound
The Solent strait U.K. 49 F8
Thessalon Canada 122 E5
Thessalonica Greece see Thessaloniki
Thessaloniki Greece 59 J4
The Storr hill U.K. 50 C3
Thet r. U.K. 49 H6
The Terraces hills Australia 109 C7
Thetford U.K. 49 H6
Thetford Mines Canada 123 H5
Thetkethaung r. Myanmar 70 A4
The Triangle mts Myanmar 70 B1
The Trossachs hills U.K. 50 E4
The Twins Australia 111 A6
Theva-i-Ra reef Fiji see Ceva-i-Ra

▶The Valley Anguilla 137 L5
Capital of Anguilla.

Thevenard Island Australia 108 A5
Thévenet, Lac l. Canada 123 H2
Theveste Alg. see Tébessa
The Wash b. U.K. 49 H6
The Weald reg. U.K. 49 H7
The Woodlands U.S.A. 131 E6
Thibodaux U.S.A. 131 F6
Thicket Portage Canada 121 L4
Thief River Falls U.S.A. 130 D1
Thiel Neth. see Tiel
Thiel Mountains Antarctica 152 K1
Thielsen, Mount U.S.A. 126 C4
Thielt Belgium see Tielt
Thiérache reg. France 52 D5
Thiers France 56 F4
Thiès Senegal 96 B3
Thika Kenya 98 D4
Thiladhunmathi Atoll Maldives 84 B5
Thiladunmathi Atoll Maldives see Thiladhunmathi Atoll
Thimbu Bhutan see Thimphu

▶Thimphu Bhutan 83 G4
Capital of Bhutan.

Thionville France 52 G5
Thira i. Greece 59 K6
Thirsk U.K. 48 F4
Thirty Mile Lake Canada 121 L2
Thiruvananthapuram India see Trivandrum
Thiruvannamalai India see Tiruvannamalai
Thiruvarur India 84 C4
Thiruvattiyur India see Tiruvottiyur
Thisted Denmark 45 F8
Thistle Creek Canada 120 B2
Thistle Lake Canada 121 I1
Thityabin Myanmar 70 A2
Thiu Khao Luang Phrabang mts Laos/Thai. see Luang Phrabang, Thiu Khao
Thiva Greece 59 J5
Thívai Greece see Thiva
Thlewiaza r. Canada 121 M2
Thoa r. Canada 121 I2
Thô Chu, Đao i. Vietnam 71 C5
Thoen Thai. 76 C5
Thoeng Thai. 70 C3
Thohoyandou S. Africa 101 J2
Tholen Neth. 52 E3
Tholen i. Neth. 52 E3
Tholey Germany 52 H5
Thomas Hill Reservoir U.S.A. 130 E4
Thomas Hubbard, Cape Canada 119 I1
Thomaston CT U.S.A. 135 I3
Thomaston GA U.S.A. 133 C5
Thomastown Rep. of Ireland 51 E5
Thomasville AL U.S.A. 133 C6
Thomasville GA U.S.A. 133 D6
Thommen Belgium 52 G4
Thompson Canada 121 L4
Thompson r. Canada 120 F5
Thompson U.S.A. 129 I2
Thompson r. U.S.A. 124 I4
Thompson Falls U.S.A. 126 E3
Thompson Peak U.S.A. 127 G6
Thompson's Falls Kenya see Nyahururu
Thompson Sound Canada 120 E5
Thomson U.S.A. 133 D5
Thon Buri Thai. 71 C4
Thonokied Lake Canada 121 I1
Thôn Sơn Hai Vietnam 71 E5
Thoothukudi India see Tuticorin
Thoreau U.S.A. 129 I4
Thorn Neth. 52 F3
Thorn Poland see Toruń
Thornaby-on-Tees U.K. 48 F4
Thornapple r. U.S.A. 134 C2
Thornbury U.K. 49 E7
Thorne U.K. 48 G5
Thorne U.S.A. 128 D2
Thornton r. Australia 110 B3
Thorold Canada 134 F2
Thorshavnfjella reg. Antarctica see Thorshavnheiane
Thorshavnheiane reg. Antarctica 152 C2
Thota-ea-Moli Lesotho 101 H5
Thouars France 56 D3
Thoubal India 83 H4
Thourout Belgium see Torhout
Thousand Islands Canada/U.S.A. 135 G1
Thousand Lake Mountain U.S.A. 129 H2
Thousand Oaks U.S.A. 128 D4
Thousandsticks U.S.A. 134 D5
Thrace reg. Europe 59 L4
Thraki reg. Europe see Thrace
Thrakiko Pelagos sea Greece 59 K4
Three Gorges Project resr China 77 F2
Three Hills Canada 120 H5
Three Hummock Island Australia 111 [inset]
Three Kings Islands N.Z. 113 D2
Three Oaks U.S.A. 134 B3
Three Pagodas Pass Myanmar/Thai. 70 B4
Three Points, Cape Ghana 96 C4
Three Rivers U.S.A. 134 C3
Three Sisters mt. U.S.A. 126 C3
Three Springs Australia 109 A7
Thrissur India see Trichur
Throckmorton U.S.A. 131 D5
Throssell, Lake salt flat Australia 109 D6
Throssel Range hills Australia 108 C5
Thrushton National Park Australia 112 C1
Thubun Lakes Canada 121 I2
Thu Dâu Môt Vietnam 71 D5
Thuddungra Australia 112 D5
Thuin Belgium 52 E4
Thul Pak. 89 H4
Thulaythawāt Gharbī, Jabal hill Syria 85 D2
Thule Greenland 119 L2
Thun Switz. 56 H3
Thunder Bay Canada 119 J5
Thunder Bay b. U.S.A. 134 D1
Thunder Creek r. Canada 121 J5
Thüngen Germany 53 J5
Thung Salaeng Luang National Park Thai. 70 C3
Thung Song Thai. 71 B5
Thung Yai Naresuan Wildlife Reserve nature res. Thai. 70 B4
Thüringen land Germany 53 K3
Thüringer Becken reg. Germany 53 L3
Thüringer Wald mts Germany 53 K4
Thuringia land Germany see Thüringen
Thuringian Forest mts Germany see Thüringer Wald
Thurles Rep. of Ireland 51 E5
Thurn, Pass Austria 47 N7
Thursday Island Australia 110 C1
Thurso U.K. 50 F2
Thurso r. U.K. 50 F2
Thurston Island Antarctica 152 K2
Thurston Peninsula i. Antarctica see Thurston Island
Thüster Berg hill Germany 53 J2
Thuthukudi India see Tuticorin
Thwaite U.K. 48 E4
Thwaites Glacier Tongue Antarctica 152 K1
Thyatira Turkey see Akhisar
Thyborøn Denmark 45 F8
Thymerais reg. France 52 B6
Tianchang China 77 H1
Tiancheng China see Chongyang
Tianchi China see Lezhi
Tiandeng China 76 E4
Tiandong China 76 E4
T'ianet'i Georgia 91 G2
Tianfanjie China 77 H2
Tianjin China 73 L5
Tianjin municipality China 73 L5
Tianjun China 80 I4
Tianlin China 76 E3
Tianma China see Changshan
Tianmen China 77 G2
Tianqiaoling China 74 C4
Tianquan China 76 D2
Tianshan China 73 M4
Tian Shan mts China/Kyrg. see Tien Shan
Tianshui China 76 E1
Tianshuihai Aksai Chin 82 D2
Tiantai China 77 I2
Tiantang China see Yuexi
Tianyang China 76 E4
Tianzhou China see Tianyang
Tianzhu Gansu China 72 I5
Tianzhu Guizhou China 77 F3
Tiaret Alg. 57 G6
Tiassalé Côte d'Ivoire 96 C4
Tibagi Brazil 145 A4
Tibal, Wādī watercourse Iraq 91 F4
Tibati Cameroon 96 E4
Tibba Pak. 89 H4
Tibé, Pic de mt. Guinea 96 C4
Tiber r. Italy 58 E4
Tiberias Israel 85 B3
Tiberias, Lake Israel see Galilee, Sea of
Tiber Reservoir U.S.A. 126 F2
Tibesti mts Chad 97 E2
Tibet aut. reg. China see Xizang Zizhiqu
Tibi India 89 I4
Tibooburra Australia 111 C6
Tibrikot Nepal 83 E3
Tibro Sweden 45 I7
Tibur Italy see Tivoli
Tiburón, Isla i. Mex. 127 E7
Ticehurst U.K. 49 H7
Tichborne Canada 135 G1
Tichégami r. Canada 123 G4
Tîchît Mauritania 96 C3
Tichla W. Sahara 96 B2
Ticinum Italy see Pavia
Ticonderoga U.S.A. 135 I2
Ticul Mex. 136 G4
Tidaholm Sweden 45 H7
Tiddim Myanmar 70 A2
Tiden India 71 A6
Tidjikja Mauritania 96 B3
Tiefa China 74 A4
Tiel Neth. 52 F3
Tieli China 74 B3
Tieling China 74 A4
Tielongtan Aksai Chin 82 D2
Tielt Belgium 52 D4
Tienen Belgium 52 E4
Tien Shan mts China/Kyrg. 72 D4
Tientsin municipality China see Tianjin
Tiên Yên Vietnam 70 D2
Tierp Sweden 45 J6
Tierra Amarilla U.S.A. 127 G5

▶Tierra del Fuego, Isla Grande de i. Arg./Chile 144 C8
Largest island in South America.
South America 138–139

Tierra del Fuego, Parque Nacional nat. park Arg. 144 C8
Tiétar r. Spain 57 D4
Tiétar, Valle de valley Spain 57 D3
Tietê r. Brazil 145 A3
Tieyon Australia 109 F6
Tiffin U.S.A. 134 D3
Tiflis Georgia see T'bilisi
Tifton U.S.A. 133 D6
Tiga Reservoir Nigeria 96 D3
Tigen Kazakh. 91 H1
Tīgh Āb Iran 89 F5
Tigheciului, Dealurile hills Moldova 59 M2
Tighina Moldova 59 M1
Tigiria India 84 E1
Tignère Cameroon 96 E4
Tignish Canada 123 I5
Tigranocerta Turkey see Siirt
Tigre r. Venez. 142 F2
Tigris r. Asia 91 G5
also known as Dicle (Turkey) or Nahr Dijlah (Iraq/Syria)
Tigrovaya Balka Zapovednik nature res. Tajik. 89 H2
Tiguidit, Falaise de esc. Niger 96 D3
Tīh, Gebel el plat. Egypt see Tīh, Jabal at
Tīh, Jabal at plat. Egypt 85 A5
Tijuana Mex. 128 E5
Tikamgarh India 82 D4
Tikanlik China 80 G3
Tikhoretsk Rus. Fed. 43 I7
Tikhvin Rus. Fed. 42 G4
Tikhvinskaya Gryada ridge Rus. Fed. 42 G4
Tiki Basin sea feature S. Pacific Ocean 151 L7
Tikokino N.Z. 113 F4
Tikopia i. Solomon Is 107 G3
Tikrīt Iraq 91 F4
Tikse Jammu and Kashmir 82 D2
Tiksheozero, Ozero l. Rus. Fed. 44 R3
Tiksi Rus. Fed. 65 N2
Tiladummati Atoll Maldives see Thiladhunmathi Atoll
Tilaiya Reservoir India 83 F4
Tilbeşar Ovasi plain Turkey 85 C1
Tilbooroo Australia 112 B1
Tilburg Neth. 52 F3
Tilbury Canada 134 D2
Tilbury U.K. 49 H7
Tilcara Arg. 144 C2
Tilden U.S.A. 131 D6
Tilemsès Niger 96 D3
Tilemsi, Vallée du watercourse Mali 96 D3
Tilhar India 82 D4
Tilimsen Alg. see Tlemcen
Tilin Myanmar 70 A2
Tillabéri Niger 96 D3
Tillamook U.S.A. 126 C3
Tillanchong Island India 71 A5
Tillia Niger 96 D3
Tillicoultry U.K. 50 F4
Tillsonburg Canada 134 E2
Tillyfourie U.K. 50 G3
Tilonia India 89 I5
Tilos i. Greece 59 L6
Tilothu India 83 F4
Tilpa Australia 112 B3
Tilsit Rus. Fed. see Sovetsk
Tilt r. U.K. 50 F4
Tilton IL U.S.A. 134 B3
Tilton NH U.S.A. 135 J2
Tim Rus. Fed. 43 H6
Ţimā Egypt 86 D4
Timah, Bukit hill Sing. 71 [inset]
Timakara i. India 84 B4
Timanskiy Kryazh ridge Rus. Fed. 42 K2
Timar Turkey 91 F3
Timaru N.Z. 113 C7
Timashevsk Rus. Fed. 43 H7
Timashevskaya Rus. Fed. see Timashevsk
Timbedgha Mauritania 96 C3
Timber Creek Australia 106 D3
Timber Mountain U.S.A. 128 E3
Timberville U.S.A. 135 F4
Timbuktu Mali 96 C3
Timétrine reg. Mali 96 C3
Timiaouine Alg. 96 D2
Timimoun Alg. 54 E6
Timirist, Râs pt Mauritania 96 B3
Timiskaming, Lake Canada see Témiscamingue, Lac
Timişoara Romania 59 I2
Timmins Canada 122 E4
Timms Hill hill U.S.A. 130 F2
Timon Brazil 143 J5
Timor i. East Timor/Indon. 108 D2
Timor-Leste country Asia see East Timor
Timor Loro Sae country Asia see East Timor
Timor Sea Australia/Indon. 106 C3
Timor Timur country Asia see East Timor
Timperley Range hills Australia 109 C6
Timrå Sweden 44 J5
Tīn, Ra's at pt Libya 90 A4
Ţīna, Khalīg el b. Egypt see Ţīnah, Khalīj aţ
Ţīnah Syria 85 D1
Ţīnah, Khalīj aţ b. Egypt 85 A4
Tin Can Bay Australia 111 F5
Tindivanam India 84 C3
Tindouf Alg. 54 C6
Ti-n-Essako Mali 96 D3
Tinggi i. Malaysia 71 D7
Tingha Australia 112 E2
Tingis Morocco see Tangier
Tingo Maria Peru 142 C5
Tingréla Côte d'Ivoire see Tengréla
Tingsryd Sweden 45 I8
Tingvoll Norway 44 F5
Tingwall U.K. 50 F1
Tingzhou China see Changting
Tinharé, Ilha de i. Brazil 145 D1
Tinh Gia Vietnam 70 D3
Tinian i. N. Mariana Is 69 L4
Tini Heke is N.Z. see Snares Islands
Tinnelvelly India see Tirunelveli
Tinogasta Arg. 144 C3
Tinos Greece 59 K6
Tinos i. Greece 59 K6
Tinqueux France 52 D5
Tinrhert, Plateau du Alg. 96 D2
Tinsukia India 83 H4
Tintagel U.K. 49 C8
Ţînţâne Mauritania 96 B3
Tintina Arg. 144 D3
Tintinara Australia 111 C7
Tioga U.S.A. 130 C1
Tioman i. Malaysia 71 D7
Tionesta U.S.A. 134 F3
Tionesta Lake U.S.A. 134 F3
Tipasa Alg. 57 H5
Tiphsah Syria see Dibsī
Tipperary Rep. of Ireland 51 D5
Tipton CA U.S.A. 128 D3
Tipton IA U.S.A. 130 F3
Tipton IN U.S.A. 134 B3
Tipton MO U.S.A. 130 E4
Tipton, Mount U.S.A. 129 F4
Tiptop U.S.A. 134 E5
Tip Top Hill hill Canada 122 D4
Tiptree U.K. 49 H7
Tiptur India 84 C3
Tipturi India see Tiptur
Tiracambu, Serra do hills Brazil 143 I4
Tirah reg. Pak. 89 H3

▶Tirana Albania 59 H4
Capital of Albania.

Tiranë Albania see Tirana
Tirano Italy 58 D1
Tirari Desert Australia 111 B5
Tiraspol Moldova 59 M1
Tiraz Mountains Namibia 100 C4
Tire Turkey 59 L5
Tirebolu Turkey 91 E2
Tiree i. U.K. 50 C4
Tîrgovişte Romania see Târgovişte
Tîrgu Jiu Romania see Târgu Jiu
Tîrgu Mureş Romania see Târgu Mureş
Tîrgu Neamţ Romania see Târgu Neamţ
Tîrgu Secuiesc Romania see Târgu Secuiesc
Tiri Pak. 89 G4
Tirich Mir mt. Pak. 89 H2
Tirlemont Belgium see Tienen
Tirna r. India 84 C2
Tîrnăveni Romania see Târnăveni
Tírnavos Greece see Tyrnavos
Tiros Brazil 145 B2
Tirourda, Col de pass Alg. 57 I5
Tirreno, Mare sea France/Italy see Tyrrhenian Sea
Tirso r. Sardinia Italy 58 C5
Tirthahalli India 84 B3
Tiruchchendur India 84 C4
Tiruchchirappalli India 84 C4
Tiruchengodu India 84 C4
Tirunelveli India 84 C4
Tirupati India 84 C3
Tiruppattur Tamil Nadu India 84 C3
Tiruppattur Tamil Nadu India 84 C4
Tiruppur India 84 C4
Tiruttani India 84 C3
Tirutturaippundi India 84 C4
Tiruvallur India 84 C3
Tiruvannamalai India 84 C3
Tiruvottiyur India 84 D3
Tiru Well Australia 108 D5
Tisa r. Serb. and Mont. 59 I2
also known as Tisza (Hungary), Tysa (Ukraine)
Tisdale Canada 121 J4
Tishomingo U.S.A. 131 D5
Ţisīyah Syria 85 C3
Tissemsilt Alg. 57 G6
Tisza r. Hungary see Tisa
Titalya Bangl. see Tetulia
Titan Dome ice feature Antarctica 152 H1
Titao Burkina 96 C3
Tit-Ary Rus. Fed. 65 N2
Titawin Morocco see Tétouan
Titicaca, Lago Bol./Peru see Titicaca, Lake

▶Titicaca, Lake Bol./Peru 142 E7
Largest lake in South America.
South America 138–139

Titiritea mt. N.Z. see Aspiring, Mount
Titlagarh India 84 D1
Titograd Serb. and Mont. see Podgorica
Titova Mitrovica Serb. and Mont. see Kosovska Mitrovica
Titov Drvar Bos.-Herz. 58 G2
Titovo Užice Serb. and Mont. see Užice
Titovo Velenje Slovenia see Velenje
Titov Veles Macedonia see Veles
Titov Vrbas Yugo. see Vrbas
Ti Tree Australia 108 F5
Titu Romania 59 K2
Titusville FL U.S.A. 133 D6
Titusville PA U.S.A. 134 F3
Tiu Chung Chau i. Hong Kong China 77 [inset]
Tiumpain, Rubha an hd U.K. see Tiumpan Head
Tiumpan Head hd U.K. 50 C2
Tiva watercourse Kenya 98 D4
Tivari India 82 C4
Tiverton Canada 134 E1
Tiverton U.K. 49 D8
Tivoli Italy 58 E4
Ţīwī Oman 88 E6
Ti-ywa Myanmar 71 B4
Tizi El Arba hill Alg. 57 H5
Tizimín Mex. 136 G4
Tizi N'Kouilal pass Alg. 57 I5
Tizi Ouzou Alg. 57 I5
Tiznap He r. China 82 D1
Tiznit Morocco 96 C2
Tiztoutine Morocco 57 E6
Tjaneni Swaziland 101 J3
Tjappsåive Sweden 44 K4
Tjeukemeer l. Neth. 52 F2
Tjirebon Indon. see Cirebon
Tjolotjo Zimbabwe see Tsholotsho
Tjorhom Norway 45 E7
Tkibuli Georgia see Tqibuli
Tlahualilo Mex. 131 C7
Tlaxcala Mex. 136 E5
Tl'ell Canada 120 D4
Tlemcen Alg. 57 F6
Tlhakalatlou S. Africa 100 F5
Tlholong S. Africa 101 I5
Tlokweng Botswana 101 G3
Tlyarata Rus. Fed. 91 G2

To r. Myanmar 70 B3
Toad r. Canada 120 E3
Toad River Canada 120 E3
Toamasina Madag. 99 E5
Toana mts U.S.A. 129 F1
Toano U.S.A. 135 G5
Toa Payoh Sing. 71 [inset]
Toba China 76 C2
Toba, Danau l. Indon. 71 B7
Toba, Lake Indon. see Toba, Danau
Toba and Kakar Ranges mts Pak. 89 G4
Toba Gargaji Pak. 89 I4
Tobago i. Trin. and Tob. 137 L6
Tobelo Indon. 69 H6
Tobermorey Australia 110 B4
Tobermory Australia 112 A1
Tobermory Canada 134 E1
Tobermory U.K. 50 C4
Tobi i. Palau 69 I6
Tobin, Lake salt flat Australia 108 D5
Tobin, Mount U.S.A. 128 E1
Tobin Lake Canada 121 K4
Tobin Lake l. Canada 121 K4
Tobi-shima i. Japan 75 E5
Tobol r. Kazakh./Rus. Fed. 78 F1
Tobol'sk Rus. Fed. 64 H4
Tô Bong Vietnam 71 E4
Tobruk Libya see Tubruq
Tobseda Rus. Fed. 42 L1
Tobyl r. Kazakh./Rus. Fed. see Tobol
Tobysh r. Rus. Fed. 42 K2
Tocache Nuevo Peru 142 C5
Tocantinópolis Brazil 143 I5
Tocantins r. Brazil 145 A1
Tocantins state Brazil 145 A1
Tocantinzinha r. Brazil 145 A1
Toccoa U.S.A. 133 D5
Tochi r. Pak. 89 H3
Töcksfors Sweden 45 G7
Tocopilla Chile 144 B2
Tocumwal Australia 112 B5
Tod, Mount Canada 120 G5
Todd watercourse Australia 110 A5
Todi Italy 58 E3
Todoga-saki pt Japan 75 F5
Todos Santos Mex. 136 B4
Toe Head hd U.K. 50 B3
Tofino Canada 120 E5
Toft U.K. 50 [inset]
Tofua i. Tonga 107 I3
Togatax China 82 E2
Togian i. Indon. 69 G7
Togian, Kepulauan is Indon. 69 G7
Togliatti Rus. Fed. see Tol'yatti
▶Togo country Africa 96 D4
Africa 7, 94–95
Togtoh China 73 K4
Togton He r. China 83 H2
Togton Heyan China see Tanggulashan
Tohatchi U.S.A. 129 I4
Toholampi Fin. 44 N5
Toiba China 83 G3
Toibalewe India 71 A5
Toijala Fin. 45 M6
Toili Indon. 69 G7
Toi-misaki pt Japan 75 C7
Toivakka Fin. 44 O5
Toiyabe Range mts U.S.A. 128 E2
Tojikiston country Asia see Tajikistan
Tok U.S.A. 120 A2
Tokar Sudan 86 E6
Tokara-rettō is Japan 75 C7
Tokarevka Rus. Fed. 43 I6
Tokat Turkey 90 E2
Tŏkchok-to i. S. Korea 75 B5
Tokdo i. N. Pacific Ocean see Liancourt Rocks

▶Tokelau terr. S. Pacific Ocean 107 I2
New Zealand Overseas Territory.
Oceania 8, 104–105

Tokmak Kyrg. see Tokmok
Tokmak Ukr. 43 G7
Tokmok Kyrg. 80 E3
Tokomaru Bay N.Z. 113 G4
Tokoroa N.Z. 113 E4
Tokoza S. Africa 101 I4
Toksun China 80 G3
Tok-tō i. N. Pacific Ocean see Liancourt Rocks
Toktogul Kyrg. 80 D3
Tokto-ri i. N. Pacific Ocean see Liancourt Rocks
Tokur Rus. Fed. 74 D1
Tokushima Japan 75 D6
Tokuyama Japan 75 C6

▶Tōkyō Japan 75 E6
Capital of Japan. Most populous city in the world and in Asia.

Tokzār Afgh. 89 G3
Tolaga Bay N.Z. 113 G4
Tôlañaro Madag. 99 E6
Tolbo Mongolia 80 H2
Tolbukhin Bulg. see Dobrich
Tolbuzino Rus. Fed. 74 B1
Toledo Brazil 144 F2
Toledo Spain 57 D4
Toledo IA U.S.A. 130 E3
Toledo OH U.S.A. 134 D3
Toledo OR U.S.A. 126 C3
Toledo, Montes de mts Spain 57 D4
Toledo Bend Reservoir U.S.A. 131 E6
Toletum Spain see Toledo
Toliara Madag. 99 E6
Tolitoli Indon. 69 G6
Tol'ka Rus. Fed. 64 J3
Tolleson U.S.A. 129 G5
Tollimarjon Uzbek. see Talimardzhan
Tolmachevo Rus. Fed. 45 P7
Tolo Dem. Rep. Congo 98 B4
Tolo Channel Hong Kong China 77 [inset]
Tolochin Belarus see Talachyn
Tolo Harbour b. Hong Kong China 77 [inset]
Tolosa France see Toulouse
Tolosa Spain 57 E2
Toluca Mex. 136 E5
Toluca de Lerdo Mex. see Toluca
Tol'yatti Rus. Fed. 43 K5
Tom' r. Rus. Fed. 74 B2
Tomah U.S.A. 130 F3
Tomakomai Japan 74 F4
Tomales U.S.A. 128 B2
Tomali Indon. 69 G7
Tomamae Japan 74 F3
Tomanivi mt. Fiji 107 H3
Tomar Brazil 142 F4
Tomar Port. 57 B4
Tomari Rus. Fed. 74 F3
Tomarza Turkey 90 D3
Tomaszów Lubelski Poland 43 D6
Tomaszów Mazowiecki Poland 47 R5
Tomatin U.K. 50 F3
Tomatlán Mex. 136 C5
Tomazina Brazil 145 A3
Tombador, Serra do hills Brazil 143 G6
Tombigbee r. U.S.A. 133 C6
Tomboco Angola 99 B4
Tombouctou Mali see Timbuktu
Tombstone U.S.A. 127 F7
Tombua Angola 99 B5
Tom Burke S. Africa 101 H2
Tomdibuloq Uzbek. see Tamdybulak
Tome Moz. 101 L2
Tomelilla Sweden 45 H9
Tomelloso Spain 57 E4
Tomi Romania see Constanța
Tomingley Australia 112 D4
Tomini, Teluk g. Indon. 69 G7
Tominian Mali 96 C3
Tomintoul U.K. 50 F3
Tomislavgrad Bos.-Herz. 58 G3
Tomkinson Ranges mts Australia 109 E6
Tømmerneset Norway 44 I3
Tommot Rus. Fed. 65 N4
Tomo r. Col. 142 E2
Tomóchic Mex. 127 G7
Tomortei China 73 K4
Tompkinsville U.S.A. 134 C5
Tom Price Australia 108 B5
Tomra China 83 F3
Tomsk Rus. Fed. 64 J4
Toms River U.S.A. 135 H4
Tomtabacken hill Sweden 45 I8
Tomtor Rus. Fed. 65 P3
Tomur Feng mt. China/Kyrg. see Pobeda Peak
Tomuzlovka r. Rus. Fed. 43 J7
Tom White, Mount U.S.A. 118 D3
Tonalá Mex. 136 F5
Tonantins Brazil 142 E4
Tonb-e Bozorg, Jazīreh-ye i. The Gulf see Greater Tunb
Tonb-e Kūchek, Jazīreh-ye i. The Gulf see Lesser Tunb
Tonbridge U.K. 49 H7
Tondano Indon. 69 G6
Tønder Denmark 45 F9
Tondi India 84 C4
Tone r. U.K. 49 E7
Toney Mountain Antarctica 152 K1
▶Tonga country S. Pacific Ocean 107 I4
Oceania 8, 104–105
Tongaat S. Africa 101 J5
Tongariro National Park N.Z. 113 E4
Tongatapu Group is Tonga 107 I4

▶Tonga Trench sea feature S. Pacific Ocean 150 I7
2nd deepest trench in the world.

Tongbai Shan mts China 77 G1
Tongcheng China 77 H2
T'ongch'ŏn N. Korea 75 B5
Tongchuan Shaanxi China 77 F1
Tongchuan Sichuan China see Santai
Tongdao China 77 F3
Tongde China 76 D1
Tongduch'ŏn S. Korea 75 B5
Tongeren Belgium 52 F4
Tonggu China 77 G2
Tonggu Zui pt China 77 F5
Tonghae S. Korea 75 C5
Tonghai China 76 D3
Tonghe China 74 C3
Tonghua Jilin China 74 B4
Tonghua Jilin China 74 B4
Tongi Bangl. see Tungi
Tongjiang Heilong. China 74 D3
Tongjiang Sichuan China 76 E2
Tongking, Gulf of China/Vietnam 70 E2
Tongle China see Leye
Tongliang China 76 E2
Tongliao China 73 M4
Tongling China 77 H2
Tonglu China 77 H2
Tongo Australia 112 A3
Tongo Lake salt flat Australia 112 A3
Tongren Guizhou China 77 F3
Tongren Qinghai China 76 D1
Tongres Belgium see Tongeren
Tongsa Bhutan see Trongsa
Tongshan China 77 H1
Tongshi China 77 F5
Tongta Myanmar 70 B2
Tongtian He r. Qinghai China 76 B1
Tongtian He r. Qinghai China 76 C1 see Yangtze
Tongue U.K. 50 E2
Tongue r. U.S.A. 126 G3
Tongue of the Ocean sea chan. Bahamas 133 E7
Tongxin China 72 J5
T'ongyŏng S. Korea 75 C6
Tongzi China 76 E2
Tónichi Mex. 127 F7
Tonk India 82 C4
Tonkābon Iran 88 C2
Tonkin reg. Vietnam 70 D2
Tônle Repou r. Laos 71 D4
Tônlé Sab l. Cambodia see Tonle Sap

▶Tonle Sap l. Cambodia 71 C4
Largest lake in Southeast Asia.

Tonopah AZ U.S.A. 129 G5
Tonopah NV U.S.A. 128 E2
Tønsberg Norway 45 G7
Tonstad Norway 45 E7
Tonto Creek watercourse U.S.A. 129 H5
Tonvarjeh Iran 88 E3
Tonzang Myanmar 70 A2
Tonzi Myanmar 70 A1
Toobeah Australia 112 D2
Toobli Liberia 96 C4
Tooele U.S.A. 129 G1
Toogoolawah Australia 112 F1
Tooma r. Australia 112 D6
Toompine Australia 112 B1
Toora Australia 112 C7
Tooraweenah Australia 112 D3
Toorberg mt. S. Africa 100 G7
Toowoomba Australia 112 E1
Tooxin Somalia 98 F2
Top Afgh. 89 H3
Top Boğazı Geçidi pass Turkey 85 C1

▶Topeka U.S.A. 130 E4
State capital of Kansas.

Topia Mex. 127 G8
Töplitz Germany 53 M2
Topoľčany Slovakia 47 Q6
Topolobampo Mex. 127 F8
Topolovgrad Bulg. 59 L3
Topozero, Ozero l. Rus. Fed. 44 R4
Topsfield U.S.A. 132 H2
Tor Eth. 97 G4
Tor Baldak mt. Afgh. 89 G4
Torbalı Turkey 59 L5
Torbat-e Heydarīyeh Iran 88 E3
Torbat-e Jām Iran 89 F3
Torbay Bay Australia 109 B8
Torbert, Mount U.S.A. 118 C3
Torbeyevo Rus. Fed. 43 I5
Torch r. Canada 121 K4
Tordesillas Spain 57 D3
Tordesilos Spain 57 F3
Töre Sweden 44 M4
Torelló Spain 57 H2
Torenberg hill Neth. 52 F2
Toretam Kazakh. see Baykonyr
Torgau Germany 53 M3
Torghay Kazakh. see Turgay
Torgun r. Rus. Fed. 43 J6
Torhout Belgium 52 D3
Torino Italy see Turin
Tori-shima i. Japan 75 F7
Torit Sudan 97 G4
Torkamān Iran 88 B2
Torkovichi Rus. Fed. 42 F4
Tornado Mountain Canada 120 H5
Torneå Fin. see Tornio
Torneälven r. Sweden 44 N4
Torneträsk l. Sweden 44 K2
Torngat, Monts mts Canada see Torngat Mountains
Torngat Mountains Canada 123 I2
Tornio Fin. 44 N4
Toro Spain 57 D3
Toro, Pico del mt. Mex. 131 C7
Torom Rus. Fed. 74 D1

▶Toronto Canada 134 F2
Provincial capital of Ontario and 5th most populous city in North America.

Toro Peak U.S.A. 128 E5
Toropets Rus. Fed. 42 F4
Tororo Uganda 98 D3
Toros Dağları mts Turkey see Taurus Mountains
Torphins U.K. 50 G3
Torquay Australia 112 B7
Torquay U.K. 49 D8
Torrance U.S.A. 128 D5
Torrão Port. 57 B4
Torre mt. Port. 57 C3
Torreblanca Spain 57 G3
Torre Blanco, Cerro mt. Mex. 127 E6
Torrecerredo mt. Spain 57 D2
Torre del Greco Italy 58 F4
Torre de Moncorvo Port. 57 C3
Torrelavega Spain 57 D2
Torremolinos Spain 57 D5

▶Torrens, Lake imp. l. Australia 111 B6
2nd largest lake in Oceania.

Torrens Creek Australia 110 D4
Torrent Spain 57 F4
Torrente Spain see Torrent
Torreón Mex. 131 C7
Torres Brazil 145 A5
Torres Mex. 127 F7
Torres del Paine, Parque Nacional nat. park Chile 144 B8
Torres Islands Vanuatu 107 G3
Torres Novas Port. 57 B4
Torres Strait Australia 106 E2
Torres Vedras Port. 57 B4
Torreta, Sierra hill Spain 57 G4
Torrevieja Spain 57 F5
Torrey U.S.A. 129 H2
Torridge r. U.K. 49 C8
Torridon, Loch b. U.K. 50 D3
Torrijos Spain 57 D4
Torrington Australia 112 E2
Torrington CT U.S.A. 132 F3
Torrington WY U.S.A. 126 G4
Torsby Sweden 45 H6

▶Tórshavn Faroe Is 44 [inset]
Capital of the Faroe Islands.

Tortilla Flat U.S.A. 129 H5
Törtköl Uzbek. see Turtkul'
Tortolì Sardinia Italy 58 C5
Tortona Italy 58 C2
Tortosa Spain 57 G3
Tortum Turkey 91 F2
Ţorūd Iran 88 D3
Torugart, Pereval pass China/Kyrg. see Turugart Pass
Torul Turkey 91 E2
Toruń Poland 47 Q4
Tory Island Rep. of Ireland 51 D2
Tory Sound sea chan. Rep. of Ireland 51 D2
Torzhok Rus. Fed. 42 G4
Tosa Japan 75 D6
Tosbotn Norway 44 H4
Tosca S. Africa 100 F3
Toscano, Arcipelago is Italy 58 C3
Tosham India 82 C3
Tōshima-yama mt. Japan 75 F4
Toshkent Uzbek. see Tashkent
Tosno Rus. Fed. 42 F4
Toson Hu l. China 83 I1
Tostado Arg. 144 D3
Tostedt Germany 53 J1
Tosya Turkey 90 D2
Totapola mt. Sri Lanka 84 D5
Tôtes France 52 B5
Tot'ma Rus. Fed. 42 I4
Totness Suriname 143 G2
Tottenham Australia 112 C4
Totton U.K. 49 F8
Tottori Japan 75 D6
Touba Côte d'Ivoire 96 C4
Touba Senegal 96 B3
Toubkal, Jbel mt. Morocco 54 C5
Toubkal, Parc National nat. park Morocco 54 C5
Touboro Cameroon 97 E4
Tougan Burkina 96 C3
Touggourt Alg. 54 F5
Tougué Guinea 96 B3
Touil Mauritania 96 B3
Toul France 52 F6
Touliu Taiwan 77 I4
Toulon France 56 G5
Toulon U.S.A. 130 F3
Toulouse France 56 E5
Toumodi Côte d'Ivoire 96 C4
Toungoo Myanmar 70 B3
Toupai China 77 F3
Tourane Vietnam see Đa Năng
Tourcoing France 52 D4
Tourgis Lake Canada 121 J1
Tourlaville France 49 F9
Tournai Belgium 52 D4
Tournon-sur-Rhône France 56 G4
Tournus France 58 A1
Touros Brazil 143 K5
Tours France 56 E3
Tousside, Pic mt. Chad 97 E2
Toussoro, Mont mt. Cent. Afr. Rep. 98 C3
Toutai China 74 B3
Touwsrivier S. Africa 100 E7
Toužim Czech Rep. 53 M4
Tovarkovo Rus. Fed. 43 G5
Tovil'-Dora Tajik. see Tavildara
Tovuz Azer. 91 G2
Towada Japan 74 F4
Towak Mountain hill U.S.A. 118 B3
Towanda U.S.A. 135 G3
Towaoc U.S.A. 129 I3
Towcester U.K. 49 G6
Tower Rep. of Ireland 51 D6
Towner U.S.A. 130 C1
Townes Pass U.S.A. 128 E3
Townsend U.S.A. 126 F3
Townsend, Mount Australia 112 D6
Townshend Island Australia 110 E4
Townsville Australia 110 D3
Towot Sudan 97 G4
Towr Kham Afgh. 89 H3
Towson U.S.A. 135 G4
Towyn U.K. see Tywyn
Toy U.S.A. 128 D1
Toyah U.S.A. 131 C6
Toyama Japan 75 E5
Toyama-wan b. Japan 75 E5
Toyohashi Japan 75 E6
Toyokawa Japan 75 E6
Toyonaka Japan 75 D6
Toyooka Japan 75 D6
Toyota Japan 75 E6
Tozanlı Turkey see Almus
Tozê Kangri mt. China 83 E2
Tozeur Tunisia 54 F5
Tozi, Mount U.S.A. 118 C3
Tqibuli Georgia 91 F2
Traben Germany 52 H5
Trâblous Lebanon see Tripoli
Trabotivište Macedonia 59 J4
Trabzon Turkey 91 E2
Tracy CA U.S.A. 128 C3
Tracy MN U.S.A. 130 E2
Trading r. Canada 122 C4
Traer U.S.A. 130 E3
Trafalgar U.S.A. 134 B4
Trafalgar, Cabo c. Spain 57 C5
Traffic Mountain Canada 120 D2
Trail Canada 120 G5
Traille, Rubha na pt U.K. 50 D5
Traill Island Greenland see Traill Ø
Traill Ø i. Greenland 119 P2
Trainor Lake Canada 120 F2
Trajectum Neth. see Utrecht
Trakai Lith. 45 N9
Tra Khuc, Sông r. Vietnam 70 E4
Trakiya reg. Europe see Thrace
Trakt Rus. Fed. 42 K3
Trakya reg. Europe see Thrace
Tralee Rep. of Ireland 51 C5
Tralee Bay Rep. of Ireland 51 C5
Trá Li Rep. of Ireland see Tralee
Tramandaí Brazil 145 A5
Tramán Tepuí mt. Venez. 142 F2
Trá Mhór Rep. of Ireland see Tramore
Tramore Rep. of Ireland 51 E5
Tranås Sweden 45 I7
Trancas Arg. 144 C3
Trancoso Brazil 145 D2
Tranemo Sweden 45 H8
Tranent U.K. 50 G5
Trang Thai. 71 B6
Trangan i. Indon. 108 F1
Trangie Australia 112 C4
Transantarctic Mountains Antarctica 152 H2
Trans Canada Highway Canada 121 H5
Transylvanian Alps mts Romania 59 J2
Transylvanian Basin plat. Romania 59 K1
Trapani Sicily Italy 58 E5
Trapezus Turkey see Trabzon
Trapper Peak U.S.A. 126 E3
Trappes France 52 C6
Traralgon Australia 112 C7
Trashigang Bhutan 83 G4
Trasimeno, Lago l. Italy 58 E3
Trasvase, Canal de Spain 57 E4
Trat Thai. 71 C4
Traunsee l. Austria 47 N7
Traunstein Germany 47 N7
Travellers Lake imp. l. Australia 111 C7
Travers, Mount N.Z. 113 D6
Traverse City U.S.A. 134 C1
Tra Vinh Vietnam 71 D5
Travnik Bos.-Herz. 58 G2
Trbovlje Slovenia 58 F1
Tre, Hon i. Vietnam 71 E4
Treasury Islands Solomon Is 106 F2
Trebbin Germany 53 N2
Trebević nat. park Bos.-Herz. 58 H3
Třebíč Czech Rep. 47 O6
Trebinje Bos.-Herz. 58 H3
Trebišov Slovakia 43 D6
Trebizond Turkey see Trabzon
Trebnje Slovenia 58 F2
Trebur Germany 53 I5
Tree Island India 84 B4
Trefaldwyn U.K. see Montgomery
Treffurt Germany 53 K3
Treffynnon U.K. see Holywell
Trefyclawdd U.K. see Knighton
Trefynwy U.K. see Monmouth
Tregosse Islets and Reefs Australia 110 E3
Treinta y Tres Uruguay 144 F4
Trelew Arg. 144 C6
Trelleborg Sweden 45 H9
Trélon France 52 E4
Tremblant, Mont hill Canada 122 G5
Trembleur Lake Canada 120 E4
Tremiti, Isole is Italy 58 F3
Tremont U.S.A. 135 G3
Tremonton U.S.A. 126 E4
Tremp Spain 57 G2
Trenance U.K. 49 B8
Trenary U.S.A. 132 C2
Trenche r. Canada 123 G5
Trenčín Slovakia 47 Q6
Trendelburg Germany 53 J3
Trêng Cambodia 71 C4
Trenque Lauquén Arg. 144 D5
Trent Italy see Trento
Trent r. U.K. 49 G5
Trento Italy 58 D1
Trenton Canada 135 G1
Trenton FL U.S.A. 133 D6
Trenton GA U.S.A. 133 C5
Trenton KY U.S.A. 134 B5
Trenton MO U.S.A. 130 E3
Trenton NC U.S.A. 133 E5
Trenton NE U.S.A. 130 C3

▶Trenton NJ U.S.A. 135 H3
State capital of New Jersey.

Treorchy U.K. 49 D7
Trepassey Canada 123 L5
Tres Arroyos Arg. 144 D5
Tresco i. U.K. 49 A9
Três Corações Brazil 145 B3
Tres Esquinas Col. 142 C3
Tres Forcas, Cabo c. Morocco see Trois Fourches, Cap des
Três Lagoas Brazil 145 A3
Três Marias, Represa resr Brazil 145 B2
Tres Picachos, Sierra mts Mex. 127 G7
Tres Picos, Cerro mt. Arg. 144 D5
Três Pontas Brazil 145 B3
Tres Puntas, Cabo c. Arg. 144 C7
Três Rios Brazil 145 C3
Tretten Norway 45 G6
Tretyy Severnyy Rus. Fed. see 3-y Severnyy
Treuchtlingen Germany 53 K6
Treuenbrietzen Germany 53 M2
Treungen Norway 45 F7
Treves Germany see Trier
Treviglio Italy 58 C2
Treviso Italy 58 E2
Trevose Head hd U.K. 49 B8
Tri An, Hô resr Vietnam 71 D5
Triánda Greece see Trianta
Triangle U.S.A. 135 G4
Trianta Greece 59 M6
Tribal Areas admin. div. Pak. 89 H3
Tri Brata, Gora hill Rus. Fed. 74 F1
Tribune U.S.A. 130 C4
Tricase Italy 58 H5
Trichinopoly India see Tiruchchirappalli
Trichur India 84 C4
Tricot France 52 C5
Trida Australia 112 B4
Tridentum Italy see Trento
Trier Germany 52 G5
Trieste Italy 58 E2
Trieste, Golfo di g. Europe see Trieste, Gulf of
Trieste, Gulf of Europe 58 E2
Triglav mt. Slovenia 58 E1
Triglavski Narodni Park nat. park Slovenia 58 E1
Trikala Greece 59 I5
Tríkkala Greece see Trikala

▶Trikora, Puncak mt. Indon. 69 J7
2nd highest mountain in Oceania.

Trim Rep. of Ireland 51 F4
Trincomalee Sri Lanka 84 D4
Trindade Brazil 145 A2
Trindade, Ilha da i. S. Atlantic Ocean 148 G7
Trinidad Bol. 142 F6
Trinidad Cuba 137 I4
Trinidad i. Trin. and Tob. 137 L6
Trinidad Uruguay 144 E4
Trinidad U.S.A. 127 G5
Trinidad country West Indies see Trinidad and Tobago
▶Trinidad and Tobago country West Indies 137 L6
North America 9, 116–117
Trinity U.S.A. 131 E6
Trinity r. CA U.S.A. 128 B1
Trinity r. TX U.S.A. 131 E6
Trinity Bay Canada 123 L5
Trinity Islands U.S.A. 118 C4
Trinity Range mts U.S.A. 128 D1
Trinkat Island India 71 A5
Trionto, Capo c. Italy 58 G5
Tripa r. Indon. 71 B7
Tripkau Germany 53 L1
Tripoli Greece 59 J6
Tripoli Lebanon 85 B2

▶Tripoli Libya 97 E1
Capital of Libya.

Trípolis Greece see Tripoli
Tripolis Lebanon see Tripoli
Tripunittura India 84 C4
Tripura state India 83 G5

▶Tristan da Cunha i. S. Atlantic Ocean 148 H8
Dependency of St Helena.

Trisul mt. India 82 D3
Triton Canada 123 L4
Triton Island atoll Paracel Is 68 E3
Trittau Germany 53 K1
Trittenheim Germany 52 G5
Trivandrum India 84 C4
Trivento Italy 58 F4
Trnava Slovakia 47 P6
Trobriand Islands P.N.G. 106 F2
Trochu Canada 120 H5
Trofors Norway 44 H4
Trogir Croatia 58 G3
Troia Italy 58 F4
Troisdorf Germany 53 H4
Trois Fourches, Cap des c. Morocco 57 E6
Trois-Ponts Belgium 52 F4
Trois-Rivières Canada 123 G5
Troitsko-Pechorsk Rus. Fed. 41 R3
Troitskoye Altayskiy Kray Rus. Fed. 72 E2
Troitskoye Khabarovskiy Kray Rus. Fed. 74 E2
Troitskoye Respublika Kalmykiya - Khalm'g-Tangch Rus. Fed. 43 J7
Trollhättan Sweden 45 H7
Trombetas r. Brazil 143 G4
Tromelin, Île i. Indian Ocean 149 L7
Tromelin Island Micronesia see Fais
Tromen, Volcán vol. Arg. 144 B5
Tromie r. U.K. 50 E3
Trompsburg S. Africa 101 G6
Tromsø Norway 44 K2
Trona U.S.A. 128 E4
Tronador, Monte mt. Arg. 144 B6
Trondheim Norway 44 G5
Trondheimsfjorden sea chan. Norway 44 F5
Trongsa Bhutan 83 G4
Troödos, Mount Cyprus 85 A2
Troödos Mountains Cyprus 85 A2
Troon U.K. 50 E5
Tropeiros, Serra dos hills Brazil 145 B1
Tropic U.S.A. 129 G3
Tropic of Cancer 131 B8
Tropic of Capricorn 110 G4
Trosh Rus. Fed. 42 L2
Trostan hill U.K. 51 F2
Trout r. B.C. Canada 120 E3
Trout r. N.W.T. Canada 120 G2
Trout Lake Alta Canada 120 H3
Trout Lake N.W.T. Canada 120 F2
Trout Lake l. N.W.T. Canada 120 F2
Trout Lake l. Ont. Canada 121 M5
Trout Peak U.S.A. 126 F3
Trout Run U.S.A. 135 G3
Trouville-sur-Mer France 49 H9
Trowbridge U.K. 49 E7
Troy tourist site Turkey 59 L5
Troy AL U.S.A. 133 C6
Troy KS U.S.A. 130 E4
Troy MI U.S.A. 134 D2
Troy MO U.S.A. 130 F4
Troy MT U.S.A. 126 E2
Troy NH U.S.A. 135 I2
Troy NY U.S.A. 135 I2
Troy OH U.S.A. 134 C3
Troy PA U.S.A. 135 G3
Troyan Bulg. 59 K3
Troyes France 56 G2
Troy Lake U.S.A. 128 E4
Troy Peak U.S.A. 129 F2
Trstenik Serb. and Mont. 59 I3
Truc Giang Vietnam see Bên Tre
Trucial Coast country Asia see United Arab Emirates
Trucial States country Asia see United Arab Emirates
Trud Rus. Fed. 42 G4
Trufanovo Rus. Fed. 42 J2
Trujillo Hond. 137 G5
Trujillo Peru 142 C5
Trujillo Spain 57 D4
Trujillo Venez. 142 D2
Trujillo, Monte mt. Dom. Rep. see Duarte, Pico
Truk is Micronesia see Chuuk
Trulben Germany 53 H5
Trumbull, Mount U.S.A. 129 G3
Trumon Indon. 71 B7
Trundle Australia 112 C4
Trưng Hiệp Vietnam 70 D4
Trung Khanh Vietnam 70 D2
Truong Sa is S. China Sea see Spratly Islands
Truro Canada 123 J5
Truro U.K. 49 B8
Truskmore hill Rep. of Ireland 51 D3
Trutch Canada 120 F3
Truth or Consequences U.S.A. 127 G6
Trutnov Czech Rep. 47 O5
Truuli Peak U.S.A. 118 C4
Truva tourist site Turkey see Troy
Trypiti, Akra pt Greece 59 K7
Trysil Norway 45 H6
Trzebiatów Poland 47 O3
Tsagaannuur Mongolia 80 G2
Tsagaan-Uul Mongolia see Sharga
Tsagan Aman Rus. Fed. 43 J7
Tsagan-Nur Rus. Fed. 43 J7
Tsaidam Basin China see Qaidam Pendi
Tsaka La pass China/Jammu and Kashmir 82 D2
Tsalenjikha Georgia 91 F2
Tsangbo r. China see Brahmaputra
Tsangpo r. China see Brahmaputra
Tsaratanana, Massif du mts Madag. 99 E5

Tsarevo Bulg. 59 L3
Tsaris Mountains Namibia 100 C3
Tsaritsyn Rus. Fed. see Volgograd
Tsaukaib Namibia 100 B4
Tsavo East National Park Kenya 98 D4
Tsavo West National Park Africa 98 D3
Tsefat Israel see Ẕefat
Tselinograd Kazakh. see Astana
Tsenogora Rus. Fed. 42 J2
Tses Namibia 100 D3
Tsetsegnuur Mongolia 80 H2
Tsetseng Botswana 100 F2
Tsetserleg *Arhangay* Mongolia 80 J2
Tsetserleg *Hövsgöl* Mongolia see Halban
Tshabong Botswana 100 F4
Tshad *country* Africa see Chad
Tshane Botswana 100 E3
Tshela Dem. Rep. Congo 99 B4
Tshibala Dem. Rep. Congo 99 C4
Tshikapa Dem. Rep. Congo 99 C4
Tshing S. Africa 101 H4
Tshipise S. Africa 101 J2
Tshitanzu Dem. Rep. Congo 99 C4
Tshofa Dem. Rep. Congo 99 C4
Tshokwane S. Africa 101 J3
Tsholotsho Zimbabwe 99 C5
Tshootsha Botswana 100 E2
Tshuapa *r.* Dem. Rep. Congo 97 F5
Tshwane S. Africa see Pretoria
Tsil'ma *r.* Rus. Fed. 42 K2
Tsimlyansk Rus. Fed. 43 I7
Tsimlyanskoye Vodokhranilishche *resr* Rus. Fed. 43 I7
Tsimmermanovka Rus. Fed. 74 E2
Tsinan China see Jinan
Tsineng S. Africa 100 F4
Tsinghai *prov.* China see Qinghai
Tsing Shan Wan *Hong Kong* China see Castle Peak Bay
Tsingtao China see Qingdao
Tsing Yi *i. Hong Kong* China 77 [inset]
Tsining China see Jining
Tsiombe Madag. 99 E6
Tsiroanomandidy Madag. 99 E5
Tsitsihar China see Qiqihar
Tsitsikamma Forest and Coastal National Park S. Africa 100 F8
Tsitsutl Peak Canada 120 E4
Tsivil'sk Rus. Fed. 42 J5
Tskhaltubo Georgia see Tsqaltubo
Ts'khinvali Georgia 91 F2
Tsna *r.* Rus. Fed. 43 I5
Tsnori Georgia 91 G2
Tsokar Chumo *l.* Jammu and Kashmir 82 D2
Tsolo S. Africa 101 I6
Tsomo S. Africa 101 H7
Tsona China see Cona
Tsqaltubo Georgia 91 F2
Tsu Japan 75 E6
Tsuchiura Japan 75 F5
Tsuen Wan *Hong Kong* China 77 [inset]
Tsugarū-kaikyō *strait* Japan 74 F4
Tsugaru Strait Japan see Tsugarū-kaikyō
Tsumeb Namibia 99 B5
Tsumis Park Namibia 100 C2
Tsumkwe Namibia 99 C5
Tsuruga Japan 75 E6
Tsurugi-san *mt.* Japan 75 D6
Tsurukhaytuy Rus. Fed. see Priargunsk
Tsuruoka Japan 75 E5
Tsushima *is* Japan 75 C6
Tsushima-kaikyō *strait* Japan/S. Korea see Korea Strait
Tsuyama Japan 75 D6
Tswaane Botswana 100 E2
Tswaraganang S. Africa 101 G5
Tswelelang S. Africa 101 G4
Tsyelyakhany Belarus 45 N10
Tsyp-Navolok Rus. Fed. 44 R2
Tsyurupyns'k Ukr. 59 O1
Tthenaagoo Canada see Nahanni Butte
Tua Dem. Rep. Congo 98 B4
Tual Indon. 69 I8
Tuam Rep. of Ireland 51 D4
Tuamotu, Archipel des *is* Fr. Polynesia see Tuamotu Islands
Tuamotu Islands Fr. Polynesia 151 K6
Tuân Giao Vietnam 70 C2
Tuangku *i.* Indon. 71 B7
Tuapse Rus. Fed. 90 E1
Tuas Sing. 71 [inset]
Tuath, Loch a' *b.* U.K. 50 C2
Tuba City U.S.A. 129 H3
Tubarão Brazil 145 A5
Tubarjal Saudi Arabia 85 D4
Tubbercurry Rep. of Ireland 51 D3
Tübingen Germany 47 L6
Tubmanburg Liberia 96 B4
Tubruq Libya 90 A4
Tubuai *i.* Fr. Polynesia 151 K7
Tubuai Islands Fr. Polynesia 151 J7
Tucano Brazil 143 K6
Tucavaca Bol. 143 G7
Tüchen Germany 53 M1
Tuchheim Germany 53 M2
Tuchitua Canada 120 D2
Tuchodi *r.* Canada 120 F3
Tuckerton U.S.A. 135 H4
Tucopia *i.* Solomon Is see Tikopia
Tucson U.S.A. 129 H5
Tucson Mountains U.S.A. 129 H5
Tuctuc *r.* Canada 123 I2
Tucumán Arg. see San Miguel de Tucumán
Tucumcari U.S.A. 131 C5
Tucupita Venez. 142 F2
Tucuruí Brazil 143 I4
Tucuruí, Represa *resr* Brazil 143 I4
Tudela Spain 57 F2
Tuder Italy see Todi
Tuela *r.* Port. 57 C3
Tuen Mun *Hong Kong* China 77 [inset]
Tuensang India 83 H4
Tufts Abyssal Plain *sea feature* N. Pacific Ocean 151 K2
Tugela *r.* S. Africa 101 J5
Tuglung China 76 B2
Tuguegarao Phil. 69 G3
Tugur Rus. Fed. 74 E1
Tuhemberua Indon. 71 B7
Tujiabu China see Yongxiu
Tukangbesi, Kepulauan *is* Indon. 69 G8
Tukarak Island Canada 122 F2
Ţukhmān, Banī *reg.* Saudi Arabia 88 C6
Tukituki *r.* N.Z. 113 F4
Tuktoyaktuk Canada 118 E3
Tuktut Nogait National Park Canada 118 F3
Tukums Latvia 45 M8
Tukuringra, Khrebet *mts* Rus. Fed. 74 B1
Tukuyu Tanz. 99 D4
Tula Rus. Fed. 43 H5
Tulach Mhór Rep. of Ireland see Tullamore
Tulagt Ar Gol *r.* China 83 H1
Tulak Afgh. 89 F3
Tulameen Canada 120 F5
Tula Mountains Antarctica 152 D2
Tulancingo Mex. 136 E4
Tulare U.S.A. 128 D3
Tulare Lake Bed U.S.A. 128 D4
Tularosa Mountains U.S.A. 129 I5
Tulasi *mt.* India 84 D2
Tulbagh S. Africa 100 D7
Tulcán Ecuador 142 C3
Tulcea Romania 59 M2
Tule *r.* U.S.A. 131 C5
Tuléar Madag. see Toliara
Tulemalu Lake Canada 121 L2
Tulia U.S.A. 131 C5
Tulihe China 74 A2
Tulita Canada 120 E1
Tulkarem West Bank see Ţūlkarm
Ţūlkarm West Bank 85 B3
Tulla Rep. of Ireland 51 D5
Tullahoma U.S.A. 132 C5
Tullamore Australia 112 C4
Tullamore Rep. of Ireland 51 E4
Tulle France 56 E4
Tulleråsen Sweden 44 I5
Tullibigeal Australia 112 C4
Tullow Rep. of Ireland 51 F5
Tully Australia 110 D3
Tully *r.* Australia 110 D3
Tully U.K. 51 E3
Tulos Rus. Fed. 44 Q5
Tulqarem West Bank see Ţūlkarm
Tulsa U.S.A. 131 E4
Tulsipur Nepal 83 E3
Tuluá Col. 142 C3
Tuluksak U.S.A. 153 B2
Tulūl al Ashāqif *hills* Jordan 85 C3
Tulun Rus. Fed. 72 I2
Tulu-Tuloi, Serra *hills* Brazil 142 F3
Tulu Welel *mt.* Eth. 98 D3
Tuma Rus. Fed. 43 I5
Tumaco Col. 142 C3
Tumahole S. Africa 101 H4
Tumain China 83 G2
Tumannyy Rus. Fed. 44 S2
Tumasik Sing. see Singapore
Tumba Dem. Rep. Congo 98 C4
Tumba Sweden 45 J7
Tumba, Lac *l.* Dem. Rep. Congo 98 B4
Tumbarumba Australia 112 D5
Tumbes Peru 142 B4
Tumbler Ridge Canada 120 F4
Tumby Bay Australia 111 B7
Tumcha *r.* Fin./Rus. Fed. 44 Q3 *also known as* Tuntsajoki
Tumen *Jilin* China 74 C4
Tumen *Shaanxi* China 77 F1
Tumereng Guyana 142 F2
Tumindao *i.* Phil. 68 F6
Tumiritinga Brazil 145 C2
Tumkur India 84 C3
Tummel *r.* U.K. 50 F4
Tummel, Loch *l.* U.K. 50 F4
Tumnin *r.* Rus. Fed. 74 F2
Tump Pak. 89 F5
Tumpat Malaysia 71 C6
Tumpôr, Phnum *mt.* Cambodia 71 C4
Tumshuk Uzbek. 89 G2
Tumu Ghana 96 C3
Tumucumaque, Serra *hills* Brazil 143 G3
Tumudibandh India 84 D2
Tumut Australia 112 D5
Tuna India 82 B5
Ţunb al Kubrá *i.* The Gulf see Greater Tunb
Ţunb aş Şughrá *i.* The Gulf see Lesser Tunb
Tunbridge Wells, Royal U.K. 49 H7
Tunceli Turkey 91 E3
Tunchang China 77 F5
Tuncurry Australia 112 F4
Tundun-Wada Nigeria 96 D3
Tunduru Tanz. 99 D5
Tunes Tunisia see Tunis
Tunga Nigeria 96 D4
Tungabhadra Reservoir India 80 C3
Tungi Bangl. 83 G5
Tung Lung Island *Hong Kong* China 77 [inset]
Tungnaá *r.* Iceland 44 [inset]
Tungor Rus. Fed. 74 F1
Tung Pok Liu Hoi Hap *Hong Kong* China see East Lamma Channel
Tungsten Canada 120 D2
Tung Wan *b. Hong Kong* China 77 [inset]
Tuni India 84 D2
Tunica U.S.A. 131 F5
Tūnis *country* Africa see Tunisia

▶Tunis Tunisia 58 D6
Capital of Tunisia.

Tunis, Golfe de *g.* Tunisia 58 D6
▶Tunisia *country* Africa 54 F5
Africa 7, 94–95
Tunja Col. 142 D2
Tunkhannock U.S.A. 135 H3
Tunnsjøen *l.* Norway 44 H4
Tunstall U.K. 49 I6
Tuntsa Fin. 44 P3
Tuntsajoki *r.* Fin./Rus. Fed. see Tumcha
Tunulic *r.* Canada 123 I2
Tununak U.S.A. 118 B3
Tunungayualok Island Canada 123 J2
Tunxi China see Huangshan
Tuodian China see Shuangbai
Tuojiang China see Fenghuang
Tuŏl Khpos Cambodia 71 D5
Tuoniang Jiang *r.* China 76 E3
Tuotuo He *r.* China see Togton He
Tuotuoheyan China see Tanggulashan
Tüp Kyrg. 80 E3
Tupã Brazil 145 A3
Tupelo U.S.A. 131 F5
Tupik Rus. Fed. 73 L2
Tupinambarama, Ilha *i.* Brazil 143 G4
Tupiraçaba Brazil 145 A1
Tupiza Bol. 142 E8
Tupper Canada 120 F4
Tupper Lake U.S.A. 135 H1
Tupper Lake *l.* U.S.A. 135 H1
Tüpqaraghan Tübegi *pen.* Kazakh. see Mangyshlak, Poluostrov

▶Tupungato, Cerro *mt.* Arg./Chile 144 C4
5th highest mountain in South America.

Tuqayyid *well* Iraq 88 B4
Tuquan China 73 M3
Tuqu Wan *b.* China see Lingshui Wan
Tura China 83 F1
Tura India 83 G4
Tura Rus. Fed. 65 L3
Turabah Saudi Arabia 86 F5
Turakina N.Z. 113 E5
Turan Rus. Fed. 72 G2
Turana, Khrebet *mts* Rus. Fed. 74 C2
Turan Lowland Asia 80 A4
Turan Oypaty *lowland* Asia see Turan Lowland
Turan Pasttekisligi *lowland* Asia see Turan Lowland
Turan Pesligi *lowland* Asia see Turan Lowland
Turanskaya Nizmennost' *lowland* Asia see Turan Lowland
Ţuraq al 'Ilab *hills* Syria 85 D3
Turar Ryskulov Kazakh. 80 D3
Tura-Ryskulova Kazakh. see Turar Ryskulov
Turayf Saudi Arabia 85 D4
Turba Estonia 45 N7
Turbat Pak. 89 F5
Turbo Col. 142 C2
Turda Romania 59 J1
Türeh Iran 88 C3
Turfan China see Turpan
Turfan Basin *depr.* China see Turpan Pendi
Turfan Depression China see Turpan Pendi
Turgay Kazakh. 80 B2
Turgayskaya Dolina *valley* Kazakh. 80 B2
Türgovishte Bulg. 59 L3
Turgutlu Turkey 59 L5
Turhal Turkey 90 E2
Türi Estonia 45 N7
Turia *r.* Spain 57 F4
Turin Canada 121 H5
Turin Italy 58 B2
Turiy Rog Rus. Fed. 74 C3
Turkana, Lake *salt l.* Eth./Kenya 98 D3
Turkestan Kazakh. 80 C3
Turkestan Range *mts* Asia 89 G2
▶Turkey *country* Asia/Europe 90 D3
Asia 6, 62–63
Turkey U.S.A. 134 D5
Turkey *r.* U.S.A. 130 F3
Turki Rus. Fed. 43 I6
Türkistan Kazakh. see Turkestan
Türkiye *country* Asia/Europe see Turkey
Turkmenabat Turkm. 89 F2
Türkmen Adasy *i.* Turkm. see Ogurchinskiy, Ostrov
Türkmen Aylagy *b.* Turkm. see Turkmenskiy Zaliv
Turkmenbashi Turkm. 88 D1
Türkmenbaşy Turkm. see Turkmenbashi
Türkmenbaşy Aylagy *b.* Turkm. see Krasnovodskiy Zaliv
Türkmen Dağı *mt.* Turkey 59 N5
▶Turkmenistan *country* Asia 87 I2
Asia 6, 62–63
Turkmeniya *country* Asia see Turkmenistan
Türkmenostan *country* Asia see Turkmenistan
Turkmenskaya S.S.R. *country* Asia see Turkmenistan
Turkmenskiy Zaliv *b.* Turkm. 88 D2
Türkoğlu Turkey 90 E3

▶Turks and Caicos Islands *terr.* West Indies 137 J4
United Kingdom Overseas Territory.
North America 9, 116–117

Turks Island Passage Turks and Caicos Is 133 G8
Turks Islands Turks and Caicos Is 137 J4
Turku Fin. 45 M6
Turkwel *watercourse* Kenya 98 D3
Turlock U.S.A. 128 C3
Turlock Lake U.S.A. 128 C3
Turmalina Brazil 145 C2
Turnagain *r.* Canada 120 E3
Turnagain, Cape N.Z. 113 F5
Turnberry U.K. 50 E5
Turnbull, Mount U.S.A. 129 H5
Turneffe Islands *atoll* Belize 136 G5
Turner U.S.A. 134 D1
Turner Valley Canada 120 H5
Turnhout Belgium 52 E3
Turnor Lake Canada 121 I3
Tŭrnovo Bulg. see Veliko Tŭrnovo
Turnu Măgurele Romania 59 K3
Turnu Severin Romania see Drobeta - Turnu Severin
Turon *r.* Australia 112 D4
Turones France see Tours
Turovets Rus. Fed. 42 I4
Turpan China 80 G3

▶Turpan Pendi *depr.* China 80 G3
Lowest point in northern Asia.

Turquino, Pico *mt.* Cuba 137 I4
Turriff U.K. 50 G3
Turris Libisonis *Sardinia* Italy see Porto Torres
Tursāq Iraq 91 G4
Turtkul' Uzbek. 80 B3
Turtle Island Fiji see Vatoa
Turtle Lake Canada 121 I4
Turugart Pass China/Kyrg. 80 E3
Turugart Shankou *pass* China/Kyrg. see Turugart Pass
Turuvanur India 84 C3
Turvo *r.* Brazil 145 A2
Turvo *r.* Brazil 145 A2
Tusayan U.S.A. 129 G4
Tuscaloosa U.S.A. 133 C5
Tuscarawas *r.* U.S.A. 134 E3
Tuscarora Mountains *hills* U.S.A. 135 G3
Tuscola *IL* U.S.A. 130 F4
Tuscola *TX* U.S.A. 131 D5
Tuscumbia U.S.A. 133 C5
Tuskegee U.S.A. 133 C5
Tussey Mountains *hills* U.S.A. 135 F3
Tustin U.S.A. 134 C1
Tutak Turkey 91 F3
Tutayev Rus. Fed. 42 H4
Tutera Spain see Tudela
Tuticorin India 84 C4
Tutong Brunei 68 E6
Tuttle Creek Reservoir U.S.A. 130 D4
Tuttlingen Germany 47 L7
Tuttut Nunaat *reg.* Greenland 119 P2
Tutuala East Timor 108 D2
Tutubu P.N.G. 110 E1
Tutubu Tanz. 99 D4
Tutuila *i.* American Samoa 107 I3
Tutume Botswana 99 C6
Tutwiler U.S.A. 131 F5
Tuun-bong *mt.* N. Korea 74 B4
Tuupovaara Fin. 44 Q5
Tuusniemi Fin. 44 P5
▶Tuvalu *country* S. Pacific Ocean 107 H2
Oceania 8, 104–105
Tuwayq, Jabal *hills* Saudi Arabia 86 G4
Tuwayq, Jabal *mts* Saudi Arabia 86 G5
Ţuwayyil ash Shihāq *mt.* Jordan 85 C4
Tuwwal Saudi Arabia 86 E5
Tuxpan Mex. 136 E4
Tuxtla Gutiérrez Mex. 136 F5
Tuya Lake Canada 120 D3
Tuyên Quang Vietnam 70 D2
Tuy Hoa Vietnam 71 E4
Tuz, Lake *salt l.* Turkey 90 D3
Tuz Gölü *salt l.* Turkey see Tuz, Lake
Tuzha Rus. Fed. 42 J4
Tuz Khurmātū Iraq 91 G4
Tuzla Bos.-Herz. 58 H2
Tuzla Turkey 85 B1
Tuzla Gölü *lag.* Turkey 59 L4
Tuzlov *r.* Rus. Fed. 43 I7
Tuzu *r.* Myanmar 70 A1
Tvedestrand Norway 45 F7
Tver' Rus. Fed. 42 G4
Twain Harte U.S.A. 128 C2
Tweed Canada 135 G1
Tweed *r.* U.K. 50 G5
Tweed Heads Australia 112 F2
Tweedie Canada 121 I4
Tweefontein S. Africa 100 D7
Twee Rivier Namibia 100 D3
Twentekanaal *canal* Neth. 52 G2
Twentynine Palms U.S.A. 128 E4
Twin Bridges *CA* U.S.A. 128 C2
Twin Bridges *MT* U.S.A. 126 E3
Twin Buttes Reservoir U.S.A. 131 C6
Twin Falls Canada 123 I3
Twin Falls U.S.A. 126 E4
Twin Heads *hill* Australia 108 D5
Twin Peak U.S.A. 128 C2
Twistringen Germany 53 I2
Twitchen Reservoir U.S.A. 128 C4
Twitya *r.* Canada 120 D1
Twofold Bay Australia 112 D6
Two Harbors U.S.A. 130 F2
Two Hills Canada 121 I4
Two Rivers U.S.A. 134 B1
Tyan' Shan' *mts* China/Kyrg. see Tien Shan
Tyao *r.* India/Myanmar 76 B4
Tyatya, Vulkan *vol.* Rus. Fed. 74 G3
Tydal Norway 44 G5
Tygart Valley U.S.A. 134 F4
Tygda Rus. Fed. 74 B1
Tygda *r.* Rus. Fed. 74 B1
Tyler U.S.A. 131 E5
Tylertown U.S.A. 131 F6
Tym' *r.* Rus. Fed. 74 F2
Tymovskoye Rus. Fed. 74 F2
Tynda Rus. Fed. 73 M1
Tyndall U.S.A. 130 D3
Tyndinskiy Rus. Fed. see Tynda
Tyne *r.* U.K. 50 G4
Tynemouth U.K. 48 F3
Tynset Norway 44 G5
Tyoploozyorsk Rus. Fed. see Teploozersk
Tyoploye Ozero Rus. Fed. see Teploozersk
Tyr Lebanon see Tyre
Tyras Ukr. see Bilhorod-Dnistrovs'kyy
Tyre Lebanon 85 B3
Tyree, Mount Antarctica 152 L1
Tyrma Rus. Fed. 74 D2
Tyrma *r.* Rus. Fed. 74 C2
Tyrnävä Fin. 44 N4
Tyrnavos Greece 59 J5
Tyrnyauz Rus. Fed. 91 F2
Tyrone U.S.A. 135 F3
Tyrrell *r.* Australia 112 A5
Tyrrell, Lake *dry lake* Australia 111 C7
Tyrrell Lake Canada 121 J2
Tyrrhenian Sea France/Italy 58 D4
Tyrus Lebanon see Tyre
Tysa *r.* Ukr. see Tisa
Tyukalinsk Rus. Fed. 64 I4
Tyulen'i Ostrova *is* Kazakh. 91 H1
Tyumen' Rus. Fed. 64 H4
Tyup Kyrg. see Tüp
Tyuratam Kazakh. see Baykonyr
Tywi *r.* U.K. 49 C7
Tywyn U.K. 49 C6
Tzaneen S. Africa 101 J2

U

Uaco Congo Angola see Waku-Kungo
Ualan *atoll* Micronesia see Kosrae
Uamanda Angola 99 C5
Uarc, Ras *c.* Morocco see Trois Fourches, Cap des
Uaroo Australia 109 A5
Uatumã *r.* Brazil 143 G4
Uauá Brazil 143 K5
Uaupés *r.* Brazil 142 E3
U'aylī, Wādī al *watercourse* Saudi Arabia 85 D4
U'aywij *well* Saudi Arabia 88 B4
U'aywij, Wādī al *watercourse* Saudi Arabia 91 F5
Ubá Brazil 145 C3
Ubaí Brazil 145 B2
Ubaitaba Brazil 145 D1
Ubangi *r.* Cent. Afr. Rep./Dem. Rep. Congo 98 B4
Ubangi-Shari *country* Africa see Central African Republic
Ubauro Pak. 89 H4
Ubayyiḑ, Wādī al *watercourse* Iraq/Saudi Arabia 91 F4
Ube Japan 75 C6
Úbeda Spain 57 E4
Uberaba Brazil 145 B2
Uberlândia Brazil 145 A2
Ubin, Pulau *i.* Sing. 71 [inset]
Ubly U.S.A. 134 D2
Ubolratna Reservoir Thai. 70 C3
Ubombo S. Africa 101 K4
Ubon Ratchathani Thai. 70 D4
Ubstadt-Weiher Germany 53 I5
Ubundu Dem. Rep. Congo 97 F5
Ucar Azer. 91 G2
Uçarı Turkey 85 A1
Ucayali *r.* Peru 142 D4
Uch Pak. 89 H4
Uch-Adzhi Turkm. 89 F2
Üchajy Turkm. see Uch-Adzhi
Üchān Iran 88 C2
Ucharal Kazakh. 80 F2
Uchiura-wan *b.* Japan 74 F4
Uchkeken Rus. Fed. 91 F2
Uchkuduk Uzbek. 80 B3
Uchquduq Uzbek. see Uchkuduk
Uchte Germany 53 I2
Uchte *r.* Germany 53 L2
Uchto *r.* Pak. 89 G5
Uchur *r.* Rus. Fed. 65 O4
Uckermark *reg.* Germany 53 N1
Uckfield U.K. 49 H8
Ucluelet Canada 120 E5
Ucross U.S.A. 126 G3
Uda *r.* Rus. Fed. 73 J2
Uda *r.* Rus. Fed. 74 D1
Udachnoye Rus. Fed. 43 J7
Udachnyy Rus. Fed. 153 E2
Udagamandalam India 84 C4
Udaipur *Orissa* India 83 F5
Udaipur *Rajasthan* India 82 C4
Udaipur *Tripura* India 83 G5
Udanti *r.* India/Myanmar 83 E5
Uday *r.* Ukr. 43 G6
'Udaynān *well* Saudi Arabia 88 C6
Uddevalla Sweden 45 G7
Uddingston U.K. 50 E5
Uddjaure *l.* Sweden 44 J4
'Udeid, Khōr al *inlet* Qatar 88 C5
Uden Neth. 52 F3
Udgir India 84 C2
Udhagamandalam India see Udagamandalam
Udhampur India 82 C2
Udia-Milai *atoll* Marshall Is see Bikini
Udimskiy Rus. Fed. 42 J3
Udine Italy 58 E1
Udit India 89 I5
Udjuktok Bay Canada 123 J3
Udmalaippettai India see Udumalaippettai
Udomlya Rus. Fed. 42 G4
Udon Thani Thai. 70 C3
Udskaya Guba *b.* Rus. Fed. 65 O4
Udskoye Rus. Fed. 74 D1
Udumalaippettai India 84 C4
Udupi India 84 B3
Udyl', Ozero *l.* Rus. Fed. 74 E1
Udzhary Azer. see Ucar
Udzungwa Mountains National Park Tanz. 99 D4
Uéa *atoll* New Caledonia see Ouvéa
Ueckermünde Germany 47 O4
Ueda Japan 75 E5
Uele *r.* Dem. Rep. Congo 98 C3
Uelen Rus. Fed. 65 U3
Uelzen Germany 53 K2
Uetersen Germany 53 J1
Uettingen Germany 53 J5
Uetze Germany 53 K2
Ufa Rus. Fed. 41 R5
Ufa *r.* Rus. Fed. 41 R5
Uffenheim Germany 53 K5
Uftyuga *r.* Rus. Fed. 42 J3
Ugab *watercourse* Namibia 99 B6
Ugalla *r.* Tanz. 99 D4
▶Uganda *country* Africa 98 D3
Africa 7, 94–95
Ugie S. Africa 101 I6
Ūgīnak Iran 89 F5
Uglegorsk Rus. Fed. 74 F2
Uglich Rus. Fed. 42 H4
Ugljan *i.* Croatia 58 F2
Uglovoye Rus. Fed. 74 C2
Ugol'noye Rus. Fed. 65 P3
Ugolnyy Rus. Fed. see Beringovskiy
Ugol'nyye Kopi Rus. Fed. 65 S3
Ugra Rus. Fed. 43 G5
Uherské Hradiště Czech Rep. 43 P6
Úhlava *r.* Czech Rep. 53 N5
Uhrichsville U.S.A. 134 E3
Uibhist a' Deas *i.* U.K. see South Uist
Uibhist a' Tuath *i.* U.K. see North Uist
Uig U.K. 50 C3
Uíge Angola 99 B4
Ŭijŏngbu S. Korea 75 B5
Ŭiju N. Korea 75 B4
Uimaharju Fin. 44 Q5
Uinta Mountains U.S.A. 129 H1
Uis Mine Namibia 99 B6
Uitenhage S. Africa 101 G7
Uithoorn Neth. 52 E2
Uithuizen Neth. 52 G1
Uivak, Cape Canada 123 J2
Ujhani India 82 D4
Uji Japan 75 D6
Uji-guntō *is* Japan 75 C7
Ujiyamada Japan see Ise
Ujjain India 82 C5
Ujung Pandang Indon. see Makassar
Újvidék Serb. and Mont. see Novi Sad
Ukal Sagar *l.* India 82 C5
Ukata Nigeria 96 D3
'Ukayrishah *well* Saudi Arabia 88 B5
Ukholovo Rus. Fed. 43 I5
Ukhrul India 83 H4
Ukhta *Respublika Kareliya* Rus. Fed. see Kalevala
Ukhta *Respublika Komi* Rus. Fed. 42 L3
Ukiah *CA* U.S.A. 128 B2
Ukiah *OR* U.S.A. 126 D3
Ukkusissat Greenland 119 M2
Ukmergė Lith. 45 N9

▶Ukraine *country* Europe 43 F6
2nd largest country in Europe.
Europe 5, 38–39

Ukrainskaya S.S.R. *country* Europe see Ukraine
Ukrayina *country* Europe see Ukraine
Uku-jima *i.* Japan 75 C6
Ukwi Botswana 100 E2
Ukwi Pan *salt pan* Botswana 100 E2
Ulaanbaatar Mongolia see Ulan Bator
Ulaangom Mongolia 80 H2
Ulan Australia 112 D4

▶Ulan Bator Mongolia 72 J3
Capital of Mongolia.

Ulanbel' Kazakh. 80 D3
Ulan Erge Rus. Fed. 43 J7
Ulanhad China see Chifeng
Ulanhot China 74 A3
Ulan Hua China 73 K4
Ulan-Khol Rus. Fed. 43 J7
Ulan-Ude Rus. Fed. 73 J2
Ulan Ul Hu *l.* China 83 G2
Ulaş Turkey 90 E3
Ulawa Island Solomon Is 107 G2
Ulayyah *reg.* Saudi Arabia 88 B6
Ul'banskiy Zaliv *b.* Rus. Fed. 74 E1
Ulchin S. Korea 75 C5
Uldz *r.* Mongolia 73 L3
Uleåborg Fin. see Oulu
Ulefoss Norway 45 F7
Ülenurme Estonia 45 O7
Ulety Rus. Fed. 73 K2
Ulhasnagar India 84 B2
Uliastai China 73 L3
Uliastay Mongolia 80 I2
Uliatea *i.* Fr. Polynesia see Raiatea
Ulicoten Neth. 52 E3
Ulie *atoll* Micronesia see Woleai
Ulita *r.* Rus. Fed. 44 R2
Ulithi *atoll* Micronesia 69 J4
Ulladulla Australia 112 E5
Ullapool U.K. 50 D3
Ulla Ulla, Parque Nacional *nat. park* Bol. 142 E6
Ullava Fin. 44 M5
Ullersuaq *c.* Greenland 119 K2
Ullswater *l.* U.K. 48 E4
Ullŭng-do *i.* S. Korea 75 C5
Ulm Germany 47 L6
Ulmarra Australia 112 F2
Ulmen Germany 52 G4
Uloowaranie, Lake *salt flat* Australia 111 B5
Ulricehamn Sweden 45 H8
Ulrum Neth. 52 G1
Ulsan S. Korea 75 C6
Ulsberg Norway 44 F5
Ulster *reg.* Rep. of Ireland/U.K. 51 E3
Ulster U.S.A. 135 G3
Ulster Canal Rep. of Ireland/U.K. 51 E3
Ultima Australia 112 A5
Ulubat Gölü *l.* Turkey 59 M4
Ulubey Turkey 59 M5
Uluborlu Turkey 59 N5
Uludağ *mt.* Turkey 59 M4
Uludağ Milli Parkı *nat. park* Turkey 59 M4
Ulugqat China see Wuqia
Ulu Kali, Gunung *mt.* Malaysia 71 C7
Ulukışla Turkey 90 D3
Ulundi S. Africa 101 J5
Ulungur Hu *l.* China 80 G2
Ulunkhan Rus. Fed. 73 K2
Uluqsaqtuuq Canada see Holman
Uluru *hill* Australia 109 E6
Uluru - Kata Tjuta National Park Australia 109 E6
Uluru National Park Australia see Uluru - Kata Tjuta National Park
Ulutau Kazakh. see Ulytau
Ulutau, Gory *mts* Kazakh. see Ulytau, Gory
Uluyatır Turkey 85 C1
Ulva *i.* U.K. 50 C4
Ulvenhout Neth. 52 E3
Ulverston U.K. 48 D4
Ulvsjön Sweden 45 I6
Ul'yanov Kazakh. see Ul'yanovskiy
Ul'yanovsk Rus. Fed. 43 K5
Ul'yanovskiy Kazakh. 80 D1
Ul'yanovskoye Kazakh. see Ul'yanovskiy
Ulysses *KS* U.S.A. 130 C4
Ulysses *KY* U.S.A. 134 D5
Ulytau Kazakh. 80 C2
Ulytau, Gory *mts* Kazakh. 80 C2
Uma Rus. Fed. 74 A1
Umaltinskiy Rus. Fed. 74 D2
'Umān *country* Asia see Oman
Uman' Ukr. 43 F6
Umarao Pak. 89 G4
'Umarī, Qa' al *salt pan* Jordan 85 C4
Umaria India 82 E5
Umarkhed India 84 C2
Umarkot India 84 D2
Umarkot Pak. 89 H5
Umaroona, Lake *salt flat* Australia 111 B5
Umarpada India 82 C5
Umatilla U.S.A. 126 D3
Umba Rus. Fed. 42 G2
Umbagog Lake U.S.A. 135 J1

Umbeara Australia 109 F6
Umboi i. P.N.G. 69 L8
Umeå Sweden 44 L5
Umeälven r. Sweden 44 L5
Umfolozi r. S. Africa 101 K5
Umfreville Lake Canada 121 M5
Umhlanga Rocks S. Africa 101 J5
Umiiviip Kangertiva inlet Greenland 119 N3
Umingmaktok Canada 153 L2
Umirzak Kazakh. 91 H2
Umiujaq Canada 122 F2
Umkomaas S. Africa 101 J6
Umlaiteng India 83 H4
Umlazi S. Africa 101 J5
Umm ad Daraj, Jabal mt. Jordan 85 B3
Umm al 'Amad Syria 85 C2
Umm al Jamājim well Saudi Arabia 88 B5
Umm al Qaiwain U.A.E. see Umm al Qaywayn
Umm al Qaywayn U.A.E. 88 D5
Umm ar Raqabah, Khabrat imp. l. Saudi Arabia 85 C5
Umm at Qalbān Saudi Arabia 91 F6
Umm az Zumūl well Oman 88 D6
Umm Bāb Qatar 88 C5
Umm Bel Sudan 86 C7
Umm Keddada Sudan 86 C7
Umm Lajj Saudi Arabia 86 E4
Umm Nukhaylah hill Saudi Arabia 85 D5
Umm Qaşr Iraq 91 G5
Umm Quşur i. Saudi Arabia 90 D6
Umm Ruwaba Sudan 86 D7
Umm Sa'ad Libya 90 B5
Umm Sa'id Qatar 88 C5
Umm Shugeira Sudan 86 C7
Umm Wa'āl hill Saudi Arabia 85 D4
Umm Wazīr well Saudi Arabia 88 B6
Umnak Island U.S.A. 118 B4
Um Phang Wildlife Reserve nature res. Thai. 70 B4
Umpqua r. U.S.A. 126 B4
Umpulo Angola 99 B5
Umraniye Turkey 59 N5
Umred India 84 C1
Umri India 82 D4
Umtali Zimbabwe see Mutare
Umtata S. Africa 101 I6
Umtentweni S. Africa 101 J6
Umuahia Nigeria 96 D4
Umuarama Brazil 144 F2
Umvuma Zimbabwe see Mvuma
Umzimkulu S. Africa 101 I6
Una r. Bos.-Herz./Croatia 58 G2
Una Brazil 145 D1
Una India 82 D3
'Unāb, Jabal al hill Jordan 85 C5
'Unāb, Wādī al watercourse Jordan 85 C4
Unaí Brazil 145 B2
Unai Pass Afgh. 89 H3
Unalaska Island U.S.A. 118 B4
Unapool U.K. 50 D2
'Unayzah Saudi Arabia 86 F4
'Unayzah, Jabal hill Iraq 91 E4
Uncia Bol. 142 E7
Uncompahgre Peak U.S.A. 129 J2
Uncompahgre Plateau U.S.A. 129 I2
Undara National Park Australia 110 D3
Underberg S. Africa 101 I5
Underbool Australia 111 C7
Underwood U.S.A. 134 C4
Undur Indon. 69 I7
Unecha Rus. Fed. 43 G5
Ungama Bay Kenya see Ungwana Bay
Ungarie Australia 112 C4
Ungava, Baie d' b. Canada see Ungava Bay
Ungava, Péninsule d' pen. Canada 122 G1
Ungava Bay Canada 123 I2
Ungava Peninsula Canada see Ungava, Péninsule d'
Ungeny Moldova see Ungheni
Unggi N. Korea 74 C4
Ungheni Moldova 59 L1
Unguana Moz. 101 L2
Unguja i. Tanz. see Zanzibar Island
Unguz, Solonchakovyye Vpadiny salt flat Turkm. 88 E2
Üngüz Angyrsyndaky Garagum des. Turkm. see Zaunguzskiye Karakumy
Ungvár Ukr. see Uzhhorod
Ungwana Bay Kenya 98 E4
Uni Rus. Fed. 42 K4
União Brazil 143 J4
União da Vitória Brazil 145 A4
União dos Palmares Brazil 143 K5
Unimak Island U.S.A. 118 B4
Unini r. Brazil 142 F4
Union MO U.S.A. 130 F4
Union WV U.S.A. 134 E5
Union, Mount U.S.A. 129 G4
Union City OH U.S.A. 134 C3
Union City PA U.S.A. 134 F3
Union City TN U.S.A. 131 F4
Uniondale S. Africa 100 F7
Unión de Reyes Cuba 133 D8

▶Union of Soviet Socialist Republics
Divided in 1991 into 15 independent nations: Armenia, Azerbaijan, Belarus, Estonia, Georgia, Kazakhstan, Kyrgyzstan, Latvia, Lithuania, Moldova, the Russian Federation, Tajikistan, Turkmenistan, Ukraine and Uzbekistan.

Union Springs U.S.A. 133 C5
Uniontown U.S.A. 134 F4
Unionville U.S.A. 135 G3
▶United Arab Emirates country Asia 88 D6
Asia 6, 62–63
United Arab Republic country Africa see Egypt

▶United Kingdom country Europe 46 G3
3rd most populous country in Europe.
Europe 5, 38–39

United Provinces state India see Uttar Pradesh

▶United States of America country N. America 124 F3
Most populous country in North America and 3rd in the world. 3rd largest country in the world and 2nd in North America.
North America 9, 116–117

United States Range mts Canada 119 L1
Unity Canada 121 I4
Unjha India 82 C5
Unna Germany 53 H3
Unnao India 82 E4
Ŭnp'a N. Korea 75 B5
Unsan N. Korea 75 B4
Ŭnsan N. Korea 75 B5
Unst i. U.K. 50 [inset]
Unstrut r. Germany 53 L3
Untari India 83 E4
Untor, Ozero l. Rus. Fed. 41 T3
Unuk r. Canada/U.S.A. 120 D3
Unuli Horog China 83 G2
Unzen-dake vol. Japan 75 C6
Unzha Rus. Fed. 42 J4
Upalco U.S.A. 129 H1
Upar Ghat reg. India 83 F5
Upemba, Lac l. Dem. Rep. Congo 99 C4
Uperbada India 83 F5
Upernavik Greenland 119 M2
Upington S. Africa 100 E5
Upland U.S.A. 128 E4
Upleta India 82 B5
Upoloksha Rus. Fed. 44 Q3
Upolu i. Samoa 107 I3
Upper Arlington U.S.A. 134 D3
Upper Arrow Lake Canada 120 G5
Upper Chindwin Myanmar see Mawlaik
Upper Fraser Canada 120 F4
Upper Garry Lake Canada 121 K1
Upper Hutt N.Z. 113 E5
Upper Klamath Lake U.S.A. 126 C4
Upper Lough Erne l. U.K. 51 E3
Upper Marlboro U.S.A. 135 G4
Upper Mazinaw Lake Canada 135 G1
Upper Missouri Breaks National Monument nat. park U.S.A. 130 A2
Upper Peirce Reservoir Sing. 71 [inset]
Upper Red Lake U.S.A. 130 E1
Upper Sandusky U.S.A. 134 D3
Upper Saranac Lake U.S.A. 135 H1
Upper Seal Lake Canada see Iberville, Lac d'
Upper Tunguska r. Rus. Fed. see Angara
Upper Volta country Africa see Burkina
Upper Yarra Reservoir Australia 112 B6
Uppinangadi India 84 B3
Uppsala Sweden 45 J7
Upsala Canada 122 C4
Upshi Jammu and Kashmir 82 D2
Upton U.S.A. 135 J2
'Uqayqah, Wādī watercourse Jordan 85 B4
'Uqayribāt Syria 85 C2
Uqlat al 'Udhaybah well Iraq 91 G5
Uqturpan China see Wushi
Uracas vol. N. Mariana Is see Farallon de Pajaros
Urad Houqi China see Sain Us
Ūrāf Iran 88 E4
Urakawa Japan 74 F4
Ural hill Australia 112 C4
Ural r. Kazakh./Rus. Fed. 78 E2
Uralla Australia 112 E3
Ural Mountains Rus. Fed. 41 S2
Ural'sk Kazakh. 78 E1
Ural'skaya Oblast' admin. div. Kazakh. see Zapadnyy Kazakhstan
Ural'skiye Gory mts Rus. Fed. see Ural Mountains
Ural'skiy Khrebet mts Rus. Fed. see Ural Mountains
Urambo Tanz. 99 D4
Uran India 84 B2
Urana Australia 112 C5
Urana, Lake Australia 112 C5
Urandangi Australia 110 B4
Urandi Brazil 145 C1
Uranium City Canada 121 I3
Uranquity Australia 112 C5
Uraricoera r. Brazil 142 F3
Urartu country Asia see Armenia
Ura-Tyube Tajik. see Üroteppa
Uravakonda India 84 C3
Uravan U.S.A. 129 I2
Urawa Japan 75 E6
'Urayf an Nāqah, Jabal hill Egypt 85 B4
Uray'irah Saudi Arabia 88 C5
'Urayq ad Duḩūl des. Saudi Arabia 88 B5
'Urayq Sāqān des. Saudi Arabia 88 B5
Urbana IL U.S.A. 130 F3
Urbana OH U.S.A. 134 D3
Urbino Italy 58 E3
Urbinum Italy see Urbino
Urbs Vetus Italy see Orvieto
Urdoma Rus. Fed. 42 K3
Urdyuzhskoye, Ozero l. Rus. Fed. 42 K2
Urdzhar Kazakh. 80 F2
Ure r. U.K. 48 F4
Ureki Georgia 91 F2
Uren' Rus. Fed. 42 J4
Urengoy Rus. Fed. 64 I3
Uréparapara i. Vanuatu 107 G3
Urewera National Park N.Z. 113 F4
Urfa Turkey see Şanlıurfa
Urfa prov. Turkey see Şanlıurfa
Urga Mongolia see Ulan Bator
Urgal r. Rus. Fed. 74 D2
Urganch Uzbek. see Urgench
Urgench Uzbek. 80 B3
Ürgüp Turkey 90 D3
Urgut Uzbek. 89 G2
Urho China 80 G2
Urho Kekkosen kansallispuisto nat. park Fin. 44 O2
Urie r. U.K. 50 G3
Uril Rus. Fed. 74 C2
Urisino Australia 112 A2
Urjala Fin. 45 M6
Urk Neth. 52 F2
Urkan Rus. Fed. 74 B1
Urkan r. Rus. Fed. 74 B1
Urla Turkey 59 L5
Urlingford Rep. of Ireland 51 E5
Urluk Rus. Fed. 73 J2
Urmā aş Şughrá Syria 85 C1
Urmai China 83 F3
Urmia Iran 88 B2
Urmia, Lake salt l. Iran 88 B2
Urmston Road sea chan. Hong Kong China 77 [inset]
Uromi Nigeria 96 D4
Uroševac Serb. and Mont. 59 I3
Urosozero Rus. Fed. 42 G3
Ŭroteppa Tajik. 89 H2
Urru Co salt l. China 83 F3
Urt Moron China 80 H4
Uruáchic Mex. 124 F6
Uruaçu Brazil 145 A1
Uruana Brazil 145 A1
Uruapan Baja California Mex. 127 D7
Uruapan Michoacán Mex. 136 D5
Urubamba r. Peru 142 D6
Urucara Brazil 143 G4
Urucu r. Brazil 142 F4
Uruçuca Brazil 145 D1
Uruçuí Brazil 143 J5
Uruçuí, Serra do hills Brazil 143 I5
Urucuia Brazil 145 B2
Urucurituba Brazil 143 G4
Uruguai r. Arg./Uruguay see Uruguay
Uruguaiana Brazil 144 E3
Uruguay r. Arg./Uruguay 144 E4
also known as Uruguai
▶Uruguay country S. America 144 E4
South America 9, 140–141
Uruhe China 74 B2
Urumchi China see Ürümqi
Ürümqi China 80 G3
Urundi country Africa see Burundi
Urup, Ostrov i. Rus. Fed. 73 S3
Urusha Rus. Fed. 74 A1
Urutaí Brazil 145 A2
Uryl' Kazakh. 80 G2
Uryupino Rus. Fed. 73 M2
Uryupinsk Rus. Fed. 43 I6
Ürzhar Kazakh. see Urdzhar
Urzhum Rus. Fed. 42 K4
Urziceni Romania 59 L2
Usa Japan 75 C6
Usa r. Rus. Fed. 42 M2
Uşak Turkey 59 M5
Usakos Namibia 100 B1
Usarp Mountains Antarctica 152 H2
Usborne, Mount hill Falkland Is 144 E8
Ushakova, Ostrov i. Rus. Fed. 64 I1
Ushant i. France see Ouessant, Île d'
Üsharal Kazakh. see Ucharal
Ush-Bel'dyr Rus. Fed. 72 H2
Ushtobe Kazakh. 80 E2
Ush-Tyube Kazakh. see Ushtobe
Ushuaia Arg. 144 C8
Ushumun Rus. Fed. 74 B1
Usingen Germany 53 I4
Usinsk Rus. Fed. 41 R2
Usk U.K. 49 E7
Usk r. U.K. 49 E7
Uskhodni Belarus 45 O10
Uskoplje Bos.-Herz. see Gornji Vakuf
Üsküdar Turkey 59 M4
Uslar Germany 53 J3
Usman' Rus. Fed. 43 H5
Usmanabad India see Osmanabad
Usmas ezers l. Latvia 45 M8
Usogorsk Rus. Fed. 42 K3
Usol'ye-Sibirskoye Rus. Fed. 72 I2
Uspenovka Rus. Fed. 74 B1
Ussel France 56 F4
Ussuri r. China/Rus. Fed. 74 D2
Ussuriysk Rus. Fed. 74 C4
Ust'-Abakanskoye Rus. Fed. see Abakan
Usta Muhammad Pak. 89 H4
Ust'-Balyk Rus. Fed. see Nefteyugansk
Ust'-Donetskiy Rus. Fed. 43 I7
Ust'-Dzheguta Rus. Fed. 91 F1
Ust'-Dzhegutinskaya Rus. Fed. see Ust'-Dzheguta
Ustica, Isola di i. Sicily Italy 58 E5
Ust'-Ilimsk Rus. Fed. 65 L4
Ust'-Ilimskiy Vodokhranilishche resr Rus. Fed. 65 L4
Ust'-Ilych Rus. Fed. 41 R3
Ústí nad Labem Czech Rep. 47 O5
Ustinov Rus. Fed. see Izhevsk
Üstirt plat. Kazakh./Uzbek. see Ustyurt Plateau
Ustka Poland 47 P3
Ust'-Kamchatsk Rus. Fed. 65 R4
Ust'-Kamenogorsk Kazakh. 80 F2
Ust'-Kan Rus. Fed. 80 F1
Ust'-Koksa Rus. Fed. 80 G1
Ust'-Kulom Rus. Fed. 42 L3
Ust'-Kut Rus. Fed. 65 L4
Ust'-Kuyga Rus. Fed. 65 O2
Ust'-Labinsk Rus. Fed. 91 E1
Ust'-Labinskaya Rus. Fed. see Ust'-Labinsk
Ust'-Lyzha Rus. Fed. 42 M2
Ust'-Maya Rus. Fed. 65 O3
Ust'-Nera Rus. Fed. 65 P3
Ust'-Ocheya Rus. Fed. 42 K3
Ust'-Olenek Rus. Fed. 65 M2
Ust'-Omchug Rus. Fed. 65 P3
Ust'-Ordynskiy Rus. Fed. 72 I2
Ust'-Penzhino Rus. Fed. see Kamenskoye
Ust'-Port Rus. Fed. 64 J3
Ustrem Rus. Fed. 41 T3
Ust'-Tsil'ma Rus. Fed. 42 L2
Ust'-Uda Rus. Fed. 72 I2
Ust'-Umalta Rus. Fed. 74 D2
Ust'-Undurga Rus. Fed. 73 L2
Ust'-Ura Rus. Fed. 42 J3
Ust'-Urgal Rus. Fed. 74 D2
Ust'-Usa Rus. Fed. 42 M2
Ust'-Vayen'ga Rus. Fed. 42 I3
Ust'-Voya Rus. Fed. 41 R3
Ust'-Vyyskaya Rus. Fed. 42 J3
Ust'ya r. Rus. Fed. 42 I3
Ust'ye Rus. Fed. 42 H4
Ustyurt, Plato plat. Kazakh./Uzbek. see Ustyurt Plateau
Ustyurt Plateau Kazakh./Uzbek. 78 E2
Ustyurt Platosi plat. Kazakh./Uzbek. see Ustyurt Plateau
Ustyuzhna Rus. Fed. 42 H4
Usulután El Salvador 136 G6
Usumbura Burundi see Bujumbura
Usvyaty Rus. Fed. 42 F5
Utah state U.S.A. 126 F5
Utah Lake U.S.A. 129 H1
Utajärvi Fin. 44 O4
Utashinai Rus. Fed. see Yuzhno-Kuril'sk
'Utaybah, Buḩayrat al imp. l. Syria 85 C3
Utena Lith. 45 N9
Uterlai India 82 B4
Uthai Thani Thai. 70 C4
Uthal Pak. 89 G5
'Uthmānīyah Syria 85 C2
Utiariti Brazil 143 G6
Utica NY U.S.A. 135 H2
Utica OH U.S.A. 134 D3
Utiel Spain 57 F4
Utikuma Lake Canada 120 H4
Utlwanang S. Africa 101 G4
Utrecht Neth. 52 F2
Utrecht S. Africa 101 J4
Utrera Spain 57 D5
Utsjoki Fin. 44 O2
Utsunomiya Japan 75 E5
Utta Rus. Fed. 43 J7
Uttaradit Thai. 70 C3
Uttarakhand state India see Uttaranchal
Uttaranchal state India 82 D3
Uttar Kashi India see Uttarkashi
Uttarkashi India 82 D3
Uttar Pradesh state India 82 D4
Uttoxeter U.K. 49 F6
Uttranchal state India see Uttaranchal
Utubulak China 80 G2
Utupua i. Solomon Is 107 G3
Uummannaq Greenland see Dundas
Uummannaq Fjord inlet Greenland 153 J2
Uummannarsuaq c. Greenland see Farewell, Cape
Uurainen Fin. 44 N5
Uusikaarlepyy Fin. see Nykarleby
Uusikaupunki Fin. 45 L6
Uutapi Namibia 99 B5
Uva Rus. Fed. 42 L4
Uvalde U.S.A. 131 D6
Uval Karabaur hills Kazakh./Uzbek. 91 I2
Uval Muzbel' hills Kazakh. 91 I2
Uvarovo Rus. Fed. 43 I6
Uvéa atoll New Caledonia see Ouvéa
Uvinza Tanz. 99 D4
Uvs Nuur salt l. Mongolia 80 H1
Uwajima Japan 75 D6
'Uwayriḑ, Ḩarrat al lava field Saudi Arabia 86 E4
Uwaysiţ well Saudi Arabia 85 D4
Uweinat, Jebel mt. Sudan 86 C5
Uwi i. Indon. 71 D7
Uxbridge Canada 134 F1
Uxbridge U.K. 49 G7
Uxin Qi China see Dabqig
Uyaly Kazakh. 80 B3
Uyar Rus. Fed. 72 G1
Üydzin Mongolia 72 J4
Uyo Nigeria 96 D4
Uyu Chaung r. Myanmar 70 A1
Uyuni Bol. 142 E8
Uyuni, Salar de salt flat Bol. 138 E8
Uza r. Rus. Fed. 43 J5
▶Uzbekistan country Asia 80 B3
Asia 6, 62–63
Ŭzbekiston country Asia see Uzbekistan
Uzbekskaya S.S.R. country Asia see Uzbekistan
Uzbek S.S.R. country Asia see Uzbekistan
Uzen' Kazakh. see Kyzylsay
Uzhgorod Ukr. see Uzhhorod
Uzhhorod Ukr. 43 D6
Užhorod Ukr. see Uzhhorod
Užice Serb. and Mont. 59 H3
Uzlovaya Rus. Fed. 43 H5
Üzümlü Turkey 59 M6
Uzun Uzbek. 89 H2
Uzunköprü Turkey 59 L4
Uzynkair Kazakh. 80 B3

V

Vaaf Atoll Maldives see Felidhu Atoll
Vaajakoski Fin. 44 N5
Vaal r. S. Africa 101 F5
Vaala Fin. 44 O4
Vaalbos National Park S. Africa 100 G5
Vaal Dam S. Africa 101 I4
Vaalwater S. Africa 101 I3
Vaasa Fin. 44 L5
Vaavu Atoll Maldives see Felidhu Atoll
Vabkent Uzbek. 89 G1
Vác Hungary 47 Q7
Vacaria Brazil 145 A5
Vacaria, Campo da plain Brazil 145 A5
Vacaville U.S.A. 128 C2
Vachon r. Canada 123 H1
Vad Rus. Fed. 42 J5
Vad r. Rus. Fed. 43 I5
Vada India 84 B2
Vadla Norway 45 E7
Vadodara India 82 C5
Vadsø Norway 44 P1

▶Vaduz Liechtenstein 56 I3
Capital of Liechtenstein.

Værøy i. Norway 44 H3
Vaga r. Rus. Fed. 42 I3
Vågåmo Norway 45 F6
Vaganski Vrh mt. Croatia 58 F2
Vágar i. Faroe Is 44 [inset]
Vågsele Sweden 44 K4
Vágur Faroe Is 44 [inset]
Váh r. Slovakia 47 Q7
Vähäkyrö Fin. 44 M5

▶Vaiaku Tuvalu 107 H2
Capital of Tuvalu, on Funafuti atoll.

Vaida Estonia 45 N7
Vaiden U.S.A. 131 F5
Vail U.S.A. 124 F4
Vailly-sur-Aisne France 52 D5
Vaitupu i. Tuvalu 107 H2
Vajrakarur India see Kanur
Vakhsh Tajik. 89 H2
Vakhsh r. Tajik. 89 H2
Vakhstroy Tajik. see Vakhsh
Vakīlābād Iran 88 E4
Valbo Sweden 45 J6
Valcheta Arg. 144 C6
Valdai Hills Rus. Fed. see Valdayskaya Vozvyshennost'
Valday Rus. Fed. 42 G4
Valdayskaya Vozvyshennost' hills Rus. Fed. 42 G4
Valdecañas, Embalse de resr Spain 57 D4
Valdemārpils Latvia 45 M8
Valdemarsvik Sweden 45 J7
Valdepeñas Spain 57 E4
Val-de-Reuil France 52 B5

▶Valdés, Península pen. Arg. 144 D6
Lowest point in South America.
South America 138–139

Valdez U.S.A. 118 D3
Valdivia Chile 144 B5
Val-d'Or Canada 122 F4
Valdosta U.S.A. 133 D6
Valdres valley Norway 45 F6
Vale Georgia 91 F2
Vale U.S.A. 126 D3
Valemount Canada 120 G4
Valença Brazil 145 D1
Valence France 56 G4
Valencia Spain 57 F4
València Spain see Valencia
Valencia reg. Spain 57 F4
Valencia Venez. 142 E1
Valencia, Golfo de g. Spain 57 G4
Valencia de Don Juan Spain 57 D2
Valencia Island Rep. of Ireland 51 B6
Valenciennes France 52 D4
Valensole, Plateau de France 56 H5
Valentia Spain see Valencia
Valentin Rus. Fed. 74 D4
Valentine U.S.A. 130 C3
Våler Norway 45 G6
Valera Venez. 142 D2
Vale Verde Brazil 145 D2
Val Grande, Parco Nazionale della nat. park Italy 58 C1
Valjevo Serb. and Mont. 59 H2
Valka Latvia 45 O8
Valkeakoski Fin. 45 N6
Valkenswaard Neth. 52 F3
Valky Ukr. 43 G6
Valkyrie Dome ice feature Antarctica 152 D1
Valladolid Mex. 136 G4
Valladolid Spain 57 D3
Vallard, Lac l. Canada 123 H3
Vall de Uxó Spain 57 F4
Valle Norway 45 E7
Vallecillos Mex. 131 D7
Vallecito Reservoir U.S.A. 129 J3
Valle de la Pascua Venez. 142 E2
Valledupar Col. 142 D1
Vallée-Jonction Canada 123 H5
Valle Fértil, Sierra de mts Arg. 144 C4
Valle Grande Bol. 142 F7
Valle Hermoso Mex. 131 D7
Vallejo U.S.A. 128 B2
Vallenar Chile 144 B3

▶Valletta Malta 58 F7
Capital of Malta.

Valley r. Canada 121 L5
Valley U.K. 48 C5
Valley City U.S.A. 130 D2
Valleyview Canada 120 G4
Valls Spain 57 G3
Val Marie Canada 121 J5
Valmiera Latvia 45 N8
Valmy U.S.A. 128 E1
Valnera mt. Spain 57 E2
Valognes France 49 F9
Valona Albania see Vlorë
Valozhyn Belarus 45 O9
Val-Paradis Canada 122 F4
Valparai India 84 C4
Valparaíso Chile 144 B4
Valparaiso U.S.A. 134 B3
Valpoi India 84 B3
Valréas France 56 G4
Vals, Tanjung c. Indon. 69 J8
Valsad India 84 B1
Valspan S. Africa 100 G4
Val'tevo Rus. Fed. 42 J2
Valtimo Fin. 44 P5
Valuyevka Rus. Fed. 43 I7
Valuyki Rus. Fed. 43 H6
Vammala Fin. 45 M6
Van Turkey 91 F3
Van, Lake salt l. Turkey 91 F3
Vanadzor Armenia 91 G2
Van Buren AR U.S.A. 131 E5
Van Buren MO U.S.A. 131 F4
Van Buren OH U.S.A. see Kettering
Vanceburg U.S.A. 134 D4
Vanch Tajik. see Vanj
Vancleve U.S.A. 134 D5
Vancouver Canada 120 F5
Vancouver U.S.A. 126 C3
Vancouver, Mount Canada/U.S.A. 120 B2
Vancouver Island Canada 120 E5
Vanda Fin. see Vantaa
Vandalia IL U.S.A. 130 F4
Vandalia OH U.S.A. 134 C4
Vandekerckhove Lake Canada 121 K3
Vanderbijlpark S. Africa 101 H4
Vanderbilt U.S.A. 134 C1
Vandergrift U.S.A. 134 F3
Vanderhoof Canada 120 E4
Vanderkloof Dam resr S. Africa 100 G6
Vanderlin Island Australia 110 B2
Vanderwagen U.S.A. 129 I4
Van Diemen, Cape N.T. Australia 108 E2
Van Diemen, Cape Qld Australia 110 B3
Van Diemen Gulf Australia 108 F2
Van Diemen's Land state Australia see Tasmania
Vändra Estonia 45 N7
Väner, Lake Sweden see Vänern

▶Vänern l. Sweden 45 H7
4th largest lake in Europe.

Vänersborg Sweden 45 H7
Vangaindrano Madag. 99 E6
Van Gölü salt l. Turkey see Van, Lake
Van Horn U.S.A. 127 G7
Vanikoro Islands Solomon Is 107 G3
Vanimo P.N.G. 69 K7
Vanino Rus. Fed. 74 F2
Vanivilasa Sagara resr India 84 C3
Vaniyambadi India 84 C3
Vanj Tajik. 89 H2
Vanna i. Norway 44 K1
Vännäs Sweden 44 K5
Vannes France 56 C3
Vannes, Lac l. Canada 123 I3
Vannovka Kazakh. see Turar Ryskulov
Van Rees, Pegunungan mts Indon. 69 J7
Vanrhynsdorp S. Africa 100 D6
Vansant U.S.A. 134 D5
Vansbro Sweden 45 I6
Vansittart Island Canada 119 J3
Van Starkenborgh Kanaal canal Neth. 52 G1
Vantaa Fin. 45 N6
Van Truer Tableland reg. Australia 109 C6
Vanua Lava i. Vanuatu 107 G3
Vanua Levu i. Fiji 107 H3
▶Vanuatu country S. Pacific Ocean 107 G3
Oceania 8, 104–105
Van Wert U.S.A. 134 C3
Vanwyksvlei S. Africa 100 E6
Vanwyksvlei l. S. Africa 100 E6
Văn Yên Vietnam 70 D2
Van Zylsrus S. Africa 100 F4
Varadero Cuba 133 D8
Varahi India 82 B5
Varakļāni Latvia 45 O8
Varalé Côte d'Ivoire 96 C4
Varāmīn Iran 88 C3
Varanasi India 83 E4
Varandey Rus. Fed. 42 M1
Varangerfjorden sea chan. Norway 44 P1
Varanger Halvøya pen. Norway 41 L1
Varangerhalvøya pen. Norway 44 P1
Varaždin Croatia 58 G1
Varberg Sweden 45 H8
Vardar r. Macedonia 59 J4
Varde Denmark 45 F9
Vardenis Armenia 91 G2
Vardø Norway 44 Q1
Varel Germany 53 I1
Varėna Lith. 45 N9
Varese Italy 58 C2
Varfolomeyevka Rus. Fed. 74 D3
Vårgårda Sweden 45 H7
Varginha Brazil 145 B3
Varik Neth. 52 F3
Varillas Chile 144 B2
Varkana Iran see Gorgān
Varkaus Fin. 44 O5
Varna Bulg. 59 L3
Värnamo Sweden 45 I8
Värnäs Sweden 45 H6
Varnavino Rus. Fed. 42 J4
Várnjárg pen. Norway see Varangerhalvøya
Varpaisjärvi Fin. 44 O5
Várpalota Hungary 58 H1
Varsaj Afgh. 89 H2
Varsh, Ozero l. Rus. Fed. 42 J2
Varto Turkey 91 F3
Várzea da Palma Brazil 145 B2
Vasa Fin. see Vaasa
Vasai India 84 B2
Vashka r. Rus. Fed. 42 J2
Vasht Iran see Khāsh
Vasilkov Ukr. see Vasyl'kiv
Vasknarva Estonia 45 O7
Vaslui Romania 59 L1
Vassar U.S.A. 134 D2
Vas-Soproni-síkság hills Hungary 58 G1
Vastan Turkey see Gevaş
Västerås Sweden 45 J7
Västerdalälven r. Sweden 45 I6
Västerfjäll Sweden 44 J3
Västerhaninge Sweden 45 K7
Västervik Sweden 45 J8
Vasto Italy 58 F3
Vasyl'kiv Ukr. 43 F6
Vatan France 56 E3
Vaté i. Vanuatu see Éfaté
Vatersay i. U.K. 50 B4
Vathar India 84 B2
Vathí Greece see Vathy
Vathy Greece 59 L6

▶Vatican City Europe 58 E4
Independent papal state, the smallest country in the world.
Europe 5, 38–39

Vaticano, Città del Europe see Vatican City
Vatnajökull ice cap Iceland 40 [inset]
Vatoa i. Fiji 107 I3
Vatra Dornei Romania 59 K1
Vätter, Lake Sweden see Vättern
Vättern l. Sweden 45 I7
Vaughn U.S.A. 127 G6
Vaupés r. Col. 142 E3
Vauquelin r. Canada 122 F3
Vauvert France 56 G5
Vauxhall Canada 121 H5
Vavatenina Madag. 99 E5
Vava'u Group is Tonga 107 I3
Vavitao i. Fr. Polynesia see Raivavae
Vavoua Côte d'Ivoire 96 C4
Vavozh Rus. Fed. 42 K4
Vavuniya Sri Lanka 84 D4
Vawkavysk Belarus 45 N10
Växjö Sweden 45 I8
Vây, Đao i. Vietnam 71 C5
Vayenga Rus. Fed. see Severomorsk
Vazante Brazil 145 B2
Vazáš Sweden see Vittangi
Veaikevárri Sweden see Svappavaara
Veal Vêng Cambodia 71 C4

Vecht r. Neth. 52 G2
also known as Vechte (Germany)
Vechta Germany 53 I2
Vechte r. Germany 53 G2
also known as Vecht (Netherlands)
Veckerhagen (Reinhardshagen) Germany 53 J3
Vedaranniyam India 84 C4
Vedasandur India 84 C4
Veddige Sweden 45 H8
Vedea r. Romania 59 K3
Veedersburg U.S.A. 134 B3
Veendam Neth. 52 G1
Veenendaal Neth. 52 F2
Vega i. Norway 44 G4
Vega U.S.A. 131 C5
Vegreville Canada 121 H4
Vehkalahti Fin. 45 O6
Vehoa Pak. 89 H4
Veinticinco de Mayo Buenos Aires Arg. see 25 de Mayo
Veinticinco de Mayo La Pampa Arg. see 25 de Mayo
Veirwaro Pak. 89 H5
Veitshöchheim Germany 53 J5
Vejle Denmark 45 F9
Vekil'bazar Turkm. 89 F2
Velbert Germany 52 H3
Velbŭzhdki Prokhod pass Bulg./Macedonia 59 J3
Velddrif S. Africa 100 D7
Velebit mts Croatia 58 F2
Velen Germany 52 G3
Velenje Slovenia 58 F1
Veles Macedonia 59 I4
Vélez-Málaga Spain 57 D5
Vélez-Rubio Spain 57 E5
Velhas r. Brazil 145 B2
Velibaba Turkey see Aras
Velika Gorica Croatia 58 G2
Velika Plana Serb. and Mont. 59 I2
Velikaya r. Rus. Fed. 42 K4
Velikaya r. Rus. Fed. 45 P8
Velikaya r. Rus. Fed. 65 S3
Velikaya Kema Rus. Fed. 74 E3
Veliki Preslav Bulg. 59 L3
Velikiye Luki Rus. Fed. 42 F4
Velikiy Novgorod Rus. Fed. 42 F4
Velikiy Ustyug Rus. Fed. 42 J3
Velikonda Range hills India 84 C3
Veliko Tŭrnovo Bulg. 59 K3
Velikoye Rus. Fed. 42 H4
Velikoye, Ozero l. Rus. Fed. 43 I5
Veli Lošinj Croatia 58 F2
Velizh Rus. Fed. 42 F5
Vella Lavella i. Solomon Is 107 F2
Vellar r. India 84 C4
Vellberg Germany 53 J5
Vellmar Germany 53 J3
Vellore India 84 C3
Velpke Germany 53 K2
Vel'sk Rus. Fed. 42 I3
Velsuna Italy see Orvieto
Velten Germany 53 N2
Veluwezoom, Nationaal Park nat. park Neth. 52 F2
Velykyy Tokmak Ukr. see Tokmak
Vel'yu r. Rus. Fed. 42 L3
Vemalwada India 84 C2
Vema Seamount sea feature S. Atlantic Ocean 148 I8
Vema Trench sea feature Indian Ocean 149 M6
Vembe Nature Reserve S. Africa 101 I2
Vempalle India 84 C3
Venado Tuerto Arg. 144 D4
Venafro Italy 58 F4
Venceslau Bráz Brazil 145 A3
Vendinga Rus. Fed. 42 J3
Vendôme France 56 E3
Venegas Mex. 131 C8
Venetia Italy see Venice
Venetie Landing U.S.A. 118 D3
Venev Rus. Fed. 43 H5
Venezia Italy see Venice
Venezia, Golfo di g. Europe see Venice, Gulf of

▶Venezuela country S. America 142 E2
5th most populous country in South America.
South America 9, 140–141

Venezuela, Golfo de g. Venez. 142 D1
Venezuelan Basin sea feature S. Atlantic Ocean 148 D4
Vengurla India 84 B3
Veniaminof Volcano U.S.A. 118 C4
Venice Italy 58 E2
Venice U.S.A. 133 D7
Venice, Gulf of Europe 58 E2
Vénissieux France 56 G4
Venkatapalem India 84 D2
Venkatapuram India 84 D2
Venlo Neth. 52 G3
Vennesla Norway 45 E7
Venray Neth. 52 F3
Venta r. Latvia/Lith. 45 M8
Venta Lith. 45 M8
Ventersburg S. Africa 101 H5
Ventersdorp S. Africa 101 H4
Venterstad S. Africa 101 G6
Ventnor U.K. 49 F8
Ventotene, Isola i. Italy 58 E4
Ventoux, Mont mt. France 56 G4
Ventspils Latvia 45 L8
Ventura U.S.A. 128 D4
Venus Bay Australia 112 B7
Venustiano Carranza Mex. 131 C7
Venustiano Carranza, Presa resr Mex. 131 C7
Vera Arg. 144 D3
Vera Spain 57 F5
Vera Cruz Brazil 145 A3
Vera Cruz Mex. see Veracruz
Veracruz Mex. 136 E5
Veraval India 82 B5
Verbania Italy 58 C2
Vercelli Italy 58 C2
Vercors reg. France 56 G4
Verdalsøra Norway 44 G5
Verde r. Goiás Brazil 145 A2
Verde r. Goiás Brazil 145 A2
Verde r. Goiás Brazil 145 B2
Verde r. Minas Gerais Brazil 145 A2
Verde r. Mex. 127 G8
Verde r. U.S.A. 129 H5
Verden (Aller) Germany 53 J2
Verde Pequeno r. Brazil 145 C1
Verdi U.S.A. 128 D2
Verdon r. France 56 G5
Verdun France 52 F5
Vereeniging S. Africa 101 H4
Vereshchagino Rus. Fed. 41 Q4
Vergennes U.S.A. 135 I1
Véria Greece see Veroia
Verín Spain 57 C3
Veríssimo Brazil 145 A2
Verkhneimbatsk Rus. Fed. 64 J3
Verkhnekolvinsk Rus. Fed. 42 M2
Verkhnespasskoye Rus. Fed. 42 J4
Verkhnetulomskiy Rus. Fed. 44 Q2
Verkhnetulomskoye Vdkhr. res. Rus. Fed. 44 Q2
Verkhnevilyuysk Rus. Fed. 65 N3
Verkhneye Kuyto, Ozero l. Rus. Fed. 44 Q4
Verkhnezeysk Rus. Fed. 73 N2
Verkhniy Vyalozerskiy Rus. Fed. 42 G2
Verkhnyaya Khava Rus. Fed. 43 H6
Verkhnyaya Salda Rus. Fed. 41 S4
Verkhnyaya Tunguska r. Rus. Fed. see Angara
Verkhnyaya Tura Rus. Fed. 41 R4
Verkhoshizhem'ye Rus. Fed. 42 K4
Verkhovazh'ye Rus. Fed. 42 I3
Verkhov'ye Rus. Fed. 43 H5
Verkhoyansk Rus. Fed. 65 O3
Verkhoyanskiy Khrebet mts Rus. Fed. 65 N2
Vermand France 52 D5
Vermelho r. Brazil 145 A1
Vermilion Canada 121 I4
Vermilion Bay U.S.A. 131 F6
Vermilion Cliffs AZ U.S.A. 129 G3
Vermilion Cliffs UT U.S.A. 129 G3
Vermilion Cliffs National Monument nat. park U.S.A. 129 H3
Vermilion Lake U.S.A. 130 E2
Vermillion U.S.A. 130 D3
Vermillion Bay Canada 121 M5
Vermont state U.S.A. 135 I1
Vernadsky research station Antarctica 152 L2
Vernal U.S.A. 129 I1
Verner Canada 122 E5
Verneuk Pan salt pan S. Africa 100 E5
Vernon Canada 120 G5
Vernon France 52 B5
Vernon AL U.S.A. 131 F5
Vernon IN U.S.A. 134 C4
Vernon TX U.S.A. 131 D5
Vernon UT U.S.A. 129 G1
Vernon Islands Australia 108 E3
Vernoye Rus. Fed. 74 C2
Vernyy Kazakh. see Almaty
Vero Beach U.S.A. 133 D7
Veroia Greece 59 J4
Verona Italy 58 D2
Verona U.S.A. 134 F4
Versailles France 52 C6
Versailles IN U.S.A. 134 C4
Versailles KY U.S.A. 134 C4
Versailles OH U.S.A. 134 C3
Versec Serb. and Mont. see Vršac
Versmold Germany 53 I2
Vert, Île i. Canada 123 H4
Vertou France 56 D3
Verulam S. Africa 101 J5
Verulamium U.K. see St Albans
Verviers Belgium 52 F4
Vervins France 52 D5
Verwood Canada 121 J5
Verzy France 52 E5
Vescovato Corsica France 56 I5
Vesele Ukr. 43 G7
Veselyy Rus. Fed. 43 I7
Veshenskaya Rus. Fed. 43 I6
Vesle r. France 52 D5
Veslyana r. Rus. Fed. 42 L3
Vesontio France see Besançon
Vesoul France 56 H3
Vesselyy Yar Rus. Fed. 74 D4
Vessem Neth. 52 F3
Vesterålen is Norway 44 H2
Vesterålsfjorden sea chan. Norway 44 H2
Vestertana Norway 44 O1
Vestfjorddalen valley Norway 45 F7
Vestfjorden sea chan. Norway 44 H3
Véstia Brazil 145 A3
Vestmanna Faroe Is 44 [inset]
Vestmannaeyjar Iceland 44 [inset]
Vestmannaeyjar is Iceland 44 [inset]
Vestnes Norway 44 E5
Vesturhorn hd Iceland 44 [inset]
Vesuvio vol. Italy see Vesuvius
Vesuvius vol. Italy 58 F4
Ves'yegonsk Rus. Fed. 42 H4
Veszprém Hungary 58 G1
Veteli Fin. 44 M5
Veteran Canada 121 I4
Vetlanda Sweden 45 I8
Vetluga Rus. Fed. 42 J4
Vetluga r. Rus. Fed. 42 J4
Vetluzhskiy Kostromskaya Oblast' Rus. Fed. 42 J4
Vetluzhskiy Nizhegorodskaya Oblast' Rus. Fed. 42 J4
Vettore, Monte mt. Italy 58 E3
Veurne Belgium 52 C3
Vevay U.S.A. 134 C4
Vevey Switz. 56 H3
Vexin Normand reg. France 52 B5
Veyo U.S.A. 129 G3
Vézère r. France 56 E4
Vezirköprü Turkey 90 D2
Vialar Alg. see Tissemsilt
Viamao Brazil 145 A5
Viana Espírito Santo Brazil 145 C3
Viana Maranhão Brazil 143 J4
Viana do Castelo Port. 57 B3
Vianen Neth. 52 F3
Viangchan Laos see Vientiane
Viangphoukha Laos 70 C2
Vianópolis Brazil 145 A2
Viareggio Italy 58 D3
Viborg Denmark 45 F8
Viborg Rus. Fed. see Vyborg
Vibo Valentia Italy 58 G5
Vic Spain 57 H3
Vicam Mex. 127 F8
Vicecomodoro Marambio research station Antarctica see Marambio
Vicente, Point U.S.A. 128 D5
Vicente Guerrero Mex. 127 D7
Vicenza Italy 58 D2
Vich Spain see Vic
Vichada r. Col. 142 E3
Vichadero Uruguay 144 F4
Vichy France 56 F3
Vicksburg AZ U.S.A. 129 G5
Vicksburg MS U.S.A. 131 F5
Viçosa Brazil 145 C3
Victor, Mount Antarctica 152 D2
Victor Harbor Australia 111 B7
Victoria Arg. 144 D4
Victoria r. Australia 108 E3
Victoria state Australia 112 B6

▶Victoria Canada 120 F5
Provincial capital of British Columbia.

Victoria Chile 144 B5
Victoria Malaysia see Labuan
Victoria Malta 58 F6

▶Victoria Seychelles 149 L6
Capital of the Seychelles.

Victoria TX U.S.A. 131 D6
Victoria VA U.S.A. 135 F5
Victoria prov. Zimbabwe see Masvingo

▶Victoria, Lake Africa 98 D4
Largest lake in Africa and 3rd in the world.
Africa 92–93
World 12–13

Victoria, Lake Australia 111 C7
Victoria, Mount Fiji see Tomanivi
Victoria, Mount Myanmar 70 A2
Victoria, Mount P. N.G. 69 L8
Victoria and Albert Mountains Canada 119 K2
Victoria Falls Zambia/Zimbabwe 99 C5
Victoria Harbour sea chan. Hong Kong China see Hong Kong Harbour

▶Victoria Island Canada 118 H2
3rd largest island in North America.

Victoria Land coastal area Antarctica 152 H2
Victoria Peak Belize 136 G5
Victoria Peak hill Hong Kong China 77 [inset]
Victoria Range mts N.Z. 113 D6
Victoria River Downs Australia 108 E4
Victoriaville Canada 123 H5
Victoria West S. Africa 100 F6
Victorica Arg. 144 C5
Victorville U.S.A. 128 E4
Victory Downs Australia 109 F6
Vidalia U.S.A. 131 F6
Vidal Junction U.S.A. 129 F4
Videle Romania 59 K2
Vidisha India 82 D5
Vidlin U.K. 50 [inset]
Vidlitsa Rus. Fed. 42 G3
Viechtach Germany 53 M5
Viedma Arg. 144 D6
Viedma, Lago l. Arg. 144 B7
Viejo, Cerro mt. Mex. 127 E7
Vielank Germany 53 L1
Vielsalm Belgium 52 F4
Vienenburg Germany 53 K3

▶Vienna Austria 47 P6
Capital of Austria.

Vienna MO U.S.A. 130 F4
Vienna WV U.S.A. 134 E4
Vienne France 56 G4
Vienne r. France 56 E3

▶Vientiane Laos 70 C3
Capital of Laos.

Vieques i. Puerto Rico 137 K5
Vieremä Fin. 44 O5
Viersen Germany 52 G3
Vierzon France 56 F3
Viesca Mex. 131 C7
Viesīte Latvia 45 N8
Vieste Italy 58 G4
Vietas Sweden 44 K3
Viêt Nam country Asia see Vietnam
▶Vietnam country Asia 70 D3
Asia 6, 62–63
Viêt Tri Vietnam 70 D2
Vieux Comptoir, Lac du l. Canada 122 F3
Vieux-Fort Canada 123 K4
Vieux Poste, Pointe du pt Canada 123 J4
Vigan Phil. 69 G3
Vigevano Italy 58 C2
Vigia Brazil 143 I4
Vignacourt France 52 C4
Vignemale mt. France 54 D3
Vignola Italy 58 D2
Vigo Spain 57 B2
Vihanti Fin. 44 N4
Vihari Pak. 89 I4
Vihti Fin. 45 N6
Viipuri Rus. Fed. see Vyborg
Viitasaari Fin. 44 N5
Vijayadurg India 84 B2
Vijayanagaram India see Vizianagaram
Vijayapati India 84 C4
Vijayawada India 84 D2
Vík Iceland 44 [inset]
Vikajärvi Fin. 44 O3
Vikeke East Timor see Viqueque
Viking Canada 121 I4
Vikna i. Norway 44 G4
Vikøyri Norway 45 E6
Vila Vanuatu see Port Vila
Vila Alferes Chamusca Moz. see Guija
Vila Bittencourt Brazil 142 E4
Vila Bugaço Angola see Camanongue
Vila Cabral Moz. see Lichinga
Vila da Ponte Angola see Kuvango
Vila de Aljustrel Angola see Cangamba
Vila de Almoster Angola see Chiange
Vila de João Belo Moz. see Xai-Xai
Vila de María Arg. 144 D3
Vila de Trego Morais Moz. see Chókwé
Vila Fontes Moz. see Caia
Vila Franca de Xira Port. 57 B4
Vilagarcía de Arousa Spain 57 B2
Vila Gomes da Costa Moz. 101 K3
Vilalba Spain 57 C2
Vila Luísa Moz. see Marracuene
Vila Marechal Carmona Angola see Uíge
Vila Miranda Moz. see Macaloge
Vilanandro, Tanjona pt Madag. 99 E5
Vilanculos Moz. 101 L1
Vila Nova de Gaia Port. 57 B3
Vilanova i la Geltrú Spain 57 G3
Vila Pery Moz. see Chimoio
Vila Real Port. 57 C3
Vilar Formoso Port. 57 C3
Vila Salazar Angola see N'dalatando
Vila Salazar Zimbabwe see Sango
Vila Teixeira de Sousa Angola see Luau
Vila Velha Brazil 145 C3
Vilcabamba, Cordillera mts Peru 142 D6
Vil'cheka, Zemlya i. Rus. Fed. 64 H1
Viled' r. Rus. Fed. 42 J3
Vileyka Belarus see Vilyeyka
Vil'gort Rus. Fed. 42 K3
Vilhelmina Sweden 44 J4
Vilhena Brazil 142 F6
Viliya r. Belarus/Lith. see Neris
Viljandi Estonia 45 N7
Viljoenskroon S. Africa 101 H4
Vilkaviškis Lith. 45 M9
Vilkija Lith. 45 M9
Vil'kitskogo, Proliv strait Rus. Fed. 65 K2
Vilkovo Ukr. see Vylkove
Villa Abecia Bol. 142 E8
Villa Ahumada Mex. 127 G7
Villa Ángela Arg. 144 D3
Villa Bella Bol. 142 E6
Villa Bens Morocco see Tarfaya
Villablino Spain 57 C2
Villacañas Spain 57 E4
Villach Austria 47 N7
Villacidro Sardinia Italy 58 C5
Villa Cisneros W. Sahara see Ad Dakhla
Villa Constitución Mex. see Ciudad Constitución
Villa Dolores Arg. 144 C4
Villagarcía de Arosa Spain see Vilagarcía de Arousa
Villagrán Mex. 131 D7
Villaguay Arg. 144 E4
Villahermosa Mex. 136 F5
Villa Insurgentes Mex. 127 F8
Villajoyosa Spain see Villajoyosa - La Vila Joíosa
Villajoyosa - La Vila Joíosa Spain 57 F4
Villaldama Mex. 131 C7
Villa Mainero Mex. 131 D7
Villa María Arg. 144 D4
Villa Montes Bol. 142 F8
Villa Nora S. Africa 101 I2
Villanueva de la Serena Spain 57 D4
Villanueva de los Infantes Spain 57 E4
Villanueva-y-Geltrú Spain see Vilanova i la Geltrú
Villa Ocampo Arg. 144 E3
Villa Ocampo Mex. 131 B7
Villa Ojo de Agua Arg. 144 D3
Villaputzu Sardinia Italy 58 C5
Villa Regina Arg. 144 C5
Villarrica Para. 144 E3
Villarrica, Lago l. Chile 144 B5
Villarrica, Parque Nacional nat. park Chile 144 B5
Villarrobledo Spain 57 E4
Villas U.S.A. 135 H4
Villasalazar Zimbabwe see Sango
Villa San Giovanni Italy 58 F5
Villa Sanjurjo Morocco see Al Hoceima
Villa San Martín Arg. 144 D3
Villa Unión Arg. 144 C3
Villa Unión Coahuila Mex. 131 C6
Villa Unión Durango Mex. 131 B8
Villa Unión Sinaloa Mex. 136 C4
Villa Valeria Arg. 144 D4
Villavicencio Col. 142 D3
Villazon Bol. 142 E8
Villefranche-sur-Saône France 56 G4
Ville-Marie Canada see Montréal
Villena Spain 57 F4
Villeneuve-sur-Lot France 56 E4
Villeneuve-sur-Yonne France 56 F2
Villers-Cotterêts France 52 D5
Villers-sur-Mer France 49 G9
Villerupt France 52 F5
Villeurbanne France 56 G4
Villiers S. Africa 101 I4
Villingen Germany 47 L6
Villuppuram India see Villupuram
Villupuram India 84 C4
Vilna Canada 121 I4
Vilna Lith. see Vilnius

▶Vilnius Lith. 45 N9
Capital of Lithuania.

Vil'nyans'k Ukr. 43 G7
Vilppula Fin. 44 N5
Vils r. Germany 53 L5
Vils r. Germany 53 N6
Vilvoorde Belgium 52 E4
Vilyeyka Belarus 45 O9
Vilyuy r. Rus. Fed. 65 N3
Vilyuyskoye Vodokhranilishche resr Rus. Fed. 65 M3
Vimmerby Sweden 45 I8
Vimy France 52 C4
Vina r. Cameroon 97 E4
Vina U.S.A. 128 B2
Viña del Mar Chile 144 B4
Vinalhaven Island U.S.A. 132 G2
Vinaròs Spain 57 G3
Vinaroz Spain see Vinaròs
Vincelotte, Lac l. Canada 123 G3
Vincennes U.S.A. 134 B4
Vincennes Bay Antarctica 152 F2
Vinchina Arg. 144 C3
Vindelälven r. Sweden 44 K5
Vindeln Sweden 44 K4
Vindhya Range hills India 82 C5
Vindobona Austria see Vienna
Vine Grove U.S.A. 134 C5
Vineland U.S.A. 135 H4
Vinh Vietnam 70 D3
Vinh Linh Vietnam 70 D3
Vinh Long Vietnam 71 D5
Vinh Thuc, Đao i. Vietnam 70 D2
Vinita U.S.A. 131 E4
Vinjhan India 82 B5
Vinland i. Canada see Newfoundland
Vinnitsa Ukr. see Vinnytsya
Vinnytsya Ukr. 43 F6
Vinogradov Ukr. see Vynohradiv

▶Vinson Massif mt. Antarctica 152 L1
Highest mountain in Antarctica.

Vinstra Norway 45 F6
Vinton U.S.A. 130 E3
Vinukonda India 84 C2
Violeta Cuba see Primero de Enero
Vipperow Germany 53 M1
Viqueque East Timor 108 D2
Virac Phil. 69 G4
Viramgam India 82 C5
Viranşehir Turkey 91 E3
Virawah Pak. 89 H5
Virchow, Mount hill Australia 108 B5
Virdel India 82 C5
Virden Canada 121 K5
Virden U.S.A. 129 I5
Vire France 56 D2
Virei Angola 99 B5
Virgem da Lapa Brazil 145 C2
Virgilina U.S.A. 135 F5
Virgin r. U.S.A. 129 F3
Virginia Rep. of Ireland 51 E4
Virginia S. Africa 101 H5
Virginia U.S.A. 130 F4
Virginia state U.S.A. 134 F5
Virginia Beach U.S.A. 135 H5
Virginia City MT U.S.A. 126 F3
Virginia City NV U.S.A. 128 D2
Virginia Falls Canada 120 E2

▶Virgin Islands (U.K.) terr. West Indies 137 L5
United Kingdom Overseas Territory.
North America 9, 116–117

▶Virgin Islands (U.S.A.) terr. West Indies 137 L5
United States Unincorporated Territory.
North America 9, 116–117

Virgin Mountains U.S.A. 129 F3
Virginópolis Brazil 145 C2
Virkkala Fin. 45 N6
Virôchey Cambodia 71 D4
Viroqua U.S.A. 130 F3
Virovitica Croatia 58 G2
Virrat Fin. 44 M5
Virton Belgium 52 F5
Virtsu Estonia 45 M7
Virudhunagar India 84 C4
Virudunagar India see Virudhunagar
Virunga, Parc National des nat. park Dem. Rep. Congo 98 C4
Vis i. Croatia 58 G3
Visaginas Lith. 45 O9
Visakhapatnam India see Vishakhapatnam
Visalia U.S.A. 128 D3
Visapur India 84 B2
Visayan Sea Phil. 69 G4
Visbek Germany 53 I2
Visby Sweden 45 K8
Viscount Melville Sound sea chan. Canada 119 G2
Visé Belgium 52 F4
Vise, Ostrov i. Rus. Fed. 64 I2
Viseu Brazil 143 I4
Viseu Port. 57 C3
Vishakhapatnam India 84 D2
Vishera r. Rus. Fed. 41 R4
Vishera r. Rus. Fed. 42 L3
Višķi Latvia 45 O8
Visnagar India 82 C5
Viso, Monte mt. Italy 58 B2
Visoko Bos.-Herz. 58 H3
Visp Switz. 56 H3
Visselhövede Germany 53 J2
Vista U.S.A. 128 E5
Vista Lake U.S.A. 128 D4
Vistonida, Limni lag. Greece 59 K4
Vistula r. Poland 47 Q3
Vitebsk Belarus see Vitsyebsk
Viterbo Italy 58 E3
Vitichi Bol. 142 E8
Vitigudino Spain 57 C3
Viti Levu i. Fiji 107 H3
Vitimskoye Ploskogor'ye plat. Rus. Fed. 73 K2
Vitória Brazil 145 C3
Vitória da Conquista Brazil 145 C1
Vitoria-Gasteiz Spain 57 E2
Vitória Seamount sea feature S. Atlantic Ocean 148 F7
Vitré France 56 D2
Vitry-en-Artois France 52 C4
Vitry-le-François France 52 E6
Vitsyebsk Belarus 43 F5
Vittangi Sweden 44 L3
Vittel France 56 G2
Vittoria Sicily Italy 58 F6
Vittorio Veneto Italy 58 E2
Viveiro Spain 57 C2
Vivero Spain see Viveiro
Vivo S. Africa 101 I2
Vizagapatam India see Vishakhapatnam
Vizcaíno, Desierto de des. Mex. 127 E8
Vizcaíno, Sierra mts Mex. 127 E8
Vize Turkey 59 L4
Vizhas r. Rus. Fed. 42 J2
Vizianagaram India 84 D2
Vizinga Rus. Fed. 42 K3
Vlaardingen Neth. 52 E3
Vlădeasa, Vârful mt. Romania 59 J1
Vladikavkaz Rus. Fed. 91 G2
Vladimir Primorskiy Kray Rus. Fed. 74 D4
Vladimir Vladimirskaya Oblast' Rus. Fed. 42 I4
Vladimiro-Aleksandrovskoye Rus. Fed. 74 D4
Vladimir-Volynskiy Ukr. see Volodymyr-Volyns'kyy
Vladivostok Rus. Fed. 74 C4
Vlakte S. Africa 101 I3
Vlasotince Serb. and Mont. 59 J3
Vlas'yevo Rus. Fed. 74 F1
Vlieland i. Neth. 52 E1
Vlissingen Neth. 52 D3
Vlora Albania see Vlorë
Vlorë Albania 59 H4
Vlotho Germany 53 I2
Vlotslavsk Poland see Włocławek
Vltava r. Czech Rep. 47 O5
Vöcklabruck Austria 47 N6
Vodlozero, Ozero l. Rus. Fed. 42 H3
Voe U.K. 50 [inset]
Voerendaal Neth. 52 F4
Vogelkop Peninsula Indon. see Doberai, Jazirah
Vogelsberg hills Germany 53 I4
Voghera Italy 58 C2
Vohburg an der Donau Germany 53 L6
Vohémar Madag. see Iharaña
Vohenstrauß Germany 53 M5
Vohibinany Madag. see Ampasimanolotra
Vohimarina Madag. see Iharaña
Vohimena, Tanjona c. Madag. 99 E6
Vohipeno Madag. 99 E6
Vöhl Germany 53 I3
Võhma Estonia 45 N7
Voinjama Liberia 96 C4
Vojens Denmark 45 F9
Vojvodina prov. Serb. and Mont. 59 H2
Vokhma Rus. Fed. 42 J4
Voknavolok Rus. Fed. 44 Q4
Vol' r. Rus. Fed. 42 L3
Volcano Bay Japan see Uchiura-wan

▶Volcano Islands Japan 69 K2
Part of Japan.

Volda Norway 44 E5
Vol'dino Rus. Fed. 42 L3
Volendam Neth. 52 F2
Volga Rus. Fed. 42 H4

▶Volga r. Rus. Fed. 43 J7
Longest river and largest drainage basin in Europe.
Europe 36–37

Volga Upland hills Rus. Fed. see Privolzhskaya Vozvyshennost'
Volgodonsk Rus. Fed. 43 I7
Volgograd Rus. Fed. 43 J6
Volgogradskoye Vodokhranilishche resr Rus. Fed. 43 J6
Völkermarkt Austria 47 O7
Volkhov Rus. Fed. 42 G4
Volkhov r. Rus. Fed. 42 G3
Völklingen Germany 52 G5
Volkovysk Belarus see Vawkavysk
Volksrust S. Africa 101 I4
Vol'no-Nadezhdinskoye Rus. Fed. 74 C4
Volnovakha Ukr. 43 H7
Vol'nyansk Ukr. see Vil'nyans'k
Volochanka Rus. Fed. 64 K2
Volochisk Ukr. see Volochys'k
Volochys'k Ukr. 43 E6
Volodars'ke Ukr. 43 H7
Volodarskoye Kazakh. see Saumalkol'
Volodymyr-Volyns'kyy Ukr. 43 E6
Vologda Rus. Fed. 42 H4
Volokolamsk Rus. Fed. 42 G4
Volokovaya Rus. Fed. 42 K2
Volos Greece 59 J5
Volosovo Rus. Fed. 45 P7
Volot Rus. Fed. 42 F4
Volovo Rus. Fed. 43 H5
Volozhin Belarus see Valozhyn
Volsinii Italy see Orvieto
Vol'sk Rus. Fed. 43 J5

▶Volta, Lake resr Ghana 96 D4
5th largest lake in Africa.

Volta Blanche r. Burkina/Ghana see White Volta
Voltaire, Cape Australia 108 D3
Volta Redonda Brazil 145 B3
Volturno r. Italy 58 F4
Volubilis tourist site Morocco 54 C5
Volvi, Limni l. Greece 59 J4
Volzhsk Rus. Fed. 42 K5
Volzhskiy Samarskaya Oblast' Rus. Fed. 43 K5
Volzhskiy Volgogradskaya Oblast' Rus. Fed. 43 J6
Vondanka Rus. Fed. 42 J4
Vontimitta India 84 C3
Vopnafjörður Iceland 44 [inset]
Vopnafjörður b. Iceland 44 [inset]
Vörå Fin. 44 M5
Voranava Belarus 45 N9
Voreioi Sporades is Greece 59 J5
Voríai Sporádhes is Greece see Voreioi Sporades
Voring Plateau sea feature N. Atlantic Ocean 148 I1
Vorjing mt. India 83 H3
Vorkuta Rus. Fed. 64 H3
Vormsi i. Estonia 45 M7
Vorona r. Rus. Fed. 43 I6
Voronezh Rus. Fed. 43 H6

Voronezh *r.* Rus. Fed. **43** H6
Voronov, Mys *pt* Rus. Fed. **42** I2
Vorontsovo-Aleksandrovskoye Rus. Fed. *see* **Zelenokumsk**
Voroshilov Rus. Fed. *see* **Ussuriysk**
Voroshilovgrad Ukr. *see* **Luhans'k**
Voroshilovsk Rus. Fed. *see* **Stavropol'**
Voroshilovsk Ukr. *see* **Alchevs'k**
Vorotynets Rus. Fed. **42** J4
Vorozhba Ukr. **43** G6
Vorpommersche Boddenlandschaft, Nationalpark *nat. park* Germany **47** N3
Vorskla *r.* Rus. Fed. **43** G6
Võrtsjärv *l.* Estonia **45** N7
Võru Estonia **45** O8
Vorukh Tajik. **89** H2
Vosburg S. Africa **100** F6
Vose Tajik. **89** H2
Vosges *mts* France **56** H3
Voskresensk Rus. Fed. **43** H5
Voskresenskoye Rus. Fed. **42** H4
Voss Norway **45** E6
Vostochno-Sakhalinskiy Gory *mts* Rus. Fed. **74** F2
Vostochno-Sibirskoye More *sea* Rus. Fed. *see* **East Siberian Sea**
Vostochnyy *Kirovskaya Oblast'* Rus. Fed. **42** L4
Vostochnyy *Sakhalinskaya Oblast'* Rus. Fed. **74** F2
Vostochnyy Chink Ustyurta *esc.* Uzbek. **80** A3
Vostochnyy Sayan *mts* Rus. Fed. **72** G2

▶**Vostok** *research station* Antarctica **152** F1
Lowest recorded screen temperature in the world.

Vostok *Primorskiy Kray* Rus. Fed. **74** D3
Vostok *Sakhalinskaya Oblast'* Rus. Fed. *see* **Neftegorsk**
Vostok Island Kiribati **151** J6
Vostroye Rus. Fed. **42** J3
Votkinsk Rus. Fed. **41** Q4
Votkinskoye Vodokhranilishche *resr* Rus. Fed. **41** R4
Votuporanga Brazil **145** A3
Vouziers France **52** E5
Voves France **56** E2
Voyageurs National Park U.S.A. **130** E1
Voynitsa Rus. Fed. **44** Q4
Vöyri Fin. *see* **Vörå**
Voyvozh Rus. Fed. **42** L3
Vozhayel' Rus. Fed. **42** K3
Vozhe, Ozero *l.* Rus. Fed. **42** H3
Vozhega Rus. Fed. **42** I3
Vozhgaly Rus. Fed. **42** K4
Voznesens'k Ukr. **43** F7
Vozonin Trough *sea feature* Arctic Ocean **153** F1
Vozrozhdeniya, Ostrov *i.* Uzbek. **80** A3
Vozzhayevka Rus. Fed. **74** C2
Vrangel' Rus. Fed. **74** D4
Vrangelya, Mys *pt* Rus. Fed. **74** E1
Vranje Serb. and Mont. **59** I3
Vratnik *pass* Bulg. **59** L3
Vratsa Bulg. **59** J3
Vrbas Serb. and Mont. **59** H2
Vrede S. Africa **101** I4
Vredefort S. Africa **101** H4
Vredenburg S. Africa **100** C7
Vredendal S. Africa **100** D6
Vresse Belgium **52** E5
Vriddhachalam India **84** C4
Vries Neth. **52** G1
Vrigstad Sweden **45** I8
Vršac Serb. and Mont. **59** I2
Vryburg S. Africa **100** G4
Vryheid S. Africa **101** J4
Vsevidof, Mount *vol.* U.S.A. **118** B4
Vsevolozhsk Rus. Fed. **42** F3
Vu Ban Vietnam **70** D2
Vučitrn Serb. and Mont. **59** I3
Vukovar Croatia **59** H2
Vuktyl' Rus. Fed. **41** R3
Vukuzakhe S. Africa **101** I4
Vulcan Canada **120** H5
Vulcan Island P.N.G. *see* **Manam Island**
Vulcano, Isola *i.* Italy **58** F5
Vu Liêt Vietnam **70** D3
Vulture Mountains U.S.A. **129** G5
Vung Tau Vietnam **71** D5
Vuohijärvi Fin. **45** O6
Vuolijoki Fin. **44** O4
Vuollerim Sweden **44** L3
Vuostimo Fin. **44** O3
Vurnary Rus. Fed. **42** J5
Vushtri Serb. and Mont. *see* **Vučitrn**
Vvedenovka Rus. Fed. **74** C2
Vyara India **82** C5
Vyarkhowye Belarus *see* **Ruba**
Vyatka Rus. Fed. *see* **Kirov**
Vyatka *r.* Rus. Fed. **42** K5
Vyatskiye Polyany Rus. Fed. **42** K4
Vyazemskiy Rus. Fed. **74** D3
Vyaz'ma Rus. Fed. **43** G5
Vyazniki Rus. Fed. **42** I4
Vyazovka Rus. Fed. **43** J5
Vyborg Rus. Fed. **45** P6
Vychegda *r.* Rus. Fed. **42** J3
Vychegodskiy Rus. Fed. **42** J3
Vyerkhnyadzvinsk Belarus **45** O9
Vyetryna Belarus **45** P9
Vygozero, Ozero *l.* Rus. Fed. **42** G3
Vyksa Rus. Fed. **43** I5
Vylkove Ukr. **59** M2
Vym' *r.* Rus. Fed. **42** K3
Vynohradiv Ukr. **43** D6
Vypin Island India **84** C4
Vypolzovo Rus. Fed. **42** G4
Vyritsa Rus. Fed. **45** Q7
Vyrnwy, Lake U.K. **49** D6
Vyselki Rus. Fed. **43** H7
Vysha Rus. Fed. **43** I5
Vyshhorod Ukr. **43** F6
Vyshnevolotskaya Gryada *ridge* Rus. Fed. **42** G4
Vyshniy-Volochek Rus. Fed. **42** G4
Vyškov Czech Rep. **47** P6
Vysokaya Gora Rus. Fed. **42** K5
Vysokogorniy Rus. Fed. **74** E2
Vystupovychi Ukr. **43** F6
Vytegra Rus. Fed. **42** H3
Vyya *r.* Rus. Fed. **42** J3
Vyžuona *r.* Lith. **45** N9

W

Wa Ghana **96** C3
Waal *r.* Neth. **52** E3
Waalwijk Neth. **52** F3
Waat Sudan **86** D8
Wabag P.N.G. **69** K8
Wabakimi Lake Canada **122** C4
Wabasca *r.* Canada **120** H3
Wabasca-Desmarais Canada **120** H4
Wabash U.S.A. **134** C3
Wabash *r.* U.S.A. **134** A5
Wabasha U.S.A. **130** E2
Wabassi *r.* Canada **122** D4
Wabatongushi Lake Canada **122** D4
Wabē Gestro *r.* Eth. **78** D6
Wabē Shebelē Wenz *r.* Eth. **98** E3
Wabigoon Lake Canada **121** M5
Wabowden Canada **121** L4
Wabrah *well* Saudi Arabia **88** B5
Wabu China **77** H1
Wabuk Point Canada **122** D3
Wabush Canada **123** I3
Waccasassa Bay U.S.A. **133** D6
Wächtersbach Germany **53** J4
Waco Canada **123** I4
Waco U.S.A. **131** D6
Waconda Lake U.S.A. **130** D4
Wad Pak. **89** G5
Wadbilliga National Park Australia **112** D6
Waddān Libya **55** H6
Waddell Dam U.S.A. **129** G5
Waddeneilanden Neth. *see* **West Frisian Islands**
Waddenzee *sea chan.* Neth. **52** E2
Waddington, Mount Canada **120** E5
Waddinxveen Neth. **52** E2
Wadebridge U.K. **49** C8
Wadena Canada **121** K5
Wadena U.S.A. **130** E2
Wadern Germany **52** G5
Wadesville U.S.A. **134** B4
Wadeye Australia **108** E3
Wadgassen Germany **52** G5
Wadhwan India *see* **Surendranagar**
Wadi India **84** C2
Wādī as Sīr Jordan **85** B4
Wadi Halfa Sudan **86** D5
Wad Medani Sudan **86** D7
Wad Rawa Sudan **86** D6
Wadsworth U.S.A. **128** D2
Waenhuiskrans S. Africa **100** E8
Wafangdian China **73** M5
Wafra Kuwait *see* **Al Wafrah**
Wagenfeld Germany **53** I2
Wagenhoff Germany **53** K2
Wagga Wagga Australia **112** C5
Wagner U.S.A. **130** D3
Wagoner U.S.A. **131** E4
Wagon Mound U.S.A. **127** G5
Wah Pak. **89** I3
Wahai Indon. **69** H7
Wāhāt Jālū Libya **97** F2
Wahemen, Lac *l.* Canada **123** H3
Wahiawa *HI* U.S.A. **127** [inset]
Wahlhausen Germany **53** J3
Wahpeton U.S.A. **130** D2
Wahran Alg. *see* **Oran**
Wah Wah Mountains U.S.A. **125** G2
Wai India **84** B2
Waialua *HI* U.S.A. **127** [inset]
Waiau N.Z. *see* **Franz Josef Glacier**
Waiau *r.* N.Z. **113** D6
Waiblingen Germany **53** J6
Waidhofen an der Ybbs Austria **47** O7
Waigeo *i.* Indon. **69** I7
Waiheke Island N.Z. **113** E3
Waikabubak Indon. **108** B2
Waikaia *r.* N.Z. **113** B7
Waikari N.Z. **113** D6
Waikerie Australia **111** B7
Waikouaiti N.Z. **113** C7
Wailuku *HI* U.S.A. **127** [inset]
Waimangaroa N.Z. **113** C5
Waimarama N.Z. **113** F4
Waimate N.Z. **113** C7
Waimea *HI* U.S.A. **127** [inset]
Wainganga *r.* India **84** C2
Waingapu Indon. **108** C2
Wainhouse Corner U.K. **49** C8
Waini Point Guyana **143** G2
Wainwright Canada **121** I4
Wainwright U.S.A. **118** C2
Waiouru N.Z. **113** E4
Waipahi N.Z. **113** B8
Waipaoa *r.* N.Z. **113** F4
Waipara N.Z. **113** D6
Waipawa N.Z. **113** F4
Waipukurau N.Z. **113** F4
Wairarapa, Lake N.Z. **113** E5
Wairau *r.* N.Z. **113** E5
Wairoa N.Z. **113** F4
Wairoa *r.* N.Z. **113** F4
Waitahanui N.Z. **113** F4
Waitahuna N.Z. **113** B7
Waitakaruru N.Z. **113** E3
Waitaki *r.* N.Z. **113** C7
Waitangi N.Z. **107** I6
Waite River Australia **108** F5
Waiuku N.Z. **113** E3
Waiwera South N.Z. **113** B8
Waiyang China **77** H3
Wajima Japan **75** E5
Wajir Kenya **98** E3
Waka Indon. **108** C2
Wakasa-wan *b.* Japan **75** D6
Wakatipu, Lake N.Z. **113** B7
Wakaw Canada **121** J4
Wakayama Japan **75** D6
Wake Atoll *terr.* N. Pacific Ocean *see* **Wake Island**
WaKeeney U.S.A. **130** D4
Wakefield N.Z. **113** D5
Wakefield U.K. **48** F5
Wakefield *MI* U.S.A. **130** F2
Wakefield *RI* U.S.A. **135** J3
Wakefield *VA* U.S.A. **135** G5

▶**Wake Island** *terr.* N. Pacific Ocean **150** H4
United States Unincorporated Territory.

Wakema Myanmar **70** A3
Wakhan *reg.* Afgh. **89** I2
Wakkanai Japan **74** F3
Wakkerstroom S. Africa **101** J4
Wakool Australia **112** B5
Wakool *r.* Australia **112** A5
Wakuach, Lac *l.* Canada **123** I3
Waku-Kungo Angola **99** B5
Wałbrzych Poland **47** P5
Walcha Australia **112** E3
Walcott U.S.A. **126** G4
Walcourt Belgium **52** E4
Wałcz Poland **47** P4
Waldburg Range *mts* Australia **109** B6
Walden U.S.A. **135** H3
Waldenbuch Germany **53** J6
Waldenburg Poland *see* **Wałbrzych**
Waldkraiburg Germany **47** N6
Waldo U.S.A. **134** D3
Waldoboro U.S.A. **135** K1
Waldorf U.S.A. **135** G4
Waldport U.S.A. **126** B3
Waldron U.S.A. **131** E5
Waldron, Cape Antarctica **152** F2
Walebing Australia **109** B7
Walêg China **76** D2
Wales *admin. div.* U.K. **49** D6
Walgaon India **82** D5
Walgett Australia **112** D3
Walgreen Coast Antarctica **152** K1
Walhalla *MI* U.S.A. **134** B2
Walhalla *ND* U.S.A. **130** D1
Walikale Dem. Rep. Congo **97** F5
Walingai P.N.G. **69** L8
Walker *r.* Australia **110** A2
Walker *watercourse* Australia **109** F6
Walker *MI* U.S.A. **134** C2
Walker *MN* U.S.A. **130** E2
Walker *r.* U.S.A. **128** D2
Walker Bay S. Africa **100** D8
Walker Creek *r.* Australia **110** C3
Walker Lake Canada **121** L4
Walker Lake U.S.A. **128** D2
Walker Pass U.S.A. **128** D4
Walkersville U.S.A. **135** G4
Walkerton Canada **134** E1
Walkerton U.S.A. **134** B3
Wall, Mount *hill* Australia **108** B5
Wallaby Island Australia **110** C2
Wallace *ID* U.S.A. **126** D3
Wallace *NC* U.S.A. **133** E5
Wallace *VA* U.S.A. **134** D5
Wallaceburg Canada **134** D2
Wallal Downs Australia **108** C4
Wallangarra Australia **112** E2
Wallaroo Australia **111** B7
Wallasey U.K. **48** D5
Walla Walla Australia **112** C5
Walla Walla U.S.A. **126** D3
Walldürn Germany **53** J5
Wallekraal S. Africa **100** C6
Wallendbeen Australia **112** D5
Wallingford U.K. **49** F7
Wallis, Îles *is* Wallis and Futuna Is **107** I3

▶**Wallis and Futuna Islands** *terr.* S. Pacific Ocean **107** I3
French Overseas Territory.
Oceania 8, 104–105

Wallis et Futuna, Îles *terr.* S. Pacific Ocean *see* **Wallis and Futuna Islands**
Wallis Islands Wallis and Futuna Is *see* **Wallis, Îles**
Wallis Lake *inlet* Australia **112** F4
Wallops Island U.S.A. **135** H5
Wallowa Mountains U.S.A. **126** D3
Walls U.K. **50** [inset]
Walls of Jerusalem National Park Australia **111** [inset]
Wallumbilla Australia **111** E5
Walmsley Lake Canada **121** I2
Walney, Isle of *i.* U.K. **48** D4
Walnut Creek U.S.A. **128** B3
Walnut Grove U.S.A. **128** C2
Walnut Ridge U.S.A. **131** F4
Walong India **83** I3
Walpole U.S.A. **135** I2
Walsall U.K. **49** F6
Walsenburg U.S.A. **127** G5
Walsh U.S.A. **131** C4
Walsrode Germany **53** J2
Waltair India **84** D2
Walterboro U.S.A. **133** D5
Walters U.S.A. **131** D5
Walter's Range *hills* Australia **112** B2
Walthall U.S.A. **131** F5
Waltham U.S.A. **135** J2
Walton *IN* U.S.A. **134** B3
Walton *KY* U.S.A. **134** C4
Walton *NY* U.S.A. **135** H2
Walton *WV* U.S.A. **134** E4
Walvisbaai Namibia *see* **Walvis Bay**
Walvisbaai *b.* Namibia *see* **Walvis Bay**
Walvis Bay Namibia **100** B2
Walvis Bay *b.* Namibia **100** B2
Walvis Ridge *sea feature* S. Atlantic Ocean **148** H8
Wama Afgh. **89** H3
Wamba *Équateur* Dem. Rep. Congo **97** F5
Wamba *Orientale* Dem. Rep. Congo **98** C3
Wamba Nigeria **96** D4
Wampum U.S.A. **134** E3
Wampusirpi Hond. **137** H5
Wamsutter U.S.A. **126** G4
Wana Pak. **89** H3
Wanaaring Australia **112** B2
Wanaka N.Z. **113** B7
Wanaka, Lake N.Z. **113** B7
Wan'an China **77** G3
Wanapitei Lake Canada **122** E5
Wanbi Australia **111** C7
Wanbrow, Cape N.Z. **113** C7
Wanda Shan *mts* China **74** D3
Wandering River Canada **121** H4
Wandersleben Germany **53** K4
Wandlitz Germany **53** N2
Wando S. Korea **75** B6
Wandoan Australia **111** E5
Wanganui N.Z. **113** E4
Wanganui *r.* N.Z. **113** E4
Wangaratta Australia **112** C6
Wangcang China **76** E1
Wangda China *see* **Zogang**
Wangdain China **83** G3
Wangdue Phodrang Bhutan **83** G4
Wanggamet, Gunung *mt.* Indon. **108** C2
Wanggao China **77** F3
Wang Gaxun China **83** I1
Wangiwangi *i.* Indon. **69** G8
Wangkui China **74** B3
Wangmo China **76** E3
Wangqing China **74** C4
Wangwu Shan *mts* China **77** F1
Wangying China *see* **Huaiyin**
Wangziguan China **76** E2
Wanham Canada **120** G4
Wan Hsa-la Myanmar **70** B2
Wanie-Rukula Dem. Rep. Congo **98** C3
Wankaner India **82** B5
Wankie Zimbabwe *see* **Hwange**
Wanlaweyn Somalia **98** E3
Wanna Germany **53** I1
Wanna Lakes *salt flat* Australia **109** E7
Wannian China **77** H2
Wanning China **77** F5
Wanroij Neth. **52** F3
Wanshan China **77** F3
Wanshan Qundao *is* China **77** G4
Wansheng China **76** E2
Wanshengchang China *see* **Wansheng**
Wantage U.K. **49** F7
Wanxian *Chongqing* China *see* **Shahe**
Wanxian *Chongqing* China **77** F2
Wanyuan China **77** F1
Wanzai China **77** G2
Wanze Belgium **52** F4
Wapakoneta U.S.A. **134** C3
Wapawekka Lake Canada **121** J4
Wapello U.S.A. **130** F3
Wapikaimaski Lake Canada **122** C4
Wapikopa Lake Canada **122** C3
Wapiti *r.* Canada **120** G4
Wapusk National Park Canada **121** M3
Waqên China **76** D1
Waqf aş Şawwān, Jibāl *hills* Jordan **85** C4
War U.S.A. **134** E5
Warab Sudan **86** C8
Warangal India **84** C2
Waranga Reservoir Australia **112** B6
Waratah Bay Australia **112** B7
Warbreccan Australia **110** C5
Warburg Germany **53** J3
Warburton Australia **109** D6
Warburton *watercourse* Australia **111** B5
Warburton Bay Canada **121** I2
Warche *r.* Belgium **52** F4
Ward, Mount N.Z. **113** B6
Warden S. Africa **101** I4
Wardenburg Germany **53** I1
Wardha India **84** C1
Wardha *r.* India **84** C2
Ward Hill *hill* U.K. **50** F2
Ward Hunt, Cape P.N.G. **69** L8
Ware Canada **120** E3
Ware U.S.A. **135** I2
Wareham U.K. **49** E8
Waremme Belgium **52** F4
Waren Germany **53** M1
Warendorf Germany **53** H3
Warginburra Peninsula Australia **110** E4
Wargla Alg. *see* **Ouargla**
Warialda Australia **112** E2
Warin Chamrap Thai. **70** D4
Warkum Neth. *see* **Workum**
Warkworth U.K. **48** F3
Warli China *see* **Walêg**
Warloy-Baillon France **52** C4
Warman Canada **121** J4
Warmbad Namibia **100** D5
Warmbad S. Africa **101** I3
Warmbaths S. Africa *see* **Warmbad**
Warminster U.K. **49** E7
Warminster U.S.A. **135** H3
Warmond Neth. **52** E2
Warm Springs *NV* U.S.A. **128** E2
Warm Springs *VA* U.S.A. **134** F4
Warmwaterberg *mts* S. Africa **96** E7
Warner Canada **121** H5
Warner Lakes U.S.A. **126** D4
Warner Mountains U.S.A. **126** C4
Warnes Bol. **142** F7
Warning, Mount Australia **112** F2
Waronda India **84** C2
Warora India **84** C1
Warra Australia **112** E1
Warragamba Reservoir Australia **112** E5
Warragul Australia **112** B7
Warrambool *r.* Australia **112** C3
Warrandirinna, Lake *salt flat* Australia **111** B5
Warrandyte Australia **112** B6
Warrawagine Australia **108** C5
Warrego *r.* Australia **112** B3
Warrego Range *hills* Australia **110** D5
Warren Australia **112** C3
Warren *AR* U.S.A. **131** E5
Warren *MI* U.S.A. **134** D2
Warren *MN* U.S.A. **130** D1
Warren *OH* U.S.A. **134** E3
Warren *PA* U.S.A. **134** F3
Warren Hastings Island Palau *see* **Merir**
Warren Island U.S.A. **120** C4
Warrenpoint U.K. **51** F3
Warrensburg *MO* U.S.A. **130** E4
Warrensburg *NY* U.S.A. **135** I2
Warrenton S. Africa **100** G5
Warrenton *GA* U.S.A. **133** D5
Warrenton *MO* U.S.A. **130** F4
Warrenton *VA* U.S.A. **135** G4
Warri Nigeria **96** D4
Warriners Creek *watercourse* Australia **111** B6
Warrington N.Z. **113** C7
Warrington U.K. **48** E5
Warrington U.S.A. **133** C6
Warrnambool Australia **111** C8
Warroad U.S.A. **130** E1
Warrumbungle National Park Australia **112** D3

▶**Warsaw** Poland **47** R4
Capital of Poland.

Warsaw *IN* U.S.A. **134** C3
Warsaw *KY* U.S.A. **134** C4
Warsaw *MO* U.S.A. **130** E4
Warsaw *NY* U.S.A. **135** F2
Warsaw *VA* U.S.A. **135** G5
Warshiikh Somalia **98** E3
Warstein Germany **53** I3
Warszawa Poland *see* **Warsaw**
Warta *r.* Poland **47** O4
Warwick Australia **112** F2
Warwick U.K. **49** F6
Warwick U.S.A. **135** J3
Warzhong China **76** D2
Wasaga Beach Canada **134** E1
Wasatch Range *mts* U.S.A. **126** F5
Wasbank S. Africa **101** J5
Wasco U.S.A. **128** D4
Washburn *ND* U.S.A. **130** C2
Washburn *WI* U.S.A. **130** F2
Washim India **84** C1
Washimeska *r.* Canada **123** G4

▶**Washington** *DC* U.S.A. **135** G4
Capital of the United States of America.

Washington *GA* U.S.A. **133** D5
Washington *IA* U.S.A. **130** F3
Washington *IN* U.S.A. **134** B4
Washington *MO* U.S.A. **130** F4
Washington *NC* U.S.A. **132** E5
Washington *NJ* U.S.A. **135** H3
Washington *PA* U.S.A. **134** E3
Washington *UT* U.S.A. **129** G3
Washington *state* U.S.A. **126** C3
Washington, Cape Antarctica **152** H2
Washington, Mount U.S.A. **135** J1
Washington Court House U.S.A. **134** D4
Washington Island U.S.A. **132** C2
Washington Land *reg.* Greenland **119** L2
Washir Afgh. **89** F3
Washita *r.* U.S.A. **131** D5
Washpool National Park Australia **112** F2
Washtucna U.S.A. **126** D3
Washuk Pak. **89** G5
Wasi India **84** B2
Wasi' Saudi Arabia **88** B5
Wasī' *well* Saudi Arabia **88** C6
Waskaganish Canada **122** F4
Waskagheganish Canada *see* **Waskaganish**
Waskaiowaka Lake Canada **121** L3
Waskey, Mount U.S.A. **118** C4
Wassenaar Neth. **52** E2
Wasser Namibia **100** D4
Wasserkuppe *hill* Germany **53** J4
Wassertrüdingen Germany **53** K5
Wassuk Range *mts* U.S.A. **128** D2
Wasua P.N.G. **69** K8
Wasum P.N.G. **69** L8
Waswanipi *r.* Canada **122** F4
Waswanipi, Lac *l.* Canada **122** F4
Watam P.N.G. **69** K7
Watampone Indon. **69** G7
Watapi Lake Canada **121** I4
Watarrka National Park Australia **109** E6
Watenstadt-Salzgitter Germany *see* **Salzgitter**
Waterbury *CT* U.S.A. **135** I3
Waterbury *VT* U.S.A. **135** I1
Waterbury Lake Canada **121** J3
Water Cays *i.* Bahamas **133** E8
Waterdown Canada **134** F2
Wateree *r.* U.S.A. **133** D5
Waterfall U.S.A. **120** C4
Waterford Rep. of Ireland **51** E5
Waterford *PA* U.S.A. **134** F3
Waterford *WI* U.S.A. **134** A2
Waterford Harbour Rep. of Ireland **51** F5
Watergrasshill Rep. of Ireland **51** D5
Waterhen Lake Canada **121** L4
Waterloo Australia **108** E4
Waterloo Belgium **52** E4
Waterloo *Ont.* Canada **134** E2
Waterloo *Que.* Canada **135** I1
Waterloo *IA* U.S.A. **130** E3
Waterloo *IL* U.S.A. **130** F4
Waterloo *NY* U.S.A. **135** G2
Waterlooville U.K. **49** F8
Waterton Lakes National Park Canada **120** H5
Watertown *NY* U.S.A. **135** H2
Watertown *SD* U.S.A. **130** D2
Watertown *WI* U.S.A. **130** F3
Waterval-Boven S. Africa **101** J3
Water Valley U.S.A. **131** F5
Waterville *ME* U.S.A. **135** K1
Waterville *WA* U.S.A. **126** C3
Watford Canada **134** E2
Watford U.K. **49** G7
Watford City U.S.A. **130** C2
Wathaman *r.* Canada **121** K3
Wathaman Lake Canada **121** K3
Watheroo National Park Australia **109** A7
Wathlingen Germany **53** K2
Watino Canada **120** G4
Watīr, Wādī *watercourse* Egypt **85** B5
Watkins Glen U.S.A. **135** G2
Watling Island Bahamas *see* **San Salvador**
Watmuri Indon. **108** E1
Watonga U.S.A. **131** D5
Watrous Canada **121** J5
Watrous U.S.A. **127** G6
Watseka U.S.A. **134** B3
Watsi Kengo Dem. Rep. Congo **97** F5
Watson *r.* Australia **110** C2
Watson Canada **121** J4
Watson Lake Canada **120** D2
Watsontown U.S.A. **135** G3
Watsonville U.S.A. **128** C3
Watten U.K. **50** F2
Watterson Lake Canada **121** L2
Watton U.K. **49** H6
Watts Bar Lake *resr* U.S.A. **132** C5
Wattsburg U.S.A. **134** F2
Watubela, Kepulauan *is* Indon. **69** I7
Wau P.N.G. **69** L8
Wau Sudan **86** C8
Waubay Lake U.S.A. **130** D2
Wauchope *N.S.W.* Australia **108** F3
Wauchope *N.T.* Australia **108** F5
Waukaringa Australia **111** B7
Waukarlycarly, Lake *salt flat* Australia **108** C5
Waukegan U.S.A. **134** B2
Waukesha U.S.A. **134** A2
Waupaca U.S.A. **130** F2
Waupun U.S.A. **130** F3
Waurika U.S.A. **131** D5
Wausau U.S.A. **130** F2
Wausaukee U.S.A. **132** C2
Wauseon U.S.A. **134** C3
Wautoma U.S.A. **130** F2
Wave Hill Australia **108** E4
Waveney *r.* U.K. **49** I6
Waverly *IA* U.S.A. **130** E3
Waverly *NY* U.S.A. **135** G2
Waverly *OH* U.S.A. **134** D4
Waverly *TN* U.S.A. **132** C4
Waverly *VA* U.S.A. **135** G5
Wavre Belgium **52** E4
Waw Myanmar **70** B3
Wawa Canada **122** D5
Wawalalindu Indon. **69** G7
Wāw al Kabīr Libya **97** E2
Wawasee, Lake U.S.A. **134** C3
Wawo Indon. **69** G7
Waxahachie U.S.A. **131** D5
Waxü China **76** D1
Waxxari China **80** G4
Way, Lake *salt flat* Australia **109** C6
Waycross U.S.A. **133** D6
Wayland *KY* U.S.A. **134** D5
Wayland *MI* U.S.A. **134** C2
Wayne *NE* U.S.A. **130** D3
Wayne *WV* U.S.A. **134** D4
Waynesboro *GA* U.S.A. **133** D5
Waynesboro *MS* U.S.A. **131** F6
Waynesboro *TN* U.S.A. **132** C5
Waynesboro *VA* U.S.A. **135** F4
Waynesburg U.S.A. **134** E4
Waynesville *MO* U.S.A. **130** E4
Waynesville *NC* U.S.A. **132** D5
Waynoka U.S.A. **131** D4
Waza, Parc National de *nat. park* Cameroon **97** E3
Wāzah Khwāh Afgh. *see* **Wazi Khwa**
Wazi Khwa Afgh. **89** H3
Wazirabad Pak. **89** I3
W du Niger, Parcs Nationaux du *nat. park* Niger **96** D3
We, Pulau *i.* Indon. **71** A6
Weagamow Lake Canada **121** N4
Weam P.N.G. **69** K8
Wear *r.* U.K. **48** F4
Weare U.S.A. **135** J2
Weatherford U.S.A. **131** D5
Weaver Lake Canada **121** L4
Weaverville U.S.A. **126** C4
Webb, Mount *hill* Australia **108** E5
Webequie Canada **122** D3
Weber, Mount Canada **120** D4
Weber Basin *sea feature* Laut Banda **150** E6

▶**Webi Shabeelle** *r.* Somalia **98** E3
5th longest river in Africa.

Webster *IN* U.S.A. **134** C4
Webster *MA* U.S.A. **135** J2
Webster *SD* U.S.A. **130** D2
Webster City U.S.A. **130** E3
Webster Springs U.S.A. **134** E4
Wecho Lake Canada **120** H2
Wedau P.N.G. **110** E1
Weddell Abyssal Plain *sea feature* Southern Ocean **152** A2
Weddell Island Falkland Is **140** D8
Weddell Sea Antarctica **152** A2
Wedderburn Australia **112** A6
Weddin Mountains National Park Australia **112** D4
Wedel (Holstein) Germany **53** J1
Wedge Mountain Canada **120** F5
Wedowee U.S.A. **133** C5
Weedville U.S.A. **135** F3
Weenen S. Africa **101** J5
Weener Germany **53** H1
Weert Neth. **52** F3
Weethalle Australia **112** C4
Wee Waa Australia **112** D3
Wegberg Germany **52** G3
Węgorzewo Poland **47** R3
Weichang China **73** L4
Weida Germany **53** M4
Weidenberg Germany **53** L5
Weiden in der Oberpfalz Germany **53** M5
Weidongmen China *see* **Qianjin**
Weifang China **73** L5
Weihai China **73** M5
Wei He *r. Shaanxi* China **76** F1
Wei He *r.* China **77** G1
Weilburg Germany **53** I4
Weilmoringle Australia **112** C2
Weimar Germany **53** L4
Weinan China **77** F1
Weinheim Germany **53** I5
Weining China **76** E3
Weinsberg Germany **53** J5
Weipa Australia **110** C2
Weiqu China *see* **Chang'an**
Weir *r.* Australia **112** D2
Weir River Canada **121** M3
Weirton U.S.A. **134** E3
Weiser U.S.A. **126** D3
Weishan China **76** D3
Weishan Hu *l.* China **77** H1
Weishi China **77** G1
Weiße Elster *r.* Germany **53** L3
Weißenburg in Bayern Germany **53** K5

Weißenfels Germany 53 L3
Weißkugel mt. Austria/Italy 47 M7
Weissrand Mountains Namibia 100 D3
Weiterstadt Germany 53 I5
Weitzel Lake Canada 121 J3
Weixi China 76 C3
Weixin China 76 E3
Weiya China 80 H3
Weiyuan Gansu China 76 E1
Weiyuan Sichuan China 76 E2
Weiyuan Yunnan China see Jinggu
Weiyuan Jiang r. China 76 D4
Weiz Austria 47 O7
Weizhou China see Wenchuan
Weizhou Dao i. China 77 F4
Wejherowo Poland 47 Q3
Wekilbazar Turkm. see Vekil'bazar
Wekusko Canada 121 L4
Wekusko Lake Canada 121 L4
Wekweti Canada 120 H1
Welatam Myanmar 70 B1
Welbourn Hill Australia 109 F6
Welch U.S.A. 134 E5
Weld U.S.A. 135 J1
Weldiya Eth. 98 D2
Welford National Park Australia 110 C5
Welk'īt'ē Eth. 98 D3
Welkom S. Africa 101 H4
Welland Canada 134 F2
Welland r. U.K. 49 G6
Welland Canal Canada 134 F2
Wellesley Canada 134 E2
Wellesley Islands Australia 110 B3
Wellesley Lake Canada 120 B2
Wellfleet U.S.A. 135 J3
Wellin Belgium 52 F4
Wellingborough U.K. 49 G6
Wellington Australia 112 D4
Wellington Canada 135 G2

▶Wellington N.Z. 113 E5
Capital of New Zealand.

Wellington S. Africa 100 D7
Wellington England U.K. 49 D8
Wellington England U.K. 49 E6
Wellington CO U.S.A. 126 G4
Wellington IL U.S.A. 134 B3
Wellington KS U.S.A. 131 D4
Wellington NV U.S.A. 128 D2
Wellington OH U.S.A. 134 D3
Wellington TX U.S.A. 131 C5
Wellington UT U.S.A. 129 H2
Wellington, Isla i. Chile 144 B7
Wellington Range hills N.T. Australia 108 F3
Wellington Range hills W.A. Australia 109 C6
Wells Canada 120 F4
Wells U.K. 49 E7
Wells U.S.A. 126 E4
Wells, Lake salt flat Australia 109 C6
Wellsboro U.S.A. 135 G3
Wellsburg U.S.A. 134 E3
Wellsford N.Z. 113 E3
Wells-next-the-Sea U.K. 49 H6
Wellston U.S.A. 134 C1
Wellsville U.S.A. 135 G2
Wellton U.S.A. 129 F5
Wels Austria 47 O6
Welshpool U.K. 49 D6
Welsickendorf Germany 53 N3
Welwitschia Namibia see Khorixas
Welwyn Garden City U.K. 49 G7
Welzheim Germany 53 J6
Wem U.K. 49 E6
Wembesi S. Africa 101 I5
Wembley Canada 120 G4
Wemindji Canada 122 F3
Wenatchee U.S.A. 126 C3
Wenatchee Mountains U.S.A. 126 C3
Wenbu China see Nyima
Wenchang Hainan China 77 F5
Wenchang Sichuan China see Zitong
Wenchow China see Wenzhou
Wenchuan China 76 D2
Wendelstein Germany 53 L5
Wenden Germany 53 H4
Wenden Latvia see Cēsis
Wenden U.S.A. 129 G5
Wendover U.S.A. 129 F1
Weng'an China 76 E3
Wengshui China 76 C2
Wengyuan China 77 G3
Wenhua China see Weishan
Wenlan China see Mengzi
Wenling China 77 I2
Wenlock r. Australia 110 C2
Wenping China see Ludian
Wenquan Guizhou China 76 E2
Wenquan Henan China see Wenxian
Wenquan Hubei China see Yingshan

▶Wenquan Qinghai China 83 G2
Highest settlement in the world.

Wenquan Xinjiang China 80 F3
Wenshan China 76 E4
Wenshui China 76 E2
Wensum r. U.K. 49 I6
Wentorf bei Hamburg Germany 53 K1
Wentworth Australia 111 C7
Wenxi China 77 F1
Wenxian Gansu China 76 E1
Wenxian Henan China 77 G1
Wenxing China see Xiangyin
Wenzhou China 77 I3
Wenzlow Germany 53 M2
Wepener S. Africa 101 H5
Wer India 82 D4
Werben (Elbe) Germany 53 L2
Werda Botswana 100 F3
Werdau Germany 53 M4
Werdēr Eth. 98 E3
Werder Germany 53 M2
Werdohl Germany 53 H3
Werl Germany 53 H3
Wernberg-Köblitz Germany 53 M5
Werne Germany 53 H3
Wernecke Mountains Canada 120 B1
Wernigerode Germany 53 K3
Werra r. Germany 53 J3
Werris Creek Australia 112 E3
Wertheim Germany 53 J5
Wervik Belgium 52 D4
Wesel Germany 52 G3
Wesel-Datteln-Kanal canal Germany 52 G3
Wesenberg Germany 53 M1
Wesendorf Germany 53 K2
Weser r. Germany 53 I1
Weser sea chan. Germany 53 I1
Wesergebirge hills Germany 53 I2
Weslaco U.S.A. 131 D7
Weslemkoon Lake Canada 135 G1
Wesleyville Canada 123 L4
Wessel, Cape Australia 110 B1
Wessel Islands Australia 110 B1
Wesselsbron S. Africa 101 H4
Wesselton S. Africa 101 I4
Wessington Springs U.S.A. 130 D2
Westall, Point Australia 109 F8
West Allis U.S.A. 134 A2
West Antarctica reg. Antarctica 152 J1
West Australian Basin sea feature Indian Ocean 149 O7

▶West Bank terr. Asia 85 B3
Territory occupied by Israel.
Asia 6

West Bay Canada 123 K3
West Bay inlet U.S.A. 133 C6
West Bend U.S.A. 134 A2
West Bengal state India 83 F5
West Branch U.S.A. 134 C1
West Bromwich U.K. 49 F6
Westbrook U.S.A. 135 J2
West Burke U.S.A. 135 J1
West Burra i. U.K. 50 [inset]
Westbury U.K. 49 E7
West Caicos i. Turks and Caicos Is 133 F8
West Cape Howe Australia 109 B8
West Caroline Basin sea feature N. Pacific Ocean 150 F5
West Chester U.S.A. 135 H4
Westcliffe U.S.A. 127 G5
West Coast National Park S. Africa 100 D7
West End Bahamas 133 E7
Westerburg Germany 53 H4
Westerholt Germany 53 H1
Westerland Germany 47 L3
Westerlo Belgium 52 E3
Westerly U.S.A. 135 J3
Western r. Canada 121 J1
Western Australia state Australia 109 C6
Western Cape prov. S. Africa 100 E7
Western Desert Egypt 90 C6
Western Dvina r. Europe see Zapadnaya Dvina
Western Ghats mts India 84 B3
Western Port b. Australia 112 B7

▶Western Sahara terr. Africa 96 B2
Disputed territory (Morocco).
Africa 7, 94–95

Western Samoa country S. Pacific Ocean see Samoa
Western Sayan Mountains reg. Rus. Fed. see Zapadnyy Sayan
Westerschelde est. Neth. 52 D3
Westerstede Germany 53 H1
Westerville U.S.A. 134 D3
Westerwald hills Germany 53 H4
West Falkland i. Falkland Is 144 D8
West Fargo U.S.A. 130 D2
West Fayu atoll Micronesia 69 L5
Westfield IN U.S.A. 134 B3
Westfield MA U.S.A. 135 I2
Westfield NY U.S.A. 134 F2
Westfield PA U.S.A. 135 G3
West Frisian Islands Neth. 52 E1
Westgat sea chan. Neth. 52 G1
Westgate Australia 112 C1
West Glacier U.S.A. 126 E2
West Grand Lake U.S.A. 132 H2
West Hartford U.S.A. 135 I3
Westhausen Germany 53 K6
West Haven U.S.A. 135 I3
Westhill U.K. 50 G3
Westhope U.S.A. 130 C1
West Ice Shelf Antarctica 152 E2
West Indies is Caribbean Sea 137 J4
West Island India 71 A4
Westkapelle Neth. 52 D3
West Kazakhstan Oblast admin. div. Kazakh. see Zapadnyy Kazakhstan
West Kingston U.S.A. 135 J3
West Lafayette U.S.A. 134 B3
West Lamma Channel Hong Kong China 77 [inset]
Westland Australia 110 C4
Westland National Park N.Z. 113 C6
Westleigh S. Africa 101 H4
Westleton U.K. 49 I6
West Liberty U.S.A. 134 D5
West Linton U.K. 50 F5
West Loch Roag b. U.K. 50 C2
Westlock Canada 120 H4
West Lorne Canada 134 E2
West Lunga National Park Zambia 99 C5
West MacDonnell National Park Australia 109 F5
West Malaysia pen. Malaysia see Peninsular Malaysia
Westmalle Belgium 52 E3
Westmar Australia 112 D1
West Mariana Basin sea feature N. Pacific Ocean 150 F4
West Memphis U.S.A. 131 F5
Westminster U.S.A. 135 G4
Westmoreland Australia 110 B3
Westmoreland U.S.A. 134 B5
Westmorland U.S.A. 129 F5
Weston OH U.S.A. 134 D3
Weston WV U.S.A. 134 E4
Weston-super-Mare U.K. 49 E7
West Palm Beach U.S.A. 133 D7
West Plains U.S.A. 131 F4
West Point pt Australia 111 [inset]
West Point CA U.S.A. 128 C2
West Point KY U.S.A. 134 C5
West Point MS U.S.A. 131 F5
West Point NE U.S.A. 130 D3
West Point VA U.S.A. 135 G5
West Point Lake resr U.S.A. 133 C5
Westport Canada 135 G1
Westport N.Z. 113 C5
Westport Rep. of Ireland 51 C4
Westport CA U.S.A. 128 B2
Westport KY U.S.A. 134 C4
Westport NY U.S.A. 135 I1
Westray Canada 121 K4
Westray i. U.K. 50 F1
Westray Firth sea chan. U.K. 50 F1
Westree Canada 122 E5
West Rutland U.S.A. 135 I2
West Salem U.S.A. 134 D3
West Siberian Plain Rus. Fed. 64 J3
West-Skylge Neth. see West-Terschelling
West Stewartstown U.S.A. 135 J1
West-Terschelling Neth. 52 F1
West Topsham U.S.A. 135 I1
West Union IA U.S.A. 130 F3
West Union IL U.S.A. 134 B4
West Union OH U.S.A. 134 D4
West Union WV U.S.A. 134 E4
West Valley City U.S.A. 129 H1
Westville U.S.A. 134 B3
West Virginia state U.S.A. 134 E4
Westwood U.S.A. 128 C1
West Wyalong Australia 112 C4
West York U.S.A. 135 G4
Westzaan Neth. 52 E2
Wetar i. Indon. 108 D1
Wetar, Selat sea chan. East Timor/Indon. 108 D2
Wetaskiwin Canada 120 H4
Wete Tanz. 99 D4
Wetter r. Germany 53 I4
Wettin Germany 53 L3
Wetumpka U.S.A. 133 C5
Wetwun Myanmar 70 B2
Wetzlar Germany 53 I4
Wewahitchka U.S.A. 133 C6
Wewak P.N.G. 69 K7
Wewoka U.S.A. 131 D5
Wexford Rep. of Ireland 51 F5
Wexford Harbour b. Rep. of Ireland 51 F5
Weyakwin Canada 121 J4
Weybridge U.K. 49 G7
Weyburn Canada 121 K5
Weyhe Germany 53 I2
Weymouth U.K. 49 E8
Weymouth U.S.A. 135 J2
Wezep Neth. 52 G2
Whakaari i. N.Z. 113 F3
Whakatane N.Z. 113 F3
Whalan Creek r. Australia 112 D2
Whale r. Canada see La Baleine, Rivière à
Whalsay i. U.K. 50 [inset]
Whampoa China see Huangpu
Whangamata N.Z. 113 E3
Whanganui National Park N.Z. 113 E4
Whangarei N.Z. 113 E2
Whapmagoostui Canada 122 F3
Wharfe r. U.K. 48 F5
Wharfedale valley U.K. 48 F4
Wharton U.S.A. 131 D6
Wharton Lake Canada 121 L1
Wha Ti Canada 120 G2
Wheatland IN U.S.A. 134 B4
Wheatland WY U.S.A. 126 G4
Wheaton IL U.S.A. 134 A3
Wheaton MN U.S.A. 130 D2
Wheaton-Glenmont U.S.A. 135 G4
Wheeler U.S.A. 131 C5
Wheeler Lake Canada 120 H2
Wheeler Lake resr U.S.A. 133 C5
Wheeler Peak NM U.S.A. 127 G5
Wheeler Peak NV U.S.A. 129 F2
Wheelersburg U.S.A. 134 D4
Wheeling U.S.A. 134 E3
Whernside hill U.K. 48 E4
Whinham, Mount Australia 109 E6
Whiskey Jack Lake Canada 121 K3
Whitburn U.K. 50 F5
Whitby Canada 135 F2
Whitby U.K. 48 G4
Whitchurch U.K. 49 E6
Whitchurch-Stouffville Canada 134 F2
White r. Canada 122 D4
White r. Canada/U.S.A. 120 B2
White r. AR U.S.A. 125 I5
White r. AR U.S.A. 131 F5
White r. CO U.S.A. 129 I1
White r. IN U.S.A. 134 B4
White r. MI U.S.A. 134 B2
White r. NV U.S.A. 129 F3
White r. SD U.S.A. 130 D3
White r. VT U.S.A. 135 I2
White watercourse U.S.A. 129 H5
White, Lake salt flat Australia 108 E5
White Bay Canada 123 K4
White Butte mt. U.S.A. 130 C2
White Canyon U.S.A. 129 H3
White Cloud U.S.A. 134 C2
Whitecourt Canada 120 H4
Whiteface Mountain U.S.A. 135 I1
Whitefield U.S.A. 135 J1
Whitefish r. Canada 120 E1
Whitefish U.S.A. 126 E2
Whitefish Bay U.S.A. 134 B1
Whitefish Lake Canada 121 J2
Whitefish Point U.S.A. 132 C2
Whitehall Rep. of Ireland 51 E5
Whitehall U.K. 50 G1
Whitehall NY U.S.A. 135 I2
Whitehall WI U.S.A. 130 F2
Whitehaven U.K. 48 D4
Whitehead U.K. 51 G3
White Hill hill Canada 123 J5
Whitehill U.K. 49 G7

▶Whitehorse Canada 120 C2
Territorial capital of Yukon.

White Horse U.S.A. 129 J4
White Horse, Vale of valley U.K. 49 F7
White Horse Pass U.S.A. 129 F1
White House U.S.A. 134 B5
White Island Antarctica 152 D2
White Island N.Z. see Whakaari
White Lake Ont. Canada 122 D4
White Lake Ont. Canada 135 G1
White Lake LA U.S.A. 131 E6
White Lake MI U.S.A. 134 B2
Whitemark Australia 111 [inset]
White Mountain Peak U.S.A. 128 D3
White Mountains U.S.A. 135 J1
White Mountains National Park Australia 110 D4
Whitemouth Lake Canada 121 M5
Whitemud r. Canada 120 G3
White Nile r. Sudan/Uganda 86 D6
also known as Bahr el Abiad or Bahr el Jebel
White Nossob watercourse Namibia 100 D2
White Oak U.S.A. 134 D5
White Otter Lake Canada 121 N5
White Pass Canada/U.S.A. 120 C3
White Pine Range mts U.S.A. 129 F2
White Plains U.S.A. 135 I3
White River Canada 122 D4
Whiteriver U.S.A. 129 I5
White River U.S.A. 130 C3
White River Valley U.S.A. 129 F2
White Rock Peak U.S.A. 129 F2
White Russia country Europe see Belarus
Whitesail Lake Canada 120 E4
White Salmon U.S.A. 126 C3
Whitesand r. Canada 120 H2
White Sands National Monument nat. park U.S.A. 127 G6
Whitesburg U.S.A. 134 D5
White Sea Rus. Fed. 42 H2
White Stone U.S.A. 135 G5
White Sulphur Springs MT U.S.A. 126 F3
White Sulphur Springs WV U.S.A. 134 E5
Whitesville U.S.A. 134 E5
Whiteville U.S.A. 133 E5
White Volta r. Burkina/Ghana 96 C4
also known as Nakambé or Nakanbe or Volta Blanche
Whitewater U.S.A. 129 I2
Whitewater Baldy mt. U.S.A. 129 I5
Whitewater Lake Canada 122 C4
Whitewood Australia 110 C4
Whitewood Canada 121 K5
Whitfield U.K. 49 I7
Whithorn U.K. 50 E6
Whitianga N.Z. 113 E3
Whitland U.K. 49 C7
Whitley Bay U.K. 48 F3
Whitmore Mountains Antarctica 152 K1
Whitney Canada 135 F1
Whitney, Mount U.S.A. 128 D3
Whitney Point U.S.A. 135 H2
Whitstable U.K. 49 I7
Whitsunday Group is Australia 110 E4
Whitsunday Island National Park Australia 110 E4
Whitsun Island Vanuatu see Pentecost Island
Whittemore U.S.A. 134 D1
Whittlesea Australia 112 B6
Whittlesey U.K. 49 G6
Whitton Australia 112 C5
Wholdaia Lake Canada 121 J2
Why U.S.A. 129 G5
Whyalla Australia 111 B7
Wiang Sa Thai. 70 C3
Wiarton Canada 134 E1
Wibaux U.S.A. 126 G3
Wichelen Belgium 52 D3
Wichita U.S.A. 130 D4
Wichita r. U.S.A. 131 D5
Wichita Falls U.S.A. 131 D5
Wichita Mountains U.S.A. 131 D5
Wick U.K. 50 F2
Wick r. U.K. 50 F2
Wickenburg U.S.A. 129 G5
Wickes U.S.A. 131 E5
Wickford U.K. 49 H7
Wickham r. Australia 108 E4
Wickham, Cape Australia 107 [inset]
Wickham, Mount hill Australia 108 E4
Wickliffe U.S.A. 131 F4
Wicklow Rep. of Ireland 51 F5
Wicklow Head hd Rep. of Ireland 51 G5
Wicklow Mountains Rep. of Ireland 51 F5
Wicklow Mountains National Park Rep. of Ireland 51 F4
Widerøe, Mount Antarctica 148 C2
Widerøefjellet mt. Antarctica see Widerøe, Mount
Widgeegoara watercourse Australia 112 B1
Widgiemooltha Australia 109 C7
Widnes U.K. 48 E5
Wi-do i. S. Korea 75 B6
Wied r. Germany 53 H4
Wiehengebirge hills Germany 53 I2
Wiehl Germany 53 H4
Wielkopolskie, Pojezierze reg. Poland 47 O4
Wielkopolski Park Narodowy nat. park Poland 47 P4
Wieluń Poland 47 Q5
Wien Austria see Vienna
Wiener Neustadt Austria 47 P7
Wierden Neth. 52 G2
Wieren Germany 53 K2
Wieringerwerf Neth. 52 F2
Wiesbaden Germany 53 I4
Wiesenfelden Germany 53 M5
Wiesentheid Germany 53 K5
Wiesloch Germany 53 I5
Wiesmoor Germany 53 H1
Wietze Germany 53 J2
Wietzendorf Germany 53 J2
Wieżyca hill Poland 47 Q3
Wigan U.K. 48 E5
Wiggins U.S.A. 131 F6
Wight, Isle of i. England U.K. 49 F8
Wignes Lake Canada 121 J2
Wigston U.K. 49 F6
Wigton U.K. 48 D4
Wigtown U.K. 50 E6
Wigtown Bay U.K. 50 E6
Wijchen Neth. 52 F3
Wijhe Neth. 52 G2
Wilberforce, Cape Australia 110 B1
Wilbur U.S.A. 126 D3
Wilburton U.S.A. 131 E5
Wilcannia Australia 112 A3
Wilcox U.S.A. 135 F3
Wilczek Land i. Rus. Fed. see Vil'cheka, Zemlya
Wildberg Germany 53 M2
Wildcat Peak U.S.A. 128 E2
Wild Coast S. Africa 101 I6
Wilderness National Park S. Africa 100 F8
Wildeshausen Germany 53 I2
Wild Horse Hill mt. U.S.A. 130 C3
Wildspitze mt. Austria 47 M7
Wildwood FL U.S.A. 133 D6
Wildwood NJ U.S.A. 135 H4
Wilge r. S. Africa 101 I4
Wilge r. S. Africa 101 I3
Wilgena Australia 109 F7

▶Wilhelm, Mount P.N.G. 69 L8
5th highest mountain in Oceania.

Wilhelm II Land reg. Antarctica see Kaiser Wilhelm II Land
Wilhelmina Gebergte mts Suriname 143 G3
Wilhelmina Kanaal canal Neth. 52 F3
Wilhelmshaven Germany 53 I1
Wilhelmstal Namibia 100 C1
Wilkes-Barre U.S.A. 135 H3
Wilkesboro U.S.A. 132 D4
Wilkes Coast Antarctica 152 G2
Wilkes Land reg. Antarctica 152 G2
Wilkie Canada 121 I4
Wilkins Coast Antarctica 152 L2
Wilkins Ice Shelf Antarctica 152 L2
Wilkinson Lakes salt flat Australia 109 F7
Will, Mount Canada 120 D3
Willand U.K. 49 D8
Willandra Billabong watercourse Australia 112 B4
Willandra National Park Australia 112 B4
Willapa Bay U.S.A. 126 B3
Willard Mex. 127 F7
Willard NM U.S.A. 127 G6
Willard OH U.S.A. 134 D3
Willcox U.S.A. 129 I5
Willcox Playa salt flat U.S.A. 129 I5
Willebadessen Germany 53 J3
Willebroek Belgium 52 E3

▶Willemstad Neth. Antilles 137 K6
Capital of the Netherlands Antilles.

Willeroo Australia 108 E3
Willette U.S.A. 134 C5
William, Mount Australia 111 C8
William Creek Australia 111 B6
William Lake Canada 121 L4
Williams AZ U.S.A. 129 G4
Williams CA U.S.A. 128 B2
Williamsburg KY U.S.A. 134 C5
Williamsburg OH U.S.A. 134 C4
Williamsburg VA U.S.A. 135 G5
Williams Lake Canada 120 F4
William Smith, Cap c. Canada 123 I1
Williamson NY U.S.A. 135 G2
Williamson WV U.S.A. 134 D5
Williamsport IN U.S.A. 134 B3
Williamsport PA U.S.A. 135 G3
Williamston U.S.A. 132 E5
Williamstown KY U.S.A. 134 C4
Williamstown NJ U.S.A. 135 H4
Willimantic U.S.A. 135 I3
Willis Group atolls Australia 110 E3
Williston S. Africa 100 E6
Williston ND U.S.A. 130 C1
Williston SC U.S.A. 133 D5
Williston Lake Canada 120 F4
Williton U.K. 49 D7
Willits U.S.A. 128 B2
Willmar U.S.A. 130 E2
Willoughby, Lake U.S.A. 135 I1
Willow Beach U.S.A. 129 F4
Willow Bunch Canada 121 J5
Willow Hill U.S.A. 135 G3
Willow Lake Canada 120 G2
Willowlake r. Canada 120 F2
Willowmore S. Africa 100 F7
Willowra Australia 108 F5
Willows U.S.A. 128 B2
Willow Springs U.S.A. 131 F4
Willowvale S. Africa 101 I7
Wills, Lake salt flat Australia 108 E5
Wilma U.S.A. 133 C6
Wilmington DE U.S.A. 135 H4
Wilmington NC U.S.A. 133 E5
Wilmington OH U.S.A. 134 D4
Wilmore U.S.A. 134 C5
Wilmslow U.K. 48 E5
Wilno Lith. see Vilnius
Wilnsdorf Germany 53 I4
Wilpattu National Park Sri Lanka 84 D4
Wilseder Berg hill Germany 53 J1
Wilson watercourse Australia 107 C5
Wilson atoll Micronesia see Ifalik
Wilson KS U.S.A. 130 D4
Wilson NC U.S.A. 132 E5
Wilson NY U.S.A. 135 F2
Wilson, Mount CO U.S.A. 129 J3
Wilson, Mount NV U.S.A. 129 F2
Wilson, Mount OR U.S.A. 126 C3
Wilsonia U.S.A. 128 D3
Wilson's Promontory pen. Australia 112 C7
Wilson's Promontory National Park Australia 112 C7
Wilsum Germany 52 G2
Wilton r. Australia 108 F3
Wilton U.S.A. 135 J1
Wiltz Lux. 52 F5
Wiluna Australia 109 C6
Wimereux France 52 B4
Wina r. Cameroon see Vina
Winamac U.S.A. 134 B3
Winbin watercourse Australia 111 D5
Winburg S. Africa 101 H5
Wincanton U.K. 49 E7
Winchester Canada 135 H1
Winchester U.K. 49 F7
Winchester IN U.S.A. 134 C3
Winchester KY U.S.A. 134 C5
Winchester NH U.S.A. 135 I2
Winchester TN U.S.A. 133 C5
Winchester VA U.S.A. 135 F4
Wind r. Canada 120 C1
Wind r. U.S.A. 126 F4
Windau Latvia see Ventspils
Windber U.S.A. 135 F3
Wind Cave National Park U.S.A. 130 C3
Windermere U.K. 48 E4
Windermere l. U.K. 48 E4
Windham U.S.A. 120 C3

▶Windhoek Namibia 100 C2
Capital of Namibia.

Windigo Lake Canada 121 N4
Windlestraw Law hill U.K. 50 G5
Wind Mountain U.S.A. 127 G6
Windom U.S.A. 130 E3
Windom Peak U.S.A. 129 J3
Windorah Australia 110 C5
Window Rock U.S.A. 129 I4
Wind Point U.S.A. 134 B2
Wind River Range mts U.S.A. 126 F4
Windrush r. U.K. 49 F7
Windsbach Germany 53 K5
Windsor Australia 112 E4
Windsor N.S. Canada 123 I5
Windsor Ont. Canada 134 D2
Windsor U.K. 49 G7
Windsor NC U.S.A. 132 E4
Windsor NY U.S.A. 135 H2
Windsor VA U.S.A. 135 G5
Windsor VT U.S.A. 135 I2
Windsor Locks U.S.A. 135 I3
Windward Islands Caribbean Sea 137 L5
Windward Passage Cuba/Haiti 137 J5
Windy U.S.A. 118 D3
Winefred Lake Canada 121 I4
Winfield KS U.S.A. 131 D4
Winfield WV U.S.A. 134 E4
Wingate U.K. 48 F4
Wingen Australia 112 E3
Wingene Belgium 52 D3
Wingen-sur-Moder France 53 H6
Wingham Australia 112 F3
Wingham Canada 134 E2
Winisk Canada 122 D3
Winisk r. Canada 122 D3
Winisk Lake Canada 122 D3
Winkana Myanmar 70 B4
Winkelman U.S.A. 129 H5
Winkler Canada 121 L5
Winlock U.S.A. 126 C3
Winneba Ghana 96 C4
Winnebago, Lake U.S.A. 134 A1
Winnecke Creek watercourse Australia 108 E4
Winnemucca U.S.A. 128 E1
Winnemucca Lake U.S.A. 128 D1
Winner U.S.A. 130 C3
Winnett U.S.A. 126 F3
Winnfield U.S.A. 131 E6
Winnibigoshish, Lake U.S.A. 130 E2
Winnie U.S.A. 131 E6
Winning Australia 109 A5

▶Winnipeg Canada 121 L5
Provincial capital of Manitoba.

Winnipeg r. Canada 121 L5
Winnipeg, Lake Canada 121 L5
Winnipegosis Canada 121 L5
Winnipegosis, Lake Canada 121 K4
Winnipesaukee, Lake U.S.A. 135 J2
Winona AZ U.S.A. 129 H4
Winona MN U.S.A. 130 F2
Winona MO U.S.A. 131 F4
Winona MS U.S.A. 131 F5
Winschoten Neth. 52 H1
Winsen (Aller) Germany 53 J2
Winsen (Luhe) Germany 53 K1
Winsford U.K. 48 E5
Winslow AZ U.S.A. 129 H4
Winslow ME U.S.A. 135 K1
Winsop, Tanjung pt Indon. 69 I7
Winsted U.S.A. 135 I3
Winston-Salem U.S.A. 132 D4
Winterberg Germany 53 I3
Winter Haven U.S.A. 133 D6
Winters CA U.S.A. 128 C2
Winters TX U.S.A. 131 D6
Wintersville U.S.A. 134 E3
Winterswijk Neth. 52 G3
Winterthur Switz. 56 I3
Winterton S. Africa 101 I5
Winthrop U.S.A. 135 K1
Winton Australia 110 C4
Winton N.Z. 113 B8
Winton U.S.A. 132 E4
Winwick U.K. 49 G6
Wirral pen. U.K. 48 D5
Wirrulla Australia 111 A7
Wisbech U.K. 49 H6
Wiscasset U.S.A. 135 K1
Wisconsin r. U.S.A. 130 F3
Wisconsin state U.S.A. 134 A1
Wisconsin Rapids U.S.A. 130 F2
Wise U.S.A. 134 D5
Wiseman U.S.A. 118 C3
Wishaw U.K. 50 F5
Wisher U.S.A. 130 D2
Wisil Dabarow Somalia 98 E3
Wisła r. Poland see Vistula
Wismar Germany 47 M4
Wistaria Canada 120 E4
Witbank S. Africa 101 I3
Witbooisvlei Namibia 100 D3
Witham U.K. 49 H7
Witham r. U.K. 49 H6
Witherbee U.S.A. 135 I1
Withernsea U.K. 48 H5
Witjira National Park Australia 111 A5
Witmarsum Neth. 52 F1
Witney U.K. 49 F7
Witrivier S. Africa 101 J3
Witry-lès-Reims France 52 E5
Witteberg mts S. Africa 101 H6
Wittenberg Germany see Lutherstadt Wittenberg
Wittenberge Germany 53 L2
Wittenburg Germany 53 L1
Wittingen Germany 53 K2

X

Y

237

Yankton U.S.A. 130 D3
Yanling *Hunan* China 77 G3
Yanling *Sichuan* China *see* Weiyuan
Yannina Greece *see* Ioannina
Yano-Indigirskaya Nizmennost' *lowland* Rus. Fed. 65 P2
Yanovski, Mount U.S.A. 120 C3
Yanrey *r.* Australia 109 A5
Yanshan *Jiangxi* China 77 H2
Yanshan *Yunnan* China 76 E4
Yanshi China 77 G1
Yanshiping China 76 B1
Yanskiy Zaliv *g.* Rus. Fed. 65 O2
Yantabulla Australia 112 B2
Yantai China 73 M5
Yanting China 76 E2
Yantongshan China 74 B4
Yantou China 77 I2
Yanwa China 76 C3
Yany-Kurgan Kazakh. *see* Zhanakorgan
Yanyuan China 76 D3
Yao Chad 97 E3
Yao'an China 76 D3
Yaodu China *see* Dongzhi
Yaoli China 77 H2

▶Yaoundé Cameroon 96 E4
Capital of Cameroon.

Yaoxian China 77 F1
Yaoxiaoling China 74 B2
Yao Yai, Ko *i.* Thai. 71 B6
Yap *i.* Micronesia 69 J5
Yapen *i.* Indon. 69 J7
Yappar *r.* Australia 110 C3
Yap Trench *sea feature* N. Pacific Ocean 150 F5
Yaqui *r.* Mex. 127 F8
Yar Rus. Fed. 42 L4
Yaradzha Turkm. *see* Yaradzhi
Yaradzhi Turkm. 88 E2
Yaraka Australia 110 D5
Yarangüme Turkey *see* Tavas
Yaransk Rus. Fed. 42 J4
Yardea Australia 111 A7
Yardımcı Burnu *pt* Turkey 59 N6
Yardımlı Azer. 91 H3
Yardymly Azer. *see* Yardımlı
Yare *r.* U.K. 49 I6
Yarega Rus. Fed. 42 L3

▶Yaren Nauru 107 G2
Capital of Nauru.

Yarensk Rus. Fed. 42 K3
Yariga-take *mt.* Japan 75 E5
Yarīm Yemen 86 F7
Yarımca Turkey *see* Körfez
Yarkand China *see* Shache
Yarkant China *see* Shache
Yarkant He *r.* China 80 E4
Yarker Canada 135 G1
Yarkhun *r.* Pak. 89 I2
Yarlung Zangbo *r.* China 76 B2 *see* Brahmaputra
Yarmouth Canada 123 I6
Yarmouth *England* U.K. 49 F8
Yarmouth *England* U.K. *see* Great Yarmouth
Yarmouth U.S.A. 135 J2
Yarmuk *r.* Asia 85 B3
Yarnell U.S.A. 129 G4
Yaroslavl' Rus. Fed. 42 H4
Yaroslavskiy Rus. Fed. 74 D3
Yarra *r.* Australia 112 B6
Yarra Junction Australia 112 B6
Yarram Australia 112 C7
Yarraman Australia 112 E1
Yarrawonga Australia 112 B6
Yarra Yarra Lakes *salt flat* Australia 109 A7
Yarronvale Australia 112 B1
Yarrowmere Australia 110 D4
Yartö Tra La *pass* China 83 H3
Yartsevo *Krasnoyarskiy Kray* Rus. Fed. 64 J3
Yartsevo *Smolenskaya Oblast'* Rus. Fed. 43 G5
Yarumal Col. 142 C2
Yarwa China 76 C2
Yarzhong China 76 C2
Yaş Romania *see* Iaşi
Yasawa Group *is* Fiji 107 H3
Yashilkŭl *l.* Tajik. 89 I2
Yashkul' Rus. Fed. 43 J7
Yasin Jammu and Kashmir 82 C1
Yasnogorsk Rus. Fed. 43 H5
Yasnyy Rus. Fed. 74 C1
Yasothon Thai. 70 D4
Yass Australia 112 D5
Yass *r.* Australia 112 D5
Yassı Burnu *c.* Cyprus *see* Plakoti, Cape
Yāsūj Iran 88 C4
Yasuní, Parque Nacional *nat. park* Ecuador 142 C4
Yatağan Turkey 59 M6
Yaté New Caledonia 107 G4
Yates *r.* Canada 120 H2
Yates Center U.S.A. 130 E4
Yathkyed Lake Canada 121 L2
Yatsushiro Japan 75 C6
Yaṭṭa West Bank 85 B4
Yatton U.K. 49 E7
Yauca Peru 142 D7
Yau Tong *b. Hong Kong* China 77 [inset]
Yavan Tajik. *see* Yovon
Yavari *r.* Brazil/Peru 142 E4
also known as Javari (Brazil/Peru)
Yávaros Mex. 127 F8
Yavatmal India 84 C1
Yavi Turkey 91 F3
Yaví, Cerro *mt.* Venez. 142 E2
Yavoriv Ukr. 43 D6
Yavuzlu Turkey 85 C1
Yawatongguzlangar China 83 E1
Yaw Chaung *r.* Myanmar 76 B4
Yaxian China *see* Sanya
Yay Myanmar *see* Ye
Yayladağı Turkey 85 C2
Yazd Iran 88 D4
Yazdān Iran 89 F3
Yazd-e Khvāst Iran 88 D4
Yazıhan Turkey 90 E3
Yazoo City U.S.A. 131 F5
Y Bala U.K. *see* Bala
Yding Skovhøj *hill* Denmark 47 L3
Ydra *i.* Greece 59 J6
Y Drenewydd U.K. *see* Newtown
Ye Myanmar 70 B4
Yea Australia 112 B6
Yealmpton U.K. 49 D8
Yebawmi Myanmar 70 A1
Yebbi-Bou Chad 97 E2
Yecheng China 80 E4
Yécora Mex. 127 F7
Yedashe Myanmar 70 B3
Yedatore India 84 C3
Yedi Burun Başı *pt* Turkey 59 M6
Yeeda River Australia 108 C4
Yefremov Rus. Fed. 43 H5
Yêgainnyin China *see* Henan
Yeghegnadzor Armenia 91 G3
Yegindykol' Kazakh. 80 C1
Yegorlykskaya Rus. Fed. 43 I7
Yegorova, Mys *pt* Rus. Fed. 74 E3
Yegor'yevsk Rus. Fed. 43 H5
Yei Sudan 97 G4
Yei *r.* Sudan 97 G4
Yeji China 77 G2
Yejiaji China *see* Yeji
Yekaterinburg Rus. Fed. 64 H4
Yekaterinodar Rus. Fed. *see* Krasnodar
Yekaterinoslav Ukr. *see* Dnipropetrovs'k
Yekaterinoslavka Rus. Fed. 74 C2
Yekhegnadzor Armenia *see* Yeghegnadzor
Ye Kyun *i.* Myanmar 70 A3
Yelabuga *Khabarovskiy Kray* Rus. Fed. 74 D2
Yelabuga *Respublika Tatarstan* Rus. Fed. 42 K5
Yelan' Rus. Fed. 43 I6
Yelan' *r.* Rus. Fed. 43 I6
Yelandur India 84 C3
Yelantsy Rus. Fed. 72 J2
Yelarbon Australia 112 E2
Yelbarsli Turkm. 89 F2
Yelenovskiye Kar'yery Ukr. *see* Dokuchayevs'k
Yelets Rus. Fed. 43 H5
Yélimané Mali 96 B3
Yelizavetgrad Ukr. *see* Kirovohrad
Yelkhovka Rus. Fed. 43 K5
Yell *i.* U.K. 50 [inset]
Yellabina Regional Reserve *nature res.* Australia 109 F7
Yellandu India 84 D2
Yellapur India 84 B3

▶Yellow *r.* China 77 G1
4th longest river in Asia.

Yellowhead Pass Canada 120 G4

▶Yellowknife Canada 120 H2
Capital of Northwest Territories.

Yellowknife *r.* Canada 120 H2
Yellow Mountain *hill* Australia 112 C4
Yellow Sea N. Pacific Ocean 73 N5
Yellowstone *r.* U.S.A. 130 C2
Yellowstone Lake U.S.A. 126 F3
Yellowstone National Park U.S.A. 126 F3
Yell Sound *strait* U.K. 50 [inset]
Yeloten Turkm. 89 F2
Yelovo Rus. Fed. 41 Q4
Yel'sk Belarus 43 F6
Yelva *r.* Rus. Fed. 42 K3
Yematan China 76 C1
▶Yemen *country* Asia 86 G6
Asia 6, 62–63
Yemetsk Rus. Fed. 42 I3
Yemişenbükü Turkey *see* Taşova
Yemmiganur India *see* Emmiganuru
Yemtsa Rus. Fed. 42 I3
Yemva Rus. Fed. 42 K3
Yena Rus. Fed. 44 Q3
Yenagoa Nigeria 96 D4
Yenakiieve Ukr. 43 H6
Yenakiyevo Ukr. *see* Yenakiyeve
Yenangyat Myanmar 70 A2
Yenangyaung Myanmar 70 A2
Yenanma Myanmar 70 A3
Yenda Australia 112 C5
Yêndum China *see* Zhag'yab
Yengisar China 80 E4
Yengo National Park Australia 112 E4
Yenice Turkey 59 L5
Yenidamlar Turkey *see* Demirtaş
Yenihan Turkey *see* Yıldızeli
Yenije-i-Vardar Greece *see* Giannitsa
Yenişehir Greece *see* Larisa
Yenişehir Turkey 59 M4
Yenisey *r.* Rus. Fed. 64 J2

▶Yenisey-Angara-Selenga *r.* Rus. Fed. 64 J2
3rd longest river in Asia.

Yeniseysk Rus. Fed. 64 K4
Yeniseyskiy Kryazh *ridge* Rus. Fed. 64 K4
Yeniseyskiy Zaliv *inlet* Rus. Fed. 153 F2
Yeniyol Turkey *see* Borçka
Yên Minh Vietnam 70 D2
Yenotayevka Rus. Fed. 43 J7
Yeola India 84 B1
Yeo Lake *salt flat* Australia 109 D6
Yeotmal India *see* Yavatmal
Yeoval Australia 112 D4
Yeovil U.K. 49 E8
Yeo Yeo *r.* Australia *see* Bland
Yeppoon Australia 110 E4
Yeraliyev Kazakh. *see* Kuryk
Yerbent Turkm. 88 E2
Yerbogachen Rus. Fed. 65 L3
Yercaud India 84 C4

▶Yerevan Armenia 91 G2
Capital of Armenia.

Yereymentau Kazakh. 80 D1
Yergara India 84 C2
Yergeni *hills* Rus. Fed. 43 J7
Yergoğu Romania *see* Giurgiu
Yeriḥo West Bank *see* Jericho
Yerilla Australia 109 C7
Yerington U.S.A. 128 D2
Yerköy Turkey 90 D3
Yerla *r.* India 84 B2
Yermak Kazakh. *see* Aksu
Yermakovo Rus. Fed. 74 B1
Yermak Plateau *sea feature* Arctic Ocean 153 H1
Yermentau Kazakh. *see* Yereymentau
Yermo Mex. 131 B7
Yermo U.S.A. 128 E4
Yerofey Pavlovich Rus. Fed. 74 A1
Yeroham Israel 85 B4
Yerres *r.* France 52 C6
Yersa *r.* Rus. Fed. 42 L2
Yershov Rus. Fed. 43 K6
Yertsevo Rus. Fed. 42 I3
Yerupaja *mt.* Peru 142 C6
Yerushalayim Israel/West Bank *see* Jerusalem
Yeruslan *r.* Rus. Fed. 43 J6
Yesagyo Myanmar 70 A2
Yesan S. Korea 75 B5
Yesil' Kazakh. 78 F1
Yeşilhisar Turkey 90 D3
Yeşilırmak *r.* Turkey 90 E2
Yeşilova *Burdur* Turkey 59 M6
Yeşilova *Yozgat* Turkey *see* Sorgun
Yessentuki Rus. Fed. 91 F1
Yessey Rus. Fed. 65 L3
Yes Tor *hill* U.K. 49 C8
Yêtatang China *see* Baqên
Yetman Australia 112 E2
Yeu Myanmar 70 A2
Yeu, Île d' *i.* France 56 C3
Yevdokimovskoye Rus. Fed. *see* Krasnogvardeyskoye
Yevlakh Azer. *see* Yevlax
Yevlax Azer. 91 G2
Yevpatoriya Ukr. 90 D1
Yevreyskaya Avtonomnaya Oblast' *admin. div.* Rus. Fed. 74 D2
Yexian China *see* Laizhou
Yeyik China 83 E1
Yeysk Rus. Fed. 43 H7
Yeyungou China 80 G3
Yezhou China *see* Jianshi
Yezhuga *r.* Rus. Fed. 42 J2
Yezo *i.* Japan *see* Hokkaidō
Yezyaryshcha Belarus 42 F5
Y Fenni U.K. *see* Abergavenny
Y Fflint U.K. *see* Flint
Y Gelli Gandryll U.K. *see* Hay-on-Wye
Yialí *i.* Greece *see* Gyali
Yi'allaq, Gebel *mt.* Egypt *see* Yu'alliq, Jabal
Yialousa Cyprus *see* Aigialousa
Yi'an China 74 B3
Yianisádha *i.* Greece *see* Gianysada
Yiannitsá Greece *see* Giannitsa
Yibin *Sichuan* China 76 E2
Yibin *Sichuan* China 76 E2
Yibug Caka *salt l.* China 83 F2
Yichang *Hubei* China 77 F2
Yichang *Hubei* China 77 F2
Yicheng *Henan* China *see* Zhumadian
Yicheng *Hubei* China 77 G2
Yicheng *Shanxi* China 77 F1
Yichun *Heilong.* China 74 C3
Yichun *Jiangxi* China 77 G3
Yidu China *see* Zhicheng
Yidun China 76 C2
Yifeng China 77 G2
Yi He *r. Henan* China 77 G1
Yi He *r. Shandong* China 77 H1
Yihuang China 77 H3
Yijun China 77 F1
Yilaha China 74 B2
Yilan China 74 C3
Yilan Taiwan *see* Ilan
Yıldız Dağları *mts* Turkey 59 L4
Yıldızeli Turkey 90 E3
Yilehuli Shan *mts* China 74 A2
Yiliang China 76 D3
Yilong *Heilong.* China 74 B3
Yilong *Sichuan* China 76 E2
Yilong *Yunnan* China *see* Shiping
Yilong Hu *l.* China 76 D4
Yimianpo China 74 C3
Yinbaing Myanmar 70 B3
Yincheng China *see* Dexing
Yinchuan China 72 J5
Yindarlgooda, Lake *salt flat* Australia 109 C7
Yingcheng China 77 G2
Yingde China 77 G3
Yinggehai China 77 F5
Yinggen China *see* Qiongzhong
Ying He *r.* China 77 H1
Yingjing China 76 D2
Yingkou China 73 M4
Yingshan China 77 G2
Yingtan China 77 H2
Yining *Jiangxi* China *see* Xiushui
Yining *Xinjiang* China 80 F3
Yinjiang China 77 F3
Yinkeng China *see* Yinkengxu
Yinkengxu China 77 G3
Yinmabin Myanmar 70 A2
Yinnyein Myanmar 70 B3
Yin Shan *mts* China 73 J4
Yinxian China *see* Ningbo
Yipinglang China 76 D3
Yiquan China *see* Meitan
Yirga Alem Eth. 98 D3
Yirol Sudan 97 G4
Yisa China *see* Honghe
Yishan *Guangxi* China *see* Yizhou
Yishan *Jiangsu* China *see* Guanyun
Yishui China 73 L5
Yishun Sing. 71 [inset]
Yíthion Greece *see* Gytheio
Yitiaoshan China *see* Jingtai
Yitong He *r.* China 74 B3
Yi Tu, Nam *r.* Myanmar 70 B2
Yitulihe China 74 A2
Yiwu China 76 D4
Yixing China 77 H2
Yiyang China 77 G2
Yizheng China 77 H1
Yizhou China 77 F3
Yizra'el *country* Asia *see* Israel
Yläne Fin. 45 M6
Ylihärmä Fin. 44 M5
Yli-Ii Fin. 44 N4
Yli-Kärppä Fin. 44 N4
Ylikiiminki Fin. 44 O4
Yli-Kitka *l.* Fin. 44 P3
Ylistaro Fin. 44 M5
Ylitornio Fin. 44 M3
Ylivieska Fin. 44 N4
Ylöjärvi Fin. 45 M6
Ymer Ø *i.* Greenland 119 P2
Ynys Enlli *i.* U.K. *see* Bardsey Island
Ynys Môn *i.* U.K. *see* Anglesey
Yoakum U.S.A. 131 D6
Yoder U.S.A. 134 C3
Yogan, Cerro *mt.* Chile 144 B8
Yogyakarta Indon. 68 E8
Yoho National Park Canada 120 G5
Yokadouma Cameroon 97 E4
Yokkaichi Japan 75 E6
Yoko Cameroon 96 E4
Yokohama Japan 75 E6
Yokosuka Japan 75 E6
Yokote Japan 75 F5
Yola Nigeria 96 E4
Yolo U.S.A. 128 C2
Yolombo Dem. Rep. Congo 98 C4
Yolöten Turkm. *see* Yeloten
Yoluk Mex. 133 C8
Yom, Mae Nam *r.* Thai. 70 C4
Yomou Guinea 96 C4
Yomuka Indon. 69 J8
Yonaguni-jima *i.* Japan 77 I3
Yŏnan N. Korea 75 B5
Yonezawa Japan 75 F5
Yong'an *Chongqing* China *see* Fengjie
Yong'an *Fujian* China 77 H3
Yongbei China *see* Yongsheng
Yongcong China 77 F3
Yongding *Fujian* China 77 H3
Yongding *Yunnan* China *see* Yongren
Yongding *Yunnan* China *see* Fumin
Yongfeng China 77 G3
Yongfu China 77 F3
Yŏnghŭng N. Korea 75 B5
Yŏnghŭng-man *b.* N. Korea 75 B5
Yŏngil-man *b.* S. Korea 75 C6
Yongjing *Guizhou* China *see* Xifeng
Yongjing *Liaoning* China *see* Xifeng
Yŏngju S. Korea 75 C5
Yongkang *Yunnan* China 76 C3
Yongkang *Zhejiang* China 77 I2
Yongle China *see* Zhen'an
Yongning *Guangxi* China 77 F4
Yongning *Jiangxi* China *see* Tonggu
Yongning *Sichuan* China *see* Xuyong
Yongping China 76 C3
Yongqing China *see* Qingshui
Yongren China 76 D3
Yongsheng China 76 D3
Yongshou China 77 F1
Yongshun China 77 F2
Yongtai China 77 H3
Yongxi China *see* Nayong
Yongxing *Hunan* China 77 G3
Yongxing *Jiangxi* China 77 G3
Yongxiu China 77 G2
Yongyang China *see* Weng'an
Yongzhou China 77 F3
Yonkers U.S.A. 135 I3
Yopal Col. 142 D2
Yopurga China 80 E4
Yordu Jammu and Kashmir 82 C2
York Australia 109 B7
York Canada 134 F2
York U.K. 48 F5
York *AL* U.S.A. 131 F5
York *NE* U.S.A. 130 D3
York *PA* U.S.A. 135 G4
York, Cape Australia 110 C1
York, Kap *c.* Greenland *see* Innaanganeq
York, Vale of *valley* U.K. 48 F4
Yorke Peninsula Australia 111 B7
Yorkshire Dales National Park U.K. 48 E4
Yorkshire Wolds *hills* U.K. 48 G5
Yorkton Canada 121 K5
Yorktown U.S.A. 135 G5
Yorkville U.S.A. 130 F3
Yorosso Mali 96 C3
Yosemite U.S.A. 134 C5
Yosemite National Park U.S.A. 128 D3
Yoshkar-Ola Rus. Fed. 42 J4
Yos Sudarso *i.* Indon. *see* Dolak, Pulau
Yŏsu S. Korea 75 B6
Yotvata Israel 85 B5
Youbou Canada 120 E5
Youghal Rep. of Ireland 51 E6
Young Australia 112 D5
Young U.S.A. 129 H4
Younghusband, Lake *salt flat* Australia 111 B6
Younghusband Peninsula Australia 111 B7
Young Island Antarctica 152 H2
Youngstown Canada 121 I5
Youngstown U.S.A. 134 E3
You Shui *r.* China 77 F2
Youssoufia Morocco 54 C5
Youvarou Mali 96 C3
Youxi China 77 H3
Youxian China 77 G3
Youyang China 77 F2
Youyi China 74 C3
Youyi Feng *mt.* China/Rus. Fed. 80 G2
Yovon Tajik. 89 H2
Yowah *watercourse* Australia 112 B2
Yozgat Turkey 90 D3
Ypres Belgium *see* Ieper
Yreka U.S.A. 126 C4
Yrghyz Kazakh. *see* Irgiz
Yr Wyddfa *mt.* U.K. *see* Snowdon
Yser *r.* France 52 C4
also known as IJzer (Belgium)
Ysselsteyn Neth. 52 F3
Ystad Sweden 45 H9
Ystwyth *r.* U.K. 49 C6
Ysyk-Köl Kyrg. *see* Balykchy

▶Ysyk-Köl *salt l.* Kyrg. 80 E3
5th largest lake in Asia.

Ythan *r.* U.K. 50 G3
Y Trallwng U.K. *see* Welshpool
Ytyk-Kyuyel' Rus. Fed. 65 O3
Yu'alliq, Jabal *mt.* Egypt 85 A4
Yuan'an China 77 F2
Yuanbao Shan *mt.* China 77 F3
Yuanjiang *Hunan* China 77 G2
Yuanjiang *Yunnan* China 76 D4
Yuan Jiang *r. Hunan* China 77 F2
Yuan Jiang *r. Yunnan* China 76 D4
Yuanjiazhuang China *see* Foping
Yuanlin China 74 A2
Yuanling China 77 F2
Yuanma China *see* Yuanmou
Yuanmou China 76 D3
Yuanquan China *see* Anxi
Yuanshan China *see* Lianping
Yuanyang China *see* Xinjie
Yub'ā *i.* Saudi Arabia 90 D6
Yuba City U.S.A. 128 C2
Yubei China 76 E2
Yuben' Tajik. 89 I2
Yucatán *pen.* Mex. 136 F5
Yucatan Channel Cuba/Mex. 137 G4
Yucca U.S.A. 129 F4
Yucca Lake U.S.A. 128 E3
Yucca Valley U.S.A. 128 E4
Yucheng *Henan* China 77 G1
Yucheng *Sichuan* China *see* Ya'an
Yuci China *see* Jinzhong
Yudi Shan *mt.* China 74 A1
Yudu China 77 G3
Yuelai China *see* Huachuan
Yueliang Pao *l.* China 74 A3
Yuendumu Australia 108 E5
Yuen Long *Hong Kong* China 77 [inset]
Yueqing China 77 I2
Yuexi China 77 H2
Yueyang *Hunan* China 77 G2
Yueyang *Hunan* China 77 G2
Yueyang *Sichuan* China *see* Anyue
Yug *r.* Rus. Fed. 42 J3
Yugan China 77 H2
Yugorsk Rus. Fed. 41 S3
Yugoslavia *country* Europe *see* Serbia and Montenegro
Yuhang China 77 I2
Yuhu China *see* Eryuan
Yuhuan China 77 I2
Yuin Australia 109 B6
Yu Jiang *r.* China 77 F4
Yukagirskoye Ploskogor'ye *plat.* Rus. Fed. 65 Q3
Yukamenskoye Rus. Fed. 42 L4
Yukarı Sakarya Ovaları *plain* Turkey 59 N5
Yukarısarıkaya Turkey 90 D3

▶Yukon *r.* Canada/U.S.A. 120 B2
5th longest river in North America.

Yukon Crossing Canada 120 B2
Yukon Territory *admin. div.* Canada 120 C2
Yüksekova Turkey 91 G3
Yulara Australia 109 E6
Yule *r.* Australia 108 B5
Yuleba Australia 112 D1
Yulee U.S.A. 133 D6
Yulin *Guangxi* China 77 F4
Yulin *Shaanxi* China 73 J5
Yulong Xueshan *mt.* China 76 D3
Yuma *AZ* U.S.A. 129 F5
Yuma *CO* U.S.A. 130 C3
Yuma Desert U.S.A. 129 F5
Yumen China 80 I4
Yumenguan China 80 H3
Yumurtalık Turkey 85 B1
Yuna Australia 109 A7
Yunak Turkey 90 C3
Yunan China 77 F4
Yunaska Island U.S.A. 118 A4
Yuncheng China 77 F1
Yundamindera Australia 109 C7
Yunfu China 77 G4
Yungas *reg.* Bol. 142 E7
Yungui Gaoyuan *plat.* China 76 D3
Yunhe *Jiangsu* China *see* Pizhou
Yunhe *Yunnan* China *see* Heqing
Yunhe *Zhejiang* China 77 H2
Yunjinghong China *see* Jinghong
Yunkai Dashan *mts* China 77 F4
Yünlin Taiwan *see* Touliu
Yunling China *see* Yunxiao
Yun Ling *mts* China 76 C3
Yunlong China 76 C3
Yunmeng China 77 G2
Yunmenling China *see* Junmenling
Yunnan *prov.* China 76 D3
Yunta Australia 111 B7
Yunt Dağı *mt.* Turkey 85 A1
Yunxi *Hubei* China 77 F1
Yunxi *Sichuan* China *see* Yanting
Yunxian *Hubei* China 77 F1
Yunxian *Yunnan* China 76 D3
Yunxiao China 77 H4
Yunyang *Chongqing* China 77 F2
Yunyang *Henan* China 77 G1
Yuping *Guizhou* China *see* Libo
Yuping *Guizhou* China 77 F3
Yuping *Yunnan* China *see* Pingbian
Yuqing China 76 E3
Yurayqir National Park Australia 112 F2
Yurba Co *l.* China 83 F2
Yürekli Turkey 85 B1
Yurga Rus. Fed. 64 J4
Yuriria Mex. 136 D4
Yurungkax He *r.* China 82 E1
Yur'ya Rus. Fed. 42 K4
Yur'yakha *r.* Rus. Fed. 42 L2
Yuryev Estonia *see* Tartu
Yur'yevets Rus. Fed. 42 I4
Yur'yev-Pol'skiy Rus. Fed. 42 H4
Yushan China 77 H2
Yü Shan *mt.* Taiwan 77 I4
Yushino Rus. Fed. 42 L1
Yushkozero Rus. Fed. 44 R4
Yushu *Jilin* China 74 B3
Yushu *Qinghai* China 76 C1
Yushuwan China *see* Huaihua
Yusufeli Turkey 91 F2
Yus'va Rus. Fed. 41 Q4
Yuta West Bank *see* Yaṭṭa
Yutai China 77 H1
Yutan China *see* Ningxiang
Yuxi *Guizhou* China *see* Daozhen
Yuxi *Hubei* China 77 F2
Yuxi *Yunnan* China 76 D3
Yuyangguan China 77 F2
Yuyao China 77 I2
Yuzawa Japan 75 F5
Yuzha Rus. Fed. 42 I4
Yuzhno-Kamyshovyy Khrebet *ridge* Rus. Fed. 74 F3
Yuzhno-Kuril'sk Rus. Fed. 74 G3
Yuzhno-Muyskiy Khrebet *mts* Rus. Fed. 73 K1
Yuzhno-Sakhalinsk Rus. Fed. 74 F3
Yuzhno-Sukhokumsk Rus. Fed. 91 G1
Yuzhnoukrayinsk Ukr. 43 F7
Yuzhnyy Rus. Fed. *see* Adyk
Yuzhou *Chongqing* China *see* Chongqing
Yuzhou *Henan* China 77 G1
Yuzovka Ukr. *see* Donets'k
Yverdon Switz. 56 H3
Yvetot France 56 E2
Ywamun Myanmar 70 A2

Z

Zaamin Uzbek. 89 H2
Zaandam Neth. 52 E2
Zab, Monts du *mts* Alg. 57 I6
Zabānābād Iran 88 E3
Zabaykal'sk Rus. Fed. 73 L3
Zabīd Yemen 86 F7
Zābol Iran 89 F4
Zacapa Guat. 136 G5
Zacatecas Mex. 136 D4
Zacatecas *state* Mex. 131 C8
Zacharo Greece 59 I6
Zacoalco Mex. 136 D4
Zacynthus *i.* Greece *see* Zakynthos
Zadar Croatia 58 F2
Zadetkale Kyun *i.* Myanmar 71 B5
Zadetkyi Kyun *i.* Myanmar 71 B5
Zadi Myanmar 71 B4
Zadoi China 76 B1
Zadonsk Rus. Fed. 43 H5
Zadran *reg.* Afgh. 89 H3
Za'farâna Egypt *see* Za'farānah
Za'farānah Egypt 90 D5
Zafer Adaları *is* Cyprus *see* Kleides Islands
Zafer Burnu *c.* Cyprus *see* Apostolos Andreas, Cape
Zafora *i.* Greece 59 L6
Zafra Spain 57 C4
Zagazig Egypt *see* Az Zaqāzīq
Zaghdeh *well* Iran 88 E3
Zaghouan Tunisia 58 D6
Zagorsk Rus. Fed. *see* Sergiyev Posad

▶Zagreb Croatia 58 F2
Capital of Croatia.

Zagros, Kūhhā-ye *mts* Iran *see* Zagros Mountains
Zagros Mountains Iran 88 B3
Zagunao China *see* Lixian
Za'gya Zangbo *r.* China 83 G3
Zāhedān Iran 89 F4
Zaḥlah Lebanon *see* Zahlé
Zahlé Lebanon 85 B3
Zāhmet Turkm. *see* Zakhmet
Ẓahrān Saudi Arabia 86 F6
Zahrez Chergui *salt pan* Alg. 57 H6
Zahrez Rharbi *salt pan* Alg. 57 H6
Zainlha China *see* Xiaojin
Zainsk Rus. Fed. *see* Novyy Zay
Zaire *country* Africa *see* Congo, Democratic Republic of
Zaïre *r.* Congo/Dem. Rep. Congo *see* Congo
Zaječar Serb. and Mont. 59 J3
Zaka Zimbabwe 99 D6
Zakamensk Rus. Fed. 80 J1
Zakataly Azer. *see* Zaqatala
Zakháro Greece *see* Zacharo
Zakhmet Turkm. 89 F2
Zākhō Iraq 91 F3
Zakhodnyaya Dzvina *r.* Europe *see* Zapadnaya Dvina
Zákinthos *i.* Greece *see* Zakynthos
Zakopane Poland 47 Q6
Zakouma, Parc National de *nat. park* Chad 97 E3
Zakwaski, Mount Canada 120 F5
Zakynthos Greece 59 I6
Zakynthos *i.* Greece 59 I6
Zala China 76 B2
Zalaegerszeg Hungary 58 G1
Zalai-domsag *hills* Hungary 58 G1
Zalamea de la Serena Spain 57 D4
Zalantun China 74 A3
Zalari Rus. Fed. 72 I2
Zalău Romania 59 J1
Zaleski U.S.A. 134 D4
Ẓalim Saudi Arabia 86 F5
Zalingei Sudan 97 F3
Ẓalmā, Jabal aẓ *mt.* Saudi Arabia 86 E4
Zama City Canada 120 G3
Zambeze *r.* Africa 99 C5 *see* Zambezi

▶Zambezi *r.* Africa 99 C5
4th longest river in the world. Also known as Zambeze.

Zambezi Zambia 99 C5
▶Zambia *country* Africa 99 C5
Africa 7, 94–95
Zamboanga Phil. 69 G5
Zamfara *watercourse* Nigeria 96 D3
Zamīndāvar *reg.* Afgh. 89 F4
Zamkog China *see* Zamtang
Zamora Ecuador 142 C4
Zamora Spain 57 D3
Zamora de Hidalgo Mex. 136 D5
Zamość Poland 43 D6
Zamost'ye Poland *see* Zamość
Zamtang China 76 D1
Zamuro, Sierra del *mts* Venez. 142 F3

Acknowledgements

Maps and data

General

Maps designed and created by HarperCollins Reference, Glasgow, UK, www.bartholomewmaps.com
Cross-sections (pp36–37, 60–61, 92–93, 102–103, 114–115, 138–139) and globes (pp14–15, 146–147): Geo-Innovations, Llandudno, UK, www.geoinnovations.co.uk

The publishers would like to thank all national survey departments, road, rail and national park authorities, statistical offices and national place name committees throughout the world for their valuable assistance, and in particular the following:
British Antarctic Survey, Cambridge, UK
Tony Champion, Professor of Population Geography, University of Newcastle upon Tyne, UK
Mr P J M Geelan, London, UK

International Boundary Research Unit, University of Durham, UK
The Meteorological Office, Bracknell, Berkshire, UK
Permanent Committee on Geographical Names for British Official Use, London, UK

Data

Bathymetric data: The GEBCO Digital Atlas published by the British Oceanographic Data Centre on behalf of IOC and IHO, 1994
Earthquakes data (pp14–15): United States Geological Survey (USGS) National Earthquakes Information Center, Denver, USA
Coral reefs data (p18): UNEP World Conservation Monitoring Centre, Cambridge, UK and World Resources Institute (WRI), Washington DC, USA
Desertification data (p18): U.S. Department of Agriculture Natural Resources Conservation Service

Population data (pp20–21): Center for International Earth Science Information Network (CIESIN), Columbia University; International Food Policy Research Institute (IFPRI); and World Resources Institute (WRI). 2000. Gridded Population of the World (GPW), Version 2. Palisades, NY: CIESIN, Columbia University. http://sedac.ciesin.columbia.edu/plue/gpw
Company sales figures (p29): Reprinted by permission of Forbes Magazine © 2004 Forbes Inc.
Terrorism data (p31): Rand-MIPT Terrorist Incident Database (Rand Corporation, Santa Monica, Ca and Oklahoma City National Memorial Institute for the Prevention of Terrorism, 2003) db.mipt.org/mipt_rand.cfm
Antarctica (p152): Antarctic Digital Database (versions 1 and 2), © Scientific Committee on Antarctic Research (SCAR), Cambridge, UK (1993, 1998)

Photographs and images

Page	Image	Satellite/Sensor	Credit	Page	Image	Satellite/Sensor	Credit	Page	Image	Satellite/Sensor	Credit
5	The Alps	MODIS	MODIS/NASA		Tōkyō		Cities Revealed aerial photography © The GeoInformation Group, 1998		Gaza/Egypt/Israel border	Shuttle	Digital image ©1996 CORBIS; Original image courtesy of NASA/CORBIS
	Amsterdam	IKONOS	Space Imaging Europe/Science Photo Library	24–25	International telecommunications traffic map		© PriMetrica, Inc. www.telegeography.com and www.primetrica.com	92–93	Congo	Shuttle	NASA
	Italy	AVHRR	Earth Satellite Corporation/Science Photo Library						Lake Victoria	MODIS	MODIS/NASA
6	Ganges Delta	SPOT	CNES, 1987 Distribution Spot Image/Science Photo Library		Internet topology		CAIDA/Science Photo Library		Kilimanjaro	Landsat	USGS/NASA
				26–27	Health care facilities		John Cole/Science Photo Library	94–95	Cape Verde	MODIS	MODIS/NASA
	Cyprus	MODIS	MODIS/NASA		Education		Moacyr Lopes Junior/UNEP/Still Pictures		Cairo	IKONOS	IKONOS satellite imagery provided by Space Imaging, Thornton, Colorado, www.spaceimaging.com
	Indian subcontinent	AVHRR	Earth Satellite Corporation/Science Photo Library	28–29	Sudan Village		Mark Edwards/Still Pictures				
7	Victoria Falls		Roger De La Harpe, Gallo Images/CORBIS		The City		London Aerial Photo Library/CORBIS		Cape Town	IKONOS	IKONOS satellite imagery provided by Space Imaging, Thornton, Colorado, www.spaceimaging.com
	Sinai Peninsula	Shuttle	NASA	30–31	Egypt/Gaza border		Marc Schlossman/Panos Pictures	102–103	Lake Eyre	Shuttle	NASA
8	Mt Cook		Mike Schroder/Still Pictures		Spratly Islands	IKONOS	IKONOS satellite imagery provided by Space Imaging, Thornton, Colorado, www.spaceimaging.com		New Caledonia and Vanuatu	SeaWiFS	Image provided by ORBIMAGE © Orbital Imaging Corporation and processing by NASA Goddard Space Flight Center.
	Bora Bora	SPOT	CNES, Distribution Spot Image/Science Photo Library		İstanbul		Getty Images				
	Ayers Rock		ImageState	32–33	Water		Harmut Schwarzbach/Still Pictures		Banks Peninsula		Institute of Geological and Nuclear Sciences, New Zealand
	Sydney	IKONOS	IKONOS satellite imagery provided by Space Imaging, Thornton, Colorado, www.spaceimaging.com		Drugs		Getty Images	104–105	Wellington		NZ Aerial Mapping Ltd www.nzam.com
9	The Pentagon	IKONOS	IKONOS satellite imagery provided by Space Imaging, Thornton, Colorado, www.spaceimaging.com		Aids		Friedrich Stark/Still Pictures		Tasmania	SeaWiFS	Image provided by ORBIMAGE. © Orbital Imaging Corporation and processing by NASA Goddard Space Flight Center.
				34–35	Aral Sea	Landsat	Data available from the U.S. Geological Survey, EROS Data Center, Sioux Falls, SD				
	Panama Canal	Landsat	Clifton-Campbell Imaging Inc. www.tmarchive.com		Abu Dhabi 1972	Landsat	Science Photo Library		Tahiti and Moorea	SPOT	CNES, Distribution Spot Image/Science Photo Library
	Cuba	MODIS	MODIS/NASA		Abu Dhabi 2000	IKONOS	IKONOS satellite imagery provided by Space Imaging, Thornton, Colorado, www.spaceimaging.com	114–115	Mississippi	ASTER	ASTER/NASA
10–11	Dili	SPOT	CNES, Distribution Spot Image/Science Photo Library		3 Gorges Dam Before		Wolfgang Kaehler/CORBIS		Grand Canyon	SPOT	CNES, 1996 Distribution Spot Image/Science Photo Library
	Vatican City	IKONOS	IKONOS satellite imagery provided by Space Imaging, Thornton, Colorado, www.spaceimaging.com		3 Gorges Dam Construction		Reuters/CORBIS		Yucatan	MODIS	MODIS/NASA
12–13	Greenland	MODIS	MODIS/NASA		Mesopotamian marshlands		NASA/EROS Data Center	116–117	The Bahamas	MODIS	MODIS/NASA
	Nile Valley	MODIS	MODIS/NASA	36–37	Iceland	MODIS	MODIS/NASA		El Paso	Shuttle	NASA
14–15	Bam		Fatih Saribas/Reuters/CORBIS		Danube delta	MODIS	MODIS/NASA		Washington DC		US Geological Society/Science Photo Library
	Mt Etna		Bernhard Edmaier/Science Photo Library		Caucasus	MODIS	MODIS/NASA	138–139	Lake Titicaca	Shuttle	NASA
16–17	Tropical Cyclone Dina	MODIS	MODIS/NASA/GSFC	38–39	Paris	IKONOS	Space Imaging Europe/Science Photo Library		Tierra del Fuego	MODIS	MODIS/NASA
	Annual precipitation map	Microwave infrared	NASA/Goddard Space Flight Centre		Bosporus	SPOT	CNES, 1991 Distribution Spot Image/Science Photo Library		Amazon/Rio Negro	Terra/MISR	NASA
	Climate change maps		Met. Office, Hadley Centre for Climate Prediction and Research		Belgrade	SIR-C/X-SAR	NASA JPL	140–141	Galapagos Islands	SPOT	CNES, 1988 Distribution Spot Image/Science Photo Library
18–19	Snow and ice		Klaus Andrews/Still Pictures	60–61	Kamchatka Peninsula	MODIS	MODIS/NASA		Falkland Islands	MODIS	MODIS/NASA
	Urban		Ron Giling/Still Pictures		Caspian Sea	MODIS	MODIS/NASA		Rio de Janeiro	SPOT	Earth Satellite Corporation/Science Photo Library
	Forest		Wolfgang Kaehler/CORBIS		Yangtze	MODIS	MODIS/NASA	146–147	Antarctica	AVHRR	NRSC Ltd/Science Photo Library
	Barren/Shrubland		Simon Fraser/Science Photo Library	62–63	Timor	MODIS	MODIS/NASA		Novaya Zemlya	Landsat ETM	NASA
20–21	Kuna Indians		Royalty-Free/CORBIS		Beijing	IKONOS	IKONOS satellite imagery provided by Space Imaging, Thornton, Colorado, www.spaceimaging.com				
	Masai Village		Yann Arthus-Bertrand/CORBIS								
22–23	Los Angeles	SRTM/Landsat 5	NASA								